Presents

The World of Professional Golf 2007

Founded by
Mark H. McCormack

Editor: Bev Norwood
Contributors: Andy Farrell, Doug Ferguson, Donald (Doc) Giffin, Marino Parascenzo

All rights reserved
First published 2007
© IMG Operations, Inc. 2007

Designed and produced by Davis Design

ISBN-13: 978-1-878843-47-0
ISBN-10: 1-878843-47-8

Printed and bound in the United States.

Contents

	Rolex Rankings	1
	Official World Golf Ranking	6
	World's Winners of 2006	14
	Multiple Winners of 2006	22
	World Money List	23
	World Money List Leaders	30
	Career World Money List	31
	Women's World Money List	32
	Senior World Money List	35
1	The Year In Retrospect	39

THE MAJOR CHAMPIONSHIPS

2	Masters Tournament	54
3	U.S. Open Championship	61
4	The Open Championship	68
5	PGA Championship	76
6	Women's Major Championships	83

OTHER SIGNIFICANT EVENTS

7	HSBC World Match Play	96
8	The Ryder Cup	101

WORLDWIDE TOURS

9	American Tours	108
10	European Tours	162
11	Asia/Japan Tours	186
12	Australasian Tour	223
13	African Tours	229
14	Women's Tours	247
15	Senior Tours	302

APPENDIXES

U.S. PGA Tour	336
Special Events	406
Nationwide Tour	410
Canadian Tour	431
Tour de las Americas (South America)	440
European Tour	449
Challenge Tour	496
Asian Tour	515
Omega China Tour	541
Japan Tour	544
Australasian Tour	565
African Tours	572
U.S. LPGA Tour	589
Ladies European Tour	612
Japan LPGA Tour	624
Korea LPGA Tour	645
Australian Women's Tour	654
South African Women's Tour	655
Champions Tour	659
European Seniors Tour	683
Japan Senior Tour	692

Introduction

Rolex has done so many things over the years that were and are good for golf. Sponsorship of this publication is a prime example. My friends at Rolex, recognizing the historic and research value *The World of Professional Golf* has provided to the game continuously since the middle 1960s, stepped up in 2005 with the support necessary to continue its existence and the service it extends to the world of golf.

I well remember my conversations with my close friend and business manager, the late Mark McCormack, when he outlined his concept of filling a written gap in the game's history with an annual book carrying detailed stories and statistics covering every organized national and international tournament during that particular calendar year. The idea made complete sense to me and I encouraged him to proceed. He did, recruiting a group of talented golf journalists to work with him in producing the first edition that covered the 1966 season worldwide. Its publication has continued and grown in size and scope ever since, keeping pace with the tremendous growth of the game throughout the world.

Mark McCormack passed away in 2003, but his contribution to the historical record of golf did not die. Credit for this goes to IMG executives and others within the organization who considered the book an important continuing tribute to Mark and to Patrick Heiniger and his executive associates at Rolex, whose support has kept the literary chain intact.

Arnold Palmer
Orlando, Florida
January 2007

Foreword
(Written in 1968)

It has long been my feeling that a sport as compelling as professional golf is deserving of a history, and by history I do not mean an account culled years later from the adjectives and enthusiasms of on-the-spot reports that have then sat in newspaper morgues for decades waiting for some patient drudge to paste them together and call them lore. Such works can be excellent when insight and perspective are added to the research, but this rarely happens. What I am talking about is a running history, a chronology written at the time, which would serve both as a record of the sport and as a commentary upon the sport in any given year—an annual, if you will....

When I embarked on this project two years ago (the first of these annuals was published in Great Britain in 1967), I was repeatedly told that such a compendium of world golf was impossible, that it would be years out of date before it could be assembled and published, that it would be hopelessly expensive to produce and that only the golf fanatic would want a copy anyway. In the last analysis, it was that final stipulation that spurred me on. There must be a lot of golf fanatics, I decided. I can't be the only one. And then one winter day I was sitting in Arnold Palmer's den in Latrobe, Pennsylvania, going through the usual motions of spreading papers around so that Arnold and I could discuss some business project, when Arnold happened to mention that he wanted to collect a copy of each new golf book that was published from now on, in order to build a golf library of his own. "It's really too bad that there isn't a book every year on the pro tour," he said. "Ah," I thought. "Another golf fanatic. That makes two of us." So I decided to do the book. And I have. And I hope you like it. If so, you can join Arnold and me as golf fanatics.

Mark H. McCormack
Cleveland, Ohio
January 1968

Mark H. McCormack
1930 – 2003

In 1960, Mark Hume McCormack shook hands with a young golfer named Arnold Palmer. That historic handshake established a business that would evolve into today's IMG, the world's premier sports and lifestyle marketing and management company —representing hundreds of sports figures, entertainers, models, celebrities, broadcasters, television properties, and prestigious organizations and events around the world. With just a handshake Mark McCormack had invented a global industry.

Sean McManus, President of CBS News and Sports, reflects, "I don't think it's an overstatement to say that like Henry Ford and Bill Gates, Mark McCormack literally created, fostered and led an entirely new worldwide industry. There was no sports marketing before Mark McCormack. Every athlete who's ever appeared in a commercial, or every right holder who sold their rights to anyone, owes a huge debt of gratitude to Mark McCormack."

Mark McCormack's philosophy was simple. "Be the best," he said. "Learn the business and expand by applying what you already know." This philosophy served him well, not only as an entrepreneur and CEO of IMG, but also as an author, a consultant and a confidant to a host of global leaders in the world of business, politics, finance, science, sports and entertainment.

He was among the most-honored entrepreneurs of his time. *Sports Illustrated* recognized him as "The Most Powerful Man in Sports." In 1999, ESPN's Sports Century listed him as one of the century's 10 "Most Influential People in the Business of Sport."

Golf Magazine called McCormack "the most powerful man in golf" and honored him along with Arnold Palmer, Gerald Ford, Dwight D. Eisenhower, Bob Hope and Ben Hogan as one of the 100 all-time "American Heroes of Golf." *Tennis* magazine and *Racquet* magazine named him "the most powerful man in tennis." Tennis legend Billie Jean King believes, "Mark McCormack was the king of sports marketing. He shaped the way all sports are marketed around the world. He was the first in the marketplace, and his influence on the world of sports, particularly his ability to combine athlete representation, property development and television broadcasting, will forever be the standard of the industry."

The London *Sunday Times* listed him as one of the 1000 people who influenced the 20th century. Alastair Cooke on the BBC said simply that "McCormack was the Oracle; the creator of the talent industry, the maker of people famous in their profession famous to the rest of the world and making for them a fortune in the process ... He took on as clients people already famous in their profession as golfer, opera singer, author, footballer, racing car driver, violinist—and from time to time if they needed special help, a prime minister, or even the Pope."

McCormack was honored posthumously by the Golf Writers Association of America with the 2004 William D. Richardson Award, the organization's highest honor, "Given to recognize an individual who has consistently made an outstanding contribution to golf."

Among McCormack's other honors were the 2001 PGA Distinguished Service Award, given to those who have helped perpetuate the values and ideals of the PGA of America. He was also named a Commander of the Royal Order of the Polar Star by the King of Sweden (the highest honor for a person living outside of Sweden) for his contribution to the Nobel Foundation.

Journalist Frank Deford states, "There have been what we love to call dynasties in every sport. IMG has been different. What this one brilliant man, Mark McCormack, created is the only dynasty ever over all sport."

Through IMG, Mark McCormack demonstrated the value of sports and lifestyle activities as effective corporate marketing tools, but more importantly, his lifelong dedication to his vocation—begun with just a simple handshake—brought enjoyment to millions of people worldwide who watch and cheer their heroes and heroines. That is his legacy.

ROLEX

The Rolex association with golf dates from 1967 when my father, André Heiniger, presented Arnold Palmer with a gold Oyster Perpetual to honour his achievements on the golf course. This marked the beginning of a loyal and privileged relationship with him, which has now spanned 40 years.

This initial association with Arnold Palmer led to further affiliations with the sport and many players who would follow him. Today, a known and recognised supporter of men's and women's golf, Rolex sponsors many of the best-known tournaments, including the four Majors, both Men's and Ladies'.

In 2006 we began sponsoring the Rolex Rankings and have ongoing partnerships with the USGA (United States Golf Association), the PGA Tour (USA) and the World Golf Championships.

Many of the best players in the world are Rolex Testimonees. After Arnold Palmer, Gary Player, and Jack Nicklaus, other great talents became Testimonees. Today, we are pleased to have champions like Phil Mickelson and Annika Sorenstam in this select group.

It is only natural, therefore, that Rolex is associated with and committed to the publication of *The World of Professional Golf*.

A pioneer in sports sponsoring, with a particular affinity for golf, year after year, Rolex has been honoured to participate in unforgettable moments of intense emotion. We owe this to golfers whose passion and determination are equalled only by their rigour and precision, qualities held in high esteem by Rolex.

Golf is Rolex!

Patrick Heiniger
Managing Director
Chief Executive Officer
Rolex SA
February 2007

Rolex and Golf

Rolex's association with golf dates from 1967 when Andre Heiniger presented Arnold Palmer with a gold Oyster Perpetual to honor his achievements on the golf course. This marked the beginning of a loyal and privileged relationship, not only with Arnold Palmer and afterwards with two other golfing greats, Gary Player and Jack Nicklaus, but also many of the great talents who have followed them. Rolex has also established relationships with the major organizing bodies of the game.

Mark McCormack (left) and Andre Heiniger enjoyed many rounds together, including this at Turnberry, Scotland.

Courtesy of Arnold Palmer

Courtesy of Arnold Palmer

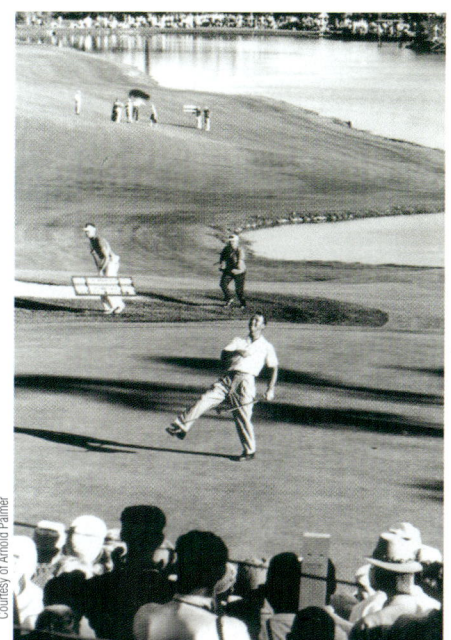

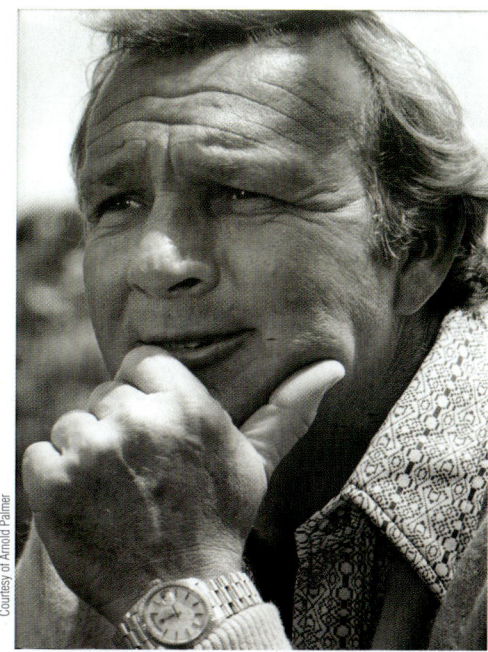

Arnold Palmer, tossing his visor at the 1960 U.S. Open (above left), has been associated with Rolex for 40 years.

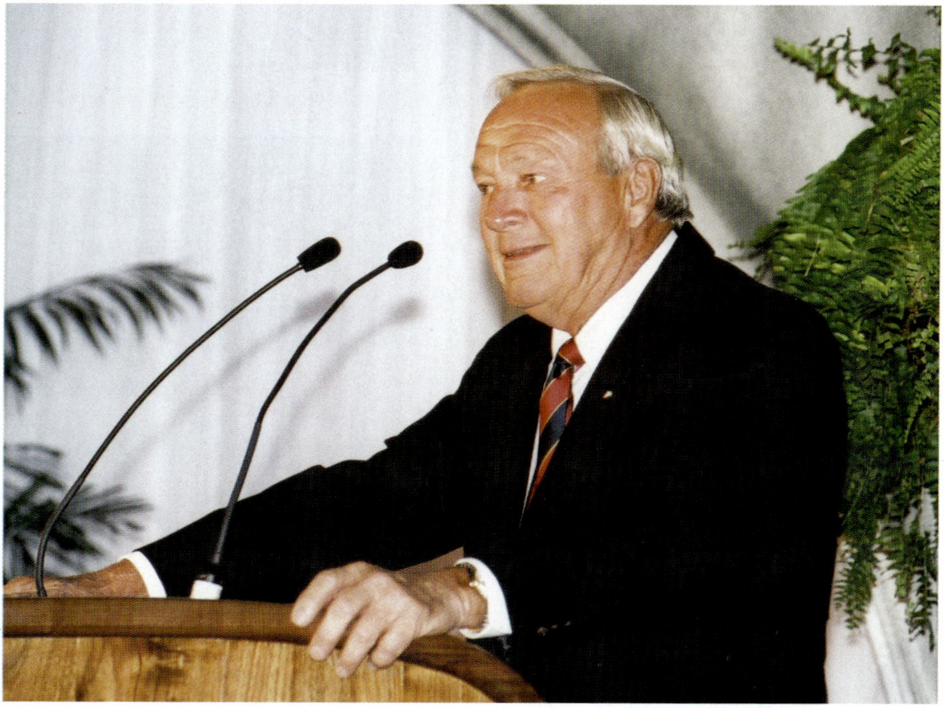

Courtesy of Arnold Palmer

Rolex's Top 10 of Women's Golf

1. Annika Sorenstam (Sweden) 14.42 points

2. Lorena Ochoa (Mexico) 11.78 points

3. Karrie Webb (Australia) 10.56 points

4. Cristie Kerr (USA) 7.64 points

5. Juli Inkster (USA) 6.86 points

7. Paula Creamer (USA) 6.22 points

6. Ai Miyazato (Japan) 6.52 points

8. Jeong Jang (Korea) 6.09 points

9. Shiho Ohyama (Japan) 5.84 points

10. Se Ri Pak (Korea) 4.98 points

Rolex and Sport

Since 1927, Rolex has been associated with the quest for excellence in sport, when it placed a Rolex Oyster on the wrist of a young swimmer, Mercedes Gleitze, as she swam across the English Channel. In 1933, Rolex began to sponsor Himalayan and polar expeditions, including the first successful ascent of Everest by Sir Edmund Hillary in 1953.

Today Rolex supports top sporting and cultural events all over the world. It is present at more than 150 events in the realms of golf, yachting, tennis, equestrian events, motor sports, exploration, culture and the arts, as well as philanthropic awards programs. Because of the commitment and continuity of these relationships, Rolex is seen not only as a sponsor … but as a real partner.

Phil Mickelson

Adam Scott

Trevor Immelman

The Ryder Cup captains Ian Woosnam (left) and Tom Lehman.

Rolex was an Official Partner of The 2006 Ryder Cup.

Butch Harmon   David Leadbetter

Lorena Ochoa

U.S. Open Championship

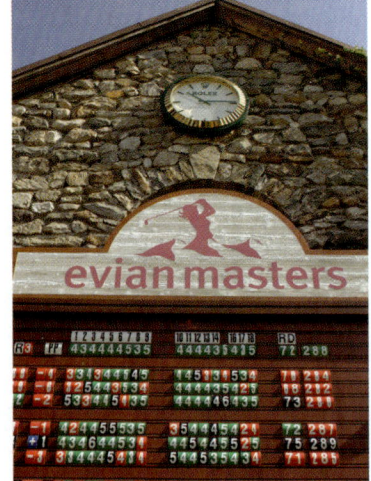

Annika Sorenstam

Evian Masters

Rolex Rankings

Annika Sorenstam ended 2006 in the same position as she began—No. 1 on the Rolex Rankings. The first official ranking system in women's golf was introduced on February 21, 2006, with Sorenstam, the 2005 LPGA Rolex Player of the Year, holding first place over Paula Creamer, the 2005 Louise Suggs Rolex Rookie of the Year, and with 16-year-old Michelle Wie in third place.

Sorenstam won five tournaments in 2006, including the U.S. Women's Open, plus the Women's World Cup of Golf for Sweden (with Liselotte Neumann) and finished the year with a 14.42 points average in the rankings. But Mexico's Lorena Ochoa climbed from No. 7 to No. 2 in the rankings with her six victories and the 2006 LPGA Rolex Player of the Year award. Whereas Sorenstam began with a margin in the rankings of almost nine points, Ochoa had closed within three points with her 11.78 average.

Karrie Webb had a comeback year with five victories worldwide including the Kraft Nabisco Championship and finished as No. 3 in the world with a 10.56 average. Cristie Kerr and Juli Inkster rounded out the top five for the year.

Other major champions of 2006 were Se Ri Pak, winner of the McDonald's LPGA Championship, who advanced from No. 90 to No. 10 in the world, and Sherri Steinhauer, winner of the Weetabix Women's British Open, who climbed from No. 105 to No. 23. Meanwhile, Creamer did not win and dropped from No. 2 to No. 7, changing places with Ochoa.

Wie's No. 3 ranking at the start was a subject of debate because she had not won a professional tournament. Her opening position was based upon the rankings protocol then in effect, requiring a minimum of 15 tournaments over a two-year rolling period, which was within the number of events Wie had played. On August 3, the Rolex Rankings Board eliminated the minimum number and instead introduced a minimum divisor of 35 tournaments over the period.

Having 16 tournaments on her record, Wie finished the year ranked No. 13 in the world. Her best was a tie for second place in the Evian Masters.

The Rolex Rankings—which was developed at the May 2004 World Congress of Women's Golf—is sanctioned by the five major women's professional golf tours: the Ladies Professional Golf Association (LPGA), Ladies European Tour (LET), Ladies Professional Golfers' Association of Japan (JLPGA), Korea Ladies Professional Golf Association (KLPGA), Australian Ladies Professional Golf (ALPG) and the Ladies' Golf Union (LGU).

The five major golf tours and the LGU developed the rankings and the protocol that governs the ranking while R2IT, an independent software development company, was retained to develop the software and to maintain the rankings on a weekly basis. The official events from all of the tours are taken into account and points are awarded according to the strength of the field, with the exception of the four major championships on the LPGA Tour schedule and the Futures Tour events, which have a fixed points distribution. The players' points averages are determined by taking the number of points awarded over a two-year rolling period and dividing that by the number of tournaments played, with a minimum divisor of 35.

The Rolex Rankings are updated and released following the completion of the previous week's tournaments around the world.

Rolex Rankings
(As of December 31, 2006)

Ranking	Player	Country	No. of Events	Total Points	Points Average
1	Annika Sorenstam	Swe	43	620.21	14.42
2	Lorena Ochoa	Mex	50	589.06	11.78
3	Karrie Webb	Aus	46	485.69	10.56
4	Cristie Kerr	USA	49	374.25	7.64
5	Juli Inkster	USA	41	281.18	6.86
6	Ai Miyazato	Jpn	53	345.68	6.52
7	Paula Creamer	USA	57	354.52	6.22
8	Jeong Jang	Kor	58	353.23	6.09
9	Shiho Ohyama	Jpn	67	391.14	5.84
10	Se Ri Pak	Kor	36	179.16	4.98
11	Pat Hurst	USA	48	236.19	4.92
12	Hee-Won Han	Kor	56	275.40	4.92
13	Michelle Wie	USA	16	171.42	4.90
14	Mi Hyun Kim	Kor	59	285.29	4.84
15	Yuri Fudoh	Jpn	50	241.75	4.84
16	Julieta Granada	Pry	42	172.15	4.10
17	Seon-Hwa Lee	Kor	53	207.88	3.92
18	Akiko Fukushima	Jpn	51	199.00	3.90
19	Sakura Yokomine	Jpn	66	254.73	3.86
20	Natalie Gulbis	USA	54	204.41	3.79
21	Jee Young Lee	Kor	39	144.23	3.70
22	Ji-Hee Lee	Kor	57	210.00	3.68
23	Sherri Steinhauer	USA	51	187.28	3.67
24	Sophie Gustafson	Swe	53	193.72	3.66
25	Morgan Pressel	USA	31	123.81	3.54
26	Mi-Jeong Jeon	Kor	63	222.01	3.52
27	Hyun-Ju Shin	Kor	63	221.31	3.51
28	Brittany Lang	USA	34	117.60	3.36
29	Brittany Lincicome	USA	44	131.62	2.99
30	Stacy Prammanasudh	USA	51	152.17	2.98
31	Miho Koga	Jpn	64	185.01	2.89
32	Meena Lee	Kor	59	164.44	2.79
33	Ji-Yai Shin	Kor	17	91.79	2.62
34	Shi-Hyun Ahn	Kor	44	112.43	2.56
35	Shinobu Moromizato	Jpn	44	110.79	2.52
36	Laura Davies	Eng	58	140.91	2.43
37	Gloria Hee Jung Park	Kor	55	130.75	2.38
38	Momoko Ueda	Jpn	36	85.31	2.37
39	Joo Mi Kim	Kor	52	122.04	2.35
40	Wendy Ward	USA	49	114.24	2.33
41	Young Kim	Kor	50	116.26	2.33
42	Yun-Jye Wei	Twn	65	147.99	2.28
43	Michele Redman	USA	43	96.35	2.24
44	Candie Kung	Twn	52	115.80	2.23
45	Gwladys Nocera	Fra	40	88.59	2.21
46	Catriona Matthew	Sco	47	101.63	2.16
47	Karine Icher	Fra	53	114.59	2.16
48	Liselotte Neumann	Swe	44	93.75	2.13
49	Mie Nakata	Jpn	59	124.11	2.10
50	Nikki Campbell	Aus	57	119.07	2.09

Ranking	Player	Country	No. of Events	Total Points	Points Average
51	Suzann Pettersen	Nor	36	74.72	2.08
52	Heather Young	USA	52	106.56	2.05
53	Kasumi Fujii	Jpn	51	103.84	2.04
54	Akane Iijima	Jpn	59	119.87	2.03
55	Sung-Ah Yim	Kor	52	104.88	2.02
56	Jin-Joo Hong	Kor	22	70.38	2.01
57	Diana D'Alessio	USA	35	69.82	1.99
58	Beth Daniel	USA	33	69.09	1.97
59	Christina Kim	USA	60	118.37	1.97
60	Michiko Hattori	Jpn	58	114.15	1.97
61	Kaori Higo	Jpn	55	107.91	1.96
62	Marisa Baena	Col	42	79.88	1.90
63	Rachel Hetherington	Aus	52	96.26	1.85
64	Helen Alfredsson	Swe	43	79.29	1.84
65	Na Yeon Choi	Kor	29	63.91	1.83
66	Angela Stanford	USA	50	89.76	1.80
67	Hiromi Mogi	Jpn	68	119.86	1.76
68	Soo-Yun Kang	Kor	52	91.33	1.76
69	Midori Yoneyama	Jpn	56	96.23	1.72
70	Nicole Castrale	USA	40	68.64	1.72
71	Hee-Young Park	Kor	29	59.45	1.70
72	Lorie Kane	Can	54	91.54	1.70
73	Carin Koch	Swe	50	83.36	1.67
74	Chieko Amanuma	Jpn	61	101.69	1.67
75	Junko Omote	Jpn	59	97.87	1.66
76	Mikiyo Nishizuka	Jpn	64	105.52	1.65
77	Laura Diaz	USA	45	73.96	1.64
78	Maria Hjorth	Swe	61	99.66	1.63
79	Michie Ohba	Jpn	51	82.86	1.62
80	Karen Stupples	Eng	49	78.60	1.60
81	Il Mi Chung	Kor	55	86.20	1.57
82	Hyun-Hee Moon	Kor	23	50.11	1.43
83	Aree Song	Kor	51	72.82	1.43
84	Kim Saiki	USA	40	57.00	1.43
85	Hiroko Yamaguchi	Jpn	65	91.13	1.40
86	Jeong-Eun Lee	Kor	63	88.05	1.40
87	Nicole Perrot	Chl	39	53.68	1.38
88	Patricia Meunier-Lebouc	Fra	45	61.40	1.36
89	Yuko Saitoh	Jpn	61	82.18	1.35
90	Kyeong Bae	Kor	53	70.53	1.33
91	Bo Bae Song	Kor	38	49.91	1.31
92	Saiki Fujita	Jpn	43	55.56	1.29
93	Veronica Zorzi	Ity	34	45.20	1.29
94	Jennifer Rosales	Phl	40	51.07	1.28
95	Lindsey Wright	Aus	51	64.81	1.27
96	Reilley Rankin	USA	46	58.16	1.26
97	Yukari Baba	Jpn	63	79.09	1.26
98	Ya Huei Lu	Twn	47	58.51	1.24
99	Rosie Jones	USA	29	43.35	1.24
100	Jae-Hee Bae	Kor	41	49.56	1.21

Ranking	Player	Country	No. of Events	Total Points	Points Average
101	Yui Kawahara	Jpn	66	79.19	1.20
102	Mitsuko Kawasaki	Jpn	65	76.43	1.18
103	Nancy Scranton	USA	49	57.55	1.17
104	Grace Park	Kor	39	45.39	1.16
105	Sarah Lee	Kor	46	52.87	1.15
106	Tamie Durdin	Aus	56	63.55	1.13
107	Silvia Cavalleri	Ity	43	48.77	1.13
108	Young Jo	Kor	52	57.74	1.11
109	Soo Young Moon	Kor	37	41.08	1.11
110	Julie Lu	Twn	58	63.56	1.10
111	Marcy Hart	USA	43	45.92	1.07
112	Iben Tinning	Den	28	35.98	1.03
113	Rui Kitada	Jpn	59	60.25	1.02
114	Sun-Ju Ahn	Kor	17	35.61	1.02
115	Birdie Kim	Kor	51	50.98	1.00
116	Yun-Hee Ku	Kor	67	66.50	0.99
117	Namika Omata	Jpn	28	33.55	0.96
118	Tina Barrett	USA	46	43.57	0.95
119	Jill McGill	USA	46	43.15	0.94
120	Kuniko Maeda	Jpn	63	58.70	0.93
121	Yuriko Ohtsuka	Jpn	61	56.66	0.93
122	Brandie Burton	USA	41	38.06	0.93
123	Jimin Kang	Kor	42	38.65	0.92
124	Sun Young Yoo	Kor	46	41.81	0.91
125	Eun-A Lim	Kor	22	31.41	0.90
126	Janice Moodie	Sco	34	31.11	0.89
127	Ayako Uehara	Jpn	61	53.55	0.88
128	Becky Morgan	Wal	50	43.53	0.87
129	Eun-Hye Lee	Kor	63	54.53	0.87
130	Young-A Yang	Kor	49	41.88	0.85
131	Nina Reis	Swe	27	29.15	0.83
132	Hsiu-Feng Tseng	Twn	39	32.29	0.83
133	Sherri Turner	USA	38	30.81	0.81
134	Karin Sjodin	Swe	26	28.22	0.81
135	Hae-Jung Kim	Kor	21	28.04	0.80
136	Mihoko Takahashi	Jpn	56	44.61	0.80
137	Dorothy Delasin	USA	49	38.92	0.79
138	Wendy Doolan	Aus	34	27.26	0.78
139	Karen Margrethe Juul	Den	36	27.70	0.77
140	Eriko Moriyama	Jpn	27	26.91	0.77
141	Miriam Nagl	Ger	41	31.51	0.77
142	Linda Wessberg	Swe	39	29.73	0.76
143	Izumi Narita	Jpn	34	26.65	0.76
144	Riikka Hakkarainen	Fin	34	26.64	0.76
145	Nobuko Kizawa	Jpn	56	42.59	0.76
146	Cecilia Ekelundh	Swe	44	33.28	0.76
147	Yun-Joo Jeong	Kor	56	42.30	0.76
148	Yuka Shiroto	Jpn	59	44.38	0.75
149	Keiko Sasaki	Jpn	65	47.71	0.73
150	Itsumi Okada	Jpn	37	26.98	0.73

ROLEX RANKINGS / 5

Ranking	Player	Country	No. of Events	Total Points	Points Average
151	Lynnette Brooky	NZl	33	25.26	0.72
152	Yeo-Jin Kang	Kor	39	28.06	0.72
153	Stephanie Arricau	Fra	38	27.07	0.71
154	Chie Arimura	Jpn	19	24.90	0.71
155	Maiko Wakabayashi	Jpn	16	24.86	0.71
156	Yuko Shinsakaue	Jpn	33	24.74	0.71
157	Tracy Hanson	USA	38	26.83	0.71
158	Becky Brewerton	Wal	32	24.59	0.70
159	Nikki Garrett	Aus	23	24.54	0.70
160	Ran Hong	Kor	29	24.50	0.70
161	Amy Yang	Kor	5	24.48	0.70
162	Eun-Hee Ji	Kor	27	24.41	0.70
163	Rebecca Hudson	Eng	30	24.39	0.70
164	Ji-Yeon Han	Kor	58	40.06	0.69
165	Yuka Irie	Jpn	58	39.98	0.69
166	Allison Hanna	USA	39	26.63	0.68
167	Kaori Nakamichi	Jpn	59	40.25	0.68
168	Anja Monke	Ger	37	25.11	0.68
169	Mineko Nasu	Jpn	61	40.86	0.67
170	Jinnie Lee	Kor	42	28.04	0.67
171	Toshimi Kimura	Jpn	59	39.30	0.67
172	Ai Ogawa	Jpn	62	40.98	0.66
173	Minea Blomqvist	Fin	39	25.75	0.66
174	Trish Johnson	Eng	31	22.83	0.65
175	Sophie Sandolo	Ity	36	22.82	0.63
176	Virginie Lagoutte	Fra	33	22.09	0.63
177	Becky Iverson	USA	39	24.42	0.63
178	Jeong-Eun Lee	Kor	24	21.86	0.62
179	Michelle Ellis	Aus	37	23.04	0.62
180	Yoko Inoue	Jpn	33	21.77	0.62
181	Tomomi Hirose	Jpn	36	22.30	0.62
182	Candy Hannemann	Bra	43	26.62	0.62
183	Amy Hung	Twn	48	28.85	0.60
184	Moira Dunn	USA	47	28.10	0.60
185	Giulia Sergas	Ity	42	25.08	0.60
186	Johanna Head	Eng	45	26.72	0.59
187	Kyoko Kadokawa	Jpn	34	20.74	0.59
188	Yuka Tonsho	Jpn	32	20.18	0.58
189	Sophie Giquel	Fra	33	19.49	0.56
190	Rebecca Stevenson	Aus	31	19.46	0.56
191	Nadina Light	Aus	48	26.50	0.55
192	Beth Bader	USA	48	26.34	0.55
193	Mayumi Shimomura	Jpn	43	23.46	0.55
194	Catherine Cartwright	USA	46	25.08	0.55
195	Virada Nirapathpongporn	Tha	38	20.72	0.55
196	Leta Lindley	USA	27	18.97	0.54
197	Joanne Mills	Aus	39	21.13	0.54
198	Noriko Aso	Jpn	60	32.42	0.54
199	Mikaela Parmlid	Swe	44	23.72	0.54
200	Meg Mallon	USA	32	18.76	0.54

Official World Golf Ranking
(As of December 31, 2006)

Ranking		Player	Country	Points Average	Total Points	No. of Events	04/05 Points Lost	2006 Points Gained
1	(1)	Tiger Woods	USA	20.41	857.41	42	-644.06	746.28
2	(7)	Jim Furyk	USA	8.88	479.58	54	-235.88	477.66
3	(3)	Phil Mickelson	USA	7.17	293.99	41	-364.08	291.82
4	(9)	Adam Scott	Aus	7.03	358.27	51	-241.21	365.29
5	(5)	Ernie Els	SAf	6.05	290.24	48	-359.71	272.52
6	(4)	Retief Goosen	SAf	5.61	336.53	60	-361.48	268.67
7	(2)	Vijay Singh	Fij	5.58	340.28	61	-554.44	278.79
8	(17)	Padraig Harrington	Ire	5.46	300.15	55	-201.94	294.03
9	(13)	Luke Donald	Eng	5.25	267.74	51	-226.83	260.65
10	(50)	Geoff Ogilvy	Aus	5.21	260.51	50	-169.78	302.56
11	(6)	Sergio Garcia	Spn	5.12	250.70	49	-269.34	187.63
12	(32)	Henrik Stenson	Swe	4.62	240.00	52	-152.58	245.54
13	(62)	Trevor Immelman	SAf	4.58	247.45	54	-125.37	263.67
14	(11)	David Howell	Eng	3.80	208.92	55	-197.54	172.93
15	(52)	Paul Casey	Eng	3.75	198.93	53	-119.19	202.89
16	(19)	Davis Love	USA	3.69	173.30	47	-163.29	150.07
17	(8)	Colin Montgomerie	Sco	3.64	211.22	58	-190.69	134.47
18	(26)	Jose M. Olazabal	Spn	3.54	183.87	52	-159.68	164.63
19	(15)	David Toms	USA	3.46	162.79	47	-214.34	166.33
20	(10)	Chris DiMarco	USA	3.46	183.14	53	-209.60	158.93
21	(24)	Nick O'Hern	Aus	3.33	166.53	50	-156.52	137.22
22	(30)	Stuart Appleby	Aus	3.33	183.05	55	-169.80	186.02
23	(20)	Tim Clark	SAf	3.24	181.61	56	-181.14	148.93
24	(39)	Shingo Katayama	Jpn	3.18	168.38	53	-111.17	141.46
25	(16)	Michael Campbell	NZl	3.17	164.66	52	-159.04	101.72
26	(27)	Stewart Cink	USA	3.12	162.10	52	-179.23	166.05
27	(38)	Chad Campbell	USA	3.10	161.07	52	-152.51	167.23
28	(12)	Angel Cabrera	Arg	3.08	154.15	50	-153.16	120.68
29	(31)	K.J. Choi	Kor	3.01	183.35	61	-146.90	154.34
30	(47)	Rod Pampling	Aus	2.93	160.91	55	-144.38	170.47
31	(216)	Robert Karlsson	Swe	2.92	166.60	57	-54.60	182.33
32	(112)	Joe Durant	USA	2.87	152.29	53	-61.67	147.92
33	(106)	Y.E. Yang	Kor	2.86	134.57	47	-64.01	124.74
34	(59)	Ian Poulter	Eng	2.82	174.67	62	-128.86	180.20
35	(18)	Darren Clarke	NIr	2.81	118.07	42	-174.34	90.77
36	(53)	Carl Pettersson	Swe	2.71	176.02	65	-127.99	167.30
37	(376)	Jeev Milkha Singh	Ind	2.63	192.07	73	-38.09	207.14
38	(65)	Lucas Glover	USA	2.61	153.74	59	-101.58	144.58
39	(71)	Rory Sabbatini	SAf	2.58	129.00	50	-129.28	169.24
40	(294)	Brett Wetterich	USA	2.56	140.74	55	-51.57	163.22
41	(34)	Ben Crane	USA	2.55	119.93	47	-99.88	85.35
42	(60)	Niclas Fasth	Swe	2.54	127.20	50	-88.33	106.73
43	(51)	Stephen Ames	Can	2.52	113.55	45	-139.70	139.13
44	(99)	Arron Oberholser	USA	2.51	110.34	44	-90.32	137.64
45	(48)	Mike Weir	Can	2.50	120.10	48	-124.73	136.82
46	(22)	Thomas Bjorn	Den	2.48	128.77	52	-148.68	100.31
47	(35)	Robert Allenby	Aus	2.47	153.01	62	-147.30	117.38
48	(410)	Johan Edfors	Swe	2.46	120.71	49	-39.31	144.69
49	(41)	Lee Westwood	Eng	2.39	128.89	54	-128.15	120.69
50	(83)	Bradley Dredge	Wal	2.37	106.68	45	-66.13	88.45

( ) Ranking in brackets indicates position as of December 31, 2005.

OFFICIAL WORLD GOLF RANKING / 7

Ranking		Player	Country	Points Average	Total Points	No. of Events	04/05 Points Lost	2006 Points Gained
51	(86)	Justin Rose	Eng	2.36	141.65	60	-83.36	130.62
52	(28)	Scott Verplank	USA	2.34	116.91	50	-143.07	106.30
53	(23)	Bart Bryant	USA	2.27	118.28	52	-128.10	69.88
54	(57)	Zach Johnson	USA	2.20	125.65	57	-140.85	138.20
55	(143)	Charl Schwartzel	SAf	2.19	131.28	60	-70.16	134.74
56	(43)	Tom Lehman	USA	2.11	92.72	44	-110.80	98.32
57	(222)	Shaun Micheel	USA	2.09	125.14	60	-50.49	136.03
58	(14)	Kenny Perry	USA	2.02	90.77	45	-156.82	47.54
59	(265)	Anthony Wall	Eng	2.02	104.82	52	-39.97	113.48
60	(151)	Brett Quigley	USA	2.02	128.99	64	-73.19	142.22
61	(69)	Tom Pernice, Jr.	USA	2.01	130.66	65	-101.20	122.44
62	(25)	Fred Couples	USA	2.01	84.40	42	-117.80	65.10
63	(337T)	Steve Stricker	USA	2.00	79.90	40	-34.83	94.45
64	(76)	Paul Broadhurst	Eng	1.99	103.34	52	-87.89	105.04
65	(70)	Richard Green	Aus	1.98	100.99	51	-101.85	108.12
66	(49)	Tim Herron	USA	1.94	106.52	55	-110.22	92.15
67	(37)	Sean O'Hair	USA	1.92	115.34	60	-81.43	87.63
68	(115)	John Senden	Aus	1.91	118.12	62	-69.79	107.30
69	(74)	Vaughn Taylor	USA	1.90	110.32	58	-93.10	103.44
70	(190)	J.J. Henry	USA	1.89	113.65	60	-67.69	130.79
71	(21)	Paul McGinley	Ire	1.89	98.03	52	-130.89	43.30
72	(213)	Dean Wilson	USA	1.88	114.49	61	-54.49	125.03
73	(40)	Miguel A. Jimenez	Spn	1.85	99.69	54	-146.19	100.47
74	(191)	Ben Curtis	USA	1.81	95.77	53	-48.65	102.23
75	(110)	Thongchai Jaidee	Tha	1.80	91.55	51	-64.52	85.52
76	(153)	Jose Manuel Lara	Spn	1.79	102.13	57	-47.47	92.02
77	(84)	Jason Bohn	USA	1.77	100.94	57	-72.90	82.96
78	(348)	Nathan Green	Aus	1.76	112.73	64	-40.75	129.84
79	(142)	Ryan Moore	USA	1.72	68.99	40	-35.91	61.06
80	(92)	Toru Taniguchi	Jpn	1.71	95.89	56	-74.38	84.91
81	(336)	Troy Matteson	USA	1.69	99.97	59	-20.55	97.17
82	(55)	Charles Howell	USA	1.69	99.48	59	-107.43	79.33
83	(117)	Simon Khan	Eng	1.65	84.10	51	-58.30	81.42
84	(123)	Jyoti Randhawa	Ind	1.64	77.00	47	-56.35	72.15
85	(45)	Fred Funk	USA	1.63	95.92	59	-135.24	86.37
86	(46)	Peter Lonard	Aus	1.61	93.25	58	-126.35	71.03
87	(170)	Aaron Baddeley	Aus	1.61	88.33	55	-54.81	92.58
88	(197)	Simon Dyson	Eng	1.59	101.82	64	-53.13	111.59
89	(79)	Stephen Dodd	Wal	1.58	74.47	47	-69.99	60.43
90	(1181T)	J.B. Holmes	USA	1.57	62.85	40	-30.42	93.27
91	(149)	Taichi Teshima	Jpn	1.56	82.53	53	-38.97	68.67
92	(72)	Billy Mayfair	USA	1.54	92.27	60	-93.46	79.27
93	(89)	S.K. Ho	Kor	1.53	81.13	53	-66.52	72.88
94	(88)	Greg Owen	Eng	1.51	80.00	53	-70.88	85.25
95	(66)	Jerry Kelly	USA	1.49	92.09	62	-107.73	89.42
96	(230T)	Hideto Tanihara	Jpn	1.47	79.27	54	-42.23	82.74
97	(107)	Jesper Parnevik	Swe	1.45	72.57	50	-75.24	78.16
98	(156)	Jonathan Byrd	USA	1.45	73.69	51	-59.34	77.53
99	(42)	Brandt Jobe	USA	1.44	79.21	55	-73.91	52.25
100	(165)	Hidemasa Hoshino	Jpn	1.43	70.23	49	-39.93	62.06

( ) Ranking in brackets indicates position as of December 31, 2005.

8 / OFFICIAL WORLD GOLF RANKING

Ranking		Player	Country	Points Average	Total Points	No. of Events	04/05 Points Lost	2006 Points Gained
101	(96)	Paul Sheehan	Aus	1.43	87.08	61	-68.93	75.19
102	(64)	Ted Purdy	USA	1.42	95.09	67	-108.97	70.89
103	(282)	Andrew Buckle	Aus	1.41	73.37	52	-32.81	84.46
104	(82)	Bo Van Pelt	USA	1.41	85.81	61	-91.02	76.35
105	(121)	Anders Hansen	Den	1.40	68.67	49	-62.88	67.60
106	(93)	Raphael Jacquelin	Frn	1.38	69.12	50	-64.87	56.50
107	(144)	Corey Pavin	USA	1.38	63.40	46	-54.53	65.94
108	(44)	Shigeki Maruyama	Jpn	1.37	80.85	59	-113.15	53.99
109	(384)	Andres Romero	Arg	1.34	59.09	44	-18.07	64.07
110	(105)	Heath Slocum	USA	1.34	79.10	59	-61.18	57.74
111	(85)	David Smail	NZl	1.34	68.24	51	-62.67	50.32
112	(234T)	Richard S. Johnson	Swe	1.33	68.07	51	-44.30	76.42
113	(125)	Jeff Sluman	USA	1.32	75.39	57	-69.59	76.06
114	(288)	Frank Lickliter	USA	1.32	81.83	62	-34.04	84.37
115	(75)	Nick Dougherty	Eng	1.30	79.49	61	-88.95	58.88
116	(68)	Kenneth Ferrie	Eng	1.29	68.61	53	-66.47	33.82
117	(307)	Camilo Villegas	Col	1.29	82.66	64	-49.92	110.59
118	(266)	Kevin Stadler	USA	1.28	84.58	66	-43.96	98.50
119	(230T)	John Bickerton	Eng	1.28	72.69	57	-39.82	75.73
120	(300T)	Marc Warren	Sco	1.28	67.58	53	-17.99	64.71
121	(207)	Ricardo Gonzalez	Arg	1.27	51.97	41	-37.04	56.19
122	(179)	Tetsuji Hiratsuka	Jpn	1.27	72.20	57	-44.14	66.12
123	(147)	Peter O'Malley	Aus	1.25	63.95	51	-44.75	57.77
124	(232)	Mathew Goggin	Aus	1.25	72.66	58	-32.46	67.73
125	(91)	David Lynn	Eng	1.24	60.97	49	-66.14	48.52
126	(33)	Justin Leonard	USA	1.23	62.88	51	-120.24	42.66
127	(180)	John Rollins	USA	1.23	72.52	59	-58.81	79.45
128	(100)	Keiichiro Fukabori	Jpn	1.23	67.58	55	-55.84	44.43
129	(148)	G. Fernandez-Castano	Spn	1.20	65.79	55	-37.61	64.24
130	(90)	Jason Gore	USA	1.19	58.42	49	-47.56	36.34
131	(175)	Daniel Chopra	Swe	1.19	88.01	74	-62.78	83.79
132	(56)	Graeme McDowell	Nir	1.18	63.89	54	-109.27	48.47
133	(114)	Bob Estes	USA	1.18	60.09	51	-63.60	59.57
134	(73)	Olin Browne	USA	1.17	69.18	59	-70.29	40.00
135	(303)	Paul Goydos	USA	1.17	46.77	40	-16.95	43.99
136	(138)	Woody Austin	USA	1.16	70.90	61	-62.80	65.26
137	(192)	Soren Kjeldsen	Den	1.16	63.87	55	-38.15	59.20
138	(101)	Steve Flesch	USA	1.16	73.05	63	-83.03	69.07
139	(157)	Billy Andrade	USA	1.16	57.79	50	-53.99	57.58
140	(194)	Liang Wen-chong	Chi	1.15	63.33	55	-33.86	58.36
141	(184)	Craig Barlow	USA	1.14	54.79	48	-48.39	60.61
142	(29)	John Daly	USA	1.14	56.79	50	-105.17	10.24
143	(63)	Mark Calcavecchia	USA	1.13	62.09	55	-76.74	34.97
144	(223)	Gary Orr	Sco	1.13	45.15	40	-25.96	43.89
145	(80)	Ryan Palmer	USA	1.13	72.12	64	-94.96	57.63
146	(129)	Fredrik Jacobson	Swe	1.12	49.42	44	-63.75	50.97
147	(311)	Francesco Molinari	Ity	1.12	63.76	57	-25.45	69.85
148	(140)	Steve Lowery	USA	1.10	69.51	63	-63.21	65.70
149	(78)	Joe Ogilvie	USA	1.10	64.72	59	-92.53	56.91
150	(102)	Harrison Frazar	USA	1.08	65.03	60	-61.28	49.06

( ) Ranking in brackets indicates position as of December 31, 2005.

Ranking		Player	Country	Points Average	Total Points	No. of Events	04/05 Points Lost	2006 Points Gained
151	(54)	Bernhard Langer	Ger	1.08	53.05	49	-72.34	36.05
152	(163)	Brett Rumford	Aus	1.08	60.34	56	-49.08	60.04
153	(333)	Chris Couch	USA	1.07	52.66	49	-26.48	58.51
154	(36)	Mark Hensby	Aus	1.07	48.31	45	-118.00	14.79
155	(58)	Steve Elkington	Aus	1.07	42.91	40	-58.96	13.41
156	(200)	Prayad Marksaeng	Tha	1.07	67.55	63	-45.09	62.53
157	(199)	Soren Hansen	Den	1.06	56.43	53	-41.16	55.89
158	(182)	Daisuke Maruyama	Jpn	1.06	59.21	56	-36.25	48.09
159	(122)	Jeff Maggert	USA	1.05	53.63	51	-62.32	58.44
160	(212)	Tomohiro Kondo	Jpn	1.04	55.26	53	-39.92	54.02
161	(241)	Darren Fichardt	SAf	1.04	54.09	52	-37.84	57.52
162	(174)	Charles Warren	USA	1.03	59.68	58	-48.09	57.19
163	(128)	Thaworn Wiratchant	Tha	1.02	59.22	58	-48.76	44.32
164	(1181T)	Martin Kaymer	Ger	1.02	40.75	40	-4.95	45.70
165	(1069)	Rafael Echenique	Arg	1.02	40.63	40	-5.31	45.30
166	(108)	Peter Hanson	Swe	1.01	49.35	49	-52.78	30.73
167	(278T)	Azuma Yano	Jpn	1.01	54.37	54	-20.16	44.04
168	(219)	Bubba Watson	USA	1.00	57.21	57	-32.21	56.83
169	(67)	Brad Faxon	USA	1.00	49.00	49	-73.16	30.29
170	(554)	Ken Duke	USA	0.98	51.89	53	-16.18	58.98
171	(259)	Nick Watney	USA	0.98	58.64	60	-35.43	60.50
172	(249)	Edward Loar	USA	0.97	38.97	40	-19.38	33.72
173	(116)	Pat Perez	USA	0.97	45.57	47	-69.69	38.53
174	(1065)	Craig Kanada	USA	0.96	38.45	40	-4.88	42.67
175	(1181T)	Alvaro Quiros	Spn	0.96	38.34	40	-5.44	43.78
176	(187T)	Katsumasa Miyamoto	Jpn	0.95	53.38	56	-35.45	43.67
177	(315)	Jean Van de Velde	Frn	0.95	38.09	40	-24.34	43.29
178	(164)	Hiroyuki Fujita	Jpn	0.95	51.18	54	-37.37	41.30
179	(296)	Jarrod Lyle	Aus	0.94	49.83	53	-25.83	55.31
180	(158)	Kaname Yokoo	Jpn	0.94	54.30	58	-41.63	42.08
181	(202)	Ryuji Imada	Jpn	0.93	54.21	58	-40.34	56.46
182	(103)	Maarten Lafeber	Hol	0.92	46.10	50	-55.46	27.11
183	(61)	Craig Parry	Aus	0.92	43.31	47	-74.91	25.83
184	(187T)	Shiv Kapur	Ind	0.89	43.84	49	-23.46	34.45
185	(386)	Prom Meesawat	Tha	0.89	43.42	49	-16.71	45.17
186	(161)	Graeme Storm	Eng	0.88	52.71	60	-46.39	42.76
187	(126)	Joey Sindelar	USA	0.87	50.63	58	-66.50	43.35
188	(929T)	Alexander Noren	Swe	0.87	34.90	40	-7.69	41.20
189	(322)	Matt Kuchar	USA	0.87	43.60	50	-21.76	42.71
190	(416)	Tsuneyuki Nakajima	Jpn	0.87	34.87	40	-10.45	33.92
191	(373)	Charlie Wi	Kor	0.87	46.09	53	-27.70	58.81
192	(169)	Paul Lawrie	Sco	0.87	39.88	46	-33.99	27.58
193	(221)	D.J. Trahan	USA	0.87	52.77	61	-31.99	46.15
194T	(473)	Eric Axley	USA	0.86	48.40	56	-10.93	50.18
194T	(328)	Markus Brier	Aut	0.86	44.94	52	-32.14	52.29
196	(131)	Richard Sterne	SAf	0.86	43.60	51	-57.11	28.97
197	(1181T)	Alejandro Canizares	Spn	0.85	34.20	40	-3.73	37.92
198	(341)	Wang Ter-chang	Twn	0.85	33.80	40	-19.08	36.47
199	(141)	Jeff Brehaut	USA	0.84	48.93	58	-46.03	30.17
200	(254)	Brian Gay	USA	0.84	53.44	64	-42.12	56.25

( ) Ranking in brackets indicates position as of December 31, 2005.

Age Groups of Current Top 100 World Ranked Players

Under 25	25-28	29-32	33-36	37-40	40-44	Over 44
			Furyk			
			Mickelson			
		Woods	Harrington			
		Donald	O'Hern	Els		
		Ogilvy	Appleby	Goosen		
		Stenson	Katayama	Olazabal		
		D. Howell	Cink	Toms		
		Casey	K.J. Choi	DiMarco		
		T. Clark	Y.E. Yang	M. Campbell		
		C. Campbell	J.M. Singh	Cabrera		
		Poulter	Wetterich	Pampling		
		Pettersson	Fasth	Karlsson		
		Sabbatini	Weir	D. Clarke		
		Crane	Bjorn	Micheel		
		Oberholser	Allenby	Quigley	V. Singh	
	Scott	Edfors	Westwood	Stricker	Love	
	Garcia	Z. Johnson	Dredge	McGinley	Montgomerie	
	Immelman	Wall	R. Green	D. Wilson	Durant	
	Glover	V. Taylor	Herron	Jaidee	Ames	
	Rose	Henry	Senden	Taniguchi	Verplank	
	Matteson	Curtis	Bohn	Lonard	Bart Bryant	Lehman
Schwartzel	C. Howell	Lara	Khan	Dodd	Broadhurst	K. Perry
O'Hair	Baddeley	N. Green	Randhawa	Teshima	Jimenez	Pernice
Moore	Tanihara	Dyson	S.K. Ho	Mayfair	Parnevik	Couples
J.B. Holmes	Byrd	Hoshino	Owen	Kelly	Jobe	Funk

2006 World Ranking Review

Major Movements

Upward

Name	Net Points Gained	Position 2005	Position 2006
Jim Furyk	242	7	2
Jeev Mikha Singh	169	376	37
Trevor Immelman	138	62	13
Geoff Ogilvy	133	50	10
Robert Karlsson	128	216	31
Adam Scott	124	9	4
Brett Wetterich	112	294	40
Johan Edfors	105	410	48
Tiger Woods	102	1	1
Henrik Stenson	93	32	12
Padraig Harrington	92	17	8
Nathan Green	89	348	78
Joe Durant	86	112	32
Shaun Micheel	86	222	57
Paul Casey	84	52	15
Troy Matteson	77	336	81
Anthony Wall	74	265	59
Dean Wilson	71	213	72
Brett Quigley	69	151	60
J.J. Henry	63	190	70
J.B. Holmes	63	–	90
Y.E. Yang	61	106	33
Camilo Villegas	61	307	117

Downward

Name	Net Points Lost	Position 2005	Position 2006
Vijay Singh	276	2	7
Kenny Perry	109	14	58
Mark Hensby	103	36	154
John Daly	95	29	142
Retief Goosen	93	4	6
Paul McGinley	88	21	71
Ernie Els	87	5	5
Darren Clarke	84	18	35
Sergio Garcia	82	6	11
Justin Leonard	78	33	126
Phil Mickelson	72	3	3

Highest-Rated Events of 2006

	Event	Top 5	Top 15	Top 30	Top 50	Top 100	World Rating Points
1	PGA Championship	5	15	29	47	93	822
2	The Open Championship	5	13	28	48	87	784
3	U.S. Open Championship	5	15	30	49	70	762
4	Masters Tournament	5	15	29	49	66	720
5	The Players Championship	5	13	28	48	81	787
6	WGC - Accenture Match Play	5	14	29	48	64	707
7	WGC - Bridgestone Invitational	5	14	28	47	65	708
8	WGC - American Express Ch.	4	13	27	42	53	608
9	Memorial Tournament	4	10	19	30	59	549
10	Barclays Classic	3	11	20	28	59	535
11	Bay Hill Invitational	4	9	16	30	60	545
12	Wachovia Championship	4	11	17	28	58	532
13	Ford Championship	5	11	18	23	48	515
14	Nissan Open	2	7	17	34	61	536
15	BMW Championship	1	6	13	18	31	306
16	HSBC Champions	2	8	13	18	27	322
17	Cialis Western Open	4	6	13	23	44	442
18	EDS Byron Nelson Champ.	2	9	15	23	47	420
19	FBR Open	2	6	10	21	49	411
20	Chrysler Championship	2	5	10	21	50	425
21	Buick Invitational	2	3	10	20	44	377
22	Verizon Heritage	1	6	12	21	45	365
23	Bank of America Colonial	1	4	10	23	45	353
24	Buick Open	3	6	7	16	34	338
25	The Tour Championship	3	8	15	22	27	335
26	The International	2	7	11	17	34	330
27	BellSouth Classic	2	7	13	20	32	324
28	Sony Open	1	4	8	16	40	312
29	Barclays Scottish Open	1	7	11	15	30	274
30	Alfred Dunhill Links Champ.	1	5	11	14	31	268
31	AT&T Pebble Beach Pro-Am	2	4	9	14	30	277
32	Dubai Desert Classic	3	5	9	11	26	262
33	Deutsche Bank Players	1	4	10	15	29	251
34	Volvo Masters	0	6	11	15	27	245
35	Funai Classic at Disney	1	2	6	13	41	268
36	Zurich Classic of New Orleans	2	4	7	12	31	264
37	Bob Hope Chrysler Classic	1	1	6	14	34	262
38	HSBC World Match Play	3	7	12	14	16	255
39	Deutsche Bank Champ.	3	3	4	9	31	251
40	Mercedes Championships	1	5	8	15	25	233

World Golf Rankings 1968-2006

Year	No. 1	No. 2	No. 3	No. 4	No. 5
1968	Nicklaus	Palmer	Casper	Player	Charles
1969	Nicklaus	Player	Casper	Palmer	Charles
1970	Nicklaus	Player	Casper	Trevino	Charles
1971	Nicklaus	Trevino	Player	Palmer	Casper
1972	Nicklaus	Player	Trevino	Crampton	Palmer
1973	Nicklaus	Weiskopf	Trevino	Player	Crampton
1974	Nicklaus	Miller	Player	Weiskopf	Trevino
1975	Nicklaus	Miller	Weiskopf	Irwin	Player
1976	Nicklaus	Irwin	Miller	Player	Green
1977	Nicklaus	Watson	Green	Irwin	Crenshaw
1978	Watson	Nicklaus	Irwin	Green	Player
1979	Watson	Nicklaus	Irwin	Trevino	Player
1980	Watson	Trevino	Aoki	Crenshaw	Nicklaus
1981	Watson	Rogers	Aoki	Pate	Trevino
1982	Watson	Floyd	Ballesteros	Kite	Stadler
1983	Ballesteros	Watson	Floyd	Norman	Kite
1984	Ballesteros	Watson	Norman	Wadkins	Langer
1985	Ballesteros	Langer	Norman	Watson	Nakajima
1986	Norman	Langer	Ballesteros	Nakajima	Bean
1987	Norman	Ballesteros	Langer	Lyle	Strange
1988	Ballesteros	Norman	Lyle	Faldo	Strange
1989	Norman	Faldo	Ballesteros	Strange	Stewart
1990	Norman	Faldo	Olazabal	Woosnam	Stewart
1991	Woosnam	Faldo	Olazabal	Ballesteros	Norman
1992	Faldo	Couples	Woosnam	Olazabal	Norman
1993	Faldo	Norman	Langer	Price	Couples
1994	Price	Norman	Faldo	Langer	Olazabal
1995	Norman	Price	Langer	Els	Montgomerie
1996	Norman	Lehman	Montgomerie	Els	Couples
1997	Norman	Woods	Price	Els	Love
1998	Woods	O'Meara	Duval	Love	Els
1999	Woods	Duval	Montgomerie	Love	Els
2000	Woods	Els	Duval	Mickelson	Westwood
2001	Woods	Mickelson	Duval	Els	Love
2002	Woods	Mickelson	Els	Garcia	Goosen
2003	Woods	Singh	Els	Love	Furyk
2004	Singh	Woods	Els	Goosen	Mickelson
2005	Woods	Singh	Mickelson	Goosen	Els
2006	Woods	Furyk	Mickelson	Scott	Els

(The World of Professional Golf 1968-1985; World Ranking 1986-2006)

Year	No. 6	No. 7	No. 8	No. 9	No. 10
1968	Boros	Coles	Thomson	Beard	Nagle
1969	Beard	Archer	Trevino	Barber	Sikes
1970	Devlin	Coles	Jacklin	Beard	Huggett
1971	Barber	Crampton	Charles	Devlin	Weiskopf
1972	Jacklin	Weiskopf	Oosterhuis	Heard	Devlin
1973	Miller	Oosterhuis	Wadkins	Heard	Brewer
1974	M. Ozaki	Crampton	Irwin	Green	Heard
1975	Green	Trevino	Casper	Crampton	Watson
1976	Watson	Weiskopf	Marsh	Crenshaw	Geiberger
1977	Marsh	Player	Weiskopf	Floyd	Ballesteros
1978	Crenshaw	Marsh	Ballesteros	Trevino	Aoki
1979	Aoki	Green	Crenshaw	Ballesteros	Wadkins
1980	Pate	Ballesteros	Bean	Irwin	Player
1981	Ballesteros	Graham	Crenshaw	Floyd	Lietzke
1982	Pate	Nicklaus	Rogers	Aoki	Strange
1983	Nicklaus	Nakajima	Stadler	Aoki	Wadkins
1984	Faldo	Nakajima	Stadler	Kite	Peete
1985	Wadkins	O'Meara	Strange	Pavin	Sutton
1986	Tway	Sutton	Strange	Stewart	O'Meara
1987	Woosnam	Stewart	Wadkins	McNulty	Crenshaw
1988	Crenshaw	Woosnam	Frost	Azinger	Calcavecchia
1989	Kite	Olazabal	Calcavecchia	Woosnam	Azinger
1990	Azinger	Ballesteros	Kite	McNulty	Calcavecchia
1991	Couples	Langer	Stewart	Azinger	Davis
1992	Langer	Cook	Price	Azinger	Love
1993	Azinger	Woosnam	Kite	Love	Pavin
1994	Els	Couples	Montgomerie	M. Ozaki	Pavin
1995	Pavin	Faldo	Couples	M. Ozaki	Elkington
1996	Faldo	Mickelson	M. Ozaki	Love	O'Meara
1997	Mickelson	Montgomerie	M. Ozaki	Lehman	O'Meara
1998	Price	Montgomerie	Westwood	Singh	Mickelson
1999	Westwood	Singh	Price	Mickelson	O'Meara
2000	Montgomerie	Love	Sutton	Singh	Lehman
2001	Garcia	Toms	Singh	Clarke	Goosen
2002	Toms	Harrington	Singh	Love	Montgomerie
2003	Weir	Goosen	Harrington	Toms	Perry
2004	Harrington	Garcia	Weir	Love	Cink
2005	Garcia	Furyk	Montgomerie	Scott	DiMarco
2006	Goosen	Singh	Harrington	Donald	Ogilvy

World's Winners of 2006

U.S. PGA TOUR

Mercedes Championships	Stuart Appleby
Sony Open in Hawaii	David Toms
Bob Hope Chrysler Classic	Chad Campbell
Buick Invitational	Tiger Woods
FBR Open	J.B. Holmes
AT&T Pebble Beach National Pro-Am	Arron Oberholser
Nissan Open	Rory Sabbatini
WGC - Accenture Match Play Championship	Geoff Ogilvy
Chrysler Classic of Tucson	Kirk Triplett
Ford Championship at Doral	Tiger Woods (3)
Honda Classic	Luke Donald
Bay Hill Invitational	Rod Pampling
The Players Championship	Stephen Ames
BellSouth Classic	Phil Mickelson
Masters Tournament	Phil Mickelson (2)
Verizon Heritage	Aaron Baddeley
Shell Houston Open	Stuart Appleby (2)
Zurich Classic of New Orleans	Chris Couch
Wachovia Championship	Jim Furyk
EDS Byron Nelson Championship	Brett Wetterich
Bank of America Colonial	Tim Herron
FedEx St. Jude Classic	Jeff Maggert
Memorial Tournament	Carl Pettersson
Barclays Classic	Vijay Singh
U.S. Open Championship	Geoff Ogilvy (2)
Booz Allen Classic	Ben Curtis
Buick Championship	J.J. Henry
Cialis Western Open	Trevor Immelman
John Deere Classic	John Senden
B.C. Open	John Rollins
U.S. Bank Championship in Milwaukee	Corey Pavin
Buick Open	Tiger Woods (5)
The International	Dean Wilson
PGA Championship	Tiger Woods (6)
WGC - Bridgestone Invitational	Tiger Woods (7)
Reno-Tahoe Open	Will MacKenzie
Deutsche Bank Championship	Tiger Woods (8)
Canadian Open	Jim Furyk (2)
84 Lumber Classic	Ben Curtis (2)
Valero Texas Open	Eric Axley
Southern Farm Bureau Classic	D.J. Trahan
Chrysler Classic of Greensboro	Davis Love
Frys.com Open	Troy Matteson
Funai Classic at the Walt Disney World Resort	Joe Durant
Chrysler Championship	K.J. Choi
The Tour Championship	Adam Scott (2)
WGC - Barbados World Cup	Bernhard Langer (2)/Marcel Siem

SPECIAL EVENTS

Tavistock Cup	Isleworth
CVS Charity Classic	Nick Price/Tim Clark
Merrill Lynch Shootout	Jerry Kelly/Rod Pampling (2)
Callaway Golf Pebble Beach Invitational	Jason Bohn
PGA Grand Slam of Golf	Tiger Woods (10)
Del Webb Father-Son Challenge	Bernhard Langer/Stefan Langer
Target World Challenge	Tiger Woods (11)

NATIONWIDE TOUR

Movistar Panama Championship	Tripp Isenhour
Chitimacha Louisiana Open	Johnson Wagner
Livermore Valley Wine Country Championship	Tripp Isenhour (2)
Athens Regional Foundation Classic	Paul Gow
BMW Charity Pro-Am at The Cliffs	Ken Duke
Virginia Beach Open	Andrew Buckle
Rheem Classic	Darron Stiles
Henrico County Open	Matt Kuchar
The Rex Hospital Open	Brenden Pappas
LaSalle Bank Open	Jason Dufner
Knoxville Open	Hunter Haas
Chattanooga Classic	Kyle Reifers
Peek'n Peak Classic	John Merrick
Scholarship America Showdown	Brandt Snedeker
Price Cutter Charity Championship	Doug LaBelle
Preferred Health Systems Wichita Open	Kevin Johnson
Cox Classic	Johnson Wagner (2)
Xerox Classic	Kevin Stadler (2)
Northeast Pennsylvania Classic	Craig Bowden
National Mining Association Pete Dye Classic	Jason Enloe
Legend Financial Group Classic	Gavin Coles
Utah Energy Solutions Championship	Craig Kanada
Albertsons Boise Open	Kevin Stadler (3)
Oregon Classic	Cliff Kresge
Mark Christopher Charity Classic	Kevin Na
Permian Basin Charity Golf Classic	Brandt Snedeker (2)
PalmettoPride Classic	Michael Sim
Miccosukee Championship	Bryce Molder
Nationwide Tour Championship	Craig Kanada (2)

CANADIAN TOUR

Yes! Golf BCR Classic	Rob Oppenheim
Yes! Golf BCR Challenge	Brian Guetz
Northern California Classic	Matt Hansen
Diablo Grande California Classic	Lee Williamson
Corona Mazatlan Classic	Rob Oppenheim (2)
Greataer Vancouver Charity Classic	Lee Williamson (2)
Times Colonist Open	Mike Grob
Telus Edmonton Open	Stephen Gangluff
MTS Classic	Josh Habig
Casino de Montreal Open	Wes Heffernan
Fallsview Casino Resort Pro-Am Classic	Stephen Gangluff (2)
Canadian Tour Championship	Stuart Anderson

TOUR DE LAS AMERICAS (SOUTH AMERICA)

Abierto Movistar de Guatemala	Miguel Carballo
Abierto del Sur Personal	Luciano Giometti
Kai Fieberg Costa Rica Open	Johan Axgren
Abierto del Centro	Angel Cabrera
Copa 3 Diamantes Mitsubishi Tour	Otto Solis
TLA Players Championship	Julio Zapata
Venezuela Open	Fabian Gomez
Colombia Open	Manuel Merizalde
Torneo de Maestros Argentina	Andres Romero
Samsung Brazil Classic	Paulo Pinto
Abierto de San Luis	Rafael Gomez
Argentina Open	Rafael Echenique (2)
Corona Mexico Open	Fabrizio Zanotti

EUROPEAN TOUR

Abu Dhabi Golf Championship	Chris DiMarco
Commercialbank Qatar Masters	Henrik Stenson
Dubai Desert Classic	Tiger Woods (2)
Madeira Island Open Caixa Geral de Depositos	Jean Van de Velde
Algarve Open de Portugal Caixa Geral de Depositos	Paul Broadhurst
Andalucia Open de Espana Valle Romano	Niclas Fasth
Telecom Italia Open	Francesco Molinari
Quinn Direct British Masters	Johan Edfors (2)
Nissan Irish Open	Thomas Bjorn
BMW Championship	David Howell
Celtic Manor Wales Open	Robert Karlsson
BA-CA Golf Open	Markus Brier
Aa St. Omer Open	Cesar Monasterio
Johnnie Walker Championship at Gleneagles	Paul Casey
Open de France ALSTOM	John Bickerton
Smurfit Kappa European Open	Stephen Dodd
Barclays Scottish Open	Johan Edfors (3)
The Open Championship	Tiger Woods (4)
Deutsche Bank Players' Championship of Europe	Robert Karlsson (2)
EnterCard Scandinavian Masters	Marc Warren
KLM Open	Simon Dyson (2)
Imperial Collection Russian Open	Alejandro Canizares
BMW International Open	Henrik Stenson (2)
Omega European Masters	Bradley Dredge
HSBC World Match Play	Paul Casey (2)
Banco Madrid Valle Romano Open de Madrid	Ian Poulter
The Ryder Cup	Europe
WGC - American Express Championship	Tiger Woods (9)
Alfred Dunhill Links Championship	Padraig Harrington
Mallorca Classic	Niclas Fasth (2)
Volvo Masters	Jeev Milkha Singh (2)

CHALLENGE TOUR

Estoril Challenge	Kyron Sullivan
Tusker Kenya Open	Johan Axgren (2)
Peugeot Challenge R.C.G. El Prat	David Drysdale
Tessali Metaponto Open di Puglia e Basilicata	Anthony Snobeck
Parco di Monza Challenge	Alvaro Salto
Telenet Trophy	Toni Karjalainen
Tikida Hotels Agadir Moroccan Classic	Adrien Mork
Morson International Pro-Am Challenge	Alvaro Quiros
Thomas Bjorn Open	Marcus Higley
Lexus Open	Kalle Brink
Credit Suisse Challenge	Francisco Cea
Open Mahou de Madrid	Juan Parron
Scottish Challenge	Sam Walker
Texbond Open	Carlos Del Moral
MAN NO Open	Rafael Cabrera Bello
Ryder Cup Wales Challenge	Sion E. Bebb
Ireland Ryder Cup Challenge	John Wade
Vodafone Challenge	Martin Kaymer
Rolex Trophy	Alexander Noren
ECCO Tour Championship	James Heath
Telia Challenge Waxolm	Rafael Echenique
Open des Volcans - Challenge de France	Martin Kaymer (2)
OKI Mahou Challenge de Espana	Adrien Mork (2)
Kazakhstan Open	Mark Pilkington
Golf Open International de Toulouse	Julien Foret
Apulia San Domenico Grand Final	James Hepworth

ASIAN TOUR

The Royal Trophy	Europe
Pakistan Open	Chris Rodgers
Maybank Malaysian Open	Charlie Wi
Enjoy Jakarta HSBC Indonesia Open	Simon Dyson
OSIM Singapore Masters	Mardan Mamat
TCL Classic	Johan Edfors
Volvo China Open	Jeev Milkha Singh
BMW Asian Open	Gonzalo Fernandez-Castano
GS Caltex Maekyung Open	Suk Jong-ryul
SK Telecom Open	Prom Meesawat
Aamby Valley Asian Masters	Hendrik Buhrmann
Macau Open	Kane Webber
Philippine Open	Scott Strange
Bangkok Airways Open	Chawalit Plaphol
Crowne Plaza Open	Chinarat Phadungsil
Brunei Open	Wang Ter-chang
Pulai Springs Malaysian Masters	Anton Haig
Barclays Singapore Open	Adam Scott
Kolon-Hana Bank Korea Open	Y.E. Yang (2)
Mercuries Taiwan Masters	Gaurav Ghei
Taiwan Open	Lin Wen-tang
Volkswagen Masters - China	Retief Goosen
Hero Honda Indian Open	Jyoti Randhawa
HSBC Champions	Y.E. Yang (3)
The Goodwill Trophy	International Team
UBS Hong Kong Open	Jose Manuel Lara
Volvo Masters of Asia	Thongchai Jaidee

OMEGA CHINA TOUR

Hainan Leg	Liang Wen-chong
Zhuhai Leg	Zhang Lian-wei
Shandong Leg	Li Chao
Shanghai Leg	Zhang Lian-wei (2)
Kunming Leg	Li Chao (2)
Omega Championship	Liang Wen-chong (2)

JAPAN TOUR

Token Homemate Cup	Wayne Perske
Tsuruya Open	Brendan Jones
The Crowns	Shingo Katayama
Japan PGA Championship	Tomohiro Kondo
Munsingwear Open KSB Cup	Toshinori Muto
Mitsubishi Diamond Cup	Kaname Yokoo
JCB Classic Sendai	Hideto Tanihara
Mandom Lucido Yomiuri Open	Nobuhiro Masuda
Gateway to the Open Mizuno Open	S.K. Ho
UBS Japan Golf Tour Championship	Tatsuhiko Takahashi
Woodone Open Hiroshima	Tetsuji Hiratsuka
Sega Sammy Cup	Yeh Wei-tze
The Golf Tournament in Omaezaki	Toru Taniguchi
Sun Chlorella Classic	Hideto Tanihara (2)
Under Armour KBC Augusta	Taichi Teshima
Fujisankei Classic	Shingo Katayama (2)
Suntory Open	Y.E. Yang
ANA Open	Tomohiro Kondo (2)
Acom International	Mamo Osanai
Coca-Cola Tokai Classic	Hidemasa Hoshino
Japan Open	Paul Sheehan (2)
Bridgestone Open	Taichi Teshima (2)
ABC Championship	Shingo Katayama (3)

Asahiryokuken Yomiuri Memorial — Tatsuhiko Ichihara
Mitsui Sumitomo Visa Taiheiyo Masters — Tsuneyuki Nakajima (2)
Dunlop Phoenix — Padraig Harrington (2)
Casio World Open — Jeev Milkha Singh (3)
Golf Nippon Series JT Cup — Jeev Milkha Singh (4)

AUSTRALASIAN TOUR

Johnnie Walker Classic — Kevin Stadler
Jacob's Creek Open — Paul Sheehan
ING New Zealand PGA Championship — Jim Rutledge
MFS Australian Open — John Senden (2)
MasterCard Masters — Justin Rose
Blue Chip New Zealand Open — Nathan Green
Cadbury Schweppes Australian PGA Champ. — Nick O'Hern

AFRICAN TOURS

Dimension Data Pro-Am — Alan McLean
Nashua Masters — Warren Abery
Telkom PGA Championship — Gregory Bourdy
Vodacom Tour Championship — Charl Schwartzel
Hassan II Trophy — Sam Torrance
Stanbic Zambia Open — Steve Basson
Vodacom Origins of Golf Tour - Western Cape — Jean Hugo
South African Airways Pro-Am - Cape Town — Jean Hugo (2)
Samsung Royal Swazi Sun Open — Thomas Aiken
Suncoast Classic — Alex Haindl
South African Airways Pro-Am - Johannesburg — Tongoona Charamba
Vodacom Origins of Golf Tour at Pretoria — Vaughn Groenewald
Vodacom Origins of Golf Tour at Kwazulu Natal — Rossouw Loubser
Vodacom Origins of Golf Tour at Bloemfontein — Rossouw Loubser (2)
Telkom PGA Pro-Am — Doug McGuigan
Eskom Power Cup — Trevor Fisher, Jr.
Vodacom Origins of Golf Tour - Eastern Cape — Kevin Stone
Seekers Travel Pro-Am — Desvonde Botes
Vodacom Origins of Golf Tour Final — Darren Fichardt
Bearingman Highveld Classic — Darren Fichardt (2)
MTC Namibia PGA Championship — Anton Haig (2)
Platinum Classic — Vaughn Groenewald (2)
Limpopo Classic — Bradford Vaughan
Coca-Cola Charity Championship — Alan Michell
Nelson Mandela Invitational — Retief Goosen (2)/Bobby Lincoln
Nedbank Golf Challenge — Jim Furyk (3)
Alfred Dunhill Championship — Alvaro Quiros (2)
South African Airways Open — Ernie Els

U.S. LPGA TOUR

SBS Open — Joo Mi Kim
Fields Open in Hawaii — Meena Lee
MasterCard Classic — Annika Sorenstam (2)
Safeway International — Juli Inkster
Kraft Nabisco Championship — Karrie Webb
LPGA Takefuji Classic — Lorena Ochoa
Florida's Natural Charity Championship — Sung Ah Yim
Ginn Clubs & Resorts Open — Mi Hyun Kim
Franklin American Mortgage Championship — Cristie Kerr
Michelob Ultra Open at Kingsmill — Karrie Webb (2)
Sybase Classic — Lorena Ochoa (2)
LPGA Corning Classic — Hee-Won Han
ShopRite LPGA Classic — Seon Hwa Lee
McDonald's LPGA Championship — Se Ri Pak
Wegmans LPGA — Jeong Jang

U.S. Women's Open — Annika Sorenstam (3)
HSBC Women's World Match Play — Brittany Lincicome
Jamie Farr Owens Corning Classic — Mi Hyun Kim (2)
CN Canadian Women's Open — Cristie Kerr (2)
Safeway Classic — Pat Hurst
Wendy's Championship for Children — Lorena Ochoa (3)
State Farm Classic — Annika Sorenstam (5)
John Q. Hammons Hotel Classic — Cristie Kerr (3)
Longs Drugs Challenge — Karrie Webb (4)
Corona Morelia Championship — Lorena Ochoa (4)
Samsung World Championship — Lorena Ochoa (5)
Honda LPGA Thailand — Hee-Won Han (2)
Mitchell Company Tournament of Champions — Lorena Ochoa (6)
ADT Championship — Julieta Granada
Lexus Cup — Asia

LADIES EUROPEAN TOUR

Princess Lalla Meriem Cup — Sophie Sandolo
Tenerife Ladies Open — Riikka Hakkarainen
Open de Espana Femenino — Lynnette Brooky
Deutsche Bank Ladies' Swiss Open — Gwladys Nocera
Vediorbis Open de France — Veronica Zorzi
KLM Ladies Open — Stephanie Arricau
BMW Ladies Italian Open — Gwladys Nocera (2)
Estoril Ladies Open of Portugal — Stephanie Arricau (2)
OTP Bank Ladies Central European Open — Rebecca Hudson (2)
Catalonia Ladies Masters — Gwladys Nocera (3)
Evian Masters — Karrie Webb (3)
Weetabix Women's British Open — Sherri Steinhauer
Scandinavian TPC Hosted by Annika — Annika Sorenstam (4)
Wales Ladies Championship of Europe — Linda Wessberg
SAS Masters — Laura Davies
Finnair Masters — Virginie Lagoutte
Nykredit Masters — Karen Margrethe Juul
Siemens Austrian Ladies Open — Sophie Gustafson
BBC Radio Kent Ladies' English Open — Cecilia Ekelundh
Dubai Ladies Masters — Annika Sorenstam (6)

JAPAN LPGA TOUR

Daikin Orchid Ladies — Mikiyo Nishizuka
Accordia Golf Ladies — Yuri Fudoh
Kinmirai Tsuushin Queens Open — Akane Iijima
Studio Alice Ladies Open — Ji-Hee Lee
Life Card Ladies — Yuri Fudoh (2)
Fujisankei Ladies Classic — Shiho Ohyama
Katokichi Queens — Mie Nakata
Salonpas World Ladies — Shiho Ohyama (2)
Vernal Ladies — Ji-Hee Lee (2)
Chukyo TV Bridgestone Ladies Open — Ji-Hee Lee (3)
Kosaido Ladies Golf Cup — Chieko Amanuma
Resort Trust Ladies — Mie Nakata (2)
We Love Kobe Suntory Ladies Open — Nikki Campbell
Nichirei Ladies — Sakura Yokomine
Promise Ladies — Saiki Fujita
Belluna Ladies Cup — Sakura Yokomine (2)
Meiji Chocolate Cup — Mi-Jeong Jeon
Stanley Ladies — Miho Koga
Philanthropy Japan LPGA Players Championship — Mi-Jeong Jeon (2)
Crystal Geyser Ladies — Shiho Ohyama (3)
NEC Karuizawa 72 — Shiho Ohyama (4)
Shin Caterpillar Mitsubishi Ladies — Mikiyo Nishizuka (2)

Yonex Ladies	Shiho Ohyama (5)
Golf 5 Ladies	Yun-Jye Wei
Japan LPGA Championship	Ai Miyazato
Munsingwear Ladies Tokai Classic	Akiko Fukushima
Miyagi TV Cup Dunlop Ladies Open	Ai Miyazato (2)
Japan Women's Open	Jeong Jang (2)
Sankyo Ladies Open	Shinobu Moromizato
Fujitsu Ladies	Mi-Jeong Jeon (3)
Masters Golf Club Ladies	Miho Koga (2)
Higuchi Hisako IDC Otsuka Kagu Ladies	Akiko Fukushima (2)
Mizuno Classic	Karrie Webb (5)
Itoen Ladies	Hyun-Ju Shin
Daiohseishi Elleair Ladies Open	Yun-Jye Wei (2)
Japan LPGA Tour Championship	Sakura Yokomine (3)
The Kyoraku Cup	Korea

KOREA LPGA TOUR

Phoenix Park Classic	Hee Young Park
KB Star Tour in Seoul	Sun Ju Ahn
Taeyoung Cup Korea Women's Open	Ji-Yai Shin
Lake Side Ladies Open	Bo-Bae Song
KB Star Tour in Busan	Soo Young Moon
Lake Hills Classic	Hee Young Park (2)
PAVV Invitational	Ji-Yai Shin (2)
SK EnClean Solux Invitational	Jin Joo Hong
Shinsegye Cup KLPGA Championship	Jee Young Lee
KB Star Tour in Hampyeong	Na Yeon Choi
Meritz Solmoro Classic	Ji Yeon Lee
Hite Cup Ladies Championship	Hyun Hee Moon
Kolon-Hana Bank Championship	Jin Joo Hong (2)
KB Star Tour in Gyeonggi	Eun-A Lim
Orient China Ladies Open	Ji-Yai Shin (3)
ADT CAPS Championship	Ji Won Yoon

AUSTRALIAN WOMEN'S TOUR

Titanium Enterprises ALPG Players Champ.	Rebecca Stevenson
ANZ Ladies Masters	*Amy Yang

SOUTH AFRICAN WOMEN'S TOUR

Women's World Cup of Golf	Annika Sorenstam/Liselotte Neumann
Pam Golding Ladies International	Nora Angehrn
Acer Women's South African Open	Rebecca Hudson
Telkom Women's Classic	Laurette Maritz
Nedbank Women's Masters	*Ashleigh Simon

CHAMPIONS TOUR

MasterCard Championship	Loren Roberts
Turtle Bay Championship	Loren Roberts (2)
ACE Group Classic	Loren Roberts (3)
Outback Steakhouse Pro-Am	Jerry Pate
AT&T Classic	Tom Kite
Toshiba Classic	Brad Bryant
Puerto Vallarta Blue Agave Golf Classic	Morris Hatalsky
Liberty Mutual Legends of Golf	Jay Haas
FedEx Kinko's Classic	Jay Haas (2)
Regions Charity Classic	Brad Bryant (2)
Boeing Championship	Bobby Wadkins
Senior PGA Championship	Jay Haas (3)
Allianz Championship	Gil Morgan
Commerce Bank Championship	John Harris
Greater Kansas City Golf Classic	Dana Quigley

U.S. Senior Open	Allen Doyle
Ford Senior Players Championship	Bobby Wadkins (2)
3M Championship	David Edwards
Boeing Greater Seattle Classic	Tom Kite (2)
JELD-WEN Tradition	Eduardo Romero (2)
Wal-Mart First Tee Open at Pebble Beach	Scott Simpson
Georgia-Pacific Grand Champions Championship	Jay Sigel
Constellation Energy Classic	Bob Gilder
Greater Hickory Classic at Rock Barn	Andy Bean
SAS Championship	Tom Jenkins
Administaff Small Business Classic	Jay Haas (4)
AT&T Championship	Fred Funk
Charles Schwab Cup Championship	Jim Thorpe

EUROPEAN SENIORS TOUR

DGM Barbados Open	Jose Rivero
Sharp Italian Seniors Open	Sam Torrance (2)
AIB Irish Seniors Open	Sam Torrance (3)
Irving Whiitlock Seniors Classic	Guillermo Encina
FirstPlus Wales Seniors Open	Jose Rivero (2)
Bendinat London Seniors Masters	Guiseppe Cali
Senior British Open	Loren Roberts (4)
Wentworth Senior Masters	Eduardo Romero
Bad Ragaz PGA Seniors Open	Juan Quiros
Scandinavian Senior Open	Katsuyoshi Tomori
PGA Seniors Championship	Sam Torrance (4)
Charles Church Scottish Seniors Open	Sam Torrance (5)
European Senior Masters	Carl Mason
The Midas Group English Seniors Open	Carl Mason (2)
OKI Castellon Open de Espana Senior	Gordon J. Brand
Estoril Seniors Open of Portugal	Carl Mason (3)
Arcapita Seniors Tour Championship	Gordon J. Brand (2)

JAPAN SENIOR TOUR

Aderans Wellness Open	Kiyoshi Murota
PGA Philanthropy Rebornest Senior Open	Tateo Ozaki
Fancl Classic	Kiyoshi Murota (2)
Japan PGA Senior Championship	Tsuneyuki Nakajima
Japan Senior Open	Tsuneyuki Nakajima (3)
Kinojyo Senior Open	Takashi Miyoshi

Multiple Winners of 2006

PLAYER	WINS	PLAYER	WINS
Tiger Woods	11	Jin Joo Hong	2
Lorena Ochoa	6	Rebecca Hudson	2
Annika Sorenstam	6	Jean Hugo	2
Shiho Ohyama	5	Tripp Isenhour	2
Sam Torrance	5	Jeong Jang	2
Karrie Webb	5	Craig Kanada	2
Jay Haas	4	Robert Karlsson	2
Loren Roberts	4	Martin Kaymer	2
Jeev Milkha Singh	4	Mi Hyun Kim	2
Johan Edfors	3	Tom Kite	2
Jim Furyk	3	Miho Koga	2
Mi-Jeong Jeon	3	Tomohiro Kondo	2
Shingo Katayama	3	Bernhard Langer	2
Cristie Kerr	3	Li Chao	2
Ji-Hee Lee	3	Liang Wen-chong	2
Carl Mason	3	Rossouw Loubser	2
Tsuneyuki Nakajima	3	Phil Mickelson	2
Gwladys Nocera	3	Ai Miyazato	2
Ji-Yai Shin	3	Adrien Mork	2
Kevin Stadler	3	Kiyoshi Murota	2
Y.E. Yang	3	Mie Nakata	2
Sakura Yokomine	3	Mikiyo Nishizuka	2
Stuart Appleby	2	Geoff Ogilvy	2
Stephanie Arricau	2	Rob Oppenheim	2
Johan Axgren	2	Rod Pampling	2
Gordon J. Brand	2	Hee Young Park	2
Brad Bryant	2	Alvaro Quiros	2
Paul Casey	2	Jose Rivero	2
Ben Curtis	2	Eduardo Romero	2
Simon Dyson	2	Adam Scott	2
Rafael Echenique	2	John Senden	2
Niclas Fasth	2	Paul Sheehan	2
Darren Fichardt	2	Brandt Snedeker	2
Yuri Fudoh	2	Henrik Stenson	2
Akiko Fukushima	2	Hideto Tanihara	2
Stephen Gangluff	2	Taichi Teshima	2
Retief Goosen	2	Bobby Wadkins	2
Vaughn Groenewald	2	Johnson Wagner	2
Anton Haig	2	Yun-Jye Wei	2
Hee-Won Han	2	Lee Williamson	2
Padraig Harrington	2	Zhang Lian-wei	2

World Money List

This list of the 400 leading money winners in the world of professional golf in 2006 was compiled from the results of men's (excluding seniors) tournaments carried in the Appendixes of this edition. This list includes tournaments with a minimum of 36 holes and four contestants and does not include such competitions as skins games, pro-ams and shootouts.

In the 41 years during which World Money Lists have been compiled, the earnings of the player in the 200th position have risen from a total of $3,326 in 1966 to $560,544 in 2006. The top 200 players in 1966 earned a total of $4,680,287. In 2006, the comparable total was $328,698,594.

The world money list of the International Federation of PGA Tours was used for the official money list events of the U.S. PGA Tour, PGA European Tour, PGA Tour of Japan, Asian Tour, Southern Africa Tour and PGA Tour of Australasia. The conversion rates used for 2006 for other events and other tours were: Euro = US$1.25; British pound = US$1.96; Japanese yen = US$0.0085; South African rand = US$0.16; Australian dollar = US$0.79; Canadian dollar = US$0.89.

POS.	PLAYER, COUNTRY	TOTAL MONEY
1	Tiger Woods, USA	$13,325,949
2	Jim Furyk, USA	9,016,397
3	Adam Scott, Australia	5,858,247
4	Geoff Ogilvy, Australia	5,583,593
5	Padraig Harrington, Ireland	4,868,184
6	Vijay Singh, Fiji	4,811,026
7	Trevor Immelman, South Africa	4,583,734
8	Luke Donald, England	4,467,204
9	Paul Casey, England	4,357,545
10	Phil Mickelson, USA	4,256,505
11	Ernie Els, South Africa	4,034,150
12	Retief Goosen, South Africa	3,952,114
13	Henrik Stenson, Sweden	3,894,787
14	Stuart Appleby, Australia	3,661,618
15	David Toms, USA	3,131,187
16	Rory Sabbatini, South Africa	3,065,918
17	Davis Love, USA	3,064,706
18	Rod Pampling, Australia	3,028,933
19	Brett Wetterich, USA	3,026,035
20	David Howell, England	2,991,103
21	Jose Maria Olazabal, Spain	2,961,916
22	Chad Campbell, USA	2,915,234
23	Carl Pettersson, Sweden	2,879,541
24	Stewart Cink, USA	2,875,494
25	Sergio Garcia, Spain	2,843,887
26	Joe Durant, USA	2,811,139
27	Chris DiMarco, USA	2,780,348
28	Jeev Milkha Singh, India	2,705,348
29	Brett Quigley, USA	2,668,669
30	Lucas Glover, USA	2,635,482
31	Colin Montgomerie, Scotland	2,617,698

POS.	PLAYER, COUNTRY	TOTAL MONEY
32	K.J. Choi, Korea	2,606,367
33	Ian Poulter, England	2,573,649
34	Dean Wilson, USA	2,509,857
35	Arron Oberholser, USA	2,477,972
36	Zach Johnson, USA	2,452,250
37	J.J. Henry, USA	2,438,563
38	Stephen Ames, Canada	2,416,405
39	Tom Pernice, Jr., USA	2,396,548
40	Tim Clark, South Africa	2,388,703
41	Shaun Micheel, USA	2,383,822
42	Mike Weir, Canada	2,345,825
43	Ben Curtis, USA	2,306,326
44	Robert Karlsson, Sweden	2,098,075
45	Jerry Kelly, USA	2,075,300
46	Nathan Green, Australia	1,970,172
47	Justin Rose, England	1,964,348
48	Johan Edfors, Sweden	1,944,359
49	Scott Verplank, USA	1,944,319
50	John Senden, Australia	1,912,814
51	Camilo Villegas, Colombia	1,864,473
52	Tom Lehman, USA	1,850,389
53	Tim Herron, USA	1,841,142
54	Steve Stricker, USA	1,811,811
55	Michael Campbell, New Zealand	1,784,525
56	Vaughn Taylor, USA	1,783,945
57	Robert Allenby, Australia	1,781,053
58	Troy Matteson, USA	1,778,597
59	Jason Bohn, USA	1,736,893
60	Angel Cabrera, Argentina	1,703,585
61	Charles Howell, USA	1,678,105
62	Y.E. Yang, Korea	1,664,728
63	Frank Lickliter, USA	1,655,678
64	Nick O'Hern, Australia	1,640,934
65	J.B. Holmes, USA	1,640,867
66	Anthony Wall, England	1,626,573
67	Shingo Katayama, Japan	1,620,492
68	Aaron Baddeley, Australia	1,603,129
69	Daniel Chopra, Sweden	1,578,316
70	Charl Schwartzel, South Africa	1,573,719
71	Richard S. Johnson, Sweden	1,555,376
72	Bernhard Langer, Germany	1,500,847
73	John Rollins, USA	1,498,828
74	Ben Crane, USA	1,489,093
75	Thomas Bjorn, Denmark	1,476,373
76	John Bickerton, England	1,456,038
77	Jeff Maggert, USA	1,430,376
78	Steve Flesch, USA	1,417,615
79	Simon Dyson, England	1,412,650
80	Sean O'Hair, USA	1,411,387
81	Bradley Dredge, Wales	1,408,868
82	Jonathan Byrd, USA	1,408,418
83	Bo Van Pelt, USA	1,393,027
84	Jeff Sluman, USA	1,382,025
85	Niclas Fasth, Sweden	1,374,964

POS.	PLAYER, COUNTRY	TOTAL MONEY
86	Greg Owen, England	1,373,140
87	Lee Westwood, England	1,373,105
88	Billy Mayfair, USA	1,367,998
89	Miguel Angel Jimenez, Spain	1,362,615
90	Jesper Parnevik, Sweden	1,361,466
91	Paul Broadhurst, England	1,358,170
92	Chris Couch, USA	1,356,731
93	Bob Estes, USA	1,340,244
94	Marc Warren, Scotland	1,326,097
95	Marcel Siem, Germany	1,319,489
96	Bart Bryant, USA	1,316,131
97	Corey Pavin, USA	1,308,084
98	Jose Manuel Lara, Spain	1,295,250
99	Simon Khan, England	1,283,585
100	Eric Axley, USA	1,282,680
101	Nick Watney, USA	1,249,016
102	Ted Purdy, USA	1,216,428
103	Darren Clarke, N. Ireland	1,205,903
104	Heath Slocum, USA	1,180,681
105	Richard Green, Australia	1,180,390
106	Woody Austin, USA	1,179,321
107	Shigeki Maruyama, Japan	1,154,115
108	Mathew Goggin, Australia	1,124,959
109	Steve Lowery, USA	1,124,950
110	Ryan Moore, USA	1,122,118
111	Charley Hoffman, USA	1,118,926
112	Billy Andrade, USA	1,114,177
113	Hunter Mahan, USA	1,107,457
114	Bubba Watson, USA	1,103,515
115	Fred Couples, USA	1,094,546
116	Ryan Palmer, USA	1,094,053
117	Hideto Tanihara, Japan	1,076,946
118	Joe Ogilvie, USA	1,073,111
119	Ryuji Imada, Japan	1,047,472
120	Daisuke Maruyama, Japan	1,047,273
121	D.J. Trahan, USA	1,037,942
122	Brian Gay, USA	1,037,600
123	Stephen Dodd, Wales	1,032,582
124	Charles Warren, USA	1,018,841
125	Craig Barlow, USA	1,006,538
126	Justin Leonard, USA	996,756
127	Peter Lonard, Australia	975,964
128	Francesco Molinari, Italy	968,675
129	Toru Taniguchi, Japan	959,834
130	Thongchai Jaidee, Thailand	948,986
131	Kenny Perry, USA	922,865
132	S.K. Ho, Korea	917,419
133	Kevin Stadler, USA	910,718
134	Harrison Frazar, USA	899,222
135	Gonzalo Fernandez-Castano, Spain	897,345
136	Will MacKenzie, USA	891,800
137	Paul Goydos, USA	890,392
138	Bill Haas, USA	887,024
139	Soren Kjeldsen, Denmark	881,591

POS.	PLAYER, COUNTRY	TOTAL MONEY
140	Anders Hansen, Denmark	868,463
141	Kent Jones, USA	860,766
142	Briny Baird, USA	844,547
143	Soren Hansen, Denmark	817,812
144	Fredrik Jacobson, Sweden	807,719
145	Joey Sindelar, USA	802,507
146	Brandt Jobe, USA	802,432
147	Paul McGinley, Ireland	801,689
148	Paul Sheehan, New Zealand	800,619
149	Tetsuji Hiratsuka, Japan	800,340
150	Taichi Teshima, Japan	799,831
151	Jeff Gove, USA	795,527
152	Philip Archer, England	793,665
153	Brian Davis, England	791,372
154	Graeme McDowell, N. Ireland	788,740
155	Raphael Jacquelin, France	788,210
156	Andres Romero, Argentina	786,011
157	Stephen Leaney, Australia	775,979
158	Mark Calcavecchia, USA	775,315
159	Kirk Triplett, USA	766,593
160	Brett Rumford, Australia	764,076
161	Dudley Hart, USA	762,736
162	Kevin Sutherland, USA	761,826
163	Olin Browne, USA	755,261
164	Jyoti Randhawa, India	747,419
165	John Cook, USA	746,638
166	Liang Wen-chong, China	740,246
167	Hidemasa Hoshino, Japan	731,923
168	Peter O'Malley, Australia	728,735
169	Jason Gore, USA	720,105
170	Pat Perez, USA	719,507
171	Arjun Atwal, India	713,035
172	David Branshaw, USA	706,346
173	J.P. Hayes, USA	704,983
174	Brad Faxon, USA	704,931
175	Paul Azinger, USA	702,090
176	Shane Bertsch, USA	699,192
177	Jarmo Sandelin, Sweden	694,402
178	Mathias Gronberg, Sweden	678,266
179	Rich Beem, USA	659,425
180	Tomohiro Kondo, Japan	657,086
181	Bubba Dickerson, USA	652,324
182	Andrew Buckle, Australia	645,954
183	Brian Bateman, USA	645,153
184	Kenneth Ferrie, England	637,394
185	Markus Brier, Austria	636,953
186	Duffy Waldorf, USA	625,513
187	Lee Janzen, USA	624,198
188	David Lynn, England	616,043
189	Graeme Storm, England	607,517
190	Omar Uresti, USA	602,980
191	Tim Petrovic, USA	601,928
192	Prayad Marksaeng, Thailand	599,979
193	Brent Geiberger, USA	590,478

POS.	PLAYER, COUNTRY	TOTAL MONEY
194	Jeff Overton, USA	587,832
195	Nick Dougherty, England	585,743
196	Jonathan Kaye, USA	578,714
197	Jerry Smith, USA	568,213
198	Ricardo Gonzalez, Argentina	565,412
199	Gary Orr, Scotland	562,917
200	Jeff Brehaut, USA	560,544
201	Bob May, USA	552,612
202	Robert Damron, USA	551,299
203	Marcus Fraser, Australia	548,753
204	Marco Dawson, Germany	545,076
205	Alex Cejka, Germany	542,101
206	Robert Garrigus, USA	537,595
207	Jose-Filipe Lima, Portugal	535,889
208	John Huston, USA	535,192
209	Nobuhiro Masuda, Japan	533,414
210	Simon Wakefield, England	533,013
211	Darren Fichardt, South Africa	530,920
212	Charlie Wi, Korea	524,263
213	Ken Duke, USA	523,037
214	Jose Coceres, Argentina	522,592
215	Damian McGrane, Ireland	521,195
216	Kaname Yokoo, Japan	518,705
217	Kris Cox, USA	517,836
218	Keiichiro Fukabori, Japan	517,375
219	David Smail, New Zealand	508,946
220	Mamoru Osanai, Japan	508,141
221	Hiroyuki Fujita, Japan	504,582
222	Robert Gamez, USA	503,841
223	Toshinori Muto, Japan	502,982
224	Azuma Yano, Japan	501,830
225	Tag Ridings, USA	498,242
226	Chris Riley, USA	495,314
227	Katsumasa Miyamoto, Japan	494,704
228	Peter Hanson, Sweden	492,668
229	Henrik Bjornstad, Norway	491,043
230	Craig Parry, Australia	487,079
231	Thaworn Wiratchant, Thailand	478,303
232	Michael Allen, Ireland	470,946
233	Jarrod Lyle, Australia	464,870
234	Jean Van de Velde, France	459,350
235	Carlos Franco, Paraguay	454,385
236	Skip Kendall, USA	453,694
237	David McKenzie, Australia	452,467
238	Edward Loar, USA	451,794
239	Mark Wilson, USA	449,868
240	Stephen Gallacher, Scotland	449,217
241	Ross Fisher, England	447,359
242	Richard Sterne, South Africa	443,823
243	John Daly, USA	442,134
244	Nick Price, Zimbabwe	439,774
245	J.L. Lewis, USA	438,669
246	Peter Lawrie, Ireland	436,424
247	Yeh Wei-tze, Taiwan	431,821

WORLD MONEY LIST

POS.	PLAYER, COUNTRY	TOTAL MONEY
248	Scott Gutschewski, USA	426,671
249	Mark O'Meara, USA	426,376
250	Wes Short, Jr., USA	422,506
251	Shiv Kapur, India	421,889
252	Maarten Lafeber, Netherlands	419,836
253	Tatsuhiko Takahashi, Japan	419,054
254	Brendan Jones, Australia	418,185
255	Emanuele Canonica, Italy	409,111
256	Kiyoshi Maita, Japan	409,012
257	D.A. Points, USA	405,984
258	Prom Meesawat, Thailand	401,341
259	Andrew Marshall, England	397,455
260	Todd Fischer, USA	395,817
261	Yusaku Miyazato, Japan	394,897
262	Paul Lawrie, Scotland	392,993
263	Bob Tway, USA	392,226
264	Cameron Beckman, USA	391,404
265	Doug Barron, USA	388,226
266	Patrick Sheehan, USA	386,797
267	Rich Bland, England	385,883
268	Danny Ellis, USA	384,450
269	Gary Emerson, England	379,825
270	Ian Leggatt, Canada	377,903
271	Johnson Wagner, USA	373,269
272	Wade Ormsby, Australia	363,606
273	Andrew Coltart, Scotland	361,343
274	Gavin Coles, Australia	354,289
275	Tatsuhiko Ichihara, Japan	353,349
276	Tommy Armour, USA	352,446
277	Jean-Francois Lucquin, France	350,201
278	Garry Houston, Wales	349,077
279	Lee Slattery, England	348,204
280	Ignacio Garrido, Spain	347,487
281	Mark Foster, England	346,630
282	Alastair Forsyth, Scotland	346,452
283	Cliff Kresge, USA	343,496
284	Alejandro Canizares, Spain	342,502
285	Takuya Taniguchi, Japan	341,508
286	Jason Dufner, USA	340,125
287	Peter Hedblom, Sweden	340,101
288	Anthony Kim, USA	339,617
289	Nozomi Kawahara, Japan	337,184
290	Lin Keng-chi, Taiwan	334,827
291	Craig Bowden, USA	334,671
292	Matt Kuchar, USA	333,297
293	Gregory Bourdy, France	332,359
294	Benn Barham, England	332,212
295	Steve Elkington, Australia	329,517
296	Unho Park, Australia	328,915
297	Jeff Quinney, USA	328,181
298	Darron Stiles, USA	325,016
299	Mathias Eliasson, Sweden	322,990
300	Christian Cevaer, France	322,901
301	Tripp Isenhour, USA	321,996

POS.	PLAYER, COUNTRY	TOTAL MONEY
302	Tom Whitehouse, England	319,662
303	Paul Stankowski, USA	319,597
304	David Duval, USA	318,276
305	Frankie Minoza, Philippines	314,603
306	Boo Weekley, USA	312,843
307	Craig Kanada, USA	308,886
308	Steve Jones, USA	308,360
309	Ron Whittaker, USA	307,046
310	Brandt Snedeker, USA	306,918
311	Jay Delsing, USA	304,603
312	Martin Erlandsson, Sweden	302,674
313	Masaya Tomida, Japan	301,805
314	Andrew McLardy, South Africa	300,317
315	Robert Rock, England	297,165
316	Alvaro Quiros, Spain	295,912
317	Alessandro Tadini, Italy	295,554
318	Brad Kennedy, Australia	293,525
319	Jim Rutledge, Canada	293,371
320	Juvic Pagunsan, Philippines	291,847
321	Gaurav Ghei, India	291,779
322	Gabriel Hjertstedt, Sweden	290,757
323	Glen Day, USA	290,635
324	Mark Hensby, Australia	290,633
325	Robert-Jan Derksen, Netherlands	290,569
326	Nicholas Thompson, USA	289,185
327	Wayne Perske, Australia	283,707
328	Steve Webster, England	281,851
329	David Griffiths, England	278,411
330	David Park, Wales	276,952
331	Chawalit Plaphol, Thailand	276,596
332	Greg Chalmers, Australia	276,426
333	Mardan Mamat, Singapore	276,268
334	Gregory Havret, France	274,679
335	Greg Kraft, USA	273,734
336	Steven Jeppesen, Sweden	273,480
337	Matthew Millar, Australia	271,860
338	Ryuichi Oda, Japan	270,459
339	Scott Strange, Australia	270,129
340	Joachim Backstom, Sweden	268,651
341	David Bransdon, Australia	264,488
342	Yoshikazu Haku, Japan	263,489
343	Cesar Monasterio, Argentina	263,360
344	Oliver Wilson, England	262,222
345	Miles Tunnicliff, England	260,881
346	David Drysdale, Scotland	259,455
347	David Carter, England	259,191
348	Ryoken Kawagishi, Japan	258,104
349	B.J. Staten, USA	256,638
350	Tjaart van der Walt, South Africa	254,623

World Money List Leaders

YEAR	PLAYER, COUNTRY	TOTAL MONEY
1966	Jack Nicklaus, USA	$168,088
1967	Jack Nicklaus, USA	276,166
1968	Billy Casper, USA	222,436
1969	Frank Beard, USA	186,993
1970	Jack Nicklaus, USA	222,583
1971	Jack Nicklaus, USA	285,897
1972	Jack Nicklaus, USA	341,792
1973	Tom Weiskopf, USA	349,645
1974	Johnny Miller, USA	400,255
1975	Jack Nicklaus, USA	332,610
1976	Jack Nicklaus, USA	316,086
1977	Tom Watson, USA	358,034
1978	Tom Watson, USA	384,388
1979	Tom Watson, USA	506,912
1980	Tom Watson, USA	651,921
1981	Johnny Miller, USA	704,204
1982	Raymond Floyd, USA	738,699
1983	Seve Ballesteros, Spain	686,088
1984	Seve Ballesteros, Spain	688,047
1985	Bernhard Langer, Germany	860,262
1986	Greg Norman, Australia	1,146,584
1987	Ian Woosnam, Wales	1,793,268
1988	Seve Ballesteros, Spain	1,261,275
1989	David Frost, South Africa	1,650,230
1990	Jose Maria Olazabal, Spain	1,633,640
1991	Bernhard Langer, Germany	2,186,700
1992	Nick Faldo, England	2,748,248
1993	Nick Faldo, England	2,825,280
1994	Ernie Els, South Africa	2,862,854
1995	Corey Pavin, USA	2,746,340
1996	Colin Montgomerie, Scotland	3,071,442
1997	Colin Montgomerie, Scotland	3,366,900
1998	Tiger Woods, USA	2,927,946
1999	Tiger Woods, USA	7,681,625
2000	Tiger Woods, USA	11,034,530
2001	Tiger Woods, USA	7,771,562
2002	Tiger Woods, USA	8,292,188
2003	Vijay Singh, Fiji	8,499,611
2004	Vijay Singh, Fiji	11,638,699
2005	Tiger Woods, USA	12,280,404
2006	Tiger Woods, USA	13,325,949

Career World Money List

Here is a list of the 50 leading money winners for their careers through the 2006 season. It includes players active on both the regular and senior tours of the world. The World Money List from this and the 40 previous editions of the annual and a table prepared for a companion book, *The Wonderful World of Professional Golf* (Atheneum, 1973) form the basis for this compilation. Additional figures were taken from official records of major golf associations, although shortcomings in records-keeping outside the United States in the 1950s and 1960s and a few exclusions from U.S. records during those years prevent these figures from being completely accurate, although the careers of virtually all of these top 50 players began after that time. Conversion of foreign currency figures to U.S. dollars is based on average values during the particular years involved.

POS.	PLAYER, COUNTRY	TOTAL MONEY
1	Tiger Woods, USA	$81,058,790
2	Vijay Singh, Fiji	59,786,184
3	Ernie Els, South Africa	57,203,115
4	Davis Love, USA	43,430,984
5	Phil Mickelson, USA	42,451,957
6	Jim Furyk, USA	37,387,886
7	Colin Montgomerie, Scotland	35,934,806
8	Hale Irwin, USA	33,708,788
9	Retief Goosen, South Africa	33,130,012
10	Nick Price, Zimbabwe	31,049,978
11	Fred Couples, USA	29,127,262
12	Bernhard Langer, Germany	28,889,872
13	Padraig Harrington, Ireland	28,156,878
14	David Toms, USA	27,996,816
15	Sergio Garcia, Spain	27,777,510
16	Darren Clarke, Northern Ireland	25,406,988
17	Tom Kite, USA	25,146,538
18	Jose Maria Olazabal, Spain	25,023,910
19	Greg Norman, Australia	24,401,664
20	Tom Lehman, USA	24,396,454
21	Gil Morgan, USA	24,105,263
22	Mark Calcavecchia, USA	23,944,964
23	Scott Hoch, USA	23,579,223
24	Justin Leonard, USA	23,495,630
25	Kenny Perry, USA	22,517,303
26	Chris DiMarco, USA	22,295,589
27	Tom Watson, USA	21,857,136
28	Masashi Ozaki, Japan	21,837,724
29	Fred Funk, USA	21,800,224
30	Stuart Appleby, Australia	21,659,358
31	Jay Haas, USA	21,389,249
32	Brad Faxon, USA	21,021,517
33	Mike Weir, Canada	20,811,849
34	Jeff Sluman, USA	20,782,818
35	Nick Faldo, England	20,534,264
36	Stewart Cink, USA	20,383,551
37	Lee Westwood, England	20,286,029
38	Mark O'Meara, USA	20,261,136

POS.	PLAYER, COUNTRY	TOTAL MONEY
39	Raymond Floyd, USA	20,259,739
40	David Duval, USA	20,123,951
41	Craig Stadler, USA	19,743,624
42	Larry Nelson, USA	19,601,949
43	Adam Scott, Australia	19,537,769
44	Loren Roberts, USA	19,498,771
45	Robert Allenby, Australia	18,980,404
46	Shigeki Maruyama, Japan	18,836,720
47	Scott Verplank, USA	18,661,975
48	Ian Woosnam, Wales	18,317,611
49	Isao Aoki, Japan	17,813,371
50	Jesper Parnevik	17,459,660

These 50 players have won $1,342,864,763 in their careers.

Women's World Money List

This list includes official earnings on the U.S. LPGA Tour, Ladies European Tour, Japan LPGA Tour and Korea LPGA Tour, along with other winnings in established unofficial events when reliable figures could be obtained.

POS.	PLAYER, COUNTRY	TOTAL MONEY
1	Lorena Ochoa, Mexico	$2,656,310
2	Annika Sorenstam, Sweden	2,367,951
3	Karrie Webb, Australia	2,133,863
4	Julieta Granada, Paraguay	1,663,586
5	Cristie Kerr, USA	1,628,182
6	Shiho Ohyama, Japan	1,427,286
7	Jeong Jang, Korea	1,425,440
8	Mi Hyun Kim, Korea	1,337,500
9	Juli Inkster, USA	1,326,442
10	Paula Creamer, USA	1,276,868
11	Hee-Won Han, Korea	1,225,276
12	Pat Hurst, USA	1,128,662
13	Ai Miyazato, Japan	1,009,363
14	Seon Hwa Lee, Korea	965,590
15	Sukura Yokomine, Japan	964,188
16	Se Ri Pak, Korea	962,586
17	Mi-Jeong Jeon, Korea	899,844
18	Brittany Lincicome, USA	894,938
19	Ji-Hee Lee, Korea	814,258
20	Hyun-Ju Shin, Korea	812,531
21	Natalie Gulbis, USA	765,218
22	Meena Lee, Korea	755,975
23	Miho Koga, Japan	747,559
24	Sherri Steinhauer, USA	745,901

POS.	PLAYER, COUNTRY	TOTAL MONEY
25	Michelle Wie, USA	735,224
26	Laura Davies, England	733,014
27	Jee Young Lee, Korea	725,551
28	Akiko Fukushima, Japan	705,377
29	Sophie Gustafson, Sweden	698,231
30	Stacy Prammanasudh, USA	683,613
31	Brittany Lang, USA	538,552
32	Gwladys Nocera, France	531,676
33	Yun-Jye Wei, Taiwan	528,692
34	Mie Nakata, Japan	523,505
35	Morgan Pressel, USA	512,936
36	Joo Mi Kim, Korea	508,466
37	Angela Stanford, USA	503,218
38	Nikki Campbell, Australia	498,102
39	Shi Hyun Ahn, Korea	488,154
40	Akane Iijima, Japan	475,240
41	Yuri Fudoh, Japan	459,646
42	Young Kim, Korea	453,676
43	Shinobu Moromizato, Japan	449,449
44	Candie Kung, Taiwan	447,235
45	Gloria Park, Korea	443,163
46	Jeong-Eun Lee, Korea	436,744
47	Ji-Yai Shin, Korea	424,123
48	Momoko Ueda, Japan	411,197
49	Karine Icher, France	403,426
50	Sung Ah Yim, Korea	385,224
51	Wendy Ward, USA	383,441
52	Hiromi Mogi, Japan	379,511
53	Nicole Castrale, USA	375,106
54	Helen Alfredsson, Sweden	371,607
55	Christina Kim, USA	360,206
56	Suzann Pettersen, Norway	344,352
57	Maria Hjorth, Sweden	343,146
58	Mikiyo Nishizuka, Japan	342,970
59	Laura Diaz, USA	342,432
60	Il Mi Chung, Korea	339,914
61	Rachel Hetherington, Australia	337,163
62	Diana D'Alessio, USA	328,396
63	Heather Young, USA	323,871
64	Michiko Hattori, Japan	321,272
65	Liselotte Neumann, Sweden	316,926
66	Kaori Higo, Japan	315,354
67	Lorie Kane, Canada	314,176
68	Yui Kawahara, Japan	312,266
69	Lindsey Wright, Australia	311,724
70	Michele Redman, USA	307,948
71	Patricia Meunier-Lebouc, France	303,924
72	Catriona Matthew, Scotland	296,542
73	Chieko Amanuma, Japan	295,814
74	Kyeong Bae, Korea	293,220
75	Karen Stupples, England	291,573
76	Aree Song, Korea	289,240
77	Michie Ohba, Japan	284,841
78	Hee Young Park, Korea	274,337

WOMEN'S WORLD MONEY LIST

POS.	PLAYER, COUNTRY	TOTAL MONEY
79	Nancy Scranton, USA	274,304
80	Saiki Fujita, Japan	265,501
81	Carin Koch, Sweden	255,052
82	Reilley Rankin, USA	254,169
83	Beth Daniel, USA	252,200
84	Marisa Baena, Colombia	252,105
85	Na Yeon Choi, Korea	242,659
86	Yuko Saitoh, Japan	238,989
87	Veronica Zorzi, Italy	238,431
88	Sarah Lee, England	236,945
89	Mitsuko Kawasaki, Japan	236,599
90	Marcy Hart, USA	235,243
91	Rui Kitada, Japan	233,738
92	Young Jo, Korea	232,862
93	Becky Morgan, Wales	232,625
94	Sun Young Yoo, Korea	231,473
95	Kim Saiki, USA	230,471
96	Midori Yoneyama, Japan	229,092
97	Yukari Baba, Japan	221,856
98	Hyun Hee Moon, Korea	218,156
99	Hiroko Yamaguchi, Japan	218,009
100	Tamie Durdin, Australia	216,968
101	Silvia Cavalleri, Italy	211,792
102	Young-A Yang, Korea	210,759
103	Ya-Huei Lu, Taiwan	210,394
104	Brandie Burton, USA	207,175
105	Catherine Cartwright, USA	202,066
106	Yuriko Ohtsuka, Japan	201,067
107	Soo Young Moon, Korea	197,814
108	Kuniko Maeda, Japan	193,984
109	Junko Omote, Japan	193,578
110	Eun-A Lim, Korea	192,886
111	Ayako Uehara, Japan	191,370
112	Yun-Hee Ku, Korea	189,094
113	Jae-Hee Bae, Korea	185,789
114	Julie Lu, Taiwan	185,553
115	Sherri Turner, USA	183,739
116	Stephanie Arricau, France	182,903
117	Linda Wessberg, Sweden	179,241
118	Becky Brewerton, Wales	175,876
119	Jin Joo Hong, Korea	175,601
120	Kasumi Fujii, Japan	175,441
121	Janice Moodie, Scotland	174,203
122	Rebecca Hudson, England	174,105
123	Mihoko Takahashi, Japan	173,627
124	Riikka Hakkarainen Finland	163,826
125	Tina Barrett, USA	161,753
126	Ai Ogawa, Japan	160,315
127	Bo-Bae Song, Korea	158,364
128	Sun Ju Ahn, Korea	158,357
129	Amy Hung, Taiwan	156,682
130	Tracy Hanson, USA	150,842
131	Anja Monke, Germany	147,301
132	Yuka Irie, Japan	145,480

POS.	PLAYER, COUNTRY	TOTAL MONEY
133	Nina Reis, Sweden	145,256
134	Miriam Nagl, Germany	143,470
135	Ji Yeon Lee, Korea	143,332
136	Virada Nirapathpongporn, Thailand	143,196
137	Karin Sjodin, Sweden	136,304
138	Dorothy Delasin, Philippines	136,098
139	Grace Park, Korea	136,099
140	Karen Margrethe Juul, Denmark	135,333
141	Allison Hanna-Williams, USA	133,480
142	Eun-Hye Lee, Korea	133,173
143	Cecilia Ekelundh, Sweden	129,784
144	Yun-Joo Jeong, Korea	129,499
145	Becky Iverson, USA	128,466
146	Keiko Sasaki, Japan	128,399
147	Ji-Yeon Han, Korea	127,960
148	Nikki Garrett, Australia	127,456
149	Sophie Giquel, France	126,112
150	Seiko Watanabe, Japan	126,104

Senior World Money List

This list includes official earnings from the world money list of the International Federation of PGA Tours, U.S. Senior PGA Tour, European Seniors Tour and Japan Senior Tour, along with other winnings in established unofficial events when reliable figures could be obtained.

POS.	PLAYER, COUNTRY	TOTAL MONEY
1	Jay Haas, USA	$2,583,626
2	Loren Roberts, USA	2,499,967
3	Fred Funk, USA	2,048,959
4	Tom Kite, USA	1,693,514
5	Brad Bryant, USA	1,692,417
6	Gil Morgan, USA	1,525,050
7	Scott Simpson, USA	1,372,876
8	Jim Thorpe, USA	1,303,284
9	Tom Jenkins, USA	1,287,666
10	David Edwards, USA	1,219,950
11	Bobby Wadkins, USA	1,193,173
12	Allen Doyle, USA	1,072,840
13	Andy Bean, USA	1,034,278
14	Eduardo Romero, Argentina	1,012,728
15	Bob Gilder, USA	994,842
16	Craig Stadler, USA	994,360
17	Tom Watson, USA	983,319
18	Hale Irwin, USA	925,475
19	Don Pooley, USA	924,614
20	Morris Hatalsky, USA	902,677
21	Keith Fergus, USA	898,531

POS.	PLAYER, COUNTRY	TOTAL MONEY
22	Tom Purtzer, USA	890,579
23	Dana Quigley, USA	884,484
24	Des Smyth, Ireland	838,181
25	D.A. Weibring, USA	783,896
26	Peter Jacobsen, USA	783,350
27	Tsuneyuki Nakajima, Japan	779,654
28	R.W. Eaks, USA	751,923
29	Bruce Lietzke, USA	724,874
30	Mark McNulty, Zimbabwe	721,459
31	Lonnie Nielsen, USA	694,212
32	Kiyoshi Murota, Japan	663,601
33	John Harris, USA	651,016
34	Sam Torrance, Scotland	610,086
35	Mark James, England	593,100
36	Jerry Pate, USA	571,358
37	Mark Johnson, USA	565,325
38	Larry Nelson, USA	564,764
39	Chip Beck, USA	525,603
40	Wayne Levi, USA	502,198
41	Masahiro Kuramoto, Japan	491,104
42	Naomichi Ozaki, Japan	480,541
43	Bruce Summerhays, USA	477,767
44	Mike Reid, USA	444,813
45	Bruce Fleisher, USA	437,233
46	Fuzzy Zoeller, USA	423,918
47	David Eger, USA	423,347
48	Danny Edwards, USA	416,623
49	Dick Mast, USA	408,900
50	Raymond Floyd, USA	385,708
51	Hajime Meshiai, Japan	380,891
52	Ben Crenshaw, USA	375,552
53	Tim Simpson, USA	359,073
54	Tom McKnight, USA	358,686
55	Curtis Strange, USA	343,252
56	Jose Rivero, Spain	339,061
57	Carl Mason, England	332,882
58	Mike McCullough, USA	319,433
59	Katsuyoshi Tomori, Japan	300,982
60	Jay Sigel, USA	298,949
61	Vicente Fernandez, Argentina	291,476
62	Ron Streck, USA	288,106
63	Walter Hall, USA	282,890
64	Dan Pohl, USA	261,666
65	Dave Eichelberger, USA	260,757
66	Doug Tewell, USA	258,091
67	Tom Wargo, USA	255,638
68	Gary McCord, USA	250,158
69	Gordon J. Brand, England	249,793
70	John Jacobs, USA	248,505
71	John Bland, South Africa	236,527
72	Ed Dougherty, USA	234,454
73	Graham Marsh, Australia	223,203
74	Stewart Ginn, Australia	221,042
75	Mitch Adcock, USA	220,780

POS.	PLAYER, COUNTRY	TOTAL MONEY
76	Isao Aoki, Japan	211,717
77	Nick Faldo, England	201,650
78	Juan Quiros, Spain	197,248
79	Leonard Thompson, USA	195,089
80	James Mason, USA	188,212
81	Horacio Carbonetti, Argentina	183,092
82	Bill Longmuir, Scotland	178,502
83	Giuseppe Cali, Italy	174,708
84	David J. Russell, England	174,572
85	Jim Ahern, USA	171,153
86	Kirk Hanefeld, USA	170,147
87	Luis Carbonetti, Argentina	169,105
88	Jack Ferenz, USA	164,084
89	Bob Eastwood, USA	162,182
90	Guillermo Encina, Chile	157,004
91	Scott Hoch, USA	149,110
92	Nick Job, England	148,821
93	Rick Karbowski, USA	147,117
94	Tony Johnstone, Zimbabwe	143,752
95	Rick Rhoden, USA	142,714
96	Dave Stockton, USA	142,286
97	Eamonn Darcy, Ireland	139,504
98	Joe Inman, USA	132,930
99	Bobby Lincoln, South Africa	132,821
100	Gery Watine, France	129,798
101	Greg Norman, Australia	127,202
102	Bertus Smit, South Africa	126,168
103	Seiji Ebihara, Japan	120,560
104	Simon Owen, New Zealand	118,298
105	Mike San Filippo, USA	117,866
106	Delroy Cambridge, Jamaica	114,177
107	Tateo Ozaki, Japan	113,956
108	Jim Dent, USA	113,912
109	Jose Maria Canizares, Spain	109,348
110	Katsunari Takahashi, Japan	108,964
111	Jim Albus, USA	108,015
112	Hugh Baiocchi, South Africa	100,962
113	Bob Cameron, England	100,242
114	Mike Sullivan, USA	92,631
115	Adan Sowa, Argentina	92,289
116	Lee Trevino, USA	91,918
117	Gary Koch, USA	89,475
118	Howard Twitty, USA	89,278
119	Bruce Heuchan, Canada	87,869
120	Doug Johnson, USA	87,794
121	Pete Oakley, USA	84,126
122	Martin Poxon, England	83,746
123	Takashi Miyoshi, Japan	83,433
124	Martin Gray, Scotland	82,419
125	Pat McGowan, USA	81,255

1. The Year in Retrospect

It all looked so familiar. On a glorious summer afternoon, Tiger Woods marched toward the 18th green at Royal Liverpool as the traditional colors of an Open Championship came to life. The grass was more brown than green, courtesy of a dry spell in the northwest of England. The men working the massive yellow-and-black scoreboard were preparing their annual message to the champion. Woods himself was easy to spot, wearing his black trousers and a red shirt, his Sunday color, with caddie Steve Williams walking at his side in his traditional Sunday black. Sergio Garcia wore a yellow outfit that led one observer to say he looked like a banana—make that second banana, given his company. Woods merely needed to finish the hole to collect the claret jug and yet another major championship.

In an instant, the routine gave way to raw emotion never seen from the world's No. 1 player. Woods tapped in for par, giving him his third Open title and making him the first player since Tom Watson in 1983 to successfully defend his title in golf's oldest championship. He stooped to pluck the ball from the cup, and instinctively thrust both arms in the air. He screamed "Yes!" But it was the way that word tore through his lips that made everyone quickly realize his 11th career major championship was so different from all the rest. It was the first one he could not share with his father, Earl Woods, who had died May 3 after a debilitating bout with cancer.

For all the great shots played in 2006, whether it was Paul Casey's ace at the Ryder Cup or Karrie Webb holing out on the 18th fairway with a wedge from 116 yards in the Kraft Nabisco Championship as she ended a four-year drought in the majors, the lasting image of 2006 was Woods in a rare moment where he lost control. Chest heaving, he sobbed on Williams's shoulder for the longest minute. His face was still contorted when he walked off the green and into the arms of his wife, Elin, where he melted in her arms and cried some more.

"I'm kind of the one who bottles things up a little bit and moves on," Woods said. "But at that moment, it just came pouring out. And of all the things that my father has meant to me and the game of golf, I just wish he would have seen it one more time."

What made that moment so relevant was that it summarized an entire year for Woods. There was the exhilaration of eight victories on the PGA Tour, including the final six starts of his 2006 campaign to match the second-longest streak in tour history. Woods also won six straight at the end of 1999 and beginning of 2000, and again he at least has raised the possibility of doing the impossible, catching Byron Nelson's record of 11 in a row. His two majors brought him to 12, leaving only Jack Nicklaus and his 18 professional majors to catch. But all those triumphs were buried in the long shadow of death.

Earl Woods was more than a father. He was the role model, confidante, swing coach, teacher and friend. Tiger spent sleepless nights over the holidays with his father until it was time to go back to work. He flew across the country from Florida to California on the eve of The Players Championship when he received word that his father was struggling. And he tried so desperately to win the Masters for him, knowing it likely would be the last major Earl Woods saw on television, that he wound up giving it too much effort. "It was the only time I saw him try too hard," Williams said. Finishing three shots behind at Augusta National haunts Woods to this day. "It was my last round that my Dad ever watched me play," Woods said. "Knowing that going into it, if I could have given him one last shot, some positive memories before he goes, it would have been huge."

Woods's final PGA Tour victory came at the American Express Championship at The Grove, outside London, where he won by eight shots for his 12th victory in a World Golf Championship event. Comparisons to his benchmark season in 2000 were starting to percolate, but when asked that afternoon how he would remember his season, Woods replied, "A loss."

"If you take into account what happened off the golf course, it's my worst year," Woods said. "People asked me, 'How do you consider the year?' I consider it as a loss. In the grand scheme of things, golf doesn't even compare to losing a parent."

TIGER WOODS

EVENT	POSITION
Buick Invitational	1
Dubai Desert Classic	1
Nissan Open	WD
WGC - Accenture Match Play	T-9
Ford Championship at Doral	1
Bay Hill Invitational	T-20
The Players Championship	T-22
Masters Tournament	T-3
U.S. Open Championship	MC
Cialis Western Open	T-2
The Open Championship	1
Buick Open	1
PGA Championship	1
WGC - Bridgestone Invitational	1
Deutsche Bank Championship	1
HSBC World Match Play	T-9
WGC - American Express Championship	1
HSBC Champions	2
Dunlop Phoenix	2
PGA Grand Slam of Golf	1
Target World Challenge	1

Returning to work after spending time with his father around the holidays, Woods got off to a blazing start, albeit with help. He won his 2006 debut at the Buick Invitational in a three-way playoff against Nathan Green of Australia and two-time Masters champion Jose Maria Olazabal. Woods won on the second extra hole when Olazabal missed a four-foot par putt.

A week later and eight time zones away in the Dubai Desert Classic, Woods drove the par-four 17th green to make birdie and closed with a birdie on the par-five 18th to get into a playoff with longtime rival Ernie

Els. The playoff didn't last long, as Els hit a four iron from a grove of palm trees into the water fronting the 18th green, and Woods only needed to make par to win.

Woods also captured the Ford Championship at Doral for the second straight year, whipping Phil Mickelson in the third round—a rematch of their final-round duel a year earlier, which Woods won—and then holding off David Toms and Colombian rookie Camilo Villegas for a one-stroke victory.

At the moment, the gap between Woods and the rest of golf was as wide as ever. Not many would have guessed that three months later, while Woods never risked losing his No. 1 ranking, he no longer was No. 1 in the eyes of so many in golf.

The turnaround began in Woods-like fashion. Mickelson prefers to play the week before a major, and he turned his tune-up at the BellSouth Classic into the largest romp on the PGA Tour since Woods's historic 15-shot victory in the 2000 U.S. Open at Pebble Beach. Mickelson, who had not come seriously close to winning all year, experimented with two drivers on the TPC at Sugarloaf and opened with 63. He proceeded to annihilate the field, winning by 13 strokes over Olazabal and taking that form down Interstate 20 to the Masters.

Mickelson didn't take the lead in the Masters until Sunday morning when the rain-delayed third round was completed, and held off Fred Couples in the final round for his second green jacket. Along with his PGA Championship victory the previous August, Mickelson joined Woods and Nick Price as the only players to capture consecutive majors in the previous 20 years.

When Mickelson arrived at Winged Foot for the U.S. Open, he was considered the favorite. "I think Phil Mickelson is the best shotmaker on tour right now," Paul Azinger said two weeks before the U.S. Open. "I think he's the most confident player in the world. And I think he's the man to beat."

Part of that was because Woods had disappeared from golf. His post-Masters break was extended when his father died, and Woods grieved privately for the month of May, even skipping the Memorial Tournament for the first time, which some thought would have been an ideal way to get ready for the U.S. Open. Woods spent nine weeks away from tournament golf and he didn't look the same when he returned at Winged Foot.

Struggling from the start, Woods opened with three straight bogeys and shot 76, matching his highest start ever in a major. He followed that with another 76 and missed the cut for the first time as a professional in a major. "I don't care if you had what transpired in my life recently or not," Woods said tersely. "Poor execution is never going to feel very good."

That left the stage to Mickelson, and he was ready to pounce. He didn't hit the ball as cleanly as he did at the Masters, but his short game was as terrific as ever, and 69 in the third round gave him a share of the lead with the unheralded Kenneth Ferrie of England and a New York crowd eager to see their man finally deliver. Euphoria swept over Winged Foot when Mickelson had a two-shot lead with four holes to play, and he arrived on the 18th tee needing a par to join Woods as the only players in the last 50 years to win three straight majors.

Mickelson hit a driver off a corporate tent and into the trees. He smacked a tree with his second shot, and a three iron for his third shot plugged into the bunker left of the green, sending him to a double bogey and these infamous words: "I am such an idiot." He was not the only player who lost the U.S. Open.

No one blew it quite like Colin Montgomerie, who got through the toughest stage by finding the 18th fairway before he hit a seven iron so fat that it came up well short of the green in thick rough. "What was that?" Montgomerie said to himself as his ball took flight, perhaps knowing the answer—"That was your best chance to win a major." He, too, made double bogey to finish one shot behind. Jim Furyk hit a beautiful bunker shot only to miss the five-foot par putt.

But this was to be Mickelson's moment. No one has his flair for the spectacular, which has hurt him as much as it has helped. Mickelson had a reputation of being too risky, too aggressive and not thinking the way a major champion should. However, this was the first time those accusations were supported by fact. One can debate whether driver was the wrong play off the 18th tee—remember, he had a one-stroke lead when he hit the first of six shots on the closing hole at Winged Foot and was trying to win with a par. But the next shot that he tried to curve around a tree brought double bogey into the equation, and that was his final answer.

He was not heard from the rest of the year, although short-game coach Dave Pelz had plenty to say. He told the *Chicago Tribune* before the PGA Championship that when Mickelson was at his best, "I'm thinking no one can beat him." Told of these comments, Woods replied, "I think I'm pretty tough to beat when I'm playing well, too."

Mickelson never had another chance to win the rest of the year, nor did he finish in the top 10. At the Ryder Cup, he failed to win a single match and went 0-4-1. "I haven't hit it the same since the Masters," he said at the Bridgestone Invitational, where he tied for 54th and finished 19 strokes behind. "I haven't been able to get my ball-striking back."

Woods was just hitting his stride at the PGA Championship. Tied for the lead with Luke Donald going into the final round at Medinah, he holed a 10-foot birdie putt at No. 1 and never looked back. It was his fifth major victory of at least five strokes. Time to reflect on a great year? Not quite yet. After winning his second straight major and third straight start, he stayed on the range until dark at Firestone, unsatisfied with a game that was unbeatable. He won the Bridgestone Invitational in a playoff over Stewart Cink, and after a two-day trip to Ireland for Ryder Cup practice, played perhaps his best round of the year.

Trailing nemesis Vijay Singh by three strokes going into the final round of the Deutsche Bank Championship outside Boston, Woods erased that deficit with two eagles in his first seven holes and closed with 63, matching the best final round of his career. His winning streak ended two weeks later when former PGA champion Shaun Micheel eliminated him in the first round of the HSBC World Match Play Championship, and he was runner-up twice in Asia at the tail end of his season, which concluded with victories in the PGA Grand Slam and the Target World Challenge.

And so, the year ended the way it began—bookend victories for Woods and no apparent challenger on the horizon, at least no one that can sustain that challenge for more than a few months at a time.

"It's mind boggling, it really is," Billy Andrade said. "Is he at that point he was in 2000? Yes. Is everybody playing for second? Well, we're not going to concede it, but he sure finishes the deal better than we do."

That hardly was the case in women's golf.

The Rolex Rankings made its debut in February, a project that had been two years in the making. There was controversy, which was to be expected any time a computer gets involved, although the biggest stir was Michelle Wie at No. 3, even though she had played only 15 women's tournaments over the last two years. The system later was altered, although one thing remained clear and allowed for no debate: Annika Sorenstam was No. 1.

Over the last five seasons, her worst year on paper was in 2003 when she won only six times. That was the year, of course, that Sorenstam became the first woman in 58 years to compete on the PGA Tour when she played in the Colonial; and two of those six victories were at the McDonald's LPGA Championship and the Weetabix Women's British Open, giving her the career Grand Slam. She was coming off 10 victories and two majors in 2005, and her No. 1 ranking was even more clear than Woods's in men's golf.

It surprised no one when Sorenstam made her 2006 debut with back-to-back victories. She teamed with Liselotte Neumann to win the Women's World Cup in South Africa, then reminded Paula Creamer who was the best in women's golf by easily beating her in the final round of the MasterCard Classic in Mexico. Surely, this year would be just like all the others.

But there was a 75 in the third round of the Safeway International outside Phoenix that derailed her chances. Then came the first LPGA major of the year, the first leg in her renewed hopes of a calendar Grand Slam, yet the Super Swede failed to break 70 all four days. Even more shocking was the Florida Natural Charity Championship in Atlanta, when Sorenstam blew a final-round lead with 75. And if that wasn't enough, she missed the cut at the Michelob Ultra Open at Kingsmill for the first time since the 2002 Weetabix Women's British Open, a streak of 69 events.

She wound up the year at No. 1, but the margin over Lorena Ochoa was shrinking fast. And some believe Ochoa was the player to beat heading into the new season. More on that later.

Sorenstam would hardly call this year a failure. Her three victories on the LPGA Tour (plus two in Europe and the Women's World Cup of Golf) were the fewest in the United States since she won only twice in 1999. But one of those was the biggest in her sport, an amazing weekend at storied Newport Country Club filled with rain, fog, a 36-hole final day and a U.S. Women's Open that was stretched over five days because of a playoff.

Fog rolled in off the Atlantic the morning of the first round, essentially wiping out the day. It gave Sorenstam one more day with swing coach Henri Reis to refine her swing, and it paid huge dividends. She opened with a two-under 69 for a share of the lead, the first time she had broken 70 in the first round of the U.S. Women's Open since she won it for the first time in 1995.

For all her monumental feats, the U.S. Women's Open had become elusive to the game's best player. She lost a two-shot lead in 2002 to Juli Inkster, took bogey on the par-five 18th hole at Pumpkin Ridge in 2003 to miss a playoff by one shot, and couldn't catch up to Meg Mallon a year later at the Orchards. Going for the third leg of the Grand Slam in 2005 at Cherry Hills, she shot herself out of contention with a four-putt double bogey.

But this was different. Sorenstam had everything fall into place at Newport, from the extra day of practice brought on by fog, to the tee times that allowed her to finish her second round Saturday morning and rest all afternoon for the 36-hole finish. She was tied for the lead with Wie and Brittany Lincicome after the third round Sunday morning, and had control of the tournament until hitting into the water on No. 7, then stumbling along with bogeys to fall behind.

A birdie on the 10th with a wedge to five feet changed everything, and Sorenstam had a 30-foot birdie putt on the 18th hole to win that dipped in and out of the cup. That put her in a playoff with Pat Hurst over 18 holes on Monday, and it was over quickly, both on the scorecard and the clock. Sorenstam opened with a birdie, built a three-shot lead through three holes and coasted to a four-shot victory. "It's fantastic," she said. "It's been a long wait, a long road. On the way, I learned a lot. The way the season has gone, up and down, to win the Open is pretty ironic."

It was her third U.S. Women's Open title, and it continued a trend of turning back the clock on the LPGA Tour, although one didn't have to rewind terribly far. Webb had gone four years without winning a major, two years since her last LPGA Tour victory, as she slowly rebuilt her swing and waited for the confidence to catch up. It caught up with one of the best shots of the year.

Starting the final round of the Kraft Nabisco Championship seven strokes behind, Webb was tied for the lead at seven under at Mission Hills Country Club when she laid up short of the water on the par-five 18th. The roar she heard a half-mile away was the 16-year-old Wie stuffing a wedge inside two feet for a birdie that would give her the lead. Webb hit a pitching wedge from 116 yards that checked up just short of the hole and trickled in for an eagle, sending her sprinting and leaping into the arms of her caddie. Before her heart rate returned to normal, however, she had to wait to see if her nine-under 279 would hold up.

Ochoa boldly hit a five wood over the water to six feet for an eagle that tied Webb. Wie had a chip from off the 18th green for an eagle to win, but she ran it 10 feet by and missed the birdie putt to finish one shot out of the playoff. Natalie Gulbis had an 18-foot birdie putt to join the playoff, but she missed. On the first extra hole, Webb and Ochoa were both over the green, but Webb holed a seven-foot birdie putt to win.

Two months later, she felt Ochoa's pain. Webb and Se Ri Pak were in a playoff at the McDonald's LPGA Championship after a thrilling back nine at Bulle Rock that featured a late charge from Sorenstam that came up short and a collapse by Wie, who was tied for the lead until making a bogey with a wedge in her hand from the 16th fairway.

Webb appeared headed for her second straight major when Pak popped up her tee shot on the 18th, leaving her 201 yards away. With a hybrid four iron, she pulled the shot slightly—this was not a problem, because Pak had been aiming right of the green to avoid water down the left side. The ball took a fortuitous hop on the green, rolled true to the cup and stopped two inches away. Flustered, Webb could only hit an eight iron to some 30 feet and missed the putt.

It was quite a resurgence for Pak, who will get into the World Golf Hall of Fame next year when she completes her 10th year on the LPGA Tour. She had not won a major since 2002 and had gone winless the last two seasons as she coped with burnout.

The only star without a major was Ochoa, although she became a star in her own right. The dynamic Mexican was a star at the University of Arizona, setting an NCAA record with eight straight victories. And while she did not win in her first full year on the LPGA Tour, she won the Rolex Rookie of the Year award by finishing ninth on the money list.

Going into the 2006 season, Ochoa was most recently known for a couple of failures. She gave up a four-shot lead with three holes to go against Annika Sorenstam, losing to her in a playoff in Phoenix. At the 2005 U.S. Women's Open at Cherry Hills, she played an hour before the leaders and was poised to take the lead until succumbing to the pressure and hitting a duck-hook into the water on her way to an "ocho"—a triple-bogey eight. But she vowed to learn from her mistakes.

Ochoa closed with 67 at the season-opening SBS Open at Turtle Bay in Hawaii before losing in a playoff. She opened with 62 in the Kraft Nabisco Championship to tie a major championship record on the LPGA, and she carried a three-shot lead over Wie into the final round. And while she lost that lead, Ochoa battled to the very end by making an eagle on the 72nd hole to force a playoff.

The loss to Webb was devastating, but Ochoa bounced back the next week with the first of her six victories in 2006, at the LPGA Takefuji Classic in Las Vegas. That was part of a string of six tournaments in which she never finished worse than second. The only tournaments where she struggled were the majors, unable to get anything going at the McDonald's LPGA Championship or the U.S. Women's Open. Her best hope was the Weetabix Women's British Open, but she closed with 73 to tie for fourth as Sherri Steinhauer won going away.

The end of the majors is not the end of the year on the LPGA Tour, perhaps because their majors have changed so much over the years, perhaps because the LPGA runs three of them (while the PGA Tour doesn't operate any of the men's majors). The benchmark in women's golf is Kathy Whitworth for her 88 career victories.

Realizing she had a good shot at winning the Rolex Player of the Year award for the first time, Ochoa ran off three straight victories to secure her first honor. Winning the Corona Morelia Championship in Mexico felt like winning a major because of the overwhelming support she had from the home crowd. And her "major" performance of the year came at the Samsung World Championship of Golf at Bighorn Golf Club in Palm Desert, California.

Sorenstam was gearing up for one last rally and took a three-stroke lead over Ochoa going into the final round. Ochoa showed why she might be the most exciting player in women's golf. Consider this: Sorenstam birdied two of the first three holes and still couldn't help but feel pressure from Ochoa. The Mexican star birdied the first hole from 25 feet and holed a 45-foot eagle putt on the par-five third. Two holes later, they were tied. Sorenstam fought back with birdies on the seventh and ninth holes, but Ochoa made a 60-foot birdie putt on the 10th that banged into the back of the cup. It sent her to a 65, a two-shot victory and what she later called "probably my best round of golf in my professional career."

Ochoa clinched the Rolex Player of the Year and the Vare Trophy for the lowest scoring average by winning The Mitchell Companies Tournament of Champions in Alabama, her sixth win of the year. A week later, she secured her first money title when the $1 million first prize at the ADT Championship went to Julieta Granada of Paraguay.

By year's end, Sorenstam was still No. 1 in the Rolex Rankings, but her lead was dwindling. The Swede had 15.24 points, with Ochoa at 12.07 and Webb in third at 11.06. But there was an unspoken feeling that Ochoa's year signaled the possibility of a change at the top on the LPGA Tour. Sorenstam was shell-shocked after the Samsung World Championship, but acknowledged Ochoa's abilities. "I really don't know what to say other than just to congratulate Lorena on a great performance and a great week and a great year," she said.

The gap in the Official World Golf Ranking for the men was as wide as it has ever been under the latest configuration. Woods was at 20.41, with Furyk securely at No. 2 with 8.88 points. Mickelson had dropped to No. 3 (7.17), followed by Adam Scott and Ernie Els, whose only victory came in the final official event of the year at the South African Airways Open. Newcomers to the top 10 were Padraig Harrington, Luke Donald and Geoff Ogilvy, while Garcia, Montgomerie and Chris DiMarco were replaced. Furyk reached his highest position in the world ranking with victories at the Wachovia Championship and the Bell Canadian Open, but it didn't mean much to him. "Rankings aren't really that important to me," he said after moving to No. 2.

Furyk has been one of the steadiest customers in golf for years, and while he didn't win a major in 2006, perhaps this was the year he finally was recognized beyond a swing that makes a peculiar loop at the top before slotting beautifully into position at impact. He isn't long, but he is long enough. Accuracy is his hallmark and he is among the best clutch putters. As far as toughness, that's why Woods asked for him as a partner at the Ryder Cup.

Furyk put all those traits to the test at the Wachovia Championship. He had wasted good opportunities to win at The Players Championship, where he had the 36-hole lead until a 75-72 weekend, and he missed a variety of short putts in the final round of the Verizon Heritage at Harbour Town, which allowed Aaron Baddeley to collect his first PGA Tour victory.

Furyk looked as though he might give away the Wachovia title at the Quail Hollow Club in Charlotte, North Carolina, when he took a one-shot lead into the final round only to get left behind by Trevor Immelman. Needing a par on the final hole to force a playoff, Furyk holed an eight-footer. On the first extra hole, he made a six-foot par for his first playoff victory on the PGA Tour in 10 years. "It didn't look good, but I stayed positive," Furyk said. "You've got to keep fighting and try to win."

Furyk won twice more, at the Canadian Open and in the Nedbank Challenge at Sun City, South Africa. Even more remarkable, and a testament to his No. 2 ranking, was that he played 14 tournaments after winning the Wachovia Championship and he finished no worse than fourth in nine of them.

None of them stung quite like Winged Foot, where Furyk had the look of a winner, even with Mickelson out front. He was closing fast until his approach to the 15th stopped only 25 feet from the hole, leaving him a difficult putt to judge over a slight ridge, although the putt isn't nearly as quick as it appears. He three-putted for bogey, then gave himself one last chance at a second U.S. Open title. From a bunker left of the 18th green, he blasted out beautifully to five feet below the hole, backed off twice to study the line, and then caught the edge. The bogey hurt even worse when Mickelson and Montgomerie each took double bogey, making the winning score of Ogilvy at five-over 285. Furyk, like the other two, finished one shot behind. "I played my heart out and it didn't work," Furyk said.

His pairing with Woods at the Ryder Cup didn't work out as well as they had hoped. They first hooked up at the Presidents Cup a year earlier and went 2-0-1 in their team matches. They drew Montgomerie and Harrington in the first match of the Ryder Cup, and while they came away with a rare point for the Americans, it wasn't always pretty. Woods hit his opening tee shot into the River Liffey.

They stayed together all four team matches with mixed results — victories in the opening fourballs Friday and the closing foursomes Saturday, with one crushing defeat in the Friday afternoon foursomes against Garcia and Donald, and another in the Saturday morning fourballs to Darren Clarke and Lee Westwood. Against Garcia and Donald, Furyk holed a 15-foot birdie on the 16th to halve the hole and keep the match all-square. After Garcia hit a wedge to three feet on the 17th to give Europe a 1-up lead, the Americans had a chance to earn a half until Furyk pulled his hybrid club from 230 yards badly into the water. "No excuses there," Furyk said. With him, there never are.

Despite winning the opening point, the rest of the Ryder Cup was a hopeless cause for the Americans. Woods went 3-2 and had a winning record for the first time in five appearances. Scott Verplank was a surprise in many ways. He was a captain's pick by Tom Lehman despite not having won in five years, but then was kept on the bench the entire day Friday. And when he did finally play, Lehman used him in fourballs, even though Verplank is best suited for foursomes because of his accuracy off the tee. No matter. He went 2-0, making an ace on the 14th hole Sunday in beating Harrington. Stewart Cink was the other captain's pick and went 1-1-3. Woods, Verplank and Cink were the only U.S. players without losing records, and they left Ireland fully aware that not only did they lose the cup, the Americans no longer had the best team.

It was a victorious year for Europe in more ways than one. The highlight, clearly, was the Ryder Cup, played for the first time ever in Ireland, and it was grandly staged, the biggest sporting event ever held in that country. Europe won for the third straight time, its longest streak since these matches began in 1927, and did so convincingly, with an 18½ to 9½ margin for the second straight match. There wasn't much second-guessing of the U.S. captain or his players this time, just the realization that Europe had the better team from top to bottom.

As the American team filed quietly out of The K Club, it occurred to them that there was no evidence the trend was about to reverse. The youngest American player was Vaughn Taylor, 30, who played for the first time and was so nervous that Lehman sat him out the first day. On the other side, Donald, Garcia and Casey were all in their 20s and big-hitting Swede Henrik Stenson was only 30.

Garcia had a poor year by his standards, failing to win anywhere in the world and taking consolation in playing in the last group with Woods at Royal Liverpool. He started the year at No. 6 in the world ranking and dipped to No. 11 by the end of the year, although at age 26, he still was considered a rising star. And while the only trophy he touched was the gold chalice shared by 11 others at the Ryder Cup, he showed his strength at The K Club by going 4-1, losing only his singles. And he played a key role in the Order of Merit.

Luke Donald, 28, cleared a big hurdle by winning the Honda Classic for his second PGA Tour victory and the most meaningful. The other was the Southern Farm Bureau Classic, held opposite the Tour Championship and shortened to 54 holes because of rain. Donald played well enough to contemplate a challenge to No. 1 in the world, although he showed how long a road that is at Medinah when he closed with a 74 and finished six shots behind Woods.

Paul Casey won four times around the world, no victory greater than the HSBC World Match Play Championship. In what can be a long week of golf with 36-hole matches each day, Casey made short work of everyone he played and crushed Micheel in the final, 10 and 8. He bulldozed over two-time U.S. Open champion Retief Goosen, former Masters champion Mike Weir and eight-time Order of Merit winner Colin Montgomerie to reach the final, and his closest match was against Weir, 5 and 3. He earned £1 million, enough of that applied as official money that he became a front-runner for the Order of Merit.

Henrik Stenson won the Qatar Masters and played well enough throughout the year that he led the Ryder Cup standings for Europe.

It was a strong season in Europe, and a pivotal time. Across the ocean, the U.S. PGA Tour revamped its schedule to create a compelling end to the season and moved The Players Championship from March to May. The European Tour was left to piece together its schedule with so many players competing in America, and tour chief George O'Grady held a players-only meeting at the Accenture Match Play Championship, reminding his players that the European Tour was worth fighting for. Its players delivered drama at nearly every turn, from David Howell winning the BMW Championship at Wentworth to Jeev Milkha Singh becoming the first Indian to win a European Tour event when he captured the season-ending Volvo Masters at Valderrama.

Indeed, the highest drama unfolded among the cork trees dotting the landscape on the Spanish golf course. Howell's position decreased as his back problems increased in the closing months. Casey, a heavy favorite to win the Order of Merit, suffered a severe stomach virus when he arrived that weakened him at a time he needed strength. Harrington, meanwhile, was looming. He had finished second in the Order of Merit twice to Retief Goosen, and a victory in the Dunhill Links Championship gave him a chance. His play in the final round was nothing short of outstanding, making a bevy of birdies early to surge into contention on a difficult course in tough conditions. He closed with a 69 and was lying second. Casey finished well back, and Harrington could only wait in the lounge to see if he earned enough money to pass Casey.

Strangely enough, it all came down to Garcia. One shot behind Singh and alone in second place, the Spaniard needed only a par on the last hole for Casey to win the Order of Merit. But he found a bunker right of the 18th green, blasted out weakly, and missed his 40-foot par putt. That dropped him into a three-way tie for second with Harrington and Donald, and giving Harrington enough money to at long last win the Harry Vardon Trophy.

It was the 30th runner-up finish for Harrington in his 11 years on tour, but none ever tasted so sweet. "It's great to finish second and yet win," he said. "It's something I've always wanted to do. As a goal at the start of the year, I always want to win the Order of Merit." Europe as a whole could claim victory. By year's end, it had eight players among the top 20 in the world.

On the U.S. PGA Tour, the strength came from Down Under. Australia had been looking for a star since Greg Norman eased into retirement, and the search soon yielded a list so large it could have been anyone. Six Australians won tournaments, with Stuart Appleby and Geoff Ogilvy each winning twice. Adam Scott was the highest-ranked Australian at the end of the year at a career-high No. 4. And perhaps it was only fitting that the season featured bookend trophies belonging to the Aussies. Stuart Appleby won the season-opening Mercedes Championships for a record third straight time, and Scott finished the year with a command performance at the Tour Championship.

But for the Australians, the year belonged to Ogilvy. Everyone knew the 29-year-old was blessed with immense talent, if only he could keep his temper at bay and not get down on himself so much. He was long and straight, a wonderful iron player and confident with the putter. And yet his only victory had been in Tucson while the stars were competing at the Accenture Match Play Championship. Oddly enough, that's where it all turned around for Ogilvy. He had reason to give up and get down, trailing the reigning U.S. Open champion, Michael Campbell of New Zealand, in the opening round at La Costa. Ogilvy rallied to win in 19 holes, and then came another comeback to beat fellow Aussie Nick O'Hern in 21 holes.

Ogilvy's real magic occurred in the third round. He was 4 down to Weir with four holes to play when he won them all to force overtime, winning in 21 holes to advance to the quarter-finals. The thrills continued with a 19-hole victory over David Howell before he got a breather against Lehman. And despite trailing early in the championship match against Davis Love, Ogilvy cruised to victory for his first World Golf Championship title. He set a record by playing 129 holes, including four straight overtime matches. And the greatest testament to his mental fortitude—with no small measure of luck—was the 10 times an opponent stood over a putt that would have sent Ogilvy home.

Ogilvy tasted true fame even before he arrived at Winged Foot. Through an arrangement he still can't explain, Ogilvy was invited to a State Dinner at the White House and found himself seated at the same table with President Bush, Australian Prime Minister John Howard, Australian media icon Rupert Murdoch, Secretary of State Condoleezza Rice and Julie Eisenhower, the daughter of former President Richard Nixon. "All he wanted to do was talk sport," Ogilvy said of the president. "No politics. Maybe that was the reason I was there. I'm an Australian and we love our sport."

Australian fans were sent into a frenzy at the U.S. Open, when Ogilvy became the first major champion from Down Under since Steve Elkington won the 1995 PGA Championship at Riviera in a playoff over Montgomerie and the first Australian to win the U.S. Open since David Graham in 1981 at Merion.

Ogilvy never dreamed it would be him, not standing over a chip from mangled rough that he holed for a par on the 17th hole; not after his tee shot on the 18th landed in a divot, causing his approach to tumble down a hill short of the green; not even after a delicate, well-played pitch to six feet. He holed the putt, presumably for second place, and became a shocked winner when Montgomerie, then Mickelson, stumbled badly.

"I think I was the beneficiary of a little bit of charity," Ogilvy said. No matter. He was the U.S. Open champion, and he showed all year long it was no fluke. Along with his two victories, he finished 16th or better in all four majors.

South Africans continued to have a presence, although the cast of characters changed. Goosen and Ernie Els were part of the Big Three, the Big Four and the Big Five over recent years, the numbers fluctuating depending on where Goosen was ranked, given that his two U.S. Open titles came with a shiny trophy but not recognition.

Els was coming off knee surgery that knocked him out of the final four months of the previous year, and his victory at the end of 2005 in South Africa renewed his hopes that he again would be capable of taking on Woods. The moment came quickly when they were in a playoff at the Dubai Desert Classic. Els did not look particularly thrilled to see Woods arrive on the 18th tee for the playoff, having finished second to him a half-dozen times, more than any other player. And when the Big Easy hit a four iron into the water on his second shot, Woods was a winner again.

Rather than seeming distraught, Els had a look that said, "This is only the start. Our real battle will come on a bigger stage." But that was as good as it got. Els failed to consistently contend on the PGA Tour, he failed to win on the European Tour, and his only shot at glory came at Royal Liverpool, when he was paired in the final group with Woods at the Open, one stroke behind. "I haven't been in this position for a while," Els said. "I'd love to play as well or even better on the weekend. Maybe I'll have to." He matched Woods's 71 in the third round, played in the group ahead of him on Sunday and failed to make a charge, finishing third.

Goosen picked up his only victory in China, failing to make a dent on the PGA Tour. He closed with a 69 to tie for third at the Masters, but never had a serious chance at winning the green jacket. He also was a distant second at The Players Championship, and hired a swing coach in October, his first one in eight years.

South African success came from Trevor Immelman, who had to overcome the perception from some players that he got his PGA Tour card by virtue of being a captain's pick for the Presidents Cup. In fact, Immelman earned his way on the U.S. tour with three top-20 finishes in the majors that were a small sign of things to come. In his first full year on the PGA Tour, he had a chance to win the Wachovia Championship until a three-putt from 50 feet on the 18th hole to fall into a playoff, won by Furyk. A week later, at the EDS Byron Nelson Championship, Immelman was tied for the lead with Scott going into the final round when both were overtaken by Brett Wetterich, whose victory helped him make the Ryder Cup team.

Immelman didn't squander his next great chance, though, at the Western Open. Woods, Singh and Furyk were among those trying to track him down at Cog Hill, but Immelman was unflappable, and he holed a 40-foot birdie putt on the 18th that dropped him to his knees in disbelief at winning his first PGA Tour event. Immelman missed the Open in Britain when his wife gave birth to their first child, but he had three more top 10s the rest of the year and set two rookie records by finishing seventh on the money list with $3,844,189.

No matter the country, the shift in power was never more evident in golf. Just look at the world ranking, a complete reversal from a generation ago. When the Official World Golf Ranking made its debut in 1986 before the Masters, the top three players were Europeans (Bernhard Langer, Seve Ballesteros and Sandy Lyle), but depth came from the Americans, with 31 represented in the top 50.

By the end of 2006, the top three spots were held by Woods, Furyk and Mickelson, but there were only 11 other Americans in the top 50. There were 17 players in the top 50 from Europe (eight of those from Britain), eight from the South Pacific (Australia, New Zealand and Fiji), five from South Africa and three from Asia, including Y.E. Yang of South Korea, whom Woods had never heard of until Yang defeated him in the HSBC Championship at Shanghai.

Such global diversity, of course, is nothing new on the LPGA Tour. It has been a truly world tour for years, especially with the recent influx of South Koreans, headed by Pak. This was supposed to be the year the Americans battled back, and LPGA officials trumpeted the arrival of 18-year-old Morgan Pressel, 19-year-old Paula Creamer and Natalie Gulbis, a California blonde who had more calendars (two) than trophies (none). But the U.S. strength came from its veterans, with Sherri Steinhauer winning the Weetabix Women's British Open and Juli Inkster winning in Phoenix at age 45.

Creamer won overseas in Japan, but she failed to win a single tournament on the LPGA a year after she was rookie of the year and starred in the Solheim Cup. Pressel rarely contended and finished 24th on the LPGA Tour money list, and Gulbis had her chances at the Kraft Nabisco, but ended 2006 still in search of her first victory.

Even an American the LPGA Tour could not officially claim—Wie, who chose not to apply for membership—failed to win. The teenager from Hawaii had at least a share of the lead on the final nine of the three U.S. majors but failed to close. The most excitement she generated all year was at Canoe Brook Country Club in Summit, New Jersey, where she tried to become the first female to qualify for the U.S. Open. She was inside the cut line after the morning round at the 36-hole sectional qualifier, but missed a half-dozen putts inside 10 feet and missed by five shots. She celebrated one small victory against the men, making the cut in the SK Telecom Open in South Korea, which was co-sanctioned by the Asian Tour.

South Korea was a strong presence again, winning nine of the 32 tournaments on the official schedule. When Pak won the McDonald's LPGA Championship, South Koreans had won seven of 14 tournaments in 2006. It was appropriate that Pak won a major, for she was the one who got it started. She was the only South Korean on the LPGA Tour in 1998 when she captured two majors. This year, there were 32 players from South Korea. "She is the face of Korean golf," Webb said. "All the young Koreans out here, if they don't already know, they should know now how much she's done for them."

Golf continued to flourish on other tours around the world. Nick O'Hern captured the Order of Merit on the Australasian Tour over Kevin Stadler, the son of former Masters champion Craig Stadler. Among the interesting stories from Down Under was Jarrod Lyle, who was ninth on the Order of Merit, but earned his PGA Tour card through the Nationwide Tour. Lyle is a leukemia survivor, whose family was helped financially by the charitable work of Robert Allenby. Seven years later, they played a practice round together at the British Open, and Lyle and Allenby can expect to see more of each other in 2007.

Along with his victory in the Volvo Masters, Jeev Milkha Singh won the Order of Merit on the Asian Tour, climbed to No. 37 in the world and qualified for the Masters for the first time. Shingo Katayama won three times on the Japan PGA Tour and led its money list.

The year in golf was not without its losses—Dick Harmon, one of Claude Harmon's four sons who went on to become notable teaching professionals, died of a heart attack in February at 58. Patty Berg, who won a record 15 majors on the LPGA Tour, died of complications from Alzheimer's disease in September at 88. And Byron Nelson died at 94, living the longest of the American triumvirate of Nelson, Sam Snead and Ben Hogan, all of whom were born in 1912.

Nelson was remarkably keen well into his 90s, and it was not unusual for him to spend the mornings in the woodshop on his ranch in Texas. His latest project was to make wood chips for the U.S. Ryder Cup team, burning their name on one side and a Bible verse on the other. He was most famous for the 1945 season when he won 11 straight PGA Tour events and 18 titles for the season. It is a year that almost certainly will never be matched, not even by Woods. For one thing, Woods only plays about 18-20 times a year.

As for the winning streak, Woods won six straight on the PGA Tour over two seasons in 2000, which caused Nelson to say, "Any time you make a record that stands for 55 years, you've done pretty good." Two days after Nelson's death in September, Woods teed off in the American Express Championship and won by eight to run his PGA Tour streak to six tournaments.

Perhaps no death drew more attention than Earl Woods because of the impact it had on his son, who by now has become the most famous athlete in the world. Stories about the two of them had become as legendary as Woods's career. Earl placed his son in a high chair before he could walk so the boy could watch him swing. He would jangle change in his pockets during rounds with his son trying to teach him mental toughness. Through it all, he was more interested in raising a good person than a champion golfer, and he succeeded on both counts.

Together they launched the Tiger Woods Foundation when Tiger became a professional in 1996, and three months before Earl died, the $25 million Tiger Woods Learning Center opened in Anaheim, California, on a small street renamed Tiger Woods Way. The goal was to get 5,000 kids through the door in the first year, and the total topped 8,000 instead.

As for the power of Tiger's mind on the golf course, one story from Earl stands out more than the others. He once told of how he tried to break down his son mentally, mentioning there was water down the right or out-of-bounds to the left when the boy was at the top of his swing. Tiger glared, but the rule was he couldn't say anything. It was a lesson in coping with frustration. Earl always gave his son an escape word if it got to be too much, but he never used it. "One day I did all my tricks, and he looked at me and smiled," Earl recalled. "At the end of the round, I told him, 'Tiger, you've completed the training.' And I made him a promise. 'You'll never run into another person as mentally tough as you.' He hasn't. And he won't."

There have been challenges, and challengers. Perhaps more than any other year since Woods turned professional, 2006 had the trappings for major movement atop the Official World Golf Ranking. Woods was firmly entrenched at No. 1, but he was followed by Singh, Mickelson, Goosen and Els. There was talk of a "Big Five," the modern version of the "Big Three" when Jack Nicklaus, Arnold Palmer and Gary Player ruled golf in the 1960s and took turns winning majors.

For this group, it was easy to call it the "Big One," for no other reason than Woods had won 10 majors and no one else had more than three. But a closer look showed more competition than many realized.

Dating to the 1999 PGA Championship, the "Big Five" had won 16 of the last 25 majors. Woods, obviously, had won the bulk of those titles, but he usually ran into one player or another along the way. And if he wasn't contending, one of the others was. At least one member of his group had won or was runner-up in 21 of those 25 majors. "He's there all the time," Els said of Woods. "The rest of us, we're in and out the rest of the time. So yes, he's winning. But there is competition."

By the end of the year—for the moment, anyway—it was back to the Big One. Mickelson won the Masters for his third major and squandered a chance to win the U.S. Open, but his success in 2006 was limited to two months, April and one week in June. Els contended at the Open in Britain, Singh didn't give himself a serious chance in any major, missing the cut in the last two. Goosen was often forgotten because of his stoic personality, and he made himself easier to ignore by disappearing for most of the year.

Woods kept marching along, living by the credo once told to him by Nicklaus about all the different rivalries through the Golden Bear's career. "Just make sure you're part of every conversation," Nicklaus said to him. That was simple. From start to finish, every conversation about the world of golf in 2006 inevitably began with two words: Tiger Woods.

2. Masters Tournament

The man who once could not win a major championship was now aiming for three in a row. "Starting tomorrow," Phil Mickelson was saying on that Sunday evening in Augusta, Georgia, "we'll start working for Winged Foot," referring to the venue for the U.S. Open Championship in June.

Mickelson had just won the Masters Tournament, the first major championship of 2006. It followed his victory in the last major of 2005, the PGA Championship. Until winning the 2004 Masters, Mickelson had been without a victory in 42 starts in the majors as a professional. "Three out of nine, that sounds better, doesn't it?" he said.

"When I won in 2004, I felt this great feeling of relief," said Mickelson, 35 years old. "This time it's a great feeling of satisfaction and accomplishment to come out on top."

Mickelson struck for four birdies in the final round at Augusta National Golf Club, posted a three-under-par 69 for a 281 total, seven under, and won by two strokes over Tim Clark, who also finished with 69 and 283 after holing out from a greenside bunker on the final hole. Five players including defending champion Tiger Woods, who shot 70, tied for third place, three strokes behind. The others at 284 were Jose Maria Olazabal (66), Retief Goosen (69), Fred Couples (71) and Chad Campbell (71).

While Mickelson needed to birdie the final hole for his first two major titles, this time he carried a three-stroke lead, was playing "stress-free" and won comfortably even with a bogey. "This is a lot better. I loved it," Mickelson said, describing his walk from the 18th tee to the green.

It was a heart-wrenching loss for Woods, who was let down by his putting on the last day, but he did not publicly reveal the depth of his feelings about the defeat. He knew his father, Earl, who had cancer and was back at home in California, probably would not live to see him win another major championship. Tiger was extremely close to his father, his mentor and best friend who had watched him become the finest golfer of his time. Earl Woods died 24 days after the Masters, on May 3.

Mickelson was the first player other than Woods to win back-to-back majors since Nick Price won the Open and PGA Championship in 1994. "When I look back on it," Mickelson said, "I think what I'm most proud of is that I didn't let other people back in it. They had to come and chase me down and make birdies to do it."

He opened the tournament with 70 to tie for fourth place (three strokes behind) and he was tied for fifth (four strokes behind) after a 72 in the second round. He led by one stroke over Couples and Campbell after 70 in the third round, which was spread over two days because of a lengthy rain delay on Saturday. Mickelson had to play 13 holes of the third round on Sunday morning.

Two drivers are not what today's golfers usually carry in their bags. But Mickelson had two drivers in his—one to draw the ball left to right, the other to fade it right to left—which helped him to counter the 155 extra yards added to the Augusta National course this year, stretching it to 7,445 yards. "It was a huge help," he said. "I got 20, 25 yards more with the driver that draws."

The two slightly different Callaway drivers had been in Mickelson's bag since the previous week's BellSouth Classic near Atlanta, where he shot a dazzling 28-under-par score and won by 13 strokes. "I had a good feeling about this tournament," Mickelson said. "Obviously, winning by 13 last week helped. But I knew I was playing well and I knew I was prepared for the tournament. But still I had to execute."

Woods said, "He continued what he had last week."

Couples, who played alongside Mickelson in the final round, said, "It was an easy 69. He didn't struggle at all." For the week, Mickelson had 43 pars, 18 birdies and 11 bogeys. "I'd like to say one thing about the course changes," he said. "I like them."

First Round

There was no rain delay in the first round for the first time since 2001, and the Augusta National course was running so dry and fast that Tiger Woods said it reminded him of the U.S. Open. The best score anyone could post was 67, five under par, by Vijay Singh, and Singh would rather have kept quiet about that. "Better not say that too loud," he said. "Maybe they will move it back 50 yards next year."

Rocco Mediate shot 68 to be one stroke behind Singh, and Arron Oberholser, playing in his first Masters, was third with 69. There were four players with 70s: Phil Mickelson, Retief Goosen, Tim Clark and Geoff Ogilvy. Former Masters champions Ben Crenshaw, Fred Couples and Mike Weir were among 11 players who shot 71s and were tied for eighth place. That group also included past major champions Ernie Els, Ben Curtis and Rich Beem, plus Chad Campbell, David Howell, Nick O'Hern, Billy Mayfair and Stuart Appleby.

Woods was in another group of 11 players who shot even-par 72s and were tied for 19th place. He rolled in a 35-foot birdie putt on the last hole that saved him from an over-par round. He said he played well, despite being five strokes behind the leader. "The golf course is playing really difficult," he said. He did enjoy one magical hole, the par-four No. 14, where he struck an eight iron from 163 yards that went into the hole for an eagle. Next to the 2 on his card, however, Woods posted a 7. On the par-five No. 15, his tee shot landed in a divot in the fairway. He dumped his second shot into the pond fronting the green and took a double bogey.

After much speculation that the leaderboard at the Masters would only hold the names of big hitters such as Singh and Woods, the list featured many styles of play.

Mediate, a hitter of average length, and with back problems at the age of 43, was on top of the leaderboard for most of the first round until Singh caught and passed him in the afternoon. Mediate made 10 consecutive pars to start his round, then poured in birdies on four of his last eight holes. In the dry conditions, with tee shots rolling well on the fairways, Mediate said he could compete with the big bombers. He did not worry about where his golf ball landed relative to those who out-drove him.

It was difficult for any of the PGA Tour players to complain about the course when Crenshaw, who plays the 50-and-over Champions Tour, shot a one-under-par round. "I felt I had a few miracles out here to happen," said Crenshaw, who had won the Masters twice. "I have to chip and putt here.

That's the only way I can get around." That, Crenshaw certainly did, nine shots better than Charles Howell, who shot 80, and 13 better than David Duval, who shot 84.

Singh, even at age 43, has always been among the Tour's strongest players, but it was a deft putter and a fluid swing that led to the day's best round. After shooting 77 in the final round of The Players Championship in March, Singh said he received several calls from friends who said his swing was out of sync. He decided to look at his swing on video. "I found out exactly what I was doing wrong," he said. "It was the same mistake that I've been doing forever. I worked really hard last week, I tried to fix it, and it's on the way, I guess."

Singh had not won a tournament since the previous August, but had posted four consecutive finishes in the top seven at Augusta, where he won in 2000. When he made seven pars to start his round, he appeared headed for an average day. Instead, he scored five birdies in a nine-hole stretch and vaulted to the top of the leaderboard.

First-Round Leaders: Vijay Singh 67, Rocco Mediate 68, Arron Oberholser 69, Tim Clark 70, Retief Goosen 70, Geoff Ogilvy 70, Phil Mickelson 70, Ben Crenshaw 71, Rich Beem 71, David Howell 71, Mike Weir 71, Fred Couples 71, Nick O'Hern 71, Ben Curtis 71, Billy Mayfair 71, Stuart Appleby 71, Chad Campbell 71, Ernie Els 71

Second Round

As the wind rustled the pine trees and bent the flagsticks around Augusta National, the leaderboard by the 18th green brought a smile to Carl Jackson, Ben Crenshaw's longtime caddie, as he studied the names of players tumbling down. Vijay Singh had made three double bogeys and Ernie Els had one. "Just look at that," Jackson said softly. The 54-year-old Crenshaw had found a place on this day with the best golfers in the world. He shot even-par 72 and finished five strokes behind the leader, Chad Campbell, who, like Crenshaw, is a Texan who is comfortable playing in the wind.

Campbell shot 67, for a total of 138, six under par, and held a three-stroke lead over Singh (74), Fred Couples (70) and Rocco Mediate (73), who all had 141 totals. Els (71) and Phil Mickelson (72) were in a group of five golfers who were four strokes behind at 142, joining Darren Clarke (70), Tim Clark (72) and David Howell. Tiger Woods (71) was with Crenshaw at 143, in a group of seven players who were five strokes behind.

Jack Nicklaus, at age 46, was the oldest player to win the Masters, in 1986, but Jackson said he had told Crenshaw, "Let's be the first player in the 50s to win." Els said, "Ben obviously loves this place. He and his caddie are such a great team around here." Jackson described Crenshaw as a player made for this course. "Once he gets it on the right position on these greens, he's dangerous," Jackson said.

Crenshaw made a mess of things on the par-four No. 17 before recovering nicely. "I hit Eisenhower's tree, first of all, and bounced all the way back," he said. "Then I half-topped a four wood out there and hit a full nine iron." He was left with a long, winding putt for par that Jackson helped him read. "It went right in the cup," Crenshaw said. He dropped his head and smiled when the putt fell, and a par on the 18th left him in the middle of a tournament he calls his favorite. He said he would like the course to remain dry, but the forecast for Saturday called for morning showers and afternoon thunderstorms.

A wet day would also make the course more difficult for Campbell, a medium-length hitter who won the Bob Hope Chrysler Classic in January. Playing in his fourth Masters, Campbell said he looked forward to the weekend but was celebrating nothing. "You don't want to get ahead of yourself," Campbell said. "It's special to be leading after two rounds. Obviously, my goal is to be leading after four rounds."

Mickelson, playing with those two drivers, said he "drove it very well" for his score of even-par 72 and a 142 total. "When I did miss a fairway, it was a yard or two in the first cut," he said. "It allowed me to be aggressive on some holes, to attack some pins, to give myself birdie opportunities. I just didn't take advantage of enough of those, but I'm in good position."

With the wind reaching 15 miles an hour and swirling, Augusta National proved a fast and difficult test, but it played shorter than its 7,445 yards. "Today was really tough out there," Woods said. "It was windy, swirly, and it just played difficult. A good shot can end up in a bad spot, and you just have to accept the consequences and move on."

Woods counted four missed putts that he said he probably should have made. "I'm in contention, so it is a good spot, I guess," he said. "With the forecast, it's as unpredictable as it's been all week."

As one of the stronger players, Woods said he preferred difficult conditions to calm ones. When it rains, Woods can carry his drives longer than most of his competitors. "I've never been a proponent of golf tournaments where you've got to shoot 20 or 30 under par just to win," Woods said. "I enjoy tournaments where if you shoot a round in the 60s, you've earned it and you're going to move up the leaderboard. You hit good shots, and you can post a good number out there."

David Duval shot 43 on the first nine—including a 10 on the par-five No. 2—then shot four-under-par 32 for the day's best score on the second nine. He missed the 36-hole cut—which fell at four-over-par 148—by 11 strokes. Other notables who missed the cut included Chris DiMarco (six over par) who lost to Woods in a playoff in 2005; Colin Montgomerie (five over), Michael Campbell (five over), Ian Woosnam (five over), David Toms (six over), Tom Lehman (seven over), John Daly (nine over) and Charles Howell (20 over). None of the five amateurs in the field made the cut.

Second-Round Leaders: Chad Campbell 67–138, Rocco Mediate 73–141, Vijay Singh 74–141, Fred Couples 70–141, Darren Clarke 70–142, Ernie Els 71–142, Phil Mickelson 72–142, Tim Clarke 72–142, David Howell 71–142, Nick O'Hern 72–143, Billy Mayfair 72–143, Padraig Harrington 70–143, Olin Browne 69–143, Ben Crenshaw 72–143, Retief Goosen 73–143, Tiger Woods 71–143

Third Round

Thunderstorms which had been forecast swept through Georgia on Saturday and delayed the Masters for more than four hours, from 1:02 p.m. to 5:20 p.m. When darkness halted play about 8 p.m., the leaderboard was slightly different than it was Friday. Chad Campbell, the 36-hole leader by three strokes, played only four holes and now led by one over Tim Clark and Rocco Mediate.

Campbell had received a preview of what would be ahead in Sunday's marathon finish. His 46-minute appearance started strong and finished with a thud. He was still the tournament leader and would have plenty of time to reverse course. "It's where I want to be," he said. Ten players were within four strokes, including the top five in the Official World Golf Ranking. "Obviously, those guys do have a lot more major experience, with the wins, but I would like to start somewhere," Campbell said.

After two closing bogeys Campbell was six under par for 40 holes. Mediate had birdies on the second and fourth holes, while Clark played five holes in three under par. Tiger Woods played nine holes and shot two-under 34, moving from five strokes behind to three. Padraig Harrington (two under in six holes) and Phil Mickelson (one under in five holes) were also three behind. Mickelson didn't have any pars. He birdied the first three holes then bogeyed the next two.

Campbell didn't tee off until 6:54 p.m. in the final group. He made birdies on the first two holes then bogeys on the third and fourth. In contrast, Mediate finished by holing a birdie putt from five feet on the par-three fourth. "I made it, which was cool because it wasn't that easy of a putt," Mediate said. "It was getting dark, but I didn't want to sit on it all night."

Clark, playing three groups ahead of Campbell and Mediate, birdied the first, second and fifth. "I couldn't be more pleased with that start," he said. By the time Campbell got on the course, Clark had birdied the first two holes, and Mickelson was on his way to making birdies on the first three before following them with two bogeys. Campbell wasn't too concerned about his two bogeys. "Honestly, even with the two bogeys, I hit two good putts," he said. "The only bad shot I hit was the second shot on No. 3."

Campbell and Mediate were facing a 32-hole day on Sunday—14 holes to complete the third round and 18 holes for the fourth round. "It's going to be a long day, it's going to be a tough day," Mediate said. "I'm looking forward to it. It's going to be challenging. I have to do something real special to win this golf tournament."

The test would be more mental than physical, according to Campbell. "It's going to be tough walking around that many times, but when you're in contention you don't really think about it," he said. "It's not like we have to run. That would be a different story."

Woods also wasn't concerned about the long day ahead. "I know I'm conditioned for it," he said. "It's just a matter of playing well, executing and making birdies. Last year, I went 54 holes on the weekend, so this is nothing new."

Last year Woods was in the 10th fairway when play started on Sunday and this time he would begin on the 10th tee. He scored birdies on the third and eighth holes, and nearly holed out with his second shot on the par-four third, his ball coming to rest near the edge of the cup. He had par saves on the first and fifth holes.

With the greens softened by the rain and more receptive to shots, Woods said that in order to keep up with the leaders on Sunday he would need to be aggressive. "It's a matter of going out there, playing well, executing and making some birdies," he said. "You know you've got to make some birdies out there with the greens so soft."

"Chad's playing great, and we've got to go out there and play well," Woods said. "On this golf course anything can happen."

Leaders When Round Suspended: Chad Campbell 6 under (after 4 holes played), Tim Clark 5 under (5 holes), Rocco Mediate 5 under (4 holes), Tiger Woods 3 under (9 holes), Padraig Harrington 3 under (6 holes), Phil Mickelson 3 under (5 holes), Stephen Ames 2 under (9 holes), Retief Goosen 2 under (9 holes), Ernie Els 2 under (5 holes), Vijay Singh 2 under (4 holes), Fred Couples 2 under (5 holes)

Fourth Round

Tied for fourth place when third-round play was suspended, Phil Mickelson went one under par for his 13 holes on Sunday morning to post 70 for his four-under 212 total. Chad Campbell was three over par on the 14 holes he played, finishing with 75 to be one stroke off the lead at 213, tied with Fred Couples, who posted 72. Six players were tied for fourth place at 214—Stephen Ames (70), Tiger Woods (71), Tim Clark (72), Darren Clarke (72), Vijay Singh (73) and Rocco Mediate (73). Rounding out the top 10 and ties at 215 were Miguel Angel Jimenez (69) and Retief Goosen (72).

At the end of the third round, a photographer distracted Mickelson as he teed off on No. 18—he ended up making a bogey—but the incident faded in the afternoon. He took the lead for good with a birdie on No. 8. He went two strokes up on Couples on No. 11, where Mickelson made par and Couples missed his third short putt of the day to take bogey. Mickelson's rivals faded the rest of the way.

The outcome was still unclear when Mickelson took a two-stroke lead over Couples into the 440-yard, par-four 14th hole. Couples hit an iron shot to four feet, and Mickelson's approach shot stopped 30 feet from the hole. Couples lipped out the short birdie attempt and was left with five feet coming back for par. He missed that too, as his putter let him down all day. "I felt like I needed to hit it firm," Couples said. "I was nervous, I got jumpy, and I hit it through the break. Then I missed the next one too. That was ballgame for me."

Mickelson did not back off. He was pin high on the par-five No. 15, nearly chipped in for eagle and made his birdie to go up by four strokes. "I'm glad I was able to finish it off on the last nine because it doesn't always happen that way," he said.

With his final-round 69, Mickelson's 281 total was two strokes better than Clark, who also shot 69 for 283 while paired with Woods. A South African, Clark joined countrymen Ernie Els and Goosen as a Masters runner-up when his 25-foot pitch from the right bunker at the 18th green tumbled into the hole. Woods was joined at 284 by Jose Maria Olazabal, Goosen, Campbell and Couples. Singh, the first-round leader, and Angel Cabrera shared eighth place at 285, and Stewart Cink was 10th at 286.

Through the round, Mickelson and Couples were encouraging each other to play well. They have been good friends and their caddies were housemates during the tournament. "Phil was smoking those two drivers that he has, and we were laughing about that," said Couples, age 46, the 1992 Masters champion. "We kept telling each other, 'Let's make birdies.'"

Couples, however, three-putted three times. "It's pretty simple to figure out," he said. "Somewhere, I needed four putts out there to beat him, and I didn't have it in me."

Earlier in the afternoon, Ben Crenshaw walked off the 18th green to a standing ovation. By his own admission, Augusta National had become too difficult for Crenshaw over the last two rounds and his scores of 78 and 79 reflected that. The two-time Masters champion, now age 54, doffed his cap and recalled his opening 71 and 72 that, for a time, had him squarely in the hunt for the title. When the rain Saturday made the course longer, he was sent tumbling down the leaderboard.

"I had a great time," Crenshaw said. "Just a great time all week." He finished 47th with a 300 total—last among those who played all four rounds.

In second place after the first round, Mediate was a bit farther up the leaderboard from Crenshaw, in a tie for 36th place at 294 after posting a closing 80. The shortest hole on the course sidetracked his run for the title. Standing on the tee of the 155-yard, par-three No. 12, Mediate was just three strokes off the lead when he dumped his shot into the pond fronting the green, then hit two shots into the water from the drop area. He made 10 on the hole.

Mediate said his back started bothering him on the long day, particularly on the ninth hole of the fourth round. "My back went psycho," he said. "I just tried to hang in there. I almost had to quit, but I couldn't do that."

Another two-time Masters champion, the 40-year-old Olazabal posted six-under-par 66, the best score of the tournament. He hit 13 greens and needed just 26 putts in the final round. "I feel at peace with myself around here," he said. "At least today."

When Woods made a birdie on the final hole, his caddie, Steve Williams, took his putter and pretended to break it over his leg. Woods seemed to think it was a good idea. "I'm probably going to snap this putter into eight pieces," Woods said. "As good as I hit it today was as bad as I putted. I putted atrociously."

His normally sharp short game abandoned him. He made three consecutive bogeys during the completion of his third round. In the final round, with a short chance for birdie on No. 12, he missed. With a short chance for eagle on No. 13, he missed again. He had 33 putts in his 70, including three three-putt greens, and he could never put pressure on the leaders.

"The way I controlled my ball flight, I thought today was the day if I'd putted normal," Woods said. "It's the most three-putts I've ever had here."

This was the first year that his father, Earl Woods, had not been able to make the trip to Augusta. "I'm sure he's watching and probably a little mad at me for the way I putted," Woods said. "I'm sure he knows what I did wrong."

The Final Leaders: Phil Mickelson 69–281, Tim Clark 69–283, Jose Maria Olazabal 66–284, Retief Goosen 69–284, Tiger Woods 70–284, Chad Campbell 71–284, Fred Couples 71–284, Angel Cabrera 68–285, Vijay Singh 71–285, Stewart Cink 70–286

3. U.S. Open Championship

Phil Mickelson's disaster on the 18th hole at Winged Foot Golf Club in the final round of the United States Open Championship will go down among the most memorable collapses along with Sam Snead's eight on the final hole of the 1939 Open when he needed a par five to win. There have been other debacles in the history of championship golf, but Snead's was most similar.

In the last pairing of the day, needing a par four to win, Mickelson ripped into his drive and pushed it so far left that it hit the roof of a hospitality tent and bounced back toward the fairway into grass worn down by the spectators. Blocking his line to the green was a tall maple tree, the same tree that cost him a stroke in the second round.

In the second round, Mickelson tried to carry his shot over the tree, but the ball hit a branch and fell straight down. He lost just one stroke then off of dirt, but here his ball lay in the trampled rough. The Open was Mickelson's to win or lose. He could win with a par, or with a bogey-five he could force a playoff with the Australian Geoff Ogilvy. Playing directly ahead of him, Ogilvy had finished with a pitch close to the hole for a par on the 18th and a score of 72 for a 285 total, five over par.

Deciding to gamble, Mickelson went for a shot he hoped would turn from right to left around the tree. It struck the tree and caromed back to about 30 feet from where his drive had finished. He then hit into a greenside bunker and, from a partially buried lie, ran his fourth shot across the green, missed the putt coming back, and lost the Open with his double-bogey six.

Stunned, Mickelson said, "I am such an idiot." He posted a 74 for a 286 total, and tied for second with Colin Montgomerie (71), who also took six at the 18th, and Jim Furyk (70), who took five there.

Ogilvy, 29 years old, became the second Australian winner of the U.S. Open, following David Graham, who won the 1981 championship. Playing on the PGA Tour since 2001, Ogilvy had won twice, once in 2005 at Tucson and the second early in 2006, when he beat Davis Love in the final of the WGC - Accenture Match Play.

Throughout his career, Ogilvy had been outshone by his countrymen. He ranked 50th in the world and sixth among Australians at the start of 2006. Now he stood eighth in the world and second among Australians to Adam Scott, who ranked sixth.

He had recently found that major championships seemed to suit his temperament and his game. "For some bizarre reason, starting at Pinehurst last year, I've played better at majors than I had up to that point," Ogilvy said. "I don't know why. I got more out of my game (in the U.S. Open) at Pinehurst than I should have and finished 25th or something (actually tied for 28th)." A month later, Ogilvy birdied three of the last four holes at St. Andrews and tied for fifth in the Open. He then tied for fifth in the PGA Championship, three strokes behind Mickelson.

Many (and probably Mickelson himself) felt Mickelson was on the cusp of providing Tiger Woods with his first genuine rival since Woods burst onto the professional circuit in the autumn of 1996 and started collecting major trophies at the 1997 Masters. After years of frustration, Mickelson, now 35 years old, had claimed his first major title in the 2004 Masters and now had won two in a row, the 2005 PGA Championship and this year's Masters. Here he was closing in on his third consecutive major.

Then it all came crashing down, and Mickelson was never the same again this year.

Woods was not there to contribute to Mickelson's demise. He had posted a pair of 76s and missed the 36-hole cut by three strokes, the first time as a professional that he had not played all four rounds in a major championship. Those two rounds on June 15-16 were Woods's first in competition since the Masters on April 9, when he tied for third place. His father, Earl, had died on May 3 after a long battle with cancer.

The qualifying tests this year drew much attention because of the presence of Michelle Wie, the 16-year-old girl from Hawaii who was already a professional and contending for the LPGA's top prizes. She advanced from local qualifying to the sectional in Summit, New Jersey, bringing with her a gallery that was limited to 3,000 and about 300 members of the media. The Golf Channel had frequent progress reports and three-hour, election-style evening coverage from all 13 qualifying sites.

Wie shot 68 and 75 and missed by five strokes, but another teenager from Hawaii, 15-year-old, 5-foot-1 Tadd Fujikawa, became the youngest ever to qualify when he shot 70 and 71 in his home state. In Columbus, Ohio, 23-year-old Madalitso Muthiya became the first-ever qualifier from Zambia, the former Northern Rhodesia. Both would miss the 36-hole cut.

First Round

Only Colin Montgomerie played under par 70 on a bright and windy first day. He finished in 69 strokes, one better than the five players who tied for second place and two better than eight others with 71s. Phil Mickelson shot 70, along with Jim Furyk, Steve Stricker, Miguel Angel Jimenez and David Howell.

Two strokes behind Montgomerie, Geoff Ogilvy came in with 71, the same score as Vijay Singh, who won the PGA Tour event a week earlier at Westchester Country Club, six miles from Winged Foot, located in Mamaroneck, New York. They and several other players had moved on to the U.S. Open without even changing hotels in nearby White Plains.

Michael Campbell began with 75, showing little of the precision he had demonstrated at Pinehurst when he won a year ago. Still, Campbell's score was one stroke better than Tiger Woods, the winner in 2000 and 2002, and two strokes better than Retief Goosen, the 2001 and 2004 champion. Winged Foot had played tough; indeed, most of the field scored 75 or higher.

The spectators were most interested in the play of Woods, competing for the first time in nine weeks. He began with a drive in the rough, then he failed to reach the green. He pitched on to 10 feet and missed the putt. Woods missed the second green as well and left a downhill six-foot putt two feet short. He reached the green on the 216-yard, par-three third hole, but was 30 feet from the hole. He missed his first putt by six feet, then missed again for his third consecutive bogey to start the round.

Woods had lost control of his driver and his short game but he fought on, and was out in 40, five over par. He played better on the second nine except for his double-bogey seven on the 12th hole, and played the last six holes in one under for his 76. He had hit just three of 14 fairways on the driving holes and 10 greens and had taken 33 putts.

Montgomerie had almost as rocky a start. He dropped strokes at the first and third holes and played an erratic first nine, making pars on just three holes. One over par at the turn, he putted spectacularly on the homeward nine, needing one putt on five holes. He holed from 25 feet on the 17th, but failed on a five-footer on the last green.

In times past that miss might have upset Montgomerie, but not this time, and he seemed to be taking whatever came in his stride. "That putt broke a mile," he said. "I can't be worried about that. I was still enjoying the putt on 17. I hit that putt, and about halfway to the hole I thought, 'Well, that has no chance.' But it kept curling and went in."

The crowd favorite was Mickelson, who had developed a strong following in this region with his runner-up performance to Woods in the 2002 U.S. Open at Bethpage State Park on Long Island, and his victory in the 2005 PGA Championship at Baltusrol Golf Club in New Jersey.

No one in the field prepared for Winged Foot so thoroughly as Mickelson, who had visited the club often leading up to the championship and who spent the previous week playing the course and working on the shots he would need. He occasionally had carried two drivers designed to shape his shots either way, including his victory in this year's Masters Tournament and the BellSouth Classic the week before that.

For Winged Foot, Mickelson decided to carry only one driver, his left-to-right club. It worked fairly well in the first round. He hit nine of 14 fairways on the driving holes. He started on the 10th tee and played an erratic first nine holes, but saved his even-par 35 with a marvelous short game. At the 18th, his ninth hole, he made a putt from 40 feet for birdie.

He played more steadily on his second nine but was let down by his putting. He lipped out a three-foot putt for par on the second hole and three-putted on the par-five fifth hole. Nevertheless, Mickelson was just one stroke behind the leader, in position to challenge for his first U.S. Open title.

First-Round Leaders: Colin Montgomerie 69, Jim Furyk 70, Phil Mickelson 70, Steve Stricker 70, Miguel Angel Jimenez 70, David Howell 70, Kenneth Ferrie 71, Graeme McDowell 71, Vijay Singh 71, Mike Weir 71, John Cook 71, Fred Funk 71, Kevin Stadler 71, Geoff Ogilvy 71

Second Round

In a surprising twist of this U.S. Open, Tiger Woods would have traded places with Steve Stricker after the second day. Each was where the other was more likely to be. Stricker was at the top of the standings with a 139 total for two rounds, while Woods was 13 strokes behind and had missed the 36-hole cut. Stricker had never led the Open, and Woods had never failed to play every round except in his first attempt as an amateur in 1995.

After an opening 70, Stricker played Winged Foot in 69 and climbed past Colin Montgomerie into first place. Montgomerie slipped to 71 after his opening 69, and at 140 stood one stroke ahead of Geoff Ogilvie and Kenneth Ferrie. Both Ogilvy and Ferrie had scores of 71 and 70. A stroke behind, tied for fifth place at 142, Jim Furyk shot 72 and Padraig Harrington, 69.

Phil Mickelson followed his opening 70 with 73 and dropped into a tie for seventh with Arron Oberholser, who won the AT&T Pebble Beach National Pro-Am earlier in the year, and two other lesser-known players, Jason Dufner, playing in his second Open, and Graeme McDowell.

There were five under-par scores in the second round. Oberholser and David Duval posted 68s, and Stricker, Harrington and Luke Donald shot 69s. Starting six strokes behind the leader, Duval displayed the skills of his earlier years and advanced from a tie for 96th into a tie for 14th place. Meanwhile, Tom Pernice and Tommy Armour avoided elimination with even-par 70s after their 79s in the first round. But Kevin Stadler, who shot 71 in the first round, fell to 81 in the second round.

Attention was focused on whether Woods would survive the 36-hole cut which would trim the field to the low 60 players and anyone tied for 60th place. Including his last two as amateur, he had made the cut in 39 consecutive majors. This time, with a second score of 76, he missed. Woods again failed to control his shots. He found the fairway with only three drives in the first round and four drives in the second.

Defending champion Michael Campbell had 77 for a 152 total, the same as Woods. Retief Goosen, who gave away the 2005 Open with 81 in the final round, played rounds of 77 and 78 here. Sergio Garcia, still seeking his first major, finished one stroke worse than Goosen, and Davis Love, who won the 1997 PGA Championship at Winged Foot, shot 154 and also missed the cut.

Stricker was out in 32 in the first round, and once again he birdied early, holing a 15-foot putt at the 14th, his fifth hole of the round. He gave back the stroke at the 15th, then recovered it with a birdie on the difficult 18th. In two days he had played Winged Foot's second nine in four under par. Now one under par for 27 holes, he had tied Montgomerie, the first-round leader.

On to his second nine, Stricker was on the verge of dropping a shot when he bunkered his approach shot to the second hole. He put his next shot into the hole, claiming a birdie-three where a five seemed likely. Then his game deserted him. Bogeys at the seventh and eighth holes wiped out his two birdies, and he was in danger of a third consecutive bogey when he found a bunker on his approach shot to the ninth green. Again Stricker pitched into the hole for a birdie. He was at even-par 35 for the nine, he shot 69 and could sit out the day as the leader.

No stranger to U.S. Open competition, Stricker tied for fifth place in 1998 and was fifth alone in 1999. He also lost by two strokes to Vijay Singh in the 1999 PGA Championship after being tied for the lead going to the final round. His game had since fallen into disrepair. He had won nothing since the 2001 Accenture Match Play and lost his PGA Tour card in 2004. And his lead was fragile because Montgomerie and Mickelson had yet to tee off.

Mickelson was observing his 36th birthday when he started the second round, June 16, although it didn't appear to be a happy birthday when he missed the fairways and greens, and bogeyed the first two holes. He settled down and made pars until the ninth hole, where he again missed the fairway and the green, taking a bogey.

Out in 38, Mickelson continued his loose play but ran in a 30-foot putt and birdied the 13th, and he saved par at the 17th with a bunker shot within a foot of the hole. He took a bogey at the 18th after a poor drive which had him blocked by the maple tree that would later cost him the championship, came back in 35 and scored 73.

Montgomerie scored pars on 17 of the 18 holes and dropped one stroke at the 14th, which ranked only behind the first hole in difficulty. He had just two birdie opportunities. He missed a makeable putt at the seventh and his 20-foot putt at the ninth glided just by the hole. Montgomerie said, "If I can hang in there the way I did today and have a chance on Sunday, one never knows."

Second-Round Leaders: Steve Stricker 69–139, Colin Montgomerie 71–140, Geoff Ogilvy 70–141, Kenneth Ferrie 70–141, Jim Furyk 72–142, Padraig Harrington 69–142, Graeme McDowell 72–143, Phil Mickelson 73–143, Arron Oberholser 68–143, Jason Dufner 71–143, Scott Hend 72–144, Bart Bryant 72–144, Phillip Archer 72–144

Third Round

With Tiger Woods out of the way, the focus was on Phil Mickelson, winner of the last two major championships, and Mickelson rose in the third round to a first-place tie with the Englishman Kenneth Ferrie. After a struggling 36 on the outward nine, Mickelson came home in 33 strokes for 69, one under par, and a 212 total, two over par. He passed five players but could not shake Ferrie, who shot his second 71.

Aside from Mickelson, only Ryuji Imada broke par, matching Mickelson's 69, and only five others shot even-par 70. This was a day when Colin Montgomerie recovered from a poor start, when Ferrie and Geoff Ogilvy showed no indication of falling away, when Vijay Singh made a move, and when Steve Stricker lost control of his driver and dropped from first place into a tie for fourth.

Ferrie could have taken first place alone if not for a bogey on the 18th. He was playing remarkable golf for someone in his first U.S. Open. Ogilvy came in with 72 and moved to third place at 213, one stroke off the lead. Singh (70) and Ian Poulter (70) shared fourth place at 215 with Montgomerie (75) and Stricker (76), who dropped four shots in the last six holes.

Jim Furyk (74), Mike Weir (71) and Padraig Harrington (74) were at 216 after all three stumbled at the end. Furyk bogeyed two of the last three holes, Weir took a double-bogey six at the 18th, and Harrington finished with a triple-bogey seven.

Peter Hedblom of Sweden scored a hole-in-one on the long 243-yard, par-three third hole with a three-iron shot that fell short, bounced a few times and rolled into the hole. He also scored an eagle-three on the fifth hole and finished with 71 for a 217 total, tied for 11th place.

Stricker was in the last pairing with Montgomerie and was hitting his drives well at the start. He ran off four pars then scored a birdie at the par-five fifth hole after reaching the green in two. Suddenly, his game deserted him. He missed the fairway and the green at the sixth hole and dropped one stroke, then took bogeys on the eighth and ninth to be out in 37 strokes. His play on the second nine was worse. He had shot 32 and 34 on the second nine in the earlier rounds, but this time he took 39 strokes for his 76. Montgomerie suddenly lost his touch as well and bogeyed five of the first six holes. He had settled down by the seventh and played the remaining 12 holes in even par.

Not many spectators had followed Ogilvy's progress, but he had played steady golf, turning in 71 and 70 the first two days, then 72 in the third round. This was his third Open. He missed he cut in 2003 and tied for 26th place in 2005. After a bogey to start the third round, he ran off eight consecutive pars then birdied the 10th hole. He took bogeys at the 13th and 14th, then finished his round with four pars.

Paired with Ogilvy, Ferrie, age 27, played a quality game of golf, breezing around Winged Foot in 71, passing Ogilvy and climbing from a tie for third into a tie for first place with Mickelson. At first this didn't look to be Mickelson's day. Through the first nine he missed all but two fairways and four greens. He lost one stroke at the third hole, a long par-three, and took it back with a birdie at the fourth, and added another birdie at the sixth. He lost those strokes with bogeys at the eighth and ninth holes, and continued missing fairways on the early holes of the second nine.

Suddenly something clicked and Mickelson couldn't miss. He hit every fairway starting at the 14th and every green from the 11th, birdied both the 14th and 16th, which together surrendered only 13 birdies during the round, came back in 33, and with 69 joined Ferrie at the top of the list.

Third-Round Leaders: Phil Mickelson 69–212, Kenneth Ferrie 71–212, Geoff Ogilvy 72–213, Ian Poulter 70–215, Vijay Singh 70–215, Colin Montgomerie 75–215, Steve Stricker 76–215, Mike Weir 71–216, Padraig Harrington 74–216, Jim Furyk 74–216, Trevor Immelman 70–217, Luke Donald 70–217, Peter Hedblom 71–217, Bart Bryant 73–217, Arron Oberholser 74–217

Fourth Round

Once again there were sunny skies as the U.S. Open entered the final day. Early starters Jeff Sluman and David Duval gave the spectators something to watch as they waited for the leaders to tee off. Sluman whipped through the first nine in 32 strokes and shot 69 for a 288 total, eight over par, that would earn him a tie for sixth place. Duval bounced back from his 75 the previous day to 71 and a tie for 16th place.

Of those who would have a role in deciding the championship, Jim Furyk and Padraig Harrington teed off first, just ahead of Steve Stricker and Mike Weir. Playing inconsistent golf, Stricker made pars on six holes, birdied three, eagled one and bogeyed the rest, as he shot 73 and tied for sixth in the group that included Sluman and Kenneth Ferrie, who began the round tied with Phil Mickelson for first place.

Ferrie began by running off six consecutive pars, then bogeyed four of the next five holes, three-putting the seventh and eighth and missing the greens of the 10th and 11th. With two more bogeys, he shot 76, five shots higher than his next worst score. But Ferrie had no strong regrets. "I'll wake up tomorrow and I'm sure I'll be really pleased with what I've done this week," he said.

Furyk and Harrington left the first tee 40 minutes ahead of Mickelson and Ferrie. Furyk cut his deficit from four to two strokes with birdies on the first hole, one of just 18 there for the week, and the fifth hole, which gave up 174 birdies. He bogeyed the seventh and ninth holes, then played the first eight holes of the second nine in one under par. He missed a putt for par of only four feet on the 18th and settled for even-par 70 and a 286 total, which came to share second place.

As so many others, Harrington had his opening as well. The Irishman played the first 15 holes in two under par. With three more pars he would have finished at 284 and won the Open. Instead he missed all three greens and fell to 287 with 71 in the final round.

The Open eventually came down to three players, in this order—Colin Montgomerie, Geoff Ogilvy and Mickelson.

This was Montgomerie's 14th Open. The Scotsman had placed second in 1994 and 1997, losing to Ernie Els both times, the first in a playoff, and third in his first Open in 1992, when Tom Kite won. He began the final round at five over par and was two under for the first nine. He then bogeyed the 10th and 14th holes to lose those strokes and was six over through No. 16. A birdie at the 17th brought him back into the hunt.

After an excellent drive on No. 18, Montgomerie first drew a six iron from his bag, then replaced it and took a seven iron instead. It was a mistake. The ball drifted right as he shouted, "What kind of shot is that?" In the rough off the green, he popped the ball out and it ran far past the hole. His first putt also was long, and he missed the second putt too, taking a six on a hole he might have birdied. Rather than the 69 within his reach, Montgomerie shot 71 for his 286 total, one too many.

Ogilvy followed Montgomerie, and at the 17th it looked that he too might throw away his opportunity. He pushed his drive far right, into heavy rough, and could not reach the fairway with his second shot. His third was in more rough left of the green. Then Ogilvy chipped in and saved his par.

On to the 18th, Ogilvy's drive rolled into a sandy divot, which could have ruined his chances. Instead, he dug the ball out with a shot that landed just short of the green, then rolled back down the steep slope. It took a delicate touch for Ogilvy to pitch the ball to three feet from the hole, and he ran that putt in for 72 and 285, and waited to see Mickelson finish.

Finding more trouble, Mickelson's drive on the 17th landed in a trash receptacle, but he salvaged a par and moved on to the final hole, which he butchered in such a painful manner. Waiting for Ferrie to putt out and end the torture, Mickelson squatted, resting his putter on his shoulder, and stared at the ground with both hands on his head.

"I thought four over would be the number," Ogilvy said, "because Monty just birdied the 17th and he and Mickelson would finish about three or four over. Then, yeah. Wow. I chipped in. Just scary. I mean a shot that you wait your whole life to chip in in a situation like that—when you need to—and then you do it." When asked his reaction to winning, Ogilvy said, "It's ridiculous. I can't even image it."

The Final Leaders: Geoff Ogilvy 72–285, Jim Furyk 70–286, Colin Montgomerie 71–286, Phil Mickelson 74–286, Padraig Harrington 71–287, Nick O'Hern 69–288, Jeff Sluman 69–288, Mike Weir 72–288, Steve Stricker 73–288, Vijay Singh 73–288, Kenneth Ferrie 76–288

4. The Open Championship

There was a sense of uncertainty entering the Open Championship five weeks later. This was due to what had happened at Winged Foot, and just as much, it was due to being at Royal Liverpool Golf Club. Venues usually are familiar places to those in the traveling party of golf's major championships, but none had been here since 1967. Much had changed in the interval.

In the village of Hoylake, on England's Wirrel peninsula west of the city, Royal Liverpool is about as close to Liverpool as the Beatles are today, as one commentator said. In miles, Hoylake could be reached by commuter train in less than 30 minutes, which is how many in the near-record of 230,000 spectators came to the championship.

As a measure of its earlier importance, through 1967 when Roberto de Vicenzo won here, the only venue that had hosted more Opens than Royal Liverpool (10) was St. Andrews (12). It was in that same summer that "Sgt. Pepper's Lonely Hearts Club Band" was released, and the hometown Beatles were having a tremendous effect on Liverpool's reputation and self-image. That was soon offset by a financial slump, strikes and skirmishes. As the city hit rock bottom, Royal Liverpool fell out of favor as well.

Construction cranes dominated the skyline this summer in the rise of a new Liverpool, and a decade-long process brought the Open back to Hoylake. The first indication came in 1995, when Royal Liverpool hosted its 17th Amateur Championship. The property was thought to be too small for a modern Open, so the club purchased more land and sent aerial photographs to the Royal and Ancient Golf Club. Hoylake Municipal joined the effort by offering its course for parking and the practice ground. The R&A agreed that the Open could return if some adjustments were made to the course and to local traffic patterns.

Despite hot weather and a dry, fast-running golf course, Royal Liverpool was a magnificent test and perhaps surprisingly so. It made a lot of critics look foolish, notably the one from *Golf Digest* who said the course was a "thing of the past," not suitable for a major championship.

This was a very different championship from the last one here. The Open had become much more international. Seventy percent of the players in 1967 were British and Irish, and this year the figure was 27 percent. There were just seven Americans in 1967, and this year there were 43 Americans, one more than the British and Irish group. This year players came from 21 overseas countries (just 10 in 1967), including 23 players from Australia, 10 from South Africa, and six each from Spain, Sweden and Japan.

There were a couple of Americans, in particular, on most observers' minds as the week began. One was Phil Mickelson, who was going for his third consecutive major championship until stumbling on the final hole of the U.S. Open at Winged Foot. Several others also fell before Geoff Ogilvy's victory, but Mickelson's was truly a debacle. The other player of great interest was the world No. 1, Tiger Woods, who had missed the 36-hole cut in a major championship for the first time in his career at Winged Foot, following the death in May of his father, Earl, after a long struggle with cancer.

What would be next for Mickelson and Woods?

Mickelson tied for 22nd place and would not have another chance to win this year, while Woods reasserted himself with a vengeance, winning the first of the final six events sanctioned by the PGA Tour that he would play in 2006, also including another major in the PGA Championship. Woods took the Open by two strokes in a tearful finish over another American who had recently lost a parent, Chris DiMarco. Tiger shot rounds of 67, 65, 71 and 67 for a total of 270, 18 under par, while defending his title and winning his third Open and 11th professional major championship.

While Mickelson famously had used two drivers in winning the Masters, Woods won this championship without his driver. In practice Woods had found that he could drive the ball 370 yards on the hard fairways but there was no way to control the ball. So Woods took the five wood out of his bag for the first time this year, replaced it with the two iron, and proceeded to wear out his long irons over the four days of the championship. He took out his driver only once, on the 16th hole of the first round, and missed the fairway that one time.

First Round

The night before the first round, in a pub called La Bodega in Hoylake, one patron approached another and said, "You're Graeme McDowell, aren't you?" Expecting to be asked for an autograph, McDowell responded in the affirmative. Then the first man said, "You get pretty laid off at the top of your backswing, don't you?" McDowell said, "Yeah, I guess I do," and the man replied, "Get a bit of work done on that, will you?"

"It was pretty funny," the Northern Irishman recalled. "Fair play to him, he knew his stuff. It's something I'm working on anyway. I was joking with the guys I was with that if I shot 66 the next day I'd want to see him on the range Friday."

A 66 was exactly what McDowell shot the next day to lead the Open. McDowell was one stroke ahead of Tiger Woods, who scored an eagle on No. 18 to finish with 67, and four others: Greg Owen, Anthony Wall, Miguel Angel Jimenez and Keiichiro Fukabori. A large group at 68 included Ernie Els, Sergio Garcia, Jim Furyk, Mike Weir, Adam Scott and Tom Lehman. Only McDowell and Lehman managed a round without a bogey.

In the days leading up to the championship, the golf course was playing as hard and fast as any in recent memory after the grass had been baked brown in the summer heat. The dry conditions finally broke in the early-morning hours before the first round, when a thunderstorm struck along with heavy rain. The early starters welcomed the sight of pitch marks for the first time in the week. When the sun came out, the course was soon dry and hard again.

Part of the intrigue about this championship concerned the lack of anyone in the field who had played in an Open at Hoylake. Some had amateur experience over the links, including Ernie Els, Padraig Harrington, David Howell, Aaron Baddeley, Nick Daugherty and Mikko Ilonen, winner of the 1995 Amateur Championship here. The last European Tour event at Hoylake was the 1991 European Pro-Celebrity, which was won by Paul Broadhurst, also a contestant here.

After all the years away, one question going into Royal Liverpool was how the scoring would be. There was talk of low numbers before the golfers arrived, and the course conditions were conducive to birdies, but perhaps Harrington said it best. "The thing about a links course, more than other courses," Harrington said, "is that you only find how hard they are when you are playing in competition."

The first 68s of the day were scored by Marcus Fraser of Australia in the second group and by Ilonen and S.K. Ho in the third group. Fraser birdied all four of the par-fives, confirming the theory that scoring would be good, but poor shots could carry a severe penalty because of Hoylake's unusual internal out of bounds at the third and 18th holes, as the course was arranged for the championship. Mark Hensby, another of the 23 Australians in the field, discovered the cost of going right on the third was a triple-bogey seven.

Els and Garcia had no such problems and posted their 68s with ease, both missing chances to go even lower. Garcia, for example, three-putted at the par-five 10th and missed a short putt at the 13th. Weir started with two bogeys and three birdies in the first five holes, while Furyk matched his four-under effort.

Of the players who had come close to winning the U.S. Open at Winged Foot, Furyk had the best return here. Phil Mickelson and Colin Montgomerie had both taken double bogeys at the 72nd hole to hand the U.S. Open trophy to Geoff Ogilvy. Montgomerie birdied the first hole, but his round stuttered after that and he posted 73. Mickelson fared better, having 69 after going four under through 10 holes. Harrington, who bogeyed the last three holes in New York, started with a double bogey and slid to 75.

Montgomerie and Harrington were not the only home players to struggle. David Howell, winner of the BMW PGA Championship, finished with 74, the same score as Luke Donald and Dougherty, and Ian Poulter shot 75, including a triple bogey at the 14th. Instead, it was England's Greg Owen, playing with Furyk, who took the early lead with 67.

Chris DiMarco started and finished his round well, with three birdies in the first four holes and three birdies in the last four, but took a triple-bogey seven in between at the seventh hole, where he drove into a bush and took two hacks to get out, then into a bunker. Had DiMarco declared an unplayable lie, the result might have been different, not just in his round of 70, but in the championship.

Woods, paired with the talkative Nick Faldo, along with Shingo Katayama, started slowly when he three-putted the first green and took two shots from a bunker at the 10th hole. But Woods went out in 34 and came back in 33, relieving any fears that he might miss the cut as he had at the U.S. Open.

First-Round Leaders: Graeme McDowell 66, Greg Owen 67, Anthony Wall 67, Miguel Angel Jimenez 67, Keiichiro Fukabori, Tiger Woods 67, Marcus Fraser 68, S.K. Ho 68, Mikko Ilonen 68, Mark Hensby 68, Sergio Garcia 68, Mike Weir 68, Ernie Els 68, Jim Furyk 68, Tom Lehman 68, Carl Pettersson 68, Adam Scott 68, Ben Crane 68, Brett Rumford 68

Second Round

It should be noted at 11:42 a.m. of the second day Tiger Woods birdied the 11th hole to take the lead for the first time this week. Thirty-five minutes later, Woods holed out with a four-iron shot for an eagle-two on the 14th. By the time he was seated in the media center, having posted a seven-under-par 65 for a 132 total and a three-stroke lead, Woods was being asked if this Open was over. "No," Woods said. "I'm not sitting here with the claret jug ... We have a long way to go." Indeed, by the end of the day, Ernie Els and Chris DiMarco had returned 65s as well. Els was then just one stroke behind Woods, and DiMarco was three back.

Of the three, Els had played the best, in the afternoon when there was more wind than in the morning, and he was the only player not to suffer a bogey. But Woods provided a stroke of brilliance that will always be associated with his triumph at Hoylake. On the 456-yard No. 14, which had a right-to-left dogleg, Woods took a two iron off the tee and was left with a shot of 212 yards to the hole, so far back that he could not see the flagstick because of mounds at the dogleg and the spectators at the green could not see him swing. Arriving unexpectedly on the green, the ball hit 10 yards short and bounced several times before dropping into the hole.

A cheer rose from the crowd at the green, and shortly after that, a roar when it became known that the shot was Tiger's. Woods and caddie Steve Williams slapped palms when the result was relayed to them by a television reporter, and then they got a standing ovation on the green.

"I had 194 yards to the front of the green," Woods said later. "I was trying to land the ball on the front edge and let chase on wherever it chases on. On the 12th I had 190 and hit a nice little four iron up on the green and I was basically hitting the same shot, just trying to hold the ball in the wind. I really hit it flush and held it nicely ... I was just trying to get my four and move on. It happened to go in."

"I can't believe it," said Graeme McDowell, who shot 73 and fell out of the lead. "I've just watched Tiger making a two at a hole where he had absolutely no right to be firing at the flag."

The leading British or Irish player was now Robert Rock, a teaching professional from Warwickshire, whose 69 for a 138 total gave him eighth place alone. Between Woods, Els, DiMarco and Rock were Retief Goosen (136) and Miguel Angel Jimenez, Adam Scott and Mikko Ilonen (all at 137).

Meanwhile, the final-hole combatants of the U.S. Open at Winged Foot were further back—Jim Furyk (139), champion Geoff Ogilvy (140), Phil Mickelson (140) and, finally, Colin Montgomerie (148) and Padraig Harrington (149), who both missed the 36-hole cut. Only Furyk would prove to be a contender here in the end.

After an early-year win in Abu Dhabi, DiMarco had experienced a terrible year. In March he injured his back and ribs while skiing, and early in July, his mother died suddenly. "I have a great peace about me this week," DiMarco said. "My mom was a huge supporter of me and she would be angry if I did not play. My dad, Rich, is here watching. It is therapeutic for me to be inside the ropes playing, and it is therapeutic for him to be outside the ropes watching."

DiMarco made 20-foot putts for birdies on the first and second holes, and his six-iron shot to eight feet at the eighth produced another birdie, the first of four in a row. He holed from 30 feet at the ninth, two-putted for a four at the 10th, and made a five-footer at the 11th. He holed from 25 feet on the 15th, then made his only bogey of the day on the 17th. He got up and down from 60 yards at the 18th for another birdie and his 65.

After DiMarco had led for much of his round, along came Woods, who produced a staggering exhibition. He took a bogey at the third hole, but regained that with a birdie at the fourth. He chipped to within a foot for his four at the par-five fifth, and holed a 60-foot putt for a birdie at the eighth. Out in 33 strokes, Woods two-putted for a birdie-four on the 10th, holed a 12-footer for birdie at the 11th, then came that eagle-three on the 14th. He got up and down for another birdie at the 16th. Woods's total of 132 for 36 holes was two off the record.

Els saw the score before he teed off. "Obviously, he's a great player," Els said, "but if he's at 12 under, I thought there must be some birdies out there. I felt I had to get my share of them ... I didn't think I was going to shoot 65, but I needed something in the 60s."

Els hit a superb seven iron to two feet at the third hole for the first of seven birdies. He holed a six-foot birdie putt on the fifth and an 18-footer on the sixth. From there, he took advantage of the par-fives. He got up and down at the 10th for a four, and two-putted the 16th and 18th holes, as well as making a three at the 14th.

Second-Round Leaders: Tiger Woods 65–132, Ernie Els 65–133, Chris DiMarco 65–135, Retief Goosen 66–136, Miguel Angel Jimenez 70–137, Adam Scott 69–137, Mikko Ilonen 69–137, Robert Rock 69–138

Third Round

There were more low scores in the third round but not from Tiger Woods or Ernie Els. Both posted 71s to allow others to challenge for the championship. Sergio Garcia equaled the course record with the fourth 65 of the week. He jumped from five to 12 under par and only a birdie at the last hole enabled Woods to preserve his lead with a 203 total, 13 under par.

This was the 11th time that Woods had held the lead or a share of it in a major championship, and he had won all the previous 10. This time Woods had a very uncharacteristic third round, three-putting three times on the second nine.

"Just take away my three-putts, three of them in eight holes, and I would have a four-shot lead," Woods said. "These were some of the most difficult pins I've ever seen in the Open Championship. It was a challenge to get the ball close. I really had to hit some quality shots. But on the greens you really had to watch your pace because every green is a slightly different speed."

By contrast, Els was kept in contention by his short game, and he shared second place with Garcia and Chris DiMarco, who shot 69. Jim Furyk and Angel Cabrera both shot 66s and were two strokes behind at 205. Also posting 66, Hideto Tanihara was in seventh place alone at 206. DiMarco said of Woods, "The guy has a knack for winning, so it's going to be tough to beat him."

Garcia and Furyk were paired for the third round and their best-ball score would have been 12 under par. Garcia got them started when he holed his second shot, with a nine iron, at the second hole for an eagle-two. Furyk rolled in a 20-footer for birdie there to get his own round going.

A beautiful recovery from under the face of a bunker enabled Garcia to save par at the fourth hole. Both Garcia and Furyk found the green at the fifth in two strokes and two-putted for birdies. Furyk then holed from 15 feet at the sixth and from 40 feet at the seventh to be out in 31 strokes.

At both the seventh and eighth holes Garcia hit approach shots with his wedge that finished six feet away. At the 198-yard ninth, he struck an eight iron to three feet, finishing the first nine with three birdies to be out in 29 strokes. It was the 11th time that nine holes had been played in an Open in 29 strokes, which was one behind the record of 28 set by Denis Durnian in 1983 at Royal Birkdale.

Furyk birdied the first two holes of the second nine and was briefly tied for the lead with Garcia, Woods and Els at 11 under par. Garcia ran off eight consecutive pars on the second nine but had one more birdie left in him, and he two-putted the 18th for his 65. Furyk missed the greens at the 12th and 14th and took bogeys at both holes. He got those strokes back with birdies on the 16th and 17th, where he holed from 25 feet, and posted 66.

None of the late starters enjoyed a really low round. From the last seven pairings, only DiMarco broke 70. After going out in one over par, DiMarco hit a marvelous wedge shot to four feet at the 11th and that sparked a run of three birdies in a row. He hit a six iron to five feet at the 12th and then a five iron to within three feet at the short 13th. An up-and-down for a birdie-four at the 16th and DiMarco shared the lead with Garcia and Woods.

Woods and Els were together in the final group, but it never amounted to a classic pairing. Els dropped a shot when he put his second shot into a bunker on the first hole, then he birdied the second hole. Woods took a bogey at the second and fell back into a share of the lead. He went in front again with a two-putt birdie at the fifth hole and struck a majestic seven iron to four feet at the short sixth hole.

Both took bogeys at the seventh. Els drove into a bush and declared an unplayable lie. His third shot found a greenside bunker and he got up and down from there for his five. Woods also hit into a greenside bunker and took three shots to get down, and his lead was cut to one stroke.

Els birdied the ninth and his short game saved him after that, and he dropped only one more shot, at the 13th. He got birdies on the last two par-fives, the 16th and 18th, to stay one behind Woods. "Somehow I hung in there," Els said. "I could have shot 76 easily and then I would have been out of it. But I find myself only one behind, so that's a bonus."

Woods began his second nine by three-putting for par at the 10th, a sign of what was to come. He did, however, hole a putt from 18 feet at the 11th which, after Garcia posted his 12-under number, got Woods back in front by one. He wasted the cushion with his three putts from four feet on the 14th, but got up and down for a birdie on the 16th. He then left his birdie effort at the 17th four feet short and missed that too. He followed that bogey with two putts from 40 feet for a birdie at the 18th, and a lot of hard work had kept him in the lead.

Third-Round Leaders: Tiger Woods 71–203, Sergio Garcia 65–204, Chris

DiMarco 69-204, Ernie Els 71-204, Jim Furyk 66-205, Angel Cabrera 66-205, Hideto Tanihara 66-206, Mark Calcavecchia 68-207, Adam Scott 70-207

Fourth Round

While Tiger Woods had so much control over his performance, this was his most emotional victory, the first since the death of his father, Earl, in May. As they approached the last green to a standing ovation, his caddie, Steve Williams, said to Woods, "This one's for dad." Woods kept his emotions in check until he had completed the round and shaken the hand of his playing companion, Sergio Garcia. Then Woods hugged Williams and his tears flowed, and did so again when he embraced his wife, Elin.

"After the last putt, I realized that my dad is never going to see this again," Woods said at the presentation ceremony. "I wish he could have seen this one last time. I tried hard at Augusta but it didn't quite happen. He was out here today keeping me calm. I had a calm feeling the entire week, especially today. I love my dad and I miss him so much. To win my first tournament after my dad passed away, and for it to be a major championship, it makes it that much more special."

Woods led by one stroke entering the final round, then matched the best score of the day with 67, five under par, for his 270 total to beat Chris DiMarco, who shot 68, by two strokes. At one point on the last nine, DiMarco got within one stroke, but Woods responded by making three birdies in a row, starting at the 14th hole.

"Hey, Tiger, would you just give me a little chance for once?" DiMarco said to Woods afterwards, and they shared a laugh. Later, DiMarco said, "He's got an uncanny ability, when someone gets close to him, to turn it up another level."

Woods became the 19th player to hold the claret jug three times, following his victories at St. Andrews in 2000 and 2005. His 11th professional major championship tied him with Walter Hagen, who also won at Hoylake, in 1924, and put him closer to his target of Jack Nicklaus's record of 18 majors.

Anthony Wall shot 69 and finished as the leading British player at eight under par, alongside Ben Crane and S.K. Ho. Hideto Tanihara shot 71 and finished in fifth place along with Sergio Garcia, who shot 73. Tanihara was one place outside the best-ever finish by a Japanese player. Andres Romero tied for eighth place with Carl Pettersson and Adam Scott, and his countryman, Angel Cabrera, was alone in seventh place. It was appropriate for Argentina to have two representatives in the top 10 at the venue of Roberto de Vicenzo's win. Jim Furyk had a poor start, bogeying the first two holes, but three birdies in the last four holes hauled Furyk up to 12 under and fourth place.

The contest came down to the final two groups on the course, DiMarco and Ernie Els, and Woods and Garcia. DiMarco dropped a shot at the first hole, but it was to be his only bogey of the day. Dressed entirely in yellow, Garcia missed a short putt and bogeyed the second hole, and unlike the American, Garcia could not limit the damage. A shorter putt slipped by the hole at the third, and all the Spaniard's confidence seemed to evaporate. "Those two three-putts put me a bit on the defensive," Garcia said. "I thought I hit good putts but they didn't go in."

Woods was putting beautifully and on the opening holes saw a number of chances just miss. He parred the first four holes, as did Els ahead of him. Els two-putted from just off the fifth green for a birdie-four and was tied with Woods at 13 under par. Woods responded immediately with a pair of two-iron shots into the fifth green and holed from 12 feet for an eagle. He was ahead by two strokes again.

DiMarco completed the first nine in 35, and was three strokes behind. That became the margin of Woods's lead when Els bogeyed the eighth. He, too, was out in 35. Woods completed pars on the next few holes for a first nine of 33, while Garcia bogeyed the eighth and ninth.

Els bogeyed the eighth and 11th holes, and his 71 left Els in third place at 13 under par. "That four-hole stretch, eighth to 11, that's where it got away," Els said. "It is not a very tough stretch, but I made two bogeys instead of two birdies. If I had played them in two under par instead of two over, I would have had half a chance. But Tiger played great today."

That left DiMarco as Woods's only challenger. At the 10th DiMarco put a three iron onto the green and two-putted for a birdie to get within two, but Woods had him covered. At that same hole, Woods had only a six iron for his approach shot and two-putted from 35 feet to reach 16 under and go three ahead again.

DiMarco made an important par save at the 11th, then holed from 20 feet at the short 13th. Woods missed the 12th green, his chip shot ran 15 feet past the hole, and he missed that putt for his only bogey of the day. Now DiMarco was only one stroke behind, but he was in trouble on the 14th when his three-iron approach went into a bank short and left of the green. He could only chop the ball out, but then he holed the putt from over 40 feet to save par.

It was Woods's turn next. On the 14th, Woods hit a five iron to nine feet and made his birdie-three. His tee shot at the short 15th finished 10 feet from the hole and he made another birdie. He then powered his ball onto the green at the par-five 16th with a three wood and seven iron, and his eagle putt from 18 feet narrowly missed. He made it three birdies in a row.

DiMarco also got a birdie at the 16th and another at the 18th for his 68, but 16 under par was not enough. Woods parred the last two holes, just missing from six feet at the 18th after a two iron off the tee and a four iron for his second shot.

Had Woods scored another birdie, he would have tied his own Open record of 19 under par, set in 2000. As it was, there was plenty of low scoring, but no records were broken during the week. It had been a triumphant return to Royal Liverpool. "This has been a fantastic week for all the players to be able to play this course," Woods said. "It has been a fantastic championship and the course was a fantastic test of golf. With the course playing this fast, it lent itself to amazing creativity."

The Final Leaders: Tiger Woods 67–270, Chris DiMarco 68–272, Ernie Els 71–275, Jim Furyk 71–276, Hideto Tanihara 71–277, Sergio Garcia 73–277, Angel Cabrera 73–278, Carl Pettersson 69–279, Andres Romero 71–279, Adam Scott 72–279

5. PGA Championship

When leading after the third round of the PGA Championship, and aiming for his second major victory of the summer, Tiger Woods was asked if he could have imagined this when he missed the 36-hole cut in the U.S. Open nine weeks earlier. "Yes," Woods said. "If you enter a tournament, your goal is to win the tournament. I figured I was going to enter a few tournaments after the U.S. Open, so yes." Asked in that same press conference what was his best attribute as a golfer, Woods quickly replied, "My mind." Indeed, no one else possessed his killer instinct on a golf course. Perhaps no one ever has.

Woods shot a total of 270 and held a five-stroke margin over the next finisher, Shaun Micheel. His score matched the PGA Championship record of 18 under par that Woods and Bob May posted in 2000, when Woods won in a playoff. He also holds the records for scores in relation to par in the other three majors (18 under par in the 1997 Masters, 12 under in the 2000 U.S. Open and 19 under in the 2000 Open).

Since this year's U.S. Open, Woods had now tied for second in the Cialis Western Open, won the Open Championship in Britain, won the Buick Open, and then the PGA Championship. He now had 12 professional major championships, six behind Jack Nicklaus's record of 18. He had done it at age 30, in 10 years and 40 major championships played. Nicklaus took 48 starts to reach his 12th major professional victory at age 33.

"It's still a long way away," Woods said of Nicklaus's record. "It took Jack over 20 years to do. It's going to take a career and I've just got to keep plugging along and keep trying. The majors are the most fun to play. I thoroughly enjoy coming down the stretch on the back nine with a chance to win. That's why I practice as hard as I do, what I live for. That to me is the ultimate rush in our sport."

In winning at Medinah Country Club, near Chicago, where he held off Sergio Garcia in the 1999 PGA Championship, Woods became the first ever to win the PGA twice at the same venue.

Woods's putter was his most important club, particularly in the first two rounds, when he hit only 15 of the 28 fairways on driving holes. He started his third round with a 35-foot putt for par, his 65 tied the course record, and he tied for the lead with Luke Donald. It was the 12th time Woods had held or shared the lead entering the final round of a major championship—and the 12th time that he won.

It appeared that Woods was back to the level of his domination of six years earlier, when he won four consecutive major championships, the last three of 2000 and the Masters of 2001. "I think he's eerily right back there," said Chris DiMarco, who was second to Woods in the recent Open and one of a large group whose chances faded in the final round of the PGA Championship.

Asked if he was playing as well or better than he was in 2000 and 2001, Woods did not hesitate. "Yes," he said. "Understanding how to get myself around the golf course, how to control things, and all the different shots I've learned since then. Yes, I feel that things are pretty darn good right now."

First Round

The winners of the year's first three major championships were in the same group for the first two rounds of the PGA Championship, and with them went a gallery of thousands to see Tiger Woods and Phil Mickelson, and some also to see Geoff Ogilvy. "Everyone and the fans have been waiting to see those two play together in a major for a while," said Ogilvy, the beneficiary of Mickelson's last-hole blunder in the U.S. Open. "And I got the best seat in the house."

The spectators had to rise early and trek out to the farthest edge of the course, because they teed off on the 10th hole at 8:30 a.m. The crowd was six deep in spots around the 10th green and some were using their periscopes to see over those in front.

"I've never seen anything like that at 8:30 in the morning on a tee that's two miles from the clubhouse," Ogilvy said. "The media presence (about 100 on the course), the photographers, were just incredible. I didn't know there were that many cameras in Illinois." Woods thought the crowd was larger on the second nine. "I think most of them got lost and couldn't find No. 10," he said.

All three turned in scores of 69, three under par, which put them in a bunch of 11 players tied for 10th place, three strokes behind the first-round leaders, Lucas Glover and Chris Riley. The Masters champion made back-to-back birdies to start the round, taking a three-stroke lead on Woods, who bogeyed the first hole. Woods climbed back with birdies on the 12th, 14th and 15th holes.

Billy Andrade was alone in third place with 67. "Those guys have all the expectations on them," Andrade said. "The rest of us are just thinking, 'Hey, maybe this will be our week to do well.'"

There wasn't much conversation between Woods and Mickelson, and Ogilvy said the round was "quite dignified inside the ropes but quite crazy outside the ropes, I'm sure." Ogilvy observed, "If I didn't know any of the back story, I would have said they were two normal guys who like each other just like any other two guys out on the tour. You wouldn't think they were the best of friends, but you wouldn't think they don't like each other, either."

Asked about the group dynamic, Woods said, "We were here to post a number. We went out there and we all hit the ball pretty good. We all kept ourselves in the ballgame." Mickelson, who missed the 36-hole cut the previous week, said, "We had a good time, and I felt like, for me, personally, I was playing a little bit better."

Ogilvy said he occasionally heard shouts that let him know he was noticed too. "There were a few 'Geoff, Geoff' calls out there, more than I could have expected," he said. "I think I might have a couple of legitimate fans."

More than half the field was at par 72 or below at Medinah, which at 7,561 yards was the longest major championship course ever. There were 60 scores under par and another 21 scores at even par. There was little wind and little resistance to the game's best players. "The greens were soft," Woods said. "Anytime the greens are soft, you're going to get low numbers on the board." Mickelson said the key was the four par-fives, three of which played under par. "They're a big factor because they're reachable," Mickelson said. "You need to take advantage of them."

Of the leaders, Glover was 14th in the Ryder Cup standings and trying to reach the top 10 to make the United States team for the first time. The team would be decided at the end of this championship. Riley had no Ryder Cup points and no chance of making the team. He was a lightning rod for criticism on the losing team in 2004, when he asked to be excused from an afternoon match because he was tired. He had not played well since.

In addition to Glover, Stewart Cink (12th on the Ryder Cup points list) and Davis Love (15th) were looking to move up after posting 68s in the first round. "We're all chasing the same goal," Glover said. "It's just like looking at the leaderboard on the 18th tee on Sunday if you are in the hunt."

Love had the best opportunity to be in the lead. He shot 30 on the first nine, including an eagle on the par-five seventh hole, and stood on the 17th tee at seven under par. He took a six iron on the 191-yard, par-three hole and hit into the rough, above a greenside bunker. He tried a delicate chip shot out of the tall grass and whiffed, then dumped his third shot into the bunker. He blasted his next shot to 10 feet from the hole, missed that putt and tapped in for a triple-bogey six.

Billy Mayfair, who shot 69, came into the championship as a sentimental favorite. He was diagnosed with testicular cancer on July 31 and on August 3, two weeks earlier, had surgery to have his right testicle removed. "I'm thrilled to be here," Mayfair said. Of the reception which he received, he said, "I almost had tears in my eyes." He was six under par through 12 holes, but tired and made three bogeys.

"I wasn't able to work out, get into shape or do my usual exercise coming into the tournament," Mayfair said. "I took two weeks off before the surgery, so mentally and physically I was worn out." Whatever happened from here, Mayfair said he would have a good week. "I was just so happy to be on the first tee," he said. "I can't explain how great it was just to be here."

First-Round Leaders: Lucas Glover 66, Chris Riley 66, Billy Andrade 67, Stewart Cink 68, Robert Allenby 68, Luke Donald 68, J.J. Henry 68, Henrik Stenson 68, Davis Love 68

Second Round

The threesome of the 2006 major champions continued to attract most of the attention in the second round, and less-regarded players and those contending to play in the Ryder Cup continued to hold the top positions on the leaderboard. American Ryder Cup hopefuls Billy Andrade, Tim Herron, and two who were already qualified for the European team, Henrik Stenson and Luke Donald, were all at 136, sharing first place at eight under par. Herron had the best round among the leaders, five-under-par 67, while Donald and Stenson posted 68s, and Andrade, 69.

Tiger Woods and Geoff Ogilvy both shot 68s and were one stroke behind at 137, along with Davis Love, who shot 69 while also seeking a place on the American team for the Ryder Cup. There were four players at 138: David Toms (67), Billy Mayfair (69), Fred Funk (69) and Chris Riley (72). Meanwhile, Phil Mickelson shot 71 and slipped to 140, tied for 18th place, four strokes off the lead.

On a rainy Friday afternoon Woods rolled in a 25-foot birdie putt on the

18th green to secure his position just off the lead. "I'm in good shape," said Woods, who had not made a bogey since the first hole of the championship.

It was on the opening hole of the second round that Woods got his biggest break of the day, this being the first hole, of course, not the 10th hole as was the case on the first day. Woods drove so far left of the fairway that his ball was headed towards a group of corporate tents, when a spectator knocked the ball back down in the rough. Woods chipped back onto the fairway and then made a par after he hit a short iron to six feet and holed the putt.

"I knew I got a weird hop," Woods said of the spectator's role. "Hey, I appreciate it. It's nice to have Shaq (Shaquille O'Neal, a basketball player) out there knocking them back."

Mickelson flirted with trouble for much of his round, hitting wild shots with his driver and loose shots with his irons. On the par-three 17th hole, Mickelson flew his tee shot into the crowd, but it bounded over the first row behind some spectators sitting behind the green. From there, Mickelson chipped onto the green and missed a six-foot putt for par. Through the two rounds, he was four over par on the par-three holes.

On the 18th hole Mickelson hit a drive far left into the trees, similar to the shot which cost him the U.S. Open title, but this time he received a kick back into the rough by the fairway. After Woods made a birdie, Mickelson holed from 18 feet for his birdie.

Mickelson said he planned to spend some time that night watching film of his swing with Rick Smith, his coach. "My ball-striking has not been very good," Mickelson said. "I'm only four back. I haven't been able to get it going, but I'm fighting. I just have to get it turned around."

Ogilvy was hitting better shots than Woods or Mickelson, and at times Ogilvy was the only one in the fairway. He appeared unfazed by being in their company, but called it a learning experience. "I'm pretty fortunate that I got to play with those guys," Ogilvy said. "Their world is a bit different from my world. They can keep their world, but it's fun for a few days."

Asked about Ogilvy, Woods said, "There is a reason why he is the U.S. Open champion. Geoff is an extremely talented player, he understands how to play major championship golf, and he's getting the job done."

Rather than with Ogilvy and Mickelson, Woods would be paired in the third round with Riley, whom he had known since their days in junior golf in southern California. After Woods finished his round, he was standing in a drizzle and being interviewed on television when Mickelson came up and held an umbrella over his head. They laughed, then Mickelson pulled the umbrella away and was gone from Woods's perspective for what would be the rest of the championship.

Another old foe, Sergio Garcia, would prove to be longer lasting. He shot 70 despite a triple-bogey seven on the 11th hole, and was now among six players at 139, three strokes off the lead and two behind Woods. It had been seven years since Garcia, now age 26, had challenged Woods in the PGA Championship at Medinah. He was paired with Woods in the final round of the Open Championship in July at Royal Liverpool and tied for fifth place, slipping from one to seven strokes behind.

"We'll see what happens," Garcia said. "There are some good scores out there, but I don't feel like I'm too far from where I want to be at the moment."

A total of 61 players were under par for the first 36 holes and the cut score was a PGA record even-par 144. Vijay Singh shot 145 and missed the cut for the second consecutive major championship. Others who missed the cut included 2005 U.S. Open champion Michael Campbell (146), Fred Couples (147), who played in the final pairing with Mickelson at this year's Masters, and Colin Montgomerie (148), one of the final-hole contenders in this year's U.S. Open, and who also missed the cut in this year's Open at Royal Liverpool.

Second-Round Leaders: Henrik Stenson 68–136, Billy Andrade 69–136, Luke Donald 68–136, Tim Herron 67–136, Davis Love 69–137, Geoff Ogilvy 68–137, Tiger Woods 68–137, Chris Riley 72–138, David Toms 67–138, Fred Funk 69–138, Billy Mayfair 69–138

Third Round

After spending Saturday morning watching on television, making mental note of hole placements and lines of putts that he saw, Tiger Woods knew that Medinah continued to play easier than expected and that he would need another low score to keep the pace. For the third day there was almost no wind and the fairways and greens were soft. "I felt like I had to go get it," said Woods, after having done just that. He matched the course record with 65, seven under par, and tied for first place with Luke Donald at 14-under 202.

Donald, who shot 66, knew as well as anyone that Woods was 11-0 when he held at least a share of the lead after 54 holes in the major championships. "His numbers are obviously impressive and that's why he's the best player in the world," Donald said. "He knows that just playing his game good is to be good enough, usually."

But this was an unusual championship for Woods and the rest of the field. "Most majors, you're just trying to survive and make pars," Woods said. "I think anyone who wants to win this championship has to make some birdies."

Former Masters champion Mike Weir posted nine birdies, matched Woods's round of 65 and was at 204, in third place alone. Current U.S. Open champion Geoff Ogilvy recovered from a double bogey on the first hole to shoot 68 and was fourth at 205. Former PGA champion Shaun Micheel and Sergio Garcia tied for fifth at 206, both recording 67s. K.J. Choi was next with 67 and 207, then Phil Mickelson was in a group of four at 208 after his 68. Tied with Mickelson were Chris DiMarco (67), Ian Poulter (68) and Tim Herron (72). Woods's pairings mate, Chris Riley, shot 73 and dropped out of the running, at 211.

All eyes would be on Woods in the final round. "It's going to take a low round because you know Tiger is playing flawless golf," Micheel said. "He's going to be a tough man to catch." But Ogilvy said, "He's not going to win them all. He's pretty special, but he's not unbeatable."

In the final round Woods would be playing alongside Donald. The Englishman was a hometown favorite of sorts because he attended Northwestern University and made his home in Chicago after graduation. "Tiger is a phenomenal player, he is the best player in the world," Donald said. "He brings a big crowd, and that can be a distraction. Tomorrow, I just have to go out and play my own game and, hopefully, I'll just keep playing the way I've been playing."

Woods started his round by slashing a three-wood shot deep into the trees to the right of the fairway. His punch shot clipped some branches and fell into thick rough short of the green. His wedge shot from there went 35 feet past the hole. But Woods holed that for a par, and followed with a tee shot on the par-three second that never left the flag, setting up a birdie from seven feet. "I was off and running," said Woods, who at that time was tied for the lead with Donald and eight others.

Midway of the second nine Woods produced a string of splendid shots, starting with a three iron from 250 yards over the lake to six feet on the par-three 13th hole. Then came a bunker shot to two feet on the par-five 14th, and a nine iron from a sand-filled divot to three feet on the 15th. On the next hole, however, Woods took a three-putt bogey, ending his streak of 50 holes at par or better.

Donald did not make a bogey and made six birdies, including five on the first nine. He added a birdie on the par-three 17th hole which tied him with Woods, who also birdied the hole.

As birdies reigned at Medinah, the 65s were the lowest round in a PGA Championship for Woods and the lowest in a major championship for Weir. In the last PGA here, Woods and Weir played in the final group, and while Woods won with 72, Weir stumbled in with 80. "It was painful," said Weir, who went on to win the Masters in 2003. "It wasn't a fun day. I just wasn't ready for it." The difference between then and now? "I think it's maturity," Weir said.

Still trying to recover from his U.S. Open debacle, Mickelson was firing at the pins and leaving himself short birdie putts that carried him into a brief share of the lead after nine holes. Then his putting let him down and he had to settle for the 68, eight strokes behind. "I'm still a low round away, and if I can just shoot seven, eight, nine under par, I should have a chance," Mickelson said. "But it's going to take a really low round coming from as far back as I am."

A closing note: Joey Sindelar achieved the rarest score in golf—a double eagle—when he holed his second shot on the 537-yard, par-five fifth hole with a three wood from 241 yards. Sindelar had a simple explanation. "They're all luck," he said. It was the third double eagle in PGA Championship history and the first in a major championship since 2004, when England's Gary Evans had one in the Open at Royal Troon. The previous double eagles in the PGA were scored by Darrell Kestner in 1993 and Per-Ulrik Johansson in 1995.

Third-Round Leaders: Tiger Woods 65–202, Luke Donald 66–202, Mike Weir 65–204, Geoff Ogilvy 68–205, Sergio Garcia 67–206, Shaun Micheel 67–206, K.J. Choi 67–207, Chris DiMarco 67–208, Phil Mickelson 68–208, Ian Poulter 68–208, Tim Herron 72–208

Fourth Round

Luke Donald came to the first tee for the final round dressed in a red shirt and white pants, the colors of the flag of his native England. Tiger Woods commented later, "I thought it was kind of weird to have a blue belt with it." Woods could not remember if another player had matched red shirts with him on Sunday, but he quickly separated himself from Donald and everyone else.

Starting the round tied with Donald, Woods hit an approach shot on No. 1 to 12 feet and made the putt for a birdie to take a one-stroke lead. His lead grew to two strokes after a two-putt birdie on the par-five fifth, and it reached three when he holed a 40-foot putt on No. 6. A 35-foot putt on No. 8 and a 12-foot putt on No. 12 made it a five-stroke lead. While Woods steamrolled toward victory with 68 and a 270 total, Donald shot 74 and finished six strokes behind, tied for third place. Shaun Micheel was second with 69 and 275, then at 276 came Donald, Adam Scott (67) and Sergio Garcia (70).

"It was a special day out there," Woods said. "I just had one of those magical days on the greens. I felt like if I could get the ball on the green, I could make it from anywhere. I felt like I could make anything.... I made some nice bombs that I probably shouldn't have made.... I just knew if I could keep doing what I was doing, the other guys were running out of holes."

Chris DiMarco, who lost to Woods in a playoff at the 2005 Masters and tied for 12th here, observed, "You would think going to the first tee that he would feel the pressure because everyone is expecting him to win, and it's the exact opposite. The guy playing with him feels the most pressure. I've never seen anybody, take away Jack Nicklaus, who looked more comfortable leading on the back nine of a major than playing the first hole of a tournament. And that's pretty scary."

Woods's caddie, Steve Williams, noted that he made just three bogeys during the week. "To make three bogeys in 72 holes, no matter how easy or hard a course is playing, is an astounding statistic," Williams said. In the end there were no tears as at Hoylake. Woods raised his fists, gave Williams a hug, and broke into a hug grin. "Overall, it wasn't the same as Hoylake, maybe just because I was in contention to win a major after my dad passed," Woods said. "It was just a totally different feeling."

Asked if he ever felt sorry for the other players, Woods smiled and said, "No." He offered no help when asked how he would approach taking on a golfer like himself. "I like it the way things are now," he said.

The Ryder Cup standings also remained unchanged when the PGA Championship ended. The 10 qualifying players for the United States team were, in order, Woods, Phil Mickelson, Jim Furyk, Chad Campbell, David Toms, DiMarco, Vaughn Taylor, J.J. Henry, Zach Johnson and Brett Wetterich. The next morning, captain Tom Lehman announced his two picks, Stewart Cink and Scott Verplank, to complete the team.

The Final Leaders: Tiger Woods 68–270, Shaun Micheel 69–275, Adam Scott 67–276, Sergio Garcia 70–276, Luke Donald 74–276, Mike Weir 73–277, Steve Stricker 69–278, K.J. Choi 71–278, Ryan Moore 69–279, Ian Poulter 71–279, Geoff Ogilvy 74–279

In other results of note, the final totals were Masters champion Phil Mickelson (282), cancer survivor Billy Mayfair (287), first round co-leaders Chris Riley (288) and Luke Glover (289), and other Ryder Cup hopefuls Tim Herron (281), Davis Love (286) and Billy Andrade (288).

6. Women's Major Championships

Kraft Nabisco Championship

Karrie Webb had fallen so far and so fast on the golf scene that she wasn't only out of sight, she was out of mind. Webb had a brilliant seven-year span from the mid-1990s, winning 30 tournaments, including six major championships. Then mysteriously, as happens in golf, her game melted away. Nothing had changed early in 2006. Then came the year's first major event, the Kraft Nabisco Championship at Mission Hills, at Rancho Mirage, California. She trailed by eight strokes in the first round, five in the second, then seven in the third. Then came the final round, and Karrie Webb was back—like a lightning strike.

Webb wiped out that seven-stroke deficit on the last day, ringing up five birdies then holing out from the fairway for a spectacular eagle at the 18th for a seven-under-par 65. Then Lorena Ochoa, who faded after leading through the first three rounds—and by a robust three strokes entering the final round—got the eagle she desperately needed at the final hole to tie Webb at nine-under 279. Then it was off to the playoff. Webb dropped a six-foot putt at the first extra hole for her first victory in two years and her first major title in four years. It also was her second Kraft Nabisco victory, her seventh major, and her career 31st victory—at the age of 31.

Was this her greatest comeback? "I have no idea," Webb said. "But just the way that I came back and holed the shot on the last to even get in a playoff was pretty spectacular."

Spectacular was the right word. Coming to the final hole, Webb was tied for the lead at seven under with whiz kid Michelle Wie, who was still playing, two groups behind her. Webb had 116 yards left to the green at the par-five 18th. She took her pitching wedge. The ball bounced twice, rolled for a few feet, and dropped for an eagle. "I think my heart just about jumped out of my chest," Webb said. "It was aching for about five minutes after." Her 65, by the way, was the second-best round of the tournament and came in a round when only two others broke 70.

Ochoa, who led through the first three rounds, was playing in the last group with Wie and Natalie Gulbis. Amazingly, she was up to Webb's challenge. At the 18th, she put her second shot eight feet from the flagstick, then holed the putt for her eagle and a par-72 to tie Webb.

Back to the 18th for the playoff: Webb hit a three-wood second into the rough behind the green and chipped up to six feet. Ochoa hit a hybrid club over the green, 30 feet from the pin, and ran her first putt 12 feet past. She two-putted from there. Then Webb dropped her six-footer for the victory. It was her first since the 2004 Kellogg-Keebler Classic.

"I'm ecstatic right now and I feel pretty lucky to be here," said Webb, who was inducted into the World Golf Hall of Fame in November. "Just a lot of hard work paid off and I'm just really enjoying the moment."

And where would this fit in her career? "It's definitely a win in 30 or

40 years that's going to stick out in my memory," Webb said. "With the fashion I won in and just the way I handled myself after having to go back and play in a playoff. It definitely ranks up there in the top couple."

Webb shot 70-68-76-65 to match Ochoa's 62-71-74-72 at 279. But it was Ochoa's tournament for three rounds. She opened with that sensational 62, 10 under par, tying the LPGA Tour record low for a major championship.

"I didn't think it was going to be this good," said Ochoa. Starting at No. 10, she birdied it from two feet, then with dazzling iron play and putting, she added the 11th, 15th, 16th and 18th from, respectively, four feet, a few inches, and seven and 10 feet. She birdied five more holes coming in, but just one from really short range, No. 7 from two feet. The others came from 20, 10, 25, and finally No. 9, her last hole, from 15 feet.

"Everything was so easy, and everything was so clear," Ochoa said. "It was fun to be out there." But not so clear to defending champion Annika Sorenstam. The best she could manage was a 71. "I wondered what course she was playing," Sorenstam said. "Because this is a difficult course."

Paula Creamer, who shot a 69, pretty much shared that view. "You can't look at the scoreboard after that," Creamer said. "You can't dwell on being seven back. We have a lot of golf left, and the course is only going to get harder."

Not lost in this shuffle was Wie, playing her first major as a professional. She missed only two fairways and hit all 18 greens in a bogey-free 66, tying her lowest score ever on the LPGA Tour to hold second place four strokes behind Ochoa. "I'm really glad I played well in the first round," Wie said. "Usually I have a little bit of trouble starting off real well. My game was really solid today."

Wie was asked why she was different from the previous year. "I'm 16, I'm not 15 anymore," Wie said patiently, explaining the obvious. "I have my driver's license. I'm a junior (in high school). That covers it."

Meanwhile, the No. 1 woman golfer in the world remained undaunted by her nine-stroke deficit to Ochoa's 62 and her chances of repeating as champion. "It's Thursday," Sorenstam said. "I have three more days. I'm looking forward to it. It's the majors. Anything can happen."

In the first two rounds, Webb gave no indication that she was on her way back. Her opening 70 left her eight behind Ochoa, and she was five behind after a second-round 68, but she at least raised some eyebrows. It included four birdies, two bogeys and an eagle at the par-four 15th, where she holed out a seven iron from 152 yards.

"It's been a long time where I felt like I've been close," Webb said. "And I'm just on the other side of playing well. When I was playing well, I was on the other side of the fine line, and things were going well. And you don't realize until you're on the wrong side of the fine line how close you really are. There are still a couple of days to go and I would like to play well and see where I end up on Sunday."

Ochoa's scores climbed, but she kept the lead. In the second round, her 71-133 left her still four ahead of Wie (71-137). The test stiffened in the third round when the winds turned chilly and blustery. Only seven out of the 70 qualifiers broke par that day. Paula Creamer, one of the sharp newcomers, shot her worst round as a professional, a 79, and six others shot 80 or higher.

Natalie Gulbis, chasing her first victory, dealt herself a hand with a 68 that put her in a tie for third place, five strokes behind Ochoa. Gulbis's card included an eagle at the par-five ninth off an eight iron from 132 yards. "It took a hop and the next thing I knew, the crowd went nuts," she said. Still, Ochoa was flying along. "As far ahead as she is," Gulbis said, "it's just going out and hit a lot of fairways. The pins—they're going to be tough on Sunday."

Wie, however, clung coolly to second place, shooting 73 and picking up a stroke to close within three of Ochoa heading into the final round. But she wasn't completely pleased. "My game felt very solid today," Wie said. "But it was kind of like a bad break kind of day—kind of two feet too long, two feet too left, too feet too right."

Webb figured she had ruined her chances with a choppy 76. She hit only 11 greens and took 33 putts, and it all added up to being seven shots out of the lead going into the final round. She was, as she said, "feeling sorry" for herself.

Ochoa shot 74, lost a stroke of her lead to Wie, and was not at all disturbed. "It was a tough day out there, I guess," Ochoa said. "I'm happy the way I finished. I still have a three-shot lead, and this course was very hard in the afternoon." She was resilient. She started with a bogey at No. 1 when she chipped poorly, but she snapped right back for a birdie at No. 2, chipping to seven feet and holing the putt. It was that way the rest of the way in the two-birdie, four-bogey day. Now came the tough question—how to sleep on the lead?

"I don't know," Ochoa said. "I've never been in this position."

But Webb had. Indeed, she had experienced all of golf's joys and pains, and at the moment, in the final round, it was joy, thanks to a steaming putter. Going out, Webb birdied No. 3 from 18 feet, No. 5 from 25 and No. 7 from 30. She got No. 10 from 12 feet, No. 11 from two. She had ventured a peek at the leaderboard.

"The first time I really looked at it, I think I was on the 17th green, and I saw I was tied for the lead," she said. "And I had made a good up-and-down on 16 before that. So that was really the first time I had taken a good look at it."

Webb turned back to her game and headed for the par-five 18th, and then came the stunner. Webb was lying two in the fairway, 116 yards from the green. She was trying to get close for a birdie. But her wedge shot hit and rolled into the hole for the eagle.

"I'm ecstatic right now," Webb said. "I feel pretty lucky to be here. Obviously, when you hit a shot at the flag on the last hole thinking you need a birdie at least, when it goes in the hole, there's always a little bit of an element of luck there. So I feel pretty fortunate."

And then Webb had to step back and wait to see what would develop with the chase at her heels, two holes behind her.

Ochoa, who had a three-shot cushion starting the final round, was in trouble. Whether it was the lack of sleep, a case of nerves or the bounce of the ball, Ochoa didn't hold that lead for long. She started strong, chipping to two feet to set up a birdie at No. 2. Then came a ruinous stretch of four bogeys in seven holes. At No. 9, she was short with a wedge shot and two-putted from 12 feet for a bogey. Then she was either in rough or trees. She bogeyed the 12th, 13th and 15th, slipping into precarious position, three over par with three holes to play. "My driver killed me on the back nine," Ochoa said. "I missed four fairways in a row."

The gallery had begun to stir when Ochoa bogeyed the ninth and Wie dropped a 15-footer for birdie to tie her. Then Gulbis joined the race with birdies at the 13th and 15th.

Webb waited nervously as they came to the 18th. Wie and Gulbis needed birdies to tie her. Ochoa needed an eagle. Gulbis missed her birdie from 18 feet, and Wie missed hers from 10. They would tie for third. But Ochoa found a spark. From 225 yards out, she put her five-wood shot eight feet beneath the hole. Then she ran in the putt for that precious eagle. She had tied Webb.

In the playoff, both hit the fairway and both put their second shots off the back edge. Ochoa sent her third 15 feet past the pin, and Webb chipped to six feet. Ochoa then missed, but Webb didn't.

Webb's earlier words still echoed. "I'm a better player than when I was playing really well," she had said. "I just don't have the confidence that I had." It seems she'd got it back.

McDonald's LPGA Championship

Se Ri Pak, a star of the 1990s and the trigger of the South Korean surge on the LPGA Tour, had seen her career plunging mysteriously into shambles. Things could have gotten much worse if she hadn't had the good fortune to injure her hand.

Pak's game had been steadily falling apart, and it seems her biggest problem was a severe case of burnout. Then came the injury in 2005. She played only 12 events. That enabled her to recharge her batteries and her spirits, and she re-broke through in the McDonald's LPGA Championship at Hamilton Farm Golf Club in Havre de Grace, Maryland. It was her first victory since 2004, the 23rd of her career, and her third LPGA title and fifth major championship. She got it the hard way—in a playoff win over Karrie Webb, herself newly returned from limbo.

"I'm very happy to be back again," Pak said. "I'm a very lucky person. I'm as happy as a person has ever been."

Pak was slow to emerge in this championship. She opened with a one-under-par 71, seven strokes behind Nicole Castrale and tied for 41st place. Castrale, playing in her second major event, was the first-round leader with 64, a record for the course. Castrale, age 27, needed three surgeries to repair a rotator cuff damaged in a car accident during her senior year at the University of Southern California. She came to the LPGA Tour after winning twice on the Futures Tour and had developed a good short game in the off-season. It showed. She got three of her birdies from inside 100 yards—chipping to four feet at the par-five 15th, flipping a wedge to within one foot at the 16th, then finessing an eight iron to eight feet at the 18th, on her first nine. The 64, her career low, gave her a two-stroke lead over Cristie Kerr and Pat Hurst.

"I had to stay patient because I know I've been playing well and just not really scoring," Castrale said.

The main attractions were well back in the field. Michelle Wie, age 16, birdied three of her final four holes for a one-under 71, tying with Pak for 41st and also with Annika Sorenstam, going not only for her fourth LPGA championship, but her fourth in a row. Sorenstam, erratic off the tee, had four birdies and three bogeys. "It kind of summarized my year a little bit, so I'm not surprised," she said.

In the rain-interrupted second round, when Castrale disappeared into the mid-70s, Wie was the story. Play was suspended for five hours by afternoon storms, and when darkness stopped play for the day, half the field was left to finish on Saturday morning. Until then, Wie was very much in the picture, chasing Dorothy Delasin into the clubhouse. Delasin rolled to a hefty lead with five birdies in six holes, then ran into trouble. She found woods off the tee and double-bogeyed, then bogeyed trying to chip out of a divot hole, and shot 71 for the clubhouse lead at six-under 138. Wie was one shot behind with 68, after missing some good opportunities, including at the par-five No. 8, where she parred after being pin-high, 30 feet away, just off the green in two. A birdie chance disappeared in a poor chip to six feet. She got the par but missed a great chance. She missed a better one at the 16th, lipping out a four-foot birdie putt.

When play was called because of darkness, Pat Hurst was eight under through the 10th hole, two strokes better than Delasin, the clubhouse leader. Could Hurst hang on?

Yes, she could. She wrapped up the second round on Saturday morning with 71 for a seven-under total of 137 and a one-stroke lead.

The attention in the third round was focused first on Sorenstam, who committed a rookie error and a fatal error. She was very much alive going into the round, just three strokes out of the lead. Then at No. 2, after a strong drive, Sorenstam removed a piece of a divot from next to her ball, then picked up the other piece, which had been loosely replaced. Karrie Webb, her playing companion, along with Pak, stopped her. That was a violation. Players are not permitted to improve the position of their ball by removing a replaced divot. It was a two-stroke penalty.

"I was next to a divot and the divot was in two pieces, and it was totally replaced in a really horrible way," Sorenstam said. "So I moved the divot, and that's against the rules." Said Webb: "I saw her remove part of the divot. I wasn't going to say anything, but then she removed the other part. I feel bad for calling it on her, but I would feel bad if she had won by one shot. I would feel bad for whoever finished second." So Sorenstam's par became a double bogey, and after a series of bad misses, she finished with 75 and was six out of the lead. The championship was pretty much out of her reach.

Sorenstam's wasn't the only embarrassing error of the third round. Hurst, who finished eight holes of the second round Saturday morning, lost control of the championship with a huge error at No. 9 in the third round. She had a 30-foot birdie putt, but left it two feet above the hole. Then she missed the par from there, sending the ball four feet past, and she missed that one, too, and double-bogeyed. She parred home, even missing a number of birdie chances along the way. "Any time you do that," Hurst said, thinking back to the destructive double bogey, "the confidence kind of goes down a little bit."

Hurst finished with 72 and a seven-under 209 total, tied for the lead by Japan's Ai Miyazato, who won six times on the Japanese Tour in 2005 and then won the LPGA qualifying tournament by a record 12 strokes. Miyazato dropped a four-foot birdie putt at No. 17 and shot 69 in the wind for her 209. Wie three-putted for bogeys three times, one from 12 feet at the fifth, but the stunner came at the par-three 17th. She missed the birdie and had about 18 inches left for her par, but missed it. She bounced back at the 18th, holing a 10-footer for birdie and 71, and was one off the lead at 210, tied for third with Shi Hyun Ahn and Mi Hyun Kim.

The first hint that Pak was coming back, though it was pretty much unnoticed, was the 69 in the second round for a four-under 140 total that put her within three of the lead. She was now in the hunt for her fifth major championship. It came down to a duel between Pak and Webb, two players who had come back to life in this season. But only after some challengers had been cleared away.

Most notable of these was the ever-dangerous Sorenstam, who had hurt herself so badly with the rules violation in the third round. Sorenstam made a good effort this time, but stumbled over a bad error. She had made four straight birdies and was looking at another from 20 feet at the final hole for a seven-under total. Somehow she ran it fully 10 feet past and three-putted for bogey instead, for 68. "I saw it was quick, but standing over it, you have to get to seven (under), and sometimes things don't compute," she said. "I just rammed it way too hard and I was thinking, 'Wow, you saw how fast it was—what are you doing?'" She tied for ninth place.

Wie also had a chance. She got within one stroke of the lead with three birdies in five holes, but she missed a par putt from four feet at the 16th, then burned the cup on a birdie try at the 17th and closed with 72 and tied for fifth place. She was still troubled by her putting, averaging 31.5 putts per round for the tournament.

Cristie Kerr, Shi Hyun Ahn and Mi Hyun Kim all needed a birdie at the 18th to join the playoff at eight-under 280. Kerr hit into the water and shot 68, and Ahn caught water, too, and shot 72 to join Hurst (73) and Wie in the tie for fifth place. Kim missed a long birdie putt, shot 71 and tied Miyazato (72) for third at 281.

It was a grand finish. Webb had been in limbo for two years, came back with a splash in the Kraft Nabisco Championship two months earlier, holing out a fairway wedge on the final hole to get into a playoff and beat Lorena Ochoa. Pak had also been in limbo for about two years, burned out by too much golf and then suffering an injury. Maybe it was fitting that it came down to a playoff.

Pak started the final round two strokes out of the lead, and Webb was three behind. Webb closed with a four-under 68, but she missed birdie putts of four feet at the 17th and 10 feet at the 18th. Pak could have won outright in regulation, but three-putted for bogey at the 18th for 69, and they tied at 280. Pak had quite an eventful round. She holed a 50-footer for birdie on the par-three 12th to take the lead. She escaped the 13th with a bogey, after driving into the rough and then hitting the green with a fairway wood out of the long grass. At the 15th, she birdied with a chip and a putt, and at the 16th she lofted a wedge from the rough to four feet and birdied. She came to the 18th with a one-stroke lead and would have won with a par. But she three-putted for the bogey and the tie.

Then both the troubled Pak and the real Pak showed up for the playoff. It was the troubled Pak off the tee, hitting her three wood fat. It ended up 70 yards short of Webb's drive. Then came the real Pak. She hit her second with a hybrid four iron, 201 yards, to within three inches of the cup. Webb was true to the green with her own second shot, but 20 feet from the hole. But when Webb missed her birdie try, Pak tapped in for her birdie and the victory.

Pak's shot made Webb think about her own wedge-eagle in the Kraft Nabisco Championship. "I thought I was getting some of my own medicine back," Webb said. "I was waiting for it to drop in the hole. I thought I had the upper hand, but then she hit an unbelievable shot, and it's just really hard to come up with the good after that."

"That was not an easy shot," Pak said, beaming. "The game of golf—you never expect it from anywhere. So that shot's going to be the best shot for the week."

Pak joined a historic group who had won the championship three times— Mickey Wright, Kathy Whitworth, Nancy Lopez and Patty Sheehan, and most recently, Sorenstam. Her comeback came at a fitting time, with the rise of South Koreans on the LPGA Tour. She was the one who started it all some eight years earlier. In 1998, her rookie year, she was the only South Korean on the tour and she won both the LPGA Championship and the U.S. Women's Open. Thanks to her inspiration, there were 32 South Koreans on the tour in 2006. But on this day, she was a kid again.

When her miracle shot ended up three inches from the cup in the playoff, she leaped into her caddie's arms.

"First time I jumped on the golf course," Pak said.

U.S. Women's Open

Annika Sorenstam wrapped up the U.S. Women's Open, beating Pat Hurst handily in a playoff, and in her acceptance speech at the 18th green, she looked at the crowd and almost with a sigh of relief said, "It's been 10 years—it's been 10 long years." Which is what other golfers might say about winning their first. But this was Sorenstam's third, and so her statement suggests that what she had expected of herself was to win, oh, every other year, at the least. But she hadn't won a Women's Open since 1996. In fact, back then, she won back-to-back, in 1995 and 1996. Then there were the missed chances that made victory seem so remote. In 2002, she gave up a two-stroke edge to Juli Inkster; in 2003, she bogeyed the 18th and missed a playoff by a stroke, and in 2004, she was outplayed by Meg Mallon.

It was also a great relief to her in another way. After dominating the LPGA Tour for so many years, she was having—for her—a down year in 2006. From 2000 through 2005, she had won, in order, five, eight, 11, six, eight and 10 tournaments. Up to this Women's Open (June 30-July 3), she had won only one, and that was some four months earlier. And more to the point, she'd been having a decidedly un-Sorenstam time of it in general. So this championship came both as a relief and a surprise to her. "I worked so hard to do it again and it just never happened," she said. "I was close a few times, but I could never get it done. So to come here this week, with not such a great season, and then to win, is pretty ironic."

There was more irony in the victory. It was her first as an American. Just 19 days before the Open, Sorenstam—the greatest and most famous of Swedish golfers—was sworn in as an American citizen. The victory also gave her a matched set of majors. She now had three Women's Opens, three Kraft Nabisco Championships and three McDonald's LPGA Championships (plus one Weetabix Women's British Open).

Her problems in 2006 all started with the grip. Sorenstam brought in her swing coach, Henri Reis, to see what was what. He concluded that her left hand had to be "stronger," meaning that it had to be turned slightly more toward her right hand on the club grip. She also put aside her new driver, which was hitting farther, in favor of her old one. "We opted for accuracy over distance," Reis said. It proved to be a prudent choice.

Thus armed, Sorenstam was ready to take on storied old Newport Country Club, in Newport, Rhode Island, site of the first U.S. Open in 1895 and also the home of the first USGA president, Theodore Havemeyer. Newport had been soaked by heavy rains, and what with fog also sitting dense the first day, the first round was put off to Friday, the second round to Saturday, and the grind of playing the final two rounds on Sunday.

The Open finally got underway on Friday, and the golfers came out to find a course of casual water and mud, and that was the occasion for a bit for the highlight film. Sorenstam found the casual water at the par-four No. 9 and was allowed to clean her ball of the mud, which was a key consideration for the 436-yard, uphill par-four, the most difficult hole on the course. Then she birdied it—the only one to do so. Her second shot was uphill, 185 yards, to a three-tiered green with the flag over a ridge. Her approach ended up just short of the green, 20 feet from the pin. She holed it. "I was lucky I was in casual water because I had a chance to clean my ball," Sorenstam said. "I had so much mud on it."

Sorenstam bogeyed once, at the tough par-four No. 6, where her seven-wood approach went through the green. She also birdied Nos. 3 and 16, for a two-under-par 69 and a tie for the lead with Hurst, South Korea's Se Ri Pak, the 1998 Women's Open champion and winner of the McDonald's LPGA Championship three weeks earlier, and amateur Jane Park, age 19, who just finished her freshman year at UCLA. They led by one stroke over a group at 70 that included Michelle Wie, age 16, who finished her round by dropping a 15-foot putt for birdie at the 18th. "I had a very solid round today, a lot of pars," Wie said. "That's what the U.S. Open is. You have to have pars when you're in trouble, and I felt like I did that today."

Only nine players broke the par of 71 in the first round, the average score was 75.95, and 21 players did not break 80.

Sorenstam played early Saturday, before the winds began tugging at Newport. She started from the 10th and parred her first 13 holes, then she was on and off the rest of the way. She birdied her 14th (No. 5), bogeyed her 15th (the tough No. 6, again), birdied the 16th, and then closed with a bogey at the tricky ninth, where she had started with a birdie the day before. She posted her par 71 and was off the course and gone. At the halfway point, she was at two-under 140 and tied with Hurst. "I'm sure she's home and just getting out from under the covers from a nice, two-hour nap," said Juli Inkster, who shot 70 in the afternoon to move to within three of Sorenstam and Hurst.

Hurst had a rockier ride than Sorenstam in the second round. She bogeyed the third, then from the fifth went birdie-bogey-birdie-birdie. Bogeys at the 12th and 13th put her back over par for the round, then a birdie at the 16th got her even, and she parred the last two for her 71. At the halfway point, Sorenstam and Hurst led by two over Wie, Shi Hyun Ahn and the amateur Park. Twenty-nine amateurs qualified for this Women's Open, the most since the 31 in 1986.

Some former champions were at least in the picture. Inkster, a two-time winner, was at 73-70–143, one over par and three strokes off the lead. The rejuvenated Karrie Webb, herself a two-time winner, shot an opening 73, but a 76 in the second round left her with a lot to do. The 2003 Women's Open champion, Hillary Lunke, was causing a little stir. She had opened with 72, then birdied the first two holes in the second round. Then she made eight on the par-four third hole, and things went worse from there. She shot 83 and missed the cut badly, and wondered out loud whether she should even keep playing the LPGA Tour. "If I left right now," she said, "it just wouldn't feel right. It would feel like I'm quitting."

Next, everyone was braced for Sunday and the two-round marathon. Not all were troubled over the prospect. "It's going to be a fun ride, playing 36 holes in one day," Wie said. "I'm not going to take it too seriously." Sorenstam works to stay in shape and took it seriously. "We know it's going to be a long weekend," she said. "You've got to be in good shape. It's going to favor the one who can handle that. There are some players out here that are in good shape, and I'd like to think I'm one of them." Maybe the message was clear to Hurst. She was the mother of two young children and not nearly as trim as Sorenstam.

Fit or not, Sorenstam shot her worst score in the third round on Sunday morning. It started with great promise, a birdie at No. 1, then nothing but three bogeys and the rest pars for a two-over 73. Hurst had the worse of it. She birdied the 10th and 11th, but scattered six bogeys and shot 75. The leaderboard changed almost completely. Sorenstam stayed tied for the lead, at even-par 213, but shared it with Wie (71) and Brittany Lincicome, with 69, the only player to break 70 in the third round. Inkster and Stacy Prammanasudh shot 71s and tied one stroke back at 214. Hurst shot 75 and drifted back to 215.

And the leaderboard changed again, abruptly, in the final round. Prammanasudh slipped back with a 72 and tied for third at 286, two strokes off the final lead, with Wie (73) and a hard-closing Se Ri Pak, who matched the day's low of 69. Wie was tied for the lead with six holes to play, but she couldn't save par from a bunker at the 13th, and she could do no better than pars the rest of the way. Inkster, age 46, bidding to become the oldest major champion in women's golf, was among five players who tied for the lead during the day. Then she three-putted for bogey at the par-three 16th. She shot 73 and finished sixth.

Sorenstam came within fractions of winning the championship outright. Her 30-foot birdie putt on the final hole rolled over the edge and stayed out. She made her 71 for an even-par 284 total. In some ways, that 71 was the measure of Sorenstam. It disguises one of the more severe stretches of the Women's Open. She had started the final round with two birdies, then double-bogeyed the par-four seventh and bogeyed the eighth and ninth. Then the other Sorenstam returned. She birdied the 10th, then at the 15th she holed an 18-foot birdie putt to tie Hurst for the lead, then holed a 20-footer at the 16th for a one-stroke lead. At the par-three 17th, her six-iron tee shot ended up over the green, 30 yards from the flag. She chipped eight feet past the pin and two-putted for a bogey and was tied going to the 18th and the near-birdie.

Hurst was more decisive in the final round. She played the first nine in four birdies and a bogey, and was even par on the back with a bogey-birdie exchange coming to the 18th. Then Hurst scrambled from a tee shot into the rough and holed a clutch five-footer for the other 69 of the day and matched the tournament-low to tie Sorenstam. "I look forward to another long day tomorrow," Sorenstam said, almost mocking herself.

Then it was off to the 18-hole playoff on Monday. The records favored Sorenstam by a landslide. She was 14-5 in playoffs and 2-0 against Hurst. And this one was over almost as soon as it began. At the par-five first hole, Hurst hit her sand-wedge approach heavy, and the ball hit near the hole but spun down off the green. Sorenstam also hit a sand wedge, and her ball landed softly and pulled back off the green, but only six feet from the pin. Hurst's birdie putt was 10 feet short, and her par putt didn't reach the hole. She bogeyed, and Sorenstam holed her six-footer for a birdie, and she led by two. Hurst missed a four-footer at No. 2, and Sorenstam two-putted from 40 feet for par.

Sorenstam birdied No. 3 and was up by three, and at No. 6, Hurst hit her tee shot into the face of a bunker, laid up in the rough, and hit a wedge to about 25 feet above the hole. Sorenstam hit into the rough, then into a muddy bunker 40 yards from the green. Worse, she came out badly, 65 feet from the cup. She two-putted for bogey, but Hurst blew a three-footer and double-bogeyed, and was four behind. The rest was a formality. Coming home, Sorenstam had a birdie-bogey back nine, and Hurst had all pars until the 18th, where she dropped a 60-footer for a birdie. She lifted her hands into the air.

"It hurts," Hurst said. "You don't know how many more chances you're going to have."

Sorenstam had won her 68th career title. But more to the point, finally, it was her third U.S. Women's Open.

Weetabix Women's British Open

If people wanted to assume her victories in the 1998 and 1999 Weetabix Women's British Open counted as major championships, Sherri Steinhauer was not going to put them right. Perception is everything. Back then the LPGA counted the du Maurier tournament as a major instead, but when Steinhauer won the British title at Royal Lytham in 2006 there was no doubting the event's major pedigree. At age 43, Steinhauer became the oldest winner of the championship, and she joined Karrie Webb as the only other three-time winner.

"People just thought they were majors," Steinhauer recalled of her previous triumphs, "so I didn't tell them they weren't. But to win this for a third time, and for it to be fully recognized as a major this time, is a great thrill. It makes the previous wins all the sweeter."

Steinhauer first won at Royal Lytham in 1998. She then won again at Woburn the following year. The Madison, Wisconsin, native has always seemed to deal in majors, even when they weren't, rather than regular tour events. Her maiden victory was the du Maurier Classic in 1992. She has only won three other times in America since. By the end of the 1990s, the Weetabix Women's British Open was a big deal on the east of the Atlantic and it was co-sanctioned by the LPGA circuit, but only since 2001, with the demise of the du Maurier, has the Weetabix event counted as a major on all tours.

Steinhauer's first victory at Lytham was extraordinary. She opened with 81. The conditions were truly horrid, heavy rain and strong, gusting winds, but, remarkably, she recovered to win the championship with rounds of 72, 70 and 69 and a four-over-par total. Her game plan after the first round was to stay out of the fairway bunkers, which she managed to do.

In 2003, when Annika Sorenstam won at Lytham, Steinhauer missed the cut, but in 2006 she again set out with the idea of missing all the fairway bunkers. She failed, but only once, on the 10th hole on the first day. In all she was in five bunkers for the week, including the last when it hardly mattered any more. Ironically, this was an area of her game that was giving her trouble earlier in the year. A lesson from her coach, Bill Harmon, helped, but twice when she found greenside bunkers in the first round she suffered double bogeys, at the fourth and the 12th.

She opened with a 73, having played in the windy conditions in the afternoon. It left her seven strokes behind the leader, Juli Inkster, who led the field by three strokes after a 66. Inkster went to the turn in 30, including an eagle at the sixth where she hit a five iron to 18 feet and holed the putt. But for a bogey at the 18th, where she found sand, Inkster would have been further ahead still.

At age 46, Inkster was attempting to become the oldest winner of a women's major championship and also to complete the Super Grand Slam. She had won each of the previous rota of four LPGA majors, including the du Maurier, but needed to add the British championship to the list. Karrie Webb remains the only player to achieve the feat, while Steinhauer would go on to become the second oldest winner of a women's major, after 45-year-old Fay Crocker.

Inkster had the advantage of playing on the first morning, when the wind had not yet got up. Only 15 players finished under par for the day and 12 of them came from the early groups. Inkster's nearest rivals were Italy's Silvia Cavalleri and Sweden's Maria Hjorth, who scored 69s.

Sorenstam, an afternoon starter, was well placed until she dropped three shots in the last two holes. Visits to greenside bunkers cost a double bogey at the 17th and a bogey at the last. The newly crowed U.S. Open champion finished at even par. One player not to take advantage of the good early conditions was Michelle Wie. She bogeyed the first three holes and recorded a 74.

Wie had finished as a runner-up to Webb at the Evian Masters the previous week. As an amateur the previous year at Royal Birkdale, she had also started poorly, with a 75, but recovered to finish third. Her two-over-par score was the highest of her rookie season as a professional on the women's circuit.

The 16-year-old was heading in the right direction the next day, one under for her round, when she came to the 14th hole. She was in a bunker short and left of the green and there was a piece of moss behind the ball. As she started her backswing, the clubhead made contact with the moss. Wie played out and made a bogey but was informed at the end of the round that she was penalized two shots for grounding her club prior to making a swing. She was in breach of rule 13-4, but what Wie, and seemingly her playing companion Laura Davies, had failed to realize was that the swing only starts with the forward movement of the club.

Wie's 72 was converted to a second 74, and at four over par she had made the cut but was 10 strokes off the lead. She scored rounds of 72 and 74 over the weekend to tie for 26th place.

At least she was around for the last two rounds. Webb missed the cut after taking an eight at the par-three ninth. The damage was done in a greenside bunker, and Cavalleri also suffered a similar fate when she had tied Inkster for the lead late in the day. At the 17th she took three shots to get out of a bunker and took a triple bogey. Inkster had added an even-par 72 and so still led at six under by three over the Italian.

Four players were a further shot behind, including Karen Stupples, the 2004 champion at Sunningdale. There she had holed out for a double eagle in the final round. Here she holed a wedge shot from 113 yards for an eagle-two at the 14th. The 33-year-old from Kent scored a 69 and still threatened after a third round of 70. But she collapsed to a 78 on the final day, one bad round being the irritating hallmark of her game since her championship success.

Sorenstam was one under par after two rounds, but also failed to challenge over the weekend after rounds of 73 and 79. Friday's best round came from Sophie Gustafson, the Swede who was runner-up at Lytham in 1998 and the champion at Birkdale in 2000. Her 67 showed what was to come on Saturday, the best weather and scoring conditions of the week. Inkster was the one not to take advantage and a 74 gave everyone else a chance.

Steinhauer, after a 70 on Friday, took over in the lead at seven under after a 66. After holing from 30 feet for a birdie at the eighth, she came home in five-under 32. It was quite a round. At the 13th she chipped in for a birdie, while at the par-five 15th she holed a putt from 50 feet from just off the back of the green for an eagle. Her confidence soaring, she hit a wedge to three feet at the 16th and made her fourth birdie of the day.

"This kind of golf suits my game," Steinhauer said. "This course requires low shots and lots of imagination. You have to run the ball up to the flags and I love that. You need experience to play here and I feel very comfortable on the course." She led by three shots over Inkster, Gustafson, Stupples and Lorena Ochoa.

Gustafson had a 69, but the best round of the day came from Ochoa, a 65 just as she had recorded in the second round at the same venue in 2003. She hit a four iron to 10 feet at the par-three first hole and then birdied the second and was off and running. It was a superb round of golf and was a quite a present for her coach, Raphael Alicone, who was celebrating his birthday.

Cristie Kerr finished a stroke behind the group at four under thanks to a 66, which was 10 shots better than the 76 she shot the day before. On Friday her shoulder was hurting and she took a painkiller but suffered an adverse reaction. "I couldn't feel my fingers and hands, and I couldn't focus," she said. The injury was related to a chronic neck problem, but had eased enough on Saturday for the American to charge into contention thanks to a run of four birdies in a row from the sixth.

On Sunday Kerr took a double bogey at the second hole and her chance looked to have gone. But she battled back so well that she was one behind Steinhauer with three holes to play. Then she tangled with Lytham's bunkers again and finished with a bogey at the 16th and a double bogey at the 18th.

Steinhauer was not to be persuaded from her steady, sensible golf. It was a brilliant piece of front-running. She birdied the fourth but otherwise collected 16 pars. She missed only two greens, at the first and last. She never overextended herself by going for the par-fives in two, and she let the pursuers make the mistakes.

Her only error came when she found a bunker at the 18th. She took a bogey, her first for 48 holes since the fifth hole on Friday. "My caddie told me after my drive on the last that I had a four-shot lead and at that point I just went limp," she said. "Up until then, whenever I started thinking ahead, I had to rewind the tape and stick to the next shot."

A closing 72 gave Steinhauer a seven-under total of 281 and a three-stroke win over Kerr and Gustafson, with Ochoa and Inkster sharing fourth place. Kerr closed with 71 and Gustafson 72, while Ochoa and Inkster both had 73s. Lorie Kane holed in one at the 12th, with a four iron from 160 yards, to finish tied for sixth place with Beth Daniel.

Although the women's game possesses some striking young talents, the four majors were all won by the experienced brigade of Webb, Se Ri Pak, Sorenstam and Steinhauer. The last achieved something never done in the men's game, winning a major while using a long putter. "I started using it about four years ago," Steinhauer said. "I've used the same putter ever since. I've only changed the grip on it once. I just was having some difficulties with my putting. I love the long putter."

7. HSBC World Match Play

In the illustrious history of the HSBC World Match Play Championship it is rare for the winner to be a non-major champion or a winner on debut that either merits distinction. In 2006 Paul Casey was both. Yet to win a major, he was playing in the HSBC World Match Play for the first time and his triumph was a considerable achievement. It was a victory remarkable for the emphatic nature of his performance on the course but, first, a little historical context is required.

Only four other winners do not currently have a major title to their name. They are Graham Marsh, Isao Aoki, Colin Montgomerie and Lee Westwood. The last two British players have hopes of removing themselves from the list, as will Casey. At age 29, he has time on his side and this was a performance that will reinforce his belief that the game's greatest prizes await.

Seven players had previously won the World Match Play on their first appearance. Arnold Palmer did so in the inaugural event in 1964. Tom Weiskopf, Hale Irwin, Aoki, Bill Rogers, Greg Norman all followed, and Ernie Els, in 1994, was the last to do so before Casey. Palmer, of course, was already a multi-major champion; Irwin and Els had won the U.S. Open earlier in the summer. The other four had not previously won a major but three of them, Weiskopf, Rogers and Norman (twice), went on to win the Open Championship in later years. Now there is a thought for Casey to hug to himself on cold winter nights.

One more note of distinction was that Casey became only the third Englishman to win this traditional event of the autumnal English sporting scene at the Wentworth Club in Virginia Water, Surrey. Nick Faldo and Westwood were the other two, with Faldo winning the title twice. On the second of those occasions, in 1992, he defeated Jeff Sluman 8 and 7 in the final. This stood as the record margin of victory in the final until Casey swept aside Shaun Micheel 10 and 8.

Three holes up at lunch, Casey sprinted for the line as he had done all week. He was not required to go past the 15th hole on any afternoon and never trailed all weekend from the afternoon of his quarter-final on Friday. "It is easier leading in match play," Casey said. "In stroke play it can be very demanding. It is much easier to chase in stroke play. But in match play it is more difficult to chase. If you get in front, and you keep putting pressure on the other guy, sticking it in the fairway, putting it on the green, that's very difficult for him to play against."

During his run, Casey defeated three major champions in Retief Goosen, Mike Weir and Micheel, as well as the eight-time European money list leader Montgomerie. All of which made his record of completing all four stages of the tournament in only 124 holes—four fewer than the previous low set by Ian Woosnam in 2001—even more impressive.

"The whole week I've been excited just to be here, to have qualified, trying to be very cool and relaxed, happy with each of my wins," Casey said. "None of the matches were easy, even if the scores don't reflect that. They all could have ended up being very tough matches. When you are playing guys like these, who have won major championships, you have to expect them to make birdies, to make putts, and to be ready to do so yourself. This is the biggest win of my career so far, financially and significance-wise, in terms of the roll of honor. I think it's just a reflection of the work I've done over the last couple of years."

Part of that work was in developing his fitness, something that certainly held him in good stead during such an exhausting week of 36-hole matches, partly it was in developing the consistency in his swing to allow him to hit the shot required at any particular moment. Throughout his amateur career, his college experiences in America and as a fledgling professional, Casey also thrived on confidence. When he had it, he would be very, very good; when it disappeared, not very good at all.

Following the Ryder Cup at Oakland Hills in 2004, Casey made some comments about the Americans which proved controversial in the media, even if by the time the media were finished with him the words were a distortion of his views. Nevertheless, he faced up to the furor, earned back the respect of his American colleagues and also took time to come to terms with the episode.

The year of 2005 was a slow one for him, not helped by injuries, but he quietly laid the foundations for better times to come. He won in China late in 2005, the first of three wins on the 2005-06 European Tour schedule. In the summer of 2006 he won the Johnnie Walker Championship at Gleneagles, and when he won at Wentworth he went to the top of the European Order of Merit, even though the massive £1 million first prize was capped for such purposes. He was edged out for the Vardon Trophy in the last week of the season by Padraig Harrington.

Victory at Wentworth was followed by a superb performance at the Ryder Cup at The K Club, adding to the perception that Casey was coming of age at the very highest level. At Oakland Hills, the story had been that he volunteered to face Tiger Woods in the singles (he lost). In truth, Casey revealed, he was volunteered by Darren Clarke. Woods was a potential opponent in the final at Wentworth, in which case the young Englishman would not have appeared in a red Nike shirt. In fact, Tiger spent the day watching an English Premiership football match at Stamford Bridge, the home of champions Chelsea. His return to the World Match Play for the first time in eight years was trumpeted loudly. The world No. 1 arrived on the back of five successive victories, including the Open and the PGA Championship.

But whereas in 1998 Woods had made it all the way to the final, only to lose to his friend Mark O'Meara, this time Tiger could not survive the first day. There were seven major champions in the starting field of 16, but only in one match did two face each other. Even then, Woods, having just collected his 12th major title, was an overwhelming favorite against Micheel, the unheralded winner of the 2003 PGA Championship. He had done little since until finishing second to Tiger at Medinah in the same championship. Before their match he joked about not being a "sacrificial lamb," but when you can putt like Micheel even a Tiger can get bitten. The only time Woods led was from the first hole until Micheel won four holes in a row from the third.

From four down after 17, Woods won the last hole before lunch and the first two afterwards but failed to birdie the par-five fourth and Micheel edged two holes clear again. Apart from the second in the afternoon, where he holed from 15 feet for a birdie-two, Tiger found no joy on the greens. Micheel birdied the seventh and then eagled the 12th from 12 feet on the way to a 4-and-3 victory. "It feels really special to beat him," Micheel said. "It shows what can happen on any given day. Typically, I am going to finish second to him more than he is going to finish second to me. If it had been a four-day championship, I suspect the outcome might have been different."

"I had a hard time with my pace on the greens," Woods said. "I felt I hit the ball decently but just didn't make the putts. I had my chances but couldn't put any pressure on Shaun. Right now I think I'm going to go and work out and get some of this frustration out." Frustration, too, for the sponsors, though they were also philosophical. "Sport has a way of writing its own script," said Giles Morgan of HSBC, "and thank goodness it does."

Little went according to the script on the first day. Jim Furyk had won the Canadian Open the week before to rise to No. 2 in the world. But he met an inspired Robert Karlsson, who never trailed during his 4-and-3 win. Karlsson, at 37, was enjoying the season of his career, his two wins setting a new record of seven by a Swedish player on the European Tour. A debut in the Ryder Cup awaited him the following week. At 6 feet, 5 inches, Karlsson towers above most opponents, but the really frightening thing about him is the streaks of birdies he is capable of producing. He had nine in the morning round, seven of them coming in nine holes from the ninth. He seemed oblivious. "When I came off the course, the BBC guy said, 'You made nine birdies,' and I was like, 'I did?' You don't really count the score when you're playing match play."

Furyk was certainly counting, and from six down after 17 holes there was no way back for the American. Karlsson's scorecard included birdie-twos at all four of the par-threes in the morning and at the second in the afternoon. At the fifth, he bunkered his tee shot but played a marvelous recovery to save par at a time when his game was wobbling ever so slightly. Bernhard Langer, in 1985, and Seve Ballesteros, in 1994, are the only other two men to have a full set of twos in one round. Seve went on to record seven twos in his match but still lost to Ernie Els.

Els, the six-time winner of the championship, was unable to play in the event in 2005 due to a knee injury. His return this time was short-lived as he too departed. He was defeated by Angel Cabrera, who showed his liking for the course by winning the BMW PGA Championship in 2005. The big-hitting Argentinean led from the 10th in the morning, and although Els took it to the 35th, Cabrera won 2 and 1.

Luke Donald and Tim Clark are good friends but Donald was being generous in losing a four-up lead with nine to play. Clark, with four birdies in six holes, squared the match at the 15th, but Donald birdied the 17th and sealed a two-hole win at the last. "I've played enough practice rounds with Tim to know he was never going to give up," Donald admitted.

Another match to go to the 36th hole was a terrific encounter between Montgomerie and David Howell. Montgomerie never trailed but it was all square at lunch before the Scot won three of the first five holes in the afternoon. However, Howell got the score back to even by the 11th and the next four holes were halved. Monty birdied the 16th, Howell the 17th, but it was Montgomerie's four at the par-five last which sealed the narrowest of victories. He shot a 65 in the afternoon to Howell's 67.

Michael Campbell, the defending champion and No. 1 seed, defeated England's Simon Khan 3 and 1, while Casey came from two down after the third, and then again after the 11th, to even the match against Goosen at lunch. He then inflicted the third South African defeat of the day by playing 14 holes in the afternoon in eight under par. Goosen birdied the second to halve the hole and the fourth, only to loose that one to an eagle from Casey, who also made six birdies. Having never managed to win a match at the Accenture Match Play in California, the former double English Amateur champion was pleased to get off the mark here. One of Adam Scott and Mike Weir had to win for the first time at Wentworth, the Australian on his third visit, the Canadian on his fourth. The honors went to Weir with a 3-and-2 victory.

After the excitements of Thursday, the quarter-finals were a more sober affair. Weir had an unfortunate end to his match against Casey when his back went into spasm and bogeys at the 14th and 15th handed the Englishman a 5-and-3 win. Weir had won the second hole of the afternoon to go one up, but it was the last time Casey trailed in a match of the rest of the tournament. He won the third and the fourth and then never looked back. In a match of poor quality, Karlsson kept his run going by defeating Cabrera 4 and 3, while for the second successive day Micheel put out the highest world-ranked player.

On Friday this was Donald, the world No. 10. Micheel's wife had been planning to go racing but was more than happy to watch her husband in action instead. He won the first two holes and the local favorite could not turn the tide. Five down at lunch, he lost the first two holes again to be seven down, and although he won some late holes, Micheel sealed a 4-and-2 win.

Montgomerie provided the day's fireworks but only after Campbell had won four of the first six holes. "You know it is going to be a long day ahead," said Monty. "It's almost five down, since it is not just getting back to level but getting ahead again. It's a hell of a place to be." Had he gone five down, the Scot admitted that would have been that, but he won the seventh and the eighth and got back to even at the 16th. It was a brave effort and in the afternoon Montgomerie went ahead, although by never more than two holes. Campbell squared the match with a brilliant chip at the 17th and then both hit their second shots into a new bunker on the left of the final green.

Montgomerie's ball was two inches closer to the hole, so he marked. Campbell was first to go and left it in the bunker. "It's a new bunker and the sand is heavy," said Montgomerie. "I would have left it in as well if I had gone first." Instead, he hit his recovery harder than he would otherwise have done and holed from eight feet for the winning birdie. Had he missed, Campbell would have had a five-footer to take the match to extra holes. "I was four down before most people were up this morning, so that's a good victory," Monty said.

But two matches of the full duration had taken their toll. He knew he had to keep the ball on the fairway to have a chance against Casey in the semi-finals. He could not and Casey was able to keep the pressure on with a superb display of driving. It got away from Montgomerie around the turn in the morning, but a 74 for the first 18 holes was never going to keep him in contention. From five up at lunch, Casey won the third and the fourth and only a couple of bogeys from the Englishman kept the game going. At the eighth Montgomerie finished at the base of a bank and, from an awkward stance with his legs at 90 degrees, he shanked his recovery.

His eyes went as sideways as the ball and almost popped out of their sockets. His third went into the water and he walked to the ninth tee. The Scot responded with a great birdie, only his third of the day, but Casey then eagled the 12th. A five iron from 210 yards to six feet was a glorious way to signal the end, which came only a hole later. In contrast, the other semi-final went the whole distance. Both Karlsson and Micheel were ahead at times but the American lunched with the lead, and although Karlsson evened the score three times in the afternoon, Micheel went to the last ahead and his birdie there gave him a two-hole win.

It would have been somewhat ironic if Micheel had won the final given his non-qualification for the American Ryder Cup team. On the other hand, might it have dented some Europe morale for a third member of their team to lose to someone who was not even in the U.S. squad at The K Club? Casey never let that scenario develop. The key moment of the final appeared to come at the 16th hole in the morning. Casey was one up but finished at the front of the green when the hole was cut right at the back. Micheel, however, hit his approach over the green, six feet down a bank.

He then thinned his chip over the green, and although Casey three-putted, Micheel lost the hole with a six to a five. Micheel said later that his caddie had given him the right yardage for the second shot, but while walking from the green to the next tee, the pair was involved in a verbal dispute which clearly unsettled the American. Casey took advantage with two mighty blows onto the 17th green to go three up. The finalists halved three holes in birdies in the morning. But Casey went out in 31 in the afternoon, for the second time in the day.

Birdies at the second and fourth put Casey five up, and as Micheel's game wilted, Casey seemed to get stronger. A succession of stunning approach shots at the seventh, eighth and ninth, none longer than six feet, gave Casey three birdies in a row, and when Micheel failed to birdie the short 10th he conceded the match. "It is disheartening when you make it this far and don't play well," said the PGA champion from 2003. "But Paul played some great golf and some great iron shots at the end."

Two years before, Casey had been the highest ranked English golfer. "That's nice," he said at the time, "but the problem is the highest ranked English golfer is only 29th in the world." He was duly overtaken by Donald and Howell, but this victory helped in the catching up. "It is all about belief," he said, "and believing that you can win world-class events. That is something Luke and David have done. Luke is very hungry for a major and David has won huge events. I am chasing those guys and need to start believing I'm capable of winning big events like this." He can because he has.

8. The Ryder Cup

Probably not even the most avid home supporters on the grounds of The K Club would have predicted what occurred in the Ryder Cup over those three days of September near Straffan in County Kildare, Ireland. It was beyond belief that the Europeans, although the favorites, could inflict another defeat on the American team of 18½ points to 9½, as they did two years earlier at Oakland Hills in the United States. That is precisely what happened, and the Irish crowds cheered themselves hoarse while doing their country proud by showing that they were great sportsmen as well as passionate fans.

The European team, led by captain Ian Woosnam, won all five series—two fourballs, two foursomes and singles—for the first time. "This is the pinnacle," said the Welshman. "I've won many tournaments around the world, I've won a major championship, I've been No. 1 in the world, and I've got to say, this is the proudest moment of my life."

It was Europe's third consecutive Ryder Cup victory and its fifth in the last six contests.

While Woosnam considered that he had "12 heroes," the heart of his team was Irishman Darren Clarke, just six weeks after the death of his wife, Heather, on August 13 because of cancer, and with the Ryder Cup being played on this island for the first time ever. The champagne and the stout had only begun to flow that Sunday night when Woosnam told the media, "Be under no illusion, every single person on this team has dedicated this win to Heather Clarke. We all miss her very much."

Clarke played three matches and won three points. The American captain, Tom Lehman, told him, "You hurt us really bad but we were glad you were on this team." Asked his memories of the week, Clarke said, "I've got too many to list. To be here all week, my team have been unbelievable. The American guys, the support they have shown me, and their wives, has just been incredible. And the crowd on Friday morning will be something I will cherish forever."

The magnitude of Clarke's performance could be judged against those of the other two Irishmen. It was not easy to carry the expectations of the country. Padraig Harrington (0-4-1) and Paul McGinley (0-1-2) did not win a point between them while losing five and collecting three halves in their eight matches.

The Spaniard Sergio Garcia won the most points for Europe, with four wins in five matches, and England's Lee Westwood had three wins and two halves. Joining Clarke with three wins and no losses were Luke Donald of England and Jose Maria Olazabal of Spain. Englishmen Paul Casey (2-0-2) and David Howell (2-0-1) were also undefeated, Scotland's Colin Montgomerie (1-1-2) provided veteran leadership, and then there were the two Swedes, Henrik Stenson (1-1-1), who secured the winning point, and Robert Karlsson (0-1-2), also a valuable contributor.

"I tip my hat to them," Lehman said. "They played inspired golf, and they never, ever did not make us pay for a mistake that we made. They made us pay every time." He was not worried about a backlash at home, saying "Quite frankly, I'm not too concerned, because I am very proud of the effort that our team gave."

Tiger Woods led the United States with three wins and two losses. Also winning two or more points were Stewart Cink (1-1-3), Jim Furyk (2-3) and Scott Verplank (2-0). The only other American to secure a point was Zach Johnson (1-2-1). The following players did not win a point while having 14 losses and six halves: Chad Campbell (0-1-2), Vaughn Taylor (0-1-1), Chris DiMarco (0-3-1), David Toms (0-3-1), Phil Mickelson (0-4-1) and Brett Wetterich (0-2-0).

The dream of a Ryder Cup for Ireland went back to the origins of the competition, and to the 1970s for Dr. Michael Smurfit, who purchased the property in 1988 and hired Arnold Palmer's company to design the golf course on the estate that once was Straffan House. It took until 1998 for The K Club to secure the Ryder Cup, that being accomplished when Smurfit also committed to Ken Schofield, then executive director of the European Tour, to 10 years of the European Open on the same course.

Asked later if that offer was excessive, Smurfit said, "On the face of it, yes. But not when I asked myself if I wanted to sponsor the European Open for 10 more years purely as a business proposition, outside the Ryder Cup. Once I decided that I did, then the obvious thing to do was to make a splash that was certain to sink everyone else. Effectively, it followed from my business decision."

It was immediately declared the greatest sporting event in the history of Ireland, and was originally scheduled for 2005 but was delayed one year after the terrorist attacks in America on September 11, 2001.

The passion that the Irish crowds brought to the Ryder Cup was on display from the moment the gates were opened Friday at 6 a.m. before a large group that rushed to claim the 1,600 seats beside the first tee. They were loud and supportive, particularly of the Europeans, but they were also impressive in that when it was any player's turn, they went quiet and gave him time to concentrate and hit the ball before resuming their cheers and chants. If it was a well-struck shot by a European, pandemonium would reign. No wonder Europe would jump to a 5-to-3 lead on the first day and never let up.

McGinley would say later, "I have been so proud of the Irish people this week, the way they have conducted themselves. And as for that first tee, I will never, ever forget it."

First Day

First off in the Friday morning fourballs were Tiger Woods and Jim Furyk, who played Padraig Harrington and Colin Montgomerie. Even Ivor Robson, the veteran first-tee starter, was affected by the occasion. The format for the first series was fourballs, but Robson announced foursomes. Whether the frenzy on the first tee was a factor, Woods hit the first shot of this Ryder Cup into the lake. Europe was one down on the 17th green with a chance to even the match, but Montgomerie left his 12-foot putt short, and the Americans won the initial point.

Paul Casey and Robert Karlsson were three up after nine holes in the second match, but Americans Stewart Cink and J.J. Henry, an impressive rookie, birdied six of the last nine holes to halve the point. The Americans went one up when they won the 14th, and things looked worse for Europe when Karlsson put his approach shot in the River Liffey, but Casey's 30-foot putt for birdie put the match back to even.

The Spanish pair of Jose Maria Olazabal and Sergio Garcia were never down in the third match against David Toms and long-hitting rookie Brett Wetterich. The Europeans were seven under par when they won, 3 and 2. Garcia opened with a birdie and scored five more birdies, leaving Olazabal to say, "The secret was playing with Sergio."

There was incredible emotion in the fourth match of the Friday morning fourballs, with Darren Clarke making his appearance, along with Lee Westwood, against Phil Mickelson and Chris DiMarco. On the tee, Clarke thought to himself, "How am I going to do this?" The Irishman then struck the shot perfectly, 320 yards down the fairway, and birdied the first hole. On the 16th, Clarke's five-wood approach set him up for the go-ahead birdie. He also birdied the last hole from 18 feet to keep the lead at one hole, then there were hugs and tears all around.

When the afternoon foursomes pairings were sent out, all 12 European and 10 American team members had played on the first day. The first three matches were halved, and the fourth match garnered the most attention, with all four players in the top 10 in the world, and Garcia and Luke Donald defeated Woods and Furyk by two holes.

Furyk drove wildly on the first hole and Woods had to hack the ball out left-handed. They were all square after Europe's bogey on the third, then Europe scored birdies on the next two holes to be two up, as Donald holed a 40-foot putt on the fifth. Another birdie by Donald from half that distance at the 12th put Europe two up again. The match was even after Furyk's 20-footer at the 13th and Woods's tee shot to three feet and Furyk's birdie putt at the par-three 14th. Europe went ahead again on the 17th, where Garcia hit his approach shot to three feet, and Furyk's 12 footer went past the hole, then Europe won the 18th after Furyk dumped his approach shot into the lake.

In the other Friday afternoon foursomes, Americans Chad Campbell and Zach Johnson came from two down with three holes to play and halved their match against Harrington and Paul McGinley. The Americans birdied the last three holes, but fortunately for the Europeans, McGinley matched the one on the 17th, holing from 10 feet to Johnson's 15 feet, to pave the way for the half.

In the second match, European David Howell's tee shot into the lake on the 15th hole enabled David Toms and Stewart Cink to pull even with Howell and Henrik Stenson and finish with a halved match. Both teams had chances to win over the closing stretch. On the 16th, Cink played a brilliant shot from a bunker that produced a conceded birdie. But Stenson made a beautiful chip from heavy rough to two feet, and Howell sank that to share the hole. Toms narrowly missed putts on the next two holes, as did Howell on the last.

In the third match, Montgomerie and Westwood earned their half for Europe against Chris DiMarco and Phil Mickelson with a birdie on the last hole. DiMarco and Mickelson posted a par-five after hitting into a bunker. Westwood had a double-breaking putt from 35 feet which he put six feet from the hole, and Montgomerie holed from there for the birdie. "How many times," asked Woosnam, "have we seen Monty hole that putt? He's got so much courage. What a man to have on your team."

Downplaying his delight with Europe's 5-to-3 lead, Woosnam said, "I would have taken a lead of any kind."

First Day Fourballs
Furyk and Woods (USA) defeated Harrington and Montgomerie (Europe), 1 hole.
Casey and Karlsson (Europe) halved with Cink and Henry (USA).
Garcia and Olazabal (Europe) defeated Toms and Wetterich (USA), 3 and 2.
Clarke and Westwood (Europe) defeated DiMarco and Mickelson (USA), 1 hole.

First Day Foursomes
Harrington and McGinley (Europe) halved with Campbell and Johnson (USA).
Howell and Stenson (Europe) halved with Cink and Toms (USA).
Montgomerie and Westwood (Europe) halved with DiMarco and Mickelson (USA).
Donald and Garcia (Europe) defeated Furyk and Woods (USA), 2 holes.

Second Day
As the fourballs and foursomes unfolded on Saturday, it became apparent that the European team was again on the right track. At the end of play, Europe had won all four series over the two days by the same score, 2½ to 1½, and now held a commanding 10-to-6 margin.

Moreover, Ian Woosnam had given each of his 12 players two matches and, as Colin Montgomerie said, "All of them have contributed and all of them have done something meaningful." In contrast, three of the Americans—Scott Verplank, Vaughn Taylor and Brett Wetterich—had been in only one match. Two had been in two matches, leaving seven to try to carry the burden.

The Europeans did not need to be reminded that they had led by the same score in 1999 at Brookline and that the Americans had come back in the singles competition for a 14½-to-13½ victory. Woosnam said, "I'm not going to get ahead of myself because we all know what this game can do." Asked if his American team could recover, captain Tom Lehman said, "It's been done before."

Down by two points, the United States needed a good start in the Saturday morning fourballs, and as it turned out, Stewart Cink and J.J. Henry were two of the Americans' most dependable players. Europe countered with Paul Casey, also playing very well, along with Robert Karlsson and the result was a halved match. Europe led through 15 holes, then Henry scored an eagle on the 16th with a 20-foot putt and a birdie on the next after an approach shot to two feet, and suddenly the Americans were in front. Finally, Casey's 12-foot birdie putt on the 18th assured the half.

"After J.J. had made that fantastic eagle at the 16th and followed it up with a birdie at the 17th," Casey said, "I thought to myself that if we could snatch the full point away from them, it would really sort of hurt. That was my goal down the last."

Next the Spaniards, Jose Maria Olazabal and Sergio Garcia, took down a pair on whom the Americans were surely depending, Phil Mickelson and Chris DiMarco, by a margin of 3 and 2. The European duo went out in 31, with Garcia's birdie on the ninth putting them three up. Olazabal sank a birdie putt on the 10th to be four up, and Garcia's sand shot at the 16th produced the birdie that won the match.

Then came Darren Clarke and Lee Westwood versus Tiger Woods and Jim Furyk—"a very special match," as Woosnam put it—which entered Ryder Cup lore when Clarke chipped in on the 16th to win by 3 and 2. "He's one for the drama, isn't he," Westwood marveled. That made Saturday morning's score 2½ to ½. Verplank and Zach Johnson supplied the American point in the last match over Padraig Harrington and Henrik Stenson.

Responding to the comment that Clarke and Westwood were making Woosnam look good in his captain's picks, Clarke said, "The people who were most certain it was not a gamble were Lee and myself. We know each other's game so well and we thrive on each other's company."

Meanwhile, Lehman didn't press the panic button, but that was being done by journalists from both sides in the media center. "Drop the world No. 1?" said Lehman, incredulously, when asked about benching Woods. Instead, Woods and Furyk went out again in the Saturday afternoon foursomes in the fourth match and defeated the Irish pair of Harrington and Paul McGinley by 3 and 2.

In the first match of the afternoon, Mickelson and David Toms had the misfortune to draw Garcia and Luke Donald. The Americans fell two behind through 11 holes but fought back to even two holes later. But Toms hit into the water on the 15th to lose the hole, Donald sank a birdie putt from 15 feet on the 16th to be two up, and Europe won by 2 and 1 at the 17th with a par. "The 14th, 15th and 16th were the holes that really hurt," Toms said. "If we had two-putted the 14th we would have won that hole. My second into the water cost us the 15th, and then, though we originally looked to have the upper hand at the 16th, they ended up beating us at that hole."

A close second match between Westwood and Montgomerie against the Americans Taylor and Chad Campbell ended in a half with two miscues by each pair over the last four holes. Taylor pushed his drive into the water on the 15th, enabling the Europeans to go one up. The Americans three-putted the 16th for a half after the Europeans were forced to lay up. On the 17th, Montgomerie's chip from the rough was too heavy and Westwood's par putt lipped out, allowing the Americans to even the match. Both teams had chances for eagles on the last, but neither converted and the match was halved.

The highlight of Saturday afternoon was produced by the Europeans' Casey in the third match with David Howell against Cink and Johnson. The Europeans went five up after 12 holes, and the result was certain, but Casey made it memorable by scoring a hole-in-one at the 213-yard 14th to end the match, 5 and 4. Casey dropped his golf club and raised his hands to the sky. "I was in shock," he said later. "The reaction of the crowd was tremendous, and then to see it on the big screen replay was another thrill."

Second Day Fourballs

Casey and Karlsson (Europe) halved with Cink and Henry (USA).
Garcia and Olazabal (Europe) defeated DiMarco and Mickelson (USA), 3 and 2.
Clarke and Westwood (Europe) defeated Furyk and Woods (USA), 3 and 2.
Johnson and Verplank (USA) defeated Harrington and Stenson (Europe), 2 and 1.

Second Day Foursomes

Donald and Garcia (Europe) defeated Mickelson and Toms (USA), 2 and 1.
Montgomerie and Westwood (Europe) halved with Campbell and Taylor (USA).
Casey and Howell (Europe) defeated Cink and Johnson (USA), 5 and 4.
Furyk and Woods (USA) defeated Harrington and McGinley (Europe), 3 and 2.

Third Day

The score was the same, 10 to 6 in Europe's favor, but there was a big difference between this and the European position entering the third-day singles in 1999 at Brookline. There, three members of the European team had not played a match in either the fourballs or foursomes, and all three would lose in the singles, effectively making the score 10 to 9, as Colin Montgomerie believed, when the day began. This year, captain Ian Woosnam had given at least two matches in the first two days to each of the 12 players, so that none would be untested—or worn out.

The result was that the Europeans won 8½ of the 12 points in the singles for the final 18½-to-9½ verdict.

It was another smart move by Woosnam that his first player off was Montgomerie, a veteran leader on the course and one who liked to play fast. It would help the team's morale starting out for European blue figures to be showing on the leaderboards. Montgomerie took the lead on David Toms at the par-three third hole, where he hit to four feet, and he recalled proudly that his score stayed "in the blue" for the rest of the day. He won by one hole.

Sergio Garcia had four wins in four matches for Europe, but in the second singles match he ran into Stewart Cink, who birdied four of the first five holes and cruised to a four-up result. Paul Casey was quick to counter that, as he scored two birdies in his first three holes and was never behind in defeating Jim Furyk by 2 and 1.

Tiger Woods went out in the fourth match, where he met Robert Karlsson. The Swede birdied the first hole from 25 feet, but Woods scored birdies on three of the next four holes to be two up and marched to a 3-and-2 victory. There was an anxious but humorous moment by the seventh green when caddie Steve Williams slipped and dropped Woods's nine iron into the lake. They played on without the club, which was recovered by a diver and returned as they closed the match, 3 up, on the 16th hole.

On the American side behind Woods, there was a sense of impending doom. Woods said, "The guys behind us have to turn it around. They're down in a lot of matches back there. It looks like the Europeans are making all the birdies."

In the very next match no birdies were being made, as Luke Donald and Chad Campbell played 10 holes in pars. Then Donald went 3-3-3 including two birdies starting at the 11th, while Campbell posted 5-5-6, and there was a three-up margin that became a 2-and-1 European victory. Campbell had defeated Donald by 5 and 3 two years earlier, but Donald said, "It wasn't about revenge, it was about getting to 14½ points as soon as possible."

As it stood, Donald had the 14th point to assure that Europe would retain the cup. Out on the course in the ninth match, David Howell had beaten Brett Wetterich 5 and 4, and now all that was needed was a half point from somewhere. It did not go according to the script Woosnam had imagined when he sent out Irishmen Paul McGinley in the sixth match and, particularly, Darren Clarke in the seventh.

Howell had disturbed the timetable, and then Henrik Stenson did also, holing a winning putt for par from five feet on the 15th green to win the eighth match by 3 and 2 over Vaughn Taylor. Europe then had 15 points—and the Ryder Cup. At first Stenson did not realize what he had done, and later said that if it had been possible, he would have waited for Clarke. "I didn't know that was the one, but I'm delighted to win my match, and more delighted that the team wins," Stenson said.

It was 3:47 p.m., and after hugging his girlfriend, Stenson was off in a cart to catch up with Clarke's match. Nine minutes later, Clarke defeated Zach Johnson 3 and 2 to put Europe ahead 16 to 8. "It was a privilege to be there, to be a part of that," Stenson said. The scene on the 16th hole was tumultuous. Clarke was crying, as was most of the huge crowd, including Woosnam, who raised Clarke's right arm like a boxing champion.

Clarke's send-off on the first tee reminded Johnson of "an 80,000-seat stadium around one tee box. I got a warm welcome too, but I felt like I was the away team." Clarke was two up through nine holes and the leaderboards were displaying European blue in as many as seven of the 12 matches. The crowd erupted when Clarke holed from 40 feet at the 10th, again from over 100 feet at the 12th, and they carried on the cheers until the end.

In the last quarter of the draw, Jose Maria Olazabal defeated Phil Mickelson 2 and 1, Lee Westwood defeated Chris DiMarco by two holes, and Scott Verplank provided the last American point by 4 and 3 over Padraig Harrington. McGinley and J.J. Henry carried the sixth match to the 18th hole, where Henry, needing a 30-foot birdie for the half, was conceded the putt.

Third Day Singles
Montgomerie (Europe) defeated Toms (USA), 1 hole.
Cink (USA) defeated Garcia (Europe), 4 and 3.
Casey (Europe) defeated Furyk (USA), 2 and 1.
Woods (USA) defeated Karlsson (Europe), 3 an 2.
Donald (Europe) defeated Campbell (USA), 2 and 1.
McGinley (Europe) halved with Henry (USA).
Clarke (Europe) defeated Johnson (USA), 3 and 2.
Stenson (Europe) defeated Taylor (USA), 4 and 3.
Howell (Europe) defeated Wetterich (USA), 5 and 4.
Olazabal (Europe) defeated Mickelson (USA), 2 and 1.
Westwood (Europe) defeated DiMarco (USA), 2 holes.
Verplank (USA) defeated Harrington (Europe), 4 and 3.

9. American Tours

The year 2006 was the Year of the Tiger X.

It always seemed to be the Year of the Tiger, and so it would simplify things just to put Roman numerals after each one, they way the National Football League does with the Super Bowl. But even by Tiger Woods's standards, the year 2006 was extraordinary. He won twice early, then endured the illness and death of his father, Earl, then rebounded and won six straight starts, including two majors, the Open Championship in Britain and the PGA Championship.

In a year of dramatic events, including another debacle for the Americans in the Ryder Cup, it would take Woods and his sensational year to push Phil Mickelson off center stage—winning the Masters, then losing the U.S. Open in one of the most amazing displays of ineptitude since Jean Van de Velde's crash in the 1999 Open. Add the slide of Vijay Singh, the swoon of Ernie Els, the attack of the Aussies, and Commissioner Tim Finchem's reshuffling of the PGA Tour, and it was a busy year.

But mostly, it was Tiger Woods's year.

With his father's condition steadily worsening, Woods won two of his first four starts, the Buick Invitational and the Ford Championship at Doral. His dad died in early May, and Woods did not play from the Masters in April until the U.S. Open in mid-June, when he missed the 36-hole cut in a major championship for the first time as a professional.

Starting in mid-July, Woods won six straight PGA Tour starts—the Open, the Buick Open, the PGA Championship, the WGC - Bridgestone Invitational, the Deutsche Bank Championship and the WGC - American Express Championship. Woods thus left those with an interest in golf primed for a debate in 2007: If Woods should keep winning, would he tie or break Byron Nelson's record of 11 straight, or do the victories have to be in the same season?

Woods won eight times in just 15 starts on the PGA Tour, and of course topped the Tour's money list with $9,941,563. He had 11 victories worldwide. Woods reaction to his year? "When you take into account what's happened off the course, it's my worst year," he said. "Golf does not compare to losing a parent."

The year was marked elsewhere by sadness. Chris DiMarco's mother, Norma, died of a heart attack in July, and Heather Clarke, wife of Northern Ireland's Darren Clarke, died in August, of cancer. Then in September, Nelson, who won 11 straight and 18 overall in 1945, died at the age of 94.

Mickelson suffered a different kind of tragedy. First, he was the great innovator, using two drivers at the Masters—one for a fade, the other for a draw. The strategy paid off in a second green jacket. Then came the meltdown at Winged Foot. Mickelson spent much of the U.S. Open searching for the fairways, but even so, seemed on the verge of winning his third straight major title. Then he staggered down the final round. One unforgettable photo shows him with his head in a trash bag, looking for his golf ball. But he came to the final hole needing just a par to win, or a bogey to have a playoff. What he produced was a scenario out of the farce movie *Caddyshack*. He bounced his tee shot off a hospitality tent, next hit a tree, then a bunker, and finally he double-bogeyed.

"I just can't believe I did that," Mickelson said. "I am such an idiot."

It didn't help that Padraig Harrington, Jim Furyk and Colin Montgomerie also fumbled the Open away. And it did help Geoff Ogilvy that he was the last man standing. Little was heard from Mickelson after that. He went on to another poor showing in the Ryder Cup, then pretty much went into seclusion.

Three former powerhouses were noticeable by their near-absences. Vijay Singh won only once, and Ernie Els and Retief Goosen went winless on the PGA Tour. The shifting spotlight caught two rookies as rising stars— South Africa's Trevor Immelman, who won the Cialis Western Open, and Colombia's Camilo Villegas, who had four top-10 finishes in 29 starts. (He joined J.B. Holmes and Bubba Watson as the new bombers, blasting the ball well over 300 yards off the tee.)

Of the PGA Tour itself, Commissioner Tim Finchem's FedEx Cup was the big news. The move was generally seen as an effort to boost television ratings. The FedEx Cup, which begins in 2007, is a season-long race for points won in competition that wraps up in a playoff series in late summer.

Finchem also negotiated new television contracts, which in themselves showed some shift in golf. ABC, which once carried three of the four major championships, along with its sister channels, ESPN and ESPN2, gave up the PGA Tour. CBS and NBC agreed to six-year contracts, and the Golf Channel signed on for 15 years.

The season was replete with those cameos that go to make up the richness of the game. Some examples:

• At the WGC - Accenture Match Play, Stephen Ames happened to answer to a golf writer that he had a chance against Tiger Woods because Woods was erratic off the tee. A resentful Woods whipped Ames, 9 and 8, a beating some thought would destroy his confidence. A month later, Ames won The Players Championship by six strokes. Said Ames: "I got my butt kicked and that was it. What am I going to do, sit down and cry about it?"

• Joe Durant, a marginal player for all of his career, spent the first part of the season worrying about keeping his playing card. He spent the latter part piling up $2.8 million.

• Jack Nicklaus, who has long been seeking a way to combat the "hot" golf ball, tried a wrinkle dating to the earlier days of Oakmont—furrowed bunkers. He used a much gentler version at his Memorial Tournament, and if players' complaints were any indication, the furrows worked. The question became, would the PGA Tour ever consider furrowing bunkers?

• Almost without anyone really taking notice, Australia was becoming a power in golf. While everyone was still thinking in terms of Greg Norman, a record six Australians out of the 23 on the PGA Tour won in 2006. Geoff Ogilvy was the headliner, winning the U.S. Open and the WGC - Accenture Match Play. Stuart Appleby also was a double winner, in the season-opening Mercedes Championship, his third straight, and the Shell Houston Open. How to explain this situation?

Robert Allenby, who wasn't among the winning Australians in 2006, offered reporters an interesting theory at the Australian Open. "We have

110 / AMERICAN TOURS

to work pretty hard to get results," he said. "Everything is handed to them on a plate."

Whatever the cause, the shift in power away from Americans was reflected in the Official World Golf Ranking. At the end of the year, Tiger Woods, Jim Furyk and Phil Mickelson were 1-2-3 on the list. The next American was Davis Love at No. 16, and overall there were only 13 Americans in the top 50. This might also explain the recent European domination in the Ryder Cup.

The Ryder Cup shifted to The K Club in Ireland, and the Europeans did it again, an 18½-to-9½ thumping. It sent the Americans off wringing their hands, wondering what went wrong. Spain's Sergio Garcia, again a spark for the Europeans, had his explanation, complete with nifty barb. "Hopefully," Garcia said, "we won't get asked if the Nationwide Tour is the second-best tour in the world anymore."

U.S. PGA Tour

Mercedes Championships
Maui, Hawaii
Winner: Stuart Appleby

Maybe they ought to put a reserved sign on the Mercedes Championships trophy and use ditto marks for the winner's name. Leading off the 2006 season, it was Stuart Appleby again, for the third straight year. "This one," he announced, "was the hardest." He blew a two-shot lead in the final round, rallied to tie Vijay Singh, then beat him with a birdie on the first playoff hole. "I had to do something special coming in," Appleby said, scolding himself. "I didn't do it, so I had to do it in the playoff."

Appleby shot 71-72-70-71 for a modest eight-under-par 284 total. Singh, finishing before him, shot 70-74-74-66.

Appleby birdied three of his first five holes for a 71 in the first round, trailing Olin Browne, whose 69 would be one of only two rounds in the 60s for the tournament. The winds were gusting to 35 mph in the second round. Appleby took the lead for good in the second with a 72 for a one-stroke edge at three-under 143. "It's more of a grind," he said. "There's no real run of birdies." He birdied the 14th and 15th, but a tee shot into high weeds cost him a bogey at the 18th. Singh birdied the 15th and 18th, both par-fives, for a 74, and was a stroke back.

Appleby inched ahead in the wind to a two-stroke lead in the third round, birdieing three of his last six holes for a 70. He holed a 12-foot putt at the 13th, a six-footer at the 15th and two-putted the 18th for his third straight round under par. Campbell, second by two strokes, acknowledged that Appleby would be tough to beat. "But I believe I've got the tools to beat him," he said. Singh (74 and five behind) was merely looking for a break. "It was a grind," he said. "Putts like three or four feet, it's like, 'Please, hit a good, solid stroke.'"

The fourth round was a reversal of form in all directions. Campbell exited the tight race on a 75, following a lost-ball double bogey at the 12th. And Singh put up a stunning seven-under 66, by far the low of the week. Said Geoff Ogilvy: "I thought we were all supposed to play the same course." Singh, starting five behind Appleby, eagled from two feet at the fifth and made the turn in 32. He birdied four times coming home, most notably the 12th, where he blasted from 50 yards out of a bunker to four inches.

Appleby eagled the fifth with a 70-foot putt, then staggered away for three bogeys and three birdies. He had to birdie the 18th to stay alive, and he did. He was 150 feet short with his approach, but he chipped to within four feet and holed it for a 71 and a tie.

In the playoff, Singh was short with his approach, short again with his eagle putt, and then wide right on a nine-footer, and parred. Appleby hit a three-iron second into the back bunker, blasted out tight, then tapped in for the birdie. Another year, another Mercedes.

Sony Open in Hawaii
Honolulu, Hawaii
Winner: David Toms

It was the Sony Open in Hawaii in mid-January and once again the Michelle Wie Show. Wie, the whiz girl, now 16, received a sponsor's exemption into her third straight Sony Open at Waialae Country Club, again trying to become the first female to make the cut in a PGA Tour event since Babe Zaharias in 1945. Then came the shock of the first round. "I can't believe I'm going this bad," Wie said, after a nine-over-par 79. A 68 in the second round left the Babe's record safe.

But Waialae wasn't safe from David Toms. Never more than a stroke off the lead all week, Toms would run off and hide by five shots. Toms opened with a 66, a stroke behind Rory Sabbatini, who birdied five of his last seven holes for a 65. With a 69 in the second round, Toms again was just a stroke off, this time behind Chad Campbell and Jim Furyk, who each shot 67–134.

In gentler winds in the third round, guys were playing well but losing ground. Furyk shot 70, and slipped back, and defending champion Vijay Singh shot 65 and also slipped. How could this be? Simple. David Toms was shooting a course-record 61, and Chad Campbell a 62, and they tied at 196. At the 18th, Toms two-putted for a birdie and Campbell's 15-footer hung on the lip, and they were tied at 14 under and leading by seven.

The Sony Open had become a two-man race for the final round, and it was over almost as soon as it started. Campbell couldn't buy a birdie, finally getting one at the 17th, when Toms had been long out of reach. "One birdie on Sunday isn't going to do it," said Campbell (70). Rory Sabbatini closed with a 62 to tie Campbell for second at 266.

Apart from Bubba Watson, a 27-year-old rookie in his debut, crushing 360-yard drives and shooting 65 for a solo fourth, it was Toms's show.

Toms sensed it was his at the first hole, when he threw an eight iron to 12 feet and holed the birdie. Said Toms: "It was like, 'Here we go again. I'm going to play well.'" And he did. He birdied the third on a 25-footer, made two good par saves, and birdied the par-five ninth, and was leading by four.

He did make a bogey at the 13th—his first in 41 holes—but he tidied things up with an up-and-down for birdie at the 18th for a 65, a 19-under 261, just a shot off the 72-hole course record, and the five-stroke win.

Bob Hope Chrysler Classic
Palm Desert, California
Winner: Chad Campbell

Chad Campbell, after squandering a chance at the Sony Open just a few days earlier, was now feeling good about things. He had just opened the Bob Hope Chrysler Classic with a 63 at Bermuda Dunes. Then his jaw dropped when he saw the scoreboard. "You expect low scores out here," Campbell said, "but you don't usually expect a 60." Instead of leading, he found himself three strokes behind. Pat Perez had shot a 12-under-par 60 at the Arnold Palmer Course at PGA West. But at least Campbell was in second place, a comfortable position for the five-round tournament played over four different courses.

Perez couldn't keep pace, then crashed to a 78 in the final round at the Classic Course, the host course, and plummeted to 73rd.

Campbell would take over in the second round and roll from there, but the big hurdle would be the final round. Could he close? Campbell, a two-time winner, hadn't won in about 21 months. He had a chance at the Sony Open the previous week. He and David Toms were tied with a seven-stroke lead going into the final round, but Campbell mustered only one birdie. He tied for second. Going into the Hope's finale, up by one, he had led from the second round.

Campbell, bogey-free in the first round, stayed that way in the blustery winds at La Quinta for a six-under 66 in the second round, and led by four over Perez and John Senden. Said Perez, after a six-bogey 73, "I've played four rounds this year, three have been in the wind, and I've shot over par every time." Senden, in contrast, shot 63 at PGA West.

It was just two holes from home in the third round that Campbell's bogey-free streak ended, but he kept his four-stroke lead with a 68 at PGA West. In the fourth round, despite a 67 at the Classic, his margin shrank to one when the seasoned Scott Verplank birdied Bermuda Dunes' 18th for a 64. Senden shot 67 at Bermuda Dunes and was third, four off the lead.

The Sony experience was just what Campbell needed. He would struggle early in the Hope's final round and was even tied with Verplank briefly. Then he went birdie-eagle into the turn, dropping a 32-foot putt for the eagle at the ninth, and led by four. But he gave two right back at the 10th, driving wildly and taking a double bogey. Then he saved bogey brilliantly at the par-four 13th. He watered his tee shot, hit his second tee shot into a fairway bunker, and from there slashed his six iron to within six feet of the cup and holed the putt for a bogey.

After making only two bogeys in the first four rounds, he had a frazzled finale at the Classic, with an eagle, three birdies, a double bogey, two singles and some tough pars for a one-under 71. His 25-under 335 gave him a three-stroke win over Verplank (73) and Parnevik (67). Phil Mickelson, making his season debut, closed with a 71 and tied for fifth.

Buick Invitational
LaJolla, California
Winner: Tiger Woods

One moment, Tiger Woods was looking down the barrel of a missed cut. The next, he was hoisting the trophy. Just another week's work in the life of the world No. 1 golfer.

This Buick Invitational was a wild one. At one point in the final round, 12 players had a share of the lead, and with six holes to play, eight were tied for the lead. But this wasn't a win that Woods would rank among his best, not after Australian rookie Nathan Green, playing in his second PGA Tour event, and two-time Masters champion Jose Maria Olazabal, made fatal errors in the two-hole playoff. But he still went into the book as the first four-time winner of the tournament.

Woods didn't begin with much promise. At Torrey Pines' North Course, the easier at some 6,800 yards, he hit only one fairway and he had to birdie his final hole for a 71, and was six off the leading seven-under 65s shot by Thomas Levet and Brandt Jobe, also on the North. The South Course measured about 7,600 yards and played about four strokes harder. Meaning that, to make the cut, Woods had work to do when he switched to the South in the second round.

Jobe, who torched the North with his putting in the first round—six of his seven birdies came from outside 15 feet—moved to the South for the second round, made the only eagle at the par-five 18th and shot a 67 for a 12-under 132 and a two-stroke lead on Tim Clark (66) and Jesper Parnevik (67).

And Woods did the job in the second round. His outward 32 included a birdie from 40 feet at the par-three third hole. Coming in, he eagled the par-five 13th from 60 feet. He shot 68–139 and was seven strokes off the lead, but he had made the cut.

Woods didn't really get his game rolling until the third round, when a seven iron at No. 8 felt just right. "That got me into the flow," he said. He shot 67, and at 206 was just a stroke behind co-leaders Sergio Garcia (68) and Rod Pampling (68). They would be the final grouping in what had become a wide open tournament when Jobe followed two quick bogeys with a double bogey. Among those now in the race was Phil Mickelson, who made up a six-shot deficit in nine holes.

The cast changed abruptly. In the final round, gone were Garcia, who shot 75, and Mickelson, who bogeyed three straight from about five feet and shot 73, and Pampling, who blew to a 76. Up popped Green and Olazabal. Olazabal two-putted the 18th for a birdie and a 69, and was leading at 10-under 178. Green led briefly after holing a 77-yard wedge shot for an eagle at the 13th, and he dropped a seven-foot putt for birdie at the 18th for a 72 to tie Olazabal. Woods, who had already three-putted three times in the final round, needed an eight-footer for a birdie at the 18th for a 72 to join the playoff. He got it.

On the first extra hole (No. 18), Woods and Olazabal both parred and Green missed the green and exited on a bogey. Then at the second, the par-three 16th, Olazabal lofted a bunker shot to four feet, but missed the putt, and Woods parred and won. But it was his birdie on the 72nd hole that set him up.

"Of all the things that happened today," Woods said, "I shouldn't have had that opportunity."

FBR Open
Scottsdale, Arizona
Winner: J.B. Holmes

First came the big-hitters, putting it out there 300 yards. Then came the bombers, topping 300. Then came J.B. Holmes ...

Case in point: In the second round of the FBR Open, Holmes—age 23, a rookie on the PGA Tour—slugged a drive 365 yards at the par-five 15th, setting up an eagle. He went on to win by seven shots, and thus won $1 million faster than anyone in Tour history. The FBR Open was the fifth tournament of the year, but it was the fourth for Holmes, who wasn't eligible for the season-opening Mercedes Championship. The $936,000 first prize gave him $1,063,500 in four events. Retief Goosen was the previous "fastest," having done it in five in 2001.

"It was one of my goals, to win out here," Holmes said. "I didn't expect it so soon. I knew I had the ability. Every tournament I played, I just got more confidence and more confidence."

Holmes shot 68-64-65-66–263, 21 under par, but as seven-stroke victories go, this one couldn't have been more deceptive. This was a duel between Holmes and Ryan Palmer to the delight of the partying fans at the par-71 TPC of Scottsdale, which was dry and running fast. But a duel only until midway through the final nine. Holmes was one up on Ryan Palmer and J.J. Henry going into the fourth round. Then Palmer took the lead by one with a downhill seven-footer for a birdie at the ninth, and Holmes tied him with a birdie at the 10th.

Everything cracked at the 522-yard, par-five 15th. Holmes overpowered the hole with a big tee shot and a 263-yard four iron to 14 feet. He got the eagle and was 20 under par. Palmer's tee shot bounced toward the water, scattering ducks along the way. Palmer hit two into the water there and three-putted for an eight. The five-stroke swing put Holmes on easy street, six shots ahead. "You hate to see anybody do that," Holmes said. "But I hit good shots and made eagle."

Holmes wasn't really noticed early. His opening 68 left him three behind Steve Lowery and Alex Cjeka, who shared the lead at 65 and had 16 others within two of them. Holmes shot 64 in the second round but slipped a stroke further back as J.J. Henry, running off a tournament-record seven straight birdies, romped to a 10-under 61 for a 128 total and a four-stroke lead.

By the third round, Holmes was getting ooohs for his power. But it was his touch that was doing the job. "I've got the putter working," Holmes said. Holmes tied a cooled-off Henry with a par at the ninth, then took the lead at the 403-yard, par-four 10th. He slugged a 341-yard drive to in front of the green, pitched to within six feet, and birdied. He also birdied the 13th and 14th and parred in for a 65, inching a stroke ahead of Henry and Palmer and setting up a dramatic fourth round that pivoted on the five-stroke swing at the 15th.

AT&T Pebble Beach National Pro-Am
Pebble Beach, California
Winner: Arron Oberholser

The longest distance in golf, it is said, is the six inches between the ears. Or as Arron Oberholser put it, "It's upstairs where I've been lacking." Oberholser, age 31 and a PGA Tour player since 2003, negotiated that dangerous stretch beautifully in the AT&T Pebble Beach National Pro-Am for his first victory, a five-stroke runaway over Rory Sabbatini.

"I think," Oberholser observed, "I can compete with the best players in the world." He reached the top of the leaderboard in the third round, sharing the lead with Mike Weir at 17 under par, the two of them six strokes ahead of Luke Donald. Then in the final round, it became Oberholser's tournament to win when Weir hit his second shot at No. 2 out of bounds and double-bogeyed. Oberholser was up by five at No. 3, but there was still a grim memory he had to hold at bay.

In the final round of this tournament in 2004, Oberholser was with Vijay Singh in the final pairing, then buckled and shot 76. "When you want something too badly," he said, "you get in your own way." This time he paved his own way, playing the three courses—Poppy Hills, then Spyglass Hill, then the last two rounds at Pebble Beach—in 65-68-66-72–271, 17 under par.

Luke Donald was the early favorite, with a record-tying, 10-under 62 at Spyglass in the first round. That was only good for a one-stroke lead over Weir, who shot an interesting 63 at Pebble Beach. After a shaky start, Weir made five straight birdies and missed only two greens and one fairway. Weir shook off the chill and fog at Poppy Hills in the second round and birdied his last three holes for a 67–130 and a three-stroke lead on Oberholser.

Oberholser, playing Pebble Beach in the third round, birdied the little par-three No. 7 from 20 feet, then No. 8, firing a five iron across the chasm to 25 feet, the two scary shots tempting the Pacific. He went from there to a 66 and a share of the 54-hole lead with Weir, who shot 69 at Spyglass Hill. They were tied at 199 and six strokes ahead of Donald, who shot 71.

In the final round, Weir's second shot at the par-five second bounced off a cart path and out of bounds, and he double-bogeyed. Then he bogeyed No. 3 and was five strokes behind Oberholser. Sabbatini, seven off the lead at the start, was closing the gap, but when he bogeyed No. 9, it was over for him.

Oberholser still wasn't in the clear. He had bogeyed the 13th from a fairway bunker and bogeyed the 14th from the rough. Then his tee shot at the 15th was even wilder. But it bounced twice on a cart path, then glanced off a tree and into an opening. He hit a wedge to eight feet and birdied. He wrapped up a par 72 to win on his 76th start.

Nissan Open
Pacific Palisades, California
Winner: Rory Sabbatini

The Nissan Open started out more like a medical report than a golf tournament. There was Ernie Els, making his first PGA Tour appearance since the previous July, coming back from knee surgery after a boating accident. Troubled David Duval, making his third cut in four events on the West Coast. Arron Oberholser, AT&T Pebble Beach National Pro-Am winner the week before, withdrawing after the third round because of illness. And Tiger Woods, making the cut, then withdrawing because of the flu.

As a companion piece to all this, Rory Sabbatini spun a pretty good yarn of his own. First, he survived weather so cold he couldn't feel his toes, a puzzling complication since this was at Riviera Country Club in southern California in February. He squandered a four-stroke lead in the final round, but recovered just in time to shoot a one-over-par 72 for a 13-under 271 total and a one-stroke victory over a charging Adam Scott, the defending champion.

"That was definitely the hardest round of golf I ever played in my life," said Sabbatini, getting his third career victory but his first since 2003.

In six outings by mid-February, Sabbatini was runner-up twice and in the top 20 four times, and now was topping the money list at over $2.1 million. He was off to a good start with a 67, three shots behind co-leaders Justin Rose and Dean Wilson. Then came a remarkable performance in the second round. Sabbatini teed off in a morning so chilly that he couldn't feel his toes. Later, a drenching rain hit. But he birdied five of the last six holes for a 65 and a four-stroke lead over Craig Barlow (69) and Thomas Levet (68).

In better weather in the third round, Sabbatini dropped a five-foot birdie putt at the 18th for a 67 and a 14-under 199 total, keeping his four-stroke lead. But it wouldn't be a comfortable one. Couples, a two-time Nissan winner, shot 31 on the back nine for a 65 and a tie for second with Barlow, who shot 67. Said Barlow: "He's going to be the favorite tomorrow, but a four-shot lead is never too much to make up." Said Couples: "If I can play a really good round, I can catch Rory."

Scott, trailing Sabbatini by nine at the start of the round, birdied seven of the last 14 holes for a 64 and a 12-under 272, and took hope from the wind getting stronger on the second nine. Both Couples and Barlow caught Sabbatini but couldn't hold on. Then Couples bogeyed the 15th from the rough, bogeyed the 16th after a poor tee shot, and three-putted the 18th for another bogey, shooting 71 and finishing fourth. Barlow bogeyed the 15th and 16th on missed short putts and shot 70 for third place. Sabbatini's chance came at the par-three 16th. There, he hit a seven iron to four feet, got the birdie, regained the lead, and two-putted the 18th from 45 feet for the par and the victory.

WGC - Accenture Match Play Championship
Carlsbad, California
Winner: Geoff Ogilvy

By any stretch of the imagination, even Geoff Ogilvy's family would have to agree that he was not among the most likely to succeed in the WGC - Accenture Match Play Championship. He came into the tournament ranked a 130-to-1 shot in Las Vegas. Even winning the Chrysler Classic of Tucson in 2005, his only victory, did little to elevate him in the eyes of the knowledgeable.

In the exclusive field of 64 at the La Costa resort in Carlsbad, California, he was seeded a lowly 52nd. And then he battled through six matches of men all seeded higher, and he won—but the hard way. He had to go extra holes through his first four matches, and the only matches ending in regulation time were the 4-and-3 decision over Tom Lehman in the semi-finals, and the 3-and-2 victory over Davis Love for the championship. The soft-spoken Aussie, who played a record 129 holes, decided the reason for his success lay somewhere else. "Something was on my side this week—keeping their putts out of the hole and making mine go," Ogilvy said.

Until Ogilvy came from nowhere to steal the show, the show was all about how Stephen Ames made the mistake of riling up the tiger. Ames, seeded dead last at 64th, was being fed to the No. 1 seed, Tiger Woods. What were his chances? "Anything can happen," Ames said, innocently. "Especially where he's hitting the ball." Result: Woods wiped him out, 9 and 8.

Woods cooled and was added to the massacre. Television's match play nightmare had come to pass—all the marquee names were gone well before the final. The first three seeds got only to the quarter-finals. Woods was ousted by Chad Campbell, 1 up; No. 2 seed Vijay Singh was beaten by Padraig Harrington in 19 holes, and No. 3 Retief Goosen by Zach Johnson, 3 and 2. No. 4 Ernie Els lost in the first round to Bernhard Langer, 1 up, and No. 5 Phil Mickelson was erased in the third round by David Howell, 3 and 1. Ogilvy, in the meantime, was making a Grand Slam of victims—a winner of each of the four majors.

In the 36-hole final, Love made two crucial errors. At the 14th in the morning, he missed a four-foot putt that would have put him 2 up. "It was a bonus at the time," Ogilvy said. "The momentum was going his way a little bit." The other mistake came in the afternoon, after he'd fought back to 1 down. At the 27th (the par-four No. 9), Love overshot the green and bogeyed when a par would have won the hole. Ogilvy accepted the gift and then went on to take command. At the 29th (No. 11), he rifled a four iron to six feet for a conceded eagle, then birdied the 12th for a 3-up lead through 30 holes.

Chrysler Classic of Tucson
Tucson, Arizona
Winner: Kirk Triplett

Kirk Triplett never did for the porkpie hat what Ben Hogan did for the flat cap, but that wasn't exactly a fashion statement he was trying to make in the Chrysler Classic of Tucson. He made his statement in the final round, opening with five straight birdies and made four straight birdies coming in, racing from six shots behind for his third PGA Tour title and his first since 2003.

At the start Triplett looked like a man trying to get the weekend off. In the first round, he smacked a ball into the water. In the second round, he hit out of bounds at one hole, and three-putted from 10 feet at another. His numbers looked reasonable, 68 and 71, but at the par-72 Catalina Course at Omni Tucson National, that was flirting with the cut. Which came in, by the way, at three-under-par 141.

"I wanted to go home," said Triplett, who lives in Scottsdale, a few hours away. "I called my wife and said I wanted to come home."

"There's nothing to do here," Cathi Triplett said. "Why don't you stay down there and practice?"

So that's what Triplett did, and it paid off handsomely. He shot 64 and 63, coming from six strokes behind in the final round, to pick off the victory at 22-under-par 266.

Triplett opened with that 68, but 17 others did better, led by Mark Wilson, who started out as though he was going to be the Chrysler Classic's 15th first-time winner. "If I could have rolled in some birdie putts early and not made a silly bogey at the 18th, this could have been something real special," said Wilson, after cruising to a 64 and a two-stroke lead. "But I'm still happy with what it is." (Wilson, who finished tied for ninth, contended until he closed with a 72, and only eight of 71 players did worse.)

Duffy Waldorf led through the middle rounds. In the second round, Waldorf birdied four of his first five holes and shot 66 for a one-stroke lead on Wilson. "It's been a long time since I've been on top—it's nice," said Waldorf, enjoying his first halfway lead since the 2000 Open in Britain. Waldorf stayed on top in the third round with a 65 for a 19-under 197 total and a two-stroke lead on Bubba Watson, the huge-hitting rookie. In the final round, Waldorf still led at the turn, birdied the 10th to get to 20 under par, but shot 72 and tied for third with Watson (70).

Triplett made the final turn at 18 under par, then birdied four straight from the 14th. That last birdie was a dazzler, a 51-foot chip from the left fringe at the 17th. Then Triplett waited. With Waldorf struggling, his main concern was Jerry Kelly. Kelly birdied the 16th from three feet and needed one more birdie to catch him. Kelly's last chance came at the 18th, from 10 feet past the hole. But his putt slipped by on the right, and Triplett then took off his porkpie hat and donned the tournament's shiny Conquistador helmet.

Ford Championship at Doral
Miami, Florida
Winner: Tiger Woods

"This guy Tiger seems to play well every day, every week," Phil Mickelson was saying at the Ford Championship at Doral early in March. "I'm just trying to keep pace. I'm trying to maybe have another shot at dueling it out with him on Sunday." The reference was to their shootout at Doral a year ago, when Tiger Woods won over the last few holes.

It was a noble ambition that lasted, oh, for the first two rounds. Others then took up the chase—Daniel Chopra and Rich Beem in the third round, then David Toms and fast-rising Colombian Camilo Villegas in the fourth. But Woods, leading or sharing the lead all the way, rang up a card of 64-67-68-69—268, 20 under par on the Doral Blue Monster, to win by one stroke over Villegas and David Toms for his third victory already this year, including one in Dubai.

Woods did wobble at the finish, and he dodged a haymaker from Toms, who had closed in with birdies at the 10th, 11th and 16th holes. Then at the 18th, he saw his four iron from the rough leave him nearly 70 feet from the pin. "I wasn't nervous all day," Toms said. "All of a sudden, I've got a putt all the way across the green, with a big break. And I'm nervous because I'm just trying to two-putt." So he ran the first putt 10 feet past and missed coming back, for his only three-putt of the tournament, and the bogey left him with a 67 and a 269 total, tied for second with Villegas (67).

Woods raced to the lead in the first round with a 64, and he needed it. The par-72 Blue Monster was more like the Blue Pussycat. Sixty players broke 70, and 116 were at par or better. The cut came in at four-under 140, the lowest in Doral's 45 years.

It started like a rematch of the Woods-Mickelson shootout last year. In the first round, Woods birdied three of his first four holes, and Mickelson made three straight birdies around his turn, and Woods was leader, 64-65 (over Mickelson and four others). The crowd thickened in the second round. Woods parred his last four holes for a 67, and Mickelson birdied two of his last three for a 66, ending at 13 under and sharing a one-stroke lead with Scott Verplank (65) and Villegas (66). It was, historians noted, the first time that Woods and Mickelson shared the 36-hole lead.

In the third round, six players shared the lead at some point, until Woods sorted things out, but only after a watery double bogey at the par-three ninth. He regrouped and powered through three straight birdies from the 13th on putts of three, 10 and eight feet, fuelling a 68 and a two-stroke lead. But he had help. Villegas was sticking with Woods until the 18th, when he had to play his second shot from behind a tree and up the first fairway. He double-bogeyed. Mickelson lost ground at the par-five 10th when he parred a hole he should have birdied, and then bogeyed the 18th, and there went the showdown. Mickelson (72) then trailed Woods by four, and would finish tied for 12th, eight behind.

It wouldn't be vintage Woods in the final round, but it would be close. He never lost the lead, but he staggered to a curious bogey-bogey finish for a 69, and it was just enough.

Honda Classic
Palm Beach Gardens, Florida
Winner: Luke Donald

Luke Donald, who looks so much younger than his 28 years, was talking of consistency. He's certainly not a big hitter and he doesn't often shoot low scores, but he always seems to be in the hunt. He hadn't missed a cut on any tour in over a year. He wrote another chapter in the Honda Classic. He didn't lead in putting, driving or anything like that. In fact, the only place where he was No. 1 was on the leaderboard—at the end of the tournament.

This was Donald's second victory, the first being the 2002 Southern Farm Bureau Classic in his rookie year. It wasn't all that satisfying, though. Bad weather had cut the tournament to 54 holes. "This one is more rewarding," Donald said. "With all the hard work I've put in the last couple years, and to finish that strongly and to finish it off in style means a lot to me."

It took some doing to get to that finish. Donald opened with a par 72 on a day when heavy winds hit the Mirasol course at Palm Beach Gardens, Florida, and lifted the scoring average to 74.277. He trailed by five strokes, and again after a 67 in the second round. He shot 68 in the third and shared the lead with Billy Mayfair, who dropped a 30-foot putt for an eagle at the 17th and a 72. Going into the final round, they led by one over Jeff Gove. Defending champion Padraig Harrington got to seven under early in the third round, but double bogeys at the seventh and eighth sent him spinning out of contention with a 74.

The last round opened in a race, with 13 players within five strokes of the Donald-Mayfair lead. But it shook itself out in a hurry. Mayfair, hoping for his first win in 228 starts, killed his chances when chip shots at No. 6 and No. 12 cost him two bogeys. A 72 would drop him to a tie for third. Geoff Ogilvy, who had a double eagle, three eagles and three double bogeys for the week, made a run with a 69, but fell two strokes short, finishing second at 278.

This was the kind of traffic Donald had to fight his way through, and he did it by giving himself a pep talk. "I knew if I just played Luke Donald golf, it'd be good enough," Donald said, and so it was. But it wasn't easy. Donald birdied two of the first four holes, then bogeyed the seventh and 10th, surrendering the lead to Gove. But Gove made a bogey and a double bogey over three holes, and Donald made his return. He holed a 10-foot birdie putt at the 13th, and regained the lead with a 25-footer at the 14th. He saved par with an 18-footer at the 16th, then fired a five iron from 203 yards to four feet at the 18th for his final birdie, a 69 and a 12-under 276 total to beat Ogilvy by two.

Bay Hill Invitational
Orlando, Florida
Winner: Rod Pampling

The golf gods were at their crazy best at the Bay Hill Invitational. First, they let Australian Rod Pampling think he was going to win. They even let him carry a four-stroke lead into the final round. Then they zapped him and let England's Greg Owen look like the winner. Then at the par-three 17th, Owen three-putted from only 40 inches for a double bogey. And there was Pampling with his second PGA Tour victory.

Said the shaken Owen: "Whatever happens with the golfing gods … It wasn't my day. I'll have to wait for my day."

"It's sad to see," said Pampling. "But it's golf."

Bay Hill was littered with victims of the gods. There was Darren Clarke. The door opened in the final round when he eagled the par-five sixth, and slammed shut when he double-bogeyed two holes later. Lucas Glover got to 12 under with birdies at the fourth and fifth in the finale, then backed up fast from the seventh with one birdie, four bogeys and two double bogeys.

In the second round, Glover suffered a watery double bogey at the 11th, but birdied the 17th with a three iron to eight feet. His 10-under total gave him a one-stroke lead on Pampling (65) and Robert Allenby (67). The leaderboard was rearranged in the third round. Clarke tied the tournament record with six straight birdies from No. 9 for a 63, tying for second with Owen and Glover at 10 under. But Pampling clinched the lead with a bold four-iron second at the 18th that just cleared the water and then settled three feet from the hole. He birdied for a 67 and a four-stroke lead. His second PGA Tour victory was all but in his pocket. But not quite.

Pampling, Owen and Clarke made up the final group. The chase thinned quickly. Glover, after two early birdies, played eight holes from No. 7 in eight over. Clarke eagled No. 6 but double-bogeyed No. 8 on his way to a 70 and a solo third place. The final round belonged to Pampling and Owen.

Owen was off and running, making six birdies over 15 holes from No. 2. Pampling birdied twice on the front and was two ahead with six holes to play, but drove out of bounds at the 13th and double-bogeyed. They jockeyed from there. Owen retook the lead at the par-five 16th, getting up and down from a bunker for a birdie, and then he was two ahead when Pampling bogeyed the 17th.

At that dangerous par-three, Owen was just short of the green and chipped to 40 inches. Then the crash: His par putt zipped two feet past. Anxiously, he popped the return. The ball lipped out. Finally, he tapped in—three putts from 40 inches for a double-bogey five. He put his face in his hands.

Pampling parred the 18th for a 72 and a 14-under 274, to win by a stroke over Owen, who bogeyed the 18th.

The Players Championship
Ponte Vedra Beach, Florida
Winner: Stephen Ames

It seems the popular belief was that Stephen Ames had been destroyed by Tiger Woods in that WGC - Accenture Match Play. Ames said that he might win because Woods had become erratic off the tee. Woods crushed him, 9 and 8, for his impertinence. Then just four weeks later, Ames, age 41 and with just one previous victory, ran away with The Players Championship by six strokes. Some raised the Woods episode again. "I got my butt kicked and that was it," Ames said. "What am I going to do, sit down and cry about it?"

The Players wasn't match play, so there was no significance attached to the fact that Woods finished 15 strokes behind Ames, who played the TPC at Sawgrass course in 71-66-70-67–274, 14 under par. Ames did it with 47 of the world's top 50 players in the field. With his opening 71, he was six strokes behind Jim Furyk and Davis Love, who shot 65s in cool, drizzly weather. "I stayed patient and just let it happen," Furyk said. Said Love, a two-time Players winner, "I feel good everywhere on this course." But not the next day. "I just kept missing fairways," he said. He shot 83, becoming the first in the tournament's 33 years to lead the first round and then miss the 36-hole cut. Furyk stayed in the hunt until shooting 75 in the third round. He would tie for third place.

The third round turned into a wild chase in the gusty winds, with eight different leaders and 19 lead changes. Ames shot a solid 70 to take the lead at nine under, one ahead of Vijay Singh and Sergio Garcia. Pressure? All told, he had 11 players within four strokes of him.

There were nightmares in the background. Adam Scott, the promising young Australian, was a shot off the lead after 36 holes and finished with 82 and 76. Arron Oberholser was leading through 52 holes, then hit his last two tee shots in the water, finished with a triple bogey and double bogey, and shot 74.

Anyone expecting Ames to fold in the final round was disappointed in a hurry. Ernie Els and Retief Goosen tried to turn the screws, but both bogeyed the 15th hole. Goosen shot 69, one of only three scores in the 60s, and finished a distant second by six strokes. Els, who did not shoot in the 60s all week, closed with 71 and tied for eighth place. With the challengers struggling in the cool winds, Ames birdied the second and sixth holes, then stretched his lead with a two-putt birdie at the 15th. On a day when the average score was 75.3, Ames closed with a brilliant, day's-low 67, for a 14-under 274 total.

BellSouth Classic
Duluth, Georgia
Winner: Phil Mickelson

"Silly Season" is the name given to a cluster of high-priced unofficial events at the end of the year that make golfers unofficially a lot richer. Phil Mickelson staged his own one-man Silly Season at the BellSouth Classic in April. It wasn't so much that he led wire-to-wire as it was that he won, absurdly enough, by 13 strokes. This he did by shooting 63-65-67-65–260, a whopping 28 under par at the par-72 TPC at Sugarloaf, near Atlanta. As a warm-up for the Masters the following week, it was a barnburner. It was also his third BellSouth title, his second in succession.

Just for the record, Jose Maria Olazabal and Zach Johnson tied for second at 15 under par, good enough to win many tournaments.

The question was, did Mickelson burn himself out for the Masters? "It was a great week, don't get me wrong," Mickelson said, "but I didn't feel like it couldn't be repeated. I feel like I'm starting to play well. I expect to do the same—or I hope to do the same, at least." In other words, there's plenty more where that came from.

That could be read as a pretty strong signal to the hopeful in the Masters because it was here in the BellSouth Classic that Mickelson tested the secret weapon he intended to turn on Augusta National. Or rather, two weapons—a pair of unmatched drivers, one for a fade, one for a draw. "I have a driver I hit a long ways that draws, and I have a driver that fades and stays in play," Mickelson said. "It's great because I only have to play with half the trouble."

The closest anyone came to Mickelson all week was in the first round, when he tied the course record with a nine-under 63. "I looked up and saw I was six under through seven," Mickelson said. But he held only a one-stroke lead on Australian Gavin Coles. Mickelson stretched things out from there. The 65 in the second round put him six ahead of J.J. Henry (65). Was he aiming at records?

"What you're thinking about is not in my mind—no," Mickelson said.

Maybe not, but he went up by eight strokes the third round, his 67 putting that cushion between him and Johnson (64) and Jonathan Byrd (66). And this despite his biggest glitch of the week. He played the last three holes in three over, including a double bogey at the 18th, where he caught water twice. It didn't faze him. "It's probably a positive because the last thing I want to do is have a record or be thinking about it," he said. "That's not my goal. It's to get my game sharp and get some momentum ... for next week." It also was a slap in the face, he said, that reminded him the tournament wasn't over. But it soon was. A closing 65 slammed the door totally.

"That's just unbelievable," Johnson said. "I mean, 13 shots better—that was complete domination." This was domination: Mickelson led the field in hitting greens in regulation, at 89 percent; he tied for sixth in putting, averaging 28 per round; and he averaged 309.1 yards on his drives, and hit 80.4 percent of the fairways.

Now golf was waiting to see whether Mickelson's two-driver show would play at Augusta.

Masters Tournament
Augusta, Georgia
Winner: Phil Mickelson

See Chapter 2.

Verizon Heritage
Hilton Head Island, South Carolina
Winner: Aaron Baddeley

Aaron Baddeley, another in the line of post-Greg Norman Aussies on the PGA Tour, was known principally for two things. First, that he was a prime talent and one of these days he'd put it all together and win something, and second, that he was the boyish guy in the television commercial where a bunch of girls were giving him the rock-star treatment and yelling his nickname, "Badds!"

Baddeley very badly wanted to live up to the first and live down the second.

One fine day in April, in his third year on the tour, he lived up to No. 1, holding on under shootout pressure against one of the toughest guys in the game, Jim Furyk, the 2003 U.S. Open champion, to score his first victory in the Verizon Heritage. Now he had an American title to go with his three Australian wins.

Anyone who believes in omens might say that was one at Harbour Town's famous 18th hole, where both made spectacular shots in the second round. Furyk sank a vastly improbable 56-foot putt for birdie. A few hours earlier, Baddeley holed out an eight iron from 164 yards for an eagle-two, capping a sharp finish off three birdies and an eagle over his last five holes. The eagle took most of the sting out of that triple bogey back at the par-four No. 8, where he knocked his approach out of bounds. Maybe that was a preview. At any rate, both shot 67, and Furyk, at 11-under 131, was two strokes up on Baddeley, Brian Gay (67), Duffy Waldorf (68) and Vaughn Taylor (70), the first-round leader.

The Furyk-Baddeley battle took real shape in the third round. Baddeley birdied the first, second and fifth, and led by one when Furyk, after two birdies, bogeyed the seventh and eighth. Furyk made a furious comeback, getting birdies at the 12th, 15th, 16th and 17th, but bogeyed the 18th for a 68 to sit at 14 under par. Baddeley bogeyed the 11th, then birdied the 12th, 13th and 16th for a 66 and tied him at 14 under. Billy Mayfair (68) was three behind, Ernie Els (65) four.

It was a slugfest in the final round. Baddeley birdied Nos. 2, 4 and 5 and took a two-stroke lead against Furyk's birdie-bogey-birdie performance over the same holes. Then the situation was reversed when Baddeley bogeyed the seventh, eighth and 11th, and Furyk birdied the 10th. The match—and it was practically match play now—was all square at the 12th when Furyk two-putted from five feet for a bogey. Baddeley, standing up under the pressure, birdied two of the toughest holes on the tour, the par-three 14th and then the par-five 15th, reaching it with a six iron from 220 yards. Baddeley was up by two at that point, but at the 17th chunked his chip shot and bogeyed. The door was open to Furyk, but he missed his 10-footer for par and stayed one behind.

It came down to the 18th. Baddeley missed the green and chipped on to six feet. Furyk had a 12-footer for his birdie for no worse than a tie. But his putt grazed the hole, and he parred. And then Baddeley tapped his six-footer, and it sneaked in from the right side. "I'm disappointed," Furyk said. "I just couldn't get a putt to go in the hole."

Baddeley, finally fulfilling the expectations, had said his piece after the third round. "I don't feel like I'm out of my element or anything like that," he said. "I'm very comfortable with where I'm at."

Shell Houston Open
Humble, Texas
Winner: Stuart Appleby

Winning doesn't get any better than this: With two holes left in the Shell Houston Open, Stuart Appleby turned to his caddie, Joe Damiano, and asked where he stood. "I knew where I was," Appleby said, with a little grin. "I just wanted to hear it from his lips."

Then Appleby became the proud and relaxed owner of a wire-to-wire, six-stroke victory with a 19-under-par total of 269 at Redstone Golf Club. He joined Tiger Woods and Phil Mickelson as two-time winners this year. "Once is nice," Appleby said. "Twice certainly shows and proves to you that what you're doing works."

This is how Appleby made it work:

First Round—Appleby's round was hardly spotless, but he did enjoy a few of what he called "bonus shots." For example, the 25-foot birdie putts at the sixth and 11th, and after his only bogey of the day, at the par-five 13th, he chipped in for birdie at the 17th and holed a 20-foot downhill putt for a birdie at the 18th. Jerry Smith, nearing age 42, and D.A. Points tied for second. Said Smith: "I think it's going to be a challenge for me all week." It was Appleby at 66, Smith and Points at 67.

Second Round—"You put it in the fairway, the game becomes a lot easier," said Appleby, who completed the rain-delayed second round on Saturday morning. Greg Owen, author of that three-putt loss on the final hole at the Bay Hill Invitational, teed off late and birdied five of his last seven holes. "I'm just trying to have a good time," Owen said, referring to a talk with his sports psychologist. Fun came in the form of a three-foot birdie putt at the 13th, a holed-out bunker shot at the 14th, and a bending 20-footer at the 18th. Appleby hit 11 of 14 fairways and 17 of 18 greens. He shot 67 for 11-under 133; Owen, 65–134; Trevor Immelman, 67–136.

Third Round—Two-time defending champion Vijay Singh shot 75 and fell out of the picture, extending his win drought to 18 starts—his longest since 2002. Owen backed out of contention with a 75. Bret Wetterich birdied four in a row on the front nine, but watered his tee shot at the 18th and shot 69. Sweden's Mathias Gronberg, who made five birdies in six holes from the eighth and finished bogey-birdie, sheltered himself from Appleby. "I didn't look too much," Gronberg said. "I never saw his score for the whole 18 holes." Appleby finished his second round Saturday morning and got the third going with a short birdie putt at No. 4. He chipped in at No. 6, and holed a 30-foot putt at No. 7. "There's a feeling," he said. "It's a confident feeling that you like the way your game feels." Appleby shot 69–202, 14 under, and Gronberg 67–204.

Fourth Round—It wasn't very deep into the finale that the tournament was Appleby's. All he had to do was hold on to it. But as he had noted: "You always feel pressure. As the week goes on, the pressure mounts. You've got to bleed it off and keep it at the level where the cooker doesn't blow." He wasted no time easing the pressure, getting a birdie at No. 1 on a 20-foot putt that curled and dropped. Gronberg missed from 15 feet. Appleby birdied the fourth, sixth and eighth. Gronberg was losing ground fast. His eagle chip at No. 8 lipped out, and he three-putted No. 9. Bob Estes, who would finish second, got within three on the first nine, then sliced his tee shot into the water at No. 8. By now, the only question was whether Appleby would break Vijay Singh's tournament record of 22 under par. He reached the par-five 13th in two and birdied, getting to 20 under. But he bogeyed the 14th, and parred in for his 19-under 269 total and the six-stroke win.

Zurich Classic of New Orleans
New Orleans, Louisiana
Winner: Chris Couch

At New Orleans, a city still reeling from Hurricane Katrina eight months earlier, Chris Couch made three great escapes at the Zurich Classic. Two of them saved him the golf tournament, the other saved his life.

Couch, nearly 33 years old, a former standout on the Nationwide Tour, was on the verge of taking his first PGA Tour victory, but he ran into big trouble over the closing holes. He fought his way through, holed a miraculous chip shot at the 18th, and there was that coveted first win. And an amazing one it was. He opened with 70-70, making the cut just on the number at four-under-par 140, then shot 64-65, leading the last two rounds, for a 19-under 269 total and a one-stroke victory over Charles Howell (65) and Fred Funk (62).

But perhaps it was providence that he even got to the tournament at all. Couch told the strange story of how, early in the week, he was lost in a seedy part of New Orleans and accepted a ride from strangers. Then things turned "weird," and fearing trouble he fled from unsavory people, running two miles through the streets until he could call police and get back to his car.

"I was just uncomfortable—that's as plain as I can tell you," Couch said. "I didn't like the situation, and I didn't like where we were going."

The same could be said for his situation toward the end of the final round. After getting a third crack at the PGA Tour, he was on the verge of taking his first win, and he was in trouble, and the closing holes at English Turn were no place to find trouble. He floated a wedge to three feet at the 16th and birdied for a two-stroke lead, and he needed it. At the par-three 17th, he bunkered his tee shot, then bladed his blast over the green and into the rough. Coming back, he pitched 12 feet past the cup. But he holed the putt and held the damage to a bogey. But now his lead was down to one stroke.

Then came the par-four 18th and another near disaster. Couch drove into the left rough, and his wedge shot flew the green and ended up against the back slope of a bunker muddy from rain. He barely got the ball out to the collar of rough. Now 55 feet from the pin, he needed to get up and down for bogey to force a playoff. But his delicate chip shot settled and rolled right into the cup for a par and his victory.

"The finish was unbelievable, but it's those things that it takes to win," said a frustrated Howell, still seeking his second tour title. Howell was just short of birdies on a 20-footer at the 17th and a 45-footer at the 18th. Funk, age 49 and two months from joining the Champions Tour, made three straight birdies but hooked his approach shot at the 16th and bogeyed. But he did roll in a 30-footer at the 18th for a birdie and the 62, then went to the range to practice for a playoff that never came, thank to Couch's clutch close.

"I'd like to make it easier the next time," Couch said. "My heart can't take much more of this."

Wachovia Championship
Charlotte, North Carolina
Winner: Jim Furyk

Not that you can ever make up for lost time and lost tournaments, but Jim Furyk did his spirits a world of good when he dropped that final six-foot putt and took the Wachovia Championship.

"It's nice to come out and get it done this time," said Furyk, after beating South Africa's Trevor Immelman on the first playoff hole. That helped ease some pains. Three weeks earlier, he let a two-stroke lead get away on the final nine and got beat by Aaron Baddeley in the Verizon Heritage. A year ago, at this very same Quail Hollow Club at Charlotte, North Carolina, Furyk lost in a playoff against Vijay Singh. "I definitely don't have the mind-set that the course owes me one," Furyk said after a 68 tied him for the first-round lead with Immelman, Rory Sabbatini and Bill Haas.

Everyone took a backseat to Bo Van Pelt, who tied the course record with a tournament-low 64 for a three-stroke lead in the rain-interrupted second round. Furyk, three behind, was unhappy with his 69. He had bogeyed the 16th and 17th. "I felt I should have played those holes better," he said. Furyk pulled it back together with 68 in the third round for an 11-under 205 total and a one-stroke lead over Immelman (66) and Retief Goosen (65). Goosen, trailing by seven going into the third round, raced to seven birdies on the second nine, but drove into a little stream at the 18th and bogeyed.

In the chill rain of the final round, it looked like another bitter pill for Furyk. He bogeyed No. 3, birdied No. 7 and bogeyed No. 8. Immelman whizzed right past him with birdies at Nos. 4, 7 and 8, and took a two-stroke lead into the final nine. It evaporated when he hit into the trees at the 11th and double-bogeyed. Then he birdied the 13th on a 12-foot putt, and also birdied the 15th, getting back to 13 under. Furyk, playing catch-up, birdied the 14th and 15th, but it seemed to be all over.

At the par-four 18th, Immelman, leading him by one, was on the green in two, but 50 feet from the cup. Furyk was in the rough. All Immelman had to do was two-putt for a par. He ran the first putt 10 feet past, missed coming back and bogeyed for 70. Furyk coolly dropped his eight-footer for a par, a 71 and a tie at 12-under 276. The playoff started and ended at the 18th. Immelman drove into the rough and had to lay up. Then his third shot spun off, and his best would be a bogey. Furyk drove into a fairway bunker and fired a three iron to the green, but the ball rolled back off. He could use his putter, but he sent the ball six feet past. Then he holed coming back. This time, he got it done.

EDS Byron Nelson Championship
Irving, Texas
Winner: Brett Wetterich

The EDS Byron Nelson Championship was a tournament no one could quite get a grip on until Brett Wetterich notched three birdies on a flawless final nine to win by one stroke. Wetterich, age 32, who had been struggling for years, finally had that first victory. He opened with 66 at Cottonwood

Valley, then closed with 64-70-68 at the TPC at Four Seasons, for a 12-under-par 268 total.

"I think if it's your time, it's your time," said Wetterich. "I just felt it was going to be my day, and it turned out." Which had to leave South Africa's Trevor Immelman feeling like an asterisk: *Finished second again. Immelman had all but won the Wachovia Championship the week before, but bogeyed the final hole then lost to Jim Furyk in a playoff. "I'm playing the best golf of my life," Immelman said. "I think for me it's just a case of trying to build on these last few achievements and hopefully close one out eventually."

Early on, it looked like Adam Scott's tournament. Scott tied for the lead in the first three rounds, first with Steve Lowery at five under par, then with Wetterich at 10 under, then with Immelman at 11 under. But Scott's game stuttered, and a closing 71 tied him for third place. Wetterich, meanwhile, was patiently putting his best showing together. He tied Scott in the second round with a bogey-free 64 punctuated by a 13-foot birdie putt at the 18th. "I had a few other putts that were close like that, so it was nice to see that one go in," Wetterich said. But who noticed? Oberholser was busy shooting 60.

Wetterich opened the third round with a bogey, because of a bad break. His approach shot to No. 1 hit the flagstick and rolled back 40 feet, into the fringe. A weak chip and two putts cost him the bogey, and ultimately 70. "I struggled a little bit today and came out even par and only one shot behind," Wetterich said. "I think that's pretty good." It wasn't early in the fourth round, however. Wetterich was disgusted over two quick bogeys. At No. 4, he came out of a bunker to 30 inches, then missed the putt, and at the par-three No. 5, he missed the green, and so he was two strokes behind Immelman and Scott. Then came the good news: At the par-three 13th, he dropped a bending eight-footer to match Immelman in birdies.

At the 15th, Immelman drove into the right rough and bogeyed. Wetterich parred and had the lead for good. Immelman drowned his last chance, watering his tee shot at the 18th. But he made an inspired par. Wetterich, on the other hand, went from fairway to green and finally just tapped in for his par and the victory.

Bank of America Colonial
Fort Worth, Texas
Winner: Tim Herron

Winning is in the eye of the winner, to borrow from an old expression. So what does it feel like to win again after seven years? Said Tim Herron, on taking the Bank of America Colonial for the fourth victory of his career but his first in 205 starts, "It feels almost like a first win." His first was in the 1996 Honda Classic and the last (before Colonial) was the 1999 Bay Hill Classic.

This one came the hard way. Herron took a share of the lead in the third round, stumbled down the final stretch, tied Sweden's Richard Johnson with a par at the 18th, then beat him on the second playoff hole. "This winning thing," said Herron, "isn't easy."

Herron trailed through the first two rounds and tied through the last two, shooting "Hogan's Alley" in 67-65-68-68–268, 12 under, to tie Johnson. They finished two better than Rod Pampling, who double-bogeyed and fell to third.

Stewart Cink opened with a six-under-par 64 and said the course "almost feels too easy to play." Five tied for second at 65 and, all told, 66 players shot par or better in the first round. Cink gradually faded and Pampling took over with 63 in the second round, including going five-for-five in sand saves. Herron (65) moved into a tie for fifth, two off the lead, with Peter Lonard, who shot a bogey-free 66 while hitting only five fairways.

Herron tied for the lead in the third round, holing out a 40-foot bunker shot for a birdie at the 14th. After two bogeys, he flipped a wedge to two feet at the 18th for a birdie and a 68 to tie Pampling (70). The round of the day, however, belonged to Stephen Ames, if one likes train wrecks. Ames started the third round just a stroke off the lead, then at No. 1 hit trees, rough and sand for a triple-bogey eight. He was on his way to 77. That cleared the way for Herron, because Ames's closing 63 only tied for fourth.

Next to self-destruct was Pampling, in the final round. In the final pairing with Herron, Pampling double-bogeyed the 15th, leaving Herron and Johnson to battle it out. They matched birdies on the first two holes, and Herron took the lead with a birdie at the fourth. It was a juggling match from there. Herron bogeyed the 16th from a greenside bunker. Johnson then birdied the 17th from 18 feet and birdied the 18th from 12 to tie. Herron missed the green at the 18th and had to hole a nine-foot putt to save par and force a playoff.

They parred the first extra hole. At the second, Johnson left his approach 25 short of the hole, and Herron put his to nine feet. Johnson missed his birdie try, but Herron didn't. "I let it slip, but I hung in there," Herron said. "... it's been seven years and I just didn't know if it was going to come."

FedEx St. Jude Classic
Memphis, Tennessee
Winner: Jeff Maggert

It was noted that Jeff Maggert's winning total in the FedEx St. Jude Classic, nine under par, was the highest in relation to par since the Memphis tournament moved to the TPC at Southwind in 1989. Maggert didn't have to point out that in golf, it's not how, but how much. And how much was three better than Tom Pernice.

Maggert, age 42, had won twice before since joining the PGA Tour in 1991, but not since 1999. It was seven years and three months, and 180 starts, between victories for him. In addition, he had missed the cut in his previous three starts, and his putter had turned sour. And this victory wasn't even on his horizon until the second nine of the final round. Then he finished eagle-birdie-par for a five-under-par 65 to top Pernice by three strokes. "I would've bet I would've won more times by now," Maggert said.

Maggert opened with 72, eight strokes behind leader Chris Smith, and made his way quietly up the board—66 in the second round, five behind Darron Stiles, and in the third round, 68 to move to three off the lead shared by Pernice and Tim Herron. They were tied at seven under heading into the final round, and eight others were within four strokes of the lead. Pernice was aiming for his first victory since 2001, and Herron now had a chance for back-to-back victories for the first time in his career. Neither would come to pass. "They have to come and get us," Herron said. "It's going to be a horse race, so I hope everybody enjoys it."

In the final round, Herron promptly plunged into a wild spree, starting with a bogey at No. 1, and when Kris Cox bogeyed No. 7, there were five tied for the lead—but none of them named Maggert. Then Herron bogeyed No. 5, double-bogeyed both No. 7 and No. 14 and was on his way to 77 and a tie for 16th place. Pernice was steadier but couldn't get going.

The way was open, and Maggert barged in. He birdied the par-three 11th on an eight-foot putt and got to six under par. Pernice, in the final pairing two groups back, also birdied it with an 18-footer, tying Maggert at six under. Maggert then led by one when Pernice bogeyed the 14th, then locked up the title with a sizzling finish. He dropped a 36-foot putt for an eagle at the par-five 16th, then a 33-footer for a birdie at the 17th for a three-stroke lead. A par at the 18th was a formality.

Maggert needed just 25 putts in the final round and only 99 for the tournament, an average of under 25. And his timing was great, too. "It's still fortunate I can come out and win at the age of 42," Maggert said.

Memorial Tournament
Dublin, Ohio
Winner: Carl Pettersson

Jack Nicklaus made loads of history in his career. Would they next be calling him revolutionary?

That might have been the kindest name the players called him when they arrived for the Memorial Tournament early in June and found the bunkers furrowed, a la Oakmont of some 60 years earlier. Nicklaus had long argued that technology, especially the modern ball, was turning golf into a pitch-and-putt game, and that something had to be done to combat the trend. And so, with the permission of the PGA Tour, he had the bunkers furrowed with big-toothed rakes. A blast from a greenside bunker no longer was almost certain to get close. Opinions varied:

"A trap is a trap—it's a hazard," said Sean O'Hair (67). "If you don't hit it there, you don't have to worry about it."

Said Phil Mickelson (69): "I don't think the bunkers are a problem. The only thing is, you can't spin it. The ball comes out fine, but you can't spin it."

Even so, Carl Pettersson, little-known Swede by way of North Carolina, stole the show. He led through the last three rounds and tacked up his second PGA Tour victory by two strokes over Brett Wetterich and Zach Johnson. No one knew much about Pettersson. "Your winner played the best golf, and that's what it boils down to," Nicklaus said. Pettersson managed a bogey-free 67 for the lead in the rain-interrupted second round. "The shots

I didn't hit quite well still went straight," he said. "My mis-hits went well and I putted well." He had more of the same in the third round (which ended Sunday morning), posting 69 to get to 11 under par and lead Woody Austin by two strokes. He wrapped up that one with a 45-foot birdie putt at the 17th and a chip from deep rough to set up a par at the sloping 18th.

Pettersson still had something to prove in the final round, and he did it with clutch golf. He holed a 20-footer for a birdie at the fourth and a 25-footer at the sixth. He saved bogey out of two bunkers at the 10th, then lit up Muirfield Village at the par-five 11th, where he lifted an exquisite chip from the rough off the back of the green, and the ball ran right into the hole for a birdie. He wrapped up a one-under 71 for a 12-under 276 total and the two-stroke victory. He won more than the $1.035 million first prize. He also won a berth in the U.S. Open. He had come to the Memorial ranked 51st in the world, just a hundredth of a point out of the top-50 ranking that would give him an automatic berth. The victory got him in.

And finally, the report card on the furrowed bunkers: Before the Memorial, Tour players were saving par from sand at an average of 49.1 percent. At the Memorial, that figure fell significantly to 43.8. Was Nicklaus on to something?

Barclays Classic
Harrison, New York
Winner: Vijay Singh

Vijay Singh was looking for answers to a decidedly un-Vijay-like year, but not the one he was getting. "This year has been horrible," Singh was saying at the Barclays Classic in June. "I don't know if it's my game or my head. People told me I should take some time off, that my golf swing is getting tired."

Fortunately for Singh, he didn't take the advice. He found the solution at Westchester Country Club in New York. Coming from behind, Singh shot 70-64-72-68, a 10-under 274 total for a two-stroke win over Adam Scott (70). This was Singh's first title after almost a year and a string of 21 tournaments. He was the first to win the Westchester tournament three times (the first two as the Buick Classic). It took him awhile to get moving.

Scott was having a holiday in the first round. He holed out twice—from 105 yards for an eagle at the par-four seventh and from 50 feet for a birdie at the 12th—then dropped birdie putts of 23 and 25 feet at the last two holes for a six-under 65 and a one-stroke lead over David Howell and Billy Andrade. Singh was five strokes back at 70. He took a share of the second-round lead with a bogey-free 64, holing a 45-foot putt for an eagle at the par-five ninth, and wrapping things up with a six-foot birdie at the 18th to join Howell (68) at eight-under 134. Howell was playing behind Singh but thinking ahead to Winged Foot the following week. "The best preparation for the U.S. Open is to have your game in shape, and I'm doing that," said Howell.

Singh trailed Billy Andrade (69) by a stroke in the third round. In the wind-swept fourth round, Singh two-putted for a birdie at the par-five fifth, then didn't birdie again until he dropped a 25-footer at the par-three 16th.

In between, Scott bogeyed the 14th, three-putting from inside five feet, and double-bogeyed the 16th while Singh birdied. Only a dynamite birdie-eagle finish gave Scott the solo second place, two strokes behind. "I saved a little bit of face at the end ... and got second place out of it," Scott said, "which is better than finishing par-par and coming in 12th or something."

Singh finished with a birdie at the 18th for a bogey-free 68, his 29th career victory and the end of a long and mysterious slump. "It was anxiety," Singh said. As to what brought the change? "My head was correct," Singh said. "I wasn't getting angry. I just played my own game."

U.S. Open Championship
Mamaroneck, New York
Winner: Geoff Ogilvy

See Chapter 3.

Booz Allen Classic
Potomac, Maryland
Winner: Ben Curtis

The Booz Allen Classic, one of the most rain-whipped tournaments on record, was a tale of hail and farewell.

The farewell, ironically, was to the tournament which, by a variety of names, had been in the Washington area since 1980. The hail was for Ben Curtis, out of sight since his career-first victory in the 2003 Open in Britain. He definitely needed another win to prove himself, and he got it wire-to-wire and by five strokes. The tournament, which took six days to play, had to survive phenomenal storms that dumped nine inches of rain on the TPC at Avenel in a day and a half by the end of play Monday. Curtis wrapped up the victory on Tuesday morning.

Imagine opening with a nine-under-par 62 and finding yourself leading by a mere stroke. That was Curtis's situation in the first round. The field found Avenel a piece of cake after the U.S. Open the week before. "After last week, the fairways look 80 yards wide, the greens look huge," Curtis said. He wasn't the only one enjoying the comfort. Jeff Gove, making his third try at getting on the PGA Tour, was right on his back with 63, and Argentina's Jose Coceres was at 64. Curtis shot 65 in the second round and kept the lead but couldn't shake Coceres (64). Then came a bizarre episode. Anticipating heavy weather, officials installed the lift-clean-place rule for the third round, and when storms didn't materialize, the golfers had the blessing of the bad-weather rule in bright, warm sunshine.

Curtis shot 67 for a tournament-record 19-under 213 total for 54 holes. "Now it (his game) seems to be going in the right direction," Curtis said. He had a comfortable five-stroke lead on Brett Quigley (67), who could only hope. "There's not a question if I'm going to shoot under par," he said. "I need to shoot five under or better." But he didn't.

By the time the storm-weary tournament approached its end on Tuesday morning, Curtis could enjoy a golfer's fantasy — waste shots and still smile.

At the 17th, he needed a 28-foot putt for par and he missed. At the 18th, he had to get up and down for par. He didn't. He bogeyed the last two holes for 70, a 20-under 264 total, and still won by five over Billy Andrade (64), Padraig Harrington (66), Nick O'Hern (67) and Steve Stricker (68). "It was just a big relief to get it done and finally get this win," Curtis said. "I've been waiting three years for it, and it finally came."

Buick Championship
Cromwell, Connecticut
Winner: J.J. Henry

It was a two-way serving of home cooking. Native son J.J. Henry, age 31, Connecticut-born-and-bred, playing to and for the folks from around Cromwell at the Buick Championship at the TPC at River Highlands. They had their native son and he had his first PGA Tour victory.

Matt Hauser, Henry's caddie, set up the triumphant moment at the 18th tee. "Matt said, 'You're one of the best drivers out here,'" Henry recounted. "'Just go out and enjoy it. Just rip it down there.'" Henry bombed a 361-yard drive to within 80 yards of the green, wedged on and got his winning par for a three-under 67 and a three-stroke victory over Hunter Mahan (65) and Ryan Moore (67). He was the PGA Tour's sixth first-time winner of the season.

While Henry was the hometown favorite, Harrison Frazar was the sentimental favorite. After what he had been through, he deserved a break. In a short span, a twin son died before birth, his wife's grandmother died, one young son had surgery and the other broke an arm. Then the surviving twin was born and nearly died. The amazing thing was that Frazar could manage 65 and tie for the first-round lead. A closing 75, however, stifled his chances.

That first round was a real pile-up—four tied for the lead and 18 others within two strokes. Darron Stiles broke the jam in the second round with a birdie at the 18th for 66 and a one-stroke lead over Peter Lonard and found 25 players within four strokes of him. Stiles's prospects? "I'm not playing those guys," he said. "I'm playing the golf course." After another 68 in the second round, Henry rode a hot putter for 63, an 11-under 199 total in the third and a two-stroke lead, his first 54-hole lead since joining the tour in 2000. He got to 12 under par with a 25-foot birdie putt at the 17th, but bogeyed the 18th after his 342-yard drive caught the right rough.

Henry led by two going into the final round and wouldn't be pressured. He birdied the third, eighth and ninth holes going out, making the turn in 14 under par with a five-stroke lead. Late moves by Ryan Moore and Hunter Mahan merely closed the gap. Mahan birdied the last two for 65. Moore birdied the 15th after just missing an eagle chip. He bogeyed the 16th after catching water, then birdied the 18th after nearly holing an approach from 110 yards for an eagle. Moore shot 67 and tied Mahan at 269, two behind. Henry, who now lives in Fort Worth, Texas, remembered his roots. "To grow up in the state of Connecticut ..." he said. "I really can't think of another event I would rather win than to get my first tour victory right here in Cromwell."

Cialis Western Open
Lemont, Illinois
Winner: Trevor Immelman

The Cialis Western Open was supposed to be the Tiger and Phil Show. It was their first appearance since the U.S. Open three weeks earlier, which was, in its way, historic for both of them—Tiger Woods having missed the cut in a major championship for the first time as a professional, and Phil Mickelson having missed winning with that debacle on the 18th hole. So why was Trevor Immelman crashing their party? Immelman, age 26, in his fourth year on the PGA Tour, was a South African who had come close enough to winning to know the pain of just missing, losing the lead at the Wachovia Championship with three putts on the final hole, and hitting his tee shot into the water at the last hole in the EDS Byron Nelson Championship.

Actually, Immelman wasn't crashing their party. He was making it his party at Cog Hill, near Chicago. That didn't really dawn on everyone until in the final round, when someone finally said, "You know, if Immelman keeps this up he could win this thing." Which he did, for his first American victory. Until then, Immelman scarcely rated a glance with his opening 69, three shots off the lead behind Joe Ogilvie, Lucas Glover, Daniel Chopra and David McKenzie, and with Vijay Singh, Davis Love and Mickelson in front of him at 67. Woods was at 72, not warmed up yet.

In the second round, Immelman shot 66 and tied for third place at 135 with Ogilvie and Stewart Cink, who tied the tournament's nine-hole record with 29 on the first nine. They were three strokes behind Chopra, who was 10 under par. In the third round, Singh shot 68 for an 11-under 202 total and led by two strokes over Carl Pettersson, Mathew Goggin, Ogilvie, Cink and Immelman, who shot 69.

The efforts of Woods and the travails of Singh and Mickelson were the main show in the fourth round until Immelman birdied the 15th and 16th holes. When his 10-foot putt dropped at the 16th, Immelman gave a big grin. He bogeyed the 17th, but came to the 18th needing par to win. Instead, he rolled in a 32-foot putt for birdie, a round of 67 and a 271 total, 13 under par, for a two-stroke victory over Woods (68) and Goggin (69). "It's an incredible feeling," Immelman said. "Obviously, it hasn't quite sunk in yet." So Woods couldn't catch up after that opening 72, and Mickelson, after starting with 67, wilted from there and tied for 68th. "Trevor's been close," Woods explained. "It was time."

Immelman was the final Western Open champion. After 103 years, the Western Open would be replaced in 2007 by the BMW Championship.

John Deere Classic
Silvis, Illinois
Winner: John Senden

Once you got past the Michelle Wie episode—she withdrew because of heat exhaustion—the attention in the John Deere Classic turned to a guy who made you wonder if just being Australian might be worth a couple of strokes. This was John Senden, age 35, who did a lot in winning the John Deere Classic. It was his first PGA Tour victory, and it gave Australians seven PGA Tour wins up to mid-July. It also put him in the Open in Britain, sending a record 23 Aussies to Royal Liverpool the following week. Senden was also the seventh player in eight years to win his first tournament in the John Deere Classic.

The par-71 TPC at Deere Run in Silvis, Illinois, was no obstacle. Senden, shooting 64-69-64-68 for a 19-under 265 total, tied for the lead in the first round, trailed Joe Ogilvie by one stroke in the second round, and led the rest of the way, wrapping up the victory coolly at the end with a birdie at the 17th hole and tap-in par at the 18th for a one-stroke margin over J.P. Hayes, who charged home in 65.

To call Senden's win a surprise was to understate. The week before Senden tied for 65th in the Cialis Western Open. In 18 previous starts, his best finishes were ties for fifth in the Bob Hope Chrysler Classic in January and for ninth in the FedEx St. Jude Classic late in May, and in between he missed six 36-hole cuts. "It's a feeling of relief that you can get it done," Senden said, and no one meant it more. This was, after all, his 139th start.

Senden took the lead in the third round with 64, leaping to birdies on the first two holes, carding seven birdies in all, and saving par at the 17th hole after his tee shot carried to the right and over a walkway. In the fourth round, Hayes, seeking his third win overall, narrowly missed an eagle at the 17th and tapped in for birdie and was tied for the lead—briefly. Senden went ahead with a birdie at the 17th, tapping in from two feet. At the 18th, Hayes's second caught a greenside bunker, and his blast out went four feet past the cup. He dropped the par putt to stay within a stroke. Senden's second shot at the 18th caught the same bunker, and he came out to five inches. He tapped in for par and his first victory. "I always thought I could do it and it probably had to be a matter of time," Senden said. "I've been dreaming of it for a long while."

The Open Championship
Hoylake, England
Winner: Tiger Woods

See Chapter 4.

B.C. Open
Verona, New York
Winner: John Rollins

Not that anyone really noticed, not with Tiger Woods in England winning the Open this week, but there was another tournament every bit as important to its field in Verona, New York—the loveable B.C. Open, and for the last time. It was especially important to John Rollins, who had been concerned that people thought his only other victory on the PGA Tour, in the 2002 Bell Canadian Open, was a fluke. "It's not like a one-time fluke anymore,"

Rollins said. "I've got that out of my own mind, if it was there, or if it was on anybody else's mind."

Rollins goes into the records book as the final B.C. Open champion. The PGA Tour ended the tournament, but it will return in 2007 on the Champions Tour as the Dick's Sporting Goods Open at En-Joie Golf Club in Endicott. That was the first and only home since the B.C. Open started in 1971, but heavy rains this year forced the tournament to move some 90 miles away. Rollins, who tied for second the year before, gave the B.C. Open a rousing sendoff, dropping a seven-foot birdie putt on the final hole for an eight-under-par 64 and a one-stroke victory over Bob May, who also closed with 64. May is remembered for forcing Woods into a playoff before bowing out in the 2000 PGA Championship. May then all but disappeared with a chronic back problem.

Mark Brooks led the first round with 65, then faded, and Sweden's Gabriel Hjertstedt, the 1997 B.C. Open winner, shared the second-round lead and led the third round. The fourth round was a leapfrog battle. Rollins made four birdies on the first nine, May made three. May eagled the par-five 12th on an 18-foot putt to tie Hjertstedt, then edged into the lead with a birdie at the 13th. Then Rollins birded the 12th and 13th holes to tie May, and Hjertstedt flubbed a chip shot at the 10th and slid two strokes behind. Rollins, playing up ahead, birdied the 14th to get to 18 under par. He saved par at the 17th after driving into a fairway bunker and then falling short of the green. It came down to the par-five 18th. May hit a 265-yard, three-wood shot to 30 feet, just missed the eagle putt, and holed a 15-incher for a birdie for his 64 to tie for the lead. Rollins then rolled in his seven-footer for his own birdie for 64 and the victory. "I just stepped up, told myself I'd made a thousand of them or more in my career," Rollins said, "and rolled it in."

U.S. Bank Championship in Milwaukee
Milwaukee, Wisconsin
Winner: Corey Pavin

According to his numbers, there was no way Corey Pavin should have won the U.S. Bank Championship, his first victory in 10 years. For that matter, there is no way he should even be competitive on the modern PGA Tour. At 5-foot-9 and 155 pounds, and now age 46, he was a bicycle in a rush of Ferraris.

Back to the tournament at Brown Deer Park in Milwaukee in late in July. These were Pavin's telling numbers: He tied for 41st in fairways hit, which is not impressive, especially for a short hitter; he tied for 16th in hitting greens in regulation, which is marginal, and he averaged only 263 yards in driving, which ranked last among those who played all four rounds. So what did Pavin have to recommend him in the tournament? The only numbers that really count: a wire-to-wire win on 61-64-68-67. That was a 20-under-par 260 total and a two-stroke victory over Wisconsin's own Jerry Kelly.

This shocking result started with a stunning first nine. "It seemed like it was a misprint up there," Pavin agreed, with a chuckle. He birdied his first six holes, holing putts of 39, 38 and 29 feet. And after a two-putt par at No. 7, he birdied the next two holes to complete the nine in 26 strokes, breaking the PGA Tour nine-hole record. He admitted that the thought of shooting 59 began haunting him. "I tried to keep it out of my mind," Pavin said. "I tried to keep the voices away." Even so, he grew edgy and managed only one birdie on the second nine, at the 16th, but he did stay bogey-free.

Pavin rolled on from there, but it wasn't easy. At one point in the third round he was still missing fairways, and it was disturbing him. He bogeyed the fourth and fifth holes, and by the seventh his six-stroke lead had shrunk to two. But Pavin is nothing if not a fighter. At the par-five No. 6 he had almost run out of gas. He caught the rough yet again, and his second shot carried only about 50 yards. Then he hit a great flop shot to four feet and saved par. "I needed something to happen right then," Pavin said, "and I got it." Then he birdied the eighth and ninth holes. "Which kind of got me back on track," he said.

Kelly could have used some of Pavin's touch. He didn't bogey in the last round, but he did miss 13 birdie putts. He did birdie the 15th to get to 18 under par, two behind Pavin, but he missed chances on the last three holes. Maybe it was just Pavin's time. Back at the par-four eighth, for example, he holed his second shot from 172 yards for an eagle. And at the 10th, just as he flipped his putter in disgust, his seven-footer dropped. It definitely was his time. "I felt so comfortable," Pavin said. "I surprised myself with how calm and even I felt."

Buick Open
Grand Blanc, Michigan
Winner: Tiger Woods

It was, as they say, the "Big Five-0" for Tiger Woods—at age 30.

Woods logged his 50th PGA Tour title in the Buick Open in August at Warwick Hills in Grand Blanc, Michigan, getting it three years younger than Jack Nicklaus was when he got his. Four six-under-par 66s gave him a season-low 264 total for a three-stroke win over a determined Jim Furyk, who closed with 64 in hot pursuit. "That's pretty cool, to get to 50," Woods said. "Never in my wildest dreams did I think I'd get to 50. I've had a lot of wonderful things happen to me in my career so far in 10 years."

Woods's main goal was to surpass Nicklaus's record of 18 major championships as a professional—Woods had 11—and with that carrot always dangling in front of him, he was also shooting at career victories. Ahead of him were Sam Snead with 82, Nicklaus (73), Ben Hogan (64), Arnold Palmer (62), Byron Nelson (52) and Billy Casper (51).

Mike Weir tied his season-best with 63—including five straight birdies on the second nine—for the first-round lead. "I didn't even really look at the leaderboard today," Weir said. "You know going into this tournament that you're going to have to be pretty close to 20 under or more." That was a good bit of fortune-telling. A 73 was his worst round and he finished at 14 under par, tied for 20th. Woods was saying the same thing as he ran off five birdies from the start for his first 66. "You know you have to go low, or else you are going to get run over," Woods said. As it turned out, Woods was the one doing the running over.

Woods's second 66 spanned two days, with a rain delay, finding him one stroke behind Brett Quigley. Then Woods pulled ahead to stay in the third round, with help from a fan at the 18th. Woods's tee shot was rocketing left for the out-of-bounds when it caromed off the man's hand and back into the fairway. Woods then put his approach to seven feet and made the birdie for his third 66 and a two-stroke lead, and gave the man an autographed glove in appreciation. "He really took one for the team," Woods said.

In the final round, Woods was in trouble once, although he didn't consider it trouble. He bogeyed the par-four 12th after a stray tee shot and was tied with Furyk. Said Woods: "I kept saying to myself, 'If Jim ties me, I'm still in the driver's seat because I have the easier holes coming up.'" Woods took the lead with a birdie at the 13th on an approach to tap-in range, then went up by two with a birdie at the 15th. Furyk gave Woods something to think about with eight birdies in 15 holes, but cooled off and shot 64.

The International
Castle Rock, Colorado
Winner: Dean Wilson

The International, held at Castle Rock near Denver, is noted for a number of oddities, such as being played for points under a modified-Stableford system, not strokes, and shots going prodigious distances in the thin air of that altitude, such as Sergio Garcia hitting a sand wedge 181 yards, and Dean Wilson getting a change of identity.

Wilson, a 36-year-old Hawaiian, was famed as "the guy who played with Annika." He was her pairings mate in the 2003 Colonial, when she lasted two rounds as the first woman in 58 years to play on the PGA Tour. He was weary of the role. "Dang," Wilson said, "I've got to win a tournament so I can be known for something else." He did, and henceforth would be known as "Winner of the 2006 International."

Wilson's first victory came the hard way. He fought his way up the points ladder, and finally had to go through a playoff with Tom Lehman, captain of the U.S. Ryder Cup team. They parred the first playoff hole. Then at the second Lehman missed a birdie try from 30 feet, and Wilson rolled in his six-footer for the win.

The vagaries of Stableford play were apparent from the start. Among those who missed the halfway cut were Phil Mickelson and Jose Maria Olazabal. Then there was Mathias Gronberg. With eight birdies and a double bogey, he led the first round by two points. But he would go on to miss the 54-hole cut. Wilson himself made a meager two points in the first round, two behind Gronberg's lead. He trailed Tom Pernice, Jr. by six in the second round (19-13 points). In the third round, Zach Johnson scored a huge 15 points, making five birdies (10 points) and an eagle (5 points). With 27 points, he led Steve Flesch by one.

In the final round, the par-five 17th was the pivotal hole. Lehman was poised to make an eagle, off a five iron to 15 feet from the cup, for his first win since the 2000 Phoenix Open. "It looked so fast and it (the grain of the grass) was so shiny going down the hill," Lehman said. "I hit a beautiful putt right on line and it came up about four inches short." He tapped in for the birdie to tie Wilson, and off they went to the playoff—Lehman to become the runner-up and Wilson to change his identity.

"It's a good thing I had this format this week," Wilson conceded. In stroke play, he would have been nine under par, but Lehman would have been 13 under, and Wilson would still be known as the guy who played with Annika.

PGA Championship
Medinah, Illinois
Winner: Tiger Woods

See Chapter 5.

WGC - Bridgestone Invitational
Akron, Ohio
Winner: Tiger Woods

When last seen getting a terrific break a week ago, Tiger Woods was the beneficiary of a fan leaping up to swat back a hooked tee shot. Woods went on to win that PGA Championship. Two weeks earlier, Woods's errant shot bounced off a fan and back into the fairway, and he proceeded to win the Buick Open. Then in the WGC - Bridgestone Invitational, Woods struck a second shot so wild that it ended up on the other side of Firestone Country Club with a baffled pie delivery man. It was about 100 yards off the golf course but it wasn't out of bounds. Not one to squander a gift, Woods—despite a staggering finish—went on to beat a frustrated Stewart Cink on the fourth playoff hole. It was his fourth consecutive win of the season, his fourth straight at Firestone South, and his fifth overall there. "I was very lucky even to be in the playoff," Woods conceded.

Not that anyone thought it would last, but Woods trailed by four strokes in the first round when Adam Scott scorched the long par-70 track for nine birdies over his last 12 holes for 63 and a two-stroke lead over Jason Gore. Woods's big break came in the second round. Woods birdied the first four holes on putts all within 15 feet, and when he came to his final hole, the par-four No. 9 that finishes at the clubhouse, he hit a nine iron out of the rough from 167 yards. The ball sailed over the green, bounced off the clubhouse roof, and ended up on the other side with the pie man in the delivery area. But the area wasn't out of bounds. After things were sorted out, Woods got a free drop back on the playing side, hit a wedge from 97 yards, and two-putted from 30 feet for his only bogey of the round, a 64 and a one-stroke lead over Davis Love (65).

Woods had another bad patch in the third round, bogeying four straight holes from No. 5, and Cink shot 64 to move ahead of him by one stroke. The fourth round was a scramble. Woods, after being two down, took a three-shot lead with a 20-foot birdie at No. 13. At the 652-yard 16th hole,

Woods drove into the trees, pitched back to the fairway, then from 230 yards went over the green, chipped back to four feet and two-putted for a bogey. Cink, making up a three-stroke deficit over the last three holes, birdied the 16th from 15 feet, then the 17th from 20 feet. They tied with pars at the 18th, Woods shooting 68, Cink 69 for 10-under 270 totals.

They halved the first three playoff holes. In the rain at the fourth extra hole, the 17th, Cink came out of a greenside bunker but never got the chance to putt for his par. Woods, standing over an eight-foot birdie putt, told himself, "Just end this thing now." And he did.

Reno-Tahoe Open
Reno, Nevada
Winner: Will MacKenzie

PGA Tour winners come in all shapes and sizes, and from all kinds of backgrounds, but free spirit Will MacKenzie, 31, was an entirely different matter. If MacKenzie was in awe of winning the Reno-Tahoe Open, then golf was in awe of him: Former standout junior golfer, golf burnout, snowboarder, kayaker, rock-climber, door-to-door hammock salesman. And don't forget that he lived out of his van in Montana after leaving home in Greenville, North Carolina. So when he shot 63 for a one-stroke lead in the Reno-Tahoe Open, the question was: "Who is Will MacKenzie?" Answer: He was the unknown second-year man who would surprise everyone and play the Montreux Golf and Country Club in 63-67-67-71, a 20-under-par 268 total, to win his first PGA Tour title by one stroke.

MacKenzie, returning to the PGA Tour after giving up the aforementioned pursuits, trailed only in the second round when Bob Estes shot 65 to take a one-stroke lead. MacKenzie still was barely noticed, what with the focus on Tiger Woods and the WGC - Bridgestone Invitational that same week. MacKenzie, however, opened with a big splash. That 63 included three eagles—one on a 293-yard approach to eight feet, one on a 15-footer, another on a 50-foot putt. "I was just hitting it pretty much wherever I wanted to the whole day, and had great speed on the greens," he said. It was the start of a two-man chase between him and Estes, who opened one stroke back.

Estes, who last won in 2002, shot a bogey-free 65 to lead MacKenzie by one in the second round and noted how tough it was to follow one good round with another. "I tried to pretend yesterday didn't happen," he said. "It's tough to win out here," said MacKenzie, after 67 in the third tied him with Estes at 19 under par, both four ahead of John Cook. "It's the dream," MacKenzie said. "I'm sure it means plenty to Bob, but it means everything to me." Estes was hoping his four career wins and 18 years' experience would give him the edge in the final round.

It almost did. MacKenzie played the first nine in two birdies and a bogey, and he was three ahead through the 13th when Estes got back-to-back birdies. Then things got sticky. At the par-five, 636-yard 17th hole, MacKenzie drove 307 yards, but to the left behind some trees. He put his third shot over the green, chipped 30 feet past, and two-putted for a bogey. Estes missed a birdie from 20 feet, but his par caught MacKenzie with one hole left. "I figured if I was there at the end, I'd win," Estes said. "But my game wasn't sharp enough." MacKenzie's was. At the 18th, Estes missed a birdie try from 16 feet, and MacKenzie holed a 10-footer for a one-under 71 and the one-stroke win.

Then MacKenzie recalled his visit in 2005, when he missed the cut. "I was gambling and losing and had a few drinks," he said. "This year, I came here to win."

Deutsche Bank Championship
Norton, Massachusetts
Winner: Tiger Woods

If ever there would be a showdown—this side of Phil Mickelson, anyway—it would be Tiger Woods against Vijay Singh. And that's the way it turned out in the final round of the Deutsche Bank Championship. Actually, it was a rematch from the Deutsche Bank tournament two years ago, when Singh beat Woods head-to-head, ending his record of 264 weeks as No. 1 in the world. This time, it was practically no contest, and Woods had his fifth consecutive PGA Tour victory.

In the final round, Woods blistered the first nine with two eagles and turned a three-shot deficit into a two-shot victory with 63 for his fifth in succession, his longest streak in a season. And this was just after Singh had turned in a career-best 61 in the third round. "Vijay played one of the great rounds of golf yesterday," Woods said. "I figured one of the hardest things to do is follow a great round with another one." Even so, Singh didn't do that badly, closing at the TPC of Boston with 68. But that was a 63 Woods put on him.

There had been a few challengers along the way, but this essentially was a Woods-Singh scrap, and it ended up that way. Woods shot 66-72-67-63–268, 16 under par; Singh shot 70-71-61-68–270. Brian Bateman finished third, six strokes behind Singh.

Woods broke on top in the first round, making six birdies for a tournament lead for the 10th time in his last 16 rounds. "I feel in control of my golf ball," Woods said. "I've still got some things to work on. It could be better." The course came under tough winds in the second round and only 11 players broke 70, and Woods (72) and Singh (71) were not among them. But there were fireworks. Robert Allenby, shooting a day's-best 66, ran off a birdie-eagle-birdie-birdie streak that included a hole-in-one at the 16th, tying for the lead with Justin Rose, who pitched in twice for birdies at par-threes for his 69.

Then the battle shaped up in the third round. Singh made his way through a light rain and soggy fairways, going five under par on his first five holes, then birdieing his last three for the 61. Was he looking for a repeat of his win over Woods two years ago? "I'm not going to be thinking about his streak or beating him," Singh said. "You worry about your own game and see what happens." Woods was trailing Singh by three when the final round started. Three holes later, he tied him. Woods's spurt included an eagle at No. 2 off a six iron to 10 feet. He holed a 25-footer for a birdie and the lead at No. 5, then got another eagle at No. 7, hitting a three wood from

266 yards to 10 feet. He had played his first seven holes in six under par. He then birdied the 15th and 17th holes for the 63. Could he match Byron Nelson's 11 straight? "If a lot of guys pull out," Woods said.

Canadian Open
Ancaster, Ontario, Canada
Winner: Jim Furyk

Jim Furyk's main fight was with the Canadian Open, but he was having a little war with the Hamilton Golf and Country Club's 13th hole, a tough par-three of a robust 235 yards. He had missed the green three days running, trying to get there with a hybrid club. In the final round, with the tournament still very much up for grabs, Furyk switched to some heavier artillery. "A soft three wood," he said, and this time the man with the loopy swing hit his target and was sitting about 12 feet from the hole. He dropped the putt for a crucial birdie.

"That's like stealing, making two there," Furyk said. He wasn't home free yet, of course. Bart Bryant and Sean O'Hair, his closest pursuers, got back to within one stroke. But Furyk slipped away with a two-putt birdie at the par-five 17th for a two-stroke lead, and then got a scary five-footer down for a par at the 18th for a five-under-par 65 and a one-stroke win over Bryant. Furyk, leading off with a course record, tying with Justin Rose, shot 63-71-67-65—266, 14 under par. It was his second win of the year and the 12th of his career.

Furyk wasn't a shoo-in. Early in the final round, three players were tied for the lead at 11 under par, and seven others were within one stroke. The heat abated somewhat when Rose, who led by one going into the final round, wilted a bit, shot 74 and slipped to a tie for 14th place. Rose, who had won twice on the European Tour, was still looking for that first win on the PGA Tour. After sharing the first-round lead, he and Furyk matched 71s and slipped a stroke off the lead in the windy second round behind a traffic jam. Jonathan Byrd birdied the final three holes for a 65 to tie at seven under par with Jesper Parnevik (68), Camilo Villegas (64) and Arron Oberholser (68), who had only two bogeys in the first 36 holes, both at the 210-yard sixth. "I don't have a club for that hole," Oberholser said. Villegas's 64 included a 30-yard chip-in at the par-four 11th and a 60-foot putt at the par-four 15th. "Might be the longest putt I ever made," Villegas said. Brett Quigley tied the fresh course record of 63 to join Furyk, Rose and six others at six under.

Rose, the teenage thriller of the 1998 British Open, birdied the first three holes on his way to the third-round lead by one over a crowd of four, and when he began slipping in the final round, Furyk stepped in over the final nine holes. He birdied the 10th from 20 feet to tie for the lead at 11 under par with Byrd, and after narrowly missing 15-foot birdie putts at the 11th and 12th, he pulled ahead with—at last—a birdie at the 13th. "That," Furyk said, "was probably the hole of the day for me."

84 Lumber Classic
Farmington, Pennsylvania
Winner: Ben Curtis

The 84 Lumber Classic was the Ben Curtis and Michelle Wie Show—Curtis because for the second time this season he won a tournament that was going out of business (the other the Booz Allen Classic in June), and Wie because she again failed in her bid to become the first woman since 1945 to make the cut in a PGA Tour event. Wie shot 77-81—158 and finished 134th, dead last in the field.

The 84 Lumber Classic, at Nemacolin Woodlands in Pennsylvania's Allegheny foothills east of Pittsburgh, had been scheduled to continue with a June date in 2007. But differences emerged between the PGA Tour and the sponsor and the tournament was dropped. It went out with a flurry. As a warm-up for the Ryder Cup the next week, it was a steeplechase all the way, ending in a final-round crush.

Curtis opened with 66, two behind leader Nicholas Thompson, then shot 69 to share the second-round lead with Ryan Moore (67). Curtis stayed on top with 69, tied with Charles Howell (68) for a one-stroke lead going into the fourth round. "There's probably 20 guys and maybe more with a legitimate chance to win," said Curtis. And it looked that way until Curtis, at the final turn, broke from a four-way tie for the lead with Howell, Moore and Robert Garrigus, a surprise contender who led the 2005 qualifying tournament.

Curtis turned things his way with three birdies in a stretch of five holes from the 12th. This included Curtis making birdie at the 15th with an eight iron out of a fairway bunker to 13 feet while Howell was three-putting from 50. Then Curtis holed a 50-footer for birdie at the par-five 16th, where Howell missed an eagle try from 14 feet. But what set Curtis up was a great save at the par-four 14th. He put his approach on a grassy uphill lie behind the green. "It was a very difficult shot, and I had three different clubs out," Curtis said. He opted for a utility wood, normally used out of rough and like a long iron. He chipped to 12 feet and holed the putt for par.

He wrapped up his 70, his 14-under-par 274 total and his two-stroke win over Howell, then considered how he would not be the defending champion in two tournaments the next year.

The Ryder Cup
Straffan, Co. Kildare, Ireland
Winners: Europe

See Chapter 8.

Valero Texas Open
San Antonio, Texas
Winner: Eric Axley

Eric Axley, age 32, a rookie on the PGA Tour via the Nationwide Tour, came to the Valero Texas Open, at LaCantera in San Antonio, having missed

13 cuts in 23 events and with the knowledge that this was a good time to get moving. If public attention might be a bother, well, the golf world was focused on the Ryder Cup in Ireland the same week. Thus inspired, Axley, a left-hander, did get moving and breezed to the victory.

"It's hard to win on any tour," Axley said. "I know a lot of this hasn't hit me yet. But, yeah—it's cool." He won by three strokes, but the margin might have been greater except for a problem—Axley himself. But first, he opened four strokes off the lead, with 68. The ubiquitous Justin Rose, fresh from three straight top-15 finishes, was nibbling at that first victory again. He made eight birdies for 64 to share the first-round lead with Alex Cjeka.

Axley charged into contention—and almost right to the win—with a pair of 63s in the middle rounds. The first tied him with D.A. Points for the halfway lead at nine under par. Points had a remarkable 66. He started par-double bogey-bogey, then birdied seven of his last 15 holes. Axley's round included three consecutive birdies from the seventh. The second 63 carried him to a four-stroke lead through the third round over Ted Purdy (64), Frank Lickliter (65) and Chris Riley (64), all tested tournament winners. At least one of them figured to hold up under the closing pressure. In fact, it was Axley himself.

In the final round, Axley enjoyed a huge leap. He arrived at the fourth tee leading by three strokes, and left the green leading by six. He had birdied, and Lickliter, his closest pursuer, double-bogeyed after blasting a bunker shot across the green. Then Purdy, in the same group, drove into an unplayable lie and made a quadruple-bogey eight. Axley could cruise home. But he didn't choose to.

He was leading by six strokes coming to the par-five, 543-yard 14th. He might have used his three wood, just to stay safe, but he used his driver instead, deciding to go for the green in two. He drove into the trees and double-bogeyed, and found his lead down to two. He had gone 53 holes without a bogey. "I didn't stick to my game plan," he admitted. "I got aggressive and I paid for it. It was a bad decision."

Axley also bogeyed the 17th, then regrouped at the 18th, hitting his approach from 143 yards to four feet and making the birdie for a 71 and a 15-under-par 265 total, and a three-stroke victory over Rose (68), Dean Wilson (69) and Anthony Kim (65), who left the University of Oklahoma before his senior year and had just made an excellent professional debut. "I've never been that great at school," Kim said. "But I felt my game was ready."

WGC - American Express Championship
Hertfordshire, England
Winner: Tiger Woods

See European Tours chapter.

Southern Farm Bureau Classic
Madison, Mississippi
Winner: D.J. Trahan

It was a year ago to the week, and the names and circumstances had changed, but the pain and uncertainty—and maybe even the fear—were still the same for D.J. Trahan. Go back to the 2005 Chrysler Classic of Greensboro. Trahan was a rookie then, trading almost shot-for-shot with the formidable K.J. Choi. He trailed Choi by one stroke in the second round, and then shot 66 and they were tied going into the fourth round. Choi won, and Trahan shot 75 and slid to a tie for 13th. Now it was the Southern Farm Bureau Classic, and the same old pressure, but more so now because Trahan, age 25, was struggling to keep his PGA Tour card.

Trahan, who led wire-to-wire, was up by two strokes going into the final round. He bogeyed twice on the first nine, but squared things with an eagle at No. 5. Trahan was battling two-time U.S. Open champion Lee Janzen most of the day. Janzen made it a three-way tie at the 12th hole, but slipped back when he hit a shot into the water at the 17th and bogeyed. But then there was Durant, who shot 74 in the third round and started the final round five strokes back. He bogeyed twice but made eight birdies, the last at the 18th, for 66 and a 13-under-par 275 total at Annandale Golf Club in Madison, Mississippi. Now catching Durant was the problem. Trahan needed some clutch play. He made a key save at the 15th, then at the 17th got up and down from 120 yards and got the 71 he needed for the tie.

The playoff was at the par-five 18th hole. They both birdied it the first two times, and on the third playing, both had birdie tries from five feet. Durant missed, but Trahan didn't. Janzen closed with 70 and finished third, one stroke behind.

The victory was a great relief for Trahan. He had been laboring. "It has been a brutal year," Trahan said. "Scoring was not going my way. The balls weren't falling the right way. If I hit good putts, or thought I hit good putts, they weren't going in. You just have to work hard and keep reassuring yourself that you're a good player, you're a good putter. Obviously, it's still inside you somewhere. You've just got to be patient and let it come to the surface."

Chrysler Classic of Greensboro
Greensboro, North Carolina
Winner: Davis Love

It was more than just the ecstasy of victory that hit Davis Love when he took the Chrysler Classic of Greensboro. There was also the agony of a lot of defeats—tournaments he might have won but that got away. He hadn't really been himself for some time, and he knew why—the Ryder Cup.

"I wanted (to play in) the Ryder Cup so badly I let it get in the way of everything else I was doing," Love said. "Grinding for the Ryder Cup was a detriment ... I'd been worried about what everybody else was doing, and (I had) expectations that didn't matter." Not only did Love not make the team, his general play suffered as well under the strain. But harmony returned early in October at Forest Oaks Country Club in Greensboro, North Carolina. This was homecooking at its finest. He had lengthened and redesigned Forest Oaks three years ago. But he rejected the notion that parenthood meant anything in the conduct of the tournament.

"When you hit that golf ball," Love said, "it doesn't know who designed the course or how much information you have." Which explains why Love, playing the par-72 course in 69-69-68-66 for a 16-under-par 272 total, had to come from behind to score his 19th career victory and his first since 2003. In the first round, he was five behind the 64s posted by Nick Watney, John Rollins and Brent Geiberger. He closed to within three of Watney (71–135) in the second round. Finally, Love broke through in the third round, tying for the third-round lead with Chris Couch (69–206) at 10 under.

Love was almost back—but not quite. He opened the last round with two birdies for a two-stroke lead. But Eric Axley, the left-handed rookie who scored his first victory two weeks earlier, also made a quick move, a first-nine 31 led by a holed-out wedge at No. 5. Love bogeyed No. 7 from a bunker, but at No. 8, he laced a three-iron shot to eight feet and birdied. "The biggest two holes, probably, of my year," Love said. "I could have gotten frustrated and disappointed and said, 'Here we go again.'"

Axley had a three-stroke lead with five holes to play. He bogeyed the 14th hole from the trees, and the par-three 17th, two-putting from eight feet. Meanwhile, Love sprinted to three straight birdies from the 13th, then parred in for 66 and a two-stroke win over Jason Bohn, who logged six birdies for 66.

Frys.com Open
Las Vegas, Nevada
Winner: Troy Matteson

Troy Matteson, age 26, a rookie on the PGA Tour, was the obedient younger brother. He was on the final hole of the Frys.com Open in Las Vegas, leading by two and facing an eight-foot putt for his first victory. And his big brother, and caddie, J.T. Matteson, knew his brother was nervous, hungry and anxious. He also knew the kid was going to try to jam this one in, to get it over. Lag putt from eight feet? Why not, when you have a two-shot cushion? So Matteson cozied his first putt to within eight inches.

Matteson could joke about it later. "I'm glad it was about eight or nine inches," Matteson said. "I can usually handle those." And he did handle that tap-in, getting it down for a par and completing a card of 67-65-64-69–265, 23 under par, to win by one stroke over Ben Crane (65), a two-time winner, and Daniel Chopra (66), who was seeking his first win. Matteson's fear of putting into the water at the 18th wasn't entirely groundless. Aaron Baddeley, tied with D.A. Points through the 16th, chipped into the water at the 18th and double-bogeyed.

Matteson surfaced in the storm-interrupted third round. Chopra had posted 64 and held the clubhouse lead at 15 under par, but still out were Charley Hoffman at 17 under with four holes to play and Matteson, who started the round at 11 under and was 16 under through 12 holes. It was going to be a long day for 22 players who had to complete their third round and then head into the final round. It would be a 24-hole day for Matteson. He finished the six holes of his third round on Sunday morning and took the 54-hole lead with a 64, getting to 19 under to lead by one over Hoffman (65). Chopra was four behind, and Crane was a stroke further back.

In the final round, Matteson shook off a bogey at the 13th and pulled away from a tie with Crane, Hoffman and Frank Lickliter with birdies at the 14th and 16th. The rookie's moment of truth came at the 444-yard, par-four 18th. Ignoring the pressure, Matteson hit his approach brilliantly to eight feet. When Chopra missed his birdie from 18 feet, Matteson had a two-stroke cushion, and that's when big brother stepped in.

"All week, what helped me was having my brother there," Matteson said. "We were walking down the gully there (at the 18th), and he goes, 'I just want to tell you, I love you, man.' He was just trying to lighten the mood a little bit. I said, 'Buddy, this has been one of the best weeks of my life. I'm glad you were right here to be part of it.'"

Funai Classic at the Walt Disney World Resort
Lake Buena Vista, Florida
Winner: Joe Durant

Joe Durant, age 42, a one-time flawed insurance agent, one-time flawed warehouse worker and one-time flawed golfer, finally found what he had been looking for in the Magic Kingdom. It was the Funai Classic at the Walt Disney World Resort in Florida, and Durant found a putting touch to go with his excellent ball-striking to score his first victory since 2001.

The tournament was played over two par-72 courses. Durant opened with 69 on the Magnolia Course and 65 at the Palm, then, as everyone moved to the Magnolia, he closed with 64-65 for a 25-under-par 263 total. He had come from behind in the final round for a four-stroke win over Frank Lickliter, who closed with a 10-under 62, and amazing rookie Troy Matteson (70). "Every birdie I made, he made a birdie to match," said Matteson, who came to Disney with a tie for eighth, sixth and a victory in the three preceding weeks. "He just kept applying pressure. Sooner or later, a guy like that is going to run away."

The tournament started with a bang when Justin Rose got a leg up on that elusive first win with 60 at the Palm Course, and he missed 59 when his birdie try from 14 feet at the 18th turned away. He led by four through the first two rounds, then his chances slipped away in the third on a par 72, the highest score among the first 10 finishers. Matteson took the lead in the third round with a 65, one ahead of Durant.

Durant found his putting touch in the final round. He birdied the third from 13 feet and tapped in for another at the par-five fourth. He moved in front for good with a birdie from the sand at the par-five 10th. At the shortish par-four 13th, he restrained the temptation to overpower it and laid up off the tee, setting up an easy wedge to two feet for another birdie. He moved to a four-stroke lead with a birdie from 11 feet at the 14th and a 20-footer at the 16th. Then he came home comfortably in pars for the 65 and the four-stroke victory.

Chrysler Championship
Palm Harbor, Florida
Winner: K.J. Choi

For a change, winning wasn't the only thing in the Chrysler Championship. This time, a high finish would also be great. This was the final full-field event of 2006, and they came to Palm Harbor, Florida, with their dreams. Some wanted to crack the top 30 on the money list to qualify for the Tour Championship the following week, others the top 40 to clinch a Masters berth, and others, more urgently, the top 125 to keep their PGA Tour playing cards.

For K.J. Choi, the goal was getting back into the top 50 in the Official World Golf Ranking, to get into the World Golf Championship series. And this he did with authority on Innisbrook's par-71 Copperhead Course, shooting 68-66-70-67—271, 13 under par, to breeze to a four-stroke victory over Brett Wetterich (66) and a rejuvenated Paul Goydos (70).

Choi launched his move on the last hole of the third round, rolling in a 10-foot birdie putt for a one-stroke lead on Ernie Els (70), Brian Gay (70) and Goydos (69). Sleeping on the lead didn't bother Choi. "When I'm in the lead on a Saturday night, I don't think much about it," Choi said. "I can only control myself."

Did Choi ever. At the par-five first hole the next day, he fired a three-wood approach to 20 feet and holed the putt for a three-stroke lead. No one came within two strokes the rest of the way, and Choi had his second Chrysler Championship in five years, winning by two over Wetterich (66) and Goydos (70). The win did the trick. Choi zoomed up the rankings from 55th to 28th. It also got him into the season-ending Tour Championship the next week and the season-opening Mercedes-Benz Championship in 2007.

Among other success stories:

• Ernie Els was flirting with falling out of the top 30, but he saved par out of a bunker at the 17th and made a heroic escape at the 18th, where he drove into the trees, pitched back to the fairway, then lofted a wedge from 51 yards for a tap-in par. His 72 and 277 total tied him for sixth place and just got him into the top 30 and the Tour Championship. "The last two up-and-downs were big," Els said. "I'll remember those for a long time."

• Goydos, who thought he would have to go back to the qualifying tournament, won $466,400, which lifted him from 160th, deep in the non-exempt area, to 97th, well inside the magic top 125. Was he expecting this surge? "No," Goydos said.

• Mark Calcavecchia was already exempt through his 2005 Canadian Open victory, but his tie for 19th moved him into the top 125, which put him into the 2007 Players Championship.

• Troy Matteson, on a hot streak for the past six weeks—including a victory in the Frys.com Open—shot a 64 in the third round, tied for ninth and finished 36th on the money list, earning his first berth in the Masters.

• Colombian rookie Camilo Villegas closed with 69, tied for 31st, and also earned a visit to the Masters.

The Tour Championship
Atlanta, Georgia
Winner: Adam Scott

Jim Furyk and Joe Durant were hot on Adam Scott's heels—or thought they were. Then they heard the gallery roar behind them, back on No. 13. "I looked at Jim and we both kind of laughed," Durant said. "We didn't have to say it, but we both knew it. That was game, set and match as far as the winner was concerned."

The roar was the sound of Scott, the bright, 26-year-old Australian, holing a 28-foot bunker shot at the 13th. The birdie gave him a five-stroke lead, which Durant and Furyk agreed was the clincher. Scott was about to make The Tour Championship, the final official PGA Tour event of 2006, his first victory of the year. It was also his fourth win on the PGA Tour, but his first in over two years. And he had come so close. He had been second three times and third three times this year. "It's been a long time since I've been here, winning on the PGA Tour," Scott said. "I had to work hard for it."

And Scott won with emphasis, by three strokes over Furyk, four over Durant, playing the East Lake course in Atlanta in an 11-under-par 269 total. With cards of 69-67-67-66, he trailed only in the opening round, and then only by one stroke. He tied for the lead with Durant in the second round, and led by three the rest of the way. It was an attention-getter, even without Tiger Woods and Phil Mickelson, who opted not to play.

Scott underlined his intentions at the par-five 15th in the second round. He was tied with Furyk and Durant at the moment, and was deflated when he caught his three-iron approach thin. But the ball kept rolling, then reached the green and stopped two feet from the cup. He got the eagle. "I thought it would be short," Scott said. "It's unexplainable." It was better than that. When Durant bogeyed the next two holes, Scott had a three-stroke lead.

Scott was pressured a few times in the final round, but responded appropriately. Vijay Singh, his pairings partner, made an early move. Scott rolled in a tricky 15-footer for birdie at No. 3. When Furyk and Durant turned up the heat, Scott chalked up three birdies in four holes around the turn. And then came that bunker shot at the 13th. "I felt all the hard work has actually paid off," Scott said. "I didn't want to throw away this opportunity … as I had done earlier this year."

There was more than a consolation prize for Furyk (65–272) and Durant (67–273). Durant went from worrying about keeping his playing card to a win and four top-10 finishes in five events, and Furyk ended the season with a 68.86 scoring average to win the Vardon Trophy.

WGC - Barbados World Cup
St. James, Barbados
Winners: Germany (Bernhard Langer and Marcel Siem)

A mixture of youth and experience proved the winning formula as Germany beat Scotland in a playoff to win the WGC - Barbados World Cup at Sandy Lane. Germany were represented by Bernhard Langer, age 49, and the 26-year-old Marcel Siem. Scotland were similarly composed with Colin Montgomerie leading the young tour winner Marc Warren.

It was Germany's second victory in the event, with Langer having partnered Torsten Gideon to the title in 1990. Both pairs tied at 16 under par, with Germany posting a best-of-the-day 66 in the final round foursomes despite an interruption due to torrential rain. They had an earlier foursomes round of 69 and fourball rounds of 65 and 68. Scotland scored 67 and 65 in the fourballs and 67 and 69 in the foursomes. At the par-three 18th in regulation, Siem missed from 12 feet to post 17 under, while Montgomerie had to hole a sliding six-footer to make the playoff. Sweden's Carl Petterssson and Henrik Stenson would have joined the playoff but for three putts at the 18th, while South Africa finished fourth and long-time contenders Argentina slipped away after missing a number of short putts.

In the playoff, both Langer and Montgomerie came up short left of the green. Warren chipped four feet past, while Siem got his chip to two feet. Montgomerie knew he needed to hole the downhill putt to extend the playoff, but the miss gave Langer the change to seal the victory. The previous week Langer had won the Del Webb Father-Son Challenge with 15-year-old Stefan, who was caddieing for him here.

"Every trophy is special and last week I won the father-and-son event, so it's two weeks in a row we have won and it's pretty neat. It's nice to be on a roll," said Langer. "To have Stefan on the bag as well was a great experience. I truly enjoyed playing with Marcel because we actually never really played much golf together, even though we are from the same country. We are from totally different generations but we had the spark, the chemistry, that you need."

Siem, winner of the 2004 Dunhill Championship, said: "It's just unbelievable. Winning a trophy with Bernard Langer is big and so much fun. I can't believe it actually. We had two legends on the tee box in the playoff with Monty and Bernhard, so that was incredible. I learned so much from Bernhard all week—like the need to stay calm and wait for chances rather than be too aggressive. He's a legend but is so nice to everyone. A great player and a great guy."

Special Events

Tavistock Cup
Orlando, Florida
Winner: Isleworth

If the Tavistock Cup was any indication, Tiger Woods was in for a dandy time at the Masters in two weeks. Woods put on one of his typical displays to lead Isleworth past Lake Nona, 17½ to 12½, in the showdown between teams of PGA Tour players who live at the two Orlando-area clubs.

Woods teamed with Mark O'Meara, captain of the Isleworth team, for a 65-66 better-ball win over Sergio Garcia and Retief Goosen, helping Isleworth to a 6-4 lead for the first day. The Tavistock Cup was billed as Woods's final tuneup before the Masters, and the first round marked a healthy improvement for him. He had three birdies and an eagle, the day after shooting 75 in the final round of The Players Championship.

In two other Isleworth better-ball wins, Robert Damron and Lee Janzen beat Ben Curtis and Justin Rose, 64-66, and Robert Allenby and Stuart Appleby sank Trevor Immelman and Lake Nona captain Ernie Els, 64-67. In Lake Nona victories, Maarten Lafeber and Graeme McDowell beat Arjun Atwal and Craig Parry, 70-72, and Mark McNulty and Ian Poulter turned back John Cook and Charles Howell, 70-71.

The second and final round was a scorekeeper's exercise, with two-man teams playing stroke play against each other, and with four points available in each of the five matches. Woods shot the low round of the day, a 65, to lead Isleworth to an 11½ to 8½ win. He beat Els, who shot 72. Cook, his partner, shot 76 and lost to both Nona opponents, Els and Mark McNulty (68). Isleworth took command when Howell (68) and Appleby (72) swept all four points from Garcia (74) and Goosen (73).

Isleworth took the bragging rights, with a 2-0-1 record in the young series. Isleworth won the first Tavistock Cup in 2004, 14½-9½, and the 2005 match ended in a tie because of darkness.

CVS Charity Classic
Barrington, Rhode Island
Winners: Nick Price and Tim Clark

The CVS Charity Classic, staged by the big pharmacy chain, proved to be the best medicine for Nick Price. Why the big grin? A 12-foot birdie putt on the second extra hole that ran obediently home and gave Price and Tim Clark the playoff victory over Brad Faxon and Mike Weir.

"This was a very big putt for me and for my self-confidence," said Price on draining the clincher after both teams finished the two-day event with nine-under-par 62s and two-round totals of 19-under 123 at Rhode Island Country Club. Maybe Price, age 49, needed a little boost. He owns the 1992

PGA Championship, and both The Open and the PGA in 1994, but the last of his 18 PGA Tour victories came in the 2002 MasterCard Colonial.

This was a superheated race from the start. Consider that Price and Clark tied in the first round at 61 with Faxon and Weir, and the big-hitting pair of Bubba Watson and J.B. Holmes. And they all trailed by a stroke. Jeff Sluman and Stewart Cink blistered the course for a 60. Pressure? Said Sluman: "There's no pressure when your partner plays like Stew. He had eight birdies and an eagle." Watson, the big-hitting rookie, stole part of the show with his eagle at the par-five No. 8, a 516-yarder. He had a mere six iron left for his second, and he hit it to 10 feet.

Power wasn't quite enough. Weir dropped a five-footer for birdie at the 18th to force the playoff. Watson and Holmes trailed by a stroke coming to the 17th, but the best they could do was par the last two holes and tie for third at 18 under. Then along came Price with the 12-footer on the second extra hole, leaving Faxon wondering what he had to do to win. This was the fourth time he finished second.

Merrill Lynch Shootout
Naples, Florida
Winners: Jerry Kelly and Rod Pampling

It was Greg Norman's old Shark Shootout under a new name, the Merrill Lynch Shootout, with two free-spirited winners—Jerry Kelly and Rod Pampling.

Pampling was a late substitute for Peter Jacobsen, who had to have hip surgery. Kelly found playing with the Australian much to his liking. "It's really fun to win with a partner," Kelly said. Said Pampling: "We had a ton of fun all day, every day," Especially the last day—when they won.

Twelve two-player teams had come to Tiburon Golf Club, in Naples, Florida, in mid-November. Kelly and Pampling got eight points in the modified alternate shot the first round, just a point off the lead. They picked up 10 in better ball the next round and with 18 were one behind the leaders, John Daly and J.B. Holmes.

In the scramble in the final round, Daly and Holmes misfired from the start and fell back. Verplank and Leonard took the lead with an eagle at the par-five 17th, where Leonard hit a four wood to 25 feet and Verplank holed the putt. Then at the 18th, Pampling hooked his approach into the water, Kelly hit just short of the green, and Pampling dropped a 20-foot putt for a birdie and the tie at 31 points.

In the playoff, at modified alternate shot, Verplank's approach was short and rolled back into the water, and Kelly put his on the green, 25 feet from the cup. Pampling then ran the birdie putt six feet past, Kelly lipped that out, and finally Pampling tapped in for a bogey and the win.

The Shootout was also highlighted by a battle to stay out of last place. It came down to the last hole. Annika Sorenstam, the first woman to play in the Shootout in its 18 years, holed a 20-foot putt for a birdie for her and partner Fred Couples. They were in great shape when Nick Faldo missed his birdie from 15. But Norman sank his, and it was Sorenstam-Couples in the cellar by one point.

The Goodwill Trophy
Shenzhen, China
Winners: International Team

See Asia/Japan Tours chapter.

Callaway Golf Pebble Beach Invitational
Pebble Beach, California
Winner: Jason Bohn

Never mind that he wasn't Tom Watson and that he wasn't beating Jack Nicklaus, as in the 1982 U.S. Open. "There's no better feeling than birdieing 17 anytime you're playing Pebble Beach," Jason Bohn said. This was the Callaway Golf Pebble Beach Invitational, and Bohn, who had one PGA Tour victory to his credit, birdied the difficult par-three hole to all but lock up the post-season event in mid-November. The tournament was also played over the Del Monte and Spyglass courses and had probably the most diverse field in the game—81 golfers from the four major tours plus mini-tour players, club pros and amateurs.

Bohn dropped a 25-foot putt for the birdie at the 17th. "I knew I had a two-stroke lead starting on the 18th," he said, "so I just laid it up on in there." Bohn finished with 71 and a 14-under-par 274 total for a one-stroke win over Scott Simpson, who birdied the 18th for 68. Bohn was on his way to a romp, leading by four strokes after No. 6, but he hit his tee shot in the water at the par-three No. 7 and made a double bogey. Jim Thorpe, who shared the second-round lead, had got to 13 under par and deep in the hunt through the 15th hole in the fourth round, but he triple-bogeyed the 16th. Simpson was a double victim. He lost a ball in the first round when he hit into the sun, and neither he nor anyone else saw where it went. Then in the final round, he missed a five-foot birdie putt at the 17th. "I could have used that," Simpson said.

PGA Grand Slam of Golf
Kauai, Hawaii
Winner: Tiger Woods

The PGA Grand Slam of Golf, the PGA of America's showdown of the winners of the four major championships, had been a foregone conclusion for so long, it was a surprise to see that Tiger Woods wasn't leading the first round. That was Jim Furyk with 67, ahead of Geoff Ogilvy by one stroke, with Woods three off the lead at 70, and finally Mike Weir at 71 at Poipu Bay in Hawaii. Then the showdown returned to the script for the second and final round, and Woods won for the seventh consecutive time.

The cast wasn't precise. Woods had won two majors, the Open and PGA Championship, so Furyk, a former U.S. Open champion, filled in. Masters champion Phil Mickelson turned down the invitation, so Weir, a former Masters champion, took his place. But it was just another Tiger Woods outing.

In the second round, Ogilvy bogeyed three of the first seven holes and was adrift. Weir triple-bogeyed the par-three No. 7 and was also out of the running. Woods soon turned up the heat in the strong winds. After three earlier birdies on the first nine, he tied Furyk with a chip-in at the ninth, then he took the lead at the 10th with a par to Furyk's bogey. Woods got to seven under par and a two-stroke lead, holing a 12-footer for birdie at the 15th. He wrapped up a six-under-par 66 for Grand Slam No. 7 and said, "I've always loved coming here."

Del Webb Father-Son Challenge
Orlando, Florida
Winners: Bernhard and Stefan Langer

It was more like instant replay—a year later—than a case of déjà vu, with the Langers coming to the final hole needing a birdie to win. This time, father Bernhard Langer reached the par-five 18th hole in two and son Stefan, with a coolness uncommon to a 16-year-old, rapped in the putt for the birdie to win the Del Webb Father-Son Challenge. The birdie wrapped up scramble-format scores of 59 and 61 for a total of 120 at ChampionsGate Golf Resort near Orlando, Florida, edging Bob and Kevin Tway (61-60) and Vijay and Qass Singh (60-61).

"It definitely was less nerve-wracking because we've been there before and knew how much fun it was to win," said Stefan. A year earlier, Stefan hit a three wood to the final hole to set up the winning birdie.

This time, the Langers shared the first-round lead with Davis Love and son Dru at 13-under-par 59. The Singhs were at 60, and the Tways and Bob and David Charles were tied at 61.

The Langers started the second round with four straight birdies and, coming in, they knew what they had to do. The Tways and the Singhs were already in the clubhouse at 121. The Tways birdied the last three holes for their 60–121, but they figured that what hurt them was not being able to do any better than three pars from the 13th. "Those three holes just killed us," Bob Tway said.

The Langers needed a birdie at the 18th. Then Bernhard, the two-time Masters champion, put his second shot 80 feet from the pin. A lag putt left a six-footer for a birdie, and Stefan stepped up and knocked in the winner.

And so Bernhard became the second father—after Raymond Floyd, who did it twice—to win consecutive titles. "If everything goes well, we should be in contention for years," said. "He's going to get better, and hopefully, I won't get a whole lot worse."

Target World Challenge
Thousand Oaks, California
Winner: Tiger Woods

Maybe Geoff Ogilvy had the secret to Tiger Woods. "I knew starting the day I would have to shoot five or six under to win," Ogilvy said. "Maybe that's why you never play well when he's there, because you try too hard to shoot a score."

If Ogilvy was right, then that was the story with Woods, host of the Target World Challenge in December. The post-season frolic with a 16-man field at Sherwood Country Club in Thousand Oaks, California, developed this way: Henrik Stenson birdied three straight holes on the second nine and took a one-shot lead with a six-under-par 66 in the first round. Woods (68) was two behind. Woods shot another 68 in the second round and took the halfway lead by one. Then Woods struggled just a bit in the third round, shot 70, and Ogilvy birdied the last hole for a 67 and a one-stroke lead over Woods.

Woods closed the gap fast in the final round. A birdie at No. 2 from 10 feet and a chip-in at No. 3, while Ogilvy bogeyed No. 2 with help from mud on his ball, and it was just about over. Before Woods knew it, he was leading by three strokes through the turn. Woods did bogey the par-three 15th, but Ogilvy got too eager at the 14th and what might have been a birdie turned into a three-putt bogey. Woods wrapped up a card of 68-68-70-66–272, 16 under par, and won comfortably by four over Ogilvy (71).

"Once you get the lead, these guys behind me, if they get aggressive, they can make mistakes," Woods said. "The whole idea is to force them to get me."

Nationwide Tour

The 2006 Nationwide Tour graduating class was a study in demographics. Of the 22 players going on to the PGA Tour, one was 47 years old, six were in their late 30s, 13 were in their 20s, and the youngest was 22, and all from a wide variety of experiences.

More to the point, there were five two-time winners, and none of them could bring in that magical third win for the "battlefield promotion," the automatic advancement to the PGA Tour. Even so, by the season's end, they had enough to make the move. Among the compelling stories out of the 2006 Nationwide Tour:

Ken Duke, 37, a former PGA Tour player, topped the money list with $382,443, but there was nothing routine about it. Duke won one tournament, the BMW Charity Pro-Am in April. Over the next three months, he had just one other top-five finish. Then he racked up four top-fives in 50 days. As Duke had said earlier, "You never know when it's going to be your turn."

Jim Rutledge, 47, the oldest of the class, scored his first career Nationwide Tour win in the ING New Zealand PGA Championship, and it almost surprised him. "If I tell the truth," the Canadian said, "it wasn't even in the back of my mind. I wanted to put together a solid round, and make a nice check and get some momentum for when the tour came back to the States." Rutledge built up some terrific momentum down the final stretch, holing out a wedge for an eagle at the par-four 17th, then dropping a 22-foot putt for birdie at the 18th. It all gave him a bogey-free, eight-under 64 and a one-stroke victory. It also made him the second-oldest rookie to play the PGA Tour. Allen Doyle was 48 when he joined in 1996.

Then the class of the Class of 2006, the five two-time winners:

• Craig Kanada, 38, who made his first start on the Nationwide Tour in 1991, first won the Utah Energy Solutions Championship in September. He came from three strokes down, birdied the par-three 15th from 40 feet, and shot 71 for a one-stroke victory. He got his second win and his pass to the big time spectacularly in the season-ending Nationwide Tour Championship. He was trailing by six strokes coming into the final round, and in the process, he did wonders for his putting average. He chipped in on the last two holes for a par-birdie finish, a score of 66 and a 13-under total of 276 for a one-stroke win over 54-hole leader Matt Kuchar. Kanada's strategy: "I decided not to use the putter anymore," he said. The victory carried him to 11th place on the money list.

• Tripp Isenhour, 38, racked up his two wins in the first five weeks. He took the season-opening Movistar Panama Championship, starting off with his best round of the year, a 63. In the final round of the Livermore Valley Wine Country Championship, he chipped to eight feet at the par-five 15th and made a birdie to tie Paul Sheehan, who had bogeyed. The issue was pretty much settled at the par-four 17th. Sheehan drove into a hazard and double-bogeyed. Isenhour put his six-iron shot 10 feet from the cup and holed the putt for a three-shot lead. After some last-minute theatrics involving a tee shot into a hazard and a scramble for a bogey, he wrapped up a 68 and a nine-under 279 total and a three-stroke win. Isenhour credited experience for the win. As he put it, "It was all these gray hairs that kept me in it."

• Johnson Wagner, 26, had to sweat out his first win at the Chitimacha Louisiana Open. First, he flew an eight-iron shot 158 yards out of a bunker to eight feet and made the putt for a one-stroke lead. Then he paced nervously as Chad Collins and Franklin Langham tried to tie him on the last hole. "I can't watch this stuff," he said. Langham three-putted for a bogey and Collins just missed his birdie from 20 feet, and Wagner had his win. He could watch his second win comfortably. In the Cox Classic, Wagner eagled the par-five 17th, then dropped an 18-foot putt for a birdie at the 18th for an eight-under 63, a 21-under 263 total and a four-stroke victory over Craig Bowden. Said Wagner: "It was a really cool feeling, coming up to that last hole knowing I had it won."

• Brandt Snedeker, 25, got both of his victories in playoffs. In the Scholarship America Showdown, he and Jeff Quinney came out of a dense pack to tie in regulation. Quinney made three straight birdies from the 15th, and Snedeker had to eagle the final hole with a 15-foot putt, both getting 67s. In the playoff at the 18th, they tied in birdies the first time, then Snedeker birdied it again the second time, two-putting from seven feet for his first career win on the tour. At the Permian Basin Charity Golf Classic, Snedeker was back from a five-tournament layoff for a broken collarbone. He holed a 15-footer on the final hole for 69 to tie Aron Price (66) at 16-under 272. Then he holed another 15-footer on the first playoff hole to win.

• Kevin Stadler, 26, son of Craig Stadler, made it look almost easy. He won his card playing in only 12 of the 31 events. Stadler first took the Xerox Classic, then five weeks later put on a closing rush to pluck the Albertsons Boise Open. And by some uncanny twist of fate, the man he beat both times was Glen Day. On the final nine of the Albertsons, he got up and down three times for pars from the 12th, then birdied three straight from the 15th. A par at the 18th gave him a five-under 66 and a 20-under 264 and a one-stroke victory, along with his ticket to the big tour.

Stadler had won the Johnnie Walker Classic in Australia early in the year, and so won exemption on the co-sponsoring European, Asian and Australasian Tours. "I can play everywhere in the world, except where I want to," Stadler had said then. And now he could play where he wants too.

Canadian Tour

Mike Weir became a national hero in Canada for winning the 2003 Masters. Wes Heffernan didn't get anywhere near that level, but there had to be a few warm thoughts for him when he kept the Americans from running the table in the 2006 Canadian Tour.

Heffernan, of Calgary, did this by taking the Casino de Montreal Open for the Players Championship early in August. And Stuart Anderson, of Edmonton, backed him up two stops later, taking the inaugural Canadian Tour Championship, which ended the season. So it wasn't a sweep, but it definitely was top-heavy with 10 American winners in the 12 events. It was also top-heavy with playoffs—six, and two of them four-way playoffs.

A win was Heffernan's main goal (he was one of six first-time winners), but another goal eluded him—Rolex Player of the Year as the money leader. He finished 13th in the Tour Championship and third on the money list with C$55,633. "But I realized most of the goals I set for myself," said Heffernan, falling just short of becoming only the third Canadian to top the money list, after Weir in 1997 and Jon Mills in 2003.

The title went to American Steve Gangluff, age 31, who lifted his total to C$67,336 with two victories in a span of four tournaments—the Telus Edmonton Open early in July, then the Fallsview Casino Resort Pro-Am Classic for his second and third career wins. Two other Americans also won twice: Rob Oppenheim, in the season-opening Yes! Golf BCR Classic and then the Corona Mazatlan Classic, and Lee Williamson, taking the Diablo Grande California Classic and the Greater Vancouver Charity Classic.

Gangluff, of Ponte Vedra Beach, Florida, took the Edmonton event in a wild finish. Brendan Steele led by two at the 18th tee. But he drove into a fairway bunker and later three-putted from 30 feet and double-bogeyed, tying with Gangluff, who had already finished. Gangluff then chipped in from 30 feet for a winning birdie on the first playoff hole. "I feel bad for Brendan," Gangluff said. "But I've been there. It was a shocker."

Gangluff's Fallsview win was another matter. He led by six going into the final round, bogeyed two of his first three holes, and won by seven.

Oppenheim, 26, from Boston, won the season-opening BCR Classic early in March and the Corona Mazatlan Classic, both with long putts on the first playoff hole. In the BCR Classic, he trailed by four strokes going into the final round, then dropped a 25-footer at the first playoff hole to beat Jim Rutledge, Omar Uresti and Craig Kanada. It was his first Canadian Tour win. His second, the Corona four stops later, was even more impressive.

Oppenheim trailed by seven in the final round, but forced the issue into a playoff and won with a 15-foot birdie putt on the first playoff hole over Gangluff. "Once you get that first win," said Oppenheim, who turned professional in 2004, "you know the feeling, and it builds your confidence."

Williamson, 26, from Crawfordsville, Indiana, also knows the feeling. He won his first in 2005, then nine months later, in April, he birdied four of his first five holes in the last round, shot 67, and rolled home by five strokes in the Diablo Grande California Classic at Patterson, California.

His win in the Greater Vancouver Charity Classic a few weeks later was considerably tighter and more routine. He did double-bogey No. 1, but retook the lead with three birdies on the front, and at the 18th, he hit over the green but chipped back to within 18 inches. "I've played better and scored worse," Williamson said. "So I'll take this one."

Heffernan, in winning his first in the Casino de Montreal Open at Quatre Domaines Golf Club, stopped the American surge with two daring approach shots and two clutch birdies. He led by a stroke going into the last round, fell behind, and came to the par-five 18th needing a birdie to tie. He powered a three-wood second from 285 yards over the back of the green, chipped to four feet, and holed the birdie putt to tie Brock Mackenzie, of Yakima, Washington. He beat the 18th again in the playoff. He went for the green from 287 yards, bunkered the shot, but got up and down for the winning birdie.

Mike Grob, drawing on his PGA and Nationwide Tour experience, picked off his fourth Canadian title in the Times Colonist Open at Royal Colwood, Victoria. Grob jumped at his chance when fourth-round leader Bret Guetz blew to a double bogey-bogey-bogey start. Grob took a two-stroke lead on a 30-foot birdie putt at the 17th, shot 67, and won by a stroke.

Brian Guetz, 27, brother of Bret, from Sacramento, California, was another first-time winner, taking the Yes! Golf BCR Challenge at Barton Creek in Austin, Texas. And also in a playoff. John Mallinger had birdied the par-five 18th and was already in at nine-under 279. Guetz had to birdie the 18th to tie him—and did. (Their birdies averted a six-way tie for first.) The playoff started and ended at the 18th. Guetz went for the green in two and won with a short birdie putt, while Mallinger's chances ended with an errant drive.

Josh Habig, 29, from Jasper, Indiana, had the longest wait of his life in the final round of the MTS Classic. Trailing by four strokes in the final round, Habig torched Pine Ridge at Winnipeg for an eight-under 63, posted a 13-under 271 total, then had to wait about an hour to see whether fourth-round leader Darren Griff or anyone else could beat it. No one could, and Habig had his first Canadian win by two shots.

Matt Hansen, from Atwater, California, dropped in from the PGA Tour for one Canadian stop—though it was the Northern California Classic at Stockton's Brookside Country Club. It proved profitable. Hansen birdied two of his last three holes for a 69 to tie at 19-under 269 with Mallinger (69), Erik Compton (67) and Jeff Quinney (67), then holed a seven-footer for a birdie and the win on the first playoff hole.

The 2006 season had been a bust for Stuart Anderson. He'd made just three of eight cuts and had only one top-20 finish. But he closed it in style, taking the Canadian Tour Championship. Holding steady with the lead down the final stretch, he finished with a three-under 67 at the damp Highlands course at the Horseshoe Resort in Barrie. It gave him a three-stroke win over fellow Canadian Matt McQuillan, who beat him at his hometown, Edmonton, last year.

And if anyone was looking for a most-likely-to-succeed for 2007, Mallinger should fit the bill. Mallinger, 24, of Long Beach, California, finished second twice—well, he lost back-to-back playoffs—made the cut in his five starts, has not missed a cut in 10 starts over two years, and had six top-10 finishes. If that's not a track record, nothing is.

Tour de las Americas (South America)

Another country heard from. This time, it was Paraguay, a South American country not exactly known as a fountainhead of golf.

What Paraguay didn't count in numbers, it could count in quality. First, there was Carlos Franco breaking through on the PGA Tour, then Julieta Granada stunning the LPGA Tour by taking the first $1 million first prize. And now Fabrizio Zanotti, age 23, surging to the top of the Tour de las Americas, scoring his first victory and winning the 2006 Order of Merit.

"I had been working hard all year and fortunately it paid off," said Zanotti, who closed the season with a huge rush, winning the season-ending Corona Mexico Open and posting four other top-10 finishes in the last six events.

Zanotti had gone three years and 27 starts on the TLA and crashed through in the final round of the Corona Mexico Open with a six-under-par 65 to edge Mexico's Daniel De Leon by a stroke. Zanotti caught fire on the last nine and ran off four straight birdies, beginning with a 10-foot putt at the 11th. "My only worry at that point was to stay cool," Zanotti said, and he did, even at the 14th where he had to rescue his ball from the rough after hitting a tree. His nine-under 275 total put him out of reach. The $49,600 first prize gave him a final $68,789 for the season, more than $24,000 ahead of Argentina's Rafael Echenique, the runner-up on the Order of Merit.

Four others, all from Argentina, also had their first victories—Miguel Carballo, Abierto Movistar de Guatemala; Luciano Giometti, Abierto del Sur Personal; Fabian Gomez, Venezuela Open, and Paulo Pinto, Samsung Brazil Classic.

The Corona Mexico Open, with the top purse on the tour at $310,000, marked the 18th time a TLA tournament was co-sanctioned by the European Challenge Tour, underlining the growing ties between the two tours. "Latin America is producing more players than ever before, and we are proud to help them develop into the stars of tomorrow," said TLA Commissioner Henrique Lavie. "We want them to reach as high as they can. With the support of international organizations such as the European Tour and the R&A, we will keep moving forward in 2007."

Pinto ended up with Juan Ignacio Gil his only challenger in the Samsung Brazil Classic. Gil led Pinto by a stroke going into the final round, but together they led by six shots and five shots, respectively. It was a two-man show, and it didn't really start until the final nine. Gil bogeyed the 10th, letting Pinto have the lead for the first time. Both birdied the 11th, then at the 13th Gil missed a birdie from eight feet but Pinto made his from seven feet and had a two-stroke lead. It was a rocking finish. Pinto missed a three-footer for par at the 16th and his lead was down to one, and when both birdied the last two holes, one was all he needed. "It feels awesome to win," Pinto said.

The tour had its touching moment. Kai Fieberg, age 42, popular founder and promoter of the Costa Rica Open, died from injuries suffered in a car accident in January, just three weeks before the tournament. He was memorialized in the name—the Kai Fieberg Costa Rica Open, also part of the European Challenge Tour. And it had a memorable all-Sweden finish. Sweden's Johan Axgren shot the final nine in five under par for 67 while Argentina's Ariel Canete, the third-round leader, slipped back with 75. Then Sweden's Alexander Noren dropped a 25-foot birdie putt on the final hole to tie Axgren and force the tournament's fourth consecutive playoff. Axgren holed a three-footer at the third extra hole for his third Challenge Tour victory.

The Rookie of the Year race ended up in a shared award between two Argentineans. No one ever made a better debut than Luciano Giometti. He made his in the Abierto del Sur Personal, and won it. And Agustin Jauretche finished third in the Venezuela Open and sixth in the Mexico Open to go with his win in the Salta Open the previous September, part of his rookie year. Jauretche totaled $15,992 and Giometti just $314 less, so the tour named them co-Rookies of the Year.

Echenique, No. 2 on the money list with $44,747, won the Most Improved Player honor and a spot on the European Tour for finishing seventh on the Challenge Tour. Echenique, age 26, won the Argentina Open and tied for fifth place and seventh in only 10 starts. In the Argentina Open, Echenique shook off a three-stroke deficit and closed with 68 for a one-stroke win over two of Argentina's finest, Ricardo Gonzalez and Angel Cabrera.

"Because of what this tournament represents and because of the fans and my family, I believe this is the most important win of my career," Echenique said. Echenique made three consecutive birdies from the second hole, then got a big boost from Gonzalez, who bogeyed the sixth and eighth. Echenique then rolled in a 35-footer for a birdie at the eighth. But Echenique had to earn the win. He bogeyed the 11th hole and double-bogeyed the 15th. They were tied, then Echenique birdied the 16th to take the lead for good.

Just behind Echenique's "most improved" effort, two others made strong enough moves to mark themselves as players to watch—Argentina's Carlos Cardeza and Guatemala's Alejandro Villavicencio. Cardeza, who tied for third at the Mexico Open, climbed 25 spots, to 10th on the Order of Merit. Villavicencio advanced 19 spots, to 17th. He made the cut in the seven events he played and finished third once and 11th twice.

They were all using Argentina's Andres Romero, the TLA's International Player of the Year, as a guiding star. Romero, the TLA Rookie of the Year in 2003 and 14th on the 2005 European Challenge Tour rankings, had a rousing debut year on the European Tour in 2006. He tied for eighth in the Open Championship, second in the Scottish Open and fourth in the Players' Championship of Europe, and was 35th on the European Order of Merit. Cabrera and Gonzalez brought to seven the number of TLA stars on the European Tour for 2007.

The TLA for 2006, which awarded $1,470,000 in prizes, consisted of 15 events held in 10 different countries. In the mix were six national opens, two qualifying schools and the World Cup qualifiers.

10. European Tours

In many ways, summing up European golf in 2006 was much the same as in 2004 and 2002—a stunning Ryder Cup victory but no major champion. The pattern of the early 21st century continued with a third successive triumph against the Americans at The K Club, the second time in a row by an 18½-to-9½ margin. It was an extraordinary week in Ireland. Not only was the quality of the play from the European players of a relentlessly high standard, but the whole atmosphere of the event was a glorious celebration of golf. The spirit between the teams was exactly right and the gallery was loud but respectful, partisan but fair.

Ian Woosnam had a problem perhaps never encountered previously by a European captain. He had 12 players all playing well and many deserved to play more than they did. But the Welshman found the right combinations and kept everyone happy. At one point, in the first series in fact, he left out three players in the top 13 in the world in Luke Donald, David Howell and Henrik Stenson. How Tom Lehman must have wished for such riches? Once more Sergio Garcia and Lee Westwood led the way in terms of points. Like Colin Montgomerie, they raise their games to heights which they have not yet managed in major championships. Above all, it was a week to celebrate the endurance of the human spirit as Darren Clarke stepped out of the shadows of the death of his wife, Heather, to record three points out of three.

There was also emotion at the summer's other great occasion, the return of the Open Championship to Hoylake for the first time in 39 years. Logistically, it all worked, the course was as hard and firm as would be wished for and Tiger Woods produced a sublime exhibition of iron play. He broke down in tears at the end, this his first win since the death of his father, Earl, but it was perhaps a week that reminded the world No. 1 that driver-wedge golf is not the area of the game where he most differentiates himself from the rest of the field. In one respect Hoylake was a disappointment, there being little challenge from the much vaunted British players, while Garcia, without his Ryder Cup putting, was no match for Woods on the final day.

At each of the last three majors a European was in the final pairing. It was Garcia at the Open, Donald, cheekily in red, with Tiger at Medinah and Kenneth Ferrie alongside Phil Mickelson at the U.S. Open. Perhaps surprisingly given the lack of a successor to Tony Jacklin, the U.S. Open represented Europe's best major performance. There were seven Europeans in the top 16, and Padraig Harrington, three bogeys to finish, and Montgomerie, a double bogey at the last, were as devastated as Mickelson in allowing Geoff Ogilvy to take the title.

Harrington gained some compensation by winning the Order of Merit for the first time. Only three men led the money list throughout the season. David Howell did so for longest, thanks to his defeat of Woods at the HSBC Champions event late in 2005 and his triumph at the BMW Championship at Wentworth, otherwise known as the PGA. When Paul Casey won the HSBC World Match Play at Wentworth he overtook Howell. It was his third win of the season, after the Volvo China Open and the Johnnie

Walker Championship, and it was a commanding display. He followed it up with a superb week at the Ryder Cup, including a hole-in-one, but got food poisoning at the Volvo Masters.

Harrington won the Dunhill Links and then finished second at Valderrama—thanks to Sergio Garcia missing a putt that would have given the Spaniard second on his own or a chance of a playoff—to defeat Casey. With two seconds and two thirds previously on the Order of Merit, it was well deserved.

Ultimately, honors were shared as Casey was voted the European Tour Golfer of the Year. It was as much a reward for salvaging his game. During 2005 he had gone for four months without making a cut. He did not qualify for the Masters but will start 2007 as one of those Europeans determined to end the major drought that dates back to Paul Lawrie's Open win at Carnoustie in 1999. Eight Europeans ended the year in the top 20 of the Official World Golf Ranking, unprecedented riches.

Sweden deserve an honorable mention. Johan Edfors arrived on the scene with three victories, including two of the biggest British events, the British Masters and the Scottish Open. A lack of consistency kept him out of the Ryder Cup, but Robert Karlsson and Henrik Stenson both made their debuts at The K Club. They also both won twice, as did Niclas Fasth. Karlsson set a new record for Sweden with a seventh European Tour title. Fasth is not far behind with five, but the suspicion is that Stenson could eclipse them all.

European Tour

The Royal Trophy
Bangkok, Thailand
Winners: Europe

See Asia/Japan Tours chapter.

Abu Dhabi Golf Championship
Abu Dhabi, United Arab Emirates
Winner: Chris DiMarco

If Chris DiMarco had one aim at the start of the 2006 season it was to get back to winning ways. It did not matter where in the world it came. The third, and last, of his three PGA Tour wins in America was the Phoenix Open in 2002. Four years later, DiMarco made the perfect start to the year by winning the inaugural Abu Dhabi Golf Championship, a new tournament on the European Tour and a new venue of Abu Dhabi Golf Club.

DiMarco made a steady start to the event with 71 on a windy opening day but then picked up the pace. The 37-year-old American scored 67 in the second round and then a superb 63 on Saturday, a score that was only bettered by Henrik Stenson's 62, a new course record. The young Swede took the 54-hole lead by one stroke over DiMarco, but it was the challenger who started impressively on the final day.

DiMarco birdied the first hole from six feet and then holed from 20 feet for an eagle at the second. At the short fourth he hit a five iron to four feet for another birdie and in the process had taken control of the tournament. Stenson, despite suffering from a slight back strain and having had a stomach bug earlier in the week, kept fighting, but DiMarco's birdie at the 16th proved a crucial moment. The powerful Stenson reached the par-five 18th in two and two-putted for a birdie, but DiMarco calmly two-putted for his par to win by a single stroke.

DiMarco's closing 67 gave him a 20-under-par total of 268. Stenson's 69 gave the Swede second place ahead of Sergio Garcia, who finished impressively with 66. Colin Montgomerie and Vijay Singh also finished in the top 10. "This is four years to the month since I have been in the winner's circle," said DiMarco, whose wife Amy caddied for him all week.

"Like I said before the start, a win, anywhere, is great and this was an unbelievable field this week."

Commercialbank Qatar Masters
Doha, Qatar
Winner: Henrik Stenson

Moving around the Gulf to Doha for the Commercialbank Qatar Masters, Henrik Stenson would have been reflecting on his fifth second place in two years. One of them came on this Doha course in 2005 when he was runner-up to Ernie Els. The 29-year-old Swede put it right in 2006 by claiming his third European Tour victory, and his first since late in 2004.

Stenson dissipated a little bit of anger at the 307-yard 16th hole on the first day. The short par-four plays as a blind hole due to a huge rock in the middle of the fairway. Stenson went straight over it and left himself only feet away for an eagle. He shared the lead after a first-round 66 with Ricardo Gonzalez of Argentina and was never headed again. He took sole possession of the lead with 68 in the second round, stayed one in front with 71 on a windy Saturday, and then closed with 68 for 15 under par and a three-stroke win over England's Paul Broadhurst.

Stenson closed out the tournament superbly with birdies at the 15th, 17th and 18th. At the 17th he holed from 30 feet and Broadhurst admitted defeat, afterwards calling the Swede "the next special one" from Europe. "The best player on the day won," he added. "I was just trying to hang in there, but his putt on the 17th killed it off. He's got a lot of chances of winning majors and stuff, he's next in the line, I think."

Dubai Desert Classic
Dubai, United Arab Emirates
Winner: Tiger Woods

There are not many places in the world where Tiger Woods has not won and the United Arab Emirates could be struck off the list after the world No. 1 completed victory in the Dubai Desert Classic. Woods had started his season the previous week by winning the Buick Invitational in a playoff in California and the 12-hour time change did not alter the result or the manner of it. Woods defeated Ernie Els at the first extra hole finally to claim a win over the Majlis course at the Emirates club.

Woods had shared the lead with Anders Hansen after 54 holes, thanks to rounds of 67, 66 and 67, but there was nothing inevitable about the victory following despite his almost automatic conversion rate. He struggled on the front nine and the leaderboard was crowed all afternoon. It was Australian left-hander Richard Green, who had upset Greg Norman and Ian Woosnam to win in 1997, who almost stole the trophy away again.

Green made four birdies in five holes to take a one-stroke lead going to the 18th hole. But his drive there finished in the trees, his attempted recovery left him completely stymied behind another tree, and he took a bogey for a 68 and a score of 18 under par. Els, the defending champion, birdied the par-five 18th as so often in the past to record a 67 and get to 19 under par. But Tiger, in the group behind, was not to be outdone. He drove the green at the short par-four 17th to make a birdie and then got up and down from the back fringe for another at the last to tie Els after a 69.

Woods played the 18th perfectly in the playoff, but Els failed to find the fairway. He attempted a four iron from the sand in the trees, but the shot came up just short in the pond in front of the green. He took a bogey and Woods made an easy par. "Today was a day that I'm very proud of, and I hung in there just like I did last week," Tiger said. "I stayed around and made some key putts and some key saves and hit some crucial shots that allowed me to get into a playoff both times."

Johnnie Walker Classic
Perth, Australia
Winner: Kevin Stadler

See Australasian Tour chapter.

Maybank Malaysian Open
Kuala Lumpur, Malaysia
Winner: Charlie Wi

See Asia/Japan Tours chapter.

Enjoy Jakarta HSBC Indonesia Open
Jakarta, Indonesia
Winner: Simon Dyson

See Asia/Japan Tours chapter.

OSIM Singapore Masters
Singapore
Winner: Mardan Mamat

See Asia/Japan Tours chapter.

TCL Classic
Sanya, Hainen Island, China
Winner: Johan Edfors

See Asia/Japan Tours chapter.

Madeira Island Open Caixa Geral de Depositos
Madeira, Portugal
Winner: Jean Van de Velde

The good news for Jean Van de Velde is that there is no water on the final hole of the Santo da Serra course, home to the Madeira Island Open. It plays severely uphill, as you might expect on the mountainous little island, and you can get in a tangle, as the 39-year-old Frenchman proved, but not as disastrously as at the 72nd hole of the 1999 Open Championship at Carnoustie. Then Van de Velde took a triple bogey and then lost a playoff to Paul Lawrie. Since then injury was added to insult as he underwent surgery for a career-threatening knee problem.

The recovery was lengthy, but in 2005 he finished 43rd on the Order of Merit, his best finish for five years. Here in Madeira he claimed his first victory on the European Tour for 13 years, and only the second of his career, the first coming at the 1993 Roma Masters. He recorded rounds of 69, 65, 71 and 68 for a 15-under-par total of 273 and a one-stroke win over England's Lee Slattery.

But that hardly tells the tale. Van de Velde shared the halfway lead and was two ahead of the field with a round to play. He made six birdies on the front nine to go five ahead and added two more coming home. He was four in front standing on the 18th tee, but ahead Slattery birdied the final hole for a second successive 66 and 14 under par. Van de Velde now had three shots in hand. His second shot came up short in a hollow in front of the green. He fluffed his first chip, sent the second 15 feet past the hole, and then two-putted for a double-bogey six.

"I was comfortable at the last and I just had to walk back up the hill, but I made the walk interesting," he said. "I found the nastiest patch of grass on the whole course and I was lucky to get it forward. But if I can't take three from 10 yards off the green, there are going to be some questions asked; I knew a six was going to win it. I wasn't nervous."

Algarve Open de Portugal Caixa Geral de Depositos
Algarve, Portugal
Winner: Paul Broadhurst

Not everyone receives a phone call from the Ryder Cup captain immediately after winning a tournament, but then Ian Woosnam was not phoning in that capacity. He is one of Paul Broadhurst's best friends and it was entirely appropriate to congratulate the 40-year-old Englishman in retaining his Algarve Open de Portugal title. Inevitably it gave Broadhurst the hope of repeating his Ryder Cup appearance of 1991, but Woosie "is a great mate and he just phoned to say well done."

Broadhurst had not won for 10 years when he triumphed in Portugal in 2005 and from the start of the 2006 tournament at Penina he was in fine form. He opened with a course-record-equaling 64 and led for the first two days. A 71 on Saturday meant he slipped one behind Ricardo Gonzalez, but the Argentinean did not maintain his charge on Sunday. Instead, Broadhurst opened the final round with five birdies in the first seven holes and he led by three shots at the turn. A double bogey at the 13th gave the rest a chance, and another Argentinean, Andres Romero, a graduate from the Challenge Tour, closed with 66 to set the clubhouse target at 15 under par.

Anthony Wall then birdied three of the last four holes for 67 to finish at 16 under and Broadhurst had to work for his sixth European Tour title. He birdied the 14th but dropped a shot at the 17th, and at the last, avoiding the trouble on the right, his second shot finished up a bank on the left of the green. It looked like a tricky shot but Broadhurst played it to perfection, the ball only just failing to go in and leaving the simplest of tap-ins for victory. He had closed with 67 for a 271 total, one ahead of Wall, whose second place was his best finish for six years.

Volvo China Open
Beijing, China
Winner: Jeev Milkha Singh

See Asia/Japan Tours chapter.

BMW Asian Open
Shanghai, China
Winner: Gonzalo Fernandez-Castano

See Asia/Japan Tours chapter.

Andalucia Open de Espana Valle Romano
Cadiz, Spain
Winner: Niclas Fasth

On his 34th birthday, Niclas Fasth scored 66 in the third round of the Andalucia Open de Espana Valle Romano. It left the Swede two behind England's David Griffiths going into the final round over the New course at San Roque. The celebrations had to wait for 24 hours but could begin in earnest after Fasth had won a four-hole playoff against John Bickerton to win the fourth title of his career. It was the third in just over a year and all three had come in extra time.

Fasth closed with 69, his worst round of the week, for a total of 270. Bickerton, playing in his 300th European Tour event and enjoying renewed confidence after winning for the first time the previous autumn, was at one point eight shots behind in the final round, but equaled the course record of 63 to set the target at 18 under par. Six players shared third place at 17 under, including Griffiths, Thomas Bjorn, Philip Archer, Mattias Eliasson of Sweden, the leading Spaniard, Jose Manuel Lara, and Scotland's Gary Orr.

Griffiths went to the turn in 39 to let the rest of the field into contention, although he had four birdies coming home to get back into the way for third place. Fasth took control of the tournament to the extent that, even when Bickerton posted the clubhouse lead, he was two clear playing the last two holes. But he took bogeys at both the 17th and 18th holes, so the pair went to a playoff. The first three holes were halved in par at the 18th, so they went to the ninth. Bickerton's second just made it over the water but stuck on the bank by a sponsor's marquee. He took a drop and chipped on, but Fasth had hit his approach with a nine iron to five feet and he holed the putt for a winning birdie.

Telecom Italia Open
Milan, Italy
Winner: Francesco Molinari

Up until now, Francesco Molinari had not been the best golfer in his own family, let alone the whole of Italy. At the age of eight Francesco started playing in his home town of Turin with his parents, grandparents and his older brother, Edoardo. As an amateur he won the Italian Strokeplay title twice, the Italian Matchplay title once and once shared the national foursomes championship with Edoardo. During his rookie season as a professional on the European Tour in 2005, he watched as Edoardo qualified for the Open Championship at St. Andrews—Francesco didn't—and then won the U.S. Amateur Championship at Merion. In April 2006 Francesco caddied for Edoardo as he played in the Masters at Augusta alongside Tiger Woods for the first two rounds.

A month later and Francesco, at 23 two years the junior, achieved something even more momentous in Italian golf. He won the Telecom Italia Open, becoming the first home player to do so for 26 years since Massimo Mannelli in 1980. Edoardo was the first to rush onto the 72nd green and douse his brother in champagne and start the joyful celebrations at Castello di Tolcinasco in Milan.

Molinari was brilliant all week, recording rounds of 68, 65, 67 and 65 for a 23-under-par 265 total and a four-stroke victory over the experienced Scandinavians Anders Hansen and Jarmo Sandelin. The pair scored rounds of 66 and 65 respectively on the final day, but could not catch the Italian. Benn Barham, the young Englishman who tied for the lead going into the last round, fell away after Molinari chipped in for an eagle at the first hole.

He added five birdies, including at the 13th, 15th and 18th after Sandelin had briefly threatened to draw even. He had made only one bogey during the week, a three-putt at the 13th in the first round.

"It's amazing," said Molinari. "I never thought I would win so early in my career. I wanted to bring some joy in Italian golf, but I didn't think that I would do it this year."

Quinn Direct British Masters
Sutton Coldfield, England
Winner: Johan Edfors

A leaderboard headed by the names of Paul Casey, Michael Campbell and Darren Clarke promised much for the final round of the Quinn Direct British Masters. There was no shortage of drama on the Brabazon course at the DeVere Belfry, but it was Sweden's Johan Edfors who proved the surprising winner. An entirely worthy one, however, for it was his second victory in two months and displayed the talent and the strength of mind that marks out a high-class performer.

Edfors, a 30-year-old from Varberg, won the Challenge Tour in 2003, played on the main tour in 2004, but was back on the Challenge Tour the following year. Earning his card for 2006 from the qualifying tournament, Edfors moved his career up a notch by winning the TCL Classic in China. The Roger Federer-lookalike moved it several notches further up with his nerveless performance here. Rounds of 68, 69, 70 and 70 left him at 11 under par and one ahead of Gary Emerson, Jarmo Sandelin and Stephen Gallacher. Campbell and Casey tied for fifth, a further shot back, after rounds of 74 and 76 respectively.

Clarke also fell away in the final round and it was Casey, two ahead of Campbell overnight, who forged clear until it came to the turn. A bogey at the ninth kept him in front, but then at the short par-four 10th he gambled on going for the green with a five wood and found the water. He took a double-bogey six and five players were then tied at the top: Casey, Campbell, Edfors, Gallacher and Sandelin.

Edfors had bogeyed the first hole to fall five behind, but then quietly collected birdies at the third, seventh, 15th and 17th holes. The last put him two ahead and he could afford to take three putts from the fringe at the last for a closing bogey. Casey, who had also bogeyed the 11th in his dreadful run, then bogeyed the last when he was looking for a birdie to tie.

Nissan Irish Open
Maynooth, Co. Kildare, Ireland
Winner: Thomas Bjorn

After experiencing near-misses, like his playoff loss at the 2003 Nissan Irish Open, and disasters aplenty at the nearby K Club, Thomas Bjorn finally won for the first time in Ireland. It was a stunningly tenacious performance by the 35-year-old Dane, who had opened with 78 but then birdied the final two holes of one of the longest weeks of the year to claim a hard-fought victory. Foul weather plagued the event and meant the final round had to be suspended on Sunday afternoon and resumed on Monday morning.

This rescheduling led to an unsettling incident for Darren Clarke. Aiming to become the first home winner of his national Open since John O'Leary in 1982, Clarke had worked himself into the lead when play was suspended overnight. He returned to the course the next morning to find his ball in the rough on the ninth hole, but discovered all the thick, long grass in which his ball had nestled down the evening before had been trampled down. A rules officials said merely this was "rub of the green," but Clarke decided to chip out as he would have done the night before rather than try for the green. He ended up with a bogey and also bogeyed the 16th and 18th holes to lose by two to Bjorn.

"A lot of people had been looking for the ball and a lot of people had flattened the grass around it," Clarke explained. "It was a much better lie than when I left it. I had the opportunity to hit it onto the green, but I felt my conscience wouldn't allow me to do that. So I decided to chip it out like I would have yesterday. Obviously, it was very disappointing to finish like that. I really wanted to win."

Bjorn had been trailing Clarke by two shots at the resumption, but got himself ahead and even. After bogeying the 16th, he came back by birdieing the 17th from 18 feet and then getting a four at the par-five 18th by getting up and down, while his playing partner, Paul Casey, could only three-putt from the front edge.

Bjorn equaled the highest first-round score by an eventual winner, the 78 of George Burns at the 1975 Kerrygold International, but responded by matching the course record on day two with a 66, and then closed with 67 and 72 to win by one over Casey. "You could say this country owes me one," Bjorn said of his ninth tour title. "After the first round I was looking at flight schedules home but then my game came good."

BMW Championship
Virginia Water, Surrey, England
Winner: David Howell

Over the winter, while he was still recuperating from his knee injury, Ernie Els masterminded a number of alternations to the West Course at Wentworth in conjunction with the head greenskeeper, Chris Kennedy. The changes added length, to take the course up to 7,308 yards, and included new bunkering to restore the challenge off the tee as Harry Colt, the original designer, intended. For usually critical professionals, the field at the BMW Championship were largely complimentary. David Howell said before the tournament began: "I think the changes are good and that Ernie has done a good job in general. I saw the majority of the course yesterday and it obviously seems more difficult; longer, tougher, better."

And right up Howell's alley. The 30-year-old Englishman made something of a mockery of the improvements, winning by five strokes over Simon Khan, but only through some stellar golf. A 65 on the second day, after an opening 68, put him three shots in front of the field, and two 69s on the weekend kept him in front. It was his fourth title on the European

Tour but his third in nine months since winning the BMW International in Germany in 2005. The run included a victory against Tiger Woods in the HSBC Champions event.

Howell finished at 17 under par, and birdies at the second, fourth and fifth quickly saw off the challenge of his playing partner, Miguel Angel Jimenez, who finished third after 72, with Brett Rumford in fourth and Richard Bland fifth. Khan finished with two birdies in a 68 to sneak one ahead of Jimenez in second place. Howell's only bogey on the final day came at the short 10th, but there were no alarms and he picked up one more shot at the par-five 12th.

Howell moved into the top 10 on the Official World Golf Ranking for the first time. He was also the first Englishman to win what was formerly called the PGA Championship since Nick Faldo won his fourth title in 1989.

Celtic Manor Wales Open
Newport, South Wales
Winner: Robert Karlsson

While the Ryder Cup course at Celtic Manor was being redeveloped ahead of the 2010 match, the Wales Open was once again played on the par-69 Roman Road course. Once again the result was some spectacular scoring from the moment Phillip Archer had a chance to shoot 59 on the first morning. The 34-year-old Englishman from Warrington had bogeyed the fourth hole but then had five birdies in a row from the fifth. He had 10 in all, then made a good putt to save par at the 17th before reaching the last. His approach shot with a wedge finished seven feet away, but the putt was downhill and right to left. He thought he had made the putt, started to turn away to celebrate, but then the ball clipped the left side of the hole and stayed out. "I read it perfectly but just hit it a little bit too hard," Archer said. "I was nervous at the end, but not over the putt. Everything was focused on it. It's a bittersweet way to end a great round."

His was the 13th round of 60 on the European Tour but it might have been the first 59. Ironically, Adrien Mork had shot the first 59 on the European Challenge Tour the week before. Archer did not go on to win the title, but Robert Karlsson, who opened with a 61, did. Rounds of 63 and 65 gave the Swede the records for the lowest 36-hole (124) and 54-hole (189) totals on the European Tour. Anything under par on the final day would have given him the all-time tournament record, but he closed with 71 for a total of 260, 16 under. He had led by six with a round to play and won by three over Paul Broadhurst, with Jose-Filipe Lima in third and Colin Montgomerie fourth. Archer finished fifth.

To make sure there was no doubt about the result, the tall Swede birdied the 13th, 15th and 16th and could then afford to bogey the last two holes. It was his sixth win on the European Tour, but came four years, and 100 tournaments, since the last one. "When I saw the leaderboard on the 17th, I had a big smile on my face," Karlsson said.

BA-CA Golf Open
Vienna, Austria
Winner: Markus Brier

Something seemed to suggest it was Markus Brier's week. He holed in one during the first round and holed another approach shot for an eagle-two during the third round. That the 38-year-old from Vienna should win the BA-CA Golf Open presented by Austrian Telecom may have been preordained. This was the first time the European Tour had returned to Austria for 10 years. It was a celebratory week with Brier playing on his home course of Fontana, just outside Vienna. Certainly the celebrations were mighty as Brier became the first player from his country to win on the European Tour.

Perhaps he had the advantage of having won the title twice, in 2002 and 2004, when it was a Challenge Tour event. Brier had been the first Austrian to play on the European Tour and the seven-year wait for a maiden victory was worthwhile. He led all week, albeit tied with Simon Dyson after 36 holes. With a round to play he was one in front, but two early bogeys meant he had to fight all the way. Colin Montgomerie had been six behind, but got five of those shots back before inexplicably dropping five shots in four holes from the 11th.

Dyson briefly caught Brier, but the Austrian birdied the ninth to go in front again. Then Denmark's Soren Hansen made four successive birdies from the eighth to draw even before bogeying the 16th. Now the pressure was off and Brier was cheered on by the large gallery. Rounds of 65, 67, 66 and 68 gave him an 18-under total of 266 and a three-shot win over Hansen. Dyson finished third, with Richard Green fourth and Montgomerie eventually finishing 13 shots behind after a 75.

Aa St. Omer Open
Lumbres, France
Winner: Cesar Monasterio

Cesar Monasterio came from five strokes behind with a round to play to win the Aa St. Omer Open and earn an exemption on the European Tour. The event is co-sanctioned with the Challenge Tour, but Monasterio took advantage to earn his playing rights on the full tour until the end of 2007. The 42-year-old from Argentina won on the Challenge Tour in Guatemala in 2005, but finished only 30th on the Order of Merit. The Aa St. Omer Open allows both full tour members and Challenge Tour players to compete against each other in the week of the U.S. Open.

Sweden's Henrik Nystrom was the third-round leader by two strokes over Martin Maritz of South Africa. But Nystrom took a double bogey at the first hole and Maritz became the frontrunner. Until, that is, Monasterio made a terrific move by birdieing the sixth hole, eagling the seventh and birdieing the eighth and 11th holes. He now led but dropped a shot at the 15th to fall into a tie with Maritz, only for the South African to bogey the 16th. At the same moment, Monasterio was playing the last hole and had a difficult lie in a greenside bunker. With a brilliant recovery he splashed to 10 feet and then holed the putt to save par.

Monasterio had rounds of 68, 68, 71 and 71 to be 10 under par. Maritz could not birdie either of the last two holes and finished one behind, with Nystrom birdieing the 18th to tie for second place. Juan Parron, of Spain, and Jean Hugo shared fourth place. "I was having a good season, but now it has become a great season," said Monasterio, who was draped in the Argentinean flag by his compatriots during the celebrations afterwards.

Johnnie Walker Championship at Gleneagles
Perthshire, Scotland
Winner: Paul Casey

Colin Montgomerie celebrated his 43rd birthday in style by shooting his second successive 68 and taking the halfway lead. But a week after losing out at the 72nd hole at the U.S. Open, Monty could not convert a victory here in front of his home supporters. Instead, Paul Casey made a raid from south of the border to win the Johnnie Walker Championship at Gleneagles.

His 66 in the third round took him from two behind Montgomerie to one in front, and Casey quickly dampened the threat from his final-round playing partner, and the enthusiasm of the gallery, by birdieing the first three holes. This was an important victory for the 28-year-old Englishman after his near-misses at the British Masters and the Irish Open when he had failed to complete the job after playing fine golf all week. Casey said: "It wasn't frustrating not to win, but I didn't want to continue to finish second or worse, because I think I am capable of winning golf events and I don't want to be seen as somebody who cannot finish them off. Therefore it was satisfying to finish it off today."

This was Casey's sixth win on the European Tour, the first having also come at Gleneagles in 2001. It was his first win of 2006, but his second on the 2005-06 European Tour after his win at the China Open the previous November. It was also his first win in Britain for three years and narrowed his deficit to David Howell at the top of the Order of Merit.

Casey came home in 38, one over par, to close with 72 and a one-stroke win at 16 under par. Montgomerie bogeyed the 15th and 17th as his challenge fizzled out. Later he bemoaned playing two of the par-fives, the ninth and the 18th, in even par and one over respectively. Monty shared fourth place with Thomas Bjorn, one behind the co-runners-up Andrew Marshall and Soren Hansen. The Dane, Hansen, was suffering from severe back pain on the final day and flew home afterwards to seek treatment.

Open de France ALSTOM
Paris, France
Winner: John Bickerton

There were celebrations aplenty for the 100th anniversary of the Open de France ALSTOM, but John Bickerton would have been happy to make the finish to this year's event as dull as possible. That was not to be the case, as the closing four holes at Le Golf National again provided plenty of drama. Bickerton arrived at the 15th tee three shots ahead of the field, but after misjudging the wind with his second shot, he found the water and took a double bogey.

Padraig Harrington had posted a total of 274, 10 under par, thanks to a 66, matching the best score of the day. Now Bickerton was only one shot ahead of Harrington, while his playing partner, Michael Campbell, also got within one by birdieing the short 16th. But Bickerton would not succumb to the pressure. He got up and down for a par at the 17th and safely two-putted for another par at the last. Water again threatens at the 18th, and this time Campbell found it to take a double bogey.

Bickerton deserved his victory after opening with a 63, one outside the course record, and then adding rounds of 70, 71 and 69 for a total of 273. Campbell took the lead away from him after the third round, even though the New Zealander took a triple-bogey seven at the 17th. He might have ended up with a nine after a bizarre rules incident involving a woman spectator kicking his ball back into play as it was headed for some merchandising tents. Campbell played the hole out for two holes before the ruling could be completed, but on the final day the 2005 U.S. Open champion struggled and he finished tied for third with Ian Poulter and Marcus Fraser.

Instead, Bickerton took control with birdies at the fourth, 11th, 12th and 14th. After Harrington's charge finished with the Irishman making birdies at the last two holes, the 36-year-old Bickerton clung on for his second tour title, the first having come the previous October in the Canaries.

Smurfit Kappa European Open
Straffan, Co. Kildare, Ireland
Winner: Stephen Dodd

Having found the key to winning late in his career, Stephen Dodd appeared not to have lost it by snatching the Smurfit Kappa European Open from a congested leaderboard. The win came a week before the Welshman's 40th birthday and was his third after winning his first in China in 2004. It was also a second title in as many seasons in Ireland after he won the 2005 Irish Open.

With the Ryder Cup due to be played on the more famous Palmer Course at The K Club later in the year, the tournament was switched to the newer Smurfit Course for only the second time. The more exposed layout was buffeted by strong winds, but Dodd used all his phlegmatic composure to await his moment. It came when he birdied the 16th and 17th holes to win by two strokes over Anthony Wall and Jose Manuel Lara.

Dodd recorded rounds of 67, 69, 73 and 70 for a nine-under score of 279. He started the final round two behind Lara, who closed with 74, while Wall, Lara's playing partner, had 73 after holing from 35 feet at the last. The putt stole a place at the Open Championship at Hoylake for Wall which would otherwise have gone to Lara if the Spaniard had finished as the sole runner-up. Paul McGinley shared fourth place after heading to the airport on Friday afternoon convinced he had missed the cut. Rounds of 67 and 69 shot him up the leaderboard alongside Lee Westwood, Jeev Milkha Singh, Simon Khan and Graeme Storm.

Barclays Scottish Open
Glasgow, Scotland
Winner: Johan Edfors

Loch Lomond in summer is a beautiful place for a celebration, which was why Johan Edfors brought over most of his family and even a Swedish chef for a week at the Barclays Scottish Open. While his father's 60th birthday and his brother-in-law's 40th birthday were duly marked in style, Edfors saved the best present until last as he won his third title of the season. After winning at the Belfry in May, this was a second high-profile victory in Britain for the 30-year-old.

It was achieved in remarkable fashion as he started six strokes behind the third-round co-leaders, Darren Clarke and Thomas Bjorn. He also started almost two hours ahead of the leaders, so they must have been somewhat shocked to find their advantage wiped out by the time they teed off, Edfors having gone to the turn in 30.

Edfors had started the tournament well with rounds of 65 and 69, but had been furious with himself after a 74 on Saturday. His run of brilliant golf continued as he birdied the 12th, 13th and 14th holes. He dropped a shot at the short 17th, which might have been crucial, but after a closing 63, he still set a demanding clubhouse target at 13 under par.

Neither Bjorn nor Clarke could reach it as they both had 72s to finish tied for fifth, alongside South African defending champion Tim Clark and England's Benn Barham. With only limited appearances during the year as he cared for his sick wife, Clarke continued to play some extraordinary golf but once again struggled on the final day.

Luke Donald's 66 and a 67 from Charl Schwartzel put them at 11 under, but the only player who seemed able to catch Edfors was the Argentinean Andres Romero. He birdied the 14th and 15th to send Edfors to the practice range for a possible playoff, but Romero bogeyed the 18th to fall back into a tie for second place, two behind Edfors. He did, however, secure both an exemption for the Open at Hoylake and his card for 2007.

The Open Championship
Hoylake, England
Winner: Tiger Woods

See Chapter 4.

Deutsche Bank Players' Championship of Europe
Hamburg, Germany
Winner: Robert Karlsson

Just as he did at Celtic Manor a couple of months before, Robert Karlsson excelled in a low-scoring week to win the Deutsche Bank Players' Championship of Europe. He did so with a tournament-record score of 25 under par at Gut Kaden. His second win of the season took him to third on the Order of Merit and into the world's top 50. It was his seventh victory, the most by a Swede on the European Tour. The previous record had been six by Anders Forsbrand.

It also virtually assured the 36-year-old of a place on the European Ryder Cup team. He certainly left an impression on captain Ian Woosnam when they were paired together in the final group of the third round: Karlsson birdied five of the first seven holes. The tall Swede is never afraid to go low when his game is in sync, and after years of being too hard on himself for his errors, Karlsson seemed to have unlocked the secret of allowing his best golf to shine through more often.

Going into the final round he was two ahead of Lee Westwood, and the Englishman immediately birdied the first. But a double bogey at the fourth halted his charge, and though others threatened throughout the day, none could get on terms with the Swede. Karlsson continued to post birdies at will, at the third, sixth, seventh, 11th, 13th, 15th and 17th before a inconsequential double bogey at the last.

His closing 67, after rounds of 64, 66 and 66, gave him a score of 263 and a four-stroke win over Westwood and Charl Schwartzel. Retief Goosen was another stroke back, sharing fourth place with Graeme McDowell, Emanuele Canonica and Andres Romero.

EnterCard Scandinavian Masters
Malmo, Sweden
Winner: Marc Warren

When Robert Karlsson led by four shots during the final round of the EnterCard Scandinavian Masters, a second victory in successive weeks and a first triumph on home soil appeared almost certain. But Karlsson's wonderful run abruptly ended when he met Marc Warren. The 25-year-old from Scotland hit a brilliant shot from the trees at the last hole to force a playoff and then won his maiden title on the European Tour.

Warren is no stranger to such tense moments. He holed the winning putt for Great Britain and Ireland at the Walker Cup in 2001. In 2005 he led the Challenge Tour with two victories, both achieved in playoffs. Not for him the fate of the previous three Challenge Tour leaders who all failed to retain their cards.

Karlsson, after his win in Germany the previous week, was suffering, rather than celebrating, with a heavy cold and nosebleeds. He started the week slowly, but in the third round, on a day of strong, swirling winds, he set a new course record at Barseback of 63. It was three shots better than anyone else in the field could manage and 10 shots better than Warren, who was two shots behind.

Warren's chances hardly improved when he three-putted at both the sixth and seventh holes. But, far from amused with himself, Warren then added four birdies in the next 11 holes. He closed with 69 for a 10-under score of 278, while Karlsson shot 71, bogeying the 17th hole. At the 18th, Warren's drive found the trees, but spotting a gap and unleashing a seven iron as if he was Seve Ballesteros in his prime, he put his second to six feet and holed the putt.

In the playoff, both players bogeyed the 18th at the first attempt before

Warren won with a par the next time around. South African Richard Sterne finished in third place, one shot outside the playoff, despite nearly missing his tee time on Saturday after becoming trapped in his hotel elevator for an hour.

KLM Open
Zandvoort, Netherlands
Winner: Simon Dyson

Simon Dyson had built up quite a reputation for winning in Asia. He won three times on the Asian Tour and when he claimed his first European Tour event it came in a co-sanctioned event at the Indonesian Open earlier in 2006. But a second win of the season, and a first in Europe, at the KLM Open was a prized achievement for the 28-year-old Yorkshireman. From a sporting family—his grandfather was a jockey and his uncle a footballer—Dyson played in the 1999 Walker Cup before turning professional.

At Kennemer he beat Australian left-hander Richard Green in a playoff. The pair had both swept past third-round leader Damian McGrane with spectacular final rounds, a 66 from Dyson and a 65 from Green. They both had stunning weekends, in fact, with Dyson scoring a brace of 66s while Green broke the course record by two strokes with a 62 on Saturday. Ireland's McGrane was three ahead of the field overnight but closed with 70 to finish one shot outside the playoff. Green, birdieing two of the last three holes, and Dyson, birdieing three of the last four, finished at 14 under par.

In the playoff, at the 18th hole, Dyson made a birdie-four by chipping to 12 feet and holing the putt for an impressive victory. "My first win felt special, but this one means so much more because of winning in Europe," Dyson said.

Green recorded his sixth second-place finish on the European Tour since winning the Dubai Classic in 1997. "I've given it as good an effort over the weekend as I could," Green said. "I know I'm now playing good enough to win another tournament soon." Players wore black armbands in the final round as a mark of respect following the death of Darren Clarke's wife Heather from cancer earlier in the morning.

Imperial Collection Russian Open
Moscow, Russia
Winner: Alejandro Canizares

Alejandro Canizares, the 23-year-old son of six-time European Tour winner Jose Maria, showed he could follow in his father's footsteps by winning the Imperial Collection Russian Open at Le Meridien Moscow Country Club. Canizares became the quickest affiliate member to win on the main tour by triumphing in only his third start. It took both Sergio Garcia, in 1999, and Graeme McDowell, in 2002, four attempts to get their maiden wins.

Canizares did it in a certain style with outstanding rounds of 66, 67, 67 and 66 for a 22-under-par total of 266. He won by four strokes over

Scotland's David Drysdale, who had 62 in the first round but closed with 69, and by five over defending champion Mikael Lundberg and Gary Murphy.

Drysdale, who played with Canizares in the final round, said: "You can't take anything away from him today, he played brilliantly. I started one behind him and levelled with him at one stage, but he never flinched. Some of his iron play was awesome."

"This is unbelievable," said Canizares. "This means everything. I was trying to get my card through exemptions and now I have done it by winning my third event, so this is way beyond my expectations."

BMW International Open
Munich, Germany
Winner: Henrik Stenson

With no dramatic late changes to the qualifying positions for the European Ryder Cup team, as so often happen every other year at Eichenried, Henrik Stenson produced plenty of drama in winning the BMW International Open. Stenson won his second title of the year in a playoff over Padraig Harrington and Retief Goosen with an eagle at the par-five 18th hole.

The trio tied at the end of 72 holes at 15 under par. Goosen set the target by making an eagle himself, holing from five feet for 67. Stenson then posted a 68, making up for a bogey at the 17th with a birdie-four at the last. Then Harrington came to the 18th with the chance to win but put his second shot into a bunker. After coming out to 12 feet he could not hole the putt. He scored 69 to join the playoff, which should also have included David Howell. The defending champion had forged ahead with rounds of 67, 69 and 66, but he closed with 72 and missed from three feet for a birdie at the last which would have got him into the playoff. He shared fourth place with Martin Erlandsson.

Back at the 18th again, Harrington found thick rough off the tee, but Stenson and Goosen were both in the fairway. The South African could not quite match his effort in regulation but found the middle of the green, pin high. Stenson hit a wonderful approach with a five iron, although it needed the gentlest of kicks off a mound to send it to four feet from the hole. He holed and the others could not match him.

"I thought I had better put it away after missing that short one on the 17th in regulation," Stenson said. "I didn't want to make the same mistake. I tugged my second shot in the playoff, but it seemed to bounce off the mound. Sometimes you need the breaks like that and it certainly feels good right now."

As well as three of the top five players, two other team members showing good form were Luke Donald and Colin Montgomerie, who shared sixth place. After the event, Ryder Cup captain Ian Woosnam announced Darren Clarke and Lee Westwood as his two wild card picks.

Omega European Masters
Crans Montana, Switzerland
Winner: Bradley Dredge

Bradley Dredge seemed to be playing a different course from everyone else at the Omega European Masters, and that included Michelle Wie. The young American had long since missed the cut when Dredge collected his second title on the European Tour. The first came at the Madeira Island Open in 2003, and although he added the World Cup title for Wales with Stephen Dodd in 2005, his improved play in recent seasons had not been reflected in the wins column. But up the mountain at Crans-sur-Sierre, Dredge just got better and better. He shared the halfway lead, was two in front after three rounds, but won by eight shots, the largest winning margin on the tour in 2006.

Dredge posted rounds of 68, 67, 65 and 67 for a 17-under-par total of 267. Francesco Molinari, in his best finish since winning the Italian Open, and Germany's Marcel Siem, the closest challenger overnight, finished at nine under par. "Bradley's score is unbelievable," said Molinari, "as there is so much trouble out there." Molinari might have claimed second place on his own but for a double bogey at the 15th. By then Dredge was long gone as he birdied the first three holes and dropped only one shot on the last day, at the 16th. Sergio Garcia, the defending champion and a resident of the Swiss resort, finished tied for fourth, nine behind, with Soren Kjeldsen and Marc Warren.

Dredge was congratulated at the prize ceremony by 1972 Apollo 17 mission commander Eugene Cernan, the last man to step foot on the moon and an ambassador for the tournament sponsors. "I'm over the moon I have won again," Dredge said.

Wie was playing in a European Tour event for the first time. But her former composure when playing against the men deserted her in the mountain air as the 16-year-old struggled to rounds of 78 and 79, finishing last of the non-qualifiers.

HSBC World Match Play
Virginia Water, Surrey, England
Winner: Paul Casey

See Chapter 7.

Banco Madrid Valle Romano Open de Madrid Masters
Madrid, Spain
Winner: Ian Poulter

Ian Poulter's disappointment at not qualifying for the Ryder Cup team was taken out on the field as he sauntered to a five-stroke win at the Banco Madrid Valle Romano Open de Madrid Masters. It was his seventh European Tour title but his first win since the Volvo Masters in 2004. It also put him back in the top 50 on the Official World Golf Ranking.

After opening with rounds of 67 and 66 at La Moraleja II, Poulter put in a brilliant 64 in the third round to take a four-stroke lead. On the final day he was never threatened and closed with 69 for a 22-under-par score of 266. Spain's Ignacio Garrido scored 66 to take second place, with Phillip Price a further shot behind and Padraig Harrington sharing fourth place with Christian L. Nilsson.

"I came here to do the job and it's good to come and do it," he said. "Today was difficult because I had the four-shot lead. I just had to keep hitting fairways and greens and roll a few putts in, which I did, and managed to keep myself well in front. I was cruising really."

As the last event before the Ryder Cup at The K Club, there was much attention on Darren Clarke. The Irishman was playing for the first time since the Open Championship two months earlier and was making his first public appearance since the death of his wife Heather. After a naturally emotional press conference, Clarke scored 68 in the first round and ended the week tied for 31st place at seven under par. "I didn't quite finish as I would want, but I know my game is in decent shape," Clarke said.

The Ryder Cup
Straffan, Co. Kildare, Ireland
Winners: Europe

See Chapter 8.

WGC - American Express Championship
Hertfordshire, England
Winner: Tiger Woods

In the week that Byron Nelson passed away at the age of 94, there was no escaping the talk of streaks. In 1945 Nelson won 11 tournaments in a row. His legend was such that he remained the first gentleman of golf 60 years after his retirement. There were probably those playing at The Grove, a new Kyle Phillips-designed course in the northwest outskirts of London, who would not mind Tiger Woods retiring. No chance. Woods led from start to finish to complete an eight-stroke victory over Ian Poulter and Adam Scott at the WGC - American Express Championship.

It was Tiger's sixth successive victory in a stroke-play event, although he did not consider it a sixth successive win as he had lost in the first round of the HSBC World Match Play Championship two weeks earlier. (There had also been the little matter of a defeat for America in the Ryder Cup the previous week.) But in terms of the PGA Tour, this was Tiger's sixth win in a row, something he also achieved in 1999-2000. While Woods finished 2006 two-thirds of the way to overhauling Jack Nicklaus's record of 18 major championships, he felt Nelson's mark was still well out of reach.

"What Byron did was absolutely remarkable," Tiger said. "If you look at it, I'm barely halfway there. Let's talk about it if the day ever comes when I get close. At the moment I'm just thrilled I've been able to win six in a row twice." This was Tiger's fifth win in seven stagings of this tournament and his 12th individual win at a World Golf Championship event. "You would think that he would lose a bit of motivation in these things by now, wouldn't you?" marveled Padraig Harrington. Apparently not.

About the only thing undecided when Woods reached the 72nd hole—in the autumnal gloaming after two interruptions of play during the final round—was whether he could eagle the 18th for the fourth day running. On the first day, he holed from 20 feet to set a new course record of 63 and jump over Harrington and Poulter into the lead. On the second day, playing it as his ninth, he hit a three wood to 10 feet during a 64 that put him five ahead of the field. On Saturday, he kept the run going by holing from 33 feet for a 67 and a six-shot lead.

On Sunday, three birdies in the first 10 holes ensured only the weather could beat him. By the time he got to the 18th, he was more than happy to take his two-putt birdie and sign for a 67 and a 23-under-par total of 261. Poulter closed with a 66 but had to settle for a tie for second after Scott got up and down at the last. Jim Furyk was fourth and Ernie Els fifth.

Alfred Dunhill Links Championship
St. Andrews, Scotland
Winner: Padraig Harrington

When Padraig Harrington won the Alfred Dunhill Links Championship in 2002, he did so only after a playoff with Eduardo Romero at the second extra hole. This victory in the same tournament four years later was a less hectic affair and the 35-year-old Irishman got to enjoy the full splendor of walking up the famous 18th fairway of the Old Course with a triumph assured. "I have a big picture of the 18th hole at St. Andrews on one wall at home, and so I look at it every day I'm there," Harrington said. "To see that scene before me on the 18th tee this afternoon and to walk up the fairway knowing that I was going to win the tournament was something to savor. There is no more special place than this."

Harrington was the only player to record four scores in the 60s at an event which for the first three days is played across three courses: Carnoustie, Kingsbarns and the Old Course at St. Andrews. He started the final round one behind Welshman Bradley Dredge, but 68 was more than good enough for a five-stroke victory over Dredge, who closed with 74, Anthony Wall and American Edward Loar.

The crucial moment came at the short 11th, where Harrington claimed a birdie but Dredge found sand for a double-bogey five and a three-shot swing. Harrington finished at 16 under par for his 10th European Tour title and his first in two years. Ernie Els eagled the 18th to finish alone in fifth place. Paul Casey shared sixth place to retain his place at the top of the Order of Merit, but Harrington's victory made it possible for him to overhaul the Englishman in the final two events of the season.

It was a double celebration for Harrington because, as in 2002, he also won the team competition with amateur J.P. McManus, the Irish businessman and racehorse owner. They won at 35 under par by five strokes over Angel Cabrera and his son, Federico.

Mallorca Classic
Mallorca, Spain
Winner: Niclas Fasth

After winning the Alfred Dunhill Links Championship, Padraig Harrington changed his schedule to include the Mallorca Classic. In order to do so, he went out to the Mediterranean island, practiced at Pula, then returned for a company day at Wentworth in England on the Wednesday and then got back in time to start the tournament. Not surprisingly, perhaps, he missed the cut. Now the Irishman's only chance to overhaul Paul Casey would be at the Volvo Masters.

Harrington's early departure left the stage clear for the rest of the field, and Niclas Fasth, having already won the Spanish Open, completed an Iberian double with a three-stroke victory over Sergio Garcia. Fasth shared the lead for the first three rounds with scores of 66, 71 and 70 and the 34-year-old Swede closed with 68 for a five-under-par total of 275. In the previous three years of the tournament, only Spaniards had won, and Garcia took the title in 2004, but his 68, while lifting him out of the pack, could not dent Fasth's path to a fifth European Tour title.

Fasth played two superb approach shots, for his third at the par-five 10th after a poor tee shot and then at the 14th from the rough to a green guarded by water. Both produced birdies and the second re-established his three-shot lead after Garcia had birdied the short 13th, almost holing in one. Jose Manuel Lara shared third place with Marc Warren, while Peter O'Malley was fifth.

Ireland's Gary Murphy entered the week 118th on the Order of Merit—the last spot to retain a card—and shared the lead with Fasth going into the final round. A 76 dropped him down to 13th but ensured his playing rights.

Volvo Masters
Sotegrande, Spain
Winner: Jeev Milkha Singh

Not just this tournament but the whole season hinged on Sergio Garcia missing a putt on the 18th green. In terms of the Volvo Masters, it meant Jeev Milkha Singh could afford to bogey the last but still claim the biggest prize of his career. In terms of the season, it took the Vardon Trophy away from Paul Casey and gave it to Padraig Harrington. Having failed to narrow the gap with Casey at the top of the Order of Merit in Mallorca, Harrington arrived at Valderrama claiming he had never done well at the course. But he got some help when Casey suffered from food poisoning on Wednesday night. Casey scored 76 in the first round, during which he was sick on the course, and although he recovered with rounds of 72, 71 and 69 to finish in 21st place, Harrington, David Howell and Robert Karlsson could all eclipse him on the final day.

Harrington it was who produced a superb run, coming home in 33 for a 69 and one under par. Over the last four holes he was incredible, birdieing the 15th and 16th holes and then saving par after he had gone in the water at the 17th and after missing the fairway at the 18th. Then the Irishman could only wait. Luke Donald had finished on the same mark, but they only rose into a tie for second place—where Harrington needed to be to dethrone Casey—when Garcia bogeyed the 18th from a bunker. He finished just €35,252 (or £23,616) ahead of Casey. "Over the last few holes every thing went right for me," Harrington said. "I was willing the ball into the hole."

The 34-year-old Singh was the first Indian to play in the Volvo Masters, let alone win it. The son of an Olympic sprinter, Singh bogeyed the 12th and 13th holes, but ahead Garcia was bogeying the 13th and 14th. The crucial shot was at the 17th, where Singh hit a six iron from 205 yards over the water to 12 feet and two-putted for a par. It gave him a two-shot lead and meant he could take a five at the last. He recorded rounds of 71, 71, 68 and 72 for a winning score of two under par.

Singh, who won the China Open earlier in the year under the same sponsors, said: "This is the biggest victory of my career so far and is going to stay with me for the rest of my life. It means a lot to me. I think this is going to be big for Indian golf. I feel more sponsors will come out and more kids will try to make a career from the sport."

HSBC Champions
Shanghai, China
Winner: Y.E. Yang

See Asia/Japan Tours chapter.

UBS Hong Kong Open
Fanling, Hong Kong
Winner: Jose Manuel Lara

See Asia/Japan Tours chapter.

MasterCard Masters
Melbourne, Australia
Winner: Justin Rose

See Australasian Tour chapter.

Blue Chip New Zealand Open
Auckland, New Zealand
Winner: Nathan Green

See Australasian Tour chapter.

Alfred Dunhill Championship
Mpumalanga, South Africa
Winner: Alvaro Quiros

See African Tours chapter.

WGC - Barbados World Cup
St. James, Barbados
Winners: Germany (Bernhard Langer and Marcel Siem)

See American Tours chapter.

South African Airways Open
Port Elizabeth, South Africa
Winner: Ernie Els

See African Tours chapter.

Challenge Tour

There was no doubting the performance of the season on the European Challenge Tour came from 26-year-old Frenchman Adrien Mork. He became the first player in any European Tour-sanctioned event, whether on the regular tour, the Challenge Tour or the Seniors Tour, to score a 59. It came in the second round of the Tikida Hotels Agadir Moroccan Classic. Starting on the back nine, Mork birdied the 10th and had five more birdies in an "outward" 29. After a par at the first, any hope of history seemed to disappear with a double bogey at the second. But he then eagled the par-five third and birdied the remaining six holes. It was at the eighth he first started thinking about 59, but at the ninth he calmly pitched to three feet and holed the putt.

Now, those are the kinds of putts you want for a 59," Mork said. "I just made sure that I wasn't going to miss it—there was no chance that I was missing that one. It feels like a dream to have done this. I honestly can't describe the way I feel because I do not think I fully realize what I have done yet, I just feel great, but also quite numb. I had never been that close to a 59 before, and this is certainly the best I have ever played, and it is an honor to break so many records for European golf."

After an opening 63, Mork was at 20 under par, the lowest 36-hole score in European golf, and his 19 birdies were also a record for two rounds. The next day, Mork was 15 shots worse off in a 74, but in the manner of a fine competitor, he closed with a 69 to win by one stroke. Tied with two holes to play, he birdied the 17th and then two-putted at the par-three 18th, knocking in a three-footer for the victory. Mork emphasized that he was not just a one-week wonder by also winning the OKI Mahou Challenge de Espana. Sweden's Johan Axgren was the only other player to win twice during the season, at the Kai Fieberg Costa Rica Open and the Tusker Kenya Open.

But Axgren was knocked off the top of the Order of Merit due to a late run from Wales' Mark Pilkington. Not only did he win the Kazakhstan Open and the biggest prize ever offered on the Challenge Tour of €48,000, but Pilkington took second place at the season-ending Apulia San Domenico Grand Final. Pilkington topped the money list with €119,152, with Axgren and fellow Swede Alexander Noren finishing second and third.

The only player at the Grand Final to jump into the top 20 places on the Order of Merit who gained cards for the main tour in 2007 was Englishman James Hepworth. He won by two stokes over Pilkington, Noren and Rafael Echenique of Argentina. Mork finished 20th on the Order of Merit, gaining the last of the available cards. Alvaro Quiros, of Spain, who was 18th on the rankings, soon found success on the main circuit by winning the Alfred Dunhill Championship in South Africa at the end of the year.

11. Asia/Japan Tours

Little wonder that Shingo Katayama dominated the Japan Tour and walked off with his third straight money-winning championship and fourth of his career in 2006. For one, he won more tournaments—three—than any other player. More impressively, though, the 33-year-old was fifth or better in 14 of his 20 starts as he piled up ¥178,402,190 in earnings on the circuit and in four World Golf Championship events. After his first No. 1 year of 2000, Katayama never wandered far from the top of the list, finishing second, third and fourth the next three seasons before leading the pack in 2004, 2005 and 2006.

Four other players picked up pairs of victories during 2006. One was Hideto Tanihara, who made a successful return to Japan after a nondescript year on the U.S. PGA Tour in 2005. His two wins helped boost him into second place on the money list. Another double victor was India's Jeev Milkha Singh, who won the last two tournaments of the season—Casio and Japan Series—and was one of eight overseas players who landed titles during the year. The others were three Australians (Wayne Perske, Brendan Jones and Paul Sheehan), two South Koreans (S.K. Ho and Y.E. Yang), Taiwan's Yeh Wei-tze and Ireland's Padraig Harrington, who beat Tiger Woods in a playoff at the Dunlop Phoenix tournament, the tour's showpiece. Sheehan won the Japan Open, Tomohiro Kondo the Japan PGA and Tatsuhiko Takahashi the Tour Championship.

Perhaps the most impressive accomplishments of 2006 were achieved by Tsuneyuki (Tommy) Nakajima, the 52-year-old all-time great of Japanese golf. Nakajima not only won on the regular tour—the Taiheiyo Club Masters—but also swept the Japan Senior Open and Senior PGA, the two majors on the Japan Senior Tour.

The Asian Tour continued to grow as a presence on the world stage, reaching 27 tournaments and US$24 million in prize money. It seemed to be making good on its new slogan—Changing the Face of Golf. "The achievements on and off the course during 2006 were beyond our greatest expectations," said Kyi Hla Han, the Asian Tour's executive chairman. "We confirmed ourselves as the fastest growing circuit in the world with a record number of tournaments offering more money than ever before. The players, led by Jeev Milkha Singh—who had a dream year rising from 319th in the world rankings to 37th with four victories worldwide—once again showed they can more than hold their own with the best in the business, and our tournaments are attracting better fields and gaining more recognition."

In the 27 tournaments of 2006, the dominant player won only two, and he came as a surprise. He was South Korea's Y.E. Yang, who took a break from the Japan Tour to win the Kolon-Hana Bank Korea Open in September and the HSBC Champions in China in early November. The HSBC Champions wasn't merely a victory, it was a statement. Behind Yang, Tiger Woods finished second and Retief Goosen and Michael Campbell tied for third.

The 35-year-old Singh was a success story in his own right. After six so-so seasons, he scored a victory in the Volvo China Open and had five other top-10 finishes in 14 starts to take the UBS Order of Merit title with record winnings of US$591,884. The Asian Tour had 14 first-time winners, none as far apart as England's Chris Rodgers, who took the Pakistan Open just a week after succeeding at the qualifying competition, and South Africa's Hendrik Buhrmann, who labored for 11 years before plucking his first, that a two-stroke victory at the inaugural Aamby Valley Asian Masters in India.

Singapore's Mardan Mamat, on winning the co-sanctioned Singapore Masters, fell into his wife's arms and wept. The joy of winning was one thing, but he also knew he had done a lot with that one victory. He was the first Singaporean to win on the European Tour. Appropriately, Mamat dedicated the victory to his countrymen. Seven events had to go extra holes, and the most gripping was the Barclays Singapore Open, limited to three rounds by weather, in which Australian Adam Scott, the defending champion, beat South African Ernie Els with a birdie on the third extra hole. Thai veteran Thongchai Jaidee, long a favorite on the tour, was in danger of being shut out for the first time since his rookie season, 1999, when he picked off the Volvo Masters of Asia—the last event on the schedule.

Asian Tour

The Royal Trophy
Bangkok, Thailand
Winner: Europe

The latest to take the stage of international competition was the inaugural Royal Trophy, pitting eight-man teams from Europe and Asia in 16 matches at the Amata Spring Golf Club in Bangkok, with the prize a trophy donated by the king of Thailand.

And to no one's surprise, the Europeans, captained by Seve Ballesteros, were the huge favorites to win.

To everyone's surprise, the Europeans, who held a huge 6-2 lead after the team matches the first day, had to hang on for dear life in the final-day singles to hold off Masahiro Kuramoto's Asian team for a narrow 9-7 victory.

Europe needed just 2½ points from the eight singles to take the trophy, but the Asians battled back, 5-3. Credit clutch play by Ireland's Graeme McDowell and Paul McGinley and Sweden's Henrik Stenson for turning the tide.

At one point in the morning, McDowell was the only European leading his match. The rest of the Europeans were either all square or trailing. It looked a little grim for Europe until McGinley closed out China's Zhang Lian-wei, 2 and 1, and McDowell stopped India's Jyoti Randhawa, 3 and 2. But the celebrating was delayed. Japan's Yasuharu Imano took a 2-up victory over England's David Howell—ironically a hero in the 2004 Ryder Cup—and Asia still had hope.

Then came the clinching points from Stenson in the final singles match against Thailand's Thongchai Jaidee, who was playing under great pressure before the homefolks. Thongchai made five bogeys, the last on the 13th, and Stenson parred for a 5-and-4 victory to give Europe three points and the first Royal Trophy.

"I am really happy with the final score today," said Ballesteros. "It has been a great two days of competition, and the Europe team played fantastic. The Asian team also showed a game and sportsmanship."

"I was happy to see the boys fight back after yesterday," Kuramoto said. "It was a very good day. For a moment it looked possible that we could upset Europe and our players grew in confidence."

Pakistan Open
Karachi, Pakistan
Winner: Chris Rodgers

It was out of the classroom and right to the head of the class for England's Chris Rodgers. No one would be keeping track of how long it took Rodgers to score his first Asian Tour victory. As they say, the ink on his diploma hadn't even dried. One week, Rodgers was topping the tour's qualifying tournament. The very next, he was at Karachi Golf Club winning the Pakistan Open, new to the Asian Tour and kicking off its season late in January.

Rodgers went into the final round with a three-stroke lead and held up under the pressure from a pair of veteran Indians, Jeev Milkha Singh and Amandeep Johl, to win by four strokes. Rodgers built up his real momentum in the second round, when he broke from the pack with a bogey-free, eight-under-par 64 to tie Welshman Mark Mouland for the halfway lead at 11-under 133. They led by two over Johl (67). Singh (69) and Pakistan's No. 2 golfer, Shabbir Iqhal (67), tied for fourth at 137, four off the lead.

Rodgers proved himself again in the third round, rebounding from a double bogey at the 16th with birdies at the last two for a 68–201, three strokes clear of Mouland (71) and Pakistan's No. 1 golfer, Muhammed Munir, who birdied five holes on the back nine for a 66.

"This is simply great, and the best part is, I'm enjoying myself," Rodgers said. He was beside himself the next day in the final round, if a wild ride can be fun. Rodgers, chased by Singh and Johl, had a classic rollercoaster round, holding together under the heat—he birdied No. 2, bogeyed No. 3, birdied No. 5, bogeyed Nos. 7 and 9, birdied No. 11, bogeyed No. 12, and finally birdied No. 15 for a 72 and a 15-under 273 total. With a four-stroke win, clearly he'd graduated with honors.

Commercialbank Qatar Masters
Doha, Qatar
Winner: Henrik Stenson

See European Tours chapter.

Johnnie Walker Classic
Perth, Australia
Winner: Kevin Stadler

See Australasian Tour chapter.

Maybank Malaysian Open
Kuala Lumpur, Malaysia
Winner: Charlie Wi

If Thailand's Thongchai Jaidee wasn't the outright favorite in the Maybank Malaysian Open, he was at least the sentimental favorite. He had won it two years running, and the fans wanted to see this bit of history made. Unfortunately for him, South Korea's Charlie Wi wasn't reading history at this time. Wi came from back in the pack to pluck the title from Thongchai's eager hands with a birdie on the last hole.

The tournament, played at the par-72 Kuala Lumpur Golf and Country Club, was disjointed over the three rounds by heavy rains and called off after 54 holes. That was just in time for Wi, formerly of Seoul and now of California, to make the clinching birdie and become the second player from the U.S. Nationwide Tour—after American Kevin Stadler in the Johnnie Walker Classic in Australia—to win an Asian-European Tour co-sponsored event in two weeks.

Spain's Miguel Angel Jimenez was eight under for 17 holes when a thunderstorm ended the first round on Thursday, and he returned Friday morning to par his last hole and post a leading 64, for a one-stroke lead on Thailand's Thaworn Wiratchant. While Jimenez was double-bogeying two holes in the second round and shooting 77, Welshman David Park took over. He shot a 64 and stood at 13 under at the halfway point, a stroke up on Thongchai and fellow Thai Thammanoon Srirot.

Attention, however, remained focused on Thongchai, who added a 63 to his opening 69 for a 132 total, just a shot off the lead. "The rain has made the course very soft and quite easy," Thongchai said. "It's easy to get the ball close, although some holes are quite tricky."

They were tricky enough to hold Ireland's Padraig Harrington, at No. 9 the highest ranked in the field, to a closing 67 and a tie for 13th. But Wi, with his 66-68-63–197 total, 19 under par, clearly wasn't fooled.

Enjoy Jakarta HSBC Indonesia Open
Jakarta, Indonesia
Winner: Simon Dyson

The way things turned out, Simon Dyson was the beneficiary of his own bright, self-fulfilling prophecy. And right on the number, as well.

The Enjoy Jakarta HSBC Indonesia Open was heading into the final round and Dyson, tied for the lead with young Australian Andrew Buckle, was asked what it might take to win.

"I think if one of us shoots four or five under tomorrow, it could take it," said Dyson.

A five under did take it—shot by Dyson himself. England's Dyson, age 29, thus had his first European Tour and fourth Asian Tour victory in the co-sanctioned event at the Emeralda Golf Club at Jakarta. His 67 gave him a 20-under-par 268 total and a two-stroke win over Buckle (69–270). Buckle, age 23 and seeking his first win, shut the door on himself with a fatal crash to a quadruple bogey. That ended a two-man chase. Tied for third six shots back were Thailand's Thongchai Jaidee (68) and Taiwan's Wang Ter-chang (70).

It had been a much tighter race. Thongchai, Wang, Dyson and Ireland's David Higgins shared the first-round lead with 66s. Wild play cost Thongchai a chance at his eighth Asian win. He was still tied with Dyson at the halfway point, both shooting 68s. But where Dyson had five birdies and a bogey, Thongchai had two more eagles and five birdies, but three bogeys and a double bogey.

Dyson and Buckle opened the third round strong and pulled away from the field. Dyson eagled No. 1 off a five iron to 20 feet, and added four birdies against a bogey for a 67. Buckle, on his way to a 65, opened with three straight birdies, and even tasted the lead briefly with a birdie at the 17th. But Dyson also birdied it, and they were tied at 15-under 201, sharing a three-shot lead. Then Buckle's crash settled it in the fourth round.

OSIM Singapore Masters
Singapore
Winner: Mardan Mamat

It dawned on Mardan Mamat when he was making the final turn that with a little grit and stick-to-it-tiveness he could actually win the OSIM Singapore Masters. Nine holes later, he was crying into his hands with joy. He had, in fact, done those very things for all four rounds, going wire-to-wire to become the first Singaporean to win a European Tour event (the tournament was co-sanctioned by the Asian and European Tours).

"Two birdies on the first and second holes, they gave me a bit of relaxation," said Mamat, who played the par-72 Laguna Golf and Country Club in 65-70-70 before closing with a 71 for a 12-under-par 276 total, beating Australia's Nick Dougherty (71), the defending champion, by one stroke.

Mamat seemed pressure-proof. In the second round, he held steady with his 70 while others were making a run at him. Australia's Marcus Both posted four birdies and an eagle in a 68 and tied for second a stroke back with Thailand's Prayad Marksaeng (69), who notched six birdies on the first nine, but then the nerves hit him and he triple-bogeyed the 17th from the water. "My palms were sweating," Prayad said.

Dougherty made a strong move at Mamat in the third round, blistering the first nine for six birdies, but he double-bogeyed No. 4 on his way to a 67 to close within a stroke. But the round of the day—of the tournament, in fact—belonged to Thailand's Chapchai Nirat. It would have been a 61—except... Chapchai ran off six straight birdies on the first nine, and got five more on the second nine, but he triple-bogeyed the par-three eighth and double-bogeyed the par-three 17th and shot 66. "Maybe the pressure got to me," Chapchai confessed.

TCL Classic
Sanya, Hainen Island, China
Winner: John Edfors

You didn't go out for a hotdog at the TCL Classic. You might come back and find the leaderboard changed from top to bottom. This was the free-for-all that delivered a battering to Yalong Bay Golf Club on the Chinese resort island of Hainan in mid-March. Consider that Liang Wen-chong, China's new golf whiz, and American Ed Loar shot 10-under-par 62s to share the first-round lead and then were barely heard from thereafter.

Consider further that Sweden's Johan Edfors did not lead in any of the rounds but won the event, his first European title, with a total of 263. That's 25 under par—an average of 6.25 under par per round.

Edfors needed just a comparatively modest four-under 68 to win, but there was nothing modest about the finish. He and Australian Andrew Buckle were tied at 24 under after they birdied the 16th, then parred the 17th and were on course for a playoff. It never happened. Buckle parred the 18th, but Edfors birdied for the win.

Edfors racked up seven birdies on the vulnerable course but also made three bogeys for his 68. Buckle, who was in the thick of it for the first three rounds, double-bogeyed the par-three No. 5 and shot 70.

The strangest story was authored by European Tour leader David Howell, who shot 63-66 in the middle rounds and led Buckle by two in the second round at 17-under 127 and by one at 23-under 193 in the third round.

"It was a little hard work, to be honest," said Howell, who paid a great visit to China in the previous November. He won the Champions Tournament in Shanghai over Tiger Woods. But this trip, Howell's putter went sour in the final round. He missed five par putts and drifted back.

Volvo China Open
Beijing, China
Winner: Jeev Milkha Singh

India's Jeev Milkha Singh, long a proponent of positive thinking—whatever name it came under—threw his mind into reverse and took a different approach in the Volvo China Open, co-sponsored by the Asian and European Tours. "I've always tried hard to win," Singh said, "and today I just went in there with reverse psychology, thinking that if it doesn't happen, never mind." Such a fatalistic approach might not be for everyone, but it seemed to work for him.

The tournament in China began as an exercise of the United Nations. France's Christian Cevaer ruled the sand, holing out of one bunker for a birdie and saving par out of four others on his way to the first-round lead on 66. Jammed a stroke behind him were England's Simon Dyson, Ross Fisher and Simon Wakefield, Portugal's Jose-Filipe Lima, Spain's Gonzalo Fernandez-Castano and Sweden's Peter Hanson. Then England's David Lynn made his move in the middle rounds. And Singh emerged in the third round through a wicked windstorm that battered the par-72 Honghua International.

Singh solved the battering elements for five birdies and the day's-low 67, barging his way into the race. The 35 mph winds whipped the course most of the day, carrying shots aside and knocking down a TV tower. "Every hole out there was tough," said Lynn, who took a one-stroke lead with a nine-birdie 67 in the second round and kept the edge with a par 72 in the blustery third round. Lynn's touch didn't last. He struggled to a 73 in the final round, clearing the way for Singh.

Singh closed with a four-birdie, two-bogey 70 for a 10-under 278, beating Fernandez-Castano by a stroke for his first victory in 13 years. Singh had taken a big step forward by going into reverse.

BMW Asian Open
Shanghai, China
Winner: Gonzalo Fernandez-Castano

Gonzalo Fernandez-Castano, a promising Spaniard, age 25, was trailing by a stroke after the third round of the BMW Asian Open. He was asked whether he could win. He found an ingenious way of ducking the question and the pressure that went with it.

"I'm not the one who has to win tomorrow," he said. The message: It was Sweden's Henrik Stenson who was leading going into the final round. Therefore, Stenson was the one who had to win. "I'll just go out and play my best golf," the Spaniard said. And so he did, and it was enough—just enough to bring in his second victory in 10 months. All it took was a tap-in birdie on the first playoff hole.

The loss was a cruel blow to Stenson. Against an Asian-European Tour co-sponsored field at the Thomson Shanghai Pudong Golf Club—a field that included Colin Montgomerie, Simon Dyson and Paul Casey—Stenson led from the start. Then leading by three into the final turn, he got crushed by a triple-bogey eight at No. 9.

At the 16th, Fernandez-Castano pitched out of one bunker, over another, and into the hole for a birdie to take the lead. Stenson caught him with a birdie at the 18th, for a 71 to Fernandez-Castano's 70 for seven-under 281. At the first playoff hole, Fernandez-Castano hooked his tee shot into the trees, then rapped a five wood through a gap and over the water. Then his chip ended up six inches from the pin, and after Stenson's birdie try lipped out, he tapped in for the birdie and the win.

GS Caltex Maekyung Open
Seoul, Korea
Winner: Suk Jong-yul

The GS Caltex Maekyung Open left a trail of some pretty happy people, even those who almost won—but didn't.

First, there was South Korea's Suk Jong-yul who did win, but who trailed most of the way and was suffering from stage fright in front of the home folks at Seoul's Lakeside Country Club. Suk, age 38, tied for the lead in the first round, trailed through the next two rounds, but closed with a bogey-free 67 for a 17-under 271 total and won by one stroke.

Then there was American Bryan Saltus, his late charge falling a stroke short to 67, leaving him second. Was he crushed? Not quite, not with that career-best $78,125 prize. Said Saltus: "I can't imagine what I'm going to buy myself." And finally crowd favorite Lee Sung, who was born deaf. Lee shared the lead in the first round with 67, led the next two rounds by two strokes (66-69), but three straight bogeys on his final back nine sent him to a par 72 and a tie for third place. "It is still a good week," said his father, Kang-kun, speaking for him.

Saltus was the man to beat in the final round, thanks to no little help from his chipping, such as the hole-out birdie at the 11th that helped him to the clubhouse lead on 67–272. Suk came to the 18th needing a birdie to win. Under this pressure, he hit a perfect tee shot, then lofted a wedge to three feet and dropped the putt. "This week, I was very nervous out there," Suk said, "as there are always high expectations from the home fans." They didn't go home disappointed. Neither did Suk.

SK Telecom Open
Seoul, Korea
Winner: Prom Meesawat

Prom Meesawat, age 23 and a rising Thai star, discovered the joys of obscurity. He was on his way to his first victory and practically no one at the Sky 72 Golf Club at Seoul, South Korea, was paying attention. The SK Telecom Open in early May was the Michelle Wie Show, with K.J. Choi, the defending champion, thrown in for good measure. "It's good playing in my group as there was no pressure, with all the attention on Michelle Wie's group and Choi's group," Prom said.

Prom blasted his way out of a tie in the final round with an eagle at No. 3 and wrapped up the storm-shortened tournament by three strokes on a card of 69-64-68–201, 15 under par. Wie had accepted another invitation to a professional men's tournament, still trying to make the 36-hole cut. This time, she did it, with 70-69–139. Wie was the second female to do it, after South Korea's Se Ri Pak in 2003. With a closing 74, Wie tied for 35th at 213.

Prom, with 69, opened four strokes behind Australian Adam Le Vesconte, then with a quiet 64 tied for the lead with Malaysia's Iain Steel (66) at 133. Prom broke away in the third round with the eagle at the par-five third hole, where he resisted the temptation to hit driver. He hit a three wood, instead, setting up a perfect second shot. "I had 230 yards to the pin, hit a good two iron which landed three feet from the pin," he said. He then birdied the fifth, and coming in birdied the 10th, 11th and 13th, and won by three over India's Jeev Milkha Singh (70) and Korea's Lee Seong-ho (70). The stage, however, still belonged to Michelle Wie.

"I passed my first goal," Wie said, "and I want to keep on going."

Aamby Valley Asian Masters
Mumbai, India
Winner: Hendrik Buhrmann

Here was one dream everyone was happy to see come true. "Before I die," Hendrik Buhrmann had proclaimed, "I want to win on the Asian Tour. That's my dream."

Buhrmann, age 42, had won eight times in his native South Africa, but never in 11 years on the Asian Tour. Then came the inaugural Aamby Valley Asian Masters in India. Buhrmann shrugged off a painful second round, and battled through wind and pressure in the fourth for a breakthrough win by two strokes.

After an opening 66 and one-stroke lead, Buhrmann stumbled to 75 and fell eight strokes behind former caddie Ashok Kumar, who shot 66–133 for a four-stroke halfway lead over England's Simon Hurd (70). "The fight is on," said Kumar, winless in his four years, "but the tournament is not over yet." He slipped to 73 in the third round, but shared the lead at 206 with Hurd (69) and Buhrmann (65). "This," said Buhrmann, "is one of my best rounds. At my age you've got to enjoy it."

Kumar was still leading with seven holes to play in the final round, then four-putted the 16th for a double bogey, shot 78, and tied for fifth. Hurd went sour on the greens, shot 73, and finished second.

Buhrmann offset three bogeys with an eagle at the 12th and two birdies, and an inspiring par save at No. 7, after hitting out of bounds. "I'm really proud of that world-class par," he said. He shot 71 for an 11-under 277 total and his first Asian victory.

Macau Open
Macau
Winner: Kane Webber

In a field loaded with veterans—including Steve Elkington, a 10-time winner on the PGA Tour—who would figure a rookie could break through in only his second outing? But that was the story with Australia's Kane Webber, age 25, in the Macau Open. Just shows what confidence can do.

"You have to come in and expect to win," said Webber, who came to the Macau Golf and Country Club fired up after tying for fifth the week before in the Aamby Valley Asian Masters. But it was a strange breakthrough. Webber never led, but he got plenty of help from leaders falling away, such as Brad Kennedy, squandering a three-stroke lead in the final round. Elkington did his bit, too, closing with two 74s.

Webber didn't surface until the second round, when a run of birdies at the 11th, 12th, 14th, 17th and 18th gave him a 65 and a tie for second a stroke behind Kennedy's lead (65–133). Kennedy widened his margin in the third round with 69–202, moving three ahead of Webber, who posted a three-birdie, three-bogey 71.

In the final round, Webber got more help, this time in the form of rain. Kennedy seemed troubled and blew to 77. Elkington shot another 74, as did Scott Strange. Webber birdied the second and third holes, and after bogeys at the 10th and 12th, he finished like a crusty veteran. At the par-five 18th, he missed the green with his second shot, 70 feet from the pin, but coolly chipped to six feet and dropped the birdie putt for his 70, a nine-under 275 total and his breakthrough victory.

"It hasn't sunk in yet," Webber said. "Maybe later today when I speak to my family."

Philippine Open
Manila, Philippines
Winner: Scott Strange

Scott Strange was talking about how he felt heading down the final stretch of the Philippine Open. The key was the difference between confidence and overconfidence. With Strange, it was just confidence. "When I made those birdies (at the 11th and 12th) and parred the 13th, I know they are not going to catch me if I play it safe the rest of the way," said Strange, whose first Asian Tour victory was in the 2005 Myanmar Open. All Strange was saying was you know what you have to do and you stay within yourself.

Which he had. Strange, who led wire-to-wire, broke open a tight chase in the final round. He led by five at the turn, posted a comfortable two-under-par 70 for an eight-under 280 total over the demanding Wack Wack Golf Club, for a five-stroke victory over South Korean rookie Park Jun-Won (67).

Strange opened with 68, leading by one shot over Taiwan's Yeh Chang-ting, the 1993 Philippine Open winner. "But I'm not going to think about winning yet," Strange said. They shared the halfway lead at 138, Strange with 70 and Yeh with 69. Strange edged ahead for good in the third, fighting the wilting heat for four birdies and four bogeys for a par 72 and a one-stroke lead.

He opened the fourth round with a birdie at the first, doubling his lead to two, and he led by five at the turn. Birdies at the 11th and 12th got him to 10 under and a seven-stroke lead. Then he turned conservative, but a couple of dropped shots didn't trouble him. Said Strange: "I thought I had done enough to win." And so he had.

Bangkok Airways Open
Koh Samui, Thailand
Winner: Chawalit Plaphol

Taiwan's Lu Wen-teh was about to win his second straight Bangkok Airways Open. He was leading by a stroke with two to play, coming to Santiburi Samui Country Club's 17th, an attention-getting par-five of 643 yards. He drove safely into the fairway, but the ball ended up in a divot. His second shot, from the dangerous lie, scooted off into the right rough. Shaken, he three-putted from 20 feet for a triple-bogey eight—enough to snuff out his chances. "I hit a good drive," Lu said, "and before I knew it, I was staggering off the green with a big number."

That opened the door to Canada's Rick Gibson, who started the final round four shots off the lead, and Thailand's Chawalit Plaphol, who was six behind and not looking like a winner. But he was stubborn. "I knew six shots back wasn't much and I just kept playing hard," he said. Not that much? Well, not when you shoot 30 on the first nine. Bogeys at the 10th and 12th cooled him, and then he birdied the 16th, finishing with a day's-best four-under 67 and a three-under 281 total to catch Gibson, who missed a short par putt at the 17th and bogeyed for 69.

Both missed the green on the first playoff hole. "I told myself that I needed to fight on and I wanted to chip in," Chawalit said. "I nearly did, but it didn't matter in the end." Gibson left his chip four feet short, then two-putted for a bogey, and Chawalit had his second Asian Tour victory. "It's not disappointing, losing in a playoff," Gibson said. "It's disappointing to lose by making a bogey."

Crowne Plaza Open
Sanya, China
Winner: Chinarat Phadungsil

They weren't calling Chinarat Phadungsil the Asian Tour's Tiger Woods, but the Thai prodigy was doing all right for himself. A year ago, as an amateur, he became the youngest ever to win on the tour. Now a professional of 17, Chinarat backed up that victory by taking the Crowne Plaza Open, touring Yalong Bay Golf Club at Sanya, China, like a seasoned veteran in 65-68-68-71–272, and winning in a playoff.

Chinarat trailed only in the second round, then won in a storybook finish. Trailing by two with three holes to play, he birdied the par-five 16th, then holed a 12-footer for a birdie at the par-four 18th to tie Taiwan's Lin Wen-tang and Thai veteran Prom Meesawat. Lin bogeyed the first extra hole out of the rough, Prom missed a four-footer for par on the second, and Chinarat parred for his second win.

Chinarat had figured this win would be tougher because the field was tougher than it was when he won the Double A International the previous November. "But," he added, "I feel I'm playing better golf now."

Chinarat opened the tournament in a hurry. He birdied the first hole, dropping a 10-footer, and raced off to a two-stroke lead on a seven-under 65, outrunning defending champion Prayad Marksaeng, who had an amazing 10 straight one-putt greens. In the second round, Chinarat bounced back from a shaky patch with six birdies in eight holes to get within two of Lin (64–131), and regained the lead in the third round.

Brunei Open
Bandar Seri Begawan, Brunei
Winner: Wang Ter-chang

Taiwan's Wang Ter-chang didn't lead the Brunei Open until it absolutely counted—the very end. This meant tying Australia's David Gleeson in the final round, then beating him in a playoff. For the 44-year-old Taiwanese veteran, it was his first Asian Tour win since the 2005 Macau Open and his fourth overall.

Until that final putt gave him a five-under-par 66 and a 16-under 268 total, Wang trailed all the way. But he staked his claim to the victory in the third round when he streaked to six birdies on the back nine and shot 64 and moved to within two strokes of co-leaders Terry Pilkadaris (64), the defending champion, and Gleeson (65), tied at 200 at Brunei's Empire Hotel and Country Club. "I only missed one green today, so I am definitely very happy with my performance," Wang said. "You have to be consistent in your putts here and thankfully I had a steady performance today."

The 65 in the third round gave Gleeson his first taste of the lead. "I made some nice birdies today," Gleeson said, "so I will head out there tomorrow and continue what I'm doing." Pilkadaris had two odd slips. He had seven birdies and an eagle, but he let two strokes slip away, bogeys at the eighth and ninth. "I'm kicking myself," he said. He was kicking harder the next day. He shot 76 and fell to a tie for 14th.

In the fourth round, Wang birdied the second and third holes, and coming in, the 12th, 13th and 15th for 66. Gleeson, after five birdies and a bogey, missed the outright win when he bogeyed again at the par-four 18th. He bogeyed it yet again on the second playoff hole, lipping out a five-foot par putt, and Wang had his win. Said Gleeson: "It was so near, yet so far."

Pulai Springs Malaysian Masters
Johor, Malaysia
Winner: Anton Haig

Anton Haig, 20, a promising South African, took that old golf commandment, "Thou shalt keep thy head down," literally and then some in the Pulai Springs Malaysian Masters. After leading all the way and what with having the Indian veteran Jyoti Randhawa breathing down his neck, Haig didn't look up until they were handing him the trophy.

"I can hardly speak ... winning my first title on the Asian Tour," said Haig. Moments earlier, he could hardly breathe. He was playing splendid golf, birdieing the 10th, 12th and 14th down the final nine. Meanwhile, Randhawa was trumping his hand. After a stretch of six birdies married by two bogeys, Randhawa took the lead with an eagle at the 16th. If ever Haig was in trouble in his young career, it was now.

Then out of nowhere, Randhawa bogeyed the last two holes. And Haig, in a performance uncommon to his age and experience, birdied both, wrapping up a card of 63-66-69-68 for a 22-under total of 266 and a one-stroke win over Scotland's Barry Hume. Hume, after a bogey at the first hole, marched home with seven birdies for a 66 to grab second place. The bogey at the 18th gave Randhawa 68 and dropped him to a tie for third. The finish left Haig wilted. "The last two holes were quite nerve-wracking," Haig said, "I don't know how I made it. The six-foot birdie putt on the final hole was just fantastic. All I needed to do," he added, "was put my head down and go for it."

Barclays Singapore Open
Singapore
Winner: Adam Scott

The Barclays Singapore Open, it can be argued, came down to one certain shot. Namely, it was Ernie Els's tee shot on the third hole of a playoff against Adam Scott. Els put it into the rough. And Scott, the rising Australian who won the title in 2005, ended it with a birdie. "I am very happy to defend this title for the first time," Scott said. "I had a real fight on my hands with Ernie. I got off to a fast start, and he didn't."

The tournament, at the par-71 Serapong Golf Club was cancelled after the third round because of storms. The play reverted to the completed scores of the third round, where Scott and Els were tied atop the leaderboard at eight-under 205, leading the field by three strokes. They halved the first two playoff holes in pars. Then came the decisive third, the par-five 18th.

There, Els made the decisive error, driving into the rough. He had to waste a shot chipping back out into the fairway, then fired his third shot to the green, about 24 feet from the pin. He left his first putt within eight feet, then missed that one and bogeyed. Scott, on the other hand, smacked his drive over the water and into the fairway. He landed his second on the sloping rough on the edge of the green, got the next shot down to six feet, and holed that for the winning birdie.

"In the playoff, I had my chances, man," Els said. "It is disappointing." It was doubly disappointing. On his last visit, in the 2003 Singapore Masters, he blew a late lead to China's Zhang Lian-wei. Scott's explanation for his win was decidedly low-key. "I hit a lot more fairways here than I normally do," he said. "I played a lot of good shots. My putting was good in spots."

Kolon-Hana Bank Korea Open
Cheonan, Korea
Winner: Y.E. Yang

It was a good time for an unheralded golfer to get stage fright, what with playing for his national championship against such heavyweights as South Africa's Retief Goosen, Bubba Watson, one of the biggest hitters on the U.S. PGA Tour, and Thai star Thaworn Wiratchant. But South Korea's Y.E. Yang kept his head down, and when he finally looked up, he had won the Kolon-Hana Bank Korea Open by three strokes at Seoul's Woo Jeong Hills Country Club, his first on Korean soil in four years.

Goosen led off with a six-under 65, including a chip-in eagle at the par-four No. 6, and tied with Yang. He blamed his putting for holding him down. Said Yang, a four-time winner in Japan: "I'm happy with my round." Then the tournament took shape. Among the challengers: Goosen slipped a tad to 72 in the second round. In the blustery third, Watson stumbled to two double bogeys and 75 while Yang was taking a three-stroke lead with a 68–200.

If the pressure was getting to Yang in the fourth round, it didn't show. He offset bogeys at Nos. 4 and 11, for example, with birdies at Nos. 8

and 10. Then came the key, a clutch 12-foot putt for birdie at the 15th. "I stroked it gently into the hole," he said, "and after that, I knew I was close to the title." A tap-in par five at the 18th wrapped up a card of 65-67-68-70 for a 14-under 270 total and the three-stroke win over countryman Kang Ji-man. The big names all closed with 70s—Thaworn and Goosen tying for sixth, and Watson for 10th. Then Yang revealed his secret. "This golf course does not favor long hitters," he said. "Good putting and accuracy off the tee are the key,"

Mercuries Taiwan Masters
Taiwan, Chinese Taipei
Winner: Gaurav Ghei

In one of the great gaffes in golf, Indian rookie S.S.P. Chowrasia held a five-stroke lead at the halfway point of the Mercuries Taiwan Masters for as long as it took him to leave the scoring table. He had forgotten to sign his scorecard. So his 64-67 scores were wiped out, leaving only a memory and the anguish. He was too crushed to speak afterward.

Then the race was wide open, and it fell to a man few had noticed until it was too late. India's Gaurav Ghei, age 38, erupted for a bogey-free 66 in the final round to score his first victory in 11 years. His 10-under 278 total at the Taiwan Golf and Country Club gave him a one-stroke win over countryman Rahil Gangjee (71), who led through the middle rounds following Chowrasia's departure.

Talk about unnoticed: Ghei (71-72-69-66) trailed by seven strokes in the first and second rounds and by four going into the last. "It's been 11 years since I won, and the way I played the last two days, without dropping a shot—it is just fantastic," he said.

In a day thick with birdies, Ghei figured his key was the par at the par-three 10th hole in the final round. He had put his tee shot into a bunker just about six feet from the cup. With no green to work with, he finessed a blast next to the cup and tapped in. And this after getting birdies at Nos. 1, 2, 4, 6 and 7 to get to five under on the front nine. "I told myself to keep it on the fairway," he said. And after the save at the 10th, he birdied the 12th and parred in. "My thoughts go out to S.S.P. (Chowrasia)," Ghei said, "but I'm very happy to have won after such a long time."

Taiwan Open
Taiwan, Chinese Taipei
Winner: Lin Wen-tang

At last, Lin Wen-tang proved something to his biggest doubter—himself. "I've had my chances to win in the past," Lin said, "but somehow I felt like I never had the mental strength to do it."

Maybe Lin had reason to. Coming into the Taiwan Open, he'd had three top-10 finishes this year and 15 in 80 previous tournaments, including two seconds. That's good work, but it could get a guy wondering. But the final round said it all. He entered it with a two-stroke lead, and a bogey at the final hole, the par-five 18th, merely cut his winning margin over Scotland's Simon Yates to three strokes. He played the Sunrise Club at Taipei in 70-68-68-69—275, 13 under par.

Lin broke through the pack in the third round with a surprise eagle at the last hole, chipping in from off the green for 68—206, to go two up on halfway leader Gary Rusnak (72). "I only wanted to get it close for a birdie," Lin said.

In the final round, Lin gave Yates only a glimmer of hope when he two-putted from four feet for a bogey at No. 2. Then he bounced back to make the turn in 34 with birdies at Nos. 5, 6 and 8. Coming home, birdies at the 13th and 17th gave him a cushion the closing bogey would only dent. "It feels wonderful—I feel great," Lin said. "I've won several local events in the past, but the Taiwan Open is my first major title. This win proves I can win and that I've got the mentality to succeed on the Asian Tour."

Volkswagen Masters - China
Sanya, China
Winner: Retief Goosen

South Africa's Retief Goosen and New Zealand's Michael Campbell found themselves in good company—each other's, that is. Just a pair of former U.S. Open champions drawing a bead on the Volkswagen Masters - China title. They tied for second with 64s, one stroke behind Taiwan's Lu Wen-teh in the first round. Goosen, the defending champion, parted company from everyone after that, and won by three strokes. But he wasn't exactly dancing after that dominating performance at Yalong Bay at Sanya. "I made a lot of bad mistakes," Goosen said after his closing 71.

Well, it was a good show anyway. He bogeyed just once in his opening round of 64. He took a three-stroke lead over Campbell on the second day with 65 off four birdies and an eagle coming home, and had a 15-under 129 total. In the third round, with an eagle and five birdies in a 67, he swept to 20-under 196 and a five-stroke lead that troubled him. "Everyone expects you to win and it puts pressure on you," he said. Lu slipped into second place on 69, leaving Campbell to go charging into the fourth round trying to catch Goosen. He kicked himself for his reckless ambition. "I pushed too hard, too soon ... and it cost me a couple of bogeys," Campbell said.

Goosen was kicking himself, too, for erratic play. He was one under on the outward nine with two birdies and a bogey, and started the back bogey-birdie. He calmed himself with a save at the par-five 13th, holing an eight-foot putt after hitting his second shot in the water. "That putt was the turnaround putt for me," he said. It helped him to his first set of back-to-back titles. "It will be great coming back next year," Goosen said, "to give myself a chance of making it a hat trick."

Hero Honda Indian Open
New Delhi, India
Winner: Jyoti Randhawa

India's Jyoti Randhawa couldn't sleep that Sunday night, thinking about missing a four-foot putt that would have won him the Hero Honda Indian Open on the first playoff hole. But he didn't miss his chance when the playoff resumed Monday, beating countryman S.S.P. Chowrasia. A third man in the playoff, India's Vijay Kumar, bowed out on the first hole on a stray tee shot. Randhawa said it was anticipation that caused him to miss the four-footer. "I thought of winning a golf tournament and I didn't think about the putt," he said.

After a leapfrog battle through the first three rounds at New Delhi's Delhi Golf Course, the three tied in regulation at 18-under-par 270, Randhawa closing with 70, Chowrasia with 69 and Kumar with 66. Chowrasia, by the way, was still living down his gaffe at the Taiwan Masters three weeks earlier when he forgot to sign his scorecard. "It's now something of the past," he insisted.

At the first playoff hole Sunday evening, Kumar was gone when he slugged his tee shot into the jungle. Chowrasia two-putted from 15 feet for par, and Randhawa missed that haunting four-foot birdie try and also parred, and play was suspended because of darkness. The playoff resumed Monday, again at the par-five 18th. Randhawa hit a good drive and fired a four iron to the green, 40 feet from the flag. Chowrasia missed in two but chipped on to 12 feet. After Randhawa got his 40-footer to within two feet, Chowrasia two-putted from 12 for his par. Randhawa then holed his short putt for a birdie, his second Indian Open, his sixth Asian Tour win and peace of mind.

"I am learning," Randhawa said, "to enjoy the walk and smell the flowers."

HSBC Champions
Shanghai, China
Winner: Y.E. Yang

Y.E. Yang would go into the record books if for no other reason than he stood up to Tiger Woods. Yang did that in the HSBC Champions in mid-November, ending Woods's string of six consecutive stroke-play events (although Woods's streak on the U.S. PGA Tour remained intact). Yang shot a final-round 69 for a two-stroke victory over Woods, who tried desperately to close the gap. "This is such a big thing that's happening to me right now," Yang said, "that it's really hard for me to explain it in words how I feel."

Yang, 34, who took the recent Korea Open and also a four-time winner in Japan, didn't win over a thin field at the co-sponsored event at Sheshan International in Shanghai. Yang also had to turn back South Africa's Retief Goosen, New Zealand's Michael Campbell and others in the world-class field. Yang shot 66-72-67-69–274, a total of 14 under par. He trailed Jyoti Randhawa by one in the first round, Randhawa by four in the second round, then Goosen by one in the third round, before rushing ahead in the final round.

"I had my chances," said Woods, seven strokes off the first-round lead with 72, "but I was too far back and Yang just went on and played some great holes."

Yang's first duel was with Goosen, who started the final round leading him by one. Goosen then went two up with birdies at the second and third. Yang answered with three straight birdies from No. 6. Then Goosen bogeyed the 10th and 11th, and Yang birdied the par-three 12th to move four strokes clear. Two late bogeys merely dented his margin. Woods took second with a 67, and Goosen (73) slipped to a tie for third with Campbell (64) at 277. The little-known South Korean hadn't just beaten Woods, he'd beaten three men who had won the U.S. Open.

The Goodwill Trophy
Shenzhen, China
Winner: International Team

Yet another of the us-against-them team matches was introduced in November 2006. The Goodwill Trophy, pitted—oddly enough—a European-American team made up of competitors from the Ryder Cup of just two months earlier, under Scotland's Colin Montgomerie, against an International team from the rest of the world, under South Africa's Retief Goosen.

After the Internationals took a one-point lead in the first-day foursome matches, the Goodwill Trophy came down to the last singles match and the very last hole. Australia's Peter Senior, of the Internationals, reached the green, but Bradley Dredge of Wales missed and took four to get on, and conceded, and the Internationals had a 6½-5½ victory. If Montgomerie's Ryder Cup magic didn't work for the entire team, it did for him. In a match of captains, he beat Goosen by one hole. Among other singles: Thailand's Thongchai Jaidee beat England's Luke Donald, 2 and 1; Swede Henrik Stenson beat Jeev Milkha Singh of India, 3 and 2, and China's Zhang Lian-wei stumbled at the 15th and lost to Spain's Alejandro Canizares.

UBS Hong Kong Open
Fanling, Hong Kong
Winner: Jose Manuel Lara

Upon taking the lead in the first round of the UBS Hong Kong Open, Spain's Jose Manuel Lara, age 29, went to countryman Miguel Angel Jimenez, a golfer of no mean accomplishments, and said, "This is my week." For a guy who had never won and who was facing a strong field in the Asian-European co-sponsored event, this was either a brash statement or pure folly. It turned out Lara knew what he was talking about. He not only won the tournament, but on a card of 64-66-66-69–265, 15 under par at the Hong Kong Golf Club, he became the first in tournament history to go wire-to-wire, outrunning Philippines' rookie Juvic Pagunsan by one stroke.

Lara had his dicey moments coming down the final stretch. When he birdied No. 3 for the fourth time, it looked like a walk in the park. But he turned wobbly. At No. 7, he made his first bogey in 25 holes, then bogeyed No. 9 as well, and they were tied. Pagunsan, age 28, took his first lead with a three-foot birdie at the 11th, and he might have run from there except he tried to hit a wood out of a fairway bunker at the par-five 13th, caught the lip, and barely reached the fairway. He made a fine par from there, but got tied by Lara's two-putt birdie.

Pagunsan retook the lead with a birdie at the 14th, and then stumbled fatally at the par-four 16th, where he drove into the left rough near a small tree and couldn't punch the ball all the way out. He bogeyed, and Lara, on in two, holed his 12-footer for a birdie and a one-stroke lead. Both parred the last two holes—Pagunsan scrambling, Lara routinely. It's not known what Jimenez might have said to Lara at the finish.

Volvo Masters of Asia
Bangkok, Thailand
Winner: Thongchai Jaidee

The Volvo Masters of Asia was the final curtain on the 2006 Asian Tour, and as such it deserved a compelling finish, with drama, tension and even some humor. The tournament got it all, and all from Thai veteran Thongchai Jaidee, though truth be known, he could have done without the humor. "I was very lucky," Thongchai said, after staggering to a Marx Brothers' finish at the final hole and still beating Philippine legend Frankie Minoza by one stroke with rounds of 68-68-69-72—277, 11 under par at the Thai Country Club in Bangkok.

Thongchai set the stage for the wild finish with some exemplary golf along the way. He led countryman Thaworn Wiratchant by one in the second round, and after the third round he led by two over Thaworn, Iain Steel and Prayad Marksaeng. In the fourth round, Thongchai got off to a blistering start with three birdies over his first four holes, but then he dropped all three shots. Thaworn and Minoza caught him at the turn, all at 11 under par. Thongchai broke away, dropping a 20-foot birdie putt at the 11th hole, then an eight-footer at the 14th. Thaworn went bogey-double bogey from the 15th, and Minoza bogeyed the 17th. Thongchai had a lock. He was up by three with one hole to play. Then came the humor—though he wasn't the one laughing.

Thongchai tried to fade a drive but pushed it into deep rough. He decided to settle for a bogey, but then hit his second into a bunker. Then came out, but into rough again. "And I said, 'let's try for a double bogey,'" he said. "Two putts for a win—it was okay." And it truly was. It was Thongchai's eighth Asian victory, his first in 22 months, and his first in 2006. It was, just in time, a great season.

Omega China Tour

To the surprise of absolutely no one, Zhang Lian-wei—long since dubbed the Father of Chinese Golf—was the star of the Omega China Tour in 2006. In this second year of the tour, Zhang, Liang Wen-chong and Li Chao dominated by winning two of the six tournaments each, but Zhang also finished in the top three in the others and topped the money list. The tour began in 2005 with four events, and had six in 2006. The plan is to add two a year so that there will be at least 10 by 2008.

The 2006 China Tour (scattered from April through October):

Hainan Leg—Liang, age 27, won not only the tournament but also the highest compliment as the protégé of Zhang, whom he beat by a whopping nine strokes. "I believe he's the best golfer in China at the moment," Zhang said. Liang closed with a one-under-par 71 to wrap up a 273 total and a nine-stroke victory over Zhang. Liang, who had back-to-back 65s, said he was actually a bit uneasy at one point in the final round, when he was leading by 10 and shanked an approach into a lake.

Zhuhai Leg—A month later, in May, it was Zhang's turn to celebrate. Zhang, age 41, hadn't won since the Volvo China Open in November 2003. His confidence suffered. Now he was in the perfect setting for a comeback—his home area. He turned a six-stroke deficit into a six-stroke victory at the Golden Gulf Golf Club. Zhang closed with a three-under-par 69 to win at a hefty total of 296, eight over par, riding in on a huge plunge by Li Chao, who after three steady rounds blew to a 12-over 84.

Shandong Leg—Li Chao bounced back and closed with a rush to end a seesaw battle and win by a stroke over Yuan Hao at the Tiger Beach Links. Actually, Li had to bounce back within the tournament, too. He was leading by three going into the final round, but the margin disappeared almost instantly. Li birdied three of the last four holes, the last the 18th, where he put his approach to about eight feet, just a little inside Yuan, and on the same line. Yuan missed, but Li didn't. He finished with a 72 for a three-over-par total, winning by one stroke.

Shanghai Leg—Zhang underlined the end to his slump with another victory, this time a playoff win over Huang Ming-jie, 25, one of the promising young players. Zhang just missed winning in regulation when his birdie putt at the par-five 18th grazed the hole. In the playoff at the 18th, both reached the island green in two. Zhang chipped to four feet, and Huang missed his par from seven feet and settled for second place, his best finish on the tour. Zhang two-putted comfortably for his second win of the season.

Kunming Leg—Li's time came in a big way at the Kunming Leg, and Huang again had to take encouragement with another second. Li raced away with a 65 in the third round and shot 71 in the fourth for an 11-under-par 277 total and a luxurious seven-stroke victory. "All I was thinking of was, just don't make mistakes," Li said. "I was actually quite nervous for the first few holes, but eventually I calmed down." Huang locked up second place with a 69 that he capped off with a 25-foot birdie putt at the final hole for a four-under 284.

Omega Championship—Liang Wen-chong wrapped up the season-ending Omega Championship, his second win, with two stunning performances. First, he ran away from the field and won by 12 shots. And then he gave back his prize money (RMB 150,000; $19,000 U.S.) "I want to offer help," Liang said. "Maybe we could set up a foundation or system to assist talented young players to go abroad and play, and to experience the high standard of events like I have done." Liang closed with a four-under-par 68 and a 15-under 273 total at Beijing's Tianan Golf Club. He finished 12 strokes ahead of Li Chao, who even with a 75 was himself six ahead of Zhang. For everyone, it was a futile chase.

Japan Tour

Token Homemate Cup
Kani, Gifu, Japan
Winner: Wayne Perske

No one was more astonished when Wayne Perske wound up in the winner's circle at the Token Homemate Cup, the mid-April Japan Tour opener, than the 31-year-old Australian himself. Things had not gone particularly well for Perske since turning professional in 2000 after a splendid amateur career. A lone victory in a secondary event that year preceded seasons marked by injuries and failures to maintain tour playing privileges and he was playing in just his 11th tournament in Japan.

"I am very surprised to win," beamed Perske after his 21-under-par 267 at Shuga Country Club, Kani, Gifu Prefecture, gave him his first title in Japan nearly three years after he was bounced from the tour for inadequate performance in 10 events. He was the fourth Australian winner in the tournament's 17-year history.

Perske began a week of low scoring with 64, trailing first-round leader Katsuya Nakagawa by two strokes. Nakagawa shot 69 Friday and was joined at 131 by Perske (67), Chang Ik-je of South Korea (68) and Akinori Tani (64). Tani, like Nakagawa a non-winner in eight seasons on the circuit, slipped a stroke in front of Perske Saturday with 68–199 despite a double bogey on the card. The Australian launched the final round with a birdie and never faltered the rest of the way en route to a bogey-free 67 and the 267. Countryman and close friend Brendan Jones, one of his playing companions Sunday, shot 68 and shared the runner-up spot with Yui Ueda, who closed with 66 for his 269.

Tsuruya Open
Kawanishi, Hyogo, Japan
Winner: Brendan Jones

A fast start in Japan helped Brendan Jones decide into which basket he would be putting most of his playing eggs during the 2006 season. With privileges on both the U.S. PGA and Japan Tours, Jones played in two early-year events in America, then went to Japan and promptly finished second-first in the initial two tournaments, following his runner-up finish in the Token Homemate Cup with his second victory in three years in the Tsuruya Open in Kawanishi, Hyogo Prefecture. It meant back-to-back wins for Australian professionals and led Jones to make 14 starts in Japan, just nine in the United States during the year.

Before Jones went in front to stay in the third round of the Tsuruya Open at the par-71 Yamanohara Golf Club, the stage was held by two seniors. Kiyoshi Murota, age 51, a six-time winner on the Japan Tour who would later in the year win twice and lead the money race on the Japan Senior Tour, led the tournament the first two days with a pair of 68s, sharing first place Thursday with Tatsuya Mitsuhashi and standing two ahead of Jones (70-68) after the second round. Meanwhile, the ageless Teruo Sugihara shot 69 Friday and made the cut with 146. At 68 years, 10 months and with eight years fighting prostate cancer behind him, Sugihara is the oldest player ever to make a cut on any tour. He finished 75-77–298, last in the field.

The long-hitting Jones followed with a five-under-par 66 Saturday despite a triple bogey at the par-four 14th hole and opened a one-stroke lead over Murota (69–205). Jones had to fight off challenges from Murota and eventual runner-up Mamo Osanai in the middle of Sunday's round, but birdies at the 13th and 15th put him comfortably in front. He posted 69 for an 11-under-par 273 in winning for the fifth time in Japan. Osanai shot 68 for 275.

The Crowns
Aichi, Japan
Winner: Shingo Katayama

Shingo Katayama launched his bid for his third straight money-winning championship with his second victory in three years in The Crowns tournament, the kingpin early-season event that began nearly a half-century ago in the circuit's founding years.

Katayama's 19th career title came relatively easily, yet a bit strangely. He won by two strokes and recorded an 18-under-par 262, just two strokes short of Masashi (Jumbo) Ozaki's course record on Nagoya Golf Club's Wago course. Early in the final round, though, Katayama sported a 10-stroke lead after runner-up Nozomi Kawahara went double bogey-bogey.

"I've never had such a huge lead before and I might have been a little too defensive," he admitted. "I played it safe from then on, trying not to shoot at the pins." In that mode, he made a lone birdie and three bogeys, shooting an even-par 70 for the two-stroke win over Kawahara. Veteran

Ryoken (Ricky) Kawagishi closed with 63 to finish third, five shots back at 269.

Although he didn't get on top until the second round, Katayama was primed for the victory from the start. He shot a bogey-free 63 Thursday to sit just a shot behind the 62 of leader Soshi Tajima, whose only win was in the 2003 KBC Augusta. Katayama kept his card clear of bogeys again Friday and shot 67–130, which put him in a first-place tie with Kawahara, who had an eagle and six birdies en route to 63–130. Tajima had 69–131.

Katayama tucked things away Saturday. He blistered Wago with a one-bogey 62 to forge a five-stroke lead at 192 over Kawahara (67) and set up the final-round show.

Japan PGA Championship
Ibigawa, Gifu, Japan
Winner: Tomohiro Kondo

Tomohiro Kondo picked a good time to end his six-year victory drought. A win in a major tournament adds a little extra luster to a player's record, so Kondo could draw a little more pride from his playoff victory in the Japan PGA Championship, just as his victim, 51-year-old Katsuyoshi Tomori, had to feel particular disappointment in having what could be one of his last chances to win on the regular tour slip away.

Both players let the title in Japan's oldest tournament (1926) escape on the final holes of regulation play. First, Tomori missed his opportunity to land his seventh career title when he bogeyed the last two holes. Then, Kondo, finishing after Tomori, blew the one-shot margin when he, too, bogeyed the 72nd hole and forced the playoff. Kondo, who started the final round four strokes behind leader Toru Taniguchi, had seized the lead Sunday with a outgoing 32 at Tanigumi Country Club in Ibigawa, Gifu Prefecture, but he also bogeyed the 16th before the overtime-forcing bogey at the last hole.

Kondo's par on the first extra hole was the winner when Tomori missed his par putt. The bonus for Kondo was the automatic five-year exemption on the tour.

Until the final round, when he struggled to a 74, Taniguchi appeared headed for his 11th career victory. With four others, Taniguchi stood two strokes off the pace of little-known Norihiro Nakata, who posted a second-nine 29 and 66. Taniguchi repeated his 68 Friday and moved into a deadlock with Nakata (70) at the head of the field. With 69 Saturday for 205, Taniguchi established a three-stroke margin over runner-up Tadahiro Takayama, a two-time winner in 2005. Kondo was then at 209, Tomori at 210, ready for their Sunday charges.

Munsingwear Open KSB Cup
Tamano, Okayama, Japan
Winner: Toshinori Muto

For the second time in eight days and third time in the young season, a first-time winner reigned on the Japan Tour. Toshinori Muto, who in five seasons had finished a tournament in the top 10 just twice, staged a mighty finish in the Munsingwear Open KSB Cup in mid-May to put a target score on the board and waited as one after another contender fell by the wayside. Starting the day seemingly out of it seven strokes behind leader Kiyoshi Miyazato, Muto racked up four birdies on the first six holes at Tojigaoka Marine Hills Golf Club in Tamano, Okayama Prefecture. He added four more coming home for 64–274 and eventually captured his initial victory by two strokes over Eiji Mizoguchi.

Muto has a modest opinion of his talents. "I had long felt that I was just a fringe member of this tour," he said. "I never thought I would get a day like this, but I'd been waiting for such a chance without hurrying."

The lead was like a hot potato through the first three rounds. Takao Nogami had it first on Thursday. He shot 64 to stand in front by two strokes over five players, including money leader Shingo Katayama and Soshi Tajima, who followed with 69s Friday to edge a stroke into the lead at 135.

Miyazato took over Saturday. The older brother of Japan LPGA star Ai Miyazato fired 67 for 203 and established a three-stroke margin over Nogami (69), Mizoguchi (70) and Tajima (71). Katayama slipped back with 73, but recovered with 69 Sunday to tie for third with Miyazato (74) and Mamo Osanai (70).

Mitsubishi Diamond Cup
Iruma, Saitama, Japan
Winner: Kaname Yokoo

Kaname Yokoo has frequently been a serious presence on the Japan Tour in recent years, best remembered for carrying Tiger Woods into a playoff before losing to him in the 2005 Dunlop Phoenix, but it had been going on four years since the international professional scored his fourth and most recent victory in that same prestigious tournament. Relying heavily on a razor-sharp short game, Yokoo emerged from a large pack of contenders and picked off the Mitsubishi Diamond Cup title in late May to end the victory drought. His five-under-par 66 and 275 gave him a two-stroke win.

"It all came down to putting and short approaches," observed Yokoo, who hit only eight greens in the final round at Sayama Golf Club at Iruma, Saitama Prefecture. "You know putts continue to fall when you win a tournament."

Until Yokoo took command Sunday, Toru Suzuki fronted a group of 10 players within three strokes of the lead overnight. The veteran, a seven-time winner, had taken the top spot in Friday's second round with birdies on three of his last five holes for 68–138, a shot ahead of Keiichiro Fukabori (68-71) and Toshinori Muto (69-70), the previous week's Munsingwear tournament winner. Suzuki shot 70–208 Saturday to retain his lead, but only by a stroke over Yokoo (71-70-68) and Shingo Katayama, who charged into the picture with 66 for his 209. Four players were at 210 and another four at 211.

Yokoo launched his run Sunday with birdies on the first two holes and broke from a tie with Suzuki with two more in the first nine, putting only eight times on that stretch. A final birdie and the absence of bogeys marked the back side, his deft chip to tap-in range some 30 yards out of heavy rough typifying his game that day.

JCB Classic Sendai
Shibata, Miyagi, Japan
Winner: Hideto Tanihara

As far as winning was concerned, it may not have made any difference, the way Hideto Tanihara was playing, but things certainly were a little easier for him when No. 1 Shingo Katayama, his playing companion and closest pursuer, developed a sore knee during the final round of the JCB Classic Sendai. Tanihara, who had spurted two shots into the lead with a fiery 63 Saturday, birdied two of the first three holes Sunday, went on to a four-under-par 71 for 266 total and a five-stroke victory on the Omotezao Kokusai Golf Club course at Shibata, Miyagi Prefecture, the first week of June. It was the third career win and first since the year-ending Asia-Japan Okinawa Open in 2003 for Tanihara, back in Japan after an unsuccessful year on the U.S. PGA Tour.

"I didn't know about his injury, though I felt something was wrong," said the 27-year-old champion. Discussing the injury, Katayama declared, "I don't want to make excuses, but I felt a sharp pain in my right knee. I just tried hard to complete my round." He shot 70, easily held second place (by five over third-place Shinichi Akiba) and continued his brilliant season. Along with his victory in The Crowns, Katayama had two thirds and two fourths in his five previous starts, as he built a commanding lead in the money race.

Tanihara and Katayama were contenders from the start. Tanihara shared the first-round lead at 67 with Taichi Teshima and Koumei Oda. Katayama was among four a stroke behind. The second day they switched positions, Katayama with 67–135 and Tanihara with 69–136. Tanihara missed the course record by a shot with his eight-birdie 63 Saturday that gave him a two-stroke lead over Katayama (66–201) as they surged away from the rest of the field and set up the Sunday duel.

Mandom Lucido Yomiuri Open
Nishinomiya, Hyogo, Japan
Winner: Nobuhiro Masuda

The most surprising element of the Mandom Lucido Yomiuri Open was not the victory of Nobuhiro Masuda after seven years of trying, but that the tournament's 72 holes were completed not only on time but at all. Wind, rain and fog descended on Yomiuri Country Club at Nishinomiya, Hyogo Prefecture, combining to bring suspensions of play in each of the first three rounds.

Sunday's weather was fine, as was the game of the 33-year-old Masuda, who won a final-round battle against Y.E. Yang, the South Korean with three titles on his record, to notch that initial win and become the Japan Tour's fourth first-time victor of 2006. Masuda closed with 68 for his 14-

under-par 274 and had a three-shot lead until he bogeyed and Yang birdied the final hole. Yang had 69–275.

Nearly half the field was still on the course when play was suspended Thursday because of blustery, wet weather, but the leader—Nobuhito Sato—posted his 67 that day. Twenty-one men failed to complete their second rounds Friday, but they were not among the four 36-hole co-leaders at 137—Tetsuji Hiratsuka (71-66), Jun Kikuchi (72-65), Katsuyoshi Tomori (69-68) and Hideto Tanihara (72-65), the 2003 Yomiuri winner coming off his JCB Sendai triumph two weeks earlier.

Again Saturday, fog prevented completion of the round, but when the results were all in Sunday morning, Masuda (69-70-67) and Yang (72-69-65) had shares of the lead. Masuda grabbed the lead quickly in the final round with birdies on two of the first three holes, made the turn with a two-stroke lead, and added birdies at the 11th and 14th holes before taking his lone bogey at the final hole.

Gateway to the Open Mizuno Open
Kasaoka, Okayama, Japan
Winner: S.K. Ho

The Japanese players should have some doubts about that old saw—"There's no place like home"—particularly as it applies to the site of the annual Gateway to the Open Mizuno Open. This should have been especially so after South Korea's S.K. Ho won the 2006 renewal of the tournament at JFE Setonaikai Golf Club in Kasaoka, Okayama Prefecture. It was the fifth consecutive year in which an overseas player landed the Mizuno title and its bonus—an invitation to the Open Championship in Britain. Ho followed Americans Dean Wilson (2002) and Todd Hamilton (2003) and Australians Brendan Jones (2004) and Chris Campbell (2005) in that achievement.

Wet weather again disrupted the flow of play, stranding half the field the first day and preventing 15 players from finishing their second rounds Friday. When everyone had posted a 36-hole score, Fiji's Dinesh Chand, a three-time winner on the tour, held the lead with a pair of 68s, one stroke in front of Ho and just two ahead of seven others at 138.

Ho, 32, a double winner in Japan in 2005 and holder of five titles on the circuit, surged into the lead Saturday with 66, the day's best score, moving three strokes ahead of runners-up Chand (70) and New Zealand's David Smail, who lost to Campbell in the 2005 Mizuno playoff. The South Korean carved out a steady one-under-par 71 Sunday on a day that saw just three men break 70, and his 274 gave him a three-shot victory.

Two of those sub-70 rounds were particularly rewarding. Tatsuhiko Ichihara, a non-winner, capped a steady tournament with 69 and tied for second with Smail, who matched Ho's 71. Wayne Perske, the Token Cup winner, stirred up a 66, tied for fourth with Kiyoshi Maita and got the fourth passport to Royal Liverpool (along with Ho, Ichihara and Smail) with his better final round than Maita's 71.

UBS Japan Golf Tour Championship
Kasama, Ibaraki, Japan
Winner: Tatsuhiko Takahashi

Tatsuhiko Takahashi came into the season a 2005 tournament winner without a title to defend and went out holding the UBS Japan Golf Tour Championship, one of the richest and most prized championships. Takahashi, who had scored his maiden victory in his 10th season in the 2005 Aiful Cup, off the schedule in 2006, carried a one-stroke lead into the final round at Shishido Hills Country Club at Kasama, Ibaraki Prefecture, fashioned a steady 68 and put away a three-stroke victory with his seven-under-par 273.

Two veterans who had leaderships roles in the early going at Shishido Hills had faded from contention by tournament's end. Kiyoshi Murota, at 50 enjoying one of his best years, fired 65 Thursday and took a two-stroke lead, but subsequent rounds of 73 and 74 led him to an 11th-place finish. Toru Taniguchi, 38, the 2002 money leader, bolted from second place into a four-stroke advantage with 66 for a 133 total Friday. The 32-year-old Takahashi, who had started the tournament with 71, matched Taniguchi's 66 and climbed into a four-way tie for second with Tsuneyuki Nakajima (70), Tetsuji Hiratsuka (68) and Toyokazu Fujishima (67).

Taniguchi had an uncharacteristic meltdown Saturday, stumbling to a 74 that cost him the lead. Takahashi took over with his second straight 68 for 205, but had the storied Nakajima (69) on his heels and three others — Taniguchi, Hiratsuka (70) and Yusaku Miyazato (68) — two off the pace.

Hiratsuka gave Takahashi a run for his money Sunday, overtaking him with his fifth birdie of the day at the 13th. But Hiratsuka lost four strokes on the next three holes, and Takahashi was in the clear as Nakajima also had a faltering finish. With 69, Hiratsuka took second place and Nakajima tied S.K. Ho for third at 277.

Woodone Open Hiroshima
Hiroshima, Japan
Winner: Tetsuji Hiratsuka

Within a single week, Tetsuji Hiratsuka twice found himself on the final holes with an opportunity to win his first tournament in two years. In the first case, he had caught leader Tatsuhiko Takahashi on the final nine of the Tour Championship only to fumble his chances away on the next three holes. Seven days later in the Woodone Open Hiroshima, Hiratsuka went to the 18th tee on the Hachihomatsu course of Hiroshima Country Club with a bare one-stroke lead on the two men who were playing with him in the final threesome. This time, Hiratsuka responded with a birdie that gave him a 68 for 19-under-par 265 and a two-stroke victory, his third in Japan.

Interestingly, his two pursuers were Shingo Katayama and S.K. Ho, who came into the Woodone Open one-two on the money list. Ho, a winner two weeks earlier in the Mizuno Open, had shot the season's first 61 — 11 birdies and a bogey — in the opening round and jumped off to a three-stroke lead, seven ahead of Hiratsuka. The South Korean standout retained the three-shot margin with a 67–128 Friday. Hiratsuka cut two strokes off his deficit with a 65, but Katayama, who hadn't finished worse than fourth all season, was nine shots off the pace at 137.

The picture changed dramatically Saturday. Hiratsuka racked up seven birdies, five on the back nine, for 64–197, while Ho was struggling to a one-over-par 72 and Katayama was charging with 65. The result was that Hiratsuka had a three-stroke lead over Ho, five over Katayama, setting up the final-holes excitement Sunday. Ho (67) and Katayama (65) tied for second.

Sega Sammy Cup
Chitose, Hokkaido, Japan
Winner: Yeh Wei-tze

How unlikely was this? Only two Taiwanese golfers teed off in the second playing of the Sega Sammy Cup tournament in the Hokkaido city of Chitose in late July. One was the defending champion, Lin Keng-chi. The other was Yeh Wei-tze, who had scored his lone victory on the Japan Tour in 2003, interestingly also in Hokkaido at the ANA Open. When the shooting was over, Yeh was a four-stroke winner. Two for two for Taiwan.

Unfamiliar names peppered the top of the leaderboard in the first round of the Sammy Cup at The North Country Golf Club. The smallest man in the field—5-foot, 2-inch Masamichi Uehira—led with a 67 that included two bogeys, and Y.E. Yang, a three-time winner in Japan, shared the 68 spot with three little-knowns—Koki Idoki, Kunihiro Kamii and Koumei Oda.

Fame was fleeting for Uehira. Rounds of 75-78-74 followed and he finished in 42nd place. The second round instead belong Yeh and Hidemasa Hoshino, whose sole victory also came in 2003 in The Crowns. Yeh had 70-68 and Hoshino 72-66 to tie for first at 138.

Scoring was high Saturday. Only one player broke 70 as Yeh took over first place when he birdied the final hole for par 72–210 and inched a stroke ahead of Hoshino (73) and Azuma Yano (70).

"I kept on attacking, especially on the par-five holes, without getting overly defensive," said the 33-year-old Taiwanese player of his closing 66 that established his four-stroke victory at 12-under-par 276. He had three early birdies and three more at the end, but probably saved the round when he salvaged a par after hitting into the water on the par-five 13th. Hoshino's 69 gave him the runner-up position, five ahead of Yano (72) and China's Liang Wen-chong.

The Golf Tournament in Omaezaki
Omaezaki, Shizuoka, Japan
Winner: Toru Taniguchi

Toru Taniguchi was experiencing a peculiarly consistent and frustrating season when he teed off at the end of July in The Golf Tournament in Omaezaki. One of Japan's most prominent and successful players, the 38-year-old Taniguchi had been a top-10 finisher in all but two of his 11 starts, yet had had only one real chance to win his 11th title on the Japan Tour when he blew a three-shot 54-hole lead in the Japan PGA Championship in May. Otherwise, it had been non-contending finishes between seventh and 10th place.

The breakthrough came in Omaezaki, but not easily. Taniguchi fought his way from a slow start into a final-round deadlock with Tomohiro Kondo and S.K. Ho, two winners earlier in 2006, and won the subsequent playoff, just the second of the season.

After 36 holes on Shizuoka Country Club's par-71 Hamaoka course, Taniguchi, with 69-70–139, trailed leader Soshi Tajima by seven strokes. Tajima, three years beyond his only tour victory, had begun the tournament with a six-under-par 65 and led by three at the halfway point when he followed with 67, 10 under par at 132. The 29-year-old began to unravel in the third round, managing just a par 71–203, then in front by just a stroke over Ho (69), Australian Paul Sheehan (67) and Thailand's Thammanoon Srirot (68).

Taniguchi and Kondo soared into contention at 205 with 66 and 65, respectively, and wound up grouped Sunday with Ho, who shot 69 for 204. The South Korean frittered away an early lead and had to birdie the last two holes for 69 to join Taniguchi and Kondo, who had 68s for their 273, in the playoff. In the overtime, Kondo went out when he missed a short putt on the second extra hole, and Taniguchi nailed down the win when he birdied the third.

Sun Chlorella Classic
Hokkaido, Japan
Winner: Hideto Tanihara

Hideto Tanihara was the object of particular attention when he began play in the rich Sun Chlorella Classic at Hokkaido's Otaru Country Club, having just returned to Japan from Britain after his fifth-place showing in the Open, matching the best finish ever by a Japanese player in the oldest championship. He responded at Otaru with his second victory of the Japan Tour season, although it was not exactly a work of art. He bogeyed two of the last three holes for a 72 and five-under-par 283 that enabled him to top five other players by a single stroke and become the first multiple winner of the year in Japan. It was his fourth career victory.

Tanihara had put himself in a hole the previous Friday after beginning the tournament in a eight-man tie for first place at 70. His second-round 74 dropped him into a tie for 17th as Masaya Tomida and Mitsuhiro Tateyama led with 72-68–140s. Tetsuji Hiratsuka took over the third day, slipping a stroke in front with 68–210, as Tanihara bounced back with 67 and tied for second at 211 with Tateyama (71).

Just as in the Tour Championship five weeks earlier, though, Hiratsuka came apart on the final nine Sunday. Riding a comfortable lead, Hiratsuka gave away four strokes on the last four holes, shot 74 and wound up in the runner-up group with Tomida (68), Katsumasa Miyamoto (69), Hiroyuki Fujita (71) and Prayad Marksaeng (72).

Under Armour KBC Augusta
Shima, Fukuoka, Japan
Winner: Taichi Teshima

Lesser-known players populated the leaderboards through much of the Under Armour KBC Augusta tournament when the Japan Tour resumed action after its usual two-week break in mid-August, but the eventual winner was quite familiar to the fans who attended the event at Keya Golf Club at Shima, Fukuoka Prefecture. Taichi Teshima, a 37-year-old Fukuoka native, rose from a mediocre start to squeeze out a one-stroke victory over Tetsuji Hiratsuka, who had to settle for a second straight runner-up finish.

Teshima shot 71 in the opening round, a distant seven strokes behind Shigemasa Higaki, a winner in 1999 (Fujisankei) but in the money just once in three 2006 starts. On Friday, Hiroo Kawai, a winless 34-year-old veteran, seized the spotlight when he shot a course-record-tying 63, eight under par, and took a one-stroke lead over Higaki (68) and Mitsuhiro Tateyama (65-67) with his 131. Kawai, who had six birdies in a first-nine 29, had never led a tournament before and didn't keep it long. In striking contrast, first place Saturday became the province of 19-year-old South Korean Lee Dong-hwan, the 2004 winner of the Japan Amateur Championship. Lee shot 65 for 201, nosing a stroke in front of Nobuhiro Masuda (63), Tateyama (70), Hiratsuka (69) and Teshima, who continued his climb with 65 following his second-round 66.

The final round became a two-man battle between Teshima and Hiratsuka. Teshima inched ahead with his sixth birdie at the 16th hole and held on with a par-par finish for 66–268 to win his fourth tour title and first in three years. His second straight second-place finish elevated Hiratsuka into the No. 1 spot on the money list.

Fujisankei Classic
Fujikawaguchiko, Yamanashi, Japan
Winner: Shingo Katayama

Shingo Katayama takes little stock in the warning to "beware of the injured player" so often heard at golf tournaments. Beset with back and knee ailments, he had fallen into his first slump of the season with a 42nd-place finish and a missed cut in his last two starts, in the latter case for the first time since 2004. Those miseries gone when he teed off in the Fujisankei Classic at the end of August, Katayama drove to a commanding three-stroke victory and regained the top spot on the money list.

Katayama was out of first place only for a few morning hours all week at Fujizakura Country Club at Fujikawaguchiko, Yamanashi Prefecture. He opened with a five-under-par 66, tied for the lead with Nobuhiro Masuda and Koichi Kashimura. He and 46 others were caught on the course as darkness fell during a rain-interrupted second round, and he found himself a stroke behind Hideto Tanihara when everybody had completed the round the next morning. He was at 66-71–137, Tanihara at 69-67–136.

Katayama quickly reclaimed the lead later that Saturday as Tanihara stumbled to a 74. Katayama ran off three birdies in a row on the second nine to score a 68 for 205 and spring five strokes into the lead over Tanihara, Jeev Milkha Singh (68), Hiroyuki Fujita (69) and Koki Idoki (69).

He put any potential challengers further at bay Sunday with two birdies on the first three holes, offset a lone bogey at the eighth hole with a birdie at the ninth, and put up nine solid pars on the back nine for 69 and the winning 10-under-par 274. He joined Tanihara as the only double winners of the season with his 20th career victory. China's Liang Wen-chong picked off the runner-up spot with 64–277, his highest finish in 46 starts in Japan, and was the only man to finish within eight shots of Katayama.

Suntory Open
Inzai, Chiba, Japan
Winner: Y.E. Yang

Two years earlier, Y.E. Yang let victory slip from his grasp in the final round of the Suntory Open and didn't want to duplicate that experience when he found himself with another chance to win on his adopted Japan Tour. Actually, the South Korean faced a tougher job at Sobu Country Club at Inzai, Chiba Prefecture, in 2006, sitting three strokes off the lead instead of entering the final round tied for the lead as he was in 2004. This time, he came up with one of the finest closing efforts of the season, exploding with a seven-under-par 63 and racing to a fourth win in Japan, his first of the year. His 266 gave him a six-stroke victory over Toru Taniguchi (71), the first-round leader, and Hidemasa Hoshino (68).

Yusaku Miyazato went in the opposite direction Sunday when it was stacking up as a day when he and his sister, the sensational Ai, might win tournaments in two different parts of Japan. Yusaku had taken over first place the second day with rounds of 66 and 67 as Taniguchi soared to 73. Miyazato shot 67 Saturday to retain a share of the lead with Shoichi Ideguchi (65) at 200, with Taniguchi at 201 after a second 64 and Yang (67-68-68) at 203.

Miyazato was in contention Sunday until his game unraveled and he lost six strokes on the last 10 holes en route to a 76. Ideguchi slipped to 74 and Yang put the win away with five birdies and a back-nine 30 for the 63.

Incidentally, Ai Miyazato won the Japan LPGA Championship that day in Hokkaido.

ANA Open
Kitahiroshima, Hokkaido, Japan
Winner: Tomohiro Kondo

By strange coincidence, Tomohiro Kondo's second win of the season in the ANA Open duplicated the victory pattern of 2005 when, over the first five months, the titles were passed around quite liberally. Just as was the case when Keiichiro Fukabori won his second title in last year's ANA Open, Kondo was just the third double victor of the 2006 campaign, joining Hideto Tanihara and Shingo Katayama in that regard.

Kondo, who scored the first victory in his seven-year career in May in a playoff in the Japan PGA Championship, had a bit easier time of it on the Wattsu course of Sapporo Golf Club. He was the co-leader after 54 holes and eked out a one-stroke triumph with his two-under-par 69 in the final round, fending off the 66s of Kaname Yokoo and Kiyoshi Maita that gave them shares of second place.

"I was eager to get my second win under my belt," said Kondo. "My putts came up a little short, but I thought I managed my game well before getting onto the greens."

Kondo took the lead Friday with nine-under-par 133 after starting with 69, four shots off the pace of Thailand's Chawalit Plaphol, the ANA victor in 2004. Kondo eagled his final hole for the 64 that gave him a one-stroke edge on Shinichi Yokota. Scoring was generally higher Saturday, and Kondo's one-over 72 was enough to leave him in co-possession of the lead with Yoshinobu Tsukada, who had 68, one of nine scores in the 60s. Kondo had his second eagle of the week Sunday in shooting the winning 69.

Acom International
Ogawa, Ibaraki, Japan
Winner: Mamo Osanai

Perhaps because it had been so long since his last previous victory, Mamo Osanai had a hard time finishing off what was on the verge of being a runaway in the Acom International in late September. The 36-year-old Osanai, who hadn't won since the now-defunct Japan Match Play Championship in 1999, never trailed at Ishioka Golf Club and led by five midway through the tournament. Yet it took an opponent's bogey in a playoff to enable him to land his third career title on the Japan Tour.

Osanai spurted to the five-stroke lead with an opening 65, a shot in front of Australian Paul Sheehan, and an eight-birdie 63 the second day, after which, in an understatement, he observed, "My putting has been good." Yoichi Shimizu was then the runner-up, also having fired 63. From there on, Osanai was a bit shaky. He came back to the field with a three-over-par 74, but still led by two strokes over Ryuichi Oda (65) and Thailand's Prayad Marksaeng (70).

He played well enough to win in regulation Sunday unless somebody close were to shoot "lights out." That's what Taichi Teshima, the KBC August champion and the 2005 runner-up in the Acom, did. Teshima produced the week's third 63 for 270 and forced a playoff when Osanai finished with 68 to match it. The playoff lasted just one hole as Teshima missed the green with his approach and failed to save par. Osanai just missed a birdie putt and tapped in for the victory.

Coca-Cola Tokai Classic
Aichi, Japan
Winner: Hidemasa Hoshino

It could be said that Hidemasa Hoshino was lurking. Although he had won just once on the Japan Tour, in 2003, Hoshino was playing like a winner up to that point in the 2006 season. With two runner-up finishes and three others in the top five, he stood 10th on the money list going into the Coca-Cola Tokai Classic. He jumped to third when he scored a two-stroke victory on the difficult West course of Miyoshi Country Club. The only player to break par for 72 holes, Hoshino came from four strokes off the lead with a final-round 67 for the winning, two-under-par 282.

Nobuhito Sato, a nine-time winner enduring a four-year victory dry spell, got off to a good start in the Tokai, leading India's Jeev Milkha Singh by one stroke with his 68. That was all for Sato, and South Korean Chang Ik-je took over the top spot Friday with 67–138, a shot in front of Katsumasa Miyamoto and Colombia's colorful Camilo Villegas, taking a break from the U.S. PGA Tour.

The revolving door continued Saturday as Hiroo Kawai, a one-round flash in the KBC Augusta earlier in the season, went in front with his third consecutive steady round (71-70-70) to head Taichi Teshima (67), Yuudai Maeda (71) and 19-year-old Lee Dong-hwan (69). Hoshino was at 215 with rounds of 70-73-72. He made his Sunday run on the back nine and built enough of a margin that he survived a double bogey before posting the 67 and waiting to see if anybody in the last two groups would catch him. Miyamoto finished with 70 for a par 284. Six players, including Villegas, Singh, Kawai and Shingo Katayama, tied for third at 286.

Japan Open
Kawagoe, Saitama, Japan
Winner: Paul Sheehan

Paul Sheehan's impressive victory in the Japan Open created options for the globe-trotting Australian beyond the prestige of the title and the permanent place it assures him in future seasons on the Japan Tour. It gave him the opportunity to pick his spots on his 2007 schedule in both Japan and America, where he played on the secondary Nationwide Tour in 2006 and did well enough in nine starts to earn playing privileges on the regular PGA Tour, as well as an invitation to the 2007 Open at Carnoustie.

With defending champion Shingo Katayama on his heels heading into the final round of the Japan Open at Kasumigaseki Country Club at Kawagoe, Saitama Prefecture, Sheehan produced a steady, near-flawless 18 holes and wound up with an even-par 71 and a three-stroke victory with his seven-under-par 277. Katayama never made a run, finishing five back after two late bogeys led to a closing 75. Though picking off the runner-up spot, lightly regarded Azuma Yano did not seriously challenge either. In fact, Sheehan led by four until making a meaningless bogey at the 72nd hole, as the seven-year professional notched his third title in Japan to go with his pair of victories in 2004. Victory in the Jacob's Creek Open in Australia came at one of the nine Nationwide Tour starts.

Considering his No. 1 position on the circuit, Katayama seemed the likely winner when he grabbed the lead Friday after trailing Jeev Milkha Singh's 65 by two strokes in the opening round. Katayama shot 69 for 136 and eased a stroke ahead of Singh (72) and South Korean amateurs Lee Won-joon (67) and Kim Kyung-tae (68). Even after Sheehan birdied two of his last four holes for 68–206, Katayama was comfortably ensconced a shot back after shooting 71 despite bogeys on the two front-nine par-threes.

Sheehan played in only two more 2006 tournaments in Japan after collecting the year's biggest check of ¥40 million, returning to America to solidify his position on the Nationwide Tour money list and the promotion to the PGA Tour.

Bridgestone Open
Chiba, Japan
Winner: Taichi Teshima

It didn't start out that way, but Taichi Teshima's second victory of the season in the Bridgestone Open came much more comfortably than at the first one two months earlier in the KBC Augusta, where he eked out a one-stroke win. In the October tournament at Sodegaura Country Club, Teshima again opened with a mediocre round, but he blitzed the field in the middle two rounds and zipped to a five-stroke triumph. The win, the fifth in the career of the 38-year-old ironman who had skipped just one tournament all year, vaulted him into second place well behind Shingo Katayama on the money list.

Kiyoshi Maita held sway the first two days. He birdied five of the first seven holes Thursday and took a two-stroke lead with his eight-under-par 64. Six back at that point after posting a 70, Teshima began his climb Friday, shooting 65 to cut his deficit in half as Maita retained the lead with 68–132. Teshima had trailed by seven at the KBC Augusta after the first round. Katayama (68-65) moved into a second-place tie with Koki Idoki (67-66) Friday at Sodegaura.

Teshima's course-record-tying 63 Saturday, highlighted by a chip-in eagle at the 16th hole, turned the tables for him. At day's end, his 198 established a four-stroke lead over Maita, five over Idoki, as both men shot 70s. Katayama fell back with 74. Teshima had total control of his game Sunday. He ran off a four-birdie 68 for 266 to establish the five-shot margin over Maita, who shot 69. Prayad Marksaeng (68), Kaname Yokoo (69) and Idoki (70) finished another two strokes back.

ABC Championship
Kato, Hyogo, Japan
Winner: Shingo Katayama

Shingo Katayama erased any doubts about his status as Japan's most talented player with his brilliant finishing kick and third victory of the season, winning the ABC Championship for the third time in four years at the ABC Golf Club at Kato in Hyogo Prefecture. The ¥24 million first prize gave him a huge lead in his quest for his third straight money title and fourth of his career. With his 21st triumph, Katayama became the fourth leading money winner of all time on the Japan Tour.

Virtually all of the excitement was packed into Sunday's finale. The lead had changed hands at the end of each of the first three rounds. Y.E. Yang, the Suntory Open winner in September, had it first, opening with 66 and a one-stroke lead over Azuma Yano, Kim Jong-duck of South Korea and 46-year-old Frankie Minoza. Yano took over Friday with 68–135, a shot ahead of Katsumune Imai (70-66) and two in front of Yang (66-71.)

At the end of 54 holes, the top spot was in the hands of Hisayuki Sasaki at 205 as he eyed his first win since 1997. Yang (69) was at 206, Yano (72) at 207, and Katayama, with 68 Saturday, trailed by four strokes. It quickly became a duel Sunday as Katayama and Yang both rolled to 31s on the first nine, Katayama starting his move with an eagle at the first hole. Still behind by three, Katayama duplicated the 31 on the second nine, and Yang, after a bogey at the 14th, had to birdie three of the last four holes just to bring about a playoff after the matching 271s. Katayama birdied the second overtime hole to record the victory.

Asahiryokuken Yomiuri Memorial
Fukuoka, Japan
Winner: Tatsuhiko Ichihara

It had been an eight-year dry spell and an unrewarding season for 27-year-old Tatsuhiko Ichihara when he began play in the Asahiryokuken Yomiuri Memorial, his 20th start of 2006. He played steadily for three days at Asoiizuka Golf Club, then burst from five strokes off the pace in the final round to land his first Japan Tour title. He more than doubled his year's earnings with the ¥20 million first-place check and won a berth in the season-ending, exclusive-field Japan Series.

Ichihara's triumph came at the expense of India's Jeev Milkha Singh, also winless in Japan but a frequent contender with eight top-10 finishes earlier in the season. Singh, fresh from his victory in the European Tour's Volvo Masters in Spain, had led the tournament through three rounds. He shot 66 the first day and shared first place with Chang Ik-je, then advanced a stroke ahead of Tetsuji Hiratsuka Friday, eagling two par-five holes on his way to 65 for 131. Chang shot 67 for 133.

A 67 Saturday gave Singh a three-stroke lead over Yoshikazu Haku at 201. Ryoken Kawagishi and Hiratsuka were at 202, and Ichihara, with his 68, shared the fifth position with Chang. Ichihara made up most of the ground Sunday with four birdies on the front nine, and the final birdie at the 15th proved the difference as he shot 67 for his 18-under-par 270. Singh, playing behind him in the last group, could manage only 73 and 271. "That helped keep me away from a pressure situation. I feel like I took advantage of that," said Ichihara, just the fifth first-time winner of the season.

Mitsui Sumitomo Visa Taiheiyo Masters
Gotemba, Shizuoka, Japan
Winner: Tsuneyuki Nakajima

Tsuneyuki (Tommy) Nakajima revived memories of the earlier years of his wonderful career in Japan and around the world and accomplished a rare feat when he stormed from far behind to capture the rich, talent-studded

Mitsui Sumitomo Visa Taiheiyo Masters in mid-November. The one-stroke victory in the Japan Tour event came just weeks after the 52-year-old ace swept the Japan Senior Open and the Senior PGA, the two major championships on the Japan Senior Tour. Only a handful of players on all of the world's tours have scored victories on the regular and senior circuits in the same season.

The win on the Gotemba course of the Taiheiyo Club in Gotemba, Shizuoka Prefecture, his career 48th, came 21 years after he won the Masters the first time and four years since his second Taiheiyo victory was his most recent one on the circuit.

Nakajima's chances seemed dim after three rounds at Gotemba. He sat in a 10th-place tie after rounds of 71-68-71, six strokes behind leader Makoto Inoue. Inoue's 67–204 had put him two shots ahead of leading money winner Shingo Katayama and three in front of Sergio Garcia. The brilliant Spanish Ryder Cupper, bent on salvaging a disappointing 2006 season, had shared the lead with Daisuke Maruyama and Katsumasa Miyamoto at 135 midway through the tournament.

None of the top contenders was a match for Nakajima Sunday, though. He ran off three birdies on the front nine and four more on the back on his way to 65, the day's best round, and 13-under-par 275 total as the big names faltered, Katayama with 73 and Garcia with 77. Toru Taniguchi produced the only challenge at the end, posting a 67 and falling a stroke short of the winner. Katayama finished three strokes further back in a third-place tie with Keiichiro Fukabori and Inoue.

Dunlop Phoenix
Miyazaki, Japan
Winner: Padraig Harrington

It will probably be remembered as a mere hiccough in the composition of his brilliant 2006 season, but Tiger Woods let a victory slip through his fingers when he made his annual trip to Japan for the Dunlop Phoenix tournament in mid-November. Seemingly headed for his 10th win of the year worldwide, Woods faltered as playing companion Padraig Harrington advanced in the final-round stretch and subsequently succumbed to a Harrington birdie on the second hole of a playoff, the fifth and last of the Japan Tour season.

The two shared the lead entering the final round at Miyazaki's Phoenix Country Club after sloshing through a rain-soaked Saturday to six-under-par 204s, Woods off a birdie on the last hole for a two-over 72 and Harrington with 71. The world No. 1 had seized the lead from Japan's No. 1, Shingo Katayama (65-70), Friday with his 67-65–132 and was one in front of Harrington (67-66) in his bid for a third straight Dunlop Phoenix title.

Katayama, the Phoenix winner in 2000, his first money title season, was just two behind Woods and Harrington at 206 going into the last 18 holes, but was the odd man out in the final threesome Sunday. Woods built a three-stroke lead through the first 12 holes, but four holes later, a three-putt bogey dropped him into a tie with the Irishman at 271. They finished par-birdie for 67s and returned to the 18th tee to settle it.

After both players birdied the par-five hole the first time, Harrington picked up his first win in Japan the second time around. Taking advantage of a break when his second shot ricocheted off a tree into play, Harrington lofted his approach two feet from the cup and tapped in after Woods missed his birdie try from 10 feet. It was just the third defeat in the 18 playoffs worldwide Woods has faced in his professional career. Keiichiro Fukabori fired a 64 Sunday, just missing a tie with his 272. Katayama (68) and Justin Rose (66) were next at 274.

Casio World Open
Kochi, Japan
Winner: Jeev Milkha Singh

India finally has a golf champion of international stature. Globe-trotting Jeev Milkha Singh, reaching the peak of his career at age 34, clearly established himself in that role when he made the Casio World Open his third victory of 2006, following his April win in the Volvo China Open and his October triumph in the Volvo Masters in Spain, an important event on the European PGA Tour.

The two-stroke victory in the Japan Tour's final full-field event of the season should not have surprised anyone. Singh nearly won the Asahiryokuken Yomiuri three weeks earlier, leading for three rounds and finishing second, his 10th top-10 finish in 15 starts in Japan in 2006.

He nearly duplicated that in the Casio World. He shot 66 in the opening round at Kochi Kuroshio Country Club, tying for the lead with Azuma Yano and Tetsuya Haraguchi, then dropped a stroke behind Haraguchi (68–134) the second day. He birdied the final hole Saturday for 69–204 and moved back into a first-place deadlock with Haraguchi (70). New Zealand's David Smail shot 67 for 206, tied for third with Toshinori Muto (69) and Hideki Kase (70). Haraguchi was no match for Singh Sunday. Singh ran off five birdies and a bogey for 68, and his 272 total bested runner-up Smail, who also shot 68 in the final round.

Michele Wie was the focus of most of the attention the first two days. The 17-year-old Hawaiian crowd-pleaser took another futile stab at making the cut, shooting 81-80 this time. She never made a birdie and missed the cut by 17 strokes.

Golf Nippon Series JT Cup
Tokyo, Japan
Winner: Jeev Milkha Singh

Jeev Milkha Singh capped his finest season by far when he followed his impressive win in the Casio World Open by outplaying the select field of 2006 winners and top-25 finishers the next Sunday in the season-finale Golf Nippon Series JT Cup. In the lead from the second round on, Singh closed with an even-par 70 at Tokyo's Yomiuri Country Club to edge Nobuhiro Masuda, the Yomiuri Open champion, by a stroke with his 269 total.

Singh positioned himself two strokes off the lead in Thursday's opening round as Wayne Perske, winner of the season-opening Token Homemate Cup in April, and Hiroyuki Fujita shot 65s. Perske slipped two back Friday as Singh and Shingo Katayama climbed into a tie for the lead at 132 with Fujita (67). Singh had a 65, Katayama 66.

The Indian player birdied his first three holes Saturday and jumped to a four-stroke lead with 67–199. Perske moved back into the runner-up slot with a second 69 for 203, as Katayama dropped five back with 72–204. Masuda and Hideto Tanihara came up with 66s Sunday and mounted the strongest challenges to Singh, who held on with his par round for 11-under-par 269 and the one-shot triumph. He was the fifth multiple winner of the Japan Tour season and the only one to do it back to back.

Katayama shot 69 Sunday and tied for seventh place at 273 as he widened the huge margin he had established in becoming the circuit's leading money winner for the fourth time and third season in a row. Tanihara was the runner-up, nearly ¥60 million behind him.

12. Australasian Tour

When Australia's leading golfers returned home for the country's leading events at the end of the year, there was certainly something to celebrate. The guest of honor was Geoff Ogilvy, the U.S. Open champion and also winner of the WGC - Accenture Match Play. But there was much more success to enjoy Down Under. Stuart Appleby wins the Mercedes Championships, the season-opening event on the PGA Tour in the United States, seemingly every year, while Adam Scott won the season-ending Tour Championship.

Scott finished the year in fourth place on the world rankings and third on the U.S. money list. Ogilvy and Appleby also featured in the top 10. With America having taken over from Europe as the place to be for young Australian golfers, there has been a definite twang to the accents on the PGA Tour. They are there in numbers but are also winning. Six players won eight titles between them. Apart from Ogilvy and Scott, Appleby won the Shell Houston Open as well as the Mercedes, Rod Pampling won the Bay Hill Invitational, Aaron Baddeley triumphed at the Verizon Heritage, while John Senden won the John Deere Classic.

"Australian golf is as strong as it's ever been and this has been the case for two or three years now," said Scott. "Our presence in the U.S. is almost unmatched. Certainly, the talk of the U.S. Tour is the dominance of the Australians out there. With Geoff claiming a major and a World Golf Championship this year, I think there's going to be a lot more to come."

Ogilvy also became a father in 2006, so the year could not have got any better. At Winged Foot, he made a brilliant up-and-down at the 72nd hole while all the rest, including Phil Mickelson, Colin Montgomerie, Jim Furyk and Padraig Harrington, were losing the plot as well as the trophy. While patently blessed with many talents, it was his composure under extreme pressure which was the hallmark of Ogilvy's success. "I made some nice putts when I needed to make them this year," he reflected. "I've probably had years where I've maybe even played better, but you make putts at the right time, get it up and down at the right time, hit the right drive at the right time, and good things happen. I could definitely play better than I did this year.

"But I could play unbelievably well next year and not have the success I've had this year. A WGC and a major, I mean, that's pretty good. I could finish top-five every week and not win but have played better. It's hard to measure. I just want to be a better player next year than I was this year, and if good things happen, that's good."

After Michael Campbell's victory the previous year, Ogilvy kept the U.S. Open in Australasian hands. He almost added his own national championship to that of America, but finished runner-up to Senden. But the reception he received was heartening given the Australasian Tour's problems to keep sponsors and tournaments. "It was big and it was good," he said. "The Australasian Tour has struggled for a bit of profile the last few years, but this year they really promoted it well. They got a lot of people in the gate. We had big crowds to play in front of and I was really well received."

Returning home was also rewarding for Nick O'Hern. The Western Australian won the Cadbury Schweppes Australian PGA Championship at the end of the year, his first victory for seven years, to claim the Order of Merit title ahead of American Kevin Stadler, who challenged after winning the Johnnie Walker Classic at the start of the season. "When I came onto the tour in 1996 it was a goal of mine to win the Order of Merit. I've been in the top five I don't know how many times. I've gone very close. To do it in this fashion is very pleasing," O'Hern said after beating Peter Lonard in a playoff at Coolum. "I had to win this week to overhaul Kevin. I've got the trophy to prove it, I've won the Order of Merit. I've tried to support the home tour and come back as much as I can and play as much as I can. Being a PGA member, not just a PGA Tour member, and to win this championship is a double whammy right there."

Johnnie Walker Classic
Perth, Western Australia
Winner: Kevin Stadler

"What is the worst thing about being Craig Stadler?" was the absent-minded question. "Exactly what you just said," replied Kevin Stadler. Winning the Johnnie Walker Classic should help the 26-year-old American distinguish himself from his father, the renowned "Walrus." The younger Stadler was in Australia ahead of two Nationwide Tour events, but first accepted an invitation to the Johnnie Walker, co-sanctioned by the European Tour. The victory gave the player ranked 256th at the time his card on two tours.

From an opening 64, which tied for the lead with Adam Scott, Stadler showed what he is capable of at the Vines resort in Perth. He slipped two shots behind K.J. Choi after a 69, but then retook the lead with 66. His closing 69 gave Stadler a 20-under-par total of 268 and a two-stroke victory over Nick O'Hern, a native Western Australian and local hero.

About the only time Stadler was rattled was when he dropped three shots in a row from the fifth in the final round. O'Hern briefly took the lead, but then Stadler rallied with birdies at the ninth and 10th holes. O'Hern bogeyed the 12th, but willed on by a large supporting gallery, he finished strongly. A seven iron from 160 yards to four feet at the 17th gave him the first of two birdies. At the par-five 18th he hit a five wood to 10 feet, but the eagle putt just missed. He had to settle for a sixth second place on the European Tour.

Stadler arrived at the 18th needing a birdie for the victory, but for the third day in a row he claimed an eagle. A superb three iron from 220 yards found the green and rode the contours perfectly to three feet. "Honestly I am kind of baffled by all his," Stadler said. "It was a great week. Except for these three holes in the middle, I felt I had total control of my game. The golf course seemed to suit me and it all worked out."

Stadler said he would now have to rearrange his schedule to include some more European Tour events, but would also keep playing on the Nationwide Tour in an effort to get his full U.S. card. Robert Allenby finished with 66 to share third place with Richard Green, four behind Stadler, while Choi was fifth.

Jacob's Creek Open
Adelaide, South Australia
Winner: Paul Sheehan

After two victories in Japan, Paul Sheehan claimed his first on the Australasian Tour by winning the Jacob's Creek Open, an event co-sanctioned with the Nationwide Tour. Sheehan, a 29-year-old from New South Wales, defeated Michael Sim at the second hole of a playoff. Sim, the third-round leader, went out of bounds with his tee shot at the deciding hole, his ball finishing between a corporate tent and a trash container to the right of the fairway. He gave himself a 15-footer to keep the playoff alive, but Sheehan's bogey was good enough to take the title.

At the first playoff hole, both men had to scramble to make pars, Sheehan from a bunker and Sim having overshot the green. Sheehan shot rounds of 73, 70, 69 and 69 to set the target at seven under par. He caught the leader with a 15-foot birdie putt at the 15th and then parred in safely. Sim, who closed with a 71, holed par-saving putts at the 16th and 17th, but could not force the birdie to win at the last.

Nick Flanagan, a former U.S. Amateur champion, chipped in for a birdie on the 18th to finish one stroke outside the playoff. Aron Price and Jarrod Lyle completed an all-Australian top five by sharing fourth place at five under. Price had briefly shared the lead with Sim after four birdies on the front nine but then fell back. Craig Bowden, the leading American, shared sixth place with Peter Senior.

ING New Zealand PGA Championship
Christchurch, New Zealand
Winner: Jim Rutledge

Jim Rutledge, the 46-year-old Canadian, rallied from nine strokes behind with a round to play to win the ING New Zealand PGA Championship at the Clearwater Resort in Christchurch. It was Rutledge's first win on the Nationwide Tour and the US$108,000 first prize was the biggest check of his 28-year professional career. He was also the fifth oldest winner ever on the Nationwide Tour.

Rutledge won by a stroke over third-round leader Jarrod Lyle and Brett Rumford after starting the final day tied for 25th place. Rutledge birdied five of the first 10 holes but finished in superb style. He eagled the 17th to tie with Lyle and then birdied the 18th to take the clubhouse lead. He had closed with a 64, eight under par, after earlier efforts of 75, 68 and 72.

He then had an hour wait as Lyle and Rumford completed their rounds. Lyle bogeyed the 18th after taking an unplayable lie in the rough to fall one behind after 74, while Rumford's bid to join the playoff from 15 feet missed on the right. He closed with a 72. Wade Ormsby finished a shot further back after a 70. Scott Gardiner and American Chad Collins shared fifth place.

It was Rutledge's first win since the 1995 Indian Open on the Asian Tour and also the third largest come-from-behind victory in the history of the Nationwide Tour. "It was just one of those days where I just got off to a good start, and I just hung in there and everything fell into place in the last few holes," said Rutledge. "This course is just not one that suits boomers. You have to be patient and just be consistent and place your shots where you can make birdies."

MFS Australian Open
Sydney, New South Wales
Winner: John Senden

John Senden added to his breakthrough year in America by winning his national championship. Senden produced a course-record 65 in the final round at Royal Sydney to win the MFS Australian Open by one stroke over U.S. Open champion Geoff Ogilvy. Half a dozen players held the lead, or a share of it, on the final day, but Senden was the last one and got to lift the Stovehaven Cup.

With his earlier rounds of 76, 72 and 67, Senden finished at eight under par. But after six holes on Saturday, he was two over for the day and six over for the championship. He would improve by 14 shots in the remaining 30 holes. He started by making seven birdies in nine holes, and then the 35-year-old made eight more in the final round. Four came on either nine, but the key was his finish as he closed with two birdies. He holed from four feet at the 18th and then saw Ogilvy's effort to catch him slide by. Ogilvy finished with 67, having spent most of the day sharing the lead. Stuart Appleby bogeyed the last to finish two behind Senden and shared third place with Gavin Coles.

Senden won the John Deere Classic for his first victory in America earlier in the year. But he said now, "This is more special, winning your national Open. It's a dream come true. It's hard to believe, really, because from the way I felt Thursday in those conditions, I'm thinking, 'Oh, just keep your head on and try and come in with a reasonable score.' And then to turn it around on the last three days was special, and it really hasn't sunk in yet, but it was a special day. Winning any event in Australia is great. I've come close before, last year I missed out by a shot from Robert Allenby and to go one better this year and finish birdie, birdie, it felt great."

MasterCard Masters
Melbourne, Victoria
Winner: Justin Rose

Justin Rose claimed his first victory in four years by winning the MasterCard Masters after an eventful final round at Huntingdale. The 26-year-old Englishman, who had a string of near-misses towards the end of the season in America, was playing in his first European Tour event since rejoining the circuit. It was also his last tournament of the year before marrying his fiancée Kate. The first prize of A$270,000 was the perfect wedding present, but for Rose, tasting victory again meant the most.

"This is great for my self-belief," said Rose. "I can't keep knocking at the door and not quite getting over the line. So I felt a little bit of added pressure that if I hadn't got over the line it would have been a positive week, but people would have been looking at it from a slightly different standpoint, like 'Why aren't you winning?'"

Rose had rounds of 69, 66, 68 and a 73 in the windy conditions on the final day for a 12-under-total of 276. He won by two strokes over Greg Chalmers and Richard Green, while amateur Aaron Pike, who equaled the course record of 64 in the opening round, was fourth. Rose led by three shots over Chalmers after birdieing the sixth, but then had a triple-bogey eight at the seventh. His second hit the lip of a bunker and rebounded into the trees where he had to take a penalty drop.

He immediately birdied the eighth before Chalmers suffered the agony of five-putting at the ninth, taking four from three feet. Pike shared the lead after holing a bunker shot for an eagle at the 14th, but Rose held on, helped along by birdies at the 14th and 16th. Chalmers holed a long putt at the 18th to get into second place, while Pike closed with 74. Rose was not safe until he had found the green from the right rough at the last.

"It was a roller-coaster. I was really pleased, though, that my emotions didn't roller-coaster," said Rose. "I stayed very calm, even when I made triple on the seventh I said, 'Well you are tied for the lead, game on,' and it was awesome to bounce back with a birdie on the eighth."

Blue Chip New Zealand Open
Auckland, New Zealand
Winner: Nathan Green

At the MFS Australian Open, Nathan Green could not hang onto the lead on the last day. At the Blue Chip New Zealand Open, he tried a different formula. Green rallied from six shots behind, having entered the final round in 39th place after 76 on the third day. In the windy conditions at Gulf Harbour in Auckland, Green set a target of five under par after a brilliant 65, which contained seven birdies. He then had to wait almost three hours to see if anyone could overtake him.

Marcus Fraser, one of three overnight leaders along with Kim Felton and England's Graeme Storm, went two clear at one point but then dropped back. Fraser closed with 73, Felton 75 and Storm 76. Michael Campbell, the 2005 U.S. Open champion, started the final day one off the lead, but three bogeys on the back nine put paid to his chances of winning on home soil.

Instead, Green completed a two-stroke victory over Campbell, Fraser, Nick Dougherty, who posted an early 67, Jarrod Moseley and Wade Ormsby. Scott Strange, Peter O'Malley, Greg Chalmers and Simon Wakefield finished a further shot behind at two under par.

Green, a 31-year-old from New South Wales, collected his first title on either the Australasian or European Tours. In his rookie season on the PGA Tour in America in 2006, Green had six top-10s, including a second place at the Buick Invitational. "It was tough to sit there and watch the guys coming in," he said. "You never wish bad on another player, but your heart is in your mouth with every putt. Luckily enough, five under ended up being good enough."

"I was actually trying not to watch the golf. It was getting to be too much. It was probably the hardest hour of my life. The last three years, my game has come together a little bit. It just feels good to be getting some good rewards for some pretty hard work. It's all falling into place and to finally win as a professional is just huge."

Cadbury Schweppes Australian PGA Championship
Coolum Beach, Queensland
Winner: Nick O'Hern

Nick O'Hern finally added a second title to his golfing resumé when he defeated Peter Lonard in a playoff to win the Cadbury Schweppes Australian PGA Championship at Coolum. The win came at the same venue as his only other victory, the Coolum Classic in 1999. After a duel over the full duration of the weekend, O'Hern holed a bunker shot at the fourth extra hole to take the title. The A$216,000 first prize meant O'Hern also won the Order of Merit.

After rounds of 66 and 69, O'Hern was two behind Lonard, who opened 68-65. In the third round, O'Hern scored a 63 to bring him even with Lonard, who had 65. The pair carded 68s on Sunday to tie at 22 under par. An eagle at the eighth hole put O'Hern into the lead and the 35-year-old Western Australian was two ahead with three to play. Twice in the last three holes he missed from three feet for par, while he also missed a birdie chance at the 17th.

The bogeys at the 16th and 18th meant a playoff, and the first three holes were halved. But at the fourth time of asking, O'Hern put his approach through the green only to hole out from the sand. There was never more than a shot between the left-handed O'Hern and Lonard over the weekend. Wade Ormsby finished in third place, three strokes behind, with Paul Gow in fourth place.

After a rash of second places in Europe and Australia, O'Hern was delighted with the long-awaited win. "It was just great to get the job done, and if it had not happened today it would have taken a long time to recover from this," said O'Hern. "I just wanted to snap my putter in half on the last green. The bunker shot was one of those things where you hit the shot you are trying to hit and if it goes in, it goes in, and luckily it went my way."

13. African Tours

If Trevor Immelman deserves the honors as South Africa's player of the year, it was Ernie Els's victory over his compatriot at the South African Airways Open that meant the year ended with an optimistic air. It was Els's last chance to continue a streak of winning somewhere in the world every year since 1992. But more importantly, it sent the three-time major champion off on his Christmas holiday in a better frame of mind than at any point in 2006.

After the knee injury that sidelined him for most of the second half of 2005, Els won the Alfred Dunhill Championship earlier in his comeback. If that win suggested it was business as usual, that was not to be the case. Els struggled all year to find the former consistency his game always possessed. At first the knee still bothered him, but even when he was physically fit, his swing suffered a bit of a hangover. It was not for the lack of effort and application, which made it all the more frustrating.

"I've been working harder than ever and felt like I was going backwards," Els said. "My wife needs a lot of credit. I've been a bear with a sore head this year." The victory at the classic links of Humewood soon had Els in a more positive frame of mind. He said his goal was to be the world No. 1 within three years.

"I need something to draw my attention," Els said. "I think some people might think it's laughable now the way Tiger is playing, but I need something to motivate me. I feel I've still got a lot to offer the game and a lot of goals to achieve. It will take a lot of good golf over the next three years, but that's my plan. I'm healthy now and can start building my swing and confidence. The way I played in this final round will give me a lot of confidence in the majors next year, so hopefully this is the little step I needed."

It was a lean year for South Africa's top two, with Retief Goosen's only victory coming at the Volkswagen Masters China. But Immelman proved the shining light. After an early win for Rory Sabbatini on the PGA Tour in America, Immelman took over.

Immelman recorded two second-place finishes at the Wachovia Championship and the Byron Nelson event and then his first victory in the United States at the Cialis Western Open, holding off Tiger Woods in the process. He went on to finish seventh on the money list and become the first South African to be the Rookie of the Year. Off the course there was even better news as his son, Jacob, was born.

"Obviously looking back now it has been one of my most incredible years personally and professionally," Immelman reflected. "The year started off quite slow in the States. But I took a lot of confidence from those second places, even if they were disappointing at the time. I started believing in myself and started to believe that I have what it takes to play with these guys week in and week out.

"I started playing consistent golf with some top 10s and top 20s, so going into the Western Open I was obviously confident in my game. The week just really panned out nicely and by Sunday I was playing in the group behind Tiger. When he's around there is always some electricity in the air and an energy about the place. It was a fantastic feeling to close that one out.

"From there I just kept putting myself in position and gained a lot of confidence. Jacob was born, so I took some time off to enjoy that. I've kept up my consistency and I am looking forward to next year. I am looking forward to the FedEx Cup. We start in Hawaii, so I don't have that much time to sit back and relax."

At home, Charl Schwartzel led the Sunshine Tour money list for the second consecutive year, thanks to his victory at the Vodacom Tour Championship. Thomas Aiken then won the winter series for the third year running. There were some remarkable stories. Rossouw Loubser, a colonel in the South African Air Force, turned professional at the age of 44 and following a distinguished amateur career and promptly won twice. Vaughn Groenewald waited 11 years for his first win and then won again.

Perhaps the most heartening victory was that of Tongoona Charamba, a 22-year-old from Zimbabwe who became only the third black golfer to win on the Sunshine Tour since 1991. "I hope that my victory will inspire the other black players on the Sunshine Tour to work hard, to persevere, to hang on when the going gets tough," said Charamba. "Victory does not come easily and you can only achieve your goals if you work hard at it." Wise words.

Dimension Data Pro-Am
Sun City, South Africa
Winner: Alan McLean

Alan McLean claimed his first victory for over seven years when he won the Dimension Data Pro-Am at the second hole of a playoff at Sun City. The 35-year-old Scot, who lives in Canada, defeated Tyrone van Aswegen after the pair tied at three under par.

The final round having to be resumed early in the morning, van Aswegen completed five holes for 67, the best score of the last round, to post the clubhouse target. He then had to wait for over an hour to see if anyone could beat him. McLean resumed tied for the lead with Ulrich van den Berg at two under par after seven holes. But he came to the last at one under and then hit a four iron from 240 yards to 18 feet and holed the putt for an eagle.

In the playoff, both players birdied the 18th, but when they played the hole again, the 24-year-old van Aswegen pulled his drive into the jungle and lost the ball. He found the green in six, while McLean was on in three and was soon declared the winner. Anton Haig and van den Berg, who led for the first three rounds, tied for third at one under, with Thomas Aiken and Hennie Otto sharing fifth at even par.

"It's beyond my wildest dream," said McLean. "I can't describe what I'm feeling right now. You keep practicing and grinding away and suddenly it happens. On the last hole before the playoff, Ulrich walked over and told me to stay calm and focused and just do the job. When I stood over the putt, I just felt incredibly calm. I came into the event knowing I needed a good finish. I lost my exemption on the Nationwide Tour and I hadn't performed well in the Dunhill or SAA Open, so I was under pressure all week."

Nashua Masters
Port Edward, Natal
Winner: Warren Abery

After winning the International Qualifier for the Open Championship a couple of weeks earlier and earning a trip to Hoylake, Warren Abery added his fourth Sunshine Tour title to a successful month with a two-stroke victory in the Nashua Masters at the Wild Coast Country Club. Abery closed with 68 to post a total of 265, 15 under par. He had started the final round tied with Scotland's Doug McGuigan, who had 70 and claimed second place one ahead of Mark Murless. Frenchman Gregory Bourdy and Switzerland's Andre Bossert were a further shot back and one better than Hennie Otto, a former winner.

In baking heat but with strong, gusting sea winds, Abery stuck to a game plan of driving aggressively off the tee but then keeping the bogeys off his card. He had two early birdies, but the crucial moment came at the short eighth. He holed out of a bunker for a two, while McGuigan found water and never recovered from the two-shot swing.

"It was mentally very tough out there," said Abery, a 32-year-old local from Umhlanga. "It's a grind, this course," he said. "I just stuck to my plan. Kept the drops and the big numbers off the card. I suppose the fact that I grew up playing on the Natal coast has helped a lot. I am used to playing in the wind and I have the patience it demands."

Telkom PGA Championship
Johannesburg, South Africa
Winner: Gregory Bourdy

Two months after losing his playing privileges on the European Tour and failing to regain his card at the qualifying tournament, Gregory Bourdy proved he had made the right decision to head to South Africa and have a crack at the Sunshine Tour. He became the first Frenchman to win on the circuit as he claimed the Telkom PGA Championship, the second oldest professional title in South Africa. His winning margin of six strokes was one outside the tour record of seven held by David Frost. His superb scoring in the first three rounds had put Bourdy well clear of the field, and a closing 69 gave the 23-year-old from Bordeaux a 21-under-par total of 267.

With three 66s in previous rounds, Bourdy tackled the final round with a comfortable six-stroke cushion over Thomas Aiken and never relinquished his lead, despite a slight stumble at the second hole, which he quickly rectified with a bounce-back birdie. He maintained the advantage through the first seven holes and, at one stage, moved as much as 10 strokes clear of the field on the second nine, but back-to-back bogeys on Nos. 15 and 16, and a late flurry of birdies from Aiken, cost him a shot at Frost's record. Aiken finished two ahead of James Kamte, a 23-year-old who birdied the last hole to claim third place on his own.

Bourdy had finished third in the South African Airways Open the month before and this win put him on top of the Order of Merit with one event remaining. "The last two months have been very special for me after what was probably the worst experience of my life when I missed my European Tour card," he said. "Golf can be like that. It's sometimes up and down."

Vodacom Tour Championship
Pretoria, South Africa
Winner: Charl Schwartzel

Charl Schwartzel became the first player since John Bland in 1990 and 1991 to win the Sunshine Tour Order of Merit two years running. In 2005, Schwartzel came to the last event with the money list title already in the bag. In 2006, he trailed Gregory Bourdy, but with the Frenchman finishing in 45th place, victory in the Vodacom Tour Championship was more than good enough for Schwartzel to finish No. 1. It was the 21-year-old's second win in just over a year after he won the Alfred Dunhill Championship at the end of 2004.

Schwartzel finished the tournament in style with a birdie at the last after dominating throughout. His closing 67 gave him a 14-under-par total of 270 and a four-stroke victory over Darren Fichardt. Thomas Aiken finished third, eight shots behind Schwartzel, while Martin Maritz, who produced a brilliant final round of 63, Dean Lambert and Warren Abery shared fourth place. The No. 1 ranking assured Schwartzel of being exempt for several prestigious events.

"When I woke up this morning I thought to myself this is the most important round of my career," Schwartzel admitted. "But I didn't want to fall into the trap of how much was riding on the round, because then the pressure can get to you. I had a three-shot lead and all I thought about was the round, and playing my own game. As it turned out, I swung it well and sunk a few putts and it all came together.

"Definitely the highlight of winning the Order of Merit is getting into the Nedbank Golf Challenge. As a little guy I used to go to the tournament with my dad and watch the guys, thinking to myself that my dream was to one day play in it. Now that dream has come true."

Hassan II Trophy
Rabat, Morocco
Winner: Sam Torrance

Sam Torrance warmed up for the start of his defense of his No. 1 position on the European Seniors Tour by defeating a number of younger contenders to win the 34th Hassan II Trophy at Royal Dar-es-Salam in Rabat, Morocco. If not for a double-bogey seven at the last hole, Torrance would have had a comfortable victory, but instead he beat France's Raphael Jacquelin at the first extra hole.

The pair tied at 11 under par after Torrance, who collected the $120,000 first prize, recorded rounds of 70, 67, 69 and 75. Jacquelin eagled the 12th hole in the final round, but also had a late double bogey, at the 16th, before recovering with birdies at the last two holes. He scored rounds of 67, 76, 69 and 69. Santiago Luna, a three-time winner of the unofficial event, finished two strokes outside the playoff alongside Jose-Filipe Lima. Next were Gordon Brand, Jr. and Carl Suneson sharing fifth place, with Peter Baker and Sandy Lyle also finishing in the top eight.

Stanbic Zambia Open
Chingola, Zambia
Winner: Steve Basson

Steve Basson got the 2006-07 season on the Sunshine Tour off to a blistering start by winning the Stanbic Zambia Open courtesy of a course record at Nchanga. Basson shot an error-free 64 to win by three shots with a nine-under-par total of 207. Zambia's Madalitso Muthiya scored 66 to share the runner-up spot at six under with veteran Chris Williams, while a group of seven players tied for fourth at four under, including overnight leaders Eugen Marugi and Ryan Tipping.

Basson, who had a five-stroke deficit to make up in the final round, got off the mark with a birdie run at the third, fourth and fifth and narrowly missed another at the par-three ninth to turn in 33. He immediately added a fourth at the 10th, followed by two more at the 13th and 15th before holing a 30-footer for an eagle at the 17th. "I fired a five iron into the green, but I just made it inside the fringe. I was left with a 30-foot putt, but the way I was putting today, I thought, 'I can hole this,'" explained Basson, who recorded his second victory in six months.

"I'm absolutely ecstatic. After my win at The Links in October, I thought I had finally arrived. Then I struggled a little through the summer and just felt that I was getting things working again this week. Courses like The Links and Nchanga this week are tailor-made for me—they reward accuracy off the tee and on the green—so I was pretty confident that my swing would hold under pressure. My wife Daphne and I recently bought a house, so I guess now we will be able to switch the electricity on and maybe give it a lick of paint."

Vodacom Origins of Golf Tour – Western Cape
Hermanus, South Africa
Winner: Jean Hugo

After several near-misses, Jean Hugo claimed his first victory in six years with a five-stroke triumph in the Vodacom Origins of Golf Tour - Western Cape at Arabella. Hugo closed with a final round of 67 to win with an eight-under-par score of 208. Chris Williams finished second at three under with 70.

Hugo's consistent performances in the Vodacom Origins of Golf series included two second places, a third and a fourth. "I've had a few close calls and narrow misses and obviously you learn from that as you go along," said Hugo. "It's been a long time from my last win. But I worked hard the last few weeks and played a lot of golf, so I thought I had prepared well for this week. I think the windy conditions also suited me more than other guys."

Hugo started a windy and wet final round one stroke off the lead of Bradford Vaughan, Titch Moore and Adilson da Silva. But the Stellenbosch professional made his move early and birdied the first, then eagled the second to take the sole lead at six under. He turned three under for his round, then reeled off three straight birdies from the 10th to put the tournament firmly within his grasp as a challenge from the rest of the field failed to materialize. This was the 30-year-old's third victory on the Sunshine Tour.

South African Airways Pro-Am Invitational - Cape Town
Cape Town, South Africa
Winner: Jean Hugo

Having ended his winless drought the week before, Jean Hugo claimed his second title in as many events, and the fourth of his career, with victory in the South African Airways Pro-Am at Paarl Golf Club. Hugo held off a challenge from overnight leader Chris Swanepoel and his former caddie, Gerlou Roux, with a four-under-par 68 to take the title with a score of 16-under-par 200.

Hugo finished two strokes ahead of 19-year-old Anton Haig, who shot to second with a final-round 65, matched by Bradford Vaughan, who took third place at 13 under. Roux (72) and Swanepoel (73) tied for fourth at 12 under alongside Lindani Ndwandwe, who carded 67.

One shot off the pace at the start of the day, Hugo avoided any drama by attacking early and coming home with uncharacteristic caution. "The turning point was really at the ninth, where Chris had an unfortunate drop," said Hugo, who started with a birdie but dropped the stroke at the next hole. "I made an eagle to catch up at the sixth, then birdied the ninth and the 10th. I had the lead, and from there on I just wanted to keep my nose in front."

He dropped a shot at the 12th, but then birdied the 14th and 16th to put the result beyond doubt. "The last two holes I played a little more conservatively, knowing I had a two-shot lead coming in. Not the best time to be a cowboy," said Hugo. "I guess the experience gained of leading by a large margin last week paid off, because I was much more focused today. I knew all the time where I was and what I wanted to do and I managed to stick to my game plan. It's great to win again, but even greater to know that I could do it back-to-back."

Samsung Royal Swazi Sun Open
Mbabane, Swaziland
Winner: Thomas Aiken

Thomas Aiken, winner of the winter series on the Sunshine Tour for the previous two years, ran away with the Samsung Royal Swazi Sun Open to record his sixth Sunshine Tour victory in under three years. Aiken had a final-round score of 18 and a winning total of 59 points in the modified-Stableford format in which players are awarded two points for a birdie, five for an eagle, eight for a double eagle and lose one point for a bogey and two for a double bogey or worse.

The 22-year-old forged ahead in a show of pure determination. He collected four birdies on the front nine, an eagle at the eighth and came home in three birdies on the closing holes, dropping only two shots all day. He won by an amazing margin of 14 points over Steve Basson. The Zambia Open champion eagled the 17th to edge out Patrick O'Brien by one point, while defending champion Hendrik Buhrmann and Dion Fourie shared fourth with 43. First-round leader Mark Murless claimed sole possession of sixth place with 42 points.

Aiken's slight frame appeared nerveless from the first stroke. "I never really felt pressure to play well this week and certainly didn't come here expecting to do well," said Aiken. "I only got back to the circuit two weeks ago and I was really still working on my game. I'm extremely pleased. I enjoyed the tournament and it means a great deal to me to win here before leaving for the Canadian Tour at the end of May."

Suncoast Classic
Durban, South Africa
Winner: Alex Haindl

Bloemfontein's Alex Haindl captured the inaugural Suncoast Classic when he sunk a mammoth 70-foot eagle putt at the second hole of a three-way playoff to win his first professional title. If the winning blow had an element of luck, the 23-year-old Haindl had produced a performance of maturity beyond his years as he calmly negotiated the daunting Durban Country Club in five-under-par 67. His score of 207 put him in a three-man playoff with Lindani Ndwandwe, who also shot 67, and overnight leader Bradford Vaughan, who staged a comeback with four birdies in his last six holes to return a 70.

"From the moment the blade hit the ball, I knew the putt would drop. But my heart still got bigger and bigger the closer it got to the hole," said Haindl, a former barman at Schoeman Park Golf Club, who had occasionally slept in his car as he followed the Sunshine Tour around the country. "It's been five years since I turned pro and it's been five long years of qualifying. That's the biggest pay-off right now—I don't have to qualify for the next two years."

Only Haindl found the green the first time at the 73rd hole, but he left his eagle putt short and matched the others for birdie. Again Haindl was the only one to reach the green of the 275-yard par-four 18th, but this time his tee shot finished on the front of the green. Vaughan's tee shot found the valley in front of the green, while Ndwandwe plugged in the greenside bunker. Vaughan's chip had all the direction and distance but stopped in the throat of the hole, causing the big man from Vanderbijlpark to fall over backwards, much to the amusement of his playing companions and the crowd alike. After Haindl holed his putt, Ndwandwe needed to hole out from the bunker but did not come close.

South African Airways Pro-Am Invitational - Johannesburg
Johannesburg, South Africa
Winner: Tongoona Charamba

Tongoona Charamba, a 22-year-old from Zimbabwe, claimed his first professional title at the South African Airways Pro-Am Invitational at Kempton Park. In the cold conditions, Charamba held off two experienced opponents in Hennie Otto and Jean Hugo, something of a hero to the youngster since he won the 1999 Zimbabwe Open.

Charamba, the 2002 Zimbabwe Amateur champion, became only the third black player to win on the Sunshine Tour in the last decade and a half, after John Mashego at the 1991 Bushveld Classic and Lindani Ndwandwe at the 2001 Western Cape Classic. He closed with a three-day total of 17-under-par 199 on rounds of 65, 67 and 67, finishing two strokes clear of Hugo, 70, and Otto, who challenged with 67. Josh Cunliffe finished fourth.

Charamba took the outright lead at 16 under at the 15th in the final round by holing a monster 40-foot putt for birdie. But, each one behind, Hugo and Otto hit their approaches to six feet at the last. Charamba was 12 feet away and calmly holed the putt to make sure there would be no playoff. Both Hugo and Otto missed their birdie chances to finish at 15 under, while the champion leapt for joy and did a quick sprint down the 18th fairway encouraged by the excited crowd, while the skilled duo were left to finish off their round.

"I hope that my victory will inspire the other black players on the Sunshine Tour to work hard, to persevere, to hang on when the going gets tough," said Charamba. "I hit the best three rounds of my golf career and I held up today, playing with two of the best on the tour. Actually, playing with Jean and Hennie was more nerve-wracking than I thought it would be. I had to work at every shot. Victory does not come easily and you can only achieve your goals if you work hard at it."

Vodacom Origins of Golf Tour at Pretoria
Pretoria, South Africa
Winner: Vaughn Groenewald

Vaughn Groenewald claimed his first victory in 11 years as a professional when he won the Vodacom Origins of Golf Tour at Pretoria Country Club by a comfortable six strokes. Groenewald started the final round with a six-stroke lead and was never challenged as he closed with 71 to win at 11 under par. Doug McGuigan and Thomas Aiken shared second place at five under with final rounds of 69.

Groenewald's win ended a frustrating period for one of South Africa's top amateurs but who had struggled to duplicate that success since turning professional. The 31-year-old spent the previous six years trying to qualify for tournaments, but victory earned him a two-year exemption.

"This is the best feeling I've had in a long time" Groenewald said. "It's taken a long time and it's always difficult to break through. But now that I have, I know I can do it and I'm just going to go forward from here. I've been waiting a long time and there's a lot more to come. At least I've got my exemption on the tour now, so I don't have to pre-qualify anymore, which is really tough."

Groenewald had the luxury of chasing his first victory without too much pressure. By birdieing the second and fourth holes he moved seven strokes clear. He also birdied the 13th to partly compensate for two dropped shots on the back nine.

"It was nice not to have too much pressure on me in the final round. But I did have a sleepless night worrying about who was going to make a charge and who wasn't," he said. "Playing the last hole I just wanted to keep it in play the whole time. It's the first time in my life I've had a chip and have never gone for the flag. I just chipped it onto the green and two-putted to make five."

Vodacom Origins of Golf Tour at Kwazulu Natal
Kwazulu Natal, South Africa
Winner: Rossouw Loubser

Rossouw Loubser, a 44-year-old South African Air Force colonel from Pretoria, won his first title as a professional at the Vodacom Origins of Golf Tour at Kwazulu Natal. After many victories as an amateur, Loubser earned his professional card at the qualifying tournament only three months before and had to pre-qualify for this tournament before recording scores of 69, 68 and 68 at Selborne Country Club.

Loubser's total of eight-under-par 205 was one shot too good for Brazil's Adilson da Silva and another recent Origins first-time winner, Vaughn Groenewald. The 44-year-old became the first rookie winner on the Sunshine Tour since Trevor Fisher at the 2003 Botswana Open, and added his name to an honors board that includes David Frost, Retief Goosen, Tim Clark, Trevor Immelman and Charl Schwartzel.

"This is incredible. I am absolutely speechless," said Loubser. "This is why I turned professional after so long as an amateur, for days like this. First and foremost, it's the satisfaction of being able to play under the gun against the best players in the world. Having played amateur golf most of my career, this is what you dream about doing. It's been a fun run and I'm thrilled with today."

Loubser started the final round in a three-way tie for the lead, but fell three behind after finding water off the 11th tee. But the bogey spurred him into action, and at the last he nervously tapped in a two-footer for the victory. "This means so much to me. This is something I dreamed of as a boy. I'm 44 now and it shows that there's still life after 44 and I can still compete," said Loubser.

Vodacom Origins of Golf Tour at Bloemfontein
Bloemfontein, South Africa
Winner: Rossouw Loubser

Making up for lost time after turning professional at the age of 44, Rossouw Loubser captured the second title of his short career at the Vodacom Origins of Golf Tour event at Bloemfontein Golf Club. He eagled the last hole to break out of a three-way tie for the lead and claim back-to-back titles.

"This is unbelievable. I'm just worried somebody is going to wake me up and say I've been dreaming," said Loubser, who closed with a solid 67 to win at 11-under-par 205, two strokes ahead of Doug McGuigan and Adilson da Silva. The victory gave Loubser full playing privileges on the more lucrative summer leg of the Sunshine Tour. "The doors that have opened for me are amazing. I'm very grateful for this. When I holed that eagle putt at the last I just stood there shaking my head because I wanted to cry like a baby. I just can't believe this is happening to me."

Loubser started the final round two strokes behind leader Leonard Loxton. But as Loxton's challenge came to an end with a triple bogey on the par-three fourth hole, Loubser worked his way into contention. Ahead of him though, McGuigan, who finished second in this event last year, and da Silva were making their own charges. McGuigan climbed from three under overnight to nine under in the clubhouse with a final round of 66, while da Silva moved from five under at the start to nine under as well with a 68.

Loubser stepped onto the 18th tee also at nine under. His drive finished on the right of the fairway, and then he cut a spectacular four iron to 12 feet. "I stood over that shot and thought that this is what I have been practicing for. I knew I just had to trust the shot and my swing," he said.

With the luxury of two putts for a win, Loubser holed his eagle putt for another remarkable victory.

Telkom PGA Pro-Am
Pretoria, South Africa
Winner: Doug McGuigan

Having finished as a runner-up twice in his previous three tournaments, Doug McGuigan held his nerve to seal his second Sunshine Tour title at the Telkom PGA Pro-Am. Starting the day only a shot ahead of Pretoria's Desvonde Botes, the 36-year-old from Kimberley scored a two-under-par 70 at the Centurion Country Club in Pretoria to top the final leaderboard with an 11-under total of 205. He won by two over Botes, who closed with a 71, and Hennie Otto, 70, the pair tying for second at nine under. Kevin Stone, playing on his home course, fired a final-round 69 to finish alone in fourth at eight under par, while Trevor Fisher, Jr. matched Stone's score to finish a stroke further back in fifth.

"This is awesome," said McGuigan, whose father, Frank, was his caddie. "We, my dad and I, have worked so hard at this. I guess I have matured. I've grown up a little even. I still have a short fuse, but mostly these days I can keep it plugged and just get on with the job. That's been a big learning curve, to move on and not fester about a missed putt or a bogey."

Otto had powered his way into contention with a second round of 63, but the final day was all about a battle between McGuigan and Botes. McGuigan holed from 40 feet for a birdie at the second hole to get back even with Botes going down the last. Botes missed the final green in a bunker and came out to 15 feet above the hole. It was a tricky putt and he ended up taking three stabs for a six. McGuigan had an 18-foot birdie putt at the last and left it a foot short, but tapped in for his first win in three years.

Eskom Power Cup
Johannesburg, South Africa
Winner: Trevor Fisher, Jr.

Trevor Fisher, Jr., who lost his playing rights after playing in America from where he had just returned, quickly found success back on the Sunshine Tour with a wire-to-wire victory at the inaugural Eskom Power Cup at Wanderers. The 27-year-old from Johannesburg produced a magnificent performance with a final-round, two-under-par 69 sealing a win by three shots over Thomas Aiken with a total of 11-under-par 202. Alan Michell and Dion Fourie finished in third place, one behind Aiken, at seven under par.

"I'm over the moon," said Fisher. "I have played so well this week, yet my game is not near where I am working towards. To win again after three years and here at the Wanderers is an unbelievable feeling. I just went out there today and tried to play the same game as I had done all week and I managed to do that. Thomas got a little close, but I managed to stay cool and stick to the game plan. I just told myself to keep focused and go on and win it."

Fisher opened with 66 and then extended his lead with 67 on the second day despite bogeying the last three holes. He began the final round a shot ahead of Alex Haindl. At the first hole, both Haindl and Michell, who was two behind, dropped shots, while Fisher parred and he never looked back. A run of birdies at the start of the back nine was ended with bogeys at the 15th and 16th holes, but he steadied himself to claim his first victory in three years.

Vodacom Origins of Golf Tour - Eastern Cape
Knysna, South Africa
Winner: Kevin Stone

With two holes to go in the final round of the Vodacom Origins of Golf Tour - Eastern Cape at Pezula, Pretoria professional and tournament leader Kevin Stone made a very important phone call from the golf course. Stone was only two strokes ahead of the field and busy weathering a strong wind, bitterly cold conditions and a charging Ian Hutchings. But he had another concern as well. He had missed the one o'clock check-out time at the Pezula Hotel.

"I had asked them for a late check-out at one p.m. But on the course I looked at my watch and saw it was 10 past one. So I quickly phoned them and said it looked like I was going to be a little bit longer," said Stone, who went on to complete a fairytale win. Stone birdied the 18th for 71 and a one-stroke victory at nine under par. The 40-year-old, who works as a club professional and admits to only playing in tournaments when he wants some time away from work, made it into the tournament as the final qualifier.

With his 13-year-old son declaring that it was his destiny to win, Stone opened with 63, then followed that up with 73 and was tied for the lead with Thabang Simon going into the final round. But with a strong wind attacking the course on the final day, Simon fell off the pace, while Stone and Hutchings, one off the lead at the start of the round, battled for the title. After a bogey at the 17th from a poor drive, Stone was only one clear of Hutchings playing the last. Hutchings then holed a magnificent 20-foot birdie putt on 18 to tie Stone at eight under, placing the pressure on his opponent to make his six-foot putt for birdie. Stone made no mistake and claimed the seventh title of his career.

Seekers Travel Pro-Am
Johannesburg, South Africa
Winner: Desvonde Botes

Desvonde Botes ended a 16-month victory drought with an emphatic three-stroke victory over Alex Haindl at the Dainfern Country Club in the Seekers Travel Pro-Am. His final-round 67 and a winning total of 20-under-par 196 made up for the double bogey that cost him the Telkom PGA Pro-Am to Doug McGuigan a month before. "This win gives me a lot of confidence, put it that way," said Botes. "This gives me that feeling that if I can get into contention, I can finish it off. Just getting into contention is a big thing out here."

Although he kept the lead all day in the final round, Botes came under fire from Haindl, who got within one shot of Botes through 12 holes. But the leader retaliated with a superb tee shot straight at the flag at the par-three 13th, holing a formality birdie to widen the gap to two. Haindl, who won his first professional title at the Suncoast Classic in May, saw his challenge end when he bogeyed the 16th, while Botes holed a superb 25-foot bunker shot for an eagle-three and a four-stroke lead.

"That's when I knew the 18th would just be a formality," said Botes, who threw his arms in the air and a wide smile to the applauding crowd. "I hit a perfect drive down the middle of the fairway and I had 110-meters to the flag. I hit a sand wedge, but I gave it a little too much and it flew over the flag into the fringe." Botes left his first putt six-feet short, then missed the second and had to settle for a bogey.

Major Champions

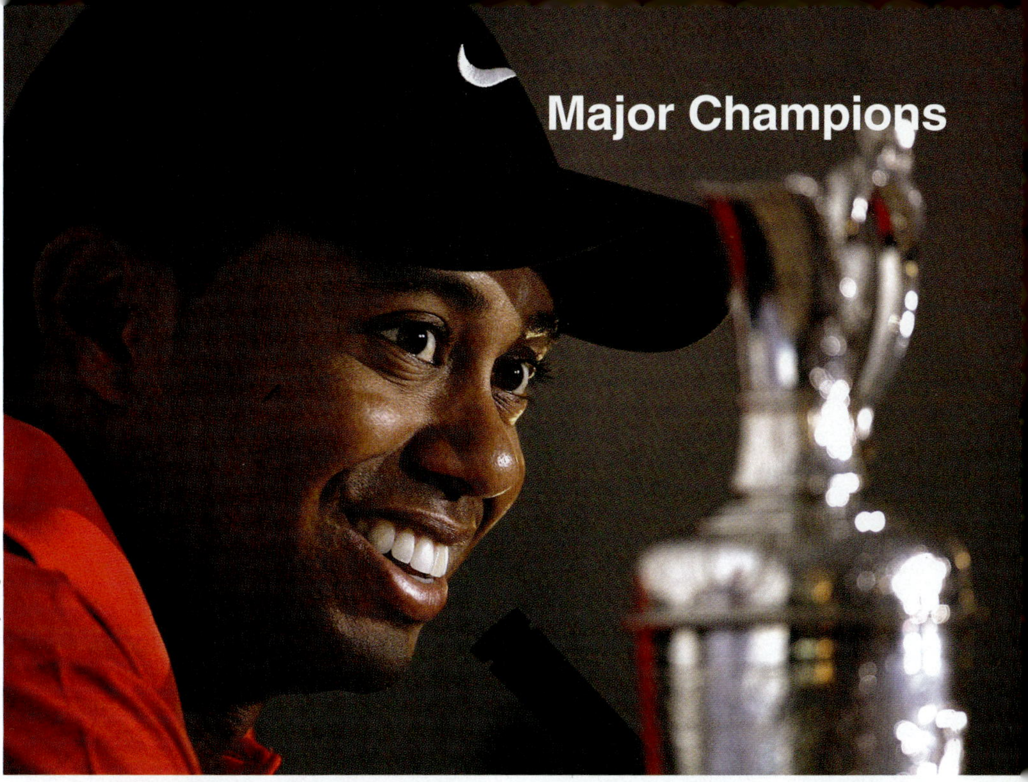

Stuart Franklin/Getty Images

Victories here at the Open and the PGA Championship brought Tiger Woods to 12 major titles.

David Cannon/Getty Images

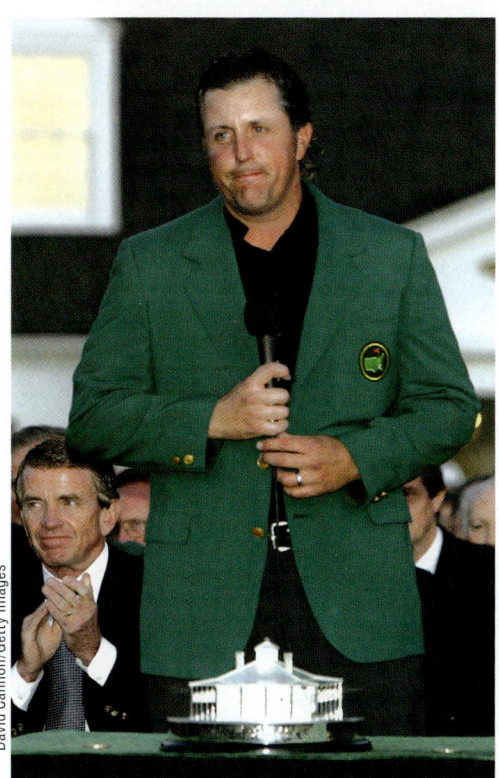

Phil Mickelson won his second Masters.

Jamie Squire/Getty Images

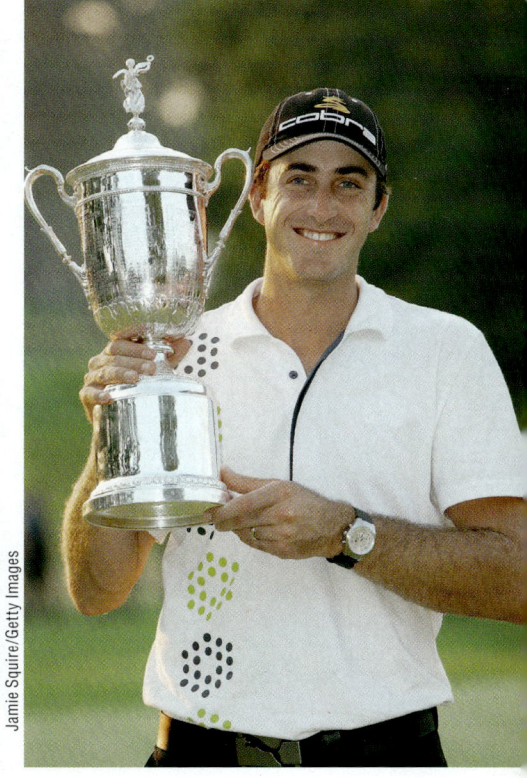

Geoff Ogilvy was a surprise at the U.S. Open.

Masters Tournament

Two drivers were the keys to Phil Mickelson's second victory in the Masters Tournament.

Fred Couples, in the last group, tied for third place.

Tim Clark was second by two strokes.

Jose Maria Olazabal shared third after his 66.

Tiger Woods was three strokes behind.

U.S. Open

While others around him collapsed, Geoff Ogilvy slipped to a one-stroke victory.

Phil Mickelson said, 'I am such an idiot.'

Jim Furyk made bogey at the 18th.

Padraig Harrington finished with three bogeys.

Colin Montgomerie double-bogeyed 18.

The Open Championship

Tiger Woods buried his head in the shoulder of caddie Steve Williams after securing the victory.

Chris DiMarco was second by two strokes.

Ernie Els placed third, five shots back.

Jim Furyk shot 71 to be fourth.

Sergio Garcia fell to share fifth place.

PGA Championship

Tiger Woods at Medinah became the first to win two PGA Championships at the same venue.

Despite 69, Shaun Micheel couldn't catch Woods.

Sergio Garcia challenged again at the PGA.

Adam Scott shot 67 to tie for third.

Luke Donald was a home favorite.

Ryder Cup

Captain Ian Woosnam held the Ryder Cup with the victorious Europeans, winners by 18½ to 9½.

Darren Clarke holed from over 100 feet in his singles victory, finishing with a 3-0 record.

Paul Casey celebrated his singles point.

Europe won on Henrik Stenson's putt.

Sergio Garcia won four of five matches.

Around the World

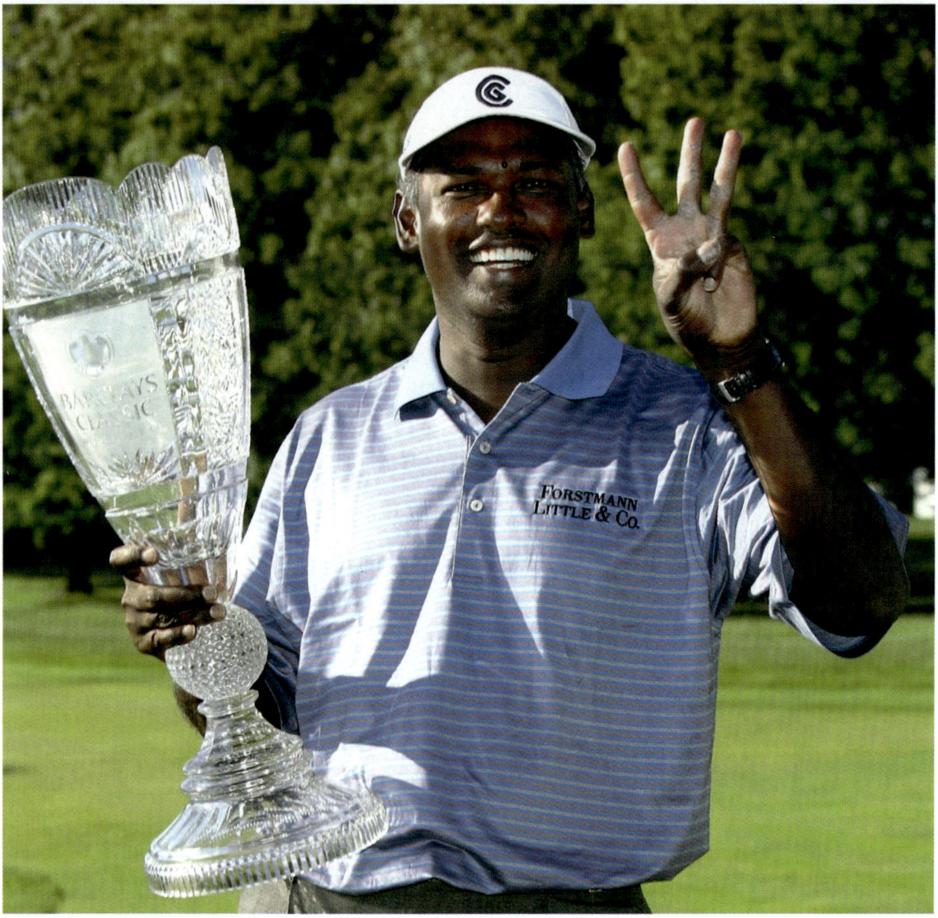

Richard Heathcote/Getty Images

Vijay Singh got his third win at Westchester in the Barclays Classic, his only victory of the year.

Doug Benc/Getty Images

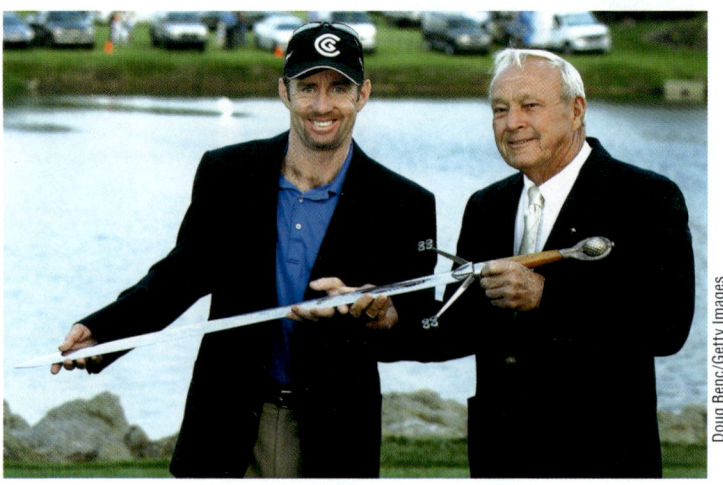

Rod Pampling accepted the Bay Hill sword from host Arnold Palmer.

Adam Scott climbed to No. 4 in the world.

Stuart Appleby won two tournaments.

Luke Donald, ranked No. 9, won the Honda Classic.

Paul Casey took the Johnnie Walker title.

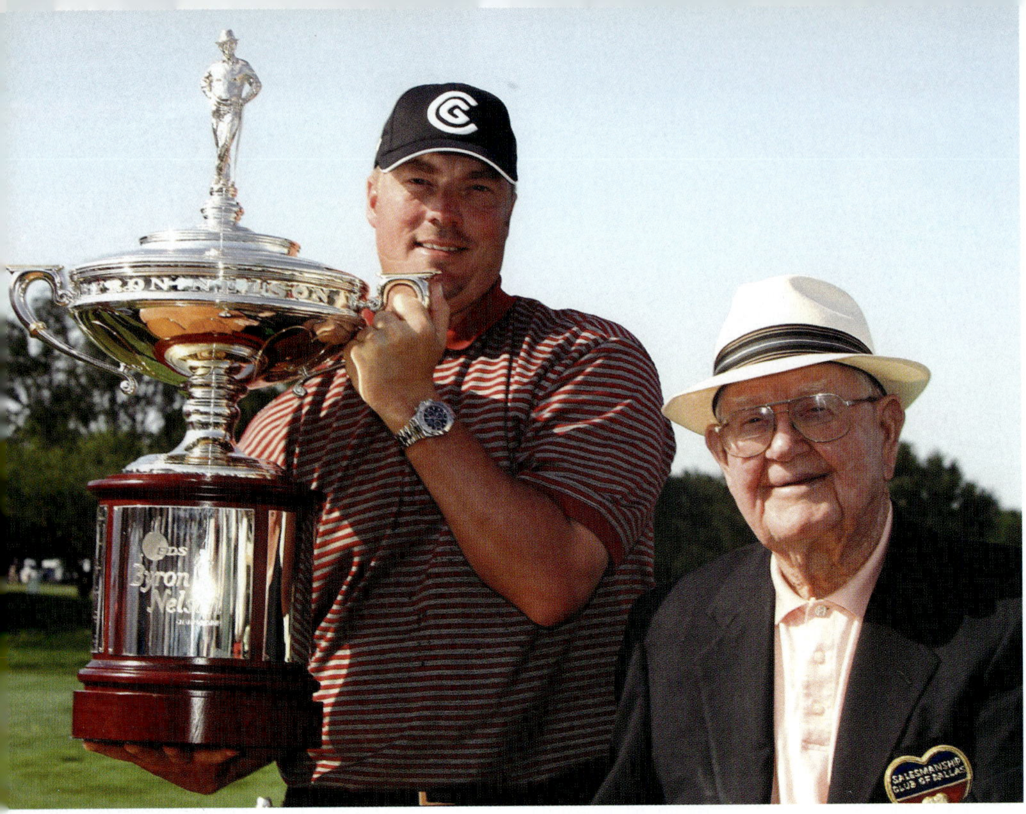
Scott Halleran/Getty Images

Brett Wetterich was the last to receive a trophy from Byron Nelson, who died at age 94.

Harry How/Getty Images

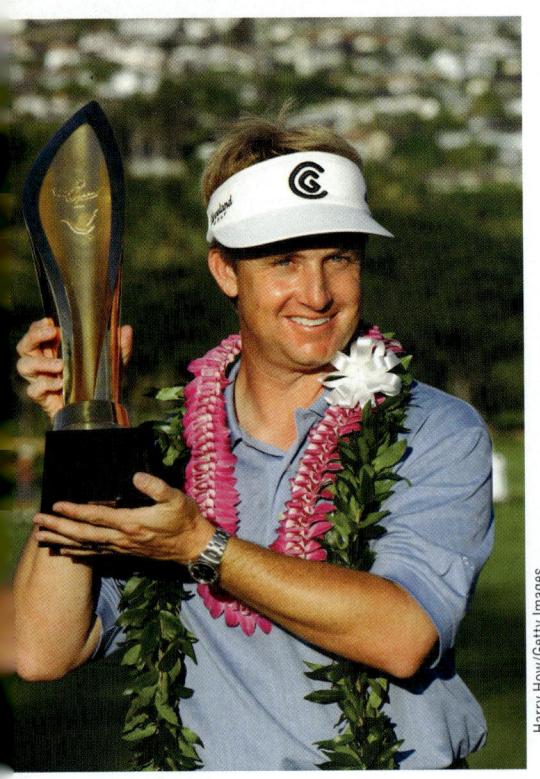

David Toms started by winning in Hawaii.

Stuart Franklin/Getty Images

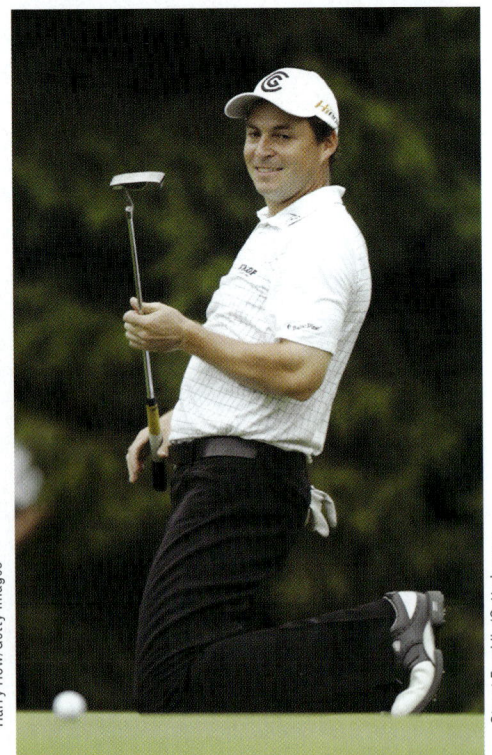

David Howell was third on the European Tour.

Padraig Harrington was the European money leader.

Stephen Ames impressed at The Players.

Carl Pettersson and Jack Nicklaus at the Memorial.

Robert Karlsson won twice in Europe.

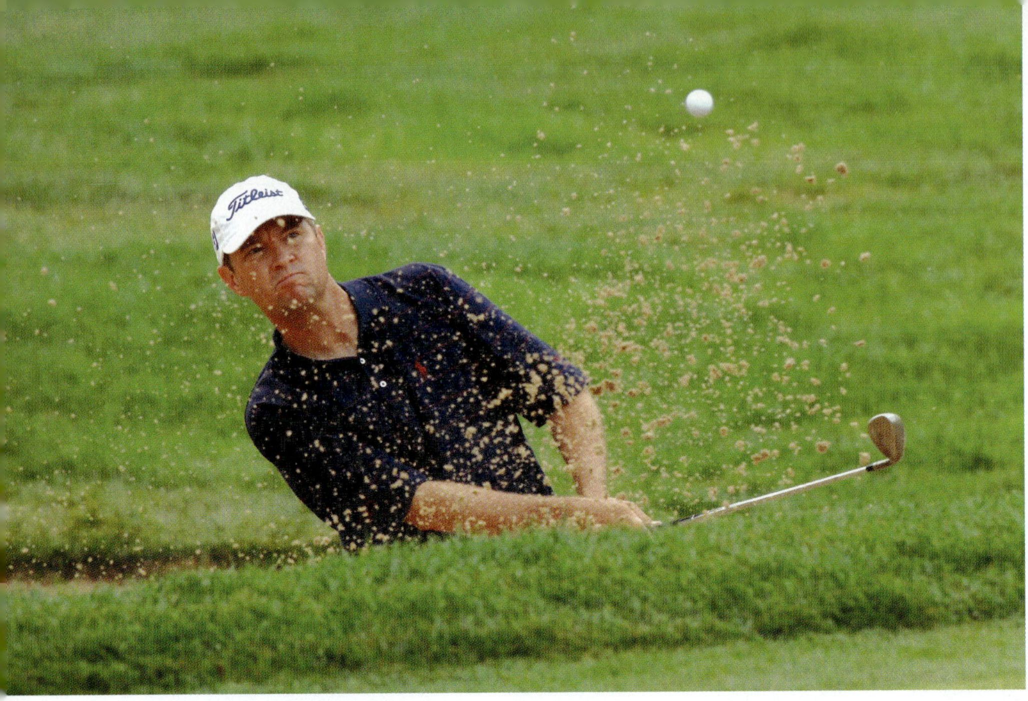

Montana Pritchard/Getty Images

Ranked No. 16 in the world, Davis Love won at Greensboro.

Warren Little/Getty Images

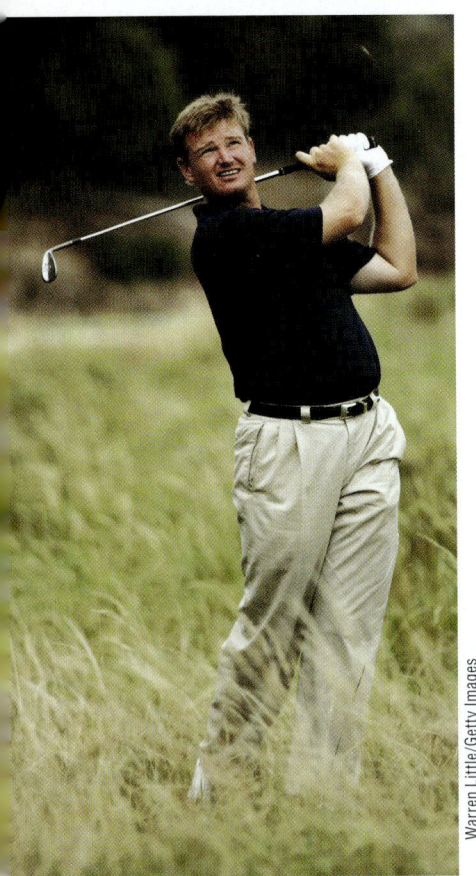

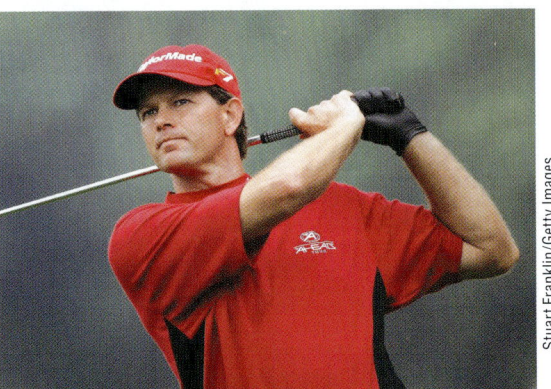

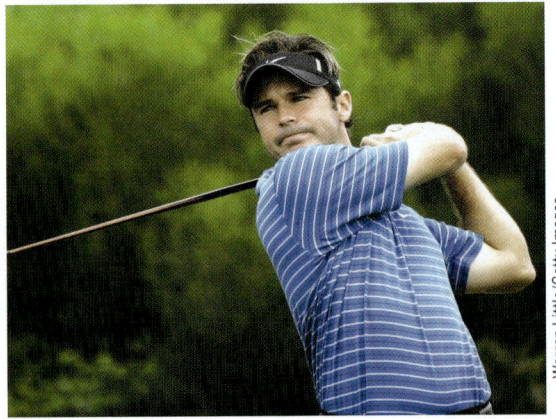

Ernie Els won his final event.

Stuart Franklin/Getty Images

Retief Goosen had a victory in China.

Warren Little/Getty Images

Trevor Immelman took the Cialis Western Open.

Vodacom Origins of Golf Tour Final
George, South Africa
Winner: Darren Fichardt

Darren Fichardt reinforced his reputation as one of the Sunshine Tour's best players by winning the Vodacom Origins of Golf Tour Final at Fancourt. Fichardt pulled out of the Alfred Dunhill Links Championship in Scotland to claim his fifth title on the Sunshine Tour, beating Bloemfontein golfer Alex Haindl by a stroke.

The 31-year-old had an indifferent season in Europe, then 72nd on the Order of Merit, and he felt he needed to return to South Africa to re-tune his game. Rounds of 71 and 69 on the first two days at the Montagu course placed him in prime position to collect the sixth and final trophy of the Vodacom series, which is dedicated to Gary Player. In the final round he turned in a steady even-par 36 going out and then mirrored that coming back to shoot 72 for a three-round total of 212.

"It's means a lot to me, this win. I haven't won in a couple of years and I didn't think I would win again. It's a really good building block and I'm glad I pulled through," Fichardt explained. "I struggled a bit today, and me and Alex had a good fight down to the end. Europe is heavy duty. Everyone's trying to kill everyone. These are my roots, and it's great to be back with my friends."

Kevin Stone, the winner at Pezula, finished third, with Leonard Loxton, Chris Swanepoel and Omar Sandys sharing fourth place. Adilson da Silva wrapped up the Vodacom Origins Points Challenge ahead of Rossouw Loubser.

Bearingman Highveld Classic
Witbank, South Africa
Winner: Darren Fichardt

Pretoria's Darren Fichardt became yet another player to win back-to-back as he defeated Alex Haindl in a playoff at the Bearingman Highveld Classic at Witbank. Fichardt tapped in a 10-foot putt at the second extra hole to deny Haindl for a second week running, claiming the trophy he won in 1997 with a winning score of 12-under-par 204. Dean Lambert delivered the low round of the day, a six-under-par 66, to tie for third with Albert Pistorius, Chris Swanepoel, Mohamed Tayob, Callie Swart and Grant Muller.

After Haindl holed a 40-foot putt for an eagle at the par-five 17th to tie Fichardt at 12 under, both players parred the par-four 18th for rounds of 71. They halved the first extra hole with pars at the 18th, then went back to the tee a second time. Fichardt drove it down the middle of the fairway, but Haindl hooked his drive and found himself in trouble among the trees separating the ninth and 18th fairways. He was left with a bump-and-run through the trees but came up 40 feet short of the green. He hit a good chip, leaving himself with a 15-foot putt for par.

Fichardt's second shot pitched to 10 feet below the hole and found almost exactly the same spot from where he missed playing the 18th the first time around. This time he made no mistake. "Once you're in a playoff, the pressure's off a little, because the worst you can do is second," said Fichardt.

MTC Namibia PGA Championship
Windhoek, Namibia
Winner: Anton Haig

Less than two months after achieving a wire-to-wire victory at the Malaysian Masters on the Asian Tour, Anton Haig repeated the feat at the MTC Namibia PGA Championship at Windhoek. Haig, who opened with a round of 62, added scores of 69 and 65 to collect his second Sunshine Tour title. His winning score of 17 under par was one better than defending champion Thomas Aiken, who repeated his second-round 63 on the final day. Aiken's putt for a birdie at the 17th lipped out and hung on the edge of the hole, which ultimately denied him a chance of a playoff.

"This victory is very special," said Haig. "I love coming to Namibia. I love the course. I knew from the moment I shot that 62 in the opening round that I had a chance to win. To have led from start to finish was an amazing experience. I wanted to give myself a low score, and as it turned out, 65 was good enough."

Haig, who at 19 became the youngest Sunshine Tour winner in 2005, had eight birdies in the final round, with four in a row from the 13th giving him a three-stroke cushion before Aiken charged back into contention. Brazil's Adilson da Silva carded a 65 to tie for third at 14 under with Grant Muller, who signed for a final-round 66. James Kingston moved up to a tie for fifth place by wiping out Haig's two-day-old course record when he navigated the par-71 layout in a flawless 10-under-par 61 that included four birdies and three exciting eagles.

Platinum Classic
Rustenburg, South Africa
Winner: Vaughn Groenewald

Vaughn Groenewald collected his second victory of the season by holing from 25 feet on the final green to win the Platinum Classic over the nine-hole Mooi Nooi course. Leading by one going into the final round, Groenewald produced a 68 to claim victory at 202, 14 under par. Thomas Aiken, hoping for a playoff until Groenewald holed at the last, was second for the second successive tournament but still won the winter series order of merit for the third year in a row. Andrew McLardy was fourth, one behind Aiken, with Marc Cayeux and Michael Kirk sharing fourth place.

"This victory means even more to me than my first," said Groenewald. "I mean, the Origins series at Pretoria Country Club was awesome, because I finally believed that I could win. But this feels amazing. To keep it together for 18 holes and beat Thomas, it feels like a real victory." Aiken took the lead early in the round, but Groenewald reclaimed the advantage at the 16th. Aiken responded by birdieing the 17th, but at the last he missed from 30 feet, opening the door for Groenewald to hole the winning putt.

"I couldn't share my first win with Karen (wife) and Kara-Lee (daughter), but they were here today," said Groenewald.

Limpopo Classic
Pietersburg, South Africa
Winner: Bradford Vaughan

Double defending champion Bradford Vaughan continued his love affair with Polokwane Golf Club when he holed a 20-foot putt at the first hole of a playoff to claim his third consecutive Limpopo Classic title. Vaughan's third victory was no walk in the park, as he had to face good friend and playing companion Warren Abery in a battle for the title.

"This is my eighth title and probably the hardest fought ever," said Vaughan. "It's been wonderful, especially after finishing last at the HSBC Champions tournament in China last week. I had very little hope coming into this week with the shoulder and neck injury that has plagued me all season. The three physiotherapists, Chantalle de Chenne, Caty Cronin and Marie Josephs, deserve all the praise for this win. They worked on me from Monday, twice a day, and every day I could feel the improvement. And my grandfather, Len, just never gave up hope that I could do it. Most importantly, I have another chance at next year's HSBC and I will guarantee you that I won't be finishing last again."

Mark Murless led until the 16th, but then Vaughan and Abery swept past, Abery holing from 15 feet at the last to tie Vaughan at 18 under par, one ahead of Murless. In the playoff at the 18th, Abery found a greenside bunker but put his recovery attempt over the green in thick rough. He chipped down to eight feet, but Vaughan had two putts for the title from 20 feet and only needed one.

Coca-Cola Charity Championship
Hermanus, South Africa
Winner: Alan Michell

Alan Michell put the seal on a magnificent performance with a final round of six-under-par 66 to run away with the inaugural Coca-Cola Charity Championship, hosted by Gary Player, at the Arabella Country Estate. From the first round, Michell proved unstoppable in his march to his first victory. After a dozen years on the professional circuit and nearly 30 top-10 finishes on the Sunshine Tour, the 33-year-old from Cape Town got the monkey off his back with an imperious eight-shot victory over Brazil's Adilson da Silva and Doug McGuigan with a winning total of 16-under-par 200.

"I am completely overwhelmed," said Michell. "What a week this has been. My mom is not well and I came into the tournament with no expectations, just worrying about her health. I had planned to spend the weekend doing some things around the house, then I'm suddenly in the lead and in contention. And here I am with a title, a trophy and a big check that will make my bank manager very happy."

Having opened the tournament with a shared course-record 64, Michell followed with 70 to move to 10 under through two rounds and started the final round one shot behind the leader, McGuigan. Six birdies, the last from 30 feet at the 14th, sped him to victory.

"I felt a little edgy at the first hole and three-putted for par, then left my second shot short at the second hole and scrambled for par," said Michell. "But I hit a great second into the third green and that settled me. I actually played quite aggressively over the first 13 or so holes. I never really thought about winning until I got to the 14th hole and realized I was five or so ahead. Then I toned it down a little, playing conservatively down the homestretch."

Nelson Mandela Invitational
Hermanus, South Africa
Winners: Retief Goosen and Bobby Lincoln

Team Lincoln captured the seventh Nelson Mandela Invitational title, presented by Coca-Cola and hosted by Gary Player, with a superb eagle on the second hole of a playoff at Arabella. Bobby Lincoln sank a two-foot putt after hitting a stunning seven-iron approach from 190 yards to the par-five 18th in the tournament's first-ever playoff.

Lincoln and playing companion Retief Goosen, who made a birdie on the last hole in regulation, ended at 16 under par after 36 holes to set up the playoff against Alan Michell and John Bland. Lincoln and Goosen had 66 in the second round but were caught by Michell and Bland's 65 after Michell, the winner of the Coca-Cola Charity Championship, eagled the 18th.

After going down the 18th the first time, the teams both birdied the hole. Michell sank a 20-foot birdie putt, leaving Lincoln to knock in a 10-footer to take the playoff back to the 18th tee and set the stage for Lincoln's heroics. "I went over to see how Retief was lying and felt he was going to make four, so I thought 'trust the wind' and took a seven iron and came up close," Lincoln said. "But that putt was a little tricky, I tell you. Retief said to me it's inside the hole, and I thought I'd hit it firm and straight. It only just sneaked into the hole."

Nedbank Golf Challenge
Sun City, South Africa
Winner: Jim Furyk

Jim Furyk successfully defended his Nedbank Golf Challenge title at Sun City and collected his second check for $1.2 million. But Furyk, by his own admission, was "leaking oil" on the final nine. He stumbled home in two-over-par 74, but retained the crystal golf ball trophy he won last year by two strokes over Sweden's Henrik Stenson.

Furyk won over the first 56 holes, in which he did not drop a shot. A birdie at the first hole in the final round increased his lead to four, but even a bogey at the third was not a problem. But none of his rivals, including Stenson, Ernie Els and Padraig Harrington, his closest pursuer overnight, could put any sustained pressure on the American.

In difficult, windy conditions, the 12 players were a cumulative 26 over par for the final round. Furyk went five clear in mid-round and only bogeys at the 11th and 12th, as well as the last, dropped the field closer. Furyk finished at 12 under par, with Stenson at 10 under after a 75 and Harrington two strokes further back.

"I was disappointed with the bogeys on 11 and 12," Furyk said. "I had to regroup and collect myself. Good pars on 13 and 14 with some really steady golf shots calmed me down a little bit. The course was set up well for me to go out there and play my game and put the ball on the fairway. The tough course set-up was definitely in my favor today. It allowed me not to play conservatively, but to make a few bogeys and not worry about it. I'm happy with the way I played the front nine, and on the back I got a little loose and hit some bad shots. I might have played a little bit conservative on the back nine at times. On the front nine I kept the peddle down and played very, very well."

Alfred Dunhill Championship
Mpumalanga, South Africa
Winner: Alvaro Quiros

Spanish rookie Alvaro Quiros attacked the Leopard Creek course with the bravado of a bullfighter to defeat South Africa's Charl Schwartzel at the Alfred Dunhill Championship. "I'm the best for a week, no?" said Quiros, flashing his smile. Quiros finished at 13-under-par 275 after a final round of 67 to beat the 2004 winner, Schwartzel, by one stroke. Schwartzel followed three 68s with a final round of 72 to finish alone in second, while Lee Westwood shot a 73 to take third at nine under. Ross Fisher and Darren Fichardt tied for fourth at eight under.

When Quiros arrived in South Africa at the start of the week, he never expected to win on his debut as a full cardholder on the European Tour, which co-sanctioned the event. The 23-year-old from the southern coastal port of Cadiz, who earned his card at the end of 2006 by finishing 18th on the final Challenge Tour standings, opened with 74, having struggled with errant drives and streaky putting. But 66 in the second round and 68 in the third gave Quiros a much needed boost on the leaderboard and he started the final round tied for fifth and just four off the pace. Out in two under par, Quiros then birdied the 13th, 14th and 15th, where he chipped in.

Quiros sealed his victory with a remarkable attempt for eagle from 65 feet on the 18th, which shaved the hole, leaving him with a simple tap-in for a birdie. Schwartzel came to the last needing a birdie to win, but put his second shot into the water and took a bogey.

"I have not been hitting the ball very straight off the tee and Saturday was terrible, I was pulling everything," said Quiros. "But with my putting, which has been very poor the last five months, I didn't miss. Today, the drives were a lot better. And when I have a six iron in my hand, I think I will go for the shot every time. Umbrellas are for ladies who can't stand the heat. When I start today, I don't think I can win. But I have to keep fighting. I'm not going to live with one win only."

South African Airways Open
Port Elizabeth, South Africa
Winner: Ernie Els

At the last possible attempt, Ernie Els claimed a victory in 2006 and kept up a record of having won at least once somewhere in the world every year since 1992. Els won the South African Airways Open for the fourth time and described it as a vital win at this stage of his career. He overturned a three-shot deficit to Trevor Immelman with a closing 65 at Humewood to finish three in front of Immelman, who signed for 71. Els finished at 24 under par with his total of 264, which was a record for the championship, three better than Tony Johnstone's effort at Durban in 1993.

It was Els's first win since the Alfred Dunhill Championship at Leopard Creek a year and a week earlier. That week came soon after he had returned to the game after recuperating from a knee injury, but 2006 was a frustrating year for the South African as he failed to recapture the game that won three major championships.

"My wife needs a lot of credit. I've been a bear with a sore head this year," said Els. "I've been working harder than ever and felt like I was going backwards. It's been a tough year for me and my family. So this win is huge for me at this stage of my career. I don't think it's really even sunk in yet."

Three birdies in the first six holes gave Els the lead, and he was two ahead at the turn. "I was happy to see a bit of breeze, because you had to be more on your game to get birdies, and I had the perfect start to my round," said Els. With five birdies in six holes from the 12th, Els made the championship his despite a bogey at the last hole. Swede Patrik Sjoland finished third at 20 under, while defending champion Retief Goosen tied for fifth at 15 under.

Goosen contended despite an extraordinary 11 at the 17th hole in the first round. He lost one ball off the tee and then had to take an unplayable in the jungle with the second ball. After dropping, Goosen watched the ball roll a few inches from where it struck the ground. He picked the ball up and re-dropped. He thought the ball had rolled more than two club lengths from the nearest point of relief, but in fact the ball was in play because it was within two club lengths of where the ball was dropped, not nearer the hole. After taking three to reach the green and then two putts for what he thought was a nine, he was handed a two-stroke penalty.

14. Women's Tours

This was supposed to be the Year of Youth in women's golf, when so much new talent was expected to blossom. That never really materialized, and before it had hardly a chance, the LPGA Tour was hit by the first of the storms that swept across the season. These had nothing to do with the weather.

Carolyn Bivens, the first female commissioner of the LPGA, was starting her first full year in the chair. In the second tournament, there was a brief but damaging boycott by the media over her new credentialing policies. Then came the real turmoil.

Three LPGA executives quit in June. Then the tournaments in Atlanta and Las Vegas folded. And then, and in a dispute with Bivens over rescheduling, the ShopRite LPGA Classic threatened legal action. Bivens declined to attend a meeting of the Tournament Owners Association, a group vital to the women's game, apparently offended that the group had met with two of the former LPGA executives who had left and formed a consulting group. The Wendy's Championship for Children withdrew over a scheduling disagreement, and the ShopRite tournament refused the dates the LPGA offered. And Bivens added tournaments in Alabama, Arkansas, South Carolina and Thailand.

Out on the golf course it turned into a year to remember, but nothing like anyone anticipated.

There was Annika Sorenstam, sinking into what was, for her, a slump. She might be the only player in women's golf for whom three LPGA victories (six overall) in a year constitutes a slump. But then, she had some opportunities that didn't used to get away. Then there was Karrie Webb, coming out of a slump that had kept her in limbo for years, winning four times. And Mexico's Lorena Ochoa, just 24 years old. She showed bright promise in 2005, then erupted in 2006, winning six times and taking all the awards that had seemed to be Sorenstam's, including the Rolex Player of the Year. Ochoa was the leading money winner at $2,592,872, a half million dollars ahead of No. 2 Webb.

Webb authored the most stunning shot of the season, holing out a pitching wedge from 116 yards on the last hole of the Kraft Nabisco Championship, the first major championship of the year. It might have been the most dramatic moment of the season. Webb had started the final round trailing by seven strokes, and the eagle finished erasing it. Then came Ochoa, playing behind Webb, and needing an eagle at the 18th to tie. Ochoa got hers, but more routinely. Webb beat her on the first playoff hole for her first victory since 2004. Webb would go on to win the Michelob Ultra, the Longs Drugs Challenge, Mizuno Classic and Evian Masters.

Ochoa bounced right back the following week and won the Takefuji Classic and through the season added the Sybase Classic, Wendy's Championship, Corona Morelia Championship (her first in her native Mexico), Samsung World Championship the next week, and Mitchell Company Tournament of Champions by 10 strokes.

It also was instructive that, despite the rise of young talent, the four major championships were taken by the established hands. After Webb's playoff win in the Kraft Nabisco Championship, South Korea's Se Ri Pak won the McDonald's LPGA Championship in a playoff against Webb. Sorenstam took her first U.S. Women's Open in 10 years in a playoff against Pat Hurst, and Sherri Steinhauer won the Weetabix Women's British Open. Oddly for Steinhauer, it was her third Women's British title, but the first two came before it had been designated a major event. "The biggest thrill for me—I won it when it was a major," Steinhauer said. "I'm absolutely stunned ... I wanted this one so badly."

Much had been expected of the hard-charging youth led by Morgan Pressel, Ai Miyazato, Natalie Gulbis and Paula Creamer, the latter the 2005 Louise Suggs Rolex Rookie of the Year. They were expected to be the new order on the LPGA. It didn't happen. But then there was the most charming story of the year. Julieta Granada was the grand irony of 2006. For all of the rising talent out there, no one noticed Granada, a rookie from Paraguay. Then came the final event of the year, the ADT Championship, and Granada, newly 20 years old at that point, became an instant millionaire. The tournament had the tour's first $1 million first prize. She was No. 4 on the money list and one of 10 who won over $1 million on the LPGA Tour for the year.

In the continuing saga of Michelle Wie, grumbling began to surface in the media. She hadn't lived up to the expectations that she, or the media, or both had established for her. In the nature of such things, anytime she played, the news was awash in hype. She began the year still wanting to become the first woman since 1945 to make the cut in a men's PGA Tour event, and she ended the year the same way. She tried four times. Wie fared much better against the women. She had five top-10 finishes, the best a tie for second in the Evian Masters. She was just 16, and still two years from being eligible to join the LPGA Tour.

U.S. LPGA Tour

Women's World Cup of Golf
Sun City, South Africa
Winners: Sweden (Annika Sorenstam and Liselotte Neumann)

See South African Women's Tour section.

SBS Open
Oahu, Hawaii
Winner: Joo Mi Kim

The 2006 season was billed as the dawning of a new age on the LPGA Tour, with possibly the strongest bunch of newcomers in history. And so it might turn out to be. But when the season started with the SBS Open in Hawaii in mid-February, center stage on the Palmer Course at Turtle Bay was taken by two unknown South Koreans. Joo Mi Kim, 21, in her second season on the tour and with a fourth as her best finish in 2005, holed a short birdie putt on the second extra hole for her first victory to beat Soo Young Moon, a fourth-year player, who also was seeking her first win.

The playoff started as a three-way. Mexico's Lorena Ochoa bowed out on the first hole, missing from six feet. Moon birdied from 20 feet, Kim from 10. On the second extra hole, Moon put her approach to 10 feet, and Kim flipped a wedge from 80 yards that rolled to within two feet of the cup. Moon missed her 10-footer, and Kim dropped the short putt for the victory.

Until the closing drama, everyone had been waiting for fireworks from the young stars. Michelle Wie, everyone's favorite teenager and not yet a member of the tour, wasn't in the field. Morgan Pressel, 17, was making her debut as the youngest player on the tour, and tied Natalie Gulbis for fifth. Paula Creamer, 19, Rookie of the Year in 2005, tied for 13th, and Japan's Ai Miyazato, 20, tied for 48th.

The final round was a scramble. It began with Kim tied with fellow Korean Sung Ah Yim and Becky Iverson at nine under. Yim and Iverson had their troubles and shot 75s and tied for eighth.

Ochoa, who had one win and four seconds in 2005, nearly put herself out of the running with an opening 74. But she rallied with a 65-67 finish, tying Kim (70-65-71) for the lead at No. 16. Moon (70-67-69) birdied four holes coming home, including the 17th on a 35-foot putt and the 18th on a tap-in to tie for the lead.

Fields Open in Hawaii
Kapolei, Hawaii
Winner: Meena Lee

The Fields Open made some remarkable history—of a sort. Since when did the media boycott a tournament? They did this time. Some newspapers and magazines boycotted the event, protesting new credentialing regulations issued by the new LPGA commissioner, Carolyn Bivens. The matter was eventually resolved, at least to the point where most of the protesting writers and photographers returned, but the episode had already marked the tournament.

Michelle Wie almost won this one. She shot 67-70-66 and trailed by three in the first round and six in the second. In the final round, she birdied Nos. 1, 3, 5, 6 and 11, bogeyed the 13th, then dropped a 17-foot putt for a birdie at the 17th. One more birdie and she would have made the eventual playoff, but she missed the 12-footer at the 18th. "I guess that wasn't meant to be," Wie said. She finished third by a stroke, at 13-under 203, and picked up her first professional paycheck, $73,227.

This was the second week of the LPGA's 2006 season, and it turned into the second week of the surprising South Koreans. Wie was the main attraction, and as expected, Morgan Pressel, Paula Creamer and Natalie Gulbis were prominent, but when it came to results, it was South Korea's Meena Lee coming from six shots off the lead in the final round to beat countrywoman Seon Hwa Lee in a playoff. Two tournaments, two South Korean champions.

Meena Lee was off and running in the final round—a birdie at the first from six feet, a hole-out eagle from 160 yards at the par-four second, then birdies at Nos. 8, 13, 16 and 18 for a bogey-free 65 and the clubhouse lead at 202. Seon Hwa Lee just missed a winning birdie at the 18th and tied with a 71. They halved the first two playoff holes in pars. At the third, the par-four 17th, both faced birdie putts. Seon Hwa Lee missed from 12 feet, but Meena Lee didn't miss from six feet, and had her second tour victory.

MasterCard Classic
Huixquilucan, Mexico
Winner: Annika Sorenstam

It was mid-March and the 2006 LPGA season had reached its third tournament, the MasterCard Classic in Mexico, and Annika Sorenstam was making her season debut. She broke from the crowd on the final nine, and she won. All was well in the world.

It was her first win since—well, her last individual outing, the ADT Championship the previous November. And it was her first competition since she teamed up with Liselotte Neumann to win the Women's World Cup in January. In other words, nothing had changed. This was the third straight time she won her season opener. She won this tournament leading off 2005, triggering a 10-win year, and this was her 11th win in 21 starts. This was also her 21st successful title defense and her 67th career win, 21 short of Kathy Whitworth's record 88.

"It is all about getting the job done," Sorenstam said. "This is what I came for, and I'm happy."

Sorenstam led wire-to-wire, but not uncontested. She was tied with Italy's Silvia Cavalleri at five-under 67 in the first round. In the second round, after two birdies and two bogeys, she fired a seven iron in tight at the

16th and got the birdie for a 71 that kept her tied for the lead with South Korea's Mi Hyun Kim (69) and Paula Creamer (67).

Fellow Swede Helen Alfredsson eagled the 12th and shot 67 to tie for second at 209 with South Korean rookie Seon Hwa Lee, who had five birdies in her 70. But Sorenstam was home free. At the 584-yard 18th, she put her wedge to 40 feet and three-putted comfortably for a bogey, a 70 and a one-stroke win at eight-under 208.

When it came to tributes, probably the best came from Natalie Gulbis, who closed with a 66 to pull within a stroke of Sorenstam, who hadn't finished. But it would take an error or two by Sorenstam to get her into a playoff. Gulbis packed and headed out anyway. "Come on," said Gulbis, who tied for fourth. "It's Annika Sorenstam."

Safeway International
Superstition, Arizona
Winner: Juli Inkster

The Safeway International had a kind of time machine feel to it. Consider that back in 1986, Aree Song was just born and Juli Inkster was 26, in her fourth year on the LPGA Tour, and winning four more tournaments. Now come forward to March 2006, and Song, now 19, was leading the tournament. And Inkster, now 45 and a Hall of Fame member, came charging from six strokes off the lead in the final round for her 31st career win. It was also, by the way, her first in 49 starts, since 2003.

"I knew I could win again," Inkster said. "I just needed the tools."

Inkster played the par-72 Superstition Mountain Golf Club, near Phoenix, in 68-68-70-67–273, 15 under par. But with all the young talent in the field, and trailing by four strokes through the first three rounds, she certainly wasn't the most likely to succeed. Song, a whiz kid from her early teens, took the first-round lead with an eight-under 64. Song, in her third year, considered newcomers like Paula Creamer and Morgan Pressel. "That's kind of cool," Song said, "to be a veteran at 19."

Sarah Lee broke into the lead on the final hole of the second round. After birdies at the 14th, 15th and 17th, she was looking at a 15-footer for eagle at the par-five 18th. "I said, 'If I make an eagle, I am going to be in the lead," Lee said. She made the putt for a 67 and jumped a stroke ahead of Song at 12-under 132. Lee still led by one through the third, matching Song with a 70, and Inkster was still four behind. Then came the unpromising start in the fourth round, where two opening pars put her six off the lead.

Then she got started. A nine iron to three feet got her a birdie at the par-three fourth, and she got another at the fifth with a sand wedge to inches. She birdied the 11th, 12th and 14th, and after a bogey at the 15th, she flipped a wedge to three feet for a birdie at the 18th for a 67 and a 15-under 273 total. Lee double-bogeyed the 14th and finished with 73–275, two strokes back, and Song also shot 73 for 276.

Kraft Nabisco Championship
Rancho Mirage, California
Winner: Karrie Webb

See Chapter 6.

LPGA Takefuji Classic
Las Vegas, Nevada
Winner: Lorena Ochoa

If it looked like a family party on Las Vegas Country Club's 18th green, that's because it was. The Ochoa family was holding a celebration for daughter Lorena, a fast-rising LPGA Tour star. Ochoa, a native of Mexico and former University of Arizona star, had just breezed wire-to-wire to a comfortable victory in the Takefuji Classic. It was the fourth win of her career, but of more immediate importance, it eased the pain of her playoff losses just weeks ago in the Fields Open and the Kraft Nabisco Championship.

"Those playoffs really taught me how to just focus and how to really be aggressive when you need to be aggressive," Ochoa said, after posting a 63-68-66 for a tournament-record 19-under-par 197 and a three-stroke win over South Korean rookie Seon Hwa Lee.

Her opening 63 was a work of art, considering that she bogeyed her first hole. She had six birdies and eagled two par-five holes off daring five-wood approaches, holing a 30-foot putt from the back fringe at the sixth and a 12-footer at the 18th, for a two-stroke lead on South Korea's Shi Hyun Ahn. Said Ochoa: "I hit all of the fairways, and I kept looking at the flag and making putts." The eagles rocked Ahn, who had run off six straight birdies from the 11th on her way to a 65.

Ochoa's 68 in the second round was much better than it looked, given the brisk April winds. Brittany Lincicome was already in with a 65. After a storm delay, Ochoa finished par-birdie-par for a two-stroke lead over Lincicome, 20, a second-year player. Paula Creamer, the 2005 Rookie of the Year, was three shots back after a 64.

No matter that Ochoa was leading Lee by three with one last hole to play, she still went after the par-five 495-yard 18th, clearing the water with her second and ending up on the back fringe. She coolly chipped to five feet and holed the putt for a birdie (Lee also birdied) that was as pleasing as it was superfluous, for a no-bogey 66.

Florida's Natural Charity Championship
Stockbridge, Georgia
Winner: Sung Ah Yim

There was a sense of disorientation about the tournament. First off, it was the Florida's Natural Charity Championship, but it was played in Georgia. Second, there was a golfer who looked like world No. 1 Annika Sorenstam, the defending champion, but she was hitting shots hither and yon, and missing putts and getting run over from behind, just like a mortal. Wait—that was Annika Sorenstam.

South Korea's Sung Ah Yim, 22, was as surprised as anyone but totally grateful. Sorenstam's errors turned into Sung's first LPGA victory. But Sung did her part. Going head-to-head with Sorenstam in the final round, Sung got up and down from the edge on three straight holes from the 15th, then birdied the 18th for a par 72, wrapping up a card of 68-64-68 for a 16-under par total of 272 at the Eagle's Landing Country Club at Stockbridge. She won by two over a faltering Sorenstam (75) and hard-closing Cristie Kerr (69) and Karrie Webb (70).

"I could hear my heart beating," Sung said. "I can't believe it right now. I'm screaming inside."

But she looked cool enough while Sorenstam was unraveling. After a 64 in the third round, Sorenstam was 17 under and leading Sung by a stroke. The tournament was all but hers. Since 2004, Sorenstam had won 11 straight times when leading going into the final round. Not this time. Among her woes: A three-putt bogey from 17 feet at No. 1, a fairway bunker, a big oak, and missing at least five putts of six feet or less.

The final blow came at the par-four 17th. Tied for the lead, she drove out of bounds and ended up two-putting from five feet for a double bogey. "There's not much to say," Sorenstam said, "other than it was a horrible day."

The tournament also got away from Kerr. She shared the first-round lead with 65 and shot another 65 in the third round, but the 75 in between stung her. Kerr took the lead in the fourth round with birdies at the 13th and 14th, but at the 15th went from gallery to rough and double-bogeyed.

Ginn Clubs & Resorts Open
Orlando, Florida
Winner: Mi Hyun Kim

Dakoda Dowd, playing in her first LPGA event, didn't figure to even make the cut. She was just age 13, and she also was under a huge emotional burden. Her mother, Kelly Jo, was dying of inoperable cancer and wanted to see her daughter play against the best in the world. Officials of the inaugural Ginn Clubs & Resorts Open gave Dakoda a sponsor's exemption. She shot 74-82 and missed the cut, but it still was a remarkable showing by a young girl in a professional field, and her mother had got her dying wish.

If expectations were low for Dakoda Dowd, they weren't much higher for Mi Hyun Kim against this field. The diminutive South Korean had won five times in her eight years on the LPGA Tour, but not since 2002. She didn't figure to bomb a drive 290 yards, either, but she did, just in time to lock up this inaugural tournament at the Reunion Resort & Club at Orlando, Florida.

It came at the 508-yard, par-five 17th in the final round. Kim's two-stroke lead had slipped to one and she needed some help. Kim, one of the shortest hitters on the tour, somehow slammed the 290-yarder. "Even a surprise to me," she said.

Kim made the most of it. She hit a seven wood to the green and two-putted from 45 feet for a birdie and a two-stroke lead with a hole to play.

The tournament was hers. Kim shot 70-66-69-71—276, 12 under par, beating two of the hottest women on tour, Karrie Webb and Lorena Ochoa, who tied for second at 10 under. "If I lost today, maybe I never win again," Kim said. "So this win is big for me."

Franklin American Mortgage Championship
Franklin, Tennessee
Winner: Cristie Kerr

You could call it a kind of hint no one could miss. Cristie Kerr came into the final round of the Franklin American Mortgage Championship trailing by four strokes and made a storybook birdie at the first hole. She hit her tee shot wide right and had to punch a four iron, just to the fringe, 50 feet from the pin. Then she rolled in the putt for a birdie. That was the hint. Said Kerr: "I just got the feeling it was going to be my day after that." It was. She went on to win by two shots.

It came down to a classic golf question for Angela Stanford, the third-round leader hoping for her second career title. Do you play conservatively to protect the lead, or do you keep on hammering? She opted for the conservative. "I'm going to make as many pars as I can," she said.

Stanford played the par-72 Vanderbilt Legends course at Franklin, Tennessee, in 65, 67 and 66, sharing the lead with Beth Barden in the first round, leading Patricia Meunier-Lebouc by one in the second, and leading by four over Kerr and Sophie Gustafson through the third. Going into the final round, Kerr (67-69-66) was not of a mind to ease up. "I'm going to sleep well tonight," she said, "and if I'm firing on all cylinders, I'll be firing at the pin."

Stanford did make her pars—15 of them. But two bogeys and a birdie for 73 tied her with Pat Hurst (68), who birdied her last five holes, and Lorena Ochoa (66), who birdied five of the last eight. Kerr kept her word and went at the pins, scattering four more birdies in her no-bogey 67. She hit an eight iron to 12 feet at the par-three fifth, a lob wedge to nine feet at the seventh, an eight iron to six inches at the 10th and a eight iron to 20 feet at the 13th. And it all started with that 50-foot hint at No. 1.

Michelob Ultra Open at Kingsmill
Williamsburg, Virginia
Winner: Karrie Webb

Suddenly, Karrie Webb, who had been struggling for years, was back on top, and Annika Sorenstam, who was dominating, was laboring. This became clear at the Michelob Ultra Open at Kingsmill. Webb ran away with the title by seven shots, and Sorenstam, the No. 1 player in the world, missed the cut for the first time since 2002, after making 68 cuts in a row. She shot 73-73—146 and missed by a stroke.

"I was hoping it was going to turn around," said Sorenstam, who won the MasterCard Classic earlier. "But then it just kept on going the way it's been going."

Webb, who started her comeback with a victory in the Kraft Nabisco Championship six weeks earlier, broke into the Michelob lead with a five-under 66 on the Kingsmill River Course at Williamsburg, Virginia. She started at No. 10 and scorched the second nine for five birdies on a 45-foot chip-in and on putts of 18 feet, two from 40 and a tap-in. Coming home, she offset three bogeys with three one-putt birdies. She was on her way to her eighth wire-to-wire victory. She was pressured only for the first two rounds, leading by one each time. Then came a no-bogey 66 in the third round on five one-putt birdies from between 10 and 25 feet for a five-stroke lead.

The final round was a formality, if an erratic one. Webb had four birdies and three bogeys for a one-under 70, a 14-under 270 total, breaking the tournament record by seven strokes and winning by seven over Lorena Ochoa (72) and Hee-Won Han (70). That gave the rejuvenated Webb two victories, two seconds and a tie for 10th in the young season. "This proved to probably a lot of people and proved to me," Webb said, "that Kraft wasn't a fluke."

Sybase Classic
New Rochelle, New York
Winner: Lorena Ochoa

The performance was what you would expect from a resurrected Australian or an awesome Swede, but this was neither Karrie Webb nor Annika Sorenstam. This was a Mexican—Lorena Ochoa, who rallied in the final round to take the Sybase Classic at Wykagl, near New York City. So in 10 starts, she had two victories, one second place and four ties for second. Ochoa opened with a pair of par 71s, then took the lead down the homestretch for a five-under 66, a five-under 208 total (it was a rain-shortened, three-round event) and a two-stroke victory over Kyeong Bae (66) and Hee-Won Han (69).

Everyone was watching the troubled Sorenstam, the world No. 1. She had even missed a cut for the first time since 2002. But her game wasn't back yet. She got to second place Saturday, a stroke behind Grace Park (67–138). "I feel my game is in me," Sorenstam said. She was encouraged. But a huge shock was waiting for her.

Ochoa, meanwhile, was in the hunt with the two 71s. Then everyone cleared out of her way in the final round. Grace Park shot 75, and Allison Hanna, who had missed five of eight cuts so far, squandered the lead down the home stretch. Sorenstam, still battling, self-destructed at the par-four No. 9, watching three shots spin back off the elevated green. She triple-bogeyed and was out of the running.

"It's been a fun tournament," Ochoa was to say, "but a really good day today." She birdied the fifth from 18 feet, the 11th and 12th from five feet, then the par-five 15th from 15 feet. Then at the par-five 18th, she missed the green by 40 yards, wedged to five feet, and got that for the 66 and the fifth victory of her career. "I think four years is a lot of years to work under pressure, manage yourself, control yourself, and that gave me confidence," Ochoa said. "I'm ready to win tournaments."

LPGA Corning Classic
Corning, New York
Winner: Hee-Won Han

The LPGA Corning Classic came down to one woman who didn't think of winning and another who thought of nothing else. If golf is a mind game, guess which one won?

South Korea's Hee-Won Han, who had four LPGA wins in her bag, came to Corning (New York) Country Club with two ties for second place in her last two outings. She had enough of second. "That's why I was thinking I just really want to win this tournament," Han said. "Three times in second place—I don't like that." Meena Lee, also a South Korean and winner of the Fields Open in February, was of another mind. "I never thought about winning," said Lee, a second-year player. "I'm satisfied with how I played."

At the fourth playoff hole, Lee missed a shortish putt and bogeyed, and Han two-putted for the win. Both came from well behind in the final round, Han trailing by four, Lee by six. They got the help they needed when Jeong Jang, leading by three, double-bogeyed the par-five No. 7 off a tree, shot 76, and tied for seventh.

Lee tied Nancy Scranton for the first-round lead at seven-under 65. Han had 66. Rookie Virada Nirapathpongporn took a one-stroke lead in the second round, and Han (70) slipped three behind and Lee (72) was four back. In the third round, they were all but out of it until Jang crashed at No. 5. Lee birdied the 12th, 16th and 17th for 66 and the clubhouse lead at 273. Han birdied the 17th from 12 feet and the 18th from three feet for 68 to force the playoff.

ShopRite LPGA Classic
Galloway Township, New Jersey
Winner: Seon Hwa Lee

Annika Sorenstam was in her customary place in the final round of the ShopRite Classic, ready to take control. But two things went wrong. First, she bogeyed two of her first three holes. And second, South Korean rookie Seon Hwa Lee, who had three seconds so far in 2006, caught fire and posted 63. So Sorenstam didn't get her second victory of the year, and Lee got her career first. "This means a lot to me," said Lee, and she didn't mean the champagne and beer shower that greeted her on the 18th green.

Lee brought a growing reputation to the Seaview Marriott Bay Course in Galloway Township, New Jersey, and she didn't let up. She opened with six-under-par 65, one stroke behind Sorenstam and Michele Redman. Now it looked like old times were back for Sorenstam, who won three of the last four ShopRite events. She birdied the third, hit the par-five fifth green in two shots and birdied again, eagled the ninth on a seven-foot putt, and made four birdies coming in for 64. "I thought I played good golf," she said.

In the second round, Sorenstam bogeyed three of her first eight holes and had to rally for 69, a stroke behind Japanese rookie Ai Miyazato. Miyazato shook off a bogey at No. 2 and carded six birdies for her second 66 and a 10-under 132 total. Lee (69) remained tied for third, two strokes back.

Sorenstam, still struggling, bogeyed two of her first three holes in the final round. That cleared the way for Lee. Lee birdied eight of the last 14 holes, including four in succession from the 10th on putts of five, 20, 18 and six feet, and then the 17th and 18th on five-footers for the 63. Sorenstam (67) tied for second by three, tied with Jeong Jang (64) and Sherri Steinhauer (66). The final irony: Lee's 16-under 197 total tied the tournament record—set by Sorenstam.

McDonald's LPGA Championship
Havre de Grace, Maryland
Winner: Se Ri Pak

See Chapter 6.

Wegmans LPGA
Pittsford, New York
Winner: Jeong Jang

When your first victory is a major, what do you do for an encore? South Korea's Jeong Jang, after taking the 2005 Weetabix Women's British Open, enjoyed high finishes for almost a year, but she was impatient for that second victory. Then she solved that problem in the Wegmans LPGA at Locust Valley, outside Rochester, New York. The Wegmans win came as a great relief. "It feels like over a year," she said. "That's why I think I'm more happy."

Jang broke from the pack in the third round on a six-under-par 66. She missed just one fairway, and speaking of touch, among her six birdies—a 15-foot putt at the second, a 45-foot chip-in at the fifth, and putts of 15 and nine feet at the 15th and 16th. She led by one stroke over fellow South Korean Mi Hyun Kim (67) and rookie Brittany Lang (69), tied at 10 under par. She predicted a low score would be needed in the final round. "Because everybody is playing good at this course," she said.

All it took was a two-under 70 by Jang. And it was a game of tag with Lang. First, Jang spotted the course a bogey at No. 1 off a tee shot into the rough, then birdied No. 2 from six feet, then No. 4, to stay ahead of Lang, and she two-putted for a birdie at the par-five eighth. Then the game was on. Lang took the lead when Jang bogeyed the 10th on two putts from 10 feet. Jang retook the lead at the 13th on a six-foot birdie putt. She bogeyed the 15th from a bunker, but birdied the 17th on a two-footer after hitting the pin with her approach. Rookie Julieta Granada, 19, of Paraguay, birdied the 18th for 67 and second place by one stroke.

"I was very nervous at the starting hole and finishing hole," Jang said. "I had a little busy day, but it's okay."

U.S. Women's Open
Newport, Rhode Island
Winner: Annika Sorenstam

See Chapter 6.

HSBC Women's World Match Play
Gladstone, New Jersey
Winner: Brittany Lincicome

Brittany Lincicome, a big-hitting, 20-year-old, came to the LPGA Tour in 2005 with a lot of promise and a lot of disappointment. Then came the HSBC Women's World Match Play at Hamilton Farm Golf Club at Gladstone, New Jersey. Lincicome, seeded 39th, outlasted Michele Redman in 20 holes, then beat Brandie Burton, 2 and 1, then Kyeong Bae, 3 and 2.

Lincicome's Cinderella story figured to end in the quarter-finals against Michelle Wie, the No. 2 seed. But Lincicome stunned everyone by breezing past Wie, 4 and 3. At the same time, Juli Inkster, the No. 8 seed, rallied from three down to oust top-seeded Annika Sorenstam, 1 up. In the semifinals, Inkster thumped Paula Creamer, 5 and 4, while Lincicome rallied from one down and beat Lorena Ochoa, the leading money winner, with a 20-foot birdie at the 19th.

Then in the final, Lincicome beat Inkster with comparative ease, 3 and 2, for her first victory. She set the tone on the 533-yard, par-five second hole, where she reached the front edge in two and two-putted for a birdie to take the lead. "On this golf course, length is huge," said Inkster, outdriven by 50 and 60 yards on some holes. "It's wide open, so you can just bomb away." Said Lincicome: "I think if someone is outdriving you by 60 yards all day ... that definitely wears on you. And having wedge into every green, that's always a good thing."

With Inkster making bogeys, Lincicome went a huge four up on a par at the par-three seventh. "I made three bogeys early," said Inkster, "and I don't think I made three bogeys in the previous three matches total." After losing the ninth, Lincicome hit a wedge tight at the par-four 10th and was back to five up. Inkster battled, but finally conceded the match on a par on the 16th.

Jamie Farr Owens Corning Classic
Sylvania, Ohio
Winner: Mi Hyun Kim

Forgive Natalie Gulbis if she's wondering that you have to do to win. Well, one answer is, if you're making birdies, keep on making them. You never know who might be gaining on you. In Gulbis's case, it was South Korea's Mi Hyun Kim gaining on her at the Jamie Farr Owens Corning Classic. After more than four years of trying, Gulbis was about to wrap up her first LPGA Tour title.

Kim and Gulbis went into the final round sharing a one-stroke lead at 12 under par. Kim took the lead on an eight-foot birdie putt at the par-three second hole. Gulbis then ran wild for her five straight birdies, starting from No. 3. She played the first nine in 29, taking a four-stroke lead. In fact, she birdied six of her first 10 holes. And then, for some reason, she couldn't make any more.

Kim, in the same group, ignored Gulbis's birdie explosion and clawed her way back. She birdied three straight from the eighth, and after Gulbis cooled off, she birdied the 16th and 17th to tie her. The final hole was pivotal. Kim, Gulbis and Paula Creamer all missed birdie putts in the 10- to-12-foot range and shot six-under 65s. Kim and Gulbis tied with 18-under 266 totals, and Creamer finished third, a stroke behind.

Kim and Gulbis halved the first two playoff holes. On the third extra hole, Kim, putting first, rolled in an 18-footer for a birdie. Gulbis, following from nine feet, missed, and Kim had her second win of the year and the seventh of her career. "I had chances—it's not like I didn't have chances," Gulbis said, chastising herself. In the playoff alone, she missed birdies from 20, 12 and nine feet. Then, reflecting, she added: "It's not like I finished last. There's a lot of positive stuff here."

"I feel a little sad (for Gulbis)," Kim said. But there were certain compensations. "I got a win and I got a trophy," Kim said, "and so I feel very happy right now."

Evian Masters
Evian-les-Bains, France
Winner: Karrie Webb

See Ladies European Tour section.

Weetabix Women's British Open
Royal Lytham and St. Annes, England
Winner: Sherri Steinhauer

See Chapter 6.

CN Canadian Women's Open
London, Ontario, Canada
Winner: Cristie Kerr

This one was so cruel, no one had the heart to trot out that old "deja vu all over again" line. Back in April, Cristie Kerr came from four strokes behind in the final round to beat Angela Stanford by one in the Franklin American Mortgage Championship. This time, Kerr came from a huge eight strokes behind, closing with 65 against Stanford's wilting 74 to win the CN Canadian Women's Open. "I feel for Angela," Kerr said. "I've been in that position many times."

Probably not exactly. Stanford, seeking her second LPGA Tour victory, was playing impressively. She opened with a bogey-free 64, tying the course record at the par-72 London (Ontario) Hunt and Country Club, and she led the first two rounds by three strokes each, and the third round by a healthy four. Kerr trailed by three in the first two rounds, then with 74, sagged to eight off for the final. That should have put her out of the running. But it only seemed to inspire her.

Back in her first-round 64, Stanford had the game that needed only nine putts for eight birdies. In the final round, it wasn't the same. This time she bogeyed No. 1, two-putting from eight feet. She made the turn in par, and managed only pars until the two closing holes. Meanwhile, Kerr had been feasting. She two-putted the par-five fourth hole from 40 feet for the toughest of her seven birdies. She got four straight from No. 7, from 12, three, six and three feet. She birdied the 12th from 12 feet and the 16th from five feet, and sat back to wait with a 276 total, 12 under par.

Stanford would have won with two closing pars, or tied with one. But she two-putted the par-three 17th hole from six feet and two-putted the 18th hole from 50 feet. "Incredible," said Kerr. "I still can't believe I won. It was just a magical day." Black magical for Stanford. "I'm not sure how I'm going to react to this one," she said. "It's probably a good thing I'm playing next week. It's probably good to keep going."

Safeway Classic
Portland, Oregon
Winner: Pat Hurst

"It's just a matter of finishing, and I haven't been able to finish," Pat Hurst was saying, putting into words the blunt tale the scoreboard had already told. This was Hurst giving herself a pep talk after the second round of the Safeway Classic at the Columbia Edgewater Country Club at Portland, Oregon. She was only one stroke out of a four-way tie for the lead going into the final round. She had five top-five finishes since May and still hadn't racked up that fifth career victory. The most recent hurt the most—a playoff loss to Annika Sorenstam in the U.S. Women's Open.

Hurst opened the Safeway tournament with 69, five adrift of South Korean rookie Jee Young Lee, who eagled the seventh, then rattled off seven straight birdies from the 10th for 64 and a two-stroke lead. Hurst's second 69 left her one stroke off the lead and in a jam of six at 207.

Next it was time for Hurst to follow her own preaching, and this she did, charging out of the blocks in the final round with four birdies in her first five holes—a three-foot putt at the first, a five-footer at the third, a 12-footer at the fourth, then two putts from 25 feet at the par-five fifth. Kim Saiki, meanwhile, birdied twice coming home in her bogey-free 67, and Jeong Jang birdied the 11th but bogeyed the 12th for 70. Hurst closed solidly if not brilliantly, getting two birdies and two bogeys on the back nine for a 68, a 10-under 206 total and a one-stroke win.

Wendy's Championship for Children
Dublin, Ohio
Winner: Lorena Ochoa

The seers at the Wendy's Championship for Children predicted it would take a score of 20 under par to win. But with Lorena Ochoa on a tear, racking up her third victory of the year, a mere 20 under par, it developed, would only have been good for fourth place.

Ochoa put on a record-setting performance at Tartan Fields, outside of Columbus, Ohio, playing the par-72 course in 67-68-64-65—264, a tournament-record 24 under par and by five strokes the lowest 72-hole score of the season. She won by three strokes over Stacy Prammanasudh and South Korea's Jee Young Lee. For a measure of Ochoa's performance, listen to the disappointed Lee: "I don't think I lost today. I played well. But Lorena played better, so I learned a lot today."

One thing Lee learned was that you could start the final round two strokes behind, make five birdies and an eagle, and make no bogeys for your first 13 holes—and still trail. Lee did catch Ochoa for a moment at the 12th, but Ochoa was off again, like the Roadrunner cartoon character.

Said Ochoa: "I thought, she's made too many birdies. It's my turn." Accordingly, she plopped an eight iron to 10 feet at the par-four 13th, then a wedge to eight feet at the par-five 14th. "So from there, I didn't even think about her or the score," Ochoa said. "Just be calm, be patient, finish strong." Which she did, closing out the day and the tournament with a seven iron to 10 feet for one last birdie.

The victory lifted her to the top in winnings with over $1.8 million by late August, and she seemed ready to dethrone Annika Sorenstam as the top money winner. But that wasn't important at the moment. What was important? "I played really smart," she said. "When I need to put a bunch of birdies together, I did." That she did, to the tune of 27 birdies and only three bogeys for the four rounds.

State Farm Classic
Springfield, Illinois
Winner: Annika Sorenstam

A Swede led the State Farm Classic wire-to-wire. Unfortunately for Maria Hjorth, she led only the first three rounds. Annika Sorenstam led the final round, posting her third LPGA Tour victory of the season. A 10-under-par 62 will do that for you. "I knew I had to post a low score," Sorenstam said. "But I didn't know how low, or how low I could go. To come from five behind and win by two, it's pretty amazing. It's something that I'm going to remember for quite some time."

Hjorth wasn't likely to forget it any time soon, either. She was seeking her third career victory and her first since 1999. She shot 65-67-70 at the par-72 Rail Golf Club at Springfield, Illinois, and led the first and third rounds and was tied with Cristie Kerr in the second round. More important, she seemed to be safe from Sorenstam, who shot 70-68-69 and trailed by five, six and five strokes. She went into the final round leading by one, with Sorenstam out of sight. "I have been working hard to get into this position," Hjorth said. "I definitely will sleep really well tonight."

The nightmare came the next day. Hjorth's troubles began at No. 9, when she went from sand to more sand and bogeyed, and ended with a double bogey at the 16th for 70 and a tie for third when Kerr closed with 67 and took second place. Sorenstam set off on her 62 by birdieing four of her first five holes on three putts (the longest from seven feet) and a chip-in. Coming in, she birdied the 11th from 12 feet, then tied for the lead at the 12th on a chip to two feet. Next, she tied Hjorth again, birdieing the 14th after hitting the pin with her approach and the par-five 15th with two putts from 29 feet. She birdied the 17th from 11 feet, then ended with a triumphant 20-footer at the 18th.

John Q. Hammons Hotel Classic
Tulsa, Oklahoma
Winner: Cristie Kerr

This time it was Cristie Kerr's turn. A week earlier, Kerr was all set to win the State Farm Classic when Annika Sorenstam vaulted over her to take it. So it was with no little satisfaction and with a great sense of accomplishment that Kerr jumped over the world No. 1 women's golfer to win the John Q. Hammons Hotel Classic.

"This was one of the only times I've gotten her," Kerr said, and there weren't many who could make that statement. But it looked like no contest starting out. Sorenstam opened with 64, seven under par at Cedar Ridge, near Tulsa, Oklahoma, and Kerr was well astern at 70. Then with Sorenstam posting 68 in the second round, Kerr scrambled to a par at No. 1, then birdied 10 of the next 13 holes for 61 and a one-stroke lead going into the final round. Then everything was up for grabs—it seemed.

Sorenstam birdied No. 1 with a nine iron to nine feet to tie Kerr, went one ahead when Kerr bogeyed No. 8 on a three-putt. Was it a sign? Kerr missed the par from three feet. Then Sorenstam went two ahead at the 10th on a nine iron to six feet, and the old scene seemed to be repeating itself. But it turned out that was Sorenstam's final birdie, and Kerr was just warming up. Against a quiet Sorenstam, Kerr scored four birdies with some of the hottest putting of her career—the 11th, 12th, 15th and 17th from, in order, 12, 24, 38 and 18 feet, wrapping up a total of 70-61-68–199, 14 under par, to beat Sorenstam by two strokes for her third victory of the year.

The story was in the putting. Sorenstam hit 51 of 54 greens in regulation, but needed 93 putts to Kerr's 85.

The victory was also the ninth of Kerr's career, and it showed how far she had come. There was a time, she conceded, that she'd been intimidated. "Well," she said, "it's something I've grown out of."

Longs Drugs Challenge
Danville, California
Winner: Karrie Webb

You could tell how things were going from the comments. Annika Sorenstam, after her eagle at No. 9: "I'm putting the pressure on Karrie … I'm sure I had her heart pumping a little." Karrie Webb, after her double bogey back at No. 7: "I knew that probably would feed Annika's aggression."

And so it went in the final round of the Longs Drugs Challenge at Blackhawk Country Club at Danville, California. It was getting to be an old story for Sorenstam—the final charge and coming up short. Sorenstam started the final round six strokes off the lead, shot 65, and finished second by one after Webb withstood the pressure for her fourth win of the year and the 34th of her career.

The showdown took time to develop. South Korea's Jeong Jang shot a course-record 64 to lead Webb by three strokes in the first round. Webb solved the wind for 70 in the second round to tie Jang (73) at seven-under-par 137. Webb then raced ahead in the third round, with 66 carrying her five ahead of Maria Hjorth (70) and Morgan Pressel (69), who went on to her career-best third place.

Webb's six-stroke lead on Sorenstam didn't last long. Webb opened the final round with two early birdies, not quite keeping pace with Sorenstam just ahead, getting three birdies in her first seven holes. Sorenstam bogeyed the eighth, but rolled in a 38-footer for eagle at the par-five ninth. Back at the par-three seventh, Webb hit her tee shot into the water and double-bogeyed. The four-stroke swing cut her lead to two. Sorenstam then birdied the 11th, 15th and 17th for 65, and stood back and waited. But Webb didn't buckle. She birdied the par-five 11th with two putts from 25 feet, and added another at the 13th off a wedge to five feet, and parred in for a 70 and the one-stroke victory.

"I was playing very solidly for the pressure Annika was putting on," Webb said. "I'm very happy I didn't succumb to that."

Corona Morelia Championship
Michoacan, Mexico
Winner: Lorena Ochoa

The Tres Marias Golf Club in Morelia was more Hollywood than Mexico for that week early in October at the Corona Morelia Championship. The script was trite but charming—local girl comes home and wins before her adoring people. But it became real when Mexico's Lorena Ochoa dropped that final putt.

"For me, it's like a U.S. Open, being able to play in my country and win in front of my people," said Ochoa, who trailed in the first round, then rocketed through the field to win by five strokes over Paraguay's Julieta Granada for her fourth victory of the season and her first in four tournaments in Mexico.

Ochoa played the par-73 Tres Marias course in 71-64-68-69—272, 20 under par. The script called for the heroine to suffer before she triumphed.

Ochoa did that for only one round, when her opening 71 left her tied for 10th place, three strokes behind Brandie Burton's 68. Ochoa couldn't wait for the final act for her grandest scene. She put on the big show in the second round. Ochoa began with two birdies, then at the par-four No. 7, she holed out an eight iron from 131 yards for an eagle. Then she birdied the next four holes, and had a total of eight birdies for a course-record 64. She also took the lead by three shots over Sun Young Yoo, and kept the three-shot cushion in the third round over Granada, who made her move with 66.

Granada made it interesting in the final round, drawing to within one when Ochoa bogeyed No. 3. Ochoa then birdied No. 8 for the fourth time and started to pull away. Said Granada: "On the back nine, I couldn't get any birdies going and that's where I lost her." Ochoa cruised home for 69 and the five-stroke win that signaled there might be a changing of the guard on the LPGA Tour. "There are those who say we are behind Annika (Sorenstam)," Ochoa said. "With all of this, maybe we are showing we are catching up with her."

Samsung World Championship
Palm Desert, California
Winner: Lorena Ochoa

If there was to be a changing of the guard in women's golf, Lorena Ochoa's performance in the Samsung World Championship will have been a big part of it. Ochoa, the Mexican whiz having a big year, came from three strokes behind in the final round to overrun Annika Sorenstam, the world No. 1 women's golfer, and win by two strokes. This was her second straight victory, her fifth of the season, but she said, "Finally, I won." Clearly, she meant she beat Sorenstam head-to-head. It worked out just as Ochoa said it would: "I believe in myself. I know I can do it."

Ochoa did it in the exclusive 20-player field at the Big Horn Golf Club in Palm Desert, California, playing in 67-73-67-65—272, 16 under par. She shared the first-round lead with Sorenstam, but trailed the rest of the way until the 11th hole in the final round. Sorenstam tied for the lead in the second round with Sophie Gustafson (70) and Paula Creamer (68), then shot 66 in the third round to take a three-stroke lead over Ochoa into the last day.

The game was on immediately. Ochoa eagled the par-five third hole and had two birdies on the first nine. Sorenstam was a bit erratic. After two birdies, she bogeyed the fifth, then took a two-stroke lead into the turn with birdies at the seventh and ninth. She bogeyed the 10th out of a bunker where Ochoa birdied, and they were tied. Ochoa took the lead with a birdie at the 11th, then locked up the tournament at the par-five 15th off a wedge to 15 feet while Sorenstam three-putted for a bogey. Sorenstam's birdie at the 16th cut Ochoa's margin to two.

"I feel very deflated at the moment," Sorenstam said. "I want those awards as much as she does." Said Ochoa, just after beating the world No. 1: "My goal is to be No. 1. I think you have to work your way up there. I think Annika is ahead. I'm fine. I'm happy. I'm patient."

Honda LPGA Thailand
Chonburi, Thailand
Winner: Hee-Won Han

There's no telling what South Korea's Hee-Won Han might have done if she had been feeling great all the way. The Honda LPGA Thailand tournament had reached just past the halfway point in the final round when Han, the defending champion, finally settled into her game. This was impressive, considering that she had started the third and final round two strokes off the pace and had already made five birdies. She did get slowed down by a bogey at the ninth, but then she rolled on. "This is my sixth title," Han said, "but it is the first time I won by five strokes."

And she did it all on the last day. The first-round lead went to Heather Young and Nicole Castrale—the latter in her first full season on the tour—with seven-under-par 65s in the deep heat of Bangkok's Amata Spring Country Club. Young had seven birdies and no bogeys, and Castrale had eight birdies and one bogey to share a one-stroke lead. Castrale quickened the pace in the second round. She birdied her first four holes with a dazzling putting show. She dropped a 20-footer at No. 1, a three-footer at No. 2, and 15-footers at the next two, on her way to 68 and an 11-under 133 total. Castrale slipped to 75 in the third round and tied for third, and Diana D'Alessio closed with 70 to finish second at 207.

Experience had proved out again. Han raced out to five birdies on the front, at Nos. 2, 4, 5, 6 and 7, and exchanged three birdies and three bogeys from there for 67, a 14-under 202 total and a five-stroke win. "I thought I played pretty good today," she said, and she got no arguments.

Kolon-Hana Bank Championship
Gyeonggi, Korea
Winner: Jin Joo Hong

Starting at the top has its noticeable benefits. For one, South Korea's Jin Joo Hong would never have to wonder whether she's ever going to win that first one. She already had. Hong, 23, was playing her first LPGA event in the Kolon-Hana Bank Championship, and she simply ran away with it. In fact, she stumbled to a double bogey at the very last hole and still had three strokes to spare.

As Hong was saying after taking the lead in the second round, "This is my first time playing in an LPGA event, and rather than feel pressure to win, I want to enjoy it." She couldn't possibly have enjoyed it more. She played the Mauna Ocean course in South Korea in 68-67-70 for an 11-under 205 total to win by three over Jeong Jang, a two-time winner on the tour. Jeong had no illusions about catching Hong, not trailing by five strokes. "I didn't think I was going to break her today," Jang said, and so she concentrated on money. A high finish would make her the ninth player of the season to top $1 million in winnings. And she did it, getting to $1,093,037.

Hong wasn't noticed early on. Her opening 68 put her in a six-way tie for third behind Joo Mi Kim. Then the 67 in the second round gave her a four-stroke lead over Kim, Karine Icher and amateur Mi Jung Hur. In the final round, Hong birdied Nos. 2, 7 and 8, then made a rare bogey at the ninth, two-putting from 12 feet. She birdied the 13th off a bunker shot to six feet and the 17th on a three-footer to go up by five. In an unceremonious finish, she three-putted the 18th from nine feet for a double-bogey six, and won by three. "It wasn't that easy," Hong said, "but I'm glad I did it."

Mizuno Classic
Mie, Japan
Winner: Karrie Webb

See Japan LPGA Tour section.

The Mitchell Company Tournament of Champions
Mobile, Alabama
Winner: Lorena Ochoa

There was only one thing left for Lorena Ochoa to do in this smashing season she was having, and that was to win the LPGA Tour's Rolex Player of the Year Award. And she did it—ending Annika Sorenstam's five-year reign—with a fury in The Mitchell Company Tournament of Champions. She crushed the field by 10 strokes for her sixth victory of the year. "Winning this tournament was very special," Ochoa said. "I think this is going to be a place I will remember for the rest of my life." The place was Magnolia Grove's Crossing at Mobile, Alabama, and she roared over it in 21-under-par 267. For the record, Juli Inkster, who closed with 68, and Paula Creamer (70) tied for second at 11-under 277.

The way was made a little clearer for Ochoa when Sorenstam and Karrie Webb skipped the tournament, but then Ochoa was on such a tear they might not have made any difference. In the first round, under lift-clean-and-place rules because of wet weather, 27 of the 39 in the winners-only field broke par. Creamer led the way with an eight-under 64, two ahead of Ochoa. Ochoa hit a rocky patch in the second round, taking a quadruple bogey at No. 1 and shooting 73 to slip three behind Inkster (69) and Moira Dunn (67). She shook off the crash and staked her claim in the third round with a nine-under 63 and a five-stroke lead. She had played the last 33 holes, since scoring the eight, in 13 under par.

"I was just tired, mentally tired," Ochoa said. "Today was the opposite. Everything was just so easy." She rode a birdie-eagle-birdie outburst from the third hole into the lead. She bogeyed the eighth, then birdied five of the next six. She might have coasted conservatively in the final round, but she turned up the heat instead, and after another bogey at the eighth, she birdied four of the next five. It was academic after that.

ADT Championship
West Palm Beach, Florida
Winner: Julieta Granada

There was a television game show called "Who Wants To Be A Millionaire?" The same question was asked at the LPGA's season-ending ADT Championship, which offered the first $1 million prize in women's golf. And Julieta Granada—a rookie from Paraguay, just two days past her 20th birthday—said, I do, thank you very much. And Granada scored her first victory and became an instant millionaire. Her first reaction? "My mom and dad made so many sacrifices for me," she said. "We went through tough times, and we managed to keep the family together. The million dollar prize—I don't even know how much that is."

The tournament, at Trump International in West Palm Beach, Florida, had a field of 32 players that was boiled down to the final eight by two cuts. Among those gone in the 36-hole cut: U.S. Women's Open champion Annika Sorenstam and Weetabix Women's British Open champion Sherri Steinhauer. And among the 54-hole victims: Juli Inkster, Cristie Kerr and Morgan Pressel. The surviving eight went into the final round with clean slates.

Granada was the total surprise of the tournament. She not only survived both cuts, she was tied for second place at eight under par coming out of the third round, a stroke behind Il Mi Chung and ahead of Karrie Webb, Paula Creamer and Player of the Year Lorena Ochoa. It didn't look promising for the unheralded Granada, who had only seven top-10 finishes in 30 events.

But Granada held them all off with a bogey-free 68, four under par, beating Ochoa by two and Webb by three. Granada scattered four birdies: the par-five third hole on a chip to one foot; at the sixth, a nine iron to 15 feet; the 10th, a seven iron to 12 feet, and the 16th, an eight iron to eight feet. She parred the 17th with a clutch five-footer, then put her eight iron at the 18th over the water and behind the hole, and two-putted for a par and a one-stroke lead. Then behind her, Ochoa and Webb both watered their tee shots at the par-three 17th, and it was all but over.

"At the end of the day, it all comes down to what you do," Granada said. And so it was for her.

Lexus Cup
Singapore
Winner: Asia

The draw for the singles matches in the Lexus Cup indicated the captains were hoping for a knockout somewhere just past the middle of the matches. Fate decreed otherwise. It would fall on the two rookies. And so they came to the par-four 17th in the final match at Singapore's Tanah Merah Country Club. Paraguay's Julieta Granada, two down, caught a greenside bunker and would have to hole her blast for a birdie. She nearly did, but then South Korea's Seon Hwa Lee, on in two, comfortably got her two-putt par to halve the hole and beat Granada 2 and 1. The Internationals had won the singles, 6½ to 5½, but Lee's win gave the Asians the Lexus Cup, 12½ to 11½.

The Lexus Cup opened with a 3-3 tie in the alternate-shot matches. Asia took the lead the second day in the fourball matches. After trailing by 2-1, Asia swept the next three matches for a 4-2 victory and the 7-5 lead going into the singles. In a battle of the captains, the Internationals' Annika Sorenstam routed Grace Park, 4 and 3, to lead off the singles. It was a struggle from there.

Ladies European Tour

Women's World Cup of Golf
Sun City, South Africa
Winner: Sweden (Annika Sorenstam and Liselotte Neumann)

See South African Women's Tour section.

ANZ Ladies Masters
Ashmore, Queensland, Australia
Winner: Amy Yang

See Australian Women's Tour section.

Princess Lalla Meriem Cup
Rabat, Morocco
Winner: Sophie Sandolo

Sophie Sandolo survived a five-hole playoff, and the flu, to win her first professional title at the Princess Lalla Meriem Cup, an unofficial invitational event played alongside the men's Hassan II Trophy, won by Sam Torrance, at the Royal Dar-es-Salam course in Rabat, Morocco. Sandolo let slip a three-stroke lead with a round to play to tie with Germany's Anja Monke at two under par for 54 holes. The pair then played five more holes in extra time before Sandolo holed from 10 feet for victory.

Stephanie Arricau, of France, was third, with Veronica Zorzi, from Italy, and another Frenchwoman, Ludivine Kreutz, fourth and fifth respectively. Sandolo, the 29-year-old who is based in Monaco, is an Italian national, born in Nice, France, of an Italian father and French mother. She was the European Amateur champion before turning professional and in 2005 and 2006 produced a calendar featuring elegant pin-up images of herself.

But before the final round in Morocco, she was not feeling well. "Before the last round I was not well at all, I had flu," she said. "The last round was very tough, it was head-to-head with Anja. After the one-and-a-half hour playoff, five long and emotional holes, I holed a putt for the victory—at last! I'm really exhausted but I'm so happy, I hope this victory will be the first of a very long series."

Tenerife Ladies Open
Tenerife, Spain
Winner: Riikka Hakkarainen

Following a winter practicing in Guatemala, where her husband Karvinen had a coaching job, Riikka Hakkarainen began her ninth season on the Ladies European Tour with a victory in the Tenerife Ladies Open at Abama. Although the 28-year-old Finn had won events in Sweden and South Africa, this was her first official tour win. She had waited since a second-place finish in 1999 and a third place in 2002 where she had double-bogeyed the final hole.

Hakkarainen became the second Finnish player to win a professional event after Minea Blomqvist. "This win will be great for Finnish golf," she said. "There are only five Finns on tour, so now I'm tied for wins with Minnie. I've been close to winning a few times, so to finally make it all the way is a fantastic feeling. I'm really relieved."

Hakkarainen scored rounds of 73, 70, 74 and 71 for an even-par 288 total to win by two strokes over Spanish rookie Tania Elosegui Mayor, who was playing in her first event on the Ladies European Tour. Five players tied for third place, including overnight leader Kirsty Taylor, Shani Waugh, Rebecca Coakley, Rebecca Hudson and Virginie Auffret. Taylor dropped out of contention with an outward 39, while Australia's Waugh claimed the lead before suffering three bogeys on the back nine. Hakkarainen had three birdies and three bogeys going out, but edged in front with birdies at the 10th and 11th holes, and after dropping a shot at the 15th, parred in for the win.

Open de Espana Feminino
San Jorge, Castellon, Spain
Winner: Lynnette Brooky

Her new philosophy not to "freak out" on the course was put to the test, but Lynnette Brooky survived to win the Open de Espana Feminino at Panoramica in Castellon. Brooky was at times brilliant, twice posting a new course record, for 66 in the first round and then for 65 in the third. The 38-year-old New Zealander went into the final round three strokes ahead of Gwladys Nocera and had increased her lead to four at the turn, and five with eight to play, before suffering two double bogeys.

The first came at the 11th hole, where she found a tricky lie in a bunker. The next came at the 17th, where she put her second shot into the water. Nocera birdied the 11th and was now within two strokes. But the Frenchwoman bogeyed the 13th and 15th and so the pressure eased on Brooky.

Both the leading two players closed with rounds of 70, giving Brooky a three-stroke victory at 13 under par. Switzerland's Nora Angehrn finished third at eight under. It was Brooky's fourth victory on the tour and her first since the 2003 French Open. "It's been a long time waiting," she said. "I knew if I didn't get a win this year I would lose my winner's status. I didn't worry about the double bogeys. I said to myself the one thing I will not do this year is freak out. Even when I hit that six iron in the water on 17 I said to myself, 'this is golf. I know I'm a good player. I can do this.'"

Deutsche Bank Ladies' Swiss Open
Gerre Losone, Switzerland
Winner: Gwladys Nocera

After finishing as a runner-up for the fourth time in just over a year in Spain the previous week, Gwladys Nocera claimed her first professional title at the Deutsche Bank Ladies' Swiss Open at Gerre Losone. It came a day before her 31st birthday as the Biarritz-based player won by three strokes over Laura Davies.

Nocera jumped into contention by scoring a course-record 63 in the third round. It left her a stroke behind England's Lisa Hall. The former two-time Solheim Cup player based in America was playing on an invitation after missing a whole season of competitive golf, and the lack of recent experience caught up with her as she closed with 76 to finished third.

Nocera compiled a final round of 71 for a 15-under-par total of 273 and was never really threatened by Davies's closing 70. Nocera already topped the money list, but her €75,000 first prize extended her lead. The last time the Swiss Open was played was in 1997 when the winner was also a Frenchwoman, Marie Laure de Lorenzi, who was watching this time.

"Last week I didn't lose the tournament, she (Lynnette Brooky) won it. So I told myself to keep going and I was thinking my time will come," Nocera said. "I'm just so happy, it's unbelievable. I tried to play as I always play. Like yesterday I was really focused on my game and trying to be more aggressive. Before, when I didn't win, I played it too cool, so I said to myself just go for it and give yourself a chance to win."

Vediorbis Open de France
Anzin St Aubin, France
Winner: Veronica Zorzi

What should have been a romp to her second successive Vediorbis Open de France title turned into a nail-biting finish for Italy's Veronica Zorzi. The 25-year-old from Verona bogeyed each of the final four holes and won by only one stroke over Laura Davies, the runner-up for the second consecutive event. Home players Stephanie Arricau and Gwladys Nocera finished third and fourth respectively.

Rounds of 71, 69 and 69 gave Zorzi a four-stroke lead going into the final round at Arras. Twice in the final round she led by five shots, after the third and the 12th, but by the time she came to the par-five 18th hole, she led by two over Davies. Her second shot then landed on a cart path and she had to lay up. With Davies looking at a six-foot birdie opportunity, Zorzi thought she had to get up and down to avoid a playoff. She could not, but Davies missed the birdie chance when the putt bobbled.

"Last year I won with a birdie and this year I won with a bogey, but it's the same result," said Zorzi, whose 72 gave her a seven-under-par total. "My heart was beating and when I hit my second shot at 18 onto the cart path I thought, 'come on, give me a chance.' I hadn't a shot from there and I made my fourth bogey in a row. I was feeling very tired and emotional, but I just kept trying to stay in the present and I just kept on fighting."

KLM Ladies Open
Valkenswaard, Netherlands
Winner: Stephanie Arricau

Returning to the Ladies European Tour, where she won twice in 2004, after an unsuccessful stint in America in 2005, Stephanie Arricau proved it was a wise decision by winning the KLM Ladies Open at Eindhovensche. It was the sixth time the title has been won by a Frenchwoman. In an exciting climax to the tournament Arricau was one of three players, along with countrywoman Gwladys Nocera and Germany's Anja Monke, tied for the lead with four holes to play. The 32-year-old from Toulouse, wearing an orange shirt in honor of the host country, made two birdies in the last three holes to claim the title, the third of her career. Playing in the group ahead, Monke missed a five-foot birdie putt at the last to ease the pressure on the leader.

Arricau recorded rounds of 67, 67 and 70 for a 204 total, 12-under-par, to win by one stroke over Monke, who closed with 69. Australian rookie Leah Hart finished third, one shot further behind, with Nocera slipping back to tie for fifth place. "Each win is difficult, but this one was the hardest," said Arricau. "There were a lot of players chasing me today and I missed quite a lot of birdie chances on the front nine. But now I think my confidence is back for the rest of the year. I feel better in Europe. I did not like the States. It's a different culture and life was tough."

BMW Ladies Italian Open
Rome, Italy
Winner: Gwladys Nocera

By winning the BMW Ladies Italian Open, Gwladys Nocera took her second title within a month, but her victory in Rome was more difficult than the one in Switzerland. With second and third rounds of 66 and 65, Nocera was three ahead going into the final day, after three holes of which she led by six. However, it got more interesting as her playing companion, Sophie Giquel, made four birdies in five holes from the eighth.

With the gap narrowed to a single shot, Nocera was having trouble converting her chances, but at the 16th she holed from six feet, which gave her an eventual two-stroke margin. Even at the last hole, though, she had to get up and down from behind the green while Giquel missed a birdie chance.

"It was harder to win today than the first time because Sophie was playing so well, and on 18 I knew she could have holed that putt to force a playoff," said Nocera. "I missed birdie chances on 14 and 15 and I knew it was time to make one at 16. The last few holes were tricky, but it was great to finally get the job done."

A 72 left Nocera at 14 under par, with her 23-year-old compatriot at 12 under after a 71. Iben Tinning, the defending champion, finished four strokes further back in a seven-way tie for third place with Elisa Serramia, Veronica Zorzi, Ana Sanchez, Laura Cabanillas, Rebecca Hudson and Linda Wessberg.

Estoril Ladies Open of Portugal
Cascais, Estoril, Portugal
Winner: Stephanie Arricau

The French dominance of the season continued with Stephanie Arricau joining Gwladys Nocera as a two-time winner. With a superb display over the second nine in the final round, Arricau won by five strokes over Nocera to take her second title of the month at the Estoril Ladies Open of Portugal at Quinta da Marinha Oitavos. After two opening rounds of 71, Arricau produced a 65 for a nine-under-par total of 207.

She went to the turn in even par and then played "the best nine holes of my life" as she came home in 29. She holed a long, downhill putt at the 10th and that sparked her into life. More birdies followed at the 11th and 13th, again from sizeable putts, then at the short 15th she hit her tee shot to two feet. She also birdied the par-five 16th before eagling the par-five 17th with an eight-foot putt.

Arricau, now just 33 years old, had started the final round one behind Australia's Sarah Kemp, who finished third, and Becky Brewerton, who slipped to fifth, with England's Rebecca Hudson taking fourth place. Nocera recorded her sixth successive top-five finish of the season but could not keep pace with Arricau. "From the 10th on I felt like I could feel the putts; it was incredible," Arricau said after her fourth career victory. "The putt definitely gave me a lot of confidence. I felt sick at the beginning of the day. Perhaps that helped me to stay cool. I usually have quite a lot of energy and that can allow me to get tense, which isn't always the best thing."

OTP Bank Ladies Central European Open
Tata, Budapest, Hungary
Winner: Rebecca Hudson

Rebecca Hudson's fourth season as a professional started well when she won the South African Open and led the Nedbank Women's Golf Tour. It improved further when the 27-year-old from Doncaster won the OTP Bank Ladies Central European Open in Hungary. It was the Englishwoman's first European success and came at the Old Lake course in Tata where she had good memories of scoring a career-low 62 the previous year.

Nothing so exceptional was required this time, but rounds of 66 and 65 left her one behind Anja Monke going into the final round. Monke let the lead slip with two early bogeys, and a closing 73 left the German two behind Hudson. Lora Fairclough and Riikka Hakkarainen shared third place a further shot behind.

Hudson's final round of 70 gave her a total of 201, 12 under par. She had only two bogeys in 54 holes, the second of them on the ninth in the final round. She still led by one and doubled the advantage with a birdie at the 11th. Her drive at the 18th, after a long wait on the tee, rebounded onto the fairway off a tree and she saved par. The win was a long time coming for the former double British Amateur champion and three-time Curtis Cup player.

"I think I was expected to come out in my first year and do this, but honestly there's such a difference between the amateur game and the professional scene," she said. "The standard out here is fantastic, and now to always be known as a tour winner, I can't explain how happy I am."

Catalonia Ladies Masters
Platja D'Aro, Girona, Costa Brava, Spain
Winner: Gwladys Nocera

Gwladys Nocera's wonderful season continued as she won the Catalonia Ladies Masters, her third title in 10 weeks, at Platja D'Aro on Spain's Costa Brava. Nocera scored three successive 69s for a nine-under-par 207 total. The first gave her a share of the first-round lead with Sophie Giquel. The second put her four strokes ahead of the field, and the third gave the 31-year-old from Biarritz a five-stroke victory over Australia's Sarah Kemp.

Five birdies in the first eight holes of the final round effectively decided the tournament and Nocera could afford a couple of dropped shots coming home, including at the 18th. Kemp secured her best finish with a closing 68 to finish one ahead of Ludivine Kreutz and Maria Hjorth.

Nocera won €55,000 to extend her lead at the top of the money list. This was her eighth top-10 finish in nine starts in 2006 and the fifth French victory in the last seven events. Her form could not be better going into the two biggest events of the season, the Evian Masters and the Women's British Open.

"It would be great to win the Evian at home in France, but the British is the one I would love to win the most. I think I still need to improve my game to win, but if I play well, I would love to finish top-10," said Nocera, who beat Cristie Kerr in the singles at the 2005 Solheim Cup.

Evian Masters
Evian-les-Bains, France
Winner: Karrie Webb

Karrie Webb utilized all her experience to triumph eventually at the Evian Masters, claiming a one-stroke victory over Laura Davies and Michelle Wie, the 16-year-old American who also finished second in the event as an amateur in 2005. Tied for the lead after a second round of 66, Wie fell behind Webb with a third round of 70. After a superb spell around the turn on the final day, including an eagle at the ninth, Wie went two ahead with seven to play.

But Webb was not to be outdone. The 31-year-old Australian birdied the 12th, 14th and 17th, and Wie dropped a shot at the 13th. Davies had the chance to eagle the 18th, which might have forced a playoff. It was Davies's third runner-up finish in Europe after a disastrous start to the season in America, but this was her best performance so far. "I couldn't be more pleased about the week apart from the fact that the putt on the last missed," said Davies, who closed with a 67. "But I've got a feeling that if I'd have holed it, Webb would have holed hers too. It's one of those things."

Webb, who collected the first prize of €380,000 for an event co-sanctioned on both the LPGA and European tours, scored wonderfully consistent rounds of 67, 68, 69 and 68 for a 16-under total of 272. "It was sort of an up-and-down day," said Webb. "I did not play the front nine as well as I did the last few days. But I played the back nine really solidly. I kind of told myself to get in there and start trusting myself a little bit more and just start believing in myself. I played extremely well the last couple of holes. I thought I was going to have to get to 17 under, but 16 ended up being good enough."

It was the 33rd career win for Webb and her third of the year, including a seventh major title at the Kraft Nabisco Championship. Mi Hyun Kim finished in fourth place, while Lorena Ochoa, who had a double-eagle two at the ninth by holing from 191 yards with a hybrid club, was fifth. Wie rued coming home in only one under par. "When I look back at it, I could not have played harder today," she said. "I played every shot as best as I could. I am getting very close."

Weetabix Women's British Open
Royal Lytham & St. Annes, England
Winner: Sherri Steinhauer

See Chapter 6.

Scandinavian TPC Hosted by Annika
Stockholm, Sweden
Winner: Annika Sorenstam

Twice the Scandinavian TPC title has been "Hosted by Annika" and now twice Annika Sorenstam has not exactly played the gracious host, instead keeping the silverware for herself. This was her third win of the season, her fifth in Sweden and the 82nd of her career, but this was extra special for coming at her home course of Bro-Balsta. At the conclusion she jumped, with her sister Charlotta and mother Gunilla, in the lake by the 18th green where she would dive for balls as a child.

It was also a special weekend for featuring a head-to-head battle between the world No. 1 and the world No. 2, Lorena Ochoa. Sorenstam set the course record of 66 in the opening round, but Ochoa bettered it by one to move into a tie for the lead with the host. They both had 69s in the third round, and then on the final day Ochoa's 66 was edged out by Sorenstam's 65 and a 21-under-par total of 271.

Sorenstam opened the final round with an eagle and birdied the second hole to move two shots ahead. Birdies at the 11th and 15th put Ochoa back even, the fifth and 14th holes being halved in birdies. Sorenstam went ahead again at the short 16th with a tee shot to two feet, but then Ochoa eagled the 17th, holing from eight feet, while Sorenstam could only birdie. At the 18th the Swede produced her third birdie in a row, making an eight-footer for victory.

"It was an incredible day," said Sorenstam. "The finish was like a fairytale. To come here at home, to play with Lorena in the last group head-to-head and in tough conditions, but to play like it was the best day ever, it doesn't get much better than that."

Wales Ladies Championship of Europe
Llanelli, Carmarthenshire, Wales
Winner: Linda Wessberg

Battling to earn her first title at the Wales Ladies Championship of Europe, Linda Wessberg did not get distracted by the brilliant scoring ahead of her. First, Gwladys Nocera posted 66 to set the clubhouse target at 12 under par. Then Laura Davies produced a 67 to get to 13 under, but ultimately it was only good enough for her fourth runner-up finish of the season.

Wessberg, the third-round leader, managed to complete a final round of 71 at the Machynys Peninsula course to claim victory with a total of 274, one ahead of Davies. Just as Davies birdied the last hole—lifting her to the top of the money list ahead of Nocera, who tied with Australian Nikki Garrett in third place—so did Wessberg to take the title. A perfect drive in the middle of the fairway gave her the opportunity to find the green at the par-five and she two-putted from 20 feet.

"I was very nervous on that last hole," said Wessberg, a 26-year-old Swede from Gothenburg in her third year on tour. "I was looking at scoreboards all day and I'm a good match player, so I would say that gave me the extra edge. I have been waiting for this for a while. I played well in my first and second seasons, but this year I have been struggling to get it all together—until this week."

SAS Masters
Oslo, Norway
Winner: Laura Davies

Laura Davies ended the longest winless drought of her career with victory at the SAS Masters in Oslo. Davies had not won for two and a half years since the 2004 Australian Open. It was the 67th win of her career and followed a season in which she started horribly in America and then suffering four runner-up finishes in Europe.

"It's been such a long time coming I'm really pleased with it," said the 42-year-old. "It's just nice to get the win, having had a few seconds and a few thirds last year. It's nice to get the win and I can't stop smiling.

"When I missed my seventh cut on the trot in America, I did wonder if I would win again. It was miserable times. But ever since those first two seconds in Europe I got all my confidence back. Obviously the Evian was the biggest performance of the year before this one. This out-rates Evian because I have finally won."

Davies led by two shots going into the final round. She eagled the second hole but then gave two shots back. There were four birdies in the round and another eagle at the 15th, where she hit a two iron to two feet, a brilliant shot. Two bogeys at the 17th and 18th holes merely cut her winning margin to six shots. She had rounds of 69, 68 and 68 for an 11-under score of 205. Ellen Smets, of Belgium, was the runner-up, with Nikki Garrett and Virginie Lagoutte sharing third place.

Finnair Masters
Helsinki, Finland
Winner: Virginie Lagoutte

Virginia Lagoutte became the third Frenchwoman to win on the European Tour in 2006, giving the country its sixth win, and claimed the second title of her own career at the Finnair Masters in Helsinki. Lagoutte won the KLM Open in 2005 in a playoff, but here won by two strokes over Sweden's Elin Ohlsson. "The first win wasn't the same," said the 27-year-old from Montpellier. "I played really well today."

After two rounds of 68, she closed with 67 for a 203 total, 10 under par. Ohlsson, who completed the tournament with a 68, finished three strokes ahead of Gwladys Nocera and American Kris Lindstrom. "I could never relax because Elin was putting so well and chasing me all the way," said Lagoutte, whose fiancé Sebastien Clement was caddying for her. "He was very stressed," she said, "but fortunately I was not."

Birdies at the 13th, 14th and 17th holes kept at bay Ohlsson, who recorded her best finish on the Ladies European Tour. "The French are playing better and better and it's boys and girls," Lagoutte said. "I think it's because it's a group thing and everybody is just helping each other." Her other secret weapons included a pink flamingo driver head cover and a faithful yellow ball marker in the shape of a teddy bear.

Nykredit Masters
Copenhagen, Denmark
Winner: Karen Margrethe Juul

Leading by two strokes with a round to play in the Nykredit Masters in her homeland of Denmark, Karen Margrethe Juul could not have had a more welcome visitor. Thomas Bjorn, the leading men's player from Denmark, shares the same management company as Juul and spoke to her after the third round. "He's been really good to me and he told me that I was stupid for not believing in myself," Juul said. "He saw it coming before I did. After this I'm going to give him a big hug."

Juul's coach, James Petts, also knew a victory was coming and informed her that he had put money on her winning at Odense Eventyr. The 30-year-old from Copenhagen duly did as she added a closing 68 to earlier rounds of 72, 67 and 66 for 15 under par. She won by four shots over the English pair of Laura Davies, gaining her fifth runner-up finish of the season after a 66, and Trish Johnson.

"It's fantastic," said Juul. "This is the best place I could ever have won a tournament. I was pretty nervous on the last few holes, but my caddie, Rasmus, helped to keep me cool." Having gone out in 33, Juul could still not shake off the pursuers until she chipped in for an eagle at the 15th. A fully qualified civil engineer, Juul was in her fifth year on tour, but this was only the second season she has been playing full-time due to her studies.

Siemens Austrian Ladies Open
Wiener Neustadt, Austria
Winner: Sophie Gustafson

Despite a brilliant charge from Laura Davies, Sophie Gustafson hung on to win the Siemens Austrian Ladies Open at Fohrenwald. It was the Swede's first win for three years and the 21st of her career. It also meant she had accumulated enough points to be considered for honorary life membership on the Ladies European Tour, which was later conferred on the 32-year-old.

Ironically, it was the victory of Davies in Norway, ending her own winless drought, that inspired Gustafson here. She was in brilliant form with 64 in the second round and 65 in the third to take a five-stroke lead. After birdies at the opening two holes on the final day, she led by seven over Davies and Anne-Marie Knight. She dropped her first shot in 34 holes at the fifth and it was all the encouragement that Davies needed.

Davies reeled off a splurge of birdies, at the 12th, 14th, 15th, 16th and 18th holes, but had to settle for her sixth second place of the season. "I didn't hole quite as many putts as I would have liked, but I gave it my best shot. I knew it was going to be almost impossible to catch Sophie. I turned out to be right," Davies said.

Gustafson had three birdies and one bogey on the back nine as a 71 left her 17 under par and two ahead of Davies. "I was reading that it was three years since Laura last won and it kind of spurred me on," she admitted. Ana Sanchez finished third, four behind Davies, with Knight back in fifth place.

BBC Radio Kent Ladies' English Open
Kent, England
Winner: Cecilia Ekelundh

For the third successive year there was a Swedish winner at Chart Hills, the Nick Faldo-designed course near the village of Biddenden in Kent. After two victories for Maria Hjorth, Cecilia Ekelundh won the BBC Radio Kent

Ladies' English Open for her third title in the last three seasons. With the tournament moved from its midsummer date due to a scheduling clash, the October weather was not great, but there was a fine battle for the title.

Ekelundh shared the lead with Denmark's Amanda Moltke-Leth going into the final round and parred the first 13 holes. The Dane had gone ahead but a bogey at the 13th meant they were tied once more. They both birdied the 14th, but at the par-five 16th Ekelundh moved ahead with a birdie while Moltke-Leth found trouble in two bunkers to take a double bogey.

Ekelundh also birdied the short 17th, where there is an island green, and could afford to three-putt the last. Her 70, for six-under-par total, gave her a one-stroke win over Germany's Martina Eberl, who had tied for the lead with five to play. Danielle Masters, who is attached to the Chart Hills club, claimed the best finish of her rookie season by finishing third, one ahead of Moltke-Leth. "This is one of my favorite courses all year, if not the favorite," said Ekelundh. "It's a good design and you never see the same hole twice. I've had some good finishes here and I hope I get to come back and play here again."

Dubai Ladies Masters
Dubai, United Arab Emirates
Winner: Annika Sorenstam

Annika Sorenstam swept to victory at the inaugural Dubai Ladies Masters with a breathtaking performance at the Emirates course. The world No. 1 opened with a 65 to lead by two shots. Two rounds of 68 put her ahead by five shots at halfway and then seven after 54 holes. She closed with a 69 for an 18-under total of 270 and a six-stroke victory over Helen Alfredsson.

"She is just such a fantastic player, she has continued to play so incredibly well in the last few years and just continues to produce and produce," said Alfredsson, the 2007 Solheim Cup captain. Karrie Webb was the nearest challenger overnight, but a 70 left her in third place, two behind Alfredsson.

"It's always nice to start a round with a seven-shot lead," Sorenstam said. "I was just solid today and I didn't really make a lot of mistakes. I was just enjoying myself and trying to avoid a big number. I think I was more nervous making a speech in front of the Royal Family than I was over the four-footers." Sorenstam finished third on the money list, which was headed by Laura Davies for the seventh time, with Gwladys Nocera second.

Amy Yang, a 17-year-old Korean who is now based in Australia, was playing in her first event as a professional and finished fourth along with Veronica Zorzi. Yang started the season by winning the ANZ Masters in Australia as an amateur. The Rolex Rookie of the Year award was won by Australia's Nikki Garrett.

Japan LPGA Tour

Daikin Orchid Ladies
Okinawa, Japan
Winner: Mikiyo Nishizuka

A little reading on the side came in handy for Mikiyo Nishizuka, helping her score her first career victory on the Japan LPGA Tour. Passages from a self-help book she had been browsing enabled Nishizuka to remain cool enough in her final-round battle with several other contenders in the traditional season-opening Daikin Orchid tournament to emerge with the one-stroke win.

Urged in the book to always look at the bright side, the 34-year-old player even said "thank you" when she took two bogeys during her final-round, three-under-par 69 that brought her from a stroke off the lead. She edged the second-round leaders—Shiho Ohyama and Ya-Huei Lu of Taiwan—and young Sakura Yokomine, one of the tour's bright new stars in 2005—with her eight-under-par 208. "I was able to relax while I played, so this book was really useful," said Nishizuka, who was happily unimpressed with her own game that day. "I almost want to apologize for winning because my shots weren't that good."

Nishizuka started the tournament with 71, four shots off the pace of Miho Koga, then shot 68 Saturday to move within a stroke of Ohyama and Lu, who both had pairs of 69s for their 138s. Yokomine was at 72-68–140 and matched Nishizuka's 68 to wind up in the runners-up grouping at Ryukyu Golf Club in Okinawa.

Accordia Golf Ladies
Miyazaki, Japan
Winner: Yuri Fudoh

New season, same old story. It only took Yuri Fudoh two tournaments into the 2006 season to put another victory on her remarkable record. Launching her bid for a seventh straight money title, the 29-year-old queen of Japanese women's golf survived a windy final round to win the resort-sponsored Accordia Ladies tournament at Aoshima Golf Club in Miyazaki by a stroke over Hiromi Mogi, the first-round leader, and veteran winner Michiko Hattori. Her one-over-par 73 for 211 gave Fudoh her 39th career victory. Mogi shot 72 and Hattori 73 as only two players broke par in the rough final-round conditions.

Mogi had six birdies and two bogeys on Friday to open the new tournament with 68 and a two-stroke lead over Hattori and Itsumi Okada. Fudoh, who started with 71, took over the lead with a 67 Saturday, one ahead of Michie Ohba, who blazed a 64, and Hattori (69). Mogi (72) was another shot back with Akiko Fukushima (72-67).

Fudoh was never seriously threatened Sunday as she matched two birdies with two bogeys and saw her winning margin slip to one when she bogeyed the last hole.

Kinmirai Tsuushin Queens Open
Kamo, Kagoshi, Japan
Winner: Akane Iijima

Akane Iijima wasted little time establishing herself as a winner, even though she wasn't really expecting it. "I never thought I could win one this early," said the surprised, second-season professional after she pulled out a two-stroke victory in the Kinmirai Tsuushin Queens Open. Iijima closed with a two-under-par 70 in the final round for the winning, five-under 211 at Kagoshima Takamaki Country Club in Kamo.

Iijima started her run to the title when she opened the tournament with 68, taking a one-stroke lead over Yuriko Ohtsuka and two over four other former circuit winners—Kasumi Fujii, Chieko Amanuma, Ikuyo Shiotani and Yumiko Baba. Fujii, who scored three of her 10 victories in 2005, repeated her 70 in a steady rain Saturday and moved a shot into the lead as Iijima shot 73 and Ohtsuka 72 for 141s. Fujii's fourth and final birdie of the day, a 25-footer on the 15th hole, gave her the narrow margin going into Sunday's action.

Iijima sputtered through the front nine, then rang up three birdies coming in for the winning 70. Hiromi Mogi matched that score to slip into second place, one ahead of Ohtsuka and two ahead of Fujii, who fell to 75 Sunday.

Studio Alice Ladies Open
Miki, Hyogo, Japan
Winner: Ji-Hee Lee

Two of the tour's more experienced winners wound up in a lengthy overtime duel in April's Studio Alice Ladies Open. South Korea's Ji-Hee Lee finally won her seventh career title with a par on the fourth extra hole to edge Akiko Fukushima on Hanayashiki Golf Club's Yokawa course at Miki in Hyogo Prefecture. Both had posted two-over-par 218s to forge the deadlock.

Shiho Ohyama, a two-time winner in 2005, launched the tournament Friday with a 70, but four players including Fukushima were at 71 and nine others including Lee were at 72. High winds ravaged the scoring Saturday and Fukushima's 73—five birdies, three bogeys and a triple bogey—was enough to boost her into the lead. She complained that her putting, not the wind, kept her from a better round. Mitsuko Kawasaki also had 73 for 145 and second place, two ahead of Lee (72-75) and four others at 147.

Lee had already posted her 218 before Fukushima rallied from a four-over-par run through 16 holes with birdies on the 17th and 18th to force the playoff. The two played the par-four 18th four times in the extra session, halving the hole three times before Lee chipped to tap-in range for par on the fourth visit and Fukushima missed her par putt after chipping 10 feet beyond the cup.

Life Card Ladies
Kikuyo, Kumamoto, Japan
Winner: Yuri Fudoh

The early weeks of the Japanese season had a familiar ring—and it came from its most dominant player. Yuri Fudoh, the money leader for the last six years, scored her second victory of the five-tournament-old season in the Life Card Ladies in mid-April.

Although she pooh-poohed her landmark 40th win—"I don't really care about having won 40 tournaments," she said afterward—it was historic on the Japan LPGA Tour. Only five other players earlier in tour history reached that total in their careers, none of them before their 30th birthday as was the case for Fudoh, only halfway through her 29th year.

Fudoh was in command of the tournament in Kunamoto, her home prefecture, the final two rounds after taking a three-stroke lead the second day at Kumamoto Airport Country Club.

Coming off her tough four-hole playoff loss to Ji-Hee Lee the previous Sunday, Akiko Fukushima joined Momoko Ueda atop the first-round standings at 67. Fudoh was just a stroke back and rose to the top Saturday in tough conditions. Her two-under-par 70 for 138, the second best score of the day, jumped her three shots in front of Ji-Yeon Han. Shiho Ohyama made a run at Fudoh Sunday, shooting 68, but the champion birdied the last two holes for another 70 and 208 total to beat her by two strokes.

Fujisankei Ladies Classic
Ito, Shizuoka, Japan
Winner: Shiho Ohyama

Shiho Ohyama had a feeling that a victory was on the horizon when she teed off in the Fujisankei Ladies Classic. "Having played well in recent weeks, I was expecting to win a tournament sometime soon," said Ohyama after she had lived up to her own expectations with a playoff victory over Akane Iijima on the hilly Kawana Hotel golf course at Ito.

Ohyama, who had two second-place finishes earlier in the season, including the previous week in the Life Card event, staged a brave finish to get into the extra-hole duel. Iijima, the 22-year-old who won the Kinmirai Queens a month earlier, was in with 68–215, and Ohyama was at even par after a double bogey at the 15th hole. She had to one-putt to save pars on the next two holes and sank a 25-foot birdie putt on the 18th green for 71–215 to bring on the playoff. Her par on the first extra hole brought Ohyama her fourth career victory when Iijima failed to convert par from a greenside bunker.

Windy conditions kept the scoring high the first two days as Yuriko Ohtsuka led Friday with a par 72, and Ohyama slipped a stroke in front with 74-70–144 Saturday to prime things for the exciting finish.

Katokichi Queens
Mure, Kagawa, Japan
Winner: Mie Nakata

The gallery of winners on the Japan LPGA Tour continued to grow at a rapid pace in its early season. Mie Nakata became the third player to notch an initial victory in the first seven events of 2006 when she posted a two-stroke triumph in the Katokichi Queens tournament. The 29-year-old, in her sixth season, joined Mikiyo Nishizuka and Akane Iijima, the earlier first-time victors.

Nakata signaled her intentions in the first round at Yashima Country Club in Kagawa Prefecture when she began the tournament with a seven-birdie, six-under-par 66 and took a one-stroke lead over South Korea's Jae-Hee Bae, the eventual runner-up Sunday evening. The seemingly ever-present Akiko Fukushima climbed into a share of the lead with Bae Saturday. Fukushima produced a 67 for her 136, and Bae, a tour rookie, added 69 for hers. Nakata slipped a stroke behind with 71–137.

"I played aggressively early in my round and it paid off nicely," said Nakata Sunday after putting together four birdies and a bogey for 69 and the winning 10-under-par 206. Interestingly, Nakata's previous best finishes were a pair of seconds in 2003, one of which came in the Katokichi Queens. With five birdies and five bogeys for 72, Bae finished second, her first career top 10.

Salonpas World Ladies
Tokyo, Japan
Winner: Shiho Ohyama

Shiho Ohyama did not have pleasant memories of the Salonpas World Ladies when she teed off in the year's first 72-hole tournament, but was all smiles at the end of the week at Tokyo's renowned Yomiuri Country Club. She had just erased the disappointment of her 2005 playoff loss in the tournament to Yuri Fudoh with a resounding six-stroke victory in one of the early-season's richest tournaments. With her fifth win, Ohyama joined Fudoh as the only other two-time victor of 2006.

Ohyama seized the lead Friday from the first-round leader, 19-year-old rookie Momoko Ueda, who had opened with 67. Ohyama bounced back from her 72 start with a blazing 66, standing a shot ahead of Ueda (72) with her 138. Strong winds inflated the scores Saturday, and Ohyama's one-over 73 was good enough to stretch her lead to five strokes over young Akane Iijima and veteran Akiko Fukushima. She was at 211.

The final six-stroke margin came with her 70 on Sunday, the product of five birdies and three bogeys. "I was able to keep my cool and thought I could get the win," said Ohyama, whose victory boosted her into first place on the money list. Hyun-Ju Shin (70) finished second and U.S. tour star Paula Creamer and Mi-Jeong Jeon, also with 70s, were two strokes further back in third place.

Vernal Ladies
Asakura, Japan
Winner: Ji-Hee Lee

Operating on the principle that a lead is never big enough until a title is secured, Ji-Hee Lee wasn't content to coast when a birdie widened her Sunday afternoon lead to three strokes with just two holes to go in the Vernal Ladies tournament. "I reached my goal of 10 under with the birdie on the 16th, but I wasn't satisfied with it," she recalled. So, she birdied the 17th and 18th to boot to register a six-stroke victory with 67 and her 12-under 204.

The South Korean, who had won earlier in the season in the Studio Alice Open and had six victories prior to that, broke from a first-round tie and never trailed at Fukuoka Century Golf Club at Asakura. She had six birdies and a bogey for 67 to share first place with Ai Ogawa, who has never finished better than fifth in 10 years on the tour.

Lee moved two shots in front Saturday. Her 70-137 established the two-stroke margin over Ogawa (72) and Michie Ohba (68-71). The issue was never in doubt Sunday as Lee became the third multiple winner of the season, joining Shiho Ohyama and Yuri Fudoh. Hyun-Ju Shin closed with 70 for 210 total, taking second place for the second week in a row.

Chukyo TV Bridgestone Ladies Open
Toyota, Aichi, Japan
Winner: Ji-Hee Lee

It had been five years since Michie Ohba won her most recent of five tournaments in Japan and she knew she had her hands full trying to land No. 6 in the Chukyo TV Bridgestone Ladies Open, even though that was the tournament she won in 2001 on the same Chukyo Golf Club course. She had only a one-stroke lead over Hyun-Ju Shin, who had finished second in the last two events, and two shots on six others.

Little did she or anybody else think Ji-Hee Lee had a chance. Lee appeared to have shot herself out of an opportunity to score back-to-back victories with a back-nine 42 and 76 Saturday that dropped her into a 20th-place tie. But the South Korean put a six-birdie 66-211 on the board early in Sunday's final round and claimed the victory when Ohba bogeyed four holes, including the 17th and 18th, for 74 and 213 total. It was Lee's third win of the season and ninth of the 27-year-old's Japan LPGA career.

Ohba had jumped off to a four-stroke lead over Lee and Shin in Friday's opening round, running off eight birdies, including five on the last six holes. Ohba's lead dwindled to a single shot Saturday when she struggled to a 74 despite two birdies on the first three holes. Shin had sole possession of second place after a 71-140, but Lee tumbled back with the 76 that brought about her early start and fast finish Sunday.

Kosaido Ladies Golf Cup
Ichihara, Chiba, Japan
Winner: Chieko Amanuma

A five-year victory drought ended in dramatic fashion for Chieko Amanuma in the Kosaido Ladies Golf Cup the last weekend of May. "I can't find words to describe how I'm feeling," said the 31-year-old golfer, who had come up empty time and again since her brilliant, three-victory season in 2001 when she finished third on the money list.

"A lot of things I've experienced the last five years came across my mind during the (Sunday) round," she related after eking out the victory with a birdie on the 72nd hole in a battle against money leader Shiho Ohyama that afternoon. In fact, although Amanuma's victory was considered wire-to-wire because she led after each of the three rounds, Ohyama twice overtook her during the final 18 holes.

Amanuma got away fast Thursday with a bogey-free, six-under-par 66 on the Kosaido Country Club course at Ichihara in Chiba Prefecture, but Ohyama was right on her heels with 67. The two remained one-two Saturday, but Amanuma extended her margin to three strokes with 71–137 as Ohyama shot 73. Amanuma followed with an unusual final round. She bogeyed the first hole, then parred the next 16 before scoring the decisive birdie on the final green for 72 and 209 total. Ohyama shot 70 and tied for second with Miho Koga.

Resort Trust Ladies
Fukushima, Japan
Winner: Mie Nakata

Mie Nakata verified her credentials at the Resort Trust Ladies tournament the first week of June. Nakata, who scored her maiden victory in her sixth season on the Japan LPGA Tour in the Katokichi Queens event earlier in the year, showed the win was no fluke when she took charge of the Resort Trust tournament from the start, shook off a sputter for a rules infraction in the final round and registered a three-stroke victory at Grandee Nasushirakawa Golf Club. It was the second consecutive wire-to-wire victory on the circuit and made Nakata the fourth multiple winner of the season.

She grabbed the lead Friday with a six-under-par 66, ringing up eight birdies as she started two strokes ahead of Kaori Higo and Nana Akahori. A 70 Saturday stretched the margin to three strokes, Miho Koga moving into second place with a 66 for 139.

Back-to-back birdies on the front nine Sunday solidified Nakata's lead. However, a bogey at the 11th preceded a double bogey at the 14th, where she incurred a two-stroke penalty when wind moved her ball and she putted from the wrong place on the green. Her lead down to one stroke, she rebounded immediately with a 17-foot birdie putt at the 15th, a five-footer for another at the 16th, and coasted home with 71–207. Koga also shot 71–210 and finished a runner-up for the second week in a row.

We Love Kobe Suntory Ladies Open
Kobe, Hyogo, Japan
Winner: Nikki Campbell

Another country was heard from in the We Love Kobe Suntory Ladies Open. Nikki Campbell, a 25-year-old from Canberra, Australia, prevailed in a final-round battle against the top two money winners of the season to collect her first title in her fourth season in Japan. She broke from a three-way deadlock with Shiho Ohyama and Ji-Hee Lee, who owned 14 titles between them, shooting a solid, four-under-par 68 for 277 total and a three-stroke victory.

Amateurs grabbed the headlines the first two days at Rokko Kokusai Golf Club in Kobe. Chie Arimura, just 18, shot 69 Thursday and led veterans Ohyama, Michiko Hattori and Ok-Hee Ku by a stroke. Next up was another 18-year-old, Maiko Wakabayashi, who fired a 66 Friday and tied Izumi Narita (72-67) for first place with 139. (Arimura and Wakabayashi ultimately tied for eighth.)

The professionals took over Saturday. Campbell, the 2002 Australian Women's Amateur champion, shot 69, and Ohyama and Lee 67s to forge the three-way tie for the lead at 209, a double bogey costing Ohyama the outright top spot despite seven birdies. Ohyama remained hot Sunday, building a three-shot lead early in the round. But Campbell stuck it out and rolled to victory with the last two of her four birdies at the 15th and 16th holes as Ohyama faltered in mid-round, giving up four strokes, and Lee fell back when she double-bogeyed the 14th hole.

Akiko Fukushima climbed into a second-place tie with Lee (71) with a closing 66 for 280 as the Australian became the season's fourth new winner.

Nichirei Ladies
Ibaraki, Japan
Winner: Sakura Yokomine

With Ai Miyazato playing in America, Sakura Yokomine was expected to pick up where Miyazato left off in the growing youth movement on the Japan LPGA Tour. Even as Miyazato, now 21, was amassing 12 victories in her first two seasons on the circuit, Yokomine, now 20, was making her presence felt with two wins and frequent challenges in 2005. The only surprise when she won the Nichirei Ladies tournament in mid-June was that it hadn't happened earlier in the season.

Her length was a big asset as she nosed out Ji-Hee Lee, the money leader, by a stroke on the Miho Golf Club course, one of the longest on the circuit at 6,403 yards. The year's third wire-to-wire champion compiled a six-under-par 210, her closing 73 just enough to edge the South Korean, already a three-time 2006 winner, who shot 70 for 211.

Another member of the young set—Kumiko Kaneda, a 16-year-old amateur—was in the mix the first two rounds, shooting 67 the first day to share second place with Hyun-Ju Shin and trail Yokomine by two. Yokomine birdied five of the last seven holes and eight in all en route to her 65. She remained two in front of the teenager after posting a 72–137 Saturday.

Sunday was an adventure, though. She had three early bogeys and double-bogeyed the 13th, but four offsetting birdies brought home the victory.

Promise Ladies
Kato, Hyogo, Japan
Winner: Saiki Fujita

The veterans had to be wondering what was going on as yet another young player—21-year-old Saiki Fujita—popped out of the blue and went on to victory in the Promise Ladies tournament. On the heels of the Nichirei win of 20-year-old Sakura Yokomine and the strong contending performances of a handful of even younger professionals and amateurs, Fujita scored her first tour victory in a playoff against Miho Koga, hardly an old-timer at age 23, although in her fifth season on the circuit.

Koga, a three-time titlist but winless for two years, started fast at Kato's Water Hills Golf Club, dropping in six birdies for 66 and a first-place tie with Ai Ogawa, who birdied her last four holes. Fujita began with a 67 and seized a two-stroke lead Saturday with a bogey-free 68–135, as Koga shot 71 and shared the runner-up spot with money leader Shiho Ohyama, who matched Fujita's 68.

Koga rallied Sunday with a 69–206 and Fujita had to birdie the final hole in regulation for 71 and the deadlock. Fujita then captured the victory when she sank a breaking 15-footer on the first extra hole after Koga missed a birdie chance from longer range. Fujita was the fourth first-time winner of 2006.

Belluna Ladies Cup
Kanra, Gunma, Japan
Winner: Sakura Yokomine

Back came Sakura Yokomine to keep the run of youthful winners going midway through the Japanese season. Two weeks after posting her first win of 2006, the talented 20-year-old made a runaway of the Belluna Ladies Cup tournament following the Promise victory of 20-year-old Saiki Fujita. Yokomine expanded a slim 36-hole lead to a five-stroke winning margin at Obatago Golf Club. "I felt a lot of pressure before winning (the Nichirei), but I was able to relax and play my golf this time around," Yokomine noted afterward.

After starting the tournament four shots off the lead, jointly held by Hiromi Mogi and Ya-Huei Lu, Yokomine shifted into high gear Saturday. Both she and Akiko Fukushima fired 64s to finish the day at 134 and 135 respectively atop the standings. Yokomine had an eagle and six birdies, while Fukushima was registering a 29 on the front nine.

Yokomine pulled away from the field quickly Sunday, fashioning a 67 for 15-under-par 201 with six birdies and a bogey. Fukushima managed just a par round and yielded the runner-up position to Yui Kawahara (68–206) and Namika Omata (70–206).

Meiji Chocolate Cup
Shimamatsu, Japan
Winner: Mi-Jeong Jeon

Another young player joined the ranks of winners in the Meiji Chocolate Cup tournament in early July. South Korea's Mi-Jeong Jeon, competing in just her second year on the circuit, came from four strokes off the pace in the final round at Sapporo International Country Club's Shimamatsu course to nose out Hiromi Mogi and become the fifth new champion of the season.

Jeon, who had been playing well earlier in the season with five top-10 finishes, started the week three shots off the pace of first-round leader Kuniko Maeda, 28, another winless campaigner. Hiromi Mogi, with one of four 69s that day, moved into first place Saturday at 137 as Maeda shot 72. Mie Nakata and Ya-Huei Lu were tied for second at 139. Mogi's third and most recent victory came nearly two years earlier.

Sitting in seventh place at 141 (71-70) going into the final round, Jeon fired a 67 to overtake Mogi and the others Sunday. Mogi and Lu had 72s to finish second and third, and Nakata skied to a 76 and tied for 10th.

Stanley Ladies
Shizuoka, Japan
Winner: Miho Koga

Miho Koga scored a spectacular as well as historic victory in the Stanley Ladies tournament in Susono. She ended her nerve-testing duel with money leader Shiho Ohyama when she holed a wedge chip for a deciding birdie the seventh time the two played Tomei Country Club's 18th hole in their playoff. The event went into the Japan LPGA Tour's record book, tying the record for the longest overtime match in the circuit's history under its current structure.

For two rounds, the tournament was in the hands of Australian Nikki Campbell, who was gunning for her second win of the season and career in Japan. Campbell, the Suntory victor in early June, jumped off a stroke in front Friday with 67, a shot ahead of Shiho Ohyama and Akiko Fukushima, and extended the margin to two over Shinobu Moromizato, back from a stint on the U.S. LPGA Tour, when she followed up with 69–136 Saturday off six birdies and three bogeys.

On Sunday, though, Campbell fell out of contention with two double bogeys on the front nine, eventually shooting 76 and tying for 10th. Both Koga and Ohyama, who started the day at 139, mustered 67s to wind up in the deadlock at 206, 10 under par. Then followed matched pars through six trips over the 18th hole before Mogi chipped in from the rough to the right of the putting surface to register her fourth career title in Japan and first in two years.

Philanthropy Japan LPGA Players Championship
Ibaraki, Japan
Winner: Mi-Jeong Jeon

At the Meiji Chocolate Cup, Mi-Jeong Jeon's thrill came in landing her first title on the Japan LPGA Tour. Two weeks later, at the Philanthropy LPGA Players Championship, the South Korean enjoyed another first—by far the largest payday of her career—when she won again. The winner's check of ¥23,400,000 at the season's third 72-hole event was the biggest of the year.

Jeon carried a four-stroke lead into the final round at Itako Country Club in Ibaraki Prefecture, but had to fight off a charge by Australian Nikki Campbell, also amid a spell of strong contention, before pulling off the two-shot win with a 71 for 277, 11 under par.

The South Korean had taken over first place from Sakura Yokomine, another recent two-time winner, who led her by two after 36 holes, having birdied three holes on the back fine for 70-69—139. Jeon conquered the incoming half Saturday with a six-birdie 30 for 65 to leap four strokes ahead of Yokomine and Campbell.

Campbell raced into the lead Sunday when she birdied five of her first seven holes and Jeon bogeyed the sixth, but fell behind to stay when the South Korean birdied the 12th and she bogeyed the 13th. Campbell shot 69—279, and Yokomine, with 71, finished in a tie for third with Shiho Ohyama.

Crystal Geyser Ladies
Chiba, Japan
Winner: Shiho Ohyama

Shiho Ohyama was ready to win again. With a playoff loss and a third-place finish right behind her, Ohyama rolled to her third victory of the season and first since early May in the Crystal Geyser Ladies tournament the first week of August. With her one-stroke win over Hsiu-Feng Tseng of Taiwan at Keiyo Country Club in Chiba Prefecture, Ohyama stretched her money race lead to more than ¥30 million.

Ohyama was out of the lead only through the middle holes of the final round. She and Tseng shared first place the first day, shooting five-under-par 67s. Ohyama eagled the final hole for hers. On Saturday, she moved two strokes in front with 69—136. Shinobu Moromizato, Momoko Ueda and Mie Nakata were next at 138, but it was Tseng who challenged Sunday after her second-round 72—139.

On her way to another 67 that day, Tseng grabbed the lead until Ohyama birdied the 15th, 16th and 17th for 69 and the one-shot win, the sixth of her career. Ueda and Yayoi Arasaki finished third at 209.

NEC Karuizawa 72
Nagano, Japan
Winner: Shiho Ohyama

Weather made a shambles of the playing schedule of the NEC Karuizawa 72, but it didn't sidetrack Shiho Ohyama's hot streak and prevent her from reaching a prized goal. Ohyama made it two in a row with her three-stroke victory in the rain-shortened tournament and became just the third player in Japan LPGA Tour history to win more than ¥100 million in a single season, joining Yuri Fudoh and Ai Miyazato in that regard.

"I knew I just had to win this tournament," Ohyama said. "To win over ¥100 million in a single year I think is really something special."

The weather became a factor the second day after veteran Akiko Fukushima, a three-time winner of the event, had opened with 66 and was tied for the lead with Namika Omata. When a severe thunderstorm struck Karuizawa 72 Golf's North course and ended play for the day, Itsumi Okada and Omata had the lead at seven under par with their incomplete rounds.

Tournament officials, realizing they couldn't get in the full 54 holes Sunday, decided to shorten the final round to nine holes. When everyone had finished 36 holes, Ohyama was tied for the lead at 137 with Omata and Fukushima. Playing the course's back nine, Ohyama birdied the 18th for 33 and 170 total to win by three over Miho Koga, Hiromi Mogi and Michiko Hattori, as Fukushima slipped to 37–174 and Omata to 40–177.

Shin Caterpillar Mitsubishi Ladies
Hakone, Kanagawa, Japan
Winner: Mikiyo Nishizuka

Mikiyo Nishizuka found that victories don't come any easier after the first one when she won the Shin Caterpillar Mitsubishi Ladies tournament in mid-August. Just as when she captured her maiden victory in the season-opening Daikin Orchid, Nishizuka had to battle from behind in the final round at Daihakone Country Club in Hakone and go extra holes to join the six other multiple winners of 2006.

Nishizuka came from four strokes off the pace in the Shin Caterpillar's final round with a 69 that thrust her into a tie at nine-under-par 210, with veteran Chieko Amanuma, who had taken her sixth career victory earlier in the year in the Kosaido Golf Cup. The playoff ended quickly when Nishizuka holed an 18-foot birdie putt on the first overtime hole.

"I didn't think too much about winning the tournament," Nishizuka said about her position after her 72-69–141, four strokes behind leader Yukari Baba and three back of Amanuma, "but thought I would have chance if I made no bogeys." She didn't, and scored four birdies for the 69–210 that matched Amanuma's 72–210. Akiko Fukushima (72), in contention all the way, and Junko Omote (69) missed the playoff by a stroke. Baba shot 75 Sunday and first-round leader Yasuko Sato, who shot 66 with the help of a hole-in-one, finished five shots off the winning score.

Yonex Ladies
Naoaoka, Niigata, Japan
Winner: Shiho Ohyama

Shiho Ohyama resumed her march toward the money title with her fifth and most exacting victory of the season in the Yonex Ladies tournament. Ohyama led from the start at Yonex Country Club at Naoaoka, Niigata Prefecture, and finished with an eight-under-par 208, three strokes clear of runner-up Jeong-Eun Lee. The ¥10.8 million check fattened her already impressive 2006 total built by the five wins and nine other top-five finishes.

Ohyama's run to the Yonex victory began Friday with a flawless, four-birdie 68, placing her one shot in front of Misato Nishikawa and Maiko Wakabayashi, the 18-year-old amateur. On Saturday, Ohyama widened her margin to two shots even though taking two bogeys and settling for 70–138. South Korea's Lee edged into second place with 69–140.

In the final round, Ohyama took the victory with another 70, and Lee held onto second place with 71–211. The win was the 29-year-old Ohyama's eighth since her tour debut in 2001.

Golf 5 Ladies
Hokkaido, Japan
Winner: Yun-Jye Wei

The Golf 5 Ladies the first weekend of September seemed a likely spot for Yuri Fudoh, striving for a seventh consecutive money title in Japan, to cut into the healthy lead Shiho Ohyama had built in the first 23 tournaments of the season.

Fudoh, who had won the Golf 5 event the last two seasons, bore up that possibility in the opening round on Alpen Golf Club's Bibai course, shooting a five-under-par 67 and establishing a one-stroke lead over Taiwan's Yun-Jye Wei. Ohyama was just three back. However, Fudoh managed just a par 72 Saturday, and South Korean Jae-Hee Bae slipped into first place ahead of her by a stroke when she fired 66 for 138. Wei also shot 72 and was at 140 with Sakura Yokomine.

It was an exciting show Sunday as four of those five leading players wound up in a deadlock at the end of 54 holes, all with 209 totals. Ohyama shot 68, Wei 69, Fudoh 70 and Bae 71. Wei then grabbed her second career win in Japan with a par-saving three-foot putt on the fifth extra hole.

Japan LPGA Championship
Tomakomai, Hokkaido, Japan
Winner: Ai Miyazato

Ai Miyazato wasted no time in picking up where she left off at the end of the 2005 season to join the richer pastures of the U.S. LPGA Tour. Making her first start following her return from a satisfactory but less than spectacular first year in America, Miyazato rolled to a three-stroke victory in the Japan LPGA Championship, the 13th of her brief and brilliant career.

Miyazato was atop the heap from the second round on at Nidom Classic course at Tomakomai, Hokkaido, as she became, at 21 years and two months, the youngest winner ever of the LPGA Championship. It gave her a second major title to go with her 2005 victory in the Japan Women's Open.

She was among the 36 players who did not finish the rain-interrupted opening round, trailing only Chiharu Yamaguchi (67) and Kaori Higo (69) when she completed it with a 70 Friday morning. She then followed with a 68–138 that day and led Higo (70–139) when the entire field completed 36 holes. Miyazato struggled with errant tee shots in difficult weather Saturday, matching three birdies and bogeys, taking a double bogey and posting 74–212. That gave her a shaky one-shot edge over Yui Kawahara and South Koreans Hyun-Ju Shin and Mi-Jeong Jeon, a two-time winner earlier in the season.

Miyazato took command on the first nine Sunday, forging a three-stroke lead by the turn, and carried that margin to victory with her 70 for a final, six-under-par 282. Shin, at 285, was the only player within seven strokes at the end.

Munsingwear Ladies Tokai Classic
Inabe, Mie, Japan
Winner: Akiko Fukushima

Akiko Fukushima, Japan's best-known international player in recent years, had won just once since leaving the U.S. LPGA Tour in mid-2004 to concentrate her efforts on her home circuit. She had gone through two years and a flock of near-misses before breaking from a 36-hole tie for the lead and seizing the title in the Munsingwear Ladies Tokai Classic in mid-September at Ryosen Golf Club, Inabe. In doing so, the 33-year-old star of the 1990s turned the tables on South Korean Ji-Hee Lee, who had defeated her in a four-hole playoff in the Studio Alice Open early in the season.

The two players had entered the final round as co-leaders with 136s after two rounds. Lee shot 66 and Fukushima 67 Saturday as they supplanted Yui Kawahara, the first-round front-runner with her 66. Fukushima was solid Sunday in shooting 66 for her 14-under-par 202 and annexing her 18th career victory on the Japan LPGA Tour. She didn't have a bogey in the last two rounds.

Lee, who had three 2006 victories on her record, strengthened her hold on the No. 2 spot on the money list as she finished second with 68–204.

Miyagi TV Cup Dunlop Ladies Open
Miyagi, Japan
Winner: Ai Miyazato

Ai Miyazato continued her triumphant return home at a tournament that had special meaning for her. Three years before, just 18 and a high school senior, Miyazato excited the Japanese golfing world when she won the Miyagi TV Cup Dunlop Ladies Open, the first amateur to win on the Japan LPGA Tour in 30 years. That convinced her to turn professional shortly thereafter. Just two weeks after capturing the 2006 Japan LPGA Championship upon her return from the U.S. LPGA Tour, Miyazato landed the Dunlop title again. That gave her 14 victories over that three-year span.

She got a little help this time from an unexpected quarter. When Takayo Bandoh, the leader through the first 36 holes, collapsed in the final round, Miyazato and money leader Shiho Ohyama stepped in. At the end of 13 holes, Ohyama led Miyazato by two strokes as she eyed her sixth win of the season. But Ohyama missed a short par putt at the next hole and went into a tailspin. Miyazato birdied the 14th and went on to post a 71 and the winning two-under-par 214 total at the Rifu Golf Club in Miyagi Prefecture. Ohyama shot 72-217 in posting her sixth runner-up finish of the season.

Bandoh, a two-time winner in her nine-year career, opened with 69 and held onto first place Saturday with 72-141, but plunged to 220 when she shot 79.

Japan Women's Open
Osaka, Japan
Winner: Jeong Jang

A player fresh from the United States and the LPGA Tour captured the most important title in women's golf in Japan—and it wasn't the defending champion, Ai Miyazato. It was Jeong Jang of South Korea, who actually has more impressive international credentials than Miyazato as the 2005 Weetabix Women's British Open champion and a mid-summer winner in an American LPGA tournament among 11 top-10 finishes.

Jang carved out the Japan Open victory at Ibaraki Country Club near Osaka with precision, taking the lead the first day and never letting go. She opened with a three-under-par 69, but faced such threats as Shiho Ohyama and Sakura Yokomine at 70 and Miyazato at 71. The South Korean pumped up her margin to three strokes Friday with another 69 and had a new set of challengers—Yun-Jye Wei, the Golf 5 winner, at 73-68-141 and Shinobu Moromizato at 72-70-142.

Miyazato, who appeared to have blown her hopes for a repeat Women's Open victory with a 75 Friday, kept her chances alive when she shot 67 Saturday to move within three of Jang, who registered a 72-210 amid generally high scoring. Hyun-Ju Shin (70) shared second place with Miyazato and finished as the runner-up Sunday. Despite wet and windy conditions, Jang rang up a 69 for a final, nine-under-par 279. Shin shot 71-284 and Miyazato took third place with 72-285.

Sankyo Ladies Open
Niisato, Gunma, Japan
Winner: Shinobu Moromizato

An unusual late-season pattern emerged again in the Sankyo Ladies Open. For the fourth time in five weeks, a player who spent most of the season competing on the LPGA Tour in America picked off a victory in Japan.

This time, it was 20-year-old Shinobu Moromizato, who spent her first full professional season in the United States with little success—nine missed cuts, no finish higher than 36th—before returning to Japan to play in the autumn tournaments there.

Although she achieved it in a 36-hole event, Moromizato's first career victory did not come easily. After heavy rains washed out play on Friday and it became a two-round tournament, Moromizato blazed Saturday with a 66 that staked her to a three-stroke lead over Shiho Ohyama. Only five others broke par 72 that day at Akagi Golf Club northwest of Tokyo.

Sunday was a different story for the young lady, though. She handled the day's strong winds well on the front nine, shooting 35 and expanding her lead to five strokes, but it was all downhill after that. Bogeys at the 12th, 13th, 14th and 16th shaved her margin to a single stroke. Then she double-bogeyed the par-three 17th, but kept the lead when Ohyama did the same thing and had to settle for a third-place finish. Moromizato parred the 18th for 77–143 and a one-stroke victory over Mi-Jeong Jeon, who shot 72. Hyun-Ju Shin, with 71–146, was the only player to break par in the Sunday gales.

Fujitsu Ladies
Chiba, Japan
Winner: Mi-Jeong Jeon

Mi-Jeong Jeon's third victory of the 2006 season had a little extra mental reward for the South Korean. Undaunted when she fell behind Ai Miyazato, the circuit's headline star, in the early going of the final round of the Fujitsu Ladies tournament in mid-October, Jeon mustered a strong finish to edge Miyazato, who also was seeking her third win of the year. The young second-year professional, trailing Miyazato by a stroke after 15 holes Sunday on Chiba's Tokyu Seven Hundred Club course, birdied Nos. 16 and 17, the latter with a 30-foot putt, and parred the final hole for 71 and a one-shot triumph with her 71–210, six under par.

Jeon trailed little-known Yuko Shinsakaue by a stroke after Friday's opening round, sharing second place with veterans Michiko Hattori and Fuki Kido at 69. Shinsakaue had no finish higher than 12th in 28 starts, missing 14 cuts, so her demise Saturday with 75 was not surprising. Jeon and Kido shot 70s for 139, and Miyazato moved into contention, running off six birdies after two early bogeys for 68–141.

Miyazato maintained the fast pace Sunday to grab the lead before succumbing to Jeon's flashy finish.

Masters Golf Club Ladies
Miki, Hyogo, Japan
Winner: Miho Koga

American star Paula Creamer, who carried home two titles after her two separate visits to Japan in 2005, went home empty-handed in 2006 following unsuccessful defenses of those two victories. In the second, Creamer made a strong showing before her third consecutive 70 on the Masters Golf Club course at Miki dropped her to fourth place.

The Masters Golf Club Ladies tournament victory went instead to Miho Koga, who strung together an eagle and three birdies on the back nine Sunday to shoot 66 and nip Akane Iijima by a stroke with her nine-under-par 207 total. Her second win of the season (career fifth) came considerably easier than the first, the seven-hole playoff win over money leader Shiho Ohyama in July.

Rui Kitada stirred memories of her splendid, three-victory 2004 season when she began the Masters with a leading, six-under-par 66, one better than Ohyama. Creamer and Iijima took over first place Saturday with their pairs of 70s, as Koga raced into contention with 68 after starting well back at 73. Iijima finished with a respectable 68, falling one short after Koga went birdie-eagle-birdie-birdie starting at the 13th hole en route to her winning 66.

Hisako Higuchi IDC Otsuka Kagu Ladies
Hanno, Saitama, Japan
Winner: Akiko Fukushima

Score another for the veteran. Akiko Fukushima, at age 33 playing in her 14th season, continued her 2006 resurgence with a playoff victory over youthful star Sakura Yokomine in the Hisako Higuchi IDC Otsuka Kagu Ladies tournament at the end of October. It was Fukushima's second win in six weeks and 19th in Japan since she landed her first win in her sophomore 1994 season when she was 20-year-old Yokomine's age.

It had been a final-round showdown between those two and 21-year-old headliner Ai Miyazato. Yokomine had jumped out in front in the opening round of the IDC Otsuka at Musashigaoka Golf Club in Hanno, Saitama Prefecture, with a six-under-par 66—an eagle, five birdies and a bogey—leading Fukushima by a stroke.

Miyazato entered the picture with a 66 in the Saturday round after beginning with a 71. That move tied her for second with Fukushima (67-70), a stroke back of Yokomine, who also shot 70 that day. Fukushima picked up the needed stroke to force the playoff Sunday, shooting 70 while Yokomine was fashioning a 71 for her 207. The overtime went just one hole as Fukushima quickly scored a winning birdie.

Mizuno Classic
Mie, Japan
Winner: Karrie Webb

A mediocre start and a brilliant performance by fellow Hall of Famer Karrie Webb brought a stunning run of five consecutive victories by Annika Sorenstam in the Mizuno Classic to a close when a sixth straight would have established a new LPGA record. Webb, enjoying her finest season in recent years, pulled away to a four-stroke victory in the late-season event that is part of both the U.S. and Japan LPGA Tours. It was her third win in Japan, the earlier ones coming in the Nichirei Cup World in 2000 and 2001.

The Australian improved each day as she picked up her fifth victory of the season. She started the tournament at its new Kintetsu Kashikojima Country Club site in a 14-player group at 69, four behind fellow Aussie Rachel Hetherington but two in front of Sorenstam, who was coming off a victory in Dubai the previous Sunday.

Sorenstam kept her title hopes alive with a 66 Saturday to move within two shots of the lead, which was acquired by 20-year-old Momoko Ueda, who stole the stars' thunder with a course- and personal-record 64 for 135. Webb slipped into sole possession of second place with 67–136. Sorenstam and Ai Miyazato were among seven players at 137.

Tied for the lead at the turn Sunday, Webb turned up the heat on the back nine, moving ahead when she holed sizeable birdie putts on the first three holes and wrapping things up with two more birdies at the 14th and 16th for 66 and the winning 14-under-par 202. Japanese veteran Kaori Higo closed with 65 to finish second at 206, and Sorenstam shot 70 for 207.

Itoen Ladies
Chonan, Chiba, Japan
Winner: Hyun-Ju Shin

Hyun-Ju Shin found light at the end of a frustrating, season-long tunnel at the Itoen Ladies tournament in mid-November. Four times earlier in the year, including at both the Women's Open and PGA Championship, the 26-year-old South Korean had to settle for second-place finishes. Finally, with just three events remaining, Shin squeezed out a one-stroke victory, a second one to go with her 2005 win in her first year in Japan.

Her final-round 71 and nine-under-par 207 total at the Great Island Club at Chonan, Chiba Prefecture, gave her the one-shot win over second-round leader Yuka Shiroto and Shiho Ohyama, the runaway money leader. Shiroto, winless through 14 seasons, had taken over first place Saturday after long-time British star Laura Davies opened the Itoen tournament with 65. With 66-69–135, Shiroto led Hyun-Ju Shin (70-66) by a stroke and Ohyama (67-70) by two going into the last round, but could do no better than 73, tying Ohyama (71) at 208.

Daioseishi Elleair Ladies Open
Matuyama, Ehime, Japan
Winner: Yun-Jye Wei

Taiwan's Yun-Jye Wei joined the unusually large list of players with multiple victories when she worked out a one-stroke victory in the Daioseishi Elleair Ladies Open at Matsuyama, Ehime Prefecture, in the year's next-to-last and final full-field event. Wei, the 10th competitor to land two or more titles during the 36-tournament season, nipped two of them—Sakùra Yokomine and Mi-Jeong Jeon—with her closing 70 for a nine-under-par 207 total. She also won the Golf 5 tournament in September.

Yokomine and Ji-Hee Lee, a three-time winner in 2006, shared first place with Izumi Marita and Ayako Uehara with 69s after the first round. Wei entered the fray Saturday with 66–137 and was tied for the lead with teenage amateur Asako Fukimoto, a stroke ahead of Yokomine, Kasumi Fujii and Chie Arimura. The Taiwanese player survived a shaky spell on the second nine Sunday as her 70 just held off Yokomine (70) and Jeon (69).

Japan LPGA Tour Championship
Miyazaki, Kyodo, Japan
Winner: Sakura Yokomine

Sakura Yokomine put an exclamation point on her superb second season at the Tour Championship. Facing the select field of the year's top 22 money winners, the 20-year-old Yokomine broke open a tight battle against fellow youngster Shinobu Moromizato in the final round and rolled to a seven-stroke victory, the most decisive margin of the 2006 season in Japan. It was her third win of the year and fifth of her young career.

Heavy rains interrupted Thursday's first round at Miyazaki Country Club in Kyodo Prefecture. But with the small field, the initial 36 holes were completed on schedule Friday with Yokomine, at 73-67–140, holding a one-stroke lead over Moromizato (69-72), technically the front-runner when all the first-round scores were in Friday.

Moromizato started with three consecutive early birdies Saturday and shot 69, which put her in a first-place deadlock with Yokomine, who posted a 70 for her 210. Shiho Ohyama, who had long ago wrapped up the money-winning crown, kept her chances for a sixth 2006 victory alive with a 69 for 213. Nobody was challenging Yokomine Sunday, though. Yokomine rang up four front-nine birdies that, coupled with the faltering game of Moromizato, enabled her to turn the competition into a rout. She finished with 67 for an 11-under-par 277 total. Ai Miyazato matched the Sunday score and wound up in a runner-up tie with Moromizato (74) and Jeong-Eun Lee (68) at 284.

Ohyama's brilliant season brought Yuri Fudoh's six-year reign as the No. 1 player to an end. Fudoh won twice early in the season to run her remarkable record of victories to 40, but played in just 16 of the 36 tournaments and finished 15th on the money list.

The Kyoraku Cup
Fukuoka, Japan
Winner: Asia

A well-balanced team of Korean all-stars rolled to a decisive victory over Japan in The Kyoraku Cup women's team match play tournament the first week of December. Jumping off to a 16-to-8 lead in the 12-match opening round, the Koreans went on to a 29-to-19 victory. All except one player contributed points to the triumph, Jee Young Lee and Meena Lee winning both of their matches to contribute four points each to the total.

Shiho Ohyama (No. 1) and Sakura Yokomine (No. 3), the top two homeland players on the final 2006 Japan LPGA Tour money list, scored double victories for Japan. Mi-Jeong Jeon, the runner-up in Japan, was one of Yokomine's victims (74-75), but rebounded in the second round, shooting 67, the lowest score of the tournament by three strokes, in routing Akane Iijima (79).

Meena Lee defeated Mikiyo Nishizuka twice, 74-78 and 71-73, and Jee Young Lee posted a 71-74 win over Shinobu Moromizato and a 72-74 victory over Hiromi Mogi.

Korea LPGA Tour

Victories were distributed quite liberally on the 2006 Korea LPGA Tour, but the season had a clear-cut standout in Ji-Yai Shin. She and two other players with two wins each were the only multiple victors during the year's 15-tournament campaign played out primarily in the spring and autumn months.

Shin landed the biggest prize—the Korea Women's Open—in mid-May at Taeyoung and the Lake Hills Classic three months later, beating American star Cristie Kerr by two shots in the Open. Beyond the victories, though, Shin finished second in five other events, including a playoff loss to Hyun Hee Moon in the Hite Cup Ladies Championship in October, and had pairs of third- and fourth-place showings. That's a remarkable 11 top-fours in 15 starts.

Hee Young Park and Jin Joo Hong were the other double winners. Park captured the season-opening Phoenix Park Open and the Lake Hills Classic in August, both by two strokes. In the latter tournament, she came from four strokes off the pace of Ji Yeon Woo in the final round with 68 for a two-shot win with her four-under-par 212.

Hong posted the most decisive triumph of 2006, rolling to a seven-stroke win in the SK EnClean Solux Invitational. No other margin was bigger than three. Her second win—by three in the Kolon-Hana Bank Championship—came against the season's strongest international field with Jeong Jang, the reigning Japan Women's Open champion, finishing second, world-class star Se Ri Pak third and American standout Paula Creamer in the top 10.

Eun-A Lim prevailed in the KB Star Tour event in Gyeonggi, the year's only 72-hole tournament, jumping off to a two-stroke lead in the first round and never trailing en route to a two-shot win. Hyun Hee Moon was the playoff victor over Ji-Yai Shin in the Hite Cup as the two players matched scores in leading each of the three rounds.

Jee Young Lee fired a final-round 66 and overcame Ran Hong's three-shot, 36-hole lead to win the Korea LPGA Championship with a 16-under-par 200. That equaled the season's lowest winning score posted by Sun Ju Ahn in her one-shot victory in the KB Star Tour event in Seoul in May.

The season's other results:

Lake Side Ladies Open—Bo-Bae Song won by a stroke over four others with her eight-under-par 208.

KB Star Tour in Busan—Soo Young Moon came from two strokes behind Na Yeon Choi after 36 holes to win by two with her 10-under-par 210.

KB Star Tour in Hampyeong—Na Yeon Choi took charge with a 68-67–135 start and, with a final-round 69, eased to a three-stroke triumph with her 12-under-par 204.

Meritz Solmoro Classic—Ji Yeon Lee fired a final-round 66 for a three-shot victory with her nine-under-par 207.

ADT CAPS Championship—Birdies were scarce as Ji Won Yoon started with 71 as co-leader with Jin Joo Hong, closed with 74, and won by a stroke with her three-under-par 213.

Australian Women's Tour

Titanium Enterprises ALPG Players Championship
Golden Beach, Queensland, Australia
Winner: Rebecca Stevenson

Rebecca Stevenson fulfilled the promise of her victory at the 1999 Australian Amateur Championship by winning her first title as a professional at the Titanium Enterprises ALPG Players Championship. Stevenson, a 27-year-old based in Perth but originally from Queensland, won by three strokes at Club Pelican on her native state's Sunshine Coast.

After rounds of 71 and 69 to get to four under par, Stevenson closed with even-par 72 for a total of 212. She lost the lead twice to Lindsey Wright, but birdied the par-three 11th and at the next short hole, the 14th, where Wright found a hazard over the green and took a double-bogey six. Stevenson hit her approach at the 15th to three feet, admitting she had thinned the shot, for another birdie. Defending champion Katherine Hull and Spain's Ana Larraneta shared second place, with Joanne Mills fourth at even par. Wright dropped back to fifth with Sara Beautell.

"Today I fought so hard," said Stevenson, who was second at the 2003 ANZ Ladies Masters. "I missed a lot of putts and I had a bad back at the end. My routine over the front nine was a little slow and I tried to speed it up a little over the back nine and it seemed to work for me."

ANZ Ladies Masters
Ashmore, Queensland, Australia
Winner: Amy Yang

Amy Yang, in her second professional event, produced a brilliant performance to win the ANZ Ladies Masters and led an extraordinary wave of amateur talent at Royal Pines. Yang, a 16-year-old schoolgirl, led the tournament after 66 on the second day and after a pair of 70s on the weekend tied at 13 under par with American Catherine Cartwright. Yang had bogeyed the 18th hole in regulation, while the 22-year-old Cartwright had birdied, but in the playoff Yang holed from 15 feet for the winning birdie.

Cartwright received the A$120,000 first prize as the leading professional. Yang's reward was not having to return to Robina High School on Queensland's Gold Coast until Tuesday. "By having a day off," Yang said via an interpreter when asked how she would celebrate. "I've put in so much effort that now I have won this, I am so happy."

Yang, from Korea, had moved with her family to Australia 14 months previously. She became the first amateur to win a professional tournament in Australia and the first on the Ladies European Tour since Gillian Stewart in 1984. Three amateurs finished in the top five places, with Ruby Tseng, a 17-year-old from Taiwan who lives in Hawaii, closing with an eight-under 64 to tie for third place with Tiffany Joh, a 19-year-old American amateur, and Louise Stahle, a professional of only a few months' standing from Sweden.

South African Women's Tour

Women's World Cup of Golf
Sun City, South Africa
Winners: Sweden (Annika Sorenstam and Liselotte Neumann)

Annika Sorenstam and Liselotte Neumann claimed a three-stroke victory for Sweden in the Women's World Cup of Golf at the Gary Player Country Club in Sun City. The Swedes had combined for 65 in the fourballs and then 69 in the foursomes and were seven shots clear with nine holes to play on the final day, which saw both players' scores counting.

Sweden dropped four strokes in four holes from the 10th, but Scotland and Korea, their nearest pursuers, also wobbled at that moment. Sorenstam steadied the ship with an eagle at the 14th and her 70 counteracted Neumann's 77. They finished with a seven-under total of 281 to share the first prize of $220,000.

"It's nice to have the No. 1 player in the world as your partner," said Neumann. "I played very good the first two days and today wasn't really my top game, but that's when Annika came in and helped, so it has been a great week."

Scotland was the only team to break par on Sunday, with 69 from Catriona Matthew and 72 from Janice Moodie. They finished second, four ahead of the Welsh pairing of Becky Morgan and Becky Brewerton, with America's Paula Creamer and Natalie Gulbis taking fourth place.

Pam Golding Ladies International
Johannesburg, South Africa
Winner: Nora Angehrn

Switzerland's Nora Angehrn earned her first victory as a professional at the Pam Golding Ladies International, the opening leg of the Nedbank Women's Golf Tour, at Dainfern near Johannesburg. Angehrn held the lead after rounds of 70 and 68, and a closing 72 gave the 25-year-old from Zurich a nine-under-par total of 210. However, on the first nine she fell behind Sweden's Helena Alterby. "I lost confidence with my putting," explained Angehrn, "the lines were really good, but I just couldn't sink them."

But Angehrn rallied superbly after the turn with birdies on the 10th hole, the 14th, thanks to a putt from 35 feet, and at the 16th, where she chipped in. Alterby fell back to close with 74, but England's Rebecca Hudson scored the lowest round of the final day with 67 to jump into a tie for second place with Bettina Hauert, of Germany, and Norway's Cecilie Lundgren, two strokes behind Angehrn. South African amateur Ashleigh Simon, the defending champion, finished with 68 to tie for fifth.

Acer Women's South African Open
Durban, South Africa
Winner: Rebecca Hudson

Rebecca Hudson enjoyed a highly successful amateur career but had to wait over three years to win her first professional title at the Acer Women's South African Open. Hudson, a 26-year-old from Doncaster, became the first Englishwoman to win in South Africa for six years. She appeared in the Curtis Cup three times and won numerous championships, but her first three seasons on the Ladies European Tour were uninspiring.

But at Durban Country Club, Hudson played wonderfully consistent golf to record rounds of 72, 73 and 72 to finish at four under par and win by four strokes over Cecilie Lundgren, with Bettina Hauert in third place. Hudson had shared second place with Lundgren and Hauert at the previous week's Pam Golding International, but here Hudson was always in control. She made two birdies on the first nine, at the par-five fifth and the ninth, and then added another at the short 12th. A dropped shot at the 17th was inconsequential as she claimed the R45,000 first prize. Ashleigh Simon, the amateur, finished as the leading home player in fourth place, while the Swedish pair of Emma Zackrisson and Elin Ohlsson shared fifth place.

Telkom Women's Classic
Pretoria, South Africa
Winner: Laurette Maritz

Rebecca Hudson's tremendous effort to win for the second week running was denied by the steady experience of Laurette Maritz, who instead won the Telkom Women's Classic for a second year in a row, the first successful defense of her career. Maritz started the event slowly with 73, but 66 in the second round put her only one behind Mandy Adamson at Zwartkop Country Club in Pretoria.

Adamson started poorly on the final day, dropping three strokes in the first three holes, and Maritz claimed a one-stroke victory after a closing 68 for a nine-under-par total of 207. It was Hudson, the South African Open champion, who became the biggest threat as the Englishwoman eagled the 11th and birdied the 14th and 16th holes to go into the lead. But Hudson dropped a shot at the 17th and could only par the par-five 18th. Maritz bogeyed the 11th and 14th holes, but her seven birdies more than made up for the errors and the seventh of those came at the last. Tied for the lead on the tee, Maritz hit a superb drive, found the green in two and two-putted for the title. Hudson closed with 68 to take second place, with Ashleigh Simon in third, while Adamson finished in sixth place. There was a remarkable performance by 12-year-old Larissa Ras, who made the cut to complete all 54 holes of the tournament.

Nedbank Women's Masters
Johannesburg, South Africa
Winner: Ashleigh Simon

Ashleigh Simon, the 16-year-old amateur, won her third professional title in as many years at the Nedbank Women's Masters at Killarney in Johannesburg. The remarkable youngster had won the South African Women's Open as a 14-year-old in 2004 and the Pam Golding International in 2005. Rounds of 70 and 69 left Simon tied for the lead with Switzerland's Florence Luscher, but she birdied three holes out of four from the sixth, also bogeying the eighth, to take a commanding lead.

Luscher, a 24-year-old from Bern, rallied with four birdies in five holes from the 11th only to falter with a bogey at the 16th and a double bogey at the last. Simon had dropped a shot at the 17th to fall back into a tie for the lead with Luscher and a playoff loomed. But her par at the 18th gave her a closing 70, for a seven-under total of 209 and a one-stroke victory over Mandy Adamson and England's Kirsty Fisher. Luscher finished two strokes behind Simon in fourth place, with Laurette Maritz and Rebecca Hudson sharing fifth place. Hudson finished top of the money list after the conclusion of the fourth and final leg of the Nedbank Women's Golf Tour.

15. Senior Tours

The battle for Player of the Year on the Champions Tour between Jay Haas and Loren Roberts came down, fittingly, to the final hole of the final tournament, the Charles Schwab Cup Championship.

Jim Thorpe was something of a disinterested spectator. His only concern was to make sure neither one got in front of him. Neither did, and Thorpe locked up his 12th Champions Tour title, and his fourth overall in northern California. "There's just something out here," the big, likeable North Carolinian said.

Meantime, there was the duel between Haas and Roberts, a pair of four-time winners in the season. At the final hole, Roberts, known as the "Boss of the Moss" for his superb putting, needed a two-putt from 56 feet. The first lipped out and stopped just over four feet away. Ordinarily, that's almost automatic for Roberts, but when he missed it, Haas had the points he needed to win the award.

"I've been second my whole career, so there you go," Roberts said.

Said Haas, "I feel bad for Loren. He played well all year."

Indeed he had. It seemed Roberts might go wire-to-wire for the whole season. He raced through the first three tournaments, taking the MasterCard Championship, Turtle Bay Championship and ACE Group Classic. He was rolling until the Outback Steakhouse Pro-Am late in February, when Jerry Pate won, and then jumped into the lake. He hadn't done that since winning The Players Championship in 1982. "And it's been a long time, so I said, 'Why not?'" Pate said. Roberts picked up the thread late in July, winning his fourth title in the Senior British Open.

Haas spread his four victories out, taking the Liberty Mutual Legends and FedEx Kinko's titles back-to-back in April, then the Senior PGA Championship in May, and finally the Administaff Small Business Classic in October.

The Rookie of the Year race was just as tight. Scott Simpson, former U.S. Open champion, took it with one victory, two runners-up and three thirds in his 18 top-25 finishes. His victory came in the Wal-Mart First Tee Open, and how many guys win while being heckled by a movie star pal? Simpson had to get up-and-down for a birdie at the final hole, with Bill Murray ribbing him from the gallery. But Simpson did it, and finished sixth on the money list, four spots ahead of David Edwards, the next-highest rookie.

Obscured by the fireworks from Haas and Roberts was the standout play of Tom Kite, Brad Bryant and Bobby Wadkins, all two-time winners. For Kite, it was two years between victories. His touch returned in March, at the AT&T Classic, and Kite ran away with it by five strokes, chalking up his eighth Champions Tour victory. Then he took the Boeing Greater Seattle Classic in a playoff against Keith Fergus.

Bryant, hiding his nervousness, holed a seven-foot putt for birdie on the final hole to take the Toshiba Classic for his second career victory. "I was more than a little excited, to say the least," Bryant admitted. A month later, he rallied in the final round to win the Regions Charity Classic. In the Boeing Championship, Wadkins started fast, then limped home to take his first Champions Tour victory since 2001. In the Ford Senior Players Championship, Wadkins didn't lead until late in the fourth round, and then made a great putt for a double bogey at the final hole to win it, and then noted: "Anyone who says they aren't feeling nerves at that stage of the game is telling a lie."

Andy Bean, who last won on the PGA Tour in 1986, scored his first Champions Tour win in the Greater Hickory Classic and heaved a sigh of relief. "You don't forget what it feels like," he said, "but it's nice to come back and experience it." And Fred Funk, frustrated so far, broke through in the AT&T Championship in October, and spoke for all newcomers to the over-50 tour: "It's not that easy."

Allen Doyle, a decided underdog when he won the U.S. Senior Open in 2005, was a decided underdog again in 2006, and he won it again, rallying in the final round.

In the Time Marches On Department: Hale Irwin, after 11 straight seasons with at least two victories each year—and a high of nine in 1997—went winless for the first time. And looking forward: Mark O'Meara, Nick Price and Nick Faldo would become eligible for the 2007 season. That should spice up the tour, though fans might not see much of Faldo, unless they are watching television. He is now well embarked on a career in PGA Tour commentary with the Golf Channel, CBS and ABC.

Champions Tour

MasterCard Championship
Ka'upulehu-Kona, Hawaii
Winner: Loren Roberts

"It's been a dream to win the first tournament of the year, some year," Don Pooley was saying. "I've played for 30 years and haven't done that. If you win the first tournament, the pressure is off and you're playing with the house's money." Pooley's chances looked great, finally. He was taking a three-stroke lead into the final round of the 2006 season-opening MasterCard Championship. And then the dream ended with just one hole to play.

Loren Roberts underlined why he's nicknamed the "Boss of the Moss." He beat Pooley by a stroke on the final hole. He rolled in a 30-foot putt for a course-record 61, 11 under par. Roberts, shooting 63-67-61 for a 191 total, set the Champions Tour record in relation to par on the Hualalai course at Kaupulehu, Hawaii. Roberts also set a tour record of 26 birdies in a three-round tournament, topping Ed Dougherty's 22 in 2001. And the 61 also broke the course record of 62, set about a half hour earlier by Gil Morgan.

Pooley hadn't been idle. He knocked in a 20-footer for birdie at the 18th for a 65. "Loren played great," Pooley said. "I shot a 65 with a three-shot lead, and normally that would be good enough. I'm disappointed, obviously."

With good reason. Pooley, seeking his third Champions Tour victory, opened with a 63, sharing the first-round lead with Roberts and Tom Watson. Roberts was fresh from an encouraging tie for 18th in the PGA Tour's Sony Open the week before. He birdied five of the first seven holes, and of his round said, "I had a pretty commercial 63."

Pooley moved ahead by three in the second round with a bogey-free 64, stringing out five birdies from No. 3 and three more from No. 11. Roberts got off to a good start, then double-bogeyed the par-three No. 5. He shot 67 and was three back going into the final round. But he blew the roof off in the finale—a chip-in eagle at the par-five 10th and nine birdies, including the clincher at the 18th, for his second Champions Tour victory.

Said Roberts, a study in understatement: "I feel really good about the way I'm playing."

Turtle Bay Championship
Oahu, Hawaii
Winner: Loren Roberts

Loren Roberts was beginning to get the hang of the Hawaiian Islands. He was also becoming quite adept at heartbreak. A week earlier he took the MasterCard Championship. And now this—in the Turtle Bay Championship, the season's first full-field event, he eagled the last hole to beat Scott Simpson. Roberts, the virtuoso putter, had regained his touch just in time.

The mild-mannered Roberts permitted himself a smile. "The name of my game is putting," he said. "If I get a little off with the putter, sometimes the rest of my game struggles, too."

He had back-to-back titles, making it three since he joined the Champions Tour the previous July. In windy weather on the Palmer Course at Turtle Bay, Roberts opened with a six-under 66 and a one-shot lead on Bruce Summerhays. Roberts seemed definitely in control with another 66 in the second round for a 12-under 132, going four up on Simpson (67). Four others were five back—R.W. Eaks, who tied the course record at 65, Isao Aoki (66), Don Pooley (69) and Summerhays (70).

Roberts had logged 14 birdies in the first two rounds but he couldn't buy one over 17 holes in the final round, opening the door to Simpson. Summerhays, deep in the race, fell out with a bogey-bogey-double bogey stretch from the 11th. Simpson started with a three-putt bogey, but birdied the fourth, 14th and 17th. Roberts, in a rare fit of three-putts, bogeyed the fifth and sixth.

Roberts's putting touch returned at the 10th. He drained an 18-footer to save par. He and Simpson were tied, going to the par-five 18th. Both reached the green in two. Simpson parred, but Roberts, after a four iron from 200 yards to nine feet, holed out for the eagle, a par 72, a 12-under 204 and the two-shot win.

"It was 17 holes of grinding and groaning, and on the last hole, everything was perfect," Roberts said. "It was worth it."

ACE Group Classic
Naples, Florida
Winner: Loren Roberts

It was becoming clear that Loren Roberts would get it done, one way or another. This time it was, by his own description, ugly. Even so, it was history. Roberts took the ACE Group Classic and thus became the first ever to win the first three Champions Tour tournaments.

"Three wins this year, and they've all come different ways," Roberts said. "This one was definitely done with an ugly stick."

And he proved he didn't have to be in Hawaii to win. This one came at the Club at TwinEagles at Naples, Florida. The interesting part about the three wins was that each came at the final hole. This time, it wasn't what he did but what others either did or didn't do. Roberts carded three birdies in the final round, at the first, third and sixth, and then parred the rest of the way for a three-under-par 69, a 14-under 202 total and a one-stroke victory.

R.W. Eaks made eight birdies, but with a bogey and a double bogey against him, he needed one more birdie at the 18th to tie. He missed the putt and shot 67. Brad Bryant birdied the 18th, but only for a 70 and tied Eaks for second at 203. Hale Irwin, who dominated the Champions Tour for years, had the best chance. He needed a birdie at the 18th to win, a par to tie. He hit his seven-iron approach into the water from 162 yards and double-bogeyed for a 68 and tied for fourth with Tom Watson at 204, two shots behind.

Roberts still needed at least a par to win. Ever the Boss of the Moss, he got it with two putts from 35 feet.

Roberts got moving in the first round when he birdied the last two holes for a 67 to pull within two of Eaks, who took a one-stroke lead with a 65. Roberts rose to the top with a 66 in the second round, tying for the lead with Don Pooley (67) and Bryant (67) at 11-under 133.

Outback Steakhouse Pro-Am
Lutz, Florida
Winner: Jerry Pate

The Outback Steakhouse Pro-Am opened in wind and drizzle late in February, but the fans turned out and the players were watching, too: Would Loren Roberts run his victory string to four straight? And the answer was no. Roberts had to be content with his record of winning the first three on the Champions Tour, but he wouldn't match Chi Chi Rodriguez's record of four wins in a row.

A streak of the opposite kind did come to an end. You could tell when Jerry Pate jumped into the lake beside the 18th green at the TPC of Tampa Bay. He hadn't taken a victory plunge since the 1982 Players Championship, taking Deane Beman, then the commissioner of the PGA Tour, and golf course architect Pete Dye with him. "I just want to have fun," Pate said. "And it's been a long time, so I said, 'Why not?'"

Once again, it was Pate's magic with the five iron to the rescue. He won the 1976 U.S. Open and the 1982 Players with a five iron for birdies on the final hole each time. This time it was a five iron to 10 feet at the 18th for the winning birdie.

Pate hung around the lead with a 68-68 start, then birdied the final hole for a five-under 66, an 11-under 202 total and a one-stroke win over defending champion Hale Irwin (68), Mark James (68) and Morris Hatalsky (64). And thus ended the 24-year drought that began with a shoulder injury in 1982. Loren Roberts shot three 69s, never led, and tied for fifth at 207.

Pate was back in the pack with his opening 68, behind Mark McNulty and Bruce Lietzke, tied for the lead at 65. Irwin, always threatening, birdied the last two holes for a 66 to tie for the second-round lead with McNulty (70) and Mark James (65) at seven-under 135. Pate moved to within a stroke with another 68.

In the closing rush, Pate broke a four-way tie with a 10-foot birdie putt at the 18th for the clubhouse lead. He was still vulnerable. Hatalsky missed a tying six-foot birdie putt at the 18th. James (68) bogeyed the par-three 17th, then failed to birdie the 18th. Irwin also bogeyed the 17th. He needed a birdie at the 18th, but drove into the rough.

AT&T Classic
Valencia, California
Winner: Tom Kite

Just when the Champions Tour was looking like a cakewalk to Tom Kite a few years earlier, it suddenly turned into a tough row to hoe. It was a long time between wins. In this case, two years. Then the touch returned in March, at the AT&T Classic, and Kite ran away with it by five shots, chalking up his eighth Champions victory.

"This was way too long of a drought," Kite said. "When I first came out here and won five or six events, I was thinking this Champions Tour was pretty easy." Kite took the AT&T Classic lead with a dazzling 64, tying the tournament record at Valencia Country Club, near Los Angeles, but that's not where the cakewalk actually began.

Andy Bean seemed finally to be getting on track for his first Champions win, and he was making a battle of it. While Kite was shooting that 64 in the second round, Bean was putting up a 65 and was just a stroke behind. Then at No. 1 in the third—he had already eagled it twice—he birdied and tied Kite. Two holes later, it was all over. Bean double-bogeyed No. 4, came undone and was on his way to a 79. Kite was four ahead after six holes, and he led by at least five on the back nine. He wrapped up his 70-64-70 for a 12-under 204 total and a five-shot victory over Gil Morgan. It was the biggest margin in the history of the tournament.

Kite was three astern in the first round, when Mitch Adcock, a Monday-qualifier, took the lead with a 67. (Adcock would self-destruct with an 80 in the third.) Kite caught fire in the second. He spotted Valencia a bogey at No. 1, then blistered the last 10 holes in nine under, including a tournament-record 29 on the second nine. Kite eagled the ninth, birdied four straight from the 10th, then birdied the last three, capping the run with a four-footer at the 18th.

Toshiba Classic
Newport Beach, California
Winner: Brad Bryant

The strange, unsettling noise Brad Bryant was hearing as he stood over that final putt was his heart. He'd never heard it beating quite that way before. "It was going 100 miles an hour," said Bryant. The occasion was the seven-foot birdie putt he was looking down on at the 18th. If he could hole it, he would have his first Champions Tour victory. He did.

"I was more than a little excited, to say the least," Bryant admitted. He was in scary territory, to be sure. He'd had only one victory in his 28-year career, and that was in the 1995 Walt Disney Classic. The final-hole birdie wrapped up a card of 68-70-66–204, nine under at the par-71 Newport Beach Country Club near Los Angeles.

Bob Eastwood, a two-time winner, capped a seven-birdie first round with a chip-in at the 18th for a 65 that gave him a one-shot lead over Graham Marsh and Bruce Lietzke. He shot a 70 in the second round and tied for the lead at 135 with Tom Purtzer, whose 67 was sparked by a 150-yard hole-out for an eagle at the 10th, and Graham Marsh, who birdied three of the final four holes for a 69. Bryant was still three off the lead with 70–138. With 19 players within four shots of the lead, the final round promised to be quite a show.

Bryant started modestly, with 10 straight pars. Then he sprinted, getting birdies at the 11th, 12th, 13th, 15th and, finally, that seven-footer at the 18th for his 204. John Harris shot 68 and tied Wadkins and Mark Johnson (68) for second at 205. Johnson and Vicente Fernandez could still tie Bryant with eagles at the 18th. But Johnson's 15-footer was a foot wide to the left and Fernandez's 63-footer was five feet short. That's when Bryant's heart quit thudding.

Puerto Vallarta Blue Agave Golf Classic
Puerto Vallarta, Mexico
Winner: Morris Hatalsky

As bogeys go, it was the finest of Morris Hatalsky's 30-year career. It was also deliberate.

Hatalsky came to the par-four 18th in the final round of the Puerto Vallarta Blue Agave Golf Classic with a two-stroke lead after Scott Simpson had bogeyed No. 17 and parred the 18th when he needed a birdie but missed a six-footer. So all Hatalsky had to do was nurse that lead home.

"That really dictated me playing way to the right, just trying to catch the green somehow and playing for three putts," Hatalsky said. He got the critical bogey, finishing a card of 70-67-70 for a nine-under-par 207 total and a one-stroke win over Simpson in the Champions Tour's sixth visit to Mexico. It was Hatalsky's first Champions victory in almost three years and his third overall. He had finally broken through for 2006 after threatening in recent weeks.

Simpson opened an early claim on the title with a five-under 67 at the Blue Agave Golf Club. Hatalsky bogeyed three times on the first nine, but the five birdies on the second, for a 70, were a sign of what was coming. In the windy second round, he birdied seven of the first 13 holes, but at the par-three 15th he hit his seven-iron tee shot into the water and double-bogeyed. His hot hand cooled to a five-under 67 for a one-stroke lead over Simpson (71), Gil Morgan (70), Tom Purtzer (67), and Dan Edwards and Masahiro Kuramoto, both with 65s.

Simpson made a run at it in the final round. He birdied the first and fourth, keeping pace with Hatalsky's birdies at the first and second. They parted company at No. 6, where Simpson double-bogeyed. He picked up the shots with three more birdies against only one by Hatalsky, and it came down to the last two holes.

Liberty Mutual Legends of Golf
Savannah, Georgia
Winner: Jay Haas

It was a fitting show—Jay Haas, fast becoming a legend, winning the Liberty Mutual Legends of Golf, the event that spawned the Champions Tour. It was a five-stroke win over Peter Jacobsen and Craig Stadler, and if it looked easy, it didn't play that way.

Haas finished with a 15-under 201 total at Savannah Harbor, Georgia, for his first victory of the year. Haas was still splitting his time between the PGA Tour and the Champions. But he did well enough in 2005—winning twice—to take Rookie of the Year honors. Coming into the Legends, his best finish in five Champions events was a tie for third. He opened the Legends with a six-under-par 66 for a two-stroke lead on Mark McNulty, Tom Wargo, Jerry Pate and Gil Morgan.

In the second round, Haas bogeyed the 18th for a 68. "The green is as big as Texas, and I missed it," he said. At 134, he still led by two over Craig Stadler (67). Jacobsen (69) was in a group at 139. Stadler was lighting up the galleries with some breezy shots. At the par-five 11th, for example, he hit driver-driver, then a wedge inside four feet. At the 16th, he holed a 58-foot putt for birdie.

Jacobsen was chewing up that five-stroke deficit fast in the final round. He birdied six of 11 holes from the fourth, and the one at the par-five 11th tied him with Haas at 10 under. Haas, playing two holes behind, came to the 11th with something of a vision. "I knew where I wanted to place the ball, and I did," he said. He hit his three wood from 237 yards to 14 feet and dropped the putt for an eagle. He birdied the 13th, 16th and 17th for his 67 and 15-under 201 total and the five-stroke win. Jacobsen bogeyed the 17th for 67–206, and Stadler tied him, bogeying the last two holes for a 70.

FedEx Kinko's Classic
Austin, Texas
Winner: Jay Haas

How does a guy feel when he's deep in the hunt? Said Jay Haas, recalling the closing holes of the FedEx Kinko's Classic, "I couldn't spit on the 17th fairway." That being the case, imagine how the contenders felt with Haas on another tear, taking his second straight Champions Tour victory. Worse, consider how Tom Kite was feeling. Haas's victory, at The Hills Country Club near Austin, was his fifth in Texas on the PGA and Champions Tours. Kite, a native son, had never won in Texas, including 0-for-12 in Champions events. And after such promise. Kite shared the first-round lead and was in the hunt the rest of the way, but he ended up tied for second place with Mark James, two behind Haas.

With an opening four-under-par 68, Kite was in a six-way tie for the lead, the largest leading group since 1999. Then Bruce Fleisher broke from the tie and took the second-round lead with 69–137, seven under, by one shot over Craig Stadler and newcomer David Edwards, both with 70–138. Kite (71) was at 139 with Ireland's Des Smyth. Haas shot a par 72 for 140, three off the lead. The tournament then developed behind him.

Edwards closed with 71, Smyth 74 and Stadler 75. James had a bogey-free 67. Then Kite blew to four bogeys and a double bogey over the last eight holes for an awkward 74, and tied for sixth at 211.

Haas, meanwhile, was on a rampage. He made five straight birdies from No. 2 on four short putts and a 50-foot chip-in at No. 6. He birdied No. 8, then bogeyed Nos. 9 and 10, the latter after driving out of bounds. At the 11th, he holed a bunker shot from 72 feet for a birdie. He birdied the 15th on a 17-foot putt and the par-three 16th from 13 to take the lead. And at the par-five 18th, he blasted out of a bunker to a foot and tapped in for his 10th birdie of the round and a 65 for an 11-under 205 and the two-stroke win.

Regions Charity Classic
Birmingham, Alabama
Winner: Brad Bryant

Brad Bryant's great shots turned a three-stroke deficit into a two-stroke victory in the final round of the Regions Charity Classic, but only with the unwitting cooperation of Mark McNulty, who hit some real clunkers at the absolutely wrong time. And so Bryant closed with an eight-under-par 64 for a 17-under 199 total. McNulty started the final round with a one-stroke lead and led by three with three holes to play, but blundered his way to a third-straight 67 and finished second by two to Bryant.

"That ending was somewhat bittersweet," said Bryant, who won his first Champions Tour event in March. "I certainly didn't expect Mark to hit a ball in the water, let alone hit it in the water twice."

"It wasn't pressure," said McNulty. "It was just two bad shots. Brad hit three great shots and I hit two bad shots."

The tournament, the former Bruno's Memorial Classic, was played at the par-72 Ross Bridge course in Hoover, Alabama. At 7,409 yards, Ross Bridge is one of the longest on the Champions Tour. Scott Simpson tied for the first-round lead on 67 with Tom McKnight, Keith Fergus and McNulty. Hale Irwin was at 68, and at 69 were Wayne Levi, Rick Rhoden and Bryant.

McNulty took the lead in the second round with another 67 and was one up on Dick Mast (66) and Bryant (67). McNulty started the final round with three straight birdies, moving Bryant to note: "It never occurred to me that I would end up winning the tournament." Especially when McNulty led by three with three holes to play. But at the 17th, he hit his second into the water for the second straight day, this time taking not a bogey but a double bogey. Then at the 18th, his approach bounced off the green and into the water, and he bogeyed.

Bryant, meanwhile, eagled the 16th with a five iron from 209 yards to three feet, and birdied the 17th on a three iron from 219 yards to four feet. "Quite possibly the best shots I've ever hit in my life," he said.

Boeing Championship
Destin, Florida
Winner: Bobby Wadkins

Bobby Wadkins broke from the starting gate like a thoroughbred and closed like something considerably less, but it was enough to turn back everything that anyone could throw at him in the Boeing Championship at the par-71 Raven Golf Club at the Sandestin resort in Florida. The big question in golf is still "how much?" And in this case it was one stroke, and it was worth Wadkins's first Champions Tour victory since 2001.

It came dramatically. Wadkins was a wire-to-wire winner, but he came down the final stretch needing a birdie to beat hot-closing Raymond Floyd. Wadkins got it, and not a moment too soon, on a seven-foot putt at the 17th—his hole—and finished with 70 for a 203 total, 10 under par.

Wadkins, age 54, set out to run away with the tournament. In the first round, when only 20 of the 78 starters could break par, he carded nine birdies against no bogeys for a course-record 62 to lead Curtis Strange and Don Pooley by four. Wadkins was eight under coming to the 17th. There, he got his ninth birdie and the 62.

Wadkins's hole got rid of some who were in pursuit in the second round. Strange had got within a shot of Wadkins, but he put two into the water at the 17th and triple-bogeyed. Craig Stadler made eight birdies in 13 holes, then hit a shot into the water and double-bogeyed. It cost Stadler a 63. Said Stadler, with a 65, "It's getting very old." Wadkins treated both the 17th and then the 18th with great courtesy. "They were making mistakes on 17," he said. "It was smart for me to try to get two pars and then get the heck out of there." So Wadkins, offsetting three bogeys with three birdies, had his 71 for a nine-under 133 total and a three-stroke lead over Stadler and John Harris (66).

Floyd, back in the pack for two rounds, came racing out in the final round with a 63. Playing more than an hour ahead of Wadkins, Floyd birdied five straight holes on the second nine and held a two-stroke lead at 10 under. Then Floyd suffered his only bogey, that at the 16th, while Wadkins birdied back at the 10th, and they were tied—until Wadkins reached the agreeable 17th.

Senior PGA Championship
Edmond, Oklahoma
Winner: Jay Haas

Jay Haas dropped the 12-foot putt, and then was puzzled. What should he do next? Well, nothing, actually. Except go receive the trophy and give an acceptance speech. It took a little while for it to dawn on him. He had just won the Senior PGA Championship. This was the third playoff hole against Brad Bryant, and after all that struggling for four days over the tough Oak Tree Golf Club, near Oklahoma City, maybe it was hard to believe it had ended so abruptly.

"I guess I wasn't expecting it," Haas said. "I was expecting to go to the next tee, and I think when Brad missed ... I didn't know what to do or where to go, who to look at, anything like that."

Haas, who won back-to-back tournaments a few weeks earlier, had just taken the first major title of his career. He had come close so many times, he couldn't believe at first that this was it. He was runner-up to Hale Irwin by a stroke in the 2004 Senior PGA, and he was third in the 2004 U.S. Senior Open, the 1999 PGA Championship and the 1995 Masters. Now he was looking up to see who just edged him out.

It was getting to be a habit with Haas, making birdies in bunches. In the Liberty Mutual Legends of Golf, he charged down the stretch to win, and in the FedEx Kinko's Classic, he charged on the first nine and then late down the second nine. This time, Haas flirted with the lead for three rounds and started the fourth round four shots off Gil Morgan's lead. Morgan suffered five bogeys over the first nine (he shot 74 and finish third). Haas, who trailed by six strokes through No. 3, exploded for five straight birdies from No. 4—from 14, 12, four, 10 and four feet, in order. He led by two strokes at the turn.

"I felt in control," Haas said. "I felt like it was my tournament." Not quite. Bryant, himself already a two-time winner by this late-May date and also looking for his first major, was having a charge of his own. Bryant, who started just a stroke off the lead, was playing behind Haas and birdied the 13th and 14th, the latter from "60 feet or some such nonsense." Bryant bogeyed the 15th, then eagled the 16th off a five iron to four feet to catch Haas. Then at the 18th, Haas dropped a 10-footer for a birdie and the lead. Bryant followed, and fired his approach from the right rough to 20 feet and holed the putt for his own birdie. Haas closed with a 68, Bryant a 71 to tie at five-under 279. The playoff went three holes.

They halved the first two, No. 18 and No. 1, in pars. Back at the 18th, both hit their tee shots into the fairway. Haas, with 182 yards to the green, put his five-iron approach into the front-right bunker. Bryant, from 157 yards, put his second on the back of the green, 70 feet from the pin. Haas blasted out to 12 feet, and Bryant rolled his 70-footer to four feet. Haas then holed his 12-footer, and when Bryant missed his par, Haas had his first major—to his surprise.

"I tried my darnedest to win a major on the PGA Tour at the PGA, the Masters, U.S. Open, British Open, whatever, but it didn't happen," Haas said. "But this is—I won't even say it's the next best thing. This is just like one of them to me."

Allianz Championship
West Des Moines, Iowa
Winner: Gil Morgan

Winning a regular tour event doesn't make up for letting a major get away, but it helps. And so Gil Morgan, who let the Senior PGA Championship slip away the week before, eased the pain by taking the Allianz Championship. But he nearly let this one slip, too. Ironically, he won because Loren Roberts, winner of a record three straight to start the Champions Tour season, dropped it.

"It's just nice to be able to come back and get a win," Morgan said. "As old as I'm getting, those are hard to find."

Morgan, age 59, started the final round leading Roberts by one, then trailed by three after the 10th, and came to the 17th down by one. There, Roberts hit his second shot into the water and double-bogeyed. Morgan dropped a 34-foot putt, his fifth birdie in seven holes, to tie. At the 18th, Roberts missed a tying birdie from nine feet, and Morgan dropped a two-footer for the par and his first Champions win since 2004 and 24th overall.

The Allianz event opened under ideal conditions at Glen Oaks Country Club at West Des Moines, Iowa. Fully 17 were within three shots of the leader, Scott Simpson (64). Morgan and Roberts were at 66.

The Morgan-Roberts battle started in the second round. Morgan started two shots off the pace and jumped into the lead with birdies at the par-five 15th and the par-three 16th, needing only 23 putts to shoot 64 for 130 and lead Roberts (65) by a stroke. Then came the curious final round. Roberts caught and passed Morgan with six birdies over 11 holes from the fourth, and twice led him by as much as three. Morgan put on his own charge, birdieing the 11th, 12th and 13th, then the 15th and 17th, the last putting him back in the lead, thanks to Roberts's double bogey. When Roberts missed the nine-footer for birdie at the 18th, Morgan parred and was in.

"I know exactly what he feels like," Morgan said. "It's not a lot of fun."

Commerce Bank Championship
East Meadow, New York
Winner: John Harris

"I knew he was going to make that putt," said John Harris, a man of no little success in amateur and collegiate golf. "But it really didn't matter. I wasn't going to give him a second chance."

That was Harris, seeking his first Champions Tour victory on the first hole of a playoff against six-time winner Tom Jenkins in the Commerce Bank Championship at the Eisenhower Park Red Course at East Meadow, New York. And Jenkins didn't get that second chance. He made his par-four, but Harris ran in a six-footer for a birdie and the victory.

Harris, age 54, had eight top-10 finishes in just over four years on the Champions Tour, and this victory was all the more impressive because he had to come from so far behind, and he did it with 64 in the final round. He had opened with a one-under 70 and was six behind Allen Doyle (64), who made nine birdies and six of them on putts of less than 10 feet. In the rain-interrupted second round, Harris shot 68, moving up to five behind Jenkins (64–133), who led by a one over Jay Haas (65) and Gil Morgan (69).

Everything had to fall into place for Harris in the final round. That meant that Haas, trying for his fourth straight win, and Andy Bean, seeking his first, and Morgan, trying for his second straight, had to miss down the stretch. They did.

Jenkins managed just two birdies and 16 pars for his 69 and 202 total, but Harris caught fire for eight birdies, three straight from the 11th. The win in regulation died with a bogey at the 18th for 64, but he tied Jenkins. In the playoff, Harris drove into the fairway and hit a five iron from 178 yards to six feet. Jenkins drove to the right and left his second short. And Harris sank his six-footer for the win.

"This," said Harris, "is what you dream about doing."

Greater Kansas City Golf Classic
Overland Park, Kansas
Winner: Dana Quigley

For Dana Quigley, Massachusetts born-and-bred, Missouri is a long way to go for a little home cooking. The man from New England in early July won his second straight tournament in Kansas City, and his third overall.

Earlier, Quigley trailed David Edwards by four strokes with 67 in the first round and by two with a 68 in the second. Then he torched LionsGate for a nine-under-par 63, a total of 18-under 198, and a three-stroke win over Edwards.

What was it about Quigley and Kansas City? "I'm just very positive when I get here," Quigley said. "It's just a great place for me to play golf."

Edwards, opening with a course-record 63, led by two over Bob Gilder, Tom Jenkins, Des Smyth and Brad Bryant. "Sometimes, when you don't expect them to go in, they start falling," he explained. He labored for 70 and a 133 total in the hot, windy second round and led Bryant by one. He didn't remember the last time he led going into the final round. It was in the 1993 Heritage, the last time he won. Not this time.

Edwards started the final round with a burst, getting three straight birdies from the second. He bogeyed the fifth, birdied three more, then bogeyed the 16th for 68.

Quigley ran him down in the early July heat. He birdied five of the first seven holes, and six of the nine, and took the lead for good with a huge putt at No. 9. About 50 feet, he first thought. Or maybe 70. "Basically, you're hoping [not to] three-putt it—and it goes in," he said. "Man, it's like one of life's unexpected pleasures." He made three more birdies coming home for a bogey-free 63 and the win. "My initial thought is, when it's your day, nothing can go wrong," he said. And nothing did.

But unfortunately for Quigley, there were no more tour stops in Kansas City for 2006.

U.S. Senior Open
Hutchison, Kansas
Winner: Allen Doyle

Maybe some fans said they were rooting for Allen Doyle in the U.S. Senior Open, but Doyle thought otherwise. "They were probably lying," he said. This was at Prairie Dunes in Hutchinson, Kansas, where Tom Watson, a native son, was the one true favorite in this field. "You know," said Doyle, "that's okay."

It would have to be. Doyle out-ran Watson in the final round to win his second straight U.S. Senior Open, his fourth senior major championship, and his 11th Champions Tour victory. Just short of age 58, Doyle became the oldest Senior Open winner.

The other prime threats didn't materialize, foiled by tricky greens and the deep, early July rough. Jay Haas, leading Champions Tour money winner, tied for the first-round lead at three-under-par 67, then slipped to finish tied for eighth, along with Loren Roberts, who had a USGA-record 62 in the third round. Fred Funk, making his Champions Tour debut, tied for 11th.

Watson thrilled the home crowd with a pair of 66s to lead through the middle rounds. Then it was a steeplechase in the final round. Peter Jacobsen took the lead with birdies at Nos. 6 and 7, then double-bogeyed No. 9. D.A. Weibring streaked to the lead on seven birdies in the first 12 holes, then went five over par from there.

Doyle had trailed all the way and was two behind Watson going into the final round. But he vaulted into the lead with two birdies in the first three holes against Watson's two bogeys. Watson's short game torpedoed him. His irons were falling short and his putts were sliding right. Doyle edged in front at the 12th, dropping a six-foot birdie putt, then birdied the 14th and 17th and shot 68 for an eight-under 272 total and a two-stroke win.

"Underdog" had struck again. And Doyle enjoys the role. "Because," Doyle said, "I am one."

Ford Senior Players Championship
Dearborn, Michigan
Winner: Bobby Wadkins

As dogfights go, they don't get any better—or worse—than this: Fully eight players, a record, tied for the second-round lead in the Ford Senior Players Championship. But none of them were named Bobby Wadkins. In fact, Wadkins trailed by four strokes in the first round, by five in that logjam second and by four again in the third. He didn't lead until late in the fourth round, and it was only through the grace of a great clutch putt for a wild double bogey at the final hole that he won at all.

"Anyone who says they aren't feeling nerves at that stage of the game is telling a lie," a relieved Wadkins said when it he had that second Champions Tour victory safely tucked away. Wadkins played the TPC of Michigan at Dearborn in 69-72-65-68 for a 14-under par 274 total and a one-stroke win over Jim Thorpe. It took some major stumbles by others to open the way for Wadkins. Loren Roberts, leading by two through the third round and by four over Wadkins, double-bogeyed the 11th and 14th and closed with a 74. Lonnie Nielsen, second when the final round started, ballooned to a 76. And so it went.

Wadkins started the final round in a four-way tie for fifth place at 10 under par, but swept past Thorpe and the others into the lead with five straight birdies from the 11th. Then came the frantic finish.

At the par-four 18th, Wadkins drove into a marsh on the left. It cost him a penalty drop. Then he hit into a greenside bunker. His sand shot rocketed across the green and hit a spectator standing on the hill. Said an embarrassed Wadkins later, "I haven't hit a bunker shot like that since I was 15." He nearly holed out his return from the rough, but it rolled 12 feet past the pin. With Thorpe three-putting for a bogey, Wadkins needed that 12-footer and a double bogey for a 68 and the win. "The tournament should have been over," Wadkins said, "and I almost gave it away."

Senior British Open
Ayrshire, Scotland
Winner: Loren Roberts

See European Seniors Tour section.

3M Championship
Blaine, Minnesota
Winner: David Edwards

It seems the short putts weren't to David Edwards's liking. He missed a couple starting the final round, and the bogeys dropped him five shots off the lead. Then he rolled in a couple of 40-footers, and Edwards, a rookie at age 50, made the 3M Championship his first Champions Tour victory. "This game is crazy," said Edwards. "I made a couple of 40-foot putts and missed a couple of two-footers. You just have to keep playing." And so he did, rolling over the TPC Twin Cities in Blaine, Minnesota, in 69-68-67–204, 12 under par, and also rolling over Craig Stadler and Brad Bryant by two strokes.

It started out like Old Home Week. Andy Bean, winless in his four years, birdied three of his last four holes for 67 and a one-stroke lead over Loren Roberts, fresh from winning the Senior British Open. The personable Bean was resurfacing after all these years. "I took 10 years off as I watched my daughters grow up," Bean explained. "When I came back out, the ball-striking was there but the putting wasn't." He credited his new "modified claw" putting grip for his improved play.

Bean faded, and Curtis Strange, the two-time U.S. Open champion, charged to four birdies over his last five holes for a 66 and a three-stroke lead over Edwards. Alas, Strange would shoot 76 in the third and final round, and Edwards didn't waste the opportunity.

Edwards missed the two short putts and bogeyed the first two holes, slipping five behind Strange, who lost the lead on a triple bogey at the 10th. Then Edwards sprinted to birdies at Nos. 8, 9, 11, 12 and 13. At the par-five 18th, when Stadler missed a 10-foot birdie putt, Edwards needed only a two-putt par for the win. But he rolled in a 10-footer for a birdie, instead, for a two-stroke victory.

At last, that first win. Said Edwards: "It's exciting, it's a relief, it's a lot of things."

Boeing Greater Seattle Classic
Snoqualmie, Washington
Winner: Tom Kite

The difference in the Boeing Greater Seattle Classic was Tom Kite's routine birdie in the playoff and Keith Fergus's adventure. Fergus started the final round five strokes off the lead and finished with an eight-under-par 64 and a 15-under 201 total at the TPC of Snoqualmie Ridge. Then he sat back as a small army battled it out.

Don Pooley led by one going into the final round and eagled No. 1. "I was trying to put some distance on the field and it didn't quite happen," Pooley said. He lost the lead on a double bogey at the par-three 13th. First-round leader Masahiro Kuramoto faded with three bogeys over the first five holes. With five holes to play, seven players were tied at 14 under par.

"I knew I had to keep rolling in birdies," said Kite, who started three off the lead. He pulled away with a birdie at the 15th, and then holed an eight-footer for another at the 16th, going to 16 under. But he three-putted from 67 feet for a bogey at the 17th, then parred the 18th for a 66 to tie the waiting Fergus.

"Going into the playoff, I felt I was at a disadvantage because Fergie is one of the longest hitters on the tour," Kite said. Even so, the playoff lasted one hole, the par-five 18th. Fergus's three-iron second bounced off the cart path and into the grandstand, where a fan caught it in his hat and dumped in out onto the hillside. Fergus's next caromed off the cart path curb and hit another fan in the grandstand and rolled back down to the cart path, from where only a miracle would save him. Kite rendered it all academic. He bunkered his second shot, blasted out to three feet, and dropped the putt for a birdie and his ninth Champions Tour title—and his third via a playoff.

JELD-WEN Tradition
Aloha, Oregon
Winner: Eduardo Romero

Argentina's Eduardo Romero could really pick his spots. Take the final round of the JELD-WEN Tradition, the last of the Champions Tour's major events for the year. "Today, before the start," Romero said, "I said, 'This is my tournament.'" That was a noble thought, and one not likely shared by many. Romero was only trailing by five strokes at the time.

But Romero got it dead right, coming from behind and beating Lonnie Nielsen with a birdie on the first playoff hole for his first victory in four Champions Tour starts. It was one of the Tradition's most memorable performances. Romero played the par-72 Reserve Vineyards Club in Aloha, Oregon, in 72-70-68-65—275, and not only did he not lead until the end, he trailed in the first three rounds, successively, by five, eight and five strokes. The outlook was not rosy.

In the last round, Romero holed out a 71-yard fairway shot for an eagle at No. 4 and closed with a 15-foot putt for a birdie for the tournament-low 65 and 13-under-par total. Back out on the course, some of the biggest names on the Champions Tour were trying to catch him. Bobby Wadkins, atop the leaderboard all the way, missed his chances at three par-fives. "If I birdie one, I'm in the playoff, make two and I win," Wadkins said. But he got none, and finished third by a stroke. Loren Roberts, a stroke off starting the final round, closed with 76.

Nielsen, who became a club professional after six winless years on the PGA Tour, was now looking for that first Champions Tour win. He gave himself a chance, tying Romero with a closing birdie for 70. The playoff at the par-five 18th was brief. Romero put his second shot 20 feet from the pin and nearly holed the putt for an eagle. He got the birdie, and Nielsen bogeyed.

Wal-Mart First Tee Open at Pebble Beach
Pebble Beach, California
Winner: Scott Simpson

This was Scott Simpson's 25th Champions Tour event, and his first victory was just within reach. He was in the fairway of the par-five 18th hole at Pebble Beach, needing to get up and down from 88 yards to win the Wal-Mart First Tee Open. Comedian Bill Murray, Simpson's longtime amateur partner in the AT&T Pebble Beach National Pro-Am, was lending his support.

"You know, I made it from here," Murray taunted, talking about an earlier event there.

"Yes," Simpson countered, "but I'm better."

And Simpson proceeded to hit a wedge to nine feet and drop the putt to wrap up a card of 67-68-68 (with Del Monte as the middle course) for a 12-under-par 204 total and a one-stroke win over David Edwards and Jay Haas. "I thought I had it going there for a while," Edwards said. "But the bogey on 15 just killed me."

D.A. Weibring had won in each of his three first years on the tour and now was looking for that one for 2006. He got a good start, with six birdies and an eagle for an eight-under 64 at Del Monte for a start, a two-shot lead in the first round. Tom Kite, a two-time winner this year, took the second-round lead with 65 at Del Monte, and he was looking forward to the final round at Pebble Beach, where he won the 1992 U.S. Open and the 1983 Bing Crosby National Pro-Am.

But it was Simpson's time. "Thirty-six holes at Pebble Beach without a bogey—that's pretty cool," said Simpson, who played there in the first and third rounds. "I was just excited to play in the tournament, let alone win it. But it was tough to make putts. It got windy, and the ball didn't stay where you hit it." Of course, he had an unsilent partner.

Georgia-Pacific Grand Champions Championship
Ball Ground, Georgia
Winner: Jay Sigel

Jay Sigel was figuring things out. "I'll probably need to shoot 67 or 68 tomorrow to win," Sigel said, heading into the second round of the Georgia-Pacific Grand Champions Championship, a two-round tournament for players age 60 and older. Sigel actually needed only 69 for a 10-under 134 and a two-stroke victory, but he had his dicey moments on his way to his first win since 2003.

Sigel had built up a good head of steam in the first round, with a nine-birdie, two-bogey 65 at the par-72 Hawks Ridge Golf Club in suburban Atlanta. He sparkled with a chip-in from a downhill lie for a birdie at No. 9, on his way to a three-stroke lead over defending champion Mike McCullough. In the second round, Sigel ran off three straight birdies from No. 6, but he wasn't home yet.

"Things tightened up on the back nine," Sigel would say. So they did. Jim Albus birdied the 12th and eagled the 13th, but a double bogey at the 17th finished him. McCullough posted four birdies coming in to get within two, but Sigel wouldn't look ahead. "I've been through this enough to know that it's not over until it's over," Sigel said.

Constellation Energy Classic
Hunt Valley, Maryland
Winner: Bob Gilder

"Now we're leaving—he's going to go into mourning," Brad Bryant was saying. "It's like the Bob Gilder Annuity Fund here."

The tournament was the Constellation Energy Classic, and the reason for all this was that Gilder won his second straight at Hayfields Country Club, near Baltimore, where he's never finished worse than 14th in five visits. And it was the end of this tournament. In 2007, the Ford Senior Players Championship would be held at nearby Baltimore Country Club.

Gilder wasn't quite as dominating this time. In 2005, he led wire-to-wire and won by four strokes. This time, he started the last round three shots off Don Pooley's lead, and was one of 15 players within four strokes of the lead. He climbed into contention with birdies at the first two holes, then sank a seven-foot birdie putt at No. 9 to move into a six-way tie for the lead. Gilder grabbed the solo lead at the 10th, hitting a nine-iron shot to six feet and dropping the putt for a birdie. He then birdied the 12th from 14 feet, the 15th from five feet and the par-five 16th with two putts, to extend his lead to two strokes. But he didn't know it. He'd avoided looking at the leaderboards.

"I asked my caddie, 'How far behind are we?'" said Gilder, at the 17th. "And he says, 'We're not.'" Gilder closed with 65 for a 14-under 202 total and a two-stroke win over Brad Bryant (68), Jay Haas (68) and Don Pooley (70). So Gilder went down as the only player in the tournament's nine years to win twice. He won nearly $600,000 at Hayfields in five appearances since becoming eligible.

Greater Hickory Classic at Rock Barn
Conover, North Carolina
Winner: Andy Bean

Everyone thought it was just a matter of time for Andy Bean, especially Bean himself. His last victory was in 1986, so it had been about 20 years. Then he finally broke through on the Champions Tour in the Greater Hickory Classic at Rock Barn, at Conover, North Carolina. Bean led wire-to-wire, but had to beat a surging R.W. Eaks in a playoff. "It's a relief to finally come out and win," said the big, outgoing Bean, age 53, an 11-time winner on the PGA Tour and making his 91st Champions Tour start. "You don't forget what it feels like, but it's nice to come back and experience it."

Bean led off with nine-under-par 63, tying his best score in four years. "I'm off to a heck of a start," Bean offered. "Now I need two more good rounds to finish the thing off." He wasn't as hot in the second round, but a two-under 70 put him at 11-under 133 with a two-stroke lead going into the final.

Eaks, whose previous best was a tie for second earlier this season, hadn't given himself much of a chance, not trailing Bean by three going into the final round and by a whopping five with nine holes to play. "I was just trying to come in second," Eaks said. He made up that five-stroke deficit in a blaze of birdies—six of them over the final seven holes for 65 to tie Bean, who bogeyed the 10th and 12th, then buckled down and birdied the 15th and 18th for a four-under 68 and a 15-under 201.

On the first playoff hole, Bean two-putted from 25 feet for a birdie, and Eaks's birdie try from four feet spun out. "You've got to feel for R.W.," Bean said, "because he kept making birdies and I kept making pars. It was a good thing I had a lead, because I was able to outlast him."

SAS Championship
Cary, North Carolina
Winner: Tom Jenkins

It was a lousy day to have to work. It was misty, and there was a penetrating chill, unusual for early October in Cary, North Carolina. It felt more like a sleeping-in day. But the show had to go on. Good thing for Tom Jenkins.

"Warming up, it was miserable," Jenkins said. "It must have been 45 (degrees) on the practice tee. I didn't think it was ever going to get warm." He turned out to be very comfortable, indeed. He shot a six-under-par 66, and when continuing rains rendered Prestonwood Country Club unplayable, Sunday's third round had to be canceled, and there was Jenkins, sitting alone atop the leaderboard at 10-under-par 134. Jenkins thus won the SAS Championship, his seventh Champions Tour title, by a stroke over Chip Beck (65) and Loren Roberts (68).

The finish was disappointing but not crushing to the two runners-up. Roberts was just back from his role as assistant captain for the U.S. Ryder Cup team. "I feel rested," Roberts said. "I hope to keep things going." And Beck, who birdied the last four holes, was making a comeback. "I thought my career was over," he said. "I thought I would never play again. I had actually surrendered to that."

Jenkins, 58, in his ninth season, had opened with 68, a stroke behind the leaders, Roberts and Mitch Adcock. Jenkins had got a new putter on Tuesday. "I rolled the ball the best I've rolled it all year," he said. "When that happens, you expect magical things." This was the magic: He had six birdies overall, and four of them came from at least 20 feet. The jewel was a 40-footer at the 10th. The clincher, the one that gave him the lead, came at the par-five 17th, where he canceled out a poor second shot by holing a 15-footer for birdie.

In shortened tournaments, the question is, always, how does it feel to win in only two rounds? Jenkins responded like legions before him. "A win," he said, "is a win."

Administaff Small Business Classic
Spring, Texas
Winner: Jay Haas

Arnold Palmer was making only his second appearance of the season, and the Administaff Small Business Classic would go down as his last hurrah. In the first round—Friday, October 13—Palmer hit two balls into the water at No. 4. Then, disheartened, announced he was withdrawing because of a sore back. Never one to walk in, he played on with Lee Trevino and John Mahaffey, but he didn't keep score. When he got in, he announced that he would no longer play on the Champions Tour.

"I've been doing this for a long time," Palmer said, "and to stand out there and not be able to make something happen is very traumatic. The people, they all want to see a good shot, and you know it and you can't give them that good shot. That's when it's time."

Jay Haas shared the first-round lead with Tom Purtzer and Dick Mast with seven-under-par 65 at Augusta Pines, near Houston. He hit almost every fairway and dropped birdie putts of 20 and 25 feet for that 65. In the second round, he pulled away with a birdie at the 10th, shot nine-under 63 for a 16-under 128 total and a five-stroke lead. But he wasn't counting his chickens. He recalled losing with big leads before. Then heavy rains hit.

Haas was at the fifth hole Sunday when officials called off the final round. It was the second straight week that a Champions Tour event had been cut after two rounds. Haas had his fourth victory of the season, winning by five over Purtzer and Bruce Lietzke. "The only way Tom and I had a chance," Lietzke said, "was for Jay to have a bad day. But he was the class of the field."

AT&T Championship
San Antonio, Texas
Winner: Fred Funk

Newcomers to the Champions Tour arrive with a monkey on their back. Blessed by youth, they're expected to win fast and often, and it was this monkey that irked Fred Funk. "They're going to hype all the new guys coming from the big tour," Funk said. "All of a sudden, I'm favored, and it's like nobody else is in the field. It's not that easy. It's something different for me, and I'm trying to minimize the pressure."

The spirited Funk, who capped his PGA Tour career with the 2005 Players Championship, tied for 11th in his only previous two Champions Tour starts in 2006. So Funk scraped off that monkey with a tight, wire-to-wire victory in the AT&T Championship at Oak Hills Country Club at San Antonio, Texas, and just in time. It was the next-to-last tournament, late in October, and there was nothing easy about the win. Funk shot 65-67-69 for a 12-under 201 total, and led by just a stroke all the way — over Scott Simpson, Dan Pohl and R.W. Eaks in the first; then Raymond Floyd, at 64 trying to become the oldest winner, and finally Chip Beck, himself a newcomer.

Funk authored some heroics along the way. In the first round, noting that he was tied for the lead at the 17th, he flipped a wedge to 10 feet and birdied. "But that didn't mean anything — I just wanted to make birdie," he said. He wasn't overly pleased with the 67 in the second round. "It's great to have a lead," Funk said, "but I was hoping for some separation." In the third, with Beck (65) the clubhouse leader, Funk calmed a wild round at the 13th by holing a bunker shot from 58 feet for a birdie.

"That was a ridiculous shot," Funk said. "It turned everything around." And, Funk hoped, maybe this win would turn everything around for him on the Champions Tour.

Charles Schwab Cup Championship
Sonoma, California
Winner: Jim Thorpe

For a guy born and raised in North Carolina and living in Florida, Jim Thorpe certainly feasted on tournaments in northern California. His latest was the Charles Schwab Cup Championship, ending the Champions Tour 2006 season. Thorpe led through three rounds and won by two strokes over Tom Kite in the 29-man field at Sonoma Golf Club, for his 12th Champions victory and his fourth in northern California. "I'm pretty much a California player," said Thorpe. And he had the figures to back him up: 66-70-67-68–271 total, 17 under par.

First, Thorpe had to weather Kite's eagles in the opening round. In a stunning spree, Kite holed out for eagle-twos at No. 9, from 57 yards, and at No. 11, from 97, sandwiched around a two-foot birdie at the 10th. "That," said Kite, "was a very enjoyable stretch." Thorpe also eagled, with a 70-yard wedge at No. 2, and needed just 23 putts for a 66 and a one-stroke lead on Kite, who eagled the 11th again in the second round, this time from 76 yards. "What are the odds?" he wondered, shaking his head. The eagle boosted him to 68–135 for a one-stroke lead over Thorpe (70) and Jay Haas (66).

In the third round, Thorpe birdied four straight from the 10th and tightened his grip on the tournament with a two-stroke lead over Kite (70), Loren Roberts (68) and Jay Haas (69). In the fourth round, Kite birdied twice just before the turn and took the lead, and Thorpe bogeyed the 10th. Things definitely didn't look good for him. Then Thorpe came to life at the par-five 13th. He smacked a 230-yard approach to 11 feet and dropped the putt for an eagle. Then he holed a 20-foot chip shot for a birdie at the 15th, and birdied the 17th. A bogey at the 18th gave him a 68.

European Seniors Tour

DGM Barbados Open
St. James, Barbados
Winner: Jose Rivero

Jose Rivero made his presence felt in the four tournaments in which he played on the European Seniors Tour after turning 50 at the tail-end of the 2005 season with two seconds, a third and a sixth-place finish. He quickly fulfilled the promise signaled by that start when he scored his first victory in the DGM Barbados Open, the 2006 opener. It didn't come easily, though. David J. Russell carried the Spaniard to a fourth extra hole before falling to Rivero's 15-foot birdie putt.

Rivero, a four-time winner in his years on the European Tour, made it hard on himself at Barbados when he bogeyed the par-four 18th hole at the end of regulation in the final round. Englishman Russell, who started the day three strokes behind Rivero, was already in with his 68–207 and the bogey dropped Jose into the deadlock and forced the playoff. Rivero snared the title on their fourth visit to the 18th when Russell missed his eight-foot birdie putt after Rivero's 15-footer went in.

Neither player was very far off the pace the first day at Royal Westmoreland Golf Club as Jim Rhodes of England and Eduardo Romero of Argentina led with 68s. Rivero shot 70 and Russell had 71. Rivero jumped into the lead with a 66 Saturday. His 136 placed him a shot in front of Delroy Cambridge and two ahead of Gavan Levenson. Russell, with 68–139, was next with Bob Cameron and Canadian Bruce Heuchan.

As always, the tour took a two-month hiatus after its sojourn to the Western Hemisphere and Barbados.

Sharp Italian Seniors Open
Venice, Italy
Winner: Sam Torrance

It was the right place for Sam Torrance to make a statement about his 2006 intentions on the European Seniors Tour. Italy had been good to Torrance in his earlier days on the European Tour. He had scored a pair of victories in the Italian Open and he did it again in May when the tour began its weekly schedule at Circolo Golf Venezia. His four-stroke victory at 11-under-par 205 confirmed that he had a repeat of his 2005 season in mind.

Torrance, who won three times the previous year to finish as the leading money winner, broke things open with a five-under-par 67 after entering the final round in a first-place tie with Eamonn Darcy (71–209), who had to settle for second place in the tournament for a second straight year.

Both players were major factors from the start on the picturesque course of the Venetian island of Lido. A run of four birdies on the back nine started Torrance with 68 and tied him for the first-round lead with Chile's Guillermo Encina, who birdied four of his last six holes. Darcy was just one back with Jamaican Delroy Cambridge and Englishman Bob Larratt.

While Torrance was shooting 70 and Darcy 69 to forge the 36-hole deadlock at 138, Stewart Ginn dazzled the field with a course-record 66 to tie for third with Cambridge (70). A 15-foot par putt on the first hole Sunday ignited Torrance's run to the title, his fifth as a senior and 37th in his career. The Scot rang up five birdies the rest of the way.

AIB Irish Seniors Open
Co. Cork, Ireland
Winner: Sam Torrance

By degree, Sam Torrance's second consecutive victory was as difficult to achieve as his one two weeks earlier had been easy. Coming off a four-stroke win in the Italian Seniors, Torrance capitalized on others' misfortunes and two solidly played overtime holes to prevail in a four-man playoff in the AIB Irish Seniors Open.

The Scot avoided the mishaps that turned things sour on the final holes of the tournament at the Fota Island Golf Club for Carl Mason, the two-time Order of Merit champion; Bobby Lincoln, the second-round leader, and Chile's Guillermo Encina.

First to have trouble was Lincoln, who absorbed a costly penalty stroke when his caddie inadvertently dropped his towel on the South African's ball. He missed the playoff by a shot. So did Mason, who had taken a two-stroke lead on the front nine Sunday. He lost six strokes on the next three holes.

Australian Stewart Ginn with a closing 67 and American Jerry Bruner and Torrance with 69s were finished with 207s, six under par, and looking on as Encina came to the 18th hole with a one-stroke lead and plunked his approach in the water. His bogey for 72 dropped him into the four-way tie and he went out, along with Ginn, on the first extra hole when they couldn't match the birdies of Torrance and Bruner.

Torrance, who began the day four shots behind leader Lincoln's 134, wrapped up his third title in an Irish Open when he holed a 14-foot eagle putt on the next hole. Torrance had won the Irish Open on the European Tour in 1981 and 1995. The victory was his sixth as a senior and 38th of his career.

Irvine Whitlock Seniors Classic
Jersey, Channel Isles
Winner: Guillermo Encina

Rather than mope about what should have been, Guillermo Encina drew a positive attitude from his final-hole slip-up that cost him victory in the Irish Seniors Open and pulled in his first European Seniors win the following Sunday in the Irvine Whitlock Seniors Classic in Jersey. He finished a solid three strokes in front of the field with a final-round 66 for a seven-under-par 209 total at La Moye Golf Club on the English island in mid-June.

"Last week was a bit of a blow, but I only hit one bad shot," he reasoned. (His shot into the water at the 72nd hole in Ireland cost him an outright victory and he lost in the subsequent playoff.) "The rest of the time I played very well, so it didn't affect my confidence."

Encina didn't reflect that in the Irvine Whitlock's opening round Friday, shooting a 72 and trailing Scotland's John Chillas, the leader, by four strokes. Defending champion Sam Torrance opened with 73 and his bid for three in a row never materialized. Bob Cameron seized the lead Saturday with a round similar to that of Chillas the day before, shooting 33 on the back nine for 71–141, a stroke better than American John Benda.

Encina entered the picture with 71–143, took over first place on the front nine at La Moye Sunday afternoon with a birdie at the second hole and an eagle at the par-five sixth, and breezed to the easy victory. Former U.S. Tour player Rex Caldwell, with 69, tied for second with fellow Yank Alan Tapie and New Zealand's Simon Owen at 212. Tapie and Owen closed with 67s.

FirstPlus Wales Seniors Open
Cardiff, Wales
Winner: Jose Rivero

Although he put a positive spin on the disappointment of his second runner-up finish of the season, David J. Russell had to be wondering what he had to do to beat Spaniard Jose Rivero, who walked off with the rich first prize in the FirstPlus Wales Seniors Open.

Englishman Russell, then with seven second-place postings in his winless, three-season senior career, had taken a four-stroke lead into the final round on the Wales National Course at the Vale Hotel Golf and Spa Resort near Cardiff, but couldn't hold on to it Sunday. Four bogeys and a double bogey in the middle of the final round did in Russell and opened the door for Rivero to capture his second Seniors Tour victory of the season, joining Sam Torrance as a double winner in 2006.

In the first one, at Barbados in the season opener, Rivero went four extra holes before defeating Russell. Another playoff loomed in Wales before Rivero holed a 12-foot birdie putt on the final green for 68 and a four-under-par 212 to snatch the one-shot victory from Russell (75), fellow Spaniard Juan Quiros (69), Frenchman Gery Watine (70) and Torrance (71).

Russell was one of the few players who managed sub-par rounds over the first two days. His three-under-par 69 staked him to a one-stroke lead over Rivero and Martin Poxon the first day and he opened the four-shot gap on Torrance Saturday when he repeated the 69. Rivero (74) and Poxon (75) fell six and seven strokes off the pace that day, but the Spaniard went on a birdie spree Sunday. He lost sole possession of the lead when he bogeyed the 17th hole, then nailed the victory with the sensational 72nd-hole birdie.

Bendinat London Seniors Masters
Ash, Kent, England
Winner: Giuseppe Cali

All signs pointed to a victory for Sam Torrance when the field teed off in the final round of the Bendinat London Seniors Masters on a hot July Sunday. Torrance, with two wins, a second and a tie for seventh in his four previous starts that put him atop the European Seniors Tour money list, had stormed to a three-stroke lead in Saturday's second round. Besides, he had won the tournament at the London Golf Club in Ash, Kent, in 2005.

It didn't work out that way.

The seasoned Scot unexpectedly stumbled over three double bogeys to a 77 Sunday that opened the way for an array of contenders. Two men took the greatest advantage—Delroy Cambridge, the Jamaican who had shared second place with Bertus Smit at five-under-par 139, and Giuseppe Cali, who had seemed out of the picture seven strokes off the lead at 69-74–143 after 36 holes.

Cambridge, a four-time winner on the tour, holed a 15-foot birdie putt on the final green for 71–210 to overtake the Italian, Cali, who had shot 67, the day's best round, for his 210. The two men then played the par-four 18th hole five more times before Cali holed a seven-foot birdie putt to end the marathon playoff and capture his second European Seniors Tour victory to go with his Mobile Cup win in 2005.

The two men parred the 18th the first two times in the overtime, matched birdies the third time, and parred it again the fourth time before Cambridge left his 17-foot birdie putt short and Cali nailed his for the victory. John Chillas, the first-round leader for the second time in three tournaments, shooting 66 for a one-stroke lead over Cambridge, faded to a 10th-place finish.

Senior British Open
Ayrshire, Scotland
Winner: Loren Roberts

Loren Roberts waved his magic wand just when he needed it as he more than made up for a shoddy overall performance in the final round and won the Senior British Open Championship, his second senior major. After squandering a four-stroke lead while struggling to a five-over-par 75, the soft-spoken Roberts, considered by many the most consistent putter in the game today, dropped in a 12-footer for par on the 18th green, the first playoff hole. Then he watched as his opponent, Eduardo Romero, missed a five-footer to three-putt and hand Roberts the title on Turnberry's Ailsa course.

The first player on either the European Seniors or Champions Tour with four 2006 titles, Roberts extended American domination of the Senior British Open, his victory following the 2003 and 2005 wins of Tom Watson and the surprise 2004 triumph of Pete Oakley. Roberts captured his first major—the JEN-WELD Tradition—in just his third start two months after turning 50 in 2005.

Roberts's faltering final round was a reversal of his performances through the first three days, particularly Saturday when his 69 in the rain and heavy winds was the only sub-par round of the day. He never trailed, putting up consecutive 65s in rather benign weather. The first one lodged him in a first-place tie with Peter Jacobsen and Craig Stadler the first day and the second forged another deadlock, this time with Romero. The Argentine professional, owner of a 2005 victory on the European Seniors Tour and eight titles in his earlier campaigning on the European Tour, shot 30 on the second nine for 63 and his share of the lead.

On Saturday, after he posted his "patient" 69, highlighted by an eagle at the par-five seventh, the Champions Tour's leading money-winner observed proudly: "That is probably in my top three rounds ever. My ball-striking was really solid today, the best yet this week." That's why his Sunday play was surprising and door-opening for Romero, who shot 73 Saturday but held second place with a four-stroke deficit.

Romero closed the gap on Roberts on the first nine Sunday, but neither man could avoid mishaps on Ailsa's demanding second nine. Even though Roberts took two double bogeys coming in, Romero had to hole an eight-footer at the 18th to force the playoff. Dick Mast, a winless American journeyman, closed with 67, the day's best round, and just missed joining the overtime combatants when, after holing a 30-foot eagle putt at the 17th, he left a 25-footer on the lip at the 18th for 275, a shot behind the 274s of Roberts and Romero.

Wentworth Senior Masters
Surrey, England
Winner: Eduardo Romero

Eduardo Romero wasted little time recovering from the disappointment of a putting fizzle and playoff loss in the important Senior British Open. The 52-year-old Argentinean, a seasoned winner in Europe, rebounded the week after losing to Loren Roberts in the Turnberry overtime with an impressive victory in defense of his only previous victory on the European Seniors Tour in the Wentworth Senior Masters.

Romero stalked the leaders for three rounds, moved in front of second-round leader Stewart Ginn after four holes in the final round at the storied Wentworth Club in Virginia Water, Surrey, and went on to victory. He closed with a two-under-par 70 and final 207, two strokes ahead of Sam Torrance, a two-time 2006 winner, and fellow Argentinean Horacio Carbonetti.

Biding his time, Romero opened the tournament Friday with a 71, trailing by five as Ginn began with a 66 that "really could have been much better" after he shot 30 on the front nine. Ginn remained in front Saturday, shooting 69 for 135, but Romero made a strong move with his 66, the day's low round, taking over second place at 137, a stroke ahead of Torrance (70-68).

Romero caught Ginn at the third hole Sunday, then went ahead to stay at the fourth when the Australian took one of several three-putts for a double bogey and ultimately shot 78. Torrance stayed close, but could never get closer than two strokes in his bid to regain the tour money lead. A birdie at the par-five 16th gave Romero the two-shot lead he carried to the finish.

Bad Ragaz PGA Seniors Open
Zurich, Switzerland
Winner: Juan Quiros

Never a winner on the European Tour, Juan Quiros became the second Spanish victor of the 2006 European Seniors Tour in just his seventh start in the Bad Ragaz PGA Seniors Open in Switzerland in August. The 50-year-old Quiros broke from a three-way, 36-hole tie to post a 65 and score a two-stroke victory over senior star Carl Mason. His 14-under-par 196 was by far the year's lowest victory total, as he followed the lead of countryman Jose Rivero, who had two 2006 wins in the books.

Quiros made the victory possible when he blistered Bad Ragaz Golf Club with a nine-under-par 61 in Saturday's second round, matching the Seniors Tour's record low round registered by Bob Cameron at the Sanremo Masters in 2004 and coming from five strokes off the first-round pace of John Bland and Stewart Ginn (65s).

Bill Longmuir, who spent a fruitless six months on the U.S. Champions Tour, nearly matched Quiros with a birdie-free 62 for his 131, and they were joined in first place by Nick Job, who shot 64.

As he did Saturday, Quiros opened the final round with birdies on the first two holes and was in control of the lead until he overshot the 15th green for his lone bogey of the day. But he bounced back immediately with a birdie at the par-five 16th and another off a seven iron to two feet at the 17th to wrap up the two-stroke victory, his first since a Challenge Tour win in 1996.

Scandinavian Senior Open
Helsingor, Denmark
Winner: Katsuyoshi Tomori

Katsuyoshi Tomori firmed up certain of next year's travel plans, thanks to a lucrative visit. When the Japanese professional capped a three-week stay in Europe with victory in the Scandinavian Senior Open, he earned, besides the first-place prize money, a two-year exemption.

Tomori, a seven-time winner on the Japan Tour, joined countrymen Seiji Ebihara, Noboru Sugai and Dragon Taki as a European Seniors winner via a splendid closing round at Denmark's Helsingor Golf Club. His five-under-par 66 brought him from two strokes off the pace at the start of the day to a two-shot triumph over Ireland's Eamonn Darcy and Spaniard Jose Rivero, a two-time 2006 winner, with his 14-under-par 199. He was the fourth first-time winner of the season.

The finish was particularly disappointing for Darcy, another in a long list of close calls without victory as the outcome. In 35 starts on the senior tour, Eamonn now had placed second seven times and in the top 10 on 10 other occasions. Rivero, the second-round leader after firing a 63 for 131, shot 70 in the Sunday round for his 201.

Tomori put himself in a contending position from the start, opening with 66 to share the lead with South Africa's Bertus Smit and added a respectable 67 Saturday to set up the Sunday charge to the championship.

PGA Seniors Championship
Colchester, England
Winner: Sam Torrance

Sam Torrance reestablished himself as the dominant player when he ground out a three-stroke victory in the storm-plagued final round of the PGA Seniors Championship. His third win of the season and seventh overall in his second full year enabled him to regain the No. 1 position on the tour's money list from Eduardo Romero.

Torrance shook off a rattling second nine that cost him the lead and left him three shots off the pace after Saturday's third round and put together a brilliant, six-under-par 66 amid two stoppages of play caused by lightning storms Sunday afternoon.

"Given the conditions, that was the best round of the week," said Torrance after his successful defense of the PGA Championship at the Stoke by Nayland Golf Club in England. He finished with a 20-under-par 268 total and the three-shot margin over Argentina's Luis Carbonetti, who closed with 69–271.

Torrance had played so well up to that point. He opened with a 65, yielding first place by a stroke to fellow Scot John Chillas, then moved in front Friday with a 66 for 131, two better than Italy's Giuseppe Cali, the London Masters winner, and three ahead of Scotland's Bill Longmuir and Ireland's Eamonn Darcy.

But his game faltered on that second nine Saturday. His three-shot lead after an outgoing 31 disappeared when he bogeyed the 10th and 12th and posted 71. Cali posted a 66 for 199 and took the three-shot margin over Torrance and Carbonetti. Torrance regained the lead Sunday with a birdie on the ninth hole, added two more at the 10th and 12th, and wrapped things up with a final birdie at the 16th.

Charles Church Scottish Seniors Open
Edinburgh, Scotland
Winner: Sam Torrance

Even as he won the PGA Seniors Championship, Sam Torrance was looking forward with delightful anticipation to the following Charles Church Scottish Seniors Open at the Marriott Dalmahoy Hotel and Country Club. "I've happy memories there," he chirped. "I think I won by 15 shots when I won the Scottish PGA Championship about 15 years ago."

It wasn't nearly that easy, but Torrance did win the tournament in his native country, his fourth title of the season and second time he put victories back to back. He had to overcome a feeble start and just managed to edge fellow Scot Bill Longmuir, a former Scottish Open winner, by a stroke at the end of the week.

Torrance struggled with his putting on the windy first day and had to settle for a 76. That left him seven strokes off the pace set by Spaniards Juan Quiros and Jose Rivero. The margin could have been greater. Quiros bogeyed and Rivero double-bogeyed the final hole for their 69s.

Foul weather Scottish-style struck Saturday, and Torrance and two other Scots handled it better than the rest of the field. Torrance shot 67 in the wind and rain and climbed within two strokes of the lead with his 143. Longmuir also finished at 143 after a 68, and Mike Miller moved within a stroke of the lead with a second 71 for 142. Quiros clung to first place with a par 72 for 141, as Rivero shot 74 to join Torrance and Longmuir at 143.

Torrance's winning 18 holes Sunday was a mixed bag on another wind-swept afternoon on Dalmahoy's East course. He had an eagle, five birdies, two bogeys and a double bogey in compiling the 70 and 213 total that gave him the one-stroke victory over Longmuir. Quiros shot 76 and tied for eighth with Rivero.

European Senior Masters
Milton Keynes, England
Winner: Carl Mason

Carl Mason's 12th European Seniors victory had special significance for him. Winless at that September point in the season and struggling a bit in the final round of the European Senior Masters, Mason pulled himself together to land the victory on one of the courses he has considered special in his native land.

"Through my career, I have always wanted to win at either Woburn or Wentworth, one of the great courses," said the 53-year-old Englishman emotionally after posting his two-stroke victory over Argentina's Horacio Carbonetti at Woburn. He finished with 69 for his seven-under-par 209 total.

Mason made up a lot of ground after getting away slowly in the opening round. He shot 73 and was seven strokes behind leader Jose Rivero, continuing his strong, two-victory season that had him second on the tour's Order of Merit behind Sam Torrance.

Mason rode a hot putter into contention Saturday. Holing four putts in the 15-to-25-foot range, he shot the day's best round, a 67, and jumped into second place, a stroke behind Carbonetti, who shot 70 for 139. Rivero slumped to 76 and slipped back into a four-way tie with Terry Gale, Noel Ratcliffe and Gery Watine at 142.

Everything clicked for Mason in the early going Sunday. With five birdies on the first eight holes, he raced to a four-stroke lead and turned in 30. But Carbonetti fought back and led briefly on the back nine before the Englishman birdied two of the last three holes to secure the victory.

The Midas Group English Seniors Open
St. Mellion, Cornwall, England
Winner: Carl Mason

Nobody was happier to see the English Seniors Open return to the schedule under the auspices of The Midas Group than Carl Mason. He had won that tournament in 2003 and 2004 before it was sidelined in 2005. So, technically, he was the defending champion when the event was staged in mid-September at St. Mellion International in Cornwall and defend it he did, making it three in a row and picking up his second straight win.

Mason carded three solid but unspectacular rounds, closing with a 71 for a four-under-par 212 and one-shot victory over Stewart Ginn, who gave it a good run with a final-round 67. It was Mason's 13th win on the European Seniors Tour and he joined Sam Torrance (four) and Jose Rivero (two) as the only multiple winners of the season.

Things started very badly for Mason in the opening round Friday. He double-bogeyed his first hole, but went on to shoot 70 and secure second place behind fellow Englishman Tony Allen (68). Mason opened his second round the same way as he did Friday, but, with three second-nine birdies, played the remaining 17 holes in three under for 71–141. Alan Mew, from Trinidad and Tobago, moved into second place with a 68 for 143.

"It was a nice, solid round," Mason said of his closing 71. He got past the troublesome first hole and held off the charge of Ginn, whose 67 left him a stroke behind Mason and a runner-up for a second time in 2006.

OKI Castellon Open de Espana Senior
Castellon, Spain
Winner: Gordon J. Brand

Gordon J. Brand had almost forgotten what it was like to win a tournament. It had been 17 years since he racked up a victory—in the Belgian Open on the European Tour—and he was 24 events into his career on the European Seniors Tour when he landed the title in the OKI Castellon Open de Espana in mid-October. He outlasted two top seniors and one of the game's biggest stars to score a two-stroke win and become the fifth first-time victor of the 2006 season.

Brand opened the Castellon Open with a bogey-free 65—"my best 18 holes of the year"—and jumped off to a one-stroke lead at Club de Campo del Mediterraneo over Carl Mason, who was gunning for his third consecutive victory in his hot pursuit of Sam Torrance for the year's money title. Torrance shot 68 and Greg Norman, making just his sixth start of the year after undergoing a second knee operation earlier in the year, shot 69.

Brand bolted to a five-shot advantage Saturday when he followed the opening 65 with a 66 for his 13-under-par 131. Torrance duplicated his 68 for 136 and Mason shot 71–137 to join Eamonn Darcy (70) and Delroy Cambridge (65) in third place. Norman remained in contention with a second 69 for 138.

Victory did not come easily Sunday for Brand. One threat eased when Torrance three-putted the 10th, and Norman fell back with bogeys at the

15th and 16th holes. Mason had the last shot at his fellow Englishman, but an errant drive into the trees at the last hole erased his chances. His 68 and Torrance's 69 for a matching 205 left them in a tie for second. Brand parred the last five holes for 72–203.

Estoril Seniors Open of Portugal
Quinta da Marinha, Portugal
Winner: Carl Mason

Even though Carl Mason realized that a third money title was out of reach, nothing was going to slow down his late-season surge, not even a drenching downpour during the last two hours of the Estoril Seniors Open of Portugal. Coming into the next-to-last tournament of the year with the hottest hand, the Englishman put on a very impressive showing, particularly in the driving rain that nearly flooded the Quinta da Marinha Oitavos Golfe course.

The leader from the outset, Mason produced three birdies at the height of the storm, and despite a double bogey on the last hole, pulled away to a four-stroke triumph over Torrance and Stewart Ginn with a closing 71 for a nine-under-par 204 total. That finish clinched a second straight money title for Torrance.

Mason's 71 Sunday in a way was more impressive than the seven-under-par 64 that jumped him off to a fast start Friday—eight birdies and a bogey—on the way to his wire-to-wire triumph, his 14th as a senior. Close behind were Spaniards Jose Rivero and Juan Quiros at 66 and Torrance and Zimbabwe's Tony Johnstone at 67.

The Englishman widened the gap to three strokes Saturday with a 69 for 133. Ginn, winless but in contention again, moved into second place with 67–136 and Torrance (70) and Rivero (71) settled in at 137.

The worse the weather, the better Mason played Sunday. Before the rains came, he struggled to a 37 on the first nine and dropped a shot out of the lead as Torrance ran off four birdies in a six-hole stretch and shot 32 going out. Mason birdied the 10th and 13th under deplorable conditions to get to 10 under par and slogged home with victory assured.

Arcapita Seniors Tour Championship
Manama, Bahrain
Winner: Gordon J. Brand

The Arcapita Seniors Tour Championship, intended to be the climax of the season, turned anticlimactic in 2006, particularly with the money-winning title already decided and after the tour's two leading players bowed out in the first round with injuries.

Still, the finale at Riffa Views in Bahrain was rewarding and meaningful to Gordon J. Brand, the winner, and Adan Sowa, the loser in the three-hole playoff that brought the season to a close. The Englishman wound up winning two of the last three events after going 17 years without a victory, while Sowa, who traveled from his native Argentina to try to salvage his playing privileges for 2007, did so handily with the runner-up money.

Brand came from five strokes off the pace in the final round with a closing 66 to set up the playoff despite having to replace his caddie/wife when she was injured on the second hole. Sowa, who had begun the final round tied for the lead with South African John Bland at 140, managed just 71 (Bland took 73) for his tying five-under-par 211. Sowa had opened with 69 and deadlocked for the lead with defending champion Des Smyth, who played most of his round with a marker after Carl Mason's nagging back ailment forced him out after two holes and Sam Torrance, the leading money winner, retired after nine with a swollen finger.

Brand and Sowa traded long halving putts on the first two extra holes before the Argentine hooked his tee shot into the water on their third go at the 18th and Brand stiffed his approach for a winning birdie.

Japan Senior Tour

Aderans Wellness Open
Nakajo, Niigata, Japan
Winner: Kiyoshi Murota

Kiyoshi Murota, the 2005 Senior PGA champion, scored his second victory since joining the over-50 ranks last year, capturing the Aderans Wellness Open, the season's opener on the Japan Senior Tour in June. Continuing the strong play he exhibited in his final years on the regular Japan Tour, Murota led from start to finish at Nakajo Golf Club in posting a one-stroke triumph with his nine-under-par 207.

Murota, who won the Taiheiyo Club Masters, one of Japan's more prestigious events, in 2003 at age 48 and two other of his six victories on that circuit after the turn of the century, jumped off to the lead in the opening round with 68, one shot better than Renkyoku Sugiyama and amateur Kenki Ito and two in front of Tateo Ozaki and Katsunari Takahashi.

He remained on top after Saturday's second round when he followed with 71–139 as Toyotake Nakao moved into second place with 69–140 and Ozaki continued two back with 71–141. Only Nakao threatened Sunday, equaling Murota's 68 for 208. Ozaki held third place, but four off the final pace with 70–211.

PGA Philanthropy Rebornest Senior Open
Miyagi, Japan
Winner: Tateo Ozaki

Tateo (Jet) Ozaki beat his more illustrious brothers to the punch on the Japan Senior Tour when he won the PGA Philanthropy Rebornest Senior Open in his third season on the circuit. Even though a 15-time victor in his regular tour career, Tateo always seemed to be in the shadow of older brother Masashi (Jumbo), the greatest winner in Japan history, and younger brother Naomichi (Joe). Playing in just his eighth Senior Tour event, the 52-year-old Ozaki cranked out a tough playoff victory over Katsunari Takahashi, the defending champion and the circuit's most successful active player, in the August tournament.

Takahashi, tied with Fujio Kobayashi as all-time senior winner with 11 titles, took the lead from Yasuo Sone in the third round at Big Raisac Country Club in Miyagi Prefecture. Sone, in front the first two days with his 67-70 rounds, slipped three strokes off the pace Saturday as Takahashi put a 69 with his earlier rounds of 68 and 70 for 207. Ozaki popped into second place with 67–209 and forged the final deadlock with 70–279 to Takahashi's 72 Sunday.

The two men played the 18th hole four times before Takahashi trapped his approach, bogeyed, and Ozaki grabbed the victory with his par.

Fancl Classic
Shizuoka, Japan
Winner: Kiyoshi Murota

Kiyoshi Murota fought off the challenge of star Tsuneyuki Nakajima and registered his second win of the season in the Fancl Classic at Susono Country Club. As in his earlier win in June in the Aderans Wellness Open, Murota led from the opening round into the final 18, but had to birdie two of the last three holes to catch Nakajima and bring on a playoff for the title.

Nakajima, who owns 48 titles from his great career on the Japan Tour, had raced home with a seven-under-par 65 after starting the final round in second place four strokes behind Murota, who built the big lead with his 66-67–133 start. The closest other contenders were at 139 (Yukio Noguchi) and 140 (five players).

Murota birdied the 16th and 18th holes Sunday for 69 and his tying 202. The playoff ended disastrously for Nakajima when he pushed his approach at the par-five 18th out of bounds. That led to a double bogey and Murota won easily with his par.

Japan PGA Senior Championship
Hokkaido, Japan
Winner: Tsuneyuki Nakajima

In other ways, Tsuneyuki (Tommy) Nakajima's record doesn't quite stack up to Masashi (Jumbo) Ozaki or Isao Aoki, the other members of Japan's great triumvirate of modern-day golf, but he laid claim to a remarkable record of career success when he won the 2006 Japan PGA Senior Championship on the first day of October at Eniwa Country Club in Hokkaido.

In his lifetime, Nakajima has won every major title available in men's golf in Japan: the Amateur and Public Amateur, the Open, PGA, Series and Match Play on the regular circuit and the Open and PGA on the Senior Tour.

Nakajima completed the impressive feat at Eniwa Country Club by handing

Katsunari Takahashi his second playoff defeat of the season after the two finished the regulation 72 holes tied with five-under-par 283s. Nakajima had taken over first place in the second round with 69-70–139 and led Takahashi by two strokes when he shot 71 Saturday. Takahashi had rounds of 68-73-71 for 212, a stroke in front of two-time 2006 winner Kiyoshi Murota.

In the playoff, after Nakajima shot 73 and Takahashi 71 Sunday for 283, the two parred the first extra hole before Nakajima birdied it the second time around for the victory.

Japan Senior Open
Mie, Japan
Winner: Tsuneyuki Nakajima

Tsuneyuki (Tommy) Nakajima extended his dominance of the major championships on the Japan Senior Tour when he repeated his 2005 victory in the Japan Senior Open in late October at Kuwana Country Club in Mie Prefecture. It was the third consecutive major title that fell into his hands following his wins in the 2005 Open and the 2006 Senior PGA earlier in the month.

Those hands were full as Kiyoshi Murota continued his brilliant, money-leading season by carrying Nakajima to the final hole before yielding by a stroke.

Katsunari Takahashi, twice a playoff loser earlier in the year, and Hajime Meshiai, who spent the season on America's Champions Tour, led Murota by one and Nakajima by two when they began the tournament with 66s. Seiji Ebihara, who has enjoyed considerable success on Europe's senior circuit, took over the lead Friday with 65–133, but Nakajima was on his heels with 68-66–134 and Murota next with 67-68–135. Scores elevated Saturday as Nakajima (72) and Murota (71) took over the lead at 216, and Nakajima pulled out the win with 69–275 to Murota's 70–276 Sunday.

Kinojyo Senior Open
Okayama, Japan
Winner: Takashi Miyoshi

Little had been heard from Takashi Miyoshi, who had dominated the 2005 campaign with three of his five victories on the over-50 circuit. He made up for that in the Kinojyo Senior Open, the year's final event in early November, rolling to a four-stroke triumph at Kinojyo Golf Club.

Miyoshi established a six-stroke lead over the first two rounds. He shot a six-under-par 66 the first day to lead by one over Kimpachi Yoshimura, then exploded to a six-stroke margin Saturday with a 64 for 130. The ever-present Kiyoshi Murota shot 66 that day to take the runner-up position at 136 and made a run at the leader on the front nine, cutting the margin to three shots. Miyoshi was not to be denied, though, and ran off four birdies on the back side to secure the four-shot win with his 200 total.

Finishing more than ¥7 million ahead of runner-up Nakajima on the final money list, Murota etched a splendid, six-tournament 2006 record of two wins, two seconds and two third-place finishes in earning ¥42,700,000.

APPENDIXES

American Tours

Mercedes Championships

Plantation Course at Kapalua, Maui, Hawaii
Par 36-37–73; 7,411 yards

January 5-8
purse, $5,400,000

	SCORES				TOTAL	MONEY
Stuart Appleby	71	72	70	71	284	$1,080,000
Vijay Singh	70	74	74	66	284	630,000
(Appleby defeated Singh on first playoff hole.)						
Jim Furyk	72	72	72	72	288	420,000
Michael Campbell	72	72	71	75	290	287,500
Vaughn Taylor	74	73	72	71	290	287,500
Lucas Glover	74	73	70	74	291	217,000
Sergio Garcia	71	74	73	75	293	195,000
Justin Leonard	72	78	72	72	294	185,000
Bart Bryant	74	72	76	73	295	175,000
Peter Lonard	74	74	73	75	296	165,000
Tim Petrovic	74	77	74	72	297	150,000
Wes Short, Jr.	73	73	75	76	297	150,000
Geoff Ogilvy	75	72	74	77	298	130,000
David Toms	71	73	79	75	298	130,000
Jason Bohn	76	70	78	75	299	110,000
Mark Calcavecchia	73	74	73	79	299	110,000
Olin Browne	69	76	76	80	301	94,000
Robert Gamez	77	76	73	75	301	94,000
K.J. Choi	75	74	77	76	302	87,000
Kenny Perry	74	77	77	74	302	87,000
Carl Pettersson	71	85	75	74	305	84,000
Ted Purdy	73	75	77	81	306	82,000
Brad Faxon	82	78	75	74	309	79,000
Heath Slocum	74	81	78	76	309	79,000
Ben Crane	79	78	78	75	310	76,000
Fred Funk	76	82	78	76	312	74,000
Sean O'Hair	77	79	80	82	318	72,000
Jason Gore	80	80	81	79	320	70,000

Sony Open in Hawaii

Waialae Country Club, Honolulu, Hawaii
Par 35-35–70; 7,060 yards

January 12-15
purse, $5,100,000

	SCORES				TOTAL	MONEY
David Toms	66	69	61	65	261	$918,000
Chad Campbell	67	67	62	70	266	448,800
Rory Sabbatini	65	72	67	62	266	448,800
Bubba Watson	67	70	66	65	268	244,800
Nathan Green	70	70	65	64	269	204,000
Vijay Singh	71	69	65	66	271	183,600
Stuart Appleby	70	66	69	67	272	158,950
Jim Furyk	67	67	70	68	272	158,950
Charles Warren	66	74	64	68	272	158,950

	SCORES				TOTAL	MONEY
Stewart Cink	71	69	66	67	273	127,500
J.B. Holmes	70	66	69	68	273	127,500
Carl Pettersson	71	68	68	66	273	127,500
Shane Bertsch	70	70	63	71	274	98,600
K.J. Choi	66	71	68	69	274	98,600
Jerry Kelly	68	69	69	68	274	98,600
Tom Byrum	68	71	68	68	275	84,150
Jerry Smith	69	67	69	70	275	84,150
Mark Calcavecchia	70	69	68	69	276	64,260
Brent Geiberger	68	73	65	70	276	64,260
Dudley Hart	69	68	69	70	276	64,260
Steve Jones	69	68	68	71	276	64,260
Loren Roberts	69	68	71	68	276	64,260
Adam Scott	71	69	70	66	276	64,260
Richard Johnson	69	71	70	67	277	40,362.86
Billy Mayfair	70	70	70	67	277	40,362.86
Arron Oberholser	70	71	68	68	277	40,362.86
Jeff Overton	72	71	66	68	277	40,362.86
John Riegger	72	71	68	66	277	40,362.86
Jason Bohn	70	72	65	70	277	40,362.85
Robert Gamez	70	69	66	72	277	40,362.85
Tommy Armour	68	74	64	72	278	30,243
David Duval	75	68	72	63	278	30,243
Troy Matteson	72	69	71	66	278	30,243
Chris Riley	76	66	68	68	278	30,243
Ron Whittaker	73	68	66	71	278	30,243
Rich Beem	71	69	71	68	279	23,502.50
David Branshaw	71	68	71	69	279	23,502.50
Jeff Gove	66	71	70	72	279	23,502.50
Ryuji Imada	72	71	69	67	279	23,502.50
Peter Lonard	67	70	68	74	279	23,502.50
Vaughn Taylor	67	72	68	72	279	23,502.50
Daniel Chopra	76	65	70	69	280	15,355.64
Fred Funk	68	71	72	69	280	15,355.64
Jonathan Kaye	73	68	71	68	280	15,355.64
Joe Ogilvie	71	72	66	71	280	15,355.64
Jesper Parnevik	72	70	68	70	280	15,355.64
Bo Van Pelt	70	73	69	68	280	15,355.64
Camilo Villegas	72	64	73	71	280	15,355.64
Arjun Atwal	70	69	69	72	280	15,355.63
Carlos Franco	70	71	67	72	280	15,355.63
Tom Lehman	71	71	66	72	280	15,355.63
Will MacKenzie	69	70	68	73	280	15,355.63
Aaron Baddeley	71	70	71	69	281	11,696
Craig Barlow	73	70	68	70	281	11,696
Joe Durant	71	72	68	70	281	11,696
Paul Goydos	69	70	74	68	281	11,696
Charles Howell	71	72	68	70	281	11,696
Jeff Maggert	69	72	68	72	281	11,696
Paul Azinger	69	72	70	71	282	10,914
Henrik Bjornstad	70	73	67	72	282	10,914
Todd Fischer	73	67	69	73	282	10,914
Jay Haas	75	66	70	71	282	10,914
Thomas Levet	71	72	70	69	282	10,914
Hunter Mahan	71	68	75	68	282	10,914
Parker McLachlin	72	71	65	74	282	10,914
Jon Mills	69	72	73	68	282	10,914
Roger Tambellini	69	73	67	73	282	10,914
Michael Allen	72	69	71	71	283	10,353
Alex Cejka	76	67	68	72	283	10,353

	SCORES				TOTAL	MONEY
Brad Faxon	71	70	71	72	284	10,149
Shigeki Maruyama	72	71	69	72	284	10,149
Woody Austin	74	68	71	72	285	9,639
Olin Browne	71	70	67	77	285	9,639
Bubba Dickerson	72	71	70	72	285	9,639
Mathew Goggin	69	72	69	75	285	9,639
Bill Haas	71	71	72	71	285	9,639
Patrick Sheehan	71	71	72	71	285	9,639
Hidemichi Tanaka	73	70	69	73	285	9,639
Vance Veazey	70	69	72	74	285	9,639
Kaname Yokoo	72	71	71	73	287	9,180
Jeff Sluman	67	73	73	75	288	9,078
James Driscoll	67	74	73	79	293	8,976

Bob Hope Chrysler Classic

The Classic Club: Par 36-36–72; 7,305 yards
Bermuda Dunes CC: Par 36-36–72; 6,927 yards
La Quinta CC: Par 36-36–72; 7,060 yards
PGA West, Palmer Course: Par 36-36–72; 6,950 yards
Palm Desert, California

January 18-22
purse, $5,000,000

	SCORES					TOTAL	MONEY
Chad Campbell	63	66	68	67	71	335	$900,000
Jesper Parnevik	69	69	71	62	67	338	440,000
Scott Verplank	68	68	65	64	73	338	440,000
John Huston	65	71	68	67	68	339	240,000
Phil Mickelson	66	69	68	67	71	341	182,500
John Senden	70	63	68	67	73	341	182,500
Mike Weir	67	69	69	66	70	341	182,500
Olin Browne	65	69	71	66	72	343	150,000
Jeff Maggert	67	71	69	64	72	343	150,000
Lucas Glover	66	75	70	67	66	344	110,833.34
Ryan Palmer	70	69	67	66	72	344	110,833.34
Bernhard Langer	70	70	67	65	72	344	110,833.33
Billy Mayfair	68	70	68	66	72	344	110,833.33
Justin Rose	70	70	64	66	74	344	110,833.33
Rory Sabbatini	71	68	68	64	73	344	110,833.33
Shane Bertsch	70	68	66	68	73	345	80,000
Brandt Jobe	72	68	68	64	73	345	80,000
Tom Pernice, Jr.	65	70	71	70	69	345	80,000
Paul Azinger	71	69	67	69	70	346	60,600
David Branshaw	69	70	72	67	68	346	60,600
John Cook	70	74	63	69	70	346	60,600
Robert Garrigus	70	71	69	70	66	346	60,600
Bill Haas	68	69	70	69	70	346	60,600
Arjun Atwal	70	67	70	70	70	347	40,500
Fred Couples	69	71	68	72	67	347	40,500
Bob Estes	69	70	67	72	69	347	40,500
Todd Fischer	68	71	67	70	71	347	40,500
Richard Johnson	67	69	69	72	70	347	40,500
Troy Matteson	73	70	65	71	68	347	40,500
Billy Andrade	68	68	67	72	73	348	31,050
Alex Cejka	69	67	68	72	72	348	31,050
Ben Crane	68	69	68	69	74	348	31,050
Tim Herron	71	69	69	66	73	348	31,050
Joe Ogilvie	66	70	68	72	72	348	31,050

	SCORES				TOTAL	MONEY
Rich Beem	70 67 69 71			72	349	22,583.34
Justin Leonard	67 72 67 71			72	349	22,583.34
Nick Watney	68 76 66 67			72	349	22,583.34
Michael Allen	70 72 66 68			73	349	22,583.34
Daniel Chopra	70 74 70 67			68	349	22,583.33
Steve Elkington	64 70 71 67			77	349	22,583.33
Ryuji Imada	71 70 72 67			69	349	22,583.33
Steve Jones	68 71 72 66			72	349	22,583.33
Carl Pettersson	71 71 69 70			68	349	22,583.33
Stephen Ames	67 72 69 70			72	350	14,177.78
Doug Barron	70 70 73 64			73	350	14,177.78
Mark Calcavecchia	69 68 72 68			73	350	14,177.78
Ben Curtis	69 71 71 65			74	350	14,177.78
Joe Durant	71 65 70 69			75	350	14,177.78
Brian Gay	72 73 67 64			74	350	14,177.78
Patrick Sheehan	66 75 64 72			73	350	14,177.78
Fred Funk	70 68 75 68			69	350	14,177.77
Tag Ridings	69 74 67 71			69	350	14,177.77
Dudley Hart	74 69 66 68			74	351	11,311.12
David Duval	69 78 69 64			71	351	11,311.11
Steve Flesch	67 76 68 69			71	351	11,311.11
Jerry Kelly	74 71 67 68			71	351	11,311.11
Shaun Micheel	67 73 70 71			70	351	11,311.11
D.A. Points	69 67 75 68			72	351	11,311.11
John Rollins	67 70 69 74			71	351	11,311.11
Kevin Sutherland	68 67 72 71			73	351	11,311.11
Dean Wilson	68 70 70 71			72	351	11,311.11
Jeff Brehaut	70 75 68 68			71	352	10,550
Tim Clark	71 68 70 70			73	352	10,550
Paul Goydos	74 70 71 63			74	352	10,550
J.L. Lewis	67 74 70 69			72	352	10,550
Greg Owen	70 71 69 67			75	352	10,550
Heath Slocum	70 71 67 72			72	352	10,550
Brian Davis	69 72 69 71			72	353	10,100
David McKenzie	69 70 70 66			78	353	10,100
Jeff Sluman	74 73 67 67			72	353	10,100
Andrew Magee	68 72 72 69			73	354	9,900
Robert Gamez	72 73 67 67			76	355	9,800
Pat Perez	60 73 70 75			78	356	9,700
Corey Pavin	73 70 69 67			78	357	9,600
Woody Austin	68 70 69 73			78	358	9,400
Craig Barlow	74 73 68 66			77	358	9,400
Mark O'Meara	69 74 70 68			77	358	9,400

Buick Invitational

Torrey Pines Golf Course, La Jolla, California
South Course: Par 36-36–72; 7,208 yards
North Course: Par 36-36–72; 6,874 yards

January 26-29
purse, $5,100,000

	SCORES			TOTAL	MONEY
Tiger Woods	71 68 67		72	278	$918,000
Nathan Green	67 70 69		72	278	448,800
Jose Maria Olazabal	74 64 71		69	278	448,800
(Woods defeated Green on first and Olazabal on second playoff hole.)					
Arjun Atwal	70 67 71		71	279	200,812.50
Lucas Glover	71 67 70		71	279	200,812.50

	SCORES				TOTAL	MONEY
Jonathan Kaye	67	73	71	68	279	200,812.50
John Rollins	69	70	71	69	279	200,812.50
Sergio Garcia	69	68	68	75	280	153,000
Phil Mickelson	71	67	69	73	280	153,000
Henrik Bjornstad	68	72	70	71	281	117,300
Tim Clark	68	66	74	73	281	117,300
Brandt Jobe	65	67	75	74	281	117,300
Rod Pampling	70	67	68	76	281	117,300
Jesper Parnevik	67	67	73	74	281	117,300
Arron Oberholser	70	70	73	69	282	91,800
Todd Fischer	71	67	72	73	283	69,232.50
Charley Hoffman	66	74	70	73	283	69,232.50
Kent Jones	66	72	75	70	283	69,232.50
Skip Kendall	66	72	75	70	283	69,232.50
Tom Lehman	74	66	73	70	283	69,232.50
Mark O'Meara	74	67	72	70	283	69,232.50
Brett Quigley	66	76	69	72	283	69,232.50
Rory Sabbatini	70	71	72	70	283	69,232.50
Stuart Appleby	66	74	71	73	284	43,477.50
Luke Donald	75	67	72	70	284	43,477.50
Davis Love	74	67	74	69	284	43,477.50
Kevin Stadler	67	72	71	74	284	43,477.50
Craig Barlow	66	71	75	73	285	33,186.43
Chad Campbell	72	66	74	73	285	33,186.43
Stewart Cink	75	68	71	71	285	33,186.43
J.B. Holmes	68	71	76	70	285	33,186.43
Shigeki Maruyama	72	65	75	73	285	33,186.43
Troy Matteson	71	68	72	74	285	33,186.43
Robert Garrigus	72	71	73	69	285	33,186.42
Ben Curtis	71	71	73	71	286	25,691.25
Mathew Goggin	73	66	74	73	286	25,691.25
Ryan Palmer	76	62	75	73	286	25,691.25
D.A. Points	68	72	71	75	286	25,691.25
Charles Howell	69	72	72	74	287	21,420
Ryuji Imada	66	72	76	73	287	21,420
Pat Perez	75	67	71	74	287	21,420
Vance Veazey	73	68	70	76	287	21,420
Tommy Armour	72	70	71	75	288	16,354
James Driscoll	71	71	73	73	288	16,354
Frank Lickliter	72	67	72	77	288	16,354
John Mallinger	72	71	71	74	288	16,354
Carl Pettersson	75	67	76	70	288	16,354
Patrick Sheehan	70	73	75	70	288	16,354
Matt Hansen	75	66	73	75	289	12,356.58
Zach Johnson	71	68	77	73	289	12,356.57
Hank Kuehne	71	69	76	73	289	12,356.57
J.L. Lewis	76	67	75	71	289	12,356.57
Ted Purdy	71	70	76	72	289	12,356.57
Vaughn Taylor	74	69	73	73	289	12,356.57
Nick Watney	66	74	72	77	289	12,356.57
Daniel Chopra	71	66	77	76	290	11,322
Brent Geiberger	72	71	75	72	290	11,322
Thomas Levet	65	73	77	75	290	11,322
Scott McCarron	74	69	73	74	290	11,322
Joey Sindelar	67	76	71	76	290	11,322
Hidemichi Tanaka	74	68	74	74	290	11,322
Bubba Watson	72	70	69	79	290	11,322
Fred Couples	74	66	80	71	291	10,608
John Daly	69	71	74	77	291	10,608
Brian Davis	68	73	75	75	291	10,608

	SCORES				TOTAL	MONEY
Daisuke Maruyama	68	75	75	73	291	10,608
Billy Mayfair	67	75	76	73	291	10,608
Chris Smith	75	68	74	74	291	10,608
Roger Tambellini	70	73	72	76	291	10,608
Shane Bertsch	67	76	70	79	292	9,945
Jonathan Byrd	67	75	72	78	292	9,945
Marco Dawson	72	68	75	77	292	9,945
Steve Lowery	67	69	76	80	292	9,945
Kevin Sutherland	75	68	74	75	292	9,945
Bob Tway	70	72	75	75	292	9,945
Chris Couch	67	74	73	79	293	9,486
Bubba Dickerson	76	66	73	78	293	9,486
Chris Riley	74	69	75	75	293	9,486
Woody Austin	69	71	75	79	294	9,231
Aaron Baddeley	73	69	75	77	294	9,231
Nicholas Thompson	67	75	78	76	296	9,078
Chris Starkjohann	72	71	83	73	299	8,976

FBR Open

TPC of Scottsdale, Scottsdale, Arizona
Par 35-36–71; 7,216 yards

February 2-5
purse, $5,200,000

	SCORES				TOTAL	MONEY
J.B. Holmes	68	64	65	66	263	$936,000
J.J. Henry	67	61	70	72	270	312,000
Steve Lowery	65	68	70	67	270	312,000
Ryan Palmer	68	66	64	72	270	312,000
Scott Verplank	69	66	67	68	270	312,000
Camilo Villegas	68	67	66	69	270	312,000
Jonathan Byrd	70	65	68	68	271	162,066.67
Phil Mickelson	69	66	70	66	271	162,066.67
Justin Leonard	69	66	65	71	271	162,066.66
Arron Oberholser	67	69	69	67	272	135,200
Dean Wilson	69	66	66	71	272	135,200
Henrik Bjornstad	67	69	68	69	273	109,200
Joe Ogilvie	67	70	67	69	273	109,200
Kenny Perry	72	65	67	69	273	109,200
Stewart Cink	69	69	68	68	274	85,800
Chris DiMarco	69	70	68	67	274	85,800
Scott Piercy	68	69	68	69	274	85,800
John Rollins	68	71	68	67	274	85,800
David Toms	68	66	66	75	275	72,800
Vijay Singh	71	68	69	68	276	54,228.58
Ben Curtis	69	71	68	68	276	54,228.57
Lucas Glover	67	71	67	71	276	54,228.57
Trevor Immelman	69	69	69	69	276	54,228.57
Geoff Ogilvy	67	72	67	70	276	54,228.57
Rory Sabbatini	69	69	64	74	276	54,228.57
Jerry Smith	66	71	68	71	276	54,228.57
Daniel Chopra	73	65	70	69	277	36,140
Brian Davis	69	68	69	71	277	36,140
Carlos Franco	70	70	69	68	277	36,140
Tim Herron	69	68	74	66	277	36,140
Tom Pernice, Jr.	69	70	65	73	277	36,140
Kirk Triplett	67	69	68	73	277	36,140
Brian Gay	69	71	68	70	278	26,891.43

	SCORES				TOTAL	MONEY
Nathan Green	69	70	69	70	278	26,891.43
Fredrik Jacobson	70	68	71	69	278	26,891.43
Jesper Parnevik	70	69	67	72	278	26,891.43
Justin Rose	69	68	71	70	278	26,891.43
Jeff Sluman	68	67	74	69	278	26,891.43
Thomas Levet	67	72	66	73	278	26,891.42
Olin Browne	70	67	69	73	279	17,752.80
Mark Calcavecchia	67	67	73	72	279	17,752.80
James Driscoll	66	72	66	75	279	17,752.80
Brent Geiberger	66	73	68	72	279	17,752.80
Charles Howell	70	68	71	70	279	17,752.80
Kent Jones	71	69	69	70	279	17,752.80
J.L. Lewis	71	67	70	71	279	17,752.80
Ryan Moore	71	65	72	71	279	17,752.80
Rod Pampling	68	73	69	69	279	17,752.80
Vaughn Taylor	70	69	71	69	279	17,752.80
Chris Couch	71	69	68	72	280	12,792
Bernhard Langer	71	68	69	72	280	12,792
John Senden	69	72	68	71	280	12,792
Alex Cejka	65	73	72	71	281	12,168
Brett Quigley	69	72	69	71	281	12,168
Robert Allenby	70	67	73	72	282	11,804
Paul Azinger	71	69	71	71	282	11,804
Scott McCarron	70	68	72	72	282	11,804
Paul Stankowski	67	66	76	73	282	11,804
Steve Flesch	71	68	72	72	283	11,336
Shigeki Maruyama	70	71	74	68	283	11,336
Heath Slocum	69	68	76	70	283	11,336
Nicholas Thompson	71	70	70	72	283	11,336
D.J. Trahan	70	69	72	72	283	11,336
Harrison Frazar	69	70	72	73	284	10,920
Hidemichi Tanaka	69	70	74	71	284	10,920
Bob Tway	70	71	71	72	284	10,920
Andrew Magee	67	73	75	70	285	10,712
Bo Van Pelt	66	73	74	73	286	10,608
Jeff Maggert	71	67	74	76	288	10,504
Jeff Brehaut	69	68	81	71	289	10,348
Chad Campbell	72	69	79	69	289	10,348

AT&T Pebble Beach National Pro-Am

Pebble Beach GL: Par 36-36–72; 6,816 yards
Poppy Hills GC: Par 36-36–72; 6,833 yards
Spyglass Hill GC: Par 36-36–72; 6,858 yards
Pebble Beach, California

February 9-12
purse, $5,400,000

	SCORES				TOTAL	MONEY
Arron Oberholser	65	68	66	72	271	$972,000
Rory Sabbatini	69	69	68	70	276	583,200
Jonathan Byrd	69	65	74	69	277	313,200
Mike Weir	63	67	69	78	277	313,200
Craig Barlow	69	68	72	69	278	205,200
Daniel Chopra	71	67	69	71	278	205,200
Brian Davis	66	72	68	73	279	157,140
Luke Donald	62	72	71	74	279	157,140
Tom Lehman	72	65	72	70	279	157,140
Vijay Singh	68	71	72	68	279	157,140

		SCORES			TOTAL	MONEY
Nick Watney	65	71	70	73	279	157,140
Tim Clark	66	71	70	73	280	118,800
Paul McGinley	71	68	71	70	280	118,800
Michael Allen	65	71	77	68	281	81,120
Chris DiMarco	68	69	73	71	281	81,120
J.L. Lewis	67	74	70	70	281	81,120
Hunter Mahan	68	73	67	73	281	81,120
Joe Ogilvie	70	71	69	71	281	81,120
Jose Maria Olazabal	71	67	72	71	281	81,120
Pat Perez	69	71	70	71	281	81,120
Steve Stricker	69	71	73	68	281	81,120
Bo Van Pelt	67	71	71	72	281	81,120
Briny Baird	70	71	72	69	282	49,680
Jason Bohn	71	69	72	70	282	49,680
Ryan Palmer	69	71	68	74	282	49,680
John Senden	72	69	68	73	282	49,680
Steve Flesch	69	72	71	71	283	37,530
Jim Furyk	68	71	74	70	283	37,530
Will MacKenzie	70	69	70	74	283	37,530
Troy Matteson	68	73	70	72	283	37,530
Duffy Waldorf	69	73	70	71	283	37,530
Mark Wilson	68	68	71	76	283	37,530
Alex Aragon	68	69	73	74	284	29,160
Shane Bertsch	72	70	70	72	284	29,160
Davis Love	69	67	75	73	284	29,160
Jerry Smith	69	68	73	74	284	29,160
Vance Veazey	71	69	71	73	284	29,160
Fredrik Jacobson	67	67	74	77	285	23,760
Brendan Jones	67	71	74	73	285	23,760
Parker McLachlin	71	69	71	74	285	23,760
Phil Mickelson	67	74	67	77	285	23,760
Brian Bateman	68	73	72	73	286	16,258.91
Mark Brooks	67	75	71	73	286	16,258.91
Robert Garrigus	68	69	74	75	286	16,258.91
Jason Gore	70	73	70	73	286	16,258.91
Lee Janzen	69	73	66	78	286	16,258.91
Steve Lowery	70	74	67	75	286	16,258.91
Jeff Maggert	71	69	72	74	286	16,258.91
Jon Mills	71	67	72	76	286	16,258.91
Craig Stadler	68	74	69	75	286	16,258.91
Darron Stiles	66	71	73	76	286	16,258.91
Charles Warren	67	75	71	73	286	16,258.90
John Cook	67	70	73	77	287	12,564
Harrison Frazar	67	72	67	81	287	12,564
Jay Williamson	69	73	70	75	287	12,564
Cameron Beckman	69	70	74	75	288	12,150
Bob May	71	67	74	76	288	12,150
Jeff Sluman	71	67	73	77	288	12,150
Paul Stankowski	69	75	68	76	288	12,150
Billy Andrade	70	73	70	76	289	11,718
Charles Howell	68	76	69	76	289	11,718
Peter Jacobsen	70	69	73	77	289	11,718
Dean Wilson	68	70	72	79	289	11,718
Charley Hoffman	68	70	74	78	290	11,394
Brett Wetterich	71	73	69	77	290	11,394
Bubba Dickerson	73	69	71	78	291	11,178
Brad Faxon	68	71	74	78	291	11,178

Nissan Open

Riviera Country Club, Pacific Palisades, California
Par 35-36–71; 6,987 yards

February 16-19
purse, $5,100,000

	SCORES				TOTAL	MONEY
Rory Sabbatini	67	65	67	72	271	$918,000
Adam Scott	68	71	69	64	272	550,800
Craig Barlow	67	69	67	70	273	346,800
Fred Couples	66	72	65	71	274	244,800
John Rollins	70	71	64	70	275	193,800
Lee Westwood	71	66	70	68	275	193,800
Trevor Immelman	67	70	67	72	276	153,637.50
Tom Lehman	67	70	70	69	276	153,637.50
Carl Pettersson	70	70	68	68	276	153,637.50
Dean Wilson	64	73	69	70	276	153,637.50
Bo Van Pelt	70	71	67	69	277	127,500
Luke Donald	69	70	71	68	278	93,985.72
Billy Mayfair	66	73	70	69	278	93,985.72
Tom Pernice, Jr.	69	73	68	68	278	93,985.72
Tim Clark	70	67	67	74	278	93,985.71
Robert Damron	72	70	67	69	278	93,985.71
Bob Estes	66	71	69	72	278	93,985.71
Jim Furyk	69	72	65	72	278	93,985.71
Harrison Frazar	67	74	71	67	279	64,005
Geoff Ogilvy	72	71	66	70	279	64,005
Paul Stankowski	70	68	71	70	279	64,005
Nick Watney	68	70	69	72	279	64,005
Jeff Brehaut	68	73	70	69	280	42,985.72
Bart Bryant	71	71	69	69	280	42,985.72
J.J. Henry	71	69	72	68	280	42,985.72
Ernie Els	70	72	71	67	280	42,985.71
Brad Faxon	69	71	68	72	280	42,985.71
Brian Gay	71	67	71	71	280	42,985.71
Corey Pavin	67	73	68	72	280	42,985.71
K.J. Choi	69	69	70	73	281	30,982.50
Steve Flesch	71	71	67	72	281	30,982.50
Brandt Jobe	68	71	71	71	281	30,982.50
Zach Johnson	71	71	66	73	281	30,982.50
Shaun Micheel	70	71	73	67	281	30,982.50
Kevin Sutherland	68	70	71	72	281	30,982.50
Mark Brooks	72	67	67	76	282	25,075
Chad Campbell	67	72	69	74	282	25,075
Tim Petrovic	70	72	72	68	282	25,075
Olin Browne	68	73	69	73	283	20,400
Yasuharu Imano	70	70	71	72	283	20,400
Greg Owen	69	71	70	73	283	20,400
Justin Rose	64	74	70	75	283	20,400
Jimmy Walker	71	71	72	69	283	20,400
Mike Weir	71	72	70	70	283	20,400
Angel Cabrera	72	71	70	71	284	14,586
Stewart Cink	71	71	70	72	284	14,586
David Duval	68	72	71	73	284	14,586
Thomas Levet	68	68	77	71	284	14,586
Rod Pampling	67	74	70	73	284	14,586
Charles Warren	70	73	70	71	284	14,586
Stuart Appleby	68	73	71	73	285	11,934
Aaron Baddeley	72	71	72	70	285	11,934
Bill Haas	71	71	74	69	285	11,934
J.B. Holmes	71	72	69	73	285	11,934

	SCORES				TOTAL	MONEY
Charles Howell	68	73	71	73	285	11,934
Paul McGinley	70	70	71	74	285	11,934
Scott Verplank	69	73	73	70	285	11,934
Ryan Palmer	71	72	71	72	286	11,322
Tag Ridings	69	72	73	72	286	11,322
Jason Schultz	67	70	76	73	286	11,322
Briny Baird	74	68	73	72	287	10,812
J.L. Lewis	70	72	72	73	287	10,812
Peter Lonard	68	74	72	73	287	10,812
Len Mattiace	71	71	74	71	287	10,812
Sean O'Hair	70	69	71	77	287	10,812
Ted Purdy	72	69	75	71	287	10,812
Bob Tway	72	69	72	74	287	10,812
Doug Barron	69	74	69	76	288	10,251
Rich Beem	75	68	69	76	288	10,251
Steve Elkington	72	71	73	72	288	10,251
Mark Hensby	74	67	69	78	288	10,251
Wes Short, Jr.	71	71	70	77	289	9,996
Joe Durant	70	70	77	73	290	9,843
Joey Sindelar	68	74	74	74	290	9,843
Jesper Parnevik	66	77	74	74	291	9,690
Scott Miller	71	72	74	75	292	9,588
Ben Curtis	74	69	74	76	293	9,384
Pat Perez	68	74	76	75	293	9,384
Henrik Stenson	71	67	80	75	293	9,384
Chris Riley	70	72	77	75	294	9,180
D.J. Trahan	70	73	79	74	296	9,078

WGC - Accenture Match Play Championship

La Costa Resort and Spa, Carlsbad, California
Par 36-36–72; 7,247 yards

February 22-26
purse, $7,500,000

FIRST ROUND

Adam Scott defeated Lucas Glover, 2 and 1.
Tom Lehman defeated Stuart Appleby, 3 and 2.
David Toms defeated Ian Poulter, 1 up.
Jose Maria Olazabal defeated Brandt Jobe, 3 and 2.
Henrik Stenson defeated Paul Casey, 1 up.
Chad Campbell defeated Tim Herron, 4 and 2.
Tiger Woods defeated Stephen Ames, 9 and 8.
Robert Allenby defeated K.J. Choi, 3 and 2.
David Howell defeated Steve Elkington, 1 up.
Scott Verplank defeated Lee Westwood, 1 up.
Phil Mickelson defeated Charles Howell, 2 up.
John Daly defeated Bart Bryant, 4 and 2.
Geoff Ogilvy defeated Michael Campbell, 1 up.
Nick O'Hern defeated Fred Funk, 5 and 3.
Bernhard Langer defeated Ernie Els, 1 up.
Mike Weir defeated Stewart Cink, 4 and 3.
Carl Pettersson defeated Kenny Perry, 1 up.
Davis Love defeated Mark Hensby, 2 and 1.
Chris DiMarco defeated Mark Calcavecchia, 2 and 1.
Arron Oberholser defeated Tim Clark, 1 up.
Angel Cabrera defeated Peter Lonard, 1 up.
Padraig Harrington defeated Rod Pampling, 4 and 2.
Vijay Singh defeated Graeme McDowell, 5 and 4.

Miguel Angel Jimenez defeated Rory Sabbatini, 2 and 1.
Colin Montgomerie defeated Niclas Fasth, 1 up.
Shingo Katayama defeated Paul McGinley, 2 and 1.
Zach Johnson defeated Jim Furyk, 1 up.
Sean O'Hair defeated Fred Couples, 1 up.
Luke Donald defeated Richard Green, 2 and 1.
Shigeki Maruyama defeated Darren Clarke, 4 and 3.
Retief Goosen defeated Paul Broadhurst, 5 and 4.
Ben Crane defeated Justin Leonard, 4 and 3.

(Each losing player received $35,000.)

SECOND ROUND

Woods defeated Allenby, 1 up.
Chad Campbell defeated Stenson, 1 up.
Toms defeated Olazabal, 2 and 1.
Lehman defeated Scott, 1 up.
Weir defeated Langer, 20 holes.
Ogilvy defeated O'Hern, 21 holes.
Mickelson defeated Daly, 2 and 1.
Howell defeated Verplank, 3 and 2.
Singh defeated Jimenez, 2 and 1.
Harrington defeated Cabrera, 19 holes.
DiMarco defeated Oberholser, 6 and 5.
Love defeated Pettersson, 1 up.
Goosen defeated Crane, 2 and 1.
Donald defeated Maruyama, 4 and 3.
Johnson defeated O'Hair, 1 up.
Katayama defeated Montgomerie, 3 and 2.

(Each losing player received $85,000.)

THIRD ROUND

Lehman defeated Toms, 4 and 3.
Chad Campbell defeated Woods, 1 up.
Howell defeated Mickelson, 3 and 1.
Ogilvy defeated Weir, 21 holes.
Love defeated DiMarco, 3 and 2.
Harrington defeated Singh, 19 holes.
Johnson defeated Katayama, 4 and 3.
Goosen defeated Donald, 1 up.

(Each losing player received $125,000.)

QUARTER-FINALS

Lehman defeated Chad Campbell, 21 holes.
Ogilvy defeated Howell, 19 holes.
Love defeated Harrington, 1 up.
Johnson defeated Goosen, 3 and 2.

(Each losing player received $240,000.)

SEMI-FINALS

Ogilvy defeated Lehman, 4 and 3.
Love defeated Johnson, 4 and 2.

PLAYOFF FOR THIRD-FOURTH PLACE

Johnson defeated Lehman, 1 up.

(Johnson earned $560,000; Lehman earned $450,000.)

FINAL

Ogilvy defeated Love, 3 and 2.

(Ogilvy earned $1,300,000; Love earned $750,000.)

Chrysler Classic of Tucson

Omni Tucson National Golf Resort, Tucson, Arizona
Par 36-36–72; 7,193 yards

February 23-26
purse, $3,000,000

	SCORES				TOTAL	MONEY
Kirk Triplett	68	71	64	63	266	$540,000
Jerry Kelly	66	68	68	65	267	324,000
Heath Slocum	67	69	65	68	269	156,000
Duffy Waldorf	66	66	65	72	269	156,000
Bubba Watson	67	67	65	70	269	156,000
David Branshaw	71	65	66	68	270	108,000
Doug Barron	66	70	67	68	271	96,750
Jason Gore	68	66	69	68	271	96,750
Cameron Beckman	72	64	70	66	272	75,000
Gabriel Hjertstedt	66	71	65	70	272	75,000
Charley Hoffman	69	68	69	66	272	75,000
Bo Van Pelt	71	69	65	67	272	75,000
Mark Wilson	64	69	67	72	272	75,000
Jason Allred	67	68	68	70	273	52,500
Ryuji Imada	70	68	69	66	273	52,500
Ted Purdy	71	68	65	69	273	52,500
Bob Tway	68	66	73	66	273	52,500
Aaron Baddeley	69	69	70	66	274	37,800
John Cook	68	69	65	72	274	37,800
Bubba Dickerson	68	68	69	69	274	37,800
Bob Estes	67	70	68	69	274	37,800
Brendan Jones	68	70	69	67	274	37,800
Justin Rose	70	68	72	64	274	37,800
Eric Axley	70	68	65	72	275	24,300
Carlos Franco	67	69	73	66	275	24,300
Brian Henninger	68	67	72	68	275	24,300
Mike Sposa	68	69	70	68	275	24,300
Vance Veazey	69	70	68	68	275	24,300
Brett Wetterich	68	69	69	69	275	24,300
Briny Baird	69	70	67	70	276	16,363.64
Kris Cox	69	67	72	68	276	16,363.64
David Edwards	69	68	68	71	276	16,363.64
Paul Goydos	68	70	69	69	276	16,363.64
Steve Jones	69	70	69	68	276	16,363.64
Steve Stricker	69	69	69	69	276	16,363.64
Don Yrene	69	70	67	70	276	16,363.64
Marco Dawson	70	67	67	72	276	16,363.63
Danny Ellis	68	69	68	71	276	16,363.63
Brian Gay	70	68	72	66	276	16,363.63
Bob May	71	69	71	65	276	16,363.63

	SCORES				TOTAL	MONEY
Jeff Gove	70	70	69	68	277	10,215
Scott Gutschewski	67	67	71	72	277	10,215
Trevor Immelman	68	70	69	70	277	10,215
Hunter Mahan	71	68	68	70	277	10,215
Daisuke Maruyama	68	71	68	70	277	10,215
Chris Riley	68	68	67	74	277	10,215
Jeff Sluman	70	68	68	71	277	10,215
Camilo Villegas	70	68	67	72	277	10,215
Gavin Coles	67	70	72	69	278	7,680
Nathan Green	67	70	66	75	278	7,680
Jeff Brehaut	71	67	71	70	279	6,946.67
Mark Brooks	71	64	68	76	279	6,946.67
Todd Fischer	71	67	68	73	279	6,946.67
Billy Mayfair	68	70	72	69	279	6,946.67
John Rollins	68	70	71	70	279	6,946.67
Kevin Sutherland	70	70	69	70	279	6,946.67
Ricky Barnes	67	72	72	68	279	6,946.66
Henrik Bjornstad	71	69	70	69	279	6,946.66
Mathias Gronberg	68	69	74	68	279	6,946.66
Michael Allen	69	68	69	74	280	6,450
Tom Byrum	71	69	73	67	280	6,450
Bill Haas	68	72	70	70	280	6,450
Jeff Overton	71	67	69	73	280	6,450
Jin Park	68	69	75	68	280	6,450
Tag Ridings	69	69	71	71	280	6,450
Alex Cejka	67	68	76	71	282	6,210
Jonathan Kaye	70	69	71	72	282	6,210
Matt Hansen	67	70	74	72	283	6,120
David Berganio, Jr.	72	68	74	70	284	6,060
Ian Leggatt	70	66	74	75	285	6,000
John Engler, Jr.	69	70	76	71	286	5,910
Wes Short, Jr.	73	67	72	74	286	5,910

Ford Championship at Doral

Doral Golf Resort & Spa, Blue Course, Miami, Florida
Par 36-36–72; 7,266 yards

March 2-5
purse, $5,500,000

	SCORES				TOTAL	MONEY
Tiger Woods	64	67	68	69	268	$990,000
David Toms	66	66	70	67	269	484,000
Camilo Villegas	65	66	71	67	269	484,000
Fredrik Jacobson	70	67	68	68	273	264,000
Lucas Glover	67	67	71	69	274	209,000
Tag Ridings	68	69	66	71	274	209,000
Rich Beem	65	67	69	74	275	160,050
Ernie Els	72	65	69	69	275	160,050
Carlos Franco	69	67	70	69	275	160,050
Jerry Kelly	69	70	68	68	275	160,050
Jeff Sluman	69	68	72	66	275	160,050
David Howell	69	70	69	68	276	115,500
Davis Love	68	69	67	72	276	115,500
Phil Mickelson	65	66	72	73	276	115,500
Harrison Frazar	69	67	71	70	277	88,000
Retief Goosen	70	69	72	66	277	88,000
Zach Johnson	69	65	71	72	277	88,000
Vijay Singh	67	73	70	67	277	88,000

	SCORES				TOTAL	MONEY
Scott Verplank	66	65	74	72	277	88,000
Stephen Ames	69	66	74	69	278	59,583.34
John Senden	70	68	72	68	278	59,583.34
Daniel Chopra	66	67	68	77	278	59,583.33
Greg Owen	70	68	68	72	278	59,583.33
Tom Pernice, Jr.	69	68	72	69	278	59,583.33
Mark Wilson	65	67	75	71	278	59,583.33
Shane Bertsch	68	67	74	70	279	37,430.56
Ken Duke	69	69	71	70	279	37,430.56
Kent Jones	71	67	71	70	279	37,430.56
Jesper Parnevik	72	66	73	68	279	37,430.56
Brett Quigley	70	70	69	70	279	37,430.56
Padraig Harrington	68	70	69	72	279	37,430.55
Lee Janzen	72	65	70	72	279	37,430.55
Shaun Micheel	69	67	70	73	279	37,430.55
Dean Wilson	66	68	69	76	279	37,430.55
Arjun Atwal	68	69	74	69	280	25,967.86
Tim Clark	68	67	74	71	280	25,967.86
Billy Mayfair	68	71	74	67	280	25,967.86
Kevin Na	69	67	72	72	280	25,967.86
Paul Stankowski	70	69	72	69	280	25,967.86
Chad Campbell	68	66	71	75	280	25,967.85
Chris DiMarco	71	68	68	73	280	25,967.85
Woody Austin	69	67	71	74	281	18,700
Briny Baird	68	67	72	74	281	18,700
Craig Barlow	68	70	72	71	281	18,700
Fred Funk	69	70	72	70	281	18,700
Kenny Perry	69	70	70	72	281	18,700
Charles Warren	69	66	73	73	281	18,700
Brian Gay	69	71	74	68	282	13,432.23
Joe Ogilvie	68	72	72	70	282	13,432.23
James Driscoll	72	67	72	71	282	13,432.22
Troy Matteson	70	64	72	76	282	13,432.22
Rocco Mediate	68	70	71	73	282	13,432.22
Sean O'Hair	70	69	70	73	282	13,432.22
Ryan Palmer	65	70	74	73	282	13,432.22
Joey Snyder	67	70	71	74	282	13,432.22
Bo Van Pelt	69	68	71	74	282	13,432.22
Angel Cabrera	70	68	72	73	283	12,375
Sergio Garcia	69	69	71	74	283	12,375
Wes Short, Jr.	73	67	72	72	284	11,990
Joey Sindelar	72	68	75	69	284	11,990
Duffy Waldorf	68	70	74	72	284	11,990
Jimmy Walker	69	70	77	68	284	11,990
Bubba Watson	69	70	68	77	284	11,990
Jeff Brehaut	70	67	72	76	285	11,605
Trevor Immelman	68	71	70	76	285	11,605
Todd Fischer	70	70	71	75	286	11,330
Todd Hamilton	69	70	76	71	286	11,330
Heath Slocum	71	69	70	76	286	11,330
Jason Bohn	67	70	80	70	287	11,000
Robert Damron	69	70	74	74	287	11,000
Justin Leonard	68	69	75	75	287	11,000
Ryuji Imada	72	68	75	73	288	10,780

Honda Classic

The Country Club at Mirasol, Sunrise Course,
Palm Beach Gardens, Florida
Par 36-36–72; 7,157 yards

March 9-12
purse, $5,500,000

	SCORES				TOTAL	MONEY
Luke Donald	72	67	68	69	276	$990,000
Geoff Ogilvy	67	71	71	69	278	594,000
Billy Mayfair	68	67	72	72	279	319,000
David Toms	67	67	76	69	279	319,000
Tom Pernice, Jr.	74	71	67	68	280	220,000
Dudley Hart	69	72	71	69	281	198,000
Stephen Ames	70	69	75	68	282	171,416.67
Frank Lickliter	71	70	70	71	282	171,416.67
Jeff Gove	68	71	69	74	282	171,416.66
Mathew Goggin	71	75	65	72	283	143,000
D.A. Points	73	71	71	68	283	143,000
Pat Perez	72	71	68	73	284	126,500
Greg Owen	71	71	72	71	285	106,333.34
Daniel Chopra	73	65	71	76	285	106,333.33
Ryuji Imada	67	73	73	72	285	106,333.33
Briny Baird	72	70	73	71	286	77,157.15
Henrik Bjornstad	71	70	75	70	286	77,157.15
Paul Azinger	72	67	74	73	286	77,157.14
Marco Dawson	74	66	73	73	286	77,157.14
Mathias Gronberg	67	71	72	76	286	77,157.14
Padraig Harrington	71	67	74	74	286	77,157.14
Bernhard Langer	74	71	70	71	286	77,157.14
Shaun Micheel	69	76	75	67	287	50,600
Kevin Na	73	74	69	71	287	50,600
Vance Veazey	76	68	70	73	287	50,600
Dean Wilson	71	71	72	73	287	50,600
John Cook	69	74	72	73	288	39,875
Bubba Dickerson	76	71	71	70	288	39,875
Carlos Franco	72	72	76	68	288	39,875
Stephen Leaney	73	72	69	74	288	39,875
Robert Allenby	75	68	71	75	289	29,260
Craig Barlow	74	68	71	76	289	29,260
Jason Caron	75	70	75	69	289	29,260
Kris Cox	73	69	76	71	289	29,260
Tim Herron	72	75	69	73	289	29,260
Charley Hoffman	72	71	74	72	289	29,260
Jesper Parnevik	71	72	75	71	289	29,260
Jerry Smith	73	70	71	75	289	29,260
Camilo Villegas	73	74	68	74	289	29,260
Jimmy Walker	72	73	71	73	289	29,260
Eric Axley	75	71	74	70	290	19,250
Mark Calcavecchia	76	69	69	76	290	19,250
Todd Fischer	72	73	72	73	290	19,250
Brian Gay	68	71	75	76	290	19,250
Scott Hend	69	70	77	74	290	19,250
Thomas Levet	74	68	78	70	290	19,250
Ian Poulter	75	72	70	73	290	19,250
Kent Jones	72	74	74	71	291	14,685
Shigeki Maruyama	71	69	76	75	291	14,685
Fred Couples	72	72	75	73	292	13,266
Danny Ellis	72	72	72	76	292	13,266
David McKenzie	74	72	70	76	292	13,266
John Rollins	72	70	76	74	292	13,266

	SCORES	TOTAL	MONEY
Paul Stankowski	70 76 71 75	292	13,266
Charles Howell	74 73 69 77	293	12,320
Hank Kuehne	70 75 72 76	293	12,320
Davis Love	70 73 76 74	293	12,320
Jon Mills	73 74 68 78	293	12,320
Carl Pettersson	76 68 73 76	293	12,320
Nicholas Thompson	73 70 71 79	293	12,320
Lee Westwood	73 66 77 77	293	12,320
Hunter Mahan	71 73 74 76	294	11,770
Daisuke Maruyama	70 70 82 72	294	11,770
Jason Schultz	68 71 75 80	294	11,770
Alex Aragon	73 74 75 73	295	11,275
Brian Davis	76 71 77 71	295	11,275
Joe Durant	73 73 77 72	295	11,275
John Huston	70 75 77 73	295	11,275
Ryan Moore	73 73 70 79	295	11,275
Nick Watney	72 72 75 76	295	11,275
Troy Matteson	71 76 72 77	296	10,890
Alex Cejka	72 71 75 79	297	10,780
Mark O'Meara	73 72 71 82	298	10,670

Bay Hill Invitational

Bay Hill Club & Lodge, Orlando, Florida
Par 36-36–72; 7,207 yards

March 16-19
purse, $5,500,000

	SCORES	TOTAL	MONEY
Rod Pampling	70 65 67 72	274	$990,000
Greg Owen	70 69 67 69	275	594,000
Darren Clarke	73 70 63 70	276	374,000
Robert Allenby	68 67 73 69	277	264,000
Ted Purdy	69 71 71 67	278	209,000
Lee Westwood	68 71 72 67	278	209,000
Vijay Singh	71 71 68 69	279	184,250
Tom Pernice, Jr.	68 73 68 71	280	165,000
Justin Rose	70 70 71 69	280	165,000
Fred Funk	69 75 68 69	281	126,500
Sergio Garcia	68 69 71 73	281	126,500
Joey Sindelar	70 73 69 69	281	126,500
Scott Verplank	72 69 70 70	281	126,500
Dean Wilson	66 70 73 72	281	126,500
Angel Cabrera	70 70 69 73	282	96,250
Carl Pettersson	74 69 68 71	282	96,250
Chad Campbell	67 71 73 72	283	82,500
Lucas Glover	67 67 72 77	283	82,500
Mike Weir	69 71 71 72	283	82,500
Charles Warren	71 72 71 70	284	59,583.34
Tiger Woods	70 71 71 72	284	59,583.34
Bart Bryant	66 71 73 74	284	59,583.33
Ben Curtis	67 73 68 76	284	59,583.33
Jim Furyk	72 69 70 73	284	59,583.33
Corey Pavin	69 69 71 75	284	59,583.33
Jason Bohn	71 68 68 78	285	38,225
Brian Gay	70 71 73 71	285	38,225
Jason Gore	67 73 73 72	285	38,225
Brandt Jobe	72 70 72 71	285	38,225
Geoff Ogilvy	70 68 70 77	285	38,225

	SCORES				TOTAL	MONEY
Jose Maria Olazabal	74	70	70	71	285	38,225
Kirk Triplett	73	70	68	74	285	38,225
Bo Van Pelt	72	68	71	74	285	38,225
Carlos Franco	68	74	74	70	286	26,033.34
Joe Ogilvie	71	72	73	70	286	26,033.34
Bubba Watson	69	75	72	70	286	26,033.34
Henrik Bjornstad	71	73	70	72	286	26,033.33
K.J. Choi	71	73	72	70	286	26,033.33
Harrison Frazar	72	66	74	74	286	26,033.33
John Huston	70	72	73	71	286	26,033.33
Pat Perez	73	72	71	70	286	26,033.33
Mark Wilson	69	70	72	75	286	26,033.33
Woody Austin	70	74	73	70	287	18,150
Bubba Dickerson	69	74	68	76	287	18,150
Billy Hurley	73	70	73	71	287	18,150
Zach Johnson	72	72	73	70	287	18,150
Bernhard Langer	70	71	73	73	287	18,150
J.B. Holmes	73	72	73	70	288	13,823.34
Nick Watney	75	70	74	69	288	13,823.34
Retief Goosen	69	73	70	76	288	13,823.33
J.J. Henry	73	71	72	72	288	13,823.33
Charles Howell	72	72	73	71	288	13,823.33
Steve Jones	71	73	68	76	288	13,823.33
Stuart Appleby	71	68	72	78	289	12,540
Ernie Els	67	73	74	75	289	12,540
Dan Forsman	71	73	67	78	289	12,540
Tom Lehman	70	72	75	72	289	12,540
Jeff Maggert	73	70	71	75	289	12,540
Daniel Chopra	71	72	69	78	290	12,100
Hunter Mahan	72	72	71	75	290	12,100
Camilo Villegas	71	69	73	77	290	12,100
Shane Bertsch	72	72	70	77	291	11,660
Patrick Damron	75	70	76	70	291	11,660
Todd Hamilton	72	73	74	72	291	11,660
Heath Slocum	72	73	70	76	291	11,660
Jeff Sluman	75	68	77	71	291	11,660
Kevin Stadler	70	72	70	80	292	11,330
David Branshaw	70	72	73	78	293	11,165
Duffy Waldorf	75	69	77	72	293	11,165
Nathan Green	74	71	73	77	295	11,000
Mark Hensby	73	70	73	82	298	10,890
Tim Petrovic	73	72	73	82	300	10,780

The Players Championship

TPC at Sawgrass, Stadium Course,
Ponte Vedra Beach, Florida
Par 36-36–72; 7,093 yards

March 23-26
purse, $8,000,000

	SCORES				TOTAL	MONEY
Stephen Ames	71	66	70	67	274	$1,440,000
Retief Goosen	69	71	71	69	280	864,000
Pat Perez	71	72	69	71	283	384,000
Jim Furyk	65	71	75	72	283	384,000
Camilo Villegas	74	70	68	71	283	384,000
Henrik Stenson	69	71	70	73	283	384,000
Jose Maria Olazabal	68	71	74	71	284	268,000

	SCORES				TOTAL	MONEY
Ernie Els	72	70	72	71	285	208,000
Vaughn Taylor	73	71	68	73	285	208,000
Bo Van Pelt	68	71	72	74	285	208,000
John Rollins	68	71	72	74	285	208,000
Carl Pettersson	71	70	70	74	285	208,000
Vijay Singh	68	70	70	77	285	208,000
Phil Mickelson	70	73	69	74	286	148,000
Sergio Garcia	70	68	70	78	286	148,000
Brad Faxon	70	69	79	69	287	124,000
K.J. Choi	69	69	77	72	287	124,000
Charles Warren	73	71	72	71	287	124,000
Fred Funk	70	69	74	74	287	124,000
Brian Davis	70	73	73	72	288	100,000
Darren Clarke	73	70	72	73	288	100,000
Greg Owen	71	68	77	73	289	76,800
Fredrik Jacobson	69	72	74	74	289	76,800
Tiger Woods	72	69	73	75	289	76,800
Craig Parry	70	73	70	76	289	76,800
Mike Weir	71	71	68	79	289	76,800
Nick Price	72	71	74	73	290	53,250
Richard S. Johnson	72	70	75	73	290	53,250
Ian Poulter	72	68	75	75	290	53,250
Jason Bohn	71	72	72	75	290	53,250
Todd Fischer	73	68	72	77	290	53,250
James Driscoll	71	72	70	77	290	53,250
Tom Lehman	71	71	70	78	290	53,250
Tom Pernice, Jr.	70	70	71	79	290	53,250
Fred Couples	69	73	75	74	291	43,200
Ben Crane	68	74	77	73	292	40,200
Joe Durant	69	72	75	76	292	40,200
Miguel Angel Jimenez	67	74	82	70	293	32,800
David Howell	71	71	81	70	293	32,800
Tim Petrovic	73	69	80	71	293	32,800
J.B. Holmes	71	73	76	73	293	32,800
Robert Allenby	67	73	78	75	293	32,800
Lee Westwood	70	73	73	77	293	32,800
Jesper Parnevik	72	72	72	77	293	32,800
Jeff Maggert	73	69	78	74	294	22,020
J.J. Henry	71	73	77	73	294	22,020
Dudley Hart	73	70	75	76	294	22,020
Jeff Sluman	70	73	75	76	294	22,020
Peter Lonard	71	73	74	76	294	22,020
Carlos Franco	71	71	75	77	294	22,020
John Daly	70	73	74	77	294	22,020
Arron Oberholser	68	71	74	81	294	22,020
Robert Gamez	71	72	78	74	295	18,613.34
Charles Howell	71	73	76	75	295	18,613.33
Adam Scott	70	67	82	76	295	18,613.33
Steve Lowery	73	70	78	75	296	18,160
Bart Bryant	73	71	74	78	296	18,160
Joey Sindelar	71	73	80	73	297	17,600
Bernhard Langer	67	75	79	76	297	17,600
Rocco Mediate	69	74	77	77	297	17,600
Sean O'Hair	73	71	75	78	297	17,600
Zach Johnson	71	73	74	79	297	17,600
Harrison Frazar	70	74	76	78	298	16,960
Kirk Triplett	70	71	76	81	298	16,960
Steve Flesch	69	70	75	84	298	16,960
Olin Browne	69	75	76	79	299	16,480
Nathan Green	72	72	75	80	299	16,480

	SCORES				TOTAL	MONEY
Rich Beem	71	72	71	85	299	16,480
Thomas Bjorn	69	73	80	78	300	16,160
Chad Campbell	70	72	79	80	301	15,920
Shingo Katayama	70	73	77	81	301	15,920
Mark Calcavecchia	69	73	81	79	302	15,680
Woody Austin	73	69	83	79	304	15,520
Mark Hensby	71	73	79	83	306	15,360

BellSouth Classic

TPC at Sugarloaf, Duluth, Georgia
Par 36-36—72; 7,259 yards

March 30-April 2
purse, $5,300,000

	SCORES				TOTAL	MONEY
Phil Mickelson	63	65	67	65	260	$954,000
Zach Johnson	69	70	64	70	273	466,400
Jose Maria Olazabal	71	64	69	69	273	466,400
Retief Goosen	69	70	69	66	274	233,200
J.J. Henry	69	65	72	68	274	233,200
Jonathan Byrd	69	68	66	73	276	190,800
Shane Bertsch	68	69	74	66	277	165,183.34
Doug Barron	74	67	65	71	277	165,183.33
Richard Johnson	73	71	66	67	277	165,183.33
Briny Baird	72	69	68	69	278	121,900
Luke Donald	68	70	74	66	278	121,900
Steve Flesch	71	68	67	72	278	121,900
Charley Hoffman	71	72	69	66	278	121,900
Ryuji Imada	71	67	72	68	278	121,900
Todd Fischer	70	71	68	70	279	87,450
Mathias Gronberg	71	73	68	67	279	87,450
Fredrik Jacobson	70	72	68	69	279	87,450
David Toms	75	68	69	67	279	87,450
Rich Beem	69	72	68	71	280	66,515
Jason Bohn	71	70	70	69	280	66,515
Brian Gay	70	69	74	67	280	66,515
Mark Wilson	68	71	70	71	280	66,515
Will MacKenzie	69	70	71	71	281	55,120
David Branshaw	72	71	70	69	282	39,220
Stewart Cink	72	69	70	71	282	39,220
Brent Geiberger	70	70	71	71	282	39,220
Dudley Hart	70	69	73	70	282	39,220
David Howell	67	72	70	73	282	39,220
Jonathan Kaye	73	70	70	69	282	39,220
Stephen Leaney	68	75	71	68	282	39,220
Larry Mize	71	69	70	72	282	39,220
Bo Van Pelt	70	74	71	67	282	39,220
Charles Warren	65	72	72	73	282	39,220
Jeff Brehaut	69	75	71	68	283	25,638.75
Alex Cejka	71	70	68	74	283	25,638.75
Bubba Dickerson	72	72	69	70	283	25,638.75
Kevin Na	73	71	72	67	283	25,638.75
Arron Oberholser	70	72	69	72	283	25,638.75
B.J. Staten	70	69	75	69	283	25,638.75
Duffy Waldorf	72	66	74	71	283	25,638.75
Ron Whittaker	72	72	72	67	283	25,638.75
Billy Andrade	70	72	70	72	284	16,642
Jeff Gove	72	71	70	71	284	16,642

	SCORES				TOTAL	MONEY
Shingo Katayama	75	67	71	71	284	16,642
Franklin Langham	70	71	73	70	284	16,642
Frank Lickliter	74	70	70	70	284	16,642
Steve Lowery	72	71	72	69	284	16,642
Ian Poulter	66	72	74	72	284	16,642
Chris Smith	69	70	74	71	284	16,642
Brett Wetterich	67	74	72	71	284	16,642
Greg Chalmers	73	71	72	69	285	12,472.67
Steve Jones	70	73	74	68	285	12,472.67
Mike Sposa	72	71	71	71	285	12,472.67
Tjaart van der Walt	75	68	73	69	285	12,472.67
Padraig Harrington	68	71	71	75	285	12,472.66
Roger Tambellini	69	71	73	72	285	12,472.66
Gavin Coles	64	72	76	74	286	11,660
Marco Dawson	72	68	72	74	286	11,660
Davis Love	71	69	75	71	286	11,660
Scott McCarron	72	71	74	69	286	11,660
Scott Parel	66	77	74	69	286	11,660
Wes Short, Jr.	69	72	74	71	286	11,660
Hidemichi Tanaka	75	69	71	71	286	11,660
Jerry Smith	70	72	74	71	287	11,183
Phil Tataurangi	71	72	78	66	287	11,183
Joe Durant	66	73	79	70	288	10,918
Sean O'Hair	72	70	70	76	288	10,918
Jeff Overton	71	72	75	70	288	10,918
Tom Byrum	69	73	76	71	289	10,494
Tim Clark	73	69	73	74	289	10,494
Robert Garrigus	75	68	73	73	289	10,494
Greg Kraft	72	72	70	75	289	10,494
Boyd Summerhays	68	72	74	75	289	10,494
Danny Ellis	68	76	72	74	290	10,176
Matt Kuchar	68	74	72	77	291	10,017
Thomas Levet	76	68	69	78	291	10,017
Dean Wilson	70	72	75	75	292	9,858
Donnie Hammond	72	70	77	74	293	9,752
Sonny Skinner	75	69	78	73	295	9,646

Masters Tournament

Augusta National Golf Club, Augusta, Georgia
Par 36-36–72; 7,445 yards

April 6-9
purse, $7,000,000

	SCORES				TOTAL	MONEY
Phil Mickelson	70	72	70	69	281	$1,260,000
Tim Clark	70	72	72	69	283	756,000
Jose Maria Olazabal	76	71	71	66	284	315,700
Retief Goosen	70	73	72	69	284	315,700
Tiger Woods	72	71	71	70	284	315,700
Fred Couples	71	70	72	71	284	315,700
Chad Campbell	71	67	75	71	284	315,700
Angel Cabrera	73	74	70	68	285	210,000
Vijay Singh	67	74	73	71	285	210,000
Stewart Cink	72	73	71	70	286	189,000
Mike Weir	71	73	73	70	287	161,000
Miguel Angel Jimenez	72	74	69	72	287	161,000
Stephen Ames	74	70	70	73	287	161,000
Arron Oberholser	69	75	73	71	288	129,500

		SCORES			TOTAL	MONEY
Billy Mayfair	71	72	73	72	288	129,500
Geoff Ogilvy	70	75	73	71	289	112,000
Scott Verplank	74	70	74	71	289	112,000
Rod Pampling	72	73	72	72	289	112,000
Nick O'Hern	71	72	76	71	290	91,000
Stuart Appleby	71	75	73	71	290	91,000
David Howell	71	71	76	72	290	91,000
Robert Allenby	73	73	74	71	291	67,200
Davis Love	74	71	74	72	291	67,200
Mark Hensby	80	67	70	74	291	67,200
Jim Furyk	73	75	68	75	291	67,200
Darren Clarke	72	70	72	77	291	67,200
Adam Scott	72	74	75	71	292	49,700
Carl Pettersson	72	74	73	73	292	49,700
Padraig Harrington	73	70	75	74	292	49,700
Shingo Katayama	75	70	73	74	292	49,700
Ernie Els	71	71	74	76	292	49,700
Brandt Jobe	72	76	77	68	293	40,512
Thomas Bjorn	73	75	76	69	293	40,512
Zach Johnson	74	72	77	70	293	40,512
Ted Purdy	72	76	74	71	293	40,512
Rory Sabbatini	76	70	74	74	294	34,416
Tim Herron	76	71	71	76	294	34,416
Rocco Mediate	68	73	73	80	294	34,416
Justin Leonard	75	70	79	71	295	30,100
Ben Curtis	71	74	77	73	295	30,100
Jason Bohn	73	71	77	74	295	30,100
Larry Mize	75	72	77	72	296	25,900
Luke Donald	74	72	76	74	296	25,900
Rich Beem	71	73	73	79	296	25,900
Olin Browne	74	69	80	74	297	23,100
Sergio Garcia	72	74	79	73	298	21,700
Ben Crenshaw	71	72	78	79	300	20,300

Out of Final 36 Holes

Bart Bryant	76	73	149
Colin Montgomerie	74	75	149
Thomas Levet	78	71	149
Ben Crane	74	75	149
Vaughn Taylor	75	74	149
Michael Campbell	75	74	149
Ian Woosnam	77	72	149
Lee Westwood	75	75	150
Peter Lonard	76	74	150
Chris DiMarco	76	74	150
Todd Hamilton	74	76	150
David Toms	72	78	150
Joe Ogilvie	74	77	151
Lucas Glover	73	78	151
Trevor Immelman	75	76	151
Tom Lehman	76	75	151
Henrik Stenson	77	74	151
Sean O'Hair	76	76	152
Shaun Micheel	82	70	152
K.J. Choi	76	76	152
Raymond Floyd	79	73	152
Bernhard Langer	79	74	153
John Daly	74	79	153
Nick Faldo	79	74	153

	SCORES	TOTAL
Thongchai Jaidee	78 75	153
Mark O'Meara	82 72	154
Tom Watson	79 75	154
Shigeki Maruyama	79 75	154
Craig Stadler	77 78	155
Paul McGinley	78 77	155
*Brian McElhinney	80 75	155
Mark Calcavecchia	80 76	156
Fred Funk	76 81	157
*Edoardo Molinari	80 77	157
David Duval	84 75	159
*Clay Ogden	83 76	159
Fuzzy Zoeller	78 81	159
*Kevin Marsh	79 81	160
Gary Player	79 81	160
*Dillon Dougherty	82 78	160
Sandy Lyle	80 81	161
Charles Coody	89 74	163
Charles Howell	80 84	164

(Professionals who did not complete 72 holes received $5,000.)

Verizon Heritage

Harbour Town Golf Links, Hilton Head Island, South Carolina
Par 35-36–71; 6,973 yards

April 13-16
purse, $5,300,000

	SCORES				TOTAL	MONEY
Aaron Baddeley	66	67	66	70	269	$954,000
Jim Furyk	64	67	68	71	270	572,400
Billy Mayfair	65	69	68	69	271	307,400
Vaughn Taylor	63	70	72	66	271	307,400
Jerry Kelly	68	69	66	70	273	201,400
Brett Quigley	68	70	68	67	273	201,400
Tim Clark	72	65	68	69	274	170,925
Ernie Els	71	67	65	71	274	170,925
Jose Coceres	69	67	68	72	276	148,400
Brian Gay	66	67	73	70	276	148,400
Geoff Ogilvy	66	68	74	69	277	132,500
Ben Crane	67	68	72	71	278	103,880
Lucas Glover	70	68	66	74	278	103,880
Stephen Leaney	71	69	70	68	278	103,880
Corey Pavin	69	69	69	71	278	103,880
Heath Slocum	71	70	65	72	278	103,880
Arjun Atwal	67	70	71	71	279	76,850
Woody Austin	68	69	70	72	279	76,850
Frank Lickliter	71	71	69	68	279	76,850
Jeff Maggert	69	66	71	73	279	76,850
Paul Azinger	68	69	73	70	280	53,000
Bart Bryant	70	69	72	69	280	53,000
Tom Pernice, Jr.	65	69	72	74	280	53,000
Joey Sindelar	69	72	68	71	280	53,000
Scott Verplank	69	71	68	72	280	53,000
Duffy Waldorf	65	68	74	73	280	53,000
Stewart Cink	70	71	72	68	281	34,538.34
Bernhard Langer	70	70	71	70	281	34,538.34
D.J. Trahan	71	69	71	70	281	34,538.34

358 / AMERICAN TOURS

	SCORES				TOTAL	MONEY
John Daly	70	67	72	72	281	34,538.33
Fred Funk	68	66	74	73	281	34,538.33
Bill Haas	70	69	70	72	281	34,538.33
Peter Jacobsen	72	70	68	71	281	34,538.33
Nick Price	70	69	71	71	281	34,538.33
Loren Roberts	68	69	73	71	281	34,538.33
Briny Baird	71	69	69	73	282	25,506.25
Chad Campbell	70	71	69	72	282	25,506.25
Joe Durant	71	69	68	74	282	25,506.25
Chris Riley	66	70	68	78	282	25,506.25
Billy Andrade	68	69	76	70	283	20,670
Ben Curtis	71	68	77	67	283	20,670
J.B. Holmes	67	69	73	74	283	20,670
Shaun Micheel	71	68	73	71	283	20,670
Rod Pampling	70	69	70	74	283	20,670
Doug Barron	72	69	69	74	284	16,960
Jeff Gove	71	67	74	72	284	16,960
Steve Flesch	71	71	72	71	285	14,013.20
Justin Leonard	70	69	74	72	285	14,013.20
Davis Love	69	70	73	73	285	14,013.20
Ian Poulter	69	70	72	74	285	14,013.20
Bob Tway	70	70	69	76	285	14,013.20
Nathan Green	72	70	73	71	286	12,235.43
Mathias Gronberg	67	71	74	74	286	12,235.43
Kevin Na	71	71	72	72	286	12,235.43
Greg Owen	70	72	74	70	286	12,235.43
Jesper Parnevik	71	70	72	73	286	12,235.43
Tim Petrovic	73	68	74	71	286	12,235.43
Chris DiMarco	69	70	71	76	286	12,235.42
Brian Davis	69	70	75	73	287	11,660
Todd Fischer	69	69	76	73	287	11,660
Peter Lonard	71	70	75	71	287	11,660
J.L. Lewis	68	73	73	74	288	11,448
Robert Gamez	70	70	76	73	289	11,130
Dudley Hart	71	71	73	74	289	11,130
Thomas Levet	71	71	76	71	289	11,130
Steve Lowery	73	67	76	73	289	11,130
Bo Van Pelt	70	70	74	75	289	11,130
Mark Calcavecchia	71	68	74	77	290	10,706
Bob Estes	70	72	71	77	290	10,706
Carl Pettersson	73	69	72	76	290	10,706
Brad Faxon	68	73	74	76	291	10,388
Ryuji Imada	73	69	80	69	291	10,388
Justin Rose	71	70	74	76	291	10,388
Brent Geiberger	76	66	76	74	292	10,176
Hidemichi Tanaka	72	67	74	81	294	10,070
Paul Stankowski	71	70	75	81	297	9,964

Shell Houston Open

Redstone Golf Club, Fall Creek Course, Humble, Texas
Par 35-37–72; 7,457 yards

April 20-23
purse, $5,500,000

	SCORES				TOTAL	MONEY
Stuart Appleby	66	67	69	67	269	$990,000
Bob Estes	71	69	66	69	275	594,000
Steve Stricker	72	70	68	66	276	374,000

	SCORES				TOTAL	MONEY
Mathias Gronberg	68	69	67	73	277	264,000
Jerry Smith	67	70	69	72	278	220,000
K.J. Choi	71	69	67	72	279	172,150
Richard Johnson	72	69	67	71	279	172,150
J.L. Lewis	71	69	68	71	279	172,150
Mike Weir	71	71	70	67	279	172,150
Brett Wetterich	70	69	69	71	279	172,150
Rich Beem	73	69	67	71	280	116,600
Paul Goydos	69	71	68	72	280	116,600
Trevor Immelman	69	67	71	73	280	116,600
Hunter Mahan	69	72	69	70	280	116,600
Nick Watney	71	69	69	71	280	116,600
Mathew Goggin	70	73	69	69	281	88,000
Jeff Gove	69	71	68	73	281	88,000
Ted Purdy	69	73	72	67	281	88,000
Jeff Overton	71	69	69	73	282	74,250
Roland Thatcher	70	70	71	71	282	74,250
Lucas Glover	71	68	74	70	283	47,750
Scott Gutschewski	73	68	70	72	283	47,750
Charley Hoffman	70	67	75	71	283	47,750
Ryan Palmer	71	69	72	71	283	47,750
Ian Poulter	72	69	70	72	283	47,750
Brett Quigley	73	70	68	72	283	47,750
John Senden	71	69	72	71	283	47,750
Wes Short, Jr.	72	68	68	75	283	47,750
Kevin Sutherland	71	70	71	71	283	47,750
Roger Tambellini	72	69	71	71	283	47,750
Charles Warren	68	73	72	70	283	47,750
Tommy Armour	73	71	73	67	284	33,275
Padraig Harrington	71	73	69	71	284	33,275
Daisuke Maruyama	73	70	69	73	285	30,387.50
Greg Owen	69	65	75	76	285	30,387.50
Daniel Chopra	74	69	71	72	286	24,234.38
Skip Kendall	70	71	72	73	286	24,234.38
Tag Ridings	70	69	75	72	286	24,234.38
Vijay Singh	69	71	75	71	286	24,234.38
Billy Andrade	73	69	70	74	286	24,234.37
Aaron Baddeley	68	70	72	76	286	24,234.37
Brent Geiberger	68	74	71	73	286	24,234.37
Stephen Leaney	68	71	72	75	286	24,234.37
Henrik Bjornstad	71	69	72	75	287	15,334
Greg Chalmers	72	69	73	73	287	15,334
Gavin Coles	75	67	74	71	287	15,334
Charles Howell	70	70	75	72	287	15,334
Brandt Jobe	73	68	76	70	287	15,334
Jerry Kelly	72	71	74	70	287	15,334
Scott McCarron	69	71	71	76	287	15,334
Jesper Parnevik	69	73	74	71	287	15,334
Duffy Waldorf	71	73	74	69	287	15,334
Jimmy Walker	71	70	72	74	287	15,334
Marco Dawson	72	70	73	73	288	12,540
Gabriel Hjertstedt	72	69	77	70	288	12,540
Blaine McCallister	71	68	76	73	288	12,540
Graeme McDowell	72	72	69	75	288	12,540
Larry Mize	73	69	72	74	288	12,540
Michael Allen	74	70	73	72	289	11,770
Paul Azinger	71	70	74	74	289	11,770
Olin Browne	70	74	70	75	289	11,770
John Daly	69	72	73	75	289	11,770
Greg Kraft	73	67	77	72	289	11,770

	SCORES	TOTAL	MONEY
Shaun Micheel	73 70 73 73	289	11,770
Chris Smith	72 72 75 70	289	11,770
B.J. Staten	73 70 69 77	289	11,770
Camilo Villegas	72 72 74 71	289	11,770
Jason Gore	71 71 74 74	290	11,165
Vance Veazey	72 71 75 72	290	11,165
Robert Damron	73 69 76 73	291	10,835
Jonathan Kaye	70 74 74 73	291	10,835
D.A. Points	67 72 78 74	291	10,835
Bo Van Pelt	76 68 72 75	291	10,835
Fredrik Jacobson	69 71 79 73	292	10,450
Frank Lickliter	69 75 78 70	292	10,450
Phil Tataurangi	73 71 72 76	292	10,450
Patrick Sheehan	70 72 75 76	293	10,230
David Branshaw	71 73 76 74	294	10,010
Lee Janzen	70 70 77 77	294	10,010
Kevin Stadler	71 68 77 78	294	10,010
Charl Schwartzel	73 71 78 75	297	9,790
Shane Bertsch	74 69 76 82	301	9,680

Zurich Classic of New Orleans

English Turn Golf & Country Club, New Orleans, Louisiana
Par 36-36–72; 7,078 yards

April 27-30
purse, $6,000,000

	SCORES	TOTAL	MONEY
Chris Couch	70 70 64 65	269	$1,080,000
Fred Funk	70 69 69 62	270	528,000
Charles Howell	70 69 66 65	270	528,000
Stuart Appleby	65 72 72 64	273	248,000
Joe Durant	68 64 73 68	273	248,000
Brett Wetterich	69 65 73 66	273	248,000
Danny Ellis	71 69 69 65	274	180,750
Lucas Glover	66 73 72 63	274	180,750
Tim Herron	67 71 69 67	274	180,750
Ian Poulter	67 68 72 67	274	180,750
Tommy Armour	66 73 69 67	275	132,000
Aaron Baddeley	69 67 75 64	275	132,000
Brian Bateman	70 67 71 67	275	132,000
Padraig Harrington	70 68 71 66	275	132,000
David Branshaw	67 71 71 67	276	81,720
Carlos Franco	69 70 68 69	276	81,720
Bill Haas	71 67 72 66	276	81,720
J.L. Lewis	70 69 69 68	276	81,720
Scott McCarron	70 69 71 66	276	81,720
Graeme McDowell	64 73 72 67	276	81,720
Phil Mickelson	68 71 68 69	276	81,720
John Senden	71 66 74 65	276	81,720
Nick Watney	66 72 70 68	276	81,720
Dean Wilson	68 72 66 70	276	81,720
Woody Austin	71 68 71 67	277	45,800
Mark Calcavecchia	71 67 71 68	277	45,800
Retief Goosen	66 69 75 67	277	45,800
J.P. Hayes	68 69 71 69	277	45,800
Jason Schultz	69 71 70 67	277	45,800
Steve Stricker	69 71 70 67	277	45,800
Cameron Beckman	67 72 67 72	278	31,920

	SCORES				TOTAL	MONEY
Stephen Leaney	68	67	72	71	278	31,920
Steve Lowery	70	69	73	66	278	31,920
Jesper Parnevik	69	68	72	69	278	31,920
Patrick Sheehan	69	71	71	67	278	31,920
Jeff Sluman	66	73	71	68	278	31,920
Jerry Smith	67	73	71	67	278	31,920
Kevin Sutherland	68	71	71	68	278	31,920
Scott Verplank	70	69	72	67	278	31,920
Bubba Watson	66	73	72	67	278	31,920
Jeff Brehaut	68	69	74	68	279	21,600
Steve Flesch	67	73	69	70	279	21,600
Charley Hoffman	66	69	76	68	279	21,600
Greg Kraft	71	69	72	67	279	21,600
Neal Lancaster	68	71	71	69	279	21,600
Darron Stiles	67	72	76	64	279	21,600
Olin Browne	66	73	72	69	280	15,620
Skip Kendall	69	70	74	67	280	15,620
Jeff Overton	73	65	71	71	280	15,620
Heath Slocum	69	71	71	69	280	15,620
David Toms	69	67	72	72	280	15,620
Mark Wilson	72	68	69	71	280	15,620
Michael Allen	68	67	78	68	281	13,960
Eric Axley	70	65	77	69	281	13,960
Matt Hansen	71	66	70	74	281	13,960
Glen Day	68	68	72	74	282	13,560
Robert Garrigus	66	72	73	71	282	13,560
Hunter Mahan	69	68	77	68	282	13,560
Paul Azinger	71	69	71	72	283	13,140
Stuart Deane	66	72	76	69	283	13,140
Roger Tambellini	70	67	74	72	283	13,140
Omar Uresti	68	72	70	73	283	13,140
Wes Short, Jr.	68	69	77	70	284	12,840
Ryan Hietala	67	68	75	75	285	12,660
Daisuke Maruyama	68	72	74	71	285	12,660
Justin Rose	69	70	75	72	286	12,420
Tjaart van der Walt	70	69	76	71	286	12,420
Kent Jones	69	70	79	69	287	12,240
Kirk Triplett	73	66	76	73	288	12,120
Larry Mize	68	71	78	72	289	12,000
Craig Perks	73	66	80	76	295	11,880

Wachovia Championship

Quail Hollow Club, Charlotte, North Carolina
Par 36-36—72; 7,438 yards

May 4-7
purse, $6,300,000

	SCORES				TOTAL	MONEY
Jim Furyk	68	69	68	71	276	$1,134,000
Trevor Immelman	68	72	66	70	276	680,400
(Furyk defeated Immelman on first playoff hole.)						
Adam Scott	71	72	66	71	280	428,400
Lucas Glover	69	73	67	72	281	277,200
Bill Haas	68	72	71	70	281	277,200
Steve Lowery	73	68	69	72	282	203,962.50
Joey Sindelar	71	74	68	69	282	203,962.50
Vaughn Taylor	70	70	71	71	282	203,962.50
Bo Van Pelt	70	64	73	75	282	203,962.50

	SCORES				TOTAL	MONEY
Retief Goosen	70	71	65	77	283	163,800
Geoff Ogilvy	71	71	70	71	283	163,800
Shaun Micheel	70	70	68	76	284	138,600
Charles Warren	73	70	70	71	284	138,600
Tim Clark	73	70	71	71	285	100,800
Ken Duke	72	71	70	72	285	100,800
Davis Love	69	69	73	74	285	100,800
Jesper Parnevik	73	71	70	71	285	100,800
Brett Quigley	74	68	69	74	285	100,800
Kevin Sutherland	71	71	70	73	285	100,800
D.J. Trahan	72	70	71	72	285	100,800
Nick Watney	72	73	71	70	286	75,600
Stephen Ames	71	73	71	72	287	63,000
David Duval	73	70	72	72	287	63,000
Jay Haas	75	71	65	76	287	63,000
John Senden	71	73	69	74	287	63,000
David Branshaw	77	68	70	73	288	46,620
Stewart Cink	70	74	71	73	288	46,620
Jason Gore	74	70	70	74	288	46,620
Shigeki Maruyama	72	71	67	78	288	46,620
Joe Ogilvie	73	73	69	73	288	46,620
Jason Bohn	71	73	73	72	289	38,193.75
J.J. Henry	73	67	71	78	289	38,193.75
Lee Janzen	72	72	72	73	289	38,193.75
Jerry Kelly	73	70	69	77	289	38,193.75
Tom Lehman	75	69	69	77	290	32,445
Phil Mickelson	71	72	73	74	290	32,445
Ted Purdy	77	66	74	73	290	32,445
Doug Barron	75	71	72	73	291	24,570
Joe Durant	74	71	73	73	291	24,570
Ernie Els	71	71	75	74	291	24,570
Bob Estes	73	72	73	73	291	24,570
Sergio Garcia	74	69	73	75	291	24,570
Charley Hoffman	72	73	72	74	291	24,570
Will MacKenzie	72	73	75	71	291	24,570
Carl Pettersson	71	74	75	71	291	24,570
Vijay Singh	71	68	71	81	291	24,570
Brad Faxon	72	73	76	71	292	16,657.20
Charles Howell	74	71	73	74	292	16,657.20
Justin Rose	70	74	68	80	292	16,657.20
Jeff Sluman	74	72	72	74	292	16,657.20
Mike Weir	73	71	72	76	292	16,657.20
Stuart Appleby	72	67	74	80	293	14,773.50
Olin Browne	71	74	72	76	293	14,773.50
Troy Matteson	72	69	75	77	293	14,773.50
Rory Sabbatini	68	73	73	79	293	14,773.50
Billy Andrade	69	73	78	74	294	14,238
Woody Austin	73	72	73	76	294	14,238
Rod Pampling	75	71	72	76	294	14,238
Tommy Armour	74	70	77	74	295	13,797
Steve Flesch	74	71	74	76	295	13,797
Robert Garrigus	70	74	71	80	295	13,797
Rocco Mediate	74	71	73	77	295	13,797
Marco Dawson	72	73	72	79	296	13,419
Jay Williamson	75	71	74	76	296	13,419
Ben Crane	71	74	74	78	297	13,167
Arron Oberholser	75	66	75	81	297	13,167
Craig Barlow	73	70	74	81	298	12,726
Mark Calcavecchia	72	73	74	79	298	12,726
Daniel Chopra	72	74	75	77	298	12,726

	SCORES				TOTAL	MONEY
Richard Johnson	74	72	77	75	298	12,726
Steve Jones	78	66	77	77	298	12,726
Ian Leggatt	75	71	75	80	301	12,348
Wes Short, Jr.	77	69	77	81	304	12,222

EDS Byron Nelson Championship

TPC Four Seasons Resort at Las Colinas: Par 35-35–70; 7,022 yards
Cottonwood Valley Course: Par 34-36–70; 6,847 yards
Irving, Texas

May 11-14
purse, $6,200,000

	SCORES				TOTAL	MONEY
Brett Wetterich	66	64	70	68	268	$1,116,000
Trevor Immelman	68	67	64	70	269	669,600
Adam Scott	65	65	69	71	270	359,600
Omar Uresti	67	66	69	68	270	359,600
Chad Campbell	72	65	65	69	271	248,000
Luke Donald	69	66	69	68	272	215,450
Shigeki Maruyama	71	68	67	66	272	215,450
Jason Bohn	70	68	68	67	273	167,400
Brian Davis	70	68	70	65	273	167,400
Dudley Hart	68	68	68	69	273	167,400
Charley Hoffman	70	67	65	71	273	167,400
Rod Pampling	71	69	67	66	273	167,400
J.J. Henry	67	70	70	67	274	109,533.34
Shaun Micheel	70	68	70	66	274	109,533.34
Ernie Els	68	69	69	68	274	109,533.33
Mathew Goggin	68	70	69	67	274	109,533.33
Arron Oberholser	74	60	72	68	274	109,533.33
Jeff Sluman	70	70	64	70	274	109,533.33
Brian Gay	69	69	68	69	275	83,700
Sean O'Hair	72	66	71	66	275	83,700
Shane Bertsch	69	70	65	72	276	64,480
Joe Ogilvie	71	62	69	74	276	64,480
Carl Pettersson	72	68	67	69	276	64,480
Wes Short, Jr.	68	71	66	71	276	64,480
Duffy Waldorf	71	68	70	67	276	64,480
K.J. Choi	69	70	67	71	277	43,090
Ben Crane	71	67	69	70	277	43,090
Bob Estes	66	69	70	72	277	43,090
Tim Herron	67	69	70	71	277	43,090
Justin Leonard	69	71	71	66	277	43,090
Peter Lonard	71	68	69	69	277	43,090
Brett Quigley	69	69	72	67	277	43,090
Bo Van Pelt	67	68	70	72	277	43,090
Kevin Sutherland	69	68	70	71	278	28,069.10
Charles Howell	69	69	71	69	278	28,069.09
Ryuji Imada	67	70	69	72	278	28,069.09
Steve Lowery	65	69	71	73	278	28,069.09
Billy Mayfair	71	67	69	71	278	28,069.09
Scott McCarron	69	69	66	74	278	28,069.09
Corey Pavin	72	66	69	71	278	28,069.09
Kenny Perry	71	69	69	69	278	28,069.09
Phil Tataurangi	68	66	74	70	278	28,069.09
Jay Williamson	69	72	70	67	278	28,069.09
Dean Wilson	67	70	73	68	278	28,069.09

	SCORES	TOTAL	MONEY
Eric Axley	73 67 68 71	279	19,220
Matt Hansen	69 70 70 70	279	19,220
Ted Purdy	70 69 65 75	279	19,220
Bubba Dickerson	67 72 68 73	280	15,141.78
Brent Geiberger	71 68 71 70	280	15,141.78
Nathan Green	67 72 70 71	280	15,141.78
Tom Lehman	70 69 71 70	280	15,141.78
Justin Rose	71 67 71 71	280	15,141.78
Vijay Singh	70 67 70 73	280	15,141.78
Ron Whittaker	72 69 68 71	280	15,141.78
Olin Browne	69 68 73 70	280	15,141.77
Patrick Sheehan	74 65 71 70	280	15,141.77
Billy Andrade	73 66 68 74	281	13,826
Chris DiMarco	74 67 69 71	281	13,826
Vaughn Taylor	71 70 71 69	281	13,826
Charles Warren	70 69 69 73	281	13,826
Richard Johnson	71 67 68 76	282	13,206
Bernhard Langer	70 70 71 71	282	13,206
Tag Ridings	71 70 67 74	282	13,206
Rory Sabbatini	71 68 69 74	282	13,206
B.J. Staten	68 73 71 70	282	13,206
Nick Watney	74 64 71 73	282	13,206
Greg Chalmers	73 67 69 74	283	12,586
Steve Jones	75 66 70 72	283	12,586
Stephen Leaney	70 70 68 75	283	12,586
Hunter Mahan	67 74 69 73	283	12,586
Robert Gamez	72 69 72 71	284	12,276
Chris Parra	73 67 74 71	285	12,152
Jeff Overton	72 68 71 75	286	11,842
Ryan Palmer	69 68 70 79	286	11,842
Tom Pernice, Jr.	68 72 73 73	286	11,842
Jimmy Walker	71 69 75 71	286	11,842
J.L. Lewis	71 70 74 74	289	11,532
Brian Bateman	72 69 74 76	291	11,408
James Driscoll	67 70 81 74	292	11,222
David McKenzie	71 70 70 81	292	11,222

Bank of America Colonial

Colonial Country Club, Fort Worth, Texas
Par 35-35–70; 7,054 yards

May 18-21
purse, $6,000,000

	SCORES	TOTAL	MONEY
Tim Herron	67 65 68 68	268	$1,080,000
Richard Johnson	68 65 68 67	268	648,000
(Herron defeated Johnson on second playoff hole.)			
Rod Pampling	67 63 70 70	270	408,000
Stephen Ames	65 66 77 63	271	209,571.43
Stewart Cink	64 67 72 68	271	209,571.43
Ben Crane	71 65 71 64	271	209,571.43
Peter Lonard	66 66 69 70	271	209,571.43
Arron Oberholser	65 68 71 67	271	209,571.43
Brett Quigley	68 70 67 66	271	209,571.43
Nathan Green	67 67 67 70	271	209,571.42
Corey Pavin	71 67 68 66	272	150,000
Brian Gay	67 67 73 66	273	117,600
Jerry Kelly	69 68 67 69	273	117,600

	SCORES				TOTAL	MONEY
Nick O'Hern	66	69	68	70	273	117,600
Bo Van Pelt	67	68	67	71	273	117,600
Dean Wilson	67	65	71	70	273	117,600
Robert Allenby	71	67	66	70	274	75,900
Woody Austin	72	65	67	70	274	75,900
K.J. Choi	70	69	72	63	274	75,900
Jim Furyk	66	67	73	68	274	75,900
Fredrik Jacobson	71	62	70	71	274	75,900
Davis Love	70	69	67	68	274	75,900
Chris Riley	68	71	66	69	274	75,900
Vaughn Taylor	70	67	67	70	274	75,900
Fred Couples	70	68	70	67	275	46,800
David Duval	70	68	69	68	275	46,800
Steve Flesch	69	68	67	71	275	46,800
Shigeki Maruyama	69	68	70	68	275	46,800
Ted Purdy	70	71	66	68	275	46,800
Brad Faxon	71	68	69	68	276	35,657.15
Bob Tway	69	70	69	68	276	35,657.15
Shane Bertsch	70	69	67	70	276	35,657.14
Chad Campbell	67	68	69	72	276	35,657.14
Charley Hoffman	65	66	71	74	276	35,657.14
Zach Johnson	65	69	70	72	276	35,657.14
David Toms	68	66	70	72	276	35,657.14
Joe Ogilvie	71	70	68	68	277	28,200
Kenny Perry	66	70	70	71	277	28,200
Wes Short, Jr.	70	68	70	69	277	28,200
Henrik Bjornstad	69	64	69	76	278	23,400
Daniel Chopra	70	64	72	72	278	23,400
Steve Lowery	70	70	69	69	278	23,400
Billy Mayfair	72	69	70	67	278	23,400
Mike Weir	66	73	72	67	278	23,400
Dudley Hart	71	70	71	67	279	15,818.19
Duffy Waldorf	72	69	72	66	279	15,818.19
Brian Bateman	72	68	67	72	279	15,818.18
Rich Beem	69	70	70	70	279	15,818.18
Fred Funk	67	70	69	73	279	15,818.18
Robert Gamez	67	71	73	68	279	15,818.18
J.L. Lewis	69	69	73	68	279	15,818.18
Scott McCarron	70	70	70	69	279	15,818.18
Justin Rose	68	69	71	71	279	15,818.18
John Senden	69	70	69	71	279	15,818.18
Camilo Villegas	68	69	73	69	279	15,818.18
Jason Bohn	72	68	72	68	280	13,260
Olin Browne	70	69	71	70	280	13,260
Ben Curtis	68	68	73	71	280	13,260
Bob Estes	69	68	71	72	280	13,260
David Frost	73	67	73	67	280	13,260
Jonathan Kaye	70	69	68	73	280	13,260
Justin Leonard	72	67	71	70	280	13,260
Ryan Palmer	66	71	75	68	280	13,260
Rory Sabbatini	72	69	70	70	281	12,720
Brandt Jobe	71	68	73	71	283	12,480
Tom Lehman	72	67	73	71	283	12,480
Ryan Moore	70	71	72	70	283	12,480
Harrison Frazar	69	70	69	76	284	12,120
J.J. Henry	70	70	73	71	284	12,120
Joey Sindelar	70	71	69	74	284	12,120
Ben Crenshaw	73	67	74	71	285	11,760
Hunter Mahan	69	72	72	72	285	11,760
Tim Petrovic	70	71	71	73	285	11,760

	SCORES				TOTAL	MONEY
Mathias Gronberg	67	71	73	75	286	11,520
Jerry Smith	71	66	73	78	288	11,400
James Driscoll	69	68	77	76	290	11,280
Bill Haas	66	75	73	78	292	11,160

FedEx St. Jude Classic

TPC at Southwind, Memphis, Tennessee
Par 35-35–70; 7,244 yards

May 25-28
purse, $5,200,000

	SCORES				TOTAL	MONEY
Jeff Maggert	72	66	68	65	271	$936,000
Tom Pernice, Jr.	67	68	68	71	274	561,600
John Cook	69	69	67	71	276	301,600
Kris Cox	74	67	63	72	276	301,600
Briny Baird	71	68	68	70	277	182,650
Jay Delsing	70	69	66	72	277	182,650
Zach Johnson	68	71	70	68	277	182,650
Daisuke Maruyama	68	73	69	67	277	182,650
John Senden	73	65	70	70	278	150,800
Brent Geiberger	69	73	70	67	279	115,266.67
Dudley Hart	74	67	70	68	279	115,266.67
Brett Quigley	69	71	71	68	279	115,266.67
Tjaart van der Walt	73	70	67	69	279	115,266.67
Ryan Palmer	69	68	69	73	279	115,266.66
David Toms	69	67	72	71	279	115,266.66
Paul Azinger	67	72	72	69	280	75,400
Fred Funk	68	75	68	69	280	75,400
Brian Gay	69	67	72	72	280	75,400
Tim Herron	70	65	68	77	280	75,400
Nick Price	68	70	69	73	280	75,400
Camilo Villegas	70	66	71	73	280	75,400
Chris DiMarco	73	70	68	70	281	48,273.34
Bob May	69	71	74	67	281	48,273.34
Ryuji Imada	71	71	68	71	281	48,273.33
Richard Johnson	72	69	69	71	281	48,273.33
Justin Leonard	72	69	67	73	281	48,273.33
Darron Stiles	69	64	77	71	281	48,273.33
Bob Burns	72	69	70	71	282	34,580
Bob Estes	71	70	69	72	282	34,580
Mathias Gronberg	71	72	67	72	282	34,580
Gabriel Hjertstedt	73	71	70	68	282	34,580
Steve Stricker	68	72	70	72	282	34,580
Duffy Waldorf	70	71	69	72	282	34,580
Doug Barron	72	70	71	70	283	27,430
Bart Bryant	71	70	71	71	283	27,430
Greg Chalmers	74	70	69	70	283	27,430
Steve Flesch	74	69	73	67	283	27,430
Michael Allen	70	69	70	75	284	20,280
Ryan Hietala	73	71	70	70	284	20,280
Greg Kraft	75	69	72	68	284	20,280
Matt Kuchar	72	68	70	74	284	20,280
Jim McGovern	73	70	70	71	284	20,280
Jeff Overton	73	68	72	71	284	20,280
D.A. Points	66	77	73	68	284	20,280
Paul Stankowski	68	76	69	71	284	20,280
Scott Sterling	74	65	71	74	284	20,280

	SCORES				TOTAL	MONEY
Robert Garrigus	69	68	76	72	285	13,988
Shigeki Maruyama	70	72	75	68	285	13,988
David Peoples	73	68	70	74	285	13,988
Chris Smith	64	71	75	75	285	13,988
Tommy Armour	72	71	71	72	286	12,168
Woody Austin	69	74	70	73	286	12,168
Jose Coceres	73	68	72	73	286	12,168
Dan Forsman	69	68	72	77	286	12,168
Matt Hansen	74	69	70	73	286	12,168
Stephen Leaney	72	68	74	72	286	12,168
Will Moore	73	71	71	71	286	12,168
Mark Calcavecchia	68	71	75	73	287	11,596
Patrick Sheehan	72	68	75	72	287	11,596
Kirk Triplett	70	72	68	79	289	11,388
Willie Wood	73	71	73	72	289	11,388
Scott Gump	71	73	71	75	290	11,128
Mike Sposa	74	68	74	74	290	11,128
Vance Veazey	73	69	74	74	290	11,128
Brian Bateman	70	72	73	76	291	10,868
Casey Wittenberg	74	65	76	76	291	10,868
Andrew Magee	70	73	71	78	292	10,712
Henrik Bjornstad	74	70	76	73	293	10,556
Danny Ellis	72	71	75	75	293	10,556
Nicholas Thompson	70	72	77	75	294	10,348
Mark Wilson	71	72	69	82	294	10,348
Paul Goydos	71	70	75	80	296	10,192
Frank Lickliter	69	72	81	75	297	10,088
Tag Ridings	76	68	83	72	299	9,984

Memorial Tournament

Muirfield Village Golf Club, Dublin, Ohio
Par 36-36–72; 7,300 yards

June 1-4
purse, $5,750,000

	SCORES				TOTAL	MONEY
Carl Pettersson	69	67	69	71	276	$1,035,000
Zach Johnson	70	68	70	70	278	506,000
Brett Wetterich	69	69	73	67	278	506,000
Brandt Jobe	70	68	74	67	279	237,666.67
Adam Scott	71	66	73	69	279	237,666.67
Phil Mickelson	69	70	70	70	279	237,666.66
Vaughn Taylor	70	72	70	68	280	179,208.34
Woody Austin	71	69	67	73	280	179,208.33
Trevor Immelman	72	70	69	69	280	179,208.33
Paul Azinger	73	71	70	67	281	155,250
Jose Maria Olazabal	74	69	71	68	282	143,750
Stewart Cink	69	74	70	70	283	126,500
Sean O'Hair	67	70	74	72	283	126,500
Craig Parry	69	72	73	70	284	100,625
Tim Petrovic	74	68	72	70	284	100,625
Ted Purdy	69	75	69	71	284	100,625
Justin Rose	75	71	67	71	284	100,625
Mark Brooks	70	71	79	66	286	63,077.50
Bart Bryant	70	75	71	70	286	63,077.50
Paul Casey	70	73	70	73	286	63,077.50
Tim Clark	69	69	75	73	286	63,077.50
Jim Furyk	73	71	72	70	286	63,077.50

	SCORES				TOTAL	MONEY
Robert Gamez	70	74	68	74	286	63,077.50
Sergio Garcia	69	74	74	69	286	63,077.50
Rod Pampling	72	73	66	75	286	63,077.50
Rory Sabbatini	74	68	71	73	286	63,077.50
Kirk Triplett	73	70	73	70	286	63,077.50
Stuart Appleby	69	71	74	73	287	42,550
Jay Haas	72	71	72	73	288	39,962.50
Davis Love	69	73	77	69	288	39,962.50
Ryan Moore	71	71	74	73	289	35,650
Geoff Ogilvy	70	72	74	73	289	35,650
Nick Price	69	74	74	72	289	35,650
J.J. Henry	70	69	75	76	290	30,331.25
Shaun Micheel	71	69	75	75	290	30,331.25
Ian Poulter	73	71	79	67	290	30,331.25
Bubba Watson	72	70	77	71	290	30,331.25
Jason Bohn	73	72	74	72	291	25,300
Vijay Singh	74	71	72	74	291	25,300
Heath Slocum	74	71	74	72	291	25,300
Bob Tway	74	74	73	70	291	25,300
Mark Calcavecchia	71	71	79	71	292	20,700
Greg Owen	70	75	70	77	292	20,700
Joey Sindelar	73	75	72	72	292	20,700
Mike Weir	71	71	74	76	292	20,700
Joe Durant	75	70	70	78	293	15,640
Brad Faxon	73	72	74	74	293	15,640
David Howell	69	70	83	71	293	15,640
Billy Mayfair	70	72	78	73	293	15,640
Bo Van Pelt	70	72	73	78	293	15,640
Duffy Waldorf	73	72	73	75	293	15,640
Chris DiMarco	72	71	73	78	294	13,409
Richard Johnson	73	71	73	77	294	13,409
Jonathan Kaye	74	73	71	76	294	13,409
J.L. Lewis	74	74	72	74	294	13,409
Scott Verplank	73	75	74	72	294	13,409
Jeff Brehaut	71	75	75	74	295	12,765
Jerry Kelly	69	72	75	79	295	12,765
Peter Lonard	75	72	76	72	295	12,765
Brett Quigley	74	71	78	72	295	12,765
Jeff Sluman	76	72	76	71	295	12,765
K.J. Choi	71	76	73	76	296	12,247.50
Retief Goosen	74	72	75	75	296	12,247.50
John Rollins	73	72	77	74	296	12,247.50
Charl Schwartzel	71	75	80	70	296	12,247.50
Aaron Baddeley	73	73	72	79	297	11,902.50
Ben Curtis	74	74	76	73	297	11,902.50
Ben Crane	73	70	76	79	298	11,500
Ernie Els	74	70	73	81	298	11,500
Steve Flesch	66	72	85	75	298	11,500
Nathan Green	74	72	78	74	298	11,500
Tim Herron	70	71	81	76	298	11,500
Kevin Stadler	74	73	78	74	299	11,155
David Duval	71	76	73	82	302	11,040

Barclays Classic

Westchester Country Club, West Course, Harrison, New York
Par 36-35–71; 6,839 yards

June 8-11
purse, $5,750,000

	SCORES				TOTAL	MONEY
Vijay Singh	70	64	72	68	274	$1,035,000
Adam Scott	65	72	69	70	276	621,000
Billy Andrade	66	70	69	72	277	333,500
Brett Quigley	71	66	70	70	277	333,500
Luke Donald	72	65	71	70	278	201,968.75
Fredrik Jacobson	67	68	72	71	278	201,968.75
Tom Pernice, Jr.	70	71	70	67	278	201,968.75
Jeff Sluman	69	69	72	68	278	201,968.75
Jason Bohn	76	64	72	67	279	155,250
Mathew Goggin	73	68	68	70	279	155,250
Ian Poulter	72	71	65	71	279	155,250
Graeme McDowell	70	68	71	71	280	132,250
David Howell	66	68	73	74	281	115,000
Trevor Immelman	72	71	67	71	281	115,000
Ryuji Imada	73	66	75	68	282	97,750
Jeff Maggert	71	71	70	70	282	97,750
David Toms	68	70	72	72	282	97,750
Brad Faxon	70	72	73	68	283	69,985.72
Tom Lehman	68	71	75	69	283	69,985.72
Geoff Ogilvy	69	68	74	72	283	69,985.72
Stuart Appleby	72	70	66	75	283	69,985.71
Phil Mickelson	70	70	71	72	283	69,985.71
John Senden	73	68	69	73	283	69,985.71
Bo Van Pelt	71	69	70	73	283	69,985.71
Steve Elkington	71	69	72	72	284	45,856.25
Joey Sindelar	68	68	73	75	284	45,856.25
Kevin Sutherland	70	67	73	74	284	45,856.25
Nick Watney	71	69	74	70	284	45,856.25
Ben Crane	71	66	77	71	285	35,773.22
Corey Pavin	73	69	72	71	285	35,773.22
Loren Roberts	71	70	73	71	285	35,773.22
Retief Goosen	71	72	69	73	285	35,773.21
Justin Leonard	72	70	68	75	285	35,773.21
Jeff Overton	75	65	73	72	285	35,773.21
Mike Weir	69	70	74	72	285	35,773.21
Michael Allen	69	70	73	74	286	26,497.92
Padraig Harrington	74	66	75	71	286	26,497.92
Sean O'Hair	70	69	74	73	286	26,497.92
Rod Pampling	72	70	72	72	286	26,497.92
Fred Funk	72	67	71	76	286	26,497.91
Peter Lonard	73	67	71	75	286	26,497.91
Chris DiMarco	70	70	75	72	287	20,125
Jonathan Kaye	73	70	69	75	287	20,125
Frank Lickliter	70	67	77	73	287	20,125
Hunter Mahan	69	69	75	74	287	20,125
John Rollins	75	68	69	75	287	20,125
Nathan Green	69	73	71	75	288	14,969.17
Kent Jones	69	71	75	73	288	14,969.17
Bernhard Langer	70	73	74	71	288	14,969.17
Kenny Perry	71	67	77	73	288	14,969.17
Paul Azinger	69	71	73	75	288	14,969.16
Arron Oberholser	68	69	74	77	288	14,969.16
John Cook	70	70	76	73	289	13,248
Todd Hamilton	71	71	75	72	289	13,248

	SCORES				TOTAL	MONEY
Joe Ogilvie	71	72	71	75	289	13,248
Ryan Palmer	71	70	78	70	289	13,248
Bob Tway	71	72	75	71	289	13,248
Craig Barlow	72	70	74	74	290	12,707.50
J.P. Hayes	70	68	72	80	290	12,707.50
Jose Maria Olazabal	72	68	75	75	290	12,707.50
Tag Ridings	71	71	70	78	290	12,707.50
Charles Howell	71	69	78	73	291	12,420
Tim Clark	70	71	78	73	292	12,190
Ian Leggatt	73	70	73	76	292	12,190
Dean Wilson	70	72	74	76	292	12,190
Robert Garrigus	74	68	77	74	293	11,787.50
Brandt Jobe	69	71	74	79	293	11,787.50
Daisuke Maruyama	68	72	78	75	293	11,787.50
Billy Mayfair	71	68	77	77	293	11,787.50
Doug Barron	69	74	73	78	294	11,270
Shane Bertsch	72	71	74	77	294	11,270
Kris Cox	73	69	76	76	294	11,270
Joe Durant	73	70	77	74	294	11,270
Lucas Glover	72	66	77	79	294	11,270
Wes Short, Jr.	72	68	77	78	295	10,867.50
Jay Williamson	72	69	77	77	295	10,867.50
Arjun Atwal	72	71	73	80	296	10,522.50
Carlos Franco	72	71	77	76	296	10,522.50
Steve Jones	69	70	79	78	296	10,522.50
Will MacKenzie	72	70	76	78	296	10,522.50
Mark Calcavecchia	71	70	80	76	297	10,177.50
Steve Flesch	72	68	79	78	297	10,177.50
Fred Couples	73	69	73	83	298	10,005
Ron Whittaker	74	69	79	77	299	9,890

U.S. Open Championship

Winged Foot Golf Club, Mamaroneck, New York
Par 35-35–70; 7,264 yards

June 15-18
purse, $6,250,000

	SCORES				TOTAL	MONEY
Geoff Ogilvy	71	70	72	72	285	$1,225,000
Jim Furyk	70	72	74	70	286	501,249
Colin Montgomerie	69	71	75	71	286	501,249
Phil Mickelson	70	73	69	74	286	501,249
Padraig Harrington	73	69	74	71	287	255,642
Nick O'Hern	75	70	74	69	288	183,255
Jeff Sluman	74	73	72	69	288	183,255
Mike Weir	71	74	71	72	288	183,255
Steve Stricker	70	69	76	73	288	183,255
Vijay Singh	71	74	70	73	288	183,255
Kenneth Ferrie	71	70	71	76	288	183,255
Ryuji Imada	76	73	69	71	289	131,670
Luke Donald	78	69	70	72	289	131,670
Ian Poulter	74	71	70	74	289	131,670
Paul Casey	77	72	72	69	290	116,735
David Howell	70	78	74	69	291	99,417
David Duval	77	68	75	71	291	99,417
Miguel Angel Jimenez	70	75	74	72	291	99,417
Robert Allenby	73	74	72	72	291	99,417
Arron Oberholser	75	68	74	74	291	99,417

	SCORES				TOTAL	MONEY
Jose Maria Olazabal	75	73	73	71	292	74,252
Tom Pernice, Jr.	79	70	72	71	292	74,252
Adam Scott	72	76	70	74	292	74,252
Peter Hedblom	72	74	71	75	292	74,252
Trevor Immelman	76	71	70	75	292	74,252
Sean O'Hair	76	72	74	71	293	52,341
Ernie Els	74	73	74	72	293	52,341
Angel Cabrera	74	73	74	72	293	52,341
Ted Purdy	78	71	71	73	293	52,341
Henrik Stenson	75	71	73	74	293	52,341
Craig Barlow	72	75	72	74	293	52,341
Rod Pampling	73	75	75	71	294	41,912
Woody Austin	72	76	72	74	294	41,912
Scott Hend	72	72	75	75	294	41,912
Steve Jones	74	74	71	75	294	41,912
Bart Bryant	72	72	73	77	294	41,912
Stewart Cink	75	71	77	72	295	36,647
Jay Haas	75	72	74	74	295	36,647
Charles Howell	77	71	73	74	295	36,647
Stephen Gangluff	76	73	77	70	296	29,459
Tommy Armour	79	70	74	73	296	29,459
John Cook	71	78	74	73	296	29,459
Jason Dufner	72	71	78	75	296	29,459
Lee Williams	75	73	73	75	296	29,459
Bo Van Pelt	72	75	73	76	296	29,459
Fred Funk	71	75	73	77	296	29,459
Chad Collins	76	71	72	77	296	29,459
Charley Hoffman	76	70	78	73	297	20,482
Charl Schwartzel	74	72	76	75	297	20,482
J.B. Holmes	74	73	75	75	297	20,482
Kent Jones	73	74	73	77	297	20,482
Phillip Archer	72	72	75	78	297	20,482
Thomas Bjorn	72	74	73	78	297	20,482
Graeme McDowell	71	72	75	79	297	20,482
Fred Couples	73	74	71	79	297	20,482
Darren Clarke	73	72	79	74	298	18,031
Ben Curtis	78	71	77	73	299	17,614
Kenny Perry	77	71	79	74	301	17,281
Jeev Milkha Singh	73	76	77	76	302	16,676
Camilo Villegas	74	72	79	77	302	16,676
Skip Kendall	73	75	76	78	302	16,676
Ben Crane	77	72	74	80	303	16,126
Tim Herron	73	76	79	77	305	15,836

Out of Final 36 Holes

Jay Delsing	78	72	150
Allen Doyle	76	74	150
Stephen Ames	72	78	150
Andrew Svoboda	75	75	150
Rory Sabbatini	74	76	150
Paul McGinley	74	76	150
Zach Johnson	73	77	150
Andrew Morse	74	76	150
*Alex Coe	77	73	150
Duffy Waldorf	75	76	151
Corey Pavin	76	75	151
Stuart Appleby	72	79	151
Mark Hensby	73	78	151
K.J. Choi	76	75	151

	SCORES		TOTAL
John Mallinger	77	74	151
Shaun Micheel	77	74	151
Tim Clark	77	74	151
Dean Wilson	76	75	151
Tadahiro Takayama	77	75	152
Bob Estes	80	72	152
Tiger Woods	76	76	152
Michael Campbell	75	77	152
Olin Browne	80	72	152
Chris DiMarco	76	76	152
Peter Jacobsen	76	76	152
Kevin Stadler	71	81	152
Taylor Wood	74	78	152
Nathan Green	77	75	152
*Billy Horschel	75	77	152
Brandt Jobe	76	76	152
Scott Verplank	76	76	152
Lucas Glover	75	77	152
Justin Leonard	77	75	152
Jyoti Randhawa	77	75	152
Brett Quigley	80	73	153
Mark Brooks	78	75	153
*Edoardo Molinari	77	76	153
Carl Pettersson	77	76	153
Tag Ridings	77	76	153
Greg Kraft	76	77	153
Dustin White	78	75	153
Chris Nallen	79	74	153
Nick Dougherty	78	75	153
Billy Mayfair	72	81	153
Chad Campbell	76	77	153
Rocco Mediate	76	77	153
Rich Beem	74	79	153
John Koskinen	79	74	153
Benjamin Hayes	76	77	153
Matt Kuchar	78	76	154
Tom Lehman	78	76	154
Niclas Fasth	78	76	154
Lee Janzen	82	72	154
J.J. Henry	77	77	154
Steve Lowery	79	75	154
Keiichiro Fukabori	75	79	154
Davis Love	76	78	154
Joey Sindelar	79	76	155
Todd Hamilton	77	78	155
Nicholas Thompson	81	74	155
Richard Green	75	80	155
Retief Goosen	77	78	155
*Jonathan Moore	77	78	155
David Berganio, Jr.	77	78	155
Oliver Wilson	80	76	156
Sergio Garcia	78	78	156
Jason Allred	78	78	156
Travis Hurst	78	78	156
D.J. Trahan	75	81	156
Shingo Katayama	81	75	156
*Patrick Nagle	81	75	156
Stephen Woodard	79	77	156
Brad Fritsch	78	78	156
Graeme Storm	81	76	157

	SCORES	TOTAL
Toru Taniguchi	75 82	157
Michael Harris	76 81	157
*Tadd Fujikawa	81 77	158
Maarten Lafeber	76 83	159
Mark Calcavecchia	80 79	159
George McNeill	77 82	159
Mathew Goggin	81 78	159
Nick Price	81 78	159
Phil Tataurangi	86 73	159
David Oh	83 77	160
*Dillon Dougherty	85 75	160
*Ryan Baca	78 83	161
Michael Derminio	81 80	161
Madalitso Muthiya	81 80	161
*Ryan Posey	84 78	162
Andy Bare	84 78	162
John Rollins	83 80	163
Rob Johnson	82 82	164
David Toms	79	WD

(Professionals who did not complete 72 holes received $2,000.)

Booz Allen Classic

TPC at Avenel, Potomac, Maryland
Par 36-35–71; 7,232 yards
(Event completed on Tuesday—rain.)

June 22-27
purse, $5,000,000

	SCORES				TOTAL	MONEY
Ben Curtis	62	65	67	70	264	$900,000
Billy Andrade	69	68	68	64	269	330,000
Padraig Harrington	70	65	68	66	269	330,000
Nick O'Hern	74	64	64	67	269	330,000
Steve Stricker	68	67	66	68	269	330,000
Ben Crane	68	68	68	66	270	167,500
Jeff Gove	63	68	71	68	270	167,500
Brett Quigley	69	63	67	71	270	167,500
Robert Allenby	68	68	66	69	271	140,000
Daniel Chopra	69	65	67	70	271	140,000
Michael Allen	70	67	68	68	273	120,000
Jose Coceres	64	64	78	67	273	120,000
Jonathan Byrd	70	66	70	68	274	83,125
Steve Flesch	65	71	72	66	274	83,125
Jonathan Kaye	68	70	70	66	274	83,125
Jerry Kelly	68	65	70	71	274	83,125
Shigeki Maruyama	72	65	67	70	274	83,125
Kenny Perry	71	67	68	68	274	83,125
Heath Slocum	68	68	69	69	274	83,125
Grant Waite	66	70	68	70	274	83,125
David Branshaw	73	67	67	68	275	52,000
Bart Bryant	66	70	66	73	275	52,000
Kris Cox	71	66	69	69	275	52,000
Mathias Gronberg	70	70	64	71	275	52,000
Frank Lickliter	68	69	69	69	275	52,000
Tommy Armour	70	70	66	70	276	34,750
K.J. Choi	68	68	68	72	276	34,750
Fred Funk	71	68	69	68	276	34,750

	SCORES				TOTAL	MONEY
J.B. Holmes	67	66	69	74	276	34,750
Hunter Mahan	69	71	69	67	276	34,750
Craig Parry	67	71	73	65	276	34,750
Kevin Sutherland	68	69	66	73	276	34,750
Charles Warren	71	68	66	71	276	34,750
Rich Beem	69	68	70	70	277	25,800
Brian Davis	70	70	70	67	277	25,800
Brian Gay	71	69	71	66	277	25,800
Jeff Overton	70	66	73	68	277	25,800
John Senden	70	69	69	69	277	25,800
Robert Damron	68	68	69	73	278	19,500
Marco Dawson	68	70	69	71	278	19,500
Steve Elkington	70	69	72	67	278	19,500
Brian Henninger	72	68	64	74	278	19,500
Thomas Levet	72	67	67	72	278	19,500
Joey Sindelar	70	70	71	67	278	19,500
Darron Stiles	69	69	68	72	278	19,500
Craig Barlow	69	67	74	69	279	13,371.43
Donnie Hammond	70	66	72	71	279	13,371.43
John Huston	67	65	73	74	279	13,371.43
Will MacKenzie	65	72	74	68	279	13,371.43
Jon Mills	69	69	67	74	279	13,371.43
Jerry Smith	68	70	71	70	279	13,371.43
Skip Kendall	72	68	72	67	279	13,371.42
Paul Azinger	69	71	72	68	280	11,520
Chris Couch	67	72	72	69	280	11,520
Glen Day	69	71	68	72	280	11,520
Spencer Levin	69	67	72	72	280	11,520
Brett Wetterich	69	71	69	71	280	11,520
Danny Ellis	72	67	68	74	281	11,150
Chris Riley	69	71	69	72	281	11,150
John Engler, Jr.	72	65	69	76	282	10,900
Greg Kraft	74	66	68	74	282	10,900
Bob May	68	71	73	70	282	10,900
J.P. Hayes	69	70	73	71	283	10,700
Brent Delahoussaye	72	68	66	78	284	10,550
Ryuji Imada	74	64	75	71	284	10,550
Charley Hoffman	70	70	76	69	285	10,400
Boyd Summerhays	72	67	73	74	286	10,300
Troy Matteson	67	71	74	76	288	10,200
Brent Geiberger	71	69	73	76	289	9,950
Scott Gutschewski	68	72	70	79	289	9,950
James McLean	66	69	78	76	289	9,950
Chris Smith	67	73	74	75	289	9,950

Buick Championship

TPC at River Highlands, Cromwell, Connecticut
Par 35-35–70; 6,820 yards

June 29-July 2
purse, $4,400,000

	SCORES				TOTAL	MONEY
J.J. Henry	68	68	63	67	266	$792,000
Hunter Mahan	69	67	68	65	269	387,200
Ryan Moore	69	66	67	67	269	387,200
Nathan Green	71	65	69	66	271	211,200
Woody Austin	67	70	68	68	273	154,550
Stewart Cink	69	65	72	67	273	154,550

	SCORES				TOTAL	MONEY
Bubba Dickerson	69	67	70	67	273	154,550
Shigeki Maruyama	74	65	68	66	273	154,550
Skip Kendall	68	67	74	65	274	101,828.58
Notah Begay	68	66	71	69	274	101,828.57
Steve Flesch	69	70	64	71	274	101,828.57
Peter Lonard	65	68	70	71	274	101,828.57
David McKenzie	69	69	67	69	274	101,828.57
Joe Ogilvie	72	63	69	70	274	101,828.57
Nick Watney	69	67	70	68	274	101,828.57
Jason Bohn	73	65	68	69	275	66,000
Brian Davis	69	71	69	66	275	66,000
Brent Geiberger	67	68	73	67	275	66,000
Trevor Immelman	70	65	68	72	275	66,000
Jonathan Kaye	69	68	70	68	275	66,000
David Branshaw	68	71	66	71	276	39,160
Ben Curtis	70	68	70	68	276	39,160
Harrison Frazar	65	71	65	75	276	39,160
Robert Gamez	71	66	68	71	276	39,160
Zach Johnson	67	69	69	71	276	39,160
Justin Leonard	67	69	69	71	276	39,160
Corey Pavin	66	73	68	69	276	39,160
Scott Verplank	65	69	71	71	276	39,160
Camilo Villegas	66	70	66	74	276	39,160
Ron Whittaker	66	70	72	68	276	39,160
Frank Lickliter	68	68	73	68	277	23,906.67
Nick O'Hern	67	72	70	68	277	23,906.67
Heath Slocum	65	71	73	68	277	23,906.67
B.J. Staten	72	68	67	70	277	23,906.67
Darron Stiles	66	66	74	71	277	23,906.67
Kirk Triplett	72	67	68	70	277	23,906.67
Marco Dawson	71	67	68	71	277	23,906.66
Todd Fischer	66	68	70	73	277	23,906.66
Carl Pettersson	66	71	73	67	277	23,906.66
Olin Browne	67	71	72	68	278	17,600
John Cook	72	65	72	69	278	17,600
Jeff Gove	72	67	69	70	278	17,600
Paul Goydos	70	67	70	71	278	17,600
K.J. Choi	71	68	69	71	279	14,080
Robert Damron	70	69	71	69	279	14,080
Billy Mayfair	69	71	70	69	279	14,080
Mike Sposa	70	70	68	71	279	14,080
Billy Andrade	69	69	73	69	280	11,193.60
Chris Couch	71	68	71	70	280	11,193.60
Fredrik Jacobson	73	67	70	70	280	11,193.60
Daisuke Maruyama	71	67	69	73	280	11,193.60
D.J. Trahan	67	68	72	73	280	11,193.60
Doug Barron	69	70	71	71	281	10,090.67
Alex Cejka	70	70	69	72	281	10,090.67
Greg Kraft	68	72	69	72	281	10,090.67
Vaughn Taylor	69	70	72	70	281	10,090.67
Fred Funk	70	69	73	69	281	10,090.66
Mathias Gronberg	68	71	65	77	281	10,090.66
Ryan Hietala	70	70	73	69	282	9,636
Will MacKenzie	68	72	73	69	282	9,636
Tim Petrovic	70	69	72	71	282	9,636
Bob Tway	67	72	74	69	282	9,636
Tag Ridings	67	69	70	77	283	9,328
Patrick Sheehan	69	69	79	66	283	9,328
Tjaart van der Walt	72	67	72	72	283	9,328
Troy Matteson	70	70	72	72	284	9,108

	SCORES				TOTAL	MONEY
Kenny Perry	67	71	75	71	284	9,108
Alex Aragon	68	72	72	73	285	8,844
Shane Bertsch	71	65	71	78	285	8,844
Joe Durant	71	69	70	75	285	8,844
John Huston	70	67	73	75	285	8,844
Jeff Overton	69	70	73	77	289	8,580
Joey Sindelar	67	72	78	72	289	8,580

Cialis Western Open

Cog Hill Golf & Country Club, Lemont, Illinois
Par 35-36–71; 7,326 yards

July 6-9
purse, $5,000,000

	SCORES				TOTAL	MONEY
Trevor Immelman	69	66	69	67	271	$900,000
Mathew Goggin	69	69	66	69	273	440,000
Tiger Woods	72	67	66	68	273	440,000
Stewart Cink	71	64	69	71	275	181,250
Tim Clark	70	71	68	66	275	181,250
Jim Furyk	69	67	69	70	275	181,250
Stephen Leaney	67	70	70	68	275	181,250
Carl Pettersson	69	70	65	71	275	181,250
Vijay Singh	67	67	68	73	275	181,250
Jason Gore	70	67	69	70	276	130,000
Scott Gutschewski	70	66	69	71	276	130,000
Stuart Appleby	68	69	72	68	277	105,000
Kenny Perry	71	69	70	67	277	105,000
Heath Slocum	70	68	69	70	277	105,000
Robert Garrigus	72	64	73	69	278	82,500
Lucas Glover	66	70	70	72	278	82,500
Steve Lowery	71	67	68	72	278	82,500
Tag Ridings	70	72	65	71	278	82,500
Daisuke Maruyama	70	71	72	66	279	67,500
Justin Rose	71	71	65	72	279	67,500
Rich Beem	72	67	70	71	280	45,666.67
Brian Davis	70	71	68	71	280	45,666.67
Bubba Dickerson	70	67	73	70	280	45,666.67
Luke Donald	70	67	71	72	280	45,666.67
Charley Hoffman	70	68	71	71	280	45,666.67
Zach Johnson	68	69	72	71	280	45,666.67
Stephen Ames	68	68	70	74	280	45,666.66
Robert Damron	69	67	71	73	280	45,666.66
Adam Scott	72	68	68	72	280	45,666.66
Robert Allenby	67	70	69	75	281	27,850
K.J. Choi	68	70	71	72	281	27,850
Daniel Chopra	66	66	76	73	281	27,850
Nathan Green	72	69	71	69	281	27,850
Bill Haas	69	70	75	67	281	27,850
Jerry Kelly	71	67	74	69	281	27,850
Shaun Micheel	69	69	70	73	281	27,850
Sean O'Hair	73	67	70	71	281	27,850
Rod Pampling	73	65	69	74	281	27,850
Scott Verplank	69	72	68	72	281	27,850
James Driscoll	73	65	74	70	282	21,000
David McKenzie	66	73	74	69	282	21,000
Shane Bertsch	68	74	70	71	283	16,087.50
Brian Gay	70	69	70	74	283	16,087.50

	SCORES				TOTAL	MONEY
Lee Janzen	73	67	73	70	283	16,087.50
Davis Love	67	70	74	72	283	16,087.50
Joe Ogilvie	66	69	69	79	283	16,087.50
Steve Stricker	71	68	71	73	283	16,087.50
Vaughn Taylor	72	69	71	71	283	16,087.50
Mike Weir	72	69	72	70	283	16,087.50
Steve Flesch	71	67	70	76	284	12,175
Dudley Hart	69	73	69	73	284	12,175
Brandt Jobe	72	70	72	70	284	12,175
Mark Wilson	69	72	73	70	284	12,175
Billy Mayfair	70	71	76	68	285	11,500
Ryan Moore	68	72	74	71	285	11,500
Patrick Sheehan	68	71	72	74	285	11,500
*Jamie Lovemark	69	72	75	69	285	
Mark Calcavecchia	71	71	68	76	286	11,000
Joe Durant	72	66	71	77	286	11,000
Jonathan Kaye	69	70	72	75	286	11,000
Skip Kendall	70	71	69	76	286	11,000
Len Mattiace	72	69	75	70	286	11,000
Paul Stankowski	70	71	71	74	286	11,000
Brett Wetterich	69	69	74	74	286	11,000
Bob Estes	72	70	74	71	287	10,350
Brent Geiberger	68	72	70	77	287	10,350
Fredrik Jacobson	72	70	66	79	287	10,350
Phil Mickelson	67	74	75	71	287	10,350
Pat Perez	69	69	70	79	287	10,350
John Senden	70	71	76	70	287	10,350
John Daly	70	72	74	72	288	9,700
Robert Gamez	73	69	73	73	288	9,700
Steve Jones	71	68	74	75	288	9,700
Peter Lonard	69	69	71	79	288	9,700
Jeff Overton	68	72	74	74	288	9,700
Jerry Smith	71	69	74	74	288	9,700
Charles Warren	67	71	75	75	288	9,700
Henrik Bjornstad	71	71	75	73	290	9,200
Tim Herron	68	74	72	76	290	9,200
Kevin Sutherland	71	71	71	77	290	9,200
Kent Jones	72	70	75	74	291	9,000
Eric Axley	70	71	73	78	292	8,850
Nick Watney	72	70	73	77	292	8,850

John Deere Classic

TPC at Deere Run, Silvis, Illinois
Par 35-36–71; 6,762 yards

July 13-16
purse, $4,000,000

	SCORES				TOTAL	MONEY
John Senden	64	69	64	68	265	$720,000
J.P. Hayes	64	71	66	65	266	432,000
Alex Cejka	69	68	64	67	268	232,000
Heath Slocum	69	65	66	68	268	232,000
John Riegger	67	69	69	64	269	152,000
B.J. Staten	66	70	66	67	269	152,000
Kent Jones	71	65	68	66	270	124,666.67
Billy Mayfair	70	70	63	67	270	124,666.67
Patrick Sheehan	68	66	66	70	270	124,666.66
Bubba Dickerson	68	68	70	65	271	85,714.29

	SCORES				TOTAL	MONEY
Jason Gore	67	69	67	68	271	85,714.29
Todd Hamilton	68	69	67	67	271	85,714.29
Jeff Overton	68	69	68	66	271	85,714.29
Daniel Chopra	64	69	68	70	271	85,714.28
Daisuke Maruyama	66	70	66	69	271	85,714.28
Joe Ogilvie	65	67	69	70	271	85,714.28
Steve Elkington	70	66	68	68	272	52,342.86
Dan Forsman	68	67	68	69	272	52,342.86
Bill Haas	70	66	69	67	272	52,342.86
Stephen Leaney	68	67	68	69	272	52,342.86
Bubba Watson	67	70	68	67	272	52,342.86
Michael Connell	66	70	67	69	272	52,342.85
Steve Jones	67	68	66	71	272	52,342.85
Jason Bohn	70	69	68	66	273	35,200
Kris Cox	65	68	70	70	273	35,200
John Huston	66	67	72	68	273	35,200
Matt Hansen	70	66	69	69	274	27,800
Ryan Moore	68	66	69	71	274	27,800
Ryan Palmer	67	68	70	69	274	27,800
Chris Smith	70	67	67	70	274	27,800
D.J. Trahan	69	67	67	71	274	27,800
Garrett Willis	70	70	66	68	274	27,800
Paul Azinger	67	70	68	70	275	21,133.34
Zach Johnson	64	72	70	69	275	21,133.34
Cameron Beckman	69	71	68	67	275	21,133.33
Mark Brooks	70	68	66	71	275	21,133.33
Steve Flesch	68	70	66	71	275	21,133.33
Jeff Maggert	73	65	65	72	275	21,133.33
Woody Austin	68	71	69	68	276	15,200
Craig Barlow	69	67	68	72	276	15,200
Henrik Bjornstad	67	69	70	70	276	15,200
Donnie Hammond	68	70	70	68	276	15,200
J.B. Holmes	75	65	65	71	276	15,200
Sean O'Hair	69	69	68	70	276	15,200
Jay Williamson	68	72	66	70	276	15,200
Dean Wilson	67	69	70	70	276	15,200
Nathan Green	68	71	68	70	277	10,760
Billy Hurley	67	72	65	73	277	10,760
Justin Rose	71	66	67	73	277	10,760
Camilo Villegas	69	70	69	69	277	10,760
Jeff Sluman	72	65	69	72	278	9,413.34
Omar Uresti	70	68	68	72	278	9,413.34
Brian Bateman	71	67	70	70	278	9,413.33
Charley Hoffman	69	69	69	71	278	9,413.33
Jerry Smith	69	69	69	71	278	9,413.33
Steve Stricker	68	70	68	72	278	9,413.33
Eric Axley	69	69	70	71	279	8,920
Paul Stankowski	72	67	70	70	279	8,920
Kevin Sutherland	69	66	71	73	279	8,920
Charles Warren	67	70	72	70	279	8,920
Arjun Atwal	71	67	70	72	280	8,520
Brian Henninger	68	72	70	70	280	8,520
Neal Lancaster	73	67	72	68	280	8,520
Chris Riley	68	70	69	73	280	8,520
John Rollins	71	69	68	72	280	8,520
Jimmy Walker	69	70	68	73	280	8,520
Jason Day	71	69	68	73	281	8,200
Matt Gogel	67	71	68	75	281	8,200
David Branshaw	69	69	73	71	282	8,000
Robert Damron	72	66	71	73	282	8,000

	SCORES				TOTAL	MONEY
Kirk Triplett	69	69	69	75	282	8,000
David McKenzie	66	74	73	70	283	7,760
Jason Schultz	66	73	74	70	283	7,760
Mike Small	67	72	72	72	283	7,760
David Duval	68	70	70	76	284	7,480
David Gossett	71	68	75	70	284	7,480
Mathias Gronberg	70	70	73	71	284	7,480
Scott Harrington	69	70	72	73	284	7,480
Will MacKenzie	67	73	75	71	286	7,280
Brendan Jones	68	72	76	76	292	7,200

The Open Championship

See European Tours chapter.

B.C. Open

Atunyote Golf Club, Verona, New York
Par 36-36–72; 7,315 yards

July 20-23
purse, $3,000,000

	SCORES				TOTAL	MONEY
John Rollins	67	70	68	64	269	$540,000
Bob May	73	66	67	64	270	324,000
Shigeki Maruyama	68	71	67	65	271	204,000
David Branshaw	71	64	68	69	272	132,000
Omar Uresti	67	71	70	64	272	132,000
Matt Gogel	67	71	67	68	273	90,750
Scott Gutschewski	67	71	68	67	273	90,750
Gabriel Hjertstedt	67	67	68	71	273	90,750
Daisuke Maruyama	67	67	71	68	273	90,750
Larry Mize	69	69	67	68	273	90,750
Nicholas Thompson	69	70	70	64	273	90,750
Jason Bohn	66	72	70	66	274	63,000
Ryuji Imada	67	70	71	66	274	63,000
Paul Stankowski	72	69	66	67	274	63,000
Mark Brooks	65	72	66	72	275	52,500
D.J. Trahan	69	68	71	67	275	52,500
Arjun Atwal	68	72	69	67	276	45,000
Scott Gump	67	67	69	73	276	45,000
Skip Kendall	69	69	72	66	276	45,000
Shane Bertsch	70	67	69	71	277	34,950
Michael Bradley	68	68	74	67	277	34,950
Mathias Gronberg	68	68	70	71	277	34,950
Ryan Palmer	73	68	70	66	277	34,950
Eric Axley	72	69	72	65	278	23,212.50
Jeff Brehaut	71	71	69	67	278	23,212.50
Bubba Dickerson	71	71	69	67	278	23,212.50
Harrison Frazar	66	71	72	69	278	23,212.50
Gary Hallberg	71	69	70	68	278	23,212.50
Dudley Hart	71	69	72	66	278	23,212.50
Jason Schultz	67	72	71	68	278	23,212.50
Chris Smith	69	68	74	67	278	23,212.50
Briny Baird	69	72	70	68	279	15,566.67
Greg Chalmers	73	69	68	69	279	15,566.67
Dan Forsman	69	70	71	69	279	15,566.67
Bill Glasson	72	69	69	69	279	15,566.67

	SCORES				TOTAL	MONEY
Esteban Toledo	69	67	75	68	279	15,566.67
Dean Wilson	69	70	71	69	279	15,566.67
Frank Lickliter	69	67	70	73	279	15,566.66
Andrew Magee	72	68	69	70	279	15,566.66
B.J. Staten	67	72	69	71	279	15,566.66
Cameron Beckman	70	66	74	70	280	11,100
Daniel Chopra	68	71	68	73	280	11,100
Will MacKenzie	74	68	69	69	280	11,100
Troy Matteson	72	70	71	67	280	11,100
Madalitso Muthiya	72	68	68	72	280	11,100
Notah Begay	69	71	71	70	281	8,505
Matthew Every	70	72	67	72	281	8,505
Neal Lancaster	74	68	67	72	281	8,505
Patrick Sheehan	68	70	70	73	281	8,505
Brian Henninger	69	68	73	72	282	7,236
Ryan Hietala	70	70	72	70	282	7,236
Joe Ogilvie	71	71	74	66	282	7,236
Chris Riley	72	69	70	71	282	7,236
Garrett Willis	73	69	71	69	282	7,236
Marco Dawson	70	70	73	70	283	6,810
Donnie Hammond	73	69	70	71	283	6,810
James McLean	71	70	70	72	283	6,810
Eli Zackheim	72	67	74	70	283	6,810
Jon Mills	69	72	71	72	284	6,630
Craig Parry	72	68	75	69	284	6,630
Mike Hulbert	68	72	74	71	285	6,540
Michael Clark	68	72	74	72	286	6,390
Jim Gallagher, Jr.	69	70	71	76	286	6,390
Wayne Levi	70	72	72	72	286	6,390
Blaine McCallister	70	68	71	77	286	6,390
Chip Beck	68	74	72	73	287	6,180
Jose Coceres	74	68	74	71	287	6,180
Joel Edwards	70	71	77	69	287	6,180
Bob Burns	69	70	71	78	288	6,030
Jay Williamson	70	68	76	74	288	6,030
Michael Allen	76	63	79	71	289	5,910
Guy Boros	70	72	74	73	289	5,910

U.S. Bank Championship in Milwaukee

Brown Deer Park Golf Course, Milwaukee, Wisconsin
Par 34-36–70; 6,759 yards

July 27-30
purse, $4,000,000

	SCORES				TOTAL	MONEY
Corey Pavin	61	64	68	67	260	$720,000
Jerry Kelly	64	67	64	67	262	432,000
Jeff Sluman	66	65	68	64	263	272,000
Frank Lickliter	66	66	64	69	265	176,000
D.J. Trahan	66	65	65	69	265	176,000
Billy Andrade	65	67	66	68	266	134,000
Woody Austin	70	68	63	65	266	134,000
Joey Sindelar	67	65	67	67	266	134,000
K.J. Choi	67	67	69	64	267	104,000
Nathan Green	67	64	67	69	267	104,000
Dicky Pride	68	67	69	63	267	104,000
Dean Wilson	66	70	68	63	267	104,000
Jason Day	68	64	70	66	268	80,000

		SCORES			TOTAL	MONEY
Shaun Micheel	68	65	65	70	268	80,000
Fred Funk	67	68	67	67	269	68,000
Bob May	66	68	67	68	269	68,000
Kenny Perry	70	68	66	65	269	68,000
Tommy Armour	66	68	68	68	270	50,400
Chris Couch	70	65	65	70	270	50,400
Jeff Gove	74	63	68	65	270	50,400
Kent Jones	68	66	71	65	270	50,400
Ian Leggatt	71	65	68	66	270	50,400
Chris Riley	67	65	70	68	270	50,400
Alex Cejka	67	70	68	66	271	31,657.15
Stewart Cink	68	68	69	66	271	31,657.15
Cameron Beckman	65	72	66	68	271	31,657.14
Jason Bohn	65	64	71	71	271	31,657.14
Nick O'Hern	71	65	67	68	271	31,657.14
Jimmy Walker	70	67	67	67	271	31,657.14
Brett Wetterich	69	69	66	67	271	31,657.14
Bill Glasson	69	69	67	67	272	22,685.72
John Huston	67	67	69	69	272	22,685.72
Tom Pernice, Jr.	72	65	69	66	272	22,685.72
Richard Johnson	69	65	67	71	272	22,685.71
Stephen Leaney	69	66	68	69	272	22,685.71
Brett Quigley	71	65	67	69	272	22,685.71
Omar Uresti	68	70	70	64	272	22,685.71
John Cook	71	64	70	68	273	16,400
David Frost	65	66	71	71	273	16,400
Len Mattiace	68	70	68	67	273	16,400
John Riegger	66	71	65	71	273	16,400
Mike Small	68	68	72	65	273	16,400
Kevin Sutherland	72	65	69	67	273	16,400
Duffy Waldorf	68	68	67	70	273	16,400
Robert Gamez	68	67	70	69	274	11,211.43
Dudley Hart	70	64	72	68	274	11,211.43
Tag Ridings	67	70	69	68	274	11,211.43
Steve Stricker	68	70	69	67	274	11,211.43
Scott Verplank	69	68	68	69	274	11,211.43
Bubba Watson	68	67	70	69	274	11,211.43
Hunter Mahan	69	69	71	65	274	11,211.42
Arjun Atwal	64	69	73	69	275	9,280
David Branshaw	69	67	68	71	275	9,280
Jay Delsing	68	70	66	71	275	9,280
Bob Estes	69	68	66	72	275	9,280
Todd Fischer	66	70	70	69	275	9,280
Matt Gogel	68	70	69	68	275	9,280
Brian Gay	70	64	72	70	276	8,840
Chris Smith	63	72	72	69	276	8,840
Paul Stankowski	70	66	67	73	276	8,840
Mark Wilson	69	66	72	69	276	8,840
Briny Baird	69	68	72	68	277	8,520
Shane Bertsch	68	70	71	68	277	8,520
Joe Durant	71	67	69	70	277	8,520
Jerry Smith	68	69	72	68	277	8,520
Bubba Dickerson	66	68	73	71	278	8,240
Lee Janzen	66	71	73	68	278	8,240
Ron Whittaker	70	67	72	69	278	8,240
Mark Calcavecchia	69	68	71	71	279	7,880
Kris Cox	70	65	73	71	279	7,880
Dan Forsman	69	69	68	73	279	7,880
David McKenzie	70	68	68	73	279	7,880
Jason Schultz	67	69	70	73	279	7,880

	SCORES				TOTAL	MONEY
Charles Warren	69	68	73	69	279	7,880
Scott Gump	66	70	72	72	280	7,560
Skip Kendall	65	70	71	74	280	7,560
Larry Mize	68	70	69	74	281	7,400
David Roesch	68	68	74	71	281	7,400
Garrett Willis	66	72	75	69	282	7,280
Matt Hansen	68	70	73	73	284	7,200
Nicholas Thompson	67	68	72	80	287	7,120

Buick Open

Warwick Hills Golf & Country Club,
Grand Blanc, Michigan
Par 36-36–72; 7,127 yards

August 3-6
purse, $4,800,000

	SCORES				TOTAL	MONEY
Tiger Woods	66	66	66	66	264	$864,000
Jim Furyk	66	68	69	64	267	518,400
Joe Durant	65	69	67	67	268	326,400
Sean O'Hair	68	68	66	67	269	198,400
Vaughn Taylor	67	71	63	68	269	198,400
Scott Verplank	68	66	66	69	269	198,400
Woody Austin	65	69	68	68	270	144,600
Harrison Frazar	70	64	69	67	270	144,600
Tom Pernice, Jr.	69	69	68	64	270	144,600
Brett Quigley	65	66	71	68	270	144,600
Craig Barlow	71	67	67	66	271	105,600
Kenny Perry	68	70	68	65	271	105,600
Vijay Singh	64	69	68	70	271	105,600
Camilo Villegas	66	72	66	67	271	105,600
Robert Allenby	67	67	66	72	272	76,800
Stephen Ames	69	66	66	71	272	76,800
Brian Gay	71	68	65	68	272	76,800
Lucas Glover	67	67	66	72	272	76,800
Skip Kendall	70	67	68	67	272	76,800
Jay Delsing	68	68	68	70	274	53,952
Charley Hoffman	68	67	67	72	274	53,952
David McKenzie	68	70	68	68	274	53,952
John Rollins	70	69	68	67	274	53,952
Mike Weir	63	70	68	73	274	53,952
Fred Funk	69	69	68	69	275	39,200
Greg Kraft	70	69	68	68	275	39,200
Charles Warren	71	68	68	68	275	39,200
Brad Faxon	72	69	69	66	276	32,640
Paul Goydos	70	66	71	69	276	32,640
J.J. Henry	72	67	68	69	276	32,640
Kent Jones	72	67	68	69	276	32,640
Dicky Pride	71	69	67	69	276	32,640
Michael Connell	70	70	68	69	277	24,822.86
Danny Ellis	71	70	70	66	277	24,822.86
Zach Johnson	71	65	70	71	277	24,822.86
Jeff Sluman	66	67	72	72	277	24,822.86
Bob Tway	71	69	70	67	277	24,822.86
Shane Bertsch	70	68	66	73	277	24,822.85
Scott Gutschewski	69	68	68	72	277	24,822.85
Jeff Brehaut	75	65	69	69	278	16,387.20
Bart Bryant	69	68	73	68	278	16,387.20

	SCORES				TOTAL	MONEY
James Driscoll	71	66	69	72	278	16,387.20
Stephen Leaney	69	66	72	71	278	16,387.20
Steve Lowery	68	68	72	70	278	16,387.20
Mark O'Meara	71	70	69	68	278	16,387.20
Jeff Overton	69	71	69	69	278	16,387.20
Corey Pavin	70	69	70	69	278	16,387.20
Jimmy Walker	72	67	70	69	278	16,387.20
Mark Wilson	72	67	69	70	278	16,387.20
David Branshaw	70	69	67	73	279	11,808
John Daly	69	69	68	73	279	11,808
Nathan Green	69	71	71	68	279	11,808
Kris Cox	68	69	72	71	280	11,059.20
Todd Fischer	67	68	74	71	280	11,059.20
Frank Lickliter	68	70	70	72	280	11,059.20
Bo Van Pelt	67	66	74	73	280	11,059.20
Nick Watney	70	68	68	74	280	11,059.20
Bob Estes	70	68	69	74	281	10,704
Jeff Gove	70	71	69	71	281	10,704
Brian Bateman	70	70	72	70	282	10,320
Olin Browne	68	69	73	72	282	10,320
Steve Flesch	72	65	73	72	282	10,320
Bob May	74	65	71	72	282	10,320
Geoff Ogilvy	72	69	69	72	282	10,320
Ryan Palmer	68	70	73	71	282	10,320
John Cook	73	67	70	73	283	9,984
Alex Cejka	71	70	71	72	284	9,792
J.P. Hayes	70	67	74	73	284	9,792
Arron Oberholser	66	75	73	70	284	9,792
Bill Haas	74	65	73	73	285	9,456
Ryuji Imada	70	69	70	76	285	9,456
Rod Pampling	73	68	71	73	285	9,456
Duffy Waldorf	71	69	71	74	285	9,456
Alex Aragon	71	69	73	74	287	9,168
Brent Geiberger	72	69	75	71	287	9,168
John Engler, Jr.	74	67	72	75	288	8,928
Ian Leggatt	69	72	71	76	288	8,928
John Riegger	69	72	72	75	288	8,928
Bubba Dickerson	71	70	79	69	289	8,736

The International

Castle Pines Golf Club, Castle Rock, Colorado
Par 36-36–72; 7,619 yards

August 10-13
purse, $5,500,000

	POINTS				TOTAL	MONEY
Dean Wilson	2	11	9	12	34	$990,000
Tom Lehman	5	11	8	10	34	594,000
(Wilson defeated Lehman on second playoff hole.)						
Steve Flesch	8	5	13	6	32	319,000
Daisuke Maruyama	2	10	7	13	32	319,000
Stewart Cink	11	6	8	6	31	220,000
Jeff Brehaut	10	2	9	9	30	184,250
Ian Leggatt	4	13	8	5	30	184,250
Bubba Watson	5	7	7	11	30	184,250
Nathan Green	7	5	9	8	29	159,500
Ernie Els	8	4	5	10	27	137,500
Rod Pampling	0	10	5	12	27	137,500

	POINTS				TOTAL	MONEY
Brett Quigley	8	8	2	9	27	137,500
Craig Barlow	(-2)	8	12	8	26	103,125
J.B. Holmes	5	4	10	7	26	103,125
Zach Johnson	9	3	15	(-1)	26	103,125
Kevin Sutherland	7	6	6	7	26	103,125
Briny Baird	4	4	12	4	24	85,250
Tim Petrovic	(-1)	9	9	7	24	85,250
Stuart Appleby	11	2	4	6	23	64,350
Olin Browne	6	2	9	6	23	64,350
Jeff Gove	9	7	7	0	23	64,350
Greg Kraft	9	3	4	7	23	64,350
Tom Pernice, Jr.	11	8	0	4	23	64,350
David Toms	9	1	6	7	23	64,350
Joe Ogilvie	3	6	6	7	22	43,862.50
Corey Pavin	7	3	8	4	22	43,862.50
Patrick Sheehan	10	8	0	4	22	43,862.50
Duffy Waldorf	3	14	2	3	22	43,862.50
Harrison Frazar	7	7	4	3	21	37,400
Sergio Garcia	6	10	6	(-1)	21	37,400
Chris Riley	6	6	6	3	21	37,400
Brian Bateman	5	1	11	1	18	33,275
Greg Chalmers	8	0	7	3	18	33,275
Billy Andrade	4	2	9	1	16	31,075
Danny Ellis	10	1	5	(-1)	15	29,700
Retief Goosen	3	12	3	(-5)	13	28,325

Out of Final 18 Holes

	POINTS				TOTAL	MONEY
Liang Wen-chong	1	6	7		14	25,850
Ryan Moore	8	5	1		14	25,850
Justin Rose	9	1	4		14	25,850
Justin Leonard	4	3	6		13	20,900
Davis Love	(-4)	11	6		13	20,900
Nicholas Thompson	8	2	3		13	20,900
Bob Tway	8	3	2		13	20,900
Tjaart van der Walt	1	9	3		13	20,900
Charles Warren	6	4	3		13	20,900
Mathias Gronberg	13	(-6)	5		12	14,960
David Howell	9	5	(-2)		12	14,960
Bernhard Langer	5	2	5		12	14,960
Shaun Micheel	2	6	4		12	14,960
Roger Tambellini	4	5	3		12	14,960
Mark Wilson	(-1)	10	3		12	14,960
John Senden	11	1	(-1)		11	13,200
Paul Casey	1	5	4		10	12,672
Lucas Glover	4	3	3		10	12,672
J.J. Henry	3	4	3		10	12,672
Ryuji Imada	6	0	4		10	12,672
Will MacKenzie	5	5	0		10	12,672
Jonathan Kaye	(-3)	10	2		9	12,320
Michael Connell	6	3	(-1)		8	12,045
Ben Crane	8	0	0		8	12,045
Heath Slocum	5	5	(-2)		8	12,045
Kane Webber	6	0	2		8	12,045
Jason Day	3	8	(-4)		7	11,660
Jay Delsing	9	4	(-6)		7	11,660
Bill Haas	8	2	(-3)		7	11,660
Daniel Chopra	(-1)	9	(-2)		6	11,440
Tag Ridings	5	3	(-3)		5	11,330
Bob May	5	2	(-6)		1	11,165

	POINTS		TOTAL	MONEY
Mike Sposa	4	5 (-8)	1	11,165
B.J. Staten	3	4 (-8)	(-1)	11,000

PGA Championship

Medinah Country Club, Medinah, Illinois
Par 36-36–72; 7,561 yards

August 17-20
purse, $6,500,000

	SCORES				TOTAL	MONEY
Tiger Woods	69	68	65	68	270	$1,224,000
Shaun Micheel	69	70	67	69	275	734,400
Adam Scott	71	69	69	67	276	353,600
Sergio Garcia	69	70	67	70	276	353,600
Luke Donald	68	68	66	74	276	353,600
Mike Weir	72	67	65	73	277	244,800
Steve Stricker	72	67	70	69	278	207,787.50
K.J. Choi	73	67	67	71	278	207,787.50
Ryan Moore	71	72	67	69	279	165,000
Ian Poulter	70	70	68	71	279	165,000
Geoff Ogilvy	69	68	68	74	279	165,000
Sean O'Hair	72	70	70	68	280	134,500
Chris DiMarco	71	70	67	72	280	134,500
Henrik Stenson	68	68	73	72	281	115,000
Tim Herron	69	67	72	73	281	115,000
Ernie Els	71	70	72	69	282	94,000
David Toms	71	67	71	73	282	94,000
Woody Austin	71	69	69	73	282	94,000
Phil Mickelson	69	71	68	74	282	94,000
Jonathan Byrd	69	72	74	68	283	71,250
Robert Allenby	68	74	71	70	283	71,250
Fred Funk	69	69	74	71	283	71,250
Harrison Frazar	69	72	69	73	283	71,250
Chad Campbell	71	72	75	66	284	53,100
Stewart Cink	68	74	73	69	284	53,100
Tim Clark	70	69	75	70	284	53,100
Anders Hansen	72	71	70	71	284	53,100
Steve Flesch	72	71	69	72	284	53,100
Dean Wilson	74	70	74	67	285	41,100
Heath Slocum	73	70	72	70	285	41,100
Robert Karlsson	71	73	69	72	285	41,100
Lee Westwood	69	72	71	73	285	41,100
Jim Furyk	70	72	69	74	285	41,100
Trevor Immelman	73	71	70	72	286	34,500
Retief Goosen	70	73	68	75	286	34,500
Davis Love	68	69	73	76	286	34,500
Richard Green	73	69	73	72	287	29,250
Graeme McDowell	75	68	72	72	287	29,250
Billy Mayfair	69	69	73	76	287	29,250
J.B. Holmes	71	70	68	78	287	29,250
Daniel Chopra	72	67	76	73	288	23,080
Billy Andrade	67	69	78	74	288	23,080
J.J. Henry	68	73	73	74	288	23,080
Justin Rose	73	70	70	75	288	23,080
Chris Riley	66	72	73	77	288	23,080
Lucas Glover	66	74	77	72	289	19,025
Olin Browne	75	66	73	75	289	19,025
Jerry Kelly	70	74	74	72	290	17,300

	SCORES				TOTAL	MONEY
Joey Sindelar	74	70	73	74	291	15,533.34
Nathan Green	71	71	74	75	291	15,533.34
Rich Beem	75	69	72	75	291	15,533.33
Corey Pavin	72	71	72	76	291	15,533.33
Ryan Palmer	70	73	72	76	291	15,533.33
Kenny Perry	72	71	71	77	291	15,533.33
Stuart Appleby	70	73	79	70	292	14,320
Hideto Tanihara	73	71	78	70	292	14,320
Aaron Baddeley	70	74	75	73	292	14,320
Stephen Ames	74	69	74	75	292	14,320
Jose Maria Olazabal	72	68	75	77	292	14,320
Steve Lowery	70	72	76	75	293	13,750
Ben Curtis	72	72	73	76	293	13,750
Jeff Maggert	75	68	78	74	295	13,425
Charles Warren	73	70	77	75	295	13,425
Jason Gore	70	73	75	77	295	13,425
Bob Tway	72	71	75	78	296	13,175
Miguel Angel Jimenez	70	73	75	78	296	13,175
David Howell	71	71	73	82	297	13,025
Don Yrene	71	72	77	80	300	12,875
Jay Haas	75	68	74	83	300	12,875
Jim Kane	71	71	80	79	301	12,725

Out of Final 36 Holes

Greg Owen	74	71		145
Zach Johnson	71	74		145
David Duval	73	72		145
Charles Howell	70	75		145
Charl Schwartzel	72	73		145
Mike Small	72	73		145
Anthony Wall	73	72		145
Brett Quigley	76	69		145
Chris Couch	74	71		145
Vijay Singh	73	72		145
Angel Cabrera	74	71		145
Rory Sabbatini	72	73		145
Arron Oberholser	75	70		145
Brad Faxon	70	76		146
Camilo Villegas	75	71		146
Michael Campbell	70	76		146
Pat Perez	73	73		146
Bob Estes	74	72		146
Andrew Buckle	73	73		146
John Rollins	73	73		146
John Daly	71	75		146
Robert Gamez	70	76		146
Justin Leonard	75	71		146
Shigeki Maruyama	76	70		146
Wes Short, Jr.	72	74		146
Bart Bryant	72	74		146
Brandt Jobe	76	70		146
Jesper Parnevik	71	75		146
Craig Thomas	76	70		146
John Senden	75	72		147
Rod Pampling	71	76		147
John Bickerton	73	74		147
Jeff Sluman	74	73		147
Paul Azinger	74	73		147
Nick O'Hern	74	73		147

	SCORES		TOTAL
Fred Couples	71	76	147
Paul Casey	74	73	147
Lee Rinker	72	75	147
Bradley Dredge	75	73	148
Scott Verplank	72	76	148
Peter Lonard	70	78	148
Craig Barlow	70	78	148
Ted Purdy	73	75	148
Kenneth Ferrie	70	78	148
Gregory Bisconti	70	78	148
Andres Romero	71	77	148
Carl Pettersson	72	76	148
Mark Brooks	73	75	148
Nick Price	75	73	148
Colin Montgomerie	77	71	148
Tom Lehman	77	71	148
Niclas Fasth	74	74	148
Stephen Dodd	73	75	148
Ben Crane	72	77	149
Johan Edfors	76	73	149
Vaughn Taylor	71	78	149
Padraig Harrington	75	74	149
Chris Wiemers	73	76	149
Gonzalo Fernandez-Castano	75	75	150
Thomas Bjorn	80	70	150
Paul Broadhurst	74	76	150
Jason Bohn	77	73	150
Kelly Mitchum	71	79	150
Steve Schneiter	72	79	151
Simon Khan	74	77	151
Tim Weinhart	77	74	151
John Aber	78	73	151
Bernhard Langer	76	75	151
Chip Sullivan	79	72	151
Nick Dougherty	80	72	152
Jeffrey Cranford	77	75	152
Alan Schulte	75	77	152
Larry Nelson	80	72	152
S.K. Ho	74	79	153
Brett Wetterich	76	77	153
Todd Hamilton	77	76	153
Tom Pernice, Jr.	77	76	153
Jerry Haas	74	79	153
Kirk Triplett	75	78	153
Ron Philo, Jr.	82	73	155
Richard S. Johnson	79	76	155
Mark Brown	80	77	157
Barry Evans	81	79	160
Sam Arnold	78	84	162
Mark Calcavecchia			WD
Dudley Hart			WD

(Professionals who did not complete 72 holes received $2,250.)

WGC - Bridgestone Invitational

Firestone Country Club, South Course, Akron, Ohio
Par 35-35–70; 7,283 yards

August 24-27
purse, $7,500,000

	SCORES				TOTAL	MONEY
Tiger Woods	67	64	71	68	270	$1,300,000
Stewart Cink	70	67	64	69	270	750,000
(Woods defeated Cink on fourth playoff hole.)						
Jim Furyk	69	65	69	68	271	450,000
Angel Cabrera	70	68	70	65	273	246,250
Paul Casey	69	69	64	71	273	246,250
Lucas Glover	66	69	69	69	273	246,250
Davis Love	67	65	70	71	273	246,250
Luke Donald	67	69	70	68	274	152,500
David Toms	67	74	65	68	274	152,500
J.J. Henry	70	68	68	69	275	120,000
Arron Oberholser	70	71	69	65	275	120,000
Adam Scott	63	71	71	70	275	120,000
Trevor Immelman	69	70	68	70	277	95,000
Ian Poulter	71	71	67	68	277	95,000
Kevin Stadler	68	67	70	72	277	95,000
Ben Crane	73	67	70	68	278	85,000
Michael Campbell	67	71	70	71	279	82,000
Stephen Ames	69	70	71	70	280	77,000
Thomas Bjorn	72	67	67	74	280	77,000
Robert Gamez	70	67	72	71	280	77,000
Vaughn Taylor	71	67	71	71	280	77,000
Robert Allenby	71	71	68	71	281	68,000
K.J. Choi	75	70	67	69	281	68,000
Sergio Garcia	69	73	68	71	281	68,000
Jose Maria Olazabal	68	70	74	69	281	68,000
Mike Weir	69	71	69	72	281	68,000
Chris DiMarco	68	72	71	71	282	60,500
Padraig Harrington	73	71	70	68	282	60,500
Kenny Perry	73	70	66	73	282	60,500
Carl Pettersson	70	72	68	72	282	60,500
Ernie Els	68	67	70	78	283	56,000
Brad Faxon	69	69	75	70	283	56,000
Justin Leonard	70	69	72	72	283	56,000
Nick O'Hern	72	69	71	71	283	56,000
Henrik Stenson	75	73	67	68	283	56,000
Jason Gore	65	76	73	70	284	50,500
Zach Johnson	71	68	72	73	284	50,500
Geoff Ogilvy	69	76	70	69	284	50,500
Rory Sabbatini	75	71	68	70	284	50,500
Charl Schwartzel	72	69	70	73	284	50,500
Brett Wetterich	72	73	71	68	284	50,500
Fred Funk	72	70	72	71	285	46,166.67
Tom Lehman	72	69	73	71	285	46,166.67
Ben Curtis	71	72	72	70	285	46,166.66
Rod Pampling	75	71	71	69	286	44,500
Vijay Singh	70	74	73	69	286	44,500
Dean Wilson	75	70	68	73	286	44,500
Retief Goosen	71	73	74	69	287	43,250
Corey Pavin	74	73	68	72	287	43,250
Olin Browne	68	75	70	75	288	41,750
Chad Campbell	68	76	72	72	288	41,750
Stephen Dodd	74	73	69	72	288	41,750
J.B. Holmes	71	72	68	77	288	41,750

	SCORES				TOTAL	MONEY
Aaron Baddeley	73	74	69	73	289	39,500
Mark Hensby	74	76	68	71	289	39,500
Miguel Angel Jimenez	70	72	77	70	289	39,500
Thomas Levet	77	69	69	74	289	39,500
Phil Mickelson	74	74	68	73	289	39,500
David Howell	67	79	71	74	291	37,500
Jeff Maggert	75	70	75	71	291	37,500
Scott Verplank	71	75	70	75	291	37,500
Bart Bryant	72	83	69	68	292	36,000
Johan Edfors	75	76	71	70	292	36,000
Robert Karlsson	75	70	73	74	292	36,000
Shiv Kapur	72	75	72	74	293	35,000
John Bickerton	74	75	70	75	294	34,250
Paul McGinley	77	75	70	72	294	34,250
Mark Calcavecchia	75	72	77	71	295	33,000
Chris Couch	72	74	72	77	295	33,000
Tim Herron	76	74	73	72	295	33,000
Stuart Appleby	76	75	76	69	296	31,750
Peter Lonard	74	73	77	72	296	31,750
Wes Short, Jr.	76	71	73	76	296	31,750
Tim Clark	68	75	80	77	300	31,250
Gonzalo Fernandez-Castano	74	76	81	70	301	31,000
Tatsuhiko Takahashi	81	73	75	75	304	30,750

Reno-Tahoe Open

Montreux Golf & Country Club, Reno, Nevada
Par 36-36–72; 7,473 yards

August 24-27
purse, $3,000,000

	SCORES				TOTAL	MONEY
Will MacKenzie	63	67	67	71	268	$540,000
Bob Estes	64	65	68	72	269	324,000
Joe Ogilvie	71	68	69	62	270	204,000
Daniel Chopra	71	67	64	69	271	144,000
Jeff Brehaut	70	68	65	69	272	105,375
Jose Coceres	72	67	67	66	272	105,375
John Cook	66	66	69	71	272	105,375
Nick Watney	66	68	71	67	272	105,375
Alex Cejka	67	67	70	69	273	84,000
Shigeki Maruyama	70	70	64	69	273	84,000
Jason Day	68	68	67	71	274	66,000
Harrison Frazar	69	72	66	67	274	66,000
Scott Gutschewski	68	67	71	68	274	66,000
Kevin Sutherland	70	67	66	71	274	66,000
Bill Haas	71	66	68	70	275	51,000
Jeff Overton	72	69	66	68	275	51,000
Pat Perez	67	71	69	68	275	51,000
Marco Dawson	71	67	68	70	276	42,000
Troy Matteson	70	71	64	71	276	42,000
Patrick Sheehan	74	66	68	68	276	42,000
Briny Baird	71	68	66	72	277	28,162.50
Craig Barlow	67	68	71	71	277	28,162.50
Shane Bertsch	68	70	69	70	277	28,162.50
Brian Gay	72	66	72	67	277	28,162.50
Kent Jones	72	68	69	68	277	28,162.50
Graeme McDowell	69	70	68	70	277	28,162.50
David McKenzie	66	68	72	71	277	28,162.50

	SCORES				TOTAL	MONEY
Yusaku Miyazato	69	66	70	72	277	28,162.50
Skip Kendall	71	71	68	68	278	21,300
Bill Glasson	69	66	73	71	279	18,225
Brian Henninger	70	68	71	70	279	18,225
Gabriel Hjertstedt	70	72	67	70	279	18,225
Spike McRoy	72	66	71	70	279	18,225
Duffy Waldorf	72	68	71	68	279	18,225
Garrett Willis	69	71	68	71	279	18,225
Eric Axley	72	71	69	68	280	13,825
Rich Beem	66	69	72	73	280	13,825
Charley Hoffman	71	66	71	72	280	13,825
Chris Riley	73	70	68	69	280	13,825
Grant Waite	74	67	69	70	280	13,825
Ron Whittaker	71	71	68	70	280	13,825
Brent Geiberger	71	69	73	68	281	10,800
Mathias Gronberg	69	70	71	71	281	10,800
Jason Schultz	72	70	70	69	281	10,800
Nicholas Thompson	73	68	68	72	281	10,800
David Branshaw	76	66	68	72	282	7,905
Mark Brooks	70	66	73	73	282	7,905
Brian Davis	71	69	70	72	282	7,905
Jay Delsing	74	68	65	75	282	7,905
Joe Durant	68	68	78	68	282	7,905
Brandt Jobe	70	69	70	73	282	7,905
Mike Sposa	72	68	70	72	282	7,905
D.J. Trahan	69	70	72	71	282	7,905
Michael Allen	71	71	71	70	283	6,840
Michael Bradley	71	70	68	74	283	6,840
Todd Fischer	69	71	71	72	283	6,840
Carlos Franco	68	71	71	73	283	6,840
Roger Tambellini	74	69	70	70	283	6,840
Jeff Gove	69	71	73	71	284	6,570
Shaun Micheel	70	68	75	71	284	6,570
Dicky Pride	70	70	69	75	284	6,570
Jerry Smith	72	68	70	74	284	6,570
Steve Elkington	70	71	72	72	285	6,300
John Engler, Jr.	68	75	68	74	285	6,300
Scott Piercy	74	64	75	72	285	6,300
Kirk Triplett	73	70	67	75	285	6,300
Tjaart van der Walt	70	70	74	71	285	6,300
Len Mattiace	70	73	71	72	286	6,090
Phil Tataurangi	73	70	71	72	286	6,090
Jon Mills	72	71	74	70	287	6,000
Arjun Atwal	71	72	71	74	288	5,910
Willie Wood	69	74	71	74	288	5,910
Jonathan Kaye	72	71	73	73	289	5,790
Jim McGovern	70	70	72	77	289	5,790
Robert Garrigus	70	71	79	70	290	5,700
Steven Bowditch	73	70	74	74	291	5,640
Joel Edwards	74	69	73	76	292	5,580

Deutsche Bank Championship

TPC of Boston, Norton, Massachusetts
Par 36-35–71; 7,415 yards

September 1-4
purse, $5,500,000

	SCORES				TOTAL	MONEY
Tiger Woods	66	72	67	63	268	$990,000
Vijay Singh	70	71	61	68	270	594,000
Brian Bateman	69	71	70	66	276	374,000
Robert Allenby	70	66	73	68	277	242,000
Justin Rose	67	69	69	72	277	242,000
J.J. Henry	68	71	68	71	278	198,000
Aaron Baddeley	67	71	71	70	279	160,050
Stephen Leaney	70	71	69	69	279	160,050
Frank Lickliter	71	72	69	67	279	160,050
Shaun Micheel	69	70	68	72	279	160,050
Steve Stricker	71	72	69	67	279	160,050
Lucas Glover	70	73	69	68	280	115,500
Ryan Moore	70	71	68	71	280	115,500
Bubba Watson	73	67	70	70	280	115,500
Nathan Green	67	74	70	70	281	93,500
Bill Haas	71	72	67	71	281	93,500
Joe Ogilvie	67	74	70	70	281	93,500
Matt Hansen	71	72	70	69	282	74,250
Charles Howell	73	69	71	69	282	74,250
Ryuji Imada	72	72	68	70	282	74,250
Steve Lowery	73	70	70	69	282	74,250
Billy Andrade	70	70	70	73	283	52,800
Bill Glasson	70	70	71	72	283	52,800
Kent Jones	69	76	67	71	283	52,800
Hunter Mahan	70	71	73	69	283	52,800
Paul Stankowski	70	71	72	70	283	52,800
Eric Axley	73	70	71	70	284	40,700
James Driscoll	69	75	71	69	284	40,700
Robert Karlsson	68	71	72	73	284	40,700
Briny Baird	75	69	70	71	285	33,412.50
Olin Browne	69	69	73	74	285	33,412.50
Steve Flesch	72	73	69	71	285	33,412.50
Brandt Jobe	70	75	66	74	285	33,412.50
Ian Leggatt	70	73	71	71	285	33,412.50
Kenny Perry	69	71	71	74	285	33,412.50
Jonathan Byrd	72	72	70	72	286	26,468.75
Jose Coceres	72	69	73	72	286	26,468.75
Harrison Frazar	72	71	73	70	286	26,468.75
Shigeki Maruyama	71	72	72	71	286	26,468.75
David Branshaw	71	71	69	76	287	22,000
Ryan Hietala	73	70	71	73	287	22,000
Jeff Overton	71	73	71	72	287	22,000
John Rollins	70	73	70	74	287	22,000
Lee Janzen	71	74	73	70	288	16,628.34
Heath Slocum	74	70	72	72	288	16,628.34
Dan Forsman	76	68	70	74	288	16,628.33
Carlos Franco	72	68	75	73	288	16,628.33
Len Mattiace	70	69	71	78	288	16,628.33
Bob May	67	72	76	73	288	16,628.33
John Riegger	73	70	73	73	289	13,074.29
Tjaart van der Walt	71	74	71	73	289	13,074.29
Bo Van Pelt	70	74	72	73	289	13,074.29
Ron Whittaker	70	75	73	71	289	13,074.29
John Huston	72	71	71	75	289	13,074.28

	SCORES				TOTAL	MONEY
Adam Scott	70	73	72	74	289	13,074.28
Kevin Sutherland	70	73	72	74	289	13,074.28
Jeff Brehaut	73	71	74	72	290	12,265
Robert Garrigus	72	72	70	76	290	12,265
Sean O'Hair	72	71	74	73	290	12,265
Jeff Sluman	70	72	72	76	290	12,265
Michael Allen	68	73	76	74	291	11,770
Brent Geiberger	72	72	76	71	291	11,770
Troy Matteson	70	73	72	76	291	11,770
John Senden	73	72	70	76	291	11,770
Nicholas Thompson	68	76	76	71	291	11,770
Brian Gay	70	74	75	73	292	11,330
D.A. Points	71	74	70	77	292	11,330
Camilo Villegas	72	69	76	75	292	11,330
Jason Bohn	72	72	73	76	293	11,000
Jay Delsing	72	73	77	71	293	11,000
Jonathan Kaye	70	74	72	77	293	11,000
Gabriel Hjertstedt	72	70	79	73	294	10,780
Henrik Bjornstad	69	75	75	76	295	10,560
Danny Ellis	74	70	75	76	295	10,560
Steve Jones	69	76	75	75	295	10,560
Jason Gore	68	77	78	73	296	10,175
Peter Lonard	68	75	77	76	296	10,175
Ryan Palmer	69	76	79	72	296	10,175
Jason Schultz	71	74	74	77	296	10,175
Todd Hamilton	68	73	75	81	297	9,900

Canadian Open

Hamilton Golf & Country Club, Ancaster, Ontario, Canada
Par 35-35–70; 6,985 yards

September 7-10
purse, $5,000,000

	SCORES				TOTAL	MONEY
Jim Furyk	63	71	67	65	266	$900,000
Bart Bryant	69	67	64	67	267	540,000
Sean O'Hair	65	69	66	68	268	340,000
Brett Quigley	71	63	67	68	269	240,000
Jonathan Byrd	65	68	67	70	270	169,500
Trevor Immelman	68	66	66	70	270	169,500
Steve Lowery	70	66	65	69	270	169,500
Rory Sabbatini	67	69	68	66	270	169,500
Camilo Villegas	69	64	69	68	270	169,500
Steve Stricker	67	69	68	67	271	135,000
Paul Azinger	69	69	68	66	272	115,000
Stewart Cink	69	69	68	66	272	115,000
Arron Oberholser	65	68	69	70	272	115,000
Tom Pernice, Jr.	66	68	70	69	273	90,000
Justin Rose	63	71	65	74	273	90,000
Bubba Watson	65	71	68	69	273	90,000
Frank Lickliter	64	72	68	70	274	75,000
Jesper Parnevik	65	68	70	71	274	75,000
Jeff Sluman	69	69	67	69	274	75,000
Aaron Baddeley	67	71	70	67	275	50,437.50
Ben Curtis	69	66	71	69	275	50,437.50
Nathan Green	64	70	69	72	275	50,437.50
David Hearn	69	67	71	68	275	50,437.50

	SCORES				TOTAL	MONEY
Ryuji Imada	66	68	71	70	275	50,437.50
Mark O'Meara	69	69	67	70	275	50,437.50
D.A. Points	68	70	70	67	275	50,437.50
Bo Van Pelt	69	71	66	69	275	50,437.50
Kevin Sutherland	71	69	63	73	276	37,000
Brian Bateman	67	70	70	70	277	31,791.67
Brian Davis	67	68	72	70	277	31,791.67
Fred Funk	67	70	71	69	277	31,791.67
Charles Warren	70	69	68	70	277	31,791.67
Eric Axley	68	66	70	73	277	31,791.66
Mark Calcavecchia	66	74	66	71	277	31,791.66
Jeff Brehaut	68	68	70	72	278	24,125
Greg Chalmers	70	70	70	68	278	24,125
Stephen Gangluff	69	68	69	72	278	24,125
Kent Jones	68	70	69	71	278	24,125
Vijay Singh	68	69	70	71	278	24,125
Omar Uresti	71	69	67	71	278	24,125
Alex Cejka	69	71	67	72	279	19,500
Rob Oppenheim	66	70	72	71	279	19,500
Nicholas Thompson	71	68	72	68	279	19,500
Olin Browne	70	70	72	68	280	14,177.78
Steve Flesch	70	70	71	69	280	14,177.78
Bill Haas	67	72	69	72	280	14,177.78
Matt Hansen	69	70	71	70	280	14,177.78
Dudley Hart	70	68	69	73	280	14,177.78
Ian Leggatt	70	70	68	72	280	14,177.78
Will MacKenzie	68	68	71	73	280	14,177.78
Robert Garrigus	68	71	68	73	280	14,177.77
Brandt Jobe	64	72	68	76	280	14,177.77
Jason Bohn	72	68	68	73	281	11,414.29
Marco Dawson	68	72	69	72	281	11,414.29
John Huston	71	68	71	71	281	11,414.29
Troy Matteson	67	73	69	72	281	11,414.29
Bob Estes	68	71	68	74	281	11,414.28
Bill Glasson	69	69	69	74	281	11,414.28
Jeff Overton	70	70	68	73	281	11,414.28
Woody Austin	72	68	71	71	282	10,650
Brent Geiberger	68	70	72	72	282	10,650
Charles Howell	70	70	70	72	282	10,650
Richard Johnson	67	72	70	73	282	10,650
Zach Johnson	70	70	69	73	282	10,650
Hunter Mahan	73	66	71	72	282	10,650
Greg Owen	68	72	73	69	282	10,650
Tim Petrovic	67	73	71	71	282	10,650
Kris Cox	68	69	70	76	283	10,100
Peter Lonard	70	70	70	73	283	10,100
Nick Price	68	72	72	71	283	10,100
*Richard Scott	69	69	70	75	283	
Billy Andrade	70	70	71	73	284	9,900
*Victor Ciesielski	68	70	69	77	284	
David Branshaw	72	67	75	72	286	9,700
David Frost	69	70	73	74	286	9,700
Jerry Smith	67	73	72	74	286	9,700
Carlos Franco	70	70	73	76	289	9,500

84 Lumber Classic

Nemacolin Woodlands Resort & Spa, Mystic Rock Course,
Farmington, Pennsylvania
Par 36-36—72; 7,516 yards

September 14-17
purse, $4,600,000

	SCORES				TOTAL	MONEY
Ben Curtis	66	69	69	70	274	$828,000
Charles Howell	67	69	68	72	276	496,800
Brett Quigley	69	70	68	70	277	312,800
Robert Garrigus	67	70	68	73	278	202,400
Ted Purdy	66	72	73	67	278	202,400
Kent Jones	69	68	75	67	279	154,100
Ryan Moore	68	67	71	73	279	154,100
Charles Warren	70	72	66	71	279	154,100
Briny Baird	73	67	67	73	280	115,000
Hunter Mahan	67	71	67	75	280	115,000
Jeff Overton	72	68	71	69	280	115,000
Greg Owen	69	68	68	75	280	115,000
Steve Stricker	70	67	70	73	280	115,000
Jeff Gove	72	67	69	73	281	78,200
Paul Goydos	69	73	71	68	281	78,200
Richard Johnson	72	72	68	69	281	78,200
Will MacKenzie	66	73	69	73	281	78,200
Justin Rose	69	71	70	71	281	78,200
Charley Hoffman	70	70	70	72	282	64,400
Robert Allenby	75	70	66	72	283	47,971.43
Marco Dawson	67	76	72	68	283	47,971.43
Harrison Frazar	71	71	69	72	283	47,971.43
Jason Gore	73	70	70	70	283	47,971.43
Jesper Parnevik	72	69	71	71	283	47,971.43
Rory Sabbatini	66	71	70	76	283	47,971.43
Michael Allen	72	68	68	75	283	47,971.42
Alex Aragon	72	71	69	72	284	28,136.67
K.J. Choi	74	68	69	73	284	28,136.67
Ben Crane	73	72	65	74	284	28,136.67
Brent Geiberger	74	69	71	70	284	28,136.67
John Huston	71	70	70	73	284	28,136.67
David McKenzie	71	72	68	73	284	28,136.67
Scott Piercy	72	70	71	71	284	28,136.67
D.A. Points	71	67	73	73	284	28,136.67
Greg Kraft	66	74	66	78	284	28,136.66
Tim Petrovic	68	74	69	73	284	28,136.66
Vijay Singh	71	71	68	74	284	28,136.66
Nicholas Thompson	64	72	71	77	284	28,136.66
Jason Bohn	69	70	69	77	285	19,320
Chris DiMarco	74	71	70	70	285	19,320
D.J. Trahan	73	69	69	74	285	19,320
Duffy Waldorf	68	76	66	75	285	19,320
Mathias Gronberg	72	72	70	72	286	16,560
Chris Smith	72	73	71	70	286	16,560
Henrik Bjornstad	75	68	74	70	287	13,156
Danny Ellis	74	70	72	71	287	13,156
John Engler, Jr.	69	73	73	72	287	13,156
Jeff Maggert	69	72	70	76	287	13,156
Patrick Sheehan	69	72	72	74	287	13,156
Mark Wilson	71	73	69	74	287	13,156
Shane Bertsch	72	70	72	74	288	10,892.80
J.B. Holmes	71	69	71	77	288	10,892.80
Sean O'Hair	67	69	78	74	288	10,892.80

	SCORES				TOTAL	MONEY
David Toms	70	74	70	74	288	10,892.80
Bo Van Pelt	72	67	67	82	288	10,892.80
Alex Cejka	71	70	74	74	289	10,304
Bubba Dickerson	72	71	71	75	289	10,304
Jerry Kelly	71	71	71	76	289	10,304
Dicky Pride	73	69	70	77	289	10,304
Jason Schultz	71	74	68	76	289	10,304
Robert Damron	71	70	71	78	290	9,752
Brian Davis	72	71	69	78	290	9,752
Todd Fischer	73	71	71	75	290	9,752
Robert Gamez	66	76	74	74	290	9,752
Mathew Goggin	74	70	71	75	290	9,752
Brian Henninger	72	73	73	72	290	9,752
Camilo Villegas	73	71	71	75	290	9,752
Bill Haas	72	73	70	76	291	9,338
Ron Whittaker	73	72	70	76	291	9,338
Nathan Green	72	72	70	78	292	9,154
Tag Ridings	67	72	74	79	292	9,154
Joe Durant	76	69	68	80	293	8,924
Skip Kendall	70	75	72	76	293	8,924
Neal Lancaster	74	71	72	76	293	8,924
Jason Day	74	71	72	77	294	8,648
Vance Veazey	72	72	72	78	294	8,648
Brett Wetterich	75	70	74	75	294	8,648
Hidemichi Tanaka	70	75	76	74	295	8,464
Mark Brooks	75	69	74	79	297	8,372
Ryan Hietala	71	74	76	78	299	8,280
Mark Calcavecchia	75	69	77	80	301	8,188

The Ryder Cup

See European Tours chapter.

Valero Texas Open

LaCantera Golf Club, Resort Course, San Antonio, Texas
Par 35-35–70; 6,881 yards

September 21-24
purse, $4,000,000

	SCORES				TOTAL	MONEY
Eric Axley	68	63	63	71	265	$720,000
Anthony Kim	69	68	66	65	268	298,666.67
Dean Wilson	66	67	66	69	268	298,666.67
Justin Rose	64	71	65	68	268	298,666.66
Frank Lickliter	67	66	65	71	269	152,000
Chris Riley	70	64	64	71	269	152,000
David McKenzie	65	68	68	69	270	134,000
Paul Goydos	69	63	69	70	271	120,000
Charley Hoffman	66	67	67	71	271	120,000
Jose Coceres	68	73	68	63	272	104,000
Harrison Frazar	69	66	70	67	272	104,000
Cameron Beckman	66	68	71	68	273	84,000
Steve Flesch	72	67	67	67	273	84,000
Daisuke Maruyama	72	69	66	66	273	84,000
Danny Ellis	68	69	65	73	275	62,000
Bob Estes	72	67	65	71	275	62,000
Brandt Jobe	69	67	65	74	275	62,000
Richard Johnson	67	69	69	70	275	62,000

	SCORES				TOTAL	MONEY
Kent Jones	69	71	65	70	275	62,000
D.A. Points	65	66	72	72	275	62,000
Robert Gamez	69	69	69	69	276	36,533.34
Brian Gay	69	67	71	69	276	36,533.34
Dudley Hart	69	69	69	69	276	36,533.34
Arjun Atwal	71	70	67	68	276	36,533.33
Steve Elkington	70	71	68	67	276	36,533.33
Fred Funk	69	71	66	70	276	36,533.33
J.P. Hayes	70	67	66	73	276	36,533.33
Bernhard Langer	68	65	69	74	276	36,533.33
Ted Purdy	65	69	64	78	276	36,533.33
Bart Bryant	69	69	66	73	277	23,771.43
Marco Dawson	68	73	66	70	277	23,771.43
Jonathan Kaye	68	70	67	72	277	23,771.43
Larry Mize	70	69	68	70	277	23,771.43
D.J. Trahan	70	70	67	70	277	23,771.43
Bob Tway	67	68	70	72	277	23,771.43
Jesper Parnevik	69	71	72	65	277	23,771.42
Olin Browne	71	70	68	69	278	17,600
David Frost	70	67	72	69	278	17,600
Greg Kraft	70	69	72	67	278	17,600
Justin Leonard	67	71	68	72	278	17,600
Wes Short, Jr.	69	70	66	73	278	17,600
Paul Stankowski	70	69	68	71	278	17,600
Robert Damron	72	67	66	74	279	12,480
Brent Geiberger	69	71	70	69	279	12,480
Gary Hallberg	68	72	67	72	279	12,480
Jerry Kelly	70	71	66	72	279	12,480
Hunter Mahan	70	71	69	69	279	12,480
John Senden	71	69	66	73	279	12,480
Tjaart van der Walt	70	68	70	71	279	12,480
Briny Baird	70	71	69	70	280	9,450
Alex Cejka	64	73	67	76	280	9,450
Shigeki Maruyama	66	73	72	69	280	9,450
Rocco Mediate	71	68	71	70	280	9,450
Shaun Micheel	71	69	69	71	280	9,450
Patrick Sheehan	70	68	72	70	280	9,450
Mike Sposa	74	66	68	72	280	9,450
Nicholas Thompson	69	70	72	69	280	9,450
Bubba Dickerson	69	67	75	70	281	8,920
Brian Henninger	70	70	69	72	281	8,920
Bob Burns	65	71	72	74	282	8,560
Michael Connell	70	69	69	74	282	8,560
Scott Gump	68	68	70	76	282	8,560
Ryan Palmer	67	72	72	71	282	8,560
Dicky Pride	68	73	70	71	282	8,560
Jimmy Walker	70	71	72	69	282	8,560
Ron Whittaker	71	69	70	72	282	8,560
Brian Davis	70	71	73	69	283	8,120
David Duval	67	73	72	71	283	8,120
Jeff Overton	69	70	67	77	283	8,120
John Rollins	73	66	73	71	283	8,120
Guy Boros	70	70	67	79	286	7,840
Omar Uresti	71	68	72	75	286	7,840
Mark Wilson	68	71	67	80	286	7,840
Ryan Hietala	67	73	69	78	287	7,680
Donnie Hammond	73	68	75	73	289	7,560
Chris Smith	72	68	68	81	289	7,560
Blaine McCallister	68	71	77	75	291	7,440
Hidemichi Tanaka	73	67	77	79	296	7,360

WGC - American Express Championship

See European Tours chapter.

Southern Farm Bureau Classic

Annandale Golf Club, Madison, Mississippi
Par 36-36–72; 7,199 yards

September 28-October 1
purse, $3,000,000

	SCORES				TOTAL	MONEY
D.J. Trahan	65	68	71	71	275	$540,000
Joe Durant	70	65	74	66	275	324,000
(Trahan defeated Durant on third playoff hole.)						
Lee Janzen	70	69	67	70	276	204,000
J.P. Hayes	73	68	68	68	277	144,000
Glen Day	67	72	73	66	278	109,500
Ted Purdy	68	70	72	68	278	109,500
Bo Van Pelt	69	70	70	69	278	109,500
Olin Browne	72	69	71	67	279	78,000
Robert Damron	69	69	71	70	279	78,000
Fred Funk	69	70	71	69	279	78,000
Jason Gore	68	71	70	70	279	78,000
Troy Matteson	72	66	71	70	279	78,000
Nick Watney	67	71	71	70	279	78,000
Marco Dawson	71	71	68	70	280	55,500
Shaun Micheel	74	67	69	70	280	55,500
Daniel Chopra	71	68	68	74	281	39,400
Brad Faxon	68	67	72	74	281	39,400
Robert Garrigus	72	71	70	68	281	39,400
Jonathan Kaye	72	70	67	72	281	39,400
Anthony Kim	73	71	67	70	281	39,400
Shigeki Maruyama	69	72	71	69	281	39,400
Rocco Mediate	72	70	67	72	281	39,400
Tim Petrovic	75	67	69	70	281	39,400
Kevin Sutherland	71	68	70	72	281	39,400
Cameron Beckman	73	69	69	71	282	21,466.67
Chris Couch	73	68	69	72	282	21,466.67
Jeff Gove	76	69	67	70	282	21,466.67
Mathias Gronberg	68	68	77	69	282	21,466.67
Skip Kendall	68	69	72	73	282	21,466.67
Bernhard Langer	74	68	68	72	282	21,466.67
Eric Axley	73	70	75	64	282	21,466.66
Ian Leggatt	70	72	67	73	282	21,466.66
Chris Riley	70	69	69	74	282	21,466.66
Michael Allen	70	71	69	73	283	15,480
Chris Smith	74	70	67	72	283	15,480
Jerry Smith	74	70	69	70	283	15,480
Mike Sposa	72	73	70	68	283	15,480
Mark Wilson	72	72	68	71	283	15,480
Henrik Bjornstad	68	76	71	69	284	12,600
John Engler, Jr.	73	72	72	67	284	12,600
Dicky Pride	71	68	74	71	284	12,600
John Senden	71	71	71	71	284	12,600
Paul Azinger	77	68	71	69	285	9,360
Kris Cox	75	67	67	76	285	9,360
Gabriel Hjertstedt	67	73	71	74	285	9,360
Ryuji Imada	73	69	72	71	285	9,360
Frank Lickliter	70	69	70	76	285	9,360

	SCORES				TOTAL	MONEY
Steve Lowery	73	71	73	68	285	9,360
Vance Veazey	73	70	72	70	285	9,360
Jason Bohn	73	67	76	70	286	7,131.43
David Duval	70	69	72	75	286	7,131.43
Todd Hamilton	73	70	72	71	286	7,131.43
Steve Jones	74	69	72	71	286	7,131.43
Neal Lancaster	72	71	74	69	286	7,131.43
Bob May	72	68	73	73	286	7,131.43
Duffy Waldorf	71	74	72	69	286	7,131.42
Mark Brooks	70	72	72	73	287	6,690
John Daly	76	65	70	76	287	6,690
Brian Davis	74	70	74	69	287	6,690
Steve Elkington	77	67	71	72	287	6,690
Charley Hoffman	74	70	73	71	288	6,390
Jerry Kelly	73	71	73	71	288	6,390
Larry Mize	73	72	71	72	288	6,390
Patrick Sheehan	72	67	78	71	288	6,390
Mike Small	70	70	73	75	288	6,390
Nicholas Thompson	71	73	72	72	288	6,390
Arjun Atwal	69	76	68	76	289	6,090
Alex Cejka	70	71	79	69	289	6,090
John Huston	69	75	68	77	289	6,090
Ron Whittaker	73	72	75	69	289	6,090
Woody Austin	74	69	78	69	290	5,940
Andrew Magee	74	71	76	70	291	5,820
Blaine McCallister	74	68	73	76	291	5,820
Darron Stiles	73	72	71	75	291	5,820
Notah Begay	71	71	77	74	293	5,700
Len Mattiace	71	72	79	72	294	5,610
Tag Ridings	73	72	77	72	294	5,610
Steven Bowditch	72	67	80	76	295	5,520
Philip Schmitt	75	70	75	79	299	5,460
Carlos Franco	73	71	81	75	300	5,400

Chrysler Classic of Greensboro

Forest Oaks Country Club, Greensboro, North Carolina
Par 36-36–72; 7,311 yards

October 5-8
purse, $5,000,000

	SCORES				TOTAL	MONEY
Davis Love	69	69	68	66	272	$900,000
Jason Bohn	69	69	70	66	274	540,000
Eric Axley	68	69	71	67	275	290,000
Steve Flesch	69	69	69	68	275	290,000
Ryan Palmer	71	65	73	67	276	200,000
Daniel Chopra	68	74	66	69	277	151,250
Joe Durant	67	71	70	69	277	151,250
Lucas Glover	73	69	66	69	277	151,250
Troy Matteson	71	68	70	68	277	151,250
Ryan Moore	67	70	71	69	277	151,250
Nick Watney	64	71	74	68	277	151,250
Brent Geiberger	64	75	71	68	278	92,142.86
Hunter Mahan	70	72	72	64	278	92,142.86
Joe Ogilvie	69	72	70	67	278	92,142.86
Greg Owen	68	69	73	68	278	92,142.86
Steve Stricker	69	70	71	68	278	92,142.86
Jonathan Byrd	67	71	71	69	278	92,142.85

	SCORES				TOTAL	MONEY
Chris Couch	69	68	69	72	278	92,142.85
Charles Howell	69	72	68	70	279	65,000
Billy Mayfair	71	70	70	68	279	65,000
Brett Quigley	69	71	68	71	279	65,000
Arjun Atwal	67	73	72	68	280	46,416.67
Briny Baird	68	72	71	69	280	46,416.67
Olin Browne	70	69	70	71	280	46,416.67
Richard Johnson	69	73	69	69	280	46,416.67
Tim Clark	67	73	69	71	280	46,416.66
John Senden	66	70	71	73	280	46,416.66
Brian Davis	69	71	74	67	281	35,500
Robert Gamez	66	74	69	72	281	35,500
Tag Ridings	66	72	74	69	281	35,500
Michael Allen	69	71	71	71	282	27,750
Aaron Baddeley	71	70	71	70	282	27,750
Jeff Brehaut	68	70	71	73	282	27,750
Jeff Gove	68	72	72	70	282	27,750
Ted Purdy	71	71	71	69	282	27,750
John Rollins	64	74	72	72	282	27,750
Vaughn Taylor	72	69	71	70	282	27,750
Bubba Watson	69	70	72	71	282	27,750
Mark Calcavecchia	69	71	76	67	283	21,000
Dudley Hart	69	70	73	71	283	21,000
Chris Smith	67	71	69	76	283	21,000
D.J. Trahan	68	73	70	72	283	21,000
Rich Beem	69	73	72	70	284	14,900
Henrik Bjornstad	68	74	73	69	284	14,900
K.J. Choi	67	73	72	72	284	14,900
John Engler, Jr.	67	75	70	72	284	14,900
Charley Hoffman	66	71	72	75	284	14,900
John Huston	72	70	73	69	284	14,900
Bob May	69	71	72	72	284	14,900
Kevin Sutherland	69	72	72	71	284	14,900
Omar Uresti	70	70	75	69	284	14,900
Doug Barron	68	71	75	71	285	11,542.86
David Branshaw	68	74	71	72	285	11,542.86
Kris Cox	67	71	76	71	285	11,542.86
Marco Dawson	73	69	71	72	285	11,542.86
Will MacKenzie	69	73	70	73	285	11,542.86
Greg Kraft	68	74	70	73	285	11,542.85
Jeff Maggert	68	72	71	74	285	11,542.85
Robert Damron	67	73	70	76	286	10,900
Brian Gay	67	73	72	74	286	10,900
Nathan Green	70	71	75	70	286	10,900
Steve Jones	68	74	72	72	286	10,900
Daisuke Maruyama	72	68	71	75	286	10,900
D.A. Points	69	73	74	71	287	10,550
Mark Wilson	70	71	76	70	287	10,550
Tim Petrovic	68	69	77	74	288	10,400
Paul Goydos	73	69	73	74	289	10,150
Steve Lowery	68	70	78	73	289	10,150
Nick O'Hern	71	71	75	72	289	10,150
Jerry Smith	70	72	74	73	289	10,150
J.P. Hayes	70	72	75	73	290	9,900
Peter Lonard	71	70	76	74	291	9,750
Mike Sposa	66	74	73	78	291	9,750
James Driscoll	66	75	75	76	292	9,550
Bernhard Langer	68	74	79	71	292	9,550
Ryuji Imada	70	72	79	72	293	9,400

Frys.com Open

TPC at Summerlin: Par 36-36–72; 7,243 yards
TPC at The Canyons: Par 36-35–71; 7,193 yards
Las Vegas, Nevada

October 12-15
purse, $4,000,000

	SCORES				TOTAL	MONEY
Troy Matteson	67	65	64	69	265	$720,000
Daniel Chopra	69	67	64	66	266	352,000
Ben Crane	66	71	64	65	266	352,000
Frank Lickliter	67	69	67	64	267	192,000
Charley Hoffman	66	66	65	71	268	152,000
Lee Janzen	70	66	66	66	268	152,000
Bubba Dickerson	65	71	66	67	269	129,000
Tom Pernice, Jr.	66	65	70	68	269	129,000
Joey Sindelar	68	66	69	67	270	112,000
Ron Whittaker	70	66	68	66	270	112,000
Rich Beem	65	69	71	66	271	84,800
Mathew Goggin	72	65	68	66	271	84,800
Bill Haas	68	65	67	71	271	84,800
Kevin Sutherland	67	69	65	70	271	84,800
Bo Van Pelt	69	64	71	67	271	84,800
Chad Campbell	70	67	68	67	272	54,300
Robert Damron	68	66	69	69	272	54,300
Jim Furyk	68	68	70	66	272	54,300
Bernhard Langer	68	68	67	69	272	54,300
Shigeki Maruyama	68	64	70	70	272	54,300
Greg Owen	66	69	69	68	272	54,300
Duffy Waldorf	65	68	68	71	272	54,300
Mark Wilson	66	71	68	67	272	54,300
Tim Petrovic	68	66	71	68	273	31,657.15
Vance Veazey	65	70	72	66	273	31,657.15
Paul Azinger	66	70	68	69	273	31,657.14
Aaron Baddeley	66	65	70	72	273	31,657.14
Harrison Frazar	68	66	70	69	273	31,657.14
Brent Geiberger	68	64	68	73	273	31,657.14
Kevin Na	68	69	67	69	273	31,657.14
Bart Bryant	67	69	66	72	274	22,200
Kris Cox	67	70	65	72	274	22,200
Jason Gore	68	67	69	70	274	22,200
Jeff Gove	69	68	68	69	274	22,200
Arron Oberholser	70	67	69	68	274	22,200
D.A. Points	65	64	72	73	274	22,200
Darron Stiles	70	68	68	68	274	22,200
Tjaart van der Walt	70	67	68	69	274	22,200
Eric Axley	68	67	72	68	275	16,400
Alex Cejka	70	68	71	66	275	16,400
Fred Funk	66	69	71	69	275	16,400
Craig Parry	67	70	69	69	275	16,400
Mike Sposa	67	71	69	68	275	16,400
Mathias Gronberg	68	67	70	71	276	11,805.72
Scott Piercy	66	68	73	69	276	11,805.72
Bubba Watson	67	66	71	72	276	11,805.72
Arjun Atwal	67	69	67	73	276	11,805.71
Todd Fischer	66	65	79	66	276	11,805.71
Brian Gay	69	67	68	72	276	11,805.71
Dean Wilson	70	66	67	73	276	11,805.71
David Branshaw	70	68	72	67	277	9,472
Olin Browne	68	68	69	72	277	9,472
Chris DiMarco	70	68	67	72	277	9,472

	SCORES				TOTAL	MONEY
Steve Flesch	64	74	69	70	277	9,472
Will MacKenzie	64	70	73	70	277	9,472
Henrik Bjornstad	71	67	68	72	278	8,880
Jonathan Byrd	68	68	72	70	278	8,880
Todd Hamilton	65	70	76	67	278	8,880
Kent Jones	70	68	69	71	278	8,880
Bob May	70	68	68	72	278	8,880
Rocco Mediate	69	69	71	69	278	8,880
Patrick Sheehan	64	73	71	70	278	8,880
Andres Gonzales	70	68	71	70	279	8,400
J.B. Holmes	66	70	73	70	279	8,400
Daisuke Maruyama	72	65	68	74	279	8,400
John Rollins	65	72	72	70	279	8,400
Jason Schultz	69	69	69	72	279	8,400
Alex Aragon	70	68	69	73	280	7,920
Bob Estes	71	65	73	71	280	7,920
Mark Hensby	74	64	67	75	280	7,920
David McKenzie	71	64	74	71	280	7,920
Jeff Overton	69	69	72	70	280	7,920
Tag Ridings	68	66	73	73	280	7,920
Scott Verplank	69	68	70	73	280	7,920
Michael Allen	70	68	72	71	281	7,480
Robert Garrigus	70	67	71	73	281	7,480
Justin Leonard	69	69	74	69	281	7,480
Nicholas Thompson	70	65	71	75	281	7,480
Bill Glasson	66	72	73	71	282	7,240
Wes Short, Jr.	68	65	74	75	282	7,240
Jonathan Kaye	71	67	72	74	284	7,080
Bob Tway	63	70	75	76	284	7,080
Nathan Green	69	65	76	79	289	6,920
Skip Kendall	68	70	75	76	289	6,920
Greg Kraft	68	69	74	79	290	6,760
Ryan Moore	71	66	74	79	290	6,760

Funai Classic at the Walt Disney World Resort

Walt Disney World Resort, Lake Buena Vista, Florida
Magnolia Course: Par 36-36–72; 7,516 yards
Palm Course: Par 36-36–72; 6,957 yards

October 19-22
purse, $4,600,000

	SCORES				TOTAL	MONEY
Joe Durant	69	65	64	65	263	$828,000
Frank Lickliter	68	70	67	62	267	404,800
Troy Matteson	67	65	65	70	267	404,800
Justin Rose	60	67	72	69	268	220,800
Marco Dawson	67	66	69	67	269	161,575
Davis Love	67	69	64	69	269	161,575
Vijay Singh	68	69	68	64	269	161,575
Nick Watney	69	68	64	68	269	161,575
Mark Calcavecchia	66	73	63	68	270	115,000
Charles Howell	65	70	65	70	270	115,000
Jerry Kelly	66	68	68	68	270	115,000
Jesper Parnevik	68	69	68	65	270	115,000
Heath Slocum	68	67	66	69	270	115,000
Woody Austin	68	66	67	70	271	82,800
Robert Damron	68	65	70	68	271	82,800
Trevor Immelman	66	69	70	66	271	82,800

	SCORES				TOTAL	MONEY
Harrison Frazar	69	67	68	68	272	66,700
Steve Lowery	69	70	66	67	272	66,700
John Rollins	73	64	66	69	272	66,700
Charles Warren	66	70	67	69	272	66,700
Jonathan Byrd	68	69	65	71	273	47,840
K.J. Choi	68	68	67	70	273	47,840
J.J. Henry	65	70	70	68	273	47,840
J.B. Holmes	68	70	68	67	273	47,840
Greg Owen	67	68	68	70	273	47,840
Michael Allen	68	69	66	71	274	34,730
Chris Couch	70	65	71	68	274	34,730
Richard Johnson	64	70	68	72	274	34,730
Ian Leggatt	66	70	68	70	274	34,730
Stuart Appleby	67	70	69	69	275	27,945
Bill Haas	66	69	70	70	275	27,945
Sean O'Hair	69	67	67	72	275	27,945
John Senden	68	67	69	71	275	27,945
Bob Tway	65	71	69	70	275	27,945
Mike Weir	70	66	67	72	275	27,945
Brian Davis	69	68	71	68	276	20,732.86
Stephen Leaney	70	67	69	70	276	20,732.86
Hunter Mahan	69	67	72	68	276	20,732.86
Tim Petrovic	70	69	70	67	276	20,732.86
Brett Quigley	70	68	68	70	276	20,732.86
Ryan Palmer	67	71	66	72	276	20,732.85
Scott Verplank	67	70	67	72	276	20,732.85
Robert Allenby	70	68	69	70	277	14,007
Chris DiMarco	67	69	68	73	277	14,007
Tag Ridings	65	66	73	73	277	14,007
Jerry Smith	71	68	68	70	277	14,007
Vaughn Taylor	72	67	66	72	277	14,007
Bubba Watson	69	68	68	72	277	14,007
Brett Wetterich	69	69	65	74	277	14,007
Azuma Yano	68	67	70	72	277	14,007
Arjun Atwal	70	69	64	75	278	10,971
Eric Axley	66	72	70	70	278	10,971
Lucas Glover	66	70	73	69	278	10,971
Nathan Green	72	67	70	69	278	10,971
Steve Flesch	65	72	71	71	279	10,534
Greg Kraft	70	67	67	75	279	10,534
Bart Bryant	72	66	70	72	280	10,212
Ryuji Imada	69	67	73	71	280	10,212
Brandt Jobe	72	65	70	73	280	10,212
Shigeki Maruyama	67	69	70	74	280	10,212
D.A. Points	67	71	71	71	280	10,212
Henrik Bjornstad	69	69	74	69	281	9,706
Ben Crane	68	67	70	76	281	9,706
Robert Gamez	68	69	70	74	281	9,706
Lee Janzen	68	69	69	75	281	9,706
Chris Riley	66	73	72	70	281	9,706
Mike Small	70	69	69	73	281	9,706
Daisuke Maruyama	69	69	71	73	282	9,338
Nicholas Thompson	71	68	75	68	282	9,338
Shaun Micheel	67	71	72	73	283	9,200
Craig Barlow	68	70	75	71	284	9,062
Bubba Dickerson	66	68	72	78	284	9,062
Rocco Mediate	69	70	72	75	286	8,924
Ron Whittaker	68	71	72	77	288	8,832

Chrysler Championship

Westin Innisbrook Resort, Copperhead Course,
Palm Harbor, Florida
Par 36-35–71; 7,295 yards

October 26-29
purse, $5,300,000

	SCORES				TOTAL	MONEY
K.J. Choi	68	66	70	67	271	$954,000
Paul Goydos	68	68	69	70	275	466,400
Brett Wetterich	72	70	67	66	275	466,400
Jonathan Byrd	68	67	73	68	276	233,200
Joe Durant	70	71	67	68	276	233,200
Ernie Els	69	66	70	72	277	177,550
Rod Pampling	69	74	69	65	277	177,550
Jesper Parnevik	72	71	68	66	277	177,550
Brian Gay	64	71	70	73	278	148,400
Troy Matteson	70	72	64	72	278	148,400
Kent Jones	70	70	70	69	279	127,200
Heath Slocum	67	72	73	67	279	127,200
Shaun Micheel	71	66	73	70	280	93,633.34
Vaughn Taylor	69	73	69	69	280	93,633.34
Jason Bohn	70	70	68	72	280	93,633.33
Ryuji Imada	72	70	68	70	280	93,633.33
Richard Johnson	69	71	69	71	280	93,633.33
Ted Purdy	69	68	73	70	280	93,633.33
Mark Calcavecchia	66	71	73	71	281	62,010
Chad Campbell	68	74	71	68	281	62,010
Stewart Cink	69	69	72	71	281	62,010
Tim Clark	70	72	69	70	281	62,010
Frank Lickliter	70	69	73	69	281	62,010
Vijay Singh	70	70	69	72	281	62,010
Ben Crane	71	73	69	69	282	40,456.67
Bernhard Langer	71	71	71	69	282	40,456.67
Justin Leonard	72	70	70	70	282	40,456.67
Justin Rose	76	66	69	71	282	40,456.67
Ryan Palmer	70	70	69	73	282	40,456.66
Mike Weir	69	72	68	73	282	40,456.66
Stuart Appleby	75	69	70	69	283	29,415
Paul Azinger	72	71	73	67	283	29,415
Lucas Glover	69	71	72	71	283	29,415
J.J. Henry	69	71	74	69	283	29,415
Stephen Leaney	72	71	72	68	283	29,415
Will MacKenzie	68	73	73	69	283	29,415
Mark O'Meara	68	74	71	70	283	29,415
Camilo Villegas	71	72	71	69	283	29,415
Jeff Brehaut	68	73	71	72	284	22,790
Tom Pernice, Jr.	69	74	72	69	284	22,790
Tim Petrovic	69	73	73	69	284	22,790
Steve Elkington	67	73	71	74	285	20,140
Peter Lonard	70	74	68	73	285	20,140
Trevor Immelman	70	74	74	68	286	15,642.58
Bart Bryant	72	71	71	72	286	15,642.57
Daniel Chopra	67	72	71	76	286	15,642.57
Lee Janzen	70	74	71	71	286	15,642.57
Brandt Jobe	74	69	74	69	286	15,642.57
Hunter Mahan	70	72	70	74	286	15,642.57
Duffy Waldorf	67	76	71	72	286	15,642.57
David Branshaw	73	64	76	74	287	12,640.50
Todd Fischer	71	72	73	71	287	12,640.50
Fred Funk	73	70	75	69	287	12,640.50

	SCORES				TOTAL	MONEY
Jeff Sluman	72	72	76	67	287	12,640.50
Bob Estes	69	74	72	73	288	12,084
Zach Johnson	73	71	72	72	288	12,084
Dean Wilson	69	74	71	74	288	12,084
Eric Axley	72	72	72	73	289	11,713
Shane Bertsch	75	67	74	73	289	11,713
Bill Haas	69	72	75	73	289	11,713
Nick Watney	71	70	74	74	289	11,713
Shigeki Maruyama	70	73	73	74	290	11,395
Rory Sabbatini	71	70	74	75	290	11,395
Scott Verplank	73	71	75	73	292	11,236
Craig Parry	70	74	75	74	293	11,077
John Rollins	71	73	77	72	293	11,077
Woody Austin	72	72	73	77	294	10,865
Steve Lowery	70	74	77	73	294	10,865
Tom Lehman	73	71	76	75	295	10,706
Tag Ridings	74	70	77	76	297	10,600

The Tour Championship

East Lake Golf Club, Atlanta, Georgia
Par 35-35–70; 7,154 yards

November 2-5
purse, $6,500,000

	SCORES				TOTAL	MONEY
Adam Scott	69	67	67	66	269	$1,170,000
Jim Furyk	69	71	67	65	272	730,000
Joe Durant	68	68	70	67	273	480,000
Retief Goosen	68	71	68	67	274	345,000
Luke Donald	73	67	69	68	277	266,000
Trevor Immelman	73	66	69	69	277	266,000
Tom Pernice, Jr.	69	72	67	69	277	266,000
Lucas Glover	73	71	66	68	278	215,000
Vijay Singh	69	72	65	72	278	215,000
Stuart Appleby	69	70	72	70	281	182,800
Ernie Els	71	72	66	72	281	182,800
J.J. Henry	71	73	69	69	282	163,150
Brett Quigley	71	68	73	70	282	163,150
Rod Pampling	73	71	73	66	283	146,900
David Toms	74	71	71	67	283	146,900
Zach Johnson	71	69	71	73	284	137,800
Arron Oberholser	71	70	72	72	285	132,600
Carl Pettersson	77	70	71	69	287	130,000
Geoff Ogilvy	74	72	71	71	288	126,100
Dean Wilson	75	72	71	70	288	126,100
Ben Curtis	73	77	66	73	289	122,200
Rory Sabbatini	74	75	71	70	290	118,300
Brett Wetterich	75	74	69	72	290	118,300
Chad Campbell	73	74	74	70	291	114,400
Stewart Cink	69	75	75	73	292	111,800
K.J. Choi	72	78	72	72	294	109,200
Davis Love	82	71	71	73	297	107,900

WGC - Barbardos World Cup

Sandy Lane Resort, Country Club Course, St. James, Barbados
Par 36-36–72; 7,173 yards

December 7-10
purse, $4,000,000

	INDIVIDUAL SCORES				TOTAL
GERMANY—$1,400,000 Bernhard Langer/Marcel Siem	65	69	68	66	268
SCOTLAND—$700,000 Colin Montgomerie/Marc Warren	67	67	65	69	268
(Germany defeated Scotland on first playoff hole.)					
SWEDEN—$400,000 Carl Pettersson/Henrik Stenson	64	70	63	72	269
SOUTH AFRICA—$200,000 Rory Sabbatini/Richard Sterne	64	71	67	68	270
SPAIN—$126,667 Gonzalo Fernandez-Castano/Miguel A. Jimenez	69	66	67	69	271
ARGENTINA—$126,667 Angel Cabrera/Andres Romero	64	67	67	73	271
UNITED STATES—$126,667 Stewart Cink/J.J. Henry	66	73	63	69	271
ITALY—$77,500 Emanuele Canonica/Francesco Molinari	68	70	64	71	273
WALES—$77,500 Stephen Dodd/Bradley Dredge	65	75	62	71	273
AUSTRALIA—$77,500 Mark Hensby/John Senden	68	72	64	69	273
MEXICO—$77,500 Octavio Gonzalez/Esteban Toledo	69	68	65	71	273
IRELAND—$57,500 Padraig Harrington/Paul McGinley	67	73	66	69	275
SWITZERLAND—$57,500 Martin Rominger/Nicolas Sulzer	73	70	64	68	275
COLOMBIA—$50,000 Manuel Merizalde/Camilo Villegas	67	74	66	70	277
ENGLAND—$48,500 Luke Donald/David Howell	66	70	70	72	278
CANADA—$48,500 Jim Rutledge/Mike Weir	69	72	66	71	278
SINGAPORE—$47,000 Lam Chih-bing/Mardan Mamat	71	72	68	69	280

	INDIVIDUAL SCORES	TOTAL
DENMARK—$46,000 Thomas Bjorn/Soren Hansen	70 70 71 70	281
KOREA—$45,000 S.K. Ho/Charlie Wi	66 72 70 75	283
FRANCE—$44,000 Raphael Jacquelin/Jean Van de Velde	68 75 65 77	285
TRINIDAD & TOBAGO—$42,500 Robert Ames/Stephen Ames	70 73 67 78	288
BARBADOS—$42,500 Roger Beale/James Johnson	69 76 71 72	288
JAPAN—$41,000 Tetsuji Hiratsuka/Hideto Tanihara	67 74 74 74	289
JAMAICA—$40,000 Delroy Cambridge/Peter Horrobin	72 76 67 80	295

Special Events

Tavistock Cup

Isleworth Country Club, Orlando, Florida
Par 36-36–72; 7,544 yards

March 27-28
purse, $2,000,000

FIRST DAY
(Team better ball; 2 points for win, 1 point for tie)

Tiger Woods and Mark O'Meara (Isleworth) defeated Sergio Garcia and Retief Goosen (Lake Nona), 65-66.
Robert Damron and Lee Janzen (Isle) defeated Ben Curtis and Justin Rose (LN), 64-66.
Mark McNulty and Ian Poulter (LN) defeated John Cook and Charles Howell (Isle), 70-71.
Maarten Lafeber and Graeme McDowell (LN) defeated Arjun Atwal and Craig Parry (Isle), 70-72.
Robert Allenby and Stuart Appleby (Isle) defeated Ernie Els and Trevor Immelman (LN), 64-67.

POINTS: Isleworth 6, Lake Nona 4

SECOND DAY
(Singles versus both players on other team; 1 point for win, ½ point for tie)

Atwal 72 and O'Meara 80 (Isle) versus Immelman 68 and Lafeber 74 (LN).
Howell 68 and Appleby 70 (Isle) versus Goosen 73 and Garcia 74 (LN).
Allenby 68 and Parry 72 (Isle) versus Poulter 72 and Rose 70 (LN).

Damron 71 and Janzen 75 (Isle) versus Curtis 73 and McDowell 74 (LN).
Woods 65 and Cook 75 (Isle) versus Els 72 and McNulty 68 (LN).

POINTS: Isleworth 11½ (Atwal 1, O'Meara 0, Howell 2, Appleby 2, Allenby 2, Parry ½, Damron 2, Janzen 0, Woods 2, Cook 0); Lake Nona 8½ (Immelman 2, Lafeber 1, Goosen 0, Garcia 0, Poulter ½, Rose 1, Curtis 1, McDowell 1, Els 1, McNulty 1)

TWO-DAY TOTAL: Isleworth 17½, Lake Nona 12½

(Each member of the winning team received $100,000; each member of the losing team received $50,000. Woods received $200,000 and Allenby, Immelman, Howell and McNulty received $25,000 each for the lowest scores on the second day.)

CVS Charity Classic

Rhode Island Country Club, Barrington, Rhode Island June 19-20
Par 35-36–71; 6,688 yards purse $1,350,000

	SCORES		TOTAL	MONEY (Team)
Nick Price/Tim Clark	61	62	123	$250,000
Brad Faxon/Mike Weir	61	62	123	175,000
(Price and Clark defeated Faxon and Weir on second playoff hole.)				
Tom Lehman/Tim Herron	63	61	124	130,000
J.B. Holmes/Bubba Watson	61	63	124	130,000
Billy Andrade/Jose Maria Olazabal	64	61	125	112,500
Stewart Cink/Jeff Sluman	60	65	125	112,500
Hale Irwin/Peter Jacobsen	65	61	126	102,500
Brett Quigley/Dana Quigley	64	62	126	102,500
Davis Love/Lucas Glover	66	62	128	95,000
Chris DiMarco/Fred Funk	63	68	131	90,000

Merrill Lynch Shootout

Tiburon Golf Course, Naples, Florida November 10-12
Par 36-36–72; 7,288 yards purse, $2,750,000

	SCORES			TOTAL	MONEY (Each)
Jerry Kelly/Rod Pampling	64	62	59	185	$337,500
Justin Leonard/Scott Verplank	63	63	59	185	215,000
(Kelly/Pampling defeated Leonard/Verplank on first playoff hole.)					
John Huston/Kenny Perry	68	61	59	188	104,166.67
Trevor Immelman/Rory Sabbatini	66	63	59	188	104,166.67
Chad Campbell/Nick Price	67	63	58	188	104,166.67
Fred Funk/Scott Hoch	68	63	58	189	80,000
John Daly/J.B. Holmes	63	62	64	189	80,000
Brad Faxon/J.J. Henry	66	65	60	191	73,750
Mark O'Meara/Jeff Sluman	66	63	62	191	73,750
Mark Calcavecchia/Steve Elkington	70	65	58	193	70,000
Nick Faldo/Greg Norman	72	65	60	197	67,500
Fred Couples/Annika Sorenstam	71	67	60	198	65,000

The Goodwill Trophy

See Asia/Japan Tours chapter.

Callaway Golf Pebble Beach Invitational

Pebble Beach GL: Par 36-36–72; 6,737 yards
Spyglass Hills GC: Par 36-36–72; 6,862 yards
Del Monte GC: Par 36-36–72; 6,357 yards
Pebble Beach, California

November 16-19
purse, $300,000

	SCORES				TOTAL	MONEY
Jason Bohn	69	69	65	71	274	$60,000
Scott Simpson	71	70	66	68	275	32,200
Parker McLachlin	67	70	68	71	276	10,200
Robert Gamez	70	73	63	70	276	10,200
Arron Oberholser	68	69	69	70	276	10,200
Harrison Frazar	73	72	63	68	276	10,200
Kevin Sutherland	72	72	66	66	276	10,200
Jim Thorpe	67	70	69	71	277	6,500
Brandt Snedeker	71	70	71	66	278	6,000
Bubba Watson	68	72	68	71	279	5,200
Rocco Mediate	70	70	70	69	279	5,200
Nick Watney	75	66	72	66	279	5,200
Michael Putnam	66	71	69	74	280	4,450
Mark Brooks	69	74	66	71	280	4,450
Charley Hoffman	72	68	70	71	281	3,733.33
Jeff Quinney	73	71	66	71	281	3,733.33
Cliff Kresge	74	69	70	68	281	3,733.33
Bo Van Pelt	68	74	65	75	282	3,100
Ricky Barnes	68	71	74	69	282	3,100
Jason Gore	70	74	69	69	282	3,100
Bruce Fleisher	70	73	70	70	283	2,700
John Merrick	69	73	71	70	283	2,700
Jeff Overton	72	69	72	70	283	2,700
D.J. Trahan	74	70	72	67	283	2,700
Ken Duke	74	66	71	73	284	2,362.50
Mark Johnson	71	69	71	73	284	2,362.50
Tom Purtzer	65	76	72	71	284	2,362.50
Shane Bertsch	71	72	70	72	285	2,132.50
John Cook	67	74	73	71	285	2,132.50
Matt Kuchar	73	70	71	71	285	2,132.50
Bryce Molder	71	71	73	70	285	2,132.50
Jeff Gove	70	74	70	72	286	2,050
Marc Lawless	73	72	72	69	286	2,050
Bubba Dickerson	70	67	76	74	287	2,010
Eric Axley	69	71	75	72	287	2,010
Brian Mogg	72	72	72	72	288	1,980
Dave Eichelberger	68	72	72	77	289	1,950
Jeff Brehaut	74	68	75	72	289	1,950
Hunter Haas	75	67	73	75	290	1,920
Laird Small	74	70	72	76	292	1,910
Jeff Hood	70	75	72	75	292	1,910
Charlie Gibson	71	68	78	82	299	1,900

PGA Grand Slam of Golf

Poipu Golf Club, Kauai, Hawaii
Par 36-36–72; 7,123 yards

November 21-22
purse, $1,250,000

	SCORES		TOTAL	MONEY
Tiger Woods	70	66	136	$500,000
Jim Furyk	67	71	138	300,000
Geoff Ogilvy	68	74	142	250,000
Mike Weir	71	74	145	200,000

Del Webb Father-Son Challenge

Champions Gate Golf Resort, Orlando, Florida
Par 37-35–72; 7,363 yards

December 2-3
purse, $1,000,000

	SCORES		TOTAL	MONEY
				(Won by professional)
Bernhard/Stefan Langer	59	61	120	$200,000
Bob/Kevin Tway	61	60	121	92,500
Vijay/Qass Singh	60	61	121	92,500
Davis/Dru Love	59	64	123	65,000
Hale/Steve Irwin	65	59	124	56,000
Tom/David Kite	62	63	125	50,166
Greg/Gregory Norman	62	63	125	50,166
Jack/Jackie Nicklaus	62	63	125	50,166
Larry/Drew Nelson	64	62	126	44,833
Johnny/Scott Miller	62	64	126	44,833
Bob/David Charles	61	65	126	44,833
Mark/Shaun O'Meara	65	62	127	43,250
Curtis/Tom Strange	64	63	127	43,250
Raymond/Ray Floyd Jr.	65	64	129	42,500
Arnold Palmer/Sam Saunders	64	68	132	42,000
Craig/Chris Stadler	66	67	133	41,500
Billy/Bob Casper	68	68	136	41,000
Lee/Daniel Trevino	70	73	143	40,500

Target World Challenge

Sherwood Country Club, Thousand Oaks, California
Par 36-36–72; 7,064 yards

December 14-17
purse, $5,750,000

	SCORES				TOTAL	MONEY
Tiger Woods	68	68	70	66	272	$1,350,000
Geoff Ogilvy	68	70	67	71	276	840,000
Chris DiMarco	70	68	68	71	277	570,000
Henrik Stenson	66	71	73	69	279	420,000
Paul Casey	69	70	70	71	280	285,000
Colin Montgomerie	69	73	72	66	280	285,000
Michael Campbell	74	69	68	71	282	240,000
Padraig Harrington	75	67	70	71	283	230,000
David Toms	73	69	68	75	285	220,000
Fred Couples	69	74	72	71	286	205,000
Davis Love	77	70	70	69	286	205,000

	SCORES	TOTAL	MONEY
Luke Donald	76 74 72 71	293	190,000
David Howell	71 75 72 77	295	185,000
Jose Maria Olazabal	70 70 78 78	296	177,500
Adam Scott	75 80 69 72	296	177,500
John Daly	69 71 77 80	297	170,000

Nationwide Tour

Movistar Panama Championship

Panama Golf Club, Panama City, Panama
Par 35-35–70; 6,818 yards

January 26-29
purse, $550,000

	SCORES	TOTAL	MONEY
Tripp Isenhour	63 67 70 69	269	$99,000
Kevin Gessino-Kraft	72 63 69 68	272	41,066.67
Parker McLachlin	66 66 71 69	272	41,066.67
Brenden Pappas	67 66 67 72	272	41,066.66
Jason Allred	71 70 66 66	273	22,000
David Hearn	67 69 69 70	275	17,215
Travis Perkins	70 64 71 70	275	17,215
Scott Petersen	70 65 70 70	275	17,215
Kyle Thompson	72 66 67 70	275	17,215
Mario Tiziani	66 67 72 70	275	17,215
Paul Claxton	68 70 69 69	276	11,660
Brad Elder	73 69 67 67	276	11,660
Tim O'Neal	73 68 63 72	276	11,660
Jim Rutledge	69 71 71 65	276	11,660
Johnson Wagner	70 70 68 68	276	11,660
Roberto Coceres	67 72 74 64	277	9,075
Kevin Durkin	71 66 68 72	277	9,075
Gavin Coles	67 73 69 69	278	6,694.29
Jason Dufner	68 71 70 69	278	6,694.29
Ken Duke	73 68 69 68	278	6,694.29
Dicky Pride	71 70 69 68	278	6,694.29
Craig Kanada	68 72 67 71	278	6,694.28
Matt Kuchar	68 70 70 70	278	6,694.28
Rick Price	69 70 69 70	278	6,694.28
Jeremy Anderson	66 68 76 69	279	4,111.25
Ryan Armour	68 72 69 70	279	4,111.25
Josh Broadaway	70 71 67 71	279	4,111.25
Gary Christian	70 70 69 70	279	4,111.25
Joe Daley	70 68 66 75	279	4,111.25
Jeff Hart	67 72 70 70	279	4,111.25
Matt Hendrix	67 70 70 72	279	4,111.25
Cliff Kresge	71 70 69 69	279	4,111.25

Jacob's Creek Open

See Australasian Tour chapter.

ING New Zealand PGA Championship

See Australasian Tour chapter.

Chitimacha Louisiana Open

Le Triomphe Country Club, Broussard, Louisiana
Par 36-35–71; 7,004 yards

March 23-26
purse, $500,000

	SCORES				TOTAL	MONEY
Johnson Wagner	67	69	69	67	272	$90,000
Chad Collins	69	68	68	68	273	54,000
Cliff Kresge	74	66	66	68	274	29,000
Franklin Langham	67	67	70	70	274	29,000
Chris Smith	69	71	69	66	275	19,000
Matt Weibring	66	72	69	68	275	19,000
Bob Heintz	71	70	68	67	276	16,750
Scott Gutschewski	68	75	70	65	278	15,500
David Edwards	68	73	69	69	279	12,500
Craig Kanada	68	74	67	70	279	12,500
Jeff Klauk	70	73	68	68	279	12,500
Deane Pappas	70	69	69	71	279	12,500
Phil Tataurangi	71	68	71	69	279	12,500
Russ Cochran	72	69	68	71	280	8,000
Gavin Coles	69	71	72	68	280	8,000
Glen Day	69	68	71	72	280	8,000
Tripp Isenhour	68	72	66	74	280	8,000
Tim O'Neal	73	70	68	69	280	8,000
Jeff Overton	71	71	67	71	280	8,000
Esteban Toledo	74	67	69	70	280	8,000
Jeff Curl	70	72	70	69	281	5,033.34
Jeff Hart	70	72	70	69	281	5,033.34
Doug LaBelle	72	70	68	71	281	5,033.33
Brian Rowell	69	69	73	70	281	5,033.33
Jim Rutledge	68	72	70	71	281	5,033.33
Ron Whittaker	70	70	70	71	281	5,033.33
Jason Allred	69	73	71	69	282	3,550
Ken Duke	75	66	71	70	282	3,550
Kevin Durkin	72	67	72	71	282	3,550
J.P. Hayes	74	69	68	71	282	3,550
Dan Olsen	70	66	72	74	282	3,550
B.J. Staten	68	72	71	71	282	3,550

Livermore Valley Wine Country Championship

The Course at Wente Vineyards, Livermore, California
Par 36-36–72; 7,185 yards

March 30-April 2
purse, $600,000

	SCORES				TOTAL	MONEY
Tripp Isenhour	67	72	72	68	279	$108,000
Paul Sheehan	72	69	70	71	282	64,800

	SCORES				TOTAL	MONEY
Jeff Quinney	67	68	74	75	284	40,800
Craig Bowden	69	71	75	70	285	24,800
Jim McGovern	71	71	74	69	285	24,800
Johnson Wagner	72	70	72	71	285	24,800
Ryan Armour	72	76	68	70	286	19,350
Jason Dufner	73	73	75	65	286	19,350
Chris Baryla	71	74	72	70	287	16,200
Ken Duke	71	71	75	70	287	16,200
Matthew Jones	72	69	73	73	287	16,200
Michael Long	72	74	69	73	288	13,800
Jeff Hart	72	76	70	71	289	11,600
Joel Kribel	71	70	75	73	289	11,600
Blaine McCallister	71	76	71	71	289	11,600
Aaron Barber	72	76	67	75	290	9,300
Brendon de Jonge	74	74	72	70	290	9,300
Jay Delsing	73	70	77	70	290	9,300
Craig Lile	73	70	72	75	290	9,300
Matt Bettencourt	70	73	74	74	291	6,500
Hunter Haas	70	75	72	74	291	6,500
Skip Kendall	72	78	69	72	291	6,500
Doug LaBelle	72	76	69	74	291	6,500
Fran Quinn	75	68	69	79	291	6,500
Jim Rutledge	74	74	72	71	291	6,500
Gabriel Hjertstedt	69	76	73	74	292	4,680
Tom Johnson	70	73	71	78	292	4,680
Dicky Pride	73	75	73	71	292	4,680
Tom Scherrer	73	70	76	73	292	4,680
Peter Tomasulo	73	77	73	70	293	4,080

Athens Regional Foundation Classic

Jennings Mill Country Club, Athens, Georgia
Par 36-36–72; 7,004 yards

April 20-23
purse, $500,000

	SCORES				TOTAL	MONEY
Paul Gow	64	67	67	69	267	$90,000
Craig Lile	65	64	69	72	270	54,000
Tom Gillis	68	67	68	69	272	29,000
Zoran Zorkic	66	64	73	69	272	29,000
Justin Bolli	66	69	68	71	274	16,950
Keoke Cotner	68	73	66	67	274	16,950
Fran Quinn	68	65	71	70	274	16,950
Jim Rutledge	69	68	71	66	274	16,950
Peter Tomasulo	71	68	66	69	274	16,950
Ken Duke	63	69	72	71	275	11,500
Jeff Hart	68	67	69	71	275	11,500
Glen Hnatiuk	68	70	71	66	275	11,500
Kevin Johnson	67	68	68	72	275	11,500
John Merrick	66	72	70	67	275	11,500
Steve Allan	68	69	71	68	276	8,250
Scott Dunlap	72	64	68	72	276	8,250
Franklin Langham	70	71	67	68	276	8,250
Parker McLachlin	70	69	67	70	276	8,250
Notah Begay	71	66	71	69	277	5,462.50
Michael Bradley	71	65	69	72	277	5,462.50
Gary Christian	70	68	69	70	277	5,462.50
Paul Claxton	70	71	70	66	277	5,462.50

	SCORES				TOTAL	MONEY
Jess Daley	72	69	65	71	277	5,462.50
Nick Flanagan	68	73	67	69	277	5,462.50
Michael Putnam	69	67	70	71	277	5,462.50
Chris Stroud	73	68	67	69	277	5,462.50
Tom Carter	69	69	68	72	278	3,800
Brandt Snedeker	70	69	70	69	278	3,800
Matt Weibring	70	69	69	70	278	3,800
Jason Allred	70	70	71	68	279	3,200
D.J. Brigman	71	70	70	68	279	3,200
Roberto Coceres	69	67	72	71	279	3,200
Bob Heintz	69	68	72	70	279	3,200
Michael Long	66	71	69	73	279	3,200

BMW Charity Pro-Am at The Cliffs

The Cliffs Golf & Country Club, Greenville, South Carolina
Cliffs Valley: Par 36-36–72; 7,023 yards
Keowee Vineyards: Par 36-35–71; 7,006 yards
Cliffs at Walnut Grove: Par 36-35–71; 7,000 yards

April 27-30
purse, $625,000

	SCORES				TOTAL	MONEY
Ken Duke	69	68	68	68	273	$112,500
Jess Daley	70	68	67	69	274	67,500
Kevin Stadler	71	66	68	70	275	36,250
Grant Waite	72	65	71	67	275	36,250
Jeff Quinney	71	68	69	68	276	21,953.13
Johnson Wagner	67	73	68	68	276	21,953.13
Richard Johnson	69	68	67	72	276	21,953.12
Chris Stroud	65	69	71	71	276	21,953.12
Steve Collins	66	72	70	69	277	16,250
Bob Heintz	69	69	70	69	277	16,250
Doug LaBelle	70	66	72	69	277	16,250
Scott Weatherly	69	66	71	71	277	16,250
Jason Allred	68	69	73	68	278	12,083.34
Ryan Armour	71	69	70	68	278	12,083.33
Mario Tiziani	72	70	66	70	278	12,083.33
Matt Hendrix	67	71	73	68	279	8,484.38
Tripp Isenhour	66	74	70	69	279	8,484.38
Craig Lile	71	71	68	69	279	8,484.38
Steve Wheatcroft	69	72	69	69	279	8,484.38
Craig Bowden	74	67	71	67	279	8,484.37
Jason Buha	68	71	68	72	279	8,484.37
Nick Malinowski	72	67	69	71	279	8,484.37
Chez Reavie	71	68	68	72	279	8,484.37
Nick Flanagan	68	71	72	69	280	5,166.67
Brad Klapprott	71	70	70	69	280	5,166.67
Cliff Kresge	69	72	70	69	280	5,166.67
Tim Wilkinson	71	67	73	69	280	5,166.67
Michael Long	72	67	73	68	280	5,166.66
Steve Schneiter	70	71	67	72	280	5,166.66
Ben Bates	71	69	69	72	281	3,750
Andrew Dahl	73	69	69	70	281	3,750
Franklin Langham	75	67	69	70	281	3,750
Deane Pappas	71	69	69	72	281	3,750
Scott Parel	70	71	71	69	281	3,750
Dicky Pride	76	67	68	70	281	3,750
Michael Putnam	69	69	71	72	281	3,750

	SCORES	TOTAL	MONEY
Boo Weekley	71 70 72 68	281	3,750
Matt Weibring	69 70 68 74	281	3,750

Virginia Beach Open

TPC of Virginia Beach, Virginia Beach, Virginia
Par 36-36–72; 7,432 yards

May 4-7
purse, $450,000

	SCORES	TOTAL	MONEY
Andrew Buckle	67 68 64 69	268	$81,000
Justin Bolli	69 66 66 72	273	48,600
Michael Long	68 68 69 69	274	30,600
Brendon de Jonge	68 68 69 70	275	19,800
Gabriel Hjertstedt	66 68 69 72	275	19,800
Kim Felton	71 67 69 69	276	15,637.50
John Merrick	66 69 68 73	276	15,637.50
Dan Olsen	71 67 69 70	277	13,050
Scott Parel	70 72 65 70	277	13,050
Darron Stiles	73 67 67 70	277	13,050
Jeremy Anderson	70 72 68 68	278	10,800
Tom Johnson	72 67 70 69	278	10,800
Ryan Armour	69 69 68 73	279	8,437.50
Steve Larick	67 72 72 68	279	8,437.50
Michael Putnam	70 68 68 73	279	8,437.50
Boo Weekley	72 67 69 71	279	8,437.50
Paul Claxton	71 71 70 68	280	5,888.58
Jason Caron	70 69 71 70	280	5,888.57
Jess Daley	70 69 69 72	280	5,888.57
Tripp Isenhour	68 70 71 71	280	5,888.57
Chris Nallen	68 71 68 73	280	5,888.57
Chez Reavie	69 69 69 73	280	5,888.57
Matt Weibring	71 71 68 70	280	5,888.57
Steve Collins	70 69 70 72	281	3,816
Matt Hendrix	69 70 69 73	281	3,816
Hiroshi Matsuo	68 73 66 74	281	3,816
Chris Stroud	72 69 71 69	281	3,816
Roland Thatcher	72 68 70 71	281	3,816
Michael Letzig	70 72 70 70	282	2,940
Craig Lile	70 71 67 74	282	2,940
David McKenzie	71 70 68 73	282	2,940
Scott Petersen	67 68 72 75	282	2,940
Fran Quinn	69 70 72 71	282	2,940
Brian Smock	71 69 66 76	282	2,940

Rheem Classic

Hardscrabble Country Club, Fort Smith, Arkansas
Par 35-35–70; 6,619 yards

May 11-14
purse, $500,000

	SCORES	TOTAL	MONEY
Darron Stiles	66 66 64 71	267	$90,000
Michael Putnam	68 67 65 67	267	54,000
(Stiles defeated Putnam on first playoff hole.)			
Deane Pappas	68 66 67 69	270	34,000

	SCORES				TOTAL	MONEY
David Hearn	66	68	69	68	271	24,000
Erik Compton	66	72	66	68	272	16,950
Jay Delsing	68	64	68	72	272	16,950
Glen Hnatiuk	68	67	68	69	272	16,950
Cliff Kresge	71	66	65	70	272	16,950
Johnson Wagner	64	72	66	70	272	16,950
Matthew Jones	69	69	69	66	273	12,000
Chris Nallen	69	67	70	67	273	12,000
Brenden Pappas	69	65	70	69	273	12,000
Tommy Tolles	70	69	63	71	273	12,000
Jason Allred	72	64	70	68	274	8,250
Ken Duke	73	65	68	68	274	8,250
Scott Dunlap	67	71	65	71	274	8,250
Scott Gutschewski	67	68	67	72	274	8,250
Brian Henninger	69	70	70	65	274	8,250
Matt Kuchar	71	67	67	69	274	8,250
John Merrick	65	72	67	71	275	6,500
Dicky Pride	67	72	68	69	276	5,033.34
Roland Thatcher	70	69	68	69	276	5,033.34
Joel Edwards	70	64	67	75	276	5,033.33
Robin Freeman	71	66	71	68	276	5,033.33
Steve Larick	68	68	69	71	276	5,033.33
Parker McLachlin	70	66	69	71	276	5,033.33
Hunter Haas	69	69	69	70	277	3,550
Franklin Langham	66	72	68	71	277	3,550
Rick Price	74	66	67	70	277	3,550
Chez Reavie	70	69	70	68	277	3,550
Brandt Snedeker	66	72	67	72	277	3,550
Tjaart van der Walt	71	66	69	71	277	3,550

Henrico County Open

The Dominion Club, Richmond, Virginia
Par 36-36–72; 6,987 yards

May 18-21
purse, $450,000

	SCORES				TOTAL	MONEY
Matt Kuchar	71	67	69	72	279	$81,000
Paul Claxton	69	68	73	69	279	48,600
(Kuchar defeated Claxton on third playoff hole.)						
Jason Caron	71	72	67	70	280	30,600
Jeff Burns	67	64	74	78	283	16,312.50
Erik Compton	72	67	68	76	283	16,312.50
Bradley Hughes	70	72	72	69	283	16,312.50
Andrew Pratt	70	73	68	72	283	16,312.50
Steve Wheatcroft	71	67	73	72	283	16,312.50
Charlie Wi	76	65	70	72	283	16,312.50
Stephen Marino	73	72	69	70	284	11,250
Fran Quinn	69	76	67	72	284	11,250
Peter Tomasulo	65	70	71	78	284	11,250
Craig Bowden	71	73	70	71	285	8,437.50
Gavin Coles	73	70	71	71	285	8,437.50
Jason Dufner	75	70	68	72	285	8,437.50
Hunter Haas	70	73	69	73	285	8,437.50
Eric Axley	69	71	75	71	286	6,090
Cliff Kresge	70	74	74	68	286	6,090
Chris Nallen	69	75	69	73	286	6,090
Chris Smith	73	69	70	74	286	6,090

	SCORES	TOTAL	MONEY
Omar Uresti	74 65 73 74	286	6,090
Zoran Zorkic	75 70 71 70	286	6,090
Joseph Alfieri	75 67 73 72	287	4,068
Matt Hendrix	69 75 70 73	287	4,068
Steve Larick	71 69 74 73	287	4,068
Bryce Molder	71 70 71 75	287	4,068
Dicky Pride	70 71 73 73	287	4,068
Dan Buchner	72 73 72 71	288	3,060
Joe Daley	70 70 78 70	288	3,060
Richard Johnson	71 74 71 72	288	3,060
David Morland	73 71 70 74	288	3,060
Brandt Snedeker	73 68 74 73	288	3,060
Johnson Wagner	69 75 73 71	288	3,060

The Rex Hospital Open

TPC at Wakefield Plantation, Raleigh, North Carolina
Par 35-36–71; 6,724 yards

June 1-4
purse, $450,000

	SCORES	TOTAL	MONEY
Brenden Pappas	66 68 65 69	268	$81,000
Charlie Wi	67 69 65 68	269	48,600
Tripp Isenhour	68 68 69 67	272	26,100
Michael Putnam	67 66 71 68	272	26,100
Brad Adamonis	72 69 67 65	273	13,275
Brendon de Jonge	68 69 68 68	273	13,275
Scott Gutschewski	68 68 69 68	273	13,275
Bob Heintz	71 69 67 66	273	13,275
Brad Klapprott	68 69 67 69	273	13,275
Neal Lancaster	69 67 69 68	273	13,275
Jim Rutledge	71 70 67 65	273	13,275
Michael Sim	66 72 70 65	273	13,275
Boo Weekley	67 69 69 68	273	13,275
Gabriel Hjertstedt	69 70 67 68	274	8,325
David Mathis	67 68 70 69	274	8,325
Johnson Wagner	67 70 69 69	275	7,650
Steve Collins	71 68 69 68	276	6,300
Kevin Durkin	71 67 70 68	276	6,300
Tim O'Neal	66 72 70 68	276	6,300
Jeff Quinney	70 67 67 72	276	6,300
Scott Weatherly	71 68 69 68	276	6,300
Notah Begay	68 72 73 64	277	4,114.29
Gary Christian	66 71 70 70	277	4,114.29
Joel Edwards	67 72 69 69	277	4,114.29
Bradley Hughes	71 70 67 69	277	4,114.29
David Hearn	69 69 68 71	277	4,114.28
Matthew Jones	67 68 70 72	277	4,114.28
Scott Parel	70 69 66 72	277	4,114.28
Paul Claxton	65 70 71 72	278	2,940
Erik Compton	67 67 72 72	278	2,940
Joe Daley	66 71 69 72	278	2,940
Ken Duke	68 72 68 70	278	2,940
Cliff Kresge	68 67 73 70	278	2,940
Chris Nallen	71 69 67 71	278	2,940

LaSalle Bank Open

The Glen Club, Glenview, Illinois
Par 36-35—71; 7,256 yards

June 8-11
purse, $750,000

	SCORES				TOTAL	MONEY
Jason Dufner	69	71	69	70	279	$135,000
Cliff Kresge	72	71	67	70	280	81,000
Cameron Beckman	69	72	68	73	282	43,500
Doug LaBelle	66	75	72	69	282	43,500
Steve Allan	71	72	65	75	283	30,000
Steve LeBrun	70	71	72	71	284	22,687.50
Parker McLachlin	73	72	71	68	284	22,687.50
Jeff Quinney	70	76	68	70	284	22,687.50
Chris Stroud	70	78	66	70	284	22,687.50
Nicholas Thompson	64	74	74	72	284	22,687.50
Chris Tidland	69	73	72	70	284	22,687.50
Nick Flanagan	68	75	72	70	285	15,187.50
Bob Heintz	70	76	67	72	285	15,187.50
Richard Johnson	69	69	72	75	285	15,187.50
Michael Sim	70	72	74	69	285	15,187.50
Roberto Coceres	71	73	74	68	286	10,875
Michael Connell	70	72	72	72	286	10,875
Hunter Haas	73	74	71	68	286	10,875
Matt Hendrix	74	70	68	74	286	10,875
Boo Weekley	69	74	71	72	286	10,875
Matt Weibring	72	73	74	67	286	10,875
Chris Baryla	71	71	71	74	287	7,260
Keoke Cotner	71	75	70	71	287	7,260
Kim Felton	74	74	71	68	287	7,260
Skip Kendall	71	76	72	68	287	7,260
Kyle Thompson	66	78	72	71	287	7,260
Andrew Buckle	73	74	70	71	288	5,550
David McKenzie	70	76	73	69	288	5,550
Tim Wilkinson	75	73	70	70	288	5,550
Mark Wilson	70	73	72	73	288	5,550

Knoxville Open

Fox Den Country Club, Knoxville, Tennessee
Par 36-36—72; 7,110 yards

June 15-18
purse, $475,000

	SCORES			TOTAL	MONEY
Hunter Haas	67	66	67	69	269	$85,500
Gary Christian	69	70	69	66	274	41,800
Parker McLachlin	67	70	68	69	274	41,800
Brendon de Jonge	70	66	74	65	275	19,633.34
Franklin Langham	72	68	68	67	275	19,633.33
Brenden Pappas	68	67	67	73	275	19,633.33
Jim Rutledge	71	68	70	67	276	14,309.38
Boo Weekley	68	70	70	68	276	14,309.38
Jason Caron	69	67	70	70	276	14,309.37
Matt Hendrix	65	71	70	70	276	14,309.37
Joel Kribel	67	70	66	74	277	11,400
Stephen Marino	68	71	69	69	277	11,400
Brad Ott	71	70	70	67	278	9,183.34
Chez Reavie	68	71	70	69	278	9,183.33

418 / AMERICAN TOURS

	SCORES				TOTAL	MONEY
Tommy Tolles	71	69	70	68	278	9,183.33
Craig Bowden	72	70	69	69	280	7,600
Jin Park	71	70	70	69	280	7,600
Tom Scherrer	71	69	72	68	280	7,600
Chris Baryla	70	71	69	71	281	5,189.38
Ryan Howison	73	68	70	70	281	5,189.38
Peter Tomasulo	71	68	71	71	281	5,189.38
Tim Wilkinson	65	71	74	71	281	5,189.38
Richard Johnson	66	71	72	72	281	5,189.37
Matthew Jones	72	70	68	71	281	5,189.37
Jarrod Lyle	72	70	68	71	281	5,189.37
Hiroshi Matsuo	67	72	70	72	281	5,189.37
D.J. Brigman	72	70	69	71	282	3,372.50
Roberto Coceres	71	68	71	72	282	3,372.50
David Morland	71	71	68	72	282	3,372.50
Tim O'Neal	68	70	71	73	282	3,372.50
Jeff Quinney	69	70	75	68	282	3,372.50
Paul Sheehan	71	71	71	69	282	3,372.50

Chattanooga Classic

Black Creek Club, Chattanooga, Tennessee
Par 36-36—72; 7,044 yards

June 22-25
purse, $475,000

	SCORES				TOTAL	MONEY
Kyle Reifers	67	69	65	61	262	$85,500
Brandt Snedeker	62	65	69	66	262	51,300
(Reifers defeated Snedeker on first playoff hole.)						
Andrew Buckle	65	65	68	65	263	27,550
Boo Weekley	65	63	66	69	263	27,550
Brad Adamonis	66	67	66	67	266	17,337.50
Scott Ford	66	68	66	66	266	17,337.50
Charlie Wi	68	64	67	67	266	17,337.50
Hunter Haas	67	66	69	66	268	13,300
Tim O'Neal	67	67	64	70	268	13,300
Anthony Painter	69	65	68	66	268	13,300
Garrett Willis	62	66	69	71	268	13,300
Chris Baryla	68	66	66	69	269	9,025
Justin Bolli	65	69	70	65	269	9,025
Jarrod Lyle	67	64	71	67	269	9,025
David Mathis	65	67	69	68	269	9,025
Andrew Pratt	68	65	68	68	269	9,025
Johnson Wagner	69	66	65	69	269	9,025
Ken Duke	67	68	70	65	270	5,985
Franklin Langham	66	69	70	65	270	5,985
Steve LeBrun	68	69	70	63	270	5,985
Michael Long	66	70	68	66	270	5,985
Nick Malinowski	68	64	69	69	270	5,985
Jeff Quinney	66	68	67	69	270	5,985
Jamie Broce	68	69	68	66	271	4,028
Brendon de Jonge	67	67	67	70	271	4,028
Chez Reavie	66	68	69	68	271	4,028
Roland Thatcher	70	67	68	66	271	4,028
Chris Tidland	67	70	69	65	271	4,028
*Thomas Hagler	67	67	69	68	271	
Craig Bowden	63	65	74	70	272	3,154
Matt Kuchar	65	71	71	65	272	3,154

	SCORES	TOTAL	MONEY
John Merrick	66 65 68 73	272	3,154
Bryce Molder	70 67 66 69	272	3,154
Dicky Pride	64 67 70 71	272	3,154

Peek'n Peak Classic

Peek'n Peak Resort, Upper Course, Findley Lake, New York
Par 36-36–72; 6,888 yards

June 29-July 2
purse, $560,000

	SCORES	TOTAL	MONEY
John Merrick	71 69 69 68	277	$100,800
Gavin Coles	72 68 70 67	277	60,480
(Merrick defeated Coles on third playoff hole.)			
Andrew Buckle	75 69 70 64	278	38,080
Craig Bowden	70 68 71 70	279	24,640
Charlie Wi	67 71 72 69	279	24,640
Kim Felton	71 73 69 67	280	19,460
Chez Reavie	70 73 69 68	280	19,460
Chris Anderson	70 73 68 70	281	13,510
Jason Caron	70 71 71 69	281	13,510
Jason Dufner	69 68 73 71	281	13,510
Craig Lile	75 66 71 69	281	13,510
Nick Malinowski	71 67 74 69	281	13,510
Andrew Pratt	70 68 70 73	281	13,510
Michael Putnam	71 69 72 69	281	13,510
Kyle Thompson	70 71 68 72	281	13,510
Tom Scherrer	67 75 68 72	282	9,240
Jaco Van Zyl	71 71 71 69	282	9,240
Glen Hnatiuk	70 70 72 71	283	7,840
Dave Rummells	66 72 76 69	283	7,840
Brandt Snedeker	71 70 71 71	283	7,840
Spike McRoy	71 70 71 72	284	6,272
Jeff Quinney	72 68 72 72	284	6,272
Peter Tomasulo	76 66 69 73	284	6,272
Scott Gardiner	71 71 76 67	285	5,152
Tom Johnson	71 70 74 70	285	5,152
Michael Bradley	71 69 75 71	286	4,004
Paul Claxton	72 70 71 73	286	4,004
Parker McLachlin	74 70 69 73	286	4,004
David Morland	67 74 71 74	286	4,004
Jin Park	70 71 73 72	286	4,004
Rick Price	68 74 70 74	286	4,004
David Roesch	71 70 73 72	286	4,004
Steve Wheatcroft	71 69 73 73	286	4,004

Scholarship America Showdown

Somerby Golf Club, Byron, Minnesota
Par 36-36–72; 7,209 yards

July 13-16
purse, $550,000

	SCORES	TOTAL	MONEY
Brandt Snedeker	70 67 68 67	272	$99,000
Jeff Quinney	67 66 72 67	272	59,400
(Snedeker defeated Quinney on second playoff hole.)			
Tim O'Neal	67 70 68 69	274	31,900

	SCORES				TOTAL	MONEY
Kyle Thompson	69	68	67	70	274	31,900
Justin Bolli	69	65	71	70	275	22,000
Jason Caron	69	69	68	70	276	19,112.50
Jon Turcott	64	67	73	72	276	19,112.50
Gary Christian	69	70	71	67	277	15,400
Michael Harris	71	70	68	68	277	15,400
Bryce Molder	69	70	65	73	277	15,400
Jin Park	67	72	69	69	277	15,400
Ricky Barnes	70	71	66	71	278	10,780
Kim Felton	69	71	67	71	278	10,780
John Mallinger	70	70	69	69	278	10,780
Brock McKenzie	69	71	70	68	278	10,780
Jim Rutledge	72	67	71	68	278	10,780
Bob Heintz	71	68	73	67	279	7,197.15
Stephen Marino	72	67	70	70	279	7,197.15
Joe Daley	70	67	71	71	279	7,197.14
John Merrick	69	66	70	74	279	7,197.14
Mike Perez	66	66	72	75	279	7,197.14
Justin Smith	72	68	68	71	279	7,197.14
Mario Tiziani	66	71	70	72	279	7,197.14
Patrick Damron	70	71	68	71	280	4,785
Doug LaBelle	71	70	70	69	280	4,785
Chris Tidland	71	70	68	71	280	4,785
Johnson Wagner	73	66	66	75	280	4,785
Joel Kribel	71	69	71	70	281	3,960
Michael Putnam	70	68	74	69	281	3,960
Boo Weekley	70	69	69	73	281	3,960

Price Cutter Charity Championship

Highland Springs Country Club, Springfield, Missouri
Par 36-36–72; 7,060 yards

July 20-23
purse, $556,000

	SCORES				TOTAL	MONEY
Doug LaBelle	63	67	67	64	261	$100,080
Nick Flanagan	69	63	64	67	263	60,048
Justin Bolli	66	66	66	66	264	32,248
Ken Duke	66	63	68	67	264	32,248
Boo Weekley	65	63	68	69	265	22,240
Ricky Barnes	65	64	69	68	266	20,016
Jess Daley	64	70	66	67	267	17,931
Jon Turcott	67	66	68	66	267	17,931
Tommy Tolles	69	64	71	64	268	16,124
Jeremy Anderson	65	70	66	68	269	12,788
Danny Briggs	68	69	66	66	269	12,788
Scott Dunlap	64	69	69	67	269	12,788
Jeff Quinney	63	68	65	73	269	12,788
Jaco Van Zyl	68	67	63	71	269	12,788
Franklin Langham	68	65	70	67	270	9,452
Scott Parel	67	69	68	66	270	9,452
Roland Thatcher	68	69	68	65	270	9,452
Craig Bowden	73	64	64	70	271	7,005.60
Jeff Burns	64	72	68	67	271	7,005.60
Craig Kanada	68	70	66	67	271	7,005.60
Matt Kuchar	66	69	71	65	271	7,005.60
Stephen Marino	66	68	65	72	271	7,005.60
Kyle Thompson	64	69	70	68	271	7,005.60

	SCORES				TOTAL	MONEY
Steve Allan	69	64	73	66	272	4,596.27
Jason Enloe	67	69	68	68	272	4,596.27
Bob Heintz	71	66	67	68	272	4,596.27
John Merrick	68	69	71	64	272	4,596.27
Ryan Armour	71	66	63	72	272	4,596.26
Hunter Haas	65	70	68	69	272	4,596.26
Steven Alker	68	67	70	68	273	3,558.40
Matt Bettencourt	71	63	69	70	273	3,558.40
Patrick Damron	70	67	71	65	273	3,558.40
Chip Deason	70	67	67	69	273	3,558.40
Chez Reavie	67	70	70	66	273	3,558.40

Preferred Health Systems Wichita Open

Crestview Country Club, Wichita, Kansas
Par 35-36–71; 6,913 yards

July 27-30
purse, $500,000

	SCORES				TOTAL	MONEY
Kevin Johnson	65	68	67	66	266	$90,000
Matt Kuchar	66	64	69	68	267	54,000
Scott Gardiner	69	67	66	67	269	29,000
Craig Lile	68	68	66	67	269	29,000
Erik Compton	67	67	69	67	270	19,000
David Hearn	66	67	69	68	270	19,000
Barry Cheesman	66	66	71	68	271	15,062.50
Jarrod Lyle	71	67	69	64	271	15,062.50
Stephen Marino	66	67	67	71	271	15,062.50
Brad Ott	66	67	68	70	271	15,062.50
Patrick Damron	66	68	68	70	272	11,500
Nick Malinowski	66	67	67	72	272	11,500
Michael Putnam	67	68	68	69	272	11,500
Steve Collins	71	65	68	69	273	8,000
Jason Dufner	65	70	68	70	273	8,000
Bradley Hughes	67	69	69	68	273	8,000
Brenden Pappas	67	68	69	69	273	8,000
Chez Reavie	65	68	71	69	273	8,000
Steve Wheatcroft	67	69	70	67	273	8,000
Charlie Wi	71	67	68	67	273	8,000
Jamie Broce	69	68	70	67	274	4,750
Dan Buchner	70	68	70	66	274	4,750
Hunter Haas	67	64	71	72	274	4,750
Matt Hendrix	66	72	67	69	274	4,750
Rich Morris	68	66	72	68	274	4,750
Brandt Snedeker	67	66	72	69	274	4,750
Jon Turcott	68	68	67	71	274	4,750
Jaco Van Zyl	67	70	65	72	274	4,750
Ryan Armour	66	71	71	67	275	3,375
Aron Price	66	71	67	71	275	3,375
Michael Sim	70	64	68	73	275	3,375
Peter Tomasulo	67	66	73	69	275	3,375

Cox Classic

Champions Run, Omaha, Nebraska
Par 35-36–71; 6,966 yards

August 3-6
purse, $650,000

	SCORES				TOTAL	MONEY
Johnson Wagner	66	70	64	63	263	$117,000
Craig Bowden	70	63	66	68	267	70,200
Paul Gow	69	67	66	66	268	29,315
Jeff Klauk	67	67	66	68	268	29,315
Cliff Kresge	69	63	71	65	268	29,315
Michael Putnam	69	67	68	64	268	29,315
Jeff Quinney	67	66	69	66	268	29,315
Chip Beck	68	64	70	67	269	16,900
Jamie Broce	69	64	67	69	269	16,900
Ken Duke	67	69	70	63	269	16,900
John Mallinger	66	65	70	68	269	16,900
Deane Pappas	67	68	66	68	269	16,900
Peter Tomasulo	64	70	67	68	269	16,900
Josh Broadaway	68	68	66	68	270	11,700
Andrew Johnson	65	68	68	69	270	11,700
Michael Long	63	70	67	70	270	11,700
Ryan Armour	64	69	66	72	271	9,100
Brendon de Jonge	65	68	68	70	271	9,100
Stephen Marino	67	67	71	66	271	9,100
Bryce Molder	65	67	69	70	271	9,100
Chez Reavie	64	67	71	69	271	9,100
Joe Daley	70	66	67	69	272	6,110
Nick Flanagan	70	65	69	68	272	6,110
Bradley Hughes	64	66	75	67	272	6,110
Matthew Jones	68	68	69	67	272	6,110
Paul Sheehan	69	63	73	67	272	6,110
Charlie Wi	67	67	70	68	272	6,110
Paul Claxton	66	71	68	68	273	4,203.34
Brad Klapprott	69	67	69	68	273	4,203.34
Michael Walton	67	70	67	69	273	4,203.34
Brad Adamonis	69	66	66	72	273	4,203.33
Andrew Buckle	69	67	70	67	273	4,203.33
Jason Dufner	69	67	70	67	273	4,203.33
Tom Johnson	66	69	69	69	273	4,203.33
Rick Price	70	65	68	70	273	4,203.33
Kevin Stadler	69	63	71	70	273	4,203.33

Xerox Classic

Irondequoit Country Club, Rochester, New York
Par 35-35–70; 6,720 yards

August 10-13
purse, $575,000

	SCORES				TOTAL	MONEY
Kevin Stadler	69	68	69	65	271	$103,500
Glen Day	66	70	68	68	272	62,100
Steven Alker	66	72	72	63	273	29,900
Chad Collins	67	72	69	65	273	29,900
Richard Johnson	66	68	73	66	273	29,900
Steve Allan	65	73	69	67	274	17,997.50
Ryan Armour	71	67	68	68	274	17,997.50
Jeff Quinney	67	72	70	65	274	17,997.50

	SCORES				TOTAL	MONEY
David Sutherland	69	71	68	66	274	17,997.50
Roland Thatcher	71	67	70	66	274	17,997.50
Pat Bates	67	70	71	67	275	13,225
Matt Kuchar	69	69	71	66	275	13,225
Fran Quinn	68	72	69	66	275	13,225
Chris Baryla	67	70	69	70	276	10,350
Matthew Jones	66	73	67	70	276	10,350
Jarrod Lyle	68	69	67	72	276	10,350
Ricky Barnes	66	75	67	69	277	7,781.67
Doug LaBelle	71	70	69	67	277	7,781.67
Rick Price	67	73	70	67	277	7,781.67
Johnson Wagner	67	73	69	68	277	7,781.67
David Hearn	69	68	67	73	277	7,781.66
Anthony Painter	68	71	68	70	277	7,781.66
Jess Daley	70	68	70	70	278	4,588.50
Joe Daley	70	68	71	69	278	4,588.50
Ken Duke	69	71	70	68	278	4,588.50
Paul Gow	73	66	68	71	278	4,588.50
Michael Long	67	73	68	70	278	4,588.50
Bryce Molder	68	70	71	69	278	4,588.50
Brenden Pappas	67	71	67	73	278	4,588.50
Chez Reavie	68	69	72	69	278	4,588.50
Grant Waite	68	73	68	69	278	4,588.50
Matt Weibring	66	73	70	69	278	4,588.50

Northeast Pennsylvania Classic

Glenmaura National Golf Club, Scranton, Pennsylvania
Par 35-36–71; 6,990 yards

August 17-20
purse, $475,000

	SCORES				TOTAL	MONEY
Craig Bowden	69	69	67	63	268	$85,500
Jess Daley	64	71	63	70	268	51,300
(Bowden defeated Daley on first playoff hole.)						
Brad Adamonis	66	65	69	69	269	27,550
Bryce Molder	70	68	64	67	269	27,550
Brendon de Jonge	71	66	65	69	271	17,337.50
Franklin Langham	68	70	68	65	271	17,337.50
Jay Williamson	68	69	66	68	271	17,337.50
Richard Johnson	66	69	67	70	272	13,775
Stephen Marino	68	70	67	67	272	13,775
Boo Weekley	70	67	64	71	272	13,775
Aaron Barber	71	67	67	68	273	10,070
Rich Barcelo	68	68	69	68	273	10,070
Scott Dunlap	68	70	70	65	273	10,070
Tom Scherrer	68	70	70	65	273	10,070
Roland Thatcher	69	69	64	71	273	10,070
Bradley Hughes	67	69	70	68	274	7,362.50
Cliff Kresge	71	68	63	72	274	7,362.50
Peter Tomasulo	68	69	67	70	274	7,362.50
Johnson Wagner	64	70	67	73	274	7,362.50
Jim McGovern	69	69	69	68	275	5,731.67
Kevin Stadler	65	70	73	67	275	5,731.67
Craig Kanada	67	70	67	71	275	5,731.66
Joe Daley	69	67	71	69	276	4,560
David Mathis	66	71	73	66	276	4,560
Esteban Toledo	68	71	71	66	276	4,560

	SCORES				TOTAL	MONEY
Dan Buchner	70	67	72	68	277	3,705
Jason Buha	69	66	70	72	277	3,705
Matt Davidson	70	70	64	73	277	3,705
John Morse	69	71	68	69	277	3,705
Paul Claxton	71	67	68	72	278	3,087.50
Doug LaBelle	69	70	65	74	278	3,087.50
David Sutherland	73	67	66	72	278	3,087.50
Steve Wheatcroft	67	68	74	69	278	3,087.50

National Mining Association Pete Dye Classic

Pete Dye Golf Club, Bridgeport, West Virginia
Par 36-36–72; 7,309 yards

August 24-27
purse, $600,000

	SCORES				TOTAL	MONEY
Jason Enloe	70	70	66	68	274	$108,000
Boo Weekley	67	67	70	70	274	64,800
(Enloe defeated Weekley on first playoff hole.)						
Jason Allred	68	71	67	70	276	40,800
Jamie Broce	69	70	68	70	277	24,800
John Mallinger	66	72	70	69	277	24,800
Jim Rutledge	71	70	72	64	277	24,800
Aron Price	71	71	66	70	278	20,100
Jeremy Anderson	71	68	69	71	279	16,800
Matthew Jones	69	72	73	65	279	16,800
Dan Olsen	72	68	70	69	279	16,800
Scott Weatherly	68	73	69	69	279	16,800
Ken Duke	73	67	68	72	280	10,400
Hunter Haas	70	69	71	70	280	10,400
Bob Heintz	69	67	72	72	280	10,400
Bradley Hughes	70	70	67	73	280	10,400
Craig Kanada	68	70	71	71	280	10,400
Brenden Pappas	73	66	71	70	280	10,400
Michael Putnam	69	70	74	67	280	10,400
Kyle Reifers	73	69	71	67	280	10,400
Tom Scherrer	69	69	71	71	280	10,400
Erik Compton	73	68	66	74	281	6,480
Scott Gardiner	75	67	68	71	281	6,480
Chris Tidland	70	71	70	70	281	6,480
Esteban Toledo	71	68	71	71	281	6,480
Steve Allan	70	69	72	71	282	4,800
Danny Briggs	71	67	71	73	282	4,800
Franklin Langham	74	67	73	68	282	4,800
Jin Park	72	68	72	70	282	4,800
Fran Quinn	73	69	69	71	282	4,800
Rich Barcelo	70	68	68	77	283	3,720
Ricky Barnes	69	72	70	72	283	3,720
Michael Long	63	77	69	74	283	3,720
David Mathis	69	70	70	74	283	3,720
Bryce Molder	70	69	74	70	283	3,720
Anthony Painter	70	69	71	73	283	3,720
Steve Wheatcroft	74	68	74	67	283	3,720

Legend Financial Group Classic

StoneWater Golf Club, Highland Heights, Ohio
Par 35-36–71; 7,045 yards

August 31-September 3
purse, $500,000

		SCORES			TOTAL	MONEY
Gavin Coles	67	71	68	68	274	$90,000
Bradley Hughes	70	63	70	72	275	54,000
Boo Weekley	70	69	69	68	276	34,000
Chris Baryla	71	67	67	72	277	24,000
Ricky Barnes	71	70	69	68	278	18,250
Ken Duke	75	67	69	67	278	18,250
Akio Sadakata	69	69	72	68	278	18,250
Craig Lile	70	68	72	69	279	15,000
Jarrod Lyle	69	71	70	69	279	15,000
Chris Anderson	69	69	74	68	280	12,500
Cameron Beckman	67	70	72	71	280	12,500
Tommy Tolles	72	70	70	68	280	12,500
D.J. Brigman	74	66	74	67	281	9,100
Glen Day	71	67	73	70	281	9,100
Jim McGovern	71	66	74	70	281	9,100
Jeff Quinney	66	70	69	76	281	9,100
Kyle Thompson	73	68	70	70	281	9,100
Josh Broadaway	69	69	72	72	282	6,750
John Merrick	75	66	73	68	282	6,750
Scott Petersen	70	71	74	67	282	6,750
Rick Price	72	65	77	68	282	6,750
Scott Gardiner	71	71	68	73	283	4,450
Kevin Gessino-Kraft	72	70	72	69	283	4,450
Brad Klapprott	70	71	72	70	283	4,450
Cliff Kresge	71	68	73	71	283	4,450
Andrew Pratt	72	70	69	72	283	4,450
Tom Scherrer	71	67	74	71	283	4,450
Chris Tidland	70	72	74	67	283	4,450
Tim Wilkinson	71	70	74	68	283	4,450
Dave Christensen	70	69	73	72	284	3,200
Darron Stiles	73	69	71	71	284	3,200
Mario Tiziani	71	67	74	72	284	3,200
Esteban Toledo	74	67	72	71	284	3,200
Grant Waite	70	72	69	73	284	3,200

Utah Energy Solutions Championship

Willow Creek Country Club, Sandy, Utah
Par 35-37–72; 7,104 yards

September 7-10
purse, $475,000

		SCORES			TOTAL	MONEY
Craig Kanada	69	67	65	71	272	$85,500
Gavin Coles	70	64	71	68	273	31,350
Ken Duke	65	70	68	70	273	31,350
Bryce Molder	64	64	70	75	273	31,350
Michael Putnam	66	71	72	64	273	31,350
Brendon de Jonge	72	67	71	64	274	15,912.50
Kevin Durkin	73	67	66	68	274	15,912.50
Matthew Jones	71	65	71	67	274	15,912.50
Craig Lile	65	69	70	71	275	12,350
Parker McLachlin	71	69	70	65	275	12,350

	SCORES				TOTAL	MONEY
Scott Parel	64	71	69	71	275	12,350
Scott Petersen	67	67	71	70	275	12,350
Gary Christian	71	69	67	69	276	8,645
Scott Gardiner	70	70	71	65	276	8,645
Scott Gutschewski	68	69	70	69	276	8,645
Gary Hallberg	71	66	71	68	276	8,645
Darron Stiles	68	67	71	70	276	8,645
Dave Christensen	70	67	70	70	277	5,404.45
Paul Gow	68	70	73	66	277	5,404.45
John Merrick	72	67	69	69	277	5,404.45
Brad Ott	71	69	71	66	277	5,404.45
Ricky Barnes	70	66	69	72	277	5,404.44
Jason Buha	72	68	67	70	277	5,404.44
Matt Hendrix	71	66	69	71	277	5,404.44
Jeff Quinney	66	67	73	71	277	5,404.44
Peter Tomasulo	70	68	68	71	277	5,404.44
Craig Bowden	70	70	68	70	278	3,515
Jamie Broce	67	71	66	74	278	3,515
Scott Hend	70	70	67	71	278	3,515
Andy Morse	69	70	68	71	278	3,515

Albertsons Boise Open

Hillcrest Country Club, Boise, Idaho
Par 36-35–71; 6,685 yards

September 14-17
purse, $650,000

	SCORES				TOTAL	MONEY
Kevin Stadler	64	64	70	66	264	$117,000
Glen Day	67	67	66	65	265	70,200
Jason Allred	65	68	68	66	267	44,200
Scott Dunlap	63	67	71	67	268	31,200
Mario Tiziani	67	64	65	73	269	26,000
Andrew Buckle	66	69	68	68	271	22,587.50
Tripp Isenhour	71	65	66	69	271	22,587.50
Jess Daley	70	68	69	65	272	16,900
Brendon de Jonge	67	68	71	66	272	16,900
Jason Dufner	68	70	69	65	272	16,900
Franklin Langham	68	71	66	67	272	16,900
Jarrod Lyle	65	67	71	69	272	16,900
Jay Williamson	69	69	64	70	272	16,900
Matt Kuchar	69	67	69	68	273	11,375
Dan Olsen	70	64	70	69	273	11,375
Jeff Quinney	69	65	67	72	273	11,375
Kyle Reifers	65	72	70	66	273	11,375
Ricky Barnes	70	65	67	72	274	9,425
Paul Gow	68	68	70	68	274	9,425
Craig Kanada	68	69	69	69	275	8,450
Hiroshi Matsuo	67	69	71	69	276	7,540
Tim Wilkinson	69	69	69	69	276	7,540
Chris Botsford	69	68	72	68	277	5,876
Jeff Freeman	64	71	72	70	277	5,876
Parker McLachlin	69	68	68	72	277	5,876
Peter Tomasulo	69	70	71	67	277	5,876
Boo Weekley	68	68	71	70	277	5,876
Steven Alker	66	71	72	69	278	4,345.72
Roberto Coceres	70	68	71	69	278	4,345.72
John Ellis	68	71	72	67	278	4,345.72

	SCORES				TOTAL	MONEY
Jamie Broce	65	66	73	74	278	4,345.71
Bob Heintz	68	68	71	71	278	4,345.71
Darron Stiles	71	65	69	73	278	4,345.71
Johnson Wagner	69	67	70	72	278	4,345.71

Oregon Classic

Shadow Hills Country Club, Junction City, Oregon
Par 36-36–72; 7,007 yards

September 21-24
purse, $450,000

	SCORES				TOTAL	MONEY
Cliff Kresge	70	67	67	67	271	$81,000
Ricky Barnes	67	68	68	68	271	48,600
(Kresge defeated Barnes on third playoff hole.)						
Tim Wilkinson	68	68	67	69	272	30,600
Chris Baryla	69	70	68	68	275	21,600
Scott Dunlap	68	69	72	67	276	18,000
Tom Johnson	69	69	73	66	277	15,637.50
Chad Collins	68	68	71	70	277	15,637.50
Bradley Hughes	70	68	72	68	278	13,050
Jarrod Lyle	69	70	70	69	278	13,050
Jason Dufner	70	72	67	69	278	13,050
Rich Barcelo	70	71	70	68	279	10,800
Fran Quinn	67	68	71	73	279	10,800
Tim O'Neal	69	72	73	66	280	7,714.29
Craig Bowden	69	73	70	68	280	7,714.29
Tom Scherrer	69	68	73	70	280	7,714.29
Jay Williamson	70	71	69	70	280	7,714.29
Roland Thatcher	71	69	69	71	280	7,714.29
Ryan Armour	66	71	71	72	280	7,714.29
John Ellis	67	71	68	74	280	7,714.29
Bryce Molder	72	71	69	69	281	4,718.58
Steve Allan	68	71	72	70	281	4,718.57
Anthony Painter	69	72	70	70	281	4,718.57
Esteban Toledo	68	73	70	70	281	4,718.57
Josh Broadaway	74	69	67	71	281	4,718.57
Boo Weekley	68	72	68	73	281	4,718.57
Stephen Marino	68	71	69	73	281	4,718.57
Andrew Buckle	69	70	77	66	282	3,420
Bob Heintz	67	76	72	67	282	3,420
Steven Alker	74	65	70	73	282	3,420
Mark Wiebe	73	69	71	70	283	3,015
Wil Collins	72	69	71	71	283	3,015

Mark Christopher Charity Classic

Empire Lakes Golf Club, Rancho Cucamonga, California
Par 35-36–71; 7,017 yards

October 5-8
purse, $500,000

	SCORES				TOTAL	MONEY
Kevin Na	62	66	71	69	268	$90,000
Jeff Quinney	67	68	65	71	271	44,000
Chris Tidland	66	68	71	66	271	44,000
Grant Waite	68	67	66	71	272	24,000

	SCORES				TOTAL	MONEY
Ken Duke	70	67	64	72	273	20,000
Ryan Armour	68	70	64	72	274	15,650
Brett Bingham	68	70	68	68	274	15,650
Josh Broadaway	67	70	68	69	274	15,650
Tim O'Neal	69	66	71	68	274	15,650
Tom Scherrer	65	71	68	70	274	15,650
Steve Allan	66	69	70	70	275	10,250
Chad Collins	69	70	66	70	275	10,250
Scott Dunlap	70	69	67	69	275	10,250
Joel Kribel	70	66	70	69	275	10,250
Deane Pappas	69	69	63	74	275	10,250
Jin Park	71	69	67	68	275	10,250
Dan Buchner	69	65	69	73	276	5,920
Bob Heintz	64	72	72	68	276	5,920
Craig Kanada	70	67	70	69	276	5,920
John Merrick	66	70	68	72	276	5,920
Scott Petersen	70	71	65	70	276	5,920
Chez Reavie	64	71	70	71	276	5,920
Roland Thatcher	67	71	68	70	276	5,920
Peter Tomasulo	68	72	69	67	276	5,920
Johnson Wagner	66	72	71	67	276	5,920
Zoran Zorkic	71	64	69	72	276	5,920
Ricky Barnes	68	73	69	67	277	3,550
Scott Gardiner	69	68	72	68	277	3,550
Brenden Pappas	66	73	68	70	277	3,550
Michael Putnam	67	73	70	67	277	3,550
Byron Schlagenhauf	68	71	69	69	277	3,550
Jimmy Walker	65	70	73	69	277	3,550

Permian Basin Charity Golf Classic

Midland Country Club, Midland, Texas
Par 36-36–72; 7,354 yards

October 12-15
purse, $475,000

	SCORES				TOTAL	MONEY
Brandt Snedeker	66	67	70	69	272	$85,500
Aron Price	73	68	65	66	272	51,300
(Snedeker defeated Price on first playoff hole.)						
Craig Bowden	67	72	68	66	273	32,300
Andrew Buckle	70	69	68	68	275	20,900
Matt Kuchar	69	67	69	70	275	20,900
Dan Buchner	68	68	73	67	276	16,506.25
Matthew Jones	72	69	68	67	276	16,506.25
John Merrick	71	65	72	69	277	13,775
Boo Weekley	74	66	71	66	277	13,775
Matt Weibring	69	69	68	71	277	13,775
Ryan Armour	74	70	70	64	278	10,925
David Hearn	71	69	70	68	278	10,925
Kyle Thompson	72	66	73	67	278	10,925
Ricky Barnes	72	72	69	66	279	8,312.50
Richard Johnson	70	71	73	65	279	8,312.50
John Mallinger	73	69	68	69	279	8,312.50
Esteban Toledo	72	70	69	68	279	8,312.50
Brad Klapprott	74	70	69	67	280	6,194
Jarrod Lyle	70	71	71	68	280	6,194
Brad Ott	72	69	71	68	280	6,194
Jeff Quinney	71	73	67	69	280	6,194

	SCORES				TOTAL	MONEY
Jaco Van Zyl	73	71	69	67	280	6,194
Tripp Isenhour	75	68	67	71	281	4,417.50
Jin Park	75	69	67	70	281	4,417.50
Chris Parra	68	70	70	73	281	4,417.50
Jim Rutledge	69	72	71	69	281	4,417.50
Kevin Johnson	69	72	71	70	282	3,705
Tim Wilkinson	70	71	72	69	282	3,705
Bradley Hughes	70	69	74	70	283	3,325
Jay Williamson	73	71	71	68	283	3,325

PalmettoPride Classic

Daniel Island Club, Charleston, South Carolina
Par 36-36—72; 7,446 yards
(Playoff completed on Monday—darkness.)

October 19-23
purse, $500,000

	SCORES				TOTAL	MONEY
Michael Sim	67	69	69	71	276	$90,000
Ken Duke	71	71	69	65	276	54,000
(Sim defeated Duke on first playoff hole.)						
Jarrod Lyle	70	69	68	71	278	34,000
Cameron Beckman	69	73	70	67	279	17,464.29
Tom Johnson	69	71	70	69	279	17,464.29
Roland Thatcher	68	71	73	67	279	17,464.29
Garrett Willis	74	69	68	68	279	17,464.29
Chad Collins	68	72	70	69	279	17,464.28
Craig Lile	66	73	70	70	279	17,464.28
Chris Tidland	67	73	70	69	279	17,464.28
Ryan Armour	74	70	70	66	280	10,600
Paul Gow	70	72	71	67	280	10,600
John Merrick	70	69	72	69	280	10,600
Michael Putnam	71	68	75	66	280	10,600
Peter Tomasulo	71	69	70	70	280	10,600
Jim McGovern	69	72	71	69	281	8,250
Kevin Stadler	71	66	68	76	281	8,250
Gary Christian	71	71	73	67	282	6,085.72
Rick Price	70	75	69	68	282	6,085.72
Jim Rutledge	71	74	68	69	282	6,085.72
Gavin Coles	68	73	69	72	282	6,085.71
Cliff Kresge	67	74	70	71	282	6,085.71
Brandt Snedeker	70	71	71	70	282	6,085.71
Matt Weibring	68	73	71	70	282	6,085.71
Jason Allred	72	71	72	68	283	3,900
Craig Bowden	69	69	72	73	283	3,900
Brendon de Jonge	70	69	70	74	283	3,900
Bradley Hughes	70	74	67	72	283	3,900
Matt Kuchar	68	72	72	71	283	3,900
Johnson Wagner	70	69	72	72	283	3,900

Miccosukee Championship

Miccosukee Golf & Country Club, Miami, Florida
Par 36-35–71; 7,200 yards

October 26-29
purse, $500,000

	SCORES				TOTAL	MONEY
Bryce Molder	65	70	67	68	270	$90,000
Boo Weekley	65	69	69	68	271	54,000
Jason Dufner	68	68	70	66	272	34,000
Cameron Beckman	68	67	69	69	273	20,666.67
Cliff Kresge	66	70	67	70	273	20,666.67
Tim O'Neal	67	66	68	72	273	20,666.66
Matt Kuchar	67	69	72	66	274	15,583.34
Chad Collins	67	67	66	74	274	15,583.33
Stephen Marino	71	66	69	68	274	15,583.33
Gary Christian	64	69	69	73	275	12,500
Parker McLachlin	67	73	69	66	275	12,500
Darron Stiles	68	70	68	69	275	12,500
Justin Bolli	71	69	68	68	276	9,666.67
Jim Rutledge	68	72	69	67	276	9,666.67
Ken Duke	66	71	70	69	276	9,666.66
Doug LaBelle	74	65	69	69	277	7,500
Michael Sim	69	70	70	68	277	7,500
Brandt Snedeker	72	66	70	69	277	7,500
Kyle Thompson	65	71	73	68	277	7,500
Steve Wheatcroft	74	63	69	71	277	7,500
Ryan Armour	67	74	68	69	278	5,400
David Hearn	66	70	74	68	278	5,400
Tripp Isenhour	70	65	73	70	278	5,400
Kyle Reifers	68	69	74	67	278	5,400
Ricky Barnes	67	73	70	69	279	3,666.67
Kevin Durkin	67	73	71	68	279	3,666.67
Hunter Haas	70	70	69	70	279	3,666.67
Craig Kanada	66	72	71	70	279	3,666.67
Jeff Quinney	69	72	71	67	279	3,666.67
Chris Tidland	69	72	67	71	279	3,666.67
Nick Flanagan	70	69	67	73	279	3,666.66
Scott Gardiner	71	67	69	72	279	3,666.66
Mark Wiebe	71	69	68	71	279	3,666.66

Nationwide Tour Championship

The Houstonian Golf & Country Club, Richmond, Texas
Par 36-36–72; 7,240 yards

November 9-12
purse, $750,000

	SCORES				TOTAL	MONEY
Craig Kanada	73	64	72	66	275	$135,000
Andrew Buckle	67	69	71	69	276	66,000
Matt Kuchar	71	65	67	73	276	66,000
Ricky Barnes	72	68	73	65	278	36,000
Doug LaBelle	70	70	72	67	279	30,000
Stephen Marino	71	68	72	69	280	26,062.50
Darron Stiles	73	70	70	67	280	26,062.50
Paul Claxton	69	70	75	67	281	22,500
Tim O'Neal	69	68	77	67	281	22,500
Chris Baryla	69	67	72	74	282	18,750
Tripp Isenhour	70	70	73	69	282	18,750

	SCORES				TOTAL	MONEY
Cliff Kresge	67	69	71	75	282	18,750
Johnson Wagner	70	67	73	73	283	15,750
Gavin Coles	72	71	71	70	284	13,125
Ken Duke	70	71	76	67	284	13,125
Craig Lile	72	69	72	71	284	13,125
Jim Rutledge	72	73	71	68	284	13,125
Jason Dufner	72	68	74	71	285	10,500
Brandt Snedeker	68	68	75	74	285	10,500
Boo Weekley	69	69	68	79	285	10,500
Ryan Armour	71	71	70	74	286	9,000
Craig Bowden	71	68	75	73	287	7,500
Gary Christian	67	76	73	71	287	7,500
Paul Gow	75	71	69	72	287	7,500
David Hearn	71	72	77	67	287	7,500
Roland Thatcher	71	73	71	73	288	6,300
Jeff Quinney	73	68	79	69	289	5,850
Peter Tomasulo	70	69	75	75	289	5,850
Steve Allan	68	73	77	72	290	5,400
Cameron Beckman	72	69	74	76	291	4,725
Nick Flanagan	71	69	79	72	291	4,725
Scott Gardiner	73	66	77	75	291	4,725
Jarrod Lyle	72	73	75	71	291	4,725
Kyle Reifers	69	70	79	73	291	4,725
Chris Tidland	68	71	74	78	291	4,725

Canadian Tour

Yes! Golf BCR Classic

Barton Creek Resort, Austin, Texas
Fazio Canyons Course: Par 36-36–72; 7,153 yards
Crenshaw Cliffside Course: Par 35-36–71; 6,553 yards

March 2-5
purse, US$100,000

	SCORES				TOTAL	MONEY
Rob Oppenheim	66	71	68	66	271	US$16,000
Omar Uresti	66	69	67	69	271	6,800
Jim Rutledge	67	72	66	66	271	6,800
Craig Kanada	63	71	67	70	271	6,800
(Oppenheim won on first playoff hole.)						
Anthony Rodriguez	71	66	67	68	272	3,800
Stephen Gangluff	69	68	68	67	272	3,800
Darren Griff	70	65	69	69	273	3,300
Lee Williamson	69	73	65	67	274	2,900
Benjamin Hayes	70	63	71	70	274	2,900
Robert Hamilton	67	74	65	68	274	2,900
Travis Johnson	72	70	64	69	275	2,500
Craig Matthew	66	71	70	69	276	2,025

	SCORES				TOTAL	MONEY
John Mallinger	69	72	67	68	276	2,025
Mike Grob	67	74	67	68	276	2,025
Steve Friesen	75	67	67	67	276	2,025
Kevin Ward	75	67	70	65	277	1,421
Alan McLean	69	69	68	71	277	1,421
Blaine McCallister	68	70	67	72	277	1,421
Rob Johnson	65	74	65	73	277	1,421
Jason Higton	68	71	69	69	277	1,421
Ryan Grant	70	67	70	70	277	1,421
Scott Ford	64	68	72	73	277	1,421
Brendan Steele	71	66	69	72	278	1,125
Chris Baryla	66	69	70	73	278	1,125
Todd Tanner	71	69	69	70	279	947
Steve Schneiter	70	72	70	67	279	947
Mike Mezei	72	68	71	68	279	947
Jim Lemon	67	74	66	72	279	947
Michael Harris	70	69	71	69	279	947
Jason Hartwick	74	68	66	71	279	947

Yes! Golf BCR Challenge

Barton Creek Resort, Fazio Foothills Course, Austin, Texas
Par 36-36–72; 7,125 yards

March 9-12
purse, US$100,000

	SCORES				TOTAL	MONEY
Brian Guetz	73	72	66	68	279	US$16,000
John Mallinger	73	71	68	67	279	9,600
(Guetz defeated Mallinger on first playoff hole.)						
Omar Uresti	73	68	71	68	280	4,600
Jim Rutledge	70	73	69	68	280	4,600
Michael Letzig	75	68	68	69	280	4,600
Craig Kanada	76	69	69	66	280	4,600
Michael Harris	71	72	68	71	282	3,200
John Ellis	70	73	66	73	282	3,200
Doug LaBelle	71	73	69	70	283	2,900
Eric Wang	76	69	67	72	284	2,600
Mike Mezei	70	70	70	74	284	2,600
Lee Williamson	72	70	70	74	286	1,960
Rob McMillan	70	72	74	70	286	1,960
Ryan Miller	78	68	69	71	286	1,960
Joseph Lanza	69	72	70	75	286	1,960
Marcus Jones	75	70	72	69	286	1,960
John Lieber	71	74	69	73	287	1,410
Robert Hamilton	76	71	68	72	287	1,410
Scott Gibson	72	74	70	71	287	1,410
Andy Doeden	71	74	69	73	287	1,410
Jason Allred	71	75	67	74	287	1,410
Anthony Rodriguez	74	72	71	71	288	1,100
Tom Kalinowski	69	71	70	78	288	1,100
Rob Johnson	71	74	70	73	288	1,100
Scott Hawley	68	75	72	73	288	1,100
Ryan Ellis	72	73	71	72	288	1,100
Will Yanagisawa	68	72	76	73	289	923
Andy Matthews	72	70	69	78	289	923
Ryan Carter	71	72	74	72	289	923
Jon Turcott	75	72	70	73	290	816
Adam Short	69	74	73	74	290	816

	SCORES				TOTAL	MONEY
Jaime Gomez	72	73	70	75	290	816
Stephen Gangluff	73	75	67	75	290	816

Northern California Classic

Brookside Golf & Country Club, Stockton, California
Par 36-36–72; 6,720 yards

March 23-26
purse, US$100,000

	SCORES				TOTAL	MONEY
Matt Hansen	67	63	70	69	269	US$16,000
Jeff Quinney	67	62	73	67	269	6,800
John Mallinger	66	65	69	69	269	6,800
Erik Compton	64	67	71	67	269	6,800
(Hansen won on first playoff hole.)						
Rob Oppenheim	72	64	70	64	270	4,000
Rob Johnson	68	66	74	65	273	3,600
Adam Speirs	68	68	69	69	274	3,300
Keith Huber	67	69	74	65	275	3,000
Ricky Barnes	67	69	72	67	275	3,000
Anthony Rodriguez	69	70	71	66	276	2,700
Eugene Smith	71	65	71	70	277	2,300
Dong Yi	72	63	73	69	277	2,300
Chris Baryla	67	71	74	65	277	2,300
Stephen Woodard	71	65	75	67	278	1,750
Jim Seki	70	66	73	69	278	1,750
Adam Short	69	69	73	67	278	1,750
Wil Collins	71	68	70	69	278	1,750
Brendan Steele	68	69	72	70	279	1,217
Chad Spencer	68	70	73	68	279	1,217
Brian Unk	71	68	72	68	279	1,217
Eric Jorgensen	69	67	74	69	279	1,217
Ron Harvey, Jr.	65	65	75	74	279	1,217
Derek Gillespie	71	66	75	67	279	1,217
Stephen Gangluff	69	70	76	64	279	1,217
Chris Cureton	69	68	76	66	279	1,217
Garrett Chaussard	68	67	74	70	279	1,217
Brian Guetz	64	71	77	68	280	923
Brad Fritsch	68	66	74	72	280	923
Ryan Carter	72	65	76	67	280	923
Scott Gibson	65	68	74	74	281	845
Eric Couture	73	67	74	67	281	845

Diablo Grande California Classic

Legends West Course at Diablo Grande, Patterson, California
Par 36-36–72; 7,100 yards

April 20-23
purse, US$100,000

	SCORES			TOTAL	MONEY
Lee Williamson	70	71	64	67	272	US$16,000
Justin Lee	70	69	69	69	277	7,800
Ben Hayes	71	68	71	67	277	7,800
Brian Guetz	68	69	72	69	278	4,400
Stephen Gangluff	69	68	68	73	278	4,400
Dustin Risdon	70	70	73	66	279	3,225

	SCORES				TOTAL	MONEY
Rob Oppenheim	67	74	69	69	279	3,225
Travis Johnson	69	70	69	71	279	3,225
Wes Heffernan	70	72	70	67	279	3,225
John Ellis	74	70	66	70	280	2,600
Brendan Steele	68	71	72	69	280	2,600
Anders Hultman	70	69	74	68	281	2,025
Ron Harvey, Jr.	68	69	70	74	281	2,025
Steve Friesen	66	74	72	69	281	2,025
Andrew Barnes	72	68	69	72	281	2,025
Eugene Smith	69	70	74	69	282	1,650
Jon Turcott	71	70	72	69	282	1,650
Byron Smith	74	71	68	70	283	1,300
Joseph Lanza	70	72	72	69	283	1,300
Michael Harris	73	72	69	69	283	1,300
Ryan Ellis	70	71	71	71	283	1,300
Stuart Anderson	68	72	71	72	283	1,300
Michael Walton	72	70	70	71	283	1,300
Brock Mackenzie	71	72	71	70	284	1,050
Lee Curry	68	74	72	70	284	1,050
Wil Collins	70	72	69	73	284	1,050
Madalitso Muthiya	71	72	72	70	285	892
Jason Hartwick	73	72	69	71	285	892
Andy Doeden	71	69	74	71	285	892
Ben Bunny	70	71	72	72	285	892
Eric Wang	71	74	72	68	285	892

Corona Mazatlan Classic

El Cid Resort, Mazatlan, Mexico
Par 36-36–72; 6,623 yards

May 11-14
purse, US$125,000

	SCORES				TOTAL	MONEY
Rob Oppenheim	73	67	69	64	273	US$20,000
Stephen Gangluff	69	66	67	71	273	12,000
(Oppenheim defeated Gangluff on first playoff hole.)						
Chris Wall	67	67	71	69	274	7,500
Michael Walton	66	70	70	70	276	5,500
Josh Habig	70	66	71	69	276	5,500
Anthony Rodriguez	68	72	70	67	277	4,167
Brian Miller	65	71	70	71	277	4,167
Wil Collins	70	67	66	74	277	4,167
Michael Harris	72	68	65	73	278	3,625
Brian Guetz	72	71	67	69	279	3,375
Adam Short	73	69	67	71	280	2,875
Kevin Pom Arleau	69	66	74	71	280	2,875
Tyler Erickson	73	64	69	74	280	2,875
Jon Turcott	70	67	73	71	281	2,312
Jim Lemon	73	70	69	69	281	2,312
Ben Weir	72	68	70	72	282	1,875
Juan Salazar	71	69	72	70	282	1,875
Gibby Martens	71	67	72	72	282	1,875
Brian Flugstad	68	69	74	71	282	1,875
Lindsay Bernakevitch	71	70	72	69	282	1,875
Craig Taylor	68	69	77	69	283	1,469
Pablo Fernandez	72	71	76	64	283	1,469
Andy Doeden	69	73	70	71	283	1,469
Matt Daniel	72	71	70	70	283	1,469

	SCORES	TOTAL	MONEY
Alejandro Villavicencio	74 68 71 71	284	1,183
Nik Tayler	75 68 71 70	284	1,183
Gordy Scutt	74 69 69 72	284	1,183
Bryan Novoa	72 72 72 68	284	1,183
Marcus Jones	74 70 70 70	284	1,183
Christo Greyling	72 71 70 71	284	1,183

Greater Vancouver Charity Classic

Hazelmere Golf Club, South Surrey, British Columbia
Par 36-36–72; 6,806 yards

June 15-18
purse, C$100,000

	SCORES	TOTAL	MONEY
Lee Williamson	68 70 70 72	280	C$16,000
Jason Hartwick	66 71 72 72	281	7,800
Andy Doeden	68 72 68 73	281	7,800
Darren Griff	69 69 73 71	282	4,800
Chad Spencer	68 71 75 69	283	3,633
Brock Mackenzie	71 71 74 67	283	3,633
Steve Friesen	70 70 71 72	283	3,633
Anders Hultman	72 72 70 71	285	2,900
Wes Heffernan	70 71 73 71	285	2,900
Brian Guetz	67 73 73 72	285	2,900
John Shin	72 71 73 70	286	2,200
Jim Lemon	68 72 70 76	286	2,200
Trevor Dodds	68 75 71 72	286	2,200
Sam Brazel	70 75 69 72	286	2,200
Brian Unk	71 72 72 72	287	1,700
James Lepp	71 70 77 69	287	1,700
George Bradford	71 71 69 76	287	1,700
Russell Surber	71 75 70 72	288	1,330
Ryan Miller	72 72 73 71	288	1,330
Rob McMillan	71 75 71 71	288	1,330
Eric Jorgensen	69 71 75 73	288	1,330
Travis Johnson	73 70 74 71	288	1,330
*Rafael Lee	72 74 74 69	289	
Marcus Jones	68 74 74 73	289	1,075
Hidemichi Haginomori	70 72 74 73	289	1,075
Patrick Ericson	71 74 71 73	289	1,075
Christopher Botsford	69 76 75 69	289	1,075
Eugene Smith	72 74 71 73	290	923
Dustin Risdon	72 74 69 75	290	923
Eric Couture	71 74 69 76	290	923

Times Colonist Open

Royal Colwood Golf Club, Victoria, British Columbia
Par 35-35–70; 6,680 yards

June 22-25
purse, C$150,000

	SCORES	TOTAL	MONEY
Mike Grob	66 71 65 67	269	C$24,000
John Lieber	67 66 72 65	270	11,700
Trevor Dodds	71 69 67 63	270	11,700
Jon Turcott	68 72 63 69	272	6,600

	SCORES				TOTAL	MONEY
Wes Heffernan	65	72	67	68	272	6,600
Dustin Risdon	70	66	67	71	274	5,175
Brad Fritsch	68	71	66	69	274	5,175
John Mallinger	70	70	66	69	275	4,350
Steve Friesen	68	68	72	67	275	4,350
Christopher Botsford	69	72	67	67	275	4,350
Jason Hartwick	66	68	70	72	276	3,600
Bret Guetz	66	67	68	75	276	3,600
Byron Smith	70	67	70	70	277	2,900
Scott Hawley	72	70	65	70	277	2,900
Wil Collins	69	68	67	73	277	2,900
Matt McQuillan	69	72	68	69	278	2,250
Justin Madison	72	67	67	72	278	2,250
Ben Greve	68	70	69	71	278	2,250
Daniel DeLeon	68	72	66	72	278	2,250
Edd Boudreau	72	67	70	69	278	2,250
Justin Snelling	72	71	68	68	279	1,688
Russell Surber	70	69	69	71	279	1,688
Mike Mezei	73	65	70	71	279	1,688
Michael Lavery	69	69	69	72	279	1,688
Andy Doeden	69	72	67	71	279	1,688
Lee Curry	74	66	71	68	279	1,688
Eric Wang	72	66	68	74	280	1,293
Lee Williamson	70	68	72	70	280	1,293
Jesse Smith	68	72	69	71	280	1,293
Jim Lemon	69	73	71	67	280	1,293
Rob Johnson	70	71	68	71	280	1,293
Christo Greyling	70	72	72	66	280	1,293
Rick Gibson	67	70	73	70	280	1,293

Telus Edmonton Open

Glendale Golf & Country Club, Edmonton, Alberta
Par 36-36—72; 6,991 yards

June 29-July 2
purse, C$150,000

	SCORES				TOTAL	MONEY
Stephen Gangluff	72	65	66	69	272	C$24,000
Brendan Steele	64	68	66	74	272	14,400
(Gangluff defeated Steele on first playoff hole.)						
Eugene Smith	67	68	67	71	273	9,000
Anthony Rodriguez	66	68	69	71	274	5,887
Michael Sims	66	69	74	65	274	5,887
Scott Gibson	65	68	68	73	274	5,887
Wil Collins	66	71	66	71	274	5,887
Tom Stankowski	70	70	66	69	275	4,500
Brien Davis	70	68	70	67	275	4,500
Darren Griff	65	66	73	72	276	4,050
Brock Mackenzie	66	72	72	67	277	3,300
Anders Hultman	71	71	70	65	277	3,300
Steve Friesen	70	70	69	68	277	3,300
Daniel DeLeon	68	69	70	70	277	3,300
Ryan Camp	71	68	71	68	278	2,625
Mike Belbin	71	72	63	72	278	2,625
David Walker	72	68	68	71	279	2,175
Alex Quiroz	68	75	70	66	279	2,175
Rob Oppenheim	67	72	70	70	279	2,175
Travis Johnson	72	70	70	67	279	2,175

	SCORES				TOTAL	MONEY
Adam Speirs	71	69	73	67	280	1,725
Dustin Risdon	73	69	69	69	280	1,725
Perry Parker	71	70	68	71	280	1,725
*Ryan Lecuyer	72	66	70	72	280	
*Jordan Irwin	72	70	70	68	280	
Jason Hartwick	72	66	73	69	280	1,725
Ryan Carter	70	69	72	69	280	1,725
Dale Vallely	70	70	71	70	281	1,414
Brad Pemberton	71	70	70	70	281	1,414
*James Love	69	74	69	69	281	
Rob Johnson	70	69	69	73	281	1,414
Paul Devenport	69	72	72	68	281	1,414

MTS Classic

Pine Ridge Golf Club, Winnipeg, Manitoba
Par 37-35–72; 6,622 yards

July 13-16
purse, C$150,000

	SCORES				TOTAL	MONEY
Josh Habig	71	66	71	63	271	C$24,000
Darren Griff	68	68	68	69	273	14,400
Chris Wall	67	71	69	68	275	7,400
Rob Oppenheim	73	68	64	70	275	7,400
Steve Friesen	68	74	70	63	275	7,400
Wes Heffernan	69	70	73	64	276	5,400
David Walker	71	70	69	67	277	4,950
Matt Seppanen	71	71	68	68	278	4,350
Lee Curry	73	68	70	67	278	4,350
Wil Collins	68	68	71	71	278	4,350
Eugene Smith	76	63	66	74	279	3,075
Byron Smith	74	67	69	69	279	3,075
Anthony Rodriguez	71	70	67	71	279	3,075
Kent Fukushima	68	69	72	70	279	3,075
Ryan Ellis	71	68	66	74	279	3,075
Chris Baryla	75	67	65	72	279	3,075
Matt McQuillan	70	69	70	71	280	2,115
Dan Roberts	68	70	70	72	280	2,115
Stuart Hendley	69	72	70	69	280	2,115
Ben Greve	73	70	68	69	280	2,115
John Ellis	71	71	71	67	280	2,115
Lee Williamson	73	69	71	68	281	1,725
Jim Lemon	69	72	68	72	281	1,725
Steve Conway	73	70	68	70	281	1,725
Michael Lavery	71	72	71	68	282	1,446
Luke Hickmott	71	72	70	69	282	1,446
Stephen Gangluff	70	71	70	71	282	1,446
Brad Fritsch	70	72	69	71	282	1,446
Matt Daniel	73	70	68	71	282	1,446
Russell Surber	71	72	70	70	283	1,166
Brian Unk	74	68	70	71	283	1,166
Chris Parra	72	71	73	67	283	1,166
Rob McMillan	73	68	73	69	283	1,166
Dustin Risdon	70	70	75	68	283	1,166
Ryan Miller	72	69	72	70	283	1,166
Lindsay Bernakevitch	72	69	72	70	283	1,166

Casino de Montreal Open

Quatre Domaines Golf Club, Montreal, Quebec
Par 36-36–72; 7,079 yards

August 3-6
purse, C$200,000

	SCORES				TOTAL	MONEY
Wes Heffernan	66	63	69	72	270	C$32,000
Brock Mackenzie	61	67	74	68	270	19,200
(Heffernan defeated Mackenzie on first playoff hole.)						
Rob Johnson	68	62	70	71	271	10,800
Darren Griff	67	64	69	71	271	10,800
Will Yanagisawa	65	70	67	70	272	7,000
Tom Stankowski	68	68	67	69	272	7,000
Brian Guetz	64	66	69	73	272	7,000
Scott Gibson	68	70	66	68	272	7,000
Lee Curry	67	65	72	69	273	5,600
Matt Bettencourt	68	68	68	69	273	5,600
Chad Spencer	69	69	72	64	274	4,600
Rob Oppenheim	66	69	71	68	274	4,600
Chris Baryla	67	66	67	74	274	4,600
Travis Johnson	69	67	64	75	275	3,700
Matt McQuillan	67	67	67	74	275	3,700
Nathan Smith	68	66	71	71	276	3,100
Hidemichi Haginomori	69	66	69	72	276	3,100
Wil Collins	69	66	73	68	276	3,100
Ben Bunny	67	67	71	71	276	3,100
Alex Quiroz	68	68	68	73	277	2,400
Jean Van de Velde	64	71	73	69	277	2,400
Adam Speirs	66	71	72	68	277	2,400
Brian Nosler	68	66	69	74	277	2,400
Brian Flugstad	68	67	68	74	277	2,400
Anthony Rodriguez	73	66	68	71	278	1,965
David Walker	72	67	69	70	278	1,965
Brad Fritsch	64	71	71	72	278	1,965
Carl Desjardins	69	68	69	72	278	1,965
Danny Sahl	69	70	70	70	279	1,720
Todd Tanner	67	72	72	68	279	1,720
Pascal Edmond	67	69	73	70	279	1,720

Fallsview Casino Resort Pro-Am Classic

Thundering Waters Golf Club, Niagara Falls, Ontario
Par 36-36–72; 7,322 yards

August 21-24
purse, C$100,000

	SCORES				TOTAL	MONEY
Stephen Gangluff	70	68	66	70	274	C$16,000
Brock Mackenzie	68	70	72	71	281	9,600
Conner Robbins	73	73	68	68	282	4,933
Lee Curry	73	73	67	69	282	4,933
Matt Bettencourt	66	76	69	71	282	4,933
Madalitso Muthiya	76	71	69	68	284	3,450
Rod Spittle	74	73	69	68	284	3,450
Chang Hong	73	72	72	68	285	2,800
Mike Grob	71	72	71	71	285	2,800
Paul Danielson	73	73	69	70	285	2,800
Lindsay Bernakevitch	70	73	70	72	285	2,800
Lee Williamson	73	69	74	70	286	2,100

	SCORES	TOTAL	MONEY
Joseph Lanza	72 72 70 72	286	2,100
Brian Guetz	75 70 71 70	286	2,100
Eugene Smith	70 73 70 74	287	1,550
Justin Snelling	74 73 68 72	287	1,550
Anthony Rodriguez	75 69 69 74	287	1,550
Alan McLean	69 72 73 73	287	1,550
Jason Hartwick	73 71 70 73	287	1,550
Bryan DeCorso	76 72 73 66	287	1,550
Rob Oppenheim	74 70 75 69	288	1,150
Wes Heffernan	73 76 70 69	288	1,150
Ian Hagen	74 71 74 69	288	1,150
Darren Griff	66 75 72 75	288	1,150
Andy Doeden	75 73 72 68	288	1,150
Richie Couglan	73 75 68 73	289	1,000
Taylor Wood	71 77 69 73	290	877
Andy Matthews	75 73 71 71	290	877
Russell Surber	68 73 75 74	290	877
Tom Stankowski	72 73 74 71	290	877
Josh Habig	71 73 68 78	290	877
Matt Daniel	73 70 77 70	290	877

Canadian Tour Championship

Highlands Golf Club at Horseshoe Resort, Barrie, Ontario
Par 36-35–71; 6,901 yards

August 31-September 3
purse, C$160,000

	SCORES	TOTAL	MONEY
Stuart Anderson	66 70 70 67	273	C$25,600
Matt McQuillan	69 75 65 67	276	15,360
Joseph Lanza	70 66 72 71	279	8,640
Brad Fritsch	72 71 72 64	279	8,640
Byron Smith	70 76 67 67	280	5,813
Eric Jorgensen	64 72 75 69	280	5,813
Joe Horowitz	73 68 70 69	280	5,813
Brendan Steele	70 71 71 70	282	4,480
Tom Stankowski	69 71 73 69	282	4,480
Anthony Rodriguez	70 71 72 69	282	4,480
Lee Curry	66 75 69 72	282	4,480
Ben Bunny	71 70 71 71	283	3,680
Michael Walton	75 67 70 72	284	3,200
Wes Heffernan	69 71 75 69	284	3,200
Jim Lemon	69 74 70 72	285	2,560
Derek Gillespie	71 73 76 65	285	2,560
Chris Cureton	70 70 75 70	285	2,560
Wil Collins	71 73 71 70	285	2,560
Lucas Bates	72 69 71 73	285	2,560
Andy Matthews	73 67 69 77	286	2,000
Anders Hultman	74 70 72 70	286	2,000
Darren Griff	70 74 73 69	286	2,000
Brian Unk	69 72 73 73	287	1,648
Adam Speirs	71 73 71 72	287	1,648
Madalitso Muthiya	69 76 71 71	287	1,648
Rob McMillan	69 74 72 72	287	1,648
Bret Guetz	75 68 67 77	287	1,648
Brian Guetz	71 74 74 68	287	1,648
Eugene Smith	74 70 73 71	288	1,400
John Ellis	69 72 78 69	288	1,400

Tour de las Americas (South America)

Abierto Movistar de Guatemala

Hacienda Neuva Country Club, Guatemala City, Guatemala
Par 36-36–72; 7,043 yards

February 2-5
purse, US$150,000

	SCORES				TOTAL	MONEY
Miguel Carballo	66	66	71	70	273	US$24,000
Gustavo Rojas	70	63	74	66	273	16,500
(Carballo defeated Rojas on first playoff hole.)						
Juan Parron	65	74	65	70	274	10,500
Felipe Aguilar	65	74	71	66	276	7,500
Sebastian Fernandez	72	70	66	68	276	7,500
Johan Axgren	67	70	68	71	276	7,500
Rafael Echenique	72	71	67	67	277	4,500
Jamie Little	71	69	68	69	277	4,500
Jean-Baptiste Gonnet	74	68	68	68	278	3,600
Kasper Jorgensen	70	68	71	70	279	3,050
Rodolfo Gonzalez	70	70	68	71	279	3,050
Hernan Rey	67	69	68	75	279	3,050
Gabriel Canizares	69	73	71	67	280	2,475
Andrew McArthur	68	75	67	70	280	2,475
Angel Romero	72	70	67	71	280	2,475
Diego Vanegas	67	68	73	72	280	2,475
Ivo Giner	70	71	70	70	281	1,893.75
Jesus Amaya	70	73	68	70	281	1,893.75
Sergio Acevedo	68	68	72	73	281	1,893.75
Mauricio Molina	73	67	66	75	281	1,893.75
Rafael Cabrera Bello	73	68	72	69	282	1,425
Gareth Davies	70	70	72	70	282	1,425
Oskar Bergman	73	68	71	70	282	1,425
Alejandro Villavicencio	71	70	71	70	282	1,425
Fabrizio Zanotti	72	70	67	73	282	1,425
Shannon Sykora	68	70	69	75	282	1,425
Marcus Higley	70	70	74	69	283	1,245
Anthony Snobeck	69	73	72	69	283	1,245
Soren Hansen	73	68	72	70	283	1,245
Brad Sutterfield	70	71	69	73	283	1,245
Olivier David	70	72	67	74	283	1,245
Miguel Guzman	71	72	65	75	283	1,245

Abierto del Sur Personal

Mar del Plata Golf Club, Mar del Plata, Argentina
Par 35-35–70

February 2-5
purse, US$55,000

	SCORES				TOTAL	MONEY
Luciano Giometti	66	70	69	73	278	US$9,233.45
Andres Romero	67	68	72	72	279	5,818.82
Matias Falaschini	68	68	71	73	280	4,111.50
Horacio Carbonetti	68	70	70	74	282	3,240.42

	SCORES				TOTAL	MONEY
Luis Carbonetti	64	72	71	75	282	2,648.08
Jorge Berendt	67	70	74	72	283	1,846.69
Martin Monguzzi	65	67	76	75	283	1,846.69
Juan Gil	69	71	71	73	284	1,358.89
*Tomas Argonz	71	72	68	74	285	
Amalio Britez	70	67	70	78	285	1,161.44
*Emilio Dominguez	67	68	75	75	285	
Sebastian Garcia Villaverde	72	66	75	72	285	1,161.44
Eduardo Romero	72	71	69	73	285	1,161.44
Cesar Costilla	71	70	72	74	287	984.32
Martin Velazquez	66	71	75	75	287	984.32
*Alan Wagner	64	74	69	80	287	
Sebastian Saavedra	70	72	76	71	289	879.79
Daniel Vancsik	66	73	74	76	289	879.79
*Estanislao Goya	66	76	76	72	290	
Ruben Alvarez	67	75	73	76	291	775.26
Agustin Jauretche	69	71	76	75	291	775.26
*Axel Ochoa	70	71	76	75	292	
Raul Perez	70	75	73	74	292	696.86
Nestor Bondarenco	76	68	76	73	293	627.18
Walter Rodriguez	72	69	74	78	293	627.18
Roberto Coceres	72	73	75	74	294	540.07
Alejandro Martinez	67	74	75	78	294	540.07
Walter Mendoza	70	72	78	74	294	540.07
*Francisco Bide	69	75	77	74	295	
Matias Gonzalez	74	71	74	76	295	477.35
Angel Monguzzi	73	71	77	74	295	477.35

Kai Fieberg Costa Rica Open

Cariari Country Club, San Jose, Costa Rica
Par 35-36–71; 6,577 yards

February 9-12
purse, US$150,000

	SCORES				TOTAL	MONEY
Johan Axgren	74	67	69	67	277	US$24,000
Alexander Noren	67	67	74	69	277	16,500
(Axgren defeated Noren on third playoff hole.)						
Gustavo Acosta	73	70	67	69	279	9,750
Jesus Amaya	72	68	67	72	279	9,750
Anthony Snobeck	70	70	68	72	280	7,500
Carlos De Corral	73	74	66	68	281	4,650
Andrew McArthur	73	71	68	69	281	4,650
Fabian Gomez	72	67	68	74	281	4,650
Ariel Canete	69	69	68	75	281	4,650
Cesar Monasterio	72	73	70	67	282	3,050
Juan Abbate	71	68	72	71	282	3,050
Clemens Prader	75	68	67	72	282	3,050
Alexandre Rocha	73	72	70	68	283	2,325
Marco Ruiz	76	70	69	68	283	2,325
Paulo Pinto	74	68	72	69	283	2,325
Miguel Fernandez	72	70	69	72	283	2,325
Eduardo Argiro	71	74	65	73	283	2,325
Van Phillips	69	68	72	74	283	2,325
Denny Lucas	72	71	68	73	284	1,762.50
Sergio Acevedo	71	70	69	74	284	1,762.50
Angel Franco	73	70	70	72	285	1,485
Jan-Are Larsen	73	70	69	73	285	1,485

	SCORES				TOTAL	MONEY
Diego Vanegas	70	74	72	70	286	1,380
Gustavo Rojas	75	69	71	71	286	1,380
Pedro Martinez	73	73	69	71	286	1,380
Ben Willman	70	74	70	72	286	1,380
Sebastian Fernandez	76	70	65	75	286	1,380
Anders Hansen	73	73	70	71	287	1,200
Bertrand Coathalem	69	73	72	73	287	1,200
Rodolfo Gonzalez	73	70	71	73	287	1,200
Rafael Gomez	71	73	70	73	287	1,200
Rafael Cabrera Bello	75	68	70	74	287	1,200
Jorge Benedetti	70	73	70	74	287	1,200
Shannon Sykora	77	67	68	75	287	1,200

Abierto del Centro

Cordoba Golf Club, Villa Allende, Argentina
Par 35-36–71; 6,824 yards

April 12-15
purse, US$60,000

	SCORES				TOTAL	MONEY
Angel Cabrera	68	67	70	70	275	US$10,756.67
Eduardo Romero	67	67	70	71	275	6,768.33
(Cabrera defeated Romero on fourth playoff hole.)						
Ricardo Gonzalez	70	71	71	66	278	4,738.67
Rodolfo Gonzalez	68	71	74	66	279	3,783
Mauricio Molina	71	73	69	68	281	2,774
Paulo Pinto	66	71	75	69	281	2,774
Emilio Dominguez	68	72	72	70	282	1,637
Hernan Rey	68	72	71	71	282	1,637
Daniel Vancsik	66	69	75	72	282	1,637
Andres Romero	69	66	74	73	282	1,637
Daniel Wardrop	70	72	73	69	284	1,298
Raul Fretes	72	75	69	69	285	1,121
Eduardo Argiro	67	72	75	71	285	1,121
Juan Abbate	72	67	74	72	285	1,121
Gustavo Rojas	76	63	78	69	286	885
Jorge Berendt	73	69	75	69	286	885
Carlos Franco	70	70	74	72	286	885
Luciano Giometti	70	74	70	72	286	885
Clodomiro Carranza	67	72	74	73	286	885
Roberto Coceres	69	71	77	70	287	708
Jesus Amaya	72	73	68	75	288	645.50
Fabian Gomez	70	65	75	78	288	645.50
Fabrizio Zanotti	72	72	75	70	289	568
Ramon Franco	68	74	76	71	289	568
Angel Franco	75	72	69	73	289	568
Gustavo Acosta	69	74	73	74	290	537
Julio Zapata	73	73	76	69	291	495.25
Nilson Cabrera	73	72	76	70	291	495.25
Ariel Canete	72	75	73	71	291	495.25
Cesar Costilla	69	73	74	75	291	495.25

Copa 3 Diamantes Mitsubishi Tour

Barquisimeto Golf Club, Barquisimeto, Venezuela
Par 36-35–71; 6,644 yards

May 4-7
purse, US$40,000

	SCORES				TOTAL
Otto Solis	73	67	69	65	274
Angel Romero	71	69	67	68	275
Alvaro Pinedo	71	70	65	69	275
Carlos Larrain	72	73	60	71	276
Diego Larrazabal	72	66	67	72	277
Miguel Martinez	70	66	77	67	280
Denis Meneghini	70	72	71	68	281
Gilberto Morales	71	67	70	73	281
Wolmer Murillo	73	68	72	69	282
Jesus Osmar	73	67	69	73	282
Juan Nutt	72	68	69	74	283
Cipriano Castro	74	71	72	68	285
Alfredo Adrian	71	71	75	69	286
Juan Berastegui	71	75	70	72	288
Manuel Bermudez	74	69	72	73	288
Rodrigo Castaneda	71	70	73	74	288
Luis Soto	73	73	70	73	289

TLA Players Championship

Mayan Golf Club, Acapulco, Mexico
Par 36-36–72; 7,019 yards

May 26-28
purse, US$60,000

	SCORES			TOTAL	MONEY
Julio Zapata	60	70	67	197	US$10,800
Fabian Gomez	67	69	63	199	5,820
Miguel Fernandez	62	68	69	199	5,820
Luis Arechiga	65	69	66	200	3,840
Miguel Guzman	67	68	67	202	2,820
Jesus Amaya	66	68	68	202	2,820
Mark Tullo	68	66	69	203	2,040
Pablo Del Grosso	67	69	68	204	1,764
Esteban Isasi	69	65	70	204	1,764
Oscar Serna	68	68	69	205	1,584
Emilio Dominguez	70	67	69	206	1,264
Otto Solis	68	68	70	206	1,264
Wilfredo Morales	66	68	72	206	1,264
Alejandro Villavicencio	67	67	72	206	1,264
Pablo Fernandez	69	73	64	206	1,264
Gustavo Acosta	64	69	73	206	1,264
Ricardo Carrillo	71	69	68	208	984
Luciano Giometti	68	69	71	208	984
David Schuster	66	70	72	208	984
Jose Trauwitz	70	69	70	209	808
Daniel Barbetti	69	69	71	209	808
Eduardo Argiro	70	67	72	209	808
Antonio Serna	71	69	70	210	704
Carlos Larrain	73	67	70	210	704
Pedro Martinez	70	69	71	210	704
Mauricio Molina	68	69	74	211	648
Antonio Maldonado	70	72	69	211	648

	SCORES	TOTAL	MONEY
Nicolas Sedler	68 76 68	212	612
Daniel De Leon	69 70 74	213	582
Fabrizio Zanotti	67 76 70	213	582
Cesar Costilla	67 76 70	213	582
Agustin Jauretche	70 72 71	213	582

Venezuela Open

Valle Arriba Golf Club, Caracas, Venezuela
Par 35-35–70; 6,372 yards

June 1-4
purse, US$65,000

	SCORES	TOTAL	MONEY
Fabian Gomez	68 65 68 64	265	US$11,700
Miguel Guzman	66 67 67 67	267	7,410
Mauricio Molina	68 67 68 65	268	3,867.50
Alejandro Villavicencio	66 71 64 67	268	3,867.50
Agustin Jauretche	66 65 68 69	268	3,867.50
Cipriano Castro	65 59 72 72	268	3,867.50
Otto Solis	68 68 66 67	269	2,093
Jose Trauwitz	64 70 67 68	269	2,093
Jose Garrido	69 65 71 65	270	1,651
Fabrizio Zanotti	75 64 65 66	270	1,651
Wilfredo Morales	67 70 66 67	270	1,651
Manuel Merizalde	67 67 67 69	270	1,651
Julio Zapata	68 64 67 73	272	1,391
Jesus Amaya	68 69 70 66	273	1,261
Wolmer Murillo	67 69 69 68	273	1,261
Pablo Del Grosso	66 69 68 70	273	1,261
Luciano Giometti	74 68 66 67	275	1,066
Nicolas Sedler	67 69 69 70	275	1,066
Miguel Martinez	71 64 69 71	275	1,066
Miguel Fernandez	73 66 70 67	276	936
Gustavo Acosta	73 68 65 71	277	871
Pablo Larrazabal	68 70 70 72	280	819
Oswaldo Villada	71 71 70 69	281	750.75
Mark Tullo	72 66 71 72	281	750.75
Alfredo Adrian	68 70 70 73	281	750.75
Cesar Costilla	73 64 69 75	281	750.75
Emilio Dominguez	69 71 72 70	282	667.33
David Shadah	75 67 68 72	282	667.33
Daniel Escalera	68 69 71 74	282	667.33
Ramon Munoz	71 71 70 71	283	630.50
Teunis Stolk	69 71 71 72	283	630.50

Colombia Open

Campestre de Cali, Cali, Colombia
Par 36-36–72

July 6-9
purse, US$90,000

	SCORES	TOTAL	MONEY
Manuel Merizalde	70 67 71 72	280	US$20,000
Alvaro Pinedo	70 68 70 74	282	11,304
Jose Trauwitz	68 75 73 69	285	6,087
*David Vanegas	74 68 71 73	286	
Gustavo Mendoza	70 70 72 74	286	4,348

	SCORES	TOTAL	MONEY
Jesus Amaya	73 71 73 70	287	2,869.75
Omar Suarez	72 72 70 73	287	2,869.75
Eduardo Argiro	70 69 75 73	287	2,869.75
Carlos Larrain	72 71 69 75	287	2,869.75
Jose Garrido	72 71 73 72	288	2,087
Raul Fretes	74 73 70 71	288	2,087
Oswaldo Villada	70 69 73 76	288	2,087
Mauricio Molina	72 71 77 69	289	1,869.50
Miguel Fernandez	76 68 76 69	289	1,869.50
Cesar Costilla	70 74 75 71	290	1,761
Wolmer Murillo	73 70 69 78	290	1,761
Clodomiro Carranza	71 74 78 68	291	1,630.50
Angel Romero	72 72 74 73	291	1,630.50
Jesus Osmar	74 70 71 77	292	1,565
Julio Zapata	74 72 77 70	293	1,500
Fernando Posada	68 78 70 77	293	1,500
Luciano Giometti	73 74 71 76	294	1,435
Paulo Pinto	74 72 73 76	295	1,369.50
Oscar Serna	71 74 73 77	295	1,369.50
Nestor Giraldo	73 72 75 76	296	1,282.50
Miguel Martinez	73 74 72 77	296	1,282.50
Bernardo Gonzalez	71 75 77 74	297	1,217
Mario Hurtado	75 72 76 75	298	1,174
*Jorge Corchuelo	75 73 77 74	299	
Mauricio Alvarado	75 73 76 75	299	1,130

Torneo de Maestros Argentina

Olivos Golf Club, Buenos Aires, Argentina
Par 36-35–71; 6,740 yards
(Final round cancelled—rain.)

November 2-5
purse, US$100,000

	SCORES	TOTAL
Andres Romero	63 73 68	204
Angel Cabrera	69 71 67	207
Daniel Vancsik	68 71 69	208
Hernan Rey	70 74 66	210
Ricardo Gonzalez	74 72 66	212
Rodolfo Gonzalez	75 69 68	212
Gustavo Rojas	70 76 67	213
Juan Abbate	72 76 66	214
Fabrizio Zanotti	73 72 69	214
Jorge Berendt	74 70 70	214
Diego Vanegas	70 72 72	214
Jose Coceres	72 71 71	214
Axel Ochoa	73 73 69	215
Sebastian Fernandez	75 71 69	215
Pablo Del Grosso	71 73 71	215
Nicolas Bollini	69 74 73	216
Tomas Argonz	71 69 76	216
Francisco Ojeda	70 78 69	217
Matias Gonzalez	76 72 69	217
Ruben Alvarez	71 71 75	217
Angel Romero	76 75 67	218
Luis Carbonetti	73 74 71	218
Oswaldo Villada	72 74 72	218
Daniel Altamirano	73 73 72	218

	SCORES	TOTAL
Raul Perez	71 73 74	218
Agustin Jauretche	76 73 70	219
Ricardo Coceres	69 77 73	219
Rafael Echenique	73 74 72	219
Fabian Gomez	73 73 73	219
Rafael Barcellos	69 76 74	219

Samsung Brazil Classic

San Fernando Golf Club, Sao Paulo, Brazil
Par 35-36–71; 7,008 yards

November 16-19
purse, US$80,000

	SCORES	TOTAL	MONEY
Paulo Pinto	70 71 67 66	274	US$14,400
Juan Ignacio Gil	69 69 69 68	275	9,120
Pedro Martinez	68 74 72 66	280	6,400
Fabrizio Zanotti	69 76 69 67	281	5,120
Pablo Del Grosso	74 70 75 63	282	3,760
Marcel Haremza	71 69 73 69	282	3,760
Gustavo Acosta	70 71 72 73	286	2,720
Christoph Guenther	69 75 69 74	287	2,240
Nilson Cabrera	76 65 79 68	288	2,080
Robert Ames	79 71 70 69	289	1,760
Daniel Nunez	72 71 73 73	289	1,760
Jose Campra	71 69 75 74	289	1,760
Joao Corteiz	71 75 74 70	290	1,440
Rafael Barcellos	72 72 75 71	290	1,440
Odair Lima	73 73 71 73	290	1,440
Tim Rice	72 74 67 78	291	1,317
Daniel Barbetti	76 70 78 68	292	1,234
Raul Fretes	75 73 70 74	292	1,234
Carlos Dluhosch	76 69 76 72	293	1,142
Ronaldo Francisco	75 71 75 73	294	1,028.50
Damiao De Lima	71 76 74 73	294	1,028.50
Bobby Jackson	74 71 78 72	295	922.33
Luis Arechiga	79 71 73 72	295	922.33
Pedro Enderle	73 74 75 73	295	922.33
Fabiano Dos Santos	76 72 72 76	296	853
Stephen Bergner	77 74 70 76	297	821
Marcelo Silva	72 79 78 69	298	762.33
Rafael Gonzalez	74 77 73 74	298	762.33
Jose Aderbal	73 77 71 77	298	762.33
Ricardo Iversson	77 76 75 72	300	717
Vinicius Muller	71 79 74 76	300	717

Abierto de San Luis

Villa Mercedes Golf Club, San Luis, Argentina
Par 71; 6,851 yards
(Fourth round cancelled—rain.)

November 23-26
purse, US$150,000

	SCORES	TOTAL	MONEY
Rafael Gomez	64 67 64	195	US$24,000
Eduardo Romero	68 65 66	199	13,500
Mark Tullo	66 64 69	199	13,500

	SCORES			TOTAL	MONEY
Julio Zapata	66	69	65	200	9,000
Rafael Echenique	68	69	64	201	6,100
Ricardo Gonzalez	68	67	66	201	6,100
Walter Miranda	68	66	67	201	6,100
Carlos Cardeza	65	69	68	202	3,900
Juan Abbate	66	67	69	202	3,900
Rodolfo Gonzalez	67	69	68	204	2,962.50
Pablo Del Grosso	66	69	69	204	2,962.50
Rafael Ponce	67	67	70	204	2,962.50
Horacio Carbonetti	67	67	70	204	2,962.50
Ruben Alvarez	69	68	68	205	2,475
Martin Monguzzi	68	68	69	205	2,475
Alvaro Pinedo	69	68	69	206	2,175
Cesar Costilla	67	70	69	206	2,175
Eduardo Argiro	71	71	65	207	1,743.75
Sergio Acevedo	70	70	67	207	1,743.75
Miguel Guzman	69	69	69	207	1,743.75
Ernesto Rivas	69	68	70	207	1,743.75
Juan Ignacio Gil	69	73	66	208	1,395
Jorge Berendt	71	70	67	208	1,395
Gustavo Acosta	71	69	68	208	1,395
Mauricio Molina	70	69	69	208	1,395
Sebastian Fernandez	72	67	69	208	1,395
Julio Noguera	68	69	71	208	1,395
Federico Pereyra	72	71	66	209	1,260
Miguel Fernandez	68	73	68	209	1,260
Francisco Ojeda	71	69	69	209	1,260

Argentina Open

Pilar Golf Club, Buenos Aires, Argentina
Par 36-35–71; 7,215 yards

November 30-December 3
purse, US$200,000

	SCORES				TOTAL	MONEY
Rafael Echenique	73	70	66	68	277	€25,479
Angel Cabrera	73	72	68	65	278	13,278
Ricardo Gonzalez	69	70	67	72	278	13,278
Ariel Canete	74	69	71	67	281	7,644
*Alan Wagner	73	75	67	70	285	
Felipe Aguilar	71	73	69	72	285	5,471
Fabrizio Zanotti	74	68	70	73	285	5,471
Daniel Barbetti	73	73	66	73	285	5,471
Jorge Berendt	74	75	66	71	286	3,615
Julio Zapata	76	73	65	72	286	3,615
Kariem Baraka	74	73	71	69	287	2,740
Andres Romero	79	69	69	70	287	2,740
Klas Eriksson	73	75	69	70	287	2,740
Juan Ignacio Gil	70	77	69	71	287	2,740
*Esteban Martinez	71	71	76	70	288	
Alvaro Velasco	72	71	74	72	289	2,201
Claudio Machado	75	70	72	72	289	2,201
Mark Tullo	67	77	70	75	289	2,201
Gustavo Acosta	78	68	68	75	289	2,201
Peter Whiteford	72	75	71	72	290	1,872
Eduardo Romero	76	74	67	73	290	1,872
Mauricio Molina	73	74	70	73	290	1,872
Raul Fretes	74	73	69	74	290	1,872

	SCORES	TOTAL	MONEY
George Murray	75 75 71 70	291	1,674
Colm Moriarty	73 74 72 72	291	1,674
Alejandro Villavicencio	76 72 68 75	291	1,674
Mikael Lundberg	72 76 68 75	291	1,674
Angel Franco	73 76 71 72	292	1,490
Carlos del Moral	75 75 71 71	292	1,490
Roberto Coceres	73 74 73 72	292	1,490
Paulo Pinto	68 74 71 79	292	1,490

Corona Mexico Open

Hacienda Golf Club, Mexico City, Mexico
Par 35-36–71; 7,306 yards

December 7-10
purse, US$310,000

	SCORES	TOTAL	MONEY
Fabrizio Zanotti	74 67 69 65	275	US$49,600
Daniel De Leon	69 69 70 68	276	34,100
Hernan Rey	75 70 70 63	278	18,600
Carlos Cardeza	69 67 73 69	278	18,600
Felipe Aguilar	69 69 69 71	278	18,600
Kieran Staunton	76 69 70 64	279	9,052
Agustin Jauretche	68 68 74 69	279	9,052
Julio Zapata	70 70 70 69	279	9,052
Pablo Del Grosso	67 73 69 70	279	9,052
Rodolfo Gonzalez	70 69 69 71	279	9,052
Fredrik Ohlsson	72 68 73 67	280	5,890
Robert Dinwiddie	73 71 68 68	280	5,890
Alejandro Villavicencio	72 70 69 69	280	5,890
Federico Garcia	70 68 72 71	281	4,805
Jorge Benedetti	73 66 71 71	281	4,805
Gustavo Rojas	71 70 69 71	281	4,805
Klas Eriksson	65 71 72 73	281	4,805
Jerome Theunis	73 70 71 68	282	3,490.60
James McLeary	69 72 72 69	282	3,490.60
Magnus A. Carlsson	71 72 70 69	282	3,490.60
Clodomiro Carranza	72 69 70 71	282	3,490.60
Sebastian Fernandez	68 73 70 71	282	3,490.60
Rafael Gomez	73 72 71 67	283	2,790
Miguel Carballo	72 72 71 68	283	2,790
Iain Pyman	71 71 72 69	283	2,790
Gary Clark	74 70 70 69	283	2,790
Mark Tullo	72 71 70 70	283	2,790
Jamie Little	71 72 70 70	283	2,790
Ricardo Carrillo	76 66 67 74	283	2,790
Miguel Guzman	72 68 77 67	284	2,325
Daniel Denison	71 72 72 69	284	2,325
Stuart Davis	70 74 70 70	284	2,325
Miguel Rodriguez	72 70 71 71	284	2,325
Matthew Abbott	73 69 71 71	284	2,325
Juan Abbate	70 73 70 71	284	2,325
Shannon Sykora	74 70 69 71	284	2,325
Manuel Inman	72 70 70 72	284	2,325

European Tours

The Royal Trophy

See Asia/Japan Tours chapter.

Abu Dhabi Golf Championship

Abu Dhabi Golf Club, Abu Dhabi, United Arab Emirates
Par 36-36–72; 7,348 yards

January 19-22
purse, €1,652,452

		SCORES			TOTAL	MONEY
Chris DiMarco	61	67	63	67	268	€275,411.70
Henrik Stenson	69	69	62	69	269	183,607.80
Sergio Garcia	60	69	65	66	270	103,445.70
Ricardo Gonzalez	68	68	67	68	271	82,624.34
Miguel Angel Jimenez	60	68	64	71	273	70,065.44
Colin Montgomerie	62	68	65	70	275	53,705.82
Jyoti Randhawa	61	70	69	65	275	53,705.82
Charl Schwartzel	69	66	68	74	277	39,163.93
Vijay Singh	68	70	69	70	277	39,163.93
David Lynn	69	69	70	70	278	31,727.74
Ian Poulter	62	69	68	69	278	31,727.74
Francois Delamontagne	61	69	69	70	279	25,580.49
Mark Foster	61	70	69	69	279	25,580.49
Thongchai Jaidee	68	69	73	69	279	25,580.49
Andrew McLardy	61	70	69	69	279	25,580.49
Zhang Lian-wei	64	69	68	68	279	25,580.49
Paul Broadhurst	63	71	68	68	280	21,372.16
Darren Fichardt	62	70	69	69	280	21,372.16
Damien McGrane	60	69	71	70	280	21,372.16
Ignacio Garrido	60	69	71	71	281	18,962.29
Richard Green	60	70	70	71	281	18,962.29
Keith Horne	66	74	71	70	281	18,962.29
Phillip Price	63	70	67	71	281	18,962.29
John Bickerton	62	70	68	72	282	16,442.24
Thomas Bjorn	63	68	71	70	282	16,442.24
Stephen Dodd	63	71	70	68	282	16,442.24
Raphael Jacquelin	64	69	67	72	282	16,442.24
Soren Kjeldsen	62	70	68	72	282	16,442.24
Jose-Filipe Lima	60	68	73	71	282	16,442.24
Marcus Fraser	63	69	68	73	283	13,715.64
Anders Hansen	63	70	72	68	283	13,715.64
Gregory Havret	60	68	74	71	283	13,715.64
Robert Karlsson	63	69	67	74	283	13,715.64
Steve Webster	63	66	72	72	283	13,715.64
Gordon Brand, Jr.	62	69	73	70	284	12,063.15
Jamie Spence	61	69	73	71	284	12,063.15
Oliver Wilson	62	69	72	71	284	12,063.15
Gary Emerson	63	69	73	70	285	10,410.67
Peter Gustafsson	69	73	73	70	285	10,410.67
Francesco Molinari	63	70	71	70	285	10,410.67
Wade Ormsby	64	70	70	71	285	10,410.67
David Park	63	66	75	71	285	10,410.67
Jean-Francois Remesy	63	70	73	69	285	10,410.67

	SCORES	TOTAL	MONEY
Simon Wakefield	65 68 68 74	285	10,410.67
Paul Casey	62 72 70 72	286	8,427.68
Marc Cayeux	61 71 72 72	286	8,427.68
Nick Dougherty	64 70 72 70	286	8,427.68
Shiv Kapur	65 66 73 72	286	8,427.68
Anthony Wall	63 70 74 69	286	8,427.68
Ross Bain	69 73 74 71	287	5,873.84
Richard Bland	60 72 74 71	287	5,873.84
Alastair Forsyth	60 74 70 73	287	5,873.84
Soren Hansen	60 66 74 77	287	5,873.84
Peter Hedblom	63 70 73 71	287	5,873.84
Barry Lane	63 71 70 73	287	5,873.84
Miguel Angel Martin	64 69 71 73	287	5,873.84
Gary Orr	64 70 69 74	287	5,873.84
Costantino Rocca	61 73 71 72	287	5,873.84
Graeme Storm	62 72 73 70	287	5,873.84
Fredrik Widmark	62 72 71 72	287	5,873.84
Ian Garbutt	63 71 71 73	288	4,296.47
Peter Hanson	63 69 71 75	288	4,296.47
Manuel Lara Jose	61 71 69 77	288	4,296.47
Gonzalo Fernandez-Castano	60 74 71 74	289	3,883.34
Richard Sterne	65 69 72 73	289	3,883.34
Mattias Eliasson	63 68 76 73	290	3,387.60
Maarten Lafeber	61 70 72 77	290	3,387.60
Stuart Little	62 72 70 76	290	3,387.60
Mikael Lundberg	62 72 73 73	290	3,387.60
Jean-Francois Lucquin	61 72 74 76	293	3,015.79

Commercialbank Qatar Masters

Doha Golf Club, Doha, Qatar
Par 36-36–72; 7,374 yards

January 26-29
purse, €1,652,721

	SCORES	TOTAL	MONEY
Henrik Stenson	66 68 71 68	273	€275,456.31
Paul Broadhurst	62 67 67 70	276	183,637.54
Darren Fichardt	67 72 70 68	277	103,462.43
Nick Dougherty	69 67 73 70	279	65,035.89
Niclas Fasth	68 70 68 73	279	65,035.89
Richard Finch	68 68 71 72	279	65,035.89
Ricardo Gonzalez	66 69 72 72	279	65,035.89
Graeme Storm	68 71 70 71	280	41,318.86
Thomas Bjorn	61 68 71 72	282	32,228.71
Maarten Lafeber	61 68 72 71	282	32,228.71
David Lynn	60 70 71 71	282	32,228.71
Paul McGinley	69 70 70 73	282	32,228.71
Ernie Els	61 71 69 72	283	25,948.24
Jarrod Lyle	62 71 71 69	283	25,948.24
Andrew Buckle	61 72 70 71	284	22,808.01
Robert Karlsson	61 69 69 75	284	22,808.01
Thammanoon Srirot	61 69 71 73	284	22,808.01
Anthony Wall	64 71 68 71	284	22,808.01
Darren Clarke	61 74 72 68	285	19,271.12
Andrew Coltart	69 72 73 71	285	19,271.12
Nick O'Hern	61 74 71 69	285	19,271.12
Unho Park	61 70 74 70	285	19,271.12
Steve Webster	62 71 71 71	285	19,271.12

	SCORES				TOTAL	MONEY
Bradley Dredge	69	72	74	71	286	15,701.17
Joakim Haeggman	60	71	75	70	286	15,701.17
David Howell	63	71	69	73	286	15,701.17
Thongchai Jaidee	60	69	73	74	286	15,701.17
Jose Manuel Lara	62	72	71	71	286	15,701.17
Charl Schwartzel	68	72	73	73	286	15,701.17
Jeev Milkha Singh	62	71	70	73	286	15,701.17
Vijay Singh	63	71	73	69	286	15,701.17
Thaworn Wiratchant	63	69	71	73	286	15,701.17
*Danny Denison	67	78	71	71	287	
Shiv Kapur	65	67	77	68	287	12,781.30
Richard Sterne	62	68	71	76	287	12,781.30
Miles Tunnicliff	61	74	72	70	287	12,781.30
Simon Dyson	64	71	70	73	288	11,238.73
Gonzalo Fernandez-Castano	67	68	73	70	288	11,238.73
Anders Hansen	61	72	74	71	288	11,238.73
Prayad Marksaeng	60	67	75	76	288	11,238.73
Damien McGrane	62	72	68	76	288	11,238.73
Angelo Que	61	72	72	73	288	11,238.73
Peter Gustafsson	60	72	70	77	289	9,090.15
Christopher Hanell	61	72	71	75	289	9,090.15
James Kingston	67	68	73	71	289	9,090.15
Ian Poulter	62	72	75	70	289	9,090.15
Chris Rodgers	63	71	72	73	289	9,090.15
Marcel Siem	69	71	74	75	289	9,090.15
Jean Van de Velde	69	71	75	74	289	9,090.15
Miguel Angel Jimenez	61	73	70	76	290	7,602.67
Andrew Oldcorn	61	74	72	73	290	7,602.67
Joakim Backstrom	61	69	75	76	291	6,776.29
John Bickerton	63	72	68	78	291	6,776.29
Peter Lawrie	62	71	72	76	291	6,776.29
Emanuele Canonica	65	68	73	76	292	5,619.37
Rahil Gangjee	65	68	70	79	292	5,619.37
Ignacio Garrido	62	73	74	73	292	5,619.37
Gaurav Ghei	62	73	74	73	292	5,619.37
Adam Fraser	62	69	78	74	293	4,792.99
Terry Pilkadaris	61	72	75	75	293	4,792.99
Scott Strange	65	70	73	75	293	4,792.99
Louis Oosthuizen	63	72	73	76	294	4,297.16
Chawalit Plaphol	67	74	71	82	294	4,297.16
Simon Yates	69	73	74	78	294	4,297.16
Kenneth Ferrie	65	70	71	79	295	3,966.61
Jyoti Randhawa	71	72	75		WD	3,801.34

Dubai Desert Classic

Emirates Golf Club, Dubai, United Arab Emirates
Par 35-37–72; 7,264 yards

February 2-5
purse, €1,958,693

	SCORES				TOTAL	MONEY
Tiger Woods	67	66	67	69	269	€329,760.30
Ernie Els	68	66	68	67	269	219,834.70
(Woods defeated Els on first playoff hole.)						
Richard Green	64	69	69	68	270	123,858
Anders Hansen	68	63	69	71	271	91,409.56
Miguel Angel Jimenez	69	67	66	69	271	91,409.56
Retief Goosen	64	67	70	71	272	69,249.67

	SCORES				TOTAL	MONEY
Darren Clarke	68	68	70	67	273	54,410.45
Henrik Stenson	67	70	68	68	273	54,410.45
Emanuele Canonica	69	68	71	66	274	41,945.51
Nick Dougherty	67	66	70	71	274	41,945.51
Niclas Fasth	67	68	73	67	275	35,218.40
Raphael Jacquelin	68	71	68	68	275	35,218.40
Bradley Dredge	60	66	68	72	276	30,403.90
Johan Edfors	69	67	72	68	276	30,403.90
Jyoti Randhawa	61	68	66	71	276	30,403.90
Paul Casey	67	69	71	70	277	26,710.59
Christopher Hanell	61	71	67	68	277	26,710.59
Richard Sterne	69	69	70	69	277	26,710.59
Simon Dyson	60	71	66	71	278	23,742.74
David Lynn	66	74	71	67	278	23,742.74
Nick O'Hern	67	72	73	66	278	23,742.74
Paul Broadhurst	69	69	67	74	279	20,873.83
Stephen Gallacher	60	69	68	72	279	20,873.83
Thongchai Jaidee	60	71	69	69	279	20,873.83
Paul Lawrie	61	70	70	68	279	20,873.83
Peter Lawrie	69	66	69	75	279	20,873.83
Damien McGrane	68	68	73	70	279	20,873.83
Andrew Coltart	61	70	67	72	280	17,015.63
Ricardo Gonzalez	69	68	70	73	280	17,015.63
David Howell	60	69	70	71	280	17,015.63
Robert Karlsson	61	67	72	70	280	17,015.63
Simon Khan	62	70	70	68	280	17,015.63
Alessandro Tadini	69	74	67	70	280	17,015.63
Lee Westwood	68	71	69	72	280	17,015.63
Jamie Donaldson	64	70	74	73	281	14,641.36
Stuart Little	69	69	71	72	281	14,641.36
Richard Finch	61	71	69	71	282	13,454.22
Ignacio Garrido	60	70	75	67	282	13,454.22
David Park	60	71	72	69	282	13,454.22
Costantino Rocca	68	73	70	71	282	13,454.22
Markus Brier	60	73	71	69	283	11,475.66
Marc Cayeux	69	66	74	74	283	11,475.66
Soren Hansen	60	65	75	73	283	11,475.66
Phillip Price	69	70	73	71	283	11,475.66
Jamie Spence	60	71	71	71	283	11,475.66
Steve Webster	60	70	69	74	283	11,475.66
Ross Bain	66	71	78	69	284	8,705.67
Thomas Bjorn	69	70	74	71	284	8,705.67
David Carter	62	71	69	72	284	8,705.67
Robert-Jan Derksen	61	72	69	72	284	8,705.67
Mark Foster	68	68	74	74	284	8,705.67
Ian Poulter	62	67	72	73	284	8,705.67
Simon Wakefield	60	70	74	70	284	8,705.67
Oliver Wilson	68	75	70	71	284	8,705.67
Phillip Archer	60	70	72	73	285	5,910.95
Joakim Backstrom	68	73	71	73	285	5,910.95
Christian Cevaer	62	71	72	70	285	5,910.95
Alastair Forsyth	60	71	72	72	285	5,910.95
Joakim Haeggman	62	71	71	71	285	5,910.95
Garry Houston	63	68	70	74	285	5,910.95
Barry Lane	68	71	70	76	285	5,910.95
Paul Sheehan	63	68	72	72	285	5,910.95
Peter O'Malley	60	72	73	71	286	4,748.55
Mark O'Meara	61	71	73	71	286	4,748.55
Gary Orr	69	74	70	73	286	4,748.55
Jonathan Lomas	62	71	72	72	287	4,154.98

	SCORES	TOTAL	MONEY
Andrew Oldcorn	61 67 70 79	287	4,154.98
Marcel Siem	61 72 71 73	287	4,154.98
Stephen Dodd	62 71 75 70	288	3,446.05
Scott Drummond	63 70 72 73	288	3,446.05
Marcus Fraser	61 71 72 74	288	3,446.05
John Bickerton	62 71 70 76	289	2,963.50
Peter Hanson	61 70 74 74	289	2,963.50
Martin Erlandsson	68 75 71 77	291	2,959
Wade Ormsby	60 73 79 70	292	2,956
Gary Emerson	63 69 74 78	294	2,953

Johnnie Walker Classic
See Australasian Tour chapter.

Maybank Malaysian Open
See Asia/Japan Tours chapter.

Enjoy Jakarta HSBC Indonesia Open
See Asia/Japan Tours chapter.

OSIM Singapore Masters
See Asia/Japan Tours chapter.

TCL Classic
See Asia/Japan Tours chapter.

Madeira Island Open Caixa Geral de Depositos

Santo da Serra Golf Club, Madeira, Portugal
Par 36-36–72; 6,826 yards

March 23-26
purse, €700,000

	SCORES	TOTAL	MONEY
Jean Van de Velde	69 65 71 68	273	€116,660
Lee Slattery	74 68 66 66	274	77,770
Pedro Linhart	71 67 69 68	275	43,820
Simon Wakefield	72 68 68 68	276	35,000
Mattias Eliasson	74 69 71 64	278	27,090
Richard Finch	70 69 72 67	278	27,090
David Griffiths	72 69 71 67	279	18,060
Jarmo Sandelin	66 68 74 71	279	18,060
Tom Whitehouse	73 65 71 70	279	18,060
Damien McGrane	68 69 71 72	280	14,000
Warren Abery	69 70 74 68	281	11,725
Christian Cevaer	74 69 68 70	281	11,725
Ian Garbutt	72 69 70 70	281	11,725
Garry Houston	68 69 72 72	281	11,725
Marcus Higley	72 69 71 70	282	10,080
Francesco Molinari	70 73 69 70	282	10,080
Fredrik Andersson Hed	76 67 74 66	283	8,890
Martin Erlandsson	70 73 69 71	283	8,890
Niclas Fasth	70 73 67 73	283	8,890
Mark Roe	74 68 73 68	283	8,890

	SCORES				TOTAL	MONEY
Fredrik Henge	68	75	75	66	284	7,490
David Lynn	72	68	74	70	284	7,490
Gary Orr	74	68	69	73	284	7,490
Magnus Persson	73	69	67	75	284	7,490
Iain Pyman	71	69	74	70	284	7,490
Alessandro Tadini	73	68	72	71	284	7,490
Oliver Wilson	71	71	74	68	284	7,490
Andrew Coltart	75	66	75	69	285	5,923.75
Tiago Cruz	71	71	69	74	285	5,923.75
Bradley Dredge	72	65	77	71	285	5,923.75
Alastair Forsyth	72	70	69	74	285	5,923.75
Mark Foster	69	73	73	70	285	5,923.75
Paul Lawrie	68	69	77	71	285	5,923.75
Steven O'Hara	72	71	76	66	285	5,923.75
Louis Oosthuizen	74	68	73	70	285	5,923.75
Felipe Aguilar	72	72	73	69	286	4,830
John Bickerton	74	70	75	67	286	4,830
Ariel Canete	71	69	72	74	286	4,830
Ben Mason	69	73	71	73	286	4,830
Oliver Whiteley	70	73	68	75	286	4,830
Johan Axgren	70	70	71	76	287	4,200
Gordon Brand, Jr.	71	72	72	72	287	4,200
Stephen Gallacher	69	70	71	77	287	4,200
Santiago Luna	73	71	72	71	287	4,200
Peter Baker	71	73	74	70	288	3,500
Robert-Jan Derksen	71	71	74	72	288	3,500
Ross Fisher	70	74	76	68	288	3,500
Sam Little	75	69	75	69	288	3,500
Christian L. Nilsson	75	67	74	72	288	3,500
Hennie Otto	70	74	72	72	288	3,500
Wilhelm Schauman	73	68	71	77	289	2,870
Francisco Valera	73	68	77	71	289	2,870
Sam Walker	69	69	76	75	289	2,870
Gregory Bourdy	72	69	78	71	290	2,324
Gareth Davies	73	71	71	75	290	2,324
Gary Emerson	68	75	76	71	290	2,324
Jose-Filipe Lima	72	72	75	71	290	2,324
David Patrick	73	71	78	68	290	2,324
David Dixon	72	72	75	72	291	1,995
Simon Khan	76	68	76	71	291	1,995
Gary Murphy	69	75	74	74	292	1,855
Raymond Russell	76	67	76	73	292	1,855
Anders Schmidt Hansen	71	73	71	79	294	1,750
Nicolas Colsaerts	70	67	81	77	295	1,645
Stuart Little	74	70	74	77	295	1,645
Ricardo Santos	72	71	77	76	296	1,540
Fredrik Widmark	70	72	76		DQ	1,470

Algarve Open de Portugal Caixa Geral de Depositos

Le Meridien Penina Golf & Resort, Algarve, Portugal
Par 35-37–72; 6,799 yards

March 30-April 2
purse, €1,250,000

	SCORES				TOTAL	MONEY
Paul Broadhurst	64	69	71	67	271	€208,330
Anthony Wall	71	67	67	67	272	138,880
Andres Romero	69	70	68	66	273	78,250

	SCORES				TOTAL	MONEY
Ricardo Gonzalez	73	66	64	71	274	57,750
Charl Schwartzel	69	70	67	68	274	57,750
Jose Manuel Lara	71	70	68	66	275	43,750
Markus Brier	72	70	66	69	277	34,375
Mattias Eliasson	70	67	71	69	277	34,375
Jarmo Sandelin	67	70	68	73	278	28,000
Brian Davis	70	71	67	71	279	24,000
Niclas Fasth	71	68	67	73	279	24,000
Alastair Forsyth	73	71	65	71	280	19,781.25
Christian L. Nilsson	65	71	71	73	280	19,781.25
Carl Suneson	67	72	66	75	280	19,781.25
Tom Whitehouse	72	72	68	68	280	19,781.25
Richard Bland	74	70	69	68	281	16,875
Christian Cevaer	66	69	72	74	281	16,875
Daniel Vancsik	70	72	73	66	281	16,875
Nick Dougherty	69	74	70	69	282	14,575
Soren Hansen	69	71	67	75	282	14,575
Paul Lawrie	68	70	76	68	282	14,575
Alessandro Tadini	69	73	69	71	282	14,575
Ian Woosnam	70	74	69	69	282	14,575
Peter Baker	72	72	71	68	283	12,062.50
Kenneth Ferrie	75	67	72	69	283	12,062.50
Ross Fisher	70	71	72	70	283	12,062.50
Peter Lawrie	73	68	67	75	283	12,062.50
Stuart Little	68	73	72	70	283	12,062.50
Gary Murphy	72	72	69	70	283	12,062.50
Simon Wakefield	70	71	72	70	283	12,062.50
Steve Webster	70	73	70	70	283	12,062.50
Warren Abery	72	66	75	71	284	9,843.75
Gary Clark	71	67	75	71	284	9,843.75
Robert Karlsson	69	73	70	72	284	9,843.75
Louis Oosthuizen	71	71	72	70	284	9,843.75
Joakim Backstrom	70	71	71	73	285	8,375
Nicolas Colsaerts	68	71	69	77	285	8,375
Steven Jeppesen	70	71	69	75	285	8,375
David Lynn	71	72	69	73	285	8,375
Miguel Angel Martin	72	72	69	72	285	8,375
Matthew Millar	73	68	72	72	285	8,375
Fredrik Widmark	75	69	72	69	285	8,375
Miguel Carballo	69	71	70	76	286	6,250
Mark Foster	74	70	70	72	286	6,250
Rafael Gomez	68	72	72	74	286	6,250
David Griffiths	69	73	75	69	286	6,250
Michael Hoey	73	67	70	76	286	6,250
Toni Karjalainen	72	70	70	74	286	6,250
Soren Kjeldsen	74	65	73	74	286	6,250
Jonathan Lomas	72	69	73	72	286	6,250
Steven O'Hara	71	67	75	73	286	6,250
Lee Slattery	70	71	73	72	286	6,250
Phillip Archer	72	71	73	71	287	4,178.57
Andre Bossert	70	73	68	76	287	4,178.57
Paul Dwyer	70	72	73	72	287	4,178.57
Gonzalo Fernandez-Castano	71	70	75	71	287	4,178.57
Peter Hedblom	69	72	73	73	287	4,178.57
Simon Khan	69	73	73	72	287	4,178.57
Sam Little	70	71	71	75	287	4,178.57
John Bickerton	70	73	71	74	288	3,375
Gary Emerson	70	73	74	71	288	3,375
Peter Hanson	70	73	71	74	288	3,375
Andrew Butterfield	73	71	71	74	289	2,937.50

	SCORES	TOTAL	MONEY
Scott Drummond	73 71 73 72	289	2,937.50
Richard Finch	67 73 73 76	289	2,937.50
Andrew Marshall	69 72 78 70	289	2,937.50
Robert Coles	73 71 68 78	290	2,447.50
Tiago Cruz	72 72 76 70	290	2,447.50
Michael Jonzon	73 71 75 71	290	2,447.50
Francisco Valera	70 71 74 75	290	2,447.50
Raul Ballesteros	76 68 73 74	291	1,872
Anders Hansen	71 70 77 73	291	1,872
Stuart Manley	72 69 76 74	291	1,872
Michael Kirk	71 73 73 76	293	1,866
Martin Erlandsson	70 74 76 74	294	1,863
David Drysdale	72 71 75 79	297	1,860

Volvo China Open

See Asia/Japan Tours chapter.

BMW Asian Open

See Asia/Japan Tours chapter.

Andalucia Open de Espana Valle Romano

San Roque Club, Cadiz, Spain
Par 36-36–72; 7,115 yards

April 27-30
purse, €1,650,000

	SCORES	TOTAL	MONEY
Niclas Fasth	67 68 66 69	270	€275,000
John Bickerton	68 65 74 63	270	183,330
(Fasth defeated Bickerton on third playoff hole.)			
Phillip Archer	67 69 68 67	271	67,375
Thomas Bjorn	70 64 68 69	271	67,375
Mattias Eliasson	68 68 68 67	271	67,375
David Griffiths	68 65 66 72	271	67,375
Jose Manuel Lara	68 66 69 68	271	67,375
Gary Orr	72 64 68 67	271	67,375
Carl Suneson	69 64 70 69	272	36,960
Robert Karlsson	70 63 68 72	273	33,000
Peter Hanson	67 69 68 70	274	28,435
Juan Parron	66 72 70 66	274	28,435
Miles Tunnicliff	66 71 69 68	274	28,435
Louis Oosthuizen	70 65 69 71	275	24,750
Charl Schwartzel	68 70 71 66	275	24,750
David Bransdon	71 65 69 71	276	21,417
David Dixon	67 70 72 67	276	21,417
Jose-Filipe Lima	65 73 69 69	276	21,417
Francesco Molinari	67 71 70 68	276	21,417
Graeme Storm	65 67 70 74	276	21,417
Stephen Browne	67 70 71 69	277	18,645
Santiago Luna	71 70 69 67	277	18,645
Fredrik Widmark	69 65 73 70	277	18,645
*Jordi Garcia Del Moral	68 68 70 72	278	
James Hepworth	68 68 69 73	278	17,160
Jarmo Sandelin	68 71 74 65	278	17,160

	SCORES				TOTAL	MONEY
Lee Slattery	67	71	70	70	278	17,160
Rafael Gomez	74	65	73	67	279	15,427.50
Colin Montgomerie	68	68	72	71	279	15,427.50
Mark Roe	71	69	72	67	279	15,427.50
Kieran Staunton	69	71	68	71	279	15,427.50
Ross Fisher	68	73	67	72	280	12,846.43
Soren Kjeldsen	69	71	68	72	280	12,846.43
Peter Lawrie	67	71	70	72	280	12,846.43
Titch Moore	66	67	75	72	280	12,846.43
Alexandre Rocha	70	68	73	69	280	12,846.43
Raymond Russell	70	69	70	71	280	12,846.43
Leif Westerberg	69	72	68	71	280	12,846.43
David Carter	68	69	75	69	281	10,560
Darren Fichardt	71	68	71	71	281	10,560
Miguel Angel Jimenez	66	74	72	69	281	10,560
Magnus Persson	70	69	72	70	281	10,560
Alvaro Quiros	68	70	71	72	281	10,560
Oliver Wilson	71	69	72	69	281	10,560
Robert-Jan Derksen	68	71	71	72	282	8,580
Johan Edfors	72	69	68	73	282	8,580
Ricardo Gonzalez	72	68	71	71	282	8,580
Peter Hedblom	68	70	70	74	282	8,580
David Higgins	70	68	72	72	282	8,580
Maarten Lafeber	70	71	72	69	282	8,580
Raul Ballesteros	66	71	71	75	283	6,765
Ivo Giner	72	69	74	68	283	6,765
Michael Kirk	72	67	71	73	283	6,765
Marco Ruiz	71	69	71	72	283	6,765
Jean Van de Velde	68	71	75	69	283	6,765
Gary Emerson	72	67	70	75	284	5,115
Gonzalo Fernandez-Castano	71	69	71	73	284	5,115
Sebastian Fernandez	73	68	70	73	284	5,115
Ignacio Garrido	70	71	72	71	284	5,115
Hennie Otto	68	73	74	69	284	5,115
Fernando Roca	67	72	74	71	284	5,115
Barry Lane	68	68	77	72	285	4,207.50
Pedro Linhart	70	68	70	77	285	4,207.50
Francisco Valera	69	69	73	74	285	4,207.50
Steve Webster	67	71	72	75	285	4,207.50
Robert Rock	71	68	72	75	286	3,795
Fredrik Henge	70	70	74	73	287	3,382.50
Christian L. Nilsson	70	71	73	73	287	3,382.50
Andrew Oldcorn	72	68	73	74	287	3,382.50
Sam Walker	69	71	74	73	287	3,382.50
Benn Barham	70	71	73	75	289	2,652.33
Klas Eriksson	71	68	72	78	289	2,652.33
Ian Garbutt	70	71	69	79	289	2,652.33
Andrew Butterfield	70	69	76	75	290	2,469

Telecom Italia Open

Castello di Tolcinasco Golf & Country Club, Milan, Italy
Par 36-36–72; 7,225 yards

May 4-7
purse, €1,400,000

	SCORES				TOTAL	MONEY
Francesco Molinari	68	65	67	65	265	€233,330
Anders Hansen	70	67	66	66	269	121,595

	SCORES				TOTAL	MONEY
Jarmo Sandelin	69	68	67	65	269	121,595
Soren Kjeldsen	63	70	69	68	270	70,000
Benoit Teilleria	69	68	65	69	271	59,360
Phillip Archer	66	67	68	71	272	45,500
Bradley Dredge	67	69	68	68	272	45,500
Peter Fowler	68	67	68	70	273	30,030
Garry Houston	70	70	65	68	273	30,030
Alessandro Tadini	66	72	67	68	273	30,030
Marc Warren	69	68	70	66	273	30,030
Nicolas Colsaerts	70	68	64	72	274	22,155
David Drysdale	67	64	73	70	274	22,155
Steven Jeppesen	67	71	67	69	274	22,155
Andrew McLardy	67	69	72	66	274	22,155
Benn Barham	65	68	67	75	275	17,290
John Bickerton	69	69	71	66	275	17,290
David Griffiths	70	68	69	68	275	17,290
Gregory Havret	66	68	73	68	275	17,290
Raphael Jacquelin	70	67	68	70	275	17,290
Jonathan Lomas	67	68	71	69	275	17,290
Titch Moore	71	67	67	70	275	17,290
Brad Sutterfield	70	70	69	66	275	17,290
Alessio Bruschi	68	70	69	69	276	14,140
Andrew Butterfield	66	68	74	68	276	14,140
Richard Green	67	69	68	72	276	14,140
Steven O'Hara	72	68	67	69	276	14,140
Mark Roe	69	66	71	70	276	14,140
Peter Gustafsson	70	67	68	72	277	12,250
Richard McEvoy	71	69	66	71	277	12,250
Alexandre Rocha	68	66	72	71	277	12,250
Francisco Valera	69	70	70	68	277	12,250
Gregory Bourdy	66	70	69	73	278	10,240
David Bransdon	69	69	69	71	278	10,240
Emanuele Canonica	69	69	70	70	278	10,240
Miguel Carballo	67	70	66	75	278	10,240
Marco Crespi	71	67	68	72	278	10,240
Hennie Otto	69	68	67	74	278	10,240
Lee Slattery	69	71	69	69	278	10,240
Mark Foster	69	67	74	69	279	7,980
Marcus Fraser	71	66	70	72	279	7,980
Santiago Luna	72	68	67	72	279	7,980
David Lynn	71	69	68	71	279	7,980
Sven Struver	70	65	73	71	279	7,980
Anthony Wall	70	65	73	71	279	7,980
Shaun P. Webster	70	69	72	68	279	7,980
Leif Westerberg	69	65	74	71	279	7,980
Ian Woosnam	70	66	73	70	279	7,980
Ricardo Gonzalez	74	65	70	71	280	6,440
Magnus Persson	69	71	70	70	280	6,440
*Matteo Delpodio	67	69	70	75	281	
Paul Dwyer	73	67	67	74	281	5,460
Sebastian Fernandez	68	67	75	71	281	5,460
James Hepworth	66	71	74	70	281	5,460
Michael Kirk	66	72	70	73	281	5,460
Christian L. Nilsson	70	69	71	71	281	5,460
Fredrik Henge	72	67	71	72	282	4,620
Gary Orr	73	67	71	72	283	4,270
Stephen Scahill	70	67	71	75	283	4,270
Rafael Gomez	67	70	73	74	284	3,990
Tom Whitehouse	70	68	72	74	284	3,990
Louis Oosthuizen	67	68	75	76	286	3,780

	SCORES	TOTAL	MONEY
Stephen Dodd	69 67 73 79	288	3,570
Andrea Maestroni	72 67 74 75	288	3,570
Richard Bland	71 67 77 74	289	3,360
Christopher Hanell	67 70 75	WD	3,220

Quinn Direct British Masters

The De Vere Belfry, Sutton Coldfield, England
Par 36-36–72; 7,157 yards

May 11-14
purse, €2,622,910

	SCORES	TOTAL	MONEY
Johan Edfors	68 69 70 70	277	€437,949
Gary Emerson	68 70 73 67	278	195,948.10
Stephen Gallacher	71 66 70 71	278	195,948.10
Jarmo Sandelin	67 71 70 70	278	195,948.10
Michael Campbell	67 70 68 74	279	101,691.80
Paul Casey	67 66 70 76	279	101,691.80
Paul Broadhurst	70 72 70 68	280	78,830.82
Jonathan Lomas	70 73 68 70	281	59,035.53
Graeme McDowell	70 68 73 70	281	59,035.53
Tom Whitehouse	70 71 69 71	281	59,035.53
Darren Clarke	66 70 70 76	282	45,283.93
David Howell	70 72 72 68	282	45,283.93
Oliver Wilson	68 74 68 72	282	45,283.93
Joakim Backstrom	71 73 68 71	283	34,981.18
Emanuele Canonica	72 72 74 65	283	34,981.18
Gonzalo Fernandez-Castano	71 71 72 69	283	34,981.18
Richard Green	70 69 73 71	283	34,981.18
Anders Hansen	73 69 69 72	283	34,981.18
Padraig Harrington	75 66 74 68	283	34,981.18
Soren Kjeldsen	68 74 73 68	283	34,981.18
Ian Poulter	68 69 74 72	283	34,981.18
David Bransdon	69 72 74 69	284	28,116.33
Ross Fisher	73 70 73 68	284	28,116.33
Steven Jeppesen	72 70 71 71	284	28,116.33
Miguel Angel Jimenez	70 70 73 71	284	28,116.33
Peter O'Malley	71 66 74 73	284	28,116.33
Stephen Dodd	74 70 71 70	285	23,780.63
Robert Karlsson	71 73 69 72	285	23,780.63
Wade Ormsby	73 71 70 71	285	23,780.63
Charl Schwartzel	71 69 72 73	285	23,780.63
Jean Van de Velde	72 72 73 68	285	23,780.63
Simon Wakefield	71 73 70 71	285	23,780.63
Robert-Jan Derksen	72 72 70 72	286	19,219.71
Bradley Dredge	71 71 71 73	286	19,219.71
Simon Dyson	71 73 71 71	286	19,219.71
David Lynn	70 72 72 72	286	19,219.71
Andrew Marshall	71 72 72 71	286	19,219.71
Graeme Storm	74 64 74 74	286	19,219.71
Anthony Wall	75 68 72 71	286	19,219.71
David Carter	71 73 72 71	287	16,291.70
Peter Hedblom	70 71 73 73	287	16,291.70
Jose-Filipe Lima	70 74 70 73	287	16,291.70
Christian L. Nilsson	69 72 74 72	287	16,291.70
Marcus Fraser	69 74 72 73	288	14,452.32
David Higgins	68 75 71 74	288	14,452.32
Gary Orr	70 73 71 74	288	14,452.32

	SCORES				TOTAL	MONEY
Warren Abery	71	68	73	77	289	11,824.62
Kenneth Ferrie	70	73	74	72	289	11,824.62
Gregory Havret	72	70	75	72	289	11,824.62
Simon Khan	74	68	75	72	289	11,824.62
Jean-Francois Lucquin	69	72	76	72	289	11,824.62
Carlos Rodiles	74	70	72	73	289	11,824.62
Daniel Vancsik	74	65	75	75	289	11,824.62
Peter Hanson	66	72	72	80	290	9,196.93
Jyoti Randhawa	70	72	72	76	290	9,196.93
Ian Woosnam	69	71	73	77	290	9,196.93
Jamie Donaldson	72	71	77	71	291	7,883.08
Barry Lane	75	67	74	75	291	7,883.08
Leif Westerberg	69	73	75	74	291	7,883.08
Miguel Carballo	71	73	75	73	292	7,094.77
Niclas Fasth	73	71	73	75	292	7,094.77
Ricardo Gonzalez	74	70	73	75	292	7,094.77
Thomas Bjorn	75	69	79	70	293	6,437.85
Richard McEvoy	76	68	78	71	293	6,437.85
*Lloyd Saltman	69	75	76	73	293	
Gary Evans	69	75	77	74	295	5,912.31
Steven O'Hara	70	74	77	74	295	5,912.31
Phillip Price	70	73	77	77	297	5,386.77
Fredrik Widmark	69	74	80	74	297	5,386.77
Shiv Kapur	70	74	80	75	299	4,992.62

Nissan Irish Open

Carton House Golf Club, Maynooth, Co. Kildare, Ireland
Par 36-36—72; 7,301 yards
(Event completed on Monday—rain.)

May 18-22
purse, €2,200,000

	SCORES				TOTAL	MONEY
Thomas Bjorn	78	66	67	72	283	€366,660
Paul Casey	73	70	68	73	284	244,440
Darren Clarke	75	70	67	73	285	137,720
Peter Hedblom	72	70	70	74	286	110,000
Bradley Dredge	71	73	72	71	287	64,093.33
Ross Fisher	73	70	69	75	287	64,093.33
Robert Karlsson	74	68	72	73	287	64,093.33
Maarten Lafeber	71	74	71	71	287	64,093.33
Robert Rock	75	73	68	71	287	64,093.33
Anthony Wall	73	68	70	76	287	64,093.33
Padraig Harrington	71	74	69	74	288	40,480
Michael Campbell	72	73	71	73	289	35,640
Robert-Jan Derksen	72	74	68	75	289	35,640
Jarrod Lyle	72	70	71	76	289	35,640
Phillip Archer	75	69	70	76	290	30,360
Christian Cevaer	70	71	74	75	290	30,360
Gregory Havret	76	71	68	75	290	30,360
Stuart Little	74	74	70	72	290	30,360
Richard Bland	76	72	69	74	291	24,273.33
Stephen Browne	78	69	72	72	291	24,273.33
Nick Dougherty	75	72	72	72	291	24,273.33
Martin Erlandsson	73	71	72	75	291	24,273.33
Niclas Fasth	72	74	75	70	291	24,273.33
Steven Jeppesen	72	71	72	76	291	24,273.33
Peter Lawrie	75	68	75	73	291	24,273.33

	SCORES				TOTAL	MONEY
Damien McGrane	75	69	74	73	291	24,273.33
Colm Moriarty	77	71	70	73	291	24,273.33
Gary Orr	77	71	72	72	292	20,570
Tom Whitehouse	73	69	72	78	292	20,570
David Dixon	74	70	74	75	293	17,694.29
Ignacio Garrido	70	77	72	74	293	17,694.29
Barry Lane	73	74	70	76	293	17,694.29
Sam Little	75	73	71	74	293	17,694.29
Andres Romero	75	73	68	77	293	17,694.29
Marc Warren	75	72	72	74	293	17,694.29
Ian Woosnam	77	70	75	71	293	17,694.29
Angel Cabrera	75	68	73	78	294	14,300
Francois Delamontagne	76	72	72	74	294	14,300
Ricardo Gonzalez	71	72	73	78	294	14,300
David Higgins	74	74	74	72	294	14,300
Raphael Jacquelin	73	70	72	79	294	14,300
Paul Lawrie	75	68	71	80	294	14,300
Henrik Stenson	75	70	73	76	294	14,300
Gonzalo Fernandez-Castano	71	76	72	76	295	11,660
Stephen Gallacher	77	71	74	73	295	11,660
Wade Ormsby	79	69	72	75	295	11,660
Iain Pyman	70	73	77	75	295	11,660
Alexandre Rocha	74	73	74	74	295	11,660
Emanuele Canonica	76	70	76	74	296	9,680
Ian Garbutt	74	72	72	78	296	9,680
Peter Gustafsson	75	69	76	76	296	9,680
Christian L. Nilsson	74	71	73	78	296	9,680
Nicolas Colsaerts	73	67	74	83	297	8,140
Matthew Millar	75	72	72	78	297	8,140
Brett Rumford	74	74	73	76	297	8,140
Ariel Canete	76	68	75	79	298	6,765
David Griffiths	77	70	72	79	298	6,765
David Lynn	74	74	72	78	298	6,765
Francesco Molinari	75	73	75	75	298	6,765
Simon Dyson	76	72	78	73	299	5,610
Johan Edfors	69	78	75	77	299	5,610
Alastair Forsyth	74	74	77	74	299	5,610
Ian Poulter	71	70	73	85	299	5,610
Marcel Siem	79	68	68	84	299	5,610
Carl Suneson	77	71	73	78	299	5,610
Rafael Gomez	75	72	74	79	300	4,620
Soren Hansen	76	70	74	80	300	4,620
Steve Webster	72	76	77	75	300	4,620
Mark Foster	76	72	73	80	301	4,180
Mikael Lundberg	75	72	76	80	303	3,660
Richard McEvoy	76	71	76	80	303	3,660
Anders Hansen	70	75	77		WD	

BMW Championship

Wentworth Club, Virginia Water, Surrey, England
Par 35-37–72; 7,308 yards

May 25-28
purse, €4,216,750

	SCORES				TOTAL	MONEY
David Howell	68	65	69	69	271	€708,330
Simon Khan	70	68	70	68	276	472,220
Miguel Angel Jimenez	71	69	65	72	277	266,050

	SCORES				TOTAL	MONEY
Brett Rumford	72	73	69	65	279	212,500
Richard Bland	73	68	71	68	280	180,200
Andrew Coltart	71	72	69	69	281	112,540
Padraig Harrington	72	70	68	71	281	112,540
Trevor Immelman	70	73	73	65	281	112,540
Gary Orr	71	70	73	67	281	112,540
Anthony Wall	71	71	73	66	281	112,540
Paul Casey	67	72	69	74	282	73,241.67
Soren Hansen	70	72	69	71	282	73,241.67
Garry Houston	69	72	71	70	282	73,241.67
Richard Green	70	71	72	70	283	59,925
Robert Karlsson	69	68	74	72	283	59,925
Maarten Lafeber	71	71	71	70	283	59,925
Jean-Francois Lucquin	76	70	67	70	283	59,925
Jose Maria Olazabal	69	74	72	68	283	59,925
Emanuele Canonica	72	71	72	69	284	48,875
Ernie Els	69	74	69	72	284	48,875
Retief Goosen	70	71	73	70	284	48,875
Raphael Jacquelin	68	72	75	69	284	48,875
Henrik Stenson	73	73	68	70	284	48,875
Steve Webster	71	70	74	69	284	48,875
Luke Donald	67	72	74	72	285	42,287.50
Kenneth Ferrie	69	73	73	70	285	42,287.50
Peter Lawrie	68	72	74	71	285	42,287.50
Nick O'Hern	72	72	68	73	285	42,287.50
Angel Cabrera	68	69	75	74	286	35,912.50
Francois Delamontagne	69	70	71	76	286	35,912.50
Niclas Fasth	70	70	71	75	286	35,912.50
Andrew McLardy	67	74	75	70	286	35,912.50
David Park	76	69	70	71	286	35,912.50
Miles Tunnicliff	72	73	70	71	286	35,912.50
Nicolas Colsaerts	70	72	70	75	287	31,450
Thaworn Wiratchant	71	71	75	70	287	31,450
Michael Campbell	72	73	73	70	288	28,900
Nick Dougherty	67	69	74	78	288	28,900
Simon Dyson	73	73	70	72	288	28,900
Paul Lawrie	69	73	73	73	288	28,900
David Carter	73	71	73	72	289	24,650
Bradley Dredge	75	71	72	71	289	24,650
Ross Fisher	71	72	75	71	289	24,650
Mark Foster	71	71	74	73	289	24,650
Jean Van de Velde	75	69	66	79	289	24,650
Ian Woosnam	71	74	74	70	289	24,650
Paul Broadhurst	71	71	73	75	290	19,550
Alastair Forsyth	71	72	72	75	290	19,550
Ian Garbutt	73	71	74	72	290	19,550
Ignacio Garrido	76	70	70	74	290	19,550
Graeme McDowell	71	70	73	76	290	19,550
Wade Ormsby	74	69	69	78	290	19,550
Markus Brier	70	76	72	73	291	14,875
Colin Montgomerie	73	72	74	72	291	14,875
Phillip Price	69	77	72	73	291	14,875
Jarmo Sandelin	77	69	75	70	291	14,875
Alessandro Tadini	77	68	69	77	291	14,875
Phillip Archer	72	73	79	68	292	12,112.50
Peter Gustafsson	72	70	75	75	292	12,112.50
Steven Jeppesen	71	74	74	73	292	12,112.50
Jyoti Randhawa	71	72	76	73	292	12,112.50
Simon Edwards	71	75	74	73	293	11,050
Graeme Storm	71	75	76	72	294	10,625

	SCORES	TOTAL	MONEY
Soren Kjeldsen	70 75 72 79	296	10,200
Darren Prosser	72 71 78 77	298	9,775
John Wells	69 77 82 72	300	9,350

Celtic Manor Wales Open

Celtic Manor Resort, Newport, South Wales
Par 35-34–69; 6,743 yards

June 1-4
purse, €2,177,970

	SCORES	TOTAL	MONEY
Robert Karlsson	61 63 65 71	260	€364,352.49
Paul Broadhurst	64 64 67 68	263	242,891.95
Jose-Filipe Lima	69 61 70 64	264	136,850.80
Colin Montgomerie	63 66 69 67	265	109,305.75
Phillip Archer	60 68 71 67	266	84,602.65
Johan Skold	65 66 67 68	266	84,602.65
Bradley Dredge	67 70 66 64	267	46,564.25
Simon Dyson	66 62 69 70	267	46,564.25
Henrik Nystrom	66 67 64 70	267	46,564.25
Gary Orr	68 63 65 71	267	46,564.25
Marcel Siem	65 66 68 68	267	46,564.25
Lee Slattery	64 67 69 67	267	46,564.25
Graeme Storm	65 67 68 67	267	46,564.25
Jyoti Randhawa	67 70 66 65	268	32,791.72
Anthony Wall	72 63 63 70	268	32,791.72
Stephen Dodd	66 68 68 67	269	28,375.77
Graeme McDowell	68 67 64 70	269	28,375.77
Matthew Millar	69 62 67 71	269	28,375.77
Simon Wakefield	69 66 67 67	269	28,375.77
Marc Warren	67 68 67 67	269	28,375.77
Francois Delamontagne	63 67 70 70	270	24,375.18
Michael Hoey	64 68 68 70	270	24,375.18
Paul Lawrie	71 66 68 65	270	24,375.18
Jeev Milkha Singh	68 69 69 64	270	24,375.18
Alastair Forsyth	67 68 67 69	271	22,079.76
Wade Ormsby	68 67 65 71	271	22,079.76
David Park	66 68 64 73	271	22,079.76
Andrew Butterfield	66 68 69 69	272	19,128.51
David Higgins	68 66 71 67	272	19,128.51
Peter Lawrie	66 68 70 68	272	19,128.51
Jean-Francois Lucquin	71 66 69 66	272	19,128.51
Brett Rumford	71 66 69 66	272	19,128.51
Alessandro Tadini	68 65 70 69	272	19,128.51
Richard Bland	70 66 71 66	273	15,302.80
Robert-Jan Derksen	66 70 68 69	273	15,302.80
Mark Foster	70 67 68 68	273	15,302.80
Stephen Gallacher	68 65 72 68	273	15,302.80
Per-Ulrik Johansson	70 65 72 66	273	15,302.80
Steven O'Hara	69 64 69 71	273	15,302.80
Andrew Oldcorn	65 70 71 67	273	15,302.80
Richard Sterne	69 67 67 70	273	15,302.80
Martin Erlandsson	68 68 69 69	274	12,023.63
David Griffiths	69 65 70 70	274	12,023.63
Garry Houston	72 65 69 68	274	12,023.63
Thongchai Jaidee	66 67 70 71	274	12,023.63
Stuart Little	68 66 69 71	274	12,023.63
Andrew Marshall	67 70 71 66	274	12,023.63

	SCORES				TOTAL	MONEY
Francisco Valera	69	66	69	70	274	12,023.63
David Dixon	67	69	72	67	275	8,963.07
Niclas Fasth	68	67	72	68	275	8,963.07
Ian Garbutt	69	65	66	75	275	8,963.07
Peter Hedblom	69	67	70	69	275	8,963.07
Alexandre Rocha	68	69	68	70	275	8,963.07
Stephen Scahill	64	71	70	70	275	8,963.07
Carl Suneson	66	70	71	68	275	8,963.07
Ignacio Garrido	66	67	70	74	277	6,602.07
Barry Lane	66	70	72	69	277	6,602.07
David Lynn	69	66	73	69	277	6,602.07
Peter O'Malley	67	69	70	71	277	6,602.07
Miles Tunnicliff	69	67	70	71	277	6,602.07
Gary Clark	66	70	72	70	278	5,683.90
Soren Hansen	68	69	70	71	278	5,683.90
Mark Roe	70	66	71	71	278	5,683.90
Nicolas Colsaerts	71	65	66	78	280	4,918.76
Jamie Donaldson	67	67	73	73	280	4,918.76
Maarten Lafeber	67	69	70	74	280	4,918.76
Phillip Price	69	66	75	70	280	4,918.76
Andrew McLardy	67	68	77	72	284	4,372.23

BA-CA Golf Open

Fontana Golf Club, Vienna, Austria
Par 35-36–71; 7,059 yards

June 8-11
purse, €1,300,000

	SCORES				TOTAL	MONEY
Markus Brier	65	67	66	68	266	€216,660
Soren Hansen	68	67	69	65	269	144,440
Simon Dyson	66	66	67	71	270	81,380
Richard Green	71	67	70	63	271	65,000
Gary Murphy	68	70	71	65	274	55,120
Miguel Angel Jimenez	67	67	74	67	275	42,250
Jean-Francois Lucquin	68	69	69	69	275	42,250
Emanuele Canonica	70	66	70	71	277	29,206.67
Darren Fichardt	69	73	69	66	277	29,206.67
Steven Jeppesen	68	67	75	67	277	29,206.67
Gregory Bourdy	67	70	70	71	278	23,140
Gregory Havret	69	68	78	63	278	23,140
Gary Emerson	70	64	74	71	279	19,162
Colin Montgomerie	67	68	69	75	279	19,162
Steven O'Hara	68	70	71	70	279	19,162
Mark Roe	72	69	70	68	279	19,162
Oliver Whiteley	66	73	70	70	279	19,162
Alexandre Rocha	68	69	71	72	280	16,445
Richard Sterne	71	66	76	67	280	16,445
Miguel Carballo	69	69	74	69	281	14,516.67
Alastair Forsyth	67	74	71	69	281	14,516.67
Philip Golding	71	68	71	71	281	14,516.67
David Higgins	67	68	72	74	281	14,516.67
Toni Karjalainen	69	71	71	70	281	14,516.67
Pedro Linhart	70	71	73	67	281	14,516.67
Thomas Bjorn	70	71	71	70	282	11,960
Robert Coles	72	68	70	72	282	11,960
Simon Hurd	69	71	69	73	282	11,960
Mikko Ilonen	72	69	76	65	282	11,960

	SCORES				TOTAL	MONEY
Titch Moore	72	67	74	69	282	11,960
Michele Reale	70	69	72	71	282	11,960
Tom Whitehouse	71	70	72	69	282	11,960
David Griffiths	69	66	73	75	283	9,776
Peter Senior	72	64	75	72	283	9,776
Lee Slattery	70	67	74	72	283	9,776
Kieran Staunton	70	68	72	73	283	9,776
Phil Worthington	71	69	73	70	283	9,776
Jorge Benedetti	66	73	74	71	284	8,450
Peter Fowler	69	70	73	72	284	8,450
Jose Manuel Lara	69	72	73	70	284	8,450
Terry Pilkadaris	71	70	73	70	284	8,450
Sven Struver	66	73	74	71	284	8,450
Per-Ulrik Johansson	70	69	75	71	285	7,410
Nicolas Meitinger	75	66	71	73	285	7,410
Benoit Teilleria	71	72	74	68	285	7,410
David Bransdon	69	74	71	72	286	6,500
Gary Clark	71	71	71	73	286	6,500
Richard McEvoy	69	72	74	71	286	6,500
Anders Sjostrand	74	68	70	74	286	6,500
Scott Drummond	69	68	75	75	287	5,460
Martin Erlandsson	68	71	79	69	287	5,460
Paul McGinley	71	71	73	72	287	5,460
Marcel Siem	71	70	74	72	287	5,460
Wilhelm Schauman	72	70	75	71	288	4,680
Jamie Spence	69	73	72	74	288	4,680
Benn Barham	67	75	74	73	289	3,926
Garry Houston	69	70	78	72	289	3,926
Ben Mason	72	71	73	73	289	3,926
Carl Suneson	71	70	72	76	289	3,926
Brad Sutterfield	73	69	75	72	289	3,926
Matthew Millar	72	71	72	75	290	3,380
Marten Olander	70	71	78	71	290	3,380
Andrew Oldcorn	72	71	76	71	290	3,380
Stephen Browne	70	70	78	73	291	3,055
David Dixon	72	70	76	73	291	3,055
Marc Cayeux	73	70	73	76	292	2,730
Cedric Menut	69	74	78	71	292	2,730
Robert Rock	70	73	79	70	292	2,730
John Bickerton	70	72	79	72	293	2,266.67
Neil Cheetham	71	71	77	74	293	2,266.67
Alvaro Salto	73	70	80	70	293	2,266.67
Alfredo Garcia-Heredia	70	72	80	73	295	1,947
Thomas Feyrsinger	70	73	84	76	303	1,944

Aa St. Omer Open

Aa St. Omer Golf Club, Lumbres, France
Par 36-35–71; 6,836 yards

June 15-18
purse, €400,000

	SCORES				TOTAL	MONEY
Cesar Monasterio	68	68	71	67	274	€66,660
Martin Maritz	71	67	66	71	275	34,740
Henrik Nystrom	69	65	68	73	275	34,740
Jean Hugo	67	69	71	69	276	18,480
Juan Parron	68	71	69	68	276	18,480
David Dixon	68	71	68	70	277	13,000

	SCORES				TOTAL	MONEY
Jamie Little	72	72	64	69	277	13,000
Paul Dwyer	70	66	73	69	278	9,480
Pedro Linhart	71	70	69	68	278	9,480
Jesus Maria Arruti	70	69	71	69	279	6,960
Klas Eriksson	67	71	68	73	279	6,960
Mikko Ilonen	72	68	66	73	279	6,960
Raymond Russell	70	70	66	73	279	6,960
Shaun P. Webster	71	68	66	74	279	6,960
Gregory Bourdy	73	71	70	66	280	5,640
Fredrik Henge	74	71	67	68	280	5,640
Christian L. Nilsson	76	68	65	71	280	5,640
Rafael Echenique	71	72	68	70	281	4,890
James Hepworth	71	69	67	74	281	4,890
Stephen Scahill	72	68	70	71	281	4,890
Nicolas Vanhootegem	69	69	70	73	281	4,890
Chris Gane	69	70	69	74	282	4,340
Gustavo Rojas	73	68	72	69	282	4,340
Lee Slattery	69	70	72	71	282	4,340
Sam Walker	72	71	68	71	282	4,340
Felipe Aguilar	66	73	74	70	283	3,680
Alessio Bruschi	69	73	71	70	283	3,680
Neil Cheetham	75	69	68	71	283	3,680
Raphael Eyraud	71	70	73	69	283	3,680
Simon Hurd	69	76	66	72	283	3,680
Terry Pilkadaris	70	70	73	70	283	3,680
Inder Van Weerelt	71	73	71	68	283	3,680
Denny Lucas	71	72	71	70	284	3,008
Alexandre Rocha	71	73	70	70	284	3,008
Kieran Staunton	71	73	71	69	284	3,008
Benoit Teilleria	71	73	69	71	284	3,008
Ben Willman	71	70	71	72	284	3,008
Adrien Mork	68	71	72	74	285	2,600
Gareth Paddison	72	70	72	71	285	2,600
Mark Pilkington	70	74	73	68	285	2,600
Michele Reale	69	73	73	70	285	2,600
Tom Whitehouse	69	72	71	73	285	2,600
Oskar Bergman	70	73	71	72	286	2,200
Jean-Baptiste Gonnet	70	73	67	76	286	2,200
Malcolm Mackenzie	73	70	71	72	286	2,200
Marco Ruiz	73	72	70	71	286	2,200
Kyron Sullivan	72	71	75	68	286	2,200
Peter Baker	73	69	73	72	287	1,800
Julien Foret	72	71	73	71	287	1,800
Graham Fox	74	68	73	72	287	1,800
James Heath	72	70	71	74	287	1,800
Massimo Scarpa	73	71	71	72	287	1,800
Joakim Backstrom	74	71	70	73	288	1,366.67
Andre Bossert	70	72	71	75	288	1,366.67
Titch Moore	74	70	72	72	288	1,366.67
Alexander Noren	73	72	71	72	288	1,366.67
Alvaro Quiros	73	71	75	69	288	1,366.67
Christian Reimbold	72	73	74	69	288	1,366.67
Iain Steel	73	69	73	74	289	1,160
Jorge Benedetti	71	68	71	80	290	1,080
David Drysdale	69	75	73	73	290	1,080
Ilya Goroneskoul	72	73	73	72	290	1,080
Miguel Carballo	73	72	73	73	291	940
Anders Schmidt Hansen	70	74	75	72	291	940
Cedric Menut	68	77	71	75	291	940
Alvaro Salto	73	72	72	74	291	940

	SCORES				TOTAL	MONEY
Roger Chapman	74	69	73	76	292	820
Hennie Otto	73	69	76	74	292	820
Johan Axgren	72	72	75	75	294	760
Phil Worthington	73	69	79	75	296	740
Thomas Nielsen	73	72	77	80	302	600

Johnnie Walker Championship at Gleneagles

Gleneagles Hotel, Perthshire, Scotland
Par 36-37–73; 7,260 yards

June 22-25
purse, €2,059,250

	SCORES				TOTAL	MONEY
Paul Casey	67	71	66	72	276	€341,667.46
Soren Hansen	69	70	68	70	277	178,052.78
Andrew Marshall	72	67	69	69	277	178,052.78
Thomas Bjorn	65	75	67	71	278	94,711.57
Colin Montgomerie	68	68	69	73	278	94,711.57
Alastair Forsyth	72	69	67	71	279	71,751.19
Fredrik Henge	69	71	72	68	280	56,375.94
Brett Rumford	69	71	67	73	280	56,375.94
Kenneth Ferrie	68	73	71	69	281	43,460.72
Robert Karlsson	71	68	73	69	281	43,460.72
Felipe Aguilar	74	68	71	69	282	34,338.07
Peter Baker	73	68	69	72	282	34,338.07
Simon Dyson	72	72	69	69	282	34,338.07
Robert Rock	72	73	68	69	282	34,338.07
David Park	74	72	71	66	283	28,905.48
Carl Suneson	71	70	70	72	283	28,905.48
Francis Valera	68	75	71	69	283	28,905.48
Steven Jeppesen	70	74	72	68	284	26,445.44
Gary Orr	73	72	70	70	285	24,600.41
Sam Torrance	69	74	69	73	285	24,600.41
Marc Warren	73	72	71	69	285	24,600.41
Paul McGinley	70	73	72	71	286	21,627.86
Andrew McLardy	67	76	70	73	286	21,627.86
Henrik Nystrom	69	75	71	71	286	21,627.86
Stephen Scahill	76	69	69	72	286	21,627.86
Peter Senior	74	69	75	68	286	21,627.86
Steve Webster	75	71	72	68	286	21,627.86
Ross Fisher	70	70	71	76	287	18,552.81
Peter Lawrie	71	72	71	73	287	18,552.81
Jose-Filipe Lima	71	73	73	70	287	18,552.81
David Lynn	71	74	70	72	287	18,552.81
Stephen Browne	68	74	71	75	288	14,821.75
Ariel Canete	73	72	74	69	288	14,821.75
Emanuele Canonica	70	73	69	76	288	14,821.75
Marcus Fraser	71	68	74	75	288	14,821.75
David Griffiths	73	73	70	72	288	14,821.75
Miguel Angel Martin	68	77	74	69	288	14,821.75
Matthew Millar	73	72	74	69	288	14,821.75
Cesar Monasterio	74	70	75	69	288	14,821.75
Graeme Storm	69	72	73	74	288	14,821.75
Tom Whitehouse	71	74	69	74	288	14,821.75
Christian Cevaer	73	73	71	72	289	11,685.19
Peter Hanson	74	68	70	77	289	11,685.19
Soren Kjeldsen	74	72	72	71	289	11,685.19
Jason McCreadie	71	72	77	69	289	11,685.19

	SCORES				TOTAL	MONEY
Anthony Wall	71	74	73	71	289	11,685.19
Robert-Jan Derksen	74	70	71	75	290	9,635.16
David Drysdale	76	70	71	73	290	9,635.16
David Higgins	74	69	76	71	290	9,635.16
Jyoti Randhawa	72	71	74	73	290	9,635.16
Jamie Spence	73	71	75	71	290	9,635.16
Richard Bland	75	68	72	76	291	7,790.13
Stuart Davis	72	69	77	73	291	7,790.13
Bradley Dredge	69	75	75	72	291	7,790.13
Santiago Luna	73	73	72	73	291	7,790.13
Sam Little	72	72	75	73	292	6,303.85
Sandy Lyle	75	71	71	75	292	6,303.85
Wade Ormsby	68	77	73	74	292	6,303.85
Lee Slattery	73	73	72	74	292	6,303.85
Andres Romero	67	73	77	76	293	5,535.09
Raymond Russell	73	73	73	74	293	5,535.09
Miles Tunnicliff	70	76	73	74	293	5,535.09
Damien McGrane	75	71	74	74	294	4,920.08
Alexandre Rocha	70	72	76	76	294	4,920.08
Shaun P. Webster	72	73	72	77	294	4,920.08
Sion E. Bebb	72	72	73	78	295	4,510.08
Ben Mason	72	74	77	73	296	4,305.07
Philip Golding	71	75	73	78	297	3,914.59
Mark Loftus	69	75	77	76	297	3,914.59
Benoit Teilleria	71	74	73	79	297	3,914.59
Robert Arnott	71	74	74	79	298	3,075
Toni Karjalainen	72	72	78	78	300	3,072
Michele Reale	72	71	74	85	302	3,069

Open de France ALSTOM

Le Golf National, Paris, France
Par 36-35–71; 7,225 yards

June 29-July 2
purse, €4,000,000

	SCORES				TOTAL	MONEY
John Bickerton	63	70	71	69	273	€666,660
Padraig Harrington	69	70	69	66	274	444,440
Michael Campbell	65	70	68	73	276	206,666.67
Marcus Fraser	70	68	69	69	276	206,666.67
Ian Poulter	68	70	69	69	276	206,666.67
Anders Hansen	70	68	68	71	277	140,000
Andrew Coltart	68	73	70	67	278	103,200
Richard Green	71	70	68	69	278	103,200
Peter O'Malley	71	68	71	68	278	103,200
Alastair Forsyth	69	69	70	71	279	76,800
Jose Maria Olazabal	74	68	70	67	279	76,800
Paul Broadhurst	68	70	75	67	280	61,920
Angel Cabrera	73	67	74	66	280	61,920
Simon Khan	74	67	71	68	280	61,920
Soren Kjeldsen	70	71	66	73	280	61,920
Paul Lawrie	69	68	75	68	280	61,920
Bradley Dredge	69	66	71	75	281	50,800
Darren Fichardt	67	70	71	73	281	50,800
Robert Karlsson	69	72	68	72	281	50,800
Jean Van de Velde	69	70	70	72	281	50,800
Stephen Dodd	69	71	71	71	282	42,200
Mattias Eliasson	69	70	69	74	282	42,200

	SCORES				TOTAL	MONEY
Mark Foster	67	71	71	73	282	42,200
Jean-Francois Lucquin	69	71	73	69	282	42,200
Francesco Molinari	71	70	71	70	282	42,200
Adrien Mork	76	66	70	70	282	42,200
Jamie Spence	69	70	70	73	282	42,200
Graeme Storm	74	69	67	72	282	42,200
Phillip Archer	70	71	70	72	283	32,750
Markus Brier	68	68	78	69	283	32,750
Ricardo Gonzalez	75	67	71	70	283	32,750
Phillip Price	70	68	70	75	283	32,750
Mark Roe	70	70	68	75	283	32,750
Eduardo Romero	71	67	72	73	283	32,750
Henrik Stenson	67	70	70	76	283	32,750
Lee Westwood	71	71	73	68	283	32,750
Joakim Backstrom	66	69	78	71	284	27,600
Robert Coles	73	68	71	72	284	27,600
David Lynn	71	72	70	71	284	27,600
Jose Manuel Lara	67	68	78	72	285	23,200
Peter Lawrie	70	69	75	71	285	23,200
Malcolm Mackenzie	70	70	70	75	285	23,200
Gary Murphy	71	70	69	75	285	23,200
Jean-Francois Remesy	68	75	69	73	285	23,200
Charl Schwartzel	70	72	72	71	285	23,200
Simon Wakefield	73	70	75	67	285	23,200
Anthony Wall	74	67	70	74	285	23,200
Andrew Butterfield	70	70	72	74	286	18,000
Kenneth Ferrie	70	73	72	71	286	18,000
Richard Finch	68	74	74	70	286	18,000
Ross Fisher	69	70	73	74	286	18,000
*Alexandre Kaleka	74	69	73	70	286	
David Park	68	69	70	79	286	18,000
Gregory Bourdy	73	70	72	72	287	14,000
Nicolas Colsaerts	71	72	71	73	287	14,000
Niclas Fasth	69	73	69	76	287	14,000
Peter Hanson	70	71	67	79	287	14,000
Steve Webster	72	71	72	72	287	14,000
Gary Orr	70	64	76	78	288	12,000
David Carter	67	70	73	79	289	10,800
Simon Dyson	73	69	70	77	289	10,800
Peter Fowler	75	68	75	71	289	10,800
Peter Gustafsson	68	68	74	79	289	10,800
Alessandro Tadini	71	71	72	75	289	10,800
James Kingston	72	69	70	80	291	9,600
Soren Hansen	68	74	70	80	292	9,000
Nicolas Joakimides	71	72	70	79	292	9,000
Paul McGinley	72	71	73	77	293	8,400
Benn Barham	67	69	77	81	294	8,000
Michael Kirk	75	68	79	76	298	7,450
Sandy Lyle	71	70	76	81	298	7,450
Marcel Siem	71	71	84	73	299	6,000

Smurfit Kappa European Open

The K Club, Straffan, Co. Kildare, Ireland
Par 36-36–72; 7,313 yards

July 6-9
purse, €3,472,719

	SCORES				TOTAL	MONEY
Stephen Dodd	67	69	73	70	279	€578,792
Jose Manuel Lara	72	68	67	74	281	301,622.98
Anthony Wall	70	68	70	73	281	301,622.98
Simon Khan	68	73	68	73	282	126,685.99
Paul McGinley	75	71	67	69	282	126,685.99
Jeev Milkha Singh	70	68	74	70	282	126,685.99
Graeme Storm	70	73	69	70	282	126,685.99
Lee Westwood	70	75	67	70	282	126,685.99
Bradley Dredge	65	70	75	73	283	67,718.66
Simon Dyson	69	74	71	69	283	67,718.66
Peter Hanson	68	74	69	72	283	67,718.66
Colin Montgomerie	69	71	72	71	283	67,718.66
Robert Karlsson	73	69	75	67	284	54,522.21
Steven O'Hara	71	69	70	74	284	54,522.21
Darren Clarke	69	68	72	76	285	50,007.63
Thongchai Jaidee	69	74	71	71	285	50,007.63
Angel Cabrera	66	78	69	73	286	44,914.26
Anders Hansen	69	72	74	71	286	44,914.26
Jamie Spence	68	72	69	77	286	44,914.26
Paul Casey	66	73	71	77	287	38,779.06
Richard Green	73	68	73	73	287	38,779.06
Padraig Harrington	70	75	69	73	287	38,779.06
Maarten Lafeber	70	73	70	74	287	38,779.06
Tom Lehman	71	70	70	76	287	38,779.06
Peter O'Malley	67	74	73	73	287	38,779.06
Emanuele Canonica	72	70	71	76	289	32,991.14
Kenneth Ferrie	73	72	70	74	289	32,991.14
Sam Little	72	70	74	73	289	32,991.14
Jean-Francois Lucquin	71	73	73	72	289	32,991.14
Graeme McDowell	69	76	72	72	289	32,991.14
Soren Hansen	72	70	77	71	290	28,302.93
Damien McGrane	69	72	73	76	290	28,302.93
Henrik Stenson	71	70	74	75	290	28,302.93
Simon Wakefield	70	72	74	74	290	28,302.93
Markus Brier	73	71	72	75	291	24,309.26
Stephen Browne	73	67	72	79	291	24,309.26
Niclas Fasth	65	75	74	77	291	24,309.26
Retief Goosen	69	72	74	76	291	24,309.26
Soren Kjeldsen	69	69	79	74	291	24,309.26
Steve Webster	70	73	77	71	291	24,309.26
Phillip Archer	72	70	74	76	292	21,531.06
Louis Oosthuizen	70	71	71	80	292	21,531.06
Nicolas Colsaerts	67	76	75	75	293	19,794.69
Andres Romero	71	75	68	79	293	19,794.69
Marcel Siem	71	72	72	78	293	19,794.69
Christian Cevaer	71	69	78	76	294	16,669.21
Jamie Donaldson	70	73	75	76	294	16,669.21
David Griffiths	71	75	71	77	294	16,669.21
Francesco Molinari	70	73	71	80	294	16,669.21
Charl Schwartzel	73	72	73	76	294	16,669.21
Alessandro Tadini	77	68	71	78	294	16,669.21
Peter Baker	70	74	71	80	295	13,196.46
Mark Foster	73	71	76	75	295	13,196.46
David Park	72	73	73	77	295	13,196.46

	SCORES				TOTAL	MONEY
Ian Poulter	72	72	75	76	295	13,196.46
Andrew Coltart	70	75	76	75	296	10,487.71
David Higgins	74	72	73	77	296	10,487.71
Eduardo Romero	71	72	77	76	296	10,487.71
Peter Senior	73	73	70	80	296	10,487.71
Tom Whitehouse	72	74	75	75	296	10,487.71
Mattias Eliasson	71	73	74	79	297	9,029.16
Andrew Marshall	74	72	73	78	297	9,029.16
Jyoti Randhawa	68	78	73	78	297	9,029.16
Leif Westerberg	70	73	76	79	298	8,334.60
Gonzalo Fernandez-Castano	75	71	74	79	299	7,987.33
Gary Emerson	70	71	77	82	300	7,292.78
Marcus Fraser	72	73	79	76	300	7,292.78
Philip Golding	71	74	75	80	300	7,292.78
Peter Gustafsson	70	75	74	82	301	6,468
Steven Jeppesen	75	70	79	77	301	6,468
Marc Cayeux	73	71	80	78	302	5,207.50
Michael Kirk	74	69	78	81	302	5,207.50
Miguel Carballo	73	73	76	81	303	5,200
David Dixon	75	71	74	83	303	5,200
Simon Thornton	76	70	76	81	303	5,200

Barclays Scottish Open

Loch Lomond Golf Club, Glasgow, Scotland
Par 36-35–71; 7,139 yards

July 13-16
purse, €3,452,332

	SCORES				TOTAL	MONEY
Johan Edfors	65	69	74	63	271	€577,540.02
Luke Donald	68	69	70	66	273	258,401.03
Andres Romero	72	64	68	69	273	258,401.03
Charl Schwartzel	68	66	72	67	273	258,401.03
Benn Barham	71	68	65	70	274	114,699.45
Thomas Bjorn	72	64	66	72	274	114,699.45
Tim Clark	69	67	69	69	274	114,699.45
Darren Clarke	66	65	71	72	274	114,699.45
Ernie Els	70	69	67	69	275	70,228.87
Sergio Garcia	71	67	69	68	275	70,228.87
Raphael Jacquelin	68	72	65	70	275	70,228.87
Kenneth Ferrie	71	69	71	65	276	57,696.25
Thongchai Jaidee	72	69	66	69	276	57,696.25
Angel Cabrera	71	66	70	70	277	44,632.29
Mark Foster	70	68	68	71	277	44,632.29
Ian Garbutt	71	67	69	70	277	44,632.29
Retief Goosen	70	69	71	67	277	44,632.29
Anders Hansen	74	66	70	67	277	44,632.29
Soren Hansen	73	66	71	67	277	44,632.29
David Lynn	70	68	69	70	277	44,632.29
Greg Owen	74	66	69	68	277	44,632.29
Ian Poulter	70	67	70	70	277	44,632.29
Jean-Francois Remesy	73	65	67	72	277	44,632.29
Phillip Archer	72	67	70	69	278	34,479.14
Stephen Gallacher	70	71	67	70	278	34,479.14
Paul Lawrie	70	71	70	67	278	34,479.14
Tom Lehman	69	72	66	71	278	34,479.14
Damien McGrane	68	66	71	73	278	34,479.14
Colin Montgomerie	72	66	69	71	278	34,479.14

	SCORES				TOTAL	MONEY
David Drysdale	65	70	69	75	279	30,320.85
Lee Westwood	69	67	71	72	279	30,320.85
David Bransdon	67	71	73	69	280	27,721.92
Richard Finch	70	69	69	72	280	27,721.92
Marcel Siem	69	69	72	70	280	27,721.92
David Howell	69	72	68	72	281	24,949.73
Simon Khan	69	72	69	71	281	24,949.73
Carl Pettersson	68	70	71	72	281	24,949.73
Oliver Wilson	74	65	72	70	281	24,949.73
Jamie Donaldson	68	67	71	76	282	20,791.44
Soren Kjeldsen	70	69	73	70	282	20,791.44
Maarten Lafeber	71	69	69	73	282	20,791.44
Jose-Filipe Lima	68	70	71	73	282	20,791.44
Jean-Francois Lucquin	71	70	68	73	282	20,791.44
Peter O'Malley	69	69	74	70	282	20,791.44
Brett Rumford	72	67	75	68	282	20,791.44
Simon Wakefield	70	69	71	72	282	20,791.44
Paul Broadhurst	69	71	70	73	283	15,593.58
Andrew Butterfield	67	73	73	70	283	15,593.58
Gary Clark	69	71	72	71	283	15,593.58
Gonzalo Fernandez-Castano	69	68	71	75	283	15,593.58
Paul McGinley	69	71	69	74	283	15,593.58
Jose Maria Olazabal	67	74	69	73	283	15,593.58
Jarmo Sandelin	74	67	70	72	283	15,593.58
Simon Dyson	70	70	69	75	284	11,504.60
Gregory Havret	69	67	73	75	284	11,504.60
Garry Houston	68	71	72	73	284	11,504.60
Jose Manuel Lara	68	70	73	73	284	11,504.60
*Edoardo Molinari	71	70	71	72	284	
Steve Webster	73	68	71	72	284	11,504.60
Shiv Kapur	72	69	72	72	285	9,875.93
Raymond Russell	67	69	75	74	285	9,875.93
Richard Bland	71	69	75	71	286	9,182.89
David Griffiths	70	71	70	75	286	9,182.89
Barry Lane	68	72	72	75	287	8,489.84
Jonathan Lomas	69	71	74	73	287	8,489.84
Hale Irwin	68	72	72	76	288	7,970.05
Nicolas Colsaerts	69	70	79	71	289	7,623.53
Joakim Haeggman	72	69	72	80	293	7,277
David Higgins	71	70	74	80	295	6,930.48

The Open Championship

Royal Liverpool Golf Club, Hoylake, England
Par 35-37–72; 7,258 yards

July 20-23
purse, €5,524,699

	SCORES				TOTAL	MONEY
Tiger Woods	67	65	71	67	270	€1,045,965.60
Chris DiMarco	70	65	69	68	272	624,673.90
Ernie Els	68	65	71	71	275	399,500.75
Jim Furyk	68	71	66	71	276	305,073.30
Sergio Garcia	68	71	65	73	277	231,710.44
Hideto Tanihara	72	68	66	71	277	231,710.44
Angel Cabrera	71	68	66	73	278	185,949.44
Carl Pettersson	68	72	70	69	279	138,493.59
Andres Romero	70	70	68	71	279	138,493.59
Adam Scott	68	69	70	72	279	138,493.59
Ben Crane	68	71	71	70	280	100,722.61

		SCORES			TOTAL	MONEY
S.K. Ho	68	73	69	70	280	100,722.61
Anthony Wall	67	73	71	69	280	100,722.61
Retief Goosen	70	66	72	73	281	82,079.25
Sean O'Hair	69	73	72	67	281	82,079.25
Robert Allenby	69	70	69	74	282	65,372.85
Mikko Ilonen	68	69	73	72	282	65,372.85
Peter Lonard	71	69	68	74	282	65,372.85
Geoff Ogilvy	71	69	70	72	282	65,372.85
Robert Rock	69	69	73	71	282	65,372.85
Brett Rumford	68	71	72	71	282	65,372.85
Mark Hensby	68	72	74	69	283	51,390.32
Phil Mickelson	69	71	73	70	283	51,390.32
Greg Owen	67	73	68	75	283	51,390.32
Charl Schwartzel	74	66	72	71	283	51,390.32
Paul Broadhurst	71	71	73	69	284	42,274.44
Jerry Kelly	72	67	69	76	284	42,274.44
Hunter Mahan	73	70	68	73	284	42,274.44
Rory Sabbatini	69	70	73	72	284	42,274.44
Lee Slattery	69	72	71	72	284	42,274.44
Simon Khan	70	72	68	75	285	35,591.89
Scott Verplank	70	73	67	75	285	35,591.89
Lee Westwood	69	72	75	69	285	35,591.89
Thaworn Wiratchant	71	68	74	72	285	35,591.89
Michael Campbell	70	71	75	70	286	28,509.83
Luke Donald	74	68	73	71	286	28,509.83
Marcus Fraser	68	71	72	75	286	28,509.83
Robert Karlsson	70	71	71	74	286	28,509.83
Rodney Pampling	69	71	74	72	286	28,509.83
John Senden	70	73	73	70	286	28,509.83
Stephen Ames	70	71	72	74	287	21,583.42
Thomas Bjorn	72	71	73	71	287	21,583.42
Mark Calcavecchia	71	68	68	80	287	21,583.42
Miguel Angel Jimenez	67	70	76	74	287	21,583.42
Brandt Jobe	69	71	75	72	287	21,583.42
Soren Kjeldsen	71	71	71	74	287	21,583.42
Jeff Sluman	71	72	68	76	287	21,583.42
John Bickerton	72	70	70	76	288	16,862.04
Simon Dyson	74	69	70	75	288	16,862.04
Gonzalo Fernandez-Castano	70	69	73	76	288	16,862.04
Andrew Marshall	72	71	68	77	288	16,862.04
Henrik Stenson	72	71	74	71	288	16,862.04
*Marius Thorp	71	71	75	71	288	
Simon Wakefield	72	71	70	75	288	16,862.04
Tom Watson	72	70	75	71	288	16,862.04
Tim Clark	72	69	69	79	289	14,963.12
David Duval	70	70	78	71	289	14,963.12
Keiichiro Fukabori	67	73	70	79	289	14,963.12
Jose Maria Olazabal	73	68	76	72	289	14,963.12
Mike Weir	68	72	73	76	289	14,963.12
Andrew Buckle	72	69	72	77	290	14,454.66
Graeme McDowell	66	73	72	79	290	14,454.66
Mark O'Meara	71	70	77	73	291	14,164.12
Marco Ruiz	71	70	80	70	291	14,164.12
Chad Campbell	70	73	74	75	292	13,946.21
Fred Funk	69	74	75	76	294	13,728.30
Vaughn Taylor	72	71	77	74	294	13,728.30
Todd Hamilton	72	71	74	78	295	13,510.39
*Edoardo Molinari	73	70	77	75	295	
Bart Bryant	69	74	77	76	296	13,365.12
Paul Casey	72	70	79	77	298	13,219.84

Out of Final 36 Holes

Rich Beem	71	73	144	4,358.19
Markus Brier	71	73	144	4,358.19
Bradley Dredge	70	74	144	4,358.19
Scott Drummond	73	71	144	4,358.19
Niclas Fasth	69	75	144	4,358.19
Mathew Goggin	75	69	144	4,358.19
Jarrod Lyle	74	70	144	4,358.19
Jeff Maggert	75	69	144	4,358.19
Paul McGinley	71	73	144	4,358.19
Tom Pernice	71	73	144	4,358.19
Mark Pilkington	76	68	144	4,358.19
Phillip Price	74	70	144	4,358.19
John Daly	72	73	145	3,631.83
Steve Elkington	71	74	145	3,631.83
Lucas Glover	72	73	145	3,631.83
Shiv Kapur	72	73	145	3,631.83
Tom Lehman	68	77	145	3,631.83
Nick O'Hern	70	75	145	3,631.83
Ted Purdy	74	71	145	3,631.83
Thomas Aiken	72	74	146	3,631.83
Stuart Appleby	74	72	146	3,631.83
Aaron Baddeley	70	76	146	3,631.83
K.J. Choi	72	74	146	3,631.83
Fred Couples	70	76	146	3,631.83
Ben Curtis	73	73	146	3,631.83
Stephen Dodd	73	73	146	3,631.83
Richard Green	71	75	146	3,631.83
J.J. Henry	73	73	146	3,631.83
Zach Johnson	73	73	146	3,631.83
Sandy Lyle	73	73	146	3,631.83
Vijay Singh	70	76	146	3,631.83
David Smail	76	70	146	3,631.83
Bo Van Pelt	74	72	146	3,631.83
Brett Wetterich	74	72	146	3,631.83
Billy Andrade	72	75	147	3,268.64
Adam Bland	73	74	147	3,268.64
Nick Dougherty	74	73	147	3,268.64
*Julien Guerrier	72	75	147	
Bradley Hughes	72	75	147	3,268.64
Davis Love	75	72	147	3,268.64
Shaun Micheel	72	75	147	3,268.64
Louis Oosthuizen	78	69	147	3,268.64
Darren Parris	75	72	147	3,268.64
Kenny Perry	73	74	147	3,268.64
Michael Wright	72	75	147	3,268.64
Nick Faldo	77	71	148	3,268.64
Shingo Katayama	74	74	148	3,268.64
Bernhard Langer	74	74	148	3,268.64
Colin Montgomerie	73	75	148	3,268.64
Arron Oberholser	73	75	148	3,268.64
Ross Wellington	75	73	148	3,268.64
Stewart Cink	72	77	149	3,268.64
Johan Edfors	75	74	149	3,268.64
Padraig Harrington	75	74	149	3,268.64
Tim Herron	76	73	149	3,268.64
J.B. Holmes	74	75	149	3,268.64
Toshinori Muto	75	74	149	3,268.64
Jim Payne	73	76	149	3,268.64
Richard Sterne	76	73	149	3,268.64

	SCORES		TOTAL	MONEY
Peter Hedblom	73	77	150	2,905.46
David Howell	74	76	150	2,905.46
Barry Lane	75	75	150	2,905.46
Paul Lawrie	76	74	150	2,905.46
Brett Quigley	79	71	150	2,905.46
Seve Ballesteros	74	77	151	2,905.46
Darren Clarke	69	82	151	2,905.46
Jamie Donaldson	75	76	151	2,905.46
Yasuharu Imano	73	78	151	2,905.46
Nick Ludwell	75	76	151	2,905.46
Ian Poulter	75	76	151	2,905.46
Warren Bladon	76	76	152	2,905.46
Adam Frayne	71	81	152	2,905.46
Tatsuhiko Ichihara	78	74	152	2,905.46
Bruce Vaughan	75	77	152	2,905.46
Warren Abery	76	77	153	2,905.46
*Daniel Denison	78	76	154	
Gary Lockerbie	78	76	154	2,905.46
Wayne Perske	76	79	155	2,905.46
Unho Park	82	74	156	2,905.46
Ben Bunny	74	83	157	2,905.46
Sam Little	83	74	157	2,905.46
Carlos Rodiles	81	76	157	2,905.46
Gary Day	82	76	158	2,905.46
Jon Bevan	82	81	163	2,905.46
Kenneth Ferrie	76		WD	2,905.46

Deutsche Bank Players' Championship of Europe

Gut Kaden, Hamburg, Germany
Par 36-36–72; 7,290 yards

July 27-30
purse, €3,600,000

	SCORES				TOTAL	MONEY
Robert Karlsson	64	66	66	67	263	€600,000
Charl Schwartzel	68	64	68	67	267	312,680
Lee Westwood	63	68	67	69	267	312,680
Emanuele Canonica	67	68	66	67	268	141,660
Retief Goosen	64	68	69	67	268	141,660
Graeme McDowell	68	70	65	65	268	141,660
Andres Romero	70	65	67	66	268	141,660
Gary Orr	67	64	70	68	269	90,000
Sergio Garcia	69	66	67	68	270	76,320
Soren Hansen	70	67	66	67	270	76,320
Niclas Fasth	68	66	70	68	272	62,040
Christian L. Nilsson	67	66	73	66	272	62,040
Ian Woosnam	65	66	69	72	272	62,040
Tim Clark	68	69	68	68	273	55,080
Angel Cabrera	66	71	69	68	274	50,760
Luke Donald	67	66	71	70	274	50,760
Mikko Ilonen	68	69	66	71	274	50,760
Paul McGinley	70	66	69	70	275	44,010
Jarmo Sandelin	71	68	71	65	275	44,010
Daniel Vancsik	69	66	67	73	275	44,010
Anthony Wall	72	66	69	68	275	44,010
Garry Houston	66	68	69	73	276	37,980
Shiv Kapur	72	66	71	67	276	37,980
Matthew Millar	67	69	68	72	276	37,980

	SCORES				TOTAL	MONEY
Ian Poulter	68	67	70	71	276	37,980
Jyoti Randhawa	68	69	73	66	276	37,980
Henrik Stenson	70	70	66	70	276	37,980
Markus Brier	74	65	67	71	277	31,500
Todd Hamilton	71	69	68	69	277	31,500
Padraig Harrington	68	65	72	72	277	31,500
Simon Khan	67	70	73	67	277	31,500
Damien McGrane	69	66	70	72	277	31,500
Sven Struver	68	70	70	69	277	31,500
Mark Foster	70	70	72	66	278	27,000
Stephen Gallacher	66	72	70	70	278	27,000
Louis Oosthuizen	69	67	72	70	278	27,000
Mattias Eliasson	69	69	72	69	279	23,040
Gary Emerson	68	69	70	72	279	23,040
Darren Fichardt	71	68	69	71	279	23,040
Thongchai Jaidee	67	71	69	72	279	23,040
Soren Kjeldsen	68	67	69	75	279	23,040
Jean-Francois Remesy	65	70	73	71	279	23,040
Graeme Storm	67	69	75	68	279	23,040
Leif Westerberg	70	69	70	70	279	23,040
Christian Cevaer	67	71	69	73	280	18,000
Johan Edfors	68	67	69	76	280	18,000
Anders Hansen	69	66	71	74	280	18,000
Mikael Lundberg	69	68	71	72	280	18,000
Richard McEvoy	71	69	68	72	280	18,000
Steven O'Hara	71	69	69	71	280	18,000
Phillip Price	70	70	70	71	281	14,760
Alessandro Tadini	70	70	70	71	281	14,760
Tom Whitehouse	74	65	72	70	281	14,760
Nicolas Colsaerts	70	70	70	72	282	11,952
Alastair Forsyth	68	72	72	70	282	11,952
Gregory Havret	65	70	70	77	282	11,952
Jean-Francois Lucquin	67	72	68	75	282	11,952
Andrew McLardy	68	69	73	72	282	11,952
Phillip Archer	68	71	70	74	283	9,360
Joakim Backstrom	71	68	69	75	283	9,360
Michael Campbell	70	69	71	73	283	9,360
Peter Gustafsson	68	71	71	73	283	9,360
Bernhard Langer	71	69	74	69	283	9,360
Jamie Spence	72	68	70	73	283	9,360
Fredrik Widmark	70	70	74	69	283	9,360
Jose Manuel Lara	70	70	71	73	284	7,740
Tino Schuster	71	69	70	74	284	7,740
Francois Delamontagne	72	68	74	71	285	7,020
Robert Rock	68	68	71	78	285	7,020
Jonathan Lomas	68	72	72	74	286	6,560
Alejandro Canizares	69	70	71	79	289	5,400

EnterCard Scandinavian Masters

Barseback Golf & Country Club, Malmo, Sweden
Par 36-36–72; 7,365 yards

August 3-6
purse, €1,600,000

	SCORES				TOTAL	MONEY
Marc Warren	67	69	73	69	278	€266,660
Robert Karlsson	75	69	63	71	278	177,770

(Warren defeated Karlsson on second playoff hole.)

	SCORES				TOTAL	MONEY
Richard Sterne	70	68	72	69	279	100,160
Marcel Siem	72	71	69	68	280	80,000
Peter Gustafsson	73	69	67	72	281	61,920
Raphael Jacquelin	68	71	72	70	281	61,920
Simon Dyson	71	71	71	70	283	41,280
Jesper Parnevik	72	70	72	69	283	41,280
Tom Whitehouse	68	70	73	72	283	41,280
Benn Barham	67	73	74	70	284	27,840
Gregory Bourdy	69	72	71	72	284	27,840
David Carter	73	66	70	75	284	27,840
Santiago Luna	71	69	73	71	284	27,840
Jarmo Sandelin	69	73	66	76	284	27,840
Felipe Aguilar	72	69	74	70	285	20,177.78
Martin Erlandsson	70	72	74	69	285	20,177.78
Niclas Fasth	71	70	74	70	285	20,177.78
Jose Manuel Lara	72	73	70	70	285	20,177.78
Peter Lawrie	70	72	72	71	285	20,177.78
Jose-Filipe Lima	73	70	73	69	285	20,177.78
Cesar Monasterio	71	71	72	71	285	20,177.78
Wade Ormsby	72	71	72	70	285	20,177.78
Mark Roe	69	65	75	76	285	20,177.78
Nicolas Colsaerts	67	67	73	79	286	16,640
Mattias Eliasson	70	71	72	73	286	16,640
Ian Garbutt	74	70	70	72	286	16,640
Fredrik Jacobson	69	67	76	75	287	14,720
*Jesper Kennegard	72	69	73	73	287	
Maarten Lafeber	73	71	71	72	287	14,720
David Lynn	69	71	74	73	287	14,720
Peter O'Malley	71	73	72	71	287	14,720
Daniel Vancsik	72	70	76	69	287	14,720
Phillip Archer	70	71	75	72	288	11,568
Richard Bland	73	71	74	70	288	11,568
Michael Campbell	68	75	75	70	288	11,568
Klas Eriksson	70	71	70	77	288	11,568
Joakim Haeggman	74	69	72	73	288	11,568
Peter Hanson	69	75	72	72	288	11,568
Gregory Havret	75	69	72	72	288	11,568
Steven O'Hara	75	69	72	72	288	11,568
Jamie Spence	70	70	75	73	288	11,568
Oliver Whiteley	74	71	70	73	288	11,568
Markus Brier	72	71	73	73	289	8,480
Francois Delamontagne	71	73	71	74	289	8,480
Robert-Jan Derksen	72	72	75	70	289	8,480
Stephen Gallacher	74	70	72	73	289	8,480
James Kingston	70	71	76	72	289	8,480
Andrew McLardy	69	73	76	71	289	8,480
Matthew Millar	72	72	72	73	289	8,480
Leif Westerberg	71	74	72	72	289	8,480
Oliver Wilson	72	73	71	73	289	8,480
Ignacio Garrido	72	71	75	72	290	6,080
David Higgins	72	73	72	73	290	6,080
Sam Little	72	70	77	71	290	6,080
Alexander Noren	73	71	72	74	290	6,080
Iain Pyman	72	73	68	77	290	6,080
Miles Tunnicliff	74	71	72	73	290	6,080
Richard Finch	72	73	72	74	291	4,720
Adam Mednick	71	74	73	73	291	4,720
Christian L. Nilsson	73	72	73	73	291	4,720
Magnus Persson	71	72	73	75	291	4,720
David Bransdon	69	70	77	76	292	4,160

	SCORES				TOTAL	MONEY
Peter Fowler	73	72	68	79	292	4,160
Fredrik Widmark	76	68	74	74	292	4,160
Andrew Butterfield	73	69	76	75	293	3,600
Michael Hoey	73	72	70	78	293	3,600
Miguel Angel Martin	72	71	74	76	293	3,600
Alexandre Rocha	72	69	74	78	293	3,600
Johan Axgren	76	69	72	77	294	3,120
Christian Cevaer	72	73	73	76	294	3,120
Michael Jonzon	74	70	75	76	295	2,575.67
Marco Ruiz	72	72	79	72	295	2,575.67
Shaun P. Webster	71	74	73	77	295	2,575.67
Fredrik Andersson Hed	68	71	81	77	297	2,389.50
Ariel Canete	74	71	77	75	297	2,389.50
Pelle Edberg	76	69	79	73	297	2,389.50
Mikael Lundberg	71	73	76	77	297	2,389.50
David Drysdale	70	74	79	75	298	2,380.50
Francesco Molinari	70	74	77	77	298	2,380.50
Louis Oosthuizen	72	70	80	81	303	2,376
Janne Martikainen	73	71	80	80	304	2,373

KLM Open

Kennemer Golf & Country Club, Zandvoort, Netherlands
Par 36-35—71; 6,862 yards

August 10-13
purse, €1,600,000

	SCORES				TOTAL	MONEY
Simon Dyson	67	71	66	66	270	€266,660
Richard Green	73	70	62	65	270	177,770
(Dyson defeated Green on first playoff hole.)						
Damien McGrane	69	68	64	70	271	100,160
Christian Cevaer	65	71	69	67	272	80,000
Garry Houston	72	68	67	66	273	67,840
Peter Lawrie	69	71	64	70	274	56,000
Phillip Archer	68	68	70	69	275	35,466.67
Markus Brier	66	73	68	68	275	35,466.67
Alejandro Canizares	67	73	66	69	275	35,466.67
Anders Hansen	65	72	71	67	275	35,466.67
David Lynn	75	65	71	64	275	35,466.67
Andrew McLardy	68	71	69	67	275	35,466.67
David Drysdale	68	70	72	66	276	25,760
David Carter	70	71	67	69	277	21,300
Soren Kjeldsen	68	68	69	72	277	21,300
Colin Montgomerie	70	71	67	69	277	21,300
Gary Murphy	69	70	70	68	277	21,300
Steven O'Hara	71	70	69	67	277	21,300
Jean-Francois Remesy	72	65	67	73	277	21,300
Marco Ruiz	69	72	67	69	277	21,300
Lee Slattery	69	72	67	69	277	21,300
Rafael Gomez	68	73	67	70	278	17,120
Jonathan Lomas	72	67	69	70	278	17,120
Paul McGinley	72	70	66	70	278	17,120
Alessandro Tadini	68	70	69	71	278	17,120
Tom Whitehouse	70	73	65	70	278	17,120
Klas Eriksson	69	71	72	67	279	14,720
Alastair Forsyth	71	69	67	72	279	14,720
Ian Garbutt	70	70	69	70	279	14,720
Miles Tunnicliff	72	70	70	67	279	14,720

	SCORES				TOTAL	MONEY
Ian Woosnam	72	70	67	70	279	14,720
Warren Abery	70	70	66	74	280	12,068.57
Gregory Bourdy	67	74	69	70	280	12,068.57
Neil Cheetham	68	71	68	73	280	12,068.57
Andrew Coltart	75	68	69	68	280	12,068.57
Richard McEvoy	71	68	68	73	280	12,068.57
Raymond Russell	67	69	72	72	280	12,068.57
Shaun P. Webster	71	69	70	70	280	12,068.57
Benn Barham	73	68	70	70	281	10,400
Adam Mednick	69	71	74	67	281	10,400
Matthew Millar	70	68	73	70	281	10,400
Marc Cayeux	72	71	69	70	282	9,120
Ignacio Garrido	68	67	73	74	282	9,120
Sam Little	72	71	71	68	282	9,120
Santiago Luna	71	72	68	71	282	9,120
Peter O'Malley	72	71	72	67	282	9,120
Felipe Aguilar	73	69	71	70	283	7,520
Robert-Jan Derksen	69	71	70	73	283	7,520
Ross Fisher	70	71	71	71	283	7,520
Stuart Little	73	69	70	71	283	7,520
Cesar Monasterio	70	72	71	70	283	7,520
Andrew Marshall	73	68	71	72	284	6,560
David Bransdon	68	71	71	75	285	5,348.57
Gary Emerson	74	69	73	69	285	5,348.57
Thongchai Jaidee	71	71	69	74	285	5,348.57
Barry Lane	68	73	74	70	285	5,348.57
Christian L. Nilsson	71	70	74	70	285	5,348.57
David Park	68	74	71	72	285	5,348.57
*Tim Sluiter	69	70	73	73	285	
Daniel Vancsik	73	69	67	76	285	5,348.57
Richard Bland	72	71	71	72	286	4,400
Jamie Donaldson	69	71	72	74	286	4,400
Edoardo Molinari	76	67	72	72	287	4,000
Phillip Price	73	69	70	75	287	4,000
Sven Struver	68	75	72	72	287	4,000
Niels Kraaij	72	70	76	70	288	3,600
Alexandre Rocha	75	67	74	72	288	3,600
Brian Akstrup	73	69	73	74	289	3,200
James Kingston	69	73	74	73	289	3,200
Robert Rock	66	76	73	74	289	3,200
Leif Westerberg	73	68	77	73	291	2,930
Carlos Rodiles	69	73	79	74	295	2,400

Imperial Collection Russian Open

Le Meridien Moscow Country Club, Moscow, Russia
Par 36-36–72; 7,154 yards

August 17-20
purse, €787,399

	SCORES				TOTAL	MONEY
Alejandro Canizares	66	67	67	66	266	€130,641.50
David Drysdale	62	70	69	69	270	87,096.94
Mikael Lundberg	68	67	70	66	271	44,132.46
Gary Murphy	67	68	68	68	271	44,132.46
Leif Westerberg	68	71	63	70	272	33,236.53
Alexandre Rocha	69	68	69	67	273	27,435.81
Carlos Rodiles	63	69	69	73	274	23,516.41
James Heath	71	67	69	68	275	18,577.96

	SCORES				TOTAL	MONEY
Jarrod Moseley	75	68	65	67	275	18,577.96
Jorge Benedetti	69	69	71	67	276	12,967.62
*Seve Benson	71	70	69	66	276	
David Dixon	69	69	70	68	276	12,967.62
Ian Garbutt	71	70	68	67	276	12,967.62
Fredrik Henge	71	67	69	69	276	12,967.62
Adrien Mork	68	69	72	67	276	12,967.62
Massimo Scarpa	70	67	69	70	276	12,967.62
Lee Slattery	72	71	65	68	276	12,967.62
Felipe Aguilar	72	70	70	65	277	9,782.83
Fredrik Andersson Hed	66	69	73	69	277	9,782.83
Stephen Browne	70	69	67	71	277	9,782.83
Andrew Butterfield	68	67	71	71	277	9,782.83
Marco Ruiz	68	69	70	70	277	9,782.83
Benn Barham	69	69	68	72	278	7,917.19
Rodolfo Gonzalez	67	69	70	72	278	7,917.19
James Kingston	65	69	73	71	278	7,917.19
Richard McEvoy	72	69	67	70	278	7,917.19
Mark Mouland	72	68	67	71	278	7,917.19
Christian L. Nilsson	72	68	69	69	278	7,917.19
Magnus Persson	69	70	68	71	278	7,917.19
Iain Pyman	76	67	68	67	278	7,917.19
Benoit Teilleria	70	68	68	72	278	7,917.19
Klas Eriksson	68	70	70	71	279	6,506.21
Toni Karjalainen	69	70	68	72	279	6,506.21
Cedric Menut	66	72	68	73	279	6,506.21
Robert Coles	73	68	69	70	280	5,722.33
Philip Golding	67	72	72	69	280	5,722.33
David Higgins	70	67	72	71	280	5,722.33
Carl Suneson	72	68	69	71	280	5,722.33
Francis Valera	65	67	74	74	280	5,722.33
Ariel Canete	72	70	69	70	281	4,624.89
Luis Claverie	72	69	70	70	281	4,624.89
Mikko Ilonen	68	73	74	66	281	4,624.89
Jonathan Lomas	68	72	72	69	281	4,624.89
Claes Nilsson	71	67	68	75	281	4,624.89
Henrik Nystrom	71	72	69	69	281	4,624.89
Terry Pilkadaris	72	69	68	72	281	4,624.89
Johan Skold	71	70	72	68	281	4,624.89
Sean Whiffin	71	69	70	71	281	4,624.89
Gustavo Acosta	70	72	69	71	282	3,292.30
Gregory Bourdy	69	72	70	71	282	3,292.30
Gary Clark	73	70	69	70	282	3,292.30
Sebastien Delagrange	73	66	71	72	282	3,292.30
Jamie Donaldson	73	70	67	72	282	3,292.30
Michael Hoey	70	69	73	70	282	3,292.30
Roope Kakko	70	71	74	67	282	3,292.30
Titch Moore	69	73	71	69	282	3,292.30
Garry Houston	67	74	71	71	283	2,508.42
Pedro Linhart	73	69	71	70	283	2,508.42
Oskar Henningsson	69	71	73	71	284	2,273.25
Tuomas Tuovinen	75	68	65	76	284	2,273.25
Daniel Vancsik	68	71	73	72	284	2,273.25
Santiago Luna	70	70	71	74	285	2,077.28
Sam Osborne	72	70	74	69	285	2,077.28
Matt Dearden	72	70	72	72	286	1,842.12
Pelle Edberg	73	70	69	74	286	1,842.12
Stephen Scahill	72	71	71	72	286	1,842.12
Thomas Sundstrom	71	71	72	72	286	1,842.12
Peter Gustafsson	75	68	73	71	287	1,606.95

Women's Tours

Her victory at the Mitchell Tournament was Lorena Ochoa's sixth of the year.

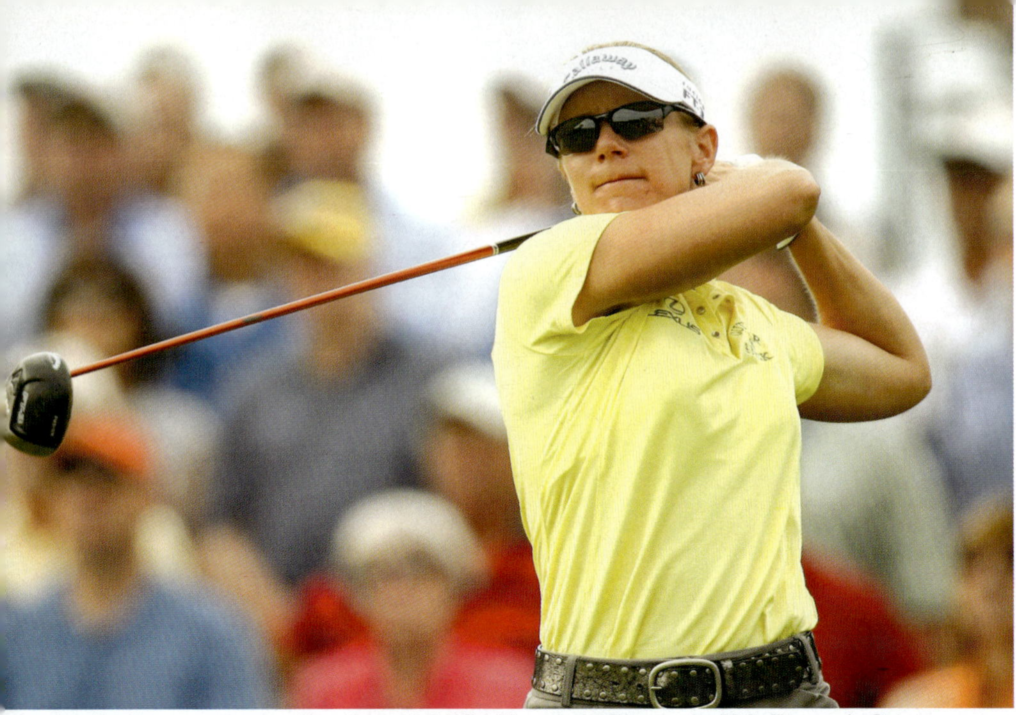

Nick Laham/Getty Images

Annika Sorenstam was eclipsed on the LPGA Tour, but still won the U.S. Women's Open.

Jeff Gross/Getty Images

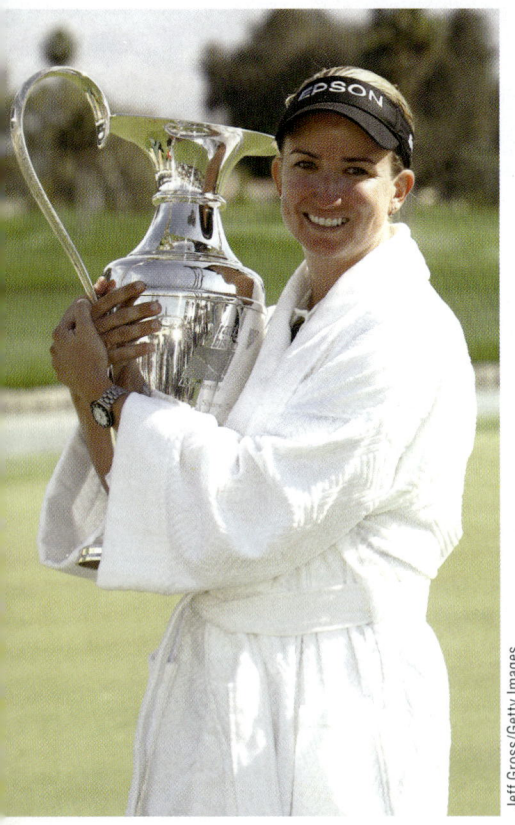

Karrie Webb took the traditional dive after winning at Kraft Nabisco.

Andy Lyons/Getty Images

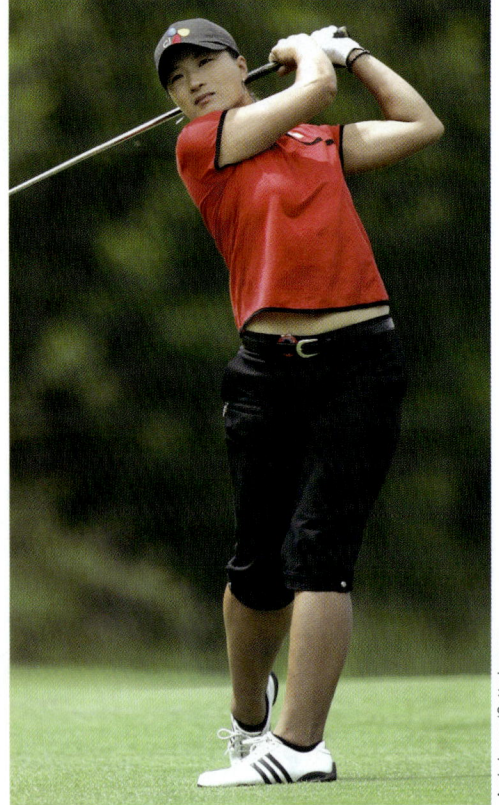

Se Ri Pak signaled her comeback at the McDonalds LPGA.

Michelle Wie shared second at the Evian Masters.

Sherri Steinhauer won a major in Britain.

Julieta Granada's ADT victory was worth $1 million.

Cristie Kerr posted three victories.

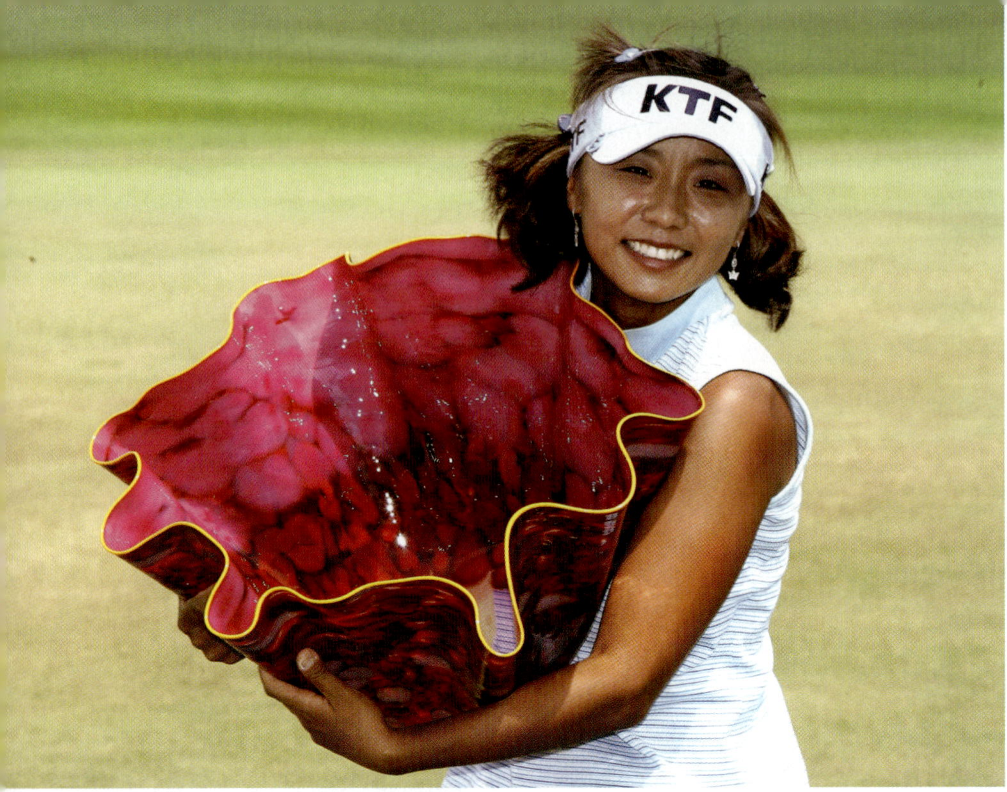

Doug Benc/Getty Images

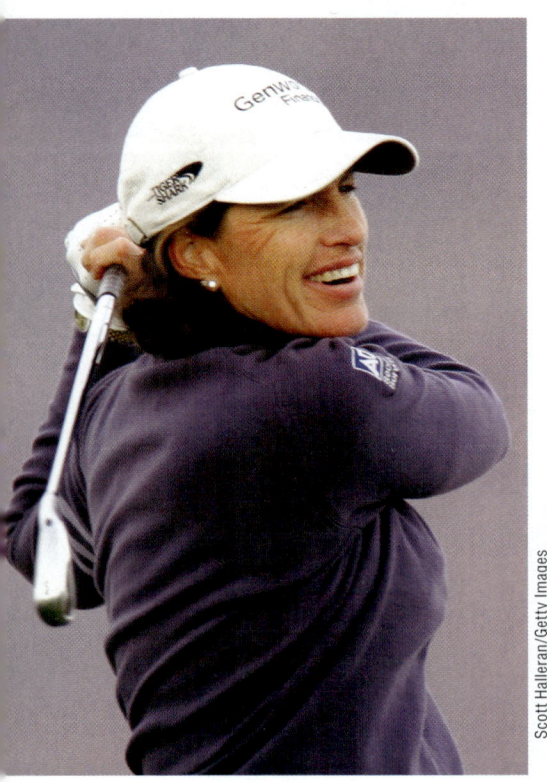

Mi Hyun Kim won two events, including the Ginn Clubs & Resorts Open in Orlando.

Scott Halleran/Getty Images

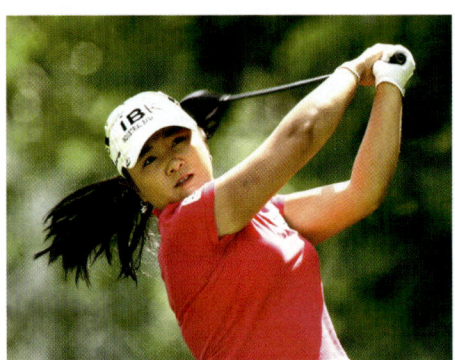

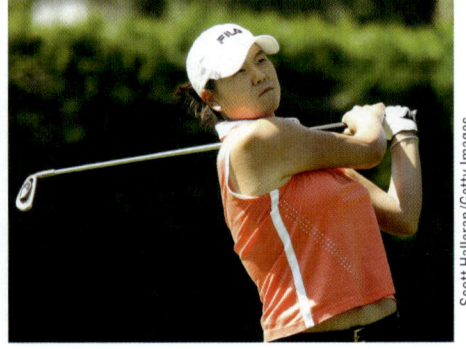

Juli Inkster claimed the Safeway International.

Nick Laham/Getty Images

Jeong Jang won twice.

Scott Halleran/Getty Images

Hee-Won Han had two victories.

Pat Hurst held the Safeway Classic trophy.

Brittany Lincicome won the HSBC Women's World Match Play.

Paula Creamer did not win in 2006.

Seon Hwa Lee was 12th in LPGA money.

Shiho Ohyama had five wins in Japan.

Senior Tours

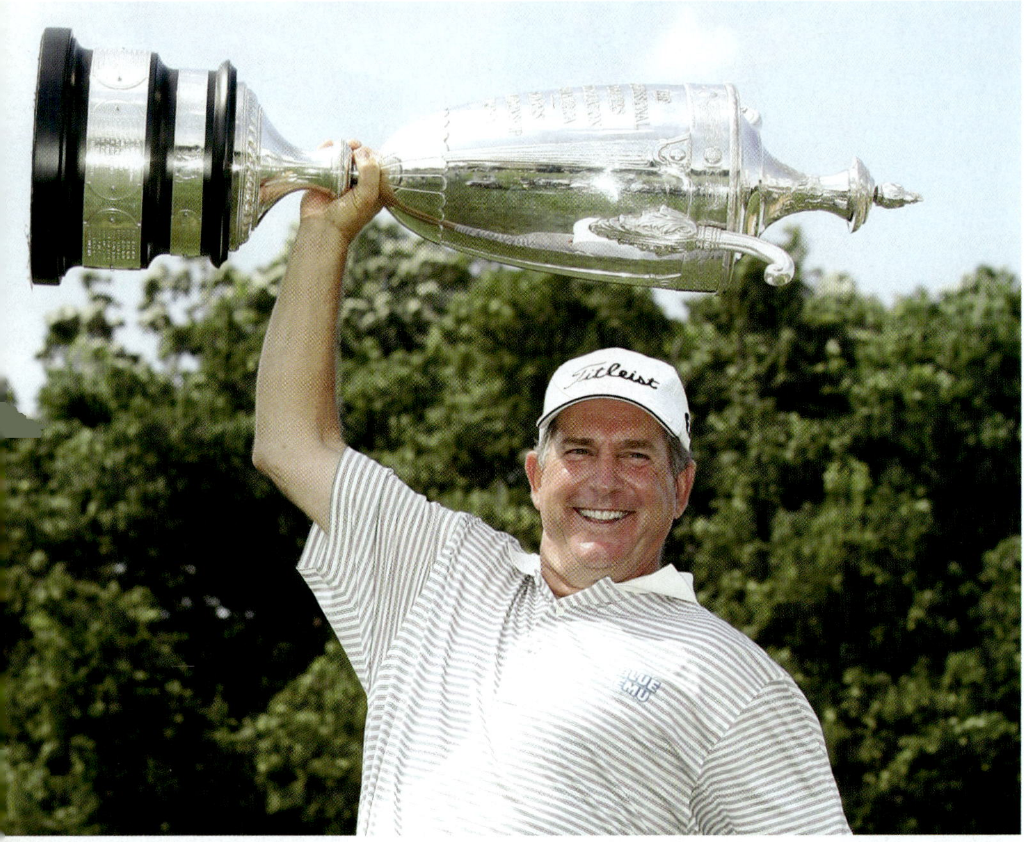

Scott Halleran/Getty Images

The four senior victories by Jay Haas included the Senior PGA Championship.

Phil Inglis/Getty Images

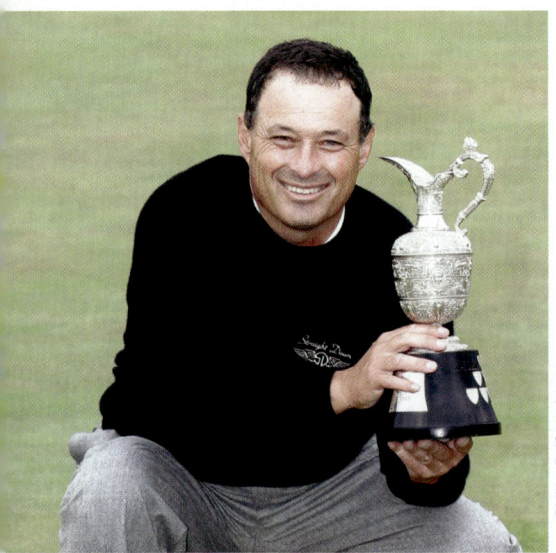

Loren Roberts won the Senior British title.

Streeter Lecka/Getty Images

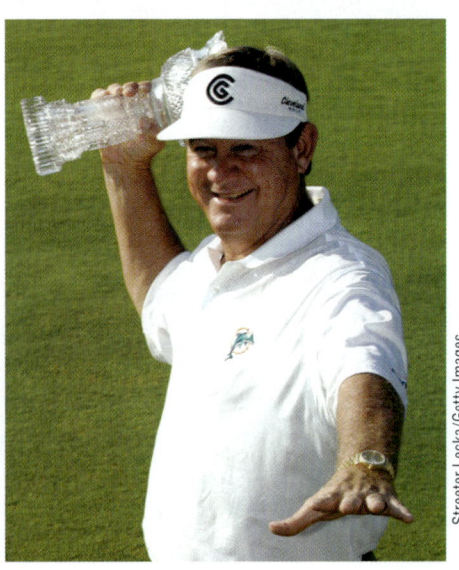

Bobby Wadkins got his major at the Players.

Scott Halleran/Getty Images

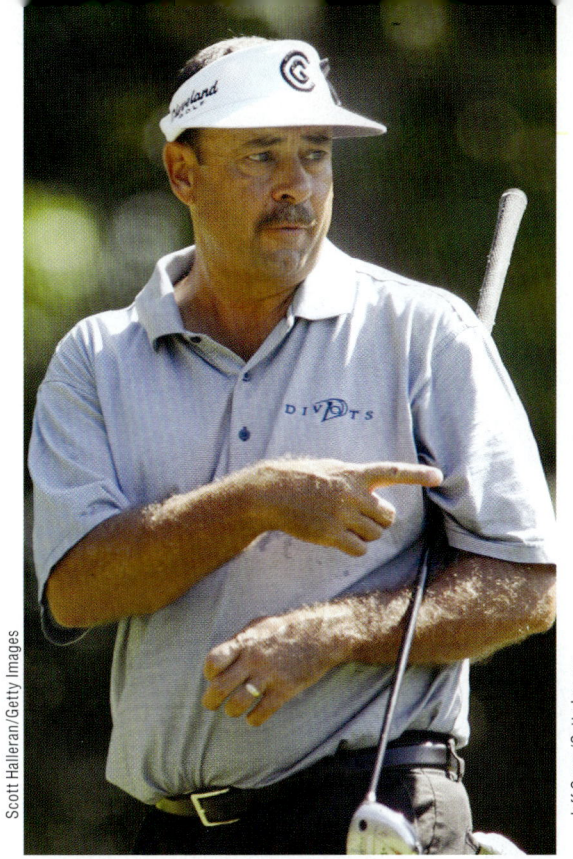

Brad Bryant posted two senior victories.

Jeff Gross/Getty Images

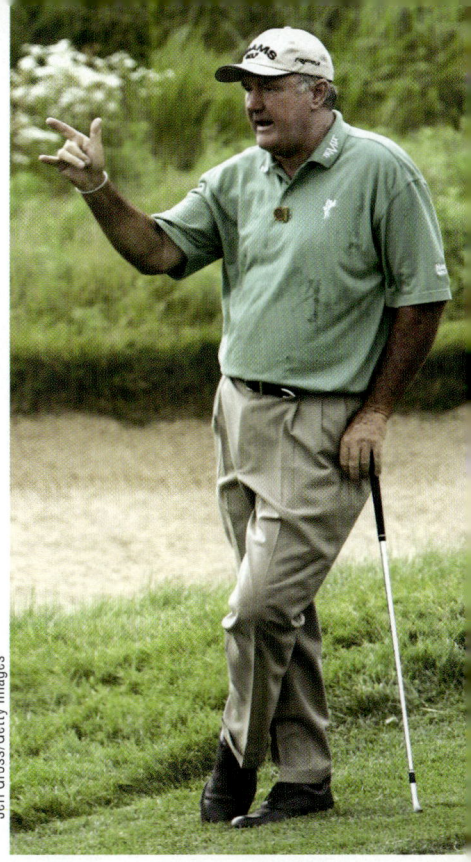

Allen Doyle won the Senior Open.

Jonathan Ferrey/Getty Images

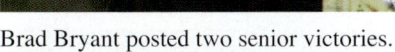

Tom Kite was fourth on the Champions Tour money list and won twice.

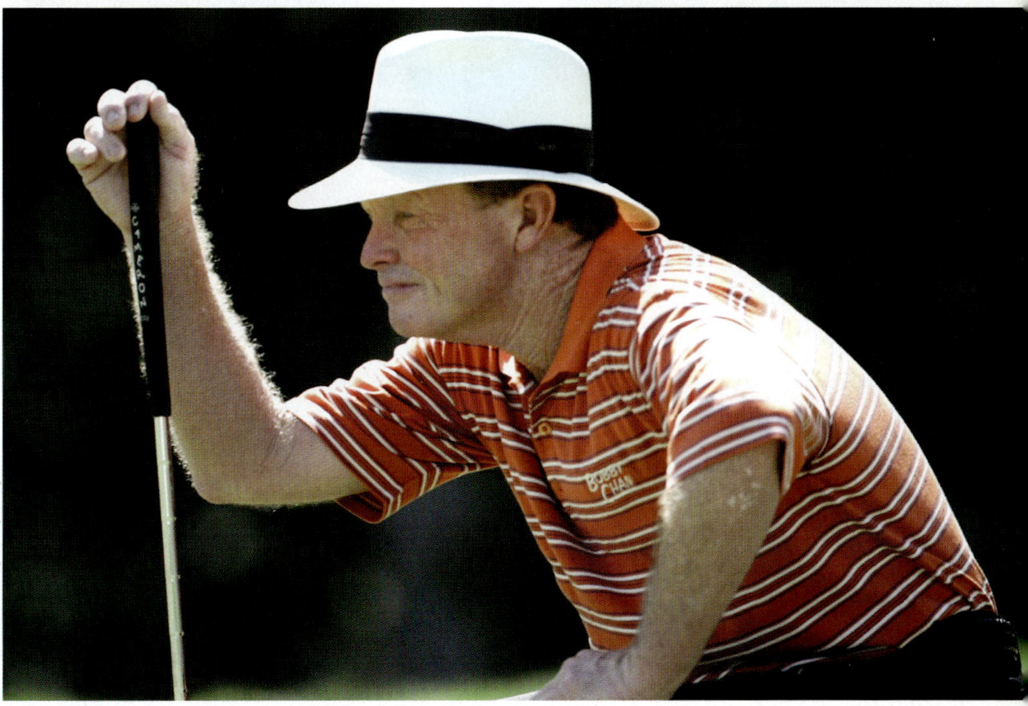

Scott Simpson claimed a Pebble Beach win.

Jim Thorpe took the Charles Schwab event.

Sam Torrance won five times, four in Europe.

Hale Irwin had no senior wins for the first time.

Gil Morgan was the Allianz victor.

	SCORES				TOTAL	MONEY
Oliver Whiteley	71	70	73	73	287	1,606.95
Carlos Del Moral	69	71	68	80	288	1,489.37
Marco Bernardini	71	72	71	75	289	1,305.25
Kalle Brink	73	70	74	72	289	1,305.25
Markus Westerberg	72	71	74	73	290	1,173
Robert Wragg	70	69	76	76	291	1,170

BMW International Open

Golfclub Munchen Nord-Eichenreid, Munich, Germany
Par 36-36–72; 6,963 yards

August 31-September 3
purse, €2,000,000

	SCORES				TOTAL	MONEY
Henrik Stenson	71	68	66	68	273	€333,330
Retief Goosen	73	66	67	67	273	173,710
Padraig Harrington	70	70	64	69	273	173,710

(Stenson defeated Goosen and Harrington on first playoff hole.)

Martin Erlandsson	67	68	69	70	274	92,400
David Howell	67	69	66	72	274	92,400
Luke Donald	68	69	71	67	275	65,000
Colin Montgomerie	70	68	66	71	275	65,000
Markus Brier	71	69	70	67	277	41,200
Robert-Jan Derksen	69	68	70	70	277	41,200
Peter Gustafsson	72	71	64	70	277	41,200
Alexandre Rocha	73	67	70	67	277	41,200
Simon Wakefield	69	69	68	71	277	41,200
Thomas Bjorn	71	69	71	67	278	29,480
Paul Casey	70	67	71	70	278	29,480
Bernhard Langer	70	69	71	68	278	29,480
David Lynn	69	70	67	72	278	29,480
Marcel Siem	68	70	70	70	278	29,480
Marc Cayeux	71	66	72	70	279	23,400
Christian Cevaer	73	69	68	69	279	23,400
Bradley Dredge	68	70	69	72	279	23,400
Ricardo Gonzalez	69	69	70	71	279	23,400
Soren Hansen	70	66	71	72	279	23,400
Garry Houston	67	70	72	70	279	23,400
Anthony Wall	72	71	67	69	279	23,400
Alejandro Canizares	71	65	71	73	280	20,200
Peter Hedblom	68	72	66	74	280	20,200
Soren Kjeldsen	72	71	66	71	280	20,200
Stephen Gallacher	72	68	69	72	281	16,666.67
Ian Garbutt	70	72	69	70	281	16,666.67
Peter Hanson	71	70	67	73	281	16,666.67
Peter O'Malley	71	68	67	75	281	16,666.67
Andres Romero	69	74	69	69	281	16,666.67
Graeme Storm	70	72	70	69	281	16,666.67
Marc Warren	73	68	72	68	281	16,666.67
Lee Westwood	68	71	68	74	281	16,666.67
Fredrik Widmark	69	69	73	70	281	16,666.67
David Drysdale	68	71	73	70	282	13,400
Jose-Filipe Lima	68	72	70	72	282	13,400
Sam Little	71	69	71	71	282	13,400
Damien McGrane	69	68	69	76	282	13,400
Jarrod Moseley	71	71	69	71	282	13,400
David Bransdon	70	69	77	67	283	11,400
Gary Evans	67	73	75	68	283	11,400

	SCORES				TOTAL	MONEY
Niclas Fasth	70	70	72	71	283	11,400
James Kingston	70	71	71	71	283	11,400
Alessandro Tadini	70	70	68	75	283	11,400
David Carter	73	69	70	72	284	9,600
Darren Fichardt	69	72	71	72	284	9,600
Miguel Angel Jimenez	71	70	71	72	284	9,600
Simon Khan	70	69	66	79	284	9,600
Phillip Archer	71	71	73	70	285	7,225
Mattias Eliasson	70	66	78	71	285	7,225
Marcus Fraser	72	71	72	70	285	7,225
Gregory Havret	73	70	72	70	285	7,225
Steven Jeppesen	70	71	67	77	285	7,225
Massimo Scarpa	72	70	72	71	285	7,225
Jean Van de Velde	73	68	72	72	285	7,225
Leif Westerberg	70	73	73	69	285	7,225
Paul Broadhurst	72	71	67	76	286	5,300
Nicolas Colsaerts	70	68	75	73	286	5,300
Richard Finch	74	69	68	75	286	5,300
Matthew Millar	68	70	72	76	286	5,300
Brett Rumford	72	68	76	70	286	5,300
Miles Tunnicliff	70	70	70	76	286	5,300
Joakim Backstrom	73	68	71	75	287	4,500
Raphael Jacquelin	73	70	70	74	287	4,500
Andrew Marshall	72	71	73	72	288	4,200
Scott Drummond	74	69	74	72	289	3,816.67
Johan Edfors	72	69	72	76	289	3,816.67
Joakim Haeggman	70	71	73	75	289	3,816.67
Emanuele Canonica	70	73	71	77	291	2,998.50
Wolfgang Huget	72	70	73	76	291	2,998.50
Daniel Vancsik	71	70	74	77	292	2,994
Jorge Benedetti	71	72	70	82	295	2,991

Omega European Masters

Crans-sur-Sierre Golf Club, Crans Montana, Switzerland
Par 36-35–71; 6,857 yards

September 7-10
purse, €2,000,000

	SCORES				TOTAL	MONEY
Bradley Dredge	68	67	65	67	267	€333,330
Francesco Molinari	68	68	70	69	275	173,710
Marcel Siem	68	67	67	73	275	173,710
Sergio Garcia	68	69	68	71	276	84,933.33
Soren Kjeldsen	70	69	67	70	276	84,933.33
Marc Warren	69	71	69	67	276	84,933.33
Ariel Canete	72	70	69	66	277	46,320
Martin Erlandsson	70	68	70	69	277	46,320
Mikko Ilonen	73	67	71	66	277	46,320
Andrew McLardy	70	65	71	71	277	46,320
Cesar Monasterio	74	69	68	66	277	46,320
Phillip Archer	68	72	72	66	278	30,960
Simon Dyson	68	74	68	68	278	30,960
Johan Edfors	73	67	67	71	278	30,960
Miles Tunnicliff	67	73	69	69	278	30,960
Simon Wakefield	68	75	65	70	278	30,960
Peter Hedblom	71	72	69	67	279	24,200
Jose Manuel Lara	69	72	71	67	279	24,200
Sam Little	67	73	71	68	279	24,200

	SCORES				TOTAL	MONEY
Richard McEvoy	70	72	71	66	279	24,200
Christian L. Nilsson	71	67	69	72	279	24,200
Anthony Wall	66	73	69	71	279	24,200
Oliver Wilson	68	69	67	75	279	24,200
Miguel Carballo	72	70	68	70	280	21,100
Eduardo Romero	70	70	72	68	280	21,100
David Carter	66	74	69	72	281	18,400
Darren Fichardt	71	72	72	66	281	18,400
Rafael Gomez	67	70	75	69	281	18,400
Ricardo Gonzalez	69	71	71	70	281	18,400
Gary Orr	69	73	69	70	281	18,400
Jean-Francois Remesy	72	67	69	73	281	18,400
Robert Rock	72	67	70	72	281	18,400
Joakim Backstrom	72	66	69	75	282	15,250
Paul Broadhurst	71	69	69	73	282	15,250
Andrew Marshall	68	72	71	71	282	15,250
Wade Ormsby	70	73	71	68	282	15,250
Miguel Angel Jimenez	70	69	75	69	283	13,800
Alessandro Tadini	69	71	71	72	283	13,800
Leif Westerberg	71	71	69	72	283	13,800
David Bransdon	68	71	68	77	284	12,400
Robert-Jan Derksen	74	69	72	69	284	12,400
Jarmo Sandelin	71	67	71	75	284	12,400
Carl Suneson	70	70	71	73	284	12,400
Robert Coles	66	72	73	74	285	10,800
Graeme McDowell	71	71	69	74	285	10,800
Matthew Millar	70	69	74	72	285	10,800
Brett Rumford	71	71	64	79	285	10,800
Marc Farry	70	73	68	75	286	9,200
David Higgins	71	72	66	77	286	9,200
Raphael Jacquelin	74	69	72	71	286	9,200
Jamie Spence	72	69	72	73	286	9,200
Peter Lawrie	74	69	72	72	287	8,200
Andrew Butterfield	68	74	73	73	288	7,400
Gary Clark	73	70	72	73	288	7,400
Philip Golding	71	72	75	70	288	7,400
Ignacio Garrido	71	68	75	75	289	6,400
Tom Whitehouse	71	70	72	76	289	6,400
James Kingston	71	71	75	73	290	6,000
Augustin Domingo	68	73	76	74	291	5,600
Gonzalo Fernandez-Castano	70	70	76	75	291	5,600
Michael Hoey	72	71	73	75	291	5,600
Anders Hansen	71	69	76	76	292	5,100
Gregory Havret	72	71	79	70	292	5,100
Francois Delamontagne	71	71	74	77	293	4,800
David Lynn	72	71	74	78	295	4,600

HSBC World Match Play

Wentworth Club, West Course, Virginia Water, Surrey, England September 14-17
Par 434 534 444–35; 345 434 455–37–72; 7,308 yards purse, £2,440,000

FIRST ROUND

Michael Campbell defeated Simon Khan, 3 and 1.
| Campbell | 4 | 3 | 5 | 5 | 4 | 4 | 4 | 4 | 4 | 3 | 4 | 5 | 3 | 3 | 4 | 3 | 5 | 3 |
| Khan | 4 | 3 | 4 | 5 | 3 | 4 | 4 | 5 | 3 | 4 | 4 | 5 | 4 | 4 | 4 | 3 | 5 | 6 |

Campbell leads, 2 up
| Campbell | 5 | 2 | 5 | 5 | 3 | 5 | 4 | 4 | 4 | 3 | 5 | 4 | 4 | 3 | 4 | 4 | 4 | |
| Khan | 5 | 4 | 3 | 5 | 2 | 4 | 5 | 4 | 4 | 3 | 4 | 4 | 4 | 4 | 4 | 4 | 5 | 5 |

Colin Montgomerie defeated David Howell, 1 up.
| Montgomerie | 4 | 3 | 5 | 3 | 3 | 4 | 4 | 4 | 5 | 3 | 4 | 4 | 4 | 2 | 5 | 4 | 4 | 5 |
| Howell | 4 | 3 | 5 | 4 | 4 | 4 | 4 | 4 | 4 | 3 | 4 | 4 | 4 | 3 | 4 | 3 | 6 | 4 |

Match all-square
| Montgomerie | 3 | 2 | 4 | 4 | 2 | 5 | 3 | 4 | 4 | 3 | 4 | 4 | 4 | 3 | 4 | 3 | 5 | 4 |
| Howell | 5 | 3 | 4 | 4 | 3 | 4 | 3 | 4 | 3 | 3 | 3 | 4 | 4 | 3 | 4 | 4 | 4 | 5 |

Paul Casey defeated Retief Goosen, 6 and 4.
| Casey | 4 | 3 | 4 | 4 | 3 | 3 | 4 | 4 | 3 | 3 | 5 | 5 | 4 | 3 | 4 | 3 | 6 | 4 |
| Goosen | 4 | 2 | 3 | 5 | 3 | 3 | 4 | 4 | 3 | 3 | 4 | 6 | 4 | 3 | 4 | 5 | 5 | 5 |

Match all-square
| Casey | 3 | 2 | 4 | 3 | 2 | 3 | 4 | 4 | 3 | 3 | 5 | 4 | 3 | | | | | |
| Goosen | 4 | 2 | 4 | 4 | 3 | 4 | 4 | 4 | 4 | 3 | 4 | 5 | 4 | 4 | | | | |

Mike Weir defeated Adam Scott, 3 and 2.
| Weir | 5 | 2 | 4 | 4 | 2 | 4 | 4 | 3 | 4 | 3 | 3 | 5 | 3 | 3 | 4 | 5 | 5 | 5 |
| Scott | 4 | 3 | 5 | 4 | 3 | 4 | 3 | 3 | 4 | 4 | 4 | 5 | 4 | 4 | 3 | 5 | 4 | |

Weir leads, 2 up
| Weir | 4 | 3 | 3 | 4 | 4 | 5 | 4 | 3 | 3 | 3 | 3 | 5 | 4 | 3 | 4 | 4 | | |
| Scott | 4 | 2 | 4 | 4 | 4 | 5 | 4 | 4 | 4 | 2 | 4 | 4 | 4 | 3 | 4 | 4 | | |

Robert Karlsson defeated Jim Furyk, 4 and 3.
| Karlsson | 4 | 2 | 5 | 5 | 2 | 4 | 4 | 4 | 3 | 2 | 3 | 4 | 4 | 2 | 4 | 3 | 4 | 5 |
| Furyk | 4 | 3 | 4 | 5 | 3 | 4 | 4 | 4 | 4 | 2 | 4 | 5 | 4 | 3 | 3 | 4 | 5 | 4 |

Karlsson leads, 5 up
| Karlsson | 4 | 2 | 4 | 5 | 3 | 5 | 4 | 4 | 3 | 4 | 4 | 4 | 3 | 4 | | | | |
| Furyk | 4 | 2 | 4 | 4 | 3 | 4 | 5 | 4 | 4 | 3 | 4 | 4 | 4 | 3 | 4 | | | |

Angel Cabrera defeated Ernie Els, 2 and 1.
| Cabrera | 4 | 4 | 4 | 4 | 3 | 4 | 4 | 3 | 4 | 2 | 4 | 4 | 4 | 3 | 4 | 3 | 4 | 5 |
| Els | 4 | 3 | 5 | 4 | 2 | 4 | 5 | 3 | 4 | 3 | 4 | 4 | 4 | 3 | 4 | 3 | 6 | 4 |

Cabrera leads, 1 up
| Cabrera | 4 | 3 | 4 | 4 | 3 | 3 | 5 | 3 | 4 | 3 | 4 | 4 | 3 | 3 | 4 | 4 | W | |
| Els | 4 | 3 | 4 | 4 | 3 | 4 | 4 | 3 | 4 | 3 | 4 | 5 | 5 | 3 | 3 | 3 | C | |

Luke Donald defeated Tim Clark, 2 up.
| Donald | 4 | 3 | 4 | 4 | 4 | 4 | 4 | 4 | 4 | 3 | 4 | 4 | 4 | 2 | 3 | 4 | 5 | 4 |
| Clark | 4 | 3 | 4 | 4 | 2 | 4 | 4 | 4 | 4 | 3 | 4 | 4 | 4 | 3 | 4 | 4 | 5 | 4 |

Donald leads, 1 up
| Donald | 4 | 3 | 4 | 4 | 3 | 4 | 3 | 3 | 4 | 3 | 4 | 5 | 4 | 3 | 4 | 4 | 4 | 3 |
| Clark | 4 | 3 | 4 | 4 | 4 | 4 | 5 | 5 | 4 | 2 | 4 | 4 | 3 | 3 | 3 | 4 | 5 | 4 |

Shaun Micheel defeated Tiger Woods, 4 and 3.
| Micheel | 5 | 3 | 3 | 4 | 2 | 4 | 5 | 4 | 4 | 3 | 4 | 4 | 4 | 3 | 4 | 4 | 4 | 6 |
| Woods | 4 | 3 | 4 | 5 | 3 | 5 | 4 | 4 | 5 | 3 | 4 | 4 | 4 | 3 | 5 | 3 | 5 | 4 |

Micheel leads, 3 up
| Micheel | 5 | 3 | 4 | 4 | 3 | 4 | 3 | 4 | 4 | 3 | 4 | 3 | 4 | | | | | |
| Woods | 4 | 2 | 4 | 5 | 3 | 4 | 4 | 4 | 4 | 3 | 4 | 4 | 4 | 3 | 4 | | | |

QUARTER-FINALS

Colin Montgomerie defeated Michael Campbell, 1 up.
Montgomerie	4	3	4	C	4	5	3	3	4	3	4	5	4	2	4	3	5	4
Campbell	3	3	4	3	3	3	4	4	4	3	4	4	4	3	6	4	5	4

Match all-square
Montgomerie	4	3	3	C	2	4	4	3	C	3	4	5	4	3	4	4	5	4
Campbell	4	4	3	3	3	4	4	4	W	4	4	4	3	4	4	4	4	5

Paul Casey defeated Mike Weir, 5 and 3.
Casey	4	3	5	5	3	3	4	4	4	3	4	4	5	3	4	4	5	5
Weir	4	3	5	4	3	5	3	4	5	3	4	4	4	3	5	4	5	5

Match all-square
Casey	4	3	4	5	3	4	3	4	4	3	4	4	3	4
Weir	4	2	5	6	3	4	4	4	4	3	4	5	4	4	5

Robert Karlsson defeated Angel Cabrera, 4 and 3.
Karlsson	5	3	3	5	3	5	4	4	5	2	4	5	4	3	5	4	5	5
Cabrera	5	3	4	5	3	4	4	4	4	3	4	6	4	3	5	4	6	4

Karlsson leads, 1 up
Karlsson	3	3	4	3	3	5	3	4	4	4	5	4	3	3	5
Cabrera	4	3	3	4	4	4	4	3	4	4	4	6	6	3	6

Shaun Micheel defeated Luke Donald, 4 and 2.
Micheel	3	2	4	5	3	3	4	3	4	3	3	4	5	3	4	3	5	4
Donald	4	3	4	4	3	4	4	4	3	4	5	4	3	4	4	4	4	5

Micheel leads, 5 up
Micheel	4	2	4	4	3	4	4	4	3	5	5	4	4	5	3
Donald	5	3	4	4	3	4	4	3	4	3	4	4	4	4

SEMI-FINALS

Shaun Micheel defeated Robert Karlsson, 2 up.
Micheel	5	3	4	6	3	4	4	4	4	3	4	5	3	3	6	3	5	4
Karlsson	4	3	4	3	4	4	3	5	4	3	4	6	4	3	5	4	4	5

Micheel leads, 1 up
Micheel	4	2	4	5	3	3	4	4	6	2	4	4	3	3	4	4	4	4
Karlsson	4	3	4	4	3	3	4	4	5	3	3	5	4	2	5	4	4	5

Paul Casey defeated Colin Montgomerie, 6 and 5.
Casey	4	3	5	4	3	4	4	4	3	2	5	4	4	3	4	4	3	5
Montgomerie	4	4	4	5	3	5	4	5	4	3	4	4	4	3	5	4	5	4

Casey leads, 5 up
Casey	4	3	4	4	4	5	3	4	3	4	3	4
Montgomerie	4	3	5	5	3	4	4	C	3	3	4	4

FINAL

Paul Casey defeated Shaun Micheel, 10 and 8
Casey	4	3	4	4	3	3	3	4	3	5	5	4	4	4	5	4	4
Micheel	4	3	4	5	3	3	4	3	4	3	3	6	4	3	4	6	5	4

Casey leads, 3 up
Casey	4	2	5	4	3	4	3	3	2
Micheel	4	3	5	5	3	5	4	4	3

PRIZE MONEY: Casey £1,000,000; Micheel £400,000; Karlsson, Montgomerie £120,000 each; Cabrera, Campbell, Donald, Weir £80,000 each; Clark, Els, Furyk, Goosen, Howell, Khan, Scott, Woods £60,000 each.

LEGEND: C—conceded hole to opponent; W—won hole by concession without holing out; X—no total score.

Banco Madrid Valle Romano Open de Madrid Masters

La Moraleja II, Madrid, Spain
Par 36-36–72; 7,018 yards

September 14-17
purse, €1,000,000

		SCORES			TOTAL	MONEY
Ian Poulter	67	66	64	69	266	€166,660
Ignacio Garrido	68	66	71	66	271	111,110
Phillip Price	70	67	68	67	272	62,600
Padraig Harrington	67	65	72	69	273	46,200
Christian L. Nilsson	68	66	68	71	273	46,200
Ricardo Gonzalez	67	67	67	73	274	32,500
Raphael Jacquelin	68	68	67	71	274	32,500
David Griffiths	70	69	67	69	275	22,466.67
Jose Maria Olazabal	71	70	67	67	275	22,466.67
Steve Webster	71	68	67	69	275	22,466.67
Joakim Backstrom	67	69	67	73	276	16,340
Darren Fichardt	66	72	70	68	276	16,340
Jean-Francois Lucquin	65	69	72	70	276	16,340
Gary Orr	67	65	70	74	276	16,340
Jean-Francois Remesy	72	65	70	69	276	16,340
Gregory Bourdy	69	70	69	70	278	12,750
David Carter	70	71	65	72	278	12,750
Gary Evans	69	70	65	74	278	12,750
*Jose Luis Gomez	69	70	68	71	278	
Alexandre Rocha	71	67	68	72	278	12,750
Jarmo Sandelin	70	72	68	68	278	12,750
Miles Tunnicliff	69	70	72	67	278	12,750
Niclas Fasth	70	66	72	71	279	10,850
Ian Garbutt	72	68	68	71	279	10,850
David Higgins	70	68	73	68	279	10,850
Damien McGrane	68	68	74	69	279	10,850
Gonzalo Fernandez-Castano	70	66	75	69	280	9,650
Mark Foster	71	68	73	68	280	9,650
Sam Little	72	71	68	69	280	9,650
Simon Wakefield	74	67	69	70	280	9,650
Warren Abery	72	70	69	70	281	7,925
Thomas Bjorn	69	69	72	71	281	7,925
Andrew Butterfield	70	71	69	71	281	7,925
Darren Clarke	68	72	69	72	281	7,925
Richard Finch	69	69	70	73	281	7,925
Ross Fisher	70	70	72	69	281	7,925
Stephen Gallacher	71	72	66	72	281	7,925
Jose Manuel Lara	73	69	72	67	281	7,925
Phillip Archer	72	70	72	68	282	5,800
Gary Clark	70	71	72	69	282	5,800
Gary Emerson	69	68	76	69	282	5,800
Peter Gustafsson	72	71	64	75	282	5,800
Garry Houston	70	68	74	70	282	5,800
Peter Lawrie	74	69	69	70	282	5,800
Jose-Filipe Lima	71	69	69	73	282	5,800
Jose Rivero	71	68	71	72	282	5,800
Robert Rock	71	70	72	69	282	5,800
Anders Sjostrand	69	69	72	72	282	5,800
Johan Skold	71	71	69	71	282	5,800
Leif Westerberg	72	71	71	68	282	5,800
Felipe Aguilar	73	67	72	71	283	4,200
Benn Barham	70	71	70	72	283	4,200
Peter Hedblom	71	70	71	71	283	4,200
Maarten Lafeber	73	68	70	72	283	4,200

	SCORES				TOTAL	MONEY
Philip Golding	71	72	71	70	284	3,700
John Bickerton	72	67	72	74	285	2,933.33
Stephen Browne	71	72	71	71	285	2,933.33
Mattias Eliasson	69	72	75	69	285	2,933.33
Alfredo Garcia-Heredia	70	73	70	72	285	2,933.33
Soren Hansen	71	69	74	71	285	2,933.33
Mikko Ilonen	71	70	68	76	285	2,933.33
Andrew McLardy	74	69	73	69	285	2,933.33
Steven O'Hara	71	71	70	73	285	2,933.33
Iain Pyman	68	73	75	69	285	2,933.33
Gabriel Canizares	70	69	71	76	286	2,250
Neil Cheetham	72	70	73	71	286	2,250
Cesar Monasterio	73	69	75	69	286	2,250
Francis Valera	71	72	74	69	286	2,250
Peter Fowler	70	69	76	72	287	2,000
Carlos De Corral	74	68	74	72	288	1,865
Alessandro Tadini	70	72	72	74	288	1,865
Miguel Angel Martin	66	74	77	72	289	1,495.50
Edoardo Molinari	69	73	74	73	289	1,495.50
Jamie Spence	69	72	73	75	289	1,495.50
Benoit Teilleria	73	70	74	72	289	1,495.50
David Bransdon	69	74	77	70	290	1,488
Oliver Wilson	69	70	76	77	292	1,485

The Ryder Cup

The K Club, Palmer Course, Straffan, Co. Kildare, Ireland　　　　　September 22-24
Par 443 544 434–35, 543 434 545–37–72; 7,335 yards

FIRST DAY
Morning Fourballs

Tiger Woods and Jim Furyk (USA) defeated Padraig Harrington and Colin Montgomerie (Europe), 1 up.

Harrington	4				4	4		3	4	5		4			4		
Montgomerie		4	3	4			4				4	3		2	4		4 4
Woods	5		3			4	5	2			3	2		3	4	5	
Furyk	3	4		4	5			3	5				4				4 4

Paul Casey and Robert Karlsson (Europe) halved with Stewart Cink and J.J. Henry (USA).

Casey	4	4		3	4		5	3		5				3	4	4	4
Karlsson			2			4	4		3	4	4	3	4				
Cink	4			4	4	4				4	4			2		4	
Henry	4	3	3				5	3				3	2	4		3 5	4

Sergio Garcia and Jose Maria Olazabal (Europe) defeated David Toms and Brett Wetterich (USA), 3 and 2.

Garcia	3		3	4		3	4	3			3	3		3	3	4
Olazabal		4	3			4			3	5		4				
Toms			3	3	4	4	3	4		4		3	3	5	3	4 4
Wetterich	4								3		4					

Darren Clarke and Lee Westwood (Europe) defeated Phil Mickelson and Chris DiMarco (USA), 1 up.

Clarke	3	4			4			3			4	3	3		4	4	4
Westwood	4		3	5		4	4		4	4				3	4		
Mickelson	4	4	3	4	4	4				4			3		3	4 5	
DiMarco							4	3		5	3		3			4	4

TOTAL: Europe 2½, United States 1½

Afternoon Foursomes

Padraig Harrington and Paul McGinley (Europe) halved with Chad Campbell and Zach Johnson (USA).

Harrington/McGinley	5	4	2	5	4	4	4	3	5	5	4	3	4	4	4	5	3	5
Campbell/Johnson	3	4	3	5	4	5	4	3	3	5	5	3	4	4	5	4	3	4

David Howell and Henrik Stenson (Europe) halved with Stewart Cink and David Toms (USA).

Howell/Stenson	4	4	2	4	4	4	4	3	4	4	4	3	4	3	5	4	4	5
Cink/Toms	4	3	3	5	3	4	4	3	4	5	4	3	4	3	3	4	4	5

Lee Westwood and Colin Montgomerie (Europe) halved with Phil Mickelson and Chris DiMarco (USA).

Westwood/Montgomerie	4	3	3	4	5	5	3	3	4	5	4	3	3	4	4	5	4	4
Mickelson/DiMarco	3	4	3	5	4	4	4	3	4	5	4	3	5	3	4	4	4	5

Luke Donald and Sergio Garcia (Europe) defeated Tiger Woods and Jim Furyk (USA), 2 up.

Donald/Garcia	4	4	4	4	3	5	4	3	4	5	5	2	4	3	4	4	3	5
Woods/Furyk	6	4	3	5	4	4	4	3	4	6	4	3	3	2	4	4	4	6

TOTAL: Europe 5, United States 3

SECOND DAY
Morning Fourballs

Paul Casey and Robert Karlsson (Europe) halved with Stewart Cink and J.J. Henry (USA).

Casey			3	4		4	2				3		3		4	4	4	
Karlsson	4	3			4	5			4	5	4		4		4			
Cink	4		3	5	4			3		4	4	3		3	4			
Henry		4				4	4		4				4			3	3	5

Sergio Garcia and Jose Maria Olazabal (Europe) defeated Phil Mickelson and Chris DiMarco (USA), 3 and 2.

Garcia	4	3	3					3					3	4	4	
Olazabal				4	4	4	2		4	4	3	4				
Mickelson				5	4	4		3	4	5		3	4	2		
DiMarco	4	4	2				4				4				4	4

Darren Clarke and Lee Westwood (Europe) defeated Tiger Woods and Jim Furyk (USA), 3 and 2.

Clarke		4	3	4	3	4	4				3	3	4	4	4
Westwood	3							3	4	5			2		
Woods			3	5		4				5	4	3	4	3	
Furyk	3	4			4		4	3	4					3	4

Scott Verplank and Zach Johnson (USA) defeated Henrik Stenson and Padraig Harrington (Europe), 2 and 1.

Stenson	4	3	3		4		4	4	5	4	3	4				
Harrington				4	3	4							3	3	4	4
Verplank			3			5	4	3	4				3			
Johnson	3	3		4	3					4	4	3	4		3	5	3

TOTAL: Europe 7½, United States 4½

Afternoon Foursomes

Sergio Garcia and Luke Donald (Europe) defeated Phil Mickelson and David Toms (USA), 2 and 1.

Garcia/Donald	4	4	3	4	4	5	4	2	3	5	4	3	4	4	4	4
Mickelson/Toms	4	4	3	4	4	5	6	2	4	5	4	2	3	4	5	5	4

Colin Montgomerie and Lee Westwood (Europe) halved with Chad Campbell and Vaughn Taylor (USA).

Montgomerie/Westwood	4	3	3	5	4	4	5	3	3	6	4	2	4	3	4	5	5	4
Campbell/Taylor	4	4	3	4	4	6	4	3	3	5	4	3	4	3	5	5	4	4

Paul Casey and David Howell (Europe) defeated Stewart Cink and Zach Johnson (USA), 5 and 4.

Casey/Howell	5	3	2	4	4	4	3	3	4	5	4	2	4	1
Cink/Johnson	5	4	3	5	5	4	4	3	4	5	4	4	4	1

Jim Furyk and Tiger Woods (USA) defeated Padraig Harrington and Paul McGinley (Europe), 3 and 2.

Harrington/McGinley	4	4	2	5	6	4	4	2	5	5	3	2	5	3	4	5
Furyk/Woods	4	4	2	4	4	4	3	3	4	5	3	3	4	3	3	5

TOTAL: Europe 10, United States 6

THIRD DAY
Singles

Colin Montgomerie (Europe) defeated David Toms (USA), 1 up.

Montgomerie	4	4	2	4	6	4	4	3	4	5	4	3	4	2	4	5	4	4
Toms	4	4	3	6	5	4	4	3	4	5	4	3	4	3	4	5	3	4

Stewart Cink (USA) defeated Sergio Garcia (Europe), 4 and 3.

Garcia	4	4	2	5	4	5	5	3	4	5	3	3	3	3	3
Cink	3	3	3	4	3	4	4	4	4	5	4	2	3	3	3

Paul Casey (Europe) defeated Jim Furyk (USA), 2 and 1.

Casey	3	4	2	6	3	4	3	3	4	4	4	3	4	2	4	4	3
Furyk	4	4	3	5	4	4	4	4	4	4	3	4	2	4	3	3

Tiger Woods (USA) defeated Robert Karlsson (Europe), 3 and 2.

Karlsson	3	4	3	5	4	4	4	3	4	4	3	3	4	3	5	5
Woods	4	3	3	4	3	5	4	3	3	6	3	3	4	3	4	4

Luke Donald (Europe) defeated Chad Campbell (USA), 2 and 1.

Donald	4	4	3	5	4	4	4	3	4	5	3	3	3	3	4	5	4
Campbell	4	4	3	5	4	4	4	3	4	5	5	5	6	3	3	4	5

Paul McGinley (Europe) halved with J.J. Henry (USA).

McGinley	4	4	2	5	5	4	4	3	5	5	5	3	4	3	4	5	4	4
Henry	4	5	3	5	3	5	4	3	4	4	3	3	5	3	4	5	4	4

Darren Clarke (Europe) defeated Zach Johnson (USA), 3 and 2.

Clarke	4	4	3	4	4	4	4	3	4	4	4	2	5	3	4	5
Johnson	4	4	3	6	3	5	X	3	4	5	4	3	4	3	4	5

Henrik Stenson (Europe) defeated Vaughn Taylor (USA), 4 and 3.

Stenson	4	4	3	4	4	3	3	3	4	5	4	3	4	3	4
Taylor	3	4	3	4	4	6	4	3	5	5	4	4	4	4	4

David Howell (Europe) defeated Brett Wetterich (USA), 5 and 4.
| Howell | 4 | 4 | 3 | 4 | 4 | 4 | 4 | 3 | 4 | 5 | 3 | 2 | 3 | 2 |
| Wetterich | 4 | 4 | 3 | 5 | 4 | 4 | 6 | 3 | 3 | 5 | 4 | 3 | 4 | 3 |

Jose Maria Olazabal (Europe) defeated Phil Mickelson (USA), 2 and 1.
| Olazabal | 4 | 4 | 2 | 4 | 4 | 4 | 4 | 2 | 4 | 5 | 4 | 2 | 4 | 3 | 4 | 5 | 4 |
| Mickelson | 4 | 4 | 3 | 4 | 3 | 6 | 4 | 2 | 4 | 5 | 4 | X | 4 | 3 | 4 | 5 | 4 |

Lee Westwood (Europe) defeated Chris DiMarco (USA), 2 up.
| Westwood | 3 | 4 | 2 | 4 | 4 | 3 | 3 | 3 | 5 | 5 | 4 | 4 | 5 | 3 | 4 | 5 | 4 | W |
| DiMarco | 4 | 5 | 2 | 6 | 4 | 4 | 4 | 3 | 5 | 5 | 4 | 2 | 4 | 3 | 4 | 4 | 3 | X |

Scott Verplank (USA) defeated Padraig Harrington (Europe), 4 and 3.
| Verplank | 4 | 3 | 3 | 5 | 3 | 4 | 4 | 3 | 4 | 5 | 4 | 4 | 4 | 2 | 4 |
| Harrington | 3 | 4 | 2 | 5 | 3 | 4 | 3 | 3 | 4 | 5 | 4 | 3 | 4 | 1 | 4 |

TOTAL: Europe 18½, United States 9½

WGC - American Express Championship

The Grove, Chandlers Cross, Hertfordshire, England September 28-October 1
Par 35-36–71; 7,152 yards purse, US$7,500,000

	SCORES				TOTAL	MONEY
Tiger Woods	63	64	67	67	261	$1,300,000
Ian Poulter	64	71	68	66	269	610,000
Adam Scott	67	68	65	69	269	610,000
Jim Furyk	67	65	69	69	270	345,000
Ernie Els	65	70	69	67	271	290,000
Stuart Appleby	71	66	70	66	273	216,666.67
Brett Wetterich	70	66	69	68	273	216,666.67
Luke Donald	68	70	67	68	273	216,666.66
Brett Quigley	70	64	67	73	274	150,000
Trevor Immelman	68	68	68	70	274	150,000
Thongchai Jaidee	71	67	71	65	274	150,000
Arron Oberholser	69	72	66	68	275	120,000
Stewart Cink	65	67	70	74	276	98,375
David Howell	66	66	71	73	276	98,375
Henrik Stenson	68	67	68	73	276	98,375
Lucas Glover	69	68	68	71	276	98,375
Jose Maria Olazabal	70	67	71	69	277	85,000
Padraig Harrington	64	69	71	73	277	85,000
Jyoti Randhawa	66	71	71	69	277	85,000
Carl Pettersson	69	70	67	71	277	85,000
Robert Karlsson	67	76	72	64	279	80,000
Chris DiMarco	69	70	70	71	280	75,000
Dean Wilson	71	70	70	69	280	75,000
Michael Campbell	69	71	69	71	280	75,000
Johan Edfors	70	68	71	71	280	75,000
Bart Bryant	70	74	67	70	281	66,666.67
Robert Allenby	69	73	69	70	281	66,666.66
Darren Clarke	68	71	72	70	281	66,666.67
Angel Cabrera	71	70	67	73	281	66,666.66
Nick O'Hern	67	69	75	70	281	66,666.67
Tim Clark	68	70	73	70	281	66,666.67
Chad Campbell	67	70	73	72	282	61,000
Lee Westwood	71	66	73	72	282	61,000
Sergio Garcia	69	73	71	69	282	61,000

	SCORES				TOTAL	MONEY
K.J. Choi	72	66	73	71	282	61,000
Louis Oosthuizen	71	70	72	69	282	61,000
J.J. Henry	70	70	70	73	283	58,000
Scott Verplank	70	68	73	73	284	56,000
Rod Pampling	70	69	72	73	284	56,000
Simon Dyson	67	69	75	73	284	56,000
Colin Montgomerie	72	67	69	77	285	52,500
Thomas Bjorn	70	71	73	71	285	52,500
Rory Sabbatini	73	67	73	72	285	52,500
Charl Schwartzel	73	69	70	73	285	52,500
Retief Goosen	71	70	75	71	287	49,000
John Bickerton	72	73	75	67	287	49,000
Zach Johnson	70	71	73	73	287	49,000
Tom Pernice, Jr.	69	70	71	78	288	46,500
Tim Herron	73	69	71	75	288	46,500
Paul Broadhurst	74	72	70	73	289	44,000
Anthony Wall	71	76	68	74	289	44,000
Tetsuji Hiratsuka	73	69	71	76	289	44,000
David Toms	73	75	69	73	290	42,000
Thaworn Wiratchant	71	71	75	74	291	40,500
Sean O'Hair	70	75	71	75	291	40,500
Vijay Singh	73	75	72	72	292	38,500
Paul Casey	74	75	72	71	292	38,500
Craig Parry	74	74	70	75	293	37,000
Toru Taniguchi	73	73	76	75	297	35,500
Gregory Bourdy	74	77	71	75	297	35,500

Alfred Dunhill Links Championship

St. Andrews Old Course: Par 36-36–72; 7,279 yards
Carnoustie Championship Course: Par 36-35–71; 7,316 yards
Kingsbarns Golf Links: Par 36-36–72; 7,099 yards
St. Andrews, Scotland

October 5-8
purse, €3,783,362

	SCORES				TOTAL	MONEY
Padraig Harrington	66	69	68	68	271	€630,566.36
Bradley Dredge	64	67	71	74	276	282,128.53
Edward Loar	70	66	70	70	276	282,128.53
Anthony Wall	70	70	69	67	276	282,128.53
Ernie Els	69	67	71	70	277	160,416.08
Paul Casey	63	74	73	68	278	122,960.44
Peter Hanson	68	68	75	67	278	122,960.44
Paul Broadhurst	70	69	72	68	279	72,641.24
Simon Dyson	66	68	75	70	279	72,641.24
Johan Edfors	64	70	76	69	279	72,641.24
James Kingston	71	65	74	69	279	72,641.24
Soren Kjeldsen	69	68	73	69	279	72,641.24
Henrik Stenson	68	70	71	70	279	72,641.24
Lee Westwood	68	75	71	65	279	72,641.24
Joakim Backstrom	71	70	67	72	280	49,292.27
Robert Karlsson	68	69	71	72	280	49,292.27
Simon Khan	68	70	71	71	280	49,292.27
Paul Lawrie	71	65	72	72	280	49,292.27
Damien McGrane	70	67	74	69	280	49,292.27
Mark Roe	67	70	76	67	280	49,292.27
Richard Sterne	68	71	74	67	280	49,292.27
Phillip Archer	72	69	72	68	281	40,482.36

	SCORES				TOTAL	MONEY
Raphael Jacquelin	67	70	74	70	281	40,482.36
Ian Poulter	75	65	74	67	281	40,482.36
Charl Schwartzel	67	67	77	70	281	40,482.36
Vijay Singh	65	70	72	74	281	40,482.36
Thomas Bjorn	70	71	71	70	282	34,807.26
Nick Dougherty	66	72	71	73	282	34,807.26
Gary Evans	65	71	76	70	282	34,807.26
Hennie Otto	69	69	71	73	282	34,807.26
David Park	68	71	72	71	282	34,807.26
Peter Baker	70	71	70	72	283	28,943
Niclas Fasth	69	75	70	69	283	28,943
Ignacio Garrido	68	70	76	69	283	28,943
Joakim Haeggman	73	67	72	71	283	28,943
Graeme Storm	72	69	72	70	283	28,943
Oliver Wilson	72	72	69	70	283	28,943
Angel Cabrera	72	68	73	71	284	24,213.75
Alejandro Canizares	69	69	76	70	284	24,213.75
Ricardo Gonzalez	70	69	75	70	284	24,213.75
Thongchai Jaidee	71	70	72	71	284	24,213.75
Miguel Angel Jimenez	67	69	75	73	284	24,213.75
Jose Manuel Lara	69	73	71	71	284	24,213.75
Robert Coles	71	67	76	71	285	19,295.33
Anders Hansen	65	72	74	74	285	19,295.33
Mikko Ilonen	66	69	76	74	285	19,295.33
Maarten Lafeber	71	71	71	72	285	19,295.33
Barry Lane	68	71	73	73	285	19,295.33
Jose Maria Olazabal	70	68	75	72	285	19,295.33
Phillip Price	71	71	70	73	285	19,295.33
David Carter	71	70	72	73	286	15,133.59
Gregory Havret	72	69	73	72	286	15,133.59
Jonathan Lomas	69	76	68	73	286	15,133.59
David Lynn	67	71	76	72	286	15,133.59
Marcus Both	73	70	71	73	287	12,863.55
Scott Drummond	66	69	76	76	287	12,863.55
Mattias Eliasson	70	70	74	74	288	11,539.36
Anton Haig	71	70	73	74	288	11,539.36
Mikael Lundberg	71	72	71	75	289	10,971.85
Tjaart van der Walt	70	69	72	78	289	10,971.85

Mallorca Classic

Pula Golf Club, Mallorca, Spain
Par 35-35–70; 6,850 yards

October 19-22
purse, €1,750,000

	SCORES				TOTAL	MONEY
Niclas Fasth	66	71	70	68	275	€291,660
Sergio Garcia	70	70	70	68	278	194,440
Jose Manuel Lara	69	72	71	67	279	98,525
Marc Warren	70	68	71	70	279	98,525
Peter O'Malley	70	70	68	72	280	74,200
Soren Kjeldsen	72	68	71	70	281	56,875
Paul McGinley	75	70	69	67	281	56,875
Benn Barham	70	71	72	69	282	36,050
Robert-Jan Derksen	76	69	67	70	282	36,050
Ricardo Gonzalez	68	74	72	68	282	36,050
Gregory Havret	75	70	66	71	282	36,050
Robert Karlsson	71	71	70	70	282	36,050

	SCORES				TOTAL	MONEY
Phillip Archer	68	75	68	72	283	26,337.50
Peter Hanson	71	70	68	74	283	26,337.50
Gary Murphy	66	71	70	76	283	26,337.50
Jeev Milkha Singh	71	75	69	68	283	26,337.50
Peter Fowler	69	78	67	70	284	22,225
Steven Jeppesen	72	69	69	74	284	22,225
Carlos Rodiles	75	73	64	72	284	22,225
Jamie Spence	78	69	66	71	284	22,225
Emanuele Canonica	71	73	72	69	285	18,987.50
Maarten Lafeber	72	76	68	69	285	18,987.50
Andrew McLardy	66	76	73	70	285	18,987.50
Carl Suneson	74	73	70	68	285	18,987.50
Alessandro Tadini	74	70	70	71	285	18,987.50
Miles Tunnicliff	73	71	75	66	285	18,987.50
Joakim Backstrom	74	70	69	73	286	16,100
Markus Brier	75	70	69	72	286	16,100
David Carter	71	73	69	73	286	16,100
Martin Erlandsson	73	73	72	68	286	16,100
David Park	69	76	70	71	286	16,100
Diego Borrego	71	68	75	73	287	13,387.50
Gary Evans	70	76	69	72	287	13,387.50
Simon Khan	70	74	69	74	287	13,387.50
Andrew Marshall	70	70	72	75	287	13,387.50
Francesco Molinari	73	73	68	73	287	13,387.50
Francis Valera	72	75	71	69	287	13,387.50
Robert Coles	75	69	73	71	288	11,025
Alastair Forsyth	73	73	70	72	288	11,025
Sam Little	72	73	70	73	288	11,025
Jonathan Lomas	68	73	74	73	288	11,025
Matthew Millar	73	75	68	72	288	11,025
Gary Orr	71	72	72	73	288	11,025
Brett Rumford	73	74	71	70	288	11,025
Richard Bland	73	73	68	75	289	9,100
David Bransdon	79	68	70	72	289	9,100
Marc Cayeux	75	70	70	74	289	9,100
Jarmo Sandelin	70	74	73	72	289	9,100
Stephen Gallacher	71	74	72	73	290	7,525
Alfredo Garcia-Heredia	72	68	77	73	290	7,525
Christian L. Nilsson	69	75	71	75	290	7,525
Jean Van de Velde	75	73	72	70	290	7,525
Oliver Wilson	74	71	74	71	290	7,525
Thomas Bjorn	73	73	69	76	291	5,366.67
Andrew Butterfield	70	73	69	79	291	5,366.67
Mark Foster	71	71	73	76	291	5,366.67
Jose-Filipe Lima	75	71	73	72	291	5,366.67
Henrik Nystrom	74	74	71	72	291	5,366.67
Wade Ormsby	75	73	71	72	291	5,366.67
Terry Price	71	76	70	74	291	5,366.67
Benoit Teilleria	76	72	73	70	291	5,366.67
Tom Whitehouse	68	78	71	74	291	5,366.67
Michael Hoey	71	74	72	75	292	4,375
Ian Garbutt	77	71	74	71	293	4,112.50
Andrew Oldcorn	73	75	70	75	293	4,112.50
Jamie Donaldson	72	74	72	76	294	3,675
Edoardo Molinari	72	75	71	76	294	3,675
Tomas Jesus Munoz	71	76	79	68	294	3,675
Carlos De Corral	74	73	74	74	295	3,050
Barry Lane	72	70	78	75	295	3,050
Jean-Francois Lucquin	76	72	74	73	295	3,050
Carlos Del Moral	75	73	73	75	296	2,620.50

	SCORES				TOTAL	MONEY
Graeme Storm	71	73	75	77	296	2,620.50
David Dixon	75	73	73	81	302	2,614.50
Richard Finch	72	76	75	79	302	2,614.50

Volvo Masters

Club de Golf Valderrama, Sotegrande, Spain
Par 35-36–71; 6,952 yards

October 26-29
purse, €3,912,700

	SCORES				TOTAL	MONEY
Jeev Milkha Singh	71	71	68	72	282	€666,660
Luke Donald	69	71	74	69	283	298,280
Sergio Garcia	71	70	70	72	283	298,280
Padraig Harrington	73	69	72	69	283	298,280
Niclas Fasth	67	75	71	71	284	154,800
David Howell	70	73	70	71	284	154,800
Jose Maria Olazabal	74	71	71	69	285	110,000
Lee Westwood	69	70	72	74	285	110,000
Phillip Archer	69	71	77	69	286	68,122.22
Raphael Jacquelin	71	73	69	73	286	68,122.22
Jose Manuel Lara	66	76	77	67	286	68,122.22
David Lynn	69	71	72	74	286	68,122.22
Peter O'Malley	70	78	66	72	286	68,122.22
Gary Orr	72	74	72	68	286	68,122.22
Ian Poulter	70	75	70	71	286	68,122.22
Marcel Siem	69	72	72	73	286	68,122.22
Henrik Stenson	70	68	73	75	286	68,122.22
Anders Hansen	72	72	72	71	287	51,533.33
Soren Kjeldsen	73	75	68	71	287	51,533.33
Paul McGinley	73	72	70	72	287	51,533.33
John Bickerton	71	71	70	76	288	44,842.86
Paul Casey	76	72	71	69	288	44,842.86
Johan Edfors	68	74	69	77	288	44,842.86
Gonzalo Fernandez-Castano	75	75	69	69	288	44,842.86
Soren Hansen	71	72	73	72	288	44,842.86
Miguel Angel Jimenez	68	74	72	74	288	44,842.86
Robert Karlsson	69	74	70	75	288	44,842.86
Paul Broadhurst	73	74	71	71	289	38,100
Angel Cabrera	71	71	72	75	289	38,100
Richard Green	67	73	74	75	289	38,100
Colin Montgomerie	77	73	69	70	289	38,100
Thongchai Jaidee	79	71	71	69	290	34,500
Graeme McDowell	67	78	74	71	290	34,500
Jarmo Sandelin	70	73	72	75	290	34,500
Simon Dyson	73	69	74	75	291	31,800
Kenneth Ferrie	77	69	73	72	291	31,800
Anthony Wall	71	77	69	74	291	31,800
Thomas Bjorn	78	72	72	70	292	29,100
Simon Khan	74	70	72	76	292	29,100
Simon Wakefield	69	76	75	72	292	29,100
Charl Schwartzel	74	73	75	72	294	26,850
Marc Warren	74	74	71	75	294	26,850
Ricardo Gonzalez	71	78	74	72	295	25,050
Peter Hanson	74	75	72	74	295	25,050
Markus Brier	73	74	73	76	296	22,800
Nick Dougherty	77	76	71	72	296	22,800
Graeme Storm	72	79	76	69	296	22,800

	SCORES				TOTAL	MONEY
Damien McGrane	76	76	74	71	297	21,000
Francesco Molinari	81	70	73	74	298	20,100
Stephen Dodd	80	76	70	73	299	18,750
Bradley Dredge	77	75	73	74	299	18,750
Emanuele Canonica	76	75	78	71	300	17,500
Brett Rumford	73	79	75	75	302	16,800
Andres Romero	78	79	78	74	309	16,300

HSBC Champions
See Asia/Japan Tours chapter.

UBS Hong Kong Open
See Asia/Japan Tours chapter.

MasterCard Masters
See Australasian Tour chapter.

Blue Chip New Zealand Open
See Australasian Tour chapter.

Alfred Dunhill Championship
See African Tours chapter.

WGC - Barbados World Cup
See American Tours chapter.

South African Airways Open
See African Tours chapter.

Challenge Tour

Abierto Movistar de Guatemala
See American Tours chapter.

Kai Fieberg Costa Rica Open
See American Tours chapter.

Estoril Challenge

Penha Longa Hotel & Golf Resort, Sintra, Portugal
Par 36-36–72; 6,876 yards

February 23-26
purse, €120,000

	SCORES				TOTAL	MONEY
Kyron Sullivan	70	69	71	74	284	€19,200
Ben Mason	70	72	71	71	284	13,200
(Sullivan defeated Mason on first playoff hole.)						
Oskar Bergman	67	72	73	73	285	8,400
Jan-Are Larsen	74	74	69	70	287	5,040
Christian L. Nilsson	66	72	79	70	287	5,040
Alexander Noren	77	71	68	71	287	5,040
Van Phillips	72	74	73	68	287	5,040
Alvaro Velasco	74	74	71	68	287	5,040
David Drysdale	70	70	76	72	288	2,880
Eduardo De La Riva	73	71	74	71	289	2,640
Inaki Alustiza	76	70	71	73	290	2,040
Pol Bech	75	68	73	74	290	2,040
Diego Borrego	68	74	75	73	290	2,040
Stuart Manley	68	74	73	75	290	2,040
Paul Nilbrink	68	72	79	71	290	2,040
Magnus Persson	74	72	70	74	290	2,040
Ben Willman	72	73	73	72	290	2,040
Fredrik Andersson Hed	71	69	77	74	291	1,291
Jose Manuel Carriles	68	74	77	72	291	1,290.86
Pablo Larrazabal	71	74	73	73	291	1,290.86
Juan Parron	71	69	77	74	291	1,290.86
Daniel Quiros	68	75	74	74	291	1,290.86
Carlos Rodiles	73	75	71	72	291	1,290.86
Edward Rush	72	72	71	76	291	1,290.86
Johan Axgren	69	78	75	70	292	1,032
Chris Gane	74	72	75	71	292	1,032
Xavier Guzman	74	72	74	72	292	1,032
Marcus Higley	79	69	73	71	292	1,032
Michael Jonzon	69	75	78	70	292	1,032
Manuel Moreno	69	75	76	72	292	1,032
Per G. Nyman	69	72	78	73	292	1,032

Tusker Kenya Open

Karen Golf Club, Nairobi, Kenya
Par 35-35–70; 6,918 yards

March 9-12
purse, €160,000

	SCORES				TOTAL	MONEY
Johan Axgren	64	69	67	70	270	€25,600
James Hepworth	67	66	71	70	274	14,400
Gary Lockerbie	71	64	70	69	274	14,400
Anders Schmidt Hansen	70	68	66	71	275	9,600
James Kamte	67	66	71	72	276	6,506.67
Jacob Okello	69	70	73	64	276	6,506.67
Johan Skold	69	68	71	68	276	6,506.67
James Heath	66	68	69	74	277	3,946.67
Tim Milford	67	70	67	73	277	3,946.67
Alvaro Velasco	70	68	67	72	277	3,946.67
Pelle Edberg	67	70	69	72	278	2,960
Van Phillips	69	71	71	67	278	2,960
Sam Walker	74	66	68	70	278	2,960
Peter Whiteford	73	66	69	70	278	2,960
Magnus A. Carlsson	72	68	70	69	279	2,320
Mark Mouland	67	68	69	75	279	2,320
Hernan Rey	69	73	69	68	279	2,320
Kyron Sullivan	70	69	70	70	279	2,320
Klas Eriksson	72	67	70	71	280	1,692.80
Oskar Henningsson	67	71	73	69	280	1,692.80
Brandon Pieters	71	68	70	71	280	1,692.80
Nicolas Vanhootegem	71	69	68	72	280	1,692.80
Ben Willman	72	70	66	72	280	1,692.80
Kariem Baraka	72	70	70	69	281	1,440
Jason Jackson	69	72	69	71	281	1,440
Simon Robinson	76	66	70	69	281	1,440
David Skinns	69	72	66	74	281	1,440
Phil Worthington	70	68	72	71	281	1,440
Didier De Vooght	71	68	70	73	282	1,264
Chris Gane	71	69	73	69	282	1,264
Peter Jespersen	68	73	70	71	282	1,264
Cedric Menut	66	68	75	73	282	1,264
Sam Osborne	69	69	74	70	282	1,264
Gustavo Rojas	66	68	73	75	282	1,264

Peugeot Challenge R.C.G. El Prat

Real Club de Golf El Prat, Barcelona, Spain
Par 36-36–72; 7,070 yards

April 6-9
purse, €120,000

	SCORES				TOTAL	MONEY
David Drysdale	68	71	71	68	278	€19,200
Johan Axgren	69	68	70	73	280	13,200
Ivo Giner	70	73	66	72	281	8,400
Chris Gane	69	78	69	66	282	6,000
Alvaro Quiros	70	75	70	67	282	6,000
Alvaro Velasco	71	74	70	67	282	6,000
Gregory Bourdy	72	71	71	70	284	3,840
Jesus Maria Arruti	72	68	70	75	285	2,537.14
Oskar Bergman	69	73	71	72	285	2,537.14
Marcus Higley	73	74	69	69	285	2,537.14

	SCORES	TOTAL	MONEY
Jan-Are Larsen	70 74 72 69	285	2,537.14
Raymond Russell	72 71 72 70	285	2,537.14
Lee Slattery	70 68 72 75	285	2,537.14
Francisco Valera	72 71 69 73	285	2,537.14
Carlos Aguilar	68 78 69 71	286	1,630
Jose Manuel Carriles	73 68 70 75	286	1,630
Michael Jonzon	71 71 70 74	286	1,630
Santiago Luna	72 68 75 71	286	1,630
Cedric Menut	72 73 69 72	286	1,630
Benoit Teilleria	70 73 69 74	286	1,630
Pedro Linhart	70 75 69 73	287	1,176
Ben Mason	72 73 71 71	287	1,176
Michele Reale	71 71 75 70	287	1,176
Sion E. Bebb	74 72 71 71	288	1,116
Alexander Noren	73 73 69 73	288	1,116
Kalle Brink	75 70 71 73	289	996
Luis Claverie	73 71 73 72	289	996
Alfredo Garcia	73 74 70 72	289	996
Jamie Little	73 72 72 72	289	996
Gary Lockerbie	73 69 70 77	289	996
Stuart Manley	69 70 79 71	289	996
Daniel Wardrop	74 71 73 71	289	996
Leif Westerberg	73 73 69 74	289	996

Tessali Metaponto Open di Puglia e Basilicata

Riva dei Tessali: Par 35-36–71; 6,503 yards
Metaponto GC: Par 36-36–72; 6,972 yards
Tessali, Italy

April 27-30
purse, €120,000

	SCORES	TOTAL	MONEY
Anthony Snobeck	72 69 65 66	272	€19,200
Kyron Sullivan	66 67 71 68	272	13,200

(Snobeck defeated Sullivan on first playoff hole.)

	SCORES	TOTAL	MONEY
Lee S. James	65 68 72 69	274	7,800
Andrew McArthur	70 66 69 69	274	7,800
Stuart Davis	67 65 70 74	276	4,880
Julien Foret	69 65 70 72	276	4,880
Cedric Menut	72 68 66 70	276	4,880
Johan Axgren	69 69 69 70	277	2,960
James Heath	68 66 70 73	277	2,960
Gareth Wright	67 71 70 69	277	2,960
Kariem Baraka	66 72 72 68	278	2,280
Oskar Bergman	72 70 66 70	278	2,280
Massimo Scarpa	66 71 68 73	278	2,280
Marco Bernardini	70 71 68 70	279	1,800
Francois Calmels	68 71 71 69	279	1,800
Chris Gane	71 69 70 69	279	1,800
Jerome Theunis	66 70 71 72	279	1,800
Robert Wiederkehr	68 68 68 75	279	1,800
Anders Schmidt Hansen	68 74 70 68	280	1,340
Jeppe Huldahl	72 69 71 68	280	1,340
Tim Milford	73 68 71 68	280	1,340
Alessio Bruschi	71 69 71 70	281	1,152
Marcus Higley	68 70 73 70	281	1,152
Mads Vibe-Hastrup	69 68 70 74	281	1,152
Fredrik Andersson Hed	71 69 71 71	282	996

	SCORES				TOTAL	MONEY
Christophe Brazillier	74	68	75	65	282	996
Julien Clement	72	66	68	76	282	996
Jean Marc De Polo	68	73	70	71	282	996
Sebastien Delagrange	69	72	73	68	282	996
Christopher Doak	66	74	68	74	282	996
Raphael Eyraud	71	69	68	74	282	996
Oskar Henningsson	70	70	70	72	282	996
David Patrick	72	69	73	68	282	996
Phil Worthington	74	69	66	73	282	996

Parco di Monza Challenge

Milano Monza Golf Club, Monza, Italy
Par 36-35–71; 7,003 yards

May 11-14
purse, €130,000

	SCORES				TOTAL	MONEY
Alvaro Salto	65	71	66	69	271	€20,800
Gareth Davies	68	68	67	70	273	14,300
Rafael Cabrera Bello	67	70	72	65	274	8,450
Anthony Snobeck	70	66	68	70	274	8,450
Juan Parron	66	69	71	69	275	6,500
Stuart Davis	70	68	70	68	276	4,030
Sebastian Fernandez	67	71	67	71	276	4,030
Jean-Baptiste Gonnet	69	67	70	70	276	4,030
Thomas Nielsen	67	69	70	70	276	4,030
Oskar Bergman	75	68	68	66	277	2,643.33
Tiago Cruz	66	73	68	70	277	2,643.33
Cesar Monasterio	68	68	71	70	277	2,643.33
James Heath	71	71	71	65	278	2,275
Mikko Korhonen	67	71	70	70	278	2,275
Marcus Higley	68	69	70	72	279	1,820
Panu Kylliainen	72	66	72	69	279	1,820
Antonio Maldonado	71	69	71	68	279	1,820
Magnus Persson	73	68	68	70	279	1,820
Alvaro Quiros	68	68	74	69	279	1,820
Sion E. Bebb	70	70	69	71	280	1,307.80
Ivo Giner	68	71	70	71	280	1,307.80
Gary Lockerbie	68	71	72	69	280	1,307.80
Miguel Rodriguez	71	70	70	69	280	1,307.80
Alvaro Velasco	73	68	71	68	280	1,307.80
Marco Bernardini	69	72	71	69	281	1,157
Jean Marc De Polo	68	71	72	70	281	1,157
Lee S. James	70	70	70	71	281	1,157
Mark Mouland	73	68	71	69	281	1,157
Graham Fox	71	70	68	73	282	1,053
Michael Jonzon	71	71	71	69	282	1,053
Christian Reimbold	72	69	69	72	282	1,053
Paolo Terreni	71	71	72	68	282	1,053

Telenet Trophy

Limburg Golf & Country Club, Houthalen, Belgium
Par 36-36—72; 6,729 yards

May 18-21
purse, €130,000

		SCORES			TOTAL	MONEY
Toni Karjalainen	66	73	67	68	274	€20,800
Ivo Giner	66	70	73	66	275	11,700
Gary Lockerbie	68	72	69	66	275	11,700
Francois Calmels	69	68	71	69	277	7,800
Rafael Echenique	72	69	68	70	279	5,850
Jean-Baptiste Gonnet	70	71	70	68	279	5,850
Ben Mason	68	74	71	67	280	3,445
Mads Vibe-Hastrup	68	73	69	70	280	3,445
Sam Walker	70	69	71	70	280	3,445
Peter Whiteford	70	72	70	68	280	3,445
Kalle Brink	68	71	71	71	281	2,210
Sebastian Fernandez	70	71	70	70	281	2,210
Chris Gane	71	70	74	66	281	2,210
Denny Lucas	69	69	72	71	281	2,210
Mark Mouland	68	71	76	66	281	2,210
Eric Ramsay	69	71	73	68	281	2,210
Wilhelm Schauman	70	74	72	65	281	2,210
Jesus Maria Arruti	72	69	71	70	282	1,511.25
Kariem Baraka	69	73	72	68	282	1,511.25
Lars Brovold	74	67	73	68	282	1,511.25
Alessandro Napoleoni	69	74	72	67	282	1,511.25
*Quentin De Valensart	75	69	70	69	283	
Morten Hedegaard	70	68	73	72	283	1,196
John E. Morgan	66	75	73	69	283	1,196
Sam Osborne	69	71	72	71	283	1,196
Knud Storgaard	68	73	70	72	283	1,196
Guido van der Valk	71	68	71	73	283	1,196
Julien Van Hauwe	68	73	71	71	283	1,196
Daniel Wardrop	70	74	71	68	283	1,196
Neil Cheetham	69	74	71	70	284	1,079
David Drysdale	70	72	72	70	284	1,079

Tikida Hotels Agadir Moroccan Classic

Golf du Soleil, Agadir, Morocco
Par 36-35—71; 6,590 yards

May 25-28
purse, €130,000

		SCORES			TOTAL	MONEY
Adrien Mork	63	59	74	69	265	€20,800
Mark Pilkington	66	67	67	66	266	11,700
Julien Van Hauwe	68	67	64	67	266	11,700
Jorge Benedetti	68	64	68	68	268	7,150
Nicolas Vanhootegem	67	66	65	70	268	7,150
Alvaro Velasco	67	67	67	68	269	5,200
Jesus Maria Arruti	68	68	68	67	271	3,445
James Hepworth	68	66	68	69	271	3,445
Andrea Maestroni	72	66	65	68	271	3,445
Alexander Noren	69	68	67	67	271	3,445
Kariem Baraka	69	67	66	70	272	2,470
Chris Gane	72	67	66	67	272	2,470
Hernan Rey	68	68	67	69	272	2,470

	SCORES				TOTAL	MONEY
Rafael Cabrera Bello	66	66	72	69	273	1,950
Rafael Echenique	67	66	66	74	273	1,950
Sebastian Fernandez	70	69	68	66	273	1,950
Cedric Menut	67	70	68	68	273	1,950
Cesar Monasterio	66	69	71	67	273	1,950
Ivo Giner	67	68	70	69	274	1,349.83
Jean-Baptiste Gonnet	68	67	72	67	274	1,349.83
Peter Jespersen	72	66	69	67	274	1,349.83
Mikko Korhonen	67	69	70	68	274	1,349.83
David Patrick	67	70	69	68	274	1,349.83
Michele Reale	66	69	71	68	274	1,349.83
Jean-Nicolas Billot	69	67	73	66	275	1,105
Francisco Cea	69	67	69	70	275	1,105
Bertrand Cornut	68	70	69	68	275	1,105
Julien Foret	69	67	69	70	275	1,105
Michael Lorenzo-Vera	67	69	72	67	275	1,105
Nicolas Meitinger	71	67	67	70	275	1,105
Paul Nilbrink	71	68	71	65	275	1,105
Guido van der Valk	70	69	66	70	275	1,105

Morson International Pro-Am Challenge

Marriott Worsley Park Hotel & Country Club,
Manchester, England
Par 35-35–70; 6,791 yards

May 31-June 3
purse, €150,288

	SCORES				TOTAL	MONEY
Alvaro Quiros	67	68	68	64	267	€23,318.56
Mark Pilkington	62	66	71	71	270	16,031.51
Jan-Are Larsen	67	68	67	69	271	9,473.16
Nicolas Vanhootegem	71	69	65	66	271	9,473.16
Kariem Baraka	67	71	67	67	272	6,558.34
Carlos De Corral	69	67	69	67	272	6,558.34
Jean-Baptiste Gonnet	65	69	71	69	274	4,663.71
Johan Axgren	68	71	70	66	275	3,293.75
Gareth Davies	69	69	69	68	275	3,293.75
Chris Gane	66	69	69	71	275	3,293.75
Ivo Giner	66	70	71	68	275	3,293.75
Simon Lilly	65	68	72	70	275	3,293.75
Christopher Doak	69	71	69	67	276	2,331.86
Anders Schmidt Hansen	68	66	73	69	276	2,331.86
Lee S. James	70	69	67	70	276	2,331.86
Euan Little	70	68	69	69	276	2,331.86
Ben Willman	69	68	70	69	276	2,331.86
James Heath	66	70	67	74	277	1,641.04
Andrew McArthur	69	66	72	70	277	1,641.04
Tim Milford	67	69	71	70	277	1,641.04
Darren Prosser	69	69	69	70	277	1,641.04
Christian Reimbold	70	70	67	70	277	1,641.04
Miguel Rodriguez	72	68	68	70	278	1,369.97
Knud Storgaard	66	70	71	71	278	1,369.97
Sven Struver	67	69	72	70	278	1,369.97
Paul McKechnie	69	71	71	68	279	1,297.09
Hernan Rey	67	71	71	70	279	1,297.09
Lars Brovold	70	67	75	68	280	1,151.35
Daniel Gaunt	70	69	70	71	280	1,151.35
Marcus Higley	68	72	69	71	280	1,151.35

	SCORES				TOTAL	MONEY
Martin Lemesurier	69	71	68	72	280	1,151.35
Zane Scotland	64	74	71	71	280	1,151.35
Paul Streeter	70	69	71	70	280	1,151.35
John Wells	67	70	69	74	280	1,151.35
James H. Williams	66	72	76	66	280	1,151.35

Thomas Bjorn Open

Horsens Golfklub, Horsens, Denmark
Par 36-36–72; 7,035 yards

June 8-11
purse, €120,000

	SCORES				TOTAL	MONEY
Marcus Higley	69	68	73	67	277	€19,200
Michiel Bothma	68	69	70	72	279	8,700
Alessio Bruschi	74	68	69	68	279	8,700
Gareth Davies	70	74	69	66	279	8,700
Denny Lucas	70	68	74	67	279	8,700
Thomas Sundstrom	69	70	71	71	281	4,320
Jerome Theunis	73	70	68	70	281	4,320
Magnus A. Carlsson	70	70	71	72	283	2,820
Klas Eriksson	74	67	72	70	283	2,820
John E. Morgan	72	73	67	71	283	2,820
Daniel Wardrop	73	74	69	67	283	2,820
Claes Nilsson	70	74	70	70	284	2,220
Zane Scotland	72	73	67	72	284	2,220
Marco Crespi	72	69	70	74	285	1,800
Pelle Edberg	76	70	71	68	285	1,800
Anton Haig	71	74	71	69	285	1,800
Mikko Korhonen	68	72	72	73	285	1,800
Andrew McArthur	73	70	74	68	285	1,800
Mickael Dieu	70	74	69	73	286	1,340
Simon Hurley	75	69	73	69	286	1,340
Miguel Rodriguez	71	71	74	70	286	1,340
Lars Brovold	70	72	75	70	287	1,140
Peter Kaensche	71	74	73	69	287	1,140
Tim Milford	70	77	70	70	287	1,140
Mads Vibe-Hastrup	77	70	73	67	287	1,140
Robert Eriksson	75	69	71	73	288	1,008
Michael Jurgensen	73	70	73	72	288	1,008
Simon Lilly	73	71	76	68	288	1,008
Hernan Rey	74	72	71	71	288	1,008
Mark Smith	76	70	71	71	288	1,008
Erik Stenman	74	70	73	71	288	1,008
Ben Willman	71	70	71	76	288	1,008

Aa St. Omer Open

See European Tour section.

Lexus Open

Larvik Golf Club, Larvik, Norway
Par 36-36–72; 6,868 yards

June 15-18
purse, €120,000

	SCORES				TOTAL	MONEY
Kalle Brink	69	69	72	65	275	€19,200
Jose Manuel Carriles	71	70	71	66	278	8,700
Greig Hutcheon	68	71	71	68	278	8,700
Peter Kaensche	72	71	70	65	278	8,700
Jan-Are Larsen	71	68	68	71	278	8,700
Stuart Cage	67	72	71	69	279	3,171.43
Daniel Gaunt	69	70	71	69	279	3,171.43
Soren Juul Hansen	71	69	69	70	279	3,171.43
*Tage Johansen	69	69	69	72	279	
James McLeary	68	73	73	65	279	3,171.43
Tim Milford	67	74	70	68	279	3,171.43
Fredrik Soderstrom	72	71	65	71	279	3,171.43
Julio Zapata	68	70	72	69	279	3,171.43
Lars Brovold	70	67	70	73	280	1,980
Raimo Sjoberg	68	67	71	74	280	1,980
Guido van der Valk	67	75	68	70	280	1,980
James H. Williams	69	69	74	68	280	1,980
Ralf Geilenberg	71	72	69	69	281	1,560
John Kelly	70	71	70	70	281	1,560
Niki Zitny	70	68	73	70	281	1,560
Peter Ankersoe	67	69	71	75	282	1,131.60
Per Barth	71	69	68	74	282	1,131.60
Gabriel Canizares	69	71	69	73	282	1,131.60
Carlos Del Moral	70	68	70	74	282	1,131.60
Oskar Henningsson	70	68	75	69	282	1,131.60
Jeppe Huldahl	70	71	71	70	282	1,131.60
Mikko Korhonen	69	71	71	71	282	1,131.60
Panu Kylliainen	71	70	69	72	282	1,131.60
Martin Lemesurier	73	70	71	68	282	1,131.60
Claes Nilsson	66	72	75	69	282	1,131.60

Credit Suisse Challenge

Wylihof GolfKlub, Luterbach, Switzerland
Par 36-37–73; 7,202 yards

June 22-25
purse, €140,000

	SCORES			TOTAL	MONEY
Francisco Cea	73	69	69	65	276	€22,400
Tim Milford	65	72	71	68	276	15,400
(Cea defeated Milford on second playoff hole.)						
Gareth Davies	73	68	70	66	277	9,100
Mads Vibe-Hastrup	69	69	70	69	277	9,100
James Heath	71	69	67	71	278	7,000
Jesus Maria Arruti	70	71	69	69	279	4,340
Rodolfo Gonzalez	73	68	68	70	279	4,340
Simon Hurley	68	74	70	67	279	4,340
James McLeary	70	72	64	73	279	4,340
Sven Struver	69	73	70	68	280	3,080
Panu Kylliainen	68	74	70	69	281	2,590
Jan-Are Larsen	73	70	68	70	281	2,590
Andrea Maestroni	68	72	70	71	281	2,590

	SCORES				TOTAL	MONEY
Andrew McArthur	69	70	73	69	281	2,590
Gustavo Acosta	70	73	69	70	282	1,830
Jean-Baptiste Gonnet	70	70	70	72	282	1,830
Juan Parron	64	76	70	72	282	1,830
Mark Pilkington	69	72	68	73	282	1,830
Martin Rominger	70	73	71	68	282	1,830
Marco Soffietti	72	71	71	68	282	1,830
Craig Williams	71	70	71	70	282	1,830
Andre Bossert	71	72	73	67	283	1,274
Alessio Bruschi	73	71	69	70	283	1,274
Rafael Cabrera Bello	72	71	72	68	283	1,274
Jean Hugo	73	70	69	71	283	1,274
Gary Lockerbie	69	73	70	71	283	1,274
Colm Moriarty	71	73	69	70	283	1,274
Paolo Terreni	72	67	75	69	283	1,274
Julio Zapata	71	70	71	71	283	1,274
Massimo Florioli	71	71	72	70	284	1,092
Chris Gane	68	71	76	69	284	1,092
Alvaro Salto	69	70	71	74	284	1,092
Anthony Snobeck	70	74	71	69	284	1,092
Alvaro Velasco	70	74	70	70	284	1,092

Open Mahou de Madrid

Club de Golf La Herreria, Madrid, Spain
Par 35-36–71; 6,661 yards

June 29-July 2
purse, €120,000

	SCORES				TOTAL	MONEY
Juan Parron	64	68	70	69	271	€19,200
Luis Claverie	68	67	69	67	271	10,800
Santiago Luna	68	70	66	67	271	10,800
(Parron defeated Claverie on first and Luna on third playoff hole.)						
Alfredo Garcia-Heredia	67	70	67	68	272	5,460
Lee S. James	66	65	68	73	272	5,460
Pedro Linhart	68	69	71	64	272	5,460
Alvaro Quiros	74	65	68	65	272	5,460
Gustavo Acosta	68	68	66	71	273	2,960
Chris Gane	68	66	67	72	273	2,960
Rodolfo Gonzalez	67	69	68	69	273	2,960
Agustin Domingo	66	66	69	73	274	2,280
Jean Hugo	69	68	68	69	274	2,280
Alvaro Salto	69	69	69	67	274	2,280
*Jose Luis Adarraga Gomez	71	65	71	68	275	
Miguel Carballo	67	72	69	67	275	2,040
Sebastian Fernandez	69	68	67	72	276	1,740
Birgir Hafthorsson	68	69	67	72	276	1,740
Panu Kylliainen	66	67	69	74	276	1,740
Christian Reimbold	72	65	72	67	276	1,740
Mattias Damberg	71	68	71	67	277	1,207.50
Gary Lockerbie	66	68	74	69	277	1,207.50
Gregory Molteni	65	70	74	68	277	1,207.50
Magnus Persson	70	64	72	71	277	1,207.50
Ricardo Santos	73	65	68	71	277	1,207.50
Kyron Sullivan	69	66	69	73	277	1,207.50
Alvaro Velasco	69	69	69	70	277	1,207.50
Sam Walker	68	70	71	68	277	1,207.50
Carlos Balmaseda	67	68	71	72	278	972

	SCORES				TOTAL	MONEY
Kariem Baraka	71	69	69	69	278	972
Jorge Benedetti	72	64	73	69	278	972
Diego Borrego	68	65	75	70	278	972
Jose Manuel Carriles	68	68	70	72	278	972
Tiago Cruz	66	72	70	70	278	972
Jeppe Huldahl	66	70	73	69	278	972
Anthony Snobeck	68	66	73	71	278	972

Scottish Challenge

Murcar Links Golf Club, Aberdeen, Scotland
Par 36-35–71; 6,504 yards

July 6-9
purse, €200,000

	SCORES				TOTAL	MONEY
Sam Walker	68	69	64	65	266	€32,000
Gareth Wright	68	66	71	67	272	22,000
Chris Doak	70	63	73	67	273	14,000
*Richard Ramsay	77	63	73	62	275	
Gareth Paddison	67	71	67	71	276	12,000
Scott Henderson	68	66	72	71	277	9,000
Alexander Noren	72	64	70	71	277	9,000
David Drysdale	70	67	71	70	278	5,300
Colin Gillies	71	64	75	68	278	5,300
Anders Schmidt Hansen	67	67	74	70	278	5,300
Mark Pilkington	71	66	74	67	278	5,300
Mikko Ilonen	68	70	72	70	280	3,900
Eric Ramsay	69	68	73	70	280	3,900
Fredrik Andersson Hed	68	72	69	72	281	3,300
Luis Claverie	70	66	74	71	281	3,300
Birgir Hafthorsson	71	69	70	71	281	3,300
James McLeary	68	65	74	74	281	3,300
Sion E. Bebb	68	69	78	67	282	2,420
Carlos De Corral	74	67	71	70	282	2,420
Stuart Manley	67	70	77	68	282	2,420
Andrew McArthur	71	71	70	70	282	2,420
Murray Urquhart	67	68	75	72	282	2,420
Oskar Bergman	70	66	75	72	283	1,900
Ben Mason	70	70	70	73	283	1,900
Magnus Persson	75	67	70	71	283	1,900
Alvaro Velasco	68	67	74	74	283	1,900
Gustavo Acosta	73	66	73	72	284	1,740
Didier De Vooght	71	70	71	72	284	1,740
Pedro Linhart	74	66	76	68	284	1,740
David Orr	73	67	74	70	284	1,740

Texbond Open

Garda Golf, Brescia, Italy
Par 36-36–72; 7,148 yards

July 12-15
purse, €120,000

	SCORES				TOTAL	MONEY
Carlos Del Moral	69	68	63	70	270	€19,200
Lee S. James	66	65	66	73	270	13,200

(Del Moral defeated James on third playoff hole.)

	SCORES				TOTAL	MONEY
Emmanuele Lattanzi	68	67	70	66	271	7,800
Nicolas Vanhootegem	67	70	68	66	271	7,800
Marcus Higley	72	65	68	67	272	6,000
Magnus A. Carlsson	70	66	66	72	274	3,320
Chris Gane	66	71	69	68	274	3,320
Stuart Manley	66	69	65	74	274	3,320
Martin Maritz	67	69	68	70	274	3,320
Alessandro Napoleoni	66	71	66	71	274	3,320
Gareth Paddison	69	67	66	72	274	3,320
Denny Lucas	67	67	71	70	275	2,280
Johan Axgren	67	66	70	73	276	2,040
Simon Hurd	67	70	70	69	276	2,040
Nicola Maestroni	69	69	68	70	276	2,040
Brian Akstrup	71	66	70	70	277	1,462.29
Clemens Prader	71	70	69	67	277	1,462.29
Knud Storgaard	70	68	67	72	277	1,462.29
Kyron Sullivan	68	70	70	69	277	1,462.29
Tuomas Tuovinen	70	70	71	66	277	1,462.29
Craig Williams	70	68	68	71	277	1,462.29
Gareth Wright	70	69	68	70	277	1,462.29
Jamie Elson	71	69	67	71	278	1,116
Nicolas Meitinger	66	69	70	73	278	1,116
Johan Skold	69	67	70	72	278	1,116
Mads Vibe-Hastrup	76	65	68	69	278	1,116
Anders Schmidt Hansen	71	67	72	69	279	1,044
Andrew McArthur	73	64	72	70	279	1,044
Kariem Baraka	68	71	69	72	280	984
Rafael Cabrera Bello	68	69	71	72	280	984
Jean Marc De Polo	70	68	68	74	280	984

MAN NO Open

Golfclub Adamstal, Austria
Par 35-35–70; 6,141 yards

July 20-23
purse, €130,000

	SCORES				TOTAL	MONEY
Rafael Cabrera Bello	61	68	66	69	264	€20,800
Niki Zitny	69	66	64	67	266	14,300
Johan Skold	67	68	65	67	267	8,450
Mads Vibe-Hastrup	71	66	63	67	267	8,450
Fredrik Andersson Hed	66	70	67	66	269	5,850
Mikko Korhonen	70	69	65	65	269	5,850
Marcus Higley	68	73	64	65	270	3,640
Toni Karjalainen	70	67	65	68	270	3,640
Shaun P. Webster	69	68	65	68	270	3,640
Jesus Maria Arruti	70	66	65	70	271	2,496
Jamie Elson	63	69	69	70	271	2,496
Martin Maritz	71	66	68	66	271	2,496
Nicolas Vanhootegem	67	68	68	68	271	2,496
Oliver Whiteley	67	69	66	69	271	2,496
David Drysdale	65	68	70	69	272	1,885
Simon Lilly	66	70	68	68	272	1,885
Tim Milford	68	67	65	72	272	1,885
Inder Van Weerelt	67	69	67	69	272	1,885
Kalle Brink	70	71	66	66	273	1,349.83
Gabriel Canizares	63	71	71	68	273	1,349.83
Klas Eriksson	71	67	69	66	273	1,349.83

	SCORES				TOTAL	MONEY
Soren Juul	64	75	66	68	273	1,349.83
Ajay Shah	70	71	65	67	273	1,349.83
Craig Smith	71	70	65	67	273	1,349.83
Greig Hutcheon	73	66	64	71	274	1,157
Cedric Menut	70	67	67	70	274	1,157
Tino Schuster	72	68	68	66	274	1,157
Zane Scotland	69	69	66	70	274	1,157
Wolfgang Huget	72	66	69	68	275	1,027
Michael Jurgensen	69	72	68	66	275	1,027
Antonio Maldonado	68	72	65	70	275	1,027
Manuel Quiros	71	69	67	68	275	1,027
Christian Reimbold	71	66	70	68	275	1,027
Martin Wiegele	68	70	66	71	275	1,027

Ryder Cup Wales Challenge

Nefyn Golf Club, Gwynedd, Wales
Par 35-36–71; 6,759 yards

July 27-30
purse, €130,000

	SCORES				TOTAL	MONEY
Sion E. Bebb	68	64	73	69	274	€20,800
Jean-Baptiste Gonnet	69	62	71	73	275	14,300
Lee S. James	68	68	73	68	277	8,450
Stuart Manley	69	68	71	69	277	8,450
Olivier David	65	64	80	69	278	5,850
Rafael Echenique	68	67	75	68	278	5,850
Jean Hugo	67	66	75	71	279	4,160
Murray Urquhart	68	70	73	69	280	3,380
Craig Williams	67	68	74	71	280	3,380
Peter Baker	68	70	75	68	281	2,730
Paul Streeter	73	65	75	68	281	2,730
Felipe Aguilar	68	68	75	71	282	2,210
Neil Cheetham	69	66	73	74	282	2,210
Andrew McArthur	72	63	74	73	282	2,210
Brian McElhinney	68	69	74	71	282	2,210
John Wells	65	67	77	73	282	2,210
David Drysdale	70	71	71	71	283	1,573
Daniel Gaunt	64	71	76	72	283	1,573
*Cenydd Mills	68	68	74	73	283	
Iain Pyman	69	71	74	69	283	1,573
Hernan Rey	69	68	76	70	283	1,573
Inder Van Weerelt	69	68	74	72	283	1,573
Stuart Davis	67	70	75	72	284	1,209
Chris Doak	75	65	75	69	284	1,209
Adam Frayne	70	70	75	69	284	1,209
Roope Kakko	70	67	76	71	284	1,209
Zane Scotland	67	66	75	76	284	1,209
Knud Storgaard	71	68	76	69	284	1,209
Jonathan Cheetham	69	68	73	75	285	1,092
Massimo Florioli	67	70	75	73	285	1,092
Mark Pilkington	68	71	78	68	285	1,092

Ireland Ryder Cup Challenge

Killarney Golf & Fishing Club, Ireland
Par 35-35–70; 6,742 yards

August 3-6
purse, €130,000

	SCORES				TOTAL	MONEY
John Wade	69	64	65	63	261	€20,800
Sebastian Fernandez	66	62	65	69	262	11,700
Michael McGeady	66	63	66	67	262	11,700
Juan Parron	64	63	65	71	263	7,800
Peter Kaensche	66	65	65	68	264	6,500
Gabriel Canizares	67	63	67	68	265	4,030
Lee S. James	67	69	64	65	265	4,030
Denny Lucas	66	67	65	67	265	4,030
Simon Robinson	67	66	64	68	265	4,030
Magnus A. Carlsson	65	67	68	66	266	2,496
Raphael Eyraud	66	69	69	62	266	2,496
James Hepworth	66	66	67	67	266	2,496
Sam Osborne	62	70	64	70	266	2,496
Miguel Rodriguez	66	63	68	69	266	2,496
Chris Doak	66	70	66	65	267	1,765.83
Robert Giles	66	66	70	65	267	1,765.83
Gary Lockerbie	67	66	67	67	267	1,765.83
Edward Rush	65	69	66	67	267	1,765.83
Murray Urquhart	66	65	67	69	267	1,765.83
James H. Williams	63	71	63	70	267	1,765.83
Euan Little	69	65	67	67	268	1,287
Hernan Rey	68	68	66	66	268	1,287
Chris Gane	64	67	70	68	269	1,196
Mark Pilkington	68	68	67	66	269	1,196
Julien Quesne	66	67	69	67	269	1,196
Craig Williams	63	71	67	68	269	1,196
Ben Willman	69	67	63	70	269	1,196
Stuart Davis	67	69	67	67	270	1,053
Didier De Vooght	67	69	67	67	270	1,053
Sebastien Delagrange	68	69	64	69	270	1,053
Michael McDermott	63	72	68	67	270	1,053
Mark O'Sullivan	67	69	66	68	270	1,053
Simon Thornton	64	72	67	67	270	1,053

Vodafone Challenge

Golf Club Elfrather Muhle, Dusseldorf, Germany
Par 36-36–72; 6,859 yards

August 10-13
purse, €120,000

	SCORES				TOTAL	MONEY
Martin Kaymer	70	67	63	70	270	€19,200
Matthew King	74	68	66	64	272	10,800
Alvaro Quiros	69	68	69	66	272	10,800
Roope Kakko	70	71	63	70	274	6,600
Jerome Theunis	71	70	66	67	274	6,600
Alexander Noren	69	66	67	73	275	4,800
Jean-Baptiste Gonnet	72	68	68	68	276	3,024
Jeppe Huldahl	71	72	65	68	276	3,024
Pablo Larrazabal	70	70	69	67	276	3,024
Mark Pilkington	67	69	69	71	276	3,024
Sam Walker	67	70	66	73	276	3,024

	SCORES	TOTAL	MONEY
Gary Lockerbie	69 69 70 69	277	2,220
Edward Rush	74 67 66 70	277	2,220
Benjamin Miarka	63 69 73 73	278	2,040
Rafael Cabrera Bello	72 71 68 68	279	1,478.67
Carlos Del Moral	69 65 74 71	279	1,478.67
Chris Doak	68 67 71 73	279	1,478.67
Raphael Eyraud	73 69 71 66	279	1,478.67
Julien Foret	70 72 66 71	279	1,478.67
Magnus Persson	73 70 68 68	279	1,478.67
Hernan Rey	66 73 68 72	279	1,478.67
Wilhelm Schauman	72 71 64 72	279	1,478.67
Martin Wiegele	71 70 69 69	279	1,478.67
Sergio Acevedo	69 70 68 73	280	1,080
Jan-Are Larsen	68 71 72 69	280	1,080
Murray Urquhart	70 70 69 71	280	1,080
Mads Vibe-Hastrup	69 69 71 71	280	1,080
Ben Willman	71 69 68 72	280	1,080
Sion E. Bebb	72 70 70 69	281	948
Michiel Bothma	69 68 69 75	281	948
Marco Crespi	70 70 70 71	281	948
Anders Schmidt Hansen	72 70 70 69	281	948
Lee S. James	73 70 69 69	281	948
Pedro Linhart	72 68 70 71	281	948

Rolex Trophy

Golf Club de Geneve, Geneva, Switzerland
Par 36-36–72; 6,746 yards

August 17-20
purse, €163,500

	SCORES	TOTAL	MONEY
Alexander Noren	66 67 62 71	266	€17,000
Johan Axgren	66 66 68 69	269	10,250
Gareth Davies	65 67 68 69	269	10,250
Rafael Cabrera Bello	69 70 65 67	271	8,000
Rafael Echenique	67 65 68 71	271	8,000
Hernan Rey	64 73 67 68	272	6,750
Mads Vibe-Hastrup	66 71 63 72	272	6,750
Marcus Higley	71 69 67 67	274	5,900
Kyron Sullivan	68 69 68 69	274	5,900
Jan-Are Larsen	67 71 68 69	275	5,600
Anthony Snobeck	71 71 64 70	276	5,400
Oskar Bergman	68 67 65 77	277	5,200
Jean-Baptiste Gonnet	72 68 68 70	278	5,000
Ivo Giner	72 69 68 71	280	4,650
James Hepworth	70 65 69 76	280	4,650
Mark Pilkington	66 70 73 71	280	4,650
Nicolas Vanhootegem	68 69 71 72	280	4,650
Anders Schmidt Hansen	68 73 66 75	282	4,400

ECCO Tour Championship

Odense Golfklub, Odense, Denmark
Par 36-34–70; 6,623 yards

August 24-27
purse, €130,000

		SCORES			TOTAL	MONEY
James Heath	65	67	67	62	261	€20,800
Thomas Norret	69	66	61	68	264	14,300
Felipe Aguilar	65	67	65	68	265	8,450
Roope Kakko	66	69	67	63	265	8,450
Birgir Hafthorsson	66	66	67	67	266	5,850
Sam Walker	70	66	64	66	266	5,850
Rafael Echenique	65	67	67	68	267	3,276
Oskar Henningsson	63	68	70	66	267	3,276
Mikko Korhonen	66	69	66	66	267	3,276
Manuel Quiros	67	68	64	68	267	3,276
Edward Rush	65	70	65	67	267	3,276
Martin Kaymer	68	66	65	69	268	2,405
Martin Maritz	65	67	70	66	268	2,405
Peter Ankersoe	67	70	63	69	269	2,080
Rafael Cabrera Bello	71	66	64	68	269	2,080
Janne Martikainen	67	63	71	68	269	2,080
Liam Bond	70	67	65	68	270	1,374.45
Sebastian Fernandez	64	71	69	66	270	1,374.45
Marcus Higley	67	69	64	70	270	1,374.45
Michael Jurgensen	64	71	67	68	270	1,374.45
Soren Juul	67	71	62	70	270	1,374.45
Jamie Little	68	70	67	65	270	1,374.45
Gary Lockerbie	69	68	66	67	270	1,374.45
Magnus Persson	64	65	68	73	270	1,374.45
Hernan Rey	64	72	66	68	270	1,374.45
Simon Robinson	74	64	66	66	270	1,374.45
Gustavo Rojas	69	68	68	65	270	1,374.45
Michiel Bothma	66	68	67	70	271	1,053
Gareth Davies	70	67	64	70	271	1,053
Carlos Del Moral	68	69	65	69	271	1,053
Raphael Eyraud	71	66	62	72	271	1,053
Rodolfo Gonzalez	69	69	65	68	271	1,053
Anders Schmidt Hansen	69	67	65	70	271	1,053

Telia Challenge Waxholm

Waxholm Golf Club, Stockholm, Sweden
Par 37-36–73; 7,318 yards

August 31-September 3
purse, €122,140

		SCORES			TOTAL	MONEY
Rafael Echenique	65	68	66	71	270	€19,547.03
Martin Kaymer	72	67	66	67	272	13,438.58
Kyron Sullivan	69	67	69	69	274	8,551.83
Alexander Noren	71	68	65	71	275	6,719.29
Sam Walker	74	66	68	67	275	6,719.29
Felipe Aguilar	69	68	67	72	276	4,886.76
Roope Kakko	71	67	69	70	277	3,909.41
Klas Eriksson	68	73	68	69	278	3,176.39
Iain Pyman	71	72	66	69	278	3,176.39
Peter Kaensche	73	67	69	70	279	2,484.10
Alvaro Salto	75	66	69	69	279	2,484.10

	SCORES	TOTAL	MONEY
Mads Vibe-Hastrup	68 70 67 74	279	2,484.10
Johan Axgren	71 68 71 70	280	2,137.96
Marcus Higley	70 69 69 72	280	2,137.96
Jan-Are Larsen	72 66 70 73	281	1,710.37
Manuel Quiros	71 71 67 72	281	1,710.37
Wilhelm Schauman	68 73 71 69	281	1,710.37
Patrik Sjoland	72 71 67 71	281	1,710.37
Johan Skold	70 72 68 71	281	1,710.37
Bjorn Pettersson	70 73 67 72	282	1,404.94
Per Barth	69 73 70 71	283	1,148.39
Matthew King	73 70 69 71	283	1,148.39
Stuart Manley	69 73 70 71	283	1,148.39
Ake Nilsson	69 74 69 71	283	1,148.39
Linus Pettersson	69 74 69 71	283	1,148.39
Tuomas Tuovinen	72 68 72 71	283	1,148.39
Markus Westerberg	71 72 69 71	283	1,148.39
Oskar Bergman	72 70 72 70	284	1,001.79
*Johan Carlsson	69 71 73 71	284	
Mattias Damberg	71 70 72 71	284	1,001.79
Michael Jonzon	70 71 72 71	284	1,001.79
Gustavo Rojas	70 71 67 76	284	1,001.79
Erik Stenman	71 69 72 72	284	1,001.79

Open des Volcans - Challenge de France

Golf des Volcans, Clermont Ferrand, France
Par 36-35–71; 7,054 yards

September 14-17
purse, €120,000

	SCORES	TOTAL	MONEY
Martin Kaymer	67 64 69 71	271	€19,200
Michael Lorenzo-Vera	69 69 66 73	277	13,200
Sion E. Bebb	67 70 71 71	279	7,800
Tim Milford	74 66 68 71	279	7,800
Jean-Nicolas Billot	72 67 71 70	280	3,702.86
Chris Gane	71 69 70 70	280	3,702.86
James Heath	72 67 69 72	280	3,702.86
Jean Hugo	70 70 71 69	280	3,702.86
Alexander Noren	74 70 66 70	280	3,702.86
Alvaro Quiros	70 69 71 70	280	3,702.86
Nicolas Vanhootegem	71 69 69 71	280	3,702.86
Magnus A. Carlsson	72 69 69 71	281	2,220
Lee S. James	76 66 70 69	281	2,220
Gareth Davies	71 71 71 69	282	1,740
Carlos Del Moral	69 72 71 70	282	1,740
Chris Doak	72 70 68 72	282	1,740
Gareth Paddison	74 69 70 69	282	1,740
Magnus Persson	70 69 71 72	282	1,740
Manuel Quiros	73 69 69 71	282	1,740
Michiel Bothma	69 72 72 70	283	1,190
Raphael Eyraud	69 72 65 77	283	1,190
Thomas Feyrsinger	71 68 71 73	283	1,190
Julien Foret	67 71 73 72	283	1,190
Nicolas Joakimides	71 71 68 73	283	1,190
Michael McGeady	72 70 73 68	283	1,190
Jeppe Huldahl	72 69 71 72	284	1,032
Cedric Menut	70 65 76 73	284	1,032
Hernan Rey	67 68 76 73	284	1,032

	SCORES	TOTAL	MONEY
Wilhelm Schauman	73 70 73 68	284	1,032
Kyron Sullivan	71 72 71 70	284	1,032

OKI Mahou Challenge de Espana

Centro Nacional de Golf, Madrid, Spain
Par 36-36–72; 7,113 yards

September 21-24
purse, €130,000

	SCORES	TOTAL	MONEY
Adrien Mork	73 67 69 62	271	€20,800
Kyron Sullivan	68 68 66 71	273	14,300
Vicente Blazquez	69 70 68 68	275	9,100
Martin Kaymer	73 64 69 70	276	7,150
Mads Vibe-Hastrup	69 71 69 67	276	7,150
Olivier David	67 67 72 71	277	4,680
Miguel Angel Martin-Lopez	68 68 70 71	277	4,680
Johan Axgren	69 71 70 68	278	3,055
Rafael Gomez	66 68 69 75	278	3,055
Johan Skold	69 64 74 71	278	3,055
Inder Van Weerelt	71 69 66 72	278	3,055
Gary Lockerbie	70 70 65 74	279	2,405
Edward Rush	70 70 73 66	279	2,405
Rafael Echenique	76 66 68 70	280	2,080
Stuart Manley	70 71 71 68	280	2,080
Clemens Prader	71 64 69 76	280	2,080
Felipe Aguilar	72 68 67 74	281	1,523.17
Neil Cheetham	69 72 71 69	281	1,523.17
Jean Hugo	68 71 69 73	281	1,523.17
Roope Kakko	69 67 72 73	281	1,523.17
Miguel Rodriguez	70 70 70 71	281	1,523.17
Julio Zapata	70 71 68 72	281	1,523.17
Manuel Quiros	68 69 75 70	282	1,222
Carlos Rodiles	71 68 71 72	282	1,222
Alvaro Salto	73 68 73 68	282	1,222
Carlos Balmaseda	73 68 69 73	283	1,079
Magnus A. Carlsson	72 68 73 70	283	1,079
Carlos Garcia	71 71 66 75	283	1,079
Alfredo Garcia-Heredia	72 71 69 71	283	1,079
Denny Lucas	71 70 73 69	283	1,079
Magnus Persson	76 66 70 71	283	1,079
Michele Reale	67 71 74 71	283	1,079
Kieran Staunton	70 70 72 71	283	1,079

Kazakhstan Open

Nurtau Golf Club, Almaty, Kazakhstan
Par 36-36–72; 7,301 yards

September 28-October 1
purse, €300,000

	SCORES	TOTAL	MONEY
Mark Pilkington	70 66 67 69	272	€48,000
Shaun P. Webster	72 66 70 66	274	33,000
Jesus Maria Arruti	69 72 66 69	276	18,000
Martin Kaymer	71 67 70 68	276	18,000
Gary Lockerbie	68 71 69 68	276	18,000
Alvaro Salto	68 70 66 73	277	12,000

	SCORES				TOTAL	MONEY
Magnus A. Carlsson	70	70	69	69	278	9,000
Kyron Sullivan	69	75	65	69	278	9,000
Neil Cheetham	72	71	66	70	279	6,180
James Hepworth	73	71	70	65	279	6,180
Wilhelm Schauman	69	75	70	65	279	6,180
Zane Scotland	70	70	66	73	279	6,180
Gareth Wright	72	64	74	69	279	6,180
Juan Abbate	69	74	70	67	280	4,221.43
Johan Axgren	70	71	73	66	280	4,221.43
Kariem Baraka	73	68	73	66	280	4,221.43
Luis Claverie	71	69	67	73	280	4,221.43
Paul Dwyer	70	68	69	73	280	4,221.43
Peter Kaensche	68	72	66	74	280	4,221.43
Denny Lucas	67	72	72	69	280	4,221.43
Gabriel Canizares	69	71	70	71	281	2,910
Gareth Davies	73	67	72	69	281	2,910
Jean-Baptiste Gonnet	69	71	70	71	281	2,910
Kieran Staunton	68	70	71	72	281	2,910
Fredrik Andersson Hed	74	69	68	71	282	2,640
Chris Gane	67	74	71	70	282	2,640
Marcus Higley	73	70	69	70	282	2,640
Jean Hugo	72	67	73	70	282	2,640
Lee S. James	71	67	75	69	282	2,640
Miguel Carballo	70	69	74	70	283	2,370
Stuart Davis	73	71	71	68	283	2,370
Sebastian Fernandez	69	71	70	73	283	2,370
Martin Wiegele	72	72	71	68	283	2,370

Golf Open International de Toulouse

Golf de Toulouse-Seilh, Toulouse, France
Par 36-36–72; 6,942 yards

October 5-8
purse, €120,000

	SCORES				TOTAL	MONEY
Julien Foret	72	67	69	66	274	€19,200
Shaun P. Webster	71	64	70	69	274	13,200
(Foret defeated Webster on first playoff hole.)						
Martin Kaymer	71	68	65	71	275	8,400
Johan Skold	67	71	67	71	276	7,200
Felipe Aguilar	72	67	70	68	277	4,500
Rodolfo Gonzalez	69	69	68	71	277	4,500
Alexander Noren	73	69	66	69	277	4,500
Peter Whiteford	69	66	74	68	277	4,500
Sion E. Bebb	70	69	69	70	278	2,550
Kalle Brink	70	66	75	67	278	2,550
Klas Eriksson	67	70	70	71	278	2,550
Rafael Gomez	71	68	70	69	278	2,550
Olivier David	68	70	71	70	279	1,860
Anthony Grenier	67	68	69	75	279	1,860
Mark Pilkington	70	72	69	68	279	1,860
Hernan Rey	70	69	72	68	279	1,860
Miguel Rodriguez	69	71	69	70	279	1,860
Sam Walker	70	70	71	68	279	1,860
Miguel Carballo	69	69	72	70	280	1,410
Paul Dwyer	70	68	70	72	280	1,410
Rafael Cabrera Bello	73	68	71	69	281	1,140
Rafael Echenique	72	68	72	69	281	1,140

	SCORES				TOTAL	MONEY
Sebastian Fernandez	70	68	75	68	281	1,140
Stuart Manley	68	72	70	71	281	1,140
Benoit Teilleria	71	68	69	73	281	1,140
John Wade	71	71	69	70	281	1,140
Magnus A. Carlsson	75	68	70	69	282	1,032
James Hepworth	75	68	68	71	282	1,032
Andrew McArthur	68	72	72	70	282	1,032
Fredrik Andersson Hed	68	67	75	73	283	972
Stephen Scahill	73	66	73	71	283	972

Apulia San Domenico Grand Final

San Domenico Golf Club, Puglia, Italy
Par 34-37–71; 6,998 yards

October 18-21
purse, €250,000

	SCORES				TOTAL	MONEY
James Hepworth	69	65	68	69	271	€42,800
Rafael Echenique	65	75	67	66	273	19,156.67
Alexander Noren	69	65	75	64	273	19,156.67
Mark Pilkington	67	68	71	67	273	19,156.67
James Heath	69	66	71	68	274	10,456
Jean Hugo	68	71	69	66	274	10,456
Rafael Cabrera Bello	69	72	68	66	275	7,871.60
Ivo Giner	69	69	72	65	275	7,871.60
Lee S. James	71	66	69	69	275	7,871.60
Sam Walker	68	70	69	68	275	7,871.60
Shaun P. Webster	67	70	68	70	275	7,871.60
Felipe Aguilar	66	70	72	68	276	6,067
Martin Kaymer	71	67	72	67	277	5,527
Chris Gane	73	72	68	65	278	4,756
Marcus Higley	69	69	69	71	278	4,756
Rafael Gomez	68	71	72	68	279	3,534.50
Andrew McArthur	69	69	69	72	279	3,534.50
Alvaro Salto	72	68	70	69	279	3,534.50
Mads Vibe-Hastrup	69	71	71	68	279	3,534.50
Jesus Maria Arruti	69	71	72	68	280	2,969
David Drysdale	70	70	72	68	280	2,969
Alvaro Quiros	67	72	73	69	281	2,750.50
Hernan Rey	67	75	69	70	281	2,750.50
Gareth Davies	72	70	72	68	282	2,596
Denny Lucas	70	73	72	68	283	2,480.50
Juan Parron	72	71	72	68	283	2,480.50
Martin Maritz	71	74	71	68	284	2,326.50
Adrien Mork	73	68	71	72	284	2,326.50
Anders Schmidt Hansen	69	75	70	71	285	2,141.67
Gary Lockerbie	74	71	72	68	285	2,141.67
Nicolas Vanhootegem	71	69	74	71	285	2,141.67

Argentina Open

See American Tours chapter.

Corona Mexico Open

See American Tours chapter.

Asian Tour

The Royal Trophy

Amata Spring Country Club, Bangkok, Thailand
Par 36-36–72; 7,322 yards

January 7-8
purse US$1,500,000

FIRST DAY
Alternate Shot

David Howell and Kenneth Ferrie (Europe) defeated S.K. Ho and Keiichiro Fukabori, 2 up.
Paul McGinley and Graeme McDowell (Europe) defeated Arjun Atwal and Jyoti Randhawa, 4 and 3.
Thomas Bjorn and Henrik Stenson (Europe) defeated Yasuharu Imano and Zhang Lianwei, 1 up.
Thaworn Wiratchant and Thongchai Jaidee (Asia) defeated Nick Faldo and Ian Woosnam, 6 and 5.

POINTS: Europe 3, Asia 1

Best Ball

Atwal and Randhawa (Asia) defeated Howell and Ferrie, 1 up.
McGinley and McDowell (Europe) defeated Ho and Zhang, 2 and 1.
Woosnam and Bjorn (Europe) defeated Thaworn and Thongchai, 3 and 2.
Stenson and Faldo (Europe) defeated Fukabori and Imano, 1 up.

POINTS: Europe 3, Asia 1

SECOND DAY
Singles

Imano (Asia) defeated Howell, 2 up.
McGinley (Europe) defeated Zhang, 2 and 1.
McDowell (Europe) defeated Randhawa, 3 and 2.
Atwal (Asia) defeated Faldo, 3 and 2.
Thaworn (Asia) defeated Woosnam, 2 and 1.
Ho (Asia) defeated Ferrie, 2 and 1.
Fukabori (Asia) defeated Bjorn, 4 and 3.
Stenson (Europe) defeated Thongchai, 5 and 4.

POINTS: Europe 3, Asia 5
TOTAL POINTS: Europe 9, Asia 7

(Each member of the European team received US$125,000; each member of the Asian team received US$62,500.)

Pakistan Open

Karachi Golf Club, Karachi, Pakistan
Par 36-36–72; 6,893 yards

January 19-22
purse US$200,000

	SCORES				TOTAL	MONEY
Chris Rodgers	69	64	68	72	273	US$31,700
Jeev Milkha Singh	68	69	71	69	277	16,950

516 / ASIA/JAPAN TOURS

	SCORES				TOTAL	MONEY
Amandeep Johl	68	67	73	69	277	16,950
Frankie Minoza	72	73	69	65	279	8,280
Iain Steel	73	66	69	71	279	8,280
Muhammed Munir	70	68	66	75	279	8,280
Jochen Lupprian	72	68	70	70	280	5,420
Ashok Kumar	68	70	70	72	280	5,420
Marcus Both	70	71	71	69	281	4,170
Barry Hume	70	72	66	73	281	4,170
Arjun Singh	69	69	75	69	282	3,130
Anura Rohana	71	70	71	70	282	3,130
Shabbir Iqbal	70	67	73	72	282	3,130
Imdad Hussain	68	72	71	71	282	3,130
Matloob Ahmed	70	70	70	72	282	3,130
Mark Mouland	68	65	71	78	282	3,130
Simon Hurd	73	72	68	70	283	2,480
Unho Park	71	69	72	71	283	2,480
Digvijay Singh	71	69	70	73	283	2,480
Akinori Tani	69	72	68	74	283	2,480
Felix Casas	76	68	71	69	284	2,250
Richard Moir	73	69	71	71	284	2,250
Sushi Ishigaki	71	72	73	69	285	2,010
Olle Nordberg	69	75	71	70	285	2,010
Mardan Mamat	76	67	71	71	285	2,010
Vivek Bhandari	72	70	71	72	285	2,010
Brad Kennedy	73	67	73	72	285	2,010
Jeremy Kavanagh	70	69	73	73	285	2,010
Zaw Moe	74	71	71	70	286	1,740
Daniel Wardrop	74	70	70	72	286	1,740
Yasin Ali	74	71	68	73	286	1,740
Anthony Kang	72	73	72	70	287	1,560

Commercialbank Qatar Masters
See European Tours Chapter.

Johnnie Walker Classic
See Australasian Tour Chapter.

Maybank Malaysian Open

Kuala Lumpur Golf & Country Club, Kuala Lumpur, Malaysia February 16-19
Par 36-36—72; 6,938 yards purse, US$1,210,000
(Event shortened to 54 holes—rain.)

	SCORES			TOTAL	MONEY
Charlie Wi	66	68	63	197	US$208,330
Thongchai Jaidee	69	63	66	198	138,880
Raphael Jacquelin	72	65	62	199	78,250
Mark Foster	71	66	63	200	57,750
John Bickerton	66	68	66	200	57,750
Gary Simpson	67	68	67	202	40,625
Chinarat Phadungsil	70	66	66	202	40,625
Graeme Storm	70	68	65	203	26,812
Mattias Eliasson	70	67	66	203	26,812

	SCORES			TOTAL	MONEY
Francesco Molinari	66	67	70	203	26,812
David Park	67	64	72	203	26,812
Keith Horne	68	67	69	204	21,500
Jean-Francois Lucquin	72	66	67	205	18,425
Padraig Harrington	69	69	67	205	18,425
Chapchai Nirat	69	69	67	205	18,425
Gary Murphy	66	68	71	205	18,425
Thammanoon Srirot	67	65	73	205	18,425
Prom Meesawat	68	70	68	206	14,421
Philip Archer	72	66	68	206	14,421
Marcus Fraser	69	69	68	206	14,421
Sam Little	70	68	68	206	14,421
Scott Strange	72	67	67	206	14,421
Simon Dyson	68	70	68	206	14,421
Gaurav Ghei	68	71	67	206	14,421
Shiv Kapur	72	68	66	206	14,421
Richard Finch	66	72	69	207	11,875
Lin Keng-chi	69	69	69	207	11,875
Steven O'Hara	72	66	69	207	11,875
Andrew Butterfield	69	70	68	207	11,875
Marcel Siem	71	70	66	207	11,875
Shaaban Hussein	71	67	70	208	9,875
Alexandre Rocha	70	69	69	208	9,875
Lu Wen-teh	68	71	69	208	9,875
Mikael Lundberg	68	69	71	208	9,875
Thaworn Wiratchant	65	71	72	208	9,875
Danny Chia	70	67	71	208	9,875
Emanuele Canonica	72	67	70	209	7,875
Unho Park	72	65	72	209	7,875
Wang Ter-chang	73	66	70	209	7,875
Amandeep Johl	71	69	69	209	7,875
Johan Edfors	70	70	69	209	7,875
Jyoti Randhawa	68	72	69	209	7,875
Ross Fisher	69	71	69	209	7,875
Ted Oh	72	69	68	209	7,875
Soren Kjeldsen	70	63	76	209	7,875
Airil Rizman Zahari	74	64	72	210	5,625
Robert-Jan Derksen	68	72	70	210	5,625
Tom Whitehouse	69	67	74	210	5,625
Fredrik Widmark	67	69	74	210	5,625
Mahal Pearce	70	70	70	210	5,625
Garry Houston	66	69	75	210	5,625
Miguel Angel Jimenez	64	77	69	210	5,625
Benn Barham	73	68	69	210	5,625
Chawalit Plaphol	70	71	69	210	5,625
Simon Wakefield	70	69	72	211	3,734
David Higgins	70	68	73	211	3,734
Christian Cevaer	71	68	72	211	3,734
Marco Ruiz	71	68	72	211	3,734
Anthony Kang	69	70	72	211	3,734
Paul Dwyer	71	66	74	211	3,734
Adam Blyth	69	72	70	211	3,734
Marc Warren	70	71	70	211	3,734
Frankie Minoza	69	69	74	212	2,937
Francois Delamontagne	68	70	74	212	2,937
Stephen Dodd	67	69	76	212	2,937
Leif Westerberg	69	71	72	212	2,937
Adam Le Vesconte	66	72	75	213	2,500
Gerry Norquist	68	72	73	213	2,500
David Carter	70	71	72	213	2,500

	SCORES	TOTAL	MONEY
Hendrik Buhrmann	69 68 77	214	2,082
Yeh Wei-tze	69 70 75	214	2,082
Prayad Marksaeng	72 68 75	215	1,871

Enjoy Jakarta HSBC Indonesia Open

Emeralda Golf Club, Jakarta, Indonesia
Par 36-36–72; 7,082 yards

March 2-5
purse, US$1,000,000

	SCORES	TOTAL	MONEY
Simon Dyson	66 68 67 67	268	US$166,660
Andrew Buckle	67 69 65 69	270	111,110
Thongchai Jaidee	66 68 72 68	274	56,300
Wang Ter-chang	66 68 70 70	274	56,300
Scott Strange	71 67 70 67	275	38,700
Matthew Millar	71 66 70 68	275	38,700
Shiv Kapur	72 68 66 71	277	27,500
David Higgins	66 71 69 71	277	27,500
Steven O'Hara	71 71 70 66	278	17,728
Brad Kennedy	67 72 73 66	278	17,728
Jose Manuel Lara	70 72 69 67	278	17,728
Anders Hansen	69 69 70 70	278	17,728
Peter Gustafsson	72 65 70 71	278	17,728
Terry Pilkadaris	72 68 68 70	278	17,728
Lu Wei-chih	71 70 66 71	278	17,728
Andrew Marshall	73 67 71 68	279	13,500
Thammanoon Srirot	68 69 72 70	279	13,500
Stephen Dodd	69 63 74 73	279	13,500
Leif Westerberg	70 67 76 67	280	11,187
Liang Wen-chong	68 73 72 67	280	11,187
Garry Houston	72 69 71 68	280	11,187
Sam Little	70 69 72 69	280	11,187
Thaworn Wiratchant	72 67 71 70	280	11,187
Anthony Kang	67 70 71 72	280	11,187
Steven Jeppesen	67 72 69 72	280	11,187
Rahil Gangjee	69 67 71 73	280	11,187
Boonchu Ruangkit	73 70 69 69	281	9,050
Charlie Wi	72 70 70 69	281	9,050
Benn Barham	70 67 74 70	281	9,050
Iain Steel	72 68 71 70	281	9,050
David Bransdon	73 66 71 71	281	9,050
David Griffiths	69 69 71 72	281	9,050
Scott Barr	70 73 72 67	282	7,314
Peter Lawrie	73 69 73 67	282	7,314
Adam Groom	72 70 71 69	282	7,314
Prayad Marksaeng	71 70 72 69	282	7,314
Jamie Donaldson	72 66 74 70	282	7,314
Lee Sung-man	72 67 72 71	282	7,314
Mahal Pearce	71 69 70 72	282	7,314
Jeev Milkha Singh	72 71 73 67	283	5,700
Richard Moir	72 71 70 70	283	5,700
Gary Rusnak	70 73 69 71	283	5,700
Andrew Butterfield	72 70 70 71	283	5,700
Robert Karlsson	72 70 70 71	283	5,700
Miles Tunnicliff	71 71 70 71	283	5,700
Felipe Aguilar	74 68 70 71	283	5,700
Keith Horne	70 70 72 71	283	5,700

	SCORES				TOTAL	MONEY
Unho Park	68	71	69	75	283	5,700
Philip Golding	69	74	73	68	284	4,200
Mo Joong-kyung	71	68	75	70	284	4,200
David Carter	69	73	71	71	284	4,200
Simon Yates	71	69	71	73	284	4,200
Wilhelm Schauman	68	68	74	74	284	4,200
Alexandre Rocha	70	72	67	75	284	4,200
Wade Ormsby	69	74	73	69	285	3,300
Rick Gibson	72	71	72	70	285	3,300
Zhang Lian-wei	72	70	71	72	285	3,300
Jason Dawes	71	72	76	67	286	2,900
Henrik Nystrom	72	71	75	68	286	2,900
David Dixon	70	71	74	71	286	2,900
Marcus Fraser	77	66	78	66	287	2,500
Carl Suneson	72	71	71	73	287	2,500
Prom Meesawat	72	67	76	72	287	2,500
Jyoti Randhawa	71	71	72	73	287	2,500
Damien McGrane	69	71	72	75	287	2,500
Robert Rock	70	73	73	72	288	2,200
Chinarat Phadungsil	69	73	77	72	291	1,957
Jarmo Sandelin	70	69	78	74	291	1,957
Chapchai Nirat	73	68	76	74	291	1,957
Fredrik Widmark	72	71	72	76	291	1,957
Ron Won	73	69	76	74	292	1,497
Marten Olander	72	68	77	75	292	1,497
Anthony Brown	69	74	77	73	293	1,490
Andrew Pitts	73	70	74	76	293	1,490
Angelo Que	70	70	74	80	294	1,485
Paul Dwyer	73	70	76	76	295	1,481

OSIM Singapore Masters

Laguna National Golf & Country Club, Singapore
Par 36-36–72; 7,207 yards

March 9-12
purse, US$1,000,000

	SCORES				TOTAL	MONEY
Mardan Mamat	65	70	70	71	276	US$166,660
Nick Dougherty	69	70	67	71	277	111,110
Ross Fisher	71	68	68	71	278	56,300
Charlie Wi	69	73	65	71	278	56,300
Jonathan Lomas	71	74	68	66	279	38,700
Chapchai Nirat	73	69	66	71	279	38,700
Jyoti Randhawa	74	68	71	68	281	27,500
Andrew Butterfield	74	69	66	72	281	27,500
Marcus Both	68	68	77	69	282	19,500
Marcus Fraser	65	76	70	71	282	19,500
Anders Hansen	69	74	66	73	282	19,500
Prayad Marksaeng	67	69	74	72	282	19,500
Thaworn Wiratchant	76	68	72	67	283	13,875
Ahmad Bateman	70	69	74	70	283	13,875
Francois Delamontagne	71	70	72	70	283	13,875
Wang Ter-chang	72	70	71	70	283	13,875
Lu Wei-chih	69	72	71	71	283	13,875
Peter Hanson	70	69	72	72	283	13,875
Joakim Haeggman	72	70	69	72	283	13,875
Wade Ormsby	67	71	72	73	283	13,875
Keith Horne	72	72	71	69	284	11,150

	SCORES				TOTAL	MONEY
Stuart Little	71	69	72	72	284	11,150
Simon Yates	72	71	69	72	284	11,150
Prom Meesawat	73	71	67	73	284	11,150
Liang Wen-chong	73	72	70	70	285	9,950
Chris Rodgers	72	70	71	72	285	9,950
Anthony Kang	75	70	67	73	285	9,950
Danny Chia	75	68	68	74	285	9,950
Jose Manuel Lara	70	74	72	70	286	8,750
Soren Hansen	71	74	70	71	286	8,750
Thammanoon Srirot	73	72	67	74	286	8,750
Andrew Marshall	73	70	69	74	286	8,750
Gary Rusnak	72	73	72	70	287	7,625
Peter Hedblom	71	70	73	73	287	7,625
Lu Wen-teh	70	71	72	74	287	7,625
Matthew Millar	73	69	70	75	287	7,625
Boonchu Ruangkit	67	73	76	72	288	6,900
Soren Kjeldsen	72	71	72	73	288	6,900
Robert Karlsson	72	73	70	73	288	6,900
Steven O'Hara	72	73	76	68	289	5,900
Jean Van de Velde	70	72	77	70	289	5,900
Lee Sung	72	71	75	71	289	5,900
Simon Dyson	73	67	78	71	289	5,900
Gary Evans	68	72	77	72	289	5,900
Unho Park	67	72	74	76	289	5,900
Charl Schwartzel	71	69	73	76	289	5,900
Ignacio Garrido	74	70	75	71	290	4,700
Edward Loar	74	68	75	73	290	4,700
Chinarat Phadungsil	70	73	73	74	290	4,700
Gaurav Ghei	73	72	69	76	290	4,700
Fredrik Widmark	69	74	70	77	290	4,700
Brett Rumford	73	69	77	72	291	3,514
David Higgins	71	72	76	72	291	3,514
Barry Lane	71	69	78	73	291	3,514
Jason Knutzon	73	72	74	72	291	3,514
Simon Khan	73	71	74	73	291	3,514
Miguel Angel Martin	69	73	73	76	291	3,514
Michael Hoey	75	65	74	77	291	3,514
Jean-Francois Lucquin	74	71	77	70	292	2,800
Simon Wakefield	72	71	76	73	292	2,800
Raymond Russell	70	72	74	76	292	2,800
Daniel Vancsik	73	71	76	73	293	2,450
Scott Strange	70	74	76	73	293	2,450
Robert Rock	70	73	76	74	293	2,450
Peter Lawrie	72	69	76	76	293	2,450
Peter Gustafsson	71	74	75	74	294	2,100
Amandeep Johl	72	73	74	75	294	2,100
Jason Dawes	74	71	73	76	294	2,100
Mike Cunning	75	70	77	73	295	1,743
Rahil Gangjee	77	68	75	75	295	1,743
Marc Cayeux	73	72	75	75	295	1,743
Christopher Hanell	73	72	77	74	296	1,496
Miles Tunnicliff	73	72	77	75	297	1,492
Bill Fung	72	72	75	79	298	1,489
Bryan Saltus	72	73	77	77	299	1,485
Shiv Kapur	71	73	80	76	300	1,481
Martin Erlandsson	70	74	76	81	301	1,478
Kyi Hla Han	72	73	79	81	305	1,474
Jarmo Sandelin	70	72			WD	

TCL Classic

Yalong Bay Golf Club, Sanya, Hainen Island, China
Par 36-36–72; 7,172 yards

March 16-19
purse, US$1,000,000

	SCORES				TOTAL	MONEY
Johan Edfors	66	66	63	68	263	US$166,660
Andrew Buckle	63	66	65	70	264	111,110
Prayad Marksaeng	66	66	68	65	265	62,600
Nick Dougherty	66	67	64	69	266	50,000
Lu Wen-teh	69	68	64	66	267	38,700
Gaurav Ghei	67	69	65	66	267	38,700
Warren Abery	63	68	71	66	268	25,800
Jeev Milkha Singh	69	63	66	70	268	25,800
David Howell	64	63	66	75	268	25,800
Paul Casey	65	68	68	68	269	19,200
Edward Loar	62	69	68	70	269	19,200
Ariel Canete	65	66	70	69	270	17,200
Matthew Millar	68	67	68	68	271	15,366
Wang Ter-chang	66	67	69	69	271	15,366
Charl Schwartzel	65	67	69	70	271	15,366
Anthony Kang	68	71	69	64	272	13,225
Prom Meesawat	68	70	68	66	272	13,225
Paul McGinley	69	65	68	70	272	13,225
Lin Keng-chi	67	67	67	71	272	13,225
Scott Strange	68	64	71	70	273	12,000
Alexandre Rocha	70	69	66	69	274	11,150
Amandeep Johl	70	63	69	72	274	11,150
Daniel Vancsik	66	65	70	73	274	11,150
Joakim Haeggman	63	69	68	74	274	11,150
Simon Yates	67	72	71	65	275	9,350
Unho Park	71	64	73	67	275	9,350
Li Chao	70	67	71	67	275	9,350
Brad Kennedy	68	66	73	68	275	9,350
David Bransdon	70	68	68	69	275	9,350
Simon Hurd	69	68	68	70	275	9,350
Thaworn Wiratchant	69	70	65	71	275	9,350
Christopher Hanell	67	68	68	72	275	9,350
Phillip Archer	66	72	70	68	276	7,212
Chris Rodgers	67	72	69	68	276	7,212
Rafael Gomez	71	68	69	68	276	7,212
Mahal Pearce	68	68	69	71	276	7,212
Gregory Havret	67	66	72	71	276	7,212
Jamie Donaldson	68	68	69	71	276	7,212
David Griffiths	68	67	69	72	276	7,212
Soren Hansen	66	69	67	74	276	7,212
Lee Sung	68	69	72	68	277	5,700
Richard McEvoy	68	71	70	68	277	5,700
Wilhelm Schauman	66	69	73	69	277	5,700
Marco Ruiz	67	70	70	70	277	5,700
Hendrik Buhrmann	71	68	67	71	277	5,700
Shiv Kapur	71	68	67	71	277	5,700
Rahil Gangjee	66	69	69	73	277	5,700
Thammanoon Srirot	69	70	74	65	278	4,600
Jarrod Lyle	68	65	75	70	278	4,600
Hennie Otto	69	68	68	73	278	4,600
Ignacio Garrido	66	73	66	73	278	4,600
Iain Pyman	69	70	70	70	279	3,900
Liang Wen-chong	62	74	71	72	279	3,900
Jason Dawes	68	67	71	73	279	3,900

	SCORES				TOTAL	MONEY
Thongchai Jaidee	70	68	72	70	280	3,042
Ross Bain	70	67	72	71	280	3,042
Angelo Que	71	67	71	71	280	3,042
Gary Clark	70	69	69	72	280	3,042
Keith Horne	72	67	69	72	280	3,042
Adam Blyth	67	66	73	74	280	3,042
Ari Savolainen	66	69	67	78	280	3,042
Terry Pilkadaris	69	68	69	75	281	2,600
Brian Akstrup	69	69	73	71	282	2,450
Stephen Scahill	71	66	70	75	282	2,450
Johan Skold	68	70	72	74	284	2,200
Raymond Russell	70	67	72	75	284	2,200
Richard Moir	69	68	71	76	284	2,200
Marcel Siem	70	68	71	78	287	2,000

Volvo China Open

Honghua International Golf Club, Beijing, China
Par 36-36–72; 7,203 yards

April 13-16
purse, US$1,800,000

	SCORES				TOTAL	MONEY
Jeev Milkha Singh	72	69	67	70	278	US$300,000
Gonzalo Fernandez-Castano	67	74	68	70	279	200,000
David Lynn	68	67	72	73	280	112,680
Jarrod Lyle	68	71	72	70	281	70,830
Peter Fowler	71	70	69	71	281	70,830
Simon Wakefield	67	73	70	71	281	70,830
Paul Casey	71	68	70	72	281	70,830
Peter O'Malley	72	72	70	68	282	42,660
Wang Ter-chang	69	72	71	70	282	42,660
Paul Lawrie	73	70	73	67	283	32,265
Simon Dyson	67	72	73	71	283	32,265
Peter Hanson	67	72	73	71	283	32,265
Prayad Marksaeng	69	67	72	75	283	32,265
Brett Rumford	69	75	71	69	284	27,540
Richard Sterne	72	72	70	71	285	24,336
Prom Meesawat	71	72	71	71	285	24,336
Jose-Filipe Lima	67	69	77	72	285	24,336
Peter Lawrie	71	70	72	72	285	24,336
Marcus Fraser	70	71	69	75	285	24,336
Christian Cevaer	66	72	79	69	286	19,552
Amandeep Johl	75	70	72	69	286	19,552
Marc Cayeux	71	65	80	70	286	19,552
Henrik Stenson	73	68	74	71	286	19,552
Damien McGrane	72	70	73	71	286	19,552
Jean Van de Velde	74	68	73	71	286	19,552
Chawalit Plaphol	72	70	72	72	286	19,552
Hendrik Buhrmann	72	68	71	75	286	19,552
Miles Tunnicliff	68	74	70	75	287	16,560
Soren Kjeldsen	71	70	71	75	287	16,560
Soren Hansen	72	70	70	75	287	16,560
Lin Wen-tang	71	73	73	71	288	14,014
Barry Lane	72	68	75	73	288	14,014
Jamie Spence	70	71	74	73	288	14,014
Jason Knutzon	70	71	74	73	288	14,014
Gregory Havret	71	72	72	73	288	14,014
Nick Dougherty	72	70	72	74	288	14,014

	SCORES				TOTAL	MONEY
Stephen Gallacher	73	70	69	76	288	14,014
Stuart Little	71	73	76	69	289	11,880
Terry Pilkadaris	72	67	76	74	289	11,880
Raphael Jacquelin	72	70	73	74	289	11,880
Ross Fisher	67	73	74	75	289	11,880
Joakim Backstrom	69	72	77	72	290	10,080
Thaworn Wiratchant	72	71	75	72	290	10,080
Scott Drummond	71	67	78	74	290	10,080
Robert Coles	70	69	77	74	290	10,080
Simon Yates	69	70	77	74	290	10,080
Nico van Rensburg	75	64	76	75	290	10,080
Fredrik Widmark	73	68	77	73	291	8,820
Adam Groom	75	70	74	73	292	8,280
Johan Edfors	72	71	75	74	292	8,280
Charlie Wi	72	69	81	71	293	7,380
Lu Wen-teh	71	70	77	75	293	7,380
Gary Emerson	71	70	73	79	293	7,380
Jose Manuel Lara	71	69	80	74	294	5,850
Harmeet Kahlon	76	67	75	76	294	5,850
Alessandro Tadini	76	67	75	76	294	5,850
Alistair Presnell	72	72	73	77	294	5,850
Li Chao	72	72	72	78	294	5,850
Robert-Jan Derksen	70	75	71	78	294	5,850
Rick Gibson	72	72	77	74	295	4,680
Rahil Gangjee	68	70	82	75	295	4,680
Frankie Minoza	71	72	76	76	295	4,680
Jason Dawes	71	70	78	76	295	4,680
Mahal Pearce	71	71	76	77	295	4,680
Scott Strange	74	71	74	77	296	3,960
Richard Bland	70	72	76	78	296	3,960
Kenneth Ferrie	74	69	75	78	296	3,960
Angelo Que	71	73	79	75	298	3,600
Paul Dwyer	70	75	76	79	300	3,420

BMW Asian Open

Tomson Shanghai Pudong Golf Club, Shanghai, China
Par 36-36–72; 7,300 yards

April 20-23
purse, US$1,800,000

	SCORES				TOTAL	MONEY
Gonzalo Fernandez-Castano	71	71	69	70	281	US$300,000
Henrik Stenson	67	72	71	71	281	200,000
(Fernandez-Castano defeated Stenson on first playoff hole.)						
Jose-Filipe Lima	71	70	73	68	282	101,340
Colin Montgomerie	69	74	71	68	282	101,340
Simon Dyson	72	71	72	68	283	64,440
Paul Casey	72	71	69	71	283	64,440
Mahal Pearce	72	72	68	71	283	64,440
Terry Pilkadaris	73	73	74	65	285	38,610
David Bransdon	72	74	73	66	285	38,610
Paul Lawrie	70	70	73	72	285	38,610
Peter O'Malley	73	70	69	73	285	38,610
Barry Lane	74	71	72	69	286	30,960
Brett Rumford	75	70	75	67	287	24,975
Steven Jeppesen	73	73	72	69	287	24,975
Christian Cevaer	73	72	73	69	287	24,975
Ignacio Garrido	75	71	71	70	287	24,975

	SCORES				TOTAL	MONEY
Charlie Wi	69	73	74	71	287	24,975
Peter Lawrie	69	72	75	71	287	24,975
Thaworn Wiratchant	73	70	73	71	287	24,975
Graeme Storm	74	69	72	72	287	24,975
Francois Delamontagne	70	73	76	69	288	19,800
Jean Van de Velde	68	78	71	71	288	19,800
Frankie Minoza	69	72	76	71	288	19,800
Andrew Marshall	71	73	73	71	288	19,800
Simon Wakefield	73	70	73	72	288	19,800
Shiv Kapur	71	74	76	68	289	16,290
Nick Dougherty	73	73	74	69	289	16,290
Jeev Milkha Singh	72	75	72	70	289	16,290
Chawalit Plaphol	73	71	75	70	289	16,290
Alex Cejka	71	74	74	70	289	16,290
Thomas Bjorn	69	78	71	71	289	16,290
Richard Bland	71	72	74	72	289	16,290
Chapchai Nirat	70	75	72	72	289	16,290
Ted Oh	70	77	73	70	290	12,780
Miles Tunnicliff	72	70	76	72	290	12,780
Marcus Fraser	69	76	73	72	290	12,780
Chris Rodgers	72	72	73	73	290	12,780
Jarrod Lyle	71	71	74	74	290	12,780
David Higgins	73	70	73	74	290	12,780
Markus Brier	72	71	70	77	290	12,780
Scott Drummond	70	75	75	71	291	10,440
Sven Struver	77	69	73	72	291	10,440
Garry Houston	71	71	76	73	291	10,440
Damien McGrane	72	74	72	73	291	10,440
Danny Chia	71	70	76	74	291	10,440
Jose Manuel Lara	74	69	72	76	291	10,440
Robert-Jan Derksen	75	71	78	68	292	9,000
Shaun Webster	73	71	77	71	292	9,000
Miguel Angel Jimenez	71	75	76	71	293	7,380
Raphael Jacquelin	72	72	78	71	293	7,380
Christopher Hanell	72	74	74	73	293	7,380
Jason Knutzon	71	73	76	73	293	7,380
Liang Wen-chong	70	74	76	73	293	7,380
Lu Wen-teh	75	70	75	73	293	7,380
Jarmo Sandelin	73	71	75	74	293	7,380
Johan Edfors	71	74	78	71	294	5,436
Prom Meesawat	73	74	75	72	294	5,436
Lee Sung	75	72	74	73	294	5,436
Stephen Gallacher	68	77	76	73	294	5,436
Simon Yates	73	74	72	75	294	5,436
Oliver Wilson	74	73	78	70	295	4,590
David Dixon	71	76	76	72	295	4,590
Jean-Francois Lucquin	71	76	75	73	295	4,590
Richard Sterne	73	73	74	75	295	4,590
Bryan Saltus	71	73	75	77	296	4,140
Kenneth Ferrie	72	75	77	73	297	3,780
Boonchu Ruangkit	70	76	78	73	297	3,780
Marc Cayeux	75	72	75	75	297	3,780
Jamie Spence	73	72	80	73	298	3,420
Adam Groom	71	75	78	76	300	3,280
Stuart Little	73	71	81	76	301	2,699
Alistair Presnell	74	73	80	76	303	2,696
Alessandro Tadini	70	77	77	80	304	2,692

GS Caltex Maekyung Open

Lakeside Country Club, Seoul, Korea
Par 36-36–72; 6,935 yards

April 27-30
purse, US$600,000

	SCORES				TOTAL	MONEY
Suk Jong-yul	67	69	68	67	271	US$125,000
Bryan Saltus	69	68	68	67	272	78,125
*Noh Seung-yul	69	69	70	66	274	
Amandeep Johl	69	69	70	66	274	34,375
Lee Sung	67	66	69	72	274	34,375
Kim Dae-sub	68	70	68	69	275	25,000
Scott Hend	70	72	67	67	276	17,447
Park Boo-won	70	71	68	67	276	17,447
Scott Barr	68	73	71	65	277	12,638
Shin Yong-jin	70	68	71	68	277	12,638
Charlie Wi	69	70	70	68	277	12,638
Iain Steel	70	70	68	70	278	10,000
Jarrod Lyle	71	72	64	72	279	9,375
Mo Joong-kyung	72	72	69	67	280	8,263
Choi Jin-ho	71	70	71	68	280	8,263
Kim Chang-yoon	71	70	71	68	280	8,263
Park Sang-eon	75	68	68	69	280	8,263
J.B. Holmes	71	71	63	75	280	8,263
Chung Joon	69	70	69	72	280	8,263
Kang Ji-man	75	67	71	68	281	7,291
Kim Sang-ki	70	65	72	74	281	7,291
Chung Jae-hoon	71	73	69	69	282	6,805
Kang Wook-soon	73	69	70	70	282	6,805
Lee Seong-ho	68	68	73	73	282	6,805
Gary Rusnak	74	70	69	70	283	6,171
*Eric Chun	69	71	72	71	283	
Lee In-woo	67	75	70	71	283	6,171
Gaurav Ghei	72	70	69	72	283	6,171
Hong Soon-sang	70	68	70	75	283	6,171
*Hur Won-kyung	70	69	74	71	284	
Richard Lee	69	74	70	71	284	5,057
Prom Meesawat	70	71	72	71	284	5,057
Lu Wei-chih	72	72	70	70	284	5,057
Park Do-kyu	73	69	70	72	284	5,057
Choi Hyuk-jae	72	69	74	69	284	5,057
Rick Gibson	74	69	72	69	284	5,057
Brad Kennedy	74	70	72	68	284	5,057
David Oh	72	72	74	66	284	5,057

SK Telecom Open

Sky 72 Golf Club, Seoul, Korea
Par 36-36–72; 7,152 yards
(Third round cancelled—rain.)

May 4-7
purse, US$600,000

	SCORES			TOTAL	MONEY
Prom Meesawat	69	64	68	201	US$127,523
Lee Seong-ho	67	67	70	204	53,134
Jeev Milkha Singh	68	66	70	204	53,134
K.J. Choi	68	72	65	205	31,880
Hong Soon-sang	71	66	69	206	23,910

	SCORES			TOTAL	MONEY
Chapchai Nirat	68	67	71	206	23,910
Kang Kyung-nam	69	68	70	207	17,800
Iain Steel	67	66	74	207	17,800
Jang Ik-jae	70	71	68	209	10,885
Moon Ji-wook	70	71	68	209	10,885
Angelo Que	71	69	69	209	10,885
Hwang In-choon	69	70	70	209	10,885
Chinarat Phadungsil	71	68	70	209	10,885
Choi Ho-sung	70	68	71	209	10,885
Lu Wei-lan	72	66	71	209	10,885
*Lee Won-jun	69	67	73	209	
Ari Savolainen	69	72	69	210	8,076
Michael Wright	73	67	70	210	8,076
Kim Chang-min	72	72	66	210	8,076
*Mang Dong-sub	68	73	70	211	
*Hur In-hoi	68	73	70	211	
Adam Blyth	69	72	70	211	6,865
Eiji Mizoguchi	71	72	68	211	6,865
Chris Rodgers	71	72	68	211	6,865
Park Boo-won	71	68	72	211	6,865
Choi Jin-ho	70	68	73	211	6,865
Kim Hong-sik	70	71	71	212	5,433
Simon Nash	70	71	71	212	5,433
Kim Chang-yoon	76	66	70	212	5,433
Kim Dae-sub	71	71	70	212	5,433
Charlie Wi	70	73	69	212	5,433
Anthony Kang	70	68	74	212	5,433
Adam Le Vesconte	65	71	76	212	5,433
Brad Kennedy	67	68	77	212	5,433

Aamby Valley Asian Masters

Aamby Valley Golf Club, Mumbai, India
Par 36-36–72; 7,087 yards

May 11-14
purse, US$400,000

	SCORES				TOTAL	MONEY
Hendrik Buhrmann	66	75	65	71	277	US$63,400
Simon Hurd	67	70	69	73	279	43,400
Terry Pilkadaris	72	71	67	70	280	24,400
Marcus Both	70	71	70	72	283	19,720
Garth Mulroy	74	68	70	72	284	12,910
Simon Griffiths	68	72	67	77	284	12,910
Kane Webber	69	74	66	75	284	12,910
Ashok Kumar	67	66	73	78	284	12,910
Anthony Brown	73	71	73	69	286	7,966
Rahil Gangjee	73	69	74	70	286	7,966
Gaurav Ghei	74	69	68	75	286	7,966
Bryan Saltus	71	70	76	70	287	6,205
Michael Wright	71	77	69	70	287	6,205
Craig Warren	73	75	68	71	287	6,205
Keith Horne	68	75	72	72	287	6,205
Anthony Kang	74	74	69	71	288	5,400
Rahul Ganapathy	74	69	69	76	288	5,400
Amandeep Johl	71	75	74	69	289	4,853
Darren Griff	73	71	70	75	289	4,853
Barry Hume	70	72	72	75	289	4,853
Jason King	71	72	76	71	290	4,500

	SCORES				TOTAL	MONEY
Yasin Ali	71	72	71	76	290	4,500
Iain Steel	72	72	69	78	291	4,320
Luke Hickmott	69	75	75	73	292	4,020
Gurbaaz Mann	71	74	72	75	292	4,020
S.S.P. Chowrasia	70	74	71	77	292	4,020
Corey Harris	69	73	71	79	292	4,020
C. Muniyappa	72	76	72	73	293	3,660
Gerald Rosales	74	70	74	75	293	3,660
Chris Gill	76	71	75	72	294	3,177
Kevin Chun	73	70	79	72	294	3,177
Robin Hodgetts	75	73	73	73	294	3,177
Tony Carolan	75	71	73	75	294	3,177
Ari Savolainen	74	70	74	76	294	3,177
Airil Rizman Zahari	69	74	73	78	294	3,177
Olle Nordberg	73	70	72	79	294	3,177

Macau Open

Macau Golf & Country Club, Macau
Par 35-36–71; 6,027 yards

May 18-21
purse, US$300,000

	SCORES				TOTAL	MONEY
Kane Webber	69	65	71	70	275	US$47,550
Scott Barr	71	68	69	70	278	32,550
Peter Karmis	71	64	72	72	279	16,545
Brad Kennedy	68	65	69	77	279	16,545
Terry Pilkadaris	72	72	66	71	281	12,300
Scott Strange	70	64	74	74	282	10,170
Gerald Rosales	72	68	71	72	283	6,837
Pat Giles	70	70	71	72	283	6,837
Lu Wei-chih	69	74	68	72	283	6,837
Jason Knutzon	71	69	69	74	283	6,837
Chinarat Phadungsil	69	68	70	76	283	6,837
Chen Yuan-chi	74	68	68	74	284	4,897
Anthony Kang	69	67	72	76	284	4,897
Steve Elkington	71	66	74	74	285	4,320
Barry Hume	74	66	70	75	285	4,320
Chris Rodgers	70	72	67	76	285	4,320
Wang Ter-chang	73	68	71	74	286	3,870
Ari Savolainen	70	69	71	76	286	3,870
Bryan Saltus	75	67	73	72	287	3,334
Tony Carolan	71	71	72	73	287	3,334
Lin Wen-tang	67	72	74	74	287	3,334
Michael Wright	69	69	74	75	287	3,334
Lu Wei-lan	71	70	71	75	287	3,334
Hong Chia-yuh	70	70	70	77	287	3,334
Jochen Lupprian	70	71	69	77	287	3,334
Simon Griffiths	75	69	73	71	288	2,880
Jarrod Moseley	75	66	70	77	288	2,880
Alistair Presnell	72	68	69	79	288	2,880
Iain Steel	72	70	75	72	289	2,490
Zhang Lian-wei	72	70	72	75	289	2,490
Martin Rominger	72	72	68	77	289	2,490
Kevin Chun	72	71	68	78	289	2,490
Park Jun-won	72	69	69	79	289	2,490
Marcus Both	66	70	72	81	289	2,490

Philippine Open

Wack Wack Golf & Country Club, Manila, Philippines
Par 36-36–72; 7,053 yards

May 25-28
purse, US$200,000

	SCORES				TOTAL	MONEY
Scott Strange	68	70	72	70	280	US$31,700
Park Jun-won	75	74	69	67	285	21,700
Chris Rodgers	70	69	75	72	286	10,086
Lu Wei-lan	69	74	72	71	286	10,086
Yeh Chang-ting	69	69	73	75	286	10,086
Juvic Pagunsan	72	70	74	72	288	6,300
Unho Park	72	71	73	72	288	6,300
Jason Dawes	70	75	74	70	289	4,242
Gary Simpson	71	72	74	72	289	4,242
Hsieh Chin-sheng	71	73	71	74	289	4,242
Cookie Lao	70	74	70	75	289	4,242
Gerald Rosales	73	72	74	71	290	3,176
S.S.P. Chowrasia	74	72	71	73	290	3,176
Adam Porker	73	72	71	74	290	3,176
Adam Le Vesconte	74	76	70	71	291	2,760
Jason Knutzon	73	71	76	71	291	2,760
Barry Hume	69	76	74	72	291	2,760
Alistair Presnell	73	75	72	72	292	2,260
Jochen Lupprian	72	76	72	72	292	2,260
Gary Rusnak	73	74	73	72	292	2,260
Anthony Kang	72	72	74	74	292	2,260
Marcus Both	73	70	74	75	292	2,260
Rick Gibson	70	72	75	75	292	2,260
Richard Moir	77	69	71	75	292	2,260
Angelo Que	71	75	70	76	292	2,260
Marciano Pucay	72	75	74	73	294	1,860
Airil Rizman Zahari	73	70	78	73	294	1,860
Wang Ter-chang	74	72	76	72	294	1,860
Elmer Salvador	78	70	71	75	294	1,860
Uttam Singh Mundy	75	74	69	76	294	1,860

Bangkok Airways Open

Santiburi Samui Country Club, Koh Samui, Thailand
Par 36-36–72; 6,881 yards

June 8-11
purse, US$300,000

	SCORES				TOTAL	MONEY
Chawalit Plaphol	71	70	73	67	281	US$47,550
Rick Gibson	69	72	71	69	281	32,550
(Chawalit defeated Gibson on first playoff hole.)						
Mardan Mamat	70	69	72	71	282	18,300
Lu Wen-teh	68	68	72	75	283	14,790
Iain Steel	66	78	72	68	284	11,235
Prayad Marksaeng	67	70	74	73	284	11,235
Lee Sung	71	71	70	74	286	8,730
S.S.P. Chowrasia	73	71	74	69	287	6,680
Thongchai Jaidee	74	73	68	72	287	6,680
Thaworn Wiratchant	68	73	72	74	287	6,680
Chen Yuan-chi	74	73	68	73	288	5,415
Anthony Kang	73	71	76	70	290	4,897
Digvijay Singh	81	67	72	70	290	4,897

	SCORES	TOTAL	MONEY
Simon Nash	74 77 70 71	292	4,320
P. Gunasegaran	73 69 76 74	292	4,320
Garth Mulroy	72 75 69 76	292	4,320
Wang Ter-chang	72 73 74 74	293	3,870
Juvic Pagunsan	73 70 74 76	293	3,870
Somkiat Srisanga	71 72 80 71	294	3,472
Amandeep Johl	75 76 72 71	294	3,472
Park Jun-won	72 73 75 74	294	3,472
Prom Meesawat	72 70 76 76	294	3,472
Yeh Chang-ting	73 78 72 72	295	3,150
Simon Griffiths	72 73 76 74	295	3,150
Rashid Ismail	75 70 75 75	295	3,150
Yasin Ali	75 69 80 72	296	2,970
Martin Maritz	72 75 76 74	297	2,835
Unho Park	71 71 78 77	297	2,835
Brad Iles	74 74 82 68	298	2,526
Lin Wen-hong	74 75 76 73	298	2,526
Brad Kennedy	74 73 77 74	298	2,526
Banlue Maneerat	71 76 75 76	298	2,526
Michael Wright	73 70 75 80	298	2,526

Crowne Plaza Open

Yalong Bay Golf Club, Sanya, China
Par 36-36–72; 7,176 yards

August 17-20
purse, US$200,000

	SCORES	TOTAL	MONEY
Chinarat Phadungsil	65 68 68 71	272	US$31,700
Prom Meesawat	69 71 67 65	272	16,950
Lin Wen-tang	67 64 74 67	272	16,950
(Chinarat defeated Lin on first and Prom on second playoff hole.)			
Adam Blyth	67 67 70 70	274	8,280
Thaworn Wiratchant	68 67 68 71	274	8,280
Unho Park	73 64 66 71	274	8,280
Alistair Presnell	71 71 65 68	275	5,420
Anthony Kang	74 68 64 69	275	5,420
Amandeep Johl	67 69 70 70	276	4,400
Kao Bo-song	69 69 71 68	277	3,775
Anton Haig	71 69 67 70	277	3,775
Garth Mulroy	70 71 67 70	278	3,374
Brad Iles	71 72 70 66	279	3,078
Sung Mao-chang	72 70 67 70	279	3,078
Simon Yates	73 70 70 67	280	2,507
Ross Bain	67 72 72 69	280	2,507
Rahil Gangjee	70 70 71 69	280	2,507
S.S.P. Chowrasia	70 72 68 70	280	2,507
Lin Keng-chi	69 71 68 72	280	2,507
Gaurav Ghei	71 67 70 72	280	2,507
Yasin Ali	71 69 67 73	280	2,507
Robin Hodgetts	67 71 68 74	280	2,507
Prayad Marksaeng	68 69 75 69	281	2,100
Scott Taylor	74 69 70 68	281	2,100
Wisut Artjanawat	71 72 68 70	281	2,100
Artemio Murakami	71 71 71 69	282	1,860
Martin Rominger	70 72 70 70	282	1,860
Simon Dunn	71 68 74 69	282	1,860
Lam Chih Bing	71 68 74 69	282	1,860
Kim Tae-jin	71 66 76 69	282	1,860

Brunei Open

Empire Hotel & Country Club,
Bandar Seri Begawan, Brunei
Par 36-35–71; 7,259 yards

August 24-27
purse, US$300,000

	SCORES				TOTAL	MONEY
Wang Ter-chang	68	70	64	66	268	US$47,550
David Gleeson	67	68	65	68	268	32,550
(Wang defeated Gleeson on second playoff hole.)						
Rahil Gangjee	64	71	69	68	272	15,130
Anthony Kang	70	67	66	69	272	15,130
Juvic Pagunsan	66	68	67	71	272	15,130
Chapchai Nirat	68	71	68	66	273	9,450
Lin Wen-tang	70	63	70	70	273	9,450
Jyoti Randhawa	73	67	68	66	274	7,065
Clay Devers	70	69	65	70	274	7,065
Edward Loar	71	70	70	64	275	5,280
Simon Griffiths	68	72	70	65	275	5,280
Simon Hurd	70	69	66	70	275	5,280
Michael Wright	67	66	72	70	275	5,280
Airil Rizman Zahari	72	68	69	67	276	3,977
Corey Harris	74	67	67	68	276	3,977
Rick Gibson	67	69	71	69	276	3,977
Lee Sung	70	68	69	69	276	3,977
Richard Moir	69	68	67	72	276	3,977
Ross Bain	67	68	68	73	276	3,977
Terry Pilkadaris	67	69	64	76	276	3,977
Brad Iles	70	68	70	69	277	3,240
Garth Mulroy	68	68	72	69	277	3,240
Tony Carolan	70	68	68	71	277	3,240
Boonchu Ruangkit	67	70	69	71	277	3,240
Jason King	68	69	66	74	277	3,240
Shabbir Iqbal	70	68	71	69	278	2,790
Marcus Both	70	69	69	70	278	2,790
Arjun Singh	71	68	69	70	278	2,790
Suk Jong-yul	70	68	69	71	278	2,790
Jason Knutzon	68	68	66	76	278	2,790

Pulai Springs Malaysian Masters

Pulai Springs Resort, Johor, Malaysia
Par 36-36–72; 6,906 yards

August 31-September 3
purse, US$300,000

	SCORES				TOTAL	MONEY
Anton Haig	63	66	69	68	266	US$47,550
Barry Hume	67	67	67	66	267	32,550
Yasin Ali	68	67	66	67	268	16,545
Jyoti Randhawa	70	64	66	68	268	16,545
Lin Chie-hsiang	68	69	63	71	271	12,300
Park Jun-won	71	67	68	66	272	8,257
Richard Moir	69	67	68	68	272	8,257
Jason Knutzon	69	66	68	69	272	8,257
Chapchai Nirat	65	65	70	72	272	8,257
David Gleeson	72	65	70	66	273	5,462
Kao Bo-song	69	62	74	68	273	5,462
Chan Song	68	70	67	68	273	5,462

	SCORES				TOTAL	MONEY
Zaw Moe	66	67	73	68	274	4,152
Eddie Lee	68	69	69	68	274	4,152
Edward Loar	69	69	67	69	274	4,152
Matt Keegan	67	68	70	69	274	4,152
Chinarat Phadungsil	69	67	69	69	274	4,152
Gaurav Ghei	71	66	67	70	274	4,152
Thaworn Wiratchant	69	67	67	71	274	4,152
Corey Harris	68	71	69	67	275	3,420
Juvic Pagunsan	72	64	70	69	275	3,420
Adam Blyth	66	71	68	70	275	3,420
Tony Carolan	70	68	68	70	276	3,105
Gary Rusnak	68	70	67	71	276	3,105
Marcus Both	63	69	69	75	276	3,105
Ross Bain	67	69	67	73	276	3,105
Chris Rodgers	69	67	71	70	277	2,700
Digvijay Singh	68	68	71	70	277	2,700
Michael Wright	68	71	72	66	277	2,700
Muhammed Munir	72	67	65	73	277	2,700
Shiv Kapur	68	68	68	73	277	2,700

Barclays Singapore Open

Sentosa Golf Club, Singapore
Par 36-35–71; 7,169 yards
(Fourth round cancelled—rain.)

September 7-10
purse, US$3,000,000

	SCORES			TOTAL	MONEY
Adam Scott	70	69	66	205	US$475,500
Ernie Els	71	65	69	205	325,500
(Scott defeated Els on third playoff hole.)					
Brad Kennedy	71	67	70	208	183,000
Liang Wen-chong	73	68	68	209	147,900
Shiv Kapur	70	69	72	211	123,000
Prom Meesawat	72	70	70	212	94,500
Anthony Kang	70	71	71	212	94,500
Lee Westwood	73	69	71	213	63,600
Unho Park	72	69	72	213	63,600
Jyoti Randhawa	68	73	72	213	63,600
Angel Cabrera	69	68	76	213	63,600
Mardan Mamat	72	69	73	214	47,500
Shingo Katayama	69	69	76	214	47,500
Scott Strange	67	69	78	214	47,500
Rashid Ismail	71	74	70	215	40,500
Yasin Ali	74	70	71	215	40,500
Lee Sung	72	71	72	215	40,500
Charl Schwartzel	70	72	73	215	40,500
Lin Keng-chi	71	73	72	216	33,800
S.S.P. Chowrasia	72	71	73	216	33,800
Adam Blyth	72	70	74	216	33,800
Edward Loar	73	68	75	216	33,800
Nick O'Hern	69	72	75	216	33,800
Arjun Singh	74	67	75	216	33,800
Jason Knutzon	74	73	70	217	28,350
Jeev Milkha Singh	71	76	70	217	28,350
Gaurav Ghei	74	71	72	217	28,350
Yeh Chang-ting	73	71	73	217	28,350
Juvic Pagunsan	67	76	74	217	28,350
Chan Song	73	67	77	217	28,350

Kolon-Hana Bank Korea Open

Woo Jeong Hills Country Club, Cheonan, Korea
Par 36-35–71; 7,086 yards

September 21-24
purse, US$700,000

	SCORES				TOTAL	MONEY
Y.E. Yang	65	67	68	70	270	US$205,128
Kang Ji-man	67	63	73	70	273	64,615
Rahil Gangjee	70	70	67	68	275	33,162
David Oh	74	66	68	67	275	33,162
Kang Kyung-nam	68	63	72	72	275	33,162
Thaworn Wiratchant	69	66	71	70	276	20,615
Nam Young-woo	66	69	71	70	276	20,615
Retief Goosen	65	72	69	70	276	20,615
Chapchai Nirat	71	71	69	66	277	16,820
*Noh Seung-yul	69	67	73	69	278	
Bubba Watson	67	66	75	70	278	14,051
Kwon Myung-ho	66	69	69	74	278	14,051
Lu Wei-chih	73	67	73	66	279	10,974
Choi Hyun	68	70	72	69	279	10,974
*Kim Do-hoon I	70	67	69	73	279	
Lee Jin-won	67	72	72	69	280	8,143
Park Young-soo	70	71	74	65	280	8,143
Shin Yong-jin	67	68	74	71	280	8,143
Kong Young-joon	67	72	69	72	280	8,143
Chung Joon	68	66	70	76	280	8,143
Chinarat Phadungsil	71	71	71	68	281	7,384
*Hur Won-kyung	71	72	69	70	282	
Yoo Jong-koo	72	67	71	72	282	6,769
Yasin Ali	69	72	73	68	282	6,769
Kim Hyung-sung	67	72	71	72	282	6,769
Marc Leishman	70	70	72	71	283	5,709
Edward Loar	69	70	74	70	283	5,709
Ted Oh	70	73	69	71	283	5,709
Simon Yates	66	76	73	68	283	5,709
*Kim Kyung-tae	70	68	72	73	283	
Suk Jong-yul	70	67	72	74	283	5,709
*Kim Do-hoon II	69	69	70	75	283	
Kim Hyung-tae	70	70	68	75	283	5,709

Mercuries Taiwan Masters

Taiwan Golf & Country Club, Taiwan, Chinese Taipei
Par 36-36–72; 6,915 yards

September 28-October 1
purse, US$500,000

	SCORES				TOTAL	MONEY
Gaurav Ghei	71	72	69	66	278	US$100,000
Rahil Gangjee	66	70	72	71	279	60,000
Ted Oh	70	68	72	72	282	35,000
Adam Groom	73	69	72	70	284	19,375
Park Jun-won	70	72	73	69	284	19,375
Jason Knutzon	67	70	76	71	284	19,375
Bryan Saltus	69	69	73	73	284	19,375
Yeh Wei-tze	71	70	71	73	285	12,500
Lin Wen-tang	72	71	67	76	286	10,000
Chris Rodgers	74	72	69	72	287	9,000
Eddie Lee	72	73	74	69	288	7,500

	SCORES				TOTAL	MONEY
Simon Hurd	73	73	70	72	288	7,500
Lin Keng-chi	72	73	72	71	288	7,500
Lu Wei-chih	71	72	71	74	288	7,500
Lin Wen-hong	72	73	64	79	288	7,500
Gerry Norquist	74	70	74	71	289	5,750
Shiv Kapur	73	71	71	74	289	5,750
Amandeep Johl	72	71	72	74	289	5,750
Lu Wen-teh	74	68	73	74	289	5,750
Chung Chun-hsing	68	71	73	77	289	5,750
Gary Rusnak	73	73	74	70	290	4,920
Richard Lee	69	73	75	73	290	4,920
Gerald Rosales	70	70	78	72	290	4,920
Hsieh Chin-sheng	71	72	71	76	290	4,920
Yasin Ali	72	73	70	75	290	4,920
Digvijay Singh	73	72	76	70	291	4,450
Rick Gibson	71	70	75	75	291	4,450
Adam Blyth	66	75	73	77	291	4,450
Simon Nash	69	72	72	78	291	4,450
Eiji Mizoguchi	72	73	75	72	292	4,100
Prom Meesawat	74	69	77	72	292	4,100
Chang Tse-peng	70	72	73	77	292	4,100

Taiwan Open

Sunrise Golf & Country Club, Taiwan, Chinese Taipei
Par 36-36–72; 7,195 yards

October 5-8
purse, US$300,000

	SCORES				TOTAL	MONEY
Lin Wen-tang	70	68	68	69	275	US$47,550
Simon Yates	70	71	69	68	278	32,550
Pat Giles	71	66	74	68	279	18,300
Thaworn Wiratchant	70	69	70	71	280	13,545
Lin Keng-chi	69	70	70	71	280	13,545
Wang Ter-chang	71	72	67	71	281	9,450
Yasin Ali	72	67	70	72	281	9,450
Richard Moir	69	72	74	67	282	7,065
Tony Carolan	75	72	66	69	282	7,065
Richard Lee	73	74	69	67	283	5,462
Clay Devers	73	71	68	71	283	5,462
Rick Gibson	71	70	70	72	283	5,462
Chinarat Phadungsil	72	71	72	69	284	4,518
Iain Steel	73	71	68	72	284	4,518
Gary Rusnak	70	66	72	76	284	4,518
Park Jun-won	72	71	67	75	285	4,140
Gurbaaz Mann	72	74	72	68	286	3,720
Chang Tse-peng	72	73	70	71	286	3,720
Chen Yuan-chi	71	70	73	72	286	3,720
Kane Webber	67	71	73	75	286	3,720
Ted Oh	71	75	69	72	287	3,150
Ari Savolainen	74	71	69	73	287	3,150
Hsieh Tung-shu	72	70	71	74	287	3,150
Brad Iles	72	69	72	74	287	3,150
Chris Rodgers	71	72	70	74	287	3,150
Tsai Chi-huang	68	77	66	76	287	3,150
Lee Sung	71	68	72	76	287	3,150
Rafael Ponce	70	74	73	71	288	2,655
Unho Park	69	74	74	71	288	2,655

	SCORES	TOTAL	MONEY
Angelo Que	69 70 74 75	288	2,655
Lu Tze-shyan	74 71 67 76	288	2,655

Volkswagen Masters - China

Yalong Bay Golf Club, Sanya, China
Par 36-36–72; 7,186 yards

October 12-15
purse, US$300,000

	SCORES	TOTAL	MONEY
Retief Goosen	64 65 67 71	267	US$47,550
Michael Campbell	64 68 70 68	270	32,550
Simon Dunn	68 69 66 68	271	18,300
Prayad Marksaeng	74 70 65 64	273	13,545
Yasin Ali	66 69 69 69	273	13,545
Lu Wen-teh	63 69 69 73	274	10,170
Chinarat Phadungsil	72 68 64 73	277	8,730
Frankie Minoza	73 69 67 69	278	7,530
Iain Steel	75 69 68 67	279	5,544
Juvic Pagunsan	72 69 70 68	279	5,544
Adam Blyth	69 71 70 69	279	5,544
Ross Bain	68 67 74 70	279	5,544
Unho Park	72 71 65 71	279	5,544
Prom Meesawat	72 69 68 71	280	4,230
Kane Webber	70 69 68 73	280	4,230
Li Chao	70 70 67 73	280	4,230
Michael Wright	70 72 65 73	280	4,230
Chapchai Nirat	73 68 72 68	281	3,485
Wang Ter-chang	74 70 69 68	281	3,485
Terry Pilkadaris	72 73 67 69	281	3,485
Lu Wei-lan	70 70 71 70	281	3,485
Anthony Kang	70 68 71 72	281	3,485
Tony Lascuna	68 72 67 74	281	3,485
Danny Chia	67 71 76 68	282	3,015
Corey Harris	73 70 70 69	282	3,015
Lam Chih Bing	72 69 70 71	282	3,015
Simon Griffiths	73 69 65 75	282	3,015
Hendrik Buhrmann	71 73 69 70	283	2,532
Barry Hume	73 72 67 71	283	2,532
Lin Wen-tang	68 71 72 72	283	2,532
Gurbaaz Mann	74 66 71 72	283	2,532
Garth Mulroy	71 72 68 72	283	2,532
Arjun Singh	70 68 72 73	283	2,532
Anthony Brown	75 69 67 72	283	2,532

Hero Honda Indian Open

Delhi Golf Club, New Delhi, India
Par 36-36–72; 6,888 yards
(Playoff completed on Monday—darkness.)

October 19-23
purse, US$400,000

	SCORES	TOTAL	MONEY
Jyoti Randhawa	69 67 64 70	270	US$63,400
Vijay Kumar	66 68 70 66	270	33,900
S.S.P. Chowrasia	69 65 67 69	270	33,900

(Randhawa defeated Kumar on first and Chowrasia on second playoff hole.)

	SCORES				TOTAL	MONEY
Simon Dyson	68	67	68	68	271	19,720
Mukesh Kumar	70	68	66	72	276	14,980
Prom Meesawat	68	68	68	72	276	14,980
Suk Jong-yul	67	73	68	69	277	10,160
Unho Park	70	65	69	73	277	10,160
Gaurav Ghei	71	68	65	73	277	10,160
*Chiragh Kumar	69	69	74	67	279	
Scott Strange	67	73	67	72	279	7,880
Mark Mouland	71	70	68	71	280	6,760
Muhammed Munir	70	69	69	72	280	6,760
Rahil Gangjee	71	66	69	74	280	6,760
Terry Pilkadaris	69	69	70	73	281	6,000
Rick Gibson	68	73	71	70	282	5,520
Thaworn Wiratchant	76	66	68	72	282	5,520
Vivek Bhandari	68	71	70	73	282	5,520
Mahal Pearce	70	69	71	73	283	4,940
Park Jun-won	72	65	72	74	283	4,940
David Gleeson	71	74	69	70	284	4,320
Somkiat Srisanga	74	70	69	71	284	4,320
Shamim Khan	70	73	70	71	284	4,320
Michael Wright	67	73	72	72	284	4,320
Shiv Kapur	74	67	69	74	284	4,320
Digvijay Singh	71	72	67	74	284	4,320
Chris Rodgers	73	71	65	75	284	4,320
Simon Dunn	66	77	71	71	285	3,720
Yasin Ali	69	73	71	72	285	3,720
Matt Holten	73	67	69	76	285	3,720

HSBC Champions

Sheshan International Golf Club, Shanghai, China
Par 36-36—72; 7,165 yards

November 9-12
purse, US$5,000,000

	SCORES				TOTAL	MONEY
Y.E. Yang	66	72	67	69	274	US$833,300
Tiger Woods	72	64	73	67	276	555,550
Retief Goosen	68	67	69	73	277	281,500
Michael Campbell	66	70	77	64	277	281,500
Marc Warren	66	71	70	71	278	213,000
Paul Casey	73	68	68	71	280	150,000
Padraig Harrington	67	70	73	70	280	150,000
Robert Karlsson	73	68	69	70	280	150,000
Jyoti Randhawa	65	69	72	75	281	94,300
Francesco Molinari	72	68	69	72	281	94,300
K.J. Choi	68	72	71	70	281	94,300
Johan Edfors	68	74	69	70	281	94,300
Jim Furyk	73	66	74	68	281	94,300
John Bickerton	68	71	71	72	282	74,100
Luke Donald	70	69	71	72	282	74,100
Colin Montgomerie	69	70	76	67	282	74,100
Jeev Milkha Singh	70	69	71	73	283	68,400
Henrik Stenson	76	64	70	74	284	64,950
Shiv Kapur	71	67	74	72	284	64,950
Bradley Dredge	71	70	70	74	285	59,300
Nick O'Hern	72	69	71	73	285	59,300
Charl Schwartzel	72	72	71	70	285	59,300
Anton Haig	71	71	72	72	286	54,100

	SCORES				TOTAL	MONEY
Kevin Stadler	74	70	71	71	286	54,100
Camilo Villegas	71	71	75	69	286	54,100
Gaurav Ghei	72	70	71	74	287	50,350
Chris DiMarco	70	74	73	70	287	50,350
Anthony Wall	73	67	78	70	288	48,100
Chinarat Phadungsil	72	69	74	74	289	45,850
Alan McLean	71	68	78	72	289	45,850
Ian Poulter	72	74	72	72	290	42,850
Mark Pilkington	74	70	75	71	290	42,850
Thaworn Wiratchant	75	67	71	78	291	39,850
Markus Brier	71	75	72	73	291	39,850
Chawalit Plaphol	67	70	82	73	292	36,850
Craig Parry	77	69	75	71	292	36,850
Scott Strange	70	76	74	73	293	35,000
Cesar Monasterio	74	68	80	72	294	34,000
Gregory Bourdy	73	68	76	78	295	31,500
Peter O'Malley	69	79	73	74	295	31,500
Jean Van de Velde	74	71	77	73	295	31,500
Simon Dyson	78	71	74	72	295	31,500
Warren Abery	74	66	76	80	296	27,500
Niclas Fasth	76	70	74	76	296	27,500
Alejandro Canizares	68	75	78	75	296	27,500
Chris Rodgers	74	76	73	73	296	27,500
Tadahiro Takayama	72	67	81	77	297	23,500
Darren Fichardt	71	69	80	77	297	23,500
David Howell	73	72	76	76	297	23,500
Gonzalo Fernandez-Castano	78	71	77	71	297	23,500
Zhang Lian-wei	72	76	73	77	298	20,000
Wang Ter-chang	71	75	76	76	298	20,000
Stephen Dodd	72	73	79	74	298	20,000
Paul Sheehan	77	72	77	73	299	16,500
Liang Wen-chong	78	75	74	72	299	16,500
Lin Wen-tang	76	75	77	71	299	16,500
Kane Webber	77	73	79	70	299	16,500
Thomas Bjorn	75	76	74	75	300	14,000
Hendrik Buhrmann	75	73	77	76	301	12,500
Adam Bland	74	77	78	72	301	12,500
Suk Jong-yul	76	75	76	75	302	11,000
Liao Gui-ming	75	74	76	78	303	10,000
Louis Oosthuizen	71	75	83	74	303	10,000
Paul Broadhurst	76	77	78	72	303	10,000
Prom Meesawat	75	75	80	74	304	9,000
Li Chao	75	78	75	79	307	8,250
Mardan Mamat	74	80	78	75	307	8,250
Qi Zeng-fa	77	77	74	81	309	7,750
Steven Bowditch	72	71	79	89	311	7,500
Huang Ming-jie	78	78	80	76	312	7,250
*Hu Mu	83	73	77	80	313	
Yuan Hao	80	74	84	75	313	7,000
Wu Wei-huang	76	78	83	79	316	6,750
Bradford Vaughan	85	73	82	77	317	6,500

The Goodwill Trophy

Mission Hills Golf Club, World Cup Course, Shenzhen, China   November 13-14
Par 36-36–72; 7,323 yards

FIRST DAY
Foursomes

Zhang Lian-wei and Jeev Milkha Singh (International Team) halved with Luke Donald and Nick Dougherty.
K.J. Choi and Thongchai Jaidee (Int'l) defeated Paul Casey and Alejandro Canizares, 3 and 2.
Henrik Stenson and Bradley Dredge (Ryder Cup Countries Team) defeated Peter Senior and Paul Sheehan, 4 and 3.
Retief Goosen and Michael Campbell (Int'l) defeated Colin Montgomerie and Chris DiMarco, 5 and 4.

POINTS: International Team 2½, Ryder Cup Countries 1½

SECOND DAY
Singles

Henrik Stenson (Ryder) defeated Jeev Milkha Singh, 3 and 2.
Paul Sheehan (Int'l) halved with Nick Dougherty.
Michael Campbell (Int'l) halved with Chris DiMarco.
K.J. Choi (Int'l) defeated Paul Casey, 1 up.
Colin Montgomerie (Ryder) defeated Retief Goosen, 1 up.
Alejandro Canizares (Ryder) defeated Zhang Lian-wei, 1 up.
Peter Senior (Int'l) defeated Bradley Dredge, 1 up.
Thongchai Jaidee (Int'l) defeated Luke Donald, 2 and 1.

TOTAL POINTS: International Team 6½, Ryder Cup Countries 5½

UBS Hong Kong Open

Hong Kong Golf Club, Fanling   November 16-19
Par 34-36–70; 6,703 yards   purse, US$2,000,000

	SCORES				TOTAL	MONEY
Jose Manuel Lara	64	66	66	69	265	US$333,330
Juvic Pagunsan	67	65	66	68	266	222,220
Jeev Milkha Singh	66	67	69	66	268	103,333
Jyoti Randhawa	64	69	69	66	268	103,333
Thongchai Jaidee	68	66	67	67	268	103,333
Soren Kjeldsen	69	68	65	67	269	65,000
Miguel Angel Jimenez	68	67	66	68	269	65,000
Francesco Molinari	68	69	67	66	270	44,933
Alejandro Canizares	71	69	63	67	270	44,933
Jean Van de Velde	68	67	67	68	270	44,933
Gregory Bourdy	65	66	69	71	271	36,800
Andrew Buckle	67	65	72	68	272	34,400
Anthony Kang	70	70	68	66	274	28,866
Raphael Jacquelin	69	67	71	67	274	28,866
Liang Wen-chong	65	72	70	67	274	28,866
Gary Simpson	69	68	69	68	274	28,866
Angelo Que	69	66	69	70	274	28,866
Simon Khan	66	68	68	72	274	28,866
Graeme Storm	65	73	71	66	275	23,000

	SCORES				TOTAL	MONEY
James Kingston	70	68	70	67	275	23,000
Bryan Saltus	68	70	69	68	275	23,000
Colin Montgomerie	69	66	70	70	275	23,000
Cesar Monasterio	68	70	67	70	275	23,000
Scott Strange	68	68	69	70	275	23,000
Thammanoon Srirot	68	66	74	68	276	19,300
Thaworn Wiratchant	68	70	69	69	276	19,300
Peter Lawrie	71	64	71	70	276	19,300
Daniel Chopra	72	67	67	70	276	19,300
Christian Cevaer	68	68	68	72	276	19,300
Matthew Millar	69	71	64	72	276	19,300
Jose-Filipe Lima	69	68	75	65	277	16,040
Lin Wen-tang	70	68	68	71	277	16,040
Gary Emerson	70	69	67	71	277	16,040
Mark Pilkington	69	67	67	74	277	16,040
Zhang Lian-wei	69	63	70	75	277	16,040
Prom Meesawat	69	69	73	67	278	13,600
Jarmo Sandelin	66	71	73	68	278	13,600
Tom Whitehouse	70	70	70	68	278	13,600
Damien McGrane	68	66	73	71	278	13,600
Rick Gibson	68	71	68	71	278	13,600
Ron Won	68	68	70	72	278	13,600
Joakim Backstrom	70	69	73	67	279	11,200
Gary Rusnak	68	71	71	69	279	11,200
K.J. Choi	71	69	70	69	279	11,200
Gaurav Ghei	70	70	69	70	279	11,200
Park Jun-won	67	69	72	71	279	11,200
Lee Sung	67	72	68	72	279	11,200
James Stewart	67	73	75	65	280	8,800
Johan Axgren	67	73	73	67	280	8,800
Kane Webber	70	70	73	67	280	8,800
Adam Le Vesconte	70	69	70	71	280	8,800
Suk Jong-yul	66	70	72	72	280	8,800
Adam Blyth	66	68	73	73	280	8,800
Robert-Jan Derksen	68	68	70	75	281	7,200
Anton Haig	69	65	71	76	281	7,200
Hendrik Buhrmann	67	71	74	70	282	5,933
Terry Pilkadaris	70	70	71	71	282	5,933
David Carter	70	69	71	72	282	5,933
Phillip Price	68	68	73	73	282	5,933
Darren Fichardt	71	68	68	75	282	5,933
Simon Yates	67	70	69	76	282	5,933
Rahil Gangjee	70	70	71	72	283	5,100
Michael Campbell	68	71	69	75	283	5,100
Clay Devers	68	72	71	74	285	4,800
Martin Rominger	68	72	72	75	287	4,600
Scott Barr	69	71	80	69	289	4,400
David Bransdon	67	73	77	75	292	4,200
Lu Wen-teh	70	70			DQ	

Volvo Masters of Asia

Thai Country Club, Bangkok, Thailand
Par 36-36–72; 7,082 yards

December 14-17
purse, US$650,000

	SCORES				TOTAL	MONEY
Thongchai Jaidee	68	68	69	72	277	US$104,000
Frankie Minoza	76	64	68	70	278	71,075
Charlie Wi	71	69	70	69	279	40,200
Thaworn Wiratchant	72	65	70	73	280	32,595
Prom Meesawat	68	70	72	71	281	27,200
Chawalit Plaphol	69	70	73	70	282	18,441
Jeev Milkha Singh	72	66	72	72	282	18,441
Edward Loar	71	68	71	72	282	18,441
David Bransdon	76	65	69	72	282	18,441
Andrew Buckle	71	70	71	71	283	12,383
S.S.P. Chowrasia	70	70	71	72	283	12,383
Prayad Marksaeng	67	72	68	76	283	12,383
Anthony Kang	76	64	73	72	285	10,554
Brad Kennedy	71	70	69	75	285	10,554
Jyoti Randhawa	72	69	73	72	286	9,910
Liang Wen-chong	74	70	73	70	287	9,325
Iain Steel	69	72	66	80	287	9,325
Thammanoon Srirot	71	74	70	73	288	8,740
Chris Rodgers	69	73	74	73	289	8,176
Simon Yates	72	71	72	74	289	8,176
Angelo Que	72	71	70	76	289	8,176
Rick Gibson	72	75	71	72	290	7,278
Barry Hume	74	71	71	74	290	7,278
Lee Sung	69	70	74	77	290	7,278
Gary Rusnak	71	72	71	76	290	7,278
Lin Keng-chi	68	73	71	78	290	7,278
Terry Pilkadaris	68	75	69	78	290	7,278
Jarrod Lyle	73	73	75	70	291	5,961
Chinarat Phadungsil	71	70	78	72	291	5,961
Wang Ter-chang	69	73	76	73	291	5,961
Adam Groom	69	75	74	73	291	5,961
Kane Webber	77	68	72	74	291	5,961
Jason Knutzon	71	70	74	76	291	5,961
Unho Park	70	70	74	77	291	5,961
Yasin Ali	72	69	71	79	291	5,961

Omega China Tour

Hainan Leg

Kangle Garden Spa & Golf Club, Hainan
Par 36-36–72

April 6-9
purse, RMB800,000

	SCORES				TOTAL	MONEY
Liang Wenchong	72	65	65	71	273	RMB150,000
Zhang Lianwei	72	72	68	70	282	90,000
Li Chao	76	67	69	71	283	50,000
Yuan Hao	66	74	76	70	286	22,000
Zheng Wengen	70	73	70	75	288	17,500
Gu Shutao	75	71	74	69	289	14,750
Xiao Zhijin	73	70	73	73	289	14,750
Huang Mingjie	78	68	72	72	290	13,750
Wu Weihuang	75	72	78	65	290	13,750
Xia Zhengrong	75	76	70	70	291	13,000
*Wu Ashun	78	72	70	71	291	
Lai Yuanlang	70	76	73	73	292	12,600
Qi Zengfa	74	72	72	74	292	12,600
Zheng Shaoguang	75	75	71	71	292	12,600
Huang Yonghuan	76	73	72	72	293	12,100
Tan Yongzong	74	75	70	74	293	12,100
Gu Cuilin	75	71	74	74	294	11,400
Liu Qiang	76	74	73	71	294	11,400
Liu Guojie	74	72	71	77	294	11,400
Shang Lei	77	74	70	73	294	11,400
Xing Xiaoxuan	74	70	75	75	294	11,400
Liao Guiming	73	69	80	73	295	10,500
Wu Xujun	74	75	72	74	295	10,500
Deng Yonghong	75	74	71	75	295	10,500
Yuan Zheng	75	73	74	73	295	10,500
Tan Guohua	76	68	74	78	296	10,000
Zhang Chengwei	81	67	75	74	297	9,800
Qiu Zhifeng	78	75	75	70	298	9,600
Chen Dongsheng	74	72	74	79	299	8,900
Gao Lei	76	76	72	75	299	8,900
Liu Anda	78	73	72	76	299	8,900
Chen Yong	73	77	75	74	299	8,900
Zhou Xunshu	76	77	71	75	299	8,900
Wang Lei	74	78	75	72	299	8,900

Zhuhai Leg

Golden Gulf Golf Club, Zhuhai
Par 36-36–72

May 11-14
purse, RMB800,000

	SCORES				TOTAL	MONEY
Zhang Lianwei	75	74	78	69	296	RMB150,000
Zheng Wengen	79	80	71	72	302	90,000
Wu Weihuang	73	78	80	72	303	50,000

	SCORES				TOTAL	MONEY
Qi Zengfa	74	73	79	78	304	36,000
Li Chao	69	74	78	84	305	22,000
Yuan Hao	72	74	86	75	307	18,000
Shang Lei	74	78	78	78	308	17,400
Chen Yu	83	76	72	78	309	16,550
Xia Zhengrong	79	80	79	71	309	16,550
Huang Yonghuan	79	76	80	75	310	15,550
Wu Xujun	80	78	74	78	310	15,550
Xiao Zhijin	75	79	83	74	311	14,800
Zheng Shaoguang	77	78	78	79	312	14,300
Zhang Jun	79	77	82	75	313	13,800
Liu Qiang	75	78	81	80	314	12,800
Tan Yongzong	75	80	82	77	314	12,800
*Ye Jianfeng	79	78	81	76	314	
Yuan Tian	76	82	76	80	314	12,800
Liu Guojie	79	77	85	74	315	11,366
Yang Shengqin	77	79	79	80	315	11,366
Liu Jian	74	75	83	83	315	11,366
*Wu Ashun	76	78	84	79	317	
Liu Xin	76	76	83	83	318	10,700
Wang Huiqiang	78	80	76	84	318	10,700
Tang Jinchang	83	78	79	79	319	10,300
Zhou Xunshu	76	75	87	81	319	10,300
Cui Xiaolong	81	80	73	86	320	9,500
Feng Xu	78	77	86	79	320	9,500
Huang Zhenxiong	80	76	83	81	320	9,500
Qiu Zhifeng	72	79	82	87	320	9,500
Song Zhiqiang	81	78	82	79	320	9,500
Deng Yonghong	79	82	78	81	320	9,500

Shandong Leg

Tiger Beach Golf Links, Shandong
Par 36-36–72

June 15-18
purse, RMB800,000

	SCORES			TOTAL	MONEY
Li Chao	75	71	71	74	291	RMB150,000
Yuan Hao	71	73	76	72	292	90,000
Zhang Lianwei	75	80	73	68	296	50,000
Huang Mingjie	71	79	75	73	298	29,000
Qiu Zhifeng	78	72	75	73	298	29,000
Liu Qiang	74	73	78	74	299	18,000
Huang Yonghuan	75	78	76	72	301	17,400
Gu Cuilin	76	74	75	77	302	16,800
Qi Zengfa	77	79	71	76	303	16,050
Zheng Shaoguang	73	79	76	75	303	16,050
*Wu Ashun	71	77	78	77	303	
Liu Anda	74	76	79	75	304	15,050
Xiao Zhijin	81	73	76	74	304	15,050
Gu Shutao	81	74	78	74	307	14,050
Song Qingli	77	80	72	78	307	14,050
Liao Guiming	78	81	73	76	308	12,800
Wu Weihuang	76	78	78	76	308	12,800
Cui Xiaolong	79	79	75	76	309	11,800
Tan Yongzong	81	78	77	73	309	11,800
Chen Xiaoma	82	77	78	72	309	11,800
Liu Guojie	76	74	80	80	310	10,900

	SCORES	TOTAL	MONEY
Xing Xiaoxuan	80 79 76 75	310	10,900
Chen Yu	79 73 80 79	311	10,500
Qing Sanyong	77 77 78 79	311	10,500
Deng Yuchao	77 78 79 78	312	10,200
Liu Xin	78 78 81 78	315	9,800
Lv Wenxu	78 78 80 79	315	9,800
Deng Yonghong	78 81 83 73	315	9,800
Fu Xin	80 78 77 81	316	9,000
Liu Junfeng	76 83 78 79	316	9,000
Meng Qingpeng	80 77 74 85	316	9,000
Wu Xujun	77 81 84 74	316	9,000
Liu Jian	78 83 76 79	316	9,000

Shanghai Leg

Grand Shanghai Golf & Holiday Resort, Shanghai
Par 36-36–72

August 31-September 3
purse, RMB800,000

	SCORES	TOTAL	MONEY
Zhang Lianwei	69 71 70 72	282	RMB150,000
Huang Mingjie	74 72 66 70	282	90,000
(Zhang defeated Huang on second playoff hole.)			
Qi Zengfa	72 70 68 73	283	50,000
Li Chao	69 70 72 73	284	36,000
*Fan Zhipeng	69 70 73 73	285	
Shang Lei	70 75 71 70	286	22,000
Xiao Zhijin	70 72 72 73	287	18,000
Cui Xiaolong	73 72 70 73	288	16,575
Gu Cuilin	70 75 74 69	288	16,575
Qiu Zhifeng	70 78 69 71	288	16,575
Wu Weihuang	69 73 68 78	288	16,575
Chen Yu	71 72 74 72	289	15,050
Liao Guiming	69 74 73 73	289	15,050
Meng Qingpeng	73 72 73 72	290	14,300
Gu Shutao	73 73 75 70	291	13,550
Yuan Hao	75 71 71 74	291	13,550
Sun Peng	75 73 71 73	292	12,300
Xia Zhengrong	72 76 71 73	292	12,300
Zheng Shaoguang	74 75 73 70	292	12,300
Chen Jian	75 71 78 70	294	11,300
Liu Peiguo	73 73 76 73	295	10,600
Shi Ningjie	77 74 71 73	295	10,600
Xing Xiaoxuan	78 69 74 74	295	10,600
Deng Yonghong	74 76 72 73	295	10,600
Yuan Tian	72 75 74 74	295	10,600
Liu Junfeng	76 75 74 71	296	9,900
Liu Anda	73 75 76 72	296	9,900
Zhang Meng	75 77 73 72	297	9,500
Ye Xionghui	76 71 74 76	297	9,500
Liu Guojie	72 73 77 76	298	9,200
*Wei Wei	76 72 75 75	298	

Kunming Leg

Kunming Country Golf Club, Kunming
Par 36-36–72

September 21-24
purse, RMB800,000

	SCORES			TOTAL	MONEY
Li Chao	68 73 65 71			277	RMB150,000
Huang Mingjie	76 71 68 69			284	90,000
Zhang Lianwei	74 72 72 68			286	50,000
Liao Guiming	73 72 74 69			288	36,000
Huang Yonghuan	74 70 76 70			290	22,000
Shang Lei	74 73 71 73			291	17,400
Xiao Zhijin	75 73 74 69			291	17,400
Yuan Hao	77 71 70 73			291	17,400
*Wu Kangchun	75 73 71 72			291	
Gu Cuilin	75 73 75 69			292	16,300
Gu Shutao	76 70 72 75			293	14,800
Liu Anda	73 75 71 74			293	14,800
Zheng Shaoguang	72 75 70 76			293	14,800
Zhang Wei	72 77 73 71			293	14,800
Tan Yongzong	73 70 72 78			293	14,800
Zhang Chengwei	74 78 74 68			294	13,300
*Wu Ashun	75 71 76 72			294	
Wu Xujun	72 77 71 75			295	12,800
*Tang Wei	74 70 76 75			295	
*He Shaocai	75 72 74 74			295	
Chen Dongsheng	74 75 71 77			297	11,600
Liu Qiang	81 72 66 78			297	11,600
Meng Qingpeng	72 79 69 77			297	11,600
Liu Anlin	75 77 75 70			297	11,600
Qiu Zhifeng	74 78 72 74			298	10,600
Wu Weihuang	71 74 77 76			298	10,600
Gui Bing	77 71 73 77			298	10,600
Fu Xin	76 77 72 74			299	10,100
Song Zhiqiang	75 79 69 76			299	10,100
Liu Guojie	76 77 73 75			301	9,500
Xu Qin	76 75 73 77			301	9,500
Deng Yonghong	74 72 78 77			301	9,500
Yuan Tian	79 73 76 73			301	9,500

Omega Championship

Tianan Golf Club, Beijing
Par 36-36–72

October 26-29
purse, RMB800,000

	SCORES			TOTAL	MONEY
Liang Wenchong	70 68 67 68			273	RMB150,000
Li Chao	72 72 66 75			285	90,000
Zhang Lianwei	78 70 74 69			291	50,000
Liao Guiming	72 74 75 74			295	36,000
Zheng Wengen	81 69 72 75			297	22,000
Liu Anda	75 72 76 75			298	18,000
Shi Ningjie	74 73 72 80			299	16,833
Shang Lei	76 73 79 71			299	16,833
Deng Yonghong	74 72 77 76			299	16,833
Qiu Zhifeng	73 77 74 77			301	15,800
Tan Yongzong	73 76 78 75			302	15,050

	SCORES				TOTAL	MONEY
Wu Hongfu	80	71	77	74	302	15,050
Xiao Zhijin	77	74	81	71	303	14,050
Yuan Hao	78	73	74	78	303	14,050
Huang Mingjie	79	70	77	78	304	13,300
Liu Guojie	76	77	77	76	306	12,300
Qi Zengfa	75	72	79	80	306	12,300
Wu Xujun	76	72	79	79	306	12,300
Gu Cuilin	80	74	78	75	307	11,150
Chen Jian	83	72	73	79	307	11,150
Huang Yonghuan	78	75	78	78	309	10,600
Wu Weihuang	76	76	82	75	309	10,600
Zhou Xunshu	74	76	82	77	309	10,600
Meng Qingpeng	77	78	78	77	310	10,200
*Su Dong	75	76	78	81	310	
Chen Yu	77	78	78	78	311	9,600
Cui Xiaolong	79	80	75	77	311	9,600
Gu Shutao	78	77	81	75	311	9,600
Tang Jinchang	78	76	78	79	311	9,600
Yang Bing	80	79	75	77	311	9,600

Japan Tour

Token Homemate Cup

Token Shuga Country Club, Kani, Gifu
Par 36-36–72; 6,906 yards

April 13-16
purse, ¥110,000,000

	SCORES				TOTAL	MONEY
Wayne Perske	64	67	69	67	267	¥22,000,000
Yui Ueda	69	66	68	66	269	9,240,000
Brendan Jones	68	67	66	68	269	9,240,000
David Smail	68	66	68	68	270	4,317,500
Chang Ik-je	63	68	70	69	270	4,317,500
Hideto Tanihara	67	68	67	68	270	4,317,500
Hiroyuki Fujita	67	67	67	69	270	4,317,500
Mitsuhiro Tateyama	67	70	69	65	271	3,113,000
S.K. Ho	68	67	70	66	271	3,113,000
Akinori Tani	67	64	68	72	271	3,113,000
Tetsuji Hiratsuka	68	69	71	64	272	2,332,000
Toshiya Sakakura	67	68	71	66	272	2,332,000
Toshinori Muto	66	70	68	68	272	2,332,000
Katsuya Nakagawa	62	69	72	69	272	2,332,000
Masashi Ozaki	69	65	72	67	273	1,782,000
Katsumasa Miyamoto	70	67	67	69	273	1,782,000
Ryoken Kawagishi	65	70	67	71	273	1,782,000
Katsumune Imai	68	68	72	66	274	1,342,000
Naomichi Ozaki	68	66	74	66	274	1,342,000
Kouki Idoki	68	70	69	67	274	1,342,000

	SCORES				TOTAL	MONEY
Hajime Meshiai	68	69	70	67	274	1,342,000
Naoya Sugiyama	68	68	68	70	274	1,342,000
Taichi Teshima	65	71	67	71	274	1,342,000
Norihiko Nakata	69	69	70	67	275	924,000
Yoichi Shimizu	70	66	71	68	275	924,000
Paul Sheehan	69	69	69	68	275	924,000
Steven Conran	68	70	68	69	275	924,000
Gregory Meyer	68	68	70	69	275	924,000
Hidemasa Hoshino	69	69	72	65	275	924,000
Sushi Ishigaki	70	68	70	68	276	683,833
Satoshi Higashi	64	74	68	70	276	683,833
Takao Nogami	67	70	69	70	276	683,833
Satoru Hirota	68	70	67	71	276	683,833
Tadahiro Takayama	68	69	68	71	276	683,833
Yasuharu Imano	69	67	68	72	276	683,833

Tsuruya Open

Yamanohara Golf Club, Kawanishi, Hyogo
Par 35-36–71; 6,778 yards

April 20-23
purse, ¥100,000,000

	SCORES				TOTAL	MONEY
Brendan Jones	70	68	66	69	273	¥20,000,000
Mamo Osanai	70	69	68	68	275	10,000,000
Kazuhiro Shimizu	73	68	70	65	276	6,800,000
Shingo Katayama	70	71	67	69	277	4,400,000
Kiyoshi Murota	68	68	69	72	277	4,400,000
Paul Sheehan	71	68	72	67	278	3,600,000
Toru Taniguchi	70	72	71	66	279	3,056,666
David Smail	70	70	70	69	279	3,056,666
Kaname Yokoo	73	71	66	69	279	3,056,666
Kouki Idoki	73	70	68	69	280	2,420,000
Ryuichi Oda	72	68	68	72	280	2,420,000
Y.E. Yang	71	69	67	73	280	2,420,000
Soushi Tajima	73	71	71	66	281	1,740,000
Tatsuya Mitsuhashi	68	74	72	67	281	1,740,000
Tetsuji Hiratsuka	75	69	70	67	281	1,740,000
Rich Tate	73	73	67	68	281	1,740,000
Tatsu Ichihara	69	70	70	72	281	1,740,000
Tadahiro Takayama	74	67	73	68	282	1,113,333
Wayne Perske	71	72	70	69	282	1,113,333
Yoshiaki Mano	72	72	69	69	282	1,113,333
Jun Kikuchi	72	73	68	69	282	1,113,333
Toshihiro Aizawa	76	67	69	70	282	1,113,333
Nozomi Kawahara	73	69	70	70	282	1,113,333
Hisayuki Sasaki	72	71	69	70	282	1,113,333
Taichi Teshima	73	71	68	70	282	1,113,333
Hidemasa Hoshino	73	71	68	70	282	1,113,333
Katsunori Kuwabara	69	72	73	69	283	721,666
S.K. Ho	73	68	73	69	283	721,666
Mitsuhiro Tateyama	76	68	70	69	283	721,666
Masaya Tomida	75	69	70	69	283	721,666
Naomichi Ozaki	73	70	70	70	283	721,666
Toshinori Muto	74	71	72	66	283	721,666

The Crowns

Nagoya Golf Club, Wago Course, Aichi
Par 35-35–70; 6,547 yards

April 27-30
purse, ¥120,000,000

		SCORES			TOTAL	MONEY
Shingo Katayama	63	67	62	70	262	¥24,000,000
Nozomi Kawahara	67	63	67	67	264	12,000,000
Ryoken Kawagishi	70	69	67	63	269	8,160,000
Y.E. Yang	69	73	63	65	270	4,710,000
Nick Dougherty	68	69	65	68	270	4,710,000
S.K. Ho	69	67	66	68	270	4,710,000
Prayad Marksaeng	70	67	64	69	270	4,710,000
Tomohiro Kondo	67	70	68	66	271	3,522,000
Taichi Teshima	71	66	66	68	271	3,522,000
Toru Taniguchi	69	67	69	67	272	3,024,000
Jeev Milkha Singh	64	69	69	70	272	3,024,000
Keiichiro Fukabori	72	68	66	67	273	2,424,000
Steven Conran	71	71	63	68	273	2,424,000
Soushi Tajima	62	69	72	70	273	2,424,000
Kiyoshi Maita	67	72	69	66	274	1,944,000
Yoshikazu Haku	69	69	69	67	274	1,944,000
Lin Keng-chi	69	69	69	67	274	1,944,000
Thaworn Wiratchant	71	70	67	67	275	1,512,000
Hidemasa Hoshino	70	72	66	67	275	1,512,000
Toshimitsu Izawa	67	70	70	68	275	1,512,000
Mamo Osanai	71	70	66	68	275	1,512,000
Jun Kikuchi	69	66	67	73	275	1,512,000
Brendan Jones	65	67	74	70	276	1,144,000
Yeh Wei-tze	71	71	64	70	276	1,144,000
Tadahiro Takayama	68	66	71	71	276	1,144,000
Tsuneyuki Nakajima	73	69	71	64	277	912,000
Hideto Tanihara	69	72	69	67	277	912,000
Ryuichi Oda	69	70	70	68	277	912,000
Yasuharu Imano	67	70	70	70	277	912,000
Paul Sheehan	69	71	67	70	277	912,000
Hiroyuki Fujita	70	68	68	71	277	912,000

Japan PGA Championship

Tanigumi Country Club, Ibigawa, Gifu
Par 36-36–72; 7,003 yards

May 11-14
purse, ¥110,000,000

		SCORES			TOTAL	MONEY
Tomohiro Kondo	68	70	71	69	278	¥22,000,000
Katsuyoshi Tomori	71	69	70	68	278	11,000,000
(Kondo defeated Tomori on first playoff hole.)						
Shingo Katayama	69	69	72	69	279	6,380,000
Toru Taniguchi	68	68	69	74	279	6,380,000
Yoshikazu Haku	72	70	70	68	280	3,996,666
Nozomi Kawahara	69	75	67	69	280	3,996,666
Jeev Milkha Singh	71	72	68	69	280	3,996,666
Lin Keng-chi	68	69	72	72	281	3,355,000
Kenichi Kuboya	70	70	70	72	282	3,102,000
Yeh Wei-tze	71	69	72	71	283	2,772,000
Liang Wen-chong	72	68	69	74	283	2,772,000
Shinichi Akiba	70	70	73	71	284	2,222,000

	SCORES	TOTAL	MONEY
Norihiko Nakata	66 70 74 74	284	2,222,000
Tadahisa Inoue	71 68 70 75	284	2,222,000
Ryoken Kawagishi	72 67 74 72	285	1,628,000
Masaya Tomida	77 67 69 72	285	1,628,000
Toru Suzuki	70 70 72 73	285	1,628,000
Achi Sato	71 69 72 73	285	1,628,000
Eiji Mizoguchi	71 70 70 74	285	1,628,000
Gregory Meyer	73 67 70 75	285	1,628,000
Katsumune Imai	70 74 72 70	286	1,130,800
Tatsuya Mitsuhashi	72 67 74 73	286	1,130,800
Hideto Tanihara	69 74 70 73	286	1,130,800
Hidemasa Hoshino	71 71 68 76	286	1,130,800
Tadahiro Takayama	70 69 69 78	286	1,130,800
Chris Campbell	71 70 75 71	287	796,125
Yui Ueda	69 75 71 72	287	796,125
Toshimitsu Izawa	70 69 74 74	287	796,125
Yoshiaki Mano	71 70 72 74	287	796,125
Scott Laycock	70 74 69 74	287	796,125
Wayne Perske	69 72 71 75	287	796,125
Dinesh Chand	72 68 71 76	287	796,125
Chawalit Plaphol	73 67 70 77	287	796,125

Munsingwear Open KSB Cup

Tojigaoka Marine Hills Golf Club, Tamano, Okayama
Par 36-36—72; 7,017 yards

May 18-21
purse, ¥100,000,000

	SCORES	TOTAL	MONEY
Toshinori Muto	68 69 73 64	274	¥20,000,000
Eiji Mizoguchi	67 69 70 70	276	10,000,000
Shingo Katayama	66 69 73 69	277	5,200,000
Mamo Osanai	70 66 71 70	277	5,200,000
Kiyoshi Miyazato	70 66 67 74	277	5,200,000
Keiichiro Fukabori	68 70 71 69	278	3,600,000
Kim Jong-duck	68 69 74 68	279	2,842,000
S.K. Ho	71 70 70 68	279	2,842,000
Nozomi Kawahara	72 68 69 70	279	2,842,000
Hideto Tanihara	66 70 71 72	279	2,842,000
Toru Taniguchi	69 71 67 72	279	2,842,000
Brendan Jones	67 70 75 68	280	1,762,857
Liang Wen-chong	68 70 74 68	280	1,762,857
Kiyoshi Maita	70 72 69 69	280	1,762,857
Y.E. Yang	72 71 67 70	280	1,762,857
Yui Ueda	71 70 69 70	280	1,762,857
Soushi Tajima	66 69 71 74	280	1,762,857
Takao Nogami	64 73 69 74	280	1,762,857
Satoshi Higashi	70 69 73 69	281	1,220,000
Hidemasa Hoshino	67 70 73 71	281	1,220,000
Hirofumi Miyase	67 73 70 71	281	1,220,000
Akinori Tani	66 70 72 73	281	1,220,000
Nobuhito Sato	73 70 71 68	282	953,333
Nobuhiro Masuda	71 72 69 70	282	953,333
Kenichi Kuboya	70 67 74 71	282	953,333
Tatsuhiko Takahashi	70 71 72 70	283	780,000
Hiroyuki Fujita	69 71 73 70	283	780,000
Takuya Taniguchi	67 71 74 71	283	780,000
David Smail	66 72 73 72	283	780,000
Masaki Nakanishi	70 72 68 73	283	780,000

Mitsubishi Diamond Cup

Sayama Golf Club, Iruma, Saitama
Par 36-35–71; 7,118 yards

May 25-28
purse, ¥110,000,000

	SCORES				TOTAL	MONEY
Kaname Yokoo	71	70	68	66	275	¥22,000,000
Nozomi Kawahara	73	70	67	67	277	9,240,000
Toru Suzuki	70	68	70	69	277	9,240,000
Shingo Katayama	72	71	66	69	278	5,280,000
Y.E. Yang	69	72	71	67	279	4,180,000
Keiichiro Fukabori	68	71	72	68	279	4,180,000
Toru Taniguchi	73	72	69	66	280	3,242,250
Taichiro Kiyota	71	71	69	69	280	3,242,250
Toshinori Muto	69	70	71	70	280	3,242,250
Mamo Osanai	72	69	69	70	280	3,242,250
Ippei Sadanobu	73	68	71	69	281	2,332,000
Lin Keng-chi	69	72	71	69	281	2,332,000
Sushi Ishigaki	71	71	69	70	281	2,332,000
Liang Wen-chong	70	71	69	71	281	2,332,000
Hiroyuki Fujita	75	70	72	65	282	1,676,400
Yusaku Miyazato	70	73	73	66	282	1,676,400
Tomokazu Yoshinaga	69	73	74	66	282	1,676,400
Brendan Jones	71	69	71	71	282	1,676,400
Shigeru Nonaka	71	73	68	70	282	1,676,400
Tetsuya Haraguchi	71	73	73	67	284	1,254,000
Takuya Taniguchi	73	73	70	68	284	1,254,000
David Smail	76	69	70	69	284	1,254,000
Hideto Tanihara	74	69	70	71	284	1,254,000
Masaki Nakanishi	70	73	72	70	285	1,034,000
Yoshiaki Mano	73	73	68	72	286	990,000
Yasuharu Imano	74	70	73	70	287	836,000
Tatsuya Mitsuhashi	70	75	73	69	287	836,000
Steven Conran	74	71	72	70	287	836,000
Hidemasa Hoshino	75	69	74	69	287	836,000
Tetsuji Hiratsuka	72	72	71	72	287	836,000
Frankie Minoza	74	70	69	74	287	836,000

JCB Classic Sendai

Omotezao Kokusai Golf Club, Shibata, Miyagi
Par 36-35–71; 6,628 yards

June 1-4
purse, ¥100,000,000

	SCORES				TOTAL	MONEY
Hideto Tanihara	67	69	63	67	266	¥20,000,000
Shingo Katayama	68	67	66	70	271	10,000,000
Shinichi Akiba	73	70	69	64	276	6,800,000
Taichi Teshima	67	71	71	68	277	4,400,000
Azuma Yano	72	69	69	67	277	4,400,000
Tetsuji Hiratsuka	72	69	71	66	278	3,450,000
Mitsuo Harada	71	66	69	72	278	3,450,000
Toshimitsu Izawa	71	68	71	69	279	2,830,000
Shoichi Ideguchi	70	72	69	68	279	2,830,000
S.K. Ho	70	68	69	72	279	2,830,000
Kiyoshi Murota	70	69	68	73	280	2,420,000
Dinesh Chand	68	74	72	67	281	2,020,000
Kunihiro Kamii	73	69	72	67	281	2,020,000

	SCORES				TOTAL	MONEY
Steven Conran	69	71	75	66	281	2,020,000
Hiroyuki Fujita	70	70	73	69	282	1,570,000
Kenichi Kuboya	72	73	71	66	282	1,570,000
Frankie Minoza	71	70	70	71	282	1,570,000
Kaname Yokoo	70	70	69	73	282	1,570,000
Yusaku Miyazato	74	71	70	68	283	1,075,000
Tsuyoshi Yoneyama	73	71	70	69	283	1,075,000
Soushi Tajima	68	72	75	68	283	1,075,000
Takuya Taniguchi	70	70	73	70	283	1,075,000
Yoshikazu Haku	69	70	74	70	283	1,075,000
Tetsuya Haraguchi	69	73	70	71	283	1,075,000
Nozomi Kawahara	73	68	70	72	283	1,075,000
Yeh Wei-tze	71	72	67	73	283	1,075,000
Sushi Ishigaki	72	72	70	70	284	704,285
Gregory Meyer	73	68	73	70	284	704,285
Tomohiro Kondo	71	67	75	71	284	704,285
Hiroo Kawai	71	69	75	69	284	704,285
Katsumune Imai	68	73	71	72	284	704,285
Tatsuhiko Takahashi	70	68	73	73	284	704,285
Toshikazu Sugihara	72	70	69	73	284	704,285

Mandom Lucido Yomiuri Open

Yomiuri Country Club, Nishinomiya, Hyogo
Par 36-36–72; 7,161 yards

June 15-18
purse, ¥100,000,000

	SCORES				TOTAL	MONEY
Nobuhiro Masuda	69	70	67	68	274	¥20,000,000
Y.E. Yang	72	69	65	69	275	10,000,000
Yusaku Miyazato	69	70	70	68	277	5,800,000
Tetsuji Hiratsuka	71	66	71	69	277	5,800,000
Hidemasa Hoshino	69	69	69	71	278	4,000,000
*Yuki Usami	74	68	69	68	279	
Nobuhito Sato	67	74	71	67	279	3,450,000
Shinichi Akiba	68	71	70	70	279	3,450,000
Katsumasa Miyamoto	70	71	72	67	280	2,830,000
Masaya Tomida	71	68	73	68	280	2,830,000
Hideto Tanihara	72	65	70	73	280	2,830,000
Yutaka Horinouchi	74	68	68	71	281	2,120,000
Thammanoon Srirot	69	71	72	69	281	2,120,000
Azuma Yano	68	70	71	72	281	2,120,000
Jun Kikuchi	72	65	74	70	281	2,120,000
Hidezumi Shirakata	73	69	69	71	282	1,570,000
Takuya Taniguchi	72	74	69	67	282	1,570,000
Tetsuya Haraguchi	72	67	76	67	282	1,570,000
Katsuyoshi Tomori	69	68	73	72	282	1,570,000
Eiji Mizoguchi	71	71	70	71	283	1,260,000
Lee Dong-hwan	71	71	72	69	283	1,260,000
Hirofumi Miyase	76	70	73	64	283	1,260,000
Chawalit Plaphol	74	69	68	73	284	940,000
Yoshimitsu Fukuzawa	69	74	69	72	284	940,000
Toshinori Muto	72	71	68	73	284	940,000
Tomohiro Kondo	71	71	73	69	284	940,000
Ryuji Masaoka	73	69	74	68	284	940,000
S.K. Ho	69	71	71	73	284	940,000
Yeh Wei-tze	72	71	73	69	285	656,250
Hideki Kase	73	72	71	69	285	656,250

	SCORES				TOTAL	MONEY
Hiroyuki Fujita	74	70	71	70	285	656,250
Tatsuya Mitsuhashi	73	69	71	72	285	656,250
Yoshinobu Tsukada	75	70	71	69	285	656,250
Yasunori Yoshida	73	73	68	71	285	656,250
Yoshiaki Mano	69	72	74	70	285	656,250
Kazuhiko Hosokawa	80	67	67	71	285	656,250

Gateway to the Open Mizuno Open

JFE Setonaikai Golf Club, Kasaoka, Okayama
Par 36-36–72; 7,287 yards

June 22-25
purse, ¥100,000,000

	SCORES				TOTAL	MONEY
S.K. Ho	68	69	66	71	274	¥20,000,000
Tatsu Ichihara	68	70	70	69	277	8,400,000
David Smail	71	67	68	71	277	8,400,000
Wayne Perske	75	68	69	66	278	4,400,000
Kiyoshi Maita	72	66	69	71	278	4,400,000
Jeev Milkha Singh	66	73	72	69	280	3,192,500
Thammanoon Srirot	71	68	71	70	280	3,192,500
Tomohiro Kondo	72	70	68	70	280	3,192,500
Toshinori Muto	72	69	69	70	280	3,192,500
Scott Laycock	70	68	73	70	281	2,520,000
Hiroyuki Fujita	72	70	67	72	281	2,520,000
Kim Jong-duck	71	68	72	71	282	1,945,000
Taichi Teshima	75	68	68	71	282	1,945,000
Takuya Taniguchi	70	68	70	74	282	1,945,000
Kiyoshi Murota	73	67	69	73	282	1,945,000
Paul Sheehan	71	73	69	70	283	1,390,000
Chang Ik-je	73	71	68	71	283	1,390,000
Hidemasa Hoshino	72	71	68	72	283	1,390,000
Satoru Hirota	72	70	69	72	283	1,390,000
Yutaka Horinouchi	73	69	69	72	283	1,390,000
Dinesh Chand	68	68	70	77	283	1,390,000
Taichiro Kiyota	74	67	72	71	284	964,000
Shinichi Akiba	71	67	73	73	284	964,000
Shigeru Nonaka	68	71	72	73	284	964,000
Shinichi Yokota	75	68	73	68	284	964,000
Yuudai Maeda	71	69	67	77	284	964,000
Tetsuji Hiratsuka	69	71	73	72	285	780,000
Kenichi Kuboya	70	70	72	73	285	780,000
Yoshinobu Tsukada	71	71	70	73	285	780,000
Tatsuhiko Takahashi	71	68	74	73	286	577,000
Ryoken Kawagishi	70	70	73	73	286	577,000
Nozomi Kawahara	69	70	75	72	286	577,000
Y.E. Yang	69	71	74	72	286	577,000
Ryuichi Oda	73	71	70	72	286	577,000
Kaname Yokoo	72	71	69	74	286	577,000
Hiroo Kawai	70	68	73	75	286	577,000
Hidezumi Shirakata	70	71	74	71	286	577,000
Brendan Jones	71	72	72	71	286	577,000
Yeh Wei-tze	72	70	74	70	286	577,000

UBS Japan Golf Tour Championship

Shishido Hills Country Club, Kasama, Ibaraki
Par 35-35–70; 7,179 yards

June 29-July 2
purse, ¥150,000,000

	SCORES				TOTAL	MONEY
Tatsuhiko Takahashi	71	66	68	68	273	¥30,000,000
Tetsuji Hiratsuka	69	68	70	69	276	15,000,000
S.K. Ho	70	71	67	69	277	8,700,000
Tsuneyuki Nakajima	67	70	69	71	277	8,700,000
Hidemasa Hoshino	70	72	67	69	278	6,000,000
Kiyoshi Maita	71	71	69	68	279	4,975,000
Lin Keng-chi	69	71	70	69	279	4,975,000
Yusaku Miyazato	70	69	68	72	279	4,975,000
Jeev Milkha Singh	70	72	67	71	280	4,080,000
Toru Taniguchi	67	66	74	73	280	4,080,000
Paul Sheehan	73	71	69	68	281	3,180,000
Nozomi Kawahara	74	67	70	70	281	3,180,000
Y.E. Yang	73	73	65	70	281	3,180,000
Kiyoshi Murota	65	74	69	73	281	3,180,000
Masaya Tomida	69	70	73	70	282	2,355,000
Frankie Minoza	70	70	72	70	282	2,355,000
Kazuhiko Hosokawa	74	70	67	71	282	2,355,000
David Smail	76	69	66	71	282	2,355,000
Kim Jong-duck	75	70	69	69	283	1,830,000
Tomohiro Kondo	74	70	68	71	283	1,830,000
Kaname Yokoo	71	72	69	71	283	1,830,000
Scott Laycock	70	70	71	72	283	1,830,000
Jun Kikuchi	71	75	69	69	284	1,395,000
Yoshinobu Tsukada	75	71	68	70	284	1,395,000
Taichi Teshima	74	66	77	67	284	1,395,000
Hiroyuki Fujita	75	63	75	71	284	1,395,000
Katsuyoshi Tomori	71	73	71	70	285	1,200,000
Takaki Ono	70	74	69	72	285	1,200,000
Toshinori Muto	72	73	71	70	286	1,110,000
Brendan Jones	72	72	72	71	287	971,250
Dinesh Chand	75	67	73	72	287	971,250
Shintaro Kai	73	72	68	74	287	971,250
Toyokazu Fujishima	70	67	71	79	287	971,250

Woodone Open Hiroshima

Hiroshima Country Club, Hiroshima
Par 35-36–71; 6,942 yards

July 6-9
purse, ¥100,000,000

	SCORES				TOTAL	MONEY
Tetsuji Hiratsuka	68	65	64	68	265	¥20,000,000
Shingo Katayama	69	68	65	65	267	8,400,000
S.K. Ho	61	67	72	67	267	8,400,000
Hidemasa Hoshino	70	65	67	68	270	4,800,000
Jun Kikuchi	65	67	71	68	271	4,000,000
Kiyoshi Maita	68	66	71	67	272	3,600,000
Lee Dong-hwan	72	66	71	64	273	3,175,000
Tomohiro Kondo	68	69	67	69	273	3,175,000
Hiroshi Iwata	69	69	69	67	274	2,820,000
Hideto Tanihara	68	66	75	66	275	2,420,000
Toshinori Muto	69	68	70	68	275	2,420,000

	SCORES				TOTAL	MONEY
Toru Taniguchi	66	67	69	73	275	2,420,000
Hiroo Kawai	69	69	69	69	276	1,920,000
Yoshikazu Haku	66	70	70	70	276	1,920,000
Satoshi Higashi	69	71	69	68	277	1,395,000
Ryuichi Oda	69	71	68	69	277	1,395,000
Seita Matsumoto	72	67	69	69	277	1,395,000
Kaname Yokoo	67	72	69	69	277	1,395,000
Naoya Takemoto	69	68	70	70	277	1,395,000
Hidezumi Shirakata	69	70	68	70	277	1,395,000
Kiyoshi Murota	68	70	68	71	277	1,395,000
Masaya Tomida	67	71	67	72	277	1,395,000
Mamo Osanai	71	68	68	71	278	1,020,000
Takeshi Kajikawa	69	70	71	69	279	840,000
Taichi Teshima	68	68	72	71	279	840,000
Lin Keng-chi	73	65	70	71	279	840,000
Toshikazu Sugihara	70	69	73	67	279	840,000
Keiichiro Fukabori	69	65	72	73	279	840,000
Shinichi Akiba	70	67	68	74	279	840,000
Keiso Kawamoto	69	64	75	72	280	680,000
Yui Ueda	68	70	73	69	280	680,000

Sega Sammy Cup

North Country Golf Club, Chitose, Hokkaido
Par 36-36–72; 7,128 yards

July 20-23
purse, ¥120,000,000

	SCORES				TOTAL	MONEY
Yeh Wei-tze	70	68	72	66	276	¥24,000,000
Hidemasa Hoshino	72	66	73	69	280	12,000,000
Liang Wen-chong	70	71	72	70	283	6,960,000
Azuma Yano	71	70	70	72	283	6,960,000
Jeev Milkha Singh	70	71	73	71	285	4,560,000
Chawalit Plaphol	72	67	74	72	285	4,560,000
Kenichi Kuboya	70	69	75	72	286	3,810,000
Y.E. Yang	68	72	73	73	286	3,810,000
Mamo Osanai	74	69	73	71	287	3,384,000
Katsumasa Miyamoto	73	71	77	67	288	2,664,000
Craig Jones	73	70	75	70	288	2,664,000
Katsumune Imai	73	72	72	71	288	2,664,000
Toru Taniguchi	72	70	74	72	288	2,664,000
Shoichi Ideguchi	71	70	72	75	288	2,664,000
Ryuichi Oda	71	72	77	69	289	1,828,800
Lin Keng-chi	74	71	76	68	289	1,828,800
Gregory Meyer	69	70	78	72	289	1,828,800
Hidezumi Shirakata	70	73	74	72	289	1,828,800
Chris Campbell	72	73	69	75	289	1,828,800
Katsunori Kuwabara	74	70	76	70	290	1,280,000
Tsuyoshi Yoneyama	74	72	74	70	290	1,280,000
Takeshi Kajikawa	74	71	73	72	290	1,280,000
Kim Jong-duck	71	70	76	73	290	1,280,000
Ryoken Kawagishi	72	71	74	73	290	1,280,000
Chang Il-je	69	74	72	75	290	1,280,000
Yosuke Mizobuchi	74	69	76	72	291	849,333
Yoichi Shimizu	75	70	75	71	291	849,333
Soushi Tajima	73	71	75	72	291	849,333
Toyokazu Fujishima	73	70	76	72	291	849,333
Paul Sheehan	72	74	72	73	291	849,333
Frankie Minoza	72	73	76	70	291	849,333

	SCORES	TOTAL	MONEY
Yoshinobu Tsukada	70 73 75 73	291	849,333
Yuudai Maeda	72 73 77 69	291	849,333
Kiyoshi Murota	70 74 73 74	291	849,333

The Golf Tournament in Omaezaki

Shizuoka Country Golf Club, Hamaoka Course,
Omaezaki, Shizuoka
Par 35-36–71; 6,922 yards

July 27-30
purse, ¥120,000,000

	SCORES	TOTAL	MONEY
Toru Taniguchi	69 70 66 68	273	¥24,000,000
Tomohiro Kondo	69 71 65 68	273	10,080,000
S.K. Ho	67 68 69 69	273	10,080,000
(Taniguchi defeated Kondo on second and Ho on third playoff hole.)			
Sushi Ishigaki	66 73 70 65	274	4,710,000
Hiroyuki Fujita	67 72 69 66	274	4,710,000
Liang Wen-chong	67 70 70 67	274	4,710,000
Yoshinobu Tsukada	67 72 66 69	274	4,710,000
Jeev Milkha Singh	70 68 72 65	275	3,151,200
Gregory Meyer	71 70 68 66	275	3,151,200
Ryoken Kawagishi	68 69 69 69	275	3,151,200
Taichi Teshima	69 72 66 68	275	3,151,200
Thammanoon Srirot	70 66 68 71	275	3,151,200
Frankie Minoza	70 72 65 69	276	2,424,000
Chris Campbell	69 69 71 68	277	1,888,000
Tetsuya Haraguchi	70 70 69 68	277	1,888,000
Makoto Inoue	69 72 68 68	277	1,888,000
Satoru Hirota	71 66 68 72	277	1,888,000
Paul Sheehan	66 71 67 73	277	1,888,000
Soushi Tajima	65 67 71 74	277	1,888,000
Riki Ikeda	70 70 70 68	278	1,320,000
Takeshi Kibamoto	68 70 73 67	278	1,320,000
Craig Jones	68 73 68 69	278	1,320,000
Norihiko Nakata	72 70 70 66	278	1,320,000
Yui Ueda	70 69 69 70	278	1,320,000
Tadahiro Takayama	67 71 67 74	279	1,080,000
Hideki Kase	70 70 71 69	280	849,333
Yoichi Shimizu	73 67 70 70	280	849,333
Kazuhiko Hosokawa	71 70 69 70	280	849,333
Hiroshi Iwata	71 71 67 71	280	849,333
Yoshiaki Mano	70 71 71 68	280	849,333
Y.E. Yang	73 68 71 68	280	849,333
Yusaku Miyazato	68 70 74 68	280	849,333
Kazuhiro Shimizu	70 68 74 68	280	849,333
Kim Jong-duck	71 68 68 73	280	849,333

Sun Chlorella Classic

Otaru Country Club, Hokkaido
Par 36-36–72; 7,509 yards

August 3-6
purse, ¥150,000,000

	SCORES	TOTAL	MONEY
Hideto Tanihara	70 74 67 72	283	¥30,000,000
Masaya Tomida	72 68 76 68	284	8,760,000

	SCORES				TOTAL	MONEY
Katsumasa Miyamoto	76	67	72	69	284	8,760,000
Hiroyuki Fujita	73	74	66	71	284	8,760,000
Prayad Marksaeng	72	69	71	72	284	8,760,000
Tetsuji Hiratsuka	71	71	68	74	284	8,760,000
S.K. Ho	71	75	71	68	285	4,762,500
Kim Jong-duck	70	72	73	70	285	4,762,500
Lee Dong-hwan	72	73	71	70	286	4,230,000
Y.E. Yang	74	70	72	71	287	3,930,000
Hidemasa Hoshino	71	74	74	69	288	2,858,571
Takeshi Kajikawa	72	73	73	70	288	2,858,571
Kiyoshi Murota	71	71	74	72	288	2,858,571
Liang Wen-chong	70	73	73	72	288	2,858,571
Taichi Teshima	73	69	73	73	288	2,858,571
Hidezumi Shirakata	73	72	70	73	288	2,858,571
Frankie Minoza	73	70	71	74	288	2,858,571
Tetsuya Haraguchi	72	73	73	71	289	2,010,000
Satoru Hirota	72	74	69	74	289	2,010,000
Koumei Oda	70	74	68	77	289	2,010,000
Lin Keng-chi	71	73	76	70	290	1,461,428
Tatsu Ichihara	74	72	72	72	290	1,461,428
Chawalit Plaphol	73	71	73	73	290	1,461,428
Toshinori Muto	75	73	69	73	290	1,461,428
Keiichiro Fukabori	74	74	68	74	290	1,461,428
Jeev Milkha Singh	71	70	74	75	290	1,461,428
Mitsuhiro Tateyama	72	68	71	79	290	1,461,428
Tomohiro Kondo	74	74	71	72	291	1,027,500
Craig Jones	72	76	71	72	291	1,027,500
Tsuyoshi Yoneyama	74	69	75	73	291	1,027,500
Nobuhito Sato	71	76	71	73	291	1,027,500
Azuma Yano	74	69	73	75	291	1,027,500
Sushi Ishigaki	73	73	69	76	291	1,027,500

Under Armour KBC Augusta

Keya Golf Club, Shima, Fukuoka
Par 35-36–71; 7,125 yards

August 24-27
purse, ¥100,000,000

	SCORES				TOTAL	MONEY
Taichi Teshima	71	66	65	66	268	¥20,000,000
Tetsuji Hiratsuka	65	68	69	67	269	10,000,000
Nobuhiro Masuda	68	71	63	69	271	6,800,000
Gregory Meyer	70	71	65	66	272	4,133,333
Liang Wen-chong	65	69	71	67	272	4,133,333
Frankie Minoza	69	68	66	69	272	4,133,333
Prayad Marksaeng	67	68	71	67	273	3,175,000
Lee Dong-hwan	68	68	65	72	273	3,175,000
Tetsuya Haraguchi	72	66	68	68	274	2,720,000
Koumei Oda	69	68	68	69	274	2,720,000
Hidezumi Shirakata	65	70	71	69	275	2,120,000
Wayne Perske	70	67	69	69	275	2,120,000
Hiroo Kawai	68	63	73	71	275	2,120,000
Thammanoon Srirot	70	65	69	71	275	2,120,000
Craig Parry	70	71	69	66	276	1,570,000
Azuma Yano	70	68	71	67	276	1,570,000
Hiroyuki Fujita	72	68	69	67	276	1,570,000
Hiroshi Iwata	71	71	65	69	276	1,570,000
Takuya Taniguchi	69	73	68	67	277	1,220,000

	SCORES	TOTAL	MONEY
Masamichi Uehira	74 68 67 68	277	1,220,000
Makoto Inoue	69 72 67 69	277	1,220,000
Shigemasa Higaki	64 68 71 74	277	1,220,000
Toru Taniguchi	72 68 71 67	278	886,666
Satoru Hirota	67 74 70 67	278	886,666
Kiyoshi Maita	72 68 69 69	278	886,666
Craig Jones	69 68 71 70	278	886,666
Keiichiro Fukabori	71 71 70 66	278	886,666
Mitsuhiro Tateyama	65 67 70 76	278	886,666
Akinori Tani	72 69 68 70	279	666,000
Kazuhiro Shimizu	68 71 70 70	279	666,000
Katsunori Kuwabara	70 68 73 68	279	666,000
Yuudai Maeda	70 66 71 72	279	666,000
Mamo Osanai	72 67 68 72	279	666,000

Fujisankei Classic

Fujizakura Country Club, Fujikawaguchiko, Yamanashi
Par 35-36–71; 7,496 yards

August 31-September 3
purse, ¥150,000,000

	SCORES	TOTAL	MONEY
Shingo Katayama	66 71 68 69	274	¥30,000,000
Liang Wen-chong	68 70 75 64	277	15,000,000
Prayad Marksaeng	67 74 70 71	282	7,200,000
Toru Taniguchi	71 72 68 71	282	7,200,000
Jeev Milkha Singh	70 72 68 72	282	7,200,000
Hiroyuki Fujita	73 68 69 72	282	7,200,000
David Smail	71 72 71 69	283	4,762,500
Taichi Teshima	67 71 73 72	283	4,762,500
Takuya Taniguchi	69 72 74 70	285	3,630,000
Nobuhiro Masuda	66 79 67 73	285	3,630,000
Hiroo Kawai	73 69 69 74	285	3,630,000
Azuma Yano	70 69 72 74	285	3,630,000
Hideto Tanihara	69 67 74 75	285	3,630,000
Sushi Ishigaki	69 77 69 71	286	2,655,000
Daisuke Maruyama	68 72 73 73	286	2,655,000
*Ryutaro Nagano	73 73 73 68	287	
Hidemasa Hoshino	72 73 73 69	287	2,085,000
Kaname Yokoo	69 75 72 71	287	2,085,000
Toyokazu Fujishima	73 73 69 72	287	2,085,000
Naoya Takemoto	72 71 71 73	287	2,085,000
Yuudai Maeda	70 70 72 75	287	2,085,000
Kouki Idoki	71 70 69 77	287	2,085,000
Kenichi Kuboya	72 72 76 68	288	1,410,000
Frankie Minoza	72 74 73 69	288	1,410,000
Lee Dong-hwan	76 69 72 71	288	1,410,000
Craig Jones	74 69 73 72	288	1,410,000
Satoru Hirota	70 73 71 74	288	1,410,000
Thammanoon Srirot	69 75 69 75	288	1,410,000
Dinesh Chand	67 75 74 73	289	1,053,000
Tatsuya Mitsuhashi	70 75 71 73	289	1,053,000
Chris Campbell	71 72 73 73	289	1,053,000
Kiyoshi Miyazato	71 69 75 74	289	1,053,000
Yoichi Shimizu	73 71 71 74	289	1,053,000

Suntory Open

Sobu Country Club, Inzai, Chiba
Par 35-35–70; 7,143 yards

September 7-10
purse, ¥100,000,000

	SCORES				TOTAL	MONEY
Y.E. Yang	67	68	68	63	266	¥20,000,000
Hidemasa Hoshino	67	68	69	68	272	8,400,000
Toru Taniguchi	64	73	64	71	272	8,400,000
Keiichiro Fukabori	70	67	71	65	273	4,133,333
Katsumasa Miyamoto	68	68	69	68	273	4,133,333
Shoichi Ideguchi	65	70	65	73	273	4,133,333
Hideki Kase	70	69	68	67	274	3,300,000
David Smail	67	70	68	70	275	2,935,000
Hiroo Kawai	67	70	67	71	275	2,935,000
Hiroyuki Fujita	67	70	70	69	276	2,420,000
Satoru Hirota	70	70	67	69	276	2,420,000
Yusaku Miyazato	66	67	67	76	276	2,420,000
Gregory Meyer	71	69	69	68	277	1,686,666
Norihiko Nakata	71	70	67	69	277	1,686,666
Azuma Yano	69	71	68	69	277	1,686,666
Takenori Hiraishi	69	71	67	70	277	1,686,666
Tetsuya Haraguchi	67	71	68	71	277	1,686,666
Jun Kikuchi	70	66	68	73	277	1,686,666
Katsunori Kuwabara	69	72	69	68	278	1,180,000
Ryuichi Oda	71	68	72	67	278	1,180,000
Makoto Inoue	71	68	67	72	278	1,180,000
Shinichi Yokota	73	67	65	73	278	1,180,000
Lee Dong-hwan	70	71	64	73	278	1,180,000
Nobuhito Sato	67	70	72	70	279	840,000
Tadahiro Takayama	71	70	68	70	279	840,000
Ryoken Kawagishi	72	65	70	72	279	840,000
Tatsuya Mitsuhashi	70	70	67	72	279	840,000
Yasumasa Suzuki	69	69	68	73	279	840,000
Koumei Oda	70	67	68	74	279	840,000
Akinori Tani	68	66	75	71	280	647,500
Kouki Idoki	70	70	70	70	280	647,500
Tetsuji Hiratsuka	69	72	70	69	280	647,500
Yoshi Mizumaki	68	72	67	73	280	647,500

ANA Open

Sapporo Golf Club, Wattsu Course,
Kitahiroshima, Hokkaido
Par 36-35–71; 7,017 yards

September 14-17
purse, ¥100,000,000

	SCORES				TOTAL	MONEY
Tomohiro Kondo	69	64	72	69	274	¥20,000,000
Kiyoshi Maita	69	70	70	66	275	8,400,000
Kaname Yokoo	70	69	70	66	275	8,400,000
Tadahiro Takayama	72	70	67	67	276	4,800,000
Paul Sheehan	72	68	69	68	277	3,800,000
Shinichi Yokota	67	67	72	71	277	3,800,000
Makoto Inoue	72	67	72	67	278	2,635,714
Katsuya Nakagawa	72	70	69	67	278	2,635,714
Katsumasa Miyamoto	70	73	67	68	278	2,635,714
Hisayuki Sasaki	70	70	70	68	278	2,635,714

	SCORES				TOTAL	MONEY
Katsumune Imai	70	68	70	70	278	2,635,714
Ryuichi Oda	70	65	72	71	278	2,635,714
Yoshinobu Tsukada	71	66	68	73	278	2,635,714
Hiroyuki Fujita	71	71	69	68	279	1,485,000
Takashi Kanemoto	72	69	70	68	279	1,485,000
Mamo Osanai	68	68	74	69	279	1,485,000
Jeev Milkha Singh	68	70	72	69	279	1,485,000
Ryoken Kawagishi	67	70	72	70	279	1,485,000
Chawalit Plaphol	65	71	73	70	279	1,485,000
Tatsu Ichihara	69	67	72	71	279	1,485,000
Shigeru Nonaka	69	69	70	71	279	1,485,000
Katsuyoshi Tomori	67	73	71	69	280	940,000
David Smail	72	71	69	68	280	940,000
Riki Ikeda	71	72	67	70	280	940,000
Koumei Oda	69	68	73	70	280	940,000
Tetsuya Haraguchi	66	69	73	72	280	940,000
Nobuo Serizawa	73	68	66	73	280	940,000
Gregory Meyer	73	67	71	70	281	720,000
Jun Kikuchi	70	69	75	67	281	720,000
Chang Ik-je	68	72	70	71	281	720,000
Yusaku Miyazato	70	67	72	72	281	720,000

Acom International

Ishioka Golf Club, Ogawa, Ibaraki
Par 36-35–71; 7,066 yards

September 21-24
purse, ¥120,000,000

	SCORES				TOTAL	MONEY
Mamo Osanai	65	63	74	68	270	¥24,000,000
Taichi Teshima	68	67	72	63	270	12,000,000
(Osanai defeated Teshima on first playoff hole.)						
Prayad Marksaeng	67	67	70	67	271	8,160,000
Katsumune Imai	70	68	69	66	273	5,280,000
Ryuichi Oda	71	68	65	69	273	5,280,000
Paul Sheehan	66	73	70	65	274	4,140,000
Katsuyoshi Tomori	70	67	69	68	274	4,140,000
S.K. Ho	67	72	68	69	276	3,396,000
Jeev Milkha Singh	72	68	67	69	276	3,396,000
Yoshikazu Haku	69	67	70	70	276	3,396,000
Liang Wen-chong	71	66	72	68	277	2,784,000
Yoichi Shimizu	70	63	74	70	277	2,784,000
Yusaku Miyazato	69	66	77	66	278	2,088,000
Yeh Wei-tze	72	69	70	67	278	2,088,000
Tatsuya Mitsuhashi	67	70	72	69	278	2,088,000
Tetsuji Hiratsuka	68	68	72	70	278	2,088,000
Kaname Yokoo	68	70	71	69	278	2,088,000
Lee Dong-hwan	72	69	70	68	279	1,656,000
Chang Ik-je	69	68	71	71	279	1,656,000
Ryoken Kawagishi	71	73	68	68	280	1,244,571
Makoto Inoue	74	68	70	68	280	1,244,571
Chris Campbell	68	73	71	68	280	1,244,571
Jun Kikuchi	71	69	71	69	280	1,244,571
Gregory Meyer	71	69	71	69	280	1,244,571
Kiyoshi Murota	71	65	74	70	280	1,244,571
Keiichiro Fukabori	72	69	69	70	280	1,244,571
Kiyoshi Maita	68	74	71	69	282	912,000
Hidemasa Hoshino	68	72	72	70	282	912,000

	SCORES	TOTAL	MONEY
Koumei Oda	73 71 70 68	282	912,000
Hiroyuki Fujita	71 70 71 70	282	912,000

Coca-Cola Tokai Classic

Miyoshi Country Club, West Course, Aichi
Par 35-36–71; 7,240 yards

September 28-October 1
purse, ¥120,000,000

	SCORES	TOTAL	MONEY
Hidemasa Hoshino	70 73 72 67	282	¥24,000,0000
Katsumasa Miyamoto	70 69 75 70	284	12,000,000
Nobuhiro Masuda	76 73 71 66	286	5,110,000
Ryuichi Oda	70 73 74 69	286	5,110,000
Jeev Milkha Singh	69 72 75 70	286	5,110,000
Camilo Villegas	70 69 76 71	286	5,110,000
Shingo Katayama	75 71 68 72	286	5,110,000
Hiroo Kawai	71 70 70 75	286	5,110,000
Kiyoshi Maita	71 74 70 72	287	3,384,000
Yoichi Shimizu	73 74 73 68	288	2,904,000
Tsuyoshi Yoneyama	73 71 72 72	288	2,904,000
Taichi Teshima	72 74 67 75	288	2,904,000
Tatsu Ichihara	75 71 74 69	289	2,224,000
Chang Ik-je	71 67 77 74	289	2,224,000
Lee Dong-hwan	74 70 69 76	289	2,224,000
Tatsuhiko Takahashi	72 74 74 70	290	1,476,000
Katsuya Nakagawa	71 76 73 70	290	1,476,000
Thammanoon Srirot	70 78 71 71	290	1,476,000
Hisayuki Sasaki	73 74 71 72	290	1,476,000
Takuya Taniguchi	73 72 73 72	290	1,476,000
Hiroyuki Fujita	73 72 73 72	290	1,476,000
Gregory Meyer	74 74 74 68	290	1,476,000
Toshiya Sakakura	72 73 72 73	290	1,476,000
Keiichiro Fukabori	74 69 74 73	290	1,476,000
Shigeru Nonaka	71 71 74 74	290	1,476,000
Masaya Tomida	74 73 73 71	291	912,000
Paul Sheehan	73 74 72 72	291	912,000
Satoru Hirota	70 71 76 74	291	912,000
Takenori Hiraishi	72 73 72 74	291	912,000
Katsumune Imai	74 72 71 74	291	912,000
S.K. Ho	74 69 72 76	291	912,000

Japan Open

Kasumingaseki Country Club, West Course,
Kawagoe, Saitama
Par 35-36–71; 7,068 yards

October 12-15
purse, ¥200,000,000

	SCORES	TOTAL	MONEY
Paul Sheehan	68 70 68 71	277	¥40,000,000
Azuma Yano	69 74 66 71	280	22,000,000
Katsumasa Miyamoto	75 71 66 69	281	12,700,000
Takuya Taniguchi	71 69 68 73	281	12,700,000
Yeh Wei-tze	70 70 73 69	282	6,200,000
S.K. Ho	71 71 70 70	282	6,200,000
Masaya Tomida	71 72 67 72	282	6,200,000

	SCORES				TOTAL	MONEY
Hiroshi Iwata	71	67	71	73	282	6,200,000
Shingo Katayama	67	69	71	75	282	6,200,000
Toshinori Muto	71	73	71	68	283	3,144,000
Hideki Kase	71	70	70	72	283	3,144,000
Hidemasa Hoshino	73	65	72	73	283	3,144,000
Yoshiaki Mano	68	73	69	73	283	3,144,000
Kiyoshi Murota	73	69	68	73	283	3,144,000
Masamichi Uehira	71	73	70	70	284	2,060,000
Liang Wen-chong	71	72	69	72	284	2,060,000
Nobuhiro Masuda	71	70	70	73	284	2,060,000
Toru Taniguchi	72	67	71	74	284	2,060,000
Tetsuji Hiratsuka	68	70	72	74	284	2,060,000
Y.E. Yang	69	70	70	75	284	2,060,000
David Smail	71	71	72	71	285	1,686,666
Kiyoshi Maita	71	71	71	72	285	1,686,666
Jeev Milkha Singh	65	72	74	74	285	1,686,666
Hideto Tanihara	70	72	74	70	286	1,540,000
Keiichiro Fukabori	72	69	74	71	286	1,540,000
Satoshi Oide	70	71	74	71	286	1,540,000
Hidezumi Shirakata	75	67	72	72	286	1,540,000
*Lee Won-joon	70	67	72	77	286	
Kiyotaka Inoue	74	72	76	65	287	1,400,000
Ryoken Kawagishi	71	72	72	72	287	1,400,000
Norihiko Furusho	71	71	71	74	287	1,400,000

Bridgestone Open

Sodegaura Country Club, Chiba
Par 36-36–72; 7,138 yards

October 19-22
purse, ¥110,000,000

	SCORES				TOTAL	MONEY
Taichi Teshima	70	65	63	68	266	¥22,000,000
Kiyoshi Maita	64	68	70	69	271	11,000,000
Prayad Marksaeng	67	69	69	68	273	5,720,000
Kaname Yokoo	70	66	68	69	273	5,720,000
Kouki Idoki	67	66	70	70	273	5,720,000
Yusaku Miyazato	68	68	71	67	274	3,960,000
Toru Taniguchi	69	69	69	68	275	3,126,200
Makoto Inoue	69	73	65	68	275	3,126,200
Takuya Taniguchi	71	67	68	69	275	3,126,200
Masaya Tomida	68	66	71	70	275	3,126,200
Toshinori Muto	72	64	70	69	275	3,126,200
Steven Conran	70	66	71	69	276	2,442,000
Keiichiro Fukabori	70	68	74	65	277	2,038,666
Lee Dong-hwan	68	70	72	67	277	2,038,666
Yui Ueda	67	71	70	69	277	2,038,666
Y.E. Yang	74	67	70	67	278	1,483,428
Tsuneyuki Nakajima	72	70	68	68	278	1,483,428
Tatsu Ichihara	67	71	71	69	278	1,483,428
Hisayuki Sasaki	66	68	75	69	278	1,483,428
Shingo Katayama	68	65	74	71	278	1,483,428
Naomichi Ozaki	71	69	67	71	278	1,483,428
Mitsuhiro Tateyama	69	67	70	72	278	1,483,428
Hideto Tanihara	70	70	70	69	279	998,800
Tadahiro Takayama	70	71	68	70	279	998,800
Yoichi Shimizu	69	68	71	71	279	998,800
Hiroyuki Fujita	69	69	70	71	279	998,800

	SCORES				TOTAL	MONEY
Katsuya Nakagawa	69	69	67	74	279	998,800
Chris Campbell	69	71	71	69	280	707,666
Hidemasa Hoshino	73	68	70	69	280	707,666
Koumei Oda	72	70	69	69	280	707,666
Hidezumi Shirakata	72	71	69	68	280	707,666
David Smail	72	66	72	70	280	707,666
Katsumune Imai	70	66	73	71	280	707,666
Brendan Jones	72	71	70	67	280	707,666
Hiroo Kawai	70	69	70	71	280	707,666
Tomohiro Kondo	68	70	70	72	280	707,666

ABC Championship

ABC Golf Club, Kato, Hyogo
Par 36-36–72; 7,217 yards

October 26-29
purse, ¥120,000,000

	SCORES				TOTAL	MONEY
Shingo Katayama	71	70	68	62	271	¥24,000,000
Y.E. Yang	66	71	69	65	271	12,000,000
(Katayama defeated Yang on second playoff hole.)						
Hisayuki Sasaki	71	67	67	70	275	8,160,000
Yusaku Miyazato	70	70	68	68	276	5,760,000
Taichi Teshima	69	70	70	68	277	4,800,000
Hiroyuki Fujita	70	74	69	65	278	4,320,000
Hidemasa Hoshino	69	70	74	66	279	3,810,000
Toru Taniguchi	71	69	70	69	279	3,810,000
Lee Dong-hwan	71	70	75	64	280	3,264,000
Azuma Yano	67	68	72	73	280	3,264,000
Gregory Meyer	68	74	70	69	281	2,784,000
Satoru Hirota	70	73	67	71	281	2,784,000
Yoshikazu Haku	70	70	73	69	282	2,304,000
Katsumune Imai	70	66	73	73	282	2,304,000
Frankie Minoza	67	74	74	68	283	1,776,000
Tetsuya Haraguchi	69	72	73	69	283	1,776,000
Brendan Jones	72	70	70	71	283	1,776,000
Katsumasa Miyamoto	72	70	70	71	283	1,776,000
Mamo Osanai	70	71	70	72	283	1,776,000
Toshinori Muto	72	73	66	72	283	1,776,000
Prayad Marksaeng	70	75	71	69	285	1,200,000
Yasuharu Imano	72	69	74	70	285	1,200,000
Makoto Inoue	70	73	73	69	285	1,200,000
Nobuhiro Masuda	72	72	70	71	285	1,200,000
Kaname Yokoo	70	72	70	73	285	1,200,000
Takuya Taniguchi	73	70	67	75	285	1,200,000
Sushi Ishigaki	70	72	74	70	286	888,000
Chang Ik-je	73	69	73	71	286	888,000
Mitsuhiro Tateyama	75	71	67	73	286	888,000
Masaya Tomida	71	70	71	74	286	888,000
Yoshinobu Tsukada	72	75	72	67	286	888,000

Asahiryokuken Yomiuri Memorial

Asoiizuka Golf Club, Fukuoka
Par 36-36–72; 7,106 yards

November 2-5
purse, ¥100,000,000

	SCORES				TOTAL	MONEY
Tatsuhiko Ichihara	69	66	68	67	270	¥20,000,000
Jeev Milkha Singh	66	65	67	73	271	10,000,000
Toru Suzuki	73	69	63	67	272	6,800,000
Hiroyuki Fujita	68	68	68	69	273	4,400,000
Chang Ik-je	66	67	70	70	273	4,400,000
Chawalit Plaphol	71	68	70	65	274	3,316,666
Masaya Tomida	70	66	69	69	274	3,316,666
Hiroshi Iwata	69	67	68	70	274	3,316,666
Tetsuji Hiratsuka	67	65	70	73	275	2,820,000
Nobuhiro Masuda	69	71	70	66	276	2,136,666
Ryuji Imada	77	64	67	68	276	2,136,666
Prayad Marksaeng	67	74	67	68	276	2,136,666
Hideki Kase	71	69	68	68	276	2,136,666
Ryoken Kawagishi	67	68	67	74	276	2,136,666
Yoshikazu Haku	68	66	67	75	276	2,136,666
Mitsuhiro Tateyama	73	64	74	66	277	1,520,000
Satoru Hirota	67	71	70	69	277	1,520,000
Yui Ueda	70	69	68	70	277	1,520,000
Nobuhito Sato	70	69	71	68	278	1,140,000
Toshikazu Sugihara	69	70	70	69	278	1,140,000
Katsuya Nakagawa	69	70	70	69	278	1,140,000
Ryuichi Oda	68	68	72	70	278	1,140,000
Gregory Meyer	70	71	67	70	278	1,140,000
Yeh Wei-tze	70	64	73	71	278	1,140,000
Shoichi Ideguchi	71	70	68	70	279	860,000
Tetsuya Haraguchi	68	71	70	70	279	860,000
Katsumune Imai	71	69	68	71	279	860,000
Tateo Ozaki	72	67	72	69	280	685,000
Tatsuya Tanioka	70	69	72	69	280	685,000
Kaname Yokoo	71	67	71	71	280	685,000
Seita Matsumoto	68	68	72	72	280	685,000
Katsuyoshi Tomori	71	71	70	68	280	685,000
Tatsuhiko Takahashi	73	68	74	65	280	685,000

Mitsui Sumitomo Visa Taiheiyo Masters

Taiheiyo Golf Club, Gotemba Course, Gotemba, Shizuoka
Par 36-36–72; 7,246 yards

November 9-12
purse, ¥150,000,000

	SCORES				TOTAL	MONEY
Tsuneyuki Nakajima	71	68	71	65	275	¥30,000,000
Toru Taniguchi	67	72	70	67	276	15,000,000
Keiichiro Fukabori	67	72	71	69	279	7,800,000
Makoto Inoue	70	67	67	75	279	7,800,000
Shingo Katayama	70	68	68	73	279	7,800,000
Yoshikazu Haku	70	74	69	67	280	5,175,000
Mitsuhiro Tateyama	72	68	69	71	280	5,175,000
Hideto Tanihara	75	67	71	68	281	3,787,500
Yusaku Miyazato	71	71	71	68	281	3,787,500
Craig Jones	71	70	71	69	281	3,787,500
Ryoken Kawagishi	73	64	74	70	281	3,787,500

	SCORES				TOTAL	MONEY
Mamo Osanai	69	67	76	69	281	3,787,500
Daisuke Maruyama	71	64	74	72	281	3,787,500
Toru Suzuki	71	68	70	73	282	2,730,000
Kiyoshi Murota	70	73	67	73	283	2,355,000
Hideki Kase	73	69	70	71	283	2,355,000
Ryuichi Oda	66	71	74	72	283	2,355,000
Katsumasa Miyamoto	71	64	72	76	283	2,355,000
Hidemasa Hoshino	73	69	70	72	284	1,770,000
Kiyoshi Maita	72	68	72	72	284	1,770,000
Yeh Wei-tze	68	71	69	76	284	1,770,000
Shinichi Yokota	68	68	76	72	284	1,770,000
Sergio Garcia	68	67	72	77	284	1,770,000
David Smail	75	70	69	71	285	1,320,000
Tetsuji Hiratsuka	76	69	70	70	285	1,320,000
Ryuji Imada	69	72	73	71	285	1,320,000
Takuya Taniguchi	75	66	73	71	285	1,320,000
Masaya Tomida	71	72	70	73	286	1,053,000
Masashi Ozaki	76	67	70	73	286	1,053,000
Yoshiaki Mano	72	71	71	72	286	1,053,000
Kaname Yokoo	73	69	73	71	286	1,053,000
Lee Won-joon	75	73	67	71	286	1,053,000

Dunlop Phoenix

Phoenix Country Club, Miyazaki
Par 35-35–70; 6,907 yards

November 16-19
purse, ¥200,000,000

	SCORES				TOTAL	MONEY
Padraig Harrington	67	66	71	67	271	¥40,000,000
Tiger Woods	67	65	72	67	271	20,000,000
(Harrington defeated Woods on second playoff hole.)						
Keiichiro Fukabori	68	71	69	64	272	13,600,000
Justin Rose	73	63	72	66	274	8,800,000
Shingo Katayama	65	70	71	68	274	8,800,000
Ian Poulter	70	64	77	65	276	6,900,000
Toru Taniguchi	72	68	69	67	276	6,900,000
Gonzalo Fernandez-Castano	66	72	73	67	278	5,870,000
Takuya Taniguchi	70	69	68	71	278	5,870,000
Hisayuki Sasaki	67	72	74	66	279	5,040,000
Yusaku Miyazato	73	70	70	66	279	5,040,000
Azuma Yano	70	70	73	67	280	4,440,000
Shiv Kapur	70	70	73	68	281	3,706,666
Toru Suzuki	71	72	70	68	281	3,706,666
Scott Laycock	70	68	73	70	281	3,706,666
Hiroyuki Fujita	70	73	72	67	282	3,040,000
Makoto Inoue	73	68	69	72	282	3,040,000
Satoru Hirota	67	71	73	71	282	3,040,000
Thomas Bjorn	74	70	71	68	283	2,440,000
Ryuichi Oda	73	69	71	70	283	2,440,000
Toshimitsu Izawa	67	72	73	71	283	2,440,000
Shigeru Nonaka	71	68	73	71	283	2,440,000
Kaname Yokoo	73	71	69	72	285	2,040,000
Yeh Wei-tze	72	67	75	72	286	1,880,000
Kim Jong-duck	72	70	76	69	287	1,522,500
Chris Campbell	70	74	74	69	287	1,522,500
Steven Conran	73	72	73	69	287	1,522,500
David Smail	72	72	70	73	287	1,522,500

	SCORES				TOTAL	MONEY
Tomohiro Kondo	71	68	74	74	287	1,522,500
Koumei Oda	71	68	74	74	287	1,522,500
Tsuneyuki Nakajima	70	74	69	74	287	1,522,500
Yoshikazu Haku	69	74	78	66	287	1,522,500

Casio World Open

Kochi Kuroshio Country Club, Kochi
Par 36-36–72; 7,235 yards

November 23-26
purse, ¥140,000,000

	SCORES				TOTAL	MONEY
Jeev Milkha Singh	66	69	69	68	272	¥28,000,000
David Smail	72	67	67	68	274	14,000,000
Shingo Katayama	70	68	70	68	276	6,720,000
Lin Keng-chi	70	68	69	69	276	6,720,000
Toshinori Muto	69	68	69	70	276	6,720,000
Tetsuya Haraguchi	66	68	70	72	276	6,720,000
Yoshikazu Haku	68	71	68	70	277	4,620,000
Tadahiro Takayama	68	72	71	67	278	4,109,000
Hideki Kase	67	69	70	72	278	4,109,000
Steven Conran	72	70	70	67	279	3,248,000
Tetsuji Hiratsuka	70	70	70	69	279	3,248,000
Toru Taniguchi	68	71	69	71	279	3,248,000
Daisuke Maruyama	69	69	70	71	279	3,248,000
Taichi Teshima	71	71	70	68	280	2,140,000
Kenichi Kuboya	72	68	71	69	280	2,140,000
Toshimitsu Izawa	70	71	70	69	280	2,140,000
Tatsuhiko Takahashi	72	69	70	69	280	2,140,000
Soushi Tajima	70	68	72	70	280	2,140,000
Nobuhiro Masuda	72	70	68	70	280	2,140,000
Lee Won-joon	69	74	67	70	280	2,140,000
Yui Ueda	69	69	73	70	281	1,596,000
Yusaku Miyazato	70	74	66	71	281	1,596,000
Yasuharu Imano	71	69	72	70	282	1,183,000
Hidemasa Hoshino	71	70	71	70	282	1,183,000
Yeh Wei-tze	71	73	69	69	282	1,183,000
Dinesh Chand	70	73	71	68	282	1,183,000
Ryuichi Oda	69	73	69	71	282	1,183,000
Azuma Yano	66	71	73	72	282	1,183,000
Nobuhito Sato	71	70	69	72	282	1,183,000
Keiichiro Fukabori	69	70	70	73	282	1,183,000

Golf Nippon Series JT Cup

Tokyo Yomiuri Country Club, Tokyo
Par 35-35–70; 7,016 yards

November 30-December 3
purse, ¥100,000,000

	SCORES				TOTAL	MONEY
Jeev Milkha Singh	67	65	67	70	269	¥30,000,000
Nobuhiro Masuda	69	66	69	66	270	13,500,000
Hideto Tanihara	69	70	66	66	271	7,350,000
David Smail	70	72	66	64	272	4,283,333
Liang Wen-chong	66	70	68	68	272	4,283,333
Toshinori Muto	68	70	66	68	272	4,283,333

	SCORES				TOTAL	MONEY
Tomohiro Kondo	72	71	68	62	273	2,820,000
Tatsuhiko Takahashi	75	67	68	63	273	2,820,000
Toru Taniguchi	67	71	67	68	273	2,820,000
Shingo Katayama	66	66	72	69	273	2,820,000
Keiichiro Fukabori	67	66	71	69	273	2,820,000
Tadahiro Takayama	71	73	66	64	274	1,870,000
Katsumasa Miyamoto	70	74	65	65	274	1,870,000
Hiroyuki Fujita	65	67	73	69	274	1,870,000
Taichi Teshima	68	66	70	70	274	1,870,000
Wayne Perske	65	69	69	71	274	1,870,000
Paul Sheehan	70	69	68	68	275	1,350,000
Yeh Wei-tze	74	65	67	69	275	1,350,000
Kaname Yokoo	67	73	66	69	275	1,350,000
Tetsuji Hiratsuka	69	67	68	71	275	1,350,000
Brendan Jones	73	67	69	67	276	1,016,666
Yasuharu Imano	72	67	69	68	276	1,016,666
Tsuneyuki Nakajima	66	72	68	70	276	1,016,666
Hidemasa Hoshino	72	68	68	69	277	920,000
Azuma Yano	70	70	68	70	278	900,000
Tatsuhiko Ichihara	72	74	68	68	282	870,000
S.K. Ho	69	73	66	74	282	870,000

Australasian Tour

Johnnie Walker Classic

The Vines Resort, Perth, Western Australia
Par 36-36–72; 7,102 yards

February 9-12
purse, £1,250,000

		SCORES			TOTAL	MONEY
Kevin Stadler	64	69	66	69	268	US$363,535
Nick O'Hern	67	71	64	68	270	242,345
Richard Green	66	69	66	71	272	122,804
Robert Allenby	69	68	69	66	272	122,804
K.J. Choi	65	66	70	72	273	92,485
Francesco Molinari	71	65	66	72	274	65,437
Adam Scott	64	71	70	69	274	65,437
Ian Poulter	70	66	69	69	274	65,437
Gavin Flint	72	64	66	73	275	44,206
Fred Couples	71	67	65	72	275	44,206
David Diaz	69	72	64	70	275	44,206
Ross Fisher	69	67	68	72	276	35,336
Chris Campbell	71	67	67	71	276	35,336
Shiv Kapur	68	71	67	70	276	35,336
Paul Casey	68	69	67	73	277	30,755
Prayad Marksaeng	72	66	70	69	277	30,755
Andrew Buckle	73	69	67	68	277	30,755
Craig Parry	68	70	65	75	278	27,120
Lee Sung-man	71	71	64	72	278	27,120
Stephen Allan	72	69	67	70	278	27,120
Stephen Leaney	70	66	69	74	279	22,685
Peter O'Malley	69	70	67	73	279	22,685
Kim Felton	71	68	67	73	279	22,685
Nick Flanagan	72	68	66	73	279	22,685
Steve Webster	71	68	68	72	279	22,685
Peter Senior	68	68	72	71	279	22,685
Soren Kjeldsen	70	71	67	71	279	22,685
Leigh McKechnie	73	66	70	70	279	22,685
Scott Gardiner	70	66	74	69	279	22,685
Tony Carolan	66	69	75	70	280	18,758
Ian Garbutt	71	69	70	70	280	18,758
Angel Cabrera	73	68	71	68	280	18,758
Gary Simpson	75	63	67	76	281	16,177
Oliver Wilson	72	68	66	75	281	16,177
Mark Foster	70	69	69	73	281	16,177
Gary Emerson	70	70	71	70	281	16,177
Sam Little	70	71	70	70	281	16,177
Simon Yates	72	70	73	66	281	16,177
Bradley Iles	68	74	67	73	282	14,178
Terry Pilkadaris	68	72	72	70	282	14,178
Jarrod Moseley	71	70	73	68	282	14,178
Raphael Jacquelin	70	69	67	77	283	12,433
Stephen Gallacher	71	66	70	76	283	12,433
Richard Finch	72	67	71	73	283	12,433
Marcus Fraser	67	71	73	72	283	12,433
Paul Sheehan	69	70	74	70	283	12,433
Robert Karlsson	72	69	69	74	284	10,251
Peter Hanson	73	69	70	72	284	10,251
Cameron Percy	71	70	72	71	284	10,251

	SCORES	TOTAL	MONEY
Jean Van de Velde	66 76 71 71	284	10,251
Lucas Parsons	69 73 71 71	284	10,251
John Bickerton	72 69 70 74	285	8,506
Graeme Storm	74 68 71 72	285	8,506
Joakim Haeggman	70 71 73 71	285	8,506
Brett Rumford	67 71 69 79	286	7,416
Ewan Porter	67 74 69 76	286	7,416
Phillip Archer	72 70 70 75	287	6,761
Simon Wakefield	70 72 72 74	288	6,434
Michael Long	73 69 73 73	288	6,434
Anthony Wall	72 67 71 79	289	5,780
Wang Ter-chang	73 66 72 78	289	5,780
Mardan Mamat	72 70 71 76	289	5,780
Maarten Lafeber	73 69 75 72	289	5,780
Andrew Marshall	70 69 76 75	290	5,235
Ryan Haller	72 69 77 73	291	5,016

Jacob's Creek Open

Royal Adelaide Golf Club, Adelaide, South Australia
Par 36-36–72; 7,113 yards

February 16-19
purse, A$1,000,000

	SCORES	TOTAL	MONEY
Paul Sheehan	73 70 69 69	281	US$134,194.54
Michael Sim	69 69 72 71	281	76,043.57
(Sheehan defeated Sim on second playoff hole.)			
Nick Flanagan	73 72 66 71	282	50,322.95
Jarrod Lyle	69 70 73 71	283	32,803.11
Aron Price	70 71 72 70	283	32,803.11
Craig Bowden	72 73 72 67	284	25,347.86
Peter Senior	67 74 72 71	284	25,347.86
Steve Allan	72 73 70 70	285	16,827.56
Ryan Armour	70 67 77 71	285	16,827.56
Steven Jeffress	70 72 72 71	285	16,827.56
Cliff Kresge	72 70 72 71	285	16,827.56
Scott Laycock	73 72 68 72	285	16,827.56
Roland Thatcher	70 75 73 67	285	16,827.56
Euan Walters	72 71 73 69	285	16,827.56
Justin Bolli	76 69 71 70	286	9,137.34
Adam Crawford	67 73 71 75	286	9,137.34
Matthew Ecob	70 71 73 72	286	9,137.34
Eric Egloff	72 73 69 72	286	9,137.34
Spencer Levin	69 68 77 72	286	9,137.34
Wade Ormsby	72 71 71 72	286	9,137.34
Anthony Painter	72 72 71 71	286	9,137.34
Michael Wright	72 69 72 73	286	9,137.34
Kurt Barnes	72 72 70 73	287	6,914.74
Hunter Haas	68 75 71 73	287	6,914.74
Bradley Iles	66 73 73 75	287	6,914.74
Peter Tomasulo	68 70 76 73	287	6,914.74
Jason Dufner	72 71 79 66	288	5,665.99
Michael Long	66 73 73 76	288	5,665.99
Scott Gardiner	69 74 71 75	289	4,860.82
Gabriel Hjertstedt	71 74 73 71	289	4,860.82
Leigh McKechnie	71 70 75 73	289	4,860.82
David Smail	69 72 73 75	289	4,860.82
Johnson Wagner	70 72 74 73	289	4,860.82

ING New Zealand PGA Championship

Clearwater Resort, Christchurch, New Zealand
Par 36-36–72; 7,137 yards

February 23-26
purse, US$600,000

	SCORES				TOTAL	MONEY
Jim Rutledge	75	68	72	64	279	US$113,684.21
Jarrod Lyle	71	66	69	74	280	53,526.31
Brett Rumford	69	68	71	72	280	53,526.31
Wade Ormsby	75	69	67	70	281	30,315.79
Chad Collins	73	73	67	69	282	24,000
Scott Gardiner	74	69	71	68	282	24,000
Jason Dufner	67	74	71	71	283	18,526.31
Paul Gow	74	67	71	71	283	18,526.31
Paul Marantz	72	70	68	73	283	18,526.31
Peter Fowler	72	72	70	70	284	12,421.05
Bob Heintz	75	68	70	71	284	12,421.05
David Morland	73	70	69	72	284	12,421.05
Peter Senior	72	72	70	70	284	12,421.05
David Smail	73	69	74	68	284	12,421.05
Kevin Stadler	71	69	70	74	284	12,421.05
Steve Allan	71	70	74	70	285	7,762.10
Ryan Armour	74	71	67	73	285	7,762.10
D.J. Brigman	71	72	73	69	285	7,762.10
Parker McLachlin	73	71	73	68	285	7,762.10
Simon Nash	73	73	70	69	285	7,762.10
Keoke Cotner	72	69	74	71	286	5,755.26
Nick Flanagan	71	70	75	70	286	5,755.26
Tom Gillis	72	70	71	73	286	5,755.26
Scott Hend	77	67	75	67	286	5,755.26
Brad Kennedy	76	69	73	68	286	5,755.26
Michael Long	72	72	70	72	286	5,755.26
Aron Price	71	70	73	72	286	5,755.26
Paul Sheehan	73	70	68	75	286	5,755.26
Steven Alker	74	65	76	72	287	3,969.92
Andrew Buckle	73	73	70	71	287	3,969.92
Mahal Pearce	72	72	70	73	287	3,969.92
Dicky Pride	74	71	75	67	287	3,969.92
Fran Quinn	73	70	71	73	287	3,969.92
Michael Sim	72	73	72	70	287	3,969.92
Brandt Snedeker	69	75	73	70	287	3,969.92

MFS Australian Open

Royal Sydney Golf Club, Sydney, New South Wales
Par 36-36–72; 6,940 yards

November 16-19
purse, A$1,500,000

	SCORES				TOTAL	MONEY
John Senden	76	72	67	65	280	A$270,000
Geoff Ogilvy	72	72	70	67	281	153,000
Stuart Appleby	75	68	71	68	282	86,625
Gavin Coles	73	70	69	70	282	86,625
Adam Scott	74	70	69	70	283	57,000
Nathan Green	67	71	73	72	283	57,000
Steven Bowditch	72	72	73	67	284	45,750
Brett Rumford	74	70	68	72	284	45,750
Aaron Baddeley	75	72	69	69	285	40,500

	SCORES				TOTAL	MONEY
Richard Green	69	71	74	72	286	37,500
*Andrew Dodt	77	70	70	70	287	
Paul Gow	76	72	69	70	287	31,500
Nick O'Hern	73	71	72	71	287	31,500
Kevin Stadler	75	74	70	69	288	25,500
Peter Lonard	71	75	70	72	288	25,500
Peter O'Malley	73	73	70	72	288	25,500
Nick Flanagan	78	72	70	70	290	20,550
Cameron Percy	73	76	69	72	290	20,550
Ben Bunny	76	77	70	68	291	17,437
Marcus Fraser	76	71	74	70	291	17,437
Robert Allenby	77	74	74	67	292	15,700
Will MacKenzie	74	73	72	73	292	15,700
Rod Pampling	77	74	68	73	292	15,700
Andrew Martin	71	73	77	72	293	14,700
Ashley Hall	75	71	74	73	293	14,700
Paul Sheehan	74	78	73	69	294	12,650
Greg Norman	79	73	68	74	294	12,650
Jarrod Lyle	69	75	75	75	294	12,650
Peter Senior	79	72	74	70	295	10,200
Paul Marantz	80	73	69	73	295	10,200
*Stephen Dartnall	77	70	74	74	295	
Mathew Goggin	73	74	74	74	295	10,200
Marcus Cain	77	74	70	74	295	10,200
Neil Sarkies	73	72	74	76	295	10,200

MasterCard Masters

Huntingdale Golf Club, Melbourne, Victoria
Par 36-36–72; 6,980 yards

November 23-26
purse, A$1,500,000

	SCORES				TOTAL	MONEY
Justin Rose	69	66	68	73	276	€170,353
Richard Green	70	71	68	69	278	80,208
Greg Chalmers	70	67	68	73	278	80,208
*Aaron Pike	64	69	72	74	279	
Aaron Baddeley	68	71	70	71	280	45,428
Kurt Barnes	70	66	75	70	281	37,856
Mathew Goggin	74	70	71	67	282	30,601
Jarrod Lyle	72	69	69	72	282	30,601
Simon Khan	71	66	72	73	282	30,601
Matthew Millar	76	69	68	70	283	22,241
Adam Bland	72	70	67	74	283	22,241
Peter Lonard	68	71	69	75	283	22,241
Raphael Jacquelin	66	72	67	78	283	22,241
John Senden	69	68	74	73	284	16,089
Nick O'Hern	73	68	69	74	284	16,089
Peter O'Malley	74	68	68	74	284	16,089
Jarrod Moseley	73	70	71	71	285	11,984
Nathan Green	73	67	71	74	285	11,984
Craig Parry	68	72	69	76	285	11,984
Paul Casey	71	70	67	77	285	11,984
Daniel Chopra	75	69	72	70	286	9,653
Andrew Tschudin	71	73	70	72	286	9,653
Peter Wilson	65	74	72	75	286	9,653
Peter Senior	72	70	67	77	286	9,653
Rafael Cabrera Bello	74	71	70	72	287	7,571

	SCORES				TOTAL	MONEY
Brendan Chant	75	68	71	73	287	7,571
Brad Kennedy	74	70	70	73	287	7,571
Damien McGrane	76	67	69	75	287	7,571
Jarmo Sandelin	71	73	68	75	287	7,571
Gary Simpson	75	65	71	76	287	7,571
Andrew Butterfield	70	70	70	77	287	7,571
Jason Norris	74	71	73	70	288	5,489
Wade Ormsby	74	71	70	73	288	5,489
Gavin Coles	71	73	70	74	288	5,489
Steven Bowditch	68	69	75	76	288	5,489
Robert Allenby	69	71	72	76	288	5,489
Tony Carolan	68	69	72	79	288	5,489
Marcus Fraser	74	69	66	79	288	5,489
James Nitties	71	68	76	74	289	4,448
Nick Dougherty	65	77	73	74	289	4,448
Aron Price	71	71	70	77	289	4,448
Graeme Storm	71	73	68	77	289	4,448
Terry Pilkadaris	72	72	75	71	290	3,312
Steve Alker	73	72	73	72	290	3,312
Peter Fowler	71	70	74	75	290	3,312
Aaron Black	70	74	71	75	290	3,312
Steve Collins	75	70	70	75	290	3,312
Peter Nolan	71	71	72	76	290	3,312
Lee S. James	74	69	71	76	290	3,312
Simon Dyson	77	68	69	76	290	3,312
*Stephen Dartnall	70	72	74	75	291	
James Heath	75	70	73	74	292	2,082
Luke Hickmott	72	72	73	75	292	2,082
Stuart Appleby	75	67	74	76	292	2,082
Brett Rumford	75	70	68	79	292	2,082
Carl Suneson	68	71	69	84	292	2,082
Gary Murphy	74	70	71	78	293	1,656
Danny Vera	72	72	77	73	294	1,585
Marcus Cain	72	73	76	73	294	1,585
Andrew Tampion	75	69	75	76	295	1,524
Mahal Pearce	71	74	74	76	295	1,524
Adam Porker	76	69	72	78	295	1,524
Dean Kinney	74	70	76	76	296	1,486
Henry Epstein	72	70	78	77	297	1,457
Michael Wright	74	71	75	77	297	1,457
Adam Crawford	71	73	73	81	298	1,429
Denny Lucas	71	73	75	85	304	1,410

Blue Chip New Zealand Open

Gulf Harbour Country Club, Auckland, New Zealand
Par 35-36–71; 6,951 yards

November 30-December 3
purse, NZ$1,500,000

	SCORES				TOTAL	MONEY
Nathan Green	71	67	76	65	279	€145,831
Nick Dougherty	69	66	79	67	281	43,952
Wade Ormsby	72	63	76	70	281	43,952
Jarrod Moseley	68	70	73	70	281	43,952
Brett Rumford	71	70	69	71	281	43,952
Michael Campbell	71	65	73	72	281	43,952
Marcus Fraser	69	69	70	73	281	43,952
Simon Wakefield	69	73	71	69	282	20,862

	SCORES				TOTAL	MONEY
Scott Strange	67	70	74	71	282	20,862
Greg Chalmers	68	70	72	72	282	20,862
Peter O'Malley	72	71	66	73	282	20,862
Tim Wilkinson	72	70	72	69	283	13,287
Daniel Chopra	74	68	71	70	283	13,287
Michael Long	69	70	73	71	283	13,287
Peter Lawrie	72	66	73	72	283	13,287
Damien McGrane	70	70	70	73	283	13,287
Kim Felton	68	72	68	75	283	13,287
Rafael Cabrera Bello	73	71	69	71	284	8,823
Shaun P. Webster	70	68	74	72	284	8,823
Kurt Barnes	71	70	69	74	284	8,823
Peter Senior	69	69	71	75	284	8,823
Graeme Storm	74	69	65	76	284	8,823
Jarmo Sandelin	71	71	73	70	285	7,292
Mahal Pearce	72	72	70	71	285	7,292
David Griffiths	70	70	72	73	285	7,292
Gareth Paddison	73	69	69	74	285	7,292
Terry Price	70	70	76	70	286	5,469
Doug Holloway	72	70	71	73	286	5,469
Ben Bunny	70	72	71	73	286	5,469
Andrew Tschudin	72	72	69	73	286	5,469
David Bransdon	70	68	74	74	286	5,469
David Lutterus	71	70	71	74	286	5,469
Richard Green	72	70	70	74	286	5,469
Brad Kennedy	73	68	70	75	286	5,469
Terry Pilkadaris	73	69	74	71	287	3,727
Eric Egloff	70	73	72	72	287	3,727
Aron Price	72	71	72	72	287	3,727
James Heath	70	69	75	73	287	3,727
Scott Hend	76	65	73	73	287	3,727
Matthew Millar	70	72	72	73	287	3,727
Andrew W. Johnson	73	67	73	74	287	3,727
Lee S. James	69	72	72	74	287	3,727
Jason Norris	71	71	70	75	287	3,727
Doug Batty	70	74	68	75	287	3,727
Daniel Vancsik	71	68	71	77	287	3,727
Marc Leishman	71	70	75	72	288	2,593
Henry Epstein	75	69	72	72	288	2,593
Craig Parry	69	71	71	77	288	2,593
Denny Lucas	70	69	79	71	289	2,106
Stephen Scahill	69	71	75	74	289	2,106
Andrew Raitt	71	67	74	77	289	2,106
Chris Downes	76	68	72	74	290	1,701
Carl Suneson	70	70	69	81	290	1,701
Tim Milford	71	71	74	75	291	1,398
Phil Tataurangi	78	66	72	75	291	1,398
James Nitties	71	69	74	77	291	1,398
Gavin Coles	75	65	72	79	291	1,398
Christian Nilsson	77	67	75	73	292	1,296
Mark Purser	69	72	77	74	292	1,296
Steven Jeffress	73	71	73	75	292	1,296
Aaron Townsend	74	68	71	79	292	1,296
David McKenzie	71	72	72	78	293	1,248
Hamish Robertson	76	68	71	78	293	1,248
Tony Christie	70	73	76	75	294	1,215
Marcus Higley	74	66	75	79	294	1,215
James Hepworth	74	70	74	77	295	1,191
Brendan Chant	71	73	71	82	297	1,175

Cadbury Schweppes Australian PGA Championship

Hyatt Regency Coolum Resort, Coolum Beach, Queensland
Par 36-36–72; 7,246 yards

December 7-10
purse, A$1,200,000

	SCORES				TOTAL	MONEY
Nick O'Hern	66	69	63	68	266	A$216,000
Peter Lonard	68	65	65	68	266	122,400
(O'Hern defeated Lonard on fourth playoff hole.)						
Wade Ormsby	68	66	68	67	269	81,000
Paul Gow	69	65	69	67	270	57,600
Peter O'Malley	66	69	66	71	272	48,000
David Smail	69	67	68	69	273	43,200
Nathan Green	70	64	71	69	274	38,400
Michael Wright	68	68	72	67	275	30,900
Stuart Appleby	67	71	70	67	275	30,900
James Nitties	64	74	68	69	275	30,900
Geoff Ogilvy	68	71	67	69	275	30,900
Peter Senior	69	69	73	65	276	22,800
David McKenzie	67	73	71	65	276	22,800
Matthew Millar	68	73	69	67	277	19,800
Rod Pampling	67	67	71	72	277	19,800
Robert Allenby	70	69	72	67	278	14,748
Chris Campbell	72	68	70	68	278	14,748
Jarrod Lyle	66	74	69	69	278	14,748
Peter Wilson	69	69	69	71	278	14,748
Ryan Haller	70	71	65	72	278	14,748
Brad Kennedy	72	68	72	67	279	12,240
Richard Green	69	71	72	67	279	12,240
Steven Jones	73	68	71	67	279	12,240
Kevin Stadler	71	71	72	66	280	11,160
Craig Parry	68	70	71	71	280	11,160
Gavin Coles	68	70	73	70	281	8,820
Adam Bland	72	68	71	70	281	8,820
Scott Gardiner	72	68	71	70	281	8,820
Steven Jeffress	69	67	74	71	281	8,820
Terry Pilkadaris	72	68	70	71	281	8,820
Kim Felton	69	72	69	71	281	8,820

African Tours

Dimension Data Pro-Am

Gary Player Country Club: Par 36-36–72; 7,831 yards
Lost City Golf Course: Par 36-36–72; 6,983 yards
Sun City, South Africa

January 26-29
purse, R1,000,000

	SCORES				TOTAL	MONEY
Alan McLean	68	74	72	71	285	R158,500
Tyrone van Aswegen	75	71	72	67	285	115,000
(McLean defeated van Aswegen on second playoff hole.)						
Anton Haig	73	69	74	71	287	59,100
Ulrich van den Berg	70	70	72	75	287	59,100
Thomas Aiken	68	76	72	72	288	38,100
Hennie Otto	69	73	72	74	288	38,100
Justin Walters	73	74	70	72	289	23,350
Titch Moore	70	74	75	70	289	23,350
Hendrik Buhrmann	76	71	71	71	289	23,350
Bruce Vaughan	73	72	70	74	289	23,350
Edrich Jansen	74	73	73	70	290	16,600
Kevin Stone	81	69	70	70	290	16,600
Chris Williams	73	71	74	72	290	16,600
Bradford Vaughan	75	70	71	75	291	14,350
Tjaart van der Walt	73	75	71	72	291	14,350
Barry Painting	73	74	73	72	292	13,100
Martin Maritz	72	74	73	73	292	13,100
Ian Hutchings	75	69	75	73	292	13,100
Michael Kirk	69	76	73	75	293	11,360
Leonard Loxton	73	77	71	72	293	11,360
Andre Cruse	73	72	73	75	293	11,360
Tongoona Charamba	72	73	74	74	293	11,360
Doug McGuigan	73	74	72	74	293	11,360

Nashua Masters

Wild Coast Sun Country Club, Port Edward, Natal
Par 35-35–70; 6,351 yards

February 2-5
purse, R1,000,000

	SCORES				TOTAL	MONEY
Warren Abery	67	63	67	68	265	R158,500
Doug McGuigan	69	64	64	70	267	115,000
Mark Murless	65	68	65	70	268	69,100
Gregory Bourdy	73	65	67	67	272	45,100
Andre Bossert	69	66	68	69	272	45,100
Hennie Otto	70	68	68	67	273	35,100
Jaco Van Zyl	69	68	69	68	274	26,600
Grant Muller	69	65	70	70	274	26,600
Adilson da Silva	69	68	69	69	275	21,100
Charl Schwartzel	72	68	68	68	276	19,100
Bruce Vaughan	74	64	72	67	277	15,700
Vaughn Groenewald	74	64	71	68	277	15,700
Alan Michell	71	65	71	70	277	15,700
Des Terblanche	71	68	68	70	277	15,700

	SCORES				TOTAL	MONEY
Dion Fourie	72	65	67	73	277	15,700
Theunis Spangenberg	70	70	69	69	278	12,850
Nic Henning	69	65	74	70	278	12,850
Alan McLean	72	67	68	71	278	12,850
Michael du Toit	70	66	70	72	278	12,850
Ulrich van den Berg	69	72	70	68	279	11,020
Jean Hugo	69	69	72	69	279	11,020
Jakobus Roos	74	66	69	70	279	11,020
Ian Hutchings	73	69	67	70	279	11,020
Bafana Hlophe	67	69	71	72	279	11,020

Telkom PGA Championship

Country Club Johannesburg, Johannesburg, South Africa
Par 36-36–72; 7,478 yards

February 16-19
purse, R2,000,000

	SCORES				TOTAL	MONEY
Gregory Bourdy	66	66	66	69	267	R317,000
Thomas Aiken	70	64	70	69	273	230,000
James Kamte	67	69	71	68	275	138,200
Tyrone van Aswegen	70	66	70	70	276	90,200
Justin Walters	73	64	68	71	276	90,200
Brandon Pieters	73	67	70	67	277	54,700
Richard Sterne	72	69	69	67	277	54,700
Michiel Bothma	69	68	70	70	277	54,700
Charl Schwartzel	69	69	69	70	277	54,700
Jaco Van Zyl	73	68	69	68	278	34,450
Andre Bossert	72	70	68	68	278	34,450
Josh Cunliffe	67	71	70	70	278	34,450
Hennie Otto	71	68	69	70	278	34,450
Grant Muller	72	68	72	67	279	28,200
Ryan Tipping	69	71	72	67	279	28,200
Henk Alberts	70	69	66	74	279	28,200
Alan McLean	71	70	71	68	280	24,750
Nico Le Grange	67	69	74	70	280	24,750
Chris Swanepoel	71	73	66	70	280	24,750
Louis Oosthuizen	72	72	65	71	280	24,750

Vodacom Tour Championship

Pretoria Country Club, Pretoria, South Africa
Par 35-36–71; 7,063 yards

February 23-26
purse, R2,000,000

	SCORES				TOTAL	MONEY
Charl Schwartzel	68	70	65	67	270	R317,000
Darren Fichardt	69	67	70	68	274	230,000
Thomas Aiken	71	70	70	67	278	138,200
Martin Maritz	69	71	76	63	279	83,533.33
Dean Lambert	71	72	70	66	279	83,533.33
Warren Abery	69	70	70	70	279	83,533.33
Hennie Otto	67	74	69	70	280	58,200
James Kamte	63	72	76	70	281	48,200
Louis Oosthuizen	74	70	67	71	282	40,200
Desvonde Botes	68	72	70	72	282	40,200

	SCORES				TOTAL	MONEY
*Charl Coetzee	67	73	70	72	282	
James Kingston	73	73	69	68	283	34,200
Justin Walters	69	71	73	70	283	34,200
Ian Hutchings	71	71	73	69	284	29,533.33
Werner Geyer	73	72	70	69	284	29,533.33
Jean Hugo	71	72	69	72	284	29,533.33
Adilson da Silva	71	73	73	68	285	26,700
Ross Wellington	69	68	73	75	285	26,700
Nic Henning	73	72	72	69	286	24,266.66
Des Terblanche	73	75	67	71	286	24,266.66
Michiel Bothma	73	69	68	76	286	24,266.66

Hassan II Trophy

Dar-es-Salam Golf Club, Red Course, Rabat, Morocco
Par 36-37–73; 7,307 yards

February 23-26
purse, US$500,000

	SCORES				TOTAL	MONEY
Sam Torrance	70	67	69	75	281	US$120,000
Raphael Jacquelin	67	76	69	69	281	70,000
(Torrance defeated Jacquelin on first playoff hole.)						
Jose-Filipe Lima	72	70	67	74	283	37,500
Santiago Luna	66	72	71	74	283	37,500
Gordon Brand, Jr.	73	72	65	74	284	18,750
Carl Suneson	73	71	71	69	284	18,750
Peter Baker	73	70	70	73	286	15,000
Sandy Lyle	73	70	73	72	288	13,500
Jean-Francois Remesy	72	71	74	72	289	12,000
Roger Chapman	76	70	70	75	291	10,500
Casey Wittenberg	76	73	70	73	292	9,500
Alessandro Tadini	72	74	73	74	293	8,750
Miguel Angel Martin	74	74	72	73	293	8,750
Younes El Hassani	73	75	73	72	293	8,750
Erik Compton	78	66	74	76	294	8,125
Costantino Rocca	75	73	73	73	294	8,125
Gregory Havret	75	76	68	76	295	7,500
Jose Manuel Lara	75	72	73	75	295	7,500
Mark Roe	76	74	71	74	295	7,500
Scott Drummond	73	72	74	78	297	7,000

Stanbic Zambia Open

Nchanga Golf Club, Chingola, Zambia
Par 36-36–72; 6,918 yards

March 17-19
purse, R750,000

	SCORES			TOTAL	MONEY
Steve Basson	72	71	64	207	R100,000
Madalitso Muthiya	72	72	66	210	62,500
Chris Williams	69	72	69	210	62,500
Omar Sandys	70	75	67	212	23,767.85
Ross Wellington	71	73	68	212	23,767.85
Rossouw Loubser	72	70	70	212	23,767.85
Mark Williams	74	67	71	212	23,767.85
Jason Jackson	70	70	72	212	23,767.85

	SCORES			TOTAL	MONEY
Ryan Tipping	68	72	72	212	23,767.85
Eugen Marugi	70	68	74	212	23,767.85
Werner Geyer	69	75	69	213	13,325
Kevin Stone	68	71	74	213	13,325
Bafana Hlophe	69	74	71	214	11,700
David Ryan	71	72	71	214	11,700
Trevor Fisher, Jr.	75	70	70	215	10,925
Bradford Vaughan	72	73	71	216	10,000
Doug McGuigan	78	67	71	216	10,000
Mark Murless	73	70	73	216	10,000
Sammy Daniels	73	68	75	216	10,000
Johan Etsebeth	73	72	72	217	8,108.33
Josh Cunliffe	76	70	71	217	8,108.33
Ian Hutchings	72	73	72	217	8,108.33
Tongoona Charamba	73	73	71	217	8,108.33
Sean Farrell	75	71	71	217	8,108.33
Des Terblanche	73	72	72	217	8,108.33
John Bele	75	72	70	217	8,108.33
Adilson da Silva	70	73	74	217	8,108.33
Brett Liddle	73	70	74	217	8,108.33

Vodacom Origins of Golf Tour - Western Cape

Arabella Country Club, Hermanus, South Africa
Par 36-36–72; 6,976 yards

April 19-21
purse, R360,000

	SCORES			TOTAL	MONEY
Jean Hugo	71	70	67	208	R56,520
Chris Williams	71	72	70	213	41,400
James Kamte	67	75	72	214	25,020
Adilson da Silva	67	73	74	214	25,020
Titch Moore	68	72	75	215	16,200
Andrew Curlewis	75	71	71	217	9,282
Rossouw Loubser	73	75	69	217	9,282
Desvonde Botes	74	74	69	217	9,282
Peter Karmis	70	75	72	217	9,282
Steve van Vuuren	72	72	73	217	9,282
Bradford Vaughan	68	72	77	217	9,282
Mike Michell	75	72	71	218	6,732
Dijon Tintinger	76	72	71	219	5,575.50
Omar Sandys	73	75	71	219	5,575.50
Alex Baillie	70	76	73	219	5,575.50
Hennie Otto	73	72	74	219	5,575.50
Grant Muller	74	71	74	219	5,575.50
Doug McGuigan	76	69	74	219	5,575.50
Kevin Stone	73	71	75	219	5,575.50
Lindani Ndwandwe	70	73	76	219	5,575.50

South African Airways Pro-Am Invitational - Cape Town

Paarl Golf Club, Cape Town, South Africa
Par 36-36–72; 6,734 yards

April 27-29
purse, R350,000

	SCORES			TOTAL	MONEY
Jean Hugo	68	64	68	200	R54,950
Anton Haig	69	68	65	202	40,250
Bradford Vaughan	70	68	65	203	28,000
Lindani Ndwandwe	70	67	67	204	16,216.66
Gerlou Roux	70	62	72	204	16,216.66
Chris Swanepoel	67	64	73	204	16,216.66
Chris Williams	68	67	70	205	10,500
Robert Wragg	69	69	68	206	8,575
Dion Fourie	68	68	70	206	8,575
Alan Michell	70	68	69	207	6,755
Michiel Bothma	69	68	70	207	6,755
Adilson da Silva	67	70	70	207	6,755
Doug McGuigan	65	71	71	207	6,755
Thomas Aiken	68	70	70	208	5,716.66
Andrew Curlewis	68	69	71	208	5,716.66
Steve Basson	69	67	72	208	5,716.66
Sammy Daniels	69	69	71	209	4,907
James Kamte	68	69	72	209	4,907
Jaco Van Zyl	69	72	68	209	4,907
Merrick Bremner	69	67	73	209	4,907
Albert Pistorius	66	69	74	209	4,907

Samsung Royal Swazi Sun Open

Royal Swazi Sun Country Club, Mbabane, Swaziland
Par 36-36–72; 5,983 yards

May 3-6
purse, R550,000

	POINTS				TOTAL	MONEY
Thomas Aiken	8	24	9	18	59	R87,175
Steve Basson	14	9	12	15	50	63,250
Patrick O'Brien	12	11	10	12	45	39,270
Dion Fourie	4	12	12	16	44	25,547.50
Hendrik Buhrmann	12	7	11	14	44	25,547.50
Mark Murless	18	8	9	7	42	19,965
Michiel Bothma	14	8	10	9	41	16,610
Omar Sandys	9	13	11	7	40	12,952.50
Jaco Van Zyl	11	12	15	2	40	12,952.50
Desvonde Botes	-2	18	11	12	39	10,945
Bradford Vaughan	5	12	11	10	38	10,010
Chris Williams	13	7	7	9	36	9,295
Chris Swanepoel	5	9	14	7	35	8,745
Des Terblanche	13	7	5	8	33	8,057.50
Grant Muller	4	16	8	5	33	8,057.50
Jean Hugo	6	12	9	4	31	7,370
Alan Michell	13	9	1	8	31	7,370
Adilson da Silva	15	10	5	1	31	7,370
Ashley Roestoff	7	5	13	5	30	6,765
James Kamte	4	10	8	8	30	6,765

Suncoast Classic

Durban Country Club, Durban, South Africa
Par 36-36–72; 6,732 yards

May 11-13
purse, R350,000

	SCORES			TOTAL	MONEY
Alex Haindl	70	70	67	207	R54,950
Lindani Ndwandwe	69	71	67	207	34,125
Bradford Vaughan	67	70	70	207	34,125
(Haindl defeated Ndwandwe and Vaughan on second playoff hole.)					
Wayne de Haas	71	68	69	208	20,650
Werner Geyer	73	71	66	210	14,000
Desvonde Botes	68	71	71	210	14,000
Brett Liddle	71	69	71	211	9,800
Jaco Van Zyl	70	69	72	211	9,800
Titch Moore	74	69	69	212	8,050
Steve Basson	69	73	72	214	6,930
Josh Cunliffe	68	74	72	214	6,930
Alan Michell	67	72	75	214	6,930
Mike Lamb	74	71	70	215	5,961.66
Adilson da Silva	71	73	71	215	5,961.66
Chris Williams	71	73	71	215	5,961.66
Sean Farrell	71	74	71	216	5,390
Michiel Bothma	70	74	72	216	5,390
Thomas Aiken	74	75	68	217	4,725
Chris Swanepoel	72	74	71	217	4,725
Gary Thain	74	71	72	217	4,725
Ian Hutchings	73	70	74	217	4,725
Ross Wellington	72	69	76	217	4,725

South African Airways Pro-Am Invitational - Johannesburg

Kempton Park Golf Club, Johannesburg, South Africa
Par 36-36–72; 6,879 yards

May 18-20
purse, R350,000

	SCORES			TOTAL	MONEY
Tongoona Charamba	65	67	67	199	R54,950
Hennie Otto	64	70	67	201	34,125
Jean Hugo	67	64	70	201	34,125
Josh Cunliffe	68	67	69	204	20,650
Chris Williams	69	68	68	205	15,750
Rossouw Loubser	71	68	67	206	9,024.16
Steve van Vuuren	70	69	67	206	9,024.16
Merrick Bremner	69	70	67	206	9,024.16
Bradford Vaughan	73	65	68	206	9,024.16
Mark Murless	67	70	69	206	9,024.16
James Kamte	67	68	71	206	9,024.16
Werner Geyer	67	73	67	207	6,107.50
Brandon Pieters	69	70	68	207	6,107.50
Alex Haindl	71	67	69	207	6,107.50
Chris Swanepoel	71	67	69	207	6,107.50
Gary Thain	71	71	66	208	5,495
Alan Michell	68	73	68	209	5,086.66
Jaco Van Zyl	73	68	68	209	5,086.66
Ross Wellington	71	67	71	209	5,086.66
John Bele	72	71	67	210	4,230
Ian Hutchings	69	72	69	210	4,230

	SCORES	TOTAL	MONEY
Andre Cruse	69 72 69	210	4,230
Patrick O'Brien	73 67 70	210	4,230
Desvonde Botes	68 71 71	210	4,230
Doron Mommsen	69 70 71	210	4,230
Des Terblanche	66 71 73	210	4,230

Vodacom Origins of Golf Tour at Pretoria

Pretoria Country Club, Pretoria, South Africa
Par 36-36–72; 7,063 yards

May 24-26
purse, R360,000

	SCORES	TOTAL	MONEY
Vaughn Groenewald	69 65 71	205	R56,520
Doug McGuigan	73 69 69	211	35,100
Thomas Aiken	73 69 69	211	35,100
Adilson da Silva	72 70 71	213	18,720
Brett Liddle	71 70 72	213	18,720
Desvonde Botes	68 75 71	214	11,700
Steve Basson	70 71 73	214	11,700
Nico van Rensburg	72 72 71	215	8,073
Omar Sandys	69 75 71	215	8,073
Hennie Otto	74 68 73	215	8,073
Keith Horne	70 70 75	215	8,073
Jean Hugo	75 69 73	217	6,420
Mark Murless	75 67 75	217	6,420
Grant Muller	71 70 76	217	6,420
David Ryan	74 72 72	218	5,250.85
Dean Lambert	72 74 72	218	5,250.85
Lindani Ndwandwe	69 76 73	218	5,250.85
Ross Wellington	74 73 71	218	5,250.85
Jason Jackson	75 69 74	218	5,250.85
Alan Michell	74 74 70	218	5,250.85
Brandon Pieters	70 72 76	218	5,250.85

Vodacom Origins of Golf Tour at Kwazulu Natal

Selborne Golf Club, Kwazulu Natal, South Africa
Par 35-36–71; 6,670 yards

June 28-30
purse, R360,000

	SCORES	TOTAL	MONEY
Rossouw Loubser	69 68 68	205	R56,520
Vaughn Groenewald	68 71 67	206	35,100
Adilson da Silva	69 69 68	206	35,100
Chris Swanepoel	69 74 65	208	18,720
Mike Lamb	70 67 71	208	18,720
Grant Veenstra	70 69 70	209	11,700
Ryan Tipping	70 69 70	209	11,700
Desvonde Botes	75 71 64	210	8,400
Doug McGuigan	71 67 72	210	8,400
Bafana Hlophe	68 69 73	210	8,400
Keith Horne	71 73 67	211	7,092
Alex Haindl	68 75 69	212	6,282
Mohamed Tayob	70 72 70	212	6,282
Barry Painting	71 71 70	212	6,282

	SCORES			TOTAL	MONEY
Chris Williams	69	72	71	212	6,282
Doron Mommsen	74	68	71	213	5,652
Ian Hutchings	75	68	71	214	5,436
Grant Muller	78	67	70	215	5,130
Werner Geyer	70	73	72	215	5,130
John Bele	73	73	70	216	4,860

Vodacom Origins of Golf Tour at Bloemfontein

Bloemfontein Golf Club, Bloemfontein, South Africa
Par 36-36–72; 7,302 yards

August 16-18
purse, R360,000

	SCORES			TOTAL	MONEY
Rossouw Loubser	66	72	67	205	R56,520
Doug McGuigan	69	72	66	207	35,100
Adilson da Silva	72	67	68	207	35,100
Leonard Loxton	68	68	72	208	21,240
Dean Lambert	69	69	72	210	16,200
Johan Etsebeth	72	70	69	211	11,700
Gerlou Roux	68	71	72	211	11,700
Henk Alberts	71	72	69	212	8,073
Tongoona Charamba	74	68	70	212	8,073
Divan van den Heever	68	74	70	212	8,073
Brett Liddle	71	69	72	212	8,073
Sean Farrell	73	71	69	213	6,156
Alex Haindl	72	72	69	213	6,156
Doron Mommsen	73	72	68	213	6,156
Omar Sandys	71	70	72	213	6,156
Josh Cunliffe	68	71	74	213	6,156
Chris Williams	76	69	69	214	4,956
Jean Hugo	71	70	73	214	4,956
Wayne de Haas	72	69	73	214	4,956
Desvonde Botes	70	70	74	214	4,956
Gary Thain	70	69	75	214	4,956
Des Terblanche	65	73	76	214	4,956

Telkom PGA Pro-Am

Centurion Country Club, Pretoria, South Africa
Par 36-36–72; 7,328 yards

August 23-25
purse, R330,000

	SCORES			TOTAL	MONEY
Doug McGuigan	68	67	70	205	R51,810
Hennie Otto	74	63	70	207	32,175
Desvonde Botes	67	69	71	207	32,175
Kevin Stone	67	72	69	208	19,470
Trevor Fisher, Jr.	72	68	69	209	14,850
Rossouw Loubser	69	72	70	211	11,550
Darren Fichardt	75	70	67	212	9,900
Kenneth Dube	70	73	70	213	7,154.40
Callie Swart	71	70	72	213	7,154.40
James Kamte	67	73	73	213	7,154.40
Adilson da Silva	70	70	73	213	7,154.40
Alex Haindl	70	69	74	213	7,154.40

	SCORES	TOTAL	MONEY
Dean Lambert	73 72 69	214	5,511
Thabang Simon	73 70 71	214	5,511
Steve Basson	76 66 72	214	5,511
Jean Hugo	69 70 75	214	5,511
Chris Williams	70 73 72	215	4,884
Ross Wellington	72 70 73	215	4,884
Clinton Whitelaw	71 74 71	216	4,139.14
Jakobus Roos	72 72 72	216	4,139.14
Tongoona Charamba	72 72 72	216	4,139.14
Wayne de Haas	70 75 71	216	4,139.14
Brett Liddle	73 72 71	216	4,139.14
Leonard Loxton	71 71 74	216	4,139.14
Irvin Mosate	76 70 70	216	4,139.14

Eskom Power Cup

Wanderers Golf Club, Johannesburg, South Africa
Par 36-35–71; 7,159 yards

August 31-September 2
purse, R350,000

	SCORES	TOTAL	MONEY
Trevor Fisher, Jr.	66 67 69	202	R54,950
Thomas Aiken	67 70 68	205	40,250
Dion Fourie	71 67 68	206	24,325
Alan Michell	69 66 71	206	24,325
Tongoona Charamba	72 69 66	207	14,000
Adilson da Silva	71 66 70	207	14,000
Alex Haindl	69 65 74	208	10,500
Brandon Pieters	67 71 71	209	9,100
Doug McGuigan	70 70 70	210	7,700
Ian Hutchings	69 70 71	210	7,700
Ross Wellington	74 68 69	211	6,405
Brett Liddle	71 71 69	211	6,405
Hennie Otto	72 70 69	211	6,405
Gian-Carlo Scarola	70 70 71	211	6,405
Wayne de Haas	71 71 70	212	5,600
Des Terblanche	74 67 71	212	5,600
Steve Basson	74 70 69	213	5,180
Lindani Ndwandwe	75 70 68	213	5,180
Clinton Whitelaw	72 71 71	214	4,637.50
Omar Sandys	70 74 70	214	4,637.50
Jakobus Roos	73 71 70	214	4,637.50
James Kamte	72 67 75	214	4,637.50

Vodacom Origins of Golf Tour - Eastern Cape

Pezula Championship Course, Knysna, South Africa
Par 36-36–72; 6,951 yards

September 13-15
purse, R360,000

	SCORES	TOTAL	MONEY
Kevin Stone	63 73 71	207	R56,520
Ian Hutchings	70 67 71	208	41,400
Jaco Ahlers	69 73 69	211	28,800
Hennie Otto	71 71 70	212	21,240
Keith Horne	71 70 72	213	16,200

	SCORES			TOTAL	MONEY
Thomas Aiken	71	72	71	214	12,600
Johan Kok	72	72	71	215	9,480
Jakobus Roos	68	75	72	215	9,480
Louis Oosthuizen	70	72	73	215	9,480
Grant Muller	70	73	73	216	7,560
Patrick O'Brien	70	73	74	217	6,588
Mike Lamb	74	73	70	217	6,588
Des Terblanche	66	74	77	217	6,588
Grant Veenstra	71	69	77	217	6,588
Mark Murless	70	74	74	218	5,443.20
Ulrich van den Berg	72	74	72	218	5,443.20
Clinton Whitelaw	72	75	71	218	5,443.20
Adilson da Silva	75	72	71	218	5,443.20
Thabang Simon	67	69	82	218	5,443.20
Alan Michell	73	71	75	219	4,507.20
Andre Cruse	76	70	73	219	4,507.20
Billy Valentyn	68	74	77	219	4,507.20
Brett Liddle	72	75	72	219	4,507.20
Darren Holder	74	74	71	219	4,507.20

Seekers Travel Pro-Am

Dainfern Country Club, Johannesburg, South Africa
Par 36-36–72; 7,258 yards

September 28-30
purse, R300,000

	SCORES			TOTAL	MONEY
Desvonde Botes	67	62	67	196	R54,950
Alex Haindl	68	64	67	199	40,250
Hennie Otto	67	67	66	200	28,000
Mark Murless	67	67	67	201	18,200
James Kamte	64	68	69	201	18,200
Darren Fichardt	66	67	70	203	11,375
Rossouw Loubser	69	64	70	203	11,375
Ashley Roestoff	67	69	68	204	9,100
Chris Williams	70	68	67	205	7,700
Anton Haig	70	65	70	205	7,700
Eugen Marugi	70	67	69	206	6,556.66
John Bele	67	67	72	206	6,556.66
Michael Kirk	70	64	72	206	6,556.66
James Kingston	68	71	68	207	5,401.66
Johan Kok	66	73	68	207	5,401.66
Doug McGuigan	69	69	69	207	5,401.66
Chris Swanepoel	72	66	69	207	5,401.66
Adilson da Silva	68	67	72	207	5,401.66
Titch Moore	67	67	73	207	5,401.66
Jaco Ahlers	68	72	68	208	4,305
Wallie Coetsee	68	71	69	208	4,305
Mohamed Tayob	69	68	71	208	4,305
Simon Smart	71	65	72	208	4,305
Marc Cayeux	68	67	73	208	4,305
Ulrich van den Berg	67	65	76	208	4,305

Vodacom Origins of Golf Tour Final

Montagu Golf Course, Fancourt, George, South Africa
Par 36-36–72; 7,342 yards

October 4-6
purse, R360,000

	SCORES			TOTAL	MONEY
Darren Fichardt	71	69	72	212	R56,520
Alex Haindl	68	73	72	213	41,400
Kevin Stone	75	72	69	216	28,800
Leonard Loxton	76	72	69	217	16,680
Chris Swanepoel	72	73	72	217	16,680
Omar Sandys	70	74	73	217	16,680
Grant Muller	74	74	70	218	9,000
Gary Thain	73	73	72	218	9,000
Adilson da Silva	68	77	73	218	9,000
Albert Pistorius	73	72	73	218	9,000
Steve van Vuuren	71	76	72	219	6,912
Mike Lamb	73	72	74	219	6,912
Divan van den Heever	78	70	72	220	6,408
Des Terblanche	77	74	71	222	5,769
Barry Painting	75	75	72	222	5,769
Wayne de Haas	70	79	73	222	5,769
Ian Hutchings	74	74	74	222	5,769
Werner Geyer	78	75	70	223	5,040
Rossouw Loubser	77	75	71	223	5,040
Ulrich van den Berg	75	77	71	223	5,040

Bearingman Highveld Classic

Witbank Golf Club, Witbank, South Africa
Par 36-36–72; 6,753 yards

October 13-15
purse, R400,000

	SCORES			TOTAL	MONEY
Darren Fichardt	66	67	71	204	R62,800
Alex Haindl	69	64	71	204	46,000
(Fichardt defeated Haindl on second playoff hole.)					
Dean Lambert	71	68	66	205	18,333.33
Albert Pistorius	70	68	67	205	18,333.33
Chris Swanepoel	68	69	68	205	18,333.33
Mohamed Tayob	69	66	70	205	18,333.33
Callie Swart	69	65	71	205	18,333.33
Grant Muller	65	69	71	205	18,333.33
Kevin Stone	68	72	66	206	8,800
Andrew Curlewis	68	71	67	206	8,800
Mawonga Nomwa	73	69	65	207	7,320
Desvonde Botes	73	66	68	207	7,320
Dion Fourie	68	68	71	207	7,320
Adilson da Silva	69	67	71	207	7,320
Clinton Whitelaw	72	70	66	208	6,160
Louis Oosthuizen	71	68	69	208	6,160
Doug McGuigan	72	67	69	208	6,160
Ross Wellington	68	65	75	208	6,160
Hennie Otto	67	75	67	209	4,930
Trevor Fisher, Jr.	72	68	69	209	4,930
Steve van Vuuren	68	72	69	209	4,930
Sean Farrell	72	68	69	209	4,930
Des Terblanche	69	71	69	209	4,930

	SCORES	TOTAL	MONEY
Michiel Bothma	68 70 71	209	4,930
Omar Sandys	68 69 72	209	4,930
Andre Cruse	71 66 72	209	4,930

MTC Namibia PGA Championship

Windhoek Country Club, Namibia
Par 35-36–71; 7,106 yards

October 19-21
purse, R600,000

	SCORES	TOTAL	MONEY
Anton Haig	62 69 65	196	R95,100
Thomas Aiken	71 63 63	197	69,000
Adilson da Silva	68 66 65	199	36,570
Grant Muller	64 69 66	199	36,570
James Kingston	70 69 61	200	23,590
Ross Wellington	66 68 66	200	23,590
Alex Haindl	67 67 67	201	15,460
Hennie Otto	68 65 68	201	15,460
Vaughn Groenewald	66 66 69	201	15,460
Titch Moore	69 70 63	202	11,000
Mark Murless	68 68 66	202	11,000
Keith Horne	69 66 67	202	11,000
Alan Michell	71 66 66	203	9,040
Ryan Tipping	67 66 70	203	9,040
Des Terblanche	65 67 71	203	9,040
Brandon Pieters	70 68 66	204	8,040
Rudy Whitfield	68 69 67	204	8,040
Bradley Davison	69 67 68	204	8,040
Trevor Fisher, Jr.	70 71 64	205	7,380
Darren Fichardt	70 68 67	205	7,380

Platinum Classic

Mooi Nooi Golf Club, Rustenburg, South Africa
Par 36-36–72; 6,835 yards

October 26-28
purse, R550,000

	SCORES	TOTAL	MONEY
Vaughn Groenewald	68 66 68	202	R95,100
Thomas Aiken	67 68 68	203	69,000
Andrew McLardy	68 70 66	204	42,840
Michael Kirk	65 71 69	205	27,850
Marc Cayeux	68 67 70	205	27,850
Michiel Bothma	70 68 69	207	18,320
Gary Thain	65 72 70	207	18,320
Mark Williams	71 66 70	207	18,320
Doug McGuigan	68 72 68	208	12,570
James Kingston	66 73 69	208	12,570
James Kamte	74 69 66	209	10,920
Mark Murless	71 74 65	210	9,120
Bobby Lincoln	70 73 67	210	9,120
Richard Sterne	70 71 69	210	9,120
Omar Sandys	67 72 71	210	9,120
Des Terblanche	70 68 72	210	9,120
Werner Geyer	74 72 65	211	7,400

	SCORES			TOTAL	MONEY
Nic Henning	72	73	66	211	7,400
Wallie Coetsee	70	73	68	211	7,400
Ulrich van den Berg	68	73	70	211	7,400
Steve van Vuuren	70	70	71	211	7,400
Jean Hugo	64	74	73	211	7,400

Limpopo Classic

Polokwane Golf Club, Pietersburg, South Africa
Par 35-36–71; 7,101 yards

November 16-19
purse, R1,000,000

	SCORES				TOTAL	MONEY
Bradford Vaughan	68	65	66	67	266	R158,500
Warren Abery	63	69	65	69	266	115,000

(Vaughan defeated Abery on first playoff hole.)

Mark Murless	65	65	66	71	267	69,100
Adilson da Silva	69	67	68	67	271	45,100
Divan van den Heever	67	65	71	68	271	45,100
Dion Fourie	70	66	67	69	272	29,433.33
Wayne de Haas	69	65	67	71	272	29,433.33
Ryan Tipping	65	68	67	72	272	29,433.33
Henk Alberts	68	67	73	65	273	20,100
Bobby Lincoln	70	65	68	70	273	20,100
Callie Swart	73	67	68	66	274	16,600
Wallie Coetsee	67	67	72	68	274	16,600
Michael Kirk	68	67	71	68	274	16,600
Des Terblanche	72	69	68	66	275	13,850
Richard Sterne	68	68	69	70	275	13,850
Hennie Otto	69	69	67	70	275	13,850
Ross Wellington	64	72	68	71	275	13,850
Steve Basson	69	68	70	69	276	12,133.33
Jakobus Roos	67	70	68	71	276	12,133.33
Ryan Reid	69	71	65	71	276	12,133.33

Coca-Cola Charity Championship

Arabella Country Club, Hermanus, South Africa
Par 36-36–72; 6,976 yards

November 21-23
purse, R500,000

	SCORES			TOTAL	MONEY
Alan Michell	64	70	66	200	R79,250
Adilson da Silva	73	69	66	208	45,300
Doug McGuigan	64	69	75	208	45,300
Vaughn Groenewald	67	70	72	209	24,550
Rossouw Loubser	73	71	66	210	18,300
James Kamte	70	73	67	210	18,300
Alex Haindl	73	68	69	210	18,300
Chris Swanepoel	67	73	71	211	15,700
Mark Murless	72	73	67	212	14,350
Thabang Simon	67	70	75	212	14,350
Des Terblanche	70	74	69	213	13,300
Jean Hugo	75	72	67	214	12,300
Werner Geyer	69	74	71	214	12,300
Hennie Otto	69	70	76	215	11,400

	SCORES	TOTAL	MONEY
Mike Lamb	76 69 71	216	10,800
Tongoona Charamba	75 72 70	217	10,200
Brett Liddle	71 72 74	217	10,200
Bradford Vaughan	74 73 71	218	9,600
Grant Muller	73 76 71	220	9,100
Kevin Stone	73 75 72	220	9,100
Ian Hutchings	72 75 73	220	9,100
Chris Williams	73 71 76	220	9,100

Nelson Mandela Invitational

Arabella Country Club, Hermanus, South Africa
Par 36-36–72; 6,976 yards

November 25-26
purse, R250,000

	SCORES	TOTAL	MONEY (Each)
Retief Goosen/Bobby Lincoln	62 66	128	R125,000
John Bland/Alan Michell	64 64	128	
(Goosen/Lincoln defeated Bland/Michell on second playoff hole.)			
Hugh Baiocchi/James Kamte	65 65	130	
Sandy Lyle/Omar Sandys	65 65		
Mark McNulty/Charl Schwartzel	65 65		
Mokgeteng J. Mashego/Adilson da Silva	67 64	131	
Vincent Tshabalala/Doug McGuigan	68 66	134	
Gary Player/Trevor Immelman	68 66		
Tony Johnstone/Helen Alfredsson	68 67	135	
Sally Little/Paul Lawrie	68 68	136	

Nedbank Golf Challenge

Gary Player Country Club, Sun City, South Africa
Par 36-36–72; 7,590 yards

November 30-December 3
purse, US$4,385,000

	SCORES	TOTAL	MONEY
Jim Furyk	68 66 68 74	276	$1,200,000
Henrik Stenson	67 71 71 69	278	600,000
Padraig Harrington	69 71 65 75	280	400,000
Ernie Els	72 67 70 72	281	300,000
Charl Schwartzel	70 69 71 72	282	275,000
Retief Goosen	70 70 71 75	286	260,000
Sergio Garcia	72 76 68 71	287	245,000
Trevor Immelman	71 69 73 74	287	245,000
Chris DiMarco	74 75 66 73	288	230,000
David Howell	69 73 73 76	291	220,000
Jose Maria Olazabal	71 73 69 79	292	210,000
Colin Montgomerie	75 77 70 76	298	200,000

Alfred Dunhill Championship

Leopard Creek Country Club, Mpumalanga, South Africa
Par 35-37–72; 7,249 yards

December 7-10
purse, €1,000,000

	SCORES				TOTAL	MONEY
Alvaro Quiros	74	66	68	67	275	€158,500
Charl Schwartzel	68	68	68	72	276	115,000
Lee Westwood	73	66	67	73	279	69,100
Darren Fichardt	72	70	69	69	280	45,100
Ross Fisher	73	69	68	70	280	45,100
Hennie Otto	71	69	69	72	281	32,100
Mark Pilkington	70	71	65	75	281	32,100
Ernie Els	72	72	69	69	282	21,433
Alan McLean	77	69	69	67	282	21,433
Alessandro Tadini	68	74	71	69	282	21,433
Phillip Archer	68	72	74	69	283	15,350
Scott Drummond	71	70	73	69	283	15,350
Titch Moore	76	64	73	70	283	15,350
Alexandre Rocha	74	67	70	72	283	15,350
Edward Rush	73	72	71	67	283	15,350
Des Terblanche	70	72	65	76	283	15,350
Johan Axgren	70	74	68	72	284	12,600
Robert Rock	70	74	71	69	284	12,600
Jaco Van Zyl	73	69	72	70	284	12,600
Liam Bond	71	71	70	73	285	11,020
Simon Nash	69	75	70	71	285	11,020
Henrik Nystrom	75	70	69	71	285	11,020
Sven Struver	76	70	70	69	285	11,020
Steve Van Vuuren	69	74	73	69	285	11,020
Jesus Maria Arruti	73	72	71	70	286	9,214
Rafael Cabrera Bello	69	69	77	71	286	9,214
Andre Cruse	71	73	72	70	286	9,214
David Drysdale	73	73	68	72	286	9,214
Ian Hutchings	70	70	75	71	286	9,214
Euan Little	72	70	70	74	286	9,214
Lee Slattery	72	73	69	72	286	9,214
Fredrik Andersson Hed	74	72	74	67	287	7,600
Michiel Bothma	73	73	71	70	287	7,600
Pelle Edberg	70	76	68	73	287	7,600
Anton Haig	78	68	70	71	287	7,600
Gregory Havret	73	68	71	75	287	7,600
Alan Michell	69	73	73	72	287	7,600
Oliver Wilson	68	70	72	77	287	7,600
Joakim Backstrom	73	72	70	73	288	6,700
Grant Muller	71	73	69	75	288	6,700
Benn Barham	70	72	72	75	289	6,100
Andrew Coltart	69	76	71	73	289	6,100
Rafael Echenique	72	74	70	73	289	6,100
Vaughn Groenewald	71	73	75	70	289	6,100
Marc Cayeux	74	69	74	73	290	5,400
Werner Geyer	71	74	73	72	290	5,400
Jean-Baptiste Gonnet	75	69	76	70	290	5,400
Keith Horne	72	71	75	73	291	4,700
Sam Little	74	70	74	73	291	4,700
Brandon Pieters	70	71	74	76	291	4,700
Patrik Sjoland	72	72	72	75	291	4,700
Neil Cheetham	73	72	70	77	292	3,700
Adilson Da Silva	72	72	74	74	292	3,700
Mattias Eliasson	73	69	68	82	292	3,700

	SCORES				TOTAL	MONEY
Andrew McLardy	70	75	69	78	292	3,700
Tyrone Van Aswegen	73	70	72	77	292	3,700
Tom Whitehouse	71	73	76	72	292	3,700
Wayne De Haas	68	72	75	78	293	2,750
Richard Finch	78	66	74	75	293	2,750
Oliver Fisher	71	70	77	75	293	2,750
Trevor Fisher, Jr.	71	72	78	72	293	2,750
James Kamte	71	74	71	77	293	2,750
Juan Parron	75	70	70	78	293	2,750
Sam Walker	69	74	71	79	293	2,750
Ross Wellington	75	71	76	71	293	2,750
Jean Hugo	73	73	74	74	294	2,300
Gareth Davies	73	68	77	77	295	2,150
Jonathan Lomas	73	73	74	75	295	2,150
Lee S. James	72	73	73	78	296	2,000
Mark Murless	74	71	77	75	297	1,900
Hendrik Buhrmann	71	75	75	77	298	1,750
Jean-Francois Lucquin	76	70	77	75	298	1,750

South African Airways Open

Humewood Golf Club, Port Elizabeth, South Africa
Par 35-37–72; 6,963 yards

December 14-17
purse, €1,000,000

	SCORES				TOTAL	MONEY
Ernie Els	67	66	66	65	264	R1,498,475
Trevor Immelman	67	66	63	71	267	1,087,222
Patrik Sjoland	68	64	69	67	268	653,278
Darren Fichardt	72	67	65	68	272	464,196
Louis Oosthuizen	71	65	70	67	273	331,839
Retief Goosen	69	66	68	70	273	331,839
Andrew Raitt	67	68	68	70	273	331,839
Gary Lockerbie	73	66	70	65	274	213,663
Lee Westwood	68	68	68	70	274	213,663
Robert Rock	70	68	69	68	275	162,846.75
Gregory Bourdy	71	68	68	68	275	162,846.75
Lee S. James	71	69	67	68	275	162,846.75
Charl Schwartzel	71	69	65	70	275	162,846.75
Jaco Van Zyl	71	65	72	68	276	138,030
Ross Fisher	70	69	66	72	277	133,303
Richard Finch	71	71	70	66	278	113,567.50
Justin Walters	73	67	71	67	278	113,567.50
Pelle Edberg	69	68	73	68	278	113,567.50
Lee Slattery	71	70	69	68	278	113,567.50
Bradford Vaughan	70	68	71	69	278	113,567.50
Angel Cabrera	75	65	69	69	278	113,567.50
Richard Sterne	73	69	66	70	278	113,567.50
James Kamte	69	68	69	72	278	113,567.50
Sam Walker	72	69	72	66	279	95,486.33
Benn Barham	71	71	68	69	279	95,486.33
Alan McLean	69	68	71	71	279	95,486.33
Nic Henning	71	68	70	71	280	85,559.50
Keith Horne	73	68	68	71	280	85,559.50
Carl Suneson	67	76	65	72	280	85,559.50
Edward Rush	70	67	70	73	280	85,559.50
James Heath	70	70	74	67	281	71,851.22
Mattias Eliasson	75	69	70	67	281	71,851.22

	SCORES				TOTAL	MONEY
Chris Swanepoel	73	70	70	68	281	71,851.22
Juan Parron	71	72	70	68	281	71,851.22
Eirik Tage Johansen	75	66	71	69	281	71,851.22
Tongoona Charamba	75	69	67	70	281	71,851.22
Des Terblanche	68	70	71	72	281	71,851.22
Steve Basson	71	69	69	72	281	71,851.22
David Frost	72	69	68	72	281	71,851.22
Mark Murless	72	71	70	69	282	55,779.12
Andrew McLardy	71	71	70	70	282	55,779.12
Chris Williams	72	70	70	70	282	55,779.12
Ulrich van den Berg	72	70	69	71	282	55,779.12
*Branden Grace	73	71	67	71	282	
Warren Bennett	73	69	68	72	282	55,779.12
Fredrik Andersson Hed	69	67	73	73	282	55,779.12
Oliver Fisher	77	67	65	73	282	55,779.12
Rafael Cabrera Bello	72	69	66	75	282	55,779.12
Michiel Bothma	75	69	72	67	283	41,598.14
Andre Cruse	72	70	73	68	283	41,598.14
Adilson da Silva	71	71	73	68	283	41,598.14
Desvonde Botes	73	68	72	70	283	41,598.14
Ian Hutchings	73	70	70	70	283	41,598.14
Hennie Otto	70	73	68	72	283	41,598.14
Edoardo Molinari	70	69	66	78	283	41,598.14
Johan Axgren	72	70	72	70	284	29,712.85
Oliver Wilson	74	69	71	70	284	29,712.85
Mathias Gronberg	72	70	70	72	284	29,712.85
Phillip Archer	75	68	69	72	284	29,712.85
Sam Little	73	71	68	72	284	29,712.85
Andrew Tampion	72	67	72	73	284	29,712.85
Ross Wellington	76	67	67	74	284	29,712.85
Alessandro Tadini	74	70	71	70	285	22,217.12
Divan van den Heever	71	73	70	71	285	22,217.12
Titch Moore	71	69	73	72	285	22,217.12
Sean Farrell	75	69	69	72	285	22,217.12
Gareth Davies	69	75	69	72	285	22,217.12
*Nigel Edwards	73	68	71	73	285	
Alexandre Rocha	74	70	67	74	285	22,217.12
Nico van Rensburg	70	70	70	75	285	22,217.12
Mike Lamb	76	68	66	75	285	22,217.12
Dion Fourie	72	70	73	71	286	16,072
Steve van Vuuren	71	65	77	73	286	16,072
Wade Ormsby	71	69	73	73	286	16,072
Gregory Havret	73	68	71	74	286	16,072
David Carter	74	69	69	74	286	16,072
Garry Houston	71	72	76	68	287	13,179
Julien Foret	75	69	74	69	287	13,179
Joachim Backstrom	72	72	73	70	287	13,179
Grant Muller	73	71	72	71	287	13,179
Thomas Aiken	76	68	71	72	287	13,179
*Christiaan Basson	73	70	73	72	288	
Birgir Hafthorsson	74	69	70	75	288	13,094
Tony Johnstone	72	72	74	71	289	13,051.50
Daniel Vancsik	71	71	75	72	289	13,051.50
Anton Haig	75	68	71	76	290	13,009
Trevor Fisher, Jr.	79	65	75	72	291	12,966
Werner Geyer	73	71	74	73	291	12,966
Scott Drummond	73	67	70	85	295	12,924
Matthew Richardson	74	68	78	76	296	12,895

Women's Tours

Women's World Cup of Golf

See South African Women's Tour section.

SBS Open

Turtle Bay Resort, Palmer Course, Oahu, Hawaii
Par 36-36–72; 6,578 yards

February 16-18
purse, $1,000,000

	SCORES			TOTAL	MONEY
Joo Mi Kim	70	65	71	206	$150,000
Lorena Ochoa	74	65	67	206	77,722
Soo Young Moon	70	67	69	206	77,722
(Kim defeated Ochoa on first and Moon on second playoff hole.)					
Karen Stupples	71	70	67	208	50,558
Miriam Nagl	74	67	68	209	33,952
Natalie Gulbis	72	67	70	209	33,952
Morgan Pressel	70	69	70	209	33,952
Juli Inkster	73	69	68	210	20,421
Cristie Kerr	71	71	68	210	20,421
Johanna Head	69	71	70	210	20,421
Sung Ah Yim	69	66	75	210	20,421
Becky Iverson	66	69	75	210	20,421
Paula Creamer	74	67	70	211	13,142
Seon Hwa Lee	73	68	70	211	13,142
Michele Redman	71	70	70	211	13,142
Julieta Granada	70	71	70	211	13,142
Christina Kim	72	68	71	211	13,142
Pat Hurst	71	69	71	211	13,142
Maria Hjorth	70	70	71	211	13,142
Grace Park	66	74	71	211	13,142
Stacy Prammanasudh	69	67	75	211	13,142
Allison Hanna	68	75	69	212	9,976
Jee Young Lee	75	67	70	212	9,976
Sae-Hee Son	71	70	71	212	9,976
Hee-Won Han	72	67	73	212	9,976
Karrie Webb	74	72	67	213	8,082
Dawn Coe-Jones	71	71	71	213	8,082
Heather Daly-Donofrio	73	68	72	213	8,082
Lorie Kane	72	69	72	213	8,082
Nicole Castrale	73	67	73	213	8,082
Meena Lee	68	72	73	213	8,082
Kyeong Bae	67	71	75	213	8,082

Fields Open in Hawaii

Kolina Golf Club, Kapolei, Hawaii
Par 36-36–72; 6,519 yards

February 23-25
purse, $1,100,000

	SCORES			TOTAL	MONEY
Meena Lee	69	68	65	202	$165,000
Seon Hwa Lee	65	66	71	202	100,942
(Meena Lee defeated Seon Hwa Lee on third playoff hole.)					

	SCORES			TOTAL	MONEY
Michelle Wie	67	70	66	203	73,227
Nicole Castrale	68	68	69	205	42,693
Lorena Ochoa	64	71	70	205	42,693
Julieta Granada	69	65	71	205	42,693
Natalie Gulbis	67	66	72	205	42,693
Karin Sjodin	68	70	68	206	27,357
Cristie Kerr	67	71	69	207	23,488
Lindsey Wright	71	66	70	207	23,488
Paula Creamer	72	69	67	208	16,808
Angela Stanford	71	70	67	208	16,808
Jeong Jang	68	72	68	208	16,808
Sophie Gustafson	70	69	69	208	16,808
Sakura Yokomine	70	68	70	208	16,808
Morgan Pressel	67	70	71	208	16,808
Aree Song	69	67	72	208	16,808
Wendy Ward	65	71	72	208	16,808
Rachel Hetherington	72	68	69	209	12,269
Brittany Lang	69	69	71	209	12,269
Il Mi Chung	69	69	71	209	12,269
Liselotte Neumann	68	69	72	209	12,269
Nicole Perrot	67	69	73	209	12,269
Dawn Coe-Jones	71	71	68	210	9,976
Heather Young	67	75	68	210	9,976
Carin Koch	72	69	69	210	9,976
Brittany Lincicome	72	69	69	210	9,976
Soo-Yun Kang	71	68	71	210	9,976
Ai Miyazato	68	71	71	210	9,976
Mikaela Parmlid	74	68	69	211	8,180
Marisa Baena	71	71	69	211	8,180
Mi Hyun Kim	69	73	69	211	8,180
Miriam Nagl	74	66	71	211	8,180

MasterCard Classic

Bosque Real Country Club, Huixquilucan, Mexico
Par 36-36–72; 6,906 yards

March 10-12
purse, $1,200,000

	SCORES			TOTAL	MONEY
Annika Sorenstam	67	71	70	208	$180,000
Helen Alfredsson	72	70	67	209	95,966
Seon Hwa Lee	70	69	70	209	95,966
Natalie Gulbis	70	74	66	210	51,259
Paula Creamer	71	67	72	210	51,259
Mi Hyun Kim	69	69	72	210	51,259
Katie Futcher	75	70	66	211	32,278
Suzann Pettersen	68	75	68	211	32,278
Tina Barrett	74	70	68	212	25,883
Cristie Kerr	71	69	72	212	25,883
Stacy Prammanasudh	73	72	68	213	20,722
Hee-Won Han	71	72	70	213	20,722
Meena Lee	70	73	70	213	20,722
Candie Kung	72	68	73	213	20,722
Virada Nirapathpongporn	74	75	66	215	15,956
Sherri Steinhauer	72	73	70	215	15,956
Carin Koch	69	76	70	215	15,956
Jee Young Lee	75	69	71	215	15,956
Siew-Ai Lim	72	68	75	215	15,956

	SCORES	TOTAL	MONEY
Julieta Granada	77 69 70	216	12,572
Brittany Lang	74 72 70	216	12,572
Maggie Will	73 73 70	216	12,572
Nadina Light	73 72 71	216	12,572
Brooke Tull	72 73 71	216	12,572
Lorie Kane	69 75 72	216	12,572
Catriona Matthew	71 70 75	216	12,572
Patricia Meunier-Lebouc	78 69 70	217	9,775
*Sophia Sheridan	73 74 70	217	
Diana D'Alessio	72 75 70	217	9,775
Young-A Yang	74 71 72	217	9,775
Teresa Lu	71 74 72	217	9,775
Amy Hung	75 69 73	217	9,775
Nancy Scranton	71 71 75	217	9,775

Safeway International

Superstition Mountain Golf Club, Superstition, Arizona
Par 36-36–72; 6,629 yards

March 16-19
purse, $1,400,000

	SCORES	TOTAL	MONEY
Juli Inkster	68 68 70 67	273	$210,000
Sarah Lee	65 67 70 73	275	128,161
Aree Song	64 69 70 73	276	92,972
Cristie Kerr	71 68 69 69	277	59,058
Catriona Matthew	70 66 72 69	277	59,058
Jeong Jang	69 72 66 70	277	59,058
Young-A Yang	68 69 72 69	278	37,189
Paula Creamer	67 67 74 70	278	37,189
Patricia Meunier-Lebouc	67 71 73 68	279	28,652
Candy Hannemann	68 72 68 71	279	28,652
Stacy Prammanasudh	68 71 69 71	279	28,652
Nicole Castrale	69 73 70 68	280	20,630
Joo Mi Kim	73 66 73 68	280	20,630
Shi Hyun Ahn	70 69 72 69	280	20,630
Young Jo	70 68 72 70	280	20,630
Hee-Won Han	71 70 68 71	280	20,630
Rachel Hetherington	73 69 66 72	280	20,630
Sophie Gustafson	69 70 68 73	280	20,630
Annika Sorenstam	69 71 75 66	281	15,577
Birdie Kim	69 73 71 68	281	15,577
Marcy Hart	68 72 71 70	281	15,577
Il Mi Chung	70 71 67 73	281	15,577
Michele Redman	66 74 66 75	281	15,577
Lorena Ochoa	67 71 75 69	282	12,911
Natalie Gulbis	70 73 68 71	282	12,911
Karrie Webb	70 70 71 71	282	12,911
Sherri Steinhauer	72 71 67 72	282	12,911
Suzann Pettersen	69 65 74 74	282	12,911
Carin Koch	69 68 75 71	283	11,016
Brooke Tull	67 72 72 72	283	11,016
Angela Stanford	70 69 71 73	283	11,016

Kraft Nabisco Championship

Mission Hills Country Club, Dinah Shore Course,
Rancho Mirage, California
Par 36-36—72; 6,569 yards

March 30-April 2
purse, $1,800,000

	SCORES				TOTAL	MONEY
Karrie Webb	70	68	76	65	279	$270,000
Lorena Ochoa	62	71	74	72	279	168,226
(Webb defeated Ochoa on first playoff hole.)						
Natalie Gulbis	73	71	68	68	280	108,222
Michelle Wie	66	71	73	70	280	108,222
Juli Inkster	69	73	74	68	284	75,985
Annika Sorenstam	71	72	73	70	286	57,104
Hee-Won Han	75	72	68	71	286	57,104
Brittany Lang	70	74	72	71	287	41,293
Helen Alfredsson	70	72	72	73	287	41,293
Shi Hyun Ahn	70	71	71	75	287	41,293
Michele Redman	72	72	72	72	288	33,388
Stacy Prammanasudh	67	73	76	72	288	33,388
Beth Daniel	72	72	72	73	289	29,289
Morgan Pressel	69	76	70	74	289	29,289
Yuri Fudoh	75	73	69	73	290	26,710
*Angela Park	68	73	75	74	290	
Pat Hurst	73	73	73	72	291	24,592
Karen Stupples	69	74	72	76	291	24,592
Jeong Jang	71	75	76	70	292	21,221
Tina Barrett	72	75	74	71	292	21,221
Veronica Zorzi	74	72	75	71	292	21,221
Young Kim	74	73	70	75	292	21,221
Seon Hwa Lee	69	69	74	80	292	21,221
Karine Icher	73	73	77	70	293	17,610
Candie Kung	72	75	72	74	293	17,610
Paula Creamer	69	71	79	74	293	17,610
Dorothy Delasin	72	72	74	75	293	17,610
Carin Koch	70	72	76	75	293	17,610
Jennifer Rosales	72	76	73	73	294	14,199
Becky Morgan	76	70	75	73	294	14,199
Patricia Meunier-Lebouc	77	67	77	73	294	14,199
Meena Lee	72	76	72	74	294	14,199
Young Jo	72	73	75	74	294	14,199
Ai Miyazato	70	77	72	75	294	14,199

LPGA Takefuji Classic

Las Vegas Country Club, Las Vegas, Nevada
Par 36-36—72; 6,550 yards

April 13-15
purse, $1,100,000

	SCORES			TOTAL	MONEY
Lorena Ochoa	63	68	66	197	$165,000
Seon Hwa Lee	67	67	66	200	99,316
Brittany Lincicome	68	65	69	202	72,046
Juli Inkster	68	72	63	203	55,734
Mi Hyun Kim	67	70	67	204	44,859
Ai Miyazato	69	70	66	205	33,713
Paula Creamer	70	64	71	205	33,713
Nancy Scranton	68	70	68	206	26,915

	SCORES	TOTAL	MONEY
Jeong Jang	70 71 66	207	22,202
Jimin Kang	67 72 68	207	22,202
Dorothy Delasin	69 68 70	207	22,202
Cristie Kerr	68 71 69	208	19,031
Catriona Matthew	69 71 69	209	16,312
Pat Hurst	68 72 69	209	16,312
Jee Young Lee	67 72 70	209	16,312
Wendy Ward	67 71 71	209	16,312
Young Jo	73 68 69	210	12,568
Janice Moodie	71 70 69	210	12,568
Ji Yeon Lee	69 72 69	210	12,568
Natalie Gulbis	71 69 70	210	12,568
Beth Bader	72 66 72	210	12,568
Liselotte Neumann	69 68 73	210	12,568
Maria Hjorth	67 70 73	210	12,568
Aree Song	73 69 69	211	9,815
Sarah Lee	73 67 71	211	9,815
Angela Stanford	69 70 72	211	9,815
Jamie Hullett	70 67 74	211	9,815
Young Kim	69 68 74	211	9,815
Shi Hyun Ahn	65 70 76	211	9,815
Julieta Granada	69 75 68	212	7,884
Tina Fischer	73 69 70	212	7,884
Brooke Tull	68 74 70	212	7,884
Hee-Won Han	71 70 71	212	7,884
Miriam Nagl	67 70 75	212	7,884

Florida's Natural Charity Championship

Eagle's Landing Country Club, Stockbridge, Georgia
Par 36-36–72; 6,408 yards

April 20-23
purse, $1,400,000

	SCORES	TOTAL	MONEY
Sung Ah Yim	68 64 68 72	272	$210,000
Cristie Kerr	65 75 65 69	274	96,775
Karrie Webb	67 67 70 70	274	96,775
Annika Sorenstam	66 69 64 75	274	96,775
Suzann Pettersen	67 74 69 65	275	47,849
Juli Inkster	67 70 70 68	275	47,849
Hee-Won Han	70 64 72 69	275	47,849
Karine Icher	68 68 71 69	276	31,165
Sherri Turner	71 70 63 72	276	31,165
Jeong Jang	69 68 67 72	276	31,165
Beth Daniel	70 66 68 73	277	25,198
Brittany Lang	68 67 69 73	277	25,198
Kyeong Bae	73 66 71 68	278	21,457
Pat Hurst	67 71 71 69	278	21,457
Julieta Granada	67 70 69 72	278	21,457
Seon Hwa Lee	73 68 68 70	279	17,726
Morgan Pressel	69 72 68 70	279	17,726
Patricia Meunier-Lebouc	66 70 73 70	279	17,726
Jee Young Lee	68 65 76 70	279	17,726
Paula Creamer	68 70 75 67	280	14,350
Shi Hyun Ahn	70 72 69 69	280	14,350
Michele Redman	71 70 70 69	280	14,350
Ai Miyazato	69 69 73 69	280	14,350
Maria Hjorth	65 73 73 69	280	14,350

	SCORES	TOTAL	MONEY
Natalie Gulbis	67 69 73 71	280	14,350
Brandie Burton	68 68 72 72	280	14,350
Michelle Ellis	68 70 73 70	281	11,592
Jamie Hullett	70 69 71 71	281	11,592
Meena Lee	68 69 73 71	281	11,592
Rachel Hetherington	68 72 69 72	281	11,592

Ginn Clubs & Resorts Open

Reunion Resort & Club, Orlando, Florida
Par 36-36—72; 6,531 yards

April 27-30
purse, $2,500,000

	SCORES	TOTAL	MONEY
Mi Hyun Kim	70 66 69 71	276	$375,000
Lorena Ochoa	67 70 75 66	278	193,477
Karrie Webb	75 67 69 67	278	193,477
Annika Sorenstam	72 70 74 67	283	125,855
Hee-Won Han	74 71 73 66	284	78,582
Michele Redman	71 73 73 67	284	78,582
Christina Kim	74 67 69 74	284	78,582
Ai Miyazato	70 68 70 76	284	78,582
Janice Moodie	71 74 73 67	285	50,137
Se Ri Pak	72 74 70 69	285	50,137
Heather Young	73 72 70 70	285	50,137
Juli Inkster	71 74 71 70	286	36,099
Virada Nirapathpongporn	73 72 70 71	286	36,099
Brittany Lang	76 68 71 71	286	36,099
Liselotte Neumann	74 70 71 71	286	36,099
Lindsey Wright	72 72 69 73	286	36,099
Pat Hurst	71 73 69 73	286	36,099
Seon Hwa Lee	72 67 72 75	286	36,099
Shi Hyun Ahn	74 70 75 68	287	27,257
Meena Lee	73 75 70 69	287	27,257
Miriam Nagl	74 70 73 70	287	27,257
Laura Diaz	67 72 76 72	287	27,257
Cristie Kerr	65 74 74 74	287	27,257
Candy Hannemann	75 71 72 70	288	23,453
Stacy Prammanasudh	70 74 74 70	288	23,453
Lee Ann Walker-Cooper	74 74 69 71	288	23,453
Katie Futcher	72 75 71 71	289	20,088
Natalie Gulbis	71 76 71 71	289	20,088
Nicole Castrale	76 69 73 71	289	20,088
Grace Park	74 71 73 71	289	20,088
Karine Icher	71 70 77 71	289	20,088

Franklin American Mortgage Championship

Vanderbilt Legends Club, Ironhorse Course,
Franklin, Tennessee
Par 36-36—72; 6,458 yards

May 4-7
purse, $1,100,000

	SCORES	TOTAL	MONEY
Cristie Kerr	67 69 66 67	269	$165,000
Lorena Ochoa	67 71 67 66	271	77,322

	SCORES				TOTAL	MONEY
Pat Hurst	70	67	66	68	271	77,322
Angela Stanford	65	67	66	73	271	77,322
Ji Yeon Lee	68	68	67	69	272	45,821
Marisa Baena	69	73	68	63	273	34,436
Sophie Gustafson	71	63	68	71	273	34,436
Young Kim	67	69	73	65	274	26,105
Patricia Meunier-Lebouc	67	66	70	71	274	26,105
Candy Hannemann	69	69	70	67	275	20,245
Karrie Webb	67	68	70	70	275	20,245
Brittany Lincicome	69	69	66	71	275	20,245
Lindsey Wright	69	67	68	71	275	20,245
Gloria HeeJung Park	68	72	68	68	276	16,607
Karine Icher	68	70	68	70	276	16,607
Laura Diaz	67	72	71	67	277	14,163
Stacy Prammanasudh	70	69	70	68	277	14,163
Carri Wood	71	69	67	70	277	14,163
Karin Sjodin	71	64	71	71	277	14,163
Diana D'Alessio	72	69	69	68	278	12,330
Karen Stupples	70	70	70	68	278	12,330
Young Jo	72	70	66	70	278	12,330
Grace Park	66	72	70	71	279	11,441
Minea Blomqvist	67	72	74	67	280	10,414
Christa Johnson	69	73	70	68	280	10,414
Katie Futcher	71	69	70	70	280	10,414
Wendy Ward	69	66	73	72	280	10,414
Marcy Hart	71	73	70	67	281	8,563
Joo Mi Kim	70	73	70	68	281	8,563
Teresa Lu	71	69	72	69	281	8,563
Sherri Turner	68	69	75	69	281	8,563
Suzanne Strudwick	70	72	67	72	281	8,563
Christina Kim	73	70	64	74	281	8,563

Michelob Ultra Open at Kingsmill

Kingsmill Resort & Spa, River Course, Williamsburg, Virginia
Par 36-35–71; 6,306 yards

May 11-14
purse, $2,200,000

	SCORES				TOTAL	MONEY
Karrie Webb	66	68	66	70	270	$330,000
Hee-Won Han	71	67	69	70	277	175,038
Lorena Ochoa	73	67	65	72	277	175,038
Paula Creamer	70	72	67	69	278	93,495
Pat Hurst	68	68	69	73	278	93,495
Cristie Kerr	69	66	70	73	278	93,495
Mi Hyun Kim	73	69	69	69	280	55,727
Reilley Rankin	70	69	72	69	280	55,727
Jeong Jang	68	70	70	72	280	55,727
Jee Young Lee	72	69	73	67	281	41,841
Shi Hyun Ahn	70	69	75	67	281	41,841
Joo Mi Kim	71	68	70	72	281	41,841
Il Mi Chung	73	69	72	68	282	33,325
Stacy Prammanasudh	73	69	70	70	282	33,325
Natalie Gulbis	72	69	71	70	282	33,325
Juli Inkster	70	67	73	72	282	33,325
Helen Alfredsson	70	74	69	70	283	26,141
Wendy Ward	72	71	69	71	283	26,141
Alena Sharp	70	73	68	72	283	26,141

	SCORES				TOTAL	MONEY
Heather Young	71	71	69	72	283	26,141
Sun Young Yoo	74	66	70	73	283	26,141
Yu Ping Lin	68	74	67	74	283	26,141
Brittany Lincicome	74	70	70	70	284	22,439
Angela Stanford	72	67	70	75	284	22,439
Se Ri Pak	73	72	69	71	285	21,217
Kim Saiki	71	72	73	70	286	18,906
Kristi Albers	71	71	74	70	286	18,906
Brandie Burton	69	72	73	72	286	18,906
Suzann Pettersen	73	67	73	73	286	18,906
Brittany Lang	69	70	72	75	286	18,906

Sybase Classic

Wykagyl Country Club, New Rochelle, New York
Par 35-36–71; 6,223 yards
(Event shortened to 54 holes — rain.)

May 18-21
purse, $1,300,000

	SCORES			TOTAL	MONEY
Lorena Ochoa	71	71	66	208	$195,000
Kyeong Bae	71	73	66	210	103,431
Hee-Won Han	68	73	69	210	103,431
Allison Hanna	69	71	71	211	67,281
Juli Inkster	72	69	71	212	54,153
Paula Creamer	72	71	70	213	37,962
Annika Sorenstam	72	67	74	213	37,962
Gloria HeeJung Park	71	67	75	213	37,962
Julieta Granada	76	69	69	214	27,897
Jill McGill	72	73	69	214	27,897
Beth Bauer	68	74	73	215	23,040
Laura Diaz	73	68	74	215	23,040
Seon Hwa Lee	70	71	74	215	23,040
Jeong Jang	71	72	73	216	19,626
Nancy Scranton	69	74	73	216	19,626
Ai Miyazato	74	73	70	217	17,110
Natalie Gulbis	68	74	75	217	17,110
Helen Alfredsson	75	66	76	217	17,110
Virada Nirapathpongporn	74	73	71	218	14,572
Stephanie Louden	77	69	72	218	14,572
Lee Ann Walker-Cooper	74	70	74	218	14,572
Beth Daniel	71	73	74	218	14,572
Marisa Baena	72	71	75	218	14,572
Janice Moodie	77	71	71	219	12,537
Nicole Castrale	75	72	72	219	12,537
Young Jo	71	73	75	219	12,537
Amy Hung	74	76	70	220	10,133
Kristi Albers	73	76	71	220	10,133
Patricia Baxter-Johnson	72	76	72	220	10,133
Cindy Rarick	74	73	73	220	10,133
Michele Redman	74	73	73	220	10,133
Kris Tamulis	73	74	73	220	10,133
Giulia Sergas	71	75	74	220	10,133
Young Kim	71	73	76	220	10,133

LPGA Corning Classic

Corning Country Club, Corning, New York
Par 36-36–72; 6,132 yards

May 25-28
purse, $1,200,000

	SCORES				TOTAL	MONEY
Hee-Won Han	66	70	69	68	273	$180,000
Meena Lee	65	72	70	66	273	110,392
(Han defeated Lee on fourth playoff hole.)						
Brandie Burton	66	68	70	70	274	80,081
Mhairi McKay	70	67	70	68	275	61,950
Laura Diaz	71	68	67	70	276	45,329
Virada Nirapathpongporn	66	67	71	72	276	45,329
Reilley Rankin	70	71	69	67	277	26,543
Natalie Gulbis	68	71	70	68	277	26,543
Giulia Sergas	71	68	68	70	277	26,543
Morgan Pressel	74	64	68	71	277	26,543
Nancy Scranton	65	69	70	73	277	26,543
Jeong Jang	66	69	66	76	277	26,543
Mi Hyun Kim	68	71	72	67	278	18,655
Audra Burks	69	68	72	69	278	18,655
Tina Barrett	69	69	70	70	278	18,655
Pat Hurst	68	73	71	67	279	15,754
Liselotte Neumann	67	69	74	69	279	15,754
Kris Tamulis	66	71	69	73	279	15,754
Il Mi Chung	74	69	67	70	280	13,659
Joanne Morley	71	69	69	71	280	13,659
Sherri Turner	73	67	68	72	280	13,659
Stephanie Louden	68	69	70	73	280	13,659
Jackie Gallagher-Smith	71	72	70	68	281	11,343
Candie Kung	74	67	68	72	281	11,343
Stacy Prammanasudh	69	68	72	72	281	11,343
Seon Hwa Lee	69	73	66	73	281	11,343
Julieta Granada	70	69	69	73	281	11,343
Beth Bader	71	69	67	74	281	11,343
Lorie Kane	73	70	68	71	282	9,126
Nina Reis	70	71	70	71	282	9,126
Vicki Goetze-Ackerman	67	68	76	71	282	9,126
Heather Young	72	70	68	72	282	9,126
Kris Tschetter	70	68	72	72	282	9,126

ShopRite LPGA Classic

Seaview Marriott Resort & Spa, Bay Course,
Galloway Twp., New Jersey
Par 37-34–71; 6,071 yards

June 2-4
purse, $1,500,000

	SCORES			TOTAL	MONEY
Seon Hwa Lee	65	69	63	197	$225,000
Jeong Jang	67	69	64	200	104,167
Sherri Steinhauer	68	66	66	200	104,167
Annika Sorenstam	64	69	67	200	104,167
Sophie Gustafson	66	71	64	201	56,118
Morgan Pressel	66	69	66	201	56,118
Becky Morgan	67	70	67	204	39,657
Gloria Hee Jung Park	66	70	68	204	39,657
Paula Creamer	70	67	68	205	29,462

	SCORES			TOTAL	MONEY
Julieta Granada	69	68	68	205	29,462
Mi Hyun Kim	67	70	68	205	29,462
Patricia Meunier-Lebouc	67	68	70	205	29,462
Karrie Webb	70	69	67	206	21,300
Cristie Kerr	69	70	67	206	21,300
Christina Kim	74	64	68	206	21,300
Amy Hung	65	70	71	206	21,300
Laura Diaz	65	69	72	206	21,300
Ai Miyazato	66	66	74	206	21,300
Young-A Yang	70	72	65	207	16,312
Shi Hyun Ahn	71	70	66	207	16,312
Natalie Gulbis	71	70	66	207	16,312
Michelle McGann	71	68	68	207	16,312
Eva Dahllof	69	70	68	207	16,312
Angela Stanford	69	69	69	207	16,312
Juli Inkster	72	69	67	208	11,604
Karine Icher	71	70	67	208	11,604
Wendy Ward	71	69	68	208	11,604
Moira Dunn	71	68	69	208	11,604
Vicki Goetze-Ackerman	70	69	69	208	11,604
Aram Cho	67	72	69	208	11,604
Minea Blomqvist	67	72	69	208	11,604
Erica Blasberg	66	73	69	208	11,604
Rosie Jones	71	67	70	208	11,604
Laura Davies	69	68	71	208	11,604
Se Ri Pak	68	69	71	208	11,604
Catriona Matthew	66	69	73	208	11,604

McDonald's LPGA Championship

Bulle Rock Golf Course, Havre de Grace, Maryland
Par 36-36–72; 6,596 yards

June 8-11
purse, $1,800,000

	SCORES				TOTAL	MONEY
Se Ri Pak	71	69	71	69	280	$270,000
Karrie Webb	70	70	72	68	280	163,998
(Pak defeated Webb on first playoff hole.)						
Mi Hyun Kim	68	71	71	71	281	105,501
Ai Miyazato	68	72	69	72	281	105,501
Cristie Kerr	66	74	74	68	282	57,464
Michelle Wie	71	68	71	72	282	57,464
Shi Hyun Ahn	69	70	71	72	282	57,464
Pat Hurst	66	71	72	73	282	57,464
Reilley Rankin	68	73	74	68	283	34,174
Annika Sorenstam	71	69	75	68	283	34,174
Young Kim	69	72	73	69	283	34,174
Sung Ah Yim	72	68	74	69	283	34,174
Lorena Ochoa	68	72	71	72	283	34,174
Meena Lee	71	72	69	72	284	26,847
Jee Young Lee	70	71	70	73	284	26,847
Seon Hwa Lee	67	74	75	69	285	22,896
Wendy Ward	69	74	70	72	285	22,896
Sherri Steinhauer	70	71	71	73	285	22,896
Silvia Cavalleri	69	71	72	73	285	22,896
Natalie Gulbis	72	73	72	69	286	19,215
Suzann Pettersen	70	72	74	70	286	19,215
Young Jo	72	72	70	72	286	19,215

	SCORES				TOTAL	MONEY
Yuri Fudoh	69	74	71	72	286	19,215
Lindsey Wright	72	73	68	73	286	19,215
Laura Diaz	71	74	72	70	287	16,207
Heather Young	71	75	70	71	287	16,207
Hee-Won Han	68	73	75	71	287	16,207
Minea Blomqvist	71	71	70	75	287	16,207
Nancy Scranton	73	73	73	69	288	13,558
Kris Tamulis	73	71	75	69	288	13,558
Angela Stanford	70	76	72	70	288	13,558
Il Mi Chung	71	72	75	70	288	13,558
Liselotte Neumann	69	74	75	70	288	13,558

Wegmans LPGA

Locust Hill Country Club, Pittsford, New York
Par 35-37–72; 6,221 yards

June 22-25
purse, $1,800,000

	SCORES				TOTAL	MONEY
Jeong Jang	69	70	66	70	275	$270,000
Julieta Granada	72	70	67	67	276	166,003
Marcy Hart	70	72	66	69	277	106,791
Brittany Lang	66	71	69	71	277	106,791
Mi Hyun Kim	72	67	67	72	278	74,981
Gloria Hee Jung Park	68	74	72	65	279	49,533
Lorena Ochoa	70	69	71	69	279	49,533
Sherri Steinhauer	72	68	69	70	279	49,533
Wendy Ward	70	68	70	71	279	49,533
Karine Icher	72	68	71	69	280	32,101
Hee-Won Han	72	70	68	70	280	32,101
Seon Hwa Lee	70	67	73	70	280	32,101
Rachel Hetherington	69	69	71	71	280	32,101
Silvia Cavalleri	71	69	68	72	280	32,101
Giulia Sergas	72	69	71	69	281	25,630
Aree Song	72	68	69	72	281	25,630
*Amanda Blumenherst	70	74	70	68	282	
Laura Diaz	71	70	71	70	282	22,176
Helen Alfredsson	70	69	73	70	282	22,176
Shi Hyun Ahn	65	71	75	71	282	22,176
Becky Iverson	69	70	71	72	282	22,176
Meg Mallon	75	68	71	69	283	18,404
Young Jo	70	72	71	70	283	18,404
Michele Redman	72	70	69	72	283	18,404
Brittany Lincicome	70	69	71	73	283	18,404
Hilary Lunke	73	71	65	74	283	18,404
Sun Young Yoo	73	69	66	75	283	18,404
Marisa Baena	71	71	73	69	284	14,587
Candy Hannemann	70	73	71	70	284	14,587
Yu Ping Lin	71	68	74	71	284	14,587
Candie Kung	75	70	67	72	284	14,587
Alena Sharp	74	69	68	73	284	14,587
Jamie Hullett	71	67	72	74	284	14,587

U.S. Women's Open

Newport Country Club, Newport, Rhode Island
Par 36-35—71; 6,616 yards

June 29-July 3
purse, $3,100,000

	SCORES				TOTAL	MONEY
Annika Sorenstam	69	71	73	71	284	$560,000
Pat Hurst	69	71	75	69	284	335,000
(Sorenstam defeated Hurst in 18-hole Monday playoff, 70-74.)						
Se Ri Pak	69	74	74	69	286	156,038
Stacy Prammanasudh	72	71	71	72	286	156,038
Michelle Wie	70	72	71	73	286	156,038
Juli Inkster	73	70	71	73	287	103,575
Brittany Lincicome	72	72	69	78	291	93,026
Rachel Hetherington	74	72	73	73	292	82,460
Shi Hyun Ahn	71	71	74	76	292	82,460
*Amanda Blumenherst	70	77	73	73	293	
Young Kim	75	69	75	74	293	66,174
Patricia Meunier-Lebouc	72	73	73	75	293	66,174
*Jane Park	69	73	75	76	293	
Jee Young Lee	71	75	70	77	293	66,174
Sophie Gustafson	72	72	71	78	293	66,174
Sherri Turner	72	74	76	72	294	53,577
Natalie Gulbis	76	71	74	73	294	53,577
Paula Creamer	71	72	76	75	294	53,577
Catriona Matthew	74	76	72	73	295	48,007
Gloria Hee Jung Park	70	78	76	72	296	41,654
Lorena Ochoa	71	73	77	75	296	41,654
Karen Stupples	78	72	70	76	296	41,654
Kristina Tucker	72	74	74	76	296	41,654
Amy Hung	76	72	77	72	297	32,873
Shani Waugh	77	72	73	75	297	32,873
Lorie Kane	73	72	75	77	297	32,873
Sherri Steinhauer	72	75	72	78	297	32,873
Morgan Pressel	76	74	75	73	298	22,529
Tracy Hanson	75	71	78	74	298	22,529
Suzann Pettersen	73	74	75	76	298	22,529
Cristie Kerr	73	74	75	76	298	22,529
Candie Kung	74	70	77	77	298	22,529
Becky Morgan	70	74	77	77	298	22,529
Carin Koch	74	73	73	78	298	22,529
Ai Miyazato	74	75	70	79	298	22,529
Jeong Jang	72	71	75	80	298	22,529

HSBC Women's World Match Play

Hamilton Farm Golf Club, Gladstone, New Jersey
Par 36-36—72; 6,598 yards

July 6-9
purse, $2,000,000

FIRST ROUND

Annika Sorenstam defeated Virada Nirapathpongporn, 3 and 2.
Heather Young defeated Sung Ah Yim, 19 holes.
Seon Hwa Lee defeated Aree Song, 3 and 2.
Brittany Lang defeated Patricia Meunier-Lebouc, 3 and 2.
Juli Inkster defeated Tina Barrett, 2 and 1.
Catriona Matthew defeated Beth Daniel, 21 holes.
Marcy Hart defeated Jeong Jang, 2 up.

Liselotte Neumann defeated Karen Stupples, 3 and 1.
Karrie Webb defeated Nancy Scranton, 4 and 2.
Gloria Hee Jung Park defeated Rachel Hetherington, 1 up.
Pat Hurst defeated Reilley Rankin, 21 holes.
Helen Alfredsson defeated Julieta Granada, 3 and 2.
Paula Creamer defeated Miriam Nagl, 2 and 1.
Marisa Baena defeated Wendy Ward, 21 holes.
Morgan Pressel defeated Sarah Lee, 20 holes.
Meena Lee defeated Sherri Steinhauer, 2 and 1.
Michelle Wie defeated Candy Hannemann, 5 and 3.
Christina Kim defeated Joo Mi Kim, 2 and 1.
Se Ri Pak defeated Angela Stanford, 5 and 4.
Lorie Kane defeated Natalie Gulbis, 3 and 2.
Brandie Burton defeated Yuri Fudoh, 4 and 3.
Brittany Lincicome defeated Michele Redman, 20 holes.
Kyeong Bae defeated Ai Miyazato, 2 up.
Suzann Pettersen defeated Young Kim, 2 and 1.
Lorena Ochoa defeated Il Mi Chung, 3 and 1.
Karine Icher defeated Stacy Prammanasudh, 4 and 3.
Mi Hyun Kim defeated Nicole Castrale, 4 and 2.
Laura Davies defeated Jee Young Lee, 2 and 1.
Cristie Kerr defeated Young Jo, 1 up.
Sophie Gustafson defeated Gwladys Nocera, 3 and 2.
Lindsey Wright defeated Hee-Won Han, 5 and 4.
Laura Diaz bye.

(Each losing player received $5,161.)

SECOND ROUND

Sorenstam defeated Heather Young, 3 and 2.
Lang defeated Seon Hwa Lee, 3 and 2.
Inkster defeated Matthew, 4 and 3.
Hart defeated Neumann, 4 and 3.
Webb defeated Park, 5 and 4.
Hurst defeated Alfredsson, 4 and 2.
Creamer defeated Baena, 5 and 3.
Pressel defeated Meena Lee, 2 and 1.
Wie defeated Christina Kim, 3 and 2.
Pak defeated Kane, 1 up.
Lincicome defeated Burton, 2 and 1.
Bae defeated Pettersen, 1 up.
Ochoa defeated Icher, 1 up.
Mi Hyun Kim defeated Davies, 5 and 4.
Gustafson defeated Kerr, 4 and 2.
Diaz defeated Wright, 2 up.

(Each losing player received $10,000.)

THIRD ROUND

Sorenstam defeated Lang, 6 and 5.
Inkster defeated Hart, 3 and 2.
Webb defeated Hurst, 3 and 2.
Creamer defeated Pressel, 3 and 1.
Wie defeated Pak, 2 and 1.
Lincicome defeated Bae, 3 and 2.
Ochoa defeated Mi Hyun Kim, 3 and 2.
Gustafson defeated Diaz, 2 and 1.

(Each losing player received $25,000.)

QUARTER-FINALS

Inkster defeated Sorenstam, 1 up.
Creamer defeated Webb, 3 and 2.
Lincicome defeated Wie, 4 and 3.
Ochoa defeated Gustafson, 3 and 2.

(Each losing player received $50,000.)

SEMI-FINALS

Inkster defeated Creamer, 5 and 4.
Lincicome defeated Ochoa, 19 holes.

PLAYOFF FOR THIRD-FOURTH PLACE

Ochoa defeated Creamer, 3 and 2.

(Ochoa earned $200,000; Creamer earned $150,000.)

FINAL

Lincicome defeated Inkster, 3 and 2.

(Lincicome earned $500,000; Inkster earned $300,000.)

Jamie Farr Owens Corning Classic

Highland Meadows Golf Club, Sylvania, Ohio
Par 34-37–71; 6,408 yards

July 13-16
purse, $1,200,000

	SCORES				TOTAL	MONEY
Mi Hyun Kim	68	66	67	65	266	$180,000
Natalie Gulbis	67	66	68	65	266	106,155
(Kim defeated Gulbis on third playoff hole.)						
Paula Creamer	67	67	68	65	267	77,007
Se Ri Pak	68	68	66	66	268	59,570
Reilley Rankin	66	68	68	70	272	47,949
Brittany Lang	71	68	69	66	274	36,034
Sung Ah Yim	66	69	69	70	274	36,034
Annika Sorenstam	69	68	68	70	275	28,768
Nicole Castrale	68	70	71	67	276	25,860
Sherri Steinhauer	73	71	68	65	277	21,891
Jackie Gallagher-Smith	73	68	68	68	277	21,891
Diana D'Alessio	67	69	69	72	277	21,891
Beth Daniel	71	70	70	67	278	16,971
Christina Kim	68	73	67	70	278	16,971
Liselotte Neumann	65	70	72	71	278	16,971
Rachel Hetherington	70	67	69	72	278	16,971
Laura Davies	67	71	65	75	278	16,971
Jee Young Lee	71	68	69	71	279	14,124
Young Jo	69	68	66	76	279	14,124
Juli Inkster	72	70	69	69	280	10,960
Nina Reis	70	74	66	70	280	10,960
Aree Song	72	69	69	70	280	10,960
Kim Saiki	70	70	70	70	280	10,960
Nancy Scranton	69	70	71	70	280	10,960
Karen Weiss	67	69	74	70	280	10,960

	SCORES				TOTAL	MONEY
Vicki Goetze-Ackerman	72	68	69	71	280	10,960
Ashli Bunch	67	71	71	71	280	10,960
Meg Mallon	68	73	67	72	280	10,960
Il Mi Chung	71	69	68	72	280	10,960
Jessica Reese-Quayle	68	68	72	72	280	10,960
Marcy Hart	69	67	71	73	280	10,960

Evian Masters

See Ladies European Tour section.

Weetabix Women's British Open

See Ladies European Tour section.

CN Canadian Women's Open

London Hunt Club, London, Ontario, Canada
Par 36-36—72; 6,611 yards

August 10-13
purse, $1,700,000

	SCORES				TOTAL	MONEY
Cristie Kerr	67	70	74	65	276	$255,000
Angela Stanford	64	70	69	74	277	152,823
Pat Hurst	69	71	70	68	278	110,863
Meena Lee	68	73	66	74	281	85,762
Jee Young Lee	67	70	71	74	282	69,028
Sun Young Yoo	72	73	69	69	283	51,876
Lindsey Wright	71	72	70	70	283	51,876
Il Mi Chung	68	74	72	70	284	39,326
Young Kim	72	72	67	73	284	39,326
Laura Diaz	72	71	73	69	285	28,671
Gloria Park	70	73	72	70	285	28,671
Jeong Jang	73	69	73	70	285	28,671
Nadina Light	70	72	73	70	285	28,671
Young Jo	70	73	69	73	285	28,671
Nicole Castrale	73	69	69	74	285	28,671
Jamie Hullett	74	71	70	71	286	21,336
Sophie Gustafson	72	69	72	73	286	21,336
Vicki Goetze-Ackerman	67	73	72	74	286	21,336
Lorie Kane	68	70	73	75	286	21,336
Se Ri Pak	70	74	75	68	287	18,910
Stacy Prammanasudh	73	70	72	72	287	18,910
Christina Kim	70	74	75	69	288	16,316
Amy Hung	72	72	74	70	288	16,316
Silvia Cavalleri	76	70	71	71	288	16,316
Tracy Hanson	71	74	71	72	288	16,316
Wendy Ward	70	72	74	72	288	16,316
Becky Iverson	72	70	72	74	288	16,316
Rachel Hetherington	73	73	74	69	289	12,900
Libby Smith	75	71	73	70	289	12,900
Beth Daniel	72	74	72	71	289	12,900
Karine Icher	71	74	73	71	289	12,900
Lee Ann Walker-Cooper	70	75	73	71	289	12,900
Mikaela Parmlid	74	73	69	73	289	12,900

Safeway Classic

Columbia Edgewater Country Club, Portland, Oregon
Par 36-36–72; 6,377 yards

August 18-20
purse, $1,400,000

	SCORES			TOTAL	MONEY
Pat Hurst	69	69	68	206	$210,000
Kim Saiki	68	72	67	207	109,291
Jeong Jang	69	68	70	207	109,291
Juli Inkster	71	67	70	208	71,092
Gloria Park	71	69	70	210	52,019
Jee Young Lee	64	75	71	210	52,019
Karrie Webb	75	70	66	211	29,358
Becky Iverson	71	73	67	211	29,358
Meena Lee	71	71	69	211	29,358
Mi Hyun Kim	67	72	72	211	29,358
Nancy Scranton	70	68	73	211	29,358
Christina Kim	66	72	73	211	29,358
Morgan Pressel	68	69	74	211	29,358
Diana Ramage	68	76	68	212	19,628
Tina Barrett	68	74	70	212	19,628
Carin Koch	71	69	72	212	19,628
Hee-Won Han	70	68	74	212	19,628
Seon Hwa Lee	71	72	70	213	15,417
Paula Creamer	72	70	71	213	15,417
Kim Hall	71	71	71	213	15,417
Stacy Prammanasudh	71	70	72	213	15,417
Nicole Castrale	71	70	72	213	15,417
Lindsey Wright	69	72	72	213	15,417
Joo Mi Kim	68	70	75	213	15,417
Dina Ammaccapane	73	73	68	214	11,821
Young Kim	71	71	72	214	11,821
Ai Miyazato	71	70	73	214	11,821
Karine Icher	69	72	73	214	11,821
Hana Kim	69	72	73	214	11,821
Candie Kung	71	66	77	214	11,821
Jenna Daniels	66	71	77	214	11,821

Wendy's Championship for Children

Tartan Fields Golf Club, Dublin, Ohio
Par 36-36–72; 6,509 yards

August 24-27
purse, $1,100,000

	SCORES				TOTAL	MONEY
Lorena Ochoa	67	68	64	65	264	$165,000
Stacy Prammanasudh	66	70	67	64	267	87,085
Jee Young Lee	66	67	68	66	267	87,085
Ai Miyazato	68	68	67	68	271	56,647
Diana D'Alessio	69	68	69	67	273	45,594
Jeong Jang	72	66	70	67	275	31,962
Karrie Webb	67	68	71	69	275	31,962
Michele Redman	70	68	67	70	275	31,962
Tina Barrett	67	72	69	68	276	22,567
Morgan Pressel	68	72	67	69	276	22,567
Cristie Kerr	70	67	69	70	276	22,567
Kyeong Bae	71	67	68	71	277	18,164
Paula Creamer	68	68	69	72	277	18,164

	SCORES				TOTAL	MONEY
Marisa Baena	69	65	71	72	277	18,164
Sophie Gustafson	74	69	72	63	278	13,651
Kris Tschetter	67	70	73	68	278	13,651
Natalie Gulbis	67	70	73	68	278	13,651
Catherine Cartwright	72	70	67	69	278	13,651
Aree Song	72	69	67	70	278	13,651
Soo-Yun Kang	67	66	75	70	278	13,651
Michelle Ellis	69	71	67	71	278	13,651
Mikaela Parmlid	67	67	72	72	278	13,651
Dina Ammaccapane	71	73	68	67	279	9,627
Paige MacKenzie	77	66	68	68	279	9,627
Heather Young	75	67	68	69	279	9,627
Beth Allen	69	70	70	70	279	9,627
Wendy Doolan	69	68	72	70	279	9,627
Brittany Lincicome	67	68	74	70	279	9,627
Karine Icher	72	70	66	71	279	9,627
Joo Mi Kim	71	65	72	71	279	9,627
Brittany Lang	70	71	66	72	279	9,627
Birdie Kim	68	69	70	72	279	9,627

State Farm Classic

Rail Golf Club, Springfield, Illinois
Par 36-36–72; 6,666 yards

August 31-September 3
purse, $1,300,000

	SCORES				TOTAL	MONEY
Annika Sorenstam	70	68	69	62	269	$195,000
Cristie Kerr	68	64	72	67	271	120,827
Seon Hwa Lee	67	67	69	69	272	70,011
Il Mi Chung	67	66	70	69	272	70,011
Maria Hjorth	65	67	70	70	272	70,011
Brittany Lang	66	72	69	66	273	38,258
Kyeong Bae	68	69	68	68	273	38,258
Nancy Scranton	73	68	63	69	273	38,258
Brittany Lincicome	72	68	68	66	274	28,115
Nina Reis	66	68	72	68	274	28,115
Julieta Granada	67	70	71	67	275	23,980
Lorena Ochoa	67	70	70	68	275	23,980
Karen Stupples	71	71	69	65	276	20,419
Angela Stanford	70	68	69	69	276	20,419
Lindsey Wright	72	67	67	70	276	20,419
Kelli Kuehne	67	72	71	67	277	17,244
Laura Diaz	72	67	70	68	277	17,244
Kris Tschetter	71	68	70	68	277	17,244
Jamie Hullett	70	71	71	66	278	15,480
Alena Sharp	71	70	67	70	278	15,480
Nicole Castrale	71	68	72	68	279	13,892
Hee-Won Han	72	68	70	69	279	13,892
Young Jo	72	68	70	69	279	13,892
Sophie Gustafson	67	69	73	70	279	13,892
Young-A Yang	73	68	71	68	280	12,172
Diana D'Alessio	69	71	71	69	280	12,172
Wendy Ward	71	69	70	70	280	12,172
Marisa Baena	71	70	74	66	281	10,601
Jee Young Lee	70	70	71	70	281	10,601
Young Kim	67	69	74	71	281	10,601
Erica Blasberg	68	68	73	72	281	10,601

John Q. Hammons Hotel Classic

Cedar Ridge Country Club, Tulsa, Oklahoma
Par 36-35–71; 6,602 yards

September 8-10
purse, $1,000,000

	SCORES			TOTAL	MONEY
Cristie Kerr	70	61	68	199	$150,000
Annika Sorenstam	64	68	69	201	91,766
Lorena Ochoa	69	69	65	203	66,570
Diana D'Alessio	66	72	66	204	51,498
Jenna Daniels	74	67	67	208	37,681
Sun Young Yoo	71	69	68	208	37,681
Candie Kung	71	72	66	209	22,961
Karine Icher	71	70	68	209	22,961
Meena Lee	70	69	70	209	22,961
Karin Sjodin	69	70	70	209	22,961
Allison Hanna	68	69	72	209	22,961
Beth Bader	74	69	67	210	15,575
Dorothy Delasin	71	72	67	210	15,575
Laura Diaz	71	71	68	210	15,575
Wendy Ward	70	72	68	210	15,575
Julieta Granada	70	71	69	210	15,575
Hana Kim	72	70	69	211	12,494
Maggie Will	70	70	71	211	12,494
Becky Iverson	70	70	71	211	12,494
Michelle Ellis	71	71	70	212	10,559
Sherri Steinhauer	71	71	70	212	10,559
Carin Koch	71	71	70	212	10,559
Hee-Won Han	70	72	70	212	10,559
Marcy Hart	72	69	71	212	10,559
Michele Redman	68	73	71	212	10,559
Suzann Pettersen	72	72	69	213	8,551
Nicole Castrale	72	71	70	213	8,551
Catherine Cartwright	72	71	70	213	8,551
Heather Young	72	68	73	213	8,551
Nancy Scranton	69	70	74	213	8,551

Longs Drugs Challenge

Blackhawk Golf & Country Club, Danville, California
Par 37-35–72; 6,212 yards

September 21-24
purse, $1,100,000

	SCORES				TOTAL	MONEY
Karrie Webb	67	70	66	70	273	$165,000
Annika Sorenstam	70	70	69	65	274	101,192
Morgan Pressel	71	68	69	68	276	73,408
Lorena Ochoa	68	72	72	66	278	42,798
Stacy Prammanasudh	70	68	72	68	278	42,798
Cristie Kerr	69	70	71	68	278	42,798
Mi Hyun Kim	70	72	67	69	278	42,798
Maria Hjorth	70	68	70	71	279	27,424
Il Mi Chung	71	71	69	69	280	24,654
Sarah Lee	73	73	68	67	281	20,868
Meredith Duncan	73	72	69	67	281	20,868
Lorie Kane	67	71	71	72	281	20,868
Pat Hurst	73	73	69	67	282	17,101
Brittany Lang	70	70	73	69	282	17,101

	SCORES				TOTAL	MONEY
Kelli Kuehne	69	71	71	71	282	17,101
Paula Creamer	69	74	72	68	283	13,851
Becky Morgan	72	71	70	70	283	13,851
Mikaela Parmlid	70	72	71	70	283	13,851
Nicole Castrale	72	71	67	73	283	13,851
Jimin Kang	69	73	68	73	283	13,851
Eva Dahllof	71	74	70	70	285	11,635
Young Jo	72	72	71	70	285	11,635
Nancy Scranton	69	74	71	71	285	11,635
Jeong Jang	64	73	74	74	285	11,635
Nadina Light	71	70	76	69	286	10,388
Reilley Rankin	71	77	71	67	286	10,388
Meena Lee	75	71	72	69	287	8,892
Jill McGill	68	71	76	72	287	8,892
Hee-Won Han	69	77	72	69	287	8,892
Wendy Ward	73	71	74	69	287	8,892
Gloria Park	69	74	70	74	287	8,892
Dorothy Delasin	77	66	69	75	287	8,892

Corona Morelia Championship

Tres Marias Residential Golf Club, Michoacan, Mexico
Par 36-37–73; 6,600 yards

October 5-8
purse, $1,000,000

	SCORES				TOTAL	MONEY
Lorena Ochoa	71	64	68	69	272	$150,000
Julieta Granada	70	70	66	71	277	92,698
Paula Creamer	76	66	71	65	278	67,246
Young-A Yang	70	73	70	69	282	52,020
Silvia Cavalleri	72	69	72	70	283	30,502
Kelli Kuehne	69	70	75	69	283	30,502
Becky Morgan	74	70	69	70	283	30,502
Morgan Pressel	69	72	71	71	283	30,502
Wendy Ward	72	69	71	71	283	30,502
Stacy Prammanasudh	72	72	69	71	284	19,793
Brandie Burton	68	75	67	74	284	19,793
Brittany Lang	74	72	72	67	285	16,190
Karin Sjodin	74	73	69	69	285	16,190
Wendy Doolan	74	70	71	70	285	16,190
Liselotte Neumann	75	70	68	72	285	16,190
Johanna Head	73	72	73	68	286	12,688
Nicole Castrale	76	68	72	70	286	12,688
Suzann Pettersen	74	72	69	71	286	12,688
Sun Young Yoo	71	67	76	72	286	12,688
Young Jo	72	70	69	75	286	12,688
Tracy Hanson	73	71	74	69	287	10,465
Giulia Sergas	70	72	74	71	287	10,465
Hye Choi	76	71	69	71	287	10,465
Carin Koch	73	73	69	72	287	10,465
Christina Kim	74	72	65	76	287	10,465
Beth Bader	74	76	71	67	288	8,638
Mi Hyun Kim	71	72	75	70	288	8,638
Teresa Lu	74	71	73	70	288	8,638
Jean Bartholomew	73	72	72	71	288	8,638
Aram Cho	73	72	70	73	288	8,638

Samsung World Championship

Bighorn Golf Course, Palm Desert, California
Par 36-36–72; 6,644 yards

October 12-15
purse, $875,000

	SCORES				TOTAL	MONEY
Lorena Ochoa	67	73	67	65	272	$218,750
Annika Sorenstam	67	71	66	70	274	136,718
Sophie Gustafson	68	70	70	69	277	92,968
Stacy Prammanasudh	70	72	67	70	279	54,688
Paula Creamer	70	68	72	71	281	43,750
Juli Inkster	75	70	73	65	283	30,078
Cristie Kerr	71	71	68	73	283	30,078
Seon Hwa Lee	68	74	71	71	284	22,969
Pat Hurst	72	70	71	71	284	22,969
Sherri Steinhauer	72	67	71	74	284	22,969
Natalie Gulbis	74	72	75	67	288	18,047
Se Ri Pak	71	74	71	72	288	18,047
Brittany Lincicome	76	71	72	70	289	15,860
Karrie Webb	71	69	75	74	289	15,860
Jeong Jang	78	73	70	69	290	13,672
Hee-Won Han	76	68	73	73	290	13,672
Michelle Wie	74	72	72	75	293	12,578
Meena Lee	74	69	79	72	294	12,032
Mi Hyun Kim	74	74	71	76	295	11,484
Gwladys Nocera	79	72	74	82	307	10,937

Honda LPGA Thailand

Amata Spring Country Club, Chonburi, Thailand
Par 36-36–72; 6,392 yards

October 20-22
purse, $1,300,000

	SCORES			TOTAL	MONEY
Hee-Won Han	67	68	67	202	$195,000
Diana D'Alessio	68	69	70	207	124,591
Candie Kung	72	67	69	208	72,192
Gloria Park	69	68	71	208	72,192
Nicole Castrale	65	68	75	208	72,192
Carin Koch	69	72	68	209	37,176
Cristie Kerr	71	68	70	209	37,176
Brittany Lang	69	70	70	209	37,176
Christina Kim	70	66	73	209	37,176
Young Kim	70	71	69	210	26,603
Sherri Turner	73	66	71	210	26,603
Shi Hyun Ahn	71	72	69	212	21,146
Jee Young Lee	72	70	70	212	21,146
Sarah Lee	71	71	70	212	21,146
Laura Diaz	71	71	70	212	21,146
Patricia Meunier-Lebouc	68	73	71	212	21,146
Laura Davies	73	70	70	213	15,484
Stacy Prammanasudh	72	71	70	213	15,484
Maria Hjorth	72	70	71	213	15,484
Reilley Rankin	71	71	71	213	15,484
Brandie Burton	70	72	71	213	15,484
Tracy Hanson	71	70	72	213	15,484
Marisa Baena	70	70	73	213	15,484
Meena Lee	66	73	74	213	15,484

	SCORES			TOTAL	MONEY
Beth Bader	73	72	69	214	12,790
Kim Saiki	68	72	74	214	12,790
Lindsey Wright	69	73	73	215	11,375
Nancy Scranton	71	70	74	215	11,375
Helen Alfredsson	68	73	74	215	11,375
Lorie Kane	69	71	75	215	11,375

Kolon-Hana Bank Championship

See Korea LPGA Tour section.

Mizuno Classic

See Japan LPGA Tour section.

The Mitchell Company Tournament of Champions

Robert Trent Jones Golf Trail, Magnolia Grove,
Mobile, Alabama
Par 36-36–72; 6,253 yards

November 9-12
purse, $1,000,000

	SCORES				TOTAL	MONEY
Lorena Ochoa	66	73	63	65	267	$150,000
Juli Inkster	67	69	73	68	277	92,177
Paula Creamer	64	74	69	70	277	92,177
Angela Stanford	69	71	71	70	281	59,959
Joo Mi Kim	66	76	70	72	284	48,260
Jeong Jang	73	72	72	68	285	33,831
Sherri Steinhauer	71	71	73	70	285	33,831
Dorothy Delasin	71	74	66	74	285	33,831
Soo-Yun Kang	72	73	72	69	286	24,861
Cristie Kerr	71	66	80	69	286	24,861
Candie Kung	70	71	75	71	287	19,316
Rachel Hetherington	71	71	71	74	287	19,316
Marisa Baena	67	75	70	75	287	19,316
Karen Stupples	69	70	72	76	287	19,316
Stacy Prammanasudh	68	71	71	77	287	19,316
Grace Park	70	75	72	71	288	15,248
Jin Joo Hong	73	71	70	74	288	15,248
Jee Young Lee	68	76	69	75	288	15,248
Carin Koch	72	71	75	71	289	13,688
Patricia Meunier-Lebouc	67	76	75	71	289	13,688
Wendy Ward	70	73	72	75	290	12,752
Moira Dunn	69	67	78	76	290	12,752
Sophie Gustafson	69	74	72	76	291	11,816
Liselotte Neumann	66	77	70	78	291	11,816
Kim Saiki	71	71	75	75	292	10,968
Seon Hwa Lee	73	72	71	76	292	10,968
Wendy Doolan	71	70	77	75	293	9,755
Sung Ah Yim	68	73	77	75	293	9,755
Jimin Kang	69	76	71	77	293	9,755
Brittany Lincicome	73	69	74	77	293	9,755

ADT Championship

Trump International Golf Club, West Palm Beach, Florida
Par 36-36–72; 6,519 yards

November 16-19
purse, $1,550,000

	SCORES			FINAL ROUND	MONEY
Julieta Granada	70	69	69	68	$1,000,000
Lorena Ochoa	75	70	67	70	100,000
Karrie Webb	69	71	70	71	20,500
Il Mi Chung	69	73	65	72	18,125
Natalie Gulbis	70	70	72	72	18,125
Mi Hyun Kim	70	73	65	72	18,125
Ai Miyazato	68	69	72	72	18,125
Paula Creamer	71	71	70	75	16,250

Players who did not advance after Round 3

	SCORES			TOTAL	MONEY
Jeong Jang	74	69	70	213	14,000
Diana D'Alessio	72	71	72	215	14,000
Juli Inkster	73	72	70	215	14,000
Cristie Kerr	73	71	71	215	14,000
Hee-Won Han	73	71	73	217	14,000
Se Ri Pak	71	71	75	217	14,000
Morgan Pressel	71	74	75	220	14,000
Wendy Ward	71	70	83	224	14,000

Players who did not advance after Round 2

	SCORES		TOTAL	MONEY
Pat Hurst	72	73	145	8,000
Brittany Lang	75	70	145	8,000
Jee Young Lee	72	73	145	8,000
Annika Sorenstam	74	72	146	8,000
Lorie Kane	78	69	147	8,000
Angela Stanford	74	73	147	8,000
Brittany Lincicome	76	72	148	8,000
Sophie Gustafson	73	76	149	8,000
Stacy Prammanasudh	76	73	149	8,000
Maria Hjorth	74	76	150	8,000
Sun Young Yoo	79	72	151	8,000
Meena Lee	76	76	152	8,000
Candie Kung	77	76	153	8,000
Seon Hwa Lee	77	76	153	8,000
Sung Ah Yim	81	72	153	8,000
Sherri Steinhauer	76	84	160	8,000

Lexus Cup

Tanah Merah Country Club, Garden Course, Singapore
Par 36-36–72; 6,620 yards

December 15-17
purse, $960,000

FIRST DAY
Alternate Shot

Young Kim and Seon Hwa Lee (Asia) defeated Laura Davies and Brittany Lincicome, 6 and 5.
Meena Lee and Jee Young Lee (Asia) defeated Paula Creamer and Natalie Gulbis, 2 up.
Grace Park and Shi Hyun Ahn (Asia) halved with Stacy Prammanasudh and Angela Stanford.
Julieta Granada and Morgan Pressel (International) defeated Hee-Won Han and Se Ri Pak, 4 and 3.
Annika Sorenstam and Carin Koch (Int'l) defeated Joo Mi Kim and Sakura Yokomine, 3 and 2.
Candie Kung and Jennifer Rosales (Asia) halved with Sherri Steinhauer and Nikki Campbell.

POINTS: Asia 3, International 3

SECOND DAY
Best Ball

Gulbis and Sorenstam (Int'l) defeated Meena Lee and Jee Young Lee, 2 up.
Park and Han (Asia) defeated Granada and Pressel, 1 up.
Creamer and Prammanasudh (Int'l) defeated Ahn and Joo Mi Kim, 3 and 2.
Kung and Rosales (Asia) defeated Campbell and Lincicome, 3 and 1.
Young Kim and Yokomine (Asia) defeated Koch and Davies, 2 up.
Pak and Seon Hwa Lee (Asia) defeated Steinhauer and Stanford, 4 and 2.

POINTS: Asia 4, International 2

THIRD DAY
Singles

Sorenstam (Int'l) defeated Park, 4 and 3.
Creamer (Int'l) defeated Kung, 1 up.
Meena Lee (Asia) halved with Stanford.
Jee Young Lee (Asia) defeated Pressel, 5 and 4.
Prammanasudh (Int'l) defeated Ahn, 4 and 3.
Young Kim (Asia) defeated Koch, 3 and 2.
Han (Asia) defeated Campbell, 3 and 2.
Steinhauer (Int'l) defeated Rosales, 4 and 3.
Yokomine (Asia) defeated Davies, 4 and 3.
Gulbis (Int'l) defeated Joo Mi Kim, 5 and 4.
Seon Hwa Lee (Asia) defeated Granada, 2 and 1.
Lincicome (Int'l) defeated Pak, 4 and 2.

TOTAL POINTS: Asia 12½, International 11½

(Each member of the Asian team received $50,000; each member of the International team received $30,000.)

Ladies European Tour

Women's World Cup of Golf
See South African Women's Tour section.

ANZ Ladies Masters
See Australian Women's Tour section.

Princess Lalla Meriem Cup

Dar-es-Salam Golf Club, Blue Course, Rabat, Morocco
Par 36-37–73; 6,780 yards

February 24-26
purse, US$60,000

	SCORES			TOTAL	MONEY
Sophie Sandolo	71	72	74	217	US$12,000
Anja Monke	73	73	71	217	7,500
(Sandolo defeated Monke on fifth playoff hole.)					
Stephanie Arricau	76	74	73	223	6,000
Veronica Zorzi	74	76	74	224	4,250
Ludivine Kreutz	72	77	75	224	4,250
Ana Belen Sanchez	80	72	73	225	3,800
Marine Monnet-Melocco	76	79	72	227	3,500
Mounya Amalou	78	77	72	227	3,500
Georgina Simpson	81	74	73	228	3,200
Tullia Calzavara	82	75	73	230	3,000
Gwladys Nocera	76	77	80	233	3,000
Ana Larraneta	75	77	82	234	3,000
Xonia Wunsch	81	80	82	243	3,000

Tenerife Ladies Open

Abama Golf, Tenerife, Spain
Par 36-36–72; 6,095 yards

April 27-30
purse, €250,000

	SCORES				TOTAL	MONEY
Riikka Hakkarainen	73	70	74	71	288	€37,500
Tania Elosegui Mayor	71	72	76	71	290	25,375
Virginie Auffret	73	76	75	67	291	11,570
Rebecca Hudson	78	76	69	68	291	11,570
Shani Waugh	73	73	74	71	291	11,570
Rebecca Coakley	74	73	73	71	291	11,570
Kirsty S. Taylor	72	69	73	77	291	11,570
Sophie Giquel	74	70	78	70	292	5,925
Georgina Simpson	73	71	75	73	292	5,925
Carlie Butler	76	76	74	69	295	4,800
Federica Piovano	77	77	69	72	295	4,800
Becky Brewerton	75	78	68	75	296	4,162.50
Karen Margrethe Juul	75	71	72	78	296	4,162.50

	SCORES				TOTAL	MONEY
Sofia Renell	74	76	76	71	297	3,725
Linda Wessberg	75	71	79	72	297	3,725
Laurette Maritz	75	71	76	75	297	3,725
Laura Cabanillas	72	82	73	71	298	3,500
Cecilia Ekelundh	73	76	77	73	299	3,115.62
Maria Boden	78	73	75	73	299	3,115.62
Gwladys Nocera	79	73	74	73	299	3,115.62
Rebecca Stevenson	72	78	80	69	299	3,115.62
Anna Knutsson	78	73	74	74	299	3,115.62
Danielle Masters	72	75	77	75	299	3,115.62
Virginie Lagoutte	74	75	74	76	299	3,115.62
Eleanor Pilgrim	78	73	71	77	299	3,115.62

Open de Espana Feminino

Panoramica Golf & Country Club, San Jorge, Castellon, Spain
Par 36-36–72; 6,252 yards

May 11-14
purse, €275,000

	SCORES				TOTAL	MONEY
Lynnette Brooky	66	74	65	70	275	€41,250
Gwladys Nocera	67	68	73	70	278	27,912.50
Nora Angehrn	71	72	66	71	280	19,250
Elisa Serramia	72	69	73	68	282	12,045
Lotta Wahlin	74	69	69	70	282	12,045
Becky Brewerton	72	68	70	72	282	12,045
Carmen Alonso	68	75	69	71	283	7,562.50
Veronica Zorzi	72	71	68	72	283	7,562.50
Eva Steinberger	71	72	74	67	284	5,175.50
Amanda Moltke-Leth	73	69	74	68	284	5,175.50
Sophie Sandolo	72	72	74	66	284	5,175.50
Asa Gottmo	73	72	68	71	284	5,175.50
Ana B. Sanchez	73	68	70	73	284	5,175.50
Lisa Holm Sorensen	74	70	73	68	285	4,235
Tullia Calzavara	69	74	73	70	286	3,855.50
Isabella Maconi	71	73	70	72	286	3,855.50
Rebecca Hudson	73	68	71	74	286	3,855.50
Shani Waugh	73	73	74	66	286	3,855.50
Anna Rawson	71	74	67	74	286	3,855.50
Karen Margrethe Juul	72	70	74	71	287	3,300
Marta Prieto	72	72	72	71	287	3,300
Beatriz Recari Eransus	71	72	72	72	287	3,300
Stefania Croce	71	73	75	68	287	3,300
Raquel Carriedo	70	74	75	68	287	3,300
Anna Knutsson	77	68	68	74	287	3,300
Virginie Auffret	69	74	70	74	287	3,300

Deutsche Bank Ladies' Swiss Open

Golf Gerre Losone, Switzerland
Par 35-37–72; 6,185 yards

May 18-21
purse, €500,000

	SCORES				TOTAL	MONEY
Gwladys Nocera	69	70	63	71	273	€75,000
Laura Davies	66	71	69	70	276	50,750

	SCORES	TOTAL	MONEY
Lisa Hall	68 67 66 76	277	35,000
Karen Margrethe Juul	67 72 68 71	278	27,000
Tania Elosegui Mayor	69 70 70 71	280	21,200
Stefanie Michl	70 72 70 69	281	17,500
Asa Gottmo	71 73 74 66	284	12,900
Eleanor Pilgrim	70 72 73 69	284	12,900
Sophie Giquel	71 74 69 70	284	12,900
Rebecca Hudson	73 71 73 68	285	8,500
Anna Rawson	71 72 70 72	285	8,500
Virginie Lagoutte	70 73 69 73	285	8,500
Becky Brewerton	72 69 68 76	285	8,500
Marta Prieto	68 74 67 76	285	8,500
Fame More	66 69 71 79	285	8,500
Anja Monke	72 71 72 71	286	7,100
Samantha Head	70 70 71 75	286	7,100
Helena Alterby	73 72 72 70	287	6,616.66
Stephanie Arricau	71 72 72 72	287	6,616.66
Eva Steinberger	73 71 71 72	287	6,616.66

Vediorbis Open de France

Le Golf d'Arras, Anzin St. Aubin, France
Par 36-36—72; 6,195 yards

May 25-28
purse, €325,000

	SCORES	TOTAL	MONEY
Veronica Zorzi	71 69 69 72	281	€48,750
Laura Davies	72 73 68 69	282	32,987.50
Stephanie Arricau	73 70 70 72	285	22,750
Gwladys Nocera	73 72 69 72	286	17,550
Anja Monke	75 71 71 70	287	11,635
Nathalie David-Mila	73 74 69 71	287	11,635
Cecilia Ekelundh	72 73 69 73	287	11,635
Asa Gottmo	73 73 76 67	289	7,702.50
Trish Johnson	69 76 71 73	289	7,702.50
Lynnette Brooky	77 71 72 70	290	6,023.33
Anna Knutsson	75 73 68 74	290	6,023.33
Kirsty S. Taylor	71 72 71 76	290	6,023.33
Linda Wessberg	74 75 74 68	291	5,118.75
Rebecca Hudson	75 71 73 72	291	5,118.75
Denise Simon	74 76 73 69	292	4,761.25
Rebecca Coakley	71 73 73 75	292	4,761.25
Riikka Hakkarainen	76 73 76 68	293	4,420
Ana B. Sanchez	74 74 73 72	293	4,420
Catrin Nilsmark	77 70 72 74	293	4,420
Nikki Garrett	77 73 75 69	294	3,900
Joanne Mills	71 75 76 72	294	3,900
Federica Piovano	73 73 75 73	294	3,900
Elisa Serramia	73 75 73 73	294	3,900
Lotta Wahlin	73 75 72 74	294	3,900
Sophie Sandolo	72 72 75 75	294	3,900
Ludivine Kreutz	70 75 74 75	294	3,900

KLM Ladies Open

Eindhovensche Golf Club, Valkenswaard, Netherlands
Par 36-36–72; 6,195 yards

June 2-4
purse, €165,000

	SCORES			TOTAL	MONEY
Stephanie Arricau	67	67	70	204	€24,750
Anja Monke	69	67	69	205	16,747.50
Leah Hart	65	71	70	206	11,550
Amanda Moltke-Leth	68	69	72	209	8,910
Sophie Giquel	69	70	71	210	6,385.50
Gwladys Nocera	71	67	72	210	6,385.50
Riikka Hakkarainen	68	72	71	211	4,950
Liza Walters	72	71	69	212	3,707
Anna Knutsson	74	68	70	212	3,707
Sophie Sandolo	70	72	70	212	3,707
Ana B. Sanchez	70	73	70	213	2,651
Anne-Marie Knight	72	70	71	213	2,651
Rebecca Coakley	71	70	72	213	2,651
Judith Van Hagen	70	71	72	213	2,651
Ludivine Kreutz	68	72	73	213	2,651
Georgina Simpson	69	70	74	213	2,651
Becky Brewerton	72	70	72	214	2,244
Nikki Garrett	73	69	72	214	2,244
Laura Terebey	69	70	75	214	2,244
Elisa Serramia	71	75	69	215	2,054.25
Laurette Maritz	75	70	70	215	2,054.25
Cherie Byrnes	70	73	72	215	2,054.25
Lisa Holm Sorensen	68	74	73	215	2,054.25

BMW Ladies Italian Open

Sheraton Golf Parco de' Medici, Rome, Italy
Par 35-37–72; 6,145 yards

June 14-17
purse, €400,000

	SCORES				TOTAL	MONEY
Gwladys Nocera	71	66	65	72	274	€60,000
Sophie Giquel	70	69	66	71	276	40,600
Elisa Serramia	68	70	73	69	280	15,931.42
Veronica Zorzi	71	72	68	69	280	15,931.42
Ana B. Sanchez	72	74	65	69	280	15,931.42
Laura Cabanillas	71	71	68	70	280	15,931.42
Rebecca Hudson	72	71	66	71	280	15,931.42
Linda Wessberg	67	72	69	72	280	15,931.42
Iben Tinning	72	69	67	72	280	15,931.42
Marta Prieto	74	69	72	66	281	7,413.33
Joanne Mills	70	70	72	69	281	7,413.33
Amanda Moltke-Leth	69	69	70	73	281	7,413.33
Ursula Wikstrom	71	69	73	69	282	6,080
Ana Larraneta	72	73	68	69	282	6,080
Nikki Garrett	70	70	72	70	282	6,080
Tullia Calzavara	68	67	75	72	282	6,080
Eleanor Pilgrim	71	68	73	71	283	5,370
Becky Brewerton	70	70	71	72	283	5,370
Trish Johnson	71	71	69	72	283	5,370
Laurette Maritz	69	73	69	72	283	5,370

Estoril Ladies Open of Portugal

Quinta da Marinha Oitavos Golfe, Cascais, Estoril, Portugal
Par 36-36–72; 6,199 yards

June 22-24
purse, €300,000

	SCORES			TOTAL	MONEY
Stephanie Arricau	71	71	65	207	€45,000
Gwladys Nocera	69	73	70	212	30,450
Sarah Kemp	69	72	72	213	21,000
Rebecca Hudson	74	71	69	214	16,200
Becky Brewerton	72	69	74	215	12,720
Helena Alterby	70	72	74	216	10,500
Marta Prieto	75	72	70	217	9,000
Carlie Butler	73	74	72	219	6,740
Stefania Croce	72	78	69	219	6,740
Lisa Jean	73	75	71	219	6,740
Rebecca Coakley	72	72	76	220	4,820
Anne-Marie Knight	67	77	76	220	4,820
Lara Tadiotto	74	71	75	220	4,820
Tania Elosegui Mayor	71	75	74	220	4,820
Katie Bakken	73	73	74	220	4,820
Leah Hart	74	78	68	220	4,820
Maria Beautell	70	76	75	221	4,080
Jehanne Jail	74	73	74	221	4,080
Laurette Maritz	67	75	79	221	4,080
Liza Walters	77	72	73	222	3,780
Pia Koivuranta	69	79	74	222	3,780
Linda Wessberg	72	77	73	222	3,780

OTP Bank Ladies Central European Open

Old Lake Golf & Country Club, Tata, Budapest, Hungary
Par 35-36–71; 6,037 yards

July 13-15
purse, €165,000

	SCORES			TOTAL	MONEY
Rebecca Hudson	66	65	70	201	€24,750
Anja Monke	64	66	73	203	16,747.50
Lora Fairclough	67	69	68	204	10,230
Riikka Hakkarainen	69	64	71	204	10,230
Sara Beautell	65	68	72	205	6,996
Sophie Sandolo	69	66	71	206	5,775
Rebecca Stevenson	69	70	68	207	4,017.75
Nora Angehrn	69	68	70	207	4,017.75
Mianne Bagger	68	68	71	207	4,017.75
Trish Johnson	66	69	72	207	4,017.75
Virginie Lagoutte	72	67	69	208	2,843.50
Karen Margrethe Juul	71	65	72	208	2,843.50
Ana B. Sanchez	64	70	74	208	2,843.50
Georgina Simpson	68	72	69	209	2,351.25
Ana Larraneta	71	69	69	209	2,351.25
Virginie Auffret	74	65	70	209	2,351.25
Karen Lunn	72	67	70	209	2,351.25
Elisa Serramia	68	70	71	209	2,351.25
Lara Tadiotto	71	67	71	209	2,351.25
Clare Queen	71	70	69	210	2,004.75
Maria Boden	68	70	72	210	2,004.75
Beatriz Recari Eransus	73	65	72	210	2,004.75

	SCORES			TOTAL	MONEY
Marta Prieto	66	71	73	210	2,004.75
Carina Vagner	72	65	73	210	2,004.75
Sophie Giquel	68	67	75	210	2,004.75

Catalonia Ladies Masters

Club Golf D'Aro, Platja D'Aro, Girona, Costa Brava, Spain
Par 36-36–72; 6,153 yards

July 21-23
purse, €190,000

	SCORES			TOTAL	MONEY
Gwladys Nocera	69	69	69	207	€55,000
Sarah Kemp	70	74	68	212	22,800
Ludivine Kreutz	75	72	66	213	11,400
Maria Hjorth	73	73	67	213	11,400
Marina Arruti	75	73	66	214	9,500
Riikka Hakkarainen	73	71	71	215	6,146.50
Lotta Wahlin	72	70	73	215	6,146.50
Lisa Hall	77	68	72	217	5,434
Nikki Garrett	75	72	71	218	4,699
Laurette Maritz	73	71	74	218	4,699
Rebecca Hudson	74	73	72	219	2,932.33
Sophie Sandolo	75	72	72	219	2,932.33
Sophie Giquel	69	76	74	219	2,932.33
Shani Waugh	76	75	70	221	2,660
Veronica Zorzi	77	72	72	221	2,660
Candy Hannemann	74	77	71	222	2,375
Amanda Moltke-Leth	76	75	71	222	2,375
Anna Rawson	80	71	71	222	2,375
Charlotta Sorenstam	76	78	69	223	2,147
Stephanie Arricau	77	73	74	224	1,817.66
Stephanie Louden	74	74	76	224	1,817.66
Tania Elosegui Mayor	74	71	79	224	1,817.66
Rebecca Coakley	79	73	73	225	1,653
Anja Monke	79	74	73	226	1,539
Elisa Serramia	77	75	74	226	1,539
Virginie Auffret	70	79	77	226	1,539
Marta Prieto	71	77	78	226	1,539
Karen Margrethe Juul	72	75	79	226	1,539
Kirsty S. Taylor	70	81	76	227	1,425
Asa Gottmo	76	75	77	228	1,368
Nora Angehrn	77	74	77	228	1,368

Evian Masters

Evian Masters Golf Club, Evians-les-Bains, France
Par 36-36–72; 6,283 yards

July 26-29
purse, €2,535,120

	SCORES				TOTAL	MONEY
Karrie Webb	67	68	69	68	272	€380,268
Laura Davies	68	71	67	67	273	215,766.59
Michelle Wie	69	66	70	68	273	215,766.59
Mi Hyun Kim	66	71	71	66	274	140,352.69
Lorena Ochoa	66	69	73	67	275	112,967.48
Se Ri Pak	68	68	70	70	276	92,427.10

	SCORES				TOTAL	MONEY
Paula Creamer	70	68	74	65	277	77,365.09
Annika Sorenstam	69	69	71	70	279	64,356.99
Jeong Jang	71	69	68	71	279	64,356.99
Cristie Kerr	73	70	73	65	281	55,455.75
Wendy Ward	69	76	69	68	282	48,062.49
Heather Young	69	74	70	69	282	48,062.49
Candie Kung	71	70	70	71	282	48,062.49
Maria Hjorth	68	72	70	73	283	42,175.09
Michele Redman	69	72	74	69	284	36,697.13
Karine Icher	75	69	71	69	284	36,697.13
Juli Inkster	74	71	70	69	284	36,697.13
Young Kim	73	72	69	70	284	36,697.13
Sophie Gustafson	71	72	71	71	285	31,493.79
Lorie Kane	70	68	74	73	285	31,493.79
Hee-Won Han	72	69	71	73	285	31,493.79
Laura Diaz	76	69	72	69	286	28,207.43
Beth Daniel	71	74	71	70	286	28,207.43
Pat Hurst	73	68	72	73	286	28,207.43
Morgan Pressel	75	75	67	70	287	25,195.14
Shi Hyun Ahn	70	73	73	71	287	25,195.14
Natalie Gulbis	71	74	70	72	287	25,195.14
Marisa Baena	74	74	72	68	288	22,365.10
Meena Lee	73	71	73	71	288	22,365.10
Sukura Yokomine	73	72	70	73	288	22,365.10

Weetabix Women's British Open

Royal Lytham & St. Annes Golf Club, England
Par 35-37–72; 6,308 yards

August 3-6
purse, £1,050,000

	SCORES				TOTAL	MONEY
Sherri Steinhauer	73	70	66	72	281	€234,880
Cristie Kerr	71	76	66	71	284	124,780
Sophie Gustafson	76	67	69	72	284	124,780
Juli Inkster	66	72	74	73	285	73,400
Lorena Ochoa	74	73	65	73	285	73,400
Lorie Kane	73	69	74	70	286	54,316
Beth Daniel	73	71	70	72	286	54,316
Julieta Granada	71	73	70	73	287	46,976
Ai Miyazato	71	75	75	67	288	42,572
Hee-Won Han	80	71	69	70	290	31,195
Joo Mi Kim	73	73	73	71	290	31,195
Karine Icher	72	73	71	74	290	31,195
Nina Reis	70	76	69	75	290	31,195
Candie Kung	72	70	71	77	290	31,195
Karen Stupples	73	69	70	78	290	31,195
Sukura Yokomine	72	73	75	71	291	20,613.16
Il Mi Chung	72	71	75	73	291	20,613.16
Laura Davies	72	72	73	74	291	20,613.16
Heather Young	72	74	70	75	291	20,613.16
Gwladys Nocera	70	73	71	77	291	20,613.16
Natalie Gulbis	72	74	67	78	291	20,613.16
Kyeong Bae	73	73	75	71	292	16,882
Jee Young Lee	72	77	69	74	292	16,882
Paula Creamer	72	71	73	76	292	16,882
Shi Hyun Ahn	75	73	69	76	293	15,560.80
Jackie Gallagher-Smith	77	74	71	72	294	13,887.28

	SCORES	TOTAL	MONEY
Tracy Hanson	74 77 70 73	294	13,887.28
Michelle Wie	74 74 72 74	294	13,887.28
Jeong Jang	78 73 68 75	294	13,887.28
Young-A Yang	72 75 68 79	294	13,887.28

Scandinavian TPC Hosted by Annika

Bro-Balsta Golf Club, Stockholm, Sweden
Par 37-36–73; 6,530 yards

August 10-13
purse, €500,000

	SCORES	TOTAL	MONEY
Annika Sorenstam	66 71 69 65	271	€75,000
Lorena Ochoa	72 65 69 66	272	50,750
Suzann Pettersen	71 69 68 68	276	35,000
Gwladys Nocera	69 69 71 71	280	27,000
Catriona Matthew	74 70 67 71	282	19,350
Laura Davies	70 75 66 71	282	19,350
Bettina Hauert	70 72 74 67	283	13,750
Veronica Zorzi	72 69 70 72	283	13,750
Iben Tinning	74 69 72 69	284	10,600
Karen Stupples	69 71 72 72	284	10,600
*Caroline Hedwall	73 70 73 69	285	
Maria Hjorth	74 70 72 69	285	8,900
Karin Sjodin	70 74 70 71	285	8,900
Sophie Sandolo	71 70 71 74	286	8,050
Liselotte Neumann	70 72 75 70	287	7,450
Marta Prieto	72 75 69 71	287	7,450
Helen Alfredsson	69 70 75 73	287	7,450
Charlotta Sorenstam	75 70 71 72	288	7,000
Sophie Giquel	74 75 70 70	289	6,700
Riikka Hakkarainen	70 72 74 73	289	6,700

Wales Ladies Championship of Europe

Machynys Peninsula Golf Club, Llanelli,
Carmarthenshire, Wales
Par 36-36–72; 6,126 yards

August 17-20
purse, €513,800

	SCORES	TOTAL	MONEY
Linda Wessberg	67 67 69 71	274	€77,070
Laura Davies	66 69 73 67	275	52,150.70
Gwladys Nocera	70 72 68 66	276	31,855.60
Nikki Garrett	69 67 69 71	276	31,855.60
Becky Brewerton	65 69 73 71	278	19,884.06
Helen Alfredsson	67 68 71 72	278	19,884.06
Lora Fairclough	73 64 74 68	279	15,414
Cherie Byrnes	66 74 70 70	280	12,177.06
Anna Knutsson	73 69 67 71	280	12,177.06
Trish Johnson	66 72 75 69	282	8,950.39
Iben Tinning	71 71 71 69	282	8,950.39
Amanda Moltke-Leth	68 67 75 72	282	8,950.39
Danielle Masters	69 67 74 72	282	8,950.39
Stephanie Arricau	72 69 69 72	282	8,950.39
Asa Gottmo	70 70 74 69	283	7,017.04

	SCORES			TOTAL	MONEY
Louise Friberg	71	70	73	69	283	7,017.04
Karen Margrethe Juul	74	68	71	70	283	7,017.04
Kiran Matharu	70	70	72	71	283	7,017.04
Denise Simon	72	69	71	71	283	7,017.04
Bettina Hauert	67	70	73	73	283	7,017.04
Lynn Brooky	68	72	70	73	283	7,017.04

SAS Masters

Oslo Golf Club, Oslo, Norway
Par 36-36–72; 6,171 yards

August 25-27
purse, €200,000

	SCORES			TOTAL	MONEY
Laura Davies	69	68	68	205	€30,000
Ellen Smets	72	69	70	211	20,300
Nikki Garrett	69	73	70	212	12,400
Virginie Lagoutte	67	74	71	212	12,400
Cecilia Ekelundh	72	71	70	213	8,480
Leah Hart	73	72	70	215	5,296
Suzann Pettersen	74	70	71	215	5,296
Rebecca Hudson	70	74	71	215	5,296
Linda Wessberg	70	74	71	215	5,296
Amanda Moltke-Leth	70	73	72	215	5,296
Karen Margrethe Juul	74	72	70	216	3,048.88
Sophie Sandolo	77	69	70	216	3,048.88
Ana B. Sanchez	71	74	71	216	3,048.88
Helen Alfredsson	73	74	69	216	3,048.88
Ludivine Kreutz	74	71	71	216	3,048.88
Lora Fairclough	73	71	72	216	3,048.88
Gwladys Nocera	74	70	72	216	3,048.88
Laurette Maritz	73	71	72	216	3,048.88
Cherie Byrnes	69	72	75	216	3,048.88
Rebecca Stevenson	74	72	71	217	2,370
Lotta Wahlin	74	72	71	217	2,370
Bettina Hauert	74	71	72	217	2,370
Sophie Giquel	75	72	70	217	2,370
Nora Angehrn	73	71	73	217	2,370
Catrin Nilsmark	72	72	73	217	2,370
Kirsty Taylor	69	74	74	217	2,370
Sarah Heath	69	74	74	217	2,370

Finnair Masters

Helsinki Golf Club, Helsinki, Finland
Par 34-37–71; 5,916 yards

September 1-3
purse, €200,000

	SCORES			TOTAL	MONEY
Virginie Lagoutte	68	68	67	203	€30,000
Elin Ohlsson	67	70	68	205	20,300
Gwladys Nocera	68	72	68	208	12,400
Kris Lindstrom	68	69	71	208	12,400
Lynn Brooky	71	67	73	211	8,480
Alison Munt	75	69	68	212	5,296
Karen Margrethe Juul	72	72	68	212	5,296

	SCORES	TOTAL	MONEY
Lisa Holm Sorensen	70 72 70	212	5,296
Catrin Nilsmark	73 68 71	212	5,296
Riikka Hakkarainen	69 72 71	212	5,296
Nikki Garrett	73 74 66	213	3,355
Rebecca Stevenson	71 71 71	213	3,355
Laura Davies	70 72 71	213	3,355
Carlie Butler	69 72 72	213	3,355
Danielle Masters	72 72 70	214	2,766.66
Lotta Wahlin	73 70 71	214	2,766.66
Anna Tybring	74 69 71	214	2,766.66
Becky Brewerton	73 70 71	214	2,766.66
Rebecca Coakley	71 70 73	214	2,766.66
Mianne Bagger	71 66 77	214	2,766.66

Nykredit Masters

Odense Eventyr Golf Klub, Copenhagen, Denmark
Par 36-36–72; 6,387 yards

September 7-10
purse, €200,000

	SCORES	TOTAL	MONEY
Karen Margrethe Juul	72 67 66 68	273	€30,000
Laura Davies	70 69 72 66	277	17,150
Trish Johnson	72 71 66 68	277	17,150
Amanda Moltke-Leth	72 71 65 71	279	10,800
Stefania Croce	65 72 70 73	280	8,480
Mianne Bagger	67 76 70 68	281	6,500
Iben Tinning	70 75 66 70	281	6,500
Danielle Masters	74 71 69 68	282	4,493.33
Gwladys Nocera	70 74 69 69	282	4,493.33
Cecilia Ekelundh	72 74 67 69	282	4,493.33
Sophie Giquel	72 70 72 69	283	3,680
Virginie Lagoutte	74 73 72 65	284	3,180
Alison Munt	71 74 71 68	284	3,180
Rebecca Stevenson	73 68 72 71	284	3,180
Virginie Auffret	72 70 70 72	284	3,180
Sara Beautell	73 75 68 69	285	2,840
Karen Lunn	72 73 69 71	285	2,840
Lisa Holm Sorensen	71 73 68 74	286	2,720
Asa Gottmo	70 74 75 68	287	2,550
Ludivine Kreutz	74 71 74 68	287	2,550
Lisa Jean	70 76 71 70	287	2,550
Kris Lindstrom	78 69 70 70	287	2,550

Siemens Austrian Ladies Open

Golfclub Fohrenwald-Wiener Neustadt, Austria
Par 37-35–72; 6,194 yards

September 14-17
purse, €250,000

	SCORES	TOTAL	MONEY
Sophie Gustafson	71 64 65 71	271	€37,500
Laura Davies	70 70 66 67	273	25,375
Ana B. Sanchez	75 66 67 69	277	17,500
Stephanie Arricau	69 71 70 68	278	13,500
Anne-Marie Knight	71 71 63 74	279	10,600

	SCORES				TOTAL	MONEY
Anja Monke	71	70	69	70	280	8,750
Asa Gottmo	70	73	70	68	281	6,875
Louise Friberg	70	72	67	72	281	6,875
Lotta Wahlin	73	73	69	67	282	5,066.66
Rebecca Hudson	72	71	68	71	282	5,066.66
Federica Piovano	71	68	71	72	282	5,066.66
Lora Fairclough	72	71	72	68	283	4,300
Ana Larraneta	73	70	71	70	284	3,866.66
Carlie Butler	75	67	71	71	284	3,866.66
Lisa Hall	69	69	68	78	284	3,866.66
Laura Cabanillas	76	68	75	66	285	3,241.66
Sofia Johansson	75	70	73	67	285	3,241.66
Virginie Auffret	72	74	71	68	285	3,241.66
Sarah Kemp	71	69	75	70	285	3,241.66
Marta Prieto	74	71	70	70	285	3,241.66
Bettina Hauert	75	70	69	71	285	3,241.66
Carmen Alonso	74	68	71	72	285	3,241.66
Mianne Bagger	73	72	68	72	285	3,241.66
Julie Forbes	76	69	68	72	285	3,241.66

BBC Radio Kent Ladies' English Open

Chart Hills Golf Club, Kent, England
Par 36-36–72; 6,158 yards

October 6-8
purse, €165,000

	SCORES			TOTAL	MONEY
Cecilia Ekelundh	71	69	70	210	€24,750
Martina Eberl	70	71	70	211	16,747.50
Danielle Masters	69	73	70	212	11,550
Amanda Moltke-Leth	68	72	73	213	8,910
Rebecca Stevenson	75	70	69	214	6,385.50
Rebecca Hudson	75	70	69	214	6,385.50
Carmen Alonso	77	68	70	215	4,257
Anna Highgate	69	73	73	215	4,257
Isabella Maconi	72	70	73	215	4,257
*Breanne Loucks	75	73	68	216	
Natalie Claire Booth	71	75	70	216	3,300
Lora Fairclough	77	70	70	217	2,706
Suzanne Dickens	76	72	69	217	2,706
Karen Lunn	76	70	71	217	2,706
Asa Gottmo	73	71	73	217	2,706
Nienke Nijenhuis	73	70	74	217	2,706
*Melissa Reid	71	71	75	217	
Melanie Holmes-Smith	78	70	70	218	2,165.62
Antonella Cvitan	74	74	70	218	2,165.62
Virginie Auffret	75	72	71	218	2,165.62
Ludivine Kreutz	79	70	69	218	2,165.62
Tania Elosegui Mayor	74	73	71	218	2,165.62
Nathalie David-Mila	75	71	72	218	2,165.62
Linda Wessberg	76	70	72	218	2,165.62
Denise Simon	76	68	74	218	2,165.62

Dubai Ladies Masters

Emirates Golf Club, Majlis Course,
Dubai, United Arab Emirates
Par 35-37–72; 6,308 yards

October 26-29
purse, €500,000

	SCORES				TOTAL	MONEY
Annika Sorenstam	65	68	68	69	270	€75,000
Helen Alfredsson	70	71	68	67	276	50,750
Karrie Webb	70	68	70	70	278	35,000
Amy Yang	69	72	70	69	280	24,100
Veronica Zorzi	69	72	69	70	280	24,100
Louise Friberg	72	72	72	65	281	17,500
Iben Tinning	72	72	73	65	282	15,000
Karen Margrethe Juul	71	69	71	72	283	11,850
Martina Eberl	70	70	70	73	283	11,850
Nikki Garrett	74	74	70	66	284	8,962.50
Becky Brewerton	73	73	71	67	284	8,962.50
Trish Johnson	72	67	71	74	284	8,962.50
Sarah Kemp	71	69	70	74	284	8,962.50
Gwladys Nocera	71	73	72	69	285	7,450
Nachiyo Ohtani	73	70	71	71	285	7,450
Sophie Sandolo	68	71	73	73	285	7,450
Sophie Giquel	73	74	68	71	286	7,000
Kirsty Taylor	68	74	75	70	287	6,800
Sofia Renell	73	71	75	69	288	6,450
Kiran Matharu	68	73	73	74	288	6,450
Tania Elosegui Mayor	69	70	73	76	288	6,450

Japan LPGA Tour

Daikin Orchid Ladies

Ryukyu Golf Club, Okinawa
Par 36-36–72; 6,376 yards

March 3-5
purse, ¥80,000,000

	SCORES			TOTAL	MONEY
Mikiyo Nishizuka	71	68	69	208	¥14,400,000
Sakura Yokomine	72	68	69	209	5,866,666
Shiho Ohyama	69	69	71	209	5,866,666
Ya-Huei Lu	69	69	71	209	5,866,666
Michiko Hattori	70	71	69	210	4,000,000
Yuri Fudoh	68	75	69	212	3,000,000
Saiki Fujita	71	70	71	212	3,000,000
Yuka Irie	70	73	70	213	1,882,000
Ji-Hee Lee	72	71	70	213	1,882,000
Junko Omote	74	69	70	213	1,882,000
Miho Koga	67	75	71	213	1,882,000
Mihoko Takahashi	76	70	68	214	1,368,000
Kaori Suzuki	74	71	69	214	1,368,000
Midori Yoneyama	73	70	71	214	1,368,000
Ikuyo Shiotani	73	73	69	215	1,088,000
Yuriko Ohtsuka	73	71	71	215	1,088,000
Michie Ohba	72	71	72	215	1,088,000
Shinobu Moromizato	71	71	73	215	1,088,000
Yun-Jye Wei	74	71	71	216	848,000
Yui Kawahara	71	73	72	216	848,000

Accordia Golf Ladies

Aoshima Golf Club, Miyazaki
Par 36-36–72; 6,424 yards

March 10-12
purse, ¥60,000,000

	SCORES			TOTAL	MONEY
Yuri Fudoh	71	67	73	211	¥10,800,000
Hiromi Mogi	68	72	72	212	4,740,000
Michiko Hattori	70	69	73	212	4,740,000
Michie Ohba	75	64	74	213	3,600,000
Mineko Nasu	74	70	70	214	2,700,000
Ai Ogawa	71	71	72	214	2,700,000
Nikki Campbell	73	71	71	215	2,100,000
Rie Murata	72	72	72	216	1,800,000
Atomi Shiota	71	72	74	217	1,224,000
Julie Lu	71	71	75	217	1,224,000
Kaori Higo	72	70	75	217	1,224,000
Akiko Fukushima	72	68	77	217	1,224,000
Hiroko Yamaguchi	76	70	72	218	918,000
Kaori Suzuki	73	72	73	218	918,000
Kasumi Fujii	73	71	74	218	918,000
Miho Koga	73	69	76	218	918,000
Ya-Huei Lu	74	72	73	219	708,000

	SCORES			TOTAL	MONEY
Yuka Irie	75	70	74	219	708,000
Chieko Amanuma	76	68	75	219	708,000
Young-Me Lee	71	75	74	220	546,000
Ji-Hee Lee	76	71	73	220	546,000
Kazu Yazaki	75	71	74	220	546,000
Mi-Jeong Jeon	74	73	73	220	546,000
Midori Yoneyama	75	71	74	220	546,000
Akane Iijima	73	74	73	220	546,000
Izumi Narita	76	69	75	220	546,000
Itsumi Okada	70	73	77	220	546,000

Kinmirai Tsuushin Queens Open

Kagoshima Takamaki Country Club, Kamo, Kagoshi
Par 36-36–72; 6,234 yards

March 17-19
purse, ¥70,000,000

	SCORES			TOTAL	MONEY
Akane Iijima	68	73	70	211	¥12,600,000
Hiromi Mogi	71	72	70	213	6,160,000
Yuriko Ohtsuka	69	72	73	214	4,900,000
Kasumi Fujii	70	70	75	215	4,200,000
Jeong-Eun Lee	74	72	70	216	3,150,000
Kaori Higo	73	71	72	216	3,150,000
Ikuyo Shiotani	70	76	71	217	2,100,000
Mi-Jeong Jeon	72	71	74	217	2,100,000
Sakura Yokomine	72	71	74	217	2,100,000
Michiko Hattori	72	74	72	218	1,400,000
Mitsuko Kawasaki	74	71	74	219	1,288,000
Chieko Amanuma	70	72	77	219	1,288,000
Akiko Fukushima	73	75	72	220	1,078,000
Tomoko Kusakabe	73	76	71	220	1,078,000
Nikki Campbell	71	78	71	220	1,078,000
Yeo-Jin Kang	75	71	74	220	1,078,000
Ya-Huei Lu	72	76	73	221	756,000
Mayumi Shimomura	72	77	72	221	756,000
Miho Koga	71	76	74	221	756,000
Yui Kawahara	73	73	75	221	756,000
Yuko Saitoh	74	76	71	221	756,000
Yumiko Baba	70	75	76	221	756,000

Studio Alice Ladies Open

Hanayashiki Golf Club, Yokawa Course, Miki, Hyogo
Par 36-36–72; 6,428 yards

April 7-9
purse, ¥60,000,000

	SCORES			TOTAL	MONEY
Ji-Hee Lee	72	75	71	218	¥10,800,000
Akiko Fukushima	71	73	74	218	5,280,000
(Lee defeated Fukushima on fourth playoff hole.)					
Kasumi Fujii	71	76	72	219	4,200,000
Michie Ohba	75	76	69	220	2,775,000
Saiki Fujita	77	75	68	220	2,775,000
Shiho Ohyama	70	77	73	220	2,775,000
Nikki Campbell	73	74	73	220	2,775,000

	SCORES			TOTAL	MONEY
Yasuko Satoh	74	76	71	221	1,500,000
Yeo-Jin Kang	76	73	72	221	1,500,000
Mitsuko Kawasaki	72	73	76	221	1,500,000
Yuriko Ohtsuka	77	74	71	222	1,038,000
Michiko Hattori	73	75	74	222	1,038,000
Hyun-Ju Shin	75	73	74	222	1,038,000
Momoko Ueda	73	78	72	223	858,000
Chieko Amanuma	74	76	73	223	858,000
Sakura Yokomine	72	77	74	223	858,000
Jae-Hee Bae	76	75	73	224	678,000
*Makoto Takemura	76	73	75	224	
Kurumi Dohi	72	76	76	224	678,000
Eriko Moriyama	75	73	76	224	678,000

Life Card Ladies

Kumamoto Airport Country Club, Kikuyo, Kumamoto
Par 36-36–72; 6,423 yards
April 14-16
purse, ¥60,000,000

	SCORES			TOTAL	MONEY
Yuri Fudoh	68	70	70	208	¥10,800,000
Shiho Ohyama	70	72	68	210	5,280,000
Akiko Fukushima	67	75	71	213	4,200,000
Sakura Yokomine	69	74	71	214	3,600,000
Ji-Yeon Han	70	71	74	215	3,000,000
Hyun-Ju Shin	73	71	72	216	1,950,000
Yuko Saitoh	71	72	73	216	1,950,000
Junko Omote	71	71	74	216	1,950,000
Akane Ohshiro	73	69	74	216	1,950,000
Kaori Nakamichi	71	75	71	217	1,200,000
Mie Nakata	75	73	70	218	1,050,000
Ya-Huei Lu	71	75	72	218	1,050,000
Ai Ogawa	71	74	73	218	1,050,000
Nikki Campbell	71	74	73	218	1,050,000
Ji-Hee Lee	73	75	71	219	870,000
Mitsuko Kawasaki	73	72	74	219	870,000
Momoko Ueda	67	82	71	220	750,000
Jae-Hee Bae	70	75	75	220	750,000
Itsumi Okada	76	73	72	221	597,600
Tamie Durdin	76	73	72	221	597,600
Eun-Hye Lee	74	75	72	221	597,600
Yuka Irie	77	72	72	221	597,600
Hiromi Mogi	75	71	75	221	597,600

Fujisankei Ladies Classic

Kawana Hotel Golf Club, Fuji Course, Ito, Shizuoka
Par 36-36–72; 6,464 yards
April 21-23
purse, ¥70,000,000

	SCORES			TOTAL	MONEY
Shiho Ohyama	74	70	71	215	¥12,600,000
Akane Iijima	75	72	68	215	6,300,000
(Ohyama defeated Iijima on first playoff hole.)					
Jeong-Eun Lee	78	72	67	217	4,900,000

	SCORES	TOTAL	MONEY
Mihoko Takahashi	73 73 72	218	4,200,000
Hiromi Mogi	75 70 75	220	3,640,000
Midori Yoneyama	74 73 74	221	2,496,666
Yuriko Ohtsuka	72 74 75	221	2,496,666
Michiko Hattori	74 72 75	221	2,496,666
Mi-Jeong Jeon	77 73 72	222	1,575,000
Kaori Nakamichi	79 70 73	222	1,575,000
Hyun-Ju Shin	75 76 72	223	1,176,000
Naoko Takasaki	77 74 72	223	1,176,000
Rui Kitada	80 71 72	223	1,176,000
Sakura Yokomine	77 73 73	223	1,176,000
Yuka Tonsho	74 75 74	223	1,176,000
Ayako Uehara	78 71 74	223	1,176,000
Yuko Saitoh	76 77 71	224	861,000
*Maiko Wakabayashi	77 75 72	224	
Michie Ohba	77 73 74	224	861,000
Junko Omote	75 74 75	224	861,000

Katokichi Queens

Yashima Country Club, Mure, Kagawa
Par 36-36–72; 6,317 yards

April 28-30
purse, ¥60,000,000

	SCORES	TOTAL	MONEY
Mie Nakata	66 71 69	206	¥10,800,000
Jae-Hee Bae	67 69 72	208	5,280,000
Eriko Moriyama	71 71 68	210	3,600,000
Midori Yoneyama	71 69 70	210	3,600,000
Akiko Fukushima	69 67 74	210	3,600,000
Yuri Fudoh	70 72 69	211	2,250,000
Mitsuko Kawasaki	72 68 71	211	2,250,000
Shiho Ohyama	71 72 69	212	1,650,000
Yuko Saitoh	70 72 70	212	1,650,000
Kaori Suzuki	74 71 68	213	1,136,000
Ya-Huei Lu	70 73 70	213	1,136,000
Sakura Yokomine	71 70 72	213	1,136,000
Jeong-Eun Lee	71 74 69	214	954,000
Yuka Shiroto	71 73 70	214	954,000
Nobuko Kizawa	70 73 71	214	954,000
Yun-Jye Wei	76 70 69	215	804,000
Eun-Hye Lee	72 70 73	215	804,000
Momoko Ueda	75 70 71	216	654,000
*Erina Hara	70 74 72	216	
Ai Ogawa	74 70 72	216	654,000
Kasumi Fujii	72 71 73	216	654,000

Salonpas World Ladies

Yomiuri Country Club, Tokyo
Par 36-36–72; 6,523 yards

May 4-7
purse, ¥100,000,000

	SCORES	TOTAL	MONEY
Shiho Ohyama	72 66 73 70	281	¥18,000,000
Hyun-Ju Shin	74 71 72 70	287	8,800,000

	SCORES				TOTAL	MONEY
Mi-Jeong Jeon	73	72	74	70	289	6,500,000
Paula Creamer	72	76	71	70	289	6,500,000
Ji-Hee Lee	74	74	73	69	290	4,500,000
Kuniko Maeda	72	72	73	73	290	4,500,000
Yuka Irie	72	74	73	72	291	2,750,000
Momoko Ueda	67	72	78	74	291	2,750,000
Ai Ogawa	70	73	74	74	291	2,750,000
Akiko Fukushima	70	74	72	75	291	2,750,000
Midori Yoneyama	70	75	74	73	292	1,540,000
Momoyo Yamazaki	71	76	72	73	292	1,540,000
Hsiu-Feng Tseng	68	73	77	74	292	1,540,000
Bo-Bae Song	72	73	73	74	292	1,540,000
Nahoko Hirao	71	73	73	75	292	1,540,000
Akane Iijima	71	73	72	76	292	1,540,000
Junko Omote	74	73	75	71	293	1,090,000
Yuri Fudoh	74	71	74	74	293	1,090,000
Sakura Yokomine	74	72	72	75	293	1,090,000
Eun-Hye Lee	73	72	76	73	294	890,000

Vernal Ladies

Fukuoka Century Golf Club, Asakura
Par 36-36–72; 6,540 yards

May 12-14
purse, ¥120,000,000

	SCORES			TOTAL	MONEY
Ji-Hee Lee	67	70	67	204	¥21,600,000
Hyun-Ju Shin	71	69	70	210	10,560,000
Michie Ohba	68	71	73	212	8,400,000
Jeong-Eun Lee	73	72	68	213	6,600,000
Shiho Ohyama	70	71	72	213	6,600,000
Akiko Fukushima	73	72	69	214	4,200,000
Midori Yoneyama	68	74	72	214	4,200,000
Ai Ogawa	67	72	75	214	4,200,000
Miho Koga	71	74	70	215	2,700,000
Tamie Durdin	73	72	70	215	2,700,000
Rui Kitada	71	75	70	216	2,088,000
Kaori Higo	72	73	71	216	2,088,000
Chihiro Nakajima	73	72	71	216	2,088,000
Momoko Ueda	72	71	73	216	2,088,000
Mitsuko Kawasaki	72	74	71	217	1,548,000
Iyoko Wada	77	69	71	217	1,548,000
Ya-Huei Lu	73	73	71	217	1,548,000
Ok-Hee Ku	71	74	72	217	1,548,000
Ji-Yeon Han	71	71	75	217	1,548,000
Ayako Uehara	76	70	72	218	1,128,000
Yasuko Satoh	75	71	72	218	1,128,000
Mineko Nasu	70	75	73	218	1,128,000
Asuka Tsujimura	76	72	70	218	1,128,000
Michiko Hattori	69	74	75	218	1,128,000
Yuri Fudoh	71	72	75	218	1,128,000

Chukyo TV Bridgestone Ladies Open

Chukyo Golf Club, Ishino Course, Toyota, Aichi
Par 36-36–72; 6,383 yards

May 19-21
purse, ¥70,000,000

	SCORES			TOTAL	MONEY
Ji-Hee Lee	69	76	66	211	¥12,600,000
Michie Ohba	65	74	74	213	6,160,000
Eun-Hye Lee	72	74	68	214	4,200,000
Asuka Tsujimura	75	70	69	214	4,200,000
Kaori Suzuki	71	72	71	214	4,200,000
Saiki Fujita	73	74	68	215	1,856,000
Yuko Saitoh	74	71	70	215	1,856,000
Sakura Yokomine	70	72	73	215	1,856,000
Mayumi Shimomura	71	71	73	215	1,856,000
Miho Koga	71	70	74	215	1,856,000
Midori Yoneyama	72	69	74	215	1,856,000
Hiroko Yamaguchi	73	68	74	215	1,856,000
Ai Ogawa	76	70	70	216	931,000
Tamie Durdin	72	74	70	216	931,000
Nobuko Kizawa	74	73	69	216	931,000
Shiho Ohyama	75	70	71	216	931,000
Mikiyo Nishizuka	71	73	72	216	931,000
Kayo Yamada	70	71	75	216	931,000
Hyun-Ju Shin	69	71	76	216	931,000
Ikuyo Shiotani	72	73	72	217	630,000
Mineko Nasu	71	76	70	217	630,000
Yeo-Jin Kang	74	70	73	217	630,000
Michiko Hattori	71	70	76	217	630,000

Kosaido Ladies Golf Cup

Chiba Kosaido Country Club, Ichihara, Chiba
Par 36-36–72; 6,333 yards

May 26-28
purse, ¥60,000,000

	SCORES			TOTAL	MONEY
Chieko Amanuma	66	71	72	209	¥10,800,000
Miho Koga	72	69	69	210	4,740,000
Shiho Ohyama	67	73	70	210	4,740,000
Akane Iijima	72	70	70	212	3,600,000
Tamie Durdin	70	73	70	213	3,000,000
Yuri Fudoh	72	71	71	214	2,400,000
Mihoko Takahashi	72	74	69	215	1,800,000
Nobuko Kizawa	69	76	70	215	1,800,000
Nikki Campbell	70	74	71	215	1,800,000
Momoko Ueda	68	78	70	216	1,004,571
Yukari Baba	72	74	70	216	1,004,571
Midori Yoneyama	71	74	71	216	1,004,571
Keiko Sasaki	72	72	72	216	1,004,571
Yun-Hee Ku	71	72	73	216	1,004,571
Natsu Nagai	70	72	74	216	1,004,571
Kuniko Maeda	73	69	74	216	1,004,571
Kasumi Fujii	70	77	70	217	651,600
Ya-Huei Lu	75	72	70	217	651,600
Izumi Narita	72	72	73	217	651,600
Itsumi Okada	72	72	73	217	651,600
Kaori Suzuki	74	69	74	217	651,600

Resort Trust Ladies

Grande Nasushirakawa Golf Club, Fukushima
Par 36-36–72; 6,502 yards

June 2-4
purse, ¥60,000,000

	SCORES			TOTAL	MONEY
Mie Nakata	66	70	71	207	¥10,800,000
Miho Koga	73	66	71	210	5,400,000
Kaori Higo	68	74	73	215	4,200,000
Mitsuko Kawasaki	76	69	71	216	3,600,000
Akane Iijima	73	73	71	217	2,540,000
Yuka Irie	74	72	71	217	2,540,000
Hiromi Mogi	73	71	73	217	2,540,000
Saiki Fujita	77	69	72	218	1,650,000
Nana Akahhori	68	75	75	218	1,650,000
Keiko Sasaki	73	74	72	219	1,148,000
Itsumi Okada	75	72	72	219	1,148,000
Michiko Hattori	69	77	73	219	1,148,000
Mikiyo Nishizuka	75	72	73	220	942,000
Junko Omote	70	76	74	220	942,000
Yuriko Ohtsuka	75	70	75	220	942,000
Akiko Fukushima	72	70	78	220	942,000
Sakura Yokomine	73	73	75	221	762,000
Shiho Ohyama	73	71	77	221	762,000
Kaori Nakamichi	73	77	72	222	609,600
Mika Saito	74	73	75	222	609,600
Asuka Tsujimura	72	74	76	222	609,600
Mineko Nasu	74	72	76	222	609,600
Momoko Ueda	74	70	78	222	609,600

We Love Kobe Suntory Ladies Open

Rokko Kokusai Golf Club, Kobe, Hyogo
Par 36-36–72; 6,457 yards

June 8-11
purse, ¥60,000,000

	SCORES				TOTAL	MONEY
Nikki Campbell	72	68	69	68	277	¥10,800,000
Akiko Fukushima	73	73	68	66	280	4,740,000
Ji-Hee Lee	71	71	67	71	280	4,740,000
Ayako Uehara	77	71	66	67	281	3,300,000
Shiho Ohyama	70	72	67	72	281	3,300,000
Sakura Yokomine	72	72	70	69	283	2,250,000
Michiko Hattori	70	73	70	70	283	2,250,000
Mie Nakata	72	70	72	70	284	1,800,000
*Chie Arimura	69	75	69	71	284	
*Maiko Wakabayashi	73	66	73	72	284	
Yuko Saitoh	73	68	75	69	285	1,350,000
Mihoko Takahashi	71	72	72	70	285	1,350,000
Atomi Shiota	72	75	71	68	286	1,068,000
Ai Ogawa	76	70	72	69	287	978,000
Yuriko Ohtsuka	73	70	72	72	287	978,000
Ok-Hee Ku	70	76	74	68	288	858,000
Kaori Nakamichi	75	72	70	71	288	858,000
Momoko Ueda	74	70	73	72	289	738,000
Chieko Amanuma	74	72	71	72	289	738,000
*Mi-Jung Hur	76	72	68	73	289	

Nichirei Ladies

Miho Golf Club, Ibaraki
Par 36-36–72; 6,403 yards

June 16-18
purse, ¥60,000,000

	SCORES			TOTAL	MONEY
Sakura Yokomine	65	72	73	210	¥10,800,000
Ji-Hee Lee	69	72	70	211	5,280,000
Kaori Nakamichi	69	74	69	212	4,200,000
Yui Kawahara	70	74	69	213	3,300,000
*Kumiko Kaneda	67	72	74	213	
Hyun-Ju Shin	67	73	73	213	3,300,000
Mie Nakata	75	70	69	214	1,950,000
Ya-Huei Lu	73	71	70	214	1,950,000
Ai Nishikawa	73	68	73	214	1,950,000
Chiharu Yamaguchi	68	72	74	214	1,950,000
Junko Omote	73	75	67	215	1,124,000
Aiko Yoshida	74	67	74	215	1,124,000
Chieko Amanuma	69	72	74	215	1,124,000
Yukari Baba	75	70	71	216	906,000
Yuriko Ohtsuka	75	70	71	216	906,000
Mikiyo Nishizuka	75	69	72	216	906,000
Momoko Ueda	72	70	74	216	906,000
Rui Kitada	73	74	70	217	756,000
Ikuyo Shiotani	75	73	70	218	584,571
Ok-Hee Ku	76	70	72	218	584,571
Miho Koga	73	73	72	218	584,571
Jae-Hee Bae	73	73	72	218	584,571
Mitsuko Kawasaki	72	72	74	218	584,571
Mi-Jeong Jeon	74	69	75	218	584,571
Yun-Jye Wei	74	69	75	218	584,571

Promise Ladies

Water Hills Golf Club, Kato, Hyogo
Par 36-36–72; 6,465 yards

June 23-25
purse, ¥80,000,000

	SCORES			TOTAL	MONEY
Saiki Fujita	67	68	71	206	¥14,400,000
Miho Koga	66	71	69	206	7,040,000
(Fujita defeated Koga on first playoff hole.)					
Yun-Joo Jeong	71	67	70	208	5,200,000
Shiho Ohyama	69	68	71	208	5,200,000
Mi-Jeong Jeon	70	71	68	209	3,600,000
Rui Kitada	70	69	70	209	3,600,000
Michiko Hattori	68	73	69	210	2,400,000
Yuriko Ohtsuka	70	70	70	210	2,400,000
Aiko Yoshida	70	69	71	210	2,400,000
Young-Me Lee	72	72	68	212	1,402,000
Sakura Yokomine	69	73	70	212	1,402,000
Yui Kawahara	72	70	70	212	1,402,000
Nobuko Kizawa	72	70	70	212	1,402,000
Chihiro Nakajima	72	71	70	213	1,136,000
Akane Iijima	71	69	73	213	1,136,000
Seiko Watanabe	71	72	71	214	896,000
Michie Ohba	74	69	71	214	896,000
Yun-Jye Wei	70	72	72	214	896,000

	SCORES			TOTAL	MONEY
Hiromi Mogi	71	71	72	214	896,000
Midori Yoneyama	72	74	69	215	648,000
Jae-Hee Bae	74	72	69	215	648,000
Momoko Ueda	76	68	71	215	648,000
Yoko Inoue	71	71	73	215	648,000
Mikiyo Nishizuka	70	71	74	215	648,000
Mizuho Ozawa	72	69	74	215	648,000
Izumi Narita	71	69	75	215	648,000

Belluna Ladies Cup

Obatago Golf Club, Kanra, Gunma
Par 36-36–72; 6,401 yards

June 30-July 2
purse, ¥60,000,000

	SCORES			TOTAL	MONEY
Sakura Yokomine	70	64	67	201	¥10,800,000
Yui Kawahara	69	69	68	206	4,740,000
Namika Omata	67	69	70	206	4,740,000
Hiromi Mogi	66	72	69	207	3,300,000
Akiko Fukushima	71	64	72	207	3,300,000
Chiharu Yamaguchi	70	72	66	208	1,800,000
Mayumi Shimomura	69	72	67	208	1,800,000
Mineko Nasu	71	70	67	208	1,800,000
Shiho Ohyama	69	71	68	208	1,800,000
Mi-Jeong Jeon	69	68	71	208	1,800,000
Kazu Yazaki	69	72	68	209	990,000
Aki Nakano	74	66	69	209	990,000
Midori Yoneyama	70	69	70	209	990,000
Miho Koga	71	68	70	209	990,000
Noriko Aso	70	66	73	209	990,000
Kuniko Maeda	69	69	72	210	810,000
*Mika Miyazato	72	66	72	210	
Yuko Saitoh	71	71	69	211	660,000
Saiki Fujita	72	69	70	211	660,000
Akane Iijima	69	71	71	211	660,000
Seiko Watanabe	70	74	67	211	660,000

Meiji Chocolate Cup

Sapporo Kokusai Country Club, Shimamatsu
Par 36-36–72; 6,518 yards

July 7-9
purse, ¥70,000,000

	SCORES			TOTAL	MONEY
Mi-Jeong Jeon	71	70	67	208	¥12,600,000
Hiromi Mogi	69	68	72	209	6,160,000
Ya-Huei Lu	73	66	72	211	4,900,000
Miho Koga	70	73	69	212	3,850,000
Hyun-Ju Shin	70	73	69	212	3,850,000
Hisako Takeda	72	72	70	214	2,275,000
Sakura Yokomine	72	70	72	214	2,275,000
Nikki Campbell	74	68	72	214	2,275,000
Chieko Amanuma	69	71	74	214	2,275,000
Aiko Yoshida	73	72	70	215	1,274,000
Yui Kawahara	69	73	73	215	1,274,000

	SCORES	TOTAL	MONEY
Yuriko Ohtsuka	70 72 73	215	1,274,000
Mie Nakata	73 66 76	215	1,274,000
Kaori Higo	70 75 71	216	952,000
Eriko Moriyama	70 74 72	216	952,000
Rui Kitada	71 72 73	216	952,000
Shiho Ohyama	74 69 73	216	952,000
Mikiyo Nishizuka	70 70 76	216	952,000
Mineko Nasu	73 73 71	217	669,200
Eun-Hye Lee	74 72 71	217	669,200
Ji-Hee Lee	72 73 72	217	669,200
Itsumi Okada	73 70 74	217	669,200
Kuniko Maeda	68 72 77	217	669,200

Stanley Ladies

Tomei Country Club, Shizuoka
Par 36-36–72; 6,509 yards

July 14-16
purse, ¥70,000,000

	SCORES	TOTAL	MONEY
Miho Koga	72 67 67	206	¥12,600,000
Shiho Ohyama	68 71 67	206	6,160,000
(Koga defeated Ohyama on seventh playoff hole.)			
Izumi Narita	72 71 66	209	4,200,000
Yun-Hee Ku	70 71 68	209	4,200,000
Rui Kitada	69 71 69	209	4,200,000
Mi-Jeong Jeon	70 72 68	210	2,450,000
*Maiko Wakabayashi	72 70 68	210	
Yun-Jye Wei	70 69 71	210	2,450,000
Shinobu Moromizato	71 67 72	210	2,450,000
Yui Kawahara	71 71 69	211	1,381,800
Ji-Yeon Han	74 68 69	211	1,381,800
Kuniko Maeda	70 71 70	211	1,381,800
Akane Iijima	73 67 71	211	1,381,800
Nikki Campbell	67 69 75	211	1,381,800
Yeo-Jin Kang	70 74 68	212	1,043,000
Mayumi Shimomura	71 72 69	212	1,043,000
Yuka Shiroto	69 73 70	212	1,043,000
Nahoko Hirao	70 73 70	213	833,000
Hiromi Mogi	71 71 71	213	833,000
Yuka Tonsho	69 70 74	213	833,000

Philanthropy Japan LPGA Players Championship

Itako Country Club, Ibaraki
Par 36-36–72; 6,504 yards

July 20-23
purse, ¥130,000,000

	SCORES	TOTAL	MONEY
Mi-Jeong Jeon	73 68 65 71	277	¥23,400,000
Nikki Campbell	69 73 68 69	279	11,440,000
Shiho Ohyama	71 75 68 67	281	8,450,000
Sakura Yokomine	70 69 71 71	281	8,450,000
Mie Nakata	70 75 70 67	282	6,500,000
Momoko Ueda	74 71 68 71	284	5,200,000
Akiko Fukushima	75 72 70 68	285	3,900,000

	SCORES				TOTAL	MONEY
Yui Kawahara	72	76	67	70	285	3,900,000
Eriko Moriyama	71	73	69	72	285	3,900,000
Kyoko Kadokawa	70	76	71	69	286	2,444,000
Hyun-Ju Shin	75	68	71	72	286	2,444,000
Yuko Shinsakaue	67	76	75	69	287	1,963,000
Miho Koga	72	74	70	71	287	1,963,000
Saiki Fujita	71	74	69	73	287	1,963,000
Shinobu Moromizato	72	72	69	74	287	1,963,000
Yun-Jye Wei	74	73	71	70	288	1,443,000
Kuniko Maeda	69	79	70	70	288	1,443,000
Junko Omote	74	74	70	70	288	1,443,000
Hiroko Yamaguchi	71	76	69	72	288	1,443,000
Hiromi Mogi	72	78	70	69	289	1,092,000
Mayumi Shimomura	74	73	72	70	289	1,092,000
Akane Iijima	70	75	71	73	289	1,092,000

Crystal Geyser Ladies

Keiyo Country Club, Chiba
Par 36-36–72; 6,384 yards

August 4-6
purse, ¥60,000,000

	SCORES			TOTAL	MONEY
Shiho Ohyama	67	69	69	205	¥10,800,000
Hsiu-Feng Tseng	67	72	67	206	5,280,000
Yayoi Arasaki	70	72	67	209	3,900,000
Momoko Ueda	69	69	71	209	3,900,000
Chihiro Nakajima	74	71	65	210	2,700,000
Hyun-Ju Shin	69	74	67	210	2,700,000
Yun-Jye Wei	69	72	70	211	1,470,000
Mi-Jeong Jeon	70	71	70	211	1,470,000
Eriko Moriyama	70	69	72	211	1,470,000
Yoko Inoue	70	69	72	211	1,470,000
Mie Nakata	68	70	73	211	1,470,000
Shinobu Moromizato	70	68	73	211	1,470,000
Tomoko Kusakabe	72	72	68	212	960,000
Michiko Mitsui	70	73	69	212	960,000
Jae-Hee Bae	68	72	72	212	960,000
Yui Kawahara	71	74	68	213	750,000
Tomomi Hirose	74	70	69	213	750,000
Yuko Saitoh	73	69	71	213	750,000
Hiromi Mogi	69	70	74	213	750,000
Julie Lu	70	75	69	214	558,000
Ayako Uehara	73	72	69	214	558,000
Jeong-Eun Lee	71	73	70	214	558,000
Michiko Hattori	74	70	70	214	558,000
Hiroko Yamaguchi	70	73	71	214	558,000
Mitsuko Kawasaki	73	70	71	214	558,000
Michie Ohba	72	69	73	214	558,000
Namika Omata	73	68	73	214	558,000

NEC Karuizawa 72

Karuizawa 72 Golf Club, Nagano
Par 36-36–72; 6,557 yards
(Final round reduced to 9 holes—rain.)

August 11-13
purse, ¥60,000,000

	SCORES			TOTAL	MONEY
Shiho Ohyama	68	69	33	170	¥10,800,000
Miho Koga	71	68	34	173	4,360,000
Hiromi Mogi	69	69	35	173	4,360,000
Michiko Hattori	69	69	35	173	4,360,000
Chiharu Yamaguchi	70	70	34	174	2,325,000
Yun-Hee Ku	71	69	34	174	2,325,000
Yun-Joo Jeong	70	69	35	174	2,325,000
Akiko Fukushima	66	71	37	174	2,325,000
Paula Creamer	71	68	36	175	1,350,000
Kaori Nakamichi	70	68	37	175	1,350,000
Rui Kitada	69	73	34	176	1,020,000
Saiki Fujita	74	68	34	176	1,020,000
Julie Lu	70	71	35	176	1,020,000
Yukari Baba	70	70	36	176	1,020,000
Itsumi Okada	70	68	38	176	1,020,000
Momoko Ueda	72	71	34	177	750,000
Mie Nakata	67	74	36	177	750,000
*Yuki Sakurai	70	70	37	177	
Tamie Durdin	68	71	38	177	750,000
Namika Omata	66	71	40	177	750,000

Shin Caterpillar Mitsubishi Ladies

Daihakone Country Club, Hakone, Kanagawa
Par 36-37–73; 6,648 yards

August 18-20
purse, ¥60,000,000

	SCORES			TOTAL	MONEY
Mikiyo Nishizuka	72	69	69	210	¥10,800,000
Chieko Amanuma	71	67	72	210	5,280,000
(Nishizuka defeated Amanuma on first playoff hole.)					
Junko Omote	74	68	69	211	3,900,000
Akiko Fukushima	68	71	72	211	3,900,000
Hyun-Ju Shin	72	72	68	212	2,500,000
Hiroko Yamaguchi	70	71	71	212	2,500,000
Yukari Baba	68	69	75	212	2,500,000
Ji-Yeon Han	74	70	69	213	1,800,000
Shiho Ohyama	76	71	67	214	1,203,000
Tomomi Hirose	71	73	70	214	1,203,000
Sakura Yokomine	72	71	71	214	1,203,000
Itsumi Okada	72	68	74	214	1,203,000
Hiromi Mogi	74	73	68	215	786,000
Young-Me Lee	73	72	70	215	786,000
Keiko Sasaki	73	71	71	215	786,000
Yuka Tonsho	73	69	73	215	786,000
Yasuko Satoh	66	75	74	215	786,000
Momoko Ueda	72	68	75	215	786,000
Mitsuko Kawasaki	70	69	76	215	786,000
Kaori Higo	72	75	69	216	510,000
Michiko Hattori	69	77	70	216	510,000
Kuniko Maeda	74	71	71	216	510,000

	SCORES			TOTAL	MONEY
Nahoko Hirao	74	70	72	216	510,000
Yuko Saitoh	72	71	73	216	510,000
Izumi Narita	74	69	73	216	510,000
Yeo-Jin Kang	74	69	73	216	510,000

Yonex Ladies

Yonex Country Club, Naoaoka, Niigata
Par 36-36–72; 6,329 yards

August 25-27
purse, ¥60,000,000

	SCORES			TOTAL	MONEY
Shiho Ohyama	68	70	70	208	¥10,800,000
Jeong-Eun Lee	71	69	71	211	5,280,000
Seiko Watanabe	72	72	69	213	4,200,000
Mie Nakata	72	71	71	214	3,600,000
Hisako Takeda	73	75	67	215	2,325,000
Mitsuko Kawasaki	72	73	70	215	2,325,000
*Mika Miyazato	70	74	71	215	
Noriko Aso	74	70	71	215	2,325,000
Yuko Saitoh	71	70	74	215	2,325,000
Kazu Yazaki	74	72	70	216	1,280,000
Tomoko Kusakabe	75	70	71	216	1,280,000
Akane Iijima	73	70	73	216	1,280,000
Keiko Sasaki	76	71	70	217	990,000
Momoko Ueda	73	73	71	217	990,000
Natsu Nagai	71	74	72	217	990,000
Hiroko Yamaguchi	72	69	76	217	990,000
Ji-Yeon Han	72	76	70	218	698,000
Kuniko Maeda	76	72	70	218	698,000
Yui Kawahara	73	75	70	218	698,000
Yun-Hee Ku	73	73	72	218	698,000
Miho Koga	71	74	73	218	698,000
Junko Omote	74	71	73	218	698,000

Golf 5 Ladies

Alpen Country Club, Bibai Course, Hokkaido
Par 36-36–72; 6,351 yards

September 1-3
purse, ¥60,000,000

	SCORES			TOTAL	MONEY
Yun-Jye Wei	68	72	69	209	¥10,800,000
Shiho Ohyama	70	71	68	209	4,400,000
Yuri Fudoh	67	72	70	209	4,400,000
Jae-Hee Bae	72	66	71	209	4,400,000

(Wei won on fifth playoff hole.)

	SCORES			TOTAL	MONEY
Ya-Huei Lu	72	73	66	211	3,000,000
Sakura Yokomine	72	68	72	212	2,400,000
Akane Iijima	73	68	72	213	2,100,000
Hiroko Yamaguchi	70	75	70	215	1,346,400
Kyoko Kadokawa	71	74	70	215	1,346,400
Mi-Jeong Jeon	75	70	70	215	1,346,400
Yuko Saitoh	73	69	73	215	1,346,400
Junko Omote	73	69	73	215	1,346,400
Yuko Shinsakaue	75	71	70	216	876,000

	SCORES	TOTAL	MONEY
Ayako Uehara	69 75 72	216	876,000
Nobuko Kizawa	76 67 73	216	876,000
Seiko Watanabe	69 73 74	216	876,000
Namika Omata	71 71 74	216	876,000
Momoko Ueda	72 70 74	216	876,000
Hyun-Ju Shin	75 72 70	217	603,600
Mayumi Shimomura	74 73 70	217	603,600
Ji-Hee Lee	73 74 70	217	603,600
Michie Ohba	73 71 73	217	603,600
Jeong-Eun Lee	72 70 75	217	603,600
Nikki Campbell	72 71 75	218	522,000

Japan LPGA Championship

Nidom Classic Course, Tomakomai, Hokkaido
Par 36-36–72; 6,526 yards
September 7-10
purse, ¥100,000,000

	SCORES	TOTAL	MONEY
Ai Miyazato	70 68 74 70	282	¥18,000,000
Hyun-Ju Shin	70 72 71 72	285	8,800,000
Yun-Jye Wei	74 70 74 71	289	7,000,000
Momoko Ueda	75 72 76 67	290	5,000,000
Julie Lu	78 68 72 72	290	5,000,000
Mi-Jeong Jeon	72 70 71 77	290	5,000,000
Shiho Ohyama	71 72 75 73	291	3,000,000
Kuniko Maeda	73 74 71 73	291	3,000,000
Shinobu Moromizato	76 72 70 73	291	3,000,000
Michiko Hattori	70 74 76 72	292	1,767,500
Akiko Fukushima	73 71 75 73	292	1,767,500
Kaori Higo	69 70 77 76	292	1,767,500
Yui Kawahara	72 68 73 79	292	1,767,500
Ji-Hee Lee	72 76 76 70	294	1,440,000
Yuri Fudoh	71 71 74 78	294	1,440,000
Mie Nakata	70 72 77 76	295	1,240,000
Yun-Joo Jeong	74 70 72 79	295	1,240,000
Tamie Durdin	73 71 79 73	296	1,090,000
Yuka Tonsho	75 71 77 74	297	916,666
Miho Koga	73 75 75 74	297	916,666
Yuka Irie	73 74 75 75	297	916,666

Munsingwear Ladies Tokai Classic

Ryosen Golf Club, Inabe, Mie
Par 36-36–72; 6,472 yards
September 15-17
purse, ¥60,000,000

	SCORES	TOTAL	MONEY
Akiko Fukushima	69 67 66	202	¥10,800,000
Ji-Hee Lee	70 66 68	204	5,280,000
Miho Koga	69 69 68	206	4,200,000
Momoko Ueda	70 71 67	208	3,000,000
Mie Nakata	68 70 70	208	3,000,000
Shinobu Moromizato	70 68 70	208	3,000,000
Mikiyo Nishizuka	74 67 68	209	1,546,800
Mi-Jeong Jeon	73 67 69	209	1,546,800
Yuko Saitoh	67 71 71	209	1,546,800

	SCORES			TOTAL	MONEY
Rui Kitada	69	69	71	209	1,546,800
Yun-Jye Wei	69	69	71	209	1,546,800
Hyun-Ju Shin	74	68	68	210	1,074,000
Shiho Ohyama	71	70	70	211	954,000
Kyoko Kadokawa	72	69	70	211	954,000
Yui Kawahara	66	71	74	211	954,000
Keiko Sasaki	71	72	69	212	744,000
Chie Arimura	69	73	70	212	744,000
Sakura Yokomine	73	69	70	212	744,000
Junko Omote	67	72	73	212	744,000
Aiko Yoshida	70	74	69	213	594,000

Miyagi TV Cup Dunlop Ladies Open

Rifu Golf Club, Miyagi
Par 36-36–72; 6,476 yards

September 22-24
purse, ¥60,000,000

	SCORES			TOTAL	MONEY
Ai Miyazato	70	73	71	214	¥10,800,000
Shiho Ohyama	71	74	72	217	5,280,000
Kasumi Fujii	73	73	73	219	4,200,000
Yukari Baba	75	72	73	220	2,775,000
Mie Nakata	78	69	73	220	2,775,000
Seiko Watanabe	71	74	75	220	2,775,000
Takayo Bandoh	69	72	79	220	2,775,000
Chie Arimura	72	76	73	221	1,396,500
Mi-Jeong Jeon	76	71	74	221	1,396,500
Yun-Hee Ku	76	70	75	221	1,396,500
Toshimi Kimura	77	66	78	221	1,396,500
Yuriko Ohtsuka	77	70	75	222	996,000
Sakura Yokomine	76	70	76	222	996,000
*Mika Miyazato	76	71	76	223	
Eriko Moriyama	75	76	72	223	846,000
Ayako Uehara	78	71	74	223	846,000
Natsuko Noro	77	70	76	223	846,000
Momoko Ueda	79	71	74	224	636,000
Yeo-Jin Kang	76	74	74	224	636,000
Kuniko Maeda	76	73	75	224	636,000
Hisako Takeda	72	73	79	224	636,000

Japan Women's Open

Ibaraki Country Club, Osaka
Par 36-36–72; 6,546 yards

September 28-October 1
purse, ¥140,000,000

	SCORES				TOTAL	MONEY
Jeong Jang	69	69	72	69	279	¥28,000,000
Hyun-Ju Shin	73	70	70	71	284	15,400,000
Ai Miyazato	71	75	67	72	285	10,780,000
Shiho Ohyama	70	74	74	70	288	6,440,000
Yun-Jye Wei	73	68	74	73	288	6,440,000
*Maiko Wakabayashi	75	74	70	71	290	
Nikki Campbell	74	70	72	75	291	4,900,000
Yui Kawahara	74	78	67	73	292	3,920,000

	SCORES	TOTAL	MONEY
Shinobu Moromizato	72 70 73 77	292	3,920,000
Mi-Jeong Jeon	70 73 73 77	292	3,080,000
Mie Nakata	73 76 72 73	294	2,555,000
Yun-Hee Ku	74 73 72 75	294	2,555,000
Ji-Hee Lee	77 73 72 73	295	1,886,500
Hiroko Yamaguchi	75 72 74 74	295	1,886,500
Yoko Inoue	75 73 73 74	295	1,886,500
Junko Omote	73 75 71 76	295	1,886,500
*Rikako Morita	74 72 71 78	295	
Mihoko Takahashi	71 73 77 75	296	1,540,000
Tamie Durdin	74 73 80 70	297	1,365,000
Jeong-Eun Lee	73 77 72 75	297	1,365,000
Yuri Fudoh	77 75 70 75	297	1,365,000
Ayako Uehara	75 73 72 77	297	1,365,000

Sankyo Ladies Open

Akagi Country Club, Niisato, Gunma
Par 36-36–72; 6,479 yards
(First round cancelled—rain.)

October 6-8
purse, ¥77,700,000

	SCORES	TOTAL	MONEY
Shinobu Moromizato	66 77	143	¥10,489,500
Mi-Jeong Jeon	72 72	144	5,128,200
Shiho Ohyama	69 76	145	4,079,250
Hyun-Ju Shin	75 71	146	3,496,500
Mitsuko Kawasaki	72 75	147	2,622,375
Chieko Amanuma	71 76	147	2,622,375
Rie Murata	75 73	148	1,172,387
Mie Nakata	74 74	148	1,172,387
Hiromi Mogi	74 74	148	1,172,387
Midori Yoneyama	74 74	148	1,172,387
Yasuko Sone	73 75	148	1,172,387
Nikki Campbell	73 75	148	1,172,387
Momoko Ueda	72 76	148	1,172,387
Michiko Hattori	72 76	148	1,172,387
Hsiu-Feng Tseng	72 76	148	1,172,387
Eun-Hye Lee	71 77	148	1,172,387
Yuko Saitoh	70 78	148	1,172,387
Kazu Yazaki	74 75	149	594,405
Kaori Suzuki	74 75	149	594,405
Hiroko Yamaguchi	74 75	149	594,405
Miho Koga	73 76	149	594,405
Rui Kitada	73 76	149	594,405
Yuka Shiroto	72 77	149	594,405

Fujitsu Ladies

Tokyu Seven Hundred Club, Chiba
Par 36-36–72; 6,583 yards

October 13-15
purse, ¥60,000,000

	SCORES	TOTAL	MONEY
Mi-Jeong Jeon	69 70 71	210	¥10,800,000
Ai Miyazato	73 68 70	211	5,280,000

	SCORES			TOTAL	MONEY
Shiho Ohyama	70	73	69	212	4,200,000
Yuko Shinsakaue	68	75	70	213	3,600,000
Ji-Hee Lee	73	69	72	214	2,700,000
Hiroko Yamaguchi	71	72	71	214	2,700,000
Sakura Yokomine	74	70	71	215	1,800,000
Jeong-Eun Lee	70	72	73	215	1,800,000
*Maiko Wakabayashi	71	75	69	215	
Kuniko Maeda	75	69	71	215	1,800,000
Yukari Baba	77	68	71	216	1,108,000
Fuki Kido	69	70	77	216	1,108,000
Yun-Jye Wei	72	70	74	216	1,108,000
Izumi Narita	72	74	71	217	882,000
Ayako Uehara	71	73	73	217	882,000
Yui Kawahara	73	71	73	217	882,000
Keiko Sasaki	72	71	74	217	882,000
Toshimi Kimura	77	69	72	218	621,600
Mitsuko Kawasaki	73	73	72	218	621,600
Kaori Higo	71	72	75	218	621,600
Yun-Hee Ku	73	72	73	218	621,600
Akiko Fukushima	72	70	76	218	621,600

Masters Golf Club Ladies

Masters Golf Club, Miki, Hyogo
Par 36-36–72; 6,510 yards

October 20-22
purse, ¥123,000,000

	SCORES			TOTAL	MONEY
Miho Koga	73	68	66	207	¥22,140,000
Akane Iijima	70	70	68	208	10,824,000
Akiko Fukushima	70	71	68	209	8,610,000
Paula Creamer	70	70	70	210	7,380,000
Shinobu Moromizato	68	75	68	211	5,535,000
Julie Lu	71	71	69	211	5,535,000
Mi-Jeong Jeon	72	70	70	212	3,997,500
Shiho Ohyama	67	74	71	212	3,997,500
Yuko Saitoh	70	72	71	213	3,075,000
Hyun-Ju Shin	72	71	71	214	2,460,000
Yun-Joo Jeong	71	75	69	215	2,029,500
Ji-Hee Lee	70	76	69	215	2,029,500
Yuka Irie	71	72	72	215	2,029,500
Morgan Pressel	72	71	72	215	2,029,500
Yun-Hee Ku	72	69	74	215	2,029,500
Yuka Shiroto	78	68	70	216	1,537,500
Yuka Tonsho	73	71	72	216	1,537,500
Yukari Baba	73	71	72	216	1,537,500
Sakura Yokomine	72	74	71	217	1,092,240
Yui Kawahara	74	72	71	217	1,092,240
Chieko Amanuma	70	75	72	217	1,092,240
Chie Arimura	72	74	71	217	1,092,240
Jeong-Eun Lee	72	73	72	217	1,092,240
Keiko Sasaki	71	75	71	217	1,092,240
Hiroko Yamaguchi	71	75	71	217	1,092,240
Yun-Jye Wei	72	72	73	217	1,092,240
Yasuko Satoh	73	71	73	217	1,092,240
Mikoko Takahashi	71	72	74	217	1,092,240

Hisako Higuchi IDC Otsuka Kagu Ladies

Musashigoaka Golf Club, Hanno, Saitama
Par 36-36–72; 6,561 yards

October 27-29
purse, ¥70,000,000

	SCORES			TOTAL	MONEY
Akiko Fukushima	67	70	70	207	¥12,600,000
Sakura Yokomine	66	70	71	207	6,160,000
(Fukushima defeated Yokomine on first playoff hole.)					
Mie Nakata	69	71	70	210	4,900,000
Mihoko Takahashi	74	70	67	211	3,500,000
Jae-Hee Bae	73	69	69	211	3,500,000
Ai Miyazato	71	66	74	211	3,500,000
Eun-Hye Lee	71	70	71	212	2,450,000
Yukari Baba	70	74	69	213	1,632,750
Momoko Ueda	74	70	69	213	1,632,750
Shiho Ohyama	71	71	71	213	1,632,750
Nobuko Kizawa	69	72	72	213	1,632,750
Natsu Nagai	70	74	70	214	1,106,000
Hyun-Ju Shin	74	69	71	214	1,106,000
Chie Arimura	71	70	73	214	1,106,000
Yuko Saitoh	70	70	74	214	1,106,000
Rui Kitada	74	73	69	216	896,000
Chieko Amanuma	73	72	71	216	896,000
Yui Kawahara	74	72	71	217	672,000
Yuka Tonsho	74	72	71	217	672,000
Young-Me Lee	73	72	72	217	672,000
Yuka Irie	71	73	73	217	672,000
Izumi Narita	69	74	74	217	672,000
Nikki Campbell	71	69	77	217	672,000

Mizuno Classic

Kinetetsu Kashikojima Country Club, Mie
Par 36-36–72; 6,506 yards

November 3-5
purse, ¥141,636,000

	SCORES			TOTAL	MONEY
Karrie Webb	69	67	66	202	¥21,245,400
Kaori Higo	73	68	65	206	12,904,573
Brittany Lang	68	69	70	207	6,800,298
Jeong-Eun Lee	72	65	70	207	6,800,298
Annika Sorenstam	71	66	70	207	6,800,298
Aree Song	69	68	70	207	6,800,298
Shinobu Moromizato	70	68	70	208	3,744,501
Ai Miyazato	69	68	71	208	3,744,501
Yun-Jye Wei	71	68	70	209	2,884,889
Rachel Hetherington	65	72	72	209	2,884,889
Momoko Ueda	71	64	74	209	2,884,889
Julieta Granada	68	72	70	210	2,190,164
Karine Icher	69	71	70	210	2,190,164
Young Kim	69	70	71	210	2,190,164
Mitsuko Kawasaki	68	70	72	210	2,190,164
Nancy Scranton	69	69	72	210	2,190,164
Ji-Hee Lee	76	67	68	211	1,603,791
Christina Kim	72	69	70	211	1,603,791
Silvia Cavalleri	72	69	70	211	1,603,791
Shiho Ohyama	72	73	66	211	1,603,791

	SCORES	TOTAL	MONEY
Sun Young Yoo	69 71 71	211	1,603,791
Diana D'Alessio	70 69 72	211	1,603,791
Akiko Fukushima	69 70 72	211	1,603,791
Hyun-Ju Shin	71 68 72	211	1,603,791
Jeong Jang	71 71 70	212	1,204,142
Michiko Hattori	71 71 70	212	1,204,142
Suzann Pettersen	69 72 71	212	1,204,142
Young-A Yang	72 69 71	212	1,204,142
Nicole Castrale	70 70 72	212	1,204,142
Yui Kawahara	70 69 73	212	1,204,142
Maria Hjorth	70 68 74	212	1,204,142

Itoen Ladies

Great Island Club, Chonan, Chiba
Par 36-36–72; 6,581 yards

November 10-12
purse, ¥70,000,000

	SCORES	TOTAL	MONEY
Hyun-Ju Shin	70 66 71	207	¥12,600,000
Shiho Ohyama	67 70 71	208	5,530,000
Yuka Shiroto	66 69 73	208	5,530,000
Yuri Fudoh	70 72 70	212	3,850,000
Tamie Durdin	69 70 73	212	3,850,000
Laura Davies	65 78 70	213	2,450,000
Akane Iijima	69 72 72	213	2,450,000
Yukari Baba	69 70 74	213	2,450,000
Momoko Ueda	71 74 69	214	1,337,000
Michie Ohba	71 73 70	214	1,337,000
Hiromi Takesue	71 73 70	214	1,337,000
Kuniko Maeda	73 69 72	214	1,337,000
Tomoko Kusakabe	69 70 75	214	1,337,000
Yun-Jye Wei	69 70 75	214	1,337,000
Hiroko Yamaguchi	74 71 70	215	973,000
Michiko Hattori	71 71 73	215	973,000
Mi-Jeong Jeon	68 72 75	215	973,000
Ji-Hee Lee	72 73 71	216	833,000
*Asako Fujimoto	76 70 71	217	
Yukiko Sakanoshita	73 73 71	217	681,333
Yeo-Jin Kang	73 73 71	217	681,333
Rui Kitada	74 72 71	217	681,333
Kasumi Fujii	74 72 71	217	681,333
Kaori Higo	71 73 73	217	681,333
Ikuyo Shiotani	71 69 77	217	681,333

Daioseishi Elleair Ladies Open

Elleair Golf Club, Matsuyama, Ehime
Par 36-36–72; 6,442 yards

November 17-19
purse, ¥100,000,000

	SCORES	TOTAL	MONEY
Yun-Jye Wei	71 66 70	207	¥18,000,000
Mi-Jeong Jeon	70 69 69	208	8,000,000
Sakura Yokomine	69 69 70	208	8,000,000
Ji-Hee Lee	69 71 70	210	5,500,000

	SCORES			TOTAL	MONEY
Chie Arimura	70	68	72	210	5,500,000
Keiko Sasaki	71	69	71	211	4,200,000
Ayako Uehara	69	73	70	212	3,000,000
Miho Koga	73	68	71	212	3,000,000
Rui Kitada	72	68	72	212	3,000,000
Shiho Ohyama	70	74	69	213	1,960,000
Hyun-Ju Shin	74	70	69	213	1,960,000
*Asako Fujimoto	72	65	76	213	
Yukari Baba	71	72	71	214	1,720,000
Shinobu Moromizato	71	72	71	214	1,720,000
Michie Ohba	73	69	72	214	1,720,000
Namika Omata	73	72	70	215	1,370,000
Yui Kawahara	72	71	72	215	1,370,000
Tamie Durdin	74	69	72	215	1,370,000
Yuka Shiroto	77	70	68	215	1,370,000
Ji-Yeon Han	71	73	72	216	1,016,000
Nobuko Kizawa	72	73	71	216	1,016,000
Nikki Campbell	75	69	72	216	1,016,000
Kaori Higo	76	70	70	216	1,016,000
*Maiko Wakabayashi	72	70	74	216	
Kasumi Fujii	71	67	78	216	1,016,000

Japan LPGA Tour Championship

Miyazaki Country Club, Miyazaki, Kyodo
Par 36-36–72; 6,445 yards

November 23-26
purse, ¥60,000,000

	SCORES				TOTAL	MONEY
Sakura Yokomine	73	67	70	67	277	¥15,000,000
Jeong-Eun Lee	76	69	71	68	284	6,500,000
Shinobu Moromizato	69	72	69	74	284	6,500,000
Ai Miyazato	72	74	71	67	284	6,500,000
Ji-Hee Lee	74	69	73	71	287	3,548,000
Momoko Ueda	75	71	72	69	287	3,548,000
Shiho Ohyama	73	71	69	74	287	3,548,000
Akane Iijima	73	73	69	73	288	2,352,000
Yuri Fudoh	75	72	72	70	289	1,764,000
Mi-Jeong Jeon	74	74	68	75	291	1,164,000
Hiromi Mogi	75	72	71	75	293	1,044,000
Kaori Higo	73	75	73	73	294	804,000
Yun-Jye Wei	74	74	73	73	294	804,000
Hyun-Ju Shin	73	73	74	74	294	804,000
Nikki Campbell	73	76	76	71	296	534,000
Chieko Amanuma	76	75	71	74	296	534,000
Mikiyo Nishizuka	74	77	73	73	297	417,000
Akiko Fukushima	82	69	76	70	297	417,000
Mie Nakata	77	72	80	72	301	336,000
Saiki Fujita	76	75	76	75	302	297,000
Miho Koga	80	76	74	72	302	297,000
Michiko Hattori	78	76	77	72	303	288,000

The Kyoraku Cup

Fukuoka Century Golf Club, Fukuoka
Par 36-36–72; 6,405 yards

December 2-3
purse, ¥61,500,000

FIRST ROUND

Shiho Ohyama (Japan) defeated Na Yeon Choi, 75-81.
Sun Hwa Lee (Korea) defeated Miho Koga, 73-74.
Ji-Hee Lee (Korea) defeated Akiko Fukushima, 76-79.
Hee-Won Han (Korea) defeated Yui Kawahara, 75-78.
Hiromi Mogi (Japan) defeated Se Ri Pak, 73-79.
Sakura Yokomine (Japan) defeated Mi-Jeong Jeon, 74-75.
Meena Lee (Korea) defeated Mikiyo Nishizuka, 74-78.
Hyun-Ju Shin (Korea) defeated Michiko Hattori, 75-77.
Jeong Jang (Korea) defeated Momoko Ueda, 72-77.
Ji-Yai Shin (Korea) defeated Mie Nakata, 74-76.
Akane Iijima (Japan) defeated Hee Young Park, 72-73.
Jee Young Lee (Korea) defeated Shinobu Moromizato, 71-74.

POINTS: Korea 16, Japan 8

SECOND ROUND

Jeong Jang (Korea) tied with Miho Koga, 72-72.
Akiko Fukushima (Japan) defeated Sun Hwa Lee, 74-78.
Hyun-Ju Shin (Korea) defeated Yui Kawahara, 72-73.
Shiho Ohyama (Japan) defeated Hee-Won Han, 71-74.
Momoko Ueda (Japan) defeated Ji-Hee Lee, 72-75.
Sakura Yokomine (Japan) defeated Mi Hyun Kim, 73-76.
Se Ri Pak (Korea) defeated Mie Nakata, 71-77.
Meena Lee (Korea) defeated Mikiyo Nishizuka, 71-73.
Shinobu Moromizato (Japan) defeated Ji-Yai Shin, 71-73.
Jee Young Lee (Korea) defeated Hiromi Mogi, 72-74.
Hee Young Park (Korea) defeated Michiko Hattori, 70-76.
Mi-Jeong Jeon (Korea) defeated Akane Iijima, 67-79.

TOTAL POINTS: Korea 29, Japan 19

(Each member of the Korean team received ¥3,250,000; each member of the Japanese team received ¥1,625,000.)

Korea LPGA Tour

Phoenix Park Classic

Phoenix Park, Gangwon
Par 36-36–72; 6,264 yards

April 26-28
purse, KRW200,000,000

	SCORES			TOTAL	MONEY
Hee Young Park	69	67	71	207	KRW36,000,000
Hae Jung Kim	69	71	69	209	20,000,000
Jeong-Eun Lee	70	72	68	210	12,000,000
Ji-Yai Shin	69	70	71	210	12,000,000
Hyun Hee Moon	69	69	74	212	8,000,000
Na Yeon Choi	71	75	67	213	7,000,000
Min Sun Lee	71	74	70	215	5,133,333
Hee Sun Hong	72	72	71	215	5,133,333
Bo Kyung Kim	72	70	73	215	5,133,333
Hye Jin Jung	74	72	70	216	3,833,333
Hey Kyung Son	73	72	71	216	3,833,333
You Jin Ji	71	72	73	216	3,833,333
Ran Hong	72	72	73	217	3,280,000
Sun Ju Ahn	69	72	76	217	3,280,000
Yu Ri Na Kim	73	76	69	218	2,560,000
Ji Won Yoon	76	71	71	218	2,560,000
Hyun Ryung Kim	71	75	72	218	2,560,000
Seong Ja Park	74	70	74	218	2,560,000
Ga Ram Son	71	72	75	218	2,560,000
Bo Mi Kim	79	72	68	219	1,870,000
Ye Sun Seo	74	76	69	219	1,870,000
Ji Hyun Lee	72	73	74	219	1,870,000
Su-Jung Yoon	70	73	76	219	1,870,000

KB Star Tour in Seoul

88 Country Club, West Course, Seoul, Gyeonggi
Par 36-36–72; 6,182 yards

May 11-13
purse, KRW200,000,000

	SCORES			TOTAL	MONEY
Sun Ju Ahn	65	66	69	200	KRW36,000,000
Na Yeon Choi	65	67	69	201	20,000,000
Ji-Yai Shin	68	66	68	202	14,000,000
Hee Young Park	68	66	72	206	10,000,000
Jeong-Eun Lee	70	70	68	208	8,000,000
Chang Kyung Woo	71	69	70	210	6,000,000
Sunny Lee	69	71	70	210	6,000,000
Jenny Lee	68	70	72	210	6,000,000
Sang Hee Kim	73	70	68	211	4,250,000
Hae Jung Kim	69	73	69	211	4,250,000
Eun Hee Ji	73	72	67	212	3,593,333
Eun-A Lim	71	72	69	212	3,593,333
Hey Kyung Son	71	71	70	212	3,593,333
Eun Jung Shin	71	73	69	213	2,477,500

	SCORES			TOTAL	MONEY
So Young Kim	71	73	69	213	2,477,500
Hee Kyung Seo	71	72	70	213	2,477,500
Min Sun Lee	71	72	70	213	2,477,500
Bo Mi Suh	68	74	71	213	2,477,500
Jong Jin Hong	72	69	72	213	2,477,500
Bo-Bae Song	68	72	73	213	2,477,500
So Hee Kim	71	67	75	213	2,477,500

Taeyoung Cup Korea Women's Open

Taeyoung Country Club, Gyeonggi
Par 36-36–72; 6,395 yards

May 19-21
purse, KRW400,000,000

	SCORES			TOTAL	MONEY
Ji-Yai Shin	67	73	65	205	KRW100,000,000
Cristie Kerr	71	70	66	207	47,000,000
Hyun Hee Moon	70	73	68	211	27,000,000
Na Yeon Choi	68	73	73	214	16,000,000
Hye Jung Choi	74	71	70	215	12,000,000
Sun Ju Ahn	73	73	71	217	9,750,000
Hae Jung Kim	76	70	71	217	9,750,000
Hee Young Park	70	75	72	217	9,750,000
Min Ji Son	75	70	72	217	9,750,000
Eun Hee Ji	73	73	72	218	8,000,000
Chae Eun Song	74	73	72	219	6,560,000
Jenny Lee	77	70	72	219	6,560,000
Su-Jung Yoon	73	74	72	219	6,560,000
Jee Young Lee	73	73	73	219	6,560,000
Bo-Bae Song	70	74	75	219	6,560,000
You Jin Ji	72	73	75	220	5,150,000
So Young Park	72	73	75	220	5,150,000
Jeong-Eun Lee	71	77	73	221	4,600,000
Eun-A Lim	76	70	75	221	4,600,000
Ga Na Lee	73	72	76	221	4,600,000

Lake Side Ladies Open

Lake Side Country Club, Gyeonggi
Par 36-36–72; 6,409 yards

May 24-26
purse, KRW220,000,000

	SCORES			TOTAL	MONEY
Bo-Bae Song	71	67	70	208	KRW39,600,000
Hee Young Park	73	70	66	209	14,300,000
Sun Ju Ahn	70	71	68	209	14,300,000
Ji-Yai Shin	72	69	68	209	14,300,000
Kyung Hee Cho	71	69	69	209	14,300,000
Hyun Hee Moon	69	72	69	210	7,150,000
Hyun-Ju Shin	70	69	71	210	7,150,000
Woo Ri Choi	68	66	78	212	5,500,000
Eun Hee Ji	72	72	69	213	4,675,000
Sang Hee Kim	70	72	71	213	4,675,000
Eun-A Lim	76	71	67	214	3,960,000
Jenny Lee	71	71	72	214	3,960,000
Mi-Hyun Cho	72	69	73	214	3,960,000

	SCORES			TOTAL	MONEY
Jong Jin Hong	73	71	71	215	3,520,000
Mi Ye Na	77	71	68	216	2,860,000
Bo Mi Kim	72	75	69	216	2,860,000
Eun Jung Shin	74	73	69	216	2,860,000
Hae Jung Kim	74	71	71	216	2,860,000
Hey Kyung Son	71	71	74	216	2,860,000
Hui Jeong Kim	73	74	70	217	2,090,000
Ji Na Lim	75	70	72	217	2,090,000
Chang Kyung Woo	75	70	72	217	2,090,000
Hae Young Jeon	75	70	72	217	2,090,000
Bo Kyung Kang	70	73	74	217	2,090,000
So Hee Kim	70	72	75	217	2,090,000

KB Star Tour in Busan

Busan Asiad, South Gyeongsang
Par 36-36–72; 6,210 yards

July 20-22
purse, KRW200,000,000

	SCORES			TOTAL	MONEY
Soo Young Moon	68	68	70	206	KRW36,000,000
Na Yeon Choi	67	67	74	208	20,000,000
Ran Hong	73	67	69	209	12,000,000
Hee Kyung Seo	66	71	72	209	12,000,000
Eun Hee Ji	69	72	69	210	7,500,000
Jenny Lee	68	72	70	210	7,500,000
Hyun Hee Moon	70	71	70	211	6,000,000
So Ra Kim	69	68	75	212	5,000,000
Seul A Yoon	76	71	66	213	3,856,000
Ji Yeon Lee	74	70	69	213	3,856,000
Yeon Mi Kim	74	70	69	213	3,856,000
Ji-Yai Shin	73	69	71	213	3,856,000
Young Ran Jo	71	70	72	213	3,856,000
Bo-Bae Song	73	74	67	214	2,768,000
Yoon Jung Won	74	70	70	214	2,768,000
Hye Jin Jung	71	72	71	214	2,768,000
Hee Young Park	71	72	71	214	2,768,000
Bo Mi Kim	71	71	72	214	2,768,000
Ye Sun Seo	73	72	70	215	1,993,333
Mi-Hyun Cho	69	74	72	215	1,993,333
Sang Hee Kim	72	71	72	215	1,993,333

Lake Hills Classic

Lake Hills Golf & Resorts, Gyeonggi
Par 36-36–72; 6,392 yards

August 25-27
purse, KRW400,000,000

	SCORES			TOTAL	MONEY
Hee Young Park	72	72	68	212	KRW100,000,000
Hyun Hee Moon	72	73	69	214	26,000,000
Hee-Won Han	72	71	71	214	26,000,000
Ji Yeon Woo	71	69	74	214	26,000,000
Jin Joo Hong	78	72	67	217	15,000,000
Sun Ju Ahn	73	72	72	217	15,000,000
Bo-Bae Song	73	71	74	218	10,000,000

	SCORES	TOTAL	MONEY
Da Ye Na	74 69 75	218	10,000,000
Min Ji Son	71 72 75	218	10,000,000
Meena Lee	74 75 70	219	5,144,000
Chang Kyung Woo	75 73 71	219	5,144,000
Jenny Lee	72 74 73	219	5,144,000
Ji Na Lim	75 70 74	219	5,144,000
Na Yeon Choi	75 69 75	219	5,144,000
Ji Hyun Lee	72 77 71	220	4,150,000
Hey Kyung Son	74 75 71	220	4,150,000
Yoon Jung Won	77 71 72	220	4,150,000
Bo Kyung Kim	73 74 73	220	4,150,000
Young Ran Jo	74 74 73	221	3,780,000
Ji-Yai Shin	77 70 74	221	3,780,000

PAVV Invitational

Phoenix Park, Gangwon
Par 36-36–72; 6,233 yards

September 6-8
purse, KRW300,000,000

	SCORES	TOTAL	MONEY
Ji-Yai Shin	68 66 70	204	KRW60,000,000
Hye Jin Jung	69 67 69	205	27,000,000
Hey Kyung Son	71 71 66	208	16,500,000
Bo Kyung Kim	69 70 69	208	16,500,000
Brittany Lincicome	71 69 69	209	11,250,000
Su-Jung Yoon	70 67 72	209	11,250,000
Soon Hee Kim	71 73 66	210	8,250,000
Jeong Jang	72 68 70	210	8,250,000
Min Gee Song	72 71 68	211	6,150,000
Kyung Sook Kim	72 69 70	211	6,150,000
Jenny Lee	71 68 72	211	6,150,000
Ji Na Lim	76 67 69	212	5,235,000
Young Ae Ham	66 72 74	212	5,235,000
So Hee Kim	71 74 68	213	3,840,000
Ran Hong	71 72 70	213	3,840,000
Haen Nim Park	70 72 71	213	3,840,000
You Jin Ji	72 70 71	213	3,840,000
Hae Jung Kim	71 71 71	213	3,840,000
Ji Hyun Lee	73 67 73	213	3,840,000
Eun Jung Shin	66 70 77	213	3,840,000

SK EnClean Solux Invitational

New Seoul, Gyeonggi
Par 36-36–72; 6,502 yards

September 15-17
purse, KRW400,000,000

	SCORES	TOTAL	MONEY
Jin Joo Hong	66 67 69	202	KRW100,000,000
Eun Jung Kong	70 71 68	209	26,000,000
Eun-A Lim	70 70 69	209	26,000,000
Ji-Yai Shin	70 69 70	209	26,000,000
Na Yeon Choi	67 72 71	210	16,000,000
So Hee Kim	69 74 68	211	10,000,000
Eun Jin Kim	70 71 70	211	10,000,000

	SCORES			TOTAL	MONEY
Hae Jung Kim	70	70	71	211	10,000,000
So Young Kim	71	68	72	211	10,000,000
Eun Hee Ji	70	69	72	211	10,000,000
Ran Hong	73	68	71	212	4,930,000
Grace Park	69	72	71	212	4,930,000
Ji Na Lim	70	70	72	212	4,930,000
Mi Hyun Kim	69	70	73	212	4,930,000
Hee Young Park	77	68	68	213	4,150,000
Soo Yun Kang	67	77	69	213	4,150,000
Yu-Jin Choi	72	70	71	213	4,150,000
Bo Mi Suh	71	71	71	213	4,150,000
Kyeong Eun Bae	74	69	71	214	3,733,333
Bo Kyung Kim	72	70	72	214	3,733,333
Sun Ju Ahn	71	70	73	214	3,733,333

Shinsegye Cup KLPGA Championship

Jayu Park, Incheon City, Gyeonggi
Par 36-36–72; 6,443 yards

September 20-22
purse, KRW300,000,000

	SCORES			TOTAL	MONEY
Jee Young Lee	68	66	66	200	KRW60,000,000
Sun Ju Ahn	67	68	67	202	22,500,000
Ran Hong	64	67	71	202	22,500,000
Hee Young Park	66	72	65	203	13,500,000
Na Yeon Choi	71	66	66	203	13,500,000
Bo-Bae Song	67	68	69	204	9,750,000
Hae Jung Kim	67	66	71	204	9,750,000
Ji-Yai Shin	72	66	67	205	7,500,000
Min Ji Son	69	69	68	206	6,375,000
Eun-A Lim	69	66	71	206	6,375,000
Young Ae Ham	72	67	68	207	5,700,000
Bo Mi Suh	70	71	67	208	4,615,000
Eun Hee Ji	69	71	68	208	4,615,000
Jeong-Eun Lee	69	67	72	208	4,615,000
Ha Na Park	68	68	72	208	4,615,000
Young Kim	67	69	72	208	4,615,000
Yoon Jung Won	66	69	73	208	4,615,000
Ga Na Lee	74	70	65	209	3,220,000
Sang Hee Kim	70	70	69	209	3,220,000
Young Ran Jo	69	70	70	209	3,220,000

KB Star Tour in Hampyeong

Dynasty Country Club, Hampyeong
Par 36-36–72; 6,297 yards

September 28-30
purse, KRW200,000,000

	SCORES			TOTAL	MONEY
Na Yeon Choi	68	67	69	204	KRW36,000,000
Ji-Yai Shin	68	70	69	207	20,000,000
Ji Yeon Woo	68	71	71	210	12,000,000
Bo Ri Lee	68	71	71	210	12,000,000
Bo-Bae Song	70	67	74	211	8,000,000
Ji Na Lim	72	70	70	212	5,300,000

	SCORES			TOTAL	MONEY
Hae Young Jeon	73	69	70	212	5,300,000
Hee Young Park	70	71	71	212	5,300,000
Su A Kim	72	68	72	212	5,300,000
Ran Hong	70	70	72	212	5,300,000
Min Gee Song	71	71	71	213	3,700,000
Woo Ri Choi	70	70	73	213	3,700,000
Bo Mi Suh	74	70	70	214	3,075,000
Jong Jin Hong	71	72	71	214	3,075,000
Ga Na Lee	68	73	73	214	3,075,000
Ha Na Park	68	70	76	214	3,075,000
Sun Ju Ahn	70	71	74	215	2,560,000
So Hee Kim	73	71	72	216	2,036,000
Seon Ah Kim	69	73	74	216	2,036,000
Jin Joo Hong	72	70	74	216	2,036,000
Jung Ah Kim	73	68	75	216	2,036,000
Chae Young Yoon	71	69	76	216	2,036,000

Meritz Solmoro Classic

Solmoro Country Club
Par 36-35–71; 6,095 yards

October 13-15
purse, KRW300,000,000

	SCORES			TOTAL	MONEY
Ji Yeon Lee	71	70	66	207	KRW60,000,000
Ji-Yai Shin	70	74	66	210	20,000,000
Jong Jin Hong	71	71	68	210	20,000,000
So Hee Kim	68	71	71	210	20,000,000
Ye Sun Seo	72	69	71	212	12,000,000
Hyun Hee Moon	73	74	67	214	7,264,286
Bo-Bae Song	72	74	68	214	7,264,286
Ga Na Lee	70	76	68	214	7,264,286
Chang Kyung Woo	73	71	70	214	7,264,286
Hui Jeong Kim	73	71	70	214	7,264,286
Min Jee Han	72	71	71	214	7,264,286
Sun Ju Ahn	71	71	72	214	7,264,286
Na Yeon Choi	72	75	68	215	4,770,000
Hyun-Ju Shin	71	71	73	215	4,770,000
Ju Mi Kim	75	66	74	215	4,770,000
Ji Yeon Woo	73	74	69	216	3,840,000
Jee Hyang Park	72	73	71	216	3,840,000
Yu Mi Yun	69	73	74	216	3,840,000
Hyun-Ji Kim	78	73	66	217	3,210,000
Hee Kyung Seo	72	74	72	218	2,880,000
You Jin Ji	70	75	73	218	2,880,000

Hite Cup Ladies Championship

Blue Heron Country Club, Gyeonggi
Par 36-36–72; 6,406 yards

October 20-22
purse, KRW400,000,000

	SCORES			TOTAL	MONEY
Hyun Hee Moon	69	69	72	210	KRW100,000,000
Ji-Yai Shin	69	69	72	210	34,000,000

(Moon defeated Shin in playoff.)

	SCORES			TOTAL	MONEY
Ju Mi Kim	74	70	67	211	24,000,000
Jeong-Eun Lee	70	71	71	212	20,000,000
Na Yeon Choi	74	71	70	215	16,000,000
Eun Hee Ji	71	72	73	216	13,000,000
Jin Joo Hong	71	70	75	216	13,000,000
Aram Cho	70	73	74	217	9,000,000
So Hee Kim	72	69	76	217	9,000,000
Soo Yun Kang	75	70	73	218	5,466,667
Hey Kyung Son	71	73	74	218	5,466,667
Ji Na Lim	75	69	74	218	5,466,667
Kyung Hee Cho	71	74	74	219	4,760,000
Sun Hwa Lee	71	77	72	220	4,373,333
Young Ran Jo	75	72	73	220	4,373,333
Bo Kyung Kim	74	69	77	220	4,373,333
Min Jee Han	74	75	72	221	3,880,000
Hyun-Ji Kim	71	78	72	221	3,880,000
Yong Nam Yeon	72	75	74	221	3,880,000
Eun-A Lim	73	71	77	221	3,880,000

Kolon-Hana Bank Championship

Mauna Ocean Country Club, Gyeonggi
Par 36-36–72; 6,381 yards

October 27-29
purse, US$1,350,000

	SCORES			TOTAL	MONEY
Jin Joo Hong	68	67	70	205	US$202,500
Jeong Jang	68	72	68	208	125,817
Se Ri Pak	74	69	67	210	91,272
Ji-Yai Shin	72	71	68	211	63,719
Karine Icher	68	71	72	211	63,719
Paula Creamer	68	72	72	212	42,708
Jee Young Lee	67	73	72	212	42,708
*Mi Jung Hur	69	70	73	212	
Gloria Park	70	72	71	213	32,376
Suzann Pettersen	69	71	73	213	32,376
Soo-Yun Kang	72	74	68	214	26,865
Na Yeon Choi	71	72	71	214	26,865
Maria Hjorth	71	76	68	215	22,640
Hee-Won Han	68	73	74	215	22,640
Joo Mi Kim	66	73	76	215	22,640
Lindsey Wright	68	79	69	216	17,680
Young Kim	72	73	71	216	17,680
Hee Kyung Seo	75	69	72	216	17,680
Mi Hyun Kim	70	74	72	216	17,680
Christina Kim	71	72	73	216	17,680
Candie Kung	73	69	74	216	17,680
Shi Hyun Ahn	77	71	69	217	14,741
Nicole Castrale	72	74	71	217	14,741
Seon-Hwa Lee	72	72	73	217	14,741
Reilley Rankin	72	77	69	218	12,202
Eun Hee Ji	73	73	72	218	12,202
Julieta Granada	74	71	73	218	12,202
Carin Koch	73	71	74	218	12,202
Hee Young Park	73	71	74	218	12,202
Brittany Lang	70	73	75	218	12,202
Patricia Meunier-Lebouc	71	71	76	218	12,202

KB Star Tour in Gyeonggi

Seven Hills Country Club, Gyeonggi
Par 36-36–72; 6,241 yards

November 9-12
purse, KRW500,000,000

	SCORES				TOTAL	MONEY
Eun-A Lim	67	71	73	70	281	KRW125,000,000
Bo Mi Kim	69	73	72	69	283	42,500,000
Soo Young Moon	72	71	72	69	284	30,000,000
Na Yeon Choi	72	71	73	69	285	20,833,333
Ji Na Lim	69	73	72	71	285	20,833,333
Ji-Yai Shin	74	71	69	71	285	20,833,333
Young Ran Jo	70	73	74	69	286	13,750,000
Sun Ju Ahn	70	73	72	71	286	13,750,000
Hee Young Park	73	71	73	70	287	8,750,000
Ran Hong	71	70	76	70	287	8,750,000
Bo Kyung Kim	69	74	74	72	289	6,500,000
Kyung Hee Cho	72	73	72	72	289	6,500,000
Bo-Bae Song	74	72	74	70	290	6,000,000
Eun Hee Ji	71	74	77	69	291	5,214,286
So Young Park	76	71	72	72	291	5,214,286
Oh Soon Lee	72	75	72	72	291	5,214,286
Bo Mi Suh	71	76	71	73	291	5,214,286
Hae Jung Kim	70	74	74	73	291	5,214,286
Woo Ri Choi	70	72	75	74	291	5,214,286
Young-A Yang	71	74	72	74	291	5,214,286

Orient China Ladies Open

Orient Golf & Country Club, Xiamen, China
Par 36-36–72; 6,489 yards

November 16-19
purse, KRW200,000,000

	SCORES				TOTAL	MONEY
Ji-Yai Shin	72	66	64	69	271	KRW28,035,000
Na Yeon Choi	75	68	67	69	279	18,690,000
Sun Ju Ahn	75	69	71	67	282	9,812,250
Bo Mi Suh	72	68	73	69	282	9,812,250
Hee Young Park	74	69	72	69	284	6,307,875
Young Ran Jo	67	72	72	73	284	6,307,875
Ga Na Lee	67	73	73	72	285	4,672,500
Russamee Gulyanamitt	70	76	69	71	286	3,738,000
Wang Chun	74	70	74	69	287	3,224,025
Eun Jung Shin	73	69	69	76	287	3,224,025
Bo Kyung Kim	70	68	75	75	288	2,943,675
Young Ae Ham	69	70	70	79	288	2,943,675
Mi-Hyun Cho	75	71	74	69	289	2,710,050
Porani Chutichai	70	71	75	73	289	2,710,050
Julie Lu	69	71	73	76	289	2,710,050
Min Jee Han	71	73	72	74	290	2,560,530
Zhang Na	74	69	72	75	290	2,560,530
Hee Kyung Seo	71	73	76	71	291	2,448,390
Hye Jin Jung	72	73	74	72	291	2,448,390
Bo Mi Kim	72	74	73	72	291	2,448,390
Chen Guanbei	71	71	74	75	291	2,448,390

ADT CAPS Championship

Sky Hill Country Club, Jeju
Par 36-36–72; 6,303 yards

November 24-26
purse, KRW300,000,000

	SCORES			TOTAL	MONEY
Ji Won Yoon	71	68	74	213	KRW60,000,000
Jin Joo Hong	71	69	74	214	27,000,000
Hee Kyung Seo	73	72	70	215	15,000,000
Min Jee Han	73	71	71	215	15,000,000
Ju Mi Kim	75	69	71	215	15,000,000
Hyun Ryung Kim	75	71	70	216	9,750,000
Ji-Yai Shin	74	70	72	216	9,750,000
Young Ran Jo	74	77	67	218	7,050,000
Soo Young Moon	72	71	75	218	7,050,000
Sun Ju Ahn	76	68	75	219	5,925,000
Bo Mi Suh	74	69	76	219	5,925,000
Mi Ri Joo	77	71	72	220	5,400,000
Na Yeon Choi	75	77	69	221	5,070,000
Young Ae Ham	75	73	74	222	4,620,000
Chae Young Yoon	73	72	77	222	4,620,000
Mi-Hyun Cho	75	77	71	223	4,020,000
Hee Young Park	74	74	75	223	4,020,000
Ga Na Lee	75	74	75	224	3,570,000
Seong Ja Park	78	73	74	225	3,050,000
Seul A Yoon	76	75	74	225	3,050,000
Ji Na Lim	74	76	75	225	3,050,000

The Kyoraku Cup

See Japan LPGA Tour section.

Australian Women's Tour

Titanium Enterprises ALPG Players Championship

Club Pelican, Golden Beach, Queensland
Par 36-36–72; 6,276 yards

January 27-29
purse, A$200,000

	SCORES			TOTAL	MONEY
Rebecca Stevenson	71	69	72	212	A$30,000
Katherine Hull	74	67	74	215	17,000
Ana Larraneta	74	70	71	215	17,000
Joanne Mills	72	74	70	216	10,000
Lindsey Wright	73	68	76	217	7,400
Sara Beautell	72	73	72	217	7,400
Nicole Lowien	70	73	75	218	5,250
Susie Parry	71	77	70	218	5,250
Sophie Sandolo	72	72	75	219	4,200
Nikki Garrett	76	74	69	219	4,200
Laura Davies	74	72	74	220	3,250
Natascha Fink	71	75	74	220	3,250
Jane Leary	75	73	74	222	2,640
Yun-Jye Wei	73	75	74	222	2,640
Anne-Marie Knight	72	72	78	222	2,640
Kathryn Imrie	77	72	74	223	2,413
Cecilia Ekelundh	73	74	76	223	2,413
Loraine Lambert	73	73	77	223	2,413
Sarah Kenyon	81	72	71	224	2,270
Catherine Cartwright	75	75	74	224	2,270

ANZ Ladies Masters

Royal Pines Resort, Ashmore, Queensland
Par 37-35–72; 6,397 yards

February 2-5
purse, A$800,000

	SCORES				TOTAL	MONEY
*Amy Yang	69	66	70	70	275	
Catherine Cartwright	70	67	70	68	275	A$120,000
(Yang defeated Cartwright on first playoff hole.)						
*Ya-Ni Tseng	73	69	70	64	276	
Louise Stahle	72	68	68	68	276	79,200
*Tiffany Joh	72	66	69	69	276	79,200
Nikki Campbell	75	67	67	68	277	48,000
Ludivine Kreutz	69	70	67	71	277	48,000
Tamie Durdin	70	74	66	68	278	29,680
Gwladys Nocera	71	68	69	70	278	29,680
Linda Wessberg	70	69	72	68	279	24,000
Hyun Hee Moon	76	68	70	66	280	16,400
Maria Hjorth	70	69	72	69	280	16,400
Nadina Light	73	69	69	69	280	16,400
Kirsty S. Taylor	71	72	68	69	280	16,400
Karin Sjodin	71	70	71	69	281	11,333.30
Hee Young Park	74	65	72	70	281	11,333.30

	SCORES				TOTAL	MONEY
Diana Luna	67	73	70	71	281	11,333.30
Teresa Lu	74	70	68	70	282	9,840
Katherine Hull	74	71	66	71	282	9,840
Lynnette Brooky	71	67	72	72	282	9,840
Nikki Garrett	73	73	71	66	283	8,980
Lindsey Wright	72	68	73	70	283	8,980
Cecilia Ekelundh	73	71	69	70	283	8,980
Sophie Sandolo	70	71	69	73	283	8,980

South African Women's Tour

Women's World Cup of Golf

Gary Player Country Club, Sun City
Par 36-36–72; 6,384 yards

January 20-22
purse, US$1,100,000

	INDIVIDUAL SCORES			TOTAL
SWEDEN—$220,000				
Annika Sorenstam/Liselotte Neumann	65	69	147	281
SCOTLAND—$160,600				
Catriona Matthew/Janice Moodie	70	73	141	284
WALES—$110,000				
Becky Brewerton/Becky Morgan	70	70	148	288
UNITED STATES—$82,500				
Paula Creamer/Natalie Gulbis	68	75	146	289
KOREA—$66,000				
Meena Lee/Bo-Bae Song	65	72	153	290
COLOMBIA—$55,000				
Marisa Baena/Cristina Baena	69	69	153	291
SOUTH AFRICA—$23,375				
Laurette Maritz/*Ashleigh Simon	69	77	146	292
FINLAND—$46,750				
Minea Blomqvist/Riikka Hakkarainen	69	69	154	292
AUSTRALIA—$35,750				
Rachel Hetherington/Shani Waugh	72	77	145	294
GERMANY—$35,750				
Anja Monke/Miriam Nagl	70	72	152	294

	INDIVIDUAL SCORES			TOTAL
ITALY—$27,500				
Veronica Zorzi/Silvia Cavalleri	73	74	148	295
JAPAN—$22,000				
Ai Miyazato/Sakura Yokomine	73	74	149	296
FRANCE—$19,800				
Gwladys Nocera/Karine Icher	72	74	152	298
BRAZIL—$17,050				
Candy Hannemann/Luciana Bemvenuti	72	77	150	299
TAIWAN—$17,050				
Amy Hung/Yu Ping Lin	67	77	155	299
ENGLAND—$15,400				
Kirsty S. Taylor/Laura Davies	71	78	152	301
CANADA—$13,750				
Lorie Kane/A.J. Eathorne	70	75	157	302
SPAIN—$13,750				
Marta Prieto/Paula Marti	69	74	159	302
PHILIPPINES—$12,100				
Dorothy Delasin/Ria Quiazon	71	82	152	305
NEW ZEALAND—$11,000				
Lynnette Brooky/Gina Scott	69	82	155	306

Pam Golding Ladies International

Dainfern Golf Club, Johannesburg
Par 36-37–73; 6,223 yards

February 23-25
purse, R300,000

	SCORES			TOTAL	MONEY
Nora Angehrn	70	68	72	210	R45,000
Rebecca Hudson	74	71	67	212	25,000
Bettina Hauert	69	74	69	212	25,000
Cecilie Lundgreen	69	74	69	212	25,000
*Ashleigh Simon	71	74	68	213	
Salimah Mussani	74	71	68	213	14,400
Marie Allen	73	70	71	214	9,150
Laurette Maritz	75	67	72	214	9,150
Morgana Robbertze	70	69	75	214	9,150
Marianne Skarpnord	71	71	72	214	9,150
Helena Alterby	70	70	74	214	9,150
Tania Elosegui	68	76	71	215	5,750
Florence Luscher	72	68	75	215	5,750
Sara Jelander	75	71	69	215	5,750
Lee-Anne Pace	72	72	72	216	4,890
Lill Kristin Saether	76	69	71	216	4,890
Johanna Waldh	74	69	73	216	4,890
Maria Boden	69	76	71	216	4,890
*Stacy Bregman	72	72	73	217	
*Tandi von Ruben	71	72	74	217	

Acer Women's South African Open

Durban Country Club, Durban
Par 37-36–73; 6,098 yards

March 2-4
purse, R300,000

	SCORES			TOTAL	MONEY
Rebecca Hudson	72	73	72	217	R45,000
Cecilie Lundgreen	74	74	73	221	33,000
Bettina Hauert	74	75	73	222	24,000
*Ashleigh Simon	74	74	75	223	
Emma Zackrisson	73	75	76	224	16,200
Elin Ohlsson	74	75	76	225	16,200
Salimah Mussani	72	82	72	226	12,150
Lee-Anne Pace	75	75	77	227	8,400
Hanna-Sofia Svenningsson	73	77	77	227	8,400
Antonella Cvitan	76	75	76	227	8,400
Michelle de Vries	76	75	76	227	8,400
*Lumien Lausberg	74	76	79	229	
Maria Boden	80	76	74	230	5,750
Laurette Maritz	74	77	79	230	5,750
*Kelli Shean	69	78	83	230	
Sofia Renell	80	74	76	230	5,055
Helena Alterby	78	72	80	230	5,750
Caryn Louw	73	80	78	231	5,055
Nora Angehrn	75	83	74	232	4,500
Eva Steinberger	81	76	75	232	4,500
Sophie Hunter	75	76	81	232	4,500
Zuzana Kamasova	81	77	74	232	4,500
Kareen Qually	75	82	75	232	4,500

Telkom Women's Classic

Zwartkop Country Club, Pretoria
Par 36-36–72; 6,215 yards

March 9-11
purse, R300,000

	SCORES			TOTAL	MONEY
Laurette Maritz	73	66	68	207	R45,000
Rebecca Hudson	71	69	68	208	33,000
*Ashleigh Simon	69	71	69	209	
Tania Elosegui	75	68	68	211	21,000
Helena Alterby	72	70	69	211	21,000
Mandy Adamson	68	70	74	212	14,400
Andrea Hirschhorn	78	71	64	213	10,450
Kirsty Fisher	72	71	70	213	10,450
Rikke Rasmussen	73	71	69	213	10,450
Sara Jelander	74	69	71	214	7,650
Emma Zackrisson	73	73	69	215	6,450
Marianne Skarpnord	68	74	73	215	6,450
Zuzana Kamasova	70	73	73	216	5,550
*Lumien Lausberg	73	72	71	216	
Lill Kristin Saether	72	71	73	216	5,550
Anne-Sophie La Nalio	72	69	76	217	4,735
Sophie Hunter	76	72	69	217	4,735
Nina Hansson	69	78	70	217	4,735
Lee-Anne Pace	72	74	71	217	4,735
Elisa Serramia	76	69	72	217	4,735
Nathalie David-Mila	73	68	76	217	4,735

Nedbank Women's Masters

Killarney Golf Club, Johannesburg
Par 36-36–72; 6,195 yards

March 15-17
purse, R300,000

	SCORES			TOTAL	MONEY
*Ashleigh Simon	70	69	70	209	
Kirsty Fisher	72	69	69	210	R39,000
Mandy Adamson	72	70	68	210	39,000
Florence Luscher	71	68	72	211	24,000
Laurette Maritz	70	71	71	212	16,200
Rebecca Hudson	70	71	71	212	16,200
*Kelli Shean	74	72	67	213	
Helena Alterby	68	75	71	214	11,250
Anne-Sophie La Nalio	73	68	73	214	11,250
Lauren Hamilton Diggle	69	73	73	215	7,020
Carina Vagner	73	73	69	215	7,020
Elisa Serramia	73	72	70	215	7,020
Marianne Skarpnord	73	71	71	215	7,020
Lotta Wahlin	73	70	72	215	7,020
Nuria Clau	71	73	72	216	5,400
Beatriz Minchiotti Fabregas	72	76	69	217	4,970
Francis Botha	74	71	72	217	4,970
Andrea Hirschhorn	74	71	72	217	4,970
Sophie Giquel	68	73	77	218	4,350
Nathalie David-Mila	78	73	67	218	4,350
Emma Zackrisson	74	74	70	218	4,350
Karen Margrethe Juul	71	76	71	218	4,350
Lee-Anne Pace	71	75	72	218	4,350

Senior Tours

MasterCard Championship

Hualalai Golf Club, Ka'upulehu-Kona, Hawaii
Par 36-36–72; 7,053 yards

January 20-22
purse, $1,700,000

	SCORES			TOTAL	MONEY
Loren Roberts	63	67	61	191	$290,000
Don Pooley	63	64	65	192	176,000
Jay Haas	67	64	63	194	120,000
D.A. Weibring	66	65	63	194	120,000
Gil Morgan	71	63	62	196	85,500
Tom Watson	63	69	64	196	85,500
David Eger	66	67	64	197	68,000
Allen Doyle	66	69	66	201	52,750
Peter Jacobsen	66	68	67	201	52,750
Tom Jenkins	66	71	64	201	52,750
Jim Thorpe	65	68	68	201	52,750
Dana Quigley	67	69	66	202	42,000
Mark Johnson	66	68	69	203	34,250
Larry Nelson	67	69	67	203	34,250
Des Smyth	69	70	64	203	34,250
Curtis Strange	64	74	65	203	34,250
Bruce Lietzke	71	66	67	204	28,250
Tom Purtzer	69	69	66	204	28,250
Bob Gilder	66	70	69	205	25,250
John Jacobs	69	69	67	205	25,250
Hale Irwin	68	69	69	206	21,500
Mark McNulty	73	66	67	206	21,500
Craig Stadler	70	65	71	206	21,500
Bruce Summerhays	69	67	70	206	21,500
Ben Crenshaw	65	72	70	207	19,000
Bruce Fleisher	68	69	71	208	17,166.67
Tom Kite	68	72	68	208	17,166.67
Fuzzy Zoeller	65	67	76	208	17,166.66
Wayne Levi	70	68	71	209	15,500
Ron Streck	70	68	71	209	15,500
Doug Tewell	68	69	72	209	15,500
Lanny Wadkins	69	72	70	211	14,500
Mike Reid	70	74	71	215	14,000
Pete Oakley	67	77	73	217	13,250
Gary Player	74	72	71	217	13,250

Turtle Bay Championship

Turtle Bay Resort, Palmer Course, Oahu, Hawaii
Par 36-36–72; 7,088 yards

January 27-29
purse, $1,500,000

	SCORES			TOTAL	MONEY
Loren Roberts	66	66	72	204	$225,000
Scott Simpson	69	67	70	206	132,000
Isao Aoki	71	66	70	207	108,000

	SCORES			TOTAL	MONEY
Don Pooley	68	69	71	208	81,000
Tom Watson	71	69	68	208	81,000
Allen Doyle	72	68	69	209	60,000
Ben Crenshaw	70	69	71	210	45,750
Keith Fergus	74	67	69	210	45,750
Jay Haas	70	68	72	210	45,750
Wayne Levi	72	69	69	210	45,750
R.W. Eaks	72	65	74	211	33,000
Danny Edwards	72	68	71	211	33,000
Bruce Summerhays	67	70	74	211	33,000
Raymond Floyd	70	73	69	212	27,750
Gil Morgan	73	70	69	212	27,750
Lonnie Nielsen	70	72	71	213	25,500
Brad Bryant	74	69	71	214	20,575
Vicente Fernandez	72	72	70	214	20,575
Tom Kite	72	70	72	214	20,575
Hajime Meshiai	72	74	68	214	20,575
Kiyoshi Murota	69	71	74	214	20,575
Des Smyth	73	66	75	214	20,575
Masahiro Kuramoto	72	71	72	215	15,750
Dana Quigley	72	68	75	215	15,750
Curtis Strange	75	67	73	215	15,750
Andy Bean	72	75	69	216	13,650
Walter Hall	72	74	70	216	13,650
Mark Johnson	69	75	72	216	13,650
David Eger	74	70	73	217	11,100
David Ishii	73	72	72	217	11,100
Jerry Pate	70	76	71	217	11,100
Mike Sullivan	73	73	71	217	11,100
Doug Tewell	72	71	74	217	11,100
Jim Thorpe	69	73	75	217	11,100
Bob Gilder	73	72	73	218	9,000
James Mason	73	71	74	218	9,000
Mike McCullough	75	74	69	218	9,000
Dave Barr	74	74	72	220	7,500
Hale Irwin	73	77	70	220	7,500
Rick Karbowski	72	72	76	220	7,500
Dick Mast	76	74	70	220	7,500
Tom McKnight	70	77	73	220	7,500
Dan Pohl	72	77	71	220	7,500

ACE Group Classic

The Club at TwinEagles, Naples, Florida
Par 36-36–72; 6,915 yards

February 17-19
purse, $1,600,000

	SCORES			TOTAL	MONEY
Loren Roberts	67	66	69	202	$240,000
Brad Bryant	66	67	70	203	128,000
R.W. Eaks	65	71	67	203	128,000
Hale Irwin	70	66	68	204	86,400
Tom Watson	66	71	67	204	86,400
Tom Jenkins	68	71	66	205	51,840
Rick Karbowski	66	68	71	205	51,840
Gary Koch	70	68	67	205	51,840
Don Pooley	66	67	72	205	51,840
Fuzzy Zoeller	67	70	68	205	51,840

	SCORES			TOTAL	MONEY
Peter Jacobsen	68	69	69	206	35,200
Tom Kite	69	69	68	206	35,200
Mark McNulty	72	67	67	206	35,200
Keith Fergus	68	69	70	207	28,800
Larry Nelson	72	68	67	207	28,800
Dana Quigley	68	69	70	207	28,800
Jerry Pate	71	70	67	208	24,800
Scott Simpson	73	66	69	208	24,800
Ed Dougherty	73	67	69	209	20,520
Danny Edwards	72	64	73	209	20,520
Dave Stockton	69	74	66	209	20,520
Bruce Summerhays	68	71	70	209	20,520
Mark Johnson	72	69	69	210	17,600
Morris Hatalsky	72	70	69	211	15,296
Gil Morgan	67	74	70	211	15,296
Mike San Filippo	68	73	70	211	15,296
Jim Thorpe	70	70	71	211	15,296
Bobby Wadkins	72	71	68	211	15,296
Isao Aoki	74	70	68	212	11,840
Allen Doyle	70	71	71	212	11,840
John Harris	69	70	73	212	11,840
John Jacobs	68	73	71	212	11,840
Doug Johnson	71	72	69	212	11,840
Gary McCord	73	69	70	212	11,840
John Bland	71	71	71	213	9,040
Raymond Floyd	74	71	68	213	9,040
Tom McKnight	73	70	70	213	9,040
Lonnie Nielsen	70	73	70	213	9,040
Dan Pohl	67	72	74	213	9,040
Des Smyth	68	75	70	213	9,040

Outback Steakhouse Pro-Am

TPC of Tampa Bay, Lutz, Florida
Par 35-36–71; 6,638 yards

February 24-26
purse, $1,600,000

	SCORES			TOTAL	MONEY
Jerry Pate	68	68	66	202	$240,000
Morris Hatalsky	71	68	64	203	117,866.67
Mark James	70	65	68	203	117,866.67
Hale Irwin	69	66	68	203	117,866.66
Bruce Fleisher	70	67	70	207	58,880
Tom Kite	68	71	68	207	58,880
Loren Roberts	69	69	69	207	58,880
Des Smyth	68	70	69	207	58,880
Leonard Thompson	70	69	68	207	58,880
David Eger	71	68	69	208	38,400
Mark McNulty	65	70	73	208	38,400
Dan Pohl	67	74	67	208	38,400
Danny Edwards	76	64	69	209	31,200
Scott Simpson	70	68	71	209	31,200
Keith Fergus	67	76	68	211	23,460
Bob Gilder	69	71	71	211	23,460
Bruce Lietzke	65	74	72	211	23,460
Tom McKnight	73	67	71	211	23,460
Larry Nelson	68	69	74	211	23,460
Mike Sullivan	73	72	66	211	23,460

	SCORES			TOTAL	MONEY
Jim Thorpe	73	69	69	211	23,460
Bobby Wadkins	68	70	73	211	23,460
Masahiro Kuramoto	69	75	68	212	16,800
Gary McCord	67	71	74	212	16,800
Dave Stockton	68	75	69	212	16,800
Brad Bryant	70	69	74	213	14,240
Vicente Fernandez	71	70	72	213	14,240
Wayne Levi	73	68	72	213	14,240
Curtis Strange	70	73	70	213	14,240
Jay Haas	72	73	69	214	12,320
Gil Morgan	70	73	71	214	12,320
Mark Johnson	68	75	72	215	11,040
Pat McGowan	71	73	71	215	11,040
Fuzzy Zoeller	76	72	67	215	11,040
Allen Doyle	69	73	74	216	9,216
Dave Eichelberger	70	74	72	216	9,216
Tom Jenkins	70	74	72	216	9,216
Doug LaCrosse	72	74	70	216	9,216
Craig Stadler	74	71	71	216	9,216
Tom Purtzer	72	73	72	217	8,160

AT&T Classic

Valencia Country Club, Valencia, California
Par 36-36–72; 6,973 yards

March 10-12
purse, $1,600,000

	SCORES			TOTAL	MONEY
Tom Kite	70	64	70	204	$240,000
Gil Morgan	69	72	68	209	140,800
Tom Jenkins	71	72	68	211	115,200
Morris Hatalsky	75	69	68	212	86,400
Peter Jacobsen	71	70	71	212	86,400
Wayne Levi	72	69	72	213	64,000
Andy Bean	70	65	79	214	48,800
Jerry Pate	71	72	71	214	48,800
Tom Purtzer	69	70	75	214	48,800
Loren Roberts	71	69	74	214	48,800
Allen Doyle	74	72	69	215	34,000
John Harris	72	71	72	215	34,000
Lonnie Nielsen	74	70	71	215	34,000
Jay Sigel	68	73	74	215	34,000
Gary McCord	73	70	73	216	28,000
Scott Simpson	74	73	69	216	28,000
Bruce Fleisher	69	76	72	217	19,258.19
Fuzzy Zoeller	71	73	73	217	19,258.19
Mitch Adcock	67	70	80	217	19,258.18
Ben Crenshaw	68	72	77	217	19,258.18
Jay Haas	73	69	75	217	19,258.18
Mark Johnson	72	72	73	217	19,258.18
Larry Nelson	70	72	75	217	19,258.18
Des Smyth	69	71	77	217	19,258.18
Jim Thorpe	71	72	74	217	19,258.18
Howard Twitty	73	70	74	217	19,258.18
Bobby Wadkins	73	69	75	217	19,258.18
Bruce Summerhays	73	73	72	218	12,137.15
Lanny Wadkins	71	75	72	218	12,137.15
Ed Dougherty	75	70	73	218	12,137.14

	SCORES	TOTAL	MONEY
R.W. Eaks	75 73 70	218	12,137.14
Walter Hall	73 68 77	218	12,137.14
Masahiro Kuramoto	74 75 69	218	12,137.14
Mark McNulty	71 72 75	218	12,137.14
John Bland	69 77 73	219	9,840
Bob Gilder	75 73 71	219	9,840
Vicente Fernandez	72 75 73	220	8,640
John Jacobs	76 71 73	220	8,640
Bruce Lietzke	72 75 73	220	8,640
Dana Quigley	70 76 74	220	8,640

Toshiba Classic

Newport Beach Country Club, Newport Beach, California
Par 35-36–71; 6,598 yards

March 17-19
purse, $1,650,000

	SCORES	TOTAL	MONEY
Brad Bryant	68 70 66	204	$247,500
John Harris	69 68 68	205	121,000
Mark Johnson	68 69 68	205	121,000
Bobby Wadkins	68 71 66	205	121,000
David Eger	68 70 68	206	68,200
Vicente Fernandez	68 68 70	206	68,200
Mike Reid	70 69 67	206	68,200
Jose Maria Canizares	71 67 69	207	43,560
Bob Gilder	70 70 67	207	43,560
Hale Irwin	71 69 67	207	43,560
Mike McCullough	71 67 69	207	43,560
Tom Wargo	69 70 68	207	43,560
Ed Dougherty	69 70 69	208	31,350
Graham Marsh	66 69 73	208	31,350
Tom Purtzer	68 67 73	208	31,350
Dave Eichelberger	67 69 73	209	23,406.43
Jay Haas	70 67 72	209	23,406.43
Tom Jenkins	72 69 68	209	23,406.43
Bruce Lietzke	66 72 71	209	23,406.43
Don Pooley	73 69 67	209	23,406.43
Craig Stadler	71 69 69	209	23,406.43
Bob Eastwood	65 70 74	209	23,406.42
Allen Doyle	70 67 73	210	16,533
R.W. Eaks	70 71 69	210	16,533
Jack Ferenz	69 73 68	210	16,533
Joe Inman	68 68 74	210	16,533
Mark McNulty	73 68 69	210	16,533
Isao Aoki	72 71 68	211	12,251.25
Andy Bean	73 71 67	211	12,251.25
Walter Hall	68 69 74	211	12,251.25
John Jacobs	70 70 71	211	12,251.25
Gary McCord	76 71 64	211	12,251.25
Larry Nelson	72 72 67	211	12,251.25
Des Smyth	71 70 70	211	12,251.25
D.A. Weibring	75 69 67	211	12,251.25
Ben Crenshaw	69 71 72	212	9,108
Morris Hatalsky	71 68 73	212	9,108
Rick Karbowski	71 68 73	212	9,108
Jay Sigel	73 68 71	212	9,108
Dave Stockton	72 70 70	212	9,108

Puerto Vallarta Blue Agave Golf Classic

Vista Vallarta Golf Club, Puerto Vallarta, Mexico
Par 36-36—72; 7,073 yards

March 31-April 2
purse, $1,600,000

	SCORES			TOTAL	MONEY
Morris Hatalsky	70	67	70	207	$240,000
Scott Simpson	67	71	70	208	140,800
Gil Morgan	68	70	71	209	105,600
Mike Reid	70	69	70	209	105,600
Tom Kite	74	67	69	210	76,800
R.W. Eaks	72	69	70	211	60,800
Mark Johnson	69	71	71	211	60,800
Danny Edwards	73	65	74	212	45,866.67
Tom Purtzer	71	67	74	212	45,866.67
Masahiro Kuramoto	73	65	74	212	45,866.66
James Mason	71	72	70	213	36,800
Lonnie Nielsen	77	67	69	213	36,800
Hale Irwin	70	70	74	214	30,400
Gary Robison	69	76	69	214	30,400
Jay Sigel	71	70	73	214	30,400
Allen Doyle	69	71	75	215	24,096
Bob Eastwood	74	69	72	215	24,096
Joe Inman	71	72	72	215	24,096
Don Pooley	69	72	74	215	24,096
Eduardo Romero	71	69	75	215	24,096
Hugh Baiocchi	73	69	74	216	17,760
Jose Maria Canizares	74	73	69	216	17,760
Mike San Filippo	70	76	70	216	17,760
Jack Spradlin	76	71	69	216	17,760
D.A. Weibring	72	70	74	216	17,760
Bob Gilder	77	67	73	217	14,240
Rick Karbowski	74	71	72	217	14,240
Gary McCord	69	75	73	217	14,240
Bobby Wadkins	75	68	74	217	14,240
Andy Bean	75	74	69	218	12,320
David Eger	68	72	78	218	12,320
Jack Ferenz	72	70	77	219	10,560
Keith Fergus	72	73	74	219	10,560
Bruce Lietzke	70	75	74	219	10,560
Curtis Strange	72	76	71	219	10,560
Doug Tewell	77	71	71	219	10,560
John Jacobs	75	73	72	220	8,320
Wayne Levi	75	75	70	220	8,320
Graham Marsh	74	71	75	220	8,320
Dan Pohl	69	71	80	220	8,320
Dave Stockton	76	68	76	220	8,320
Leonard Thompson	72	74	74	220	8,320

Liberty Mutual Legends of Golf

Westin Savannah Harbor Golf Resort & Spa, Savannah, Georgia
Par 36-36—72; 7,087 yards

April 21-23
purse, $2,500,000

	SCORES			TOTAL	MONEY
Jay Haas	66	68	67	201	$395,000
Peter Jacobsen	70	69	67	206	215,500

	SCORES			TOTAL	MONEY
Craig Stadler	69	67	70	206	215,500
Hale Irwin	70	69	68	207	155,000
Des Smyth	70	73	66	209	128,000
Tom Jenkins	71	69	70	210	91,250
Mark Johnson	70	70	70	210	91,250
Larry Nelson	71	70	69	210	91,250
Jerry Pate	68	69	73	210	91,250
Loren Roberts	72	69	70	211	72,000
Brad Bryant	72	74	66	212	64,500
Gil Morgan	68	76	68	212	64,500
Allen Doyle	71	68	74	213	49,600
Bruce Fleisher	72	70	71	213	49,600
Mark James	76	73	64	213	49,600
Jim Thorpe	72	72	69	213	49,600
Fuzzy Zoeller	73	72	68	213	49,600
Andy Bean	75	69	70	214	35,875
John Jacobs	72	69	73	214	35,875
Mark McNulty	68	76	70	214	35,875
Tom Wargo	68	73	73	214	35,875
Tom Kite	78	70	68	216	25,158.34
Curtis Strange	73	73	70	216	25,158.34
Bob Gilder	73	71	72	216	25,158.33
Wayne Levi	72	71	73	216	25,158.33
Scott Simpson	70	72	74	216	25,158.33
D.A. Weibring	73	71	72	216	25,158.33
Jim Colbert	73	70	74	217	18,450
Dave Eichelberger	71	70	76	217	18,450
Mark McCumber	74	72	71	217	18,450
Mike Reid	70	74	73	217	18,450
Jim Albus	70	73	75	218	15,600
Tom Purtzer	75	72	71	218	15,600
Morris Hatalsky	70	73	76	219	13,737.50
Bob Murphy	69	69	81	219	13,737.50
Dana Quigley	77	70	72	219	13,737.50
Jay Sigel	72	76	71	219	13,737.50
Dave Stockton	74	73	73	220	11,933.34
Bob Eastwood	75	72	73	220	11,933.33
Leonard Thompson	74	73	73	220	11,933.33

FedEx Kinko's Classic

The Hills Country Club, Austin, Texas
Par 36-36–72; 6,879 yards
April 28-30
purse, $1,600,000

	SCORES			TOTAL	MONEY
Jay Haas	68	72	65	205	$240,000
Mark James	71	69	67	207	128,000
Tom Kite	68	71	68	207	128,000
David Edwards	68	70	71	209	96,000
Tom Jenkins	71	70	69	210	76,800
Bruce Fleisher	68	69	74	211	57,600
Hale Irwin	73	70	68	211	57,600
Bruce Lietzke	71	74	66	211	57,600
Bob Gilder	71	69	72	212	43,200
Don Pooley	71	72	69	212	43,200
Brad Bryant	74	72	67	213	32,000
Ben Crenshaw	73	71	69	213	32,000

	SCORES			TOTAL	MONEY
Pat McGowan	74	69	70	213	32,000
Des Smyth	70	69	74	213	32,000
Craig Stadler	68	70	75	213	32,000
D.A. Weibring	74	71	68	213	32,000
Jerry Pate	74	71	69	214	25,600
J.C. Snead	71	73	71	215	24,000
Peter Jacobsen	72	73	71	216	21,840
Larry Nelson	75	71	70	216	21,840
John Bland	74	72	71	217	18,666.67
Scott Simpson	72	72	73	217	18,666.67
Jim Thorpe	72	70	75	217	18,666.66
Ed Dougherty	71	80	67	218	14,960
Keith Fergus	71	73	74	218	14,960
John Harris	74	70	74	218	14,960
Mark McNulty	74	71	73	218	14,960
Bobby Wadkins	75	73	70	218	14,960
Fuzzy Zoeller	73	75	70	218	14,960
Hugh Baiocchi	73	74	72	219	11,306.67
Bob Eastwood	75	74	70	219	11,306.67
Vicente Fernandez	72	79	68	219	11,306.67
Bruce Summerhays	74	74	71	219	11,306.67
Mark Lye	79	73	67	219	11,306.66
Curtis Strange	68	74	77	219	11,306.66
Dave Eichelberger	74	71	75	220	8,502.86
Morris Hatalsky	71	78	71	220	8,502.86
Wayne Levi	70	76	74	220	8,502.86
Gil Morgan	76	73	71	220	8,502.86
Tom Purtzer	71	78	71	220	8,502.86
Andy Bean	76	74	70	220	8,502.85
Mark McCumber	75	70	75	220	8,502.85

Regions Charity Classic

Robert Trent Jones Trail at Ross Bridge,
Birmingham, Alabama
Par 36-36–72; 7,509 yards

May 5-7
purse, $1,600,000

	SCORES			TOTAL	MONEY
Brad Bryant	68	67	64	199	$240,000
Mark McNulty	67	67	67	201	140,800
David Edwards	71	65	67	203	115,200
Jim Thorpe	70	71	63	204	96,000
Tom McKnight	67	70	69	206	76,800
Danny Edwards	71	67	69	207	51,840
Bob Gilder	70	70	67	207	51,840
Morris Hatalsky	72	68	67	207	51,840
Dick Mast	69	66	72	207	51,840
Loren Roberts	70	67	70	207	51,840
Allen Doyle	71	71	66	208	34,000
Keith Fergus	67	71	70	208	34,000
Hale Irwin	68	70	70	208	34,000
Mark Johnson	73	66	69	208	34,000
Dan Pohl	74	67	68	209	26,400
Don Pooley	74	65	70	209	26,400
Scott Simpson	67	70	72	209	26,400
Bobby Wadkins	69	69	71	209	26,400
John Harris	71	70	69	210	21,173.34

	SCORES			TOTAL	MONEY
Jack Ferenz	71	67	72	210	21,173.33
Des Smyth	69	68	73	210	21,173.33
Tom Kite	73	70	68	211	16,091.43
Masahiro Kuramoto	70	71	70	211	16,091.43
James Mason	72	71	68	211	16,091.43
Jerry Pate	71	71	69	211	16,091.43
Rick Rhoden	68	72	71	211	16,091.43
Jay Sigel	70	70	71	211	16,091.43
Hugh Baiocchi	70	69	72	211	16,091.42
Ben Crenshaw	72	67	73	212	12,640
Tom Jenkins	70	73	69	212	12,640
Lonnie Nielsen	72	70	70	212	12,640
Bill Longmuir	71	75	67	213	11,040
Mike Smith	71	73	69	213	11,040
Leonard Thompson	72	71	70	213	11,040
Joe Inman	74	70	70	214	9,400
Rick Karbowski	75	69	70	214	9,400
Mike Reid	71	70	73	214	9,400
Mike Sullivan	73	69	72	214	9,400
Andy Bean	72	68	75	215	7,200
Jim Dent	73	70	72	215	7,200
David Eger	70	76	69	215	7,200
Vicente Fernandez	72	71	72	215	7,200
Graham Marsh	71	74	70	215	7,200
Pat McGowan	72	71	72	215	7,200
Craig Stadler	72	70	73	215	7,200
Dave Stockton	73	72	70	215	7,200
Ron Streck	73	71	71	215	7,200

Boeing Championship

Raven Golf Club at Sandestin, Destin, Florida
Par 36-35–71; 6,931 yards

May 12-14
purse, $1,600,000

	SCORES			TOTAL	MONEY
Bobby Wadkins	62	71	70	203	$240,000
Raymond Floyd	68	73	63	204	140,800
Loren Roberts	69	68	69	206	88,000
Scott Simpson	69	70	67	206	88,000
Craig Stadler	71	65	70	206	88,000
Tom Watson	72	67	67	206	88,000
Gil Morgan	72	69	66	207	57,600
John Bland	72	69	67	208	45,866.67
Peter Jacobsen	72	70	66	208	45,866.67
Jerry Pate	71	69	68	208	45,866.66
Brad Bryant	71	70	68	209	35,200
Wayne Levi	69	70	70	209	35,200
Bruce Summerhays	72	67	70	209	35,200
David Edwards	69	73	68	210	28,000
Bruce Fleisher	73	68	69	210	28,000
Dana Quigley	74	67	69	210	28,000
D.A. Weibring	72	67	71	210	28,000
Allen Doyle	72	68	71	211	23,280
Hale Irwin	70	70	71	211	23,280
Andy Bean	72	68	72	212	18,320
Ed Dougherty	70	72	70	212	18,320
Bob Gilder	72	68	72	212	18,320

	SCORES	TOTAL	MONEY
Bruce Lietzke	72 70 70	212	18,320
Mike McCullough	67 71 74	212	18,320
Dan Pohl	70 70 72	212	18,320
Ben Crenshaw	75 70 68	213	13,600
Morris Hatalsky	69 71 73	213	13,600
Tom Jenkins	70 70 73	213	13,600
Lonnie Nielsen	70 73 70	213	13,600
Don Pooley	66 78 69	213	13,600
Doug Tewell	72 74 67	213	13,600
Hubert Green	73 68 73	214	10,800
John Harris	70 66 78	214	10,800
John Jacobs	70 74 70	214	10,800
Jim Thorpe	75 69 70	214	10,800
Jack Ferenz	72 75 68	215	8,666.67
Masahiro Kuramoto	76 72 67	215	8,666.67
Graham Marsh	75 69 71	215	8,666.67
Jay Sigel	73 71 71	215	8,666.67
Keith Fergus	70 73 72	215	8,666.66
J.C. Snead	74 70 71	215	8,666.66

Senior PGA Championship

Oak Tree Golf Club, Edmond, Oklahoma
Par 36-35–71; 7,102 yards

May 25-28
purse, $2,000,000

	SCORES	TOTAL	MONEY
Jay Haas	68 70 73 68	279	$360,000
Brad Bryant	69 67 72 71	279	216,000
(Haas defeated Bryant on third playoff hole.)			
Gil Morgan	66 70 71 74	281	136,000
Dana Quigley	69 70 72 71	282	96,000
Loren Roberts	68 71 71 73	283	76,000
Tsuneyuki Nakajima	71 70 74 69	284	66,000
Katsuyoshi Tomori	69 76 73 67	285	60,000
Peter Jacobsen	67 68 75 75	285	60,000
Doug Tewell	71 75 71 70	287	54,000
D.A. Weibring	71 71 70 76	288	50,000
Bob Gilder	70 75 78 66	289	42,333.34
Jose Rivero	70 69 78 72	289	42,333.33
Dick Mast	71 72 69 77	289	42,333.33
Kiyoshi Murota	72 72 77 69	290	32,000
Scott Simpson	72 73 72 73	290	32,000
Bruce Fleisher	73 71 73 73	290	32,000
David Edwards	72 68 74 76	290	32,000
Jim Thorpe	69 73 73 75	290	32,000
Mark McNulty	73 72 74 72	291	23,000
Kirk Hanefeld	73 71 79 68	291	23,000
Mitch Adcock	76 70 72 73	291	23,000
Sam Torrance	72 70 73 76	291	23,000
Hale Irwin	73 70 76 73	292	16,000
Allen Doyle	74 72 76 70	292	16,000
Tom Purtzer	73 67 77 75	292	16,000
Mike Reid	71 71 75 75	292	16,000
Tom Watson	68 71 74 79	292	16,000
Leonard Thompson	74 73 73 73	293	13,000
Isao Aoki	74 69 73 77	293	13,000
Mike McCullough	74 73 69 77	293	13,000

	SCORES	TOTAL	MONEY
Des Smyth	74 72 75 73	294	11,000
Rick Rhoden	72 75 76 71	294	11,000
Keith Fergus	75 73 77 69	294	11,000
Naomichi Ozaki	71 71 74 78	294	11,000
Eduardo Romero	74 71 71 78	294	11,000
Danny Edwards	70 76 75 74	295	8,825
Tom McKnight	71 76 74 74	295	8,825
Tim Simpson	71 72 74 78	295	8,825
Vicente Fernandez	73 72 71 79	295	8,825
Howard Twitty	72 74 74 76	296	6,750
Gordon Brand	72 70 78 76	296	6,750
Dave Barr	73 70 77 76	296	6,750
Morris Hatalsky	71 75 74 76	296	6,750
Tom Kite	74 69 78 75	296	6,750
Joe Inman	72 72 75 77	296	6,750
Andy Bean	73 73 77 73	296	6,750
Bruce Summerhays	73 73 81 69	296	6,750

Allianz Championship

Glen Oaks Country Club, West Des Moines, Iowa
Par 35-36–71; 6,879 yards

June 2-4
purse, $1,500,000

	SCORES	TOTAL	MONEY
Gil Morgan	66 64 67	197	$225,000
Loren Roberts	66 65 67	198	132,000
Hajime Meshiai	68 64 68	200	108,000
Keith Fergus	69 65 68	202	90,000
Allen Doyle	71 65 67	203	72,000
James Blair	69 68 67	204	51,000
Ed Dougherty	68 68 68	204	51,000
Kirk Hanefeld	67 65 72	204	51,000
Morris Hatalsky	67 67 70	204	51,000
Danny Edwards	70 66 69	205	32,250
David Edwards	66 67 72	205	32,250
John Harris	67 66 72	205	32,250
Bruce Lietzke	65 70 70	205	32,250
Tom Purtzer	68 66 71	205	32,250
Fuzzy Zoeller	67 68 70	205	32,250
Graham Marsh	66 71 69	206	21,278.58
Bruce Fleisher	70 68 68	206	21,278.57
Bob Gilder	66 69 71	206	21,278.57
Wayne Levi	67 68 71	206	21,278.57
Tim Simpson	69 71 66	206	21,278.57
Dave Stockton	67 69 70	206	21,278.57
Bruce Summerhays	70 65 71	206	21,278.57
Tom Jenkins	67 66 74	207	16,125
Lonnie Nielsen	70 66 71	207	16,125
Jack Ferenz	68 69 71	208	13,987.50
Tom McKnight	70 72 66	208	13,987.50
Mike San Filippo	70 66 72	208	13,987.50
Jim Thorpe	65 69 74	208	13,987.50
Jim Ahern	73 66 70	209	11,587.50
Dave Eichelberger	70 70 69	209	11,587.50
Joe Inman	70 68 71	209	11,587.50
Jay Sigel	72 66 71	209	11,587.50
Doug Johnson	72 69 69	210	8,887.50

	SCORES			TOTAL	MONEY
Mark McCumber	72	69	69	210	8,887.50
Mark McNulty	65	76	69	210	8,887.50
Naomichi Ozaki	70	67	73	210	8,887.50
Mike Reid	69	69	72	210	8,887.50
Scott Simpson	64	71	75	210	8,887.50
Ron Streck	70	67	73	210	8,887.50
Howard Twitty	73	67	70	210	8,887.50

Commerce Bank Championship

Eisenhower Park, Red Course, East Meadow, New York
Par 35-36–71; 6,904 yards

June 23-25
purse, $1,500,000

	SCORES			TOTAL	MONEY
John Harris	70	68	64	202	$225,000
Tom Jenkins	69	64	69	202	132,000
(Harris defeated Jenkins on first playoff hole.)					
Andy Bean	70	66	67	203	90,000
Jay Haas	69	65	69	203	90,000
Gil Morgan	65	69	69	203	90,000
Dana Quigley	71	68	65	204	60,000
Dave Eichelberger	69	67	69	205	45,750
Masahiro Kuramoto	70	66	69	205	45,750
Scott Simpson	69	67	69	205	45,750
Tom Wargo	67	68	70	205	45,750
Mitch Adcock	70	67	69	206	30,000
Allen Doyle	64	71	71	206	30,000
Bruce Fleisher	68	67	71	206	30,000
Bob Gilder	73	65	68	206	30,000
Hajime Meshiai	70	69	67	206	30,000
Naomichi Ozaki	70	66	70	206	30,000
Bruce Summerhays	68	69	70	207	24,000
Jim Ahern	67	72	69	208	19,890
Jim Chancey	72	68	68	208	19,890
David Eger	70	65	73	208	19,890
Jay Sigel	70	67	71	208	19,890
Howard Twitty	68	70	70	208	19,890
Ben Crenshaw	69	68	72	209	15,030
R.W. Eaks	70	71	68	209	15,030
Mike Hill	68	70	71	209	15,030
Mike Sullivan	73	67	69	209	15,030
Leonard Thompson	71	68	70	209	15,030
Walter Hall	72	69	69	210	12,150
Tom McKnight	71	69	70	210	12,150
Don Pooley	67	75	68	210	12,150
Mike San Filippo	71	68	71	210	12,150
Ed Dougherty	72	71	68	211	8,925
Danny Edwards	70	71	70	211	8,925
Jack Ferenz	67	72	72	211	8,925
Keith Fergus	68	73	70	211	8,925
Hale Irwin	73	66	72	211	8,925
Mark Johnson	74	66	71	211	8,925
Bill Longmuir	71	73	67	211	8,925
James Mason	70	69	72	211	8,925
Mike McCullough	69	71	71	211	8,925
Dan Pohl	71	71	69	211	8,925

Greater Kansas City Golf Classic

Nicklaus Golf Club at LionsGate, Overland Park, Kansas
Par 36-36–72; 7,251 yards

June 30-July 2
purse, $1,650,000

	SCORES			TOTAL	MONEY
Dana Quigley	67	68	63	198	$248,000
David Edwards	63	70	68	201	145,700
Brad Bryant	65	69	70	204	109,200
Naomichi Ozaki	69	69	66	204	109,200
Keith Fergus	70	65	70	205	64,350
Bob Gilder	65	71	69	205	64,350
Lonnie Nielsen	67	69	69	205	64,350
Tim Simpson	68	70	67	205	64,350
R.W. Eaks	69	68	69	206	41,250
Tom Jenkins	65	72	69	206	41,250
Masahiro Kuramoto	69	69	68	206	41,250
Gary McCord	67	68	71	206	41,250
Andy Bean	68	70	69	207	31,350
Craig Stadler	70	69	68	207	31,350
D.A. Weibring	73	69	65	207	31,350
David Eger	72	70	67	209	26,400
Bruce Lietzke	70	68	71	209	26,400
Des Smyth	65	72	72	209	26,400
Gil Morgan	68	73	69	210	23,265
Morris Hatalsky	69	70	72	211	18,432.86
Wayne Levi	72	71	68	211	18,432.86
Mark McNulty	72	70	69	211	18,432.86
Hajime Meshiai	69	71	71	211	18,432.86
Mike Reid	74	70	67	211	18,432.86
Danny Edwards	69	70	72	211	18,432.85
Bobby Wadkins	68	70	73	211	18,432.85
Mike San Filippo	68	73	71	212	15,015
Kirk Hanefeld	71	70	72	213	13,695
Bruce Summerhays	69	70	74	213	13,695
Tom Watson	71	67	75	213	13,695
Jim Dent	69	73	72	214	10,450
Bob Eastwood	75	65	74	214	10,450
Bruce Fleisher	71	72	71	214	10,450
Jay Haas	70	70	74	214	10,450
Walter Hall	71	73	70	214	10,450
Scott Masingill	71	72	71	214	10,450
Tom McKnight	71	73	70	214	10,450
Tom Purtzer	72	70	72	214	10,450
Mike Sullivan	72	71	71	214	10,450
Dan Pohl	72	72	71	215	8,415

U.S. Senior Open

Prairie Dunes Country Club, Hutchison, Kansas
Par 35-35–70; 6,646 yards

July 6-9
purse, $2,600,000

	SCORES				TOTAL	MONEY
Allen Doyle	69	68	67	68	272	$470,000
Tom Watson	70	66	66	72	274	280,000
Bruce Lietzke	69	70	70	66	275	148,567
Peter Jacobsen	72	66	68	69	275	148,567

	SCORES				TOTAL	MONEY
Scott Simpson	72	70	66	68	276	93,205
Andy Bean	71	72	64	69	276	93,205
Bob Gilder	71	66	70	70	277	78,682
D.A. Weibring	68	71	71	68	278	67,001
Jay Haas	67	75	67	69	278	67,001
Loren Roberts	72	71	62	73	278	67,001
Curtis Strange	73	70	67	69	279	54,122
Fred Funk	72	72	65	70	279	54,122
Morris Hatalsky	70	67	70	72	279	54,122
Craig Stadler	71	74	70	66	281	41,852
Mark McNulty	75	67	71	68	281	41,852
Brad Bryant	71	71	70	69	281	41,852
Ben Crenshaw	75	71	66	69	281	41,852
Dick Mast	70	73	68	70	281	41,852
Mark James	68	69	69	75	281	41,852
Masahiro Kuramoto	68	72	72	70	282	32,272
Bruce Summerhays	69	72	70	71	282	32,272
Jim Thorpe	75	71	65	71	282	32,272
Fuzzy Zoeller	74	69	71	69	283	26,920
Dave Barr	67	76	70	70	283	26,920
R.W. Eaks	72	71	76	64	283	26,920
Kirk Hanefeld	75	70	70	69	284	22,131
Graham Marsh	68	75	70	71	284	22,131
Tom Wargo	71	73	67	73	284	22,131
David Edwards	76	67	70	72	285	18,327
Mike Reid	74	69	72	70	285	18,327
Des Smyth	73	73	70	69	285	18,327
Hale Irwin	73	72	71	70	286	16,708
Gary McCord	71	72	73	70	286	16,708
Lonnie Nielsen	69	77	71	69	286	16,708
Tom McKnight	72	72	71	72	287	15,689
Hubert Green	76	71	70	71	288	14,417
Rod Spittle	74	73	71	70	288	14,417
Vicente Fernandez	70	75	73	70	288	14,417
Jon Fiedler	71	74	73	70	288	14,417
Larry Nelson	77	70	69	73	289	13,153

Ford Senior Players Championship

TPC of Michigan, Dearborn, Michigan
Par 36-36–72; 7,069 yards

July 13-16
purse, $2,500,000

	SCORES				TOTAL	MONEY
Bobby Wadkins	69	72	65	68	274	$375,000
Jim Thorpe	67	70	69	69	275	220,000
Jay Haas	68	70	70	68	276	137,500
Gil Morgan	70	66	71	69	276	137,500
Loren Roberts	71	67	64	74	276	137,500
Des Smyth	71	67	68	70	276	137,500
Brad Bryant	68	69	68	72	277	85,000
Tom Purtzer	69	67	72	69	277	85,000
Tom Kite	68	70	70	70	278	67,500
Fuzzy Zoeller	65	72	73	68	278	67,500
Fred Funk	69	70	70	70	279	50,000
Morris Hatalsky	75	65	67	72	279	50,000
Mark James	69	70	71	69	279	50,000
Dan Pohl	69	71	70	69	279	50,000

	SCORES	TOTAL	MONEY
Don Pooley	70 66 70 73	279	50,000
Dana Quigley	69 68 68 74	279	50,000
Lonnie Nielsen	73 65 66 76	280	35,350
Naomichi Ozaki	71 65 73 71	280	35,350
Jerry Pate	71 65 74 70	280	35,350
Scott Simpson	67 70 74 69	280	35,350
Tom Watson	69 67 78 66	280	35,350
Andy Bean	71 67 74 69	281	23,525
David Edwards	69 67 71 74	281	23,525
Bob Gilder	72 72 69 68	281	23,525
Tom Jenkins	68 75 68 70	281	23,525
Gary Koch	74 68 71 68	281	23,525
Gary McCord	70 68 69 74	281	23,525
Tom McKnight	71 73 67 70	281	23,525
Mike Reid	70 66 74 71	281	23,525
Bruce Summerhays	72 74 69 66	281	23,525
D.A. Weibring	69 71 71 70	281	23,525
Tim Simpson	73 71 67 71	282	17,250
Craig Stadler	72 69 69 72	282	17,250
Tom Wargo	72 69 72 69	282	17,250
John Jacobs	68 75 73 67	283	15,000
Wayne Levi	71 72 72 68	283	15,000
Bruce Lietzke	67 80 68 68	283	15,000
Keith Fergus	71 73 68 72	284	13,250
Graham Marsh	69 72 71 72	284	13,250
Dick Mast	70 67 75 72	284	13,250

Senior British Open

See European Seniors Tour section.

3M Championship

TPC of the Twin Cities, Blaine, Minnesota
Par 36-36–72; 6,909 yards

August 4-6
purse, $1,750,000

	SCORES	TOTAL	MONEY
David Edwards	69 68 67	204	$262,500
Brad Bryant	69 70 67	206	140,000
Craig Stadler	71 67 68	206	140,000
Tom Kite	74 69 64	207	94,500
Gil Morgan	72 68 67	207	94,500
Tom Purtzer	68 74 66	208	59,500
Rick Rhoden	72 67 69	208	59,500
Loren Roberts	68 71 69	208	59,500
D.A. Weibring	70 69 69	208	59,500
Hale Irwin	69 70 70	209	40,250
Wayne Levi	72 71 66	209	40,250
Chris Starkjohann	69 71 69	209	40,250
Bruce Summerhays	78 67 64	209	40,250
David Eger	71 73 66	210	32,375
Curtis Strange	68 66 76	210	32,375
Andy Bean	67 73 71	211	27,168.75
Keith Fergus	68 72 71	211	27,168.75
Walter Hall	70 72 69	211	27,168.75
Tim Simpson	73 69 69	211	27,168.75

	SCORES			TOTAL	MONEY
Bruce Lietzke	69	71	72	212	20,037.50
James Mason	69	71	72	212	20,037.50
Naomichi Ozaki	71	70	71	212	20,037.50
Mike Reid	76	68	68	212	20,037.50
Ron Streck	71	69	72	212	20,037.50
Jim Thorpe	71	70	71	212	20,037.50
Vicente Fernandez	71	70	72	213	13,650
Bruce Fleisher	70	69	74	213	13,650
Gibby Gilbert	74	69	70	213	13,650
John Harris	75	68	70	213	13,650
Morris Hatalsky	72	66	75	213	13,650
Tom McKnight	69	75	69	213	13,650
Mark McNulty	74	69	70	213	13,650
Mike San Filippo	69	73	71	213	13,650
Scott Simpson	72	70	71	213	13,650
Joe Stansberry	73	70	70	213	13,650
Hugh Baiocchi	74	66	74	214	9,843.75
Tom Jenkins	70	73	71	214	9,843.75
Graham Marsh	71	72	71	214	9,843.75
Bob Ralston	72	74	68	214	9,843.75
Jim Colbert	73	69	73	215	7,700
R.W. Eaks	70	72	73	215	7,700
Jack Ferenz	71	73	71	215	7,700
Mike McCullough	70	71	74	215	7,700
Lonnie Nielsen	74	71	70	215	7,700
Don Pooley	73	71	71	215	7,700
J.C. Snead	68	73	74	215	7,700
Leonard Thompson	75	72	68	215	7,700

Boeing Greater Seattle Classic

TPC at Snoqualmie Ridge, Snoqualmie, Washington
Par 36-36–72; 7,264 yards

August 18-20
purse, $1,600,000

	SCORES			TOTAL	MONEY
Tom Kite	71	64	66	201	$240,000
Keith Fergus	66	71	64	201	140,800
(Kite defeated Fergus on first playoff hole.)					
David Edwards	65	71	66	202	81,920
Tom Jenkins	74	67	61	202	81,920
Wayne Levi	68	68	66	202	81,920
Don Pooley	67	65	70	202	81,920
Scott Simpson	72	61	69	202	81,920
Walter Hall	68	68	67	203	51,200
Lonnie Nielsen	67	72	66	205	40,000
Tim Simpson	72	66	67	205	40,000
Bobby Wadkins	76	64	65	205	40,000
D.A. Weibring	74	65	66	205	40,000
Danny Edwards	72	69	65	206	30,400
Masahiro Kuramoto	63	70	73	206	30,400
Doug Tewell	67	69	70	206	30,400
Jim Chancey	68	71	68	207	22,697.15
Ben Crenshaw	70	72	65	207	22,697.15
Andy Bean	66	72	69	207	22,697.14
Bob Gilder	69	69	69	207	22,697.14
Morris Hatalsky	70	69	68	207	22,697.14
Rick Karbowski	70	68	69	207	22,697.14

	SCORES			TOTAL	MONEY
Graham Marsh	66	69	72	207	22,697.14
Ed Dougherty	69	70	69	208	15,337.15
Tom Purtzer	68	72	68	208	15,337.15
Jack Ferenz	73	70	65	208	15,337.14
Mark Johnson	71	65	72	208	15,337.14
Mike McCullough	69	68	71	208	15,337.14
Mike San Filippo	66	71	71	208	15,337.14
Des Smyth	69	66	73	208	15,337.14
Joe Inman	67	73	69	209	11,552
Mike Reid	70	69	70	209	11,552
Bruce Summerhays	70	69	70	209	11,552
Leonard Thompson	72	68	69	209	11,552
Jim Thorpe	71	68	70	209	11,552
Jim Albus	70	70	70	210	9,600
David Eger	71	67	72	210	9,600
Tom McKnight	70	69	71	210	9,600
Allen Doyle	67	74	70	211	8,640
Rick Rhoden	69	71	71	211	8,640
Isao Aoki	72	69	71	212	7,680
Bruce Fleisher	67	74	71	212	7,680
Gil Morgan	73	69	70	212	7,680
Naomichi Ozaki	70	72	70	212	7,680

JELD-WEN Tradition

Reserve Vineyards & Golf Club, Aloha, Oregon
Par 35-37–72; 6,998 yards

August 24-27
purse, $2,500,000

	SCORES				TOTAL	MONEY
Eduardo Romero	72	70	68	65	275	$375,000
Lonnie Nielsen	69	68	68	70	275	219,000
(Romero defeated Nielson on first playoff hole.)						
Bobby Wadkins	67	67	71	71	276	180,000
Mark James	72	72	68	67	279	115,000
Tom Kite	68	70	70	71	279	115,000
Larry Nelson	71	68	70	70	279	115,000
Tom Purtzer	70	68	71	70	279	115,000
Andy Bean	70	69	73	68	280	80,000
Keith Fergus	68	70	72	71	281	60,000
Bruce Lietzke	72	70	70	69	281	60,000
Hajime Meshiai	71	69	71	70	281	60,000
Don Pooley	73	69	71	68	281	60,000
Doug Tewell	76	68	69	68	281	60,000
Brad Bryant	75	73	67	67	282	41,266.67
David Edwards	74	68	67	73	282	41,266.67
Craig Stadler	73	72	71	66	282	41,266.67
Tom Watson	74	69	71	68	282	41,266.67
Tom Jenkins	70	68	70	74	282	41,266.66
Loren Roberts	67	71	68	76	282	41,266.66
Bruce Fleisher	71	73	66	73	283	29,350
Bob Gilder	72	70	68	73	283	29,350
Jay Haas	73	72	66	72	283	29,350
John Jacobs	72	72	66	73	283	29,350
Naomichi Ozaki	74	71	72	66	283	29,350
Allen Doyle	73	73	69	69	284	23,312.50
Tom McKnight	70	72	70	72	284	23,312.50
Tim Simpson	70	72	73	69	284	23,312.50

	SCORES				TOTAL	MONEY
Fuzzy Zoeller	74	69	69	72	284	23,312.50
Morris Hatalsky	71	69	70	75	285	19,750
Gil Morgan	73	71	72	69	285	19,750
D.A. Weibring	74	75	66	70	285	19,750
Ben Crenshaw	71	73	71	71	286	16,875
Hale Irwin	70	72	71	73	286	16,875
Dan Pohl	72	69	72	73	286	16,875
Dana Quigley	75	70	69	72	286	16,875
Bruce Summerhays	71	72	73	71	287	14,333.34
David Eger	76	68	72	71	287	14,333.33
Jim Thorpe	73	70	71	73	287	14,333.33
R.W. Eaks	73	72	74	69	288	11,750
Danny Edwards	74	73	72	69	288	11,750
Vicente Fernandez	72	70	76	70	288	11,750
Walter Hall	76	72	71	69	288	11,750
Masahiro Kuramoto	75	73	71	69	288	11,750
James Mason	72	71	73	72	288	11,750
Mike Reid	77	72	71	68	288	11,750

Wal-Mart First Tee Open at Pebble Beach

Pebble Beach Golf Links, Pebble Beach, California
Par 35-37–72; 6,822 yards
Del Monte Golf Course, Monterey, California
Par 36-36–72; 6,357 yards

September 1-3
purse, $2,000,000

	SCORES			TOTAL	MONEY
Scott Simpson	67	69	68	204	$300,000
David Edwards	67	70	68	205	160,000
Jay Haas	66	69	70	205	160,000
Masahiro Kuramoto	69	72	65	206	120,000
Tom Kite	69	65	73	207	88,000
Eduardo Romero	69	67	71	207	88,000
Mike McCullough	68	68	72	208	61,000
Loren Roberts	67	71	70	208	61,000
Des Smyth	68	70	70	208	61,000
D.A. Weibring	64	71	73	208	61,000
R.W. Eaks	69	70	70	209	44,000
Mark Johnson	70	72	67	209	44,000
Gil Morgan	69	70	70	209	44,000
Dan Pohl	69	67	74	210	36,000
Bruce Summerhays	70	68	72	210	36,000
Tom Watson	69	69	72	210	36,000
Bob Gilder	69	72	70	211	25,950
Bruce Lietzke	70	68	73	211	25,950
Gary McCord	69	70	72	211	25,950
Larry Nelson	68	72	71	211	25,950
Naomichi Ozaki	69	72	70	211	25,950
Tom Purtzer	66	70	75	211	25,950
Tim Simpson	69	71	71	211	25,950
Jim Thorpe	71	68	72	211	25,950
Keith Fergus	74	68	70	212	17,428.58
Andy Bean	68	72	72	212	17,428.57
David Eger	67	75	70	212	17,428.57
Bruce Fleisher	68	70	74	212	17,428.57
Hale Irwin	71	69	72	212	17,428.57
Wayne Levi	69	68	75	212	17,428.57

	SCORES			TOTAL	MONEY
Lonnie Nielsen	72	71	69	212	17,428.57
Vicente Fernandez	68	72	73	213	13,500
John Harris	71	69	73	213	13,500
Graham Marsh	71	73	69	213	13,500
Don Pooley	72	70	71	213	13,500
Hugh Baiocchi	70	73	71	214	11,466.67
Tom Wargo	71	71	72	214	11,466.67
Dana Quigley	76	72	66	214	11,466.66
Bob Eastwood	74	73	68	215	9,800
Danny Edwards	70	69	76	215	9,800
Mark McCumber	70	70	75	215	9,800
Tom McKnight	67	73	75	215	9,800
Mark McNulty	70	70	75	215	9,800

Georgia-Pacific Grand Champions Championship

Hawks Ridge Golf Club, Ball Ground, Georgia
Par 36-36–72; 6,826 yards

September 8-9
purse, $400,000

	SCORES		TOTAL	MONEY
Jay Sigel	65	69	134	$85,000
Mike McCullough	68	68	136	49,000
Jim Albus	69	68	137	41,000
Dave Eichelberger	69	70	139	29,750
Jim Dent	70	69	139	29,750
Tom Wargo	70	71	141	18,500
Graham Marsh	70	71	141	18,500
Dave Stockton	71	70	141	18,500
Bruce Summerhays	74	67	141	18,500
Raymond Floyd	72	70	142	12,500
John Jacobs	74	68	142	12,500
John Bland	71	73	144	11,000
Mike Hill	69	77	146	10,500
Bob Charles	76	71	147	10,000
Jim Colbert	75	73	148	9,250
Bob Eastwood	75	73	148	9,250
J.C. Snead	74	75	149	8,500
Gibby Gilbert	73	79	152	8,000

Constellation Energy Classic

Hayfields Country Club, Hunt Valley, Maryland
Par 36-36–72; 7,031 yards

September 15-17
purse, $1,700,000

	SCORES			TOTAL	MONEY
Bob Gilder	69	68	65	202	$255,000
Brad Bryant	68	68	68	204	124,666.67
Jay Haas	69	67	68	204	124,666.67
Don Pooley	70	64	70	204	124,666.66
Chip Beck	69	70	66	205	74,800
Tom Watson	70	68	67	205	74,800
R.W. Eaks	69	69	68	206	54,400
Tom Jenkins	68	68	70	206	54,400
Tom Purtzer	69	69	68	206	54,400

	SCORES			TOTAL	MONEY
Tom Kite	69	72	66	207	42,500
Bruce Summerhays	69	68	70	207	42,500
Jim Thorpe	66	72	70	208	37,400
Mark McNulty	71	69	69	209	28,924.29
Gil Morgan	71	67	71	209	28,924.29
Naomichi Ozaki	75	68	66	209	28,924.29
Ron Streck	69	72	68	209	28,924.29
Andy Bean	73	63	73	209	28,924.28
Keith Fergus	69	66	74	209	28,924.28
Masahiro Kuramoto	68	67	74	209	28,924.28
Kirk Hanefeld	73	69	68	210	18,991.43
Morris Hatalsky	71	70	69	210	18,991.43
Mark Johnson	68	72	70	210	18,991.43
Mike Reid	74	67	69	210	18,991.43
Scott Simpson	70	71	69	210	18,991.43
Rod Spittle	70	72	68	210	18,991.43
Jay Sigel	73	67	70	210	18,991.42
John Bland	76	65	70	211	14,110
Scott Hoch	72	70	69	211	14,110
Lonnie Nielsen	71	69	71	211	14,110
Tim Simpson	71	69	71	211	14,110
Bobby Wadkins	71	69	71	211	14,110
David Edwards	70	71	71	212	10,965
Walter Hall	68	74	70	212	10,965
John Harris	73	71	68	212	10,965
Joe Inman	74	70	68	212	10,965
Wayne Levi	70	75	67	212	10,965
Mark Lye	69	73	70	212	10,965
Danny Edwards	72	72	69	213	8,670
Graham Marsh	69	70	74	213	8,670
Dan Pohl	70	72	71	213	8,670
Rick Rhoden	74	69	70	213	8,670
Curtis Strange	71	70	72	213	8,670

Greater Hickory Classic at Rock Barn

Rock Barn Golf & Spa, Conover, North Carolina
Par 35-37–72; 7,039 yards

September 29-October 1
purse, $1,600,000

	SCORES			TOTAL	MONEY
Andy Bean	63	70	68	201	$240,000
R.W. Eaks	69	67	65	201	140,800
(Bean defeated Eaks on first playoff hole.)					
Chip Beck	67	69	67	203	115,200
Dana Quigley	67	71	66	204	96,000
Allen Doyle	69	66	70	205	62,400
Hajime Meshiai	70	67	68	205	62,400
Naomichi Ozaki	69	70	66	205	62,400
Tom Purtzer	68	69	68	205	62,400
Larry Nelson	70	69	67	206	44,800
Brad Bryant	69	68	70	207	38,400
Jay Haas	74	67	66	207	38,400
Walter Hall	69	72	66	207	38,400
Bob Eastwood	68	73	67	208	28,000
Bob Gilder	71	70	67	208	28,000
Tom Kite	68	68	72	208	28,000
James Mason	70	69	69	208	28,000

	SCORES			TOTAL	MONEY
Craig Stadler	71	71	66	208	28,000
Curtis Strange	70	70	68	208	28,000
David Edwards	71	72	66	209	21,173.34
John Jacobs	70	70	69	209	21,173.33
Tom McKnight	70	72	67	209	21,173.33
Danny Edwards	70	75	65	210	17,240
Wayne Levi	72	69	69	210	17,240
Gil Morgan	69	70	71	210	17,240
Jay Sigel	70	70	70	210	17,240
David Eger	71	70	70	211	13,600
Dave Eichelberger	70	74	67	211	13,600
Vicente Fernandez	69	72	70	211	13,600
Mark McNulty	73	69	69	211	13,600
Scott Simpson	72	72	67	211	13,600
Ron Streck	71	67	73	211	13,600
Keith Fergus	70	72	70	212	11,040
Lonnie Nielsen	71	69	72	212	11,040
Bruce Summerhays	71	70	71	212	11,040
Kirk Hanefeld	72	73	68	213	9,400
Morris Hatalsky	71	72	70	213	9,400
Kenny Knox	71	72	70	213	9,400
Mark Lye	69	71	73	213	9,400
Jose Maria Canizares	69	70	75	214	7,680
Ed Dougherty	70	70	74	214	7,680
Joe Inman	70	68	76	214	7,680
Tom Jenkins	72	71	71	214	7,680
Masahiro Kuramoto	69	72	73	214	7,680
Bob Murphy	71	72	71	214	7,680

SAS Championship

Prestonwood Country Club, Cary, North Carolina
Par 36-36—72; 7,197 yards
(Third round cancelled—rain.)

October 6-8
purse, $2,000,000

	SCORES		TOTAL	MONEY
Tom Jenkins	68	66	134	$300,000
Chip Beck	70	65	135	160,000
Loren Roberts	67	68	135	160,000
Mitch Adcock	67	69	136	120,000
Jay Haas	71	66	137	96,000
Jim Ahern	69	70	139	76,000
Andy Bean	70	69	139	76,000
Brad Bryant	69	71	140	55,000
Raymond Floyd	71	69	140	55,000
Scott Hoch	69	71	140	55,000
Gil Morgan	71	69	140	55,000
Bob Gilder	71	70	141	42,000
Fuzzy Zoeller	71	70	141	42,000
Danny Edwards	71	71	142	34,000
John Harris	69	73	142	34,000
Masahiro Kuramoto	71	71	142	34,000
Mark McNulty	70	72	142	34,000
Jim Thorpe	72	70	142	34,000
David Edwards	72	71	143	23,075
Vicente Fernandez	72	71	143	23,075
Tom Purtzer	71	72	143	23,075

	SCORES		TOTAL	MONEY
Mike Reid	74	69	143	23,075
Eduardo Romero	70	73	143	23,075
Tim Simpson	70	73	143	23,075
Ron Streck	71	72	143	23,075
Bobby Wadkins	73	70	143	23,075
Des Smyth	72	72	144	17,400
Chris Starkjohann	77	67	144	17,400
D.A. Weibring	72	72	144	17,400
Allen Doyle	75	70	145	14,750
David Eger	72	73	145	14,750
Pat McGowan	79	66	145	14,750
Lonnie Nielsen	71	74	145	14,750
Jose Maria Canizares	74	72	146	11,350
Jim Colbert	77	69	146	11,350
Keith Fergus	74	72	146	11,350
Vance Heafner	72	74	146	11,350
Tom Kite	71	75	146	11,350
Wayne Levi	74	72	146	11,350
Naomichi Ozaki	70	76	146	11,350
Bruce Summerhays	75	71	146	11,350

Administaff Small Business Classic

Augusta Pines Golf Club, Spring, Texas
Par 36-36—72; 7,006 yards
(Third round cancelled—rain.)

October 13-15
purse, $1,600,000

	SCORES		TOTAL	MONEY
Jay Haas	65	63	128	$240,000
Bruce Lietzke	67	66	133	128,000
Tom Purtzer	65	68	133	128,000
Dick Mast	65	69	134	96,000
Jim Thorpe	69	66	135	76,800
Des Smyth	69	67	136	64,000
Larry Nelson	70	67	137	51,200
Ron Streck	71	66	137	51,200
D.A. Weibring	69	68	137	51,200
R.W. Eaks	71	67	138	34,400
Dave Eichelberger	67	71	138	34,400
Tom Jenkins	68	70	138	34,400
Mark Johnson	71	67	138	34,400
Mike McCullough	72	66	138	34,400
Tom McKnight	69	69	138	34,400
Vicente Fernandez	70	69	139	22,697.15
Kenny Knox	71	68	139	22,697.15
Mark James	69	70	139	22,697.14
Loren Roberts	70	69	139	22,697.14
Bill Rogers	68	71	139	22,697.14
Eduardo Romero	69	70	139	22,697.14
Curtis Strange	68	71	139	22,697.14
Mitch Adcock	71	69	140	14,666.67
Chip Beck	72	68	140	14,666.67
Jim Dent	72	68	140	14,666.67
Ed Dougherty	72	68	140	14,666.67
Mike Reid	73	67	140	14,666.67
Scott Simpson	72	68	140	14,666.67
Andy Bean	69	71	140	14,666.66

	SCORES			TOTAL	MONEY
Brad Bryant	68	72		140	14,666.66
Dana Quigley	68	72		140	14,666.66
Jose Maria Canizares	73	68		141	10,102.86
Allen Doyle	72	69		141	10,102.86
Wayne Levi	72	69		141	10,102.86
Mark McNulty	71	70		141	10,102.86
Naomichi Ozaki	75	66		141	10,102.86
Walter Hall	69	72		141	10,102.85
Gil Morgan	69	72		141	10,102.85
Bob Eastwood	75	67		142	7,520
Keith Fergus	69	73		142	7,520
Morris Hatalsky	71	71		142	7,520
John Jacobs	73	69		142	7,520
Gary McCord	75	67		142	7,520
Lonnie Nielsen	72	70		142	7,520
Don Pooley	75	67		142	7,520

AT&T Championship

Oak Hills Country Club, San Antonio, Texas
Par 35-36–71; 6,670 yards

October 20-22
purse, $1,600,000

	SCORES			TOTAL	MONEY
Fred Funk	65	67	69	201	$240,000
Chip Beck	69	68	65	202	140,800
Scott Simpson	66	68	69	203	115,200
Ben Crenshaw	71	66	68	205	78,933.34
Raymond Floyd	67	66	72	205	78,933.33
Loren Roberts	68	68	69	205	78,933.33
R.W. Eaks	66	69	71	206	48,800
Jay Haas	70	64	72	206	48,800
Mark McNulty	68	70	68	206	48,800
Ron Streck	69	66	71	206	48,800
Gary McCord	69	69	69	207	36,800
Don Pooley	71	68	68	207	36,800
Walter Hall	68	69	71	208	27,222.86
Mark James	68	69	71	208	27,222.86
Tom Kite	69	70	69	208	27,222.86
D.A. Weibring	68	69	71	208	27,222.86
Fuzzy Zoeller	69	70	69	208	27,222.86
Danny Edwards	70	67	71	208	27,222.85
Jim Thorpe	69	66	73	208	27,222.85
James Mason	68	67	74	209	18,784
Dick Mast	68	68	73	209	18,784
Tom Purtzer	68	70	71	209	18,784
Craig Stadler	68	68	73	209	18,784
Bruce Summerhays	70	69	70	209	18,784
Andy Bean	71	68	71	210	13,942.86
John Bland	69	68	73	210	13,942.86
Morris Hatalsky	69	69	72	210	13,942.86
Bruce Lietzke	70	68	72	210	13,942.86
Gil Morgan	69	70	71	210	13,942.86
Keith Fergus	67	67	76	210	13,942.85
Dana Quigley	69	67	74	210	13,942.85
Tom Jenkins	70	70	71	211	11,280
Eduardo Romero	70	72	69	211	11,280
Jim Ahern	71	70	71	212	9,840

	SCORES			TOTAL	MONEY
David Edwards	71	73	68	212	9,840
David Eger	72	69	71	212	9,840
Lonnie Nielsen	67	71	74	212	9,840
Hale Irwin	68	71	74	213	8,640
Hajime Meshiai	68	72	73	213	8,640
Bob Eastwood	73	71	70	214	7,040
Kenny Knox	71	72	71	214	7,040
Mike Reid	70	74	70	214	7,040
Bill Rogers	70	71	73	214	7,040
Tim Simpson	71	69	74	214	7,040
Dave Stockton	71	72	71	214	7,040
Leonard Thompson	70	74	70	214	7,040
Lee Trevino	72	66	76	214	7,040

Charles Schwab Cup Championship

Sonoma Golf Club, Sonoma, California
Par 36-36–72; 7,012 yards

October 26-29
purse, $2,500,000

	SCORES				TOTAL	MONEY
Jim Thorpe	66	70	67	68	271	$440,000
Tom Kite	67	68	70	68	273	254,000
Keith Fergus	71	70	67	66	274	213,000
Loren Roberts	71	66	68	71	276	158,000
Eduardo Romero	73	69	66	68	276	158,000
Jay Haas	70	66	69	72	277	105,000
Craig Stadler	68	69	71	69	277	105,000
Tom Watson	70	70	67	70	277	105,000
Andy Bean	69	68	69	72	278	79,000
Des Smyth	69	70	69	70	278	79,000
R.W. Eaks	72	71	66	71	280	62,000
Hale Irwin	70	70	70	70	280	62,000
Tom Jenkins	72	67	69	72	280	62,000
Bruce Lietzke	70	70	68	72	280	62,000
Lonnie Nielsen	69	70	73	69	281	50,500
Tom Purtzer	70	72	71	68	281	50,500
Bob Gilder	68	70	68	76	282	46,000
Gil Morgan	72	66	68	77	283	43,000
Brad Bryant	71	69	71	73	284	37,125
David Edwards	72	71	73	68	284	37,125
Dana Quigley	73	71	69	71	284	37,125
Bobby Wadkins	71	66	75	72	284	37,125
Mark McNulty	72	73	70	71	286	32,000
Morris Hatalsky	71	72	70	74	287	28,666.67
D.A. Weibring	73	71	69	74	287	28,666.67
Don Pooley	72	70	70	75	287	28,666.66
John Harris	80	71	73	67	291	26,000
Scott Simpson	70	74	73	78	295	25,000
Allen Doyle	76	70	74	76	296	24,500

European Seniors Tour

DGM Barbados Open

Royal Westmoreland Golf Club, St. James, Barbados
Par 37-36–73; 6,814 yards

March 1-3
purse, €190,881

	SCORES			TOTAL	MONEY
Jose Rivero	70	66	71	207	€30,330.03
David Russell	71	68	68	207	20,220.02
(Rivero defeated Russell on fourth playoff hole.)					
Bruce Heuchan	72	67	69	208	14,154.01
Eduardo Romero	68	72	69	209	11,121.01
Sam Torrance	73	70	67	210	9,139.45
Delroy Cambridge	69	68	74	211	8,088.01
Luis Carbonetti	72	70	70	212	6,470.40
Martin Gray	70	73	69	212	6,470.40
Gavan Levenson	69	69	74	212	6,470.40
Bob Cameron	71	68	74	213	5,257.21
Bill Longmuir	72	71	71	214	4,650.60
Carl Mason	71	73	70	214	4,650.60
Hugh Baiocchi	74	66	75	215	3,841.81
John Chillas	71	69	75	215	3,841.81
David Oakley	73	75	67	215	3,841.81
Jim Rhodes	68	76	72	216	3,427.40
Gordon Brand	73	73	71	217	3,039.74
Ray Carrasco	74	70	73	217	3,039.74
Terry Gale	74	72	71	217	3,039.74
Jerry Bruner	72	72	74	218	2,436.51
Horacio Carbonetti	71	75	72	218	2,436.51
Nick Job	69	71	78	218	2,436.51
Hank Woodrome	76	72	70	218	2,436.51

Sharp Italian Seniors Open

Circolo Golf Venezia, Venice, Italy
Par 35-37–72; 6,757 yards

May 19-21
purse, €175,000

	SCORES			TOTAL	MONEY
Sam Torrance	68	70	67	205	€26,250
Eamonn Darcy	69	69	71	209	17,500
Pietro Molteni	70	72	69	211	10,937.50
Luis Carbonetti	74	68	69	211	10,937.50
Guillermo Encina	68	73	71	212	7,910
Juan Quiros	76	67	70	213	6,300
Carl Mason	72	70	71	213	6,300
Stewart Ginn	73	66	74	213	6,300
Delroy Cambridge	69	70	75	214	4,550
David J. Russell	74	71	69	214	4,550
Pete Oakley	72	72	70	214	4,550
Gordon J. Brand	70	70	75	215	3,675
Bobby Lincoln	70	72	73	215	3,675

	SCORES			TOTAL	MONEY
Martin Poxon	70	72	74	216	3,062.50
Adan Sowa	71	73	72	216	3,062.50
Bob Larratt	69	72	75	216	3,062.50
Gery Watine	72	74	70	216	3,062.50
Alan Tapie	76	71	70	217	2,467.50
Bertus Smit	72	75	70	217	2,467.50
Bruce Heuchan	73	74	70	217	2,467.50
David Good	75	70	73	218	2,041.67
Jose Rivero	77	70	71	218	2,041.67

AIB Irish Seniors Open

Sheraton Fota Island Golf Resort & Spa, Co. Cork, Ireland
Par 36-35–71; 6,820 yards

June 2-4
purse, €420,000

	SCORES			TOTAL	MONEY
Sam Torrance	70	68	69	207	€63,000
Jerry Bruner	69	69	69	207	31,500
Guillermo Encina	68	67	72	207	31,500
Stewart Ginn	67	73	67	207	31,500

(Torrance defeated Encina and Ginn on first and Bruner on second playoff hole.)

	SCORES			TOTAL	MONEY
Horacio Carbonetti	70	69	69	208	16,086
Tony Johnstone	68	71	69	208	16,086
Bobby Lincoln	67	67	74	208	16,086
Carl Mason	69	66	73	208	16,086
Bruce Heuchan	74	66	69	209	11,340
Kevin Spurgeon	72	66	71	209	11,340
Gordon J. Brand	69	70	71	210	9,660
Denis O'Sullivan	69	73	68	210	9,660
Nick Job	73	68	70	211	8,190
Manuel Pinero	70	71	70	211	8,190
Jimmy Heggarty	70	72	70	212	7,140
Simon Owen	70	71	71	212	7,140
Juan Quiros	69	70	73	212	7,140
Rex Caldwell	73	72	68	213	5,922
Eamonn Darcy	70	71	72	213	5,922
Gavan Levenson	69	73	71	213	5,922

Irvine Whitlock Seniors Classic

La Moye Golf Club, Jersey, Channel Isles
Par 36-36–72; 6,581 yards

June 9-11
purse, €174,880

	SCORES			TOTAL	MONEY
Guillermo Encina	72	71	66	209	€26,285.83
Rex Caldwell	72	71	69	212	13,142.92
Simon Owen	73	72	67	212	13,142.92
Alan Tapie	71	74	67	212	13,142.92
Bob Cameron	70	71	72	213	7,465.17
David J. Russell	72	71	70	213	7,465.17
John Chillas	68	75	71	214	5,116.97
Stewart Ginn	75	71	68	214	5,116.97
Bertus Smit	71	72	71	214	5,116.97
Kevin Spurgeon	71	73	70	214	5,116.97

	SCORES			TOTAL	MONEY
Sam Torrance	73	72	69	214	5,116.97
John Benda	71	71	73	215	3,680.01
Adan Sowa	76	70	69	215	3,680.01
Tony Allen	70	76	70	216	3,241.92
Bruce Heuchan	74	74	68	216	3,241.92
Doug Johnson	74	70	73	217	2,720.58
Martin Poxon	73	70	74	217	2,720.58
Jim Rhodes	75	75	67	217	2,720.58
Gery Watine	75	75	67	217	2,720.58
Luis Carbonetti	80	71	67	218	2,243.06
Terry Gale	75	70	73	218	2,243.06

FirstPlus Wales Seniors Open

Vale Hotel Golf & Spa Resort, Cardiff, Wales
Par 36-36–72; 6,887 yards

June 16-18
purse, €729,803

	SCORES			TOTAL	MONEY
Jose Rivero	70	74	68	212	€109,366.50
Juan Quiros	74	70	69	213	49,251.38
David J. Russell	69	69	75	213	49,251.38
Sam Torrance	74	68	71	213	49,251.38
Gery Watine	71	72	70	213	49,251.38
Martin Poxon	70	75	69	214	29,164.40
Nick Job	73	71	71	215	26,247.96
Carl Mason	73	72	71	216	23,331.52
Gordon J. Brand	76	72	69	217	20,415.08
Luis Carbonetti	74	72	72	218	18,956.86
Horacio Carbonetti	72	75	72	219	16,769.53
Des Smyth	72	72	75	219	16,769.53
Guillermo Encina	75	71	74	220	13,488.54
Tony Johnstone	71	78	71	220	13,488.54
Bobby Lincoln	73	75	72	220	13,488.54
Kevin Spurgeon	75	73	72	220	13,488.54
Giuseppe Cali	77	67	78	222	10,000.96
Bob Cameron	76	74	72	222	10,000.96
John Chillas	74	76	72	222	10,000.96
Mike Ferguson	77	71	74	222	10,000.96
Jimmy Heggarty	75	72	75	222	10,000.96
Pete Oakley	72	79	71	222	10,000.96

Bendinat London Seniors Masters

London Golf Club, Ash, Kent, England
Par 36-36–72; 7,037 yards

June 29-July 1
purse, €218,064

	SCORES			TOTAL	MONEY
Giuseppe Cali	69	74	67	210	€32,709.60
Delroy Cambridge	67	72	71	210	21,806.40
(Cali defeated Cambridge on fifth playoff hole.)					
Tony Allen	70	71	70	211	15,264.48
Nick Job	70	71	71	212	10,925.01
Juan Quiros	74	68	70	212	10,925.01
Martin Foster	69	72	72	213	8,286.43

	SCORES	TOTAL	MONEY
Sam Torrance	70 66 77	213	8,286.43
Bobby Lincoln	74 68 72	214	6,541.92
Carl Mason	69 73 72	214	6,541.92
John Chillas	66 77 72	215	5,233.54
Martin Gray	70 74 71	215	5,233.54
Bertus Smit	72 67 76	215	5,233.54
Kevin Spurgeon	68 73 75	216	4,361.28
Guillermo Encina	68 73 76	217	4,034.18
Jose Rivero	73 71 73	217	4,034.18
Gordon J. Brand	76 71 71	218	3,385.44
Terry Gale	74 72 72	218	3,385.44
John Mashego	71 74 73	218	3,385.44
David J. Russell	73 72 73	218	3,385.44
John Benda	73 71 75	219	2,878.44

Senior British Open

Westin Turnberry Resort, Ayrshire, Scotland
Par 35-35–70; 7,012 yards

July 27-30
purse, €1,473,677

	SCORES	TOTAL	MONEY
Loren Roberts	65 65 69 75	274	€231,225.91
Eduardo Romero	67 63 73 71	274	154,223.88
(Roberts defeated Romero on first playoff hole.)			
Dick Mast	71 67 70 67	275	86,819.62
Craig Stadler	65 66 77 70	278	69,382.43
Tim Simpson	66 67 72 74	279	58,788.24
Jay Haas	72 68 73 68	281	45,087.59
D.A. Weibring	72 70 71 68	281	45,087.59
David Edwards	67 65 76 75	283	32,874.23
Gil Morgan	68 65 75 75	283	32,874.23
Gordon J. Brand	67 73 75 69	284	25,672.23
John Harris	73 68 72 71	284	25,672.23
Tom Kite	69 69 74 72	284	25,672.23
Hale Irwin	73 71 71 70	285	21,759.85
Don Pooley	76 63 72 74	285	21,759.85
Mark James	67 70 75 74	286	19,089.33
Kiyoshi Murota	70 70 76 70	286	19,089.33
Tsuneyuki Nakajima	68 68 74 76	286	19,089.33
Lonnie Nielsen	71 69 75 71	286	19,089.33
James Blair	71 71 71 74	287	16,598.30
Jon Chaffee	72 70 74 71	287	16,598.30
Morris Hatalsky	73 67 75 72	287	16,598.30
Mike Reid	68 67 78 74	287	16,598.30
Eamonn Darcy	71 67 78 72	288	14,711.71
Andrew Reynolds	73 66 77 72	288	14,711.71
John Ross	67 72 76 73	288	14,711.71
Tom Watson	73 67 74 74	288	14,711.71
Stewart Ginn	69 68 78 74	289	12,061.33
Kirk Hanefeld	68 72 77 72	289	12,061.33
Carl Mason	75 66 75 73	289	12,061.33
Tom McKnight	70 70 79 70	289	12,061.33
Mark McNulty	68 68 79 74	289	12,061.33
Juan Quiros	67 76 72 74	289	12,061.33
David J. Russell	70 73 73 73	289	12,061.33
Des Smyth	66 71 82 70	289	12,061.33

Wentworth Senior Masters

Wentworth Club, Edinburgh Course, Surrey, England
Par 36-36–72; 6,873 yards

August 4-6
purse, €365,992

	SCORES			TOTAL	MONEY
Eduardo Romero	71	66	70	207	€54,846.75
Horacio Carbonetti	68	72	69	209	31,079.82
Sam Torrance	70	68	71	209	31,079.82
Giuseppe Cali	73	70	67	210	17,087.81
Terry Gale	70	72	68	210	17,087.81
Bertus Smit	70	70	70	210	17,087.81
Tony Johnstone	71	69	71	211	12,431.93
Katsuyoshi Tomori	69	71	71	211	12,431.93
Jim Rhodes	73	70	69	212	9,872.41
David J. Russell	74	68	70	212	9,872.41
Seiji Ebihara	71	72	70	213	8,044.19
Stewart Ginn	66	69	78	213	8,044.19
Juan Quiros	71	72	70	213	8,044.19
John Bland	69	73	72	214	6,215.96
Guillermo Encina	71	70	73	214	6,215.96
Bruce Heuchan	73	72	69	214	6,215.96
Martin Poxon	71	75	68	214	6,215.96
Des Smyth	69	72	73	214	6,215.96
John Chillas	73	72	70	215	4,689.40
Jeff Hawkes	73	71	71	215	4,689.40
Carl Mason	75	71	69	215	4,689.40
Emilio Rodriguez	70	72	73	215	4,689.40

Bad Ragaz PGA Seniors Open

Golf Club Bad Ragaz, Zurich, Switzerland
Par 35-35–70; 6,183 yards

August 11-13
purse, €210,000

	SCORES			TOTAL	MONEY
Juan Quiros	70	61	65	196	€31,500
Carl Mason	66	67	65	198	21,000
Stewart Ginn	65	70	64	199	11,914
Nick Job	67	64	68	199	11,914
Bill Longmuir	69	62	68	199	11,914
Luis Carbonetti	68	68	65	201	8,400
John Bland	65	68	69	202	6,405
Horacio Carbonetti	68	67	67	202	6,405
Jose Rivero	67	67	68	202	6,405
Gery Watine	73	64	65	202	6,405
Bob Cameron	70	67	66	203	4,326
Jimmy Heggarty	69	69	65	203	4,326
Doug Johnson	68	70	65	203	4,326
David J. Russell	68	66	69	203	4,326
Peter Teravainen	70	64	69	203	4,326
Giuseppe Cali	70	68	66	204	3,360
Jim Rhodes	71	66	67	204	3,360
Jean Pierre Sallat	70	70	64	204	3,360
John Chillas	67	67	71	205	2,779
Mike Miller	68	69	68	205	2,779
Bertus Smit	68	67	70	205	2,779

Scandinavian Senior Open

Helsingor Golf Club, Helsingor, Denmark
Par 36-35–71; 6,368 yards

August 17-19
purse, €250,000

	SCORES			TOTAL	MONEY
Katsuyoshi Tomori	66	67	66	199	€39,258.79
Eamonn Darcy	68	64	69	201	22,246.65
Jose Rivero	68	63	70	201	22,246.65
Giuseppe Cali	69	67	66	202	12,231.29
Simon Owen	68	65	69	202	12,231.29
Bertus Smit	66	71	65	202	12,231.29
Gordon J. Brand	67	69	67	203	8,898.66
Stewart Ginn	67	69	67	203	8,898.66
John Chillas	68	69	67	204	7,328.31
Martin Gray	69	68	68	205	6,543.14
Nick Job	69	69	67	205	6,543.14
Peter Teravainen	67	70	69	206	5,757.96
Delroy Cambridge	69	72	66	207	4,580.19
Luis Carbonetti	68	68	71	207	4,580.19
Carl Mason	69	69	69	207	4,580.19
Glenn Ralph	69	70	68	207	4,580.19
Emilio Rodriguez	67	74	66	207	4,580.19
Gery Watine	67	75	65	207	4,580.19
Jerry Bruner	72	67	69	208	3,463.50
Angel Fernandez	71	67	70	208	3,463.50
David Good	71	68	69	208	3,463.50

PGA Seniors Championship

Stoke by Nayland Golf Club, Colchester, England
Par 36-36–72; 6,589 yards

August 25-28
purse, €293,646

	SCORES				TOTAL	MONEY
Sam Torrance	65	66	71	66	268	€48,936.11
Luis Carbonetti	68	69	65	69	271	31,214.57
Giuseppe Cali	67	66	66	74	273	17,912.41
John Bland	69	68	68	70	275	12,479.96
Doug Johnson	70	65	69	71	275	12,479.96
Tony Johnstone	67	69	70	69	275	12,479.96
Bill Longmuir	67	67	70	74	278	9,249.85
Simon Owen	68	75	66	69	278	9,249.85
Bertus Smit	70	70	72	66	278	9,249.85
Nick Job	67	68	71	73	279	6,698.80
Carl Mason	71	68	73	67	279	6,698.80
Martin Poxon	68	71	69	71	279	6,698.80
Jose Rivero	70	73	68	68	279	6,698.80
Eamonn Darcy	69	65	73	73	280	4,991.98
Delroy Cambridge	70	67	74	71	282	4,037.63
Philippe Dugeny	69	73	68	72	282	4,037.63
Jean Pierre Sallat	72	68	72	70	282	4,037.63
Bob Cameron	70	72	71	70	283	3,362.25
Manuel Pinero	71	71	70	71	283	3,362.25
Seiji Ebihara	72	73	69	70	284	3,068.60
Martin Foster	71	71	69	73	284	3,068.60
Emilio Rodriguez	72	71	72	69	284	3,068.60

Charles Church Scottish Seniors Open

Marriott Dalmahoy Hotel & Country Club,
Edinburgh, Scotland
Par 35-37–72; 6,997 yards

September 1-3
purse, €295,824

	SCORES			TOTAL	MONEY
Sam Torrance	76	67	70	213	€44,373.60
Bill Longmuir	75	68	71	214	29,582.40
John Bland	76	70	69	215	14,566.37
Mike Miller	71	71	73	215	14,566.37
Glenn Ralph	71	73	71	215	14,566.37
David J. Russell	74	72	69	215	14,566.37
Bertus Smit	70	75	70	215	14,566.37
Juan Quiros	69	72	76	217	8,874.72
Jose Rivero	69	74	74	217	8,874.72
Delroy Cambridge	73	72	74	219	6,803.95
Nick Job	70	75	74	219	6,803.95
Carl Mason	72	74	73	219	6,803.95
Pete Oakley	71	76	72	219	6,803.95
Giuseppe Cali	73	76	71	220	4,886.03
Seiji Ebihara	74	71	75	220	4,886.03
Guillermo Encina	74	75	71	220	4,886.03
Martin Gray	71	75	74	220	4,886.03
Gavan Levenson	75	73	72	220	4,886.03
Bobby Lincoln	76	69	75	220	4,886.03
Eamonn Darcy	74	74	73	221	3,387.18
Terry Gale	73	72	76	221	3,387.18
Craig Maltman	74	72	75	221	3,387.18
Ian Mosey	71	76	74	221	3,387.18
Simon Owen	77	72	72	221	3,387.18
Hank Woodrome	76	73	72	221	3,387.18

European Senior Masters

Woburn Golf Club, Dukes Course, Milton Keynes, England
Par 35-37–72; 6,896 yards

September 8-10
purse, €334,321

	SCORES			TOTAL	MONEY
Carl Mason	73	67	69	209	€50,100.52
Horacio Carbonetti	69	70	72	211	33,400.35
Giuseppe Cali	74	69	69	212	18,949.13
Eamonn Darcy	74	70	68	212	18,949.13
Jose Rivero	66	76	70	212	18,949.13
Bruce Heuchan	71	73	70	214	12,692.13
Tony Johnstone	74	71	69	214	12,692.13
Pete Oakley	69	75	71	215	10,020.11
Noel Ratcliffe	73	69	73	215	10,020.11
Terry Gale	72	70	74	216	8,016.08
Bertus Smit	73	71	72	216	8,016.08
Sam Torrance	77	72	67	216	8,016.08
Bob Cameron	76	72	69	217	5,523.58
Rodger Davis	71	72	74	217	5,523.58
Angel Fernandez	71	72	74	217	5,523.58
Stewart Ginn	71	73	73	217	5,523.58
Mark James	76	74	67	217	5,523.58
Nick Job	78	71	68	217	5,523.58

	SCORES	TOTAL	MONEY
Gavan Levenson	74 74 69	217	5,523.58
Juan Quiros	70 77 70	217	5,523.58

The Midas Group English Seniors Open

St. Mellion International Hotel Golf & Country Club,
St. Mellion, Cornwall, England
Par 36-36–72; 6,854 yards

September 15-17
purse, €220,534

	SCORES	TOTAL	MONEY
Carl Mason	70 71 71	212	€33,080.17
Stewart Ginn	76 70 67	213	22,053.45
Seiji Ebihara	74 72 68	214	11,589.09
Martin Gray	73 73 68	214	11,589.09
Nick Job	71 75 68	214	11,589.09
Tony Johnstone	76 70 68	214	11,589.09
Gavan Levenson	72 76 67	215	7,057.10
Alan Mew	75 68 72	215	7,057.10
Bertus Smit	71 73 71	215	7,057.10
Bob Cameron	72 75 69	216	4,741.49
David Good	74 75 67	216	4,741.49
Bill Hardwick	73 72 71	216	4,741.49
John Mashego	75 74 67	216	4,741.49
Jim Rhodes	73 73 70	216	4,741.49
Kevin Spurgeon	74 71 71	216	4,741.49
Rex Caldwell	72 76 69	217	3,638.82
Pete Oakley	71 76 70	217	3,638.82
Giuseppe Cali	74 74 70	218	2,924.29
Horacio Carbonetti	72 75 71	218	2,924.29
Bob Lendzion	75 71 72	218	2,924.29
Simon Owen	73 73 72	218	2,924.29
Martin Poxon	74 75 69	218	2,924.29

OKI Castellon Open de Espana Senior

Club de Campo del Mediterraneo, Castellon, Spain
Par 36-36–72; 6,706 yards

October 13-15
purse, €300,000

	SCORES	TOTAL	MONEY
Gordon J. Brand	65 66 72	203	€45,000
Carl Mason	66 71 68	205	25,500
Sam Torrance	68 68 69	205	25,500
Stewart Ginn	70 70 68	208	15,030
Bobby Lincoln	68 73 67	208	15,030
Guillermo Encina	70 68 71	209	11,400
Greg Norman	69 69 71	209	11,400
Bob Cameron	73 67 70	210	8,250
Bill Hardwick	67 74 69	210	8,250
Jimmy Heggarty	71 70 69	210	8,250
Gery Watine	70 69 71	210	8,250
Delroy Cambridge	72 65 74	211	5,925
Luis Carbonetti	67 75 69	211	5,925
Eamonn Darcy	67 70 74	211	5,925
Simon Owen	71 71 69	211	5,925

	SCORES			TOTAL	MONEY
Tony Allen	68	74	70	212	4,385
John Benda	68	70	74	212	4,385
Tony Charnley	74	69	69	212	4,385
Tony Johnstone	70	70	72	212	4,385
Jean Pierre Sallat	70	70	72	212	4,385
Alan Tapie	72	71	69	212	4,385

Estoril Seniors Open of Portugal

Oitavos Golf, Quinta da Marinha, Portugal
Par 36-35–71; 6,705 yards

October 20-22
purse, €300,000

	SCORES			TOTAL	MONEY
Carl Mason	64	69	71	204	€45,000
Stewart Ginn	69	67	72	208	25,500
Sam Torrance	67	70	71	208	25,500
Tony Johnstone	67	73	70	210	15,030
Juan Quiros	66	72	72	210	15,030
Horacio Carbonetti	72	69	71	212	12,000
Delroy Cambridge	71	71	71	213	10,200
Bill Longmuir	69	73	71	213	10,200
Eamonn Darcy	71	70	74	215	7,500
Glenn Ralph	71	70	74	215	7,500
Jose Rivero	66	71	78	215	7,500
Adan Sowa	73	68	74	215	7,500
Giuseppe Cali	72	70	74	216	5,250
Terry Gale	73	73	70	216	5,250
Doug Johnson	73	73	70	216	5,250
Gavan Levenson	71	72	73	216	5,250
John Mashego	68	73	75	216	5,250
Jim Rhodes	71	74	71	216	5,250
David Good	73	72	72	217	3,847.50
Nick Job	68	72	77	217	3,847.50
Simon Owen	75	71	71	217	3,847.50
Bertus Smit	68	73	76	217	3,847.50

Arcapita Seniors Tour Championship

Riffa Views Golf Club, Manama, Bahrain
Par 36-36–72; 6,777 yards

November 9-11
purse, €393,546

	SCORES			TOTAL	MONEY
Gordon J. Brand	73	72	66	211	€63,393.34
Adan Sowa	69	71	71	211	42,262.23
(Brand defeated Sowa on third playoff hole.)					
Luis Carbonetti	72	71	69	212	29,583.56
John Bland	71	69	73	213	19,750.55
Stewart Ginn	74	71	68	213	19,750.55
Simon Owen	72	72	69	213	19,750.55
Des Smyth	69	72	73	214	15,214.40
Horacio Carbonetti	74	70	71	215	12,678.67
Jim Rhodes	73	70	72	215	12,678.67
Jimmy Heggarty	71	75	70	216	10,988.18
Bob Cameron	76	72	69	217	8,706.02

	SCORES	TOTAL	MONEY
Martin Gray	71 71 75	217	8,706.02
Gavan Levenson	72 74 71	217	8,706.02
Denis O'Sullivan	74 74 69	217	8,706.02
Gery Watine	73 73 71	217	8,706.02
Terry Gale	74 74 70	218	6,364.69
Bobby Lincoln	79 71 68	218	6,364.69
Mike Miller	73 74 71	218	6,364.69
Pete Oakley	72 76 70	218	6,364.69
Jose Rivero	78 72 68	218	6,364.69

Japan Senior Tour

Aderans Wellness Open

Nakajo Golf Club, Nakajo, Niigata
Par 36-36–72; 6,987 yards

June 9-11
purse, ¥60,000,000

	SCORES	TOTAL	MONEY
Kiyoshi Murota	68 71 68	207	¥12,000,000
Toyotake Nakao	71 69 68	208	5,700,000
Tateo Ozaki	70 71 70	211	4,050,000
Tsuneyuki Nakajima	72 71 70	213	2,383,000
Yukio Noguchi	73 70 70	213	2,383,000
Katsuyoshi Tomori	72 71 70	213	2,383,000
Hideto Shigenobu	73 69 72	214	1,581,000
Noboru Fujiike	72 71 71	214	1,581,000
Tadami Ueno	74 72 70	216	1,326,000
Takashi Miyoshi	75 69 72	216	1,326,000
Chen Tze-ming	74 69 73	216	1,326,000
Toshiaki Sudo	71 76 70	217	1,096,000
Katsunari Takahashi	70 74 73	217	1,096,000
Boonchu Ruangkit	77 67 73	217	1,096,000
Toru Nakayama	74 70 74	218	927,000
Kimpachi Yoshimura	71 75 72	218	927,000
Saburo Fujiki	75 71 73	219	792,000
Masami Ito	73 70 76	219	792,000
Kazuo Kanayama	75 72 72	219	792,000
Shuichi Sano	79 70 71	220	631,000
Yasushi Taki	77 73 70	220	631,000
Katsuji Hasegawa	74 74 72	220	631,000
Yoshikazu Yokoshima	76 75 69	220	631,000
Tadashige Kusano	76 74 70	220	631,000
Norihiko Matsumoto	76 72 72	220	631,000

PGA Philanthropy Rebornest Senior Open

Big Raisac Country Club, Miyagi
Par 36-36–72; 6,917 yards

August 10-13
purse, ¥30,000,000

	SCORES				TOTAL	MONEY
Tateo Ozaki	73	69	67	70	279	¥5,400,000
Katsunari Takahashi	68	70	69	72	279	2,700,000
(Ozaki defeated Takahashi on fourth playoff hole.)						
Kiyoshi Murota	69	70	72	72	283	1,600,000
David Ishii	72	72	71	68	283	1,600,000
Andy Bean	70	70	71	72	283	1,600,000
Yasuo Sone	67	70	73	74	284	1,125,000
Toyotake Nakao	74	68	70	72	284	1,125,000
Tadami Ueno	76	71	67	71	285	810,000
Hiroshi Fujita	67	71	74	73	285	810,000
Shoichi Sato	69	73	72	71	285	810,000
Seiji Ebihara	68	72	72	74	286	562,500
Junji Hashizoe	70	71	73	72	286	562,500
Boonchu Ruengkit	73	72	71	70	286	562,500
Yoshitaka Yamamoto	68	74	71	73	286	562,500
Katsumi Nanjo	74	70	73	71	288	450,000
Shuichi Sano	75	69	70	74	288	450,000
Chen Tze-ming	73	69	71	75	288	450,000
Toru Nakayama	74	70	71	74	289	347,250
Noboru Fujiike	69	74	72	74	289	347,250
Toshihiko Kikuichi	73	72	69	75	289	347,250
Gohei Sato	71	76	72	70	289	347,250

Fancl Classic

Susono Country Club, Shizuoka
Par 36-36–72; 6,851 yards

August 18-20
purse, ¥60,000,000

	SCORES			TOTAL	MONEY
Kiyoshi Murota	66	67	69	202	¥15,000,000
Tsuneyuki Nakajima	70	67	65	202	6,900,000
(Murota defeated Nakajima on first playoff hole.)					
Seiji Ebihara	67	73	66	206	3,900,000
Masami Ito	67	73	70	210	2,550,000
Boonchu Ruangkit	72	71	67	210	2,550,000
David Ishii	71	69	71	211	1,950,000
Noboru Fujiike	72	68	71	211	1,950,000
Yukio Noguchi	69	70	73	212	1,500,000
Koichi Suzuki	73	70	70	213	1,290,000
Toyotake Nakao	73	72	68	213	1,290,000
Katsunari Takahashi	73	71	70	214	1,170,000
Hisao Inoue	72	69	73	214	1,170,000
Takaaki Fukuzawa	71	75	69	215	960,000
Kazuo Kanayama	73	71	71	215	960,000
Hiroshi Makino	71	73	71	215	960,000
Shinji Kuraoka	75	73	67	215	960,000
Hideto Shigenobu	74	72	69	215	960,000
Takashi Miyoshi	72	71	73	216	697,500
Yoshio Fumiyama	72	70	74	216	697,500
Yoshinori Ichioka	71	74	71	216	697,500
Toshihiko Otsuka	73	76	67	216	697,500

Japan PGA Senior Championship

Eniwa Country Club, Hokkaido
Par 36-36–72; 7,012 yards

September 28-October 1
purse, ¥50,000,000

	SCORES				TOTAL	MONEY
Tsuneyuki Nakajima	69	70	71	73	283	¥10,000,000
Katsunari Takahashi	68	73	71	71	283	5,000,000
(Nakajima defeated Takahashi on second playoff hole.)						
Kiyoshi Murota	72	74	67	73	286	3,500,000
Katsuyoshi Tomori	68	72	74	73	287	2,500,000
Boonchu Ruangkit	75	70	71	73	289	2,000,000
Tateo Ozaki	73	73	75	69	290	1,425,000
Shuichi Sano	72	70	73	75	290	1,425,000
Hiroshi Makino	73	72	74	72	291	1,166,666
Hiroshi Fujita	75	72	71	73	291	1,166,666
David Ishii	76	71	71	73	291	1,166,666
Yoshitaka Yamamoto	72	71	77	72	292	1,025,000
Nichito Hashimoto	76	73	73	70	292	1,025,000
Seiji Ebihara	78	72	75	68	293	862,500
Yasushi Taki	72	73	72	76	293	862,500
Yoshinori Ichioka	72	75	72	74	293	862,500
Noboru Fujiike	73	74	75	71	293	862,500
Masami Ito	74	71	74	76	295	675,000
Noboru Sugai	74	73	72	77	296	620,000
Kimpachi Yoshmura	71	79	75	71	296	620,000
Minoru Hatsumi	74	75	72	76	297	570,000
Takashi Miyoshi	76	76	72	73	297	570,000

Japan Senior Open

Kuwana Country Club, Mie
Par 36-36–72

October 26-29
purse, ¥80,000,000

	SCORES				TOTAL	MONEY
Tsuneyuki Nakajima	68	66	72	69	275	¥16,000,000
Kiyoshi Murota	67	68	71	70	276	8,800,000
Naomichi Ozaki	67	71	70	73	281	6,160,000
Seiji Ebihara	68	65	76	73	282	3,386,666
Hiroshi Makino	71	73	70	68	282	3,386,666
Takashi Miyoshi	76	67	68	71	282	3,386,666
Katsuyoshi Tomori	70	69	73	71	283	2,240,000
Katsunari Takahashi	66	74	69	74	283	2,240,000
Hajime Meshiai	66	74	73	71	284	1,640,000
Kimpachi Yoshimura	69	75	69	71	284	1,640,000
Takeru Shibata	69	69	73	74	285	1,332,000
Isao Aoki	67	73	72	73	285	1,332,000
Tateo Ozaki	70	71	73	72	286	1,052,000
Takaaki Fukuzawa	74	69	70	73	286	1,052,000
Shinji Kuraoka	71	72	78	66	287	912,000
David Ishii	73	72	72	70	287	912,000
Toshiaki Sudo	74	68	73	73	288	840,000
Toru Nakayama	72	72	70	75	289	744,000
Bill Longmuir	72	70	75	72	289	744,000
Yoshitaka Yamamoto	73	74	72	70	289	744,000
Tsunemi Nakajima	71	72	73	73	289	744,000

Kinojyo Senior Open

Kinojyo Golf Club, Okayama
Par 36-36–72; 8,653 yards

November 3-5
purse, ¥20,000,000

	SCORES			TOTAL	MONEY
Takashi Miyoshi	66	64	70	200	¥3,600,000
Kiyoshi Murota	70	66	68	204	1,800,000
Hajime Meshiai	69	71	67	207	1,300,000
Isao Aoki	74	65	69	208	1,000,000
Yoshitaka Yamamoto	68	71	70	209	850,000
Noboru Fujiike	68	70	71	209	850,000
Tsunemi Nakajima	70	69	71	210	613,333
Katsunari Takahashi	75	67	68	210	613,333
Takaaki Fukuzawa	69	71	70	210	613,333
Yoshinori Ichioka	69	73	69	211	410,000
Seiji Ebihara	69	71	71	211	410,000
Kimpachi Yoshimura	67	76	68	211	410,000
Toshihiko Kikuichi	73	70	68	211	410,000
Koichi Suzuki	73	68	71	212	340,000
Kenshi Ikeda	69	73	71	213	290,000
Minoru Hatsumi	69	73	71	213	290,000
Koji Okuno	73	68	72	213	290,000
Kazuo Kanayama	71	71	71	213	290,000
Takeru Shibata	71	69	74	214	214,500
Kazuki Nagao	73	71	70	214	214,500
Toyotake Nakao	72	73	69	214	214,500
Yasushi Taki	69	72	73	214	214,500